THE JERUSALEM TALMUD
FIRST ORDER: ZERAÏM
TRACTATE *BERAKHOT*

STUDIA JUDAICA

FORSCHUNGEN ZUR WISSENSCHAFT
DES JUDENTUMS

HERAUSGEGEBEN VON
E. L. EHRLICH

BAND XVIII

WALTER DE GRUYTER · BERLIN · NEW YORK
2000

THE JERUSALEM TALMUD
תלמוד ירושלמי

FIRST ORDER: ZERAÏM
סדר זרעים
TRACTATE *BERAKHOT*
מסכת ברכות

EDITION, TRANSLATION, AND COMMENTARY

BY
HEINRICH W. GUGGENHEIMER

WALTER DE GRUYTER · BERLIN · NEW YORK
2000

ISBN 978-3-11-068132-1
e-ISBN (PDF) 978-3-11-080048-7

This volume is text- and page-identical with the hardback published in 2000.

Library of Congress Control Number: 2020942820

Bibliographic information published by the Deutsche Nationalbibliothek
The Deutsche Nationalbibliothek lists this publication in the
Deutsche Nationalbibliografie;
detailed bibliographic data are available on the Internet at http://dnb.dnb.de.

Printing and binding: CPI books GmbH, Leck

www.degruyter.com

Preface

The Jerusalem Talmud is the precursor and basis of the Babylonian Talmud, the Midrash literature, and much of synagogal poetry. It is no exaggeration to say that a genuine understanding of all of rabbinic literature from the first millennium C. E. requires knowledge and understanding of the Jerusalem Talmud.

The present edition is based on the *editio princeps* and manuscripts, without any emendations. A close examination of the text shows that it is in good condition and the places where an emendation would be desirable are few, even for a Tractate as large as the first one, *Berakhot*. For ease of study, the text in the present edition has been subdivided into paragraphs and vocalized following the rules of rabbinic Hebrew. An extensive commentary is given. Since most of the existing commentaries rely heavily on emendations, the commentary is based on an independent new study, using the oldest available sources. The relation of the Jerusalem to the Babylonian Talmud is discussed in the Introduction.

I wish to thank my wife, Dr. Eva Guggenheimer, who acted as critic, style editor, proof reader, and expert on the Latin and Greek vocabulary. Her own notes on some possible Latin and Greek etymologies are identified by (E. G.).

Contents

Introductions

Introduction to Talmudic Literature

Historical Background	1
Talmud, Midrash and Synagogal Poetry	11
Survey of Times of Tannaïm and Amoraïm	15
Babylonian and Jerusalem Talmud	16

Introduction to the Talmud Yerushalmi

Text of the Jerusalem Talmud	28
Order *Zeraïm*	32
This Edition of the Talmud Yerushalmi	33
Tractate Berakhot	38

Chapter 1, מאימתי

Halakhah 1	39
Halakhah 2	86
Halakhah 3	92
Halakhah 4	95
Halakhah 5	97
Halakhah 6	109
Halakhah 7	111
Halakhah 8	117
Halakhah 9	146

Chapter 2, היה קורא

Halakhah 1 156
Halakhah 2 174
Halakhah 3 175
Halakhah 4 196
Halakhah 5 217
Halakhah 6 224
Halakhah 7 231
Halakhah 8 238
Halakhah 9 251

Chapter 3, מי שמתו
Halakhah 1 256
Halakhah 2 283
Halakhah 3 288
Halakhah 4 295
Halakhah 5 308
Halakhah 6 324

Chapter 4, תפילת השחר
Halakhah 1 327
Halakhah 2 361
Halakhah 3 366
Halakhah 4 382
Halakhah 5 389
Halakhah 6 396

Chapter 5, אין עומדין
Halakhah 1 403
Halakhah 2 423
Halakhah 3 438
Halakhah 4 440
Halakhah 5 445
Halakhah 6 453

Chapter 6, כיצד מברכין
Halakhah 1 455
Halakhah 2 481
Halakhah 3 485
Halakhah 4 486
Halakhah 5 490
Halakhah 6 495
Halakhah 7 502
Halakhah 8 503

Chapter 7, שלשה שאכלו
Halakhah 1 507
Halakhah 2 521
Halakhah 3 529
Halakhah 4 536
Halakhah 5 539
Halakhah 6 542

Chapter 8, אלו דברים
Halakhah 1 550
Halakhah 2 559
Halakhah 3 571
Halakhah 4 572
Halakhah 5 576
Halakhah 6 579
Halakhah 7 583
Halakhah 8 592
Halakhah 9 594

Chapter 9, הרואה
Halakhah 1 599
Halakhah 2 620

Halakhah 3 629
Halakhah 4 661
Halakhah 5 663
Halakhah 6 667
Halakhah 7 675

INDICES
Index of Biographical Notes 689
Index of Biblical Quotations 692
Index of Greek and Latin Words 695
General Index 697

INTRODUCTIONS

Introduction to Talmudic Literature

Historical Background

We have very little detailed information on the religious life of the Jewish people between the conquest of the Land under Joshua and the Babylonian exile. From the complaints of the prophets, we see that Baal rituals were widely followed. These rituals were of a magical nature and their object was the prevention of crop failures that would imperil survival of individuals and communities. Since the prophets do not in general complain about neglect of Jewish ceremonial law, it is very likely that Jewish ritual was scrupulously followed even by Baal worshippers. The complete elimination of polytheistic tendencies from the body of Jewish practices after the Babylonian exile may be attributed to the experience of the disaster of the destruction of Jerusalem but also to the fact that, both in Babylonia and in the resettled Persian province of Yehud (after 515 B.C.E.), the Jews were part of a great empire with government roads where in case of crop failure in one province, relief could be brought in from the outside, so crop failure was no longer a matter of life and death.

The reports in the books of Ezra and Nehemiah on the organization of the new Jewish commonwealth stress the reestablishment of religious rituals, and the basic features of what today is called "rabbinic Judaism" stem from this period. For the first three hundred years of this development, our sources are very scanty. At that period also, the majority of Jews were still living in Babylonia and of their history extremely little is known, nothing at all of their intellectual history besides the fact that a thriving Jewish community persisted there in the middle of a sea of Gentiles. The persecutions that preceded the Maccabean revolt were of relatively short duration and, since they had a happy outcome, did not create a need to record religious practices for future generations. Even in the times of the First Temple, there seems to have been a division between popular-prophetic religion, depending on the traditions of the Oral Law, and the organized established Temple cult, lead by King and High Priest who insisted that only the priests were the genuine authorities for teaching the Written Law. This division becomes explicit and deep at the Return from Babylonia[1]. It will be seen from the Talmud text (9:7), that the split was already in evidence at the time of the Return. In books on Jewish history, the high-priestly party of the later Sadducees who rejected the Oral Law, is usually described as being more worldly than the representatives of the Oral Law, the later Pharisees. But the development of ultra-observant Sadducee sects, who avoided all contacts with Gentiles and the unobservant, is now known to precede the Hasmonean revolt[2]. Pharisee sects of the latter kind are known only from the last generation preceding the destruction of the Second Temple. The *Pĕrushim* or

1 Cf. H. Mantel, *The Secession of the Samaritans.* Bar Ilan Annual vii-viii (5729-5730) 162-177.

2 Detailed arguments are given by BenZion Wacholder and Martin G. Abegg in the Introduction to Fascicle 3 of *A Preliminary Edition of the Unpublished Dead Sea Scrolls*, Biblical Archeological Society, Washington D.C., 1995.

Pharisees, the later rabbinic Jews, whose main tenet was the use of rules of interpretation of the Oral Law to adapt the commands of the Torah to changing circumstances, always represented the religious majority. (Another difference was that Sadducees only believed in the survival of the soul but not in bodily resurrection, as against the Pharisees.)

In the more than 500 years of the existence of the Second Temple, a body of religious practice evolved in the implementation and extension of Torah commandments. It seems that a need for exact formulation and promulgation of accepted rules arose first in the times just preceding the Hasmonean revolt; in any case, the first such proclamation (Mishnah *Idiut* 8:4) dates from that time. In the century preceding the destruction of the Second Temple, the emerging necessity of codifying religious law put an end to the prior practice of promulgating only those rules that could be adopted unanimously. Of the emerging two schools, the one headed by the Babylonian Hillel and his descendents kept strictly to the old Pharisaic principles while the one headed by the Judean Shammai tended more towards sectarian interpretions and, in particular, stricter interpretation of rules of intercourse with Gentiles [as shown in the "eighteen rules" (Mishnah *Šabbat* 1:4), promulgated during the ascendancy of the House of Shammai, many of which were designed to make intercourse with Gentiles almost impossible.]

The catastrophy of the first war with the Romans and the destruction of the Temple (in 71 C.E.) led, shortly thereafter, to the disappearance of sects. The only permanently surviving school was that of Hillel, whose head at that time, Rabban Yoḥanan ben Zakkai, escaped from Jerusalem during the siege and requested permission from Vespasian, the commanding general of the Roman armies, to organize a Jewish place of study at Jabneh, in the plain. Jabneh had been the personal property of

Miriam, the last Hasmonean and wife of Herod. In her will, she gave Jabneh to Livia, wife of Augustus. Herod, after murdering his wife, had no choice but to execute her will. Consequently, Jabneh became the personal property of the Emperor and not part of the province of Judea; hence, it was not under martial law. [Probably, Vespasian had no direct authority to dispose of Jabneh; Rabban Yoḥanan ben Zakkai chose Jabneh because it was an oasis of peace in a country at war, and he asked for it since he considered Vespasian to be the next emperor.] Rabban Yoḥanan seems to have survived the war only for a few years. One of his great innovations was the introduction of the title "Rebbi" for a person authorized to render religious decisions. No titles are found earlier, except that for two or three generations the title "Rabban" was used for the head of the Synhedrion. In the next two generations his students, mainly R. Eliezer ben Hyrkanos and R. Joshua ben Ḥananiah and their students, were busy adapting Judaism to a permanent existence without a Temple and collecting all statements of interpretation of Biblical verses and proclamations of religious practice they could obtain. The bulk of this work must be credited to Rabbis Eliezer and Joshua. It is probable also that the opinions of the school of Shammai came to posterity through R. Eliezer.

Hillel's great-grandson, Rabban Simeon ben Gamliel I, was president of the revolutionary government in the war with the Romans. His son, Gamliel II, could become president of the Synhedrion only after a change in the Roman government (probably accession of Nerva in 96 C.E.). Rabban Gamliel died before the revolt of Bar Kokhba, but he cannot have died too long before that revolt since his son, Rabban Simeon ben Gamliel II, notes that he himself was still a child at the time of the siege of Betar. After the death of Rabban Gamliel, the leadership of the Synhedrion was in the hands of Rebbi Aqiba. Rebbi Aqiba and his older contemporary Rebbi Ismael are credited with introducing systematic and coherent methods of derivation of practical implications from Biblical verses.

Rebbi Joshua was a strong supporter of submission to Rome under all circumstances. After his death and that of Rabban Gamliel, Rebbi Aqiba became a supporter of the messianic movement of Bar Kokhba. As a consequence, Rebbi Joshua's nephew, Ḥananiah, left Judea and founded a House of Study at Nahardea, modelled after that of Jabneh. This town in Babylonia, near the lower Euphrates, was the traditional place of exile of king Joiachin, and capital of the Jews of Babylonia. Two generations later, Ḥananiah's descendant Samuel (bar Abba) was the first to make his Babylonian academy a leading institution in world Jewry. When Ḥananiah left, R. Ismael took his House of Study out of harm's way and established it at Kefar Darom, near Gaza in Philistia.

The catastrophy of the war of Bar Kokhba, culminating in the fall of Betar in 138 C.E., destroyed all Jewish learning and most of the Jewish presence in Judea. Public Jewish learning was forbidden in all of the land of Israel, now renamed Palestine, for a period of unknown length, possibly until the accession of Septimius Severus in 193 C.E. (or, at the least, until Marcus Aurelius after 161 C.E.). All we know of the intellectual activity of Jews between the canonization of the Hebrew Bible and 138 C.E. comes to us from the reconstruction of the ancient material by the leaders of the generation following Bar Kokhba (with the exception of a few Sadducee materials from the Geniza and Qumran, and from books in Greek written by Jews, also mostly of Sadducee tendencies, preserved by Gentiles, such as Siraḥ and the writings of Philo and Josephus.)

The circumstances of the transmission of all this material to the next generation are unclear. The Babylonian Talmud (*Yebamot* 62b) reports that all students of R. Aqiba, who numbered in the thousands, died and that "the world was empty of learning until R. Aqiba came to our teachers in the South: R. Meïr, R. Yehudah, R. Yose, R. Simeon, and R. Eleazar ben Shamua, and transmitted his knowledge to them." In one version of *Seder Tannaïm and Amoraïm* ascribed to R. Joseph Ṭov 'Elem, these teachers and R. Neḥemiah are called "students of R. Aqiba who after the latter's death disagreed about the meaning of his sayings," but in another version preserved in *Maḥzor Vitry* they are "students of R. Aqiba who never saw R. Aqiba and did not live in his generation.[3]" Since R. Aqiba was first imprisoned and then executed towards the end of the war of Bar Kokhba, it is unlikely that he ever went South[4], outside of Judea proper, to the House of Study of R. Ismael. Also, the chronology noted above gives support in the main to the second version of *Seder Tannaïm and Amoraïm*, which is the reading of the school of Rashi.

R. Meïr is the author of a collection of rules that one generation later became the foundation of the *Mishnah*, the authoritative source of statements proclaimed as valid by the Patriarch R. Yehudah the Prince (ben Rabban Simeon ben Gamliel II) and the basis of rabbinic Judaism to this very day. It is attested both in the Babylonian and the Jerusalem Talmudim (*Yebamot*, 121a, 12d) that R. Meïr was a personal student of R. Aqiba. Nothing is known of his ancestors.

R. Yehudah (bar Ilaï) is the author of a collection of laws derived from the verses of the book of Leviticus that in the following generations was

---

3 See *Maḥzor Vitry*, ed. S. Horovitz, Nürnberg 1923, p. 486, note ז.

4 In the Talmud Yerushalmi composed in Galilee, "South" usually means Judea, or better the only part of Judea still inhabited by Jews, the region around Lod. But since R. Aqiba lived in that region, he cannot be said to have gone there.

edited as *Sifra* (or *Torat Cohanim*). This book, while reputed to contain the teachings of R. Aqiba, follows the method of R. Ismael. This fact gives credence to the second version of *Seder Tannaïm and Amoraïm*, to the effect that the other five sages were graduates of the school of R. Ismael versed in the teachings of R. Aqiba.

R. Yose (bar Ḥalaphta) is the author of a collection that became *Seder 'Olam*, a chronology of the world starting from Creation, which is the basis of our count of "years after Creation." He did not collect statements of law but his opinion is always considered the most authoritative one in this group.

R. Simeon (bar Ioḥai) is the author of a collection that later became *Sifry*, the collection of laws derived from the books of Numbers and Deuteronomy. *Sifry* on Numbers follows the method of R. Ismael, that on Deuteronomy also the method of R. Aqiba. It is not impossible, given the preceding, that both books go back to collections of R. Simeon.

R. Neḥemiah is the reputed author of a collection of laws which later became the (or one) *Tosephta*. (The current *Tosephta* may be a much later collection.) It is known that R. Neḥemia's father was a scholar but his name is unknown. His family is said to be that of the Biblical Neḥemiah.

R. Eleazar ben Shamua' did not survive the persecutions following the war of Bar Kokhba. With R. Aqiba, and R. Yehudah ben Bava who ordained the six sages when ordination was a capital crime, he is counted among the Ten Martyrs.

The Tannaïtic corpus, the collection of works having their roots in the works of the scholars between the destruction of the Temple and the edition of the Mishnah, also contains a few minor works and the *Mekhilta*, the collection of laws (and homilies) attached to verses of

Exodus, attributed to R. Ismael (ben Elisha) of the preceding generation. (A second *Mekhilta*, falsely attributed to R. Simeon, was edited in the first post-tannaïtic period in Galilee[5]. The other collections mentioned were probably edited for posterity in Babylonia.) This is almost all we have from earlier periods. Some scholars of the last generation of Tannaïm are reported to have made collections similar to R. Meïr's; none of these have survived.

It is clear from the preceding that statements attributed to any one of these sages do not usually originate with them but are earlier traditions accepted and transmitted by these teachers. For example, the opinion ascribed by the Tosephta (*Terumot* 2:12, *Ḥallah* 2:11) to Rebbi Yehudah regarding the boundaries of the Land of Israel is already found in Josephus's *Jewish Antiquities* in his description of the boundaries of the land of Canaan[6]. [A different subject are mystical themes that in later Amoraic sources are adapted from earlier Sadducee Jewish sources. The sources of Philo and their influence on the development of Amoraic mysticism have not yet been sufficiently studied.]

When the public study of Torah was again permitted through the influence of R. Yehudah bar Ilaï with the Roman government, the Academies and Houses of Study were all in Galilee, with the exception of a small circle of students at Lod, in the plain East of Jerusalem. The population of Galilee took almost no part in either war and so came through almost unscathed, except for the severe economic circumstances.

---

5 *Mekhilta* edited by H. S. Horovitz, I. A. Rabin, Berlin 1931 (reprint Jerusalem1960.) *Mekhilta deR. Simeon bar Yoḥai*, edited by J. N. Epstein, E. Z. Melamed, Jerusalem 1955.

6 *Jewish Antiquities* I.130. The editor of the Loeb edition erroneously identified *Okeanos* not with the sea beyond the Straits of Gibraltar but with the Indian Ocean.

Historically and chronologically we are on safer ground starting with the edition of the Mishnah, since the history of Talmudic Babylonia was compiled, on the basis of documents, by the 10th Century C.E. Gaon, Sherira, in his famous "Letter". The first edition of the Mishnah was complete in 218 C.E. when Rav (Rav Abba bar Ayvo) left the Academy of R. Yehudah the Prince to return to his native Babylonia and to start his own Academy at Sura (Mata Meḥassia) in friendly competition with Samuel's Academy at Nahardea. It seems that the entire time of the Severan (Pseudo-Antoninan) dynasty (193-235 C.E.) was a very good one for Jews in general and those of the Land of Israel in particular. The title "Rav" was coined expressly for Rav by Rebbi Yehudah the Prince (who usually is just called "Rebbi") to indicate an ordination that does not include authorization to judge matters pertaining to the laws of the Land of Israel. It became the title of all ordained rabbis outside the Land.

As explained above, the Mishnah is a collection of religious traditions based on the prior collection of R. Meïr. It is authoritative but very short. Immediately after publication of the Mishnah, an intensive effort started to connect the rest of traditional rules to those of the Mishnah and to elucidate its elliptic, often cryptic, statements. That effort took place both in Galilee and in Babylonia and resulted in the "Jerusalem" (really, the Galilean) and the Babylonian Talmudim.

Rebbi must have survived several years after 218, since the Jerusalem Talmud is based on a later version of the Mishnah (although the differences between the Jerusalem and the Babylonian texts are small.) He may well have seen the start of the reign of Alexander Severus in 222 C. E. (The latter might be the emperor Antoninus, friend of Rebbi, in Jewish tradition. All emperors of the Severan dynasty and most later ones in the third century called themselves Antoninus.)

Rebbi is counted as the last of the *Tannaïm*, the "proclaimers", who formulated Jewish law in the period starting with the establishment of the Synhedrion at Jabneh. A new period starts in Jewish intellectual history with the death of Rebbi. In his will, Rebbi had appointed his son Gamliel (III) as patriarch but the presidency of his Court of Law and the House of Study was given to the Babylonian-born R. Ḥanina (bar Ḥama). From that moment on, the house of Hillel retained the political patriarchate but never regained leadership in spiritual and intellectual matters. The Academy soon moved to Tiberias while the patriarch resided in Sepphoris; other centers of study sprang up, generating a great flowering of intellectual activity under very adverse economic circumstances. A parallel activity appeared at the same time in Babylonia. The great and varied activity of the time is all based on the Mishnah edited by Rebbi; the sages of the period are called *Amoraïm*, "leaders of discussion."

The exterior circumstances of the period in Palestine were not auspicious. Alexander Severus was murdered in Germany in 235 C.E.. After his death there followed a period known as the Military Anarchy, characterized by a quick succession of mostly unsuccessful pretenders to the throne who debased the currency and thereby caused rapid inflation and general decline of commerce and wealth. At that time, the oasis state of Palmyra gained a measure of independence; Odenathus, its ruler, attempted to occupy Babylonia and destroyed Nahardea, the Jewish center. When Palmyra was subdued by Aurelianus, the only Roman emperor of the period who managed to have a stable reign, the Yeshivah of Samuel relocated from the destroyed Nahardea to Pum Beditha, where it stayed until after the Arab conquest, when it removed to the newly created capital of Baghdad. The Military Anarchy came to an end with the accession of Diocletian in 284 C.E. He reorganized the Roman state in the manner of despotic absolutism and introduced a new, stable currency based on honest gold coins. The rapid improvement of the economy was followed by the victory of the Christian church in Constantine's edict of 313 C.E.; under Constantine's sons and successors the church started an unceasing war against Jewish doctrine that became vicious under Theodosius I (from 379 C.E.) and led to the end of the patriarchate around 425 C.E. and the emigration of the last House of Study to Damascus at about that time.

The rulers of Babylonia after the destruction of the Seleucid empire by the Romans in the first century B.C.E. were the Parthians, an Afghan tribe not much interested in administration. The Parthians gave the peoples under their dominion great autonomy; Jewish courts in Parthia had full criminal jurisdiction and the Davidic Head of the Diaspora was recognized as local ruler. The Parthians were overthrown by the Persian Ardashir in 226 C.E. The Persians kings were Zoroastrians. Many were friendly to the Jews; others were Zoroastrian zealots. Troubles for the Jews were intermittent in the Talmudic period, but became permanent in the century preceding the Arab conquest in 642 C.E.

Talmud, Midrash, and Synagogal Poetry

The Galilean sages of the third century C.E., living under the difficult economic conditions described above, invented three literary forms that dominated the intellectual life of Jewry for over 1500 years: Talmud, Midrash, and synagogal poetry. [Archeological evidence shows at the same time an extraordinary growth of Jewish activity in Galilee, best represented by the building of synagogues.]

Synagogal poetry goes back at least to the last generations of Tannaïm; both Talmudim quote fragments of poetry from that time. Also, Rav, returning to Babylonia from his studies in Galilee, introduced the use of poetic inserts (*piyyuṭim*) into the liturgy of his academy of Surah. The autochthonous academy of Pum Beditha never accepted any poetic inserts, not even on the high holidays, as reported in Geonic responsa. Ashkenazic prayer traditions were originally modelled after those of Southern Italy, which in turn were patterned on Galilean usage. Southern Italy belonged to the Byzantine empire of Justinian. That emperor forbade the study of Jewish law but permitted Jewish prayer; hence, Byzantine authors used the vehicle of poetry to teach much of Talmudic and Midrashic information to the people. But the origin of this poetry goes back to Mishnaic times. [Ashkenazic liturgies were filled with poetry both of Palestinian/Syrian and Ashkenazic origin. Sephardic prayers were always patterned on the Babylonian model; while Spain produced great liturgical poets it never really accepted poetry as the body of prayer (except for penitential compositions admitted and composed also in Babylonia.) Most synagogal poetry was eliminated starting around 1800 C.E. from Ashkenazic orthodox prayers by the combined influence of Ḥasidim, who tried to follow the Sephardic pattern, the Gaon of Wilna who did not tolerate any deviation from Babylonian patterns, and Mendelssohnian reform.]

The history of the Midrash covers more than 1000 years. The Midrash in most of its forms contains outlines of homilies on Biblical verses and is the main repository of Jewish ethical teachings. The oldest Midrashim, *Bereshit Rabba* and the old *Tanḥuma*, refer mainly to Amoraïm of the last Galilean generations, R. Berekhiah and R. Tanḥuma. However, both contain examples of people who spend hundreds of thousands of sesterces for a garment, which illustrates the hyperinflation of the Military Anarchy. Rebbis Berekhiah and Tanḥuma seem to have been the first systematic collectors of homilies that have come down to us; rabbis from the time of the Military Anarchy are reported to have had their own books of sermons. The greatest flowering of Midrashic literature occured in the Byzantine empire, after the conclusion of the Talmud, but it would not exist without the collections of the Amoraïm.

The Talmud is the main creation of the last three quarters of the third century C.E. As reported earlier, after the promulgation of the Mishnah as official rule book of Jewish practice, an intense effort of clarification of its meaning began simultaneouly in Galilee and Babylonia. In the first century of this development, the two countries moved together, influenced by frequent travels of Galilean sages to Babylonia and the influx of Babylonian students to Galilean academies. The man who turned this effort into the creation of the Talmud was Rebbi Yoḥanan (bar Nappaḥa), the head of the academy of Tiberias, who died in 279 C.E. His method was to elucidate the Mishnah by referring it to related statements from other collections of tannaïtic statements, so-called *baraitot*, "external" pronouncements (i. e., external to the Mishnah) and to analyze the underlying principles. This naturally made it necessary to try to attach carefully to each statement the name of its author, to avoid comparing apples and oranges. A natural consequence was that also in amoraïc reasonings it is necessary to record the name of the person who makes the statement and the chain of transmission. It is assumed that a student follows the reasoning of his teacher unless he explicitly disclaims it; this rule is valid for both tannaïtic and amoraïc statements in both Talmudim. That gives the Talmudim the possibility to explore different chains of reasoning simultaneously without getting self-contradictory. The basic method and the basic scope are identical in both Talmudim. However, the formalized, condensed language in which the discussions are conducted is much more developed in the Babli than in the Yerushalmi; this again shows the priority in time of the Yerushalmi. Not all technical terms of the formalized language retain their exact meaning in the migration from Galilee to Babylonia; the Yerushalmi cannot be read in terms of Babylonian practice.

In addition, both Talmudim contain much extra-legal and extra-logical material, called *aggadic,* included mostly to make some point of practice that depends more on a moral than on a legal/scriptural basis.

The first written version of the Jerusalem Talmud that has come down to us is the compilation of civil law contained in the first three tractates of the order *Neziqin*, "torts". This is a short manual for lawyers and judges rather than a reasoned derivation of anything. It was probably collected in Caesarea (Philippi) at the end of the third century C.E. It is not characteristic for the other parts of the Talmud and has come to us only because the compilers of the Talmud, under pressure by a hostile government turned into an agent of the Christian church, did not have time to go over the material a second time. (R. Saul Lieberman, in תלמודה דקיסרין, Complement to *Tarbiẓ* 4, 1931, gives a detailed analysis of the differences between the redaction of *Neziqin* and the rest of the Yerushalmi in methodology, tradition, and language. He concludes that the tradition there is that of Caesarea because of the overwhelming number of quotes from sages known to have lived, taught, or studied, at Caesarea. Almost certainly, the remainder of the Yerushalmi was composed in Tiberias. The residence of R. Abbahu, and place of compilation of the oldest parts of the Yerushalmi, is usually placed at Caesarea-on-Sea. The reason for identifying Caesarea as Caesarea Philippi

(Banias) are given in the commentary to the Talmud.) We do not know when the Jerusalem Talmud was compiled in its present form. The work seems to have started at the same time that the rules of computation of the Jewish calender were published by the Academy led by R. Yose of the Fourth Generation of Galilean Amoraïm[7], sometime between 325-350 C.E. The last Amoraïm mentioned in that Talmud lived in the third quarter of the fourth century; they probably were the final editors of the text before us. The Babylonian Talmud was compiled first in the Academy of Rav Ashi, shortly after the work on the Yerushalmi had stopped. Its final edition was prepared by Rabina III and his school, almost a century later[8].

Survey of the Times of Tannaïm and Amoraïm

All dates given are of the Common Era.

Tannaïtic Era

Dates C.E.	Generation	
60-80	First	Rabban Yoḥanan ben Zakkai
	Destruction of the Temple in 71	
80-110	Second	Rebbis Eliezer and Joshua, Rabban Gamliel
110-138	Third	Rebbis Aqiba and Ismael
	Bar Kokhba revolt crushed in 138, persecution of Jewish faith	
(138-)200	Fourth	Rebbis Meïr and Yehudah, Rabban Simeon ben Gamliel
200-220	Fifth	Rebbi (Yehudah the Prince)
218-225		Transition from Tannaïm to Amoraïm
	Parthian rule in Babylonia overthrown by Persians	

7 Yerushalmi *'Eruvin* 3:11 (fol. 21c).

8 This does not exclude that some notes in that Talmud were inserted later, in Gaonic times.

Amoraïtic Era

Dates C.E.	Generation	Babylon	Israel
220-250	First	Rav and Samuel	R. Ḥanina, R. Oshaya, R. Yannai
250-290	Second	Rav Huna, Rav Yehudah	R. Yoḥanan, R. Simeon ben Laqish
		Military Anarchy in Roman Empire	
290-320	Third	Rabba and Rav Joseph	R. Zeïra, R. Ḥiyya bar Abba
		Roman Empire becomes Christian	
320-350	Fourth	Abbaie and Rava	R. Yose and R. Jonah
350-375	Fifth	Rav Papa	R. Mana, R. Yose bar Abun
	End of Patriarchate, exile of the Galilean Yeshivah to Damascus		
375-425	Sixth	Rav Ashi	
425-460	Seventh	Mar bar Rav Ashi	
460-500	Eighth	Ravina III and Rav Yose, editors of the Babli	

Babylonian and Jerusalem Talmud

The Babylonian Talmud shows two distinct phases in its development. The first one, spanning the Amoraïc period in the third century, is strictly parallel to the activities in the Land of Israel: intensive research for collections of *baraitot* and systematization based on the Mishnah. The second period was started by the heads of the academy of Pum Beditha in the first quarter of the fourth century, Rabba (Rav Abba bar Naḥmani) and Rav Joseph (bar Ḥiyya), who introduced the method of dialectical analysis to elucidate the underlying principles of chains of laws and whose goal was a unified understanding of all the vast branches of talmudic rules. This second phase is almost totally lacking in the Jerusalem Talmud. At the time of its compilation, the Galilean Amoraïm acted under enormous pressure from the Christian church and had no time to assimilate new methods. Dialectics is the distincly Babylonian contribution to Jewish thought and is the feature that brought the Babylonian Talmud to be studied exclusively in Northern, and almost exclusively in Southern, Europe. Dialectical hairsplitting, considered the trade-mark of talmudic argument, is characteristic of Babylonian talmudics. As a consequence also, the Jerusalem Talmud is lacking the long arguments that extend over several pages, so characteristic of the Babylonian Talmud. The method of presentation in the present edition of the Jerusalem Talmud, to split the text into its natural paragraphs and to give the translation following the text, would lead to unwieldy, long sections in the Babylonian Talmud.

The relationship between the Babylonian (Babli) and Jerusalem (Yerushalmi) Talmudim is a complicated one. While there is a visible influence of Babylonian teaching on the teachings in the Land of Israel, there is no influence of the Babylonian *Talmud* on the Yerushalmi since the first edition of the Babli, under Rav Ashi, only started when the work on the Yerushalmi was forcibly ended. The Babli we have today, apart from distortions introduced by Gentile censors and generations upon generations of Jewish learned emendators, is the result of a second and third going over by the later Ravina and the group of editors known as *Maranan Savoraë* (about 475-550 C.E.). Any investigation of the influence of the Yerushalmi on the editorial process of the Babli must concentrate on those parts that are recognizeable as the first level of Talmudic activity or on actual decisions, not on the dialectical part. It must also be noted that the two Talmudim are not completely parallel. The tractates on agricultural laws peculiar to the Land of Israel, including the laws of giving and receiving charity, are developed only in the Yerushalmi. The tractates on laws of sacrificing, including ritual slaughtering, are developed only in the Babli.

The influences of the Yerushalmi on the Babli have many aspects. We give examples of some of these aspects.

Babli 'Avodah Zarah 38b:

Statement of law: *Shetitaäh* (a cereal made from roasted flour), Rav permits (to buy from unsupervised Gentile vendors) but Samuel's father[9] and Levi forbid it.

Preliminary discussion: Everybody agrees that it is permitted if made from wheat or barley and that it is forbidden if it is made from peas in vinegar. (Since roasted pea meal is very sweet, it may be necessary to unsweeten it by vinegar and Gentile vinegar is forbidden if made from grapes.) The difference of opinion refers only to cereal made from pea meal with water; one party is of the opinion that one must forbid peas in water so that people would not buy peas in vinegar but the other party does not think it necessary.

Another opinion: Everybody agrees that cereal made from peas is forbidden (for the reason just stated); the disagreement is over wheat or barley. One party thinks one must forbid one because of the other, the other party does not think so.

Side remark: Rav said: Barzilai the Gileadite sent both kinds of *shetitaäh* to David, as it is written (*2Sam.* 17::27-28): "a couch, basins, pottery, wheat, barley, flour, roasted; as well as beans, peas, and roasted[10]."

Conclusion: Today, *shetitaäh* is brought in barrels to the markets of Nahardea and nobody cares for the opinion of Samuel's father and Levi, although Samuel's father was the head of the academy of Nahardea and

---

9 His name is Abba bar Abba; this shows that he was a posthumous child. Since this is a very unfortunate circumstance, such persons are usually described by circumlocutions; cf. E. Guggenheimer and H. Guggenheimer, *Etymologisches Lexikon der jüdischen Familiennamen*, München 1996, p. xviii.

10 The two mentions of "roasted" refer to the two kinds of *shetitaäh*.

his rulings should be followed in his home town. (It is clear that "today" does not mean the time of the edition of the Talmud, since Nahardea was destroyed in the middle of the third century; it refers to Rav's lifetime.)

It seems difficult to understand why Rav's side remark could take the place of a reasoned discussion on the merits of the positions of the parties. Also, the Talmud seems to approve of the actions of the populace of Nahardea even though Rav himself was known to insist that wrong actions of the unlearned should never be condoned. It follows that the side remark is no side remark at all but is Rav's proof of his position and that, in the opinion of the editors, the opposing party had no counter argument. The reason seems to be that the Yerushalmi was known to all students of the Babli. There, *Qiddushin* 2:1, fol. 45b, we find a discussion of the verses *Neh.* 7:63-65, dealing with priestly families returning from Babylonia: "The descendants of Barzilai; they married of the daughters of Barzilai and were called after them. These tried to find the documents of their [priestly] status but without success, so they were excluded from the priesthood. The governor told them not to eat most holy things until there would be a priest for Urim and Tummin[11]." The Talmud comments: "These daughters of Barzilai, did they convert honestly or with ulterior motives[12]? If they (the daughters of Barzilai) converted honestly, they (their male descendants) should eat most holy things; if they converted with ulterior motives, they should not eat any holy things[13]! Even if you

11 The divine oracle carried by the High Priest that could be asked to decide their case. But there was no oracle in the Second Temple.

12 In order to be able to marry a Jewish husband without really accepting all teachings of Judaism.

13 Since their sons would not be Jews, much less priests.

say that they converted honestly, is a convert not like a prostitute as far as marrying a Cohen goes[14]? Explain that they were not daughters but daughters of daughters[15]." The entire discussion makes sense only if we assume that Barzilai, who appears as partner of Shovi ben Naḥash the Ammonite from Rabbat Ammon, was not a Jew. Hence, the problem of Rav and the father of Samuel was decided 1200 years earlier by David, who accepted both kinds of *shetitaäh* from Gentiles. It follows that, although in general the second opinion given in the Talmud is the authoritative one, here we follow the first opinion of the preliminary discussion, and the people of Nahardea were completely right to follow the ruling of King David against that of their own rabbi, Abba bar Abba.

Both Talmudim are written in very condensed form and, in large parts, are intelligible only on the basis of orally transmitted explanations. Such an oral tradition is missing for the Yerushalmi; hence, today it is impossible to understand the Yerushalmi without first having acquired a thorough understanding of the thought processes underlying the stereotyped language of the Babli. Even so it is wrong to assume that the Yerushalmi must be understood in the sense of the Babli; quite the contrary: since the Babli assumes that one knows the Yerushalmi, it is incumbent upon the student of the Yerushalmi to analyze the formulations and to understand the modifications introduced by the editors of the Babli. Any subject discussed in the Yerushalmi and not taken up by the Babli may be considered as having been accepted in

---

14 As Ezechiel said (*Ez.* 44:22), they should only marry "virgins from the seed of the house of Israel;" i. e., born to two Jewish parents.

15 Their mothers had converted and married Jewish husbands. Then the daughters were "from the seed of the house of Israel."

practice by the editors of the Babli and represents current practice. [This is the explicit attitude of Alfassi (end of *'Eruvin*, § 687). Maimonides, who is reported to have compiled a list of the laws contained in the Yerushalmi, admits not only the Yerushalmi, but also the halakhic Midrashim as independent sources of Halakhah[16].] It must be noted that for those parts of the Mishnah for which there is only a Yerushalmi, the quotes in the Babli often are just quotes and not a reworking of the Yerushalmi. [Since Ashkenazic prayer texts are basically of Yerushalmi origin, their adaptation to Babylonian patterns was a very slow process extending over the last 1000 years; in many prayer practices we still follow Yerushalmi opinions against explicit Babylonian rules to the contrary as noted by Tosaphot, *'Arakhin* 3a, s. v. לאיתויי.]

The oral tradition of the Babli, as transmitted in the Babylonian academies during the 500 years following the edition of the Talmud, has come to us in a very fragmentary state in responsa of the Babylonian Geonim and their books, in a more complete way in the commentary of R. Ḥananel of Kairawan in Tunisia, the commentary ascribed to R. Gershom of Mayence, and, above all, in the commentary of Rashi (R. Shelomo ben Isaac of Troyes, 1040-1105). Rashi was a student of R. Jacob ben Yaqar, a student of R. Gershom ben Yehudah, who was a student of Rav Hai Gaon. Hence, he was continuing the living Babylonian tradition, just as R. Ḥananel was both through his father R. Ḥushiel who had studied

---

16 In the introduction to Mishneh Torah, he writes: "From the two Talmudim, Tosephta, Sifra, and Sifri, from all of these is made clear what is forbidden and was is permitted . . . ." For example, in Mishneh Torah, *Hilkhot Isurē Bi'ah* 21:8 he follows *Sifra Aḥarē* Parashah 9:8 [and its parallel Yerushalmi *Giṭṭin* 8:10 (fol. 49c)], with an incongruous attempt to accomodate the contrary decision of the Babli,

in Babylonia and through extensive correspondence with Rav Hai Gaon. Since Rashi always notes when his explanation deviates from that of his teachers, we may assume that his commentaries represent the historic interpretation of the Babylonian Talmud. Rabbenu Ḥananel quotes the Yerushalmi very frequently; his student R. Isaac Alfassi brought the Kairawan tradition to Spain and with it the study of the Yerushalmi as a tool for the understanding of the Babli. On the other hand, it seems that Rashi never saw a copy of the Yerushalmi except the section *Zeraïm* dealing with the laws of the Land of Israel; his quotes of Yerushalmi material in matters of *halakhah* are from sources originating in the Babylonian academies.

The commentary to the Babli tractate *Nazir,* which goes under the name of Rashi, is not by Rashi himself but by his son-in-law, Yehudah bar Natan. It may be assumed that everything R. Yehudah bar Natan knew, he learned from Rashi. At the end of chapter 3 (20b), commenting on the words of the Talmud: "Can you say that Rav formulated a stringent rule and would not agree to a simple consequence?" R. Yehudah bar Natan explained that "the stringent rule" referred to here is not found in the Babli at all, but in Yerushalmi *Sanhedrin* 5:2 (fol. 22d). Since the study of the commentary of Rabbenu Ḥananel, and with it knowledge of the Yerushalmi, came to Northern France only in the generation of Rashi's grandsons, we see not only that the Babli takes a statement in the Yerushalmi for granted but also that the corresponding tradition was preserved in the Babylonian academies.

In Babli *Sabbath* 85a, on Rebbi Ḥiyya bar Abba's discussion of the verse (*Deut.* 19:14): "Do not move the boundary of your neighbor which

---

Yebamot 76a.

the early ones designated," the Talmud explains that the 'early ones' were the Sons of Seïr called Ḥorites in *Gen.* 36:20, but a man of their tribe is called a Ḥiwwite in 36:2; otherwise Ḥiwwites appear in Genesis as inhabitants of Sichem, and neither of these groups has any connection with Amorites. Rashi explains "the early ones" as "Amorites and Ḥiwwites." The Amorites belong to the Canaanites that the same R. Ḥiyya bar Abba declares as authors of the boundaries in Yerushalmi *Kil'aim* 4:6; Rashi's explanation is based on a Yerushalmi tradition.

Aggadic parts of the Babylonian Talmud frequently are shortened versions of Yerushalmi sermons; the reader will find several examples in the present volume, *Berakhot*, e. g., in Halakhot 4:3, 5:7. In general, as explained above, Midrashim and midrashic material are from the Land of Israel. Many medieval authors, in particular Ashkenazic ones, have a tendency to call all midrashic sources "Yerushalmi."

The current text of the Babli has undergone many changes in the course of centuries, either through Christian censors [mainly the Jesuit censor of the Basel print (1578-1581) and the Russian censor of the Wilna print (1859-1866)] and 17th century Jewish emendators (those of Solomon Lurie, *Maharshal*, and Samuel Eliezer Halevi Idels, *Maharsha*, have been absorbed into the text and are now unrecognizable as such[17]). The early manuscript tradition of the Talmud is unknown; most early copies of the Talmud have been burned by the Church. In the case of reading differences between the untampered-with first Venice prints (after 1520, mainly based on Sephardic or Byzantine manuscripts) and the only

17 The process has been documented in detail by R. Raphael Rabbinovicz in the introduction to the first volume of his *Diqduqe Sopherim*, Munich 1867 (Reprint New York 1960), and in a separate volume on the printing of the Talmud.

completely preserved Talmud of the Ashkenazic tradition (Munich manuscript, written 1343), it is often difficult to decide which version is preferable. The manuscript tradition of the Yerushalmi is still poorer; there is only one reasonably complete manuscript (Leyden) that is the main *Vorlage* of the Venice print, one not very good manuscript of the first part (*Zeraïm*, agricultural laws) and *Soṭah*, and a few Genizah fragments. But the text of the Yerushalmi, not being studied very much, has escaped the hands of emendators, and, having been published before the time of the Council of Trent, also those of the Christian censors. Hence, in parallel passages, the Yerushalmi can be a valuable tool in selecting the uncorrupted reading in the Babli.

The printed editions of the Babli read in *Bava Qama* 112b: "Rav Ashi said in the name of Rebbi Sabbatai." The reading of the Munich manuscript and an Alfassi manuscript is: "Rav Joseph in the name of R. Sabbatai." Some manuscripts, as well as the printed versions of Alfassi and R. Asher ben Yeḥiel (*Rosh*) read: "Rebbi Assi in the name of R. Sabbatai." R. Raphael Rabbinovicz, the author of *Diqduqe Soferim*, already noted that the last reading is the only correct one. The parallel in the Yerushalmi (*Sanhedrin* 2:10, fol. 25d) reads: "R. Yose in the name of R. Sabbatai." R. Z. Frankel in his *Mavo Hayerushalmi* (Breslau 1870) and R. Arieh Leib Yellin in *Yefe Enaim ad loc.* (in the Wilna Talmud) note that the Babylonian Rebbi Assi, who became head of academy and famous authority in Galilee, is called R. Yose or R. Yasa in the Yerushalmi. Hence, the third reading is the only correct one and the second one resulted from a misguided "correct" writing of the shortened name Yose as Biblical Joseph (and does not refer to Rav Joseph bar Ḥiyya.)

In Babli *Sanhedrin* 51a: "Ravin (Rebbi Avin) sent in the name of R. Yose ben R. Ḥanina." In the parallel in the Yerushalmi (*Sanhedrin* 7:1, fol.

24b): "Rebbi Abbahu in the name of R. Yose ben R. Ḥanina." The Yerushalmi version is the correct one since Ravin emigrated to Babylonia and taught in the Yeshivot there; he had no need to send anything by mail.

A frequently vexing question in the Babli is the distinction to be made between sayings of רבה Rabba, Rav Abba bar Naḥmani, and those of his student רבא Rava, Rav Abba bar Rav Joseph bar Ḥama. However, many times the author of the statement in question is neither Rabba nor Rava, but rather one of the many Palestinian Amoraïm named Rebbi Abba (רבי אבא, רבי בא, רבי ווא). For example, in *Yebamot* 102a, the prints read: "Rabba said in the name of Rav Cahana who said in the name of Rav," but Alfassi and Rosh read: "Rava." In the parallel in the Yerushalmi, *Yebamot* 12:1 (fol. 12c), the statement is by "Rebbi Abba in the name of Rav Yehudah in the name of Rav." This Rebbi Abba was a Babylonian, student of Rav Huna as was Rabba, who emigrated to Galilee and there became an important teacher. Even though we cannot distinguish in the Babli between Rabba and Rebbi Abba, we can exclude the reading "Rava" with confidence.

In *Yebamot* 49a there is a question whether to read "R. Joshua" or "R. Yehudah" in the Mishnah. A parallel discussion in Yerushalmi *Qiddushin* 3:14 (fol. 64d) decides the matter clearly in favor of the first reading.

The Yerushalmi often is useful in rejecting emendations of or detecting insertions into the text of the Babli. For example, in *Avodah Zarah* 14a, a statement introduced by דתניא "for it was proclaimed in a *baraita*," is emended by the editors to דתנן "for it was proclaimed in a Mishnah," referring to the Mishnah on p. 8a. However, the Yerushalmi and the Mishnah manuscripts of the Palestinian tradition (and Alfassi manuscripts) do not have the clause in question; one must conclude that it was introduced into the Mishnah of the Babli from the later *baraita*, after the final edition of the Babli but long before any of the surviving manuscripts of the Babli were written.

In *Berakhot* 48a, in a discussion of the relationship between king Yannai and Simeon ben Shetaḥ, the printed Talmud text has: "Rebbi Abba, son of R. Ḥiyya bar Abba, said in the name of R. Yoḥanan." The last clause is missing in the Munich manuscript and this is the preferred reading of R. Rabbinovicz, and, for reasons of talmudic style, of R. Isaiah Berlin. However, the parallel in the Yerushalmi (6:2, fol. 11b), clearly designates R. Yoḥanan as author of the statement. Hence, unevenness of style is no argument in judging the text of the Talmud.

Similarly, the usual style of the Babli is to call הלכה למשה מסיני, "practice going back to Moses on Sinai" any rule that is part of the establishment of Jewish practice by Ezra and Neḥemiah, and simply הלכה, "practice," any decision inserted by the last editors. In the Yerushalmi there are no decisions inserted by the editors and "practice" there has the same meaning as "practice going back to Moses on Sinai" in the Babli. However, "practice" in Babli *Giṭṭin* 18a is the same as "practice" in Yerushalmi *Yebamot* 4:11 (fol. 6b). Hence, this is not an insertion of the last editors and, here also, stylistic uniformity is not a necessity in the Babli. [However, as mentioned earlier, R. Eliahu Raḥamim Ziani considers all or most insertions of the last editors as taken from the Yerushalmi.]

Another example of the importance of the Yerushalmi for the simple understanding of the Babli is the statement of Rava in *Berakhot* 15b: "In reading the *Shema'*, one has to be careful in the reading, among other words, of עשב בשדך *'ēsev bĕsādĕkhā*." It is known that the alternative pronunciations of בגדכפת, while their existence in ancient Hebrew speech is corroborated by Phoenician sources, were not observed in daily speech in the Talmudic period. So the fear is that one will say either *ēsev vĕsādĕkhā* or *ēseb bĕsādĕkhā* and pronounce the two words as one. Which of these possibilities is the background of the saying? Rava's statement appears as an anonymous statement in Yerushalmi *Berakhot* 2:4 (fol. 4d). It is known that during the Talmudic period in Galilee, under the influence of spoken Greek, every ב,בּ was pronounced β = /*v*/. (In later times, many Jewish communities in Arabic speaking countries lost the soft "*b*".) The statement of Rava does not give information about the phonetics of Babylonian Jewish speech.

The intricate relationship between Yerushalmi and Babli is another indication of the true historical character of the Talmudim and it shows that the thesis, that the Babli was written, not edited, by the Savoraë, has no basis in fact. The last Babylonian teacher mentioned in the Yerushalmi is Rava; this shows that the editing of the Yerushalmi came to an end long before Rav Ashi and the first collection of the Babli.

R. Eliahu Raḥamim Ziani[18] has argued recently that the *Maranan Savaraë* inserted many of the decisions of the Yerushalmi into the Babli.

There exists an extensive literature[19] but as yet no exhaustive investigation on all these problems.

---

18 רבנן סבוראי וכללי הלכה, Haifa 1992.

19 Numerous Journal articles and, among others, the books

H. Albeck, מחקרים בברייתא ותוספתא ויחסן לתלמוד, Mossad Harav Kook, Jerusalem 1969.

Zwi Moshe Dor, תורת ארץ־ישראל בבבל, Dvir, Tel Aviv 1971.

J. N. Epstein, מבואות לספרות האמוראים, Magnes-Dvir 1949.

J. N. Epstein, מבוא לנוסח המשנה, Magnes-Dvir 1964.

Z. Frankel, מבוא הירושלמי, Breslau 1870.

E. Shechter, המשנה בבבלי וירושלמי, Mossad Harav Kook, Jerusalem 1959.

Introduction to the Talmud Yerushalmi

Text of the Jerusalem Talmud

As mentioned earlier, there exists only one reasonably complete manuscript of the Yerushalmi and its text is mostly identical with that of the Venice print, 1522-23. Both in the manuscript and in the printed edition, several chapters at the end of tractates are missing; these probably were lost during the centuries. There exists one other manuscript, in Rome, containing the entire first order and tractate *Soṭah* of the third order, and some remnants of manuscripts from the Cairo Genizah. The scribe of the Rome manuscript was neither careful nor educated; nevertheless, the manuscript is useful in many places. A manuscript of the Fourth Order of the Yerushalmi is in the Escurial library in Madrid. In establishing a correct text it is useful that parallel discussions in different tractates are copied word by word from one another; hence, the text at one place can be used to check the text at another place. This is not true for the Babli; there, no two parallel discussions are identical.

In addition, quotes of the Yerushalmi in Gaonic literature can be considered verbally correct. The quotes in later medieval authors have to be used with caution. First, they often are paraphrases and not exact quotes and, second, Ashkenazic authors call "Yerushalmi" anything of Palestinian origin, including (or even, mainly) midrashic sources. Some modern authors even postulate the existence of a separate Ashkenazic "Yerushalmi book," containing practical rules from Yerushalmi and Midrashim. (Fragments that might be viewed as such a text have lately been identified by J. Sussman.) In any case, the uncertainty is so great that quotes by medieval authors may be used for meaning but not as sources of the text.

The Venice text was reprinted, with a few additional typographical errors and a very rudimentary commentary, at Cracow in 1620. This edition was later reproduced (Krotoschin 1866, New York 1948). The edition mostly in use today is the Wilna edition from the 1920's, which is indispensable because of the many commentaries added to the text. However, the text in many places has been emended, mostly following the Babli, and the division into Halakhot in many places does not follow the manuscript evidence. This is true also for an earlier Zhitomir edition. It will be seen in our text that the Yerushalmi needs no emendations.

Since there is no Babylonian Talmud on the first order of the Mishnah, *Zeraïm*, except for the first tractate, *Berakhot*, the two medieval standard commentaries on that Mishnah, those of Maimonides and of R. Simson of Sens, are based largely on the Yerushalmi and the corresponding Tosephta. In many places, R. Simson directly comments on the Yerushalmi; his readings have the weight of a minor manuscript. The present edition is intended to cover all of *Zeraïm*, complementing the Babylonian Talmud.

Two of the early modern commentators of the Yerushalmi, R. Shelomo Cirillo in Safed in the 16th century and R. Eliahu Fulda around 1700, produced their own texts of the first order of the Yerushalmi. The sources of R. Cirillo are unknown; since his text is contemporary with but independent of the Venice print, he must have had manuscripts at his disposal. It is not clear whether his deviations from the Venice text are based on manuscript evidence or are conjectural smoothings of the text and adaptations to the Babli. His spelling definitely shows a copyist used to Babylonian texts. Hence, his readings cannot be used as substitutes of the Venice text without corroborating evidence. His text in manuscript is in the British Museum; it has been partially published only in this century (the first few tractates were added to the last Wilna print.) The deviations in the text of R. Eliahu Fulda almost certainly are his own changes.

The oldest surviving commentary on the Yerushalmi after R. Cirillo, for tractate *Berakhot* only, is by R. Eleazar Ascari of Safed. This is also one of the best commentaries available and the present editor is much indebted to him. At the same time, R. Samuel Yafeh Ashkenazi in Constantinople (Istanbul) wrote a commentary on the midrashic parts of the Yerushalmi. His readings, as well as those of the seventeenth century Constantinople halakhic commentary *Sedeh Yehoshua* by R. Joshua Benvenist, seem to be based on manuscripts of the Sephardic community there; but these manuscripts have not come down to us.

In the eighteenth century, there appeared two comprehensive commentaries on the Yerushalmi. R. David Fraenkel wrote a commentary and notes on those parts not dealt with by R. Eliahu Fulda (1743-1762). R. Moses Margalit wrote a commentary on the entire Yerushalmi, published between 1750 and 1770. R. Margalit is unsurpassed in explaining the difficulties of the text; for the resolutions of the difficulties, R. David Fraenkel is a much better guide. R. Margalit is an extreme emender of the text. Somewhat later, the Gaon Eliahu of Wilna rekindled interest in the Yerushalmi among his students; he himself also wrote short commentaries on the first order of the Yerushalmi and gave many emendations of the text, practically all of them inspired by the Babli.

The most important work of the nineteenth century on the Yerushalmi is that of R. Zacharias Frankel, founder of the Rabbinical Seminary of Breslau. His "Introduction to the Yerushalmi" (Breslau 1870) is still most valuable, as are his commentaries of the first tractates of the Yerushalmi.

His successor, R. Israel Lewy, wrote the standard commentary on tractate *Bava Qama*, which was published in the annual reports of the Breslau seminary from 1895-1914. For most tractates of the Babli, the commentary *Yefe Enayim* by R. Arieh Leib Yelin (Wilna, 1880-1886, based on earlier work by Joshua Heshel, Wilna 1869) is a safe and almost complete guide to parallels found in the Yerushalmi and midrashic literature. For certain tractates, the commentaries and notes of R. Jacob David of Słuck (published 1900) are also valuable. A French translation by M. Schwab (published 1872 ff.) of the entire Jerusalem Talmud, with minimal notes and based on a text distorted by numerous emendations, is now available on a CD-ROM (*Le Talmud de Jérusalem*, Editions Les temps Qui Coulent, Paris 1998).

The quotations from the Yerushalmi in the medieval sources then known were collected by Dov Baer Ratner in the twelve volumes of his work *Ahavat Zion wiYerushalaim*, Wilna 1901-1917. However, as noted before, these quotations have to be used with caution. Earlier, two brothers-in-law, R. Mordecai Zeëv Ettinger and R. Joseph Saul Nathanson of Lviv (Lemberg), used these quotations in a reasoned approach, to try to establish the text of the Yerushalmi. Their notes were published in the Zhitomir edition, 1860-1867. A much larger work, based on their approach and the work of Ratner, was produced by Samuel Shraga Feigensohn for the Wilna edition of the Yerushalmi. Feigensohn also produced an introduction to the Yerushalmi, taken, with acknowledgement, mainly from R. Z. Frankel's work.

Of twentieth century works, the most useful, if used with proper care, are the commentary *Tevunah* by R. Isaac Eizik Krasilshchikov of Poltava, the works of R. Saul Lieberman (*Talmuda deKesarin*, Jerusalem 1931, *Tosephta kifshuṭah*, New York 1956-1988), L. Ginzburg (*A commentary on the Palestinian Talmud*, New York 1941-1961), the comparison of the Mishnah in both Talmudim by R. Dr. Elimelech Shechter (Jerusalem 1959), and the commentary on the first chapters of *Berakhot* by R. Shelomo Goren (Jerusalem 1961).

Order *Zeraïm*

The tractates of order *Zeraïm*, "Agricultural Laws", treat the following topics:

1. *Berakhot*, "Benedictions," 9 chapters. The laws of prayer, benedictions before and after meals, and sundry benedictions. It is placed at the start of the Mishnah because of the first topic and is part of the discussion of agricultural laws because of the second one.

2. *Peah*, "Corner (of the field)," 8 chapters. The obligation to leave a corner of every field for the poor to harvest, and all similar laws that favor the poor, including the general rules for giving charity and its communal organization.

3. *Demaï*, "Deficient Produce," 7 chapters. Laws about produce bought from a Jew who cannot be trusted to have given the prescribed tithes and their heave as described in the following tractates. Discussion of the relations between observant and ignorant Jews.

4. *Kilaim*, "Mixed (produce; textiles)", 9 chapters. The Biblical prohibitions to plant or sow different species on the same field, cross-breed different species of animals and plants, and to weave wool and linen together.

5. *Sheviït*, "Seventh Year," 10 chapters. The laws of the Sabbatical Year, when all planting and sowing is prohibited, and the laws on the remission of debts in that year.

6. *Terumot*, "Heaves," 11 chapters. The heaves, the obligatory gifts to the priest from any harvest, both from the farmer and from the Levite who receives the tithe, and the laws of ritual purity applying to heaves.

7. *Ma'serot*, "Tithes", 5 chapters. The tithe to be given to the Levite, the "second tithe" that in the years 1,2,4,5 of any sabbatical cycle is eaten by the farmer and his family in Jerusalem, and the "tithe of the poor" to be given in years 3,6 of that cycle.

8. *Ma'ser sheni*, "Second Tithe," 5 chapters. The rules applying in Jerusalem to all food that must be consumed there, be it the second tithe or any similar obligation such as the fruits of the fourth year of a newly planted tree or vineyard, and the redemption of such food by money.

9. *Ḥallah*, 4 chapters. The rules for taking the priest's share from any dough in ritual purity.

10. *Orlah*, 3 chapters. The rules for treating a fruit tree the first three years after its planting when its fruit may not be eaten.

11. *Bikkurim*, "First Fruits", 3 chapters. The rules of designating first fruits for dedication to the Temple and the ceremonies of their presentation in the Temple.

This Edition of the Talmud Yerushalmi

The text of the Talmud given in this edition is that of the Venice print except that in cases of obvious misprints or scribal errors a manuscript text (from the Rome manuscript or Genizah fragments) or a text from an exact parallel in another tractate has been substituted, all with due acknowledgement. The reading of the Venice print is given in a note attached to the substituted word in the text. At several places (e. g. *Peah* 1:2), it can be seen from manuscripts that the "obvious" correction of scribal errors accepted by the commentators is incorrect and that the correct term is not one the Babli would have used. Since all editors and commentators are trained in the Babli, conjectural emendations are always inadmissible in the Yerushalmi. In addition, abbreviations have been expanded into full words. Nowhere has the Venice text been changed without manuscript evidence, except in the resolution of abbreviations; in a few places where there was no manuscript evidence but readings in medieval authors, the text has been left unchanged, but the translation, as fully explained in the notes, follows the medieval interpretation.

Spelling is remarkably uniform in the several manuscript sources of the Yerushalmi. The rules of this spelling are quite different from those of the Babli. The Aramaic of the Yerushalmi is Galilean and is consistent with other Galilean sources; the Aramaic in the Babli is Babylonian. Spelling in the Babli is historical; the vowel letters (*matres lectionis*) ו,י serve to indicate long vowels *ō, ū; ī, ē*. In the Yerushalmi, spelling is phonetic with silent א,ה,ח,ע often elided; ו,י stand for long and short *o, u; i*. One also finds י consistently used as a sign for *zērē* ֵ, but since this vowel is identical with Greek η, which is *ī* in modern Greek, it is possible that ֵי was pronounced as if it were ִי. The influence of Greek is also seen in the phonetic equivalence of ו, בּ, ב, corresponding to β (*weta*), and often in the equivalence of שׂ,שׁ,ס.

Biblical quotes in the Talmud text were usually written by the scribe from memory and, hence, do not follow the masoretic rules of *plene* and defective spelling and, sometimes, not even the exact wording. These quotes have been left as they appear in the manuscript and have not been "corrected" to the official biblical spelling.

In the Venice print, the Mishnah for each chapter is given at the start of the chapter; this is also usual in manuscripts of the Babli. In the present edition, the Mishnah is given immediately before the relevant Halakhah. Inconsistent numbering of Halakhot has been made consistent wherever possible without changing the text. The text has been subdivided into logical units. Since Yerushalmi manuscripts and prints insert frequent periods, this division is easy to make and is quite natural. The logical sequence of these units is usually obvious; if not, it has been commented upon.

The English translation is the result of an independent new study of the text; the notes are addressed to a reader with a rudimentary knowledge of rabbinic literature in general and the Babli in particular. For the understanding of the text of tractate Berakhot, I found the commentary by R. Eleazar Ascari to be the most useful, but naturally I also consulted the other standard commentaries as well as the works of R. Zacharias Frankel, Levi Ginzburg, and R. Saul Lieberman. I have tried to give a consistent account of the meaning of the text; I did not try to write an encyclopedia of all proposed interpretations. Technical terms as abbreviations for long explanations have been retained as essential elements of Talmudic style. The interpretation of these terms, as well as the identification of botanical and zoological names, follows the oldest sources available.

The text has been vocalized. In the vocalization of the Aramaic portions, I have followed the language of the Jerusalem *Targumim* to the Hebrew Bible. Aramaic in the Yerushalmi is used only in the description of the speech of the unlearned and in a few aggadic inserts describing sermons. Discussions between scholars are always reported in rabbinic Hebrew. The Aramaisms (and Grecisms and Latinisms) of that language have to be considered as part of the Hebrew used, not as Aramaic or Greek, and are assumed to follow Hebrew vocalization rules.

Any attempt to vocalize rabbinic Hebrew texts raises difficult questions. As S. Morag has pointed out, vocalization of rabbinic Hebrew has never been standardized. It is inappropriate to use the rules of Biblical Hebrew for Talmudic and Medieval texts since in all dialects rabbinic Hebrew was stressed on the penultimate syllable. The traditions of Oriental communities (Yemen, Baghdad, Persia) derive from Babylonian sources as exemplified by the Babylonian supralinear punctuation. A vocalization of the Yerushalmli should be based on Occidental sources but the remnants of Palestinian supralinear punctuation in Mishnaic texts are too few to serve as guidance. Since the study of the Yerushalmi was introduced to Northern and Southern Europe by the scholars of Kairawan in Tunesia, it is appropriate that the vocalization should follow Sephardic rules.

In the present text, I did not try to reconstruct Mishnaic and Amoraic Hebrew based on one of the theories proposed on that subject, but I have followed rabbinic Sephardic tradition as expressed by eighteenth century vocalized texts from Livorno. The Livorno standard recognizes *dagesh forte*, uses *meteg* (ָֽ) only to indicate wide *qamaẓ* (ā) before *shewa*, and *maqqef* to indicate short *qamaẓ* (ŏ). *Shewa* after a long vowel is silent, otherwise the rules of Biblical Hebrew apply. In order not to change the text, the *dagesh* has been eliminated in cases where double consonants וו, יי take the place of a single Hebrew consonant with a *dagesh*. Vocalization is always added disregarding *matres lectionis*.

Ashkenazic rabbinic Hebrew had lost *meteg, maqqef*, and *dagesh forte* long before any surviving vocalized text was written. It pronounces *shewa* only if absolutely necessary for the formation of the word. The appearance of *meteg, maqqef*, and *dagesh forte* in modern Ashkenazic prayer books is a result of the return to biblical patterns demanded by

Eliahu Wilna and Moses Mendelsohn in the second half of the Eighteenth Century. An argument can be made that the pronunciation of the Yerushalmi was close to Medieval Ashkenazic rabbinic Hebrew, i. e., Ashkenazic with "Sephardic" vowels. A good sourcebook for the problems of vocalization of rabbinic texts is קובץ מאמרים בלשון חז״ל, הביא לדפוס משה בר־אשר, ירושלים תשל״ב.

All abbreviations in the text have been expanded. Where needed, the titles Rebbi, Rav have been corrected without comment. Biographical notes, as far as such details are known, have been given for all persons quoted in the Talmud with special emphasis on the time of their activity. This is important for the understanding of the sequence of statements on any topic treated.

Words of Greek and Latin origin have been identified as such; the original words are given in footnotes. Since Greek was the spoken language of most of the Gentile population in Galilee, it is the custom in "scholarly" treatment of Talmudic topics to refer Latinate words to their Byzantine Greek equivalents. But since the Eastern Roman empire (i. e., Byzantium) was administered in Latin until its destruction by the Western crusaders, there is no reason not to derive these words directly from the Latin. While the Hebrew and Aramaic spelling of the Yerushalmi often seems to defy all rules, Greek and Latin words are transcribed with astonishing fidelity.

The detailed grammar of the Yerushalmi is mostly unexplored. R. Z. Frankel, in his Introduction to the Yerushalmi (Breslau 1870), declares the Yerushalmi to be unmindful of grammatical rules. However, the most striking deviation of the Yerushalmi from normative Hebrew and Aramaic grammars, the occasional use of the third person singular form of a verb for all persons, genders, and numbers, is also found at a few places in the Jerusalem Targum and, therefore, has to be considered a characteristic feature of the speech of the times. Spelling, morphology, and syntax of the Yerushalmi should be recognized as following their own rules.

Tractate Berakhot

Tractate *Berakhot*, "benedictions," deals roughly with four different topics. i) The first three chapters deal with the rules of recitation of *Shema'*. The third chapter contains general rules of prayer for people with certain disabilities; most of these rules apply equally to the recitation of *Shema'*, prayer proper (the *'Amidah*), and reciting Grace after meals. ii) Chapters four and five deal with laws of the *'Amidah*, the eighteen benedictions on weekdays and seven on Sabbath and holidays. iii) Chapter six treats the benedictions to be recited before eating; chapter seven treats Grace after meals. These chapters justify the position of the tractate at the head of the order *Zeraïm* of the Mishnah dealing with agricultural laws in all their ritual aspects. Chapter eight treats several other subjects connected with festive dinners. iv) Chapter nine finally treats all other kinds of benedictions that appear in the Jewish prayer book.

מאימתי פרק ראשון

(fol. 2a) **משנה א**: מֵאֵימָתַי קוֹרִין אֶת שְׁמַע בָּעֲרָבִין. מִשָּׁעָה שֶׁהַכֹּהֲנִים נִכְנָסִין לוֹכֶל בִּתְרוּמָתָן עַד סוֹף הָאַשְׁמוּרָה הָרִאשׁוֹנָה דִּבְרֵי רַבִּי אֱלִיעֶזֶר. וַחֲכָמִים אוֹמְרִים עַד חֲצוֹת. רַבָּן גַּמְלִיאֵל אוֹמֵר עַד שֶׁיַּעֲלֶה עַמּוּד הַשַּׁחַר.

Mishnah 1: When does one start to read the *Shema* in the evening[1]? From the time that the priests enter to eat[2] their *Terumah*[3], until the end of the first night watch[4] are the words of Rebbi Eliezer[5]. But the Sages say until midnight. Rabban Gamliel says until the first sign of dawn[6].

1 The Mishnah presupposes that everybody knows that there is an obligation to recite the verses *Deut*. 6:4-9 since it is written (v. 7) "You shall teach them to your children and speak about them when you sit in your house, when you go on the road, and when you are lying down and when you are getting up." Since it says "when you are lying down" before "when you are getting up", the obligation of the evening is discussed before that of the morning.

2 The spelling of the Yerushalmi is largely phonetic, in contrast to the Babli whose Hebrew spelling is historical. Since the א was silent in Galilean speech of the time and had lost its role as glottal stop, the Mishnah in the Yerushalmi has לוֹכֶל for classical לֶאֱכוֹל in the Babylonian Mishnah.

3 *Terumah*, the heave, is the gift to the Cohen from agricultural produce (*Num*. 18:12) and also the Cohen's part of the tithes given to the Levites from produce (*Num*. 18:26). These gifts must be eaten in ritual purity (*Num*. 18:13: "every pure person in your family may eat it.") There are several stages in the cleansing from ritual impurity. Serious impurities (defilement by a corpse, a leper, or a sufferer from gonorrhea) need special rituals. More common defilements, such as touching a dead animal or coming in contact with a more severely impure person, need

immersion in the ritual bath (*miqweh*). This immersion removes impurity but does not yet allow a person to touch sanctified food or to enter the Temple before nightfall, as it is said (*Lev*. 22:6-7): "He may not eat of sanctified food unless he immersed himself in water. When the sun leaves he shall be purified and after that he may eat of the sanctified food." [For the more severe kinds of impurity, a sacrifice is needed before the Cohen may eat sacred food in the Temple; this does not concern us here.] The Halakhah will discuss the exact meaning of "the sun leaving" and its relation to sunset and nightfall.

Today, no Cohen may eat any *Terumah* and the minimal amount set apart for *Terumah* must be burned; it is ritually unclean from the start since nowadays everybody is defiled by the impurity of dead bodies. That impurity can be removed only by sprinkling with water treated with the ashes of the Red Heifer (*Num*. 19). The Mishnah was edited approximately between 200 and 220 C. E. It must be assumed that the rules of the Mishnah are intended to be practical. It follows that 130 years after the destruction of the Temple there were still places in Israel where the Cohanim could purify themselves by the ashes of the Red Heifer (in Galilee which was only minimally damaged by the two wars with the Romans.)

4 The night is divided either into three (Babylonian) or four (Roman) watches.

5 The name of R. Eliezer is attached only to the statement about the night watch. The start of the time of the evening *Shema* is accepted by everybody. Rebbi Eliezer ben Hyrcanus was one of the foremost students of Rabban Yoḥanan ben Zakkai, the founder of the Synhedrion of Jabneh after the destruction of the Temple. He was the most conservative of all teachers of his time and reputed to transmit old traditions most reliably.

6 It will be seen that the difference between Rabban Gamliel and the other sages is practical rather than theoretical. They agree that "when you are lying down" means "all the time that you are lying on your bed" and not "when you are ready to go to bed". The latter interpretation is that of R. Eliezer.

הלכה א. מֵאֵימָתַי קוֹרִין אֶת שְׁמַע בָּעֲרָבִין. אֲנָן תַּנִּינָן מִשָּׁעָה שֶׁהַכֹּהֲנִים נִכְנָסִין לוֹכַל בִּתְרוּמָתָן. תַּנֵּי רִבִּי חִיָּיא מִשָּׁעָה שֶׁדֶּרֶךְ בְּנֵי אָדָם נִכְנָסִין לֶאֱכוֹל פִּיתָּן

בְּלֵילֵי שַׁבָּת. וְתַנֵּי עֲלָהּ קְרוֹבִין דִּבְרֵיהֶן לִהְיוֹת שָׁוִין. אִיתָא חֲמֵי מִשָּׁעָה שֶׁהַכֹּהֲנִים נִכְנָסִין לוֹכַל בִּתְרוּמָתָן יְמָמָא הוּא וְעִם כּוֹכְבַיָּא הוּא. מִשָּׁעָה שֶׁדֶּרֶךְ בְּנֵי אָדָם נִכְנָסִין לֶאֱכוֹל פִּיתָּן בְּלֵילֵי שַׁבָּת שָׁעָה וְתַרְתֵּי לֵילְיָא הוּא. וְאַתְּ אָמַר קְרוֹבִין דִּבְרֵיהֶן לִהְיוֹת שָׁוִין. אָמַר רִבִּי יוֹסֵי תִּפְתָּר בְּאִלֵּין כּוּפְרָנַיָּא דְּקִיקַיָּא דְּאוֹרְחֵיהוֹן מִסְתַּלְּקָא עַד דְּהוּא יְמָמָא דְצָדֵי לוֹן מִקַּמֵּי חַיּוּתָא.

Halakhah 1. When does one start to read the *Shema* in the evening?. We have stated[7]: "From the time that the priests enter to eat their *Terumah*". Rebbi Ḥiyya stated[8]: "From the time that people enter their houses Friday evening to eat their meal." We have stated: "Their opinions are almost identical." Come and see: "From the time that the priests enter to eat their *Terumah*" is still daylight and the stars start to appear[9], "from the time that people enter their houses Friday evening to eat their meal" is one or two hours into the night. You want to say that the two opinions are almost identical? Rebbi Yose[10] said: Explain it by people in hamlets who usually leave the roads when there still is some daylight because they are afraid of wild beasts.

7 תני is the translation of *Targum Yerushalmi* for Hebrew הגד "to tell formally". It is a technical term that implies a statement of Tannaïm, the teachers of the oral law who were active from Maccabean times to the death of Rebbi Yehudah the Prince, the compiler of the Mishnah. The insistence on this being taught, or formulated, repeatedly, shows that a statement introduced by תני is a formal statement, carefully formulated for oral repetition, and not just an *ad hoc* statement in a discussion. The vocalization תַּנֵּי is the prevalent one in the Yerushalmi *Targumim.*

8 Rebbi Ḥiyya is R. Ḥiyya bar Abba bar Aḥa Karsala from Kufra in Babylonia, the greatest of the students and colleagues of Rebbi (Yehuda, the editor of the Mishnah). Rebbi Ḥiyya is credited with collecting the tannaitic material that Rebbi left out of the Mishnah. The collection known as the *Tosephta* is probably based on his material even though in the current form it is a Babylonian rearrangement. Now the Tosephta (*Berakhot* I,1) is

quoted in the Babli (*Berakhot* 2b): מאימתי מתחילין לקרות קרית שמע בערבית משעה שבני אדם נכנסין לאכול פתן בערבי שבתות דברי רבי מאיר וחכמים אומרים משעה שהכהנים זכאין לאכול בתרומתן. "When may one start to read the *Shema* in the evening? From the time that people enter to eat their meals on Friday Evening, says Rebbi Meïr, but the Sages say from the moment that the Cohanim are allowed to eat their *Terumah*." It seems that the Talmud does not indicate that R. Ḥiyya is reported here to quote the Tosephta but that there was a difference of opinion between Rebbi and Rebbi Ḥiyya about which opinion of those mentioned in the Tosephta should be accepted in the Mishnah as authoritative.

There is a fundamental disagreement between the two Talmudim in the interpretation of R. Meïr's opinion. The Babli quotes a second version of R. Meir, "from the time that the Cohanim immerse themselves in order to eat *Terumah*." Since the Cohanim have to concentrate on their status of purity between immersion and eating, in order not to touch unclean matter inadvertently, it is clear that they will immerse themselves at or shortly after sunset, when it is still clearly day and no stars are visible, and start to eat at the earliest moment which can be declared to be night. Hence, the other version of R. Meïr, that people start to eat Friday nights, must also mean an early time. Since people return from work early on Fridays, being notified of the approching Sabbath by the sounding of trumpets (Babli *Šabbat* 35b), they will eat early. In particular in Babylonia, where synagogues were out in the fields, Friday evening services were held so that people could return to town before the unlit roads became completely dark. In Israel, on the other hand, synagogues were in towns and often the sermon was held on Friday evening. It is told in *Lev. rabba* 9(9) that R. Meïr was preaching Friday evenings and even women came to hear the sermon at that time. Hence, the Sabbath meal was late. In Israel, R. Meïr's pronouncement was taken to indicate a very late time.

9 As noted in the preceding comment, the Cohanim start to eat when it is no longer day, but before it is completely dark. The exact definition of "day," "twilight," "night" will be given later in the present section.

10 This R. Yose is the late Galilean Amora R. Yose (probably, ben Zabida), not the Tanna R. Yose ben Ḥalaphta.

תַּנֵּי הַקּוֹרֵא קוֹדֶם לָכֵן לֹא יָצָא יְדֵי חוֹבָתוֹ. אִם כֵּן לָמָּה קוֹרִין אוֹתָהּ בְּבֵית הַכְּנֶסֶת. אָמַר רִבִּי יוֹסֵי אֵין קוֹרִין אוֹתָהּ בְּבֵית הַכְּנֶסֶת בִּשְׁבִיל לָצֵאת יְדֵי חוֹבָתוֹ אֶלָּא כְדֵי לַעֲמוֹד בִּתְפִלָּה מִתּוֹךְ דָּבָר שֶׁל תּוֹרָה:

It was stated: "He who recites (the *Shema'*) before that time did not fulfill his duty." If that is so, why does one recite (the *Shema'*) in the synagogue? Rebbi Yose said: one does not recite it to fulfill one's duty but only to stand in prayer after the study of Torah[11].

11 This section is quoted by Rashi in his commentary of the Mishnah in the Babylonian Talmud. The old Ashkenazic ritual that has preserved the Israeli usages, in contrast to the Sephardic rituals coming from Babylonia, requires that afternoon and evening prayers be said consecutively in the synagogue any time after מִנְחָה קְטַנָּה, $^{5}/_{4}$ hours before sundown (the hour computed as $^{1}/_{12}$th of daylight hours.) Hence, evening prayers with *Shema'* are recited in full daylight. R. Yose declares that after nightfall everybody has to recite the *Shema'* for himself (without benedictions) to fulfill the duty of reciting the *Shema'* at its proper time. In contrast to *Shema'*, the daily prayers are not bound rigidly to their times, as will be explained later in the Talmud.

רִבִּי זְעִירָא בְּשֵׁם רַב יִרְמְיָה סָפֵק בֵּרַךְ עַל מְזוֹנוֹ סָפֵק לֹא בֵּרַךְ צָרִיךְ לְבָרֵךְ דִּכְתִיב וְאָכַלְתָּ וְשָׂבָעְתָּ וּבֵרַכְתָּ. סָפֵק הִתְפַּלֵּל סָפֵק לֹא הִתְפַּלֵּל אַל יִתְפַּלֵּל וּדְלֹא כְּרִבִּי יוֹחָנָן דְּאָמַר רִבִּי יוֹחָנָן (fol. 2b) וּלְוַאי שֶׁיִּתְפַּלֵּל אָדָם כָּל־הַיּוֹם כֻּלּוֹ. לָמָּה שֶׁאֵין תְּפִלָּה מַפְסֶדֶת. סָפֵק קָרָא סָפֵק לֹא קָרָא נִישְׁמְעִינָהּ מֵהָדָא הַקּוֹרֵא קוֹדֶם לָכֵן לֹא יָצָא יְדֵי חוֹבָתוֹ. וְקוֹדֶם לָכֵן לָאו סָפֵק הוּא וְאַתְּ אָמַר צָרִיךְ לִקְרוֹת. הָדָא אָמְרָה סָפֵק קָרָא סָפֵק לֹא קָרָא צָרִיךְ לִקְרוֹת.

Rebbi Zeïra[12] in the name of Rav Jeremiah[13]: One who is in doubt whether he said Grace after his meal or not, must say Grace, since it is written (*Deut.* 8:10): "You will eat and be satiated, then you must praise the Eternal[14], your God[15]". One who who is in doubt whether he prayed or not, may not pray, against the opinion of Rebbi Yoḥanan[16] who said: If only one would pray the whole day long, why? Because prayer is never in vain[17]! About one who is in doubt whether he recited (the *Shema'*) or not we may hear from this: He who recites (the *Shema'*) before that time did not fulfill his duty. And before that time is it not doubtful[18]? This means that one who is in doubt whether he recited (the *Shema*) or not must recite again[19].

12 Rebbi Zeïra was a Babylonian who appears in the Babylonian Talmud as Rebbi Zera; he rose to be head of the Yeshivah of Tiberias after Rebbi Yoḥanan.

13 Rav Jeremiah appears in the Babylonian Talmud as Rav Jeremiah bar Abba, one of the outstanding students of Rav. He should not be identified with Rebbi Jeremiah, a Babylonian and student of Rebbi Zeïra in Galilee.

14 There is a problem how the Divine Name YHWH should be translated. The traditional "Lord", taken from the Septuagint, is a translation not of the Name but of its substitute *ădōnāi*. The vocalization of the Name is unknown. The root is certainly הוה "to exist". The form of the name indicates either *qal* or *pi'el*, with a meaning "Eternal" or a *hif'il*, meaning "Creator". Probably it means both but for purposes of translation it is convenient to follow Mendelssohn and use the first meaning. [The so-called "scholarly" *hif'il* vocalization, *yahweh* "Creator," is certainly false since theophorous names show that the first syllable is vocalized either *yā*, *yô*, or *yĕ*, never *yah*, and, hence, as is to be expected, the Name does not follow any normative grammatical rule.]

15 The verse quoted shows that saying Grace is a Biblical obligation (at least for people who ate to be satiated). For Biblical obligations, we always follow the rule that in doubt one has to follow the most stringent alternative.

16 Rebbi Yoḥanan is the greatest authority among the Galilean Amoraïm of the second generation. It is rare to have a decision of later generations going against him.

17 Everybody agrees that praying the *Amidah* three times a day is a rabbinic obligation. The majority opinion, reported here by R. Zeïra and anonymously in *Babli Berakhot* 21a, is that one may not recite this prayer more than three times a day (at least on weekdays) and that, therefore, when

in doubt one may not pray since rabbinic ordinances are interpreted leniently in case of doubt. The contrary opinion of Rebbi Yoḥanan is also reported in the Babylonian Talmud (*loc. cit.*) but without the argument that prayer is never in vain. Rav Haï Gaon (*Otzar HaGeonim Berakhot*, Responsa p. 50, Commentaries p. 26) explains that Rebbi Yoḥanan thinks that prayer, as a supplication for Divine grace and in imitation of sacrifices, can be offered as fulfillment of a vow. It follows that, in his opinion, anyone who is in doubt whether he prayed already, should declare that his prayer should be counted as obligatory if he did not pray but as a voluntary offering if he already had fulfilled his obligation. This opinion is not acceptable to the Yerushalmi; since prayer is never in vain it does not need a prior declaration. There is a practical difference between the two Talmudim since according to Rav Haï's interpretation, someone who started praying and remembered in the middle that he already had prayed, must stop in the middle even according to Rebbi Yoḥanan, but in the Jerusalem Talmud R. Yoḥanan is explicitly on record (*Halakhah* 4:3) that he goes on praying since prayer is never in vain.

18 Later it will be discussed that sometime between sundown and nightfall there is a time of twilight when it is doubtful whether it belongs to day or night. Hence, someone who recites the *Shema'* during twilight cannot be said to certainly have violated the rule that the evening *Shema'* must be recited in the night and his case is equivalent to the one where the person is not sure whether he had recited the *Shema'* already during the current evening.

19 Since the Talmud has to prove indirectly that in reading the *Shema'* one is stringent in case of doubt it seems that it is implied that the reading of *Shema'* is a rabbinic institution (though it might leave in doubt the status of the first sentence or the first section.)

סִימָן לְדָבָר צֵאת הַכּוֹכָבִים. וְאַף עַל פִּי שֶׁאֵין רְאָיָה לְדָבָר זֵכֶר לְדָבָר וַאֲנַחְנוּ עוֹשִׂים בַּמְּלָאכָה וְחֶצְיָם מַחֲזִיקִים בָּרְמָחִים מֵעֲלוֹת הַשַּׁחַר עַד צֵאת הַכּוֹכָבִים. וּכְתִיב וְהָיָה לָנוּ הַלַּיְלָה מִשְׁמָר וְהַיּוֹם מְלָאכָה.

A sign for it (nightfall) is after stars have become visible[20]. And though there is no proof, at least there is a hint[21] in (*Neh.* 4:15): "We were working; half of them were holding spears, from the beginning of dawn to the visibility of stars." And it is written (*v.* 16): "The night was for us for watch duty and daytime for work.[22]"

20 This is an extended quote from a parallel to the Tosephta (1:1) quoted in note 8. It is not from our Tosephta since the last sentence is missing there and the first sentence reads in the Tosephta, and in the Babylonian Talmud (2b), סימן לדבר צאת הכוכבים. Levi Ginzberg already has pointed out that the Biblical noun construction צאת הכוכבים "the emergence of stars" is never used in the Yerushalmi which prefers the verbal form. "It" referred to in this quote must be nightfall, the common time both for the criterion of R. Meïr and that of the Sages (Note 8).

21 This expression is found also in Yerushalmi *Sheviït* 9:2 (38d), *Pesaḥim* 1:1 (27a), *Moëd Qaṭan* 1:4 (80c), *Yebamot* 4:11 (6a), *Niddah* 1:4 (49a).

22 The argument goes as follows: Nehemiah's people worked from dawn to dusk (in contrast to hired workers who labor from sunrise to sunset; *Baba meẓia'* 7:1). The second verse, missing in the Tosephta, contains the proof: Neḥemiah declares that "day was for work" and, since he had defined his working day as dawn to dusk in the preceding verse, his definition at least for "day" is "dawn to dusk". This is only a "hint", not a proof, since his working day was irregular.

כַּמָּה כוֹכָבִים יֵצְאוּ וִיהֵא לַיְלָה. רִבִּי פִּינְחָס בְּשֵׁם רִבִּי אַבָּא בַּר פַּפָּא כּוֹכָב אֶחָד וַדַּאי יוֹם. שְׁנַיִם סָפֵק לַיְלָה. שְׁלֹשָׁה וַדַּאי לַיְלָה. שְׁנַיִם סָפֵק וְהָכְתִיב עַד צֵאת הַכּוֹכָבִים. אֶלָּא מִיעוּט כּוֹכָבִים שְׁנַיִם. קַדְמָיָא לָא מִתְחַשֵּׁב.

How many stars have to appear that it should be night? Rebbi Phineas[23] in the name of Rebbi Abba bar Pappus: one star (visible) is certainly daylight. Two are doubtful as night. Three is certainly night. Are two doubtful? Is it not written (*Neh.* 4:15): "To the visibility of stars?[24]" The minimum of "stars" are two! The first one does not count[25].

23 R. Pinḥas Hacohen bar Ḥama, an Israeli Amora of the fourth generation. His source R. Abba bar Pappus was a Babylonian of the second Amora

generation immigrating into Galilee. In the Babli (*Šabbat* 35b), the criterion of three stars is attributed to Samuel, one of the two foremost Babylonian authorities of the first generation. This criterion is originally Babylonian since the criterion of Cohanim eating their *Terumah* was never applicable in Babylonia.

24 The argument here is that Neḥemiah uses a plural in his definition of nightfall. So he talks about at least two stars. Now Talmudic interpretation of Scripture follows a principle that I have discussed repeatedly ("Logical Problems in Jewish Tradition" in: *Confrontations with Judaism*, ed. P. Longworth, London 1967, pp. 171-196; *Seder Olam*, Northvale NJ 1998, p. 6) that every Biblical statement must have a definite meaning. Since numbers do not have an upper bound, the only definite number indicated by a plural is 2. Hence, the plural must mean two unless it is accompanied by a description like "many", etc. The description in the Babli is: תפסת מועט תפסת תפסת מרובה לא תפסת "If you grab the minimum you have something in your hand; if you grab more you have nothing in your hand." It follows that Neḥemiah can talk only about two stars in his description of night.

25 Since Venus often is visible in daylight, it cannot count in the determination of nightfall. Later it is stated that no star visible during daytime hours can be counted for the determination of nightfall. This naturally seems to eliminate the count of stars as a practical procedure.

בְּעֶרֶב שַׁבָּת רָאָה כוֹכָב אֶחָד וְעָשָׂה מְלָאכָה פָּטוּר. שְׁנַיִם מֵבִיא אָשָׁם תָּלוּי. שְׁלֹשָׁה מֵבִיא חַטָּאת. בְּמוֹצָאֵי שַׁבָּת רָאָה כוֹכָב אֶחָד וְעָשָׂה מְלָאכָה מֵבִיא חַטָּאת. שְׁנַיִם מֵבִיא אָשָׁם תָּלוּי. שְׁלֹשָׁה פָּטוּר.

Friday night, if someone saw one star and did work (forbidden on the Sabbath), he is free from punishment. Two, he brings a trespass offering for a sin in doubt[26]. Three, he brings a sin offering. Saturday night, if someone saw one star and did (forbidden) work, he brings a sin offering. Two, he brings a trespass offering for a sin in doubt. Three, he is free from punishment.

26 The trespass offering described in *Lev.* 5:17-19 for somebody who without premeditation commits an act of which he later has doubts whether it was sinful or not. By the preceding statement, at the time when exactly two stars are visible it is impossible to know whether it is day or not. The sin offering for sins committed in error is described *Lev.* 4:27-35.

רִבִּי יוֹסֵי בַּר בּוּן בָּעֵי אִין תֵּימַר שְׁנַיִם סָפֵק. רָאָה שְׁנֵי כוֹכָבִים בְּעֶרֶב שַׁבָּת וְהִתְרוּ בוֹ וְעָשָׂה מְלָאכָה. רָאָה שְׁנֵי כוֹכָבִים בְּמוֹצָאֵי שַׁבָּת וְהִתְרוּ בוֹ וְעָשָׂה מְלָאכָה. מַה נַפְשֵׁךְ אִם הָרִאשׁוֹנִים יוֹם הֵן אַף הָאַחֲרוֹנִים יוֹם הֵן וִיהֵא חַיָּיב עַל הָאַחֲרוֹנִים. אִם הָאַחֲרוֹנִים לַיְלָה אַף הָרִאשׁוֹנִים לַיְלָה וִיהֵא חַיָּיב עַל הָרִאשׁוֹנִים. רָאָה בֹ כוֹכָבִים בְּעֶרֶב שַׁבָּת וְקָצַר כַּחֲצִי גְרוֹגֶרֶת. בְּשַׁחֲרִית וְקָצַר כַּחֲצִי גְרוֹגֶרֶת. רָאָה שְׁנֵי כוֹכָבִים בְּמוֹצָאֵי שַׁבָּת וְקָצַר כַּחֲצִי גְרוֹגֶרֶת. מַה נַפְשֵׁךְ אִם הָרִאשׁוֹנִים יוֹם הֵן אַף הָאַחֲרוֹנִים יוֹם הֵן וְיִצְטָרֵף שֶׁל שַׁחֲרִית עִם שֶׁל מוֹצָאֵי שַׁבָּת וִיהֵא חַיָּיב עַל הָאַחֲרוֹנִים. אִם הָאַחֲרוֹנִים לַיְלָה אַף הָרִאשׁוֹנִים לַיְלָה וְיִצְטָרֵף שֶׁל שַׁחֲרִית עִם שֶׁל לֵילֵי שַׁבָּת וִיהֵא חַיָּיב עַל הָרִאשׁוֹנִים.

Rebbi Yose bar Abun[27] investigated: If you say that two (stars) present a doubt, if someone saw two stars on Friday night, was warned, and did forbidden work, he also saw two stars on Saturday night, was warned, and did forbidden work, then it is logical to assert that if the first period was daytime the last period was also daytime and he would be guilty for the later work; if the last period was nighttime then the first period was also nighttime and he would be guilty for the first work[28]. If someone saw two stars on Friday night and harvested about (the volume of) half a fig, in the morning he harvested about half a fig, and he saw two stars on Saturday night and harvested about half a fig, then it is logical to assert that if the first period was daytime the last period was also daytime and one would combine daytime with Saturday night and he would be guilty for his last work; if the last period was nighttime then the first period was also nighttime and one would combine daytime with Friday night and he would be guilty for his first work[29].

27 R. Yose bar Abun was the colleague of R. Yose bar Zabida and one of the last editors of the Yerushalmi. The first conclusion of R. Yose bar Abun is reported in the Babli (*Šabbat* 35b) by R. Yose bar Zabida. The names Abun, Abba are often contracted to Bun, Ba in the Yerushalmi.

28 As Rashi points out in *Šabbat* 35b, one has to assume that the person did work the entire period during which exactly two stars were visible. Since it is not determined when exactly the changeover from Sabbath to workday occurs during this period, one has to exclude the possibility that he did the work during daytime the first time and during nighttime the second time.

The first case discussed by R. Yose bar Abun deals with a criminal trial. In Jewish law, the Biblical penalties cannot be imposed unless the accused was duly warned by witnesses not to commit the crime that he was seen to start. However, such a warning must be given unconditionally. Since nobody can assert categorically that work in twilight is a Biblical prohibition on Friday night and Saturday night, R. Yose seems to assert that two conditional warnings, given in mutually exclusive circumstances which together make a certainty of the transgression, can be counted as an unconditional warning.

29 Harvesting is forbidden on the Sabbath. Like all such work, the minimal amount of work that is punishable depends on the intention of the person acting. If the harvest is to clear the field for a new crop then the most minute amount of work is punishable. If the harvest is for human consumption then the minimal harvest punishable is the volume of a dried fig. If the harvest is for animal feed then the minimal amount is to fill the mouth of a lamb (*Tosephta Šabbat* 10:15). Here it is understood that one uses the example of one who harvests for human consumption. Any forbidden work on the Sabbath is sinful even in the tiniest of amounts; the minimal amounts determine only whether there is a criminal liability or not. If the work was done inadvertently or the person forgot that it was Sabbath, he may bring a sin offering in the Temple as soon as the Temple will be rebuilt. However, a sin offering can only be brought if the same action, done

intentionally, would have been a criminal act. Hence, no sin offering can be brought as atonement for doing less than a minimal amount of work which would qualify as criminal act. For such an action there can be no warning and the formulation of the problem also leaves out mention of due warning; one may speak here only about the obligation (or possibility) of bringing a sin-offering.

It is spelled out in *Leviticus* (5:2-4) in respect to sin offerings for transgressions by speech (by oath, or non-speech, be refusing to be a witness) that the sin offering is brought if "(he did,) and it was forgotten by him, and he remembered and was guilty." It is taken from here that in all cases there is one sin offering for all transgressions done in one forgetting; that any realization of the forbidden action in the time in between will cause a separate sin with a separate sin offering. Hence, it is assumed here that the person in question either was not aware that the day was a Sabbath or that harvesting on the Sabbath is forbidden, without any intermediate awareness of either Sabbath or the prohibition of harvesting. It is then asserted by R. Yose bar Abun that all acts committed during one forgetting do combine, since they will all be covered by one sin-offering.

The certainty of guilt on the Sabbath is then established by the same argument as in the first case under the same conditions, viz., that in both cases the action was performed exactly during the entire time that exactly two stars were visible. The practical determination of such an action is made questionable by the next action.

הֲדָא דְתֵימַר בְּאִילֵּין דְּלֵית אוֹרְחַתְהוֹן מִתְחַמְיָא בִימָמָא. בְּרַם בְּאִילֵּין דְּאוֹרְחָהוֹן מִתְחַמְיָא בִימָמָא לָא מְשַׁעֲרִין בְּהוֹן. אָמַר רִבִּי יוֹסֵי בֵּרִבִּי בּוּן וּבִלְחוּד דְּיִתְחַמּוּן תְּלָתָא כוֹכָבִין בַּר מִן הַדָּא כוֹכַבְתָּא.

That means (we judge) by those stars that are not usually seen during the day. But by those stars that are usually seen during the day we do not estimate. Rebbi Yose ben Rebbi Abun said: There must be three stars not counting Venus[30].

30 Here we take up the discussion from the penultimate section. The interpretation and the text are a matter of some controversy. Rabbenu Ḥananel

(of Kairawan, 11th Century) in his commentary to *Šabbat* 35b reads in the statement of R. Yose bar Abun: ובלחוד דיתחמון תלתא כוכבים בר מן חד כוכבתא, this is close to our text. R. Eliezer ben Joel (Ravia, Rhineland, 12th-13th Cent., § 199) reads ובלחוד דיתחמו תלתא כוכבין בדמות חד כוכבתא "only that three stars should look like one star" and explains in the name of Rebbi Yehuda (either the Pious of Regensburg or Sir Leon of Paris) that three stars have to appear in a group like feet of a tripod. The same text is quoted by the 14th cent. R. Nissim Gerondi (Ran) as דדמיין לחדא כוכבתא "which are similar to one star" and his contemporary *Hagahot Maimuniot* (*Hilkhot Šabbat*, 5:4 Note 3) that three stars should be seen כמין חד כוכבא "in the manner of one star", to which reading the explanation of Ravia applies well. In fact, R. Zachariah Frankel in his commentary on the Yerushalmi points out that the feminine כוכבתא makes sense only if it refers to Venus. A "star" in general is כוכבא, masculine, and it seems that the text of *Hagahot Maimuniot* has been corrected by German Jewish attention to grammatical correctness. However, if we accept the reading כוכבתא the statement of R. Yose bar Abun is a duplication of the earlier remark that "the first star does not count." Ran explains that the earlier statement determines the moment of nightfall from Biblical sources but that the requirement that three stars should be seen close together is a rabbinic ordinance "to add from weekday to the holy day" and, therefore, has a different status and is a legitimate addition.

רִבִּי יַעֲקֹב דְּרוֹמָאָה בְּשֵׁם רִבִּי יְהוּדָה בֶּן פָּזִי כּוֹכָב אֶחָד וַדַּאי יוֹם. שְׁנַיִם לַיְלָה. וְלֵית לֵיהּ סָפֵק. אִית לֵיהּ סָפֵק בֵּין כּוֹכָב לְכוֹכָב.

Rebbi Jacob the Southerner[31] in the name of R. Yehudah ben Pazi: One star (visible) certainly daytime. Two are night. Does he not allow for a period of doubt? He has a doubt between star and star[32].

31 Amora of the fourth generation, from the region of Lod, contemporary of R. Phineas, who transmits a conflicting Babylonian statement. His source, R. Yehudah ben Simon, of the family Ben Pazi, is a Galilean source from the school of R. Yoḥanan.

32 The interval between the moment when only one star is clearly visible and when two stars are clearly visible

is his time of dusk, of which it is not known whether it belongs to day or to night.

תַּנֵּי כָּל־זְמַן שֶׁפְּנֵי מִזְרַח מַאֲדִימוֹת זֶהוּ יוֹם. הִכְסִיפוּ זֶהוּ בֵּין הַשְּׁמָשׁוֹת. הִשְׁחִירוּ נַעֲשָׂה הָעֶלְיוֹן שָׁוֶה לַתַּחְתּוֹן זֶהוּ לַיְלָה.

It was stated: All the time that the Eastern sky is red it is certainly daylight. If it became silver colored then it is dusk. If it became black, equally from zenith to horizon, then it is night[33].

33 The Babli (*Šabbat* 34b) has a tannaitic statement: "What is dusk? From sundown all the time that the Eastern sky is red. If the lower part turns silver colored (pale grey) but the zenith is not yet silver colored, that is dusk. If the zenith is silver colored equal to the horizon then it is night; these are the words of R. Yehudah (bar Ilaï)." This statement looks somewhat garbled and it is explained in the name of Samuel as: " From sundown all the time that the Eastern sky is red it is daytime. If the lower part turns silver colored (pale grey) but the zenith is not yet silver colored, that is dusk. If the zenith is silver colored equal to the horizon, then it is night." The text of the Yerushalmi is from a tannaitic source and supports Samuel's reading. However, the Yerushalmi version is clearer since when the color of the sky at the horizon is equal to that at the zenith and is darker than pale grey, it is close to being dark.

רִבִּי אוֹמֵר הַלְּבָנָה בִתְקוּפָתָהּ הִתְחִיל גַּלְגַּל חַמָּה לְשַׁקֵּעַ וּתְחִלַּת גַּלְגַּל לְבָנָה לַעֲלוֹת זֶהוּ בֵּין הַשְּׁמָשׁוֹת. אָמַר רִבִּי חֲנִינָא סוֹף גַּלְגַּל חַמָּה לְשַׁקֵּעַ וּתְחִלַּת גַּלְגַּל לְבָנָה לַעֲלוֹת. וְתַנֵּי שְׁמוּאֵל כֵּן אֵין הַלְּבָנָה זוֹרַחַת בְּשָׁעָה שֶׁהַחַמָּה שׁוֹקַעַת וְלֹא שׁוֹקַעַת בְּשָׁעָה שֶׁהַחַמָּה זוֹרַחַת.

Rebbi says: (When) the moon is at its turning point, and the sphere of the sun has started to disappear and the sphere of the moon to rise, that is dusk. Rebbi Ḥanina said: When the solar sphere finishes disappearing and the lunar sphere starts to rise. Samuel has a tannaitic statement: The moon does not shine at the moment of the disappearance of the sun nor does it go down at the moment that the sun shines[34].

34 Rebbi is Rebbi Yehudah the Prince, the editor of the Mishnah. R. Ḥanina probably is the Amora R. Ḥanina, the student of Rebbi.

The explanation of this section depends on whether one accepts that Rebbi and R. Ḥanina speak of the same tradition, only that R. Ḥanina insists that the correct tradition of Rebbi's statement is that dusk starts only at the moment of the final disappearance of the sun and not at the moment of the disappearance of the lower rim of the solar disk as in the first tradition. This is the opinion of most commentators of the Yerushalmi; in the language of the Babli it means that two tradents, the first one anonymous and the second R. Ḥanina, give their versions of what Rebbi really said. [Nachmanides (*Writings of Rabbenu Moshe ben Naḥman*, ed. Chavel, Jerusalem 1964, *Torat Haädam*, p. 154-251) insists that R. Ḥanina only explains Rebbi's statement in popular terms. Since the Talmud quotes a teaching accepted by Samuel the astronomer as confirmation of R. Ḥanina's position, it is difficult to accept that the first tradent and R. Ḥanina should have completely parallel statements.]

A reasonable explanation of this section must start with a discussion of "the turning point of the moon." Usually this is taken as the moment of the full moon, when the moon changes from increasing to decreasing. However, this interpretation is impossible since the orbit of the moon usually deviates from the ecliptic and only about every 223 months the full moon is in the ecliptic in opposition to the sun. Hence, the "turning point of the moon" is the only time when there is a possibility of a lunar eclipse and the full moon is directly opposite to the sun. R. Ḥanina and Samuel express the view of geometric astronomy, i.e., that the full moon cannot rise as long as the sun is still visible. The anonymous first tradent notes that in rare cases the refraction of the earth's atmosphere can lead to a situation where the full moon starts to rise while the sun, geometrically below the horizon, is still visible. [In science, this phenomenon was first studied by Ibn al Haytham in the tenth Cent.; cf. R. Rashed, *Optique et mathématiques*, Variorum: Ashgate Publ. Co., Brookfield Vt, 1992] For practical purposes, both teachers seem to agree that in the consideration of "sundown" for Sabbath observance, the influence of refraction in the atmosphere should be disregarded.

רִבִּי שְׁמוּאֵל בַּר חִיָּא בַּר יְהוּדָה בְּשֵׁם רִבִּי חֲנִינָא הִתְחִיל גַּלְגַּל חַמָּה לִשְׁקוֹעַ אָדָם עוֹמֵד בְּרֹאשׁ הַר הַכַּרְמֶל וְיוֹרֵד וְטוֹבֵל בְּיַם הַגָּדוֹל וְעוֹלֶה וְאוֹכֵל בִּתְרוּמָתוֹ חֲזָקָה בְּיוֹם טָבַל. הָדָא דְתֵימַר בְּהַהוּא דְּאָזִיל לֵיהּ בְּקָפּוֹנְדָּרָא. בְּרַם הַהוּא דְּאָזַל לֵיהּ בְּאִיסְרָטָא לָא בְדָא.

Rebbi Samuel bar Ḥiyya bar Yehudah in the name of Rebbi Ḥanina: When the solar disk starts to sink and a man is standing on top of Mount Carmel, he descends and immerses himself in the ocean, ascends and eats his *Terumah*, one may assume that he immersed himself during daytime[35]. Than is, if he used a shortcut[36] but when he went on the road[37] this does not apply.

35 Therefore, he was cleansed from impurity at nightfall and is justified in eating *Terumah*.

36 Latin *compendiarium* (scil. *iter*) "short cut". The text cannot really mean "the top of mount Carmel" since even running down in a straight line from today's Haifa University to the shore would take about an hour. The "top of Mount Carmel" here is more likely to be at today's "Elijah's cave".

In the Babylonian Talmud (*Šabbat* 35a) the statement of R. Ḥanina is given as illustration of the notion of dusk of R. Neḥemiah mentioned here in the next section. In the interpretation of Tosaphot (*l. c., s. v.* וירד), the statement means that just when the Cohen emerges from the sea then dusk starts.

37 Latin *strata* (scil. *via*), "paved road, pavement".

אֵיזֶהוּא בֵּין הַשְּׁמָשׁוֹת. אָמַר רִבִּי תַנְחוּמָא לְטִיפָּה שֶׁל דָּם שֶׁהִיא נְתוּנָה עַל גַּבֵּי חוּדּוֹ שֶׁל סַיִיף נֶחְלְקָה הַטִּיפָּה לְכַאן וּלְכַאן זֶהוּ בֵּין הַשְּׁמָשׁוֹת. אֵיזֶהוּא בֵּין הַשְּׁמָשׁוֹת. מִשֶּׁתִּשְׁקַע הַחַמָּה כְּדֵי שֶׁיְּהַלֵּךְ אָדָם חֲצִי מִיל דִּבְרֵי רִבִּי נְחֶמְיָה. רִבִּי יוֹסֵי אוֹמֵר בֵּין הַשְּׁמָשׁוֹת כְּהֶרֶף עַיִן וְלֹא יָכְלוּ לַעֲמוֹד עָלָיו חֲכָמִים.

What is dusk? Rebbi Tanḥuma[38] said (it is comparable) to a drop of blood on the tip of a sword. The drop splits here and there, that is dusk. What is dusk?[39] From after sundown the time a man needs to walk half a *mil*, the words of Rebbi Neḥemiah. Rebbi Yose said: dusk is a moment and the sages could not determine it.

38 One of the latest authorities mentioned in the Yerushalmi, renowned as a preacher, and author of the basic *Yelammedenu* Midrash. His simile here is also of the nature of a sermon, illustrating the opinion of R. Yose that there is no real extended dusk but only day and night with a fleeting moment in between, the blinking of an eye in the terminology of R. Yose and the splitting of a drop of blood on the tip of a sword for R. Tanḥuma.

39 While the first statement here was a homily by a late Amora , now we are dealing with a legal statement by two of the outstanding students of Rebbi Akiba, of the fourth generation of Tannaim. Rebbi Yose here is Rebbi Yose bar Ḥalaphta, the highest authority in his generation.

In the Babli (*Šabbat* 34b), the previous statement describing dusk as the time between the end of a reddish glow in the East to uniform dark greyness from Eastern horizon to zenith is attributed to Rebbi Yehudah (bar Ilaï), followed by the statements of R. Neḥemiah and R. Yose here, making the definition of dusk a triple disagreement. By contrast, it seems that the Yerushalmi accepts the criterion of the color of the Eastern sky as universally valid, only that Rebbi Neḥemiah qualifies it in time. The relationship between the statements of R. Neḥemiah and R. Yose is discussed in the next section. Since the standard for a normal person is to walk 10 *parasangs* [= 40 miles (*mil*)] in a day of 12 hours, the time allocated to a *mil* is $^{12}/_{40}$ hours or $(12\times60)/40 = 18$ minutes. [Maimonides counts the 10 *parasangs* from beginning of dawn to the end of dusk; his time for walking a *mil* is 24 minutes.] This refers to a day of 12 hours between sunrise and sunset, i.e., for the equinoxes if constant hours are used. In addition, the determination of time is valid only for the Land of Israel or other countries of the same latitude. For other latitudes, the length of dusk has to be determined by the angle of depression of the sun at the end of 9 or 12 minutes after sunset in Israel on March 21. The Babylonian Talmud (*Šabbat* 34b) replaces the time of $^1/_2$ (Roman?) *mil* in Galilee by $^2/_3$ Babylonian?) *mil* in Babylonia on the lower Euphrates.

רִבִּי יוֹסֵי וְרִבִּי אַחָא הֲווּ יָתְבִין. אָמַר רִבִּי יוֹסֵי לְרִבִּי אָחָא לָא מִסְתַּבְּרָא סוֹף חֲצִי מִיל דְּרִבִּי נְחֶמְיָה כְּהֶרֶף עַיִן אָמַר לֵיהּ אוּף אֲנָא סָבַר כֵּן. רִבִּי חִזְקִיָּה לָא אָמַר כֵּן אֶלָּא כָּל־הֶרֶף עַיִן וְהֶרֶף עַיִן שֶׁבַּחֲצִי מִיל דְּרִבִּי (fol. 2c) נְחֶמְיָה סָפֵק הוּא. אָמַר רִבִּי מָנָא קַשְׁיָיתֵיהּ קוֹמֵי רִבִּי חִזְקִיָּה כַּד תַּנִּינָן תַּמָּן רָאָה אַחַת בַּיּוֹם וְאַחַת בֵּין הַשְּׁמָשׁוֹת. אַחַת בֵּין הַשְּׁמָשׁוֹת וְאַחַת לְמָחָר אִם יוֹדֵעַ הָרְאִיָּה מֵהַיּוֹם וּמִקְצָתָהּ לְמָחָר וַדַּאי לְטוּמְאָה וּלְקָרְבָּן וְאִם סָפֵק שֶׁמִּקְצַת הָרְאִיָּה מֵהַיּוֹם וּמִקְצָתָהּ לְמָחָר וַדַּאי לְטוּמְאָה וְסָפֵק לְקָרְבָּן. רִבִּי חִייָא בַּר יוֹסֵף בָּעָא קוֹמֵי רִבִּי יוֹחָנָן מַאן תַּנָּא רְאִיָּה נֶחְלֶקֶת לִשְׁנַיִם רִבִּי יוֹסֵי. אָמַר לֵיהּ קְשָׁתָה עַל דַּעְתָּךְ דְּאַתְּ אָמַר כָּל־הֶרֶף עַיִן וְהֶרֶף עַיִן שֶׁבַּחֲצִי מִיל דְּרִבִּי נְחֶמְיָה סָפֵק הוּא. לָמָּה אָמַר לִי קְשִׁיתֵיהּ לִכְשֶׁיָּבוֹא אֱלִיָּהוּ וְיֹאמַר זֶהוּ בֵּין הַשְּׁמָשׁוֹת.

Rebbi Yose and Rebbi Aḥa[40] were sitting together. Rebbi Yose said to Rebbi Aḥa: Is it not reasonable that the end of the half a *mil* of Rebbi Neḥemiah is the moment (of Rebbi Yose)[41]? He answered: I also am of that opinion. Rebbi Ḥizqiah[42] does not say so but every single moment in the half a *mil* of Rebbi Neḥemiah is in doubt. Rebbi Mana said: I pointed out the difficulty before Rebbi Ḥizqiah from what we have taught (*Zabim* I,6): "He saw one emission during daytime and one at dusk or one at dusk and the next one the next day; if he knows that the emission at dusk was partially during daytime and partially during nighttime, he certainly is impure and needs a sacrifice but if it is questionable whether the emission occured partially during daytime and partially during nighttime he certainly is impure but it is questionable whether he owes a sacrifice.[43]" Rebbi Ḥiyya bar Josef[44] asked before Rebbi Yoḥanan: Who is the Tanna who will split an emission into two? Rebbi Yose![45] I said to him: Here is your problem since you say that every single moment in the half a *mil* of Rebbi Neḥemiah is in doubt.[46] What is his question good for? For the time when Elijah will come and say: that is dusk[47].

40 Rebbi Aḥa was an Amora of the fourth generation, older than the Amora Rebbi Yose.

41 R. Yose considers all of Rebbi Neḥemiah's "dusk" as being part of daytime and that the change-over to night comes instantly at an undefined time shortly after the end of R. Neḥemiah's "dusk". With Rebbi Yehudah instead of Rebbi Neḥemiah, this is the opinion of Samuel, the astronomical authority of the first Amoraic generation in Babylonia, in the Babylonian Talmud (*Šabbat* 35a).

42 Amora of the fourth generation in Galilee. R. Mana (II) is his only known student.

43 Tractate *Zabim* deals with men suffering from gonorrhea or any other sexually related effluent (*Lev.* 15:1-15). In the interpretation of the school of Hillel there are three stages in the uncleanness of a *zab*. If he had one episode, he is unclean but may cleanse himself by immersion in water as with any other defilement. If he had two episodes not separated by a full day, he can cleanse himself only by immersion in running water after being free of symptoms for a full seven days. If he had three episodes (again, not separated by a full day from dusk to dusk without incident) then he not only has to immerse himself in running water after seven days but he also has to bring a purifying sacrifice (if there is a Temple.) There is a standard duration that is counted as an episode and a continuous emission during a longer period is counted as two (or more, depending on length) emissions. The Mishnah here states that an episode during dusk will be counted as two even if it is relatively short if part of the episode happened during the previous day and part during the following night. Hence, the exact determination of the boundary between day and night is essential.

44 A Babylonian, student of Rab and Samuel at the start of the Amoraic period, who at an advanced age emigrated to Israel and became a member of the Academy of R. Yoḥanan.

45 Rebbi Yose mentioned here is the Tanna, ben Ḥalaphta. His opinion is given based on an explicit *Tosefta Zabim* I,12-13: "If he had one long emission such that he would have had

time to immerse himself in a ritual bath and dry himself then it is counted as two episodes; shorter than that it is only counted as one. Rebbi Yose says it is always counted as only one episode. However, Rebbi Yose agrees that if he had an emission during dusk, even though its duration was not long enough for immersion and drying himself, it is counted for two since it happened on different days. In this sense did R. Yose say: If he had an emission during twilight he is possibly defiled (unclean for seven days) but not obliged to bring a sacrifice. If he had two emissions during twilight he is possibly defiled and possibly obligated to a sacrifice. If he had one emission at another (certain) time and one during twilight or one during twilight and one at another time he is certainly defiled (for seven days) and questionable for a sacrifice. If he had two emissions at other times and one at twilight or two at twilight and one at another time he is certainly defiled and certainly must bring a sacrifice."

46 Up to here, everything is R. Mana's question to R. Ḥizqiah: Since the Tosephta clearly states that the Mishnah quoted is R. Yose's opinion, if every moment of R. Neḥemiah's twilight is questionable for R. Yose then the statement of the Mishnah: "if he knows that the emission at dusk was partially during daytime and partially during nighttime" is meaningless since it is never knowable by anybody whether anything occurred partially during daytime and partially during nighttime.

47 While the prophet Elijah has no authority to change religious rulings he has transcendental knowledge of the true state of things. Hence, for someone instructed by Elijah the doubt of R. Yose does not apply and the Mishnah, while unlikely to be practical, is neither impossible nor void.

This is the end of the discussion in the Yerushalmi, seemingly accepting R. Ḥizqiah's position. In the Babylonian Talmud the decision is left explicitly open so that in any case one has to go with the more stringent rule (earlier start of Sabbath, later nightfall for *Terumah* and end of Sabbath.)

מַאן פַּלִּיג. רִבִּי חֲנִינָה חֲבֵרֵהוֹן דְּרַבָּנָן בָּעֵי כְּמָה דְאַתְּ אָמַר בְּעַרְבִית נִרְאוּ שְׁלֹשָׁה כוֹכָבִים אַף עַל פִּי שֶׁהַחַמָּה נְתוּנָה בְּאֶמְצַע הָרָקִיעַ לַיְלָה הוּא. וָמַר אַף בְּשַׁחֲרִית כֵּן. אָמַר רִבִּי אַבָּא כְּתִיב הַשֶּׁמֶשׁ יָצָא עַל הָאָרֶץ וְלוֹט בָּא צוֹעֲרָה.

וּכְתִיב וּבָא הַשֶּׁמֶשׁ וְטָהֵר. מַקִּישׁ יְצִיאָתוֹ לְבִיאָתוֹ. מַה בִּיאָתוֹ מִשֶּׁיִּתְכַּסֶּה מִן הַבְּרִיאוֹת. אַף יְצִיאָתוֹ לִכְשֶׁיִּתְוַדָּע לַבְּרִיּוֹת. אָמַר רִבִּי אַבָּא כְּתִיב הַבּוֹקֶר אוֹר. הַתּוֹרָה קְרָאָהּ לְאוֹר בּוֹקֶר. תַּנֵּי רִבִּי יִשְׁמָעֵאל בַּבּוֹקֶר בַּבּוֹקֶר כְּדֵי לִיתֵּן תְּחוּם לְבוֹקְרוֹ שֶׁל בּוֹקֶר.

Who disagrees?[48] Rebbi Ḥanina the Colleague of the Rabbis[49] asked: Just as you say in the evening that it is night if three stars are visible even though the sun is in the middle of the sky it is night, so you must say the same thing in the morning. Rebbi Abba[50] said: It is written (*Gen.* 19:23): "The sun *went out* over the earth and Lot came to Zoar." And it is written (*Lev.* 22:7): "The sun will *come* and he shall be pure." He brackets going out and coming. Since coming means that it is hidden from the creatures so also its coming out when it will be ascertained by the creatures. Rebbi Abba[51] said, it is written (*Gen.* 43:3): "In the morning it was light." The Torah called the light morning.[52] Rebbi Ismael[53] stated: (*Ex.* 12:10) "In the morning, in the morning," to give a domain to the very early morning.

48 With the criterion of three stars for the start of night.

49 He usually goes by the name of R. Ḥananiah the Colleague of the Rabbis, a Babylonian who was an important teacher of the leaders of the fourth generation of Amoraim but who never headed a talmudic academy. He insists that it is logical to assert that as long as three stars can still be seen at dawn it is night even though it is relatively light and (Mishnah 5) one may well distinguish between dark blue and white, or between dark blue and dark green. Hence, since the theory of the three stars contradicts the Mishnah it must be invalid.

50 R. Abba also was a Babylonian, a student of Rav Huna and Rav Yehudah in Babylonia, who went to Israel and became a rich silk merchant and talmudic authority of the third generation of Amoraim, a contemporary of R. Ḥanina the Colleague of the Rabbis. His argument parallels the previous one but, since it is based on Biblical verses, it seems to be an attack on the Mishnah which gives different treatments to dawn and dusk.

The first verse asserts that Lot came

to Zoar at sunrise. The second verse asserts that the Cohen who had cleansed himself from impurity is purified at nightfall as explained earlier. The argument seems to center on the ambiguous statement "the sun will come and he will be pure." Everywhere, the "coming" of the sun is its going, sundown or nightfall. In the first verse, the coming of Lot to Zoar is real coming, parallel to the going out of the sun. Hence, in the first verse coming and going out are the same. It would follow that, in the second verse also, coming must have the same status as going out since it is one of the principles of Rabbinic interpretation that Biblical expressions have the same meaning at every occurrence (a principle known as *gĕzērāh šāwāh*.) Hence, the different treatment of dawn and dusk in the Mishnah seems to contradict the principles of Rabbinic Bible interpretation.

51 It is not known if this Rebbi Abba, solving the puzzle, is the same as the author of the preceding question or another sage of the same name. The editorial principle of the Babli, to quote an authority the first time as פלוני אמר and the following times as אמר פלוני or ואמר פלוני does not apply to the Yerushalmi.

52 The Biblical text tells of Joseph's brothers leaving Egypt to return to Canaan. Hence, it means the first dawn which was the first possible time for their leaving, and the Biblical verse connects the technical meaning of "morning" with the first light of dawn. Hence, the asymmetry of treating dawn and dusk is Biblical and Rebbi Ḥanina's and Rebbi Abba's arguments are unjustified.

53 He is a Tanna, an older contemporary of Rebbi Akiba and head of his own school. The sentence is a quote from an anonymous statement in *Mekhilta dĕRibbi Ishmaël, Bo*, 6): "'They shall eat the meat during that night'; from here I understand during the entire night. The verse says 'do not leave any leftovers until morning; but anything left over until morning you shall burn in fire.' Why does the verse repeat 'until morning'? To give a domain to the earliest part of morning. From here they said (*Mishnah* 3-4): 'The consumption of the Passover sacrifice and all other sacrifices, the burning of their parts on the altar can be done until the start of dawn and all sacrifices that must be eaten within one day can be eaten until the start of dawn.' Why did the Sages decree (that all must be done) until midnight? To remove people from transgression and to make a fence around the Torah."

This is an additional indication that the earliest possible sign of dawn is the Biblical start of a new day.

אָמַר רִבִּי יוֹסֵי בֵּי רִבִּי בּוּן אִם אוֹמֵר לִיתֵּן עוֹבְיוֹ שֶׁל רָקִיעַ לְלַיְלָה בֵּין בָּעֲרָבִין בֵּין בְּשַׁחֲרִית נִמְצֵאת אוֹמֵר שֶׁאֵין הַיּוֹם וְהַלַּיְלָה שָׁוִין. וְתַנֵּי בְּאֶחָד בִּתְקוּפַת נִיסָן וּבְאֶחָד בִּתְקוּפַת תִּשְׁרֵי הַיּוֹם וְהַלַּיְלָה שָׁוִין. אָמַר רִבִּי הוּנָא נַלְפִינָן מִדֶּרֶךְ הָאָרֶץ שְׁרֵי מַלְכָּא נְפַק אַף עַל גַּב דְּלָא נְפַק אָמְרִין דְּנָפַק. שָׁרֵי עָלֵיל לָא אָמְרִין דְּעָל עַד שַׁעֲתָא דְיֵעוּל.

Rebbi Yose bar Abun said: If you say to give the thickness of the sky[54] to the night both in the evening and in the morning then you must say that day and night are not of equal length; but we have stated: On the days of the vernal and autumnal equinoxes, day and night have equal length. Rebbi Huna[55] said: We may learn from the ways of the world since if the king leaves [his palace] one already states that he left before he left but when he returns one does not say that he did return until he actually entered [the palace].

54 The "thickness of the sky" is twilight, the time that the sun is no longer seen over the earth before it has disappeared behind the gates of heaven that are closed for the night.

R. Yose bar Abun argues that if twilight is treated the same way for dawn and dusk then at the equinox the days are not evenly split between day and night. Since it is accepted that at the equinox day and night are equal it follows that any part of twilight given to the night at dusk must be given to the day at dawn.

55 A Babylonian who in most other tractates of the Yerushalmi appears as Rebbi Ḥuna (רבי חונא, חונה), a student of Rav Yosef in Babylonia, who emigrated to Israel. His argument is from popular usage, that as the king is said to be leaving before he left, so the sun is said to be setting although three stars can still be seen; but the king is not reported to have returned until he actually did. Hence, day cannot end before the sun has disappeared beyond the heavenly gates and three stars are visible. [The Babylonian Talmud

(*Pesaḥim* 53b) is strictly of the opinion that the twilights of dawn and dusk are of equal length.]

זֶה שֶׁעוֹמֵד לְהִתְפַּלֵּל צָרִיךְ לְהַשְׁווֹת אֶת רַגְלָיו. תְּרֵין אֲמוֹרָיִן ר׳ לֵוִי וְר׳ סִימוֹן חַד אָמַר כְּמַלְאָכִים וְחַד אָמַר כְּכֹהֲנִים. מַאן דְּאָמַר כְּכֹהֲנִים לֹא תַעֲלֶה בְמַעֲלוֹת עַל מִזְבְּחִי. שֶׁהָיוּ מְהַלְּכִין עֲקֵב בְּצַד גּוֹדֶל וְגוֹדֶל בְּצַד עֲקֵב. וּמַאן דְּאָמַר כְּמַלְאָכִים וְרַגְלֵיהֶם רֶגֶל יְשָׁרָה. ר׳ חֲנִינָא בַר אַנְדְּרֵיי בְּשֵׁם ר׳ שְׁמוּאֵל בַּר סוֹטֵר הַמַּלְאָכִים אֵין לָהֵן קְפִיצִין וּמַה טַעֲמָא קִרְבֵת אַל חַד מִן קָמַיָּא קַיָּמַיָּא.

He who prepares to pray must equalize his feet[56]. Two Amoraim, Rebbi Levi[57] and Rebbi Simon[58]; one of them says like angels[59] and one of them says like priests. He who says like priests, (*Ex.* 20:26): "You shall not ascend my alter by stairs;" that means that they were walking with their heel next to the great toe and great toe next to the heel. He who says like angels (*Ez.* 1:7)" "Their feet were a straight foot." Rebbi Ḥanina bar Andrei in the name of R. Samuel ben Soṭar[60]: angels have no moving joints. What is the reason? (*Dan.* 7:16) "I approached one of those standing," the fixed ones[61].

56 The Babli (*Berakhot* 10b) brings only the opinion that in praying the *'Amidah* prayer one has to equalize one's feet like the angels; and this is the name of R. Yose bar Ḥanina in the name of R. Eliezer ben Jacob.

57 A preacher in the Academy of R. Yoḥanan.

58 An older preacher, R. Simon ben Pazi, student of R. Joshua ben Levi.

59 It is usually explained that this means that both legs have to be parallel and together so that they would look like one foot, from the verse quoted: "their *feet* were one straight *foot*." However, *Sefer Haëshkol* (part 1, p. 17) quotes an opinion, possibly of Rav Hai Gaon, that the heels should be together but the toes separated to form a semicircle since the verse quoted from Ezechiel continues "the sole of their feet was like the foot sole of a calf."

60 Rebbi Ḥanina bar Andrei seems to have been a contemporary of R. Levi and R. Yose bar Ḥanina; he is

mentioned only two times in Talmudic literature. R. Samuel bar Soṭar seems to be identical with R. Samuel bar Sosarṭa, another contemporary of the preceding. The entire discussion in the Yerushalmi is between sages of the same generation.

61 In *Midrash Bereshit rabba* 65(17), the lexical note is attributed to the slightly older authority R. Reuben: Rebbi Reuben said: It is written (*Ez.* 1:25) "When they were standing their wings became limp." Is there any sitting in heaven (that standing should be remarkable)? Does not R. Samuel say: there is no sitting in heaven since it says (*Ez.* 1:7) "their feet were a straight foot." They have no moving joints: (*Dan.* 7:16) "I approached one of those standing קאמיה," the fixed ones קיימיא. It also says (*Is.* 6:2): "Seraphim are standing over Him;" (*2Chr.* 18:18): "All the hosts of Heaven were standing," and here it says "when they are standing"; this is astonishing. What really means "when they are standing" (בעמדם), it means "the people come, silence" (בא עם דם), i.e., when Israel are saying "Hear o Israel" the angels are silent and then their wings drop.

Midrash Bereshit rabba is an old Yerushalmi source and one may speculate that the Midrash precedes the editing of the Talmud; otherwise it would be incomprehensible why a statement on the Amidah prayer intrudes on the discussion of the rules of *Shema'*.

אָמַר רִבִּי הוּנָא זֶה שֶׁרוֹאֶה אֶת הַכֹּהֲנִים בְּבֵית הַכְּנֶסֶת בִּבְרָכָה רִאשׁוֹנָה צָרִיךְ לוֹמַר בָּרְכוּ אֶת יי מַלְאָכָיו. בִּשְׁנִיָּה בָּרְכוּ אֶת יי כָּל־צְבָאָיו. בִּשְׁלִישִׁית בָּרְכוּ אֶת יי כָּל־מַעֲשָׂיו. בְּמוּסָף בִּבְרָכָה רִאשׁוֹנָה צָרִיךְ לוֹמַר שִׁיר הַמַּעֲלוֹת הִנֵּה בָּרְכוּ אֶת יי כָּל־עַבְדֵי יי הָעוֹמְדִים בְּבֵית יי בַּלֵּילוֹת. בִּשְׁנִיָּה שְׂאוּ יְדֵיכֶם קֹדֶשׁ. בִּשְׁלִישִׁית יְבָרֶכְךָ יי מִצִּיּוֹן. אִם הָיוּ אַרְבַּע חוֹזֵר תְּלִיתָאָה בְקַדְמִיתָא וּרְבִיעָתָא בִתְנִיָּאתָא.

Rebbi Huna said: He who sees the priests in the synagogue, at the first blessing he must say (*Ps.* 103:20) "praise the Lord, His messengers." At the second blessing (*v.* 21) "praise the Lord all His hosts." At the third blessing (*v.* 22) "praise the Lord all His creatures." At *Musaf* at the first blessing he must say (*Ps.* 134:1) "A song of ascent. Praise the Lord all servants of the Lord, who are standing in the Lord's House in the nights."

At the second blessing (*v.* 2) "lift your hands in holiness." At the third blessing (*v.* 3) "May the Lord bless you from Zion." When there are four blessings then for the third he repeats the first, for the fourth the second[62].

62 Since the priestly blessing is regular part of the morning *Amidah*, the instruction on how to behave during the blessing is added here. The Babli (*Soṭa* 39b) gives separate verses also for days of three and four blessings and rejects the last selection of the Yerushalmi.

אָמַר רִבִּי חִנְּנָא מֵאַיֶּלֶת הַשַּׁחַר עַד שֶׁיֵּאוֹר הַמִּזְרַח אָדָם מְהַלֵּךְ אַרְבָּעַת מִילִין. מִשֶּׁיֵּאוֹר הַמִּזְרַח עַד שֶׁתֵּנֵץ הַחַמָּה אַרְבָּעַת מִיל. וּמְנַיִין מִשֶּׁיֵּאוֹר הַמִּזְרַח עַד שֶׁתֵּנֵץ הַחַמָּה אַרְבָּעַת מִיל דִּכְתִיב וּכְמוֹ הַשַּׁחַר עָלָה וגו׳. וּכְתִיב הַשֶּׁמֶשׁ יָצָא עַל הָאָרֶץ וְלוֹט בָּא צוֹעֲרָה. וּמִן סְדוֹם לְצוֹעַר אַרְבָּעַת מִיל. יוֹתֵר הֲווֹן. אָמַר רִבִּי זְעִירָא הַמַּלְאָךְ הָיָה מְקַדֵּר לִפְנֵיהֶם הַדֶּרֶךְ. וּמְנַיִין מֵאַיֶּלֶת הַשַּׁחַר עַד שֶׁיֵּאוֹר הַמִּזְרַח אַרְבָּעַת מִיל. כְּמוֹ וּכְמוֹ מִילָּה מְדַמְיָא לַחֲבֵרְתָהּ.

Rebbi Ḥinnena[63] said: From the appearance of the "morning hind[64]" until the first rays of light in the East a man can walk four *mil*[65]. From the first rays of light in the East until sunrise four *mil*[66]. From where do we know that from the first rays of light in the East until sunrise there are four *mil?* Since it is written (*Gen.* 19:15) "about when the morning came etc.[67]" And it is written (*v.* 23) "the sun rose over the land and Lot arrived at Zoär." From Sodom to Zoär there are four *mil*. It is farther than that.[68] Rebbi Zeïra said: the angel was flattening[69] the road before them. And from where do we know that from the appearance of "the morning hind" until the first rays of light at the East there are four *mil*? "About when", "when", compares one thing to another[70].

63 The prints and the Leyden manuscript have ר׳ חצנ׳, referring to an otherwise unknown scholar. The reading chosen is that of the Rome manuscript. The bearer of that name was a Galilean Amora of the third

generation.

64 This Biblical allusion (*Psalm* 22) denotes the zodiacal light; see the next section.

65 For the determination of the time implied by the distance, see the paragraph after the next.

66 This statement is found also in the Babylonian Talmud (*Pesaḥim* 94a), there one speaks of עלות השחר, "the coming up of the morning". איילת השחר is not a technical term used in the Babli.

67 The verse describes the time when the angels pushed Lot to leave Sodom.

68 In absence of a reliable tradition about the locations of Zoar and Sodom, it is difficult to know the real distances. In the documents found with the Bar Kochba letters in the desert of Judea, a locality Zoar is mentioned. Hence, in Mishnaic times the location of Zoar was still known. In the Babli (*Pesaḥim* 93b), Rebbi Ḥanina testifies that he checked out the distance and found it to be five *mil*. The Babli finds that the time of an average person walking five *mil* is too long for dawn but he does not try to harmonize the interpretation of the verses with the current observations of twilight.

69 The verb מקדר is used in tractate *Eruvin* in the technical sense of "levelling" by surveyors who for exact measurements use only yardsticks that are exactly horizontal. R. Zeïra wants to say that they walked only absolutely flat roads where the usual speed is higher.

70 One can apply the principle of גזרה שוה, that in general a certain expression has the same meaning in all contexts.

אָמַר רִבִּי יוֹסֵי בֵּי רִבִּי בוּן הֲדָא אַיַּלְתָּא דְשַׁחֲרָא מַאן דְּאָמַר כּוֹכַבְתָּא הִיא טָעֲיָא זִמְנִין דְּהִיא מְקַדְּמָא וְזִמְנִין דְּהִיא מְאַחֲרָא. מַאי כְּדוֹן כְּמִין תְּרֵין דִּקוֹרְנִין דִּנְהוֹרָא דְסַלְּקִין מִן מַדִּינְחָא וּמְנַהֲרִין. דִּלְמָא רִבִּי חִייָא רַבָּא וְרִבִּי שִׁמְעוֹן בֶּן חֲלַפְתָּא הֲווּ מְהַלְּכִין בְּהָדָא בִקְעַת אַרְבֶּל בִּקְרִיצְתָּא וְרָאוּ אַיֶּלֶת הַשַּׁחַר שֶׁבָּקַע אוֹרָהּ. אָמַר רִבִּי חִייָא רַבָּא לְרִבִּי שִׁמְעוֹן בֶּן חֲלַפְתָּא בִּירִבִּי כַּךְ הִיא גְאֻלָּתָן שֶׁל יִשְׂרָאֵל בַּתְּחִילָּה קִמְאָה קִמְאָה כָּל־מָה שֶׁהִיא הוֹלֶכֶת הִיא רָבָה וְהוֹלֶכֶת. מַאי טַעְמָא כִּי אֵשֵׁב בַּחֹשֶׁךְ יי אוֹר לִי. כֵּן בַּתְּחִילָּה וּמָרְדְּכַי יֹשֵׁב בְּשַׁעַר הַמֶּלֶךְ. וְאַחַר כַּךְ וַיִּקַּח הָמָן אֶת הַלְּבוּשׁ וְאֶת הַסּוּס. וְאַחַר כַּךְ וַיָּשָׁב מָרְדְּכַי אֶל שַׁעַר הַמֶּלֶךְ. וְאַחַר כַּךְ וּמָרְדְּכַי יָצָא מִלִּפְנֵי הַמֶּלֶךְ בִּלְבוּשׁ מַלְכוּת. וְאַחַר כַּךְ לַיְּהוּדִים הָיְתָה אוֹרָה וְשִׂמְחָה.

Rebbi Yose bar Abun said: Anybody who identifies the "morning hind" with the planet Venus is in error; that planet sometimes is too early and sometimes too late[71]. What is it? It is like two double horns of light that arise from the East and give light. Explanation[72]: The great Rebbi Ḥiyya and Rebbi Simeon ben Ḥalaphta[73] were walking in the valley of Arbela before morning and saw "the morning hind" that started radiating. The great Rebbi Ḥiyya said to Rebbi Simeon ben Ḥalaphta, the great man: so will be the deliverance of Israel; it starts out very little and grows and longer as it goes on. What is the reason (*Micha* 7:8): "When I shall dwell in darkness, the Lord is my light." So also at the start (*Esther* 2:21): "Mordocai was sitting at the king's gate." After that (6:11): "Haman took the garment and the horse." After that (6.12): "Mordocai returned to the king's gate." After that (8:15): "Mordocai left the king's presence in royal garb." After that (8.16): "The Jews had light and joy."

71 That means, sometimes Venus sets still during the night and sometimes it is still seen after sunrise.

72 This is the explanation of Frankel in his "Introduction to the Yerushalmi", from Greek δήλωμα. Levy in his dictionary refers to Greek δίλημμα, which means only "proposition of two difficult alternatives." Brüll in his critique of Levy's dictionary proposes Greek δράμα "action". Frankel's choice is difficult since both long vowels should be expressed, דילומא. (In Midrashim, the spelling דילמא is found.) Brüll's explanation is more difficult to accept since substitutions of the liquids *l,r* for one another are extremely rare in Greek words coming into Aramaic. Also, no action is reported here.

73 Rebbi Ḥiyya the Great is Rebbi Ḥiyya, the student and colleague of Rebbi, the collector of the Tosephtah. Rebbi Simeon ben Ḥalaphta is a contemporary who like Rebbi Ḥiyya does not appear in the Mishnah (except for the aggadic very last Mishnah.)

וְאַתְיָא דְרִבִּי חֲנִינָה כְּרִבִּי יוּדָה דְּתַנֵּי בְשֵׁם רִבִּי יוּדָה עוֹבְיוֹ שֶׁל רָקִיעַ מַהֲלַךְ חֲמִשִּׁים שָׁנָה. אָדָם בֵּינוֹנִי מְהַלֵּךְ אַרְבָּעִים מִיל בַּיּוֹם. עַד שֶׁהַחַמָּה נוֹסֶרֶת בָּרָקִיעַ מַהֲלַךְ חֲמִשִּׁים שָׁנָה אָדָם מְהַלֵּךְ אַרְבַּעַת מִיל נִמְצֵאת אוֹמֵר שֶׁעוֹבְיוֹ שֶׁל רָקִיעַ אֶחָד מֵעֲשָׂרָה בַיּוֹם. וּכְשֵׁם שֶׁעוֹבְיוֹ שֶׁל רָקִיעַ מַהֲלַךְ חֲמִשִּׁים שָׁנָה כָּךְ עוֹבְיָהּ שֶׁל הָאָרֶץ וְעוֹבְיוֹ שֶׁל תְּהוֹם מַהֲלַךְ חֲמִשִּׁים שָׁנָה וּמַה טַעַם הַיּוֹשֵׁב עַל חוּג הָאָרֶץ וּכְתִיב וְחוּג שָׁמַיִם יִתְהַלָּךְ. וּכְתִיב בְּחֻקּוֹ חוּג עַל פְּנֵי תְהוֹם. חוּג חוּג לִגְזֵרָה שָׁוָה.

The statement of Rebbi Ḥanina[74] is parallel to that of Rebbi Yehudah since it was stated in the name of Rebbi Yehudah: the thickness of the sky is a walk of 50 years[75]. An average person walks 40 *mil* during a day[76]. Until the sun breaks through in the sky it passes the distance of 50 years; during that time a man can walk four *mil*. If follows that the thickness of the sky is one tenth [of the path of the sun] in one day. And just as the thickness of the sky is a walk of 50 years so the thickness of the earth and that of the abyss is a walk of 50 years[77]. What is the reason? (*Is.* 40:22) "He Who thrones over the circle of the earth," and it is written (*Job* 22:14): "He passes by the circle of the sky." And it is written (*Prov.* 8:27) "When He carved out a circle on the face of the abyss." "Circle" (חוג) always has the same meaning.

74 Here the argument returns to the prior statement of R. Ḥanina, that the twilight at dawn is the time to walk four *mil*. In the Leyden ms. and the prints, the reference here is to R. Ḥiyya; the correct reading is in the Rome ms. and the commentary of R. Eleazar Askari.

75 In the parallel version of this argument in the Babli, Rebbi Yehudah is quoted only as saying that the thickness of the sky, the distance the sun covers between the start and the end of dawn, is one-tenth of the entire day (from beginning of dawn to end of dusk). In the next section and in the parallel *Bereshit rabba* 6(9), it is asserted that the entire sky represents a distance of 500 years and that between each sky and the next there is

a distance measured by 500 years. It is not clear how the "distance of 500 years" is meant to be computed.

76 A *mil* is 2000 cubits. Therefore, the exact length of a *mil* depends on the length of a cubit. Based on a length of 55 cm for a cubit, the *mil* would be 1100 meters. The Roman mile was 1473.2 m. A *mil* of 1100 m would give a daily trip of 27.34 English miles. Determination of the *mil* by modern Rabbinic authorities vary from 960m (Rav Naeh) to 1152m (Ḥazon Ish) and 1296m (Ḥatam Sopher). In the Babli *Pesaḥim* 94a, Rava quotes a tradition that the circumference of the earth is 6000 *parasangs* or 24'000 mil. It is not clear at which latitude this length is computed. Based on a Greek παρασάγγης of 5.523 km, the computed 33'078 km would fit well with the circumference of the earth at about the latitude of Jerusalem or Southern Babylonia. The corresponding *mil* would be 1380 m.

77 The abyss being below the mantle of Earth.

תַּנֵּי עֵץ חַיִּים מַהֲלַךְ חֲמֵשׁ מֵאוֹת שָׁנָה. אָמַר רִבִּי יוּדָה בֵּירִבִּי אִלְעָאִי לֹא סוֹף דָּבָר נוֹפוֹ. אֶלָּא אֲפִילוּ כוֹרְתוֹ. וְכָל־פִּילוּג מֵי בְרֵאשִׁית מִתְפַּלְּגִין מִתַּחְתָּיו וּמַה טַעַם וְהָיָה כְּעֵץ שָׁתוּל עַל פַּלְגֵי מָיִם. תַּנֵּי עֵץ חַיִּים אֶחָד מִשִּׁשִּׁים לַגַּן. וְנָהָר יוֹצֵא מֵעֵדֶן לְהַשְׁקוֹת אֶת הַגָּן. תַּמְצִית כּוֹר תַּרְקָב שׁוֹתָה. תַּמְצִית כּוּשׁ מִצְרַיִם שׁוֹתָה. נִמְצֵאת אוֹמֵר מִצְרַיִם מַהֲלַךְ אַרְבָּעִים יוֹם. וְכוּשׁ מַהֲלַךְ שֶׁבַע שָׁנִים וְעוֹד. וְרַבָּנָן אָמְרִין כִּשְׁנֵי אָבוֹת הָרִאשׁוֹנִים כִּימֵי הַשָּׁמַיִם עַל הָאָרֶץ. וּכְשֵׁם שֶׁבֵּין הָאָרֶץ לָרָקִיעַ מַהֲלַךְ חֲמֵשׁ מֵאוֹת שָׁנָה. כָּךְ בֵּין רָקִיעַ לְרָקִיעַ מַהֲלַךְ חֲמֵשׁ מֵאוֹת שָׁנָה וְעוּבְיוֹ מַהֲלַךְ חֲמֵשׁ מֵאוֹת שָׁנָה. וּמַה חָמִית מֵימַר עוֹבְיוֹ שֶׁל רָקִיעַ מַהֲלַךְ חֲמֵשׁ מֵאוֹת שָׁנָה. אָמַר רִבִּי בּוּן יְהִי רָקִיעַ בְּתוֹךְ הַמַּיִם. יְהִי רַקִּיעַ בְּתָוֶךְ. רַב אָמַר לַחִים הָיוּ שָׁמַיִם בְּיוֹם הָרִאשׁוֹן וּבַשֵּׁנִי נִקְרְשׁוּ. רַב אָמַר יְהִי רָקִיעַ יְחֲזַק הָרָקִיעַ. יִקְרֵשׁ הָרָקִיעַ. יִגְלֵד הָרָקִיעַ. יִמְתַּח הָרָקִיעַ. אָמַר רִבִּי יוּדָה בֶּן פָּזִי יֵעָשֶׂה כְמִין מַטְלֵית הָרָקִיעַ. הֵיךְ מַה דְּאַתְּ אָמַר וַיְרַקְּעוּ אֶת פַּחֵי הַזָּהָב וגו׳.

Is has been stated: The Tree of Life is wide a parcourse of 500 years. Rebbi Yehudah ben Rebbi Ilaï[78] said: not only its crown but even its stem.

All the splitting of primeval waters splits under it since (*Ps.* 1:3) "He shall be like a tree planted on split waters[79]." It has been stated: The Tree of Life is one sixtieth of the Garden. (*Gen.* 2:10) "And a river originated in Eden to irrigate the Garden." The remainder of a *kur* is a triple *qab*, a sixtieth[80]. The remainder of Africa is Egypt, a sixtieth. We find that it is said that Egypt can be traversed in 40 days[81]. Black Africa can be traversed in slightly more than seven years[82]. But the teachers say [the sky is determined] by the days of the patriarchs (*Deut.* 11:21) "like the days of the sky over the earth."[83] And just as the sky over the earth is at a distance of a way of 500 years so between one sky and the next is a way of 500 years and its thickness is a way of 500 years. Why did you see fit to say the thickness of the sky is a way of 500 years?[84] Rebbi Abun said[85] (*Gen.* 1:6): "There shall exist a spread-sky within the water." The spread-sky shall be in the middle. Rav said: the sky was wet on the first day and jelled on the second day. Rav said: "There shall exist a spread-sky": the sky shall strengthen, the sky shall jell, the sky shall solidify, the sky shall be spread. Rebbi Yehudah ben Pazi said: The sky (רקיע) shall be made like a piece of cloth, just as it is said (*Ex.* 39:3) "They stretched (וירקעו) out the gold sheets."

78 He is Rebbi Yehudah quoted in both Talmudim without his father's name.

79 Taken as an allusion to paradise. It is clear from the text that the Garden of Eden and the Tree of Life are not earthly creations.

80 From here on there is a parallel in Babli *Taänit* 10a. Rashi explains there that with what remains in watering vessels used for a *kur* of grain one can still irrigate three *qab*. (A *kur* is 180 *qab*.)

81 Egypt is defined as the country between the Mediterranean and Aswan (Syene). The distance was determined by the Alexandrian astronomer Eratosthenes to be approximately 5000 stadia. The length of the Greek stadion is no better defined than the

Jewish *mil*. The distance is in the order of magnitude of 1000 km or about 650 miles.

82 All commentators are at a loss here since it should say "slightly less than seven years" (2400 days) but there is no manuscript evidence for such a reading.

83 The full verse reads: "that your days and the days of your descendants should increase on the Land that the Eternal had sworn to your forefathers to give to them, like the days of the sky over the earth." The days of the forefathers were 175 years for Abraham, 180 for Isaac, and 147 for Jacob, together 502 years. The time when Abraham recognized God as the Creator is a matter of controversy in midrashic sources; our source here seems to side with the opinion that Abraham recognized the futility of idol worship at age 3; then his years as the Lord's servant were 173 and the sum is 500.

84 I.e., to take the part of R. Yehudah against the anonymous Sages who had earlier defined the thickness of the sky as the equivalent of 50 years. The question remains unanswered.

85 This section is given in greater detail in *Bereshit rabba* 4(1). There we read: "The rabbis say in the names of R. Ḥanina, R. Pinḥas, R. Jacob bar Abun, in the name of R. Shemuel bar Naḥman: When the Holy One, praise to Him, said: 'there should be a spread', the middle drop jelled and separated upper and lower waters." After that the opinion of Rav is quoted.

The opinion of R. Yehudah ben Pazi is given there by R. Yehudah bar Simon (the full name is R. Yehudah ben R. Simon ben Pazi where either "ben Pazi" is a family name or Pazi is one of R. Ḥiyya's twin daughters, Pazi and Martha). So possibly R. Abun here is the father of R. Jacob bar Abun in the second generation of Amoraïm and not the late R. Abun.

תַּנֵּי בְּשֵׁם רִבִּי יְהוֹשֻׁעַ עוֹבְיוֹ שֶׁל רָקִיעַ כִּשְׁתֵּי אֶצְבָּעַיִים. מִלְּתֵיהּ דְּרִבִּי חֲנִינָא פְּלִיגָא דְּאָמַר רִבִּי אָחָא בְּשֵׁם רִבִּי חֲנִינָא תַּרְקִיעַ עִמּוֹ לִשְׁחָקִים חֲזָקִים כִּרְאִי מוּצָק. תַּרְקִיעַ מְלַמֵּד שֶׁהֵן עֲשׂוּיִין כְּטָס. יָכוֹל שֶׁאֵינָן בְּרִיאִין תַּלְמוּד לוֹמַר חֲזָקִים. יָכוֹל שֶׁהֵן נִתְרָפִין תַּלְמוּד לוֹמַר כִּרְאִי מוּצָק. בְּכָל־שָׁעָה וְשָׁעָה נִרְאִין מוּצָקִים.

It has been stated in the name of Rebbi Joshua[86]: the thickness of the sky is two fingers wide. The words of Rebbi Ḥanina[87] disagree, as Rebbi

Aḥa said in the name of Rebbi Ḥanina (*Job* 37:18) "Go to spread the skies with Him; they are strong like a cast mirror." "Go to spread", that shows that they are made like sheet metal. I could think that they are not sturdy but the verse says "strong". I could think that they might weaken[88], the verse says "like a cast mirror;" at every moment they appear recast.

86 Rebbi Joshua ben Ḥananiah, one of the two foremost students of Rabban Yoḥanan ben Zakkai, of the first generation after the destruction of the Second Temple. He is known for his cosmological opinion, explained in the first chapters of *Seder 'Olam*, that the world was created in Nisan. Here he disagrees with the opinion of the later rabbis, discussed up to now, that the width of the sky is a parcourse of several years. In the Babylonian Talmud *Ḥagigah* 15a, R. Joshua seems to oppose the opinion of Simeon ben Zoma who defines the spread between the lower (terrestrian) and the upper (heavenly) waters to be three digits; smaller measures there are only given by late Amoraïm.

87 Even though his words are reported by Rebbi Aḥa of the fourth generation of Amoraïm, R. Ḥanina here is R. Ḥanina bar Ḥama of the first generation. The verse from Job is ambiguous as are most verses of that book. The verb תרקיע is usually taken to mean "to reach the sky"; here it is taken in the sense "to work metal into thin sheets" indicated in the previous section by R. Yehudah ben Pazi.

88 At some time in the future. The *Targum* to *Job* translates "mirror of refined metal". The implication here seems to be from the passive participle מוצק "being cast" (or "refined") in a timeless manner.

רִבִּי יוֹחָנָן וְרִבִּי שִׁמְעוֹן בֶּן לָקִישׁ. רִבִּי יוֹחָנָן אָמַר (fol. 2d) בְּנוֹהֵג שֶׁבְּעוֹלָם אָדָם מֹתֵחַ אוֹהֶל עַל יְדֵי שֶׁהוּת רָפֶה. בְּרַם הָכָא וַיִּמְתָּחֵם כְּאוֹהֶל לָשֶׁבֶת. וּכְתִיב חֲזָקִים. רִבִּי שִׁמְעוֹן בֶּן לָקִישׁ אָמַר בְּנוֹהֵג שֶׁבְּעוֹלָם אָדָם נוֹסֵךְ כֵּלִים עַל יְדֵי שֶׁהוּת מַעֲלֶה חֲלוּדָה בְּרַם הָכָא כִּרְאִי מוּצָק. בְּכָל־שָׁעָה וְשָׁעָה הֵן נִרְאִין כִּשְׁעַת יְצִיקָתָן. רִבִּי עֲזַרְיָה אָמַר עַל הָא דְּרִבִּי שִׁמְעוֹן בֶּן לָקִישׁ וַיְכֻלּוּ הַשָּׁמַיִם וְהָאָרֶץ וְכָל־צְבָאָם. וַיְכַל אֱלֹהִים בַּיּוֹם הַשְּׁבִיעִי. וַיְבָרֶךְ אֱלֹהִים אֶת יוֹם הַשְּׁבִיעִי. מַה כְתִיב בַּתְרֵיהּ אֵלֶּה תוֹלְדוֹת הַשָּׁמַיִם. וְכִי מַה עִנְיָן זֶה אֵצֶל זֶה. אֶלָּא יוֹם נִכְנַס

וְיוֹם יוֹצֵא. שַׁבָּת נִכְנַס וְשַׁבָּת יוֹצֵא. חוֹדֶשׁ נִכְנַס וְחוֹדֶשׁ יוֹצֵא. שָׁנָה נִכְנַס וְשָׁנָה יוֹצְאָה. וּכְתִיב אֵלֶּה תוֹלְדוֹת הַשָּׁמַיִם וְהָאָרֶץ בְּהִבָּֽרְאָם בְּיוֹם עֲשׂוֹת יי אֱלֹהִים אֶרֶץ וְשָׁמָיִם.

Rebbi Yoḥanan and Rebbi Simeon ben Laqish[89]. Rebbi Yoḥanan said: Usually when someone stretches the ropes of a tent, in time the ropes will loosen. But here (*Is*. 40:22) "He stretched them like a tent to sit in," and it said (*Job* 37:18): "they are strong." Rebbi Simeon ben Laqish said: "Usually if someone casts a vessel, in time it will rust. But here "like a cast mirror," all the time they look like newly cast. Rebbi Azariah[90] comments on the remark of Rebbi Simeon ben Laqish (*Gen*. 2:1-3) "The sky and the earth and all their hosts were completed. God finished on the Seventh Day . . . and God blessed the Seventh Day." What is written after that? (*Gen*. 2:4) "These are the generations of the skies." What has one to do with the other? Only that a day comes and goes, a week comes and goes, a month comes and goes, a year comes and goes[91]. And it is written (*Gen*. 2:4) "These are the generations of the skies and the earth when they were created, on the day that the Eternal, God, created earth and heaven."

89 The brother-in-law and, according to Babylonian tradition, student of R. Yoḥanan. They both elaborate on the verse from Job treated by R. Yoḥanan's teacher R. Ḥanina.

90 One of the teachers of the fifth generation of Galilean Amoraïm. In *Bereshit rabba* 12, R. Azariah explicitly objects to the opinion that everything that has generations will wilt and die, including sky and earth. His statement here seems to say that the generations of the sky are the astronomical periods and that nevertheless everything is as on the day when sky and earth were created.

91 The use of masculine forms for both masculine and feminine is not uncommon in the Yerushalmi.

רִבִּי אוֹמֵר אַרְבַּע אַשְׁמוּרוֹת בַּיּוֹם וְאַרְבַּע אַשְׁמוּרוֹת בַּלַּיְלָה. הָעוֹנָה אֶחָד מֵעֶשְׂרִים וְאַרְבָּעָה לְשָׁעָה. הָעֵת אֶחָד מֵעֶשְׂרִים וְאַרְבָּעָה לְעוֹנָה. הָרֶגַע אֶחָד מֵעֶשְׂרִים וְאַרְבָּעָה לָעֵת. כַּמָּה הוּא הָרֶגַע. רִבִּי בֶּרֶכְיָה בְּשֵׁם רִבִּי חֶלְבּוֹ אָמַר כְּדֵי לְאוֹמְרוֹ. וְרַבָּנָן אָמְרִין הָרֶגַע כְּהֶרֶף עַיִן. תַּנֵּי שְׁמוּאֵל הָרֶגַע אֶחָד מֵחֲמֶשֶׁת רִבּוֹא וְשֵׁשֶׁת אֲלָפִים וּשְׁמוֹנֶה מֵאוֹת וְאַרְבָּעִים וּשְׁמוֹנֶה לְשָׁעָה. רִבִּי נָתָן אוֹמֵר שָׁלוֹשׁ רֹאשׁ הָאַשְׁמוֹרֶת הַתִּיכוֹנָה.

Rebbi[92] said: There are four watches during daytime and four at nighttime. The period is one twenty-fourth of an hour. The time is one twenty-fourth of a period. The moment is one twenty-fourth of a time. How much is a moment? Rebbi Berekhiah in the name of Rebbi Ḥelbo said: as long as one needs to pronounce it. The Sages say the moment is like the blink of an eyelash. Samuel did formulate: the moment is one in 56,848 of an hour[93]. Rebbi Nathan said three: (*Jud.* 7:19) "at the start of the middle watch."

92 Since Rebbi Eliezer in the Mishnah had defined the time of the recital of *Shema'* as the first watch in the night, the discussion of the Mishnah now turns to the legal determination of the length of a nightwatch. The text here is composed of two sources. The statement about the number of watches in a night according to Rebbi and Rebbi Nathan is a Tosephta (*Berakhot* 1:1). This Tosephta also has the division of the hour and its subdivisions by 24 parts each. This seems to belong to Rebbi's statement since this subdivision and the division of the night (and possibly the day) is Roman practice. Rebbi Nathan, a contemporary of Rebbi known as "the Babylonian", follows a Babylonian tradition that also seems to have been the old Israelite practice since the verse from Judges speaks of one "middle watch" which is possible only if there are an odd number of watches in the night. According to Rebbi, a watch is three hours and it has been noted that R. Joshua, who allows *Shema'* to be recited during the first three hours of daylight, follows Rebbi in the division of the day.

93 Of this part there exist three Yerushalmi sources [the Talmud here,

Midrash Ekha rabbati on *Threni* 2:19. *Midrash Samuel* 3(1)], all of which have an identical text and the definition of the number of moments in an hour by Rebbi as $24^3 = 13824$, by Samuel as 56848, and by others either as the time needed to say the word or as the blinking of an eye. In Babylonian sources (*Berakhot* 7a, *Abodah zarah* 4a) the numbers are quoted anonymously and are given as 58888 (printed editions), 56880 (Munich manuscript), 56800 (Koronel manuscript) in *Berakhot* and 53848 (printed editions), 56884 (R. Ḥananel), 56888 (Munich ms.) in *Abodah zarah*. In *Sefer Agadot Hatalmud* the reading is 5845. The opinion that a moment is the length of time needed to pronounce the word is attributed in the Babli to Rebbi Abin (who might be identical with Rabin, a Galilean authority who escaped persecution by an emperor and became an authority in Babylonia.) Only the numbers given in the Yerushalmi tradition are composites of simple numbers; Samuel's number is $16 \times 11 \times 17 \times 19$, whereas the Babylonian numbers have no decomposition into small factors. Now most of the numbers in the Babylonian sources (who have beeen copied and edited much more than the Yerushalmi and, therefore, are more likely to contain scribal errors) are close to Samuel's number. One may, therefore, assume that the original number in all Talmud texts was 56848.

In the Babylonian Talmud, the number given is from an anonymous Tannaïtic source which also adds: "Nobody can determine the moment exactly; only Bileam the sorcerer could do that." In Antiquity (and the Middle Ages), all astronomical computations were done in the technique of the old Babylonians, in a number system based on subdivisions by 60. In general, divisions were executed only for numbers that have an easy reciprocal in the sexagesimal system, i.e., they are composed by factors of 60 (2, 3, 5, and their multiples). Instead of dividing, people looked up the reciprocal in a table and then multiplied. Samuel is the astronomer of most authority in the Talmud. Hence, it is reasonable to assume that his number, which is not invertible by the Babylonian method, is a good example that "nobody can exactly determine the moment" because 1/56848 is an infinite sexagesimal fraction. Hence, the comment of the Tanna, that "nobody can determine the moment exactly," is implied in the number of Samuel and the Babylonian text is a derivative of the Yerushalmi text here.

רִבִּי זְרִיקָן וְרִבִּי אַמִּי בְּשֵׁם רִבִּי שִׁמְעוֹן בֶּן לָקִישׁ טַעֲמֵיהּ דְּרִבִּי חֲצוֹת לַיְלָה אָקוּם לְהוֹדוֹת לָךְ עַל מִשְׁפְּטֵי צִדְקֶךָ. וּכְתִיב קִדְּמוּ עֵינַי אַשְׁמֻרוֹת. רִבִּי חִזְקִיָּה אָמַר רִבִּי זְרִיקָן רִבִּי בָּא חַד אָמַר טַעֲמֵיהּ דְּרִבִּי וְחָרִינָה אָמַר טַעֲמֵיהּ דְּרִבִּי נָתָן. מַאן דָּמַר טַעֲמֵי דְּרִבִּי חֲצוֹת לַיְלָה. וּמַאן דָּמַר טַעֲמֵיהּ דְּרִבִּי נָתָן רֹאשׁ הָאַשְׁמוֹרֶת הַתִּיכוֹנָה. מָן מְקַיֵּים רִבִּי נָתָן טַעֲמֵיהּ דְּרִבִּי חֲצוֹת לַיְלָה. פְּעָמִים חֲצוֹת לַיְלָה. וּפְעָמִים קִדְּמוּ עֵינַי אַשְׁמֻרוֹת. הָא בְאֵי זֶה צַד בְּשָׁעָה שֶׁהָיָה דָוִד סוֹעֵד סְעוּדַת מְלָכִים חֲצוֹת לַיְלָה. וּבְשָׁעָה שֶׁהָיָה סוֹעֵד סְעוּדַת עַצְמוֹ קִדְּמוּ עֵינַי אַשְׁמֻרוֹת. מִכָּל־מָקוֹם לָא הֲוָה אֶרְתָּא אַתְיָא וּמַשְׁכַּח לְדָוִד דָּמִיךְ. הוּא שֶׁדָּוִד אָמַר עוּרָה כְבוֹדִי עוּרָה הַנֵּבֶל וְכִנּוֹר אָעִירָה שָּׁחַר. אִתְעִיר יְקָרִי מִן קוֹמֵי אִיקָרֵיהּ דִּבְרָאִי. אִיקָרִי לָא חָשִׁיב כְּלוּם מִן קֳדָם אִיקָרֵיהּ דִּבְרָאִי. אָעִירָה שָׁחַר. אֲנָא הֲוֵינָא מְעוֹרֵר שַׁחְרָא. שַׁחְרָא לָא הֲוָא מְעוֹרֵר לִי. וְהָיָה יִצְרוֹ מְקַטְרְגוֹ וְאוֹמֵר לוֹ דָּוִד דַּרְכָּן שֶׁל מְלָכִים לִהְיוֹת הַשַּׁחַר מְעוֹרְרָן. וְאַתְּ אָמַר אָעִירָה שָׁחַר. דַּרְכָּן שֶׁל מְלָכִים לִהְיוֹת יְשֵׁנִין עַד שָׁלֹשׁ שָׁעוֹת. וְאַתְּ אָמַר חֲצוֹת לַיְלָה אָקוּם. וְהוּא אוֹמֵר עַל מִשְׁפְּטֵי צִדְקֶךָ. וּמַה הָיָה דָוִד עוֹשֶׂה. רִבִּי פִינְחָס בְּשֵׁם רִבִּי אֶלְעָזָר בְּרִבִּי מְנַחֵם הָיָה נוֹטֵל נֶבֶל וְכִנּוֹר וְנוֹתְנוֹ מֵרַאֲשׁוֹתָיו וְעוֹמֵד בַּחֲצִי הַלַּיְלָה וּמְנַגֵּן בָּהֶם שֶׁיִּשְׁמְעוּ חֲבֵירֵי תוֹרָה. וּמַה הָיוּ חֲבֵירֵי תוֹרָה אוֹמְרִין וּמַה אִם דָּוִד הַמֶּלֶךְ עוֹסֵק בַּתּוֹרָה אָנוּ עַל אַחַת כַּמָּה וְכַמָּה. אָמַר רִבִּי לֵוִי כִּנּוֹר הָיָה תָלוּי כְּנֶגֶד חַלּוֹנוֹתָיו שֶׁל דָּוִד וְהָיָה רוּחַ צְפוֹנִית מְנַשֶּׁבֶת בַּלַּיְלָה וּמְנַפְנֶפֶת בּוֹ וְהָיָה מְנַגֵּן מֵאֵילָיו. הַהוּא דִכְתִיב וְהָיָה כְּנַגֵּן הַמְנַגֵּן. כְּנַגֵּן בַּמְנַגֵּן אֵין כָּתוּב כַּאן אֶלָּא כְּנַגֵּן הַמְנַגֵּן. הַכִּנּוֹר הָיָה מְנַגֵּן מֵאֵילָיו.

Rebbi Zeriqan and Rebbi Ammi[94] in the name of Rebbi Simeon ben Laqish: The reason of Rebbi is (*Ps.* 119:62): "At midnight I get up to thank You for Your just laws." And it is written (*Ps.* 119:148): "My eyes preceded night watches." Rebbi Ḥizqiah said: Rebbi Zeriqan and Rebbi Abba, one explained the reason of Rebbi, the other the reason of Rebbi Nathan. He who explained the reason of Rebbi: "at midnight". He who explained the reason of Rebbi Nathan (*Jud.* 7:19): "at the start of the middle watch."[95] How does Rebbi Nathan uphold the basis of Rebbi's reason, "at midnight"? Sometimes "at midnight," sometimes "my eyes preceded night watches." How is that? When David had a state dinner, "at midnight." When he ate by himself, "my eyes preceded night watches." In no case did dawn come and found David asleep. That is what David said (*Ps.* 57:9): "Wake up, my honor, wake up, o harp and lute, I shall awake dawn." My honor has to be awake because of the honor of my Creator. My honor counts for nothing before the honor of my Creator. I shall awake dawn, dawn will not awake me. His evil instinct was trying to seduce him and told him: David, usually dawn awakes kings and you say "I shall awake dawn!" Usually kings sleep until three hours into the day and you say "at midnight I get up!" But he answers, "for Your just laws." What did David do? Rebbi Phineas in the name of Rebbi Eleazar ben Rebbi Menaḥem[96]: He took a harp, put it on his headboard, got up at midnight and started playing on it so that his companions in the study of Torah should hear it. What were his companions in the study of Torah saying? When king David studies Torah, certainly we have to do it also! Rebbi Levi[97] said: a lute was hanging in David's window and in the night the North wind was blowing and moving it and it was playing by itself. This refers to what is written (*2Kings* 3:15): "It happened when the musical instrument was playing." It does not say "when he played on the musical instrument" but "when the instrument was playing"; it was playing by itself.

94 Rebbi Ammi (or Immi) was the successor of Rebbi Yoḥanan as head of the academy of Tiberias. Rebbi Zeriqan was another student of Rebbi Yoḥanan. Their argument goes as follows: King David declares that he is used to get up at midnight and also that he gets up at the start of some night watch. But if midnight is the start of a watch then the number of watches has

to be even. [The parallel in the Babli (*Berakhot* 3b) is a shortened version of the Yerushalmi (in particular, in the Ashkenazic manuscript tradition.)]

95 See the preceding paragraph.

96 Rebbi Eleazar ben Rebbi Menaḥem was an Aggadist of the generation of Rebbi Ammi; Rebbi Phineas belongs to the following generation. A parallel Babylonian tradition is given in *Babli Berakhot* 4a. The Yerushalmi version is also found in *Pesiqta dRav Kahana*, ויהי בחצי הלילה, 13 and in *Midrash Tehillim* 119.

97 The preacher in the academy of R. Yoḥanan. A shortened version, without the reference to the story of Elisha, is a Babylonian tradition, by contemporary Babylonian teachers, in Babli *Berakhot* 3b. The verse quoted talks about the prophetic extasy of Elisha before king Jehoshaphat. R. Elazar Azkari explains that the verse from Kings can be taken to be parallel to *Psalms* 57:9 since in the latter verse the harp is also adressed directly, as a living being.

מַה מְקַיֵּם רִבִּי טַעֲמָא דְרִבִּי נָתָן רֹאשׁ הָאַשְׁמוֹרֶת הַתִּיכוֹנָה. אָמַר רִבִּי הוּנָא סוֹפָהּ שֶׁל שְׁנִיָּה וְרֹאשָׁהּ שֶׁל שְׁלִישִׁית הֵן מְתַוְּכוֹת אֶת הַלַּיְלָה. אָמַר רִבִּי מָנָא וְיֵאוֹת. מִי כְתִיב תִּיכוֹנוֹת לֹא תִיכוֹנָה. קַדְמִיתָא לָא מִתְחַשְּׁבָא דְּעַד כְּדוֹן בְּרִייָתָא עֵירִין.

How does Rebbi uphold the basis of Rebbi Nathan's reason, "at the start of the middle watch"?[98] Rebbi Huna said: the end of the second and the start of the third split the night into two. Rebbi Mana said: Is this true? Does it say "watches"? No, it says "watch"! The first watch does not count since there the creatures are still awake.

98 This is the logical end of the previous discussion that was interrupted by the aggadic interpretations of the verses sustaining the opinion of Rebbi. Both Rebbi Huna and Rebbi Mana belong to the fourth generation of Galilean Amoraïm, rather later than the authors of the previous section.

פסקא. וַחֲכָמִים אוֹמְרִים עַד חֲצוֹת. רִבִּי יָסָא בְשֵׁם רִבִּי יוֹחָנָן הֲלָכָה כַּחֲכָמִים. רִבִּי יָסָא מְפַקֵּד לַחֲבֵרַיָּא אִין בָּעֵיתוּן מִתְעַסְקָא בְאוֹרַיְיתָא אַתּוּן קַרְיָיה שְׁמַע קוֹדֶם חֲצוֹת וּמִתְעַסְקִין. מִילְתֵיהּ אָמְרָה שֶׁהֲלָכָה כַּחֲכָמִים מִילְתֵיהּ אָמְרָה שֶׁאָמַר דְּבָרִים אַחַר אֱמֶת וְיַצִּיב. תַּנֵּי הַקּוֹרֵא אֶת שְׁמַע בְּבֵית הַכְּנֶסֶת בְּשַׁחַר יָצָא יְדֵי חוֹבָתוֹ. בָּעֶרֶב לֹא יָצָא יְדֵי חוֹבָתוֹ. מַה בֵין הַקּוֹרֵא בְשַׁחֲרִית. וּמַה בֵין הַקּוֹרֵא בְעַרְבִית. רִבִּי הוּנָא בְשֵׁם רַב יוֹסֵף מַה טַעַם אָמְרוּ אָדָם צָרִיךְ לִקְרוֹת שְׁמַע בְּבֵיתוֹ בָעֶרֶב בִּשְׁבִיל לְהַבְרִיחַ אֶת הַמַּזִּיקִין. מִילְתֵיהּ אָמְרָה שֶׁאֵין אוֹמֵר דְּבָרִים אַחַר אֱמֶת וְיַצִּיב. מִילְתֵיהּ דְּרִבִּי שְׁמוּאֵל בַּר נַחְמָנִי אָמַר כֵּן. רִבִּי שְׁמוּאֵל בַּר נַחְמָנִי כַּד הֲוָה נָחִית לְעִיבּוּרָה הֲוָה מִקַּבֵּל גַּבֵּי רִבִּי יַעֲקֹב גָּרוֹסָה וַהֲוָה רִבִּי זְעִירָא מִטַּמֵּר בֵּינֵי קוּפַיָּא מִשְׁמַעְנָא הֵיךְ הֲוָה קָרֵי וְחָזַר וְקָרֵי עַד דַּהֲוָא שְׁקַע מִינֵיהּ גֵו שֵׁינָתֵיהּ. וּמַאי טַעֲמָא רִבִּי אַחָא וְרִבִּי תַּחְלִיפְתָּא חָמוֹי בְּשֵׁם רִבִּי שְׁמוּאֵל בַּר נַחְמָן רִגְזוּ וְאַל תֶּחֱטָאוּ אִמְרוּ בִלְבַבְכֶם עַל מִשְׁכַּבְכֶם וְדוֹמוּ סֶלָה.

New Section.[99] "But the sages say until midnight." Rebbi Yasa[100] in the name of Rebbi Yoḥanan: Practice follows the Sages. Rebbi Yasa commanded his colleagues: if you want to study Torah then you should recite the *Shema'* before midnight and then study[101]. His words imply that the practice follows the Sages. His words imply that one may speak after *Emet Weyaẓiv*[102]. It was stated: He who reads the *Shema'* in the synagogue during the morning service has fulfilled his duty; during the evening service he did not fulfill his duty[103]. What is the difference between him who reads in the morning and him who reads in the evening?[104] Rebbi Huna in the name of Rav Joseph:[105] Why did they say, a man has to read the *Shema'* in his house in the evening? In order to make evil spirits flee. His words imply that one may not speak after *Emet Weyaẓiv*. The words of Rebbi Samuel ben Naḥmani say the same. When R. Samuel ben Naḥmani descended for the intercalation[106], he was received by Rebbi Jacob the groats miller. Rebbi Zeïra was hiding among the crates to hear how he read [the *Shema'*]; he read it over and over again until he drifted away in sleep. What is the reason? Rebbi Aḥa and his father-in-law Rebbi Taḥlifa in the name of Rebbi Samuel bar Naḥmani (*Ps*. 4:5): "Tremble, do not sin, talk in your hearts on your couches and be silent, Selah."[107]

99 Quote from the next part of the Mishnah that is going to be discussed.

100 Rebbi Yasa in the Yerushalmi is Rabbi Assi in the Babli, the head of the Academy at Tiberias after the death of R. Yoḥanan. It seems that the procedures which R. Yasa recommended to his colleagues were not explicitly given by Rebbi Yoḥanan but reflected the general tradition of the Academy of Tiberias. In the Babli (*Berakhot* 8b), Rav Yehudah says in the name of Samuel that practice follows Rabban Gamliël who allows the recital of *Shema'* after midnight in emergency cases. From the next "New Section" in the Yerushalmi it is clear that this is not the Israeli position; they forbid the recitation of the *Shema'* after midnight. The opinion of Samuel represents either the autochthonous Babylonian practice or the teaching of the Academy of Nahardea founded by Ḥananiah ben Ḥananiah, the nephew of Rebbi Joshua, at the time of the revolt of Bar Kokhba.

101 One talks here about studying in the night. It is stated in Mishnah *Šabbat* 1:2 that one interrupts everything he is doing to recite *Shema'* at its proper time. Hence, we may assume that all these scholars did recite *Shema'* in the synagogue. It was stated at the start that one reads *Shema'* in the synagogue, when Minḥa and Maäriv services are held together while it is still before sundown, to stand in prayer after studying words of Torah. [This Israeli practice was followed by Ashkenazic Jewry, whose ritual basically was Galilean, until the sixteenth Century as can be seen from Rashi to the first Mishnah, *Ṭur Oraḥ Ḥayyim* 235 and the glosses of R. Moshe Isserls *Oraḥ Ḥayyim* 235. Because of the disapproval of the main commentators of *Shulḥan Arukh*, *Magen Abraham* and *TaZ*, the practice has disappeared in all Ashkenazic congregations except those of the old German rite.] The question here is whether the recitation of *Shema'* after nightfall is needed in order to fulfill the obligation of *Shema'* or whether it is needed to protect one's

sleep from evil influences. In the first case, one recites *Shema'* as soon as possible and then continues one's normal activities; in the second case one may say *Shema'* only when one actually goes to sleep and then cannot say anything anymore before actually sleeping.

102 In the Babylonian ritual followed today, the benediction after *Shema'* in the morning is אמת ויציב but in the evening אמת ואמונה ; in Israel the same version, אמת ויציב, was recited morning and evening.

We find a disagreement between Rashi and his grandson Rabbenu Tam about the practice of praying Maäriv immediately after Minḥah, before sundown. According to Rashi on the Mishnah, the practice of reciting the *Shema'* is exclusively to start the *Amidah* prayer after words of Torah. Hence, the only valid recitation is in the night. According to Rabbenu Tam (*Tosafot Berakhot* 2a), the prayers are held after *plag haminḥah*, not more than 1.25 variable hours before sundown, and according to an opinion of R. Yehudah mentioned later in the Mishnah, both *Amidah* and *Shema'* are valid prayers. According to Rashi, it is possible that the original *minhag* of the Jews in Israel did not imply that the benedictions before and after *Shema'* were recited in the synagogue and that, therefore, they had to be recited at home and could be combined with other prayers. It follows that "one may speak after אמת ויציב" can mean that one does not have to mention the praise of God for the redemption of Israel from Egypt immediately before starting the *Amidah* prayer. This interpretation is given by several commentators of the Yerushalmi, foremost among them R. Eleazar Askari. However, since the obligation to "connect the redemption to the *Amidah*" in evening prayers is given in the name of R. Yoḥanan in the Babylonian Talmud (*Berakhot* 9b) it is difficult to state the opposite opinion here in the name of R. Yoḥanan.

103 This supports Rashi's opinion. However, *Raviah*, the foremost Ashkenazic authority of the early thirteenth century, writes that "I have received in tradition from Rabbenu Tam that practice does not follow any of these statements but R. Yehudah in Mishnah *Berakhot* 4:1."

104 This question has no answer in the text and seems to be a marginal gloss copied into the text since the quotes of this section in *Raviah* (#1, vol. 1, p.5) and in *Midrash Tehillim* (4[9]) do not contain the sentence.

105 Rebbi Ḥuna is a younger Ga-

lilean Amora and is not to be confused with Rav Ḥuna, the student of Rav and leader of the second generation of Babylonian Amoraïm. Rav Joseph is the Babylonian (bar Ḥiyya), leader of the third generation in Babylonia. Rebbi Ḥuna often quotes Babylonian authorities and, therefore, possibly was a Babylonian immigrant to Israel.

106 Rebbi Shemuël bar Naḥmani (or Naḥman) was a student of the early Israeli Amora Rebbi Jonathan and one of the creators of the Midrash. The declaration of the addition of a month to the twelve month lunar year before the publication of the computed calendar was always made by an assembly of the leaders of the generation at a place called Callirrhoe (Ḥamat Gader). Rebbi Zeïra probably was too young at that time to be invited to the procedings but came to attend the gathering of the Sages, in order to learn from their ways.

While in the Babylonian Talmud נחת means "to leave the Land of Israel", in the Yerushalmi it can mean simply "to descend", in this case into the Jordan valley from his residence in Lod.

107 This paragraph is the basis of *Rema*'s notes in *Shulḥan Arukh Oraḥ Ḥayyim* 239,1, as noted by the Gaon of Wilna.

מִילְּתֵיהּ דְּרִבִּי יְהוֹשֻׁעַ בֶּן לֵוִי פְּלִיגָא דְּרִבִּי יְהוֹשֻׁעַ בֶּן לֵוִי קָרֵי מִזְמוֹרֵי בַּתְרֵיהּ. וְהָא תַנֵּי אֵין אוֹמֵר דְּבָרִים אַחַר אֱמֶת וְיַצִּיב. פָּתַר לָהּ בֶּאֱמֶת וְיַצִּיב שֶׁל שַׁחֲרִית. דָּמַר רִבִּי זְעִירָא בְשֵׁם רַב אַבָּא בַּר יִרְמְיָה שָׁלֹשׁ תְּכֵיפוֹת הֵן. תֵּכֶף לִסְמִיכָה שְׁחִיטָה. תֵּכֶף לִנְטִילַת יָדַיִם בְּרָכָה. תֵּכֶף לִגְאוּלָּה תְּפִילָּה. תֵּכֶף לִסְמִיכָה שְׁחִיטָה וְסָמַךְ וְשָׁחַט. תֵּכֶף לִנְטִילַת יָדַיִם בְּרָכָה שְׂאוּ יְדֵיכֶם קֹדֶשׁ וּבָרְכוּ אֶת יי. תֵּכֶף לִגְאוּלָּה תְּפִילָּה יִהְיוּ לְרָצוֹן אִמְרֵי פִי. מַה כְתִיב בַּתְרֵיהּ יַעַנְךָ יי בְּיוֹם צָרָה. אָמַר רִבִּי יוֹסֵי בֵּי רִבִּי בּוּן כָּל־מִי שֶׁהוּא תוֹקֵף סְמִיכָה לִשְׁחִיטָה אֵין פְּסוּל נוֹגֵעַ בְּאוֹתוֹ קָרְבָּן. וְכָל־מִי שֶׁהוּא תוֹקֵף לִנְטִילַת יָדַיִם בְּרָכָה אֵין הַשָּׂטָן מְקַטְרֵג בְּאוֹתָהּ סְעוּדָה. וְכָל־מִי שֶׁהוּא תוֹקֵף גְאוּלָּה לִתְפִילָּה אֵין הַשָּׂטָן מְקַטְרֵג בְּאוֹתוֹ הַיּוֹם. אָמַר רִבִּי זְעִירָא אֲנָא תְכֵפִית גְּאוּלָּה לִתְפִילָּה וְאִיתְצְדֵית בְּאַנְגָּרְיָא מוֹבִילָה הֲדַס לְפַלָּטִין אָמְרוּ לֵיהּ רַבֵּנוּ רִבּוּ הִיא. אִית בְּנֵי אִינְשֵׁי הָבִין פְּרִיטִין מַחְכִּים פַּלָּטִין. אָמַר רִבִּי אִמִּי כָּל־מִי שֶׁאֵינוֹ תוֹקֵף לִגְאוּלָּה תְּפִילָּה לְמַה הוּא דוֹמֶה. לְאוֹהֲבוֹ שֶׁל מֶלֶךְ שֶׁבָּא וְהִרְחִיק עַל פִּתְחוֹ שֶׁל מֶלֶךְ. יָצָא לֵידַע מַה הוּא מְבַקֵּשׁ וּמְצָאוֹ שֶׁהִפְלִיג עוֹד הוּא הִפְלִיג.

The behavior of Rebbi Joshua ben Levi[108] disagrees since Rebbi Joshua ben Levi read psalms afterwards. But have we not stated: One does not say words after *Emet Weyaẓiv*? He explains that as relating to *Emet Weyaẓiv* of the morning prayers[109], since Rebbi Zeïra said in the name of Rav Abba bar Jeremiah[110]: There are three immediacies: immediately after leaning comes slaughtering[111], immediately after hand-washing comes benediction[112], immediately after redemption comes prayer[113]. Immediately after leaning comes slaughtering: "He shall lean . . . he shall slaughter" (*Lev.* 1:4-5)[114]. Immediately after hand-washing comes benediction, (*Ps.* 134:2) "Lift your hands in holiness and bless the Lord.[115]" Immediately after redemption comes prayer, (*Ps.* 19:15) "May the words of my mouth be for goodwill" and it is written after that (*Ps.* 20:2) "May the Lord answer you on the day of worry."[116] Rebbi Yose ben Rebbi Abun said: For anyone who immediately slaughters after leaning, no disqualification will appear regarding his sacrifice. For anyone who immediately pronounces the benediction after washing his hands, Satan will not find anything to accuse about at that meal. For anyone who immediately prays after mentioning redemption, Satan will not find anything to accuse him of the entire day[117]. Rebbi Zeïra said, I am used to immediately pray after mentioning redemption and I was conscripted to forced labor, to bring myrrh to the Palace. They said to him: our teacher, that is an honor. There are people who pay money to see the inside of the Palace. Rebbi Immi[118] said: Anyone who does not immediately pray after mentioning redemption, whom is he to be likened to? To an acquaintance of the king who comes from afar to the king's door. When the king comes to see what he wants, he finds that the person left. Hence, the king also leaves.

108 One of the great sages of the first generation of Amoraïm. He lived in the valley of Beth Shean (*Demay* 2:1). It follows that his way of reading the nightly *Shema'*, which is the one followed today, is the oldest. In the Babylonian Talmud (*Berakhot* 4b) he is only reported to have stated the duty to read the *Shema'* before sleeping, with the reason of R. Samuel ben Naḥmani given by a Galilean Amora by the name of R. Yose or R. Assi. The psalms read by R. Joshua ben Levi are detailed in Babli *Shevuöt* 15b where it is noted that, while it is forbiddden to use Biblical verses as charms in healing, it is admissible to recite them for protection.

109 Here it is obvious that "words after *Emet Weyaẓiv*" mean any insertion between the benediction גאל ישראל and the *Amidah* prayer. It does not follow that the expression must have the same meaning in the preceding section.

110 R. Abba bar Jeremiah seems to have been a Babylonian whose father (or uncle) was a contemporary of Rav and who was the teacher of Rebbi Zeïra (Rebbi Zera in the Babli) when the latter was still in Babylonia. The parallel teaching is mentioned, in the same wording but with a different meaning, in the Babylonian Talmud (*Berakhot* 42a) in the name of Rav.

111 In the usual process of bringing a sacrifice in the temple, the votary has to press with his hand on the head of the sacrifice before the slaughter.

112 It is clear from the following that the meaning here is that immediately after washing one's hands, while drying them, one has to pronounce the appropriate benediction. [Possibly, it could mean that immediately after washing the hands one has to pronounce the benediction over bread that starts the meal. The urgency of starting the meal directly after washing one's hands is ascribed in Babli *Berakhot* 52b to the School of Shammai; this interpretation of the Yerushalmi is implied by R. Aqiba Eiger in his notes to Babli *Berakhot* 42a.] In the Babli, *Berakhot* 42a, the same expression means that immediately after washing one's hands *after* the meal one has to say Grace and is not allowed to eat anymore.

113 This means that immediately after reciting the benediction: "Praise to You, o Lord, Who redeemed Israel," one has to start the *Amidah* prayer. This creates no problems in the morning prayers but is impossible in the evening since after the benediction (starting *Emet Weëmunah* or *Emet Weyaẓiv*) there follows at least one

more benediction and a *Qaddish* to separate the recital of *Shema'* and its benedictions, an unconditional obligation at least from the institutions of the Men of the Great Assembly, and the *Amidah* prayer that in the night is of conditional Rabbinical character. When the principle "immediately after redemption comes prayer" was adopted also for the evening prayers (see preceding section), the intermediate pieces were declared to be "extensions of the thanksgiving for redemption." The benediction immediately preceding the *Qaddish* was fixed by Babylonian Gaonim to be a benediction for future redemption. The *Qaddish* itself may be a Gaonic institution.

114 Leaning and slaughtering are two obligations of the votary given in two consecutive verses. (However, leaning must be performed by the votary himself but slaughtering can be delegated to a third party.)

115 Hands lifted in holiness are washed hands. An allusion to this is found in the benediction that does not read "to wash the hands" but "to lift the hands."

116 This derivation is a good example for the tendency of the Talmud to assume that everybody knows his Bible by heart and that it is enough to quote the start of a sentence in order to recall the entire sentence. The last sentence of Psalm 19 reads in its entirety: "May the words of my mouth be for goodwill before You, o Lord, my Rock and *my Redeemer*". The next psalm, disregarding the title "For the director, a psalm of David," starts: "May the Lord answer you on the day of worry." Since psalms in ancient manuscripts were written without paragraph divisions, the description of God as redeemer and the mention of help through prayer are consecutive.

117 This third statement is quoted in the Babli (*Berakhot* 9b), in the name of the holy congregation of Jerusalem, i.e., the Tanna R. Yose ben Hammeshullam. To it is appended the story about Rebbi Zera (Zeïra)'s complaint, only there he had to bring myrrh to the king himself. Since R. Zeïra was a Babylonian immigrant to Israel, it is not clear whether his forced labor occured in Babylonia, on the occasion of a visit of the Persian king, or in Galilee where he only had the opportunity to see the interior of the governor's residence. The language of the story in the Yerushalmi points to its happening in Israel, while the language of the Babli points to the Persian empire. It cannot be decided where the incident happened.

118 In the Babylonian Talmud, he

appears as Rebbi Ammi, colleague of Rebbi Assi/Yasa. In the Yerushalmi, his name usually is Immi. His simile is quoted by Rashi, *Berakhot* 4b.

פסקא. רַבָּן גַּמְלִיאֵל אוֹמֵר עַד שֶׁיַּעֲלֶה עַמּוּד הַשַּׁחַר: אַתְיָא דְרַבָּן גַּמְלִיאֵל כְּרַבִּי שִׁמְעוֹן דְּתַנֵּי בְּשֵׁם רִבִּי שִׁמְעוֹן פְּעָמִים שֶׁאָדָם קוֹרֵא אֶת שְׁמַע אַחַת לִפְנֵי עַמּוּד הַשַּׁחַר וְאַחַת לְאַחַר עַמּוּד הַשַּׁחַר וְנִמְצָא יוֹצֵא חוֹבָתוֹ שֶׁל יוֹם (fol. 3a) וְשֶׁל לַיְלָה. הָא רַבָּן גַּמְלִיאֵל כְּרַבִּי שִׁמְעוֹן בְּעַרְבִית אַף בְּשַׁחֲרִית כֵּן. אוֹ יְהֵא בָהּ כַּיי דָּמַר רִבִּי זְעִירָא תַּנָּאֵי אַחֲוֹי דְּרַב חִיָּא בַּר אַשִׁיא וּדְרַב אַבָּא בַּר חָנָה הַקּוֹרֵא עִם אַנְשֵׁי מִשְׁמָר לֹא יָצָא כִּי מַשְׁכִּימִין הָיוּ.

New Section. "Rabban Gamliel says until the first sign of dawn." The statement of Rabban Gamliel is parallel to that of Rebbi Simeon, as we have stated in the name of Rebbi Simeon[119]: "Sometimes a person reads the *Shema'* [twice], once before dawn and once at dawn, and has fulfilled his obligation for day and night." Hence Rabban Gamliel is like Rebbi Simeon for evening prayers, is he also like him in the morning? His position might be that expressed[120] by Rebbi Zeïra the Tanna[121], the brother of Rav Ḥiyya bar Ashi[122], and of Rav Abba bar Ḥana[123]: He who reads with the men of the *Mishmar* did not fulfill his duty because they were too early[124].

119 He is Rebbi Simeon bar Yoḥay, one of the students of R. Aqiba. In the Babli (*Berakhot* 8b), the statement occurs in two versions, either "sometimes a person reads the *Shema'* twice during the night", or "sometimes a person reads the *Shema'* twice during the day" and there they have to explain that either the few minutes before the start of dawn are already counted as day because some people already get up or that the first minutes of dawn are counted as night because most people still are asleep. The statement in its Babylonian form is also in the Tosephta (*Berakhot* 1:1); in general, our Tosephta seems to be a Babylonian version. The Yerushalmi version avoids the ambiguity but in parallel to the Babli one has to assume that R. Simeon accepts that one may read *Shema'* twice within the span of a few minutes and

fulfill two distinct obligations by the readings.

120 The Aramaic/Hebrew כיי דמר should be read as equivalent of Babylonian: בְּהַאי דְּאָמַר.

121 Meaning a person specializing in the memorizing and recitation of tannaïtic statements in the amoraïc period. A Tanna of the tannaïtic period never has the title "Tanna".

122 One of the foremost students of Rav in Babylonia.

123 First cousin and colleague of Rav and student of their common uncle Rebbi Ḥiyya. Their statement, slightly enlarged, appears as an anonymous *baraita* in the Babli *Yoma* 37b. It seems to be a Tosephta from the collection of the Academy of Rav.

124 The *Mishmar* were the priests who kept watch during the night at the Temple service. Since the Temple service started at the first signs of dawn, the men of the *Mishmar* [and the laymen accompanying them, the *Maämad*], had to *finish* their prayers before the start of service, i. e., before the first sign of dawn.

The Yerushalmi does not try to answer the question raised, whether Rabban Gamliel and Rebbi Simeon are of the same opinion for morning prayers, since it already had decided in the preceding section that the practice follows the Sages and, therefore, one may not recite the *Shema'* after midnight. Hence, the opinions of both Rebbi Simeon and Rabban Gamliel are of purely theoretical interest and no answer is required. In the Babli, the quote from Rebbi Simeon is given as a support to their decision that practice follows Rabban Gamliel. It seems to be the position of the Yerushalmi that in Temple times practice followed Rabban Gamliel in the Temple precinct and the Sages everywhere else.

משנה ב: מַעֲשֶׂה שֶׁבָּאוּ בָנָיו מִבֵּית הַמִּשְׁתֶּה אָמְרוּ לוֹ לֹא קָרִינוּ אֶת שְׁמַע. אָמַר לָהֶן אִם לֹא עָלָה עַמּוּד הַשַּׁחַר חַיָּבִין אַתֶּם לִקְרוֹת.

Mishnah 2: It happened that his (Rabban Gamliel's) sons returned from a wedding feast and told him: We did not recite the *Shema'*. He said to them: If dawn has not yet come then you are obligated to recite.

הלכה ב: וְרַבָּן גַּמְלִיאֵל פָּלִיג עַל רַבָּנִין וְעָבֵד עוּבְדָא כְוָתֵיהּ. וְהָא רִבִּי מֵאִיר פָּלִיג עַל רַבָּנִין וְלָא עָבֵד עוּבְדָא כְוָתֵיהּ. וְהָא רִבִּי עֲקִיבָא פָּלִיג עַל רַבָּנִין וְלָא עָבֵד עוּבְדָא כְוָתֵיהּ:

Halakhah 2. Rabban Gamliel disagrees with the Sages and acts upon his opinion?[125] Did not Rebbi Meïr disagree with the Sages and not act upon his opinion, did not Rebbi Aqiba disagree with the Sages and not act upon his opinion?

125 Since it is written (*Ex.* 23:2) "to yield to the majority", a religious authority is not allowed to act upon his personal opinion if it disagrees with the majority. This principle is then illustrated by several examples. It therefore is a big question why Rabban Gamliel's action is mentioned in the Mishnah without a disapproving remark. [The position of the Babli here is quite different: Since the action of Rabban Gamliel is mentioned in the Mishnah without a disapproving remark, it follows that general practice follows Rabban Gamliel since the practice of a religious authority overrides theoretical arguments.]

וְהֵן אַשְׁכְּחָן דְּרִבִּי מֵאִיר פָּלִיג עַל רַבָּנִין וְלָא עָבֵד עוּבְדָא כְוָתֵיהּ. דְּתַנֵּי סָכִין אַלְוונְתִּית לְחוֹלֶה בְּשַׁבָּת. אֵימָתַי שֶׁטְּרָפוֹ בְשֶׁמֶן וּבְיַיִן מֵעֶרֶב שַׁבָּת. אֲבָל אִם לֹא טְרָפוֹ מֵעֶרֶב שַׁבָּת אָסוּר. תַּנֵּי אָמַר רִבִּי שִׁמְעוֹן בֶּן אֶלְעָזָר מַתִּיר הָיָה רִבִּי מֵאִיר לִטְרוֹף יַיִן וְשֶׁמֶן וְלָסוּךְ לְחוֹלֶה בְּשַׁבָּת. וּכְבָר חָלָה וּבִקַּשְׁנוּ לַעֲשׂוֹת לוֹ כֵן וְלֹא הִנִּיחַ לָנוּ. וְאָמַרְנוּ לוֹ רִבִּי דְּבָרֶיךָ מְבַטֵּל בְּחַיֶּיךָ. וְאָמַר לָן אַף עַל פִּי שֶׁאֲנִי מֵקֵל לַאֲחֵרִים מַחְמִיר אֲנִי עַל עַצְמִי דְּהָא פְלִיגֵי עָלַי חֲבֵרָי.

So we find that Rebbi Meïr disagreed with the Sages and did not act upon his opinion. We have stated: One rubs *olentia*[126] on a sick person on the Sabbath; but only if it was mixed with oil and wine before Sabbath eve. But if he did not mix it before Sabbath eve it is forbidden. We have stated: Rebbi Simeon ben Eleazar said: Rebbi Meïr did allow to mix wine and oil and to rub it onto a sick persion on Sabbath. When he fell sick, we wanted to prepare the same for him but he did not let us do it. We said to him: Our teacher, are you going to invalidate your words when your life is in danger? He said to us: even though I am lenient for others, I am stringent for myself because my colleagues disagree with me.

126 Latin *olentia* "sweet smelling things" (E. G.). There are at least two kinds, one mixture used for medical purposes, and one, mentioned in Halakhah 6:6, to be used as air freshener in a house. The Babli (*Šabbat* 140a) defines medical אלונתית as a mixture of wine, olive oil, and balsamum, used to reduce fever. [Brill derives the Hebrew word from Latin (*unguentum*) *oleamentum*, an ointment made with a base of olive oil. Jastrow (followed by Krauss, Löw, and Lieberman) derives the word from Greek οἰνάνθη, οἰνανθίς, Latin *oenanthe*, which however means only "bloom of the wild grape" and clearly is inapplicable here.]

The entire quote is from *Tosephta Šabbat* 13 where it belongs to a sequence of statements that one may not use edibles for medicinal purposes on the Sabbath except if used also as food. For example, for a toothache it is possible to rinse the tooth with vinegar on condition that the vinegar then be swallowed; it is not admissible to spit out the vinegar after use. Hence, it is not allowed to mix wine and oil with balsamum on the Sabbath since that would make it inedible. The parallel quote in the Babli is *Šabbat* 134a; the only difference in the texts is that the Babli and Tosephta have a purely Hebrew text while the Yerushalmi has the connecting remarks in Aramaic.

וְהֵן אַשְׁכְּחָן דְּרִבִּי עֲקִיבָא פַּלִּיג עַל רַבָּנִין וְלָא עָבַד עוּבְדָּא כְּוָתֵיהּ. כְּיֵי דְתַנִּינָן תַּמָּן הַשִּׁדְרָה וְהַגּוּלְגּוֹלֶת מִשְּׁנֵי מֵתִים. אֵבֶר מִן הַמֵּת מִשְּׁנֵי מֵתִים. אֵבֶר מִן הַחַי מִשְּׁנֵי אֲנָשִׁים. רִבִּי עֲקִיבָא מְטַמֵּא וַחֲכָמִים מְטַהֲרִין. תַּנֵּי מַעֲשֶׂה וְהֵבִיאוּ קוּפָּה מְלֵאָה עֲצָמוֹת מִכְּפַר טַבִּי וְהִנִּחוּהָ בָּאֲוִיר הַכְּנֶסֶת בְּלוֹד. וְנִכְנַס תּוֹדְרוֹס הָרוֹפֶא וְנִכְנְסוּ כָּל־הָרוֹפְאִים עִמּוֹ. אָמַר תּוֹדְרוֹס הָרוֹפֶא אֵין כַּאן שִׁדְרָה מִמֵּת אֶחָד וְלֹא גוּלְגּוֹלֶת מִמֵּת אֶחָד. אָמְרוּ הוֹאִיל וְיֵשׁ כַּאן מְטַהֲרִין וְיֵשׁ כַּאן מְטַמְּאִין. נַעֲמוֹד עַל הַמִּנְיָן. הִתְחִילוּ מֵרִבִּי עֲקִיבָא וְטִהֵר. אָֽמְרוּ לוֹ הוֹאִיל וְהָיִיתָ מְטַמֵּא וְטִיהַרְתָּ טָהוֹר.

So we find that Rebbi Aqiba disagreed with the Sages and did not act upon his opinion. As we have stated there (*Mishnah Ahilot* 2:6): "Spine and skull from two dead bodies, a limb composed of limbs of two dead bodies, limbs taken from two living persons, Rebbi Aqiba declares them to be impure and the Sages declare them to be pure."[127] We have stated:[128] "It happened that they brought a chest full of bones from Kefar Tabi[129] to Lod and deposited it in the open air [the courtyard] of the synagogue. Theodoros the physician entered and with him all physicians. Theodoros declared that there was no complete spine from one dead person and no complete skull from one dead person. They said: Since we have here some who declare this pure and others who declare it impure, let us vote upon it. They started with Rebbi Aqiba and he declared it to be pure. They said: Since you had declared it impure, but now you vote for it to be pure, it is pure."

127 Purity and impurity mentioned here refer to transmission of impurity by a "tent", since automatically everybody under the same roof with a corpse becomes impure; the "pure" bones mentioned here will still transmit impurity by touch. The conditions of impurity are spelled out in *Ahilot* 2:1. Flesh is causing impurity down to the volume of an olive but bones do so only if they are either the volume of a quarter *qab* (about .55 liter), most of the bones composing the skeleton in number or in importance, or skull and/or spine. [Whether one has to read שדרה וגלגולת as "skull *and* spine" or "skull *or* spine" is discussed inconclusively in *Babli Nazir* 52b ff.]

128 Tosephta *Ahilot* 4:2; there the full name Theodoros is given to the chief surgeon. The Tosephta starts: "Rebbi Yehudah said: Six cases did Rebbi Aqiba declare impure and he changed his opinion; it happened . . .", and ends: "Rebbi Simeon said: Until the time of his death did Rebbi Aqiba maintain that it should be impure; whether he changed his opinion when dying I do not know." This means that according to Rebbi Yehudah, the vote at Lod showed that Rebbi Aqiba changed his opinion but, according to

Rebbi Simeon, Rebbi Aqiba did not change his opinion, only he did not want openly to defy the opinion of the majority. We assume that the Yerushalmi here accepts the opinion of Rebbi Simeon, otherwise there is no proof here. It follows that also when the Yerushalmi quotes the Tosephta, sometimes the proof comes from the omitted parts.

129 Former Arab village Kafr Ṭab East of Lod.

וְהֵן אַשְׁכְּחָן דְּרִבִּי שִׁמְעוֹן פָּלִיג עַל רַבָּנִין וְלָא עֲבַד עוּבְדָּא כְּוָתֵיהּ. כְּיֵי דְתַנִּינָן תַּמָּן רִבִּי שִׁמְעוֹן אוֹמֵר כָּל־הַסְּפִיחִין מוּתָּרִין חוּץ מִסְּפִיחֵי כְּרוּב שֶׁאֵין כְּיוֹצֵא בָּהֶן בְּיַרְקוֹת שָׂדֶה. וַחֲכָמִים אוֹמְרִים כָּל־הַסְּפִיחִין אֲסוּרִין. ר׳ שִׁמְעוֹן בַּר יוֹחַי עֲבַד עוּבְדָּא בִּשְׁמִיטְתָא חֲמָא חַד מְלַקֵּט סְפִיחֵי שְׁבִיעִית. אָמַר לֵיהּ וְלֵית אָסוּר. וְלָאו סְפִיחַ אִינּוּן. אָמַר לֵיהּ וְלַאו אַתְּ הוּא שֶׁאַתְּ מַתִּיר. אָמַר לֵיהּ וְאֵין חֲבֵרַי חוֹלְקִין עָלַי. וְקָרֵי עֲלוֹי וּפֹרֵץ גָּדֵר יִשְּׁכֶנּוּ נָחָשׁ. וְכֵן הֲוָת לֵיהּ.

So we find that Rebbi Simeon disagreed with the Sages and did not act upon his opinion. As we have stated there (*Mishnah Ševiït* 9:1) "Rebbi Simeon says: all aftergrowth is allowed except the aftergrowth of cabbage because nothing similar grows wild[130]. But the Sages say that all aftergrowth is forbidden." Rebbi Simeon bar Yoḥai acted on this in a Sabbatical year. He saw a man harvesting aftergrowth. He said to him: Is that not forbidden, is that not aftergrowth? The man answered him back: Are you not the one who allows it? He retorted: Do not my colleagues disagree with me? He recited over him (*Eccl.* 10:6): "He who breaches a fence may be bitten by a snake", and this is what happened to that man.

130 The Mishnah deals with produce of the Seventh year offered for sale by an *Am Haärez*, a Jew who cannot be trusted with the careful fulfillment of all his religious obligations. The Torah says not only that it is forbidden to plant and sow during the Sabbatical year but also (*Lev.* 32:5): "Do not harvest the aftergrowth of your harvest," i. e., it is forbidden to commercially exploit the produce growing on one's field from the seeds of the preceding year. It is, however, acceptable to collect from one's fields

small amounts for one's daily needs (and even for storage as long as wild animals can find similar food on the fields.) Rebbi Simeon is of the opinion that a poor person may offer anything for sale since he might (or probably did) collect them from wild growing plants which do not fall under the prohibition. The only exception is produce which is never found growing wild; such vegetables are forbidden for commerce in the production of one's own field. The Sages, while agreeing that Rebbi Simeon's position is the one which follows the Biblical precept closely, nevertheless as a Rabbinic ordinance forbid any such buying from untrustworthy people since it is too difficult to enforce the fine distinction made by Rebbi Simeon.

Our example shows that Rebbi Simeon refrained from disagreeing in practice from the rest of the Sages even in purely Rabbinical ordinances. The man cursed by him probably did collect wild aftergrowth, or maybe was known to Rebbi Simeon as a landless person who, therefore, collected from growth on other people's land that was declared ownerless (הפקר), otherwise his opponent could not have invoked R. Simeon's own ruling. [This explanation follows Maimonides on the Mishnah. Babli *Pesaḥim* 51b has a different text, see the discussion in Mishnah *Ševiït* 9:1, and *Kilaim*, Halakhah 1:9, and the notes to the Mishnah edition of the Institute for the Complete Israeli Talmud, *Ševiït* 9:1. The Rome ms. has here "forbidden," influenced by the Babli.]

וְרַבָּן גַּמְלִיאֵל פָּלִיג עַל רַבָּנִין וְעָבֵד עוּבְדָא כְּוָתֵיהּ. שַׁנְיָא הָכָא שֶׁהִיא לְשִׁינּוּן. מֵעַתָּה אַף מִשֶּׁיַּעֲלֶה עַמּוּד הַשַּׁחַר. וְאִית דְּבָעֵי מֵימַר תַּמָּן הָיוּ יְכוֹלִין לְקַיֵּם דִּבְרֵי חֲכָמִים. בְּרַם הָכָא כְּבַר עָבַר חֲצוֹת וְלֹא הָיוּ יְכוֹלִין לְקַיֵּם דִּבְרֵי חֲכָמִים אָמַר לוֹן עוֹבְדִין עוֹבַד כְּוָתֵיהּ.

And Rabban Gamliel disagreed with the Sages and did act on his own opinion! There is a difference here since the recitiation of the *Shema'* is for study[131]. But then they could have read also after the start of dawn[132]. Some want to say that in the other cases it was possible to uphold the words of the Sages. But here it was after midnight and they could no longer fulfill the precept of the Sages; so he told his sons to act according to his opinion[133].

131 As explained at the end of Mishnah 5.

132 And why did he tell them only to read before dawn? [Naturally, after dawn there already is an obligation to read the morning *Shema'*; the question seems to be whether it is preferable to read the *Shema'* twice if one forgot to recite it in the preceding period.] The question remains unanswered but this cannot be taken as rejection of the explanation.

133 Since the Sages will agree in this situation.

משנה ג. וְלֹא זוֹ בִלְבַד אֶלָּא כָל־שֶׁאָמְרוּ חֲכָמִים עַד חֲצוֹת מִצְוָתָן עַד שֶׁיַּעֲלֶה עַמּוּד הַשַּׁחַר. הֶקְטֵר חֲלָבִים וְאֵיבָרִים [וַאֲכִילַת פְּסָחִים] מִצְוָתָן עַד שֶׁיַּעֲלֶה עַמּוּד הַשַּׁחַר.

Mishnah 3: Not only that, but everywhere the Sages said "until midnight", the obligation is to the start of dawn. The obligation of burning fats and limbs on the altar [and eating of the Passover sacrifice] is until the start of dawn.[134]

134 This entire Mishnah, and the following one, are still the words of Rabban Gamliel. In the Venice print and the Leyden manuscript, the Passover sacrifice is not mentioned in the Mishnah preceding the chapter but it is in the Mishnah repeated before the Halakhah. The Biblical precept is to burn the remaining parts of the sacrifices on the altar "the entire night until morning" (*Lev*. 6:1).

In the interpretation of the Mishnah, there is a fundamental disagreement between Rashi and Maimonides. Rashi (*Berakhot* 2a, *s. v.* כדי להרחיק) writes: "Concerning burning of the fats, the Sages did not restrict it to 'until midnight' at all and it is mentioned here only to emphasize that everything that has to be done in the night is *kasher* the entire night." Maimonides, in his commentary on the Mishnah, writes: "They said about all of these activities 'until midnight', even though there would be time until the first signs of dawn, as a 'fence' that no one should come to act under pressure and prolong his actions until after the start of dawn;

that is what they said 'In order to remove people from sin.'" And he formulates this in his code (*Maäse haqorbanot* 4:2): "In order to avoid wilful transgression, the Sages said to bring to the altar the parts that have to be burned only until midnight."

Neither the Yerushalmi nor the Babli discuss the burning of sacrifices during the night. However, as Rebbi Ḥuna points out in the following paragraph, in his opinion the entire discussion in the Mishnah is about Rabbinic precepts, rather than Biblical commandments. This is compatible only with the point of view of Maimonides. It is a well known principle that Maimonides follows the Yerushalmi in all points in which there is no contrary opinion indicated in the Babli; he will take the silence of the Babli in this matter as an endorsement of the interpretation of the Yerushalmi.

הלכה ג. אֲנָן תַּנִּינָן אֲכִילַת פְּסָחִים. אִית דְּלָא תַנָּא אֲכִילַת פְּסָחִים. מַאן תַּנָּא אֲכִילַת פְּסָחִים רַבָּנָן. וּמַאן דְּלָא תַּנָּא אֲכִילַת פְּסָחִים רִבִּי אֱלִיעֶזֶר. וּמַאי טַעֲמָא דְרִבִּי אֱלִיעֶזֶר נֶאֱמַר כַּאן לַיְלָה וְנֶאֱמַר לְהַלָּן לַיְלָה. מַה לַיְלָה שֶׁנֶּאֱמַר לְהַלָּן חֲצוֹת. אַף כַּאן חֲצוֹת. אָמַר רִבִּי חוּנָה וְלֵית כַּאן אֲכִילַת פְּסָחִים אֲפִילוּ כְּרַבָּנָן דְּתַנִּינָן הַפֶּסַח אַחַר חֲצוֹת מְטַמֵּא אֶת הַיָּדַיִם.

Halakhah 3: We have stated "the eating of the Passover sacrifice". Some people do not formulate "the eating of the Passover sacrifice". Who formulates "the eating of the Passover sacrifice"? The Sages. Who does not formulate "the eating of the Passover sacrifice"? Rebbi Eliezer.[135] What is the reason of Rebbi Eliezer? It is written here (*Ex.* 12:8) "in the night", and it is written there (*Ex.* 12:29) "in the night". Just as there it means midnight, so also here it means midnight. Rebbi Ḥuna[136] says: "The eating of the Passover sacrifice" cannot be here even for the Sages since we have stated (*Pesaḥim* 10:9) "the Passover sacrifice after midnight makes one's hands impure."[139]

135 For the Sages, the obligation of eating the Passover sacrifices lasts during the entire Seder night; the limitation to the first half of the night

is a Rabbinical ordinance. According to Rebbi Eliezer [and Rebbi Eleazar ben Azariah in the Babli, *Berakhot* 9a], there is a Biblical prohibition of celebrating the Exodus after midnight. (Cf. the discussion in the author's *The Scholar's Haggadah*, Northvale NJ 1995, pp. 263-264.)

Rebbi Eliezer's argument goes as follows: The Bible prescribes that the Passover sacrifice should be eaten "in that night." It also reports that the death of the Egyptian firstborn was "in the middle of the night". Since the second occurrence of "night" is qualified by "middle" but the first is left indeterminate, and we subscribe to the opinion that, unless explicitly given otherwise, words in the Pentateuch have an invariable meaning, the first occurrence must also mean "midnight." The Sages follow Rebbi Aqiba in pointing out that the first Passover had to be eaten "in a hurry", the hurry of the Exodus that happened only the following day. Hence, the notion of "night" here is opposed to "day" and not restricted to the first half.

136 This is the form in which the name of the Galilean Amora R. Ḥuna appears most frequently in the Yerushalmi. It is probable that the Babylonian Amora Rav Huna (הונא) also originally was called חונא "the gracious one", but in Babylonia every ח was pronounced as ה.

Rebbi Ḥuna points out that, since we are agreed that this Mishnah and the following one deal only with Rabbinical ordinances, the mention of the Passover sacrifice is impossible since, by Rabbinical ordinance, the Passover sacrifice is ritually impure after midnight, for the same reason that voluntary offerings cannot be eaten after midnight as explained in the next Halakhah. Here is another fundamental difference between the Yerushalmi and the Babli. According to the Yerushalmi both in *Berakhot* and in *Pesaḥim* (37d), the prohibitions mentioned in the Mishnah are Rabbinical. But the Babli in both cases (*Berakhot* 9a, *Pesaḥim* 120b) refers only to the opinions of Rebbis Eliezer and Eleazar ben Azariah that the prohibition is Biblical.

138 The reason is the same as the one given for sacrifices in the next Mishnah.

משנה ד. כָּל־הַנֶּאֱכָלִין לְיוֹם אֶחָד מִצְווֹתָן עַד שֶׁיַּעֲלֶה עֲמוּד הַשַּׁחַר. אִם כֵּן לָמָּה אָמְרוּ חֲכָמִים עַד חֲצוֹת כְּדֵי לְהַרְחִיק אֶת הָאָדָם מִן הָעֲבֵירָה.

Mishnah 4: All sacrifices that can be eaten during one full day only could be eaten until the first dawn. In that case, why did the Sages say, only until midnight? In order to remove people from sin.

הלכה ד. כָּל־הַנֶּאֱכָלִין לְיוֹם אֶחָד קָדְשֵׁי קָדָשִׁים. אִם כֵּן לָמָּה אָמְרוּ חֲכָמִים וכו׳ אִם אַתְּ אוֹמֵר עַד שֶׁיַּעֲלֶה עֲמוּד הַשַּׁחַר הוּא סָבוּר שֶׁלֹּא עָלָה עֲמוּד הַשַּׁחַר. נִמְצָא אוֹכֵל וּמִתְחַיֵּב. מִתּוֹךְ שֶׁאַתְּ אוֹמֵר לוֹ עַד חֲצוֹת. אֲפִילוּ הוּא אוֹכֵל אַחַר חֲצוֹת אֵינוֹ מִתְחַיֵּב.

Halakhah 4: "All sacrifices that can be eaten during one full day only," these are the holiest of holies.[139] "In that case, why did the Sages say, etc.?" If you would say until the start of dawn, one might think that dawn did not yet start and it would turn out that he eats in sin.[140] When you say to him: "only until midnight," even if he does eat after midnight he will not incur guilt.

139 This is the reading of the שרידי ירושלמי from the Cairo Genizah. The Leyden manuscript and the printed editions have קדשים קלים "simple sacrifices". Zachariah Frankel already conjectured that the correct reading must be the one before us, as will be explained now.

There were four kinds of animal sacrifices in the Temple. Of certain sacrifices of atonement, only the blood was sprinkled on the altar; the rest was burnt outside the Temple precinct. The flesh of the עולה, "holocaust" (totally burnt), was all burnt on the altar. The usual sacrifices of atonement had to be eaten by male Cohanim in the Temple precinct, except that blood, fat, and certain organs had to be burnt on the altar. These sacrifices are called "holiest of holies" and had to be consumed during the day of sacrifice or the following night. Family sacrifices, שלמים, "peace", or "payment", or "wholeness" sacrifices, were eaten by the family of the votary (except for the blood and fat, which was burnt on the altar, and certain parts which were to be eaten by priestly families.) These family sacrifices were called "simple sacrifices"; most of them had to be eaten during two days and the intervening night. The only "simple sacrifices" to be eaten during one day were thanksgiving sacrifices and the sacrifice of the *Nazir* at the end of his votary period when he cut his hair. Hence, *all* "holiest of holies" sacrifices are covered by our Mishnah but only a minority of "simple sacrifices". There might be some justification for the reading "simple sacrifices" referring to the obligation of laity only who never ate "holiest of holies"; but then no special determination would be necessary.

140 The determination of dawn was possible only for professional astronomers. In many cases, people would think that is was night when it was already dawn and then incur guilt by eating the sacrifices. In mid-month, with a large moon, the determination of the start of dawn is practically impossible for a non-professional. Midnight is no better defined than the start of dawn but a deviation from the true midnight would be harmless.

משנה ה. מֵאֵימָתַי קוֹרִין אֶת שְׁמַע בְּשַׁחֲרִית מִשֶּׁיַּכִּיר בֵּין תְּכֵלֶת לְלָבָן. רִבִּי אֱלִיעֶזֶר אוֹמֵר בֵּין תְּכֵלֶת לְכָרָתָן. (וְגוֹמְרָהּ) עַד הָנֵץ הַחַמָּה. וְרִבִּי יְהוֹשֻׁעַ אוֹמֵר עַד שָׁלֹשׁ שָׁעוֹת שֶׁכֵּן דֶּרֶךְ (בְּנֵי) מְלָכִים לַעֲמוֹד בְּשָׁלֹשׁ שָׁעוֹת. הַקּוֹרֵא מִכַּאן וָאֵילַךְ לֹא הִפְסִיד כְּאָדָם שֶׁהוּא קוֹרֵא בַתּוֹרָה.

Mishnah 5: From when on does one read the *Shema'* in the morning? From when one can distinguish between dark blue[141] and white; Rebbi Eliezer says, between dark blue and the color of leeks; (he may read it)[142] until sunrise. Rebbi Yehoshua says, until three hours of the day since it is the rule of (sons of)[143] kings to rise at three hours. He who reads after that did not lose, he is like a man reading in the Torah.

141 The translation of תכלת is problematic. It is defined in Babli *Menaḥot* as a color obtained by dying with the blood of some marine snail but since the snail has not been clearly identified, the color cannot be

established by experimentation. From the second paragraph in the Halakhah, it would seem that תכלת could also be green, like color of the sea or like grasses. Since both in Babli (*Soṭa* 17a, *Menaḥot* 35b, *Ḥullin* 89a, *Sifri* 115) and in Yerushalmi (here, *Bemidbar rabba* 14) sources the final comparison is with the sky, in modern Hebrew תכלת means "sky-blue" in contrast to כָּחוֹל "dark blue, color of *kohl*".

The old Greek Septuagint translation gives ὑάκινθος "hyacinth, a blue stone, perhaps aquamarine; also a blue flower." Ashkenazic tradition has the color of תכלת as almost black since the stripes of our prayer shawls that symbolize the unavailable תכלת stripes of the *tzitzit*, are traditionally dyed black. Hence the chosen translation of "dark blue".

142 The word in parentheses is found in the Mishnah preceding the chapter but is missing in the Mishnah here in the Halakhah. The word is also missing in most manuscripts of the Babli and in all early authorities, from *Halakhot Gedolot* to *Rosh*. For its meaning, I am following here Rabbenu Saadiah Gaon and Rabbenu Tam who admit לגמור את ההלל, "to read the Hallel", as benediction of the Ḥazan even if only half the Hallel is recited.

143 Here again, the word in parentheses is found in the Mishnah preceding the chapter but is missing in the Mishnah here in the Halakhah, as well as in the Mishnah in the Babli. The story of the discussion of David with his יצר הרע, fol. 2d, proves that the correct text does not contain the words "sons of".

הלכה ה. כֵּנִי מַתְנִיתָא בֵּין תְּכֵלֶת שֶׁבָּהּ לְלָבָן שֶׁבָּהּ. וּמַה טַעֲמוֹן דְּרַבָּנָן וּרְאִיתֶם אוֹתוֹ מִן הַסָּמוּךְ לוֹ. וּמַה טַעֲמֵיהּ דְּרִבִּי אֱלִיעֶזֶר וּרְאִיתֶם אוֹתוֹ כְּדֵי שֶׁיְּהֵא נִיכָּר בֵּין הַצְּבוּעִין.

Halakhah 5: So is the Mishnah: Between its[144] dark blue and its white. What is the reason of the Rabbis? (*Num.* 15:39) "You shall see it"[145], from what is close to it. What is the reason of Rebbi Eliezer? "You shall see it", that it should be recognizable among colors[146].

144 "It" is the ציצית, the fringes of the garment. We shall see later that the third section of the *Shema'*, dealing with the obligation of *tzitzit*, was in Israel recited in abridged form during evening prayers. Hence, the *tzitzit*

characterized the morning prayers. Each *tzitzit* contained three strands of white thread with one of *tĕkhēlet*.

145   I. e., the תכלת thread among the white threads of the *tzitzit*.

146   That תכלת should be recognized not only as a color, but as its specific color.

תַּנֵּי בְשֵׁם רִבִּי מֵאִיר וּרְאִיתֶם אוֹתָהּ אֵין כְּתִיב כַּאן אֶלָּא וּרְאִיתֶם אוֹתוֹ. מַגִּיד שֶׁכָּל־הַמְקַיֵּים מִצְוַת צִיצִית כְּאִילוּ מְקַבֵּל פְּנֵי שְׁכִינָה. מַגִּיד שֶׁהַתְּכֵלֶת דּוֹמֶה לְיָם. וְהַיָּם דּוֹמֶה לַעֲשָׂבִים. וַעֲשָׂבִים דּוֹמִין לָרָקִיעַ. וְרָקִיעַ דּוֹמֶה לְכִסֵּא הַכָּבוֹד. וְהַכִּסֵּא דּוֹמֶה לְסַפִּיר דִּכְתִיב וָאֶרְאֶה וְהִנֵּה עַל הָרָקִיעַ אֲשֶׁר עַל רֹאשׁ הַכְּרוּבִים כְּאֶבֶן סַפִּיר כְּמַרְאֵה דְמוּת כִּסֵּא.

We have stated in the name of Rebbi Meïr: It does not say "you shall see it"[147] but "you shall see Him". This tells you that anyone who keeps the obligation of *tzitzit* is as if he were admitted to the presence of God's glory. This tells that *tĕkhēlet* is similar to the sea. But the sea is similar to grasses, grasses are similar to the sky, the sky is similar to the Throne of Glory, and the Throne is similar to sapphire[148], as it is written (*Ez.* 10:1): "I saw, and here by the spread that was on top of the Cherubim like sapphire stone, the looks of the form of the Throne."

147   In Rabbinic Hebrew, ציצית is clearly feminine, plural ציציות. Rebbi Meïr notes that the verb referring to ציצית in this verse is in the masculine form. Usually, this is taken to mean that in Biblical Hebrew, ציצית is masculine (parallel to masculine קֹהֶלֶת "the preacher"); but many dictionaries of Biblical Hebrew refrain from assigning a gender to the word. Rebbi Meïr votes for taking ציצית as feminine; hence the suffix in "and you shall see" cannot refer to the *tzitzit*.

148   The extended list is found only here; the other sources (quoted in the discussion of תכלת) only have the comparison of sea and sky.

The Gaon of Wilna has noted that the last two items in the list are in inverted order; one should read: the sky is similar to sapphire, sapphire is similar to the Throne of Glory. We are interested in connecting *tĕkhēlet* to the

Throne of Glory, and the verse from Ezechiel provides the characterization as similar to sapphire.

אֲחֵרִים אוֹמְרִים וּרְאִיתֶם אוֹתוֹ כְּדֵי שֶׁיְּהֵא אָדָם רָחוֹק מֵחֲבֵירוֹ אַרְבַּע אַמּוֹת וּמַכִּירוֹ. רַב חִסְדָּא אָמַר כַּהֲדָא דַאֲחֵרִים. מַה אֲנָן קַיָּמִין אִם בְּרָגִיל אֲפִילוּ רָחוֹק כַּמָּן חַכִּים לֵיהּ. וְאִם בְּשֶׁאֵינוֹ רָגִיל אֲפִילוּ קָרוֹב לֵיהּ לָא חַכִּים לֵיהּ. אֶלָּא כֵּן אֲנָן קַיָּמִין בְּרָגִיל וְשֶׁאֵינוֹ רָגִיל. כְּהַהוּא דְאָזִיל לֵיהּ לְאַכְסַנְיָא וְאָתֵי.

Others say: "'You shall see it', that a man should be four *ammot*[149] distant from another man and recognize him." Rav Ḥisda[150] says: (the practice follows)[151] the statement of "Others". What are we talking about? If he knows the other person, even at a great distance he will recognize him. If he does not know him, even close by he will not recognize him. We must talk about an occasional acquaintance, like a man who visits a hostelry at intervals.

149 The size of the Talmudic *ammah* (cubit) has not been definitely established; it is between 18 and 24 inches. It is uncertain whether the Galilean and Babylonian *ammot* were the same measurements.

150 One of the greatest of the students of Rab, a leader of the second generation of Amoraïm in Babylonia.

151 אמר in the Yerushalmi often can mean "establishes practice to be followed", parallel to the statement of Rav Huna, contemporary of Rav Ḥisda, in the Babli: "The practice follows 'Others'".

אִית תְּנָיֵי תַּנֵּי בֵּין זְאֵב לְכֶלֶב בֵּין חֲמוֹר לַעֲרוֹד. וְאִית תְּנָיֵי תַּנֵּי כְּדֵי שֶׁיְּהֵא אָדָם רָחוֹק מֵחֲבֵירוֹ אַרְבַּע אַמּוֹת וּמַכִּירוֹ. הֲוָא בָעֵי מֵימַר מָן דָּמַר בֵּין זְאֵב לְכֶלֶב בֵּין חֲמוֹר לְעָרוֹד כְּמָן דָּמַר בֵּין תְּכֵלֶת לְכָרָתָן. וּמָן דָּמַר כְּדֵי שֶׁיְּהֵא אָדָם רָחוֹק מֵחֲבֵירוֹ אַרְבַּע אַמּוֹת וּמַכִּירוֹ. בֵּין תְּכֵלֶת לְלָבָן. אֲבָל אָמְרוּ מִצְוָותָהּ עִם הָנֵץ הַחַמָּה כְּדֵי שֶׁיִּסְמוֹךְ גְּאוּלָּה לִתְפִילָּה וְנִמְצָא מִתְפַּלֵּל בַּיּוֹם. אָמַר רִבִּי זְעִירָא וַאֲנָא אָמְרִית טַעֲמָא יִרָאוּךָ עִם שֶׁמֶשׁ. אָמַר מַר עוּקְבָּא הַוָּתִיקִין הָיוּ מַשְׁכִּימִים וְקוֹרִין אוֹתָהּ כְּדֵי שֶׁיִּסְמְכוּ לָהּ תְּפִילָּתָן עִם הָנֵץ הַחַמָּה.

Some Tannaïm formulate: "Between wolf and dog, between domesticated and wild donkey."[152] But some Tannaïm formulate: "That a man should be four *ammot* distant from another man and recognize him". That is what we have[153] to say that he who says between wolf and dog, between domesticated and wild donkey is parallel to him who says between dark blue and the color of leeks; he who says that a man should be four *ammot* distant from another man and recognize him is parallel to him who says between dark blue and white. But they said that its preferred obligation is at sunrise so that one may join the mention of redemption to prayer and pray at daytime[154]. Rebbi Zeïra said: I found the reason (*Ps.* 72:5): "They will fear You with the sun."[155] Mar Uqba[156] said: The very religious were getting up early and reading the *Shema'* so that they could follow it directly at sunrise with the *Amidah* prayer.

152 Meaning the earliest time for reading the *Shema'*. In the Babli (9b), the first criterion is given by Rebbi Meïr, the second one by Rebbi Aqiba, and both are given independently of the Mishnah. In the Yerushalmi, no names are attached since both opinions are identified as alternatives "between dark blue and leek colored", which is not the practice anyway.

"Others" (אחרים) usually denotes Rebbi Meïr. In the Babli, the problem remains that the statement attributed to "Others" cannot belong to Rebbi Meïr. However, in the Yerushalmi it may well be that "between wolf and dog" is Rebbi Meïr's restatement of Rebbi Eliezer's criterion in the Mishnah, and "to recognize at 4 *ammot*" the same authority's restatement of the criterion of the First Tanna in the Mishnah.

153 *Pne Mosheh* (R. Moshe Margalit) reads הוּא בָּעֵי מֵימַר "he (Rav Ḥisda, mentioned earlier) wants to say." Then the entire statement is tentative, and רב חסדא אמר will simply mean "Rav Ḥisda said", not as an authoritative statement. However, the commentary *Pne Moshe* (R. Moshe ben Ḥabib) reads הווין בעי מימר "they (or we) want to say."

154 This is from the Tosephta (1:2) and is the end of the statement that in the morning one may say the *Shema'* as soon as one recognizes a person at a

distance of 4 *ammot*. Hence, "they said" refers to those who adopt the criterion mentioned last. If one recites the *Shema'* slowly at sunrise and then says the benediction of *Emet weyaẓiv*, he will just say the *Amidah* prayer when the sun is clearly above the horizon and it is visibly day.

155 The same explanation is given in his name in the Babli, hence he is really the author and not only the tradent. Since the first section of *Shema'* is "acceptance of the yoke of the kingdom of Heaven", this is in essence fear of God, and, hence, the verse refers to the reading of *Shema'* and not the prayer. It is clear that the prayer to be performed preferably at sunrise is the recitation of *Shema'*.

156 *Resh Galuta*, the Davidic ruler of the Jews in Babylonia, in the first generation of Amoraïm. It is interesting to note that this statement of the Babylonian Mar Uqba is reported in the Babli (9b) in the name of the later Rebbi Yoḥanan. Maybe each Talmud wanted to ascribe the deeds of ותיקין to an external source, not to be held to their standards, as explained in the next section.

The explanation of ותיק has been given by A. Kohut in his ערוך השלם, from the Arabic וַתִּק "to have confidence, faith". As explained by the Babylonian Talmud, they had faith in God that all the time spent in His service would not detract from their ability to earn a livelihood, and so they were rewarded with earning enough money for their needs in the time left over after religious services and deeds.

תַּנֵּי אָמַר רִבִּי יוּדָה מַעֲשֶׂה שֶׁהָיִיתִי מְהַלֵּךְ אַחֲרֵי רִבִּי אֶלְעָזָר בֶּן עֲזַרְיָה וְאַחֲרֵי רִבִּי עֲקִיבָה וְהָיוּ עֲסוּקִין בְּמִצְוֹת וְהִגִּיעַ עוֹנַת קְרִיַּת שְׁמַע וְהָיִיתִי סָבוּר שֶׁמָּא נִתְיָאֲשׁוּ מִקְּרִיַּת שְׁמַע וְקָרִיתִי וְשָׁנִיתִי וְאַחַר כַּךְ הִתְחִילוּ הֵם. וּכְבָר הָיְתָה הַחַמָּה עַל רֹאשׁ הֶהָרִים.

We have stated[157]: Rebbi Yehudah said: It happened that once I was walking behind Rebbi Eleazar ben Azariah and Rebbi Aqiba when they were occupied with duties and time came to recite the *Shema'* and I got the opinion that maybe they had given up on reciting the *Shema'*, so I recited it and went over my studies[158]; but after that they started and the sun was already over the mountain tops.

157 Tosephta *Berakhot* 1:3; there R. Aqiba (who was the greater scholar) is mentioned before R. Eleazar ben Azariah (the vice president of the Synhedrion), and it is spelled out that they were occupied to attend to some public needs. We have a principle that he who is fulfilling a religious duty is free from engaging in any conflicting religious duty. The two sages therefore would have had the possibility of not reciting *Shema'* at all. The fact that they recited the *Shema'* shows that they considered the obligation of this recitation in full force until the end of the third hour and that, therefore, their prior occupation did not reduce the later obligation. This is explained more thoroughly in the next section.

It seems that the text of the Yerushalmi is superior to the Tosephta since the vice president has precedence over a simple member and the mention of their being engaged in religious obligations is more to the point.

158 Reciting from memory the material he had learned earlier from his teachers.

עַד הָנֵץ הַחַמָּה. רִבִּי זְבַדְיָה בְּרֵיהּ דְּרִבִּי יַעֲקֹב בַּר זַבְדִּי בְּשֵׁם רִבִּי יוֹנָה כְּדֵי שֶׁתְּהֵא הַחַמָּה (fol. 3b) מְטַפְטֶפֶת עַל רָאשֵׁי הֶהָרִים. רִבִּי יְהוֹשֻׁעַ אוֹמֵר עַד שָׁלֹשׁ שָׁעוֹת. רִבִּי אִידִי וְרַב הַמְנוּנָא וְרַב אַדָּא בַּר אַחֲוָא בְּשֵׁם רַב הֲלָכָה כְּרִבִּי יְהוֹשֻׁעַ בְּשׁוֹכֵחַ. רִבִּי חוּנָה אָמַר תְּרֵין אַמוֹרָאִין חַד אָמַר בְּשׁוֹכֵחַ. מֵגִיב לֵיהּ חַבְרֵיהּ וְכִי יֵשׁ הֲלָכָה בְּשׁוֹכֵחַ. כַּךְ הִיא הֲלָכָה. וְלָמָּה אָמְרוּ בְשׁוֹכֵחַ כְּדֵי שֶׁיְּהֵא אָדָם מְזָרֵז אַצְמוֹ לִקְרוֹתָהּ בְּעוֹנָתָהּ.

"Until sunrise." Rebbi Zabida the son of Rebbi Jacob bar Zabdi in the name of Rebbi Jonah[159]: until the sun starts to appear[160] at the mountain tops. "Rebbi Joshua says, until three hours of the day." Rebbi Idi, Rav Hamnuna, and Rav Ada bar Aḥava[161] in the name of Rav: The practice follows Rebbi Joshua for one who forgets. Rebbi Ḥuna told of two Amoraïm of whom one said 'for one who forgot.' His colleague responded: Do you ever fix practice for one who forgets[162]? In fact, it is the practice. Why did they say, for one who forgot? That everybody should make an effort and read it at its best time.

159 Of the leaders of the fourth generation of Amoraïm in Galilee. The first tradent was his student.

160 Literally: "drips", meaning that the first rays of the sun start to appear at the lower parts of the mountain silhouette.

161 The last name is correct in *Seridé Yerushalmi*. The name mentioned in the printed editions, אדא בר אחא , is not mentioned again in any Talmudic source. Rav Ada bar Aḥawa (Yerushalmi) is called Rav Ada bar Ahavah in the Babli; all teachers quoted here are students of Rav. In the Babli (10b), Rav Yehudah says in the name of Samuel: the practice follows Rebbi Joshua, without qualifications. It seems that in Israel one was reluctant to give up the recitation of the *Shema'* at sunrise but in Babylonia the practice of very early prayers was never established.

162 Since rules are made to be followed, not to be forgotten.

תַּמָּן תַּנִּינָן מַפְסִיקִין לִקְרִיַּת שְׁמַע וְאֵין מַפְסִיקִין לִתְפִילָּה. אָמַר רִבִּי אָחָא קִרְיַּת שְׁמַע דְּבַר תּוֹרָה. תְּפִילָּה אֵינָהּ דְּבַר תּוֹרָה. אָמַר רִבִּי בָּא קִרְיַּת שְׁמַע זְמַנָּהּ קָבוּעַ. תְּפִילָּה אֵין זְמַנָּהּ קָבוּעַ. אָמַר רִבִּי יוֹסֵי קִרְיַּת שְׁמַע אֵינָהּ צְרִיכָה כַוָּנָה. תְּפִילָּה צְרִיכָה כַוָּנָה. אָמַר רִבִּי מָנִי קַשִּׁיתָהּ קוֹמֵי רִבִּי יוֹסֵי וַאֲפִילוּ תֵּימַר קִרְיַּת שְׁמַע אֵינָהּ צְרִיכָה כַוָּנָה ג׳ פְּסוּקִין הָרִאשׁוֹנִין צְרִיכִין כַּוָּנָה. מִן גַּו דְּאִינּוּן צִבְחַר מִיכַּוֵּן.

There (*Šabbat* 1:2) we have stated: "One interrupts for the recitation of *Shema'* but one does not interrupt for prayer."[163] Rebbi Aḥa said: The recitation of *Shema'* is a Biblical obligation; prayer is not a Biblical obligation[164]. Rebbi Abba said: The time for the recitation of the *Shema'* is fixed, the time for prayer is not fixed.[165] Rebbi Yose said: The recitation of *Shema'* does not need concentration, prayer needs concentration.[165] Rebbi Mana said: I objected before Rebbi Yose: Even if you say that the recitation of the *Shema'* does not need concentration, the first three verses need concentration. Since they are so few, one will concentrate upon their meaning.

163 It is implied by the following discussion that one talks about groups of people engaged in the study of Torah. This situation is made explicit in Babli *Šabbat* 9b. Of those who give the reasons for the difference in the treatment of *Shema'* and *Amidah*, Rebbis Aḥa and Yose belong to the fourth generation of Amoraïm in Israel, hence Rebbi Abba will also belong to that group. [There were too many Amoraïm by the name of Rebbi Abba to clearly distinguish between them.]

The entire section here and the following one also appear in Yerushalmi *Šabbat* 1:2.

164 Everybody in this discussion seems to agree that the basis of the recitation of *Shema'* is Biblical, at least for the first verse [following the Babli (*Teshuvot ha Rashba*, #320)] or the first three verses [following the Yerushalmi, as seen here]. There is disagreement on the status of prayer. The Yerushalmi at the beginning of Chapter 4 follows the *Sifri* in the interpretation of the "service of the heart" mentioned in *Deut.* 10:12, 11:13 as prayer, which, therefore, is Biblical. Rebbi Aḥa does not accept this derivation; similarly, the Babli (*Berakhot* 21a) declares prayer to be a Rabbinical obligation.

165 Rebbi Abba is among those who accept prayer as a Biblical obligation. The clearest statement of that position is given by Maimonides (*Hilkhot Tefillah* I:1) who writes: "It is a positive commandment that one should pray every day as it is said: 'you shall serve the Eternal, your God.' Tradition teaches us that this service is prayer, as it is said: 'to serve Him with all your heart'; the sages explain that the service of the heart is prayer. But the number of prayers is not from the Torah, neither is the formulation of the prayer from the Torah. Prayer has no fixed time from the Torah." [Everybody agrees that the obligation of offering prayer three times a day is historical (*Daniel* 6:11) and the form of prayer is an institution of the Men of the Great Assembly.] This interpretation of the disagreement between Rebbis Aḥa and Abba is given by the great Sephardic commentators, Rabbis Eleazar Azkari and Moshe ben Ḥabib.

There is a different interpretation possible, namely that Rebbi Abba wants to state that the time of *Shema'* is narrowly fixed, as we have seen, and once that time is passed, the omission cannot be repaired. For prayer, however, the rules are much more elastic. First, there is much more time given for the recitation; then it is possible to pray in advance of the time (as in the evening prayers held before sundown), and a missed prayer can be compensated for by praying the next time twice. Hence, in a real sense, even prayer in the Rabbinical sense has no fixed time compared to *Shema'*.

166 Rebbi Yose, the greatest authority among the participants in this discussion, notes that one may make a distinction between *Shema'* and prayer that does not depend on whether the obligations are Biblical or Rabbinical. While it is essential that the first verse (or verses), containing the "acceptance of the yoke of the Kingdom of Heaven", should be well understood during the recitation, the rest of *Shema'*, which also counts for Torah study, is acceptable even if it is recited in mechanical repetition since this helps in memorizing the Torah text, an essential part of study. On the other hand, mechanical and unthinking prayer is a contradiction in terms and intrinsically invalid.

רִבִּי יוֹחָנָן בְּשֵׁם רִבִּי שִׁמְעוֹן בֶּן יוֹחַי כְּגוֹן אָנוּ שֶׁעוֹסְקִין בְּתַלְמוּד תּוֹרָה אֲפִילוּ לִקְרִיַּת שְׁמַע אֵין אָנוּ מַפְסִיקִין. רִבִּי יוֹחָנָן אָמְרָהּ עַל גַּרְמֵיהּ כְּגוֹן אָנוּ שֶׁאֵין אָנוּ עוֹסְקִין בְּתַלְמוּד תּוֹרָה וַאֲפִילוּ לִתְפִילָּה אָנוּ מַפְסִיקִין. דֵּין כְּדַעֲתֵיהּ וְדֵין כְּדַעֲתֵיהּ. רִבִּי יוֹחָנָן כְּדַעֲתֵיהּ דְּרִבִּי יוֹחָנָן אוֹמֵר וּלְוַאי שֶׁמִּתְפַּלֵּל אָדָם כָּל־הַיּוֹם. לָמָּה שֶׁאֵין תְּפִילָּה מַפְסֶדֶת. רִבִּי שִׁמְעוֹן בֶּן יוֹחַי כְּדַעֲתֵיהּ דְּרִבִּי שִׁמְעוֹן בֶּן יוֹחַי אָמַר אִילּוּ הֲוֵינָא קָאִים עַל טוּרָא דְסִינַי בְּשַׁעְתָּא דְאִיתְיְהִיבַת תּוֹרָה לְיִשְׂרָאֵל הֲוֵינָא מִתְבָּעֵי קוֹמוֹי רַחֲמָנָא דְּיִתְבְּרֵי לְבַר נָשָׁא תְּרֵין פּוּמִין חַד דַּהֲוָה לָעֵי בְּאוֹרָיְתָא וְחַד דַּעֲבִיד לֵיהּ כָּל־צוֹרְכֵיהּ. חָזַר וָמַר וּמַה אִין חַד הוּא לֵית עָלְמָא יָכִיל קָאִים בֵּיהּ מִן דֶּלַטוֹרְיָה דִילֵיהּ. אִילּוּ הֲווּ תְּרֵין עַל אַחַת כַּמָּה וְכַמָּה. אָמַר רִבִּי יוֹסֵי קוֹמוֹי רִבִּי יִרְמְיָה אַתְיָא דְרִבִּי יוֹחָנָן כְּרִבִּי חֲנִינָא בֶּן עֲקַבְיָה דְּתַנֵּי כּוֹתְבֵי סְפָרִים תְּפִילִּין וּמְזוּזוֹת מַפְסִיקִין לִקְרִיַּת שְׁמַע וְאֵין מַפְסִיקִין לִתְפִילָּה. רִבִּי חֲנִינָא בֶּן עֲקַבְיָה אוֹמֵר כְּשֵׁם שֶׁמַּפְסִיקִין לִקְרִיַּת שְׁמַע כָּךְ מַפְסִיקִין לִתְפִילָּה וְלִתְפִילִּין וְלִשְׁאָר מִצְווֹתֶיהָ שֶׁל תּוֹרָה. וְלֹא מוֹרֵי רִבִּי שִׁמְעוֹן בֶּן יוֹחַי שֶׁמַּפְסִיקִין לַעֲשׂוֹת סוּכָּה וְלַעֲשׂוֹת לוּלָב. וְלֵית לֵיהּ לְרִבִּי שִׁמְעוֹן בֶּן יוֹחַי הַלּוֹמֵד עַל מְנַת לַעֲשׂוֹת וְלֹא הַלּוֹמֵד שֶׁלֹּא לַעֲשׂוֹת. שֶׁהַלּוֹמֵד שֶׁלֹּא לַעֲשׂוֹת נוֹחַ לוֹ שֶׁלֹּא נִבְרָא. וְאָמַר רִבִּי יוֹחָנָן הַלּוֹמֵד שֶׁלֹּא לַעֲשׂוֹת נוֹחַ לוֹ אִילּוּ נֶהֶפְכָה שִׁלְיָתוֹ עַל פָּנָיו וְלֹא יָצָא לָעוֹלָם. טַעֲמֵיהּ דְּרִבִּי שִׁמְעוֹן בֶּן יוֹחַי זֶהוּ שִׁינּוּן וְזֶה שִׁינּוּן וְאֵין מְבַטֵּל

שִׁינּוּן מִפְּנֵי שִׁינּוּן. וְהָא תַנִּינָן הַקּוֹרֵא מִכָּן וְאֵילָךְ לֹא הִפְסִיד כְּאָדָם שֶׁהוּא קוֹרֵא בַתּוֹרָה. הָא בְעוֹנָתָהּ חֲבִיבָה מִדִּבְרֵי תוֹרָה. הִיא הִיא. אָמַר רִבִּי יוּדָן רִבִּי שִׁמְעוֹן בֶּן יוֹחַי עַל יְדֵי שֶׁהָיָה תָדִיר בְּדִבְרֵי תוֹרָה לְפִיכָךְ אֵינָהּ חֲבִיבָה יוֹתֵר מִדִּבְרֵי תוֹרָה. אָמַר רִבִּי אַבָּא מָרִי לֹא תַנִּינָן אֶלָּא כְאָדָם שֶׁהוּא קוֹרֵא בַתּוֹרָה. הָא בְעוֹנָתָהּ כְּמִשְׁנָה הִיא. רִבִּי שִׁמְעוֹן בֶּן יוֹחַי כְדַעֲתֵיהּ דְּרִבִּי שִׁמְעוֹן בֶּן יוֹחַי אָמַר הָעוֹסֵק בְּמִקְרָא מִדָּה שֶׁאֵינָהּ מִדָּה. וְרַבָּנָן עָבְדֵי מִקְרָא כְמִשְׁנָה.

Rebbi Yoḥanan in the name of Rebbi Simeon ben Yoḥai: "For example we, who are engaged in the study of Torah, we do not interrupt even for the recitation of *Shema'*." Rebbi Yoḥanan used to say about himself: "For example we, who are not engaged in the study of Torah[167], we do interrupt even for prayer."

This one follows his own opinion and that one follows his own opinion. Rebbi Yoḥanan follows his own opinion since Rebbi Yoḥanan says: "if only a man would pray the entire day. Why? Because prayer is never in vain!"[168]

Rebbi Simeon ben Yoḥai follows his own opinion since Rebbi Simeon ben Yoḥai said: "If I had stood at Mount Sinai at the moment that the Torah was given to Israel, I would have implored the All-Merciful that he should create two mouths for man; one for him to exert himself in Torah and the other one for his other needs." But he changed his mind and said: "With one mouth already the world almost cannot exist because of its denunciations[169]; if there were two how much more would there be?

Rebbi Yose said before Rebbi Jeremiah: The position of Rebbi Yoḥanan is identical with that of Rebbi Ḥanina ben Aqabiah, as we have stated: "The scribes of Torah scrolls, *Tefillin*, and *Mezuzot*, do interrupt for the recitation of *Shema'* but do not interrupt for prayer. Rebbi Ḥanina ben Aqabiah said: just as they interrupt for *Shema'*, so they interrupt for prayer, *tefillin*, and all other commandments of the Torah".[170]

Would not Rebbi Simeon ben Yoḥai agree that one interrupts to make a *sukkah* or a *lulav*? Does not Rebbi Simeon ben Yoḥai make the distinction between one who studies in order to do[171] and one who studies in order not to do? Because he who studies in order not to do would have been better off had he not been born. And did not Rebbi Yoḥanan say, he who studies in order not to do would have been better off if the afterbirth he was in was twisted around and he never would have entered the world? The reason of Rebbi Simeon ben Yoḥai is that this one is repeated study and that one is repeated study and he does not push aside one study for the other study.[172] But did we not formulate:[173] "He is like a man reading in the Torah." Hence, at the right time it is preferred to Torah. One is like the other.[174] Rebbi Yudan said that Rebbi Simeon ben Yoḥai, since he was permanently studying Torah, did not prefer *Shema'* to the study of Torah. Rebbi Abba Mari said, did we not formulate: "He who reads (*Shema'*) after that did not lose, he is only like a man reading in the Torah"? Hence, at the right time it is like Mishnah. Rebbi Simeon ben Yoḥai follows his own opinion since Rebbi Simeon ben Yoḥai said: He who studies the written Torah does himself good that is not so good. But the rabbis equate the study of the Bible with that of the oral law.[175]

167 Since we spend some time every day not studying.

168 See Note [17].

169 Latin *delatorius, a, um,* adj. to *delatio*, in late Latin *delatura* "accusation, information, denunciation," the act of a *delator*,"government informer." Because of an informer about his anti-Roman feelings, Rebbi Simeon ben Yoḥai and his son had to spend 12 years hidden in a cave (Babli *Šabbat* 33b, Yerushalmi *Ševiït* 9:1, fol. 38d). When he left the cave, he was so upset that people would engage in

farming and commerce and not study Torah all day long that a heavenly voice ordered him back to his cave for another 12 months in order to get used to the world again. Both Talmudim consider his position appropriate only for exceedingly holy people.

170 While we have the principle that "he who is engaged in the fulfillment of a commandment does not have to worry about other commandments," this does not apply to people whose entire occupation is the fulfillment of a commandment.

The source is *Tosephta Berakhot* 2:6, cf. also Babli *Sukkah* 26a. The Tosephta also brings the opinion of Rebbi, that they do not interrupt for *Shema'*, and a testimony that Rabban Gamliel and the Synhedrion at Yavneh did not interrupt sessions dealing with communal matters.

171 He who does is one who fulfills the commandments of the Torah. He who does not is one who does not fulfill the commandments of the Torah. Someone who studies Torah with the intent of not fulfilling its commandments certainly has no part in the future world since he does not have the excuse of everybody else that he did not know enough to fulfill all commandments. This is clearly spelled out in the following lines. The question here is, how can Rebbi Simeon ben Yoḥai take a position that for all practical purposes identifies the actions of the most holy man with that of the deliberate sinner?

172 But he certainly will interrupt for all other obligations. In fact, the story of his stay in the cave notes that he and his son took off their clothes and sat covered with sand up to their necks in order not to wear out the clothes, and used them only for the times of prayer. This means that Rebbi Simeon did *not* recite *Shema'* since its recitation was replaced by his studies, but he *did* pray, even though the Mishnah seems to indicate that one omits prayer more easily than *Shema'*.

173 In our Mishnah here in *Berakhot*.

174 This is a preliminary answer. Rebbi Yudan (Amora, colleague of R. Yose) tries to relativize the answer that it applies only to someone like Rebbi Simeon ben Yoḥai who spends his entire life studying and memorizing Torah. R. Abba Mari, one generation after R. Yudan, points out that this interpretation of the Mishnah is impossible but that one must take the statement of R. Simeon as an indication of his attitude in general.

175 Studying Scripture is equal to studying the Oral Law in merit. Hence, reciting the *Shema'* in its proper time

transcends both for everybody including scholars of the rank of Rebbi Simeon ben Yoḥai. Mishnah here stands for the entire Oral Law, which was called Mishnah in the time of Rebbi Simeon bar Yoḥai. (See the parallel in Babli *Baba meẓia'* 33a.)

מִשְׁנָה ו: בֵּית שַׁמַּאי אוֹמְרִים בָּעֶרֶב כָּל־אָדָם יַטּוּ וְיִקְרוּ וּבַבּוֹקֶר יַעֲמוֹדוּ שֶׁנֶּאֱמַר בְּשִׁבְתְּךָ בְּבֵיתֶךָ וּבְלֶכְתְּךָ בַדֶּרֶךְ וּבְשָׁכְבְּךָ וּבְקוּמֶךָ. וּבֵית הִלֵּל אוֹמְרִים כָּל־אָדָם קוֹרִין כְּדַרְכָּן. שֶׁנֶּאֱמַר וּבְלֶכְתְּךָ בַדֶּרֶךְ. אִם כֵּן לָמָּה נֶאֱמַר וּבְשָׁכְבְּךָ וּבְקוּמֶךָ. אֶלָּא בְּשָׁעָה שֶׁבְּנֵי אָדָם שׁוֹכְבִין וּבְשָׁעָה שֶׁבְּנֵי אָדָם עוֹמְדִין.

Mishnah 6: The school of Shammai say: In the evening, everyone must bend down[176] and recite and in the morning they should stand up since it is said (*Deut.* 6:7): "when you sit in your house or go on the road, when you are lying down and when you are getting up." But the school of Hillel say: everyone should recite in the position he is in, since it says "or go on the road." In that case, why does it say: "when you are lying down and when you are getting up;" this means the time when people go to sleep and the time when they are getting up.

176 Means to lie down on a couch, or as on a couch. "Reciting" always refers to the *Shema'* since, as a technical term, it is used only for formal recitation of Biblical texts.

הלכה ו. הָא דְבֵית הִלֵּל מְקִימוֹן תְּרֵין קְרָיָא מַה מְקַיְימִין דְּבֵית שַׁמַּאי בְּשִׁבְתְּךָ בְּבֵיתֶךָ וּבְלֶכְתְּךָ בַדֶּרֶךְ. בְּשִׁבְתְּךָ בְּבֵיתֶךָ פְּרָט לְעוֹסְקִים בְּמִצְוֹת. וּבְלֶכְתְּךָ בַדֶּרֶךְ פְּרָט לַחֲתָנִים.

Halakhah 6: They of the school of Hillel are able to explain both parts of the verse. How do those of the school of Shammai explain "when you sit in your house or go on the road"? "When you sit in your house", to exclude those who are occupied with other religious commandments, "or go on the road" to exlude bridegrooms.[177]

177 An almost exact parallel is found in the Babli, *Berakhot* 11a. The bride is exempt from reciting the *Shema'* since women are freed from all positive commandments which have to be performed at set times. The bridegroom himself fulfills a divine commandment by getting married, but that fulfillment is really restricted to the short act of actual marriage and then to the first married intercourse; the exemption of the bridegroom from saying *Shema'* refers to the entire wedding feast when he is unable to concentrate even on the first verses.

תַּנֵּי מַעֲשֶׂה בְּרַבִּי אֶלְעָזָר בֶּן עֲזַרְיָה וְרַבִּי יִשְׁמָעֵאל שֶׁהָיוּ שְׁרוּיִין בְּמָקוֹם אֶחָד וְהָיָה רִבִּי אֶלְעָזָר בֶּן עֲזַרְיָה מוּטֶּה וְרִבִּי יִשְׁמָעֵאל זָקוּף. הִגִּיעַ עוֹנַת קִרְיַת שְׁמַע נִזְקַף רִבִּי אֶלְעָזָר בֶּן עֲזַרְיָה וְהִטָּה רִבִּי יִשְׁמָעֵאל. אָמַר רִבִּי אֶלְעָזָר לְרִבִּי יִשְׁמָעֵאל אוֹמֵר לְאֶחָד בְּשׁוּק מַה לְךָ זְקָנְךָ מְגוּדָּל וְהוּא אוֹמֵר יִהְיֶה כְּנֶגֶד הַמַּשְׁחִיתִים. אֲנִי שֶׁהָיִיתִי מוּטֶּה נִזְקַפְתִּי וְאַתָּה שֶׁהָיִיתָ נִזְקַף הִטִּיתָ. אָמַר לוֹ אַתָּה נִזְקַפְתָּ כְּדִבְרֵי בֵית שַׁמַּאי. וַאֲנִי הִטִּיתִי כְּדִבְרֵי בֵית הִלֵּל. דָּבָר אַחֵר שֶׁלֹּא יִרְאוּנִי הַתַּלְמִידִים וְיַעֲשׂוּ הֲלָכָה קֶבַע כְּדִבְרֵי בֵית שַׁמַּאי.

We have stated[178]: It happened that Rebbi Eleazar ben Azariah and Rebbi Ismael stayed at the same place and Rebbi Eleazar ben Azariah was reclining while Rebbi Ismael was standing. When the time for the recital of the *Shema'* arrived did Rebbi Eleazar ben Azariah stand and Rebbi Ismael reclined. Rebbi Eleazar said to Rebbi Ismael, this is as when one says to someone in the market place, your beard is overgrown, and he says, that is against those who shave[179]. I, who was reclining, stood up and you, who were standing, went on to recline. He answered him: You stood up following the school of Shammai, I reclined following the school of Hillel. Another explanation: That the students should not see me and make it the permanent practice to follow the school of Shammai.[180]

178 In the Babylonian parallels (*Berakhot* 11a, *Tosephta Berakhot* 1:4, *Sifri Deut.* 34), R. Eleazar ben Azariah at first is sitting up and R. Ismael is reclining. This means that in the Babylonian version, the discussion was in the evening (also indicated in the Babylonian Talmud by a change in language, not "that they stayed at the same place" but that "they had dinner together.") In our version, the discussion takes place in the morning.

While R. Ismael, after R. Aqiba the greatest scholar of his generation, did certainly exceed R. Eleazar ben Azariah in scholarship, the latter was the vice president of the Synhedrion; it is more likely that R. Ismael was sitting upright at the start. They might have got up very early, before the start of dawn, when it still was possible to eat before praying. It is impossible to decide which of the two versions is the original.

179 I do it deliberately. Why did you do the opposite of what I am doing?

180 Both explanations are necessary. R. Ismael did recline, not because it was required by the school of Hillel, but to spite the followers of the school of Shammai. He had to do this, even though the school of Hillel would have allowed him to continue standing, to give an example to the students. This shows that in all cases where there is a disagreement over practice, the actions of the leading Torah scholars count more than all theoretical arguments.

מִשְׁנָה ז: אָמַר רִבִּי טַרְפוֹן אֲנִי הָיִיתִי בָא בַדֶּרֶךְ וְהִטֵּיתִי לִקְרוֹת כְּדִבְרֵי בֵית שַׁמַּאי וְסִיכַּנְתִּי בְעַצְמִי מִפְּנֵי הַלִּיסְטִין. אָמְרוּ לוֹ כְדַיי הָיִיתָ לָחוּב עַל אַצְמָךְ שֶׁעָבַרְתָּ עַל דִּבְרֵי בֵית הִלֵּל.

Mishnah 7: Rebbi Ṭarphon[181] said: I was on the road and reclined to recite the *Shema'* following the school of Shammai. There I put myself in danger because of the robbers. They told him: It would have served you right to be in mortal danger since you transgressed the words of the school of Hillel.

181 The oldest of the Tannaïm of the second generation, who started his studies still before the destruction of the Temple, at the time of the ascendency of the school of Shammai. It seems that he was slow to adapt the practices he had learned as a child to those of the school of R. Yoḥanan ben Zakkai of the school of Hillel which was the only one to survive the war against the Romans.

הלכה ז. בְּשֵׁם רִבִּי יוֹחָנָן דּוֹדִים דִּבְרֵי סוֹפְרִים לְדִבְרֵי תוֹרָה וַחֲבִיבִין כְּדִבְרֵי תוֹרָה. חִכֵּךְ כְּיֵין הַטּוֹב. שִׁמְעוֹן בַּר וָוא בְּשֵׁם רִבִּי יוֹחָנָן דּוֹדִים דִּבְרֵי סוֹפְרִים לְדִבְרֵי תוֹרָה וַחֲבִיבִין מִדִּבְרֵי תוֹרָה. כִּי טוֹבִים דוֹדֶיךָ מִיָּיִן. רִבִּי בָּא בַּר כֹּהֶן בְּשֵׁם רִבִּי יוּדָה בֶּן פָּזִי תֵּדַע לְךָ שֶׁחֲבִיבִין דִּבְרֵי סוֹפְרִים מִדִּבְרֵי תוֹרָה שֶׁהֲרֵי רִבִּי טַרְפוֹן אִילּוּ לֹא קָרָא לֹא הָיָה עוֹבֵר אֶלָּא בַעֲשֵׂה. וְעַל יְדֵי שֶׁעָבַר עַל דִּבְרֵי בֵית הִלֵּל נִתְחַיָּיב מִיתָה עַל שֵׁם וּפוֹרֵץ גָּדֵר יִשְּׁכֶנּוּ נָחָשׁ.

Halakhah 7: In the name of Rebbi Yoḥanan[182]: The words of the scribes are related to the words of Scripture and are pleasant like the words of Scripture. (*Song of Songs* 7:10) "Your throat is like the good wine"; Simeon ben Abba in the name of R. Yoḥanan[183]: The words of the scribes are related to the words of Scripture and are more pleasant than the words of Scripture. (*Song of Songs* 1:2) "Since your friendship is better than wine"; Rebbi Abba bar Cohen in the name of Rebbi Judah ben Pazi: You can know that the words of the scribes are more pleasant than those of Scripture because if Rebbi Tarphon did not recite at all he would have transgressed only a positive commandment. But because he transgressed the words of the school of Hillel he should have suffered death since it says: (*Proverbs* 10:8) "He who breaches a fence will be bitten by a snake."

182 This entire Halakhah, until the next Mishnah, really belongs to *Avodah zarah* 2:5 (fol. 41c) where *Song of Songs* 1:2, "May he kiss me with the kisses of his mouth since your friendship is better than wine", is discussed.

In the transcription here, the first word fell out. It should read: The fellows (of the Yeshivah) in the name of R. Yoḥanan.

In traditional interpretation, the Song of Songs is a dialogue between God and the people of Israel (represented by the girl); the question of the Mishnah was whether one reads דּוֹדַיִךְ (feminine) or דּוֹדֶיךָ (masculine) for "your friendship, your relations."

183 The members of the Yeshivah are of the second (colleagues of R. Yoḥanan) or the third (his students) generations of Amoraïm. R. Simeon bar Abba is one of the outstanding students of R. Yoḥanan. The two Amoraïm who explain the latter's words are of the fourth and fifth generations, respectively.

The "throat" of the Jewish people are the sayings of its sages; wine in both verses are the words of the Torah.

תַּנֵּי רִבִּי יִשְׁמָעֵאל דִּבְרֵי תוֹרָה יֵשׁ בָּהֶן אִיסּוּר וְיֵשׁ בָּהֶן הֵיתֵר. יֵשׁ בָּהֶן קוּלִּין וְיֵשׁ בָּהֶן חוּמְרִין. אֲבָל דִּבְרֵי סוֹפְרִין כּוּלָּן חֲמוּרִין הֶן. תֵּדַע לָךְ שֶׁהוּא כֵן. דְּתַנִּינָן תַּמָּן הָאוֹמֵר אֵין תְּפִילִּין לַעֲבוֹר עַל דִּבְרֵי תוֹרָה פָּטוּר. חָמֵשׁ טוֹטָפוֹת לְהוֹסִיף עַל דִּבְרֵי סוֹפְרִים חַיָּב. רִבִּי חֲנַנְיָה בְרֵיהּ דְּרִבִּי אָדָא בְּשֵׁם רִבִּי תַנְחוּם בֵּירִבִּי חִיָּא חֲמוּרִים דִּבְרֵי זְקֵנִים מִדִּבְרֵי נְבִיאִים דִּכְתִיב אַל תַּטִּפוּ יַטִּיפוּן לֹא יַטִּיפוּ לָאֵלֶּה לֹא יִסַּג כְּלִימוֹת. וּכְתִיב אַטִּף לְךָ לַיַּיִן וְלַשֵּׁכָר. וְנָבִיא וְזָקֵן לְמִי הֵן דּוֹמִין לַמֶּלֶךְ שֶׁשָּׁלַח ב׳ פַּלְמַטָּרִין שֶׁלּוֹ לִמְדִינָה. עַל אֶחָד מֵהֶן כָּתַב אִם אֵינוֹ מַרְאֶה לָכֶם חוֹתָם שֶׁלִּי וְסֵמַנְטֵרִין שֶׁלִּי אַל תַּאֲמִינוּ לוֹ. וְעַל אֶחָד מֵהֶן כָּתַב אַף עַל פִּי שֶׁאֵינוֹ מַרְאֶה לָכֶם חוֹתָם שֶׁלִּי הֶאֱמִינוּהוּ בְּלֹא חוֹתָם וְסֵמַנְטֵרִין. כַּךְ בְּנָבִיא כְתִיב וְנָתַן לְךָ אוֹת וּמוֹפֵת. בְּרַם הָכָא עַל פִּי הַתּוֹרָה אֲשֶׁר יוֹרוּךָ.

Rebbi Ismael did formulate: In the Torah there are forbidden matters and permitted matters. There are easy parts and severe parts. But in the words of the Sages all are severe[184]. You can realize that this is so since we have stated (Mishnah *Sanhedrin* 11:5): "If he[185] says there is no obligation of *Tefillin* against the words of the Torah he is not criminally liable. If he says that *Tefillin* have five sections, to add to the words of the Sages, he is guilty." Rebbi Ḥananiah, the son of Rebbi Ada[186], in the name of Rebbi Tanḥum the son of Rebbi Ḥiyya: The words of the Sages carry more weight than those of the prophets, since it is written (*Micah* 2:6): "Do not preach, they preach; Do not preach to those, that shame does not reach you.[187]" And it is written (*Micah* 2:11) "I shall preach to you for wine and liquor."[188] The relation of prophet and scholar can be compared to the case of a king who sent two of his *palmatars*[189] to a province. About one of them he wrote, if he does not show you my seal and σημαντήριον[190], do not believe him. About the other one he wrote, even if he does not show you my seal, believe him without seal and σημαντήριον. So about a prophet is written (*Deut*. 13:2) "He gives you a sign or miracle." But here it is written (*Deut*. 17:11): "According to the teachings that they will teach you"[191].

184 Since their essential duty is to build "a fence around the Law", it is in the nature of the institutions of the *Sopherim*, the men of the Great Assembly headed by Ezra and their successors before the period of the Rabbis, to be more restrictive than the original precepts of the Torah.

185 The Mishnah speaks about the זקן ממרא, the rebellious religious leader, who does not accept the rulings of the supreme court sitting in the Temple court. If he asserts something that goes against the text of the Torah, he is not dangerous and not criminally liable since every child that has learned to read realizes his error. But if he asserts something in contradiction to an authoritative teaching of the oral law asserted by the Synhedrion, then he has committed a capital crime.

In the Babli, the reference is to Mishnah *Sanhedrin* 10:5. The interpretation of the law is much more restrictive in the Babli than in the Yerushalmi.

186 A preacher of the fourth generation of Galilean Amoraïm whose name is quoted also as Ḥanina or Ḥinnena. His teacher R. Tanḥum bar Ḥiyya was from Kefar Agin (Umm Junia) South of the Sea of Galilee.

187 Only false prophets will preach to such a generation, whereas the true prophet gets his orders from God not to preach. According to Rashi, טיף means "speak about your visions", rather than the commonly used "preach".

188 The real inference is from the rest of the verse that is not quoted but assumed to be known to every student: "You shall preach to this people." It follows that the prophet sometimes is ordered to be silent and sometimes to speak but the sage is ordered to teach at all times.

189 The *Arukh* notes the word but gives no explanation. Mussaphia, in his Notes to *Arukh*, proposes the impossible Greco-Latin hybrid πόλεμο-*notarius*, "secretary of war." The best explanation seems to be that of A. Kohut, *diplomatarius*; the first syllable *di* was interpreted as Aramaic relative pronoun (Hebrew שֶׁ) and, therefore, dropped. *Diplomatarius* is a late (Byzantine) form of *diplomarius*, the holder of an imperial *diploma*, a "doubly folded" imperial order or privilege which gave its holder the right to use the imperial mails for transportation. The two *diplomatarii* arrive in the province by imperial mail but this does not imply that they are plenipotentiaries (since, sometimes, the privilege of using the mails was given to private citizens.)

190 Hebrew word (חותם) "seal" and its Greek equivalent given as parallels.

191 The reference is to the tradition attached to v. 9, that obliges one in cases of doubt to go the the Temple and ask "the judge who shall be in those days". Since it is impossible to ask a judge who does not live in one's days, this is taken to mean that any chief judge, even if not the most competent one, has the same status as any other living in another time. (Babli *Rosh Hashanah* 25b, *Sifri Devarim* 153).

הֲדָא דְתֵימַר מִשֶּׁיָּצָאת בַּת קוֹל. אֲבָל עַד שֶׁיָּצָאת בַּת קוֹל כָּל־הָרוֹצֶה לְהַחְמִיר עַל עַצְמוֹ וְלִנְהוֹג כְּחוּמְרֵי בֵית שַׁמַּאי וּכְחוּמְרֵי בֵית הִלֵּל עַל זֶה נֶאֱמַר הַכְּסִיל בַּחֹשֶׁךְ יֵלֵךְ. כְּקוּלֵּי אֵילּוּ וְאֵילּוּ נִקְרָא רָשָׁע אֶלָּא אִי כְקוּלֵּי וּכְחוּמְרֵי דְדֵין. אִי כְקוּלֵּי וּכְחוּמְרֵי דְדֵין. הָדֵין דְּתֵימַר עַד שֶׁלֹּא יָצָאת בַּת קוֹל. אֲבָל מִשֶּׁיָּצָאת בַּת קוֹל לָעוֹלָם הֲלָכָה כְדִבְרֵי בֵית הִלֵּל וְכָל־הָעוֹבֵר עַל דִּבְרֵי בֵית הִלֵּל חַייָב מִיתָה. תַּנֵּי יָצָאת בַּת קוֹל וְאָמְרָה אֵילּוּ וְאֵילּוּ דִּבְרֵי אֱלֹהִים חַיִּים אֲבָל הֲלָכָה כְדִבְרֵי בֵית הִלֵּל. אֵיכַן יָצָאת בַּת קוֹל. רִבִּי בִּיבִי בְּשֵׁם רִבִּי יוֹחָנָן בְּיַבְנֶה יָצָאת בַּת קוֹל.

That means[192] after the divine voice[193] was heard. But before the divine voice was heard, [194]it was said of anyone who wanted to restrict himself and follow the restrictions both of the school of Shammai and that of Hillel: (*Eccl.* 2:14) "the fool walks in darkness;" anyone who followed the leniencies of both of them[195] was called an evildoer. But one had to follow either the leniencies and restrictions of one school or the leniencies and restrictions of the other. That was before the divine voice was heard. But after the divine voice was heard[196], practice always follows the school of Hillel and everyone who transgresses the rulings of the school of Hillel merits death. We have stated: "A divine voice came and said: Both of them are the words of the Living God but practice follows the school of Hillel".[197] Where was the divine voice heard? Rebbi Bibi[198] in the name of Rebbi Yoḥanan: The divine voice came in Jabneh[199].

192 Referring to the statement in the Mishnah, that Rebbi Tarphon was told that he incurred guilt by following the teachings of the school of Shammai (with which he probably grew up).

193 A בת קול, "daughter of a voice", is a sound carrying information of indeterminate origin.

194 Tosephta *Idiut* 2:3 (in a different version *Sukkah* 2:3). The main discussion in the Babli is *Eruvin* 6b. The 24 instances of restrictions of the school of Hillel where the school of Shammai is more lenient are enumerated in Tosephta *Idiut* 2. It is reported there that the most conscientious one of the followers of Shammai in the years before the destruction of the Temple, R. Yoḥanan ben Haḥoranit, followed the rulings of the school of Hillel in practice. The man who rebuilt Jewish learning after the destruction of the Temple, R. Yoḥanan ben Zakkai, was a student of Hillel.

195 In the opinion of the Babli, only in the case of two leniencies whose theoretical bases contradict one another. Similarly, the fool is one who follows contradictory rigidities.

196 This is an explanation of the Tosephta, rather than a duplication of the earlier note on the Mishnah.

197 The same statement is in Babli *Eruvin* 6b. The language is tannaïtic, but the origin of the phrase is unknown.

198 Since in Talmudic times every ב or ב was pronounced /v/ in Galilee under the influence of Byzantine

Greek, his name probably is a shortening of Latin Vivianus, חַיִּים. R. Bibi was one of the notable students of R. Yoḥanan.

199 The Synhedrion was at Jabneh between the two wars against the Romans and held there its first meeting when it was reconstituted after the persecutions that followed the war of Bar Kokhba. Afterwards, it moved to Galilee permanently. This gives a *terminus ad quem* for the adoption of the rules of the school of Hillel by all of Judaism. It seems that the exact point in time was the reconstitution of the Synhedrion after the war of Bar Kokhba.

While Talmudic literature is full of disagreements on practical points of Jewish practice, there is unanimity that the principles underlying all discussions are those fixed by the school of Hillel in Rabbinic (Pharisaic) Judaism. After the war of Bar Kokhba, we do not hear of any followers of the school of Shammai in practice, nor of Jews that are Sadducees in practice. In the Talmud (Babli *Nidda* 33b), R. Yose (ben Ḥalaphta) states that the Sadducees in his time follow Rabbinic practice. We know that the sect at Qumran were Sadducees and their *Tefillin* follow Sadducee rules; characteristically, they have many more Biblical quotes in addition to the required verses (cf. Y. Yadin, *Tefillin from Qumran*, Jerusalem, 1978). The *Tefillin* found with the Bar Kokhba letters in the caves of the Judean desert are of the same type. Hence, Sadducee practice did not completely stop until the war of Bar Kokhba. As far as Sadduceeism goes, its disappearance in practice can be dated to the aftermath of the war of Bar Kokhba.

It is not believable that a man of the stature of Rebbi Tarphon would transgress a generally accepted practice supported by a divine pronouncement and by popular consent. Hence, the episode of Rebbi Tarphon must be dated in time before the *bat qol*. It is generally accepted that Rebbi Tarphon did not live to see the war of Bar Kokhba. This narrows the time of the *bat qol* to close to that war.

(fol. 3c) **משנה ח.** בְּשַׁחַר מְבָרֵךְ שְׁתַּיִם לְפָנֶיהָ וְאַחַת לְאַחֲרֶיהָ. בָּעֶרֶב מְבָרֵךְ שְׁתַּיִם לְפָנֶיהָ וּשְׁתַּיִם לְאַחֲרֶיהָ. אַחַת אֲרוּכָּה וְאַחַת קְצָרָה. מָקוֹם שֶׁאָמְרוּ

לְהַאֲרִיךְ אֵינוֹ רְשַׁאי לְקַצֵּר. לְקַצֵּר אֵינוֹ רְשַׁאי לְהַאֲרִיךְ. לַחֲתוֹם אֵינוֹ רְשַׁאי שֶׁלֹּא לַחֲתוֹם. שֶׁלֹּא לַחֲתוֹם אֵינוֹ רְשַׁאי לַחֲתוֹם.

Mishnah 8: In the morning he offers two blessings before [the *Shema'*] and one after. In the evening he offers two blessings before and two after, one long and one short. At a place where they[200] said to make it long he is not allowed to make it short, short he is not allowed to make it long. To seal[201] he is not allowed not to seal, not to seal he is not allowed to seal.

200 The men of the Great Assembly.

201 "To seal" means to start the last sentence of the benediction with the words "Praise to You, o Eternal, . . .".

הלכה ח. רִבִּי סִימוֹן בְּשֵׁם רִבִּי שְׁמוּאֵל בַּר נַחְמָן עַל שֵׁם וְהָגִיתָ בּוֹ יוֹמָם וָלַיְלָה שֶׁיְּהֵא הֲגָיַת הַיּוֹם וְהַלַּיְלָה שָׁוִין. רִבִּי יוֹסֵי בְּרִבִּי אָבִין בְּשֵׁם רִבִּי יְהוֹשֻׁעַ בֶּן לֵוִי עַל שֵׁם שֶׁבַע בַּיּוֹם הִלַּלְתִּיךָ עַל מִשְׁפְּטֵי צִדְקֶךָ. רִבִּי נַחְמָן בְּשֵׁם רִבִּי מָנִי כָּל־הַמְקַיֵּם שֶׁבַע בַּיּוֹם הִלַּלְתִּיךָ כְּאִילּוּ קִיֵּם וְהָגִיתָ בּוֹ יוֹמָם וָלַיְלָה.

Halakhah 8: Rebbi Simon in the name of Rebbi Samuel bar Naḥman: Because of[202] (*Jos.* 1:8): "You should think about it day and night", that the thinking of day and night should be equal. Rebbi Yose bar Rebbi Abin in the name of Rebbi Joshua ben Levi: Because of (*Ps.* 119:164): "Seven times a day I praise You for Your just laws." Rebbi Nachman in the name of Rebbi Mani[203]: Everybody who keeps "seven times a day I praise you" is as if he kept also "you should think about it day and night"[204].

202 The reason is sought for benedictions before and after the recitation of *Shema'*. The first opinion, ascribed to an early Amora, gives the reason why the two recitations should be parallel and why each one has to include a benediction of thanks for the Torah, since the recitation of the *Shema'* also helps to fulfill the obligation of Torah-study in a minimal

way. The second opinion, by a late Amora in the name of one of the first ones, explains the asymmetry in the numbers since they must add up to the odd number of 7.

Since in Halakhah 9 (and in the Babli, *Berakhot* 14b) it is reported that in Israel one did not recite the entire last section of *Shema'* in the evening, Rebbi Simon also gives a reason for the asymmetry: In the evening one recites 4 benedictions and 2 sections, in the morning 3 benedictions and 3 sections, for a total of 6 morning and evening. In the next section it is clear that Rebbi Simon makes a distinction between the first two and the third sections of *Shema'*, a distinction rejected by Rebbi Levi from the circle of Rebbi Yoḥanan.

203 Usually, Rebbi Mani in the Yerushalmi is R. Mana the first, an Amora of the first generation. However, Rebbi Naḥman, the preacher, is an Amora of the last generation in Galilee, a student of Rebbi Mana the second. Hence, it is reasonable to assume that R. Mani here is R. Mana the second. However, since the late R. Yose bar Abin transmits in the name of the very early R. Joshua ben Levi, it is not impossible that the name of R. Mani is transmitted correctly.

The statement of R. Mani implies that anybody who recites *Shema'* with its benedictions regularly, every evening and every morning, cannot be considered transgressing the obligation of Torah study even if he does not study otherwise. In contrast to the first two statements, this one has practical consequences.

204 In the Babli, *Menaḥot* 99b, Rebbi Yoḥanan reports in the name of R. Simeon bar Yoḥai that reading the *Shema'* alone is enough; no mention of the necessary benedictions.

מִפְּנֵי מַה קוֹרִין שְׁתֵּי פַּרְשִׁיּוֹת הַלָּלוּ בְּכָל־יוֹם. רִבִּי סִימוֹן אָמַר מִפְּנֵי שֶׁכָּתוּב בְּהֶן שְׁכִיבָה וְקִימָה. רִבִּי לֵוִי אָמַר מִפְּנֵי שֶׁעֲשֶׂרֶת הַדִּבְּרוֹת כְּלוּלִין בָּהֶן. אָנֹכִי יי אֱלֹהֶיךָ. שְׁמַע יִשְׂרָאֵל יי אֱלֹהֵינוּ. לֹא יִהְיֶה לְךָ אֱלֹהִים אֲחֵרִים עַל פָּנָי. יי אֶחָד. לֹא תִשָּׂא אֶת שֵׁם יי אֱלֹהֶיךָ לַשָּׁוְא. וְאָהַבְתָּ אֶת יי אֱלֹהֶיךָ. מַאן דְּרָחִים מַלְכָּא לֹא לִישְׁתַּבַּע בִּשְׁמֵיהּ וּמְשַׁקֵּר. זָכוֹר אֶת יוֹם הַשַּׁבָּת לְקַדְּשׁוֹ. לְמַעַן תִּזְכְּרוּ. רִבִּי אוֹמֵר זוּ מִצְוַת שַׁבָּת שֶׁהִיא שְׁקוּלָה כְּנֶגֶד כָּל־מִצְווֹתֶיהָ שֶׁל תּוֹרָה דִּכְתִיב וְאֶת שַׁבַּת קָדְשְׁךָ הוֹדַעְתָּ לָהֶם וּמִצְווֹת וְחוּקִים וְתוֹרָה צִוִּיתָ וגו' לְהוֹדִיעֲךָ שֶׁהִיא שְׁקוּלָה כְּנֶגֶד מִצְווֹתֶיהָ שֶׁל תּוֹרָה. כַּבֵּד אֶת אָבִיךָ וְאֶת אִמֶּךָ. לְמַעַן יִרְבּוּ יְמֵיכֶם

וִימֵי בְנֵיכֶם. לֹא תִרְצַח. וַאֲבַדְתֶּם מְהֵרָה. מַאן דְּקָטֵיל מִתְקַטֵיל. לֹא תִנְאַף. לֹא תָתוּרוּ אַחֲרֵי לְבַבְכֶם וְאַחֲרֵי עֵינֵיכֶם. אָמַר רִבִּי לֵוִי לִיבָּא וְעֵינָא תְּרֵין סַרְסוּרֵי דְחַטָּאָה כְּתִיב תְּנָה בְנִי לִבְּךָ לִי וְעֵינֶיךָ דְּרָכַי תִּצֹּרְנָה. אָמַר הַקָּדוֹשׁ בָּרוּךְ הוּא אִי יְהַבַת לִי לִבָּךְ וְעֵינָךְ אֲנָא יְדַע דְּאַתְּ לִי. לֹא תִגְנֹב. וְאָסַפְתָּ דְגָנֶךָ וְלֹא דְגָנוֹ שֶׁל חֲבֵרְךָ. לֹא תַעֲנֶה בְרֵעֲךָ עֵד שָׁקֶר. אֲנִי יי אֱלֹהֵיכֶם. וּכְתִיב וַיי אֱלֹהִים אֱמֶת. מַהוּ אֱמֶת אָמַר רִבִּי אַבוּן שֶׁהוּא אֱלֹהִים חַיִּים וּמֶלֶךְ עוֹלָם. אָמַר רִבִּי לֵוִי אָמַר הַקָּדוֹשׁ בָּרוּךְ הוּא אִם הֵעַדְתָּ לַחֲבֵירָךְ עֵדוּת שֶׁקֶר מַעֲלֶה אֲנִי עָלֶיךָ כְּאִילּוּ הֵיעַדְתָּ עָלַי שֶׁלֹּא בָרָאתִי שָׁמַיִם וָאָרֶץ. לֹא תַחְמוֹד בֵּית רֵעֶיךָ. וּכְתַבְתָּם עַל מְזוּזוֹת בֵּיתֶךָ. בֵּיתֶךָ וְלֹא בֵית חֲבֵירָךְ.

Why does one read these two sections every day? Rebbi Simon says because they mention lying down and getting up. Rebbi Levi said, because the Ten Commandments are contained in them[205].

"I am the Eternal, your God." - "Hear[206], o Israel, The Eternal, our God."

"You should not have any other gods before me." - "The Eternal is One."

"Do not take the name of the Eternal, your God, in vain." - "You must love the Eternal, your God." He who loves the king will not swear in his name and lie.

"Remember the Sabbath day to sanctify it." - "So that you shall remember;" Rebbi said: that is the commandment of Sabbath which is as important as all other commandments of the Torah together, as it is written (*Neh.* 9:14): "You informed them about Your Sabbath, commandments, laws, and Torah you commanded them, . . ." to show that it is as important as the other commandments of the Torah[207].

"Honor your father and mother" - "So that your days and the days of your children should increase.[208]"

"Do not murder" - "You will soon be lost." He who kills will be killed.

"Do not commit adultery" - "Do not stray after your hearts and after your eyes." Rebbi Levi said: heart and eye are the two agents of sin. It is written (*Prov.* 23:26) "My son, give Me your heart; your eyes should watch My ways." The Holy One, Praise to Him, says: If you give me your heart and eyes I know that you are mine[209].

"Do not steal" - "You shall harvest your grain, " not your neighbor's grain[210]"

"Do not testify against your neighbor as a false witness," - "I am the Lord, your God." And it is written (*Jer.* 10:10) "But the Lord is the God of truth." What is truth? Rebbi Abun said: that (*Jer.* 10:10) "He is God of life and king of the world." Rebbi Levi said: The Holy One, praise to Him, said, if you gave false testimony against your neighbor, I count that against you as if you gave testimony against Me that I did not create heaven and earth[211].

"Do not covet your neighbor's house" - "You shall write them on the doorposts of your house," your house and not your neighbor's house.

205 Since Rebbi Levi depends heavily on the third section of *Shema'*, he cannot agree that in the evening one should recite only two sections. In the Babli (*Berakhot* 12b), the third section of *Shema'* is singled out for its importance because five of the Ten Commandments are alluded to in it.

206 As R. Shelomo ben Adrat (Rashba) points out, שמע can mean "hear, understand, or accept."

207 Since the Sabbath alone is given a parallel status to "Torah" in this verse.

208 This promise is connected with honoring father and mother in the Ten Commandments of Deuteronomy.

209 The connection seems to be from the following verse: "Because a dark ditch is the harlot and a source of trouble the strange woman."

210 This contradicts the opinion of the Babli, *Sanhedrin* 86a, that the Ten commandments forbid kidnapping, a capital crime like murder and adultery. The Babli's opinion is found also in *Mekhilta deR. Ismael* (Jithro 5), which possibly was edited in the Academy of Rav in Babylonia. The same attitude as here, that all stealing is prohibited, is found in *Mekhilta deR. Simeon bar Yoḥai*, p. 153.

211 This argument is the base of Rashi's commentary on *Berakhot* 14b, on the statement that one is required to end the recitation of *Shema'* with "the Eternal is the God of truth." Rabbi Abun (Rabin) was a younger contemporary of R. Levi.

תַּמָּן תַּנֵּי אָמַר לָהֶן הַמְּמוּנֶּה בָּרְכוּ בְרָכָה אַחַת וְהֵם בֵּירְכוּ. מַה בֵּרְכוּ. רַב מַתָּנָה אָמַר בְּשֵׁם שְׁמוּאֵל זוּ בִּרְכַּת תּוֹרָה. וְקָרְאוּ עֲשֶׂרֶת הַדִּבְּרוֹת שְׁמַע וְהָיָה אִם שָׁמוֹעַ. וַיֹּאמֶר. רִבִּי אַמִּי בְּשֵׁם רִבִּי שִׁמְעוֹן בֶּן לָקִישׁ זֹאת אוֹמֶרֶת שֶׁאֵין הַבְּרָכוֹת מְעַכְּבוֹת. אָמַר רִבִּי בָּא אֵין מִן הָדָא לֵית שְׁמַע מִינָּהּ כְּלוּם שֶׁעֲשֶׂרֶת הַדִּבְּרוֹת הֵן הֵן גּוּפָהּ שֶׁל שְׁמַע. דְּרַב מַתָּנָה וְרִבִּי שְׁמוּאֵל בַּר נַחְמָן תְּרַוֵּיהוֹן אָמְרִין בְּדִין הֲוָה שֶׁיְּהוּ קוֹרִין עֲשֶׂרֶת הַדִּבְּרוֹת בְּכָל־יוֹם וּמִפְּנֵי מַה אֵין קוֹרִין אוֹתָן מִפְּנֵי טַעֲנַת הַמִּינִין שֶׁלֹּא יְהוּ אוֹמְרִין אֵלּוּ לְבַד נִיתְּנוּ לְמֹשֶׁה בְּסִינַי.

There it was stated (*Tamid* Mishnah 5:1): "The official in charge told them[212]: recite one benediction! and they recited one benediction." What benediction did they recite? Rav Mattanah in the name of Samuel[213]: that is the benediction for the Torah. "Then they recited the Ten Commandments and the three sections of *Shema'*." Rebbi Ammi in the name of Rebbi Simeon ben Laqish: that means that the benedictions are no obstacle[214]. Rebbi Abba said: From here you cannot draw any inference because the Ten Commandments contain the essence of *Shema'*[215]. Rav Mattanah and Rebbi Samuel ben Naḥman both say that it would have been logical to require that the Ten Commandments should be recited every day. Why does one not recite them? Because of the arguments of the Christians[216], that they should not say that only these were given to Moses at Sinai.

212 This Mishnah deals with the details of the Temple service, in particular the prayers of the priests before the start of dawn and beginning of services. The official in charge was one of the small permanent staff of the Temple; the priests themselves were divided into 24 "watches", one of which

served in the Temple from the placing of new show-bread on the Sabbath to its removal the next week. These "watches" are remembered in several *kinnot* for the Ninth of Av.

213 Rav Mattanah was a student of Samuel, the head of the Academy of Nahardea and representative of the Babylonian tradition in Talmudic studies.

214 Since it is implied that the priests fulfilled their duty of reciting the *Shema'*, it follows that the non-recitation of the benedictions preceding and following the *Shema'* does not invalidate the recitation of *Shema'* itself.

The Babli (11b) has a totally different approach. First, they note that Rav Mattanah did not know what benediction was recited in the Temple and then they report that Rav Yehudah said in the name of Samuel that the second of the daily benedictions preceding the *Shema'* was recited. Rebbi Ammi in the name of R. Simeon ben Laqish is quoted that "benedictions do not invalidate one another", i. e., the recitation of the second before the first is not an obstacle. The essential difference is that for the Babli, the last benediction before *Shema'*, which is praise for the Torah and its study, may take the place of the explicit benediction for the Torah (e. g., for somebody who came late to the Synagogue and is reciting that benediction before he had a chance to recite the benediction for the Torah), whereas the Yerushalmi requires two benedictions unless one starts studying after the recitation of the *Shema'* without interruption; see below and *Tosaphot Berakhot* 11b, *s. v.* שכבר.

215 Since the benedictions for the *Shema'* were instituted for *Shema'* only, they are not applicable to the Ten Commandments; hence, the Ten Commandments, if recited at the start of the service, require the benediction for the Torah. On the other hand, in the preceding section is was shown that *Shema'* contains allusions to all of the Ten Commandments. Hence, *Shema'* is in a sense a duplication of the Ten Commandments and a separate benediction would be out of place.

216 מִין always denotes a Jewish Christian. In the Babli (12a) it is said that "the reading of the Ten Commandments was stopped because of the propaganda of the (Jewish) Christians."

רִבִּי שְׁמוּאֵל בַּר נַחְמָן בְּשֵׁם רִבִּי יְהוּדָה בַּר זְבוּדָא בְּדִין הָיָה שֶׁיְּהוּ קוֹרִין פָּרָשַׁת בָּלָק וּבִלְעָם בְּכָל־יוֹם וּמִפְּנֵי מָה אֵין קוֹרִין אוֹתָם שֶׁלֹּא לְהַטְרִיחַ עַל הַצִּיבּוּר.

רִבִּי חוּנָה אָמַר מִפְּנֵי שֶׁכָּתוּב בָּהּ שְׁכִיבָה וְקִימָה. רִבִּי יוֹסֵי בֵּי רִבִּי בּוּן אָמַר מִפְּנֵי שֶׁכָּתוּב בָּהֶן יְצִיאָה וּמַלְכוּת. אָמַר רִבִּי אֶלְעָזָר מִפְּנֵי שֶׁכְּתוּבָה בַּתּוֹרָה בַנְּבִיאִים וּבַכְּתוּבִים.

Rebbi Samuel bar Naḥman in the name of Rebbi Yehudah bar Zebida[217]: It would have been logical that one also would have to recite the chapter of Balaq and Balaam every day[218]. Why does one not recite it? Not to incommodate the public too much. Rebbi Ḥuna said, because it mentions lying down and standing up[219]. Rebbi Yose bar Abun said, because it contains the Exodus and God's kingdom[220]. Rebbi Eleazar said, because it is written in the Torah, in the Prophets, and in the Hagiographs.[221]

217 A Galilean Amora of the second generation, possibly a student of Rav in Babylonia. He is also the author of the parallel statement in the Babli (12b). The statement of Rebbi Ḥuna is given in the Babli in the name of Rebbi Yose bar Abun. The reasons of Rebbi Yose bar Abun and Rebbi Eleazar in the Yerushalmi are missing in the Babli. The quotes in the Babli are all in the name of Galilean authorities.

218 The blessings of Balaam, *Num.* 23:7 - 24:25.

219 *Num.* 23:24, 24:9.

220 *Num.* 24:8, 23:21.

221 In the Torah as indicated; in the Prophets *Michah* 6:5, in the Hagiographs *Neḥemiah* 13:2

אָמַר לָהֶן הַמְּמוּנֶּה בָּֽרְכוּ בְרָכָה אַחַת וְהֵם בֵּירְכוּ. מַה בֵּֽרְכוּ. רַב מַתָּנָה אָמַר בְּשֵׁם שְׁמוּאֵל זוּ בִּרְכַּת תּוֹרָה. וַהֲלֹא לֹא בֵֽרְכוּ יוֹצֵר הַמְּאוֹרוֹת. רִבִּי שְׁמוּאֵל אָחִיו דְּרִבִּי בֶּֽרֶכְיָה עֲדַיִין לֹא יָֽצְאוּ הַמְּאוֹרוֹת וְתֵימַר יוֹצֵר הַמְּאוֹרוֹת.

[222]"The official in charge told them: recite one benediction! and they recited one benediction." What benediction did they recite? Rav Mattanah in the name of Samuel: that is the benediction for the Torah. But they did not yet recite "Creator of the Lights![223]" Rebbi Samuel, brother of Rebbi Berekhiah, said: there is no light yet and you want to recite "Creator of the Lights"?

222 In the Babli, this piece would be introduced by גופא "let us return to our main theme." Such a reference is always missing in the Yerushalmi. In the Babli, this argument is an anonymous tentative statement (12a). Rebbi Samuel, brother of Rebbi Berekhiah, is an Israeli Amora of the fourth generation. His brother, Rebbi Berekhiah, is one of the authors of the oldest sections of *Midrash Rabba*.

223 The first benediction before the *Shema'*, a celebration of God's creation of the sun. The corresponding benediction in the evening is a celebration of God's making the world revolve alternatingly into darkness and light.

וּבְשַׁבָּת מוֹסִיפִין בְּרָכָה אַחַת לְמִשְׁמָר הַיּוֹצֵא. מַהוּ בְרָכָה. אָמַר רִבִּי חֶלְבּוֹ זוֹ הִיא הַשּׁוֹכֵן בַּבַּיִת הַזֶּה יִטַּע בֵּינֵיכֶם אַחֲוָה וְאַהֲבָה שָׁלוֹם וְרֵעוּת.

(*Tamid* Mishnah 5:1) On the Sabbath they add one benediction for the departing watch. What kind of benediction? Rebbi Ḥelbo[224] said, that is it: May He Who resides in the Temple plant among you brotherliness and love, peace and neighborliness.

224 A Babylonian, student of Rav Huna and colleague of Rav Sheshet, who emigrated to Galilee and became student of Rebbi Samuel bar Naḥman and Rebbi Ammi. He was the main teacher of Rebbi Berekhiah. His statement appears in the Babli in identical form (12a).

שְׁמוּאֵל אָמַר הִשְׁכִּים לִשְׁנוֹת קוֹדֶם קִרְיַת שְׁמַע צָרִיךְ לְבָרֵךְ. לְאַחַר קִרְיַת שְׁמַע אֵין צָרִיךְ לְבָרֵךְ. אָמַר רִבִּי בָּא וְהוּא שֶׁשָּׁנָה עַל אָתָר. רִבִּי חוּנָא אָמַר נִרְאִין הַדְּבָרִים מִדְרַשׁ צָרִיךְ לְבָרֵךְ. הֲלָכוֹת אֵין צָרִיךְ לְבָרֵךְ. רִבִּי סִימוֹן בְּשֵׁם רִבִּי יְהוֹשֻׁעַ בֶּן לֵוִי בֵּין מִדְרַשׁ בֵּין הֲלָכוֹת צָרִיךְ לְבָרֵךְ. אָמַר רַב חִיָּיא בַּר אַשִׁי נְהָגִין הֲוֵינָן קוֹמוֹי רַב בֵּין מִדְרַשׁ בֵּין הֲלָכוֹת זְקָקִינָן לְמִבְרְכָה.

Samuel said: If one got up early to study before he recited the *Shema'* he has to recite the benediction. After the recitation of *Shema'* he does not have to recite the benediction. Rebbi Abba[225] said, that is only if he studied immediately. Rebbi Ḥuna[226] said: It is reasonable to say that for exegesis[227] one has to recite the benediction, for practical rules[228] one does not have to recite the benediction. Rebbi Simon in the name of Rebbi Joshua ben Levi: Both for exegesis and for practical rules one has to recite the benediction. Rav Ḥiyya bar Ashi said: When we were sitting before Rav, he always required us to recite the benediction both for exegesis and for practical rules[229].

225 The opinion of the Yerushalmi is that the benediction before *Shema'* is no substitute for the benediction on the Torah. The statement of Rebbi Abba, Babylonian immigrant to Israel, former student of Rav Yehudah, the student of Samuel, harmonizes Babylonian practice, expressed by Samuel, with Israeli theory by accepting the Babylonian practice but making it impracticable. על אתר is the same as Babylonian לאלתר "on the spot, immediately."

226 From the parallel in the Babli (11b) and the order of statements it seems that "Rebbi" here in the Yerushalmi is a scribal error for Rav; the author of the statement is Rav Huna, the student of Rav from the family of the Resh Galuta. The discussion in the Babli is much more detailed, starting with the study of Scripture and going into the details of the sections of the Oral Law.

227 It seems that here מדרש includes both exegesis of the Torah and exegesis of the Oral Law, anything that is not obvious either from a biblical verse or from a Mishnaic statement.

228 Practical rules, הלכה, refers to the memorization of fixed statements which are immediately applicable, whether a Mishnah, Tosephta, or a deciding statement of an Amora.

229 In the Babli (11b), Rav Ḥiyya bar Ashi, the student of Rav, notes that for his early morning class, Rav washed his hands, recited the benedictions, and proceeded to teach the *Midrash Halakha* on the Torah, thus combining all aspects of Torah study. In the version of the Babli, the statement of Rav Ḥiyya bar Ashi is separate from the preceding discussion and seems to indicate that the different aspects of Torah study should not be separated, in contrast to the Yerushalmi version.

תַּנֵּי הַקּוֹרֵא עִם אַנְשֵׁי מַעֲמָד לֹא יָצָא כִּי מְאַחֲרִין הָיוּ. רִבִּי זְעִירָא בְשֵׁם רִבִּי אַמִּי בְּיוֹמוֹי דְרִבִּי יוֹחָנָן הֲוִינָן נַפְקִין לְתַעֲנִיתָא וְקוֹרוֹי שְׁמַע בָּתָר תְּלַת שָׁעִין וְלֹא הֲוָה מַמְחֵי בְיָדָן. רִבִּי יוֹסֵי וְרִבִּי אָחָא נַפְקָן לְתַעֲנִיתָא אָתָא צִיבּוּרָא וּמוֹקְרֵי שְׁמַע בָּתָר תְּלַת שָׁעִין. בָּעָא רַב אָחָא מְחוּיֵי בְיָדָן. אָמַר לֵיהּ רִבִּי יוֹסֵה וַהֲלֹא כְּבַר קָרְאוּ אוֹתָהּ בְּעוֹנָתָהּ. כְּלוּם קוֹרִין אוֹתָהּ אֶלָּא כְּדֵי לַעֲמוֹד בִּתְפִילָּה מִתּוֹךְ דְּבַר תּוֹרָה. אָמַר לֵיהּ מִפְּנֵי הַהֶדְיוֹטוֹת שֶׁלֹּא יְהוּ אוֹמְרִין בְּעוֹנָתָהּ הֵן קוֹרִין אוֹתָהּ.

It was stated[230]: He who recites with the men of *Maämad*[231] has not done his duty since they were too late. Rebbi Zeïra in the name of Rebbi Ammi: In the days of Rebbi Yoḥanan we went out for a fast-day and recited *Shema'* after three hours and he did not oppose us[232]. Rebbi Yose and Rebbi Aḥa went out for a fast-day. The public came and recited *Shema'* after three hours. Rebbi[233] Aḥa wanted to oppose them. Rebbi Yose said to him: Did they not recite at its due time[234], now they only recite it in order to stand in prayer after words of the Torah. He answered back: It is because of the uneducated, who should not say that the recitation was in its correct time[235].

230 A somewhat different version of this *baraita* is in Babli *Yoma* 37b.

231 The land of Israel was divided into 24 districts, corresponding to the 24 families of priests, and every week a select group of laymen from the district in charge of the week came to Jerusalem to be present at the sacrifices. Since public sacrifices were brought on behalf of the entire people, a sacrifice must be brought with its owners being present. The lay delegation, the *Men of Maämad*, were the representatives of the Jewish people at the daily sacrifices. Since these sacrifices started very early, the men of *Maämad* had to participate before they could hold their prayers. Therefore, they started their morning prayers only after the daily morning sacrifice was completed. By that time, it was later than three hours into daylight and anyone else would be too late in their recitation.

232 In Israel, a fast day usually meant a day of fasting for rain. The services for these fast days were always held in the public square, therefore one had "to go out". Also, the sermon was given before the start of prayers since a sermon after prayers would not do much good and on fastdays the regular service, with an extended *Amidah*, was said. By the time that a great many people were assembled and the sermon was given, it was rather late, later than three variable hours (one quarter of the time between sunrise and sundown).

233 The reading רב that is found in all printed editions and manuscripts is clearly a copyist's error; the entire discussion is about rain fasts in Israel and only Israeli scholars are involved.

234 At the time of the morning benedictions that were said at home, not in the synagogue.

235 The disagreement between Rebbis Yose and Aḥa is not resolved in the Yerushalmi.

אֵלּוּ בְּרָכוֹת שֶׁמַּאֲרִיכִין בָּהֶן בִּרְכוֹת רֹאשׁ הַשָּׁנָה וְיוֹם הַכִּפּוּרִים וּבִרְכוֹת תַּעֲנִית צִיבּוּר. מִבִּרְכוֹתָיו אָדָם נִיכַּר אִם תַּלְמִיד חָכָם הוּא אִם בּוּר הוּא. אֵלּוּ בְּרָכוֹת שֶׁמְּקַצְּרִין בָּהֶן הַמְּבָרֵךְ עַל הַמִּצְוֹת וְעַל הַפֵּירוֹת וּבִרְכַּת הַזִּימּוּן וּבְרָכָה אַחֲרוֹנָה שֶׁל בִּרְכַּת הַמָּזוֹן אַחַר הַמָּזוֹן. הָא כָּל־שְׁאָר בְּרָכוֹת אָדָם מַאֲרִיךְ. אָמַר חִזְקִיָּה מִן מַה דְתַנֵּי הַמַּאֲרִיךְ הֲרֵי זֶה מְגוּנֶּה וְהַמְּקַצֵּר הֲרֵי זֶה מְשׁוּבָּח הָדָא אָמְרָה שֶׁאֵין זֶה הַכְּלָל. תַּנֵּי צָרִיךְ לְהַאֲרִיךְ בְּגוֹאֵל יִשְׂרָאֵל בְּתַעֲנִית. הָא בְשֵׁשׁ שֶׁהוּא מוֹסִיף אֵינוֹ מַאֲרִיךְ. אָמַר רִבִּי יוֹסֵה שֶׁלֹּא תֹאמַר הוֹאִיל וְהוּא מֵעֵין יֹח לֹא יַאֲרִיךְ בָּהּ. לְפוּם כֵּן צָרִיךְ מֵימַר צָרִיךְ לְהַאֲרִיךְ בְּגוֹאֵל יִשְׂרָאֵל בְּתַעֲנִית.

These are the benedictions that one makes long[236]: the benedictions for *Rosh Hashanah* and *Yom Kippur*, and the benedictions for a public fast day. From his benedictions one can tell whether someone is a scholar or is uneducated. These are the benedictions that one makes short: He who makes a benediction over a commandment and on fruits, the introductory paragraph of Grace[237], and the last benediction in Grace after the meal[238]. Hence, all other benedictions one should make long. Ḥizqiah[239] said: From what we have stated: He who makes it long is despicable, he who makes is short is praiseworthy, which means that this is not a principle[240]. We have stated: One has to make long the benediction "Who saves Israel" on a fast day[241]. Hence[242], the six additional benedictions he should not make long. Rebbi Yose said: You should not say: because this is part[243] of *Shemoneh Esreh* one should not make it long, therefore it is necessary to say: One has to make long the benediction "Who saves Israel" on a fast day.

236 In a different order (short, long, recognize) the statement is found in Tosephta *Berakhot* 1:6. In Tosephta 1:7, the list of the short benedictions is repeated as that of benedictions which do not have a separate ending (where, however, Rebbi Yose Hagalili disagrees about the fourth benediction of Grace.) Towards the end of the *Halakhah* here, Rebbi Yudan will explain that Tosephta 1:7 gives the definition of "short" in the Mishnah and Tosephta 1:6; hence, it follows that "long" is identical with "having a separate ending: Praise to You, o Eternal, . . ." That identification has been accepted by most Medieval authorities.

However, originally the definition seems to have been the one given here and in Tosephta 1:6, *viz.*, that there exist benedictions, those of *Musaph* of *Rosh Hashanah*, all prayers of *Yom Kippur* with the Confessions, and the additional benedictions in the prayer of a public fast for rain (a lengthened Seventh benediction followed by six additional ones, detailed in Mishnah *Taänit* 2:4) which were not those of the congregation, but of the cantor who in Israel at that time was supposed to present his own compositions, and those of the list had to be long. Then there exists a short list of short benedictions that may not be lengthened by poetic insertion. And finally, there exist the benedictions not mentioned here at all, like the benedictions before and after the recitation of *Shema'*, where it seems the cantor may produce poetic insertions without being characterized either as scholar or as uneducated.

237 Some Medieval authors (e. g. *Sefer Hamanhig, Hilkhot Seüdah*, #16) read "the benediction over food (מזון)" instead of *zimmun* (זימון), the introductory paragraph. This reading would explain the seemingly redundant "Grace after a meal" but is it not supported by any manuscript either of the Yerushalmi or the Tosephta. *Sefer*

Hamanhig explains this "benediction over food (מזון)" as the benediction *before* the meal.

238 The last benediction was originally only "Praise to You, o Lord, King of the Universe, Who is good and does good" (*Talmid Rabbenu Yonah, Alfassi Berakhot* 36a). The extensions that today make the benediction short in form but long in text are mainly of Babylonian origin; cf. the discussion in the author's *The Scholar's Haggadah*, pp. 358-359.

239 One of the twin sons of Rebbi Ḥiyya, collaborator of Rebbi Yehudah the Prince.

240 The benedictions not mentioned may be enlarged by poetic insertions but do not have to be long.

241 With poetic or Biblical insertions.

242 Since the next six benedictions are not mentioned in this *baraita*.

243 Of the everyday prayers. One has to assume that Rebbi Yose would classify the קרובץ insertions on Purim as short.

אֵלּוּ בְּרָכוֹת שֶׁשּׁוֹחֲחִין בָּהֶן בְּרֹאשׁוֹ תְּחִילָּה וְסוֹף. וּבְמוֹדִים תְּחִילָּה וְסוֹף. הַשּׁוֹחֵחַ עַל כָּל־בְּרָכָה וּבְרָכָה מְלַמְּדִין אוֹתוֹ שֶׁלֹּא יָשׁוּחַ. רִבִּי יִצְחָק בַּר נַחְמָן בְּשֵׁם רִבִּי יְהוֹשֻׁעַ בֶּן לֵוִי כֹּהֵן גָּדוֹל שׁוֹחֶה עַל סוֹף כָּל־בְּרָכָה וּבְרָכָה. הַמֶּלֶךְ רֹאשׁ כָּל־בְּרָכָה וּבְרָכָה וְסוֹף כָּל־בְּרָכָה וּבְרָכָה. רִבִּי סִימוֹן בְּשֵׁם רִבִּי יְהוֹשֻׁעַ בֶּן לֵוִי הַמֶּלֶךְ מִשֶּׁהוּא כּוֹרֵעַ אֵינוֹ זוֹקֵף עַד שֶׁהוּא מַשְׁלִים כָּל־תְּפִילָּתוֹ. מַאי טַעֲמָא וַיְהִי כְּכַלּוֹת שְׁלֹמֹה לְהִתְפַּלֵּל אֶל יי אֵת כָּל־הַתְּפִילָּה וְאֶת כָּל־הַתְּחִינָּה הַזֹּאת קָם מִלִּפְנֵי מִזְבַּח יי מִכְּרוֹעַ עַל בִּרְכָּיו.

These are the benedictions for which one bows down[244]: The first[245], beginning and end; "thanks", beginning and end. One who bows down for every benediction is taught that he should not bow down[246]. Rebbi Isaac bar Naḥman[247] in the name of Rebbi Joshua ben Levi: The High Priest bows down at the end of every benediction; the king at the start and the end of every benediction. Rebbi Simon in the name of Rebbi Joshua ben Levi: Once the king bows down deeply he does not get up until he finishes his entire prayer[249]. What is the reason? (*1Kings* 8:54) "It was when Solomon finished all this prayer and supplication to the Eternal, he got up before the Eternal's altar and did no longer bow down on his knees."

244 Here one does not talk about the recitation of the *Shema'* and its benedictions at all but about the eighteen benedictions of the *Amidah*, the subject of Chapters 3 and 4. In the Babli, the place of this discussion is in Chap. 4, p. 34a. The reason that the subject is taken up in this context in the Yerushalmi is that in the Tosephta (*Berakhot* 1:8) it is dealt with immediately after the discussion of short and long benedictions. (In Tosephta and Babli, the verb "to bow down" is שחה, not שחח as in the Yerushalmi. This is another indication that the Tosephta in our hands today is a Babylonian edition of an originally Israeli text.)

245 At the very start of *Shemone Esre* and before the benediction "Shield of Abraham."

246 Either because he imitates behavior reserved for the High Priest or because he is ostentatious in his religiosity, an objectionable behavior.

247 One of the students of R. Joshua ben Levi in the early Talmudic period.

248 It seems that the statements of Rebbis Simon and Isaac ben Naḥman refer to two different statements of R. Joshua ben Levi: The first one is about bowing down like everybody else, the second one is about kneeling, as in the *Musaph* prayer of *Rosh Hashanah*, when everybody can get up except for the king (according to Rashi in the Babli, 34a, because with increasing earthly power comes the need for increasing submission to God.)

אֵי זוּ הִיא כְּרִיעָה וְאֵי זוּ הִיא בְּרִיכָה. רִבִּי חִייָא רַבָּא הֶרְאָה בְּרִיכָה לִפְנֵי רִבִּי וְנִפְסַח וְנִתְרַפֵּא. רִבִּי לֵוִי בַּר סִיסִי הֶרְאָה כְּרִיעָה לִפְנֵי רִבִּי וְנִפְסַח וְלֹא נִתְרַפֵּא.

[249]What is bowing down to one's knees and what is kneeling? The great Rebbi Ḥiyya demonstrated kneeling before Rebbi, he got up lame and was healed. Rebbi Levi ben Sisi demonstrated bowing down to his knees before Rebbi, he got up lame and was not healed.

249 The origin of this short insertion is *Sukkah* 5:4 where it is reported that Rabban Gamliel, on occasion of the joyous dance for the drawing of water

on Sukkot not only had a fire dance with eight different torches swirling in the air but also showed "bowing down to one's knees" as making a push-up by supporting oneself not on two hands but only on two fingers. This introduction has fallen out here and the two terms כריעה, בריכה have been switched. What the Yerushalmi calls בריכה, the parallel in the Babli (*Megillah* 22b, also *Berakhot* 34b) calls קידה, "falling on one's face".

וְכַפָּיו פְּרוּסוֹת הַשָּׁמָיִם אָמַר רִבִּי אַיְבוּ כְּגוֹן הָדֵין נֶקְרִיס[250] הָיָה עוֹמֵד. אָמַר רִבִּי אֶלְעָזָר בַּר אֲבִינָא הִזְהִיר בַּכַּפַּיִם הַלָּלוּ שֶׁלֹּא יִנָּטְפוּ בְּבִנְיַן בֵּית הַמִּקְדָּשׁ כְּלוּם.

(*1Kings* 8:54) "His hands raised to Heaven."[251] Rebbi Ayvu said: He was standing as if inanimate. Rebbi Eleazar bar Avina said: He made clear that these palms did not get at all dirty during the building of the Temple[252].

250 Reading of the Rome manuscript; Leyden and Venice: בקדים. The word is Greek νεκρός "inanimate" (adj.).

251 This is the end of the verse quoted earlier for Solomon's prayer. The text of the Venice edition here is inferior to that of the Rome manuscript that has been followed. (In the Venice print: הזהיר is missing, נטפו for ינטפו.) As Levy recognized, נטף is the same as טנף.

252 He seems to emphasize that Solomon raised his "open hands", not his "hands", to show that from all the riches that David had assembled for the building of the Temple (*1Chr.* 29:1-9) not a penny was sticking to his own palms.

תָּנָא רִבִּי חֲלַפְתָּא בֶּן שָׁאוּל הַכֹּל שׁוֹחֲחִין עִם שְׁלִיחַ צִיבּוּר בְּהוֹדָאָה. רִבִּי זְעִירָא אָמַר וּבִלְבַד בְּמוֹדִים. רִבִּי זְעִירָא סָבַר לִקְרוֹבָה כְּדֵי לְשׁוּחַ עִמּוֹ תְּחִילָּה וְסוֹף. רִבִּי יֹסֵה כַּד דְּסַלִּיק לְהָכָא חַמְתֵּין גְּחָנִין וּמְלַחֲשִׁין. אָמַר לוֹן מַהוּ דֵין (fol. 3d) לְחִישָׁה וְלֹא שְׁמִיעַ דָּמַר רִבִּי חֶלְבּוֹ רִבִּי שִׁמְעוֹן בְּשֵׁם רִבִּי יוֹחָנָן בְּשֵׁם רִבִּי יִרְמְיָה רִבִּי חֲנִינָא בְּשֵׁם רִבִּי מְיָישָׁא רִבִּי חִיָּיא בְּשֵׁם רִבִּי סִימַאי. וְאִית דְּאָמְרִין חֲבֵרַיָּא

בְּשֵׁם רִבִּי סִימַאי מוֹדִים אֲנַחְנוּ לָךְ אֲדוֹן כָּל־הַבְּרִיּוֹת אֱלוֹהַּ הַתּוּשְׁבָּחוֹת צוּר הָעוֹלָמִים חַי הָעוֹלָם יוֹצֵר בְּרֵאשִׁית מְחַיֵּה מֵתִים שֶׁהֶחֱיִיתָנוּ וְקִייַּמְתָּנוּ וּזְכִיתָנוּ וְסִייַּעְתָּנוּ וְקֵרַבְתָּנוּ לְהוֹדוֹת לִשְׁמָךְ בָּרוּךְ אַתָּה יי אֵל הָהוֹדָאוֹת. רִבִּי בָּא בַּר זַבְדָּא בְּשֵׁם רַב מוֹדִים אֲנַחְנוּ לָךְ שֶׁאָנוּ חַייָבִין לְהוֹדוֹת לִשְׁמָךְ תְּרַנֵּנּוּ שְׂפָתַי כִּי אֲזַמְּרָה לָּךְ וְנַפְשִׁי אֲשֶׁר פָּדִיתָ בָּרוּךְ אַתָּה יי אֵל הָהוֹדָאוֹת. רִבִּי שְׁמוּאֵל בַּר אִינְיָא בְּשֵׁם רִבִּי אָחָא הוֹדָיָה וּשְׁבָח לִשְׁמָךְ לָךְ גְּדוּלָּה לָךְ גְּבוּרָה לָךְ תִּפְאֶרֶת יְהִי רָצוֹן מִלְּפָנֶיךָ יי אֱלֹהֵינוּ וֵאלֹהֵי אֲבוֹתֵינוּ שֶׁתִּסְמְכֵינוּ מִנְּפִילָתֵינוּ וְתִזְקְפֵנוּ מִכְּפִיפָתֵינוּ כִּי אַתָּה הוּא סוֹמֵךְ נוֹפְלִים וְזוֹקֵף כְּפוּפִים וּמָלֵא רַחֲמִים וְאֵין עוֹד מִלְּבַדֶּךָ בָּרוּךְ אַתָּה יי אֵל הָהוֹדָאוֹת. בַּר קַפָּרָא אָמַר לָךְ כְּרִיעָה לָךְ כְּפִיפָה לָךְ הִשְׁתַּחֲוָיָה לָךְ בְּרִיכָה לְךָ תִּכְרַע כָּל־בֶּרֶךְ תִּשָּׁבַע כָּל־לָשׁוֹן לְךָ יי הַגְּדֻלָּה וְהַגְּבוּרָה וְהַתִּפְאֶרֶת וְהַנֵּצַח וְהַהוֹד כִּי כֹל בַּשָּׁמַיִם וּבָאָרֶץ לְךָ יי הַמַּמְלָכָה וְהַמִּתְנַשֵּׂא לְכֹל לְרֹאשׁ וְהָעֹשֶׁר וְהַכָּבוֹד מִלְּפָנֶיךָ וְאַתָּה מוֹשֵׁל בַּכֹּל וּבְיָדְךָ כֹּחַ וּגְבוּרָה וּבְיָדְךָ לְגַדֵּל וּלְחַזֵּק לַכֹּל וְעַתָּה אֱלֹהֵינוּ מוֹדִים אֲנַחְנוּ לָךְ וּמְהַלְלִים לְשֵׁם תִּפְאַרְתֶּךָ בְּכָל־לֵב וּבְכָל־נֶפֶשׁ מִשְׁתַּחֲוִים כָּל עַצְמוֹתַי תֹּאמַרְנָה יי מִי כָמוֹךָ מַצִּיל עָנִי מֵחָזָק מִמֶּנּוּ וְעָנִי וְאֶבְיוֹן מִגּוֹזְלוֹ בָּרוּךְ אַתָּה יי אֵל הָהוֹדָאוֹת. אָמַר רִבִּי יוּדָן נְהִגִין רַבָּנִין אָמְרִין כּוּלְּהוֹן. וְאִית דְּאָמְרִין אוֹ הָדָא אוֹ הָדָא.

Rebbi Ḥalaphta ben Shaül[253] stated: Everybody bows down with the cantor for the benediction of thanksgiving. Rebbi Zeïra said: But only for the word *modim*. Rebbi Zeïra was attentive to the Qeroba[254] to bow his head at the beginning and at the end. Rebbi Yose when he came up here[255] saw them bowing down and whispering. He said to them: What is this whispering? He had not heard what Rebbi Ḥelbo, Rebbi Simeon said in the name of Rebbi Yoḥanan, in the name of Rebbi Jeremiah[256], Rebbi Ḥanina in the name of Rebbi Miasha[257], Rebbi Ḥiyya in the name of Rebbi Simai, and some say, the colleagues[258] in the name of Rebbi Simai: We thank You, Master of all creatures, God of praises, eternal Rock, Life of the Universe, Creator, Who resurrects the dead, that You have made us alive, kept us, gave us merit, supported us, and brought us near to give thanks to Your name; praised be You, o Eternal, God of thanksgiving. Rebbi Abba bar Zavda[259] in the name of Rav: We thank You since we are obliged to give thanks; may my lips sing, for I shall sing to You with my soul that You have redeemed; praised are You, o Eternal, God of thanksgiving. Rebbi Samuel bar Inia[260] in the name of Rebbi Aḥa: Thanksgiving and praise to Your name, Yours is greatness, Yours is strength, Yours is glory! May it please You, o Eternal, our God and God of our fathers, that You may support us in our fall, straighten us up from our bent state, because You support the falling and straighten up the bent ones, You are full of mercy and nothing exists except You; praised are You, o Eternal, God of thanksgiving. Bar Qappara[261] said: For You we fall down, for You we bend down, for You we prostrate ourselves, for You we kneel, to You every knee should fall down and every tongue swears. (*1Chr.* 29:11-13): Yours, o Eternal, is greatness, strength, glory, victory, and majesty, truly all that is in heaven and on earth; Yours, o Eternal, is the kingdom, and You lift Yourself over all as head. Riches and honor are before You, You rule over all; in Your hand is power and strength, it is in Your hand to make great and strengthen everything. And now, our God, we thank You and praise Your glorious name; with all our heart and soul we prostrate ourselves before You. (*Ps.* 35:10) My entire self shall say: O Eternal, who is like You, Who saves the destitute from one who is stronger than he is, the destitute and poor from the one who robs him. Praised are You, o Eternal, God of thanksgiving.

Rebbi Yudan said: the rabbis used to say all of these[262]. But some say, either one or the other.

253 An Amora of the first generation in Israel who occasionally is quoted as a Tanna. His opinion is the only one given here, to the effect that

one has to bow down at *modim*. The Babli (*Berakhot* 34b) quotes that Rava, Rav Naḥman and Rav Sheshet actually fell down on their knees for *modim*; the Talmud quotes a *baraita* which explicitly forbids falling down on one's knees. Louis Ginzberg assumes that in Israel, falling on one's knees was always strictly forbidden since their synagogues were built of stone with stone floors and falling on one's knees on a stone floor outside the Temple is forbidden. In Babylonia, where synagogues were brick with hardened dirt floors, falling on one's knees was permitted.

254 *Qeroba* is the cantor, the שליח ציבור, who presents his own poetic *offering* of the prayer, the *qerovut*, קרובות or קרובץ, to the congregation for the repetition of the *Amidah*, as noted by L. Ginzberg. סבר here seems to mean "to be attentive", as in the exclamation before the *qiddush* סברי "please pay attention".

It seems that Rebbi Zeïra timed his thanksgiving, one of the longer texts given here, so he could end his benediction in unison with the cantor.

255 "Coming up" means making *aliyah* from Babylonia to Israel. The Babli (*Soṭa* 40a) also reports very short texts by Rav, Samuel, Rebbi Simai (also of the generation between Tannaïm and Amoraïm) and a slightly longer one by Rav Aḥa bar Jacob (a student of Rav Huna, the student of Rav). Most of these texts are so short that they do not lead to the congregation whispering for any length of time.

256 A Tanna of the last generation, student of R. Yehudah ben Batyra.

257 One of the first Tannaïm with the title of "Rebbi", from the last times of the Second Temple.

258 The collective of scholars in the Yeshivah.

259 An Israeli Amora who received his training in the Babylonian academy of Rav.

260 A student of Rebbi Aḥa, Israeli Amora of the fourth generation. The name of his father cannot be determined with certainty; the form given here is from the Rome manuscript. In the Venice print it appears as Mina, at other places in the Yerushalmi it appears as Ina, Idi, Bina, Yonah, Yanna, Yannai. The fourth generation of Galilean Amoraïm saw the Roman empire become Christian and lived through the first persecutions that finally forced the following generation to abandon the work on the Jerusalem Talmud.

261 A contemporary of Rebbi who also made his own compilation of Mishnayot. His full name was R.

Eleazar, son of R. Eleazar the Qappar. Since his name is identical to that of his father it is clear that he was a posthumous child; cf. E. and H. Guggenheimer, *Jewish Family Names and Their Origins*, Ktav 1992, *Etymologisches Lexikon der jüdischen Familiennamen*, München 1996, both p. xviii.

While the previous texts were quoted in historical order, the text of Bar Qappara should have been the first. The reason may be his extensive use of Biblical verses that were a matter of controversy, see below (and in all Yerushalmi versions this is a formal benediction.)

262 Statement of Rav Papa in Babli *Soṭa* 40a. It appears from here that Rav Papa (fifth generation in Babylonia) had good precedent for his ruling from Rebbi Yudan (fourth generation in Israel). The method of Rebbi Yudan/Rav Papa is more adequate to a collection of short statements as given in the Babli than to the very long pieces quoted here in the Yerushalmi.

תַּנֵּי וּבִלְבַד שֶׁלֹּא יָשׁוּחַ יוֹתֵר מִדַּאי. אָמַר רִבִּי יִרְמְיָה וּבִלְחוּד דְּלֹא יַעֲבִיד כְּהָדֵין חַרְדּוֹנָה אֶלָּא כָּל עַצְמוֹתַי תֹּאמַרְנָה יי מִי כָמוֹךָ. מִילְּתָא דְּחָנָן בַּר בָּא פְּלִיגָא דְּחָנָן בַּר בָּא אָמַר לַחֲבֵרַיָּא נֵימוֹר לְכוֹן מִילְּתָא טָבָא דְּחָמִית לְרַב עָבֵיד וְאָמְרִיתָהּ קוֹמֵי שְׁמוּאֵל וְקָם וְנָשַׁק עַל פּוּמִי. בָּרוּךְ אַתָּה שׁוֹחֶה. בָּא לְהַזְכִּיר אֶת הַשֵּׁם זוֹקֵף. שְׁמוּאֵל אָמַר אֲנָא אָמְרִית טַעֲמָא יי זוֹקֵף כְּפוּפִים. אָמַר רִבִּי אַמִּי לֹא מִסְתַּבְּרָא אֶלָּא מִפְּנֵי שְׁמִי נִיחַת הוּא. אָמַר רִבִּי אָבוּן אִלּוּ הֲוָא כְתִיב בְּשְׁמִי נִיחַת הוּא יֵאוּת. לֵית כְּתִיב אֶלָּא מִפְּנֵי שְׁמִי נִיחַת הוּא. קוֹדֶם עַד שֶׁלֹּא הִזְכִּיר אֶת הַשֵּׁם כְּבָר נִיחַת הוּא.

We have stated: Only that one should not bow down too much[263]. Rebbi Jeremiah said: On condition that one should not behave like that large lizard[264], but (*Ps*. 35:10) "All my bones should say, o Eternal, who is like You?" The word of Ḥanan bar Abba[265] disagrees since Ḥanan bar Abba said to the colleagues: I shall tell you one of the good things that I saw Rav do and, when I told it before Samuel, he got up and kissed me on my mouth. At "praised are You", he bows down. When he comes to mention *Hashem*, he straightens up. Samuel said: I shall give the reason (*Ps.* 35:10): "The Eternal straightens the bent ones." Rebbi Ammi[266] said: It is not reasonable, but (*Mal.* 2:5): "Before My Name he is low."[267] Rebbi Abun said: If it were written "at My Name he is low" then you would be right, but it is written "before My Name he is low", before he mentions *Hashem* he is low.

263 After the digression about the text of the private prayer during *modim*, the discussion now returns to the statement that one has to bow twice at the beginning and the end of the *Amidah*.

264 Arabic חִרְדּוֹן, חַרְדּוֹן "large lizard". Tosafot *Berakhot* 12b in the Venice print quote this Yerushalmi as הירוגא and declares it to be the Yerushalmi translation of צָב (*Lev.* 11:29). In the Wilna Talmud Babli, the word was changed to חרדונא following our text. In the *Targum Yerushalmi* (*Pseudo-Jonathan*), the translation of צב is חֲדְרוֹנָא. It seems that the *Targum Yerushalmi* takes Hebrew צב as parallel to Arabic צׂב̱ "lizard" (of all sizes), not as "turtle" as in late Biblical and modern Hebrew.

Rebbi Jeremiah means that, while one should not bow down too much, on the other hand one should not behave like a lizard which keeps its body quiet and moves only the head when it is catching flies. He requires that one should bow down enough so that all bones of one's spine are moved in God's praise.

265 Ḥanan bar Abba appears in the Babli as Rav Ḥanan bar Rava, son-in-law of Rav and father-in-law of Rav Ḥisda. He disagrees with those who bow down at *modim* and remain bowed to the end of their private supplication, even though he formulates his statement in terms of the first benediction of *Shemone Esreh* which starts and ends with "Praised are You, *Hashem*", but his statement is applicable to all other situations, that one never should be bowed when mentioning the Name.

266 Since Rebbi Ammi and Rebbi Abun the first (Ravin) were contemporaries, R. Abun here is the first, not his posthumous son of the same name. Rebbi Ammi also is the contemporary of R. Ḥiyya bar Abba mentioned in the next section and, as successor of R. Yoḥanan as head of the Yeshivah of Tiberias, he is the higher authority.

267 The verse in Maleachi refers to Levi, son of Jacob, or Aharon, the High Priest. Most commentators of Psalms, including Rashi, derive נחת from the root חתת "to tremble" but the Amoraïm take it as derived from (Aramaic) נחת "to descend".

רִבִּי שְׁמוּאֵל בַּר נָתָן בְּשֵׁם רִבִּי חָמָא בַּר חֲנִינָא מַעֲשֶׂה בְּאֶחָד שֶׁשָּׁחַח יוֹתֵר מִדַּאי וְהֶעֱבִירוֹ רִבִּי. רִבִּי אַמִּי אָמַר רִבִּי יוֹחָנָן הֲוָה מַעֲבִיר. אָמַר לֵיהּ רִבִּי חִייָא בַּר בָּא לֹא הָיָה מַעֲבִיר אֶלָּא גּוֹעֵר.

Rebbi Samuel bar Nathan[268] in the name of Rebbi Ḥama bar Ḥanina: It happened that one bowed down too much and Rebbi removed him. Rebbi Ammi said, Rebbi Yoḥanan did remove. Rebbi Ḥiyya bar Abba said, he did not remove but scold.

268 A student of R. Ḥama bar Ḥanina, the son of R. Ḥanina ben Ḥama of the generation of Rebbi. Since Rebbi Yoḥanan did know Rebbi Samuel bar Nathan in his old age, it follows that the two stories are complementary, not that there is a difference of opinion on who removed the cantor because of his excessive bowing. It is clear that we are talking about a cantor because only he can be removed from office by the Rabbi. This does not imply that any congregant would be allowed to bow down too much, only that he cannot be removed. This is the interpretation of Maimonides (*Hilkhot Tefillah* 9:4, see *Kesef Mishneh* on that text).

It is difficult to decide the opinion of the Yerushalmi about whether in practice one removes or simply scolds such a cantor since Rebbi Ammi is in general the higher authority but Rebbi Ḥiyya bar Abba is quoted in the last, preferred, position.

אֵלּוּ בְּרָכוֹת שֶׁפּוֹתְחִין בָּהֶן בְּבָרוּךְ. כָּל־הַבְּרָכוֹת פּוֹתְחִין בָּהֶן בְּבָרוּךְ וְאִם הָיְתָה בְּרָכָה סְמוּכָה לַחֲבֵירָתָהּ כְּגוֹן קְרִיַת שְׁמַע וּתְפִילָּה אֵין פּוֹתְחִין בָּהֶן בְּבָרוּךְ.

These are the benedictions one begins with "Praised". All benedictions one begins with "Praised", but a benediction following another one, e. g., the recitation of *Shema'* and *Amidah*, one does not begin with "Praised".[269]

269 This statement exists in two additional versions. In the Babli (*Berakhot* 46a) it reads: All benedictions one begins with "Praised" except for benedictions over fruits, obligations, benedictions following another one and the last benediction of the recitation of *Shema'*. In the Tosephta (*Berakhot* 1:9) it reads: All benedictions one begins with "Praised" except for benedictions following another one and the last benediction of the recitation of *Shema'*.

The versions of the Tosephta and the Babli are essentially identical, except that the Babli for completeness includes the short benedictions of one sentence for the execution of a *mitzwah* and for eating food, whose form otherwise is taken for granted. The main difference between the Babli/Tosephta and the Yerushalmi is that the last benediction for the *Shema'*, the one recited after *Shema'*, is considered by the Yerushalmi to be the continuation of the second benediction before *Shema'* but for the Babli it needs special mention. The consequence is that for the Yerushalmi all prayer benedictions separated by Scriptural readings from a preceding benediction are considered consecutive (the benedictions after the morning Psalms and *Hallel)* whereas for the Babli each one needs special treatment. The first objection to the rule given in the next paragraph is therefore impossible for the Babli.

הָתִיב רִבִּי יִרְמְיָה וַהֲרֵי גְּאוּלָּה. שַׁנְיָא הִיא. דְּמַר רִבִּי יוֹחָנָן הַלֵּל אִם שֲׁמְעָהּ בְּבֵית הַכְּנֶסֶת יָצָא. הָתִיב רִבִּי אֶלְעָזָר בֵּי רִבִּי יוֹסֶה קוֹמֵי רִבִּי יוֹסֶה וַהֲרֵי סוֹפָהּ. אֲמַר לֵיהּ שְׁתַּיִם הֵנָּה אַחַת לָבוֹא וְאַחַת לְשֶׁעָבַר.

Rebbi Jeremiah objected: But there is "redemption"[270]. There is a difference since Rebbi Yoḥanan said[271]: If he heard *Hallel* in the synagogue he has fulfilled his obligation. Rebbi Eleazar, the son of Rebbi Yose, objected before Rebbi Yose, but there is its ending.[272] He said to him: there are two, one for the future and one for the past.[273]

270 The answer shows that the question is about the benediction at the end of the recitation of the *Haggadah* in the *Seder* night: "Praised are You, o Eternal, our God, King of the Universe, Who has redeemed us and has redeemed our forefathers from Egypt and let us attain this night to eat

mazzah and bitter herbs. May it please You, o Eternal, our God and God of our fathers, to let us attain in peace more festive seasons and holidays, when we shall rejoice in the rebuilding of Your city and enjoy Your service. There we shall eat from the family offerings and the *pesaḥ* sacrifice whose blood shall reach the wall of Your altar for goodwill. Then we shall thank You with a new song for our redemption and the liberation of our persons. Praise be to You, o Eternal, Who did save Israel."

This benediction follows the recitation of the first two Psalms of *Hallel*. It is clear from here, and from the parallel in the last Chapter of Yerushalmi *Pesaḥim* that in Israel in Talmudic times one preceded the recitation of *Hallel* by a benediction (the details are discussed in the author's *The Scholar's Haggadah*, pp. 317-318). Hence, by the principle of the Yerushalmi, this benediction should not start with "Praised".

271 *Pesaḥim* 9:1, fol. 37c. In Galilee there existed congregations which were illiterate except for the cantor, where no one could recite the *Hallel* or the entire *Haggadah* at home. For these people it was instituted that *Hallel* should be recited in the synagogue after evening prayers (with its benedictions before and after); then the people could go home and just recite the benediction for redemption, drink four cups and go to bed. The text there seems to imply that the required recital of the Exodus likewise was read to them in the synagogue. The generally accepted implication of this and the following arguments is that any benediction which under some circumstances could be recited by itself has the status of a benediction that is not following another one (*Rashba* on Babli *Berakhot* 36a).

272 There is much controversy about the meaning of this question; every commentator has another interpretation. In the author's opinion, this is a complete parallel to the identical question asked later for *Qiddush* and refers simply to the concluding statement "Praise be to You, o Eternal, Who did save Israel." Since this follows the entire text, it certainly is a benediction following another one, so why does it repeat "Praise be to You, o Eternal"?

273 A statement of Rava in Babli *Pesaḥim* 117b notes that the benediction for redemption after *Shema'* and in the *Haggadah* is גאל ישראל but that in the *Amidah* prayer is גואל ישראל. The same formulation, גאל ישראל, is found in the Mishnah *Pesaḥim* and is followed by the *Haggadah* texts with

the exception of the Yemenite ones. The unvocalized text of Mishnah and Talmud is read גָּאַל יִשְׂרָאֵל in the past tense. Then Rebbi Yose's statement makes sense. Since the text concentrates on the future after a perfunctory mention of the past, the conclusion by a benediction for the past is a change of theme and, therefore, the concluding phrase has to be considered a separate benediction. [Rebbi Yose belongs to those authorities who require that the topic of the final benediction should be repeated *immediately* before the final sentence. His opinion is superseded here by that of Rebbi Mana later in the discussion but is taken up again by Rebbi Aḥa.]

The very conservative Yemenite tradition, strictly based on the Babli, cannot be expected to disregard a prescription of that Talmud. Hence, it is possible that Rava did read גָּאֵל יִשְׂרָאֵל, a *pa'el* form of the present [cf. S. Morag, בנין פָּאֵל ובנין נִתְפָּאֵל, *Tarbiẓ 26* (1957), 349-356 and the material quoted in the author's *The Scholar's Haggadah*, p. 322.] The Yerushalmi here shows that the Israeli reading was גָּאַל יִשְׂרָאֵל. Hence, identical (consonantal) wording in Babli and Yerushalmi does not necessarily imply same text and same meaning. Since Italian and Northern European Jewry obtained their prayer texts from Israel, probably in the Mishnaic period, it is the rule that their prayer texts follow Yerushalmi sources.

הָתִיבוּן הֲרֵי הַבְדָּלָה. שַׁנְיָא הִיא. דָּמַר רִבִּי בָּא בַּר זַבְדָּא רִבִּי הָיָה מְפַזְּרָן וְחָזַר וְכוֹלְלָן עַל הַכּוֹס. רִבִּי חִייָא רַבָּא הָיָה מְכַנְּסָן.

They objected: There is *Havdalah*.[274] There is a difference since Rebbi Abba bar Zavda said that Rebbi was dispersing them and collecting them on the cup. The great Rebbi Ḥiyya was collecting them[275].

274 The *Havdalah* benediction at the end of the Sabbath is preceded by benedictions over wine, spices, and light. These are all short sentences and it is universally agreed that they should start with "praise". The only problem is the *Havdalah* benediction itself, which follows the other ones. The answer is that the benedictions over spices and fire are recited in order only for convenience, not out of necessity, and that Rebbi did recite them separately. Hence, *Havdalah* is a potentially free-standing benediction, but it follows

always the benediction for wine. The objection based on this is not raised, but it will be raised for *Qiddush* and the answer given there also applies here. It is explained in Babli *Pesaḥim* 54a that Rebbi was collecting the other benedictions on the cup for his family, not for himself.

275 Being a Babylonian, he never gave up Babylonian practices even though he spent his life in Galilee.

הָתִיבוּן הֲרֵי נְבָרֵךְ. שַׁנְיָא הִיא. שֶׁאִם הָיוּ שְׁנַיִם יוֹשְׁבִין וְאוֹכְלִין שֶׁאֵינָן אוֹמְרִים נְבָרֵךְ. הֲרֵי הַזָּן אֶת הַכֹּל. קַשְׁיָא.

They objected: There is *Nevarekh*.[276] There is a difference, because if there were two sitting together and eating they would not say *Nevarekh*. There is "He Who feeds all"[277]; that is difficult.

276 The introductory section of Grace after meals, known as ברכת הזימון, "the benediction of preparation". This introductory paragraph is recited only when at least three people are eating together who are obliged to recite Grace in the same degree of obligation. Hence, Grace itself must start with "Praised".

277 This is the concluding benediction of the first paragraph of Grace; the question is parallel to that asked for the concluding paragraphs of "redemption" and *Qiddush*. The lack of an answer here is provisional; the final answer of the Amoraïm of the last Galilean generation covers all these cases.

הֲרֵי הַטּוֹב וְהַמֵּטִיב. שַׁנְיָא הִיא. דְּאָמַר רַב הוּנָא מִשֶּׁנִּיתְּנוּ הֲרוּגֵי בֵיתַר לִקְבוּרָה נִקְבְּעָה הַטּוֹב וְהַמֵּטִיב. הַטּוֹב שֶׁלֹּא הִסְרִיחוּ. וְהַמֵּטִיב שֶׁנִּיתְּנוּ לִקְבוּרָה.

There is "He Who is good and does good"[278]. There is a difference since Rav Ḥuna said: When permission was received to bury the slain of Bethar, "He Who is good and does good" was fixed, "He Who is good" because they did not rot, "He Who does good" because permission was received to bury them.

278 The fourth section of Grace that clearly follows the third but nevertheless starts with "Praised". The answer is that the first three sections

278 The fourth section of Grace that clearly follows the third but nevertheless starts with "Praised". The answer is that the first three sections constitute Grace as required by the Torah, while the fourth starts Rabbinic Grace.

הָא קִדּוּשָׁה. שַׁנְיָא הִיא. שֶׁאִם הָיָה יוֹשֵׁב וְשׁוֹתֶה מִבְּעוֹד יוֹם וְקִדֵּשׁ עָלָיו הַיּוֹם שֶׁאֵינוֹ אוֹמֵר בּוֹרֵא פְרִי הַגֶּפֶן. וְהָא סוֹפָהּ. אָמַר רִבִּי מָנָא טוֹפֵס בְּרָכוֹת כָּךְ הוּא. אָמַר רִבִּי יוּדָן מַטְבֵּעַ קָצָר פּוֹתֵחַ בָּהֶן בְּבָרוּךְ וְאֵינוֹ חוֹתֵם בָּהֶן בְּבָרוּךְ. מַטְבֵּעַ אָרוֹךְ פּוֹתֵחַ בָּהֶן בְּבָרוּךְ וְחוֹתֵם בָּהֶן בְּבָרוּךְ.

There is *Qiddush*[279]. There is a difference since if one was sitting and drinking when it still was day and the holy day came upon him, he does not say "Creator of the fruit of the vine." But there is its final sentence? Rebbi Mana said, the type[280] of benedictions is like that. Rebbi Yudan said: A short form starts with "Praised" and does not end with "Praised", a long form starts with "Praised" and ends with "Praised".

279 The main benediction follows the benediction over wine (or over bread) and, nevertheless, starts with "Praised". The answer is that *Qiddush* during a meal does not require the benediction over wine even though there is an interruption in the meal since one is forbidden to eat and drink after sundown Friday night before making *Qiddush*. The Babli does not take up this question, hence practice follows this Yerushalmi, *Shulḥan Arukh Oraḥ Ḥayyim* 271, Sec. 4. The *Qiddush* starts with "praised" and its final sentence again starts with "praised."

280 Greek τύπος, "pattern, model, prescribed form". Rebbi Mana was a student of Rebbi Yudan who uses the Hebrew מטבע "coin" for "form". The students of Rebbi Mana were the collectors of the Yerushalmi in the form it came down to us. Hence, his answer is final: All long benedictions end with "Praise to You, o Eternal, . . ." as a matter of principle (going back to the Men of the Great Assembly). Between this sentence and the next, a "since" should be mentally interpolated.

כָּל־הַבְּרָכוֹת אַחַר חִיתוּמֵיהֶן אֵין אוֹמְרִין בְּרָכָה פָּסוּק. הֱתִיב רִבִּי יִצְחָק בֵּרִבִּי אֶלְעָזָר קוֹמוֹי רִבִּי יוֹסֵה מִכֵּיוָן דְּתֵימַר אַחַר חִיתוּמֵיהֶן אֵין אוֹמְרִין בְּרָכָה פָּסוּק. אָמְרִין חֲכִימֵי הָדֵין טַלְיָא דְּהוּא סָבַר מַהוּ אַחַר חִיתוּמֵיהֶן שֶׁאִם הָיָה עוֹמֵד בְּשַׁחֲרִית וְשָׁכַח וְהִזְכִּיר שֶׁל עַרְבִית וְחָזַר וְחָתַם בְּשֶׁל שַׁחֲרִית יָצָא. אָמַר רִבִּי אָחָא כָּל־הַבְּרָכוֹת כְּעֵין חוֹתְמוֹתֵיהֶן. וְאִילֵּין דְּאָמְרִין צַהֲלִי וָרֹנִּי יוֹשֶׁבֶת צִיּוֹן וְגוֹמֵר אֵין בּוֹ מִשּׁוּם בְּרָכָה פָּסוּק.

All benedictions after their seals[281]; one does not say a verse as benediction. Rebbi Isaac ben Rebbi Eleazar objected before Rebbi Yose: Because you say after their seals, one does not say a verse as benediction[282]? They said, that young man is intelligent because he thinks! What is the meaning of "after their seals"? It is that when he was standing in the morning prayer and forgot and mentioned the text of evening prayers but he caught himself and finished with the text of morning prayers, then he did his duty[283]. Rebbi Aḥa said, all benedictions in the kind of their seals.[284] But those who say (*Is.* 12:6): "Jubilate and sing, inhabitant of Zion . . . " do not violate the rule that no benediction is a verse[285].

281 This is a continuing discussion of the statement of Rebbi Yudan. The "seal" of a longer benediction is the last sentence "Praise to You, o Eternal, . . . " It is stated that this "seal" is what makes the benediction valid and it cannot be a Biblical verse.

282 Since the two statements appear together in one *baraita*, there should be a logical connection between them but there seems to be none.

283 "They" are the members of Rebbi Yose's Yeshivah. They do not disagree with the rule which they state, but they note that the *baraita* does not deal with it; its correct interpretation is by Rebbi Aḥa.

About the rule itself, there is disagreement between the Yerushalmi and the parallel Babli, *Berakhot* 12a, where it is stated: "If in the morning one started with 'Creator of light' and ended with 'Making evenings dark', he did not do his duty. If in the evening he starts with 'He Who makes evenings dark' and ends with 'Creator of light', he did not do his duty. But if he started with 'Creator of light' and ended with 'Making evenings dark', he did his duty. The principle is: Everything is determined by the seal." The Babli asserts that if in evening prayers one started out wrongly with the text appropriate for morning prayers then everything is O.K. if only the final doxology is correct. But the Yerushalmi speaks of one "who is standing in morning prayers and forgot", i. e., that he started out correctly, forgot himself in the middle, and remembered in time to close with the correct text. The principles of prayer texts were instituted by the Men of the Great Assembly. They determined the contents of the prayers but not, in general, their texts. (For the *Amidah*, the Mishnah even reports that Rebbi Eliezer says that one who repeats the same text for more than 30 days cannot really be an honest supplicant). The question is whether, in addition to the contents, the Men of the Great Assembly only determined the "seals" (following the Babli) or also the introductory sentences (following the Yerushalmi).

284 The language is difficult. R. Eleazar Askari explains that Rebbi Aḥa insists that only the "seal" counts and, therefore, the text preceding the "seal" is unimportant; the text of the "seal" cannot be a verse. R. Shelomo Cirillo and R. Moshe ben Ḥabib explain, on the contrary, that the "seal" must fit the text of the benediction just preceding and that this text cannot be a verse. In the Babli (*Pesaḥim* 104a) this principle is spelled out only for *Havdalah* [and in the Yerushalmi the treatment given for *Havdalah*, (*Berakhot* 5:2, fol. 9b) supports R. Eleazar Askari.] Most Medieval authorities extend the principle of the Babli to all longer benedictions.

285 Ezra Fleischer (*Tarbiẓ* 41, p. 450) has published a Yerushalmi prayer text from the Cairo Genizah which uses this verse in the third benediction of the '*Amidah*, קדושת השם. From what is left of the original Galilean *minhag* it seems clear that the standard text of longer benedictions always ended with a Biblical verse just preceding the "seal". For example, in Grace, the verses were *Ps*. 145:16, *Deut. 8:10*, Ps. 147:2. In the morning prayers, the verses have survived in the first benediction for *Shema'* in all *minhagim* and for the benediction after *Shema'* in most of them. The text states that the only acceptable place for a Biblical verse is *before* the "seal". Even the

Mishnah prescribes benedictions whose text is a Biblical verse (*Taäniot* 2:2); what is prohibited here is using a verse in the final doxology.

משנה ט. מַזְכִּירִין יְצִיאַת מִצְרַיִם בַּלֵּילוֹת. אָמַר לָהֶן רִבִּי אֶלְעָזָר בֶּן עֲזַרְיָה הֲרֵי אֲנִי כְּבֶן שִׁבְעִים שָׁנָה וְלֹא זָכִיתִי שֶׁתֵּאָמֵר יְצִיאַת מִצְרַיִם בַּלֵּילוֹת עַד שֶׁדְּרָשָׁהּ בֶּן זוֹמָא שֶׁנֶּאֱמַר לְמַעַן תִּזְכּוֹר אֶת יוֹם צֵאתְךָ מֵאֶרֶץ מִצְרַיִם כֹּל יְמֵי חַיֶּיךָ. יְמֵי חַיֶּיךָ הַיָּמִים. כֹּל יְמֵי חַיֶּיךָ הַלֵּילוֹת. וַחֲכָמִים אוֹמְרִים יְמֵי חַיֶּיךָ הָעוֹלָם הַזֶּה. כֹּל יְמֵי חַיֶּיךָ לְהָבִיא לִימוֹת הַמָּשִׁיחַ.

Mishnah 9: One must mention the Exodus in the night. Rebbi Eleazar ben Azariah[286] said to them[287]: Here I am about 70 years old and I could not succed in proving that the Exodus must be mentioned every night[288] until Ben Zoma[289] derived it from the verse (*Deut.* 16:3): ". . . that you should remember the day of your leaving Egypt the entire days of your life." The days of your life - the days. The entire days of your life - the nights. But the Sages say, the days of your life - this world; The entire days of your life - this includes the times of the Messiah.

286 A descendant of Ezra in the tenth generation who was appointed vice president of the Synhedrion at age 18 (according to the Babli) or 13 (Yerushalmi).

287 Neither the Mishnah in the Babli nor manuscripts of the Mishnah have "to them"; in the *Haggadah* the Yerushalmi text is preserved only in the text of Maimonides and the Yemenite *Haggadot*. Nevertheless, the phrase cannot refer to the discussion at Bne Beraq reported in the *Haggadah*. As R. Saul Lieberman points out, the Yerushalmi takes R. Eleazar ben Azariah at his word that he made his statement when he was close to 70 years old and it is quite impossible that R. Eliezer should still have been alive at least 50 years after the deposition of Rabban Gamliel and the elevation of Rebbi Eleazar ben Azariah. The most likely interpretation is that the Israeli *Haggadah*, but not the Mishnah, read

"to them" and that the copyist of the Yerushalmi followed his memory from the *Haggadah* instead of the text before him. For a similar occurrence in the Septuagint, see *The Scholar's Haggadah*, p. 257-258.

288 Everybody agrees that the third benediction of the *Shema'* and the mention of the Exodus are obligatory as an institution of the Men of the Great Assembly. The only question is whether the benediction was instituted as a Rabbinic ordinance or was formulated in fulfillment of a Biblical commandment.

289 A mystic of the first generation of Tannaïm who died young.

הלכה ט: אַף עַל פִּי שֶׁנִּכְנַס לִגְדוּלָּה הֶאֱרִיךְ יָמִים. הֲדָא אָמְרָה שֶׁהַגְּדוּלָּה מְקַצֶּרֶת יָמִים.

Halakha 9: Even though he entered high office he lived long. This means that high office shortens one's life.

תַּמָּן אָמְרִין לֹא יַתְחִיל וַיֹּאמֶר וְאִם הִתְחִיל גּוֹמֵר. וְרַבָּנָן דְּהָכָא אָמְרִין מַתְחִיל וְאֵינוֹ גּוֹמֵר. מַתְנִיתִין פְּלִיגָא עַל רַבָּנָן דְּהָכָא[290] מַזְכִּירִין יְצִיאַת מִצְרַיִם בַּלֵּילוֹת. רִבִּי בָּא רַב יְהוּדָה בְּשֵׁם רַב מוֹדִים אֲנַחְנוּ לָךְ שֶׁהוֹצֵאתָנוּ מִמִּצְרַיִם וּפְדִיתָנוּ מִבֵּית עֲבָדִים לְהוֹדוֹת לִשְׁמָךְ. מַתְנִיתָא פְּלִיגָא עַל רַבָּנָן דְּתַמָּן וַיֹּאמֶר אֵינוֹ נוֹהֵג אֶלָּא בַיּוֹם כָּל־פָּרָשַׁת וַיֹּאמֶר אֵינוֹ נוֹהֵג אֶלָּא בַיּוֹם.

There[291] they say one should not start *wayyomer*[292] but if one did start he has to finish. The rabbis here[293] say one starts but does not finish. The Mishnah disagrees with the rabbis here[294]: "One must mention the Exodus in the night." Rebbi Abba, Rav Yehudah in the name of Rav: We thank You that You took us out of Egypt and redeemed us from the house of slavery to give thanks to Your Name.[295] A *baraita* disagrees with the rabbis there: *Wayyomer* is used only during daytime. The entire section of *wayyomer* is used only during daytime[296].

290 דהכא is the reading of the Rome manuscript and also the reading of the prints in the next paragraph. The word דהתם of the printed editions and the Leyden ms. is impossible; it is the Babylonian Aramaic equivalent of Galilean תמן.

291 "There"always means Babylonia; "here" is the Land of Israel.

292 The third section of the *Shema'*, *Num.* 15:37-41. This is the only part of *Shema'* that mentions the Exodus. The statement of "there" is reported in the Babli by Rav Cahana in the name of Rav (*Berakhot* 14b).

293 The Israeli practice is reported in the Babli (loc. cit.) as reciting only the first and last sentences of the section; our text also requires one to start, i.e., to recite the first verse, and to mention the Exodus, the last words of the last verse.

294 Both R. David Oppenheim and R. Moshe ben Ḥabib note that in this section and the next, "here" and "there" should be switched since the first question is against those who say that one does not have to recite the third section at all, against the Babylonian practice, and the *baraita* in the next section seems to imply that one does not mention the third section at all, against Israeli practice.

295 This is the proposed text of the evening benediction after the recitation of *Shema'*. It is the answer to the objection raised in the first sentence. The obligation of mentioning the Exodus does not refer to the recitation of the third section of *Shema'* but to the benediction after the *Shema'* and, therefore, would be fulfilled even if the third section were to be omitted completely. The text in the Babli is longer.

296 But in the night one recites only first and last verses.

רִבִּי בָּא בַּר אָחָא נָחֵית לְתַמָּן חֲמֵיתוֹן מַתְחִילִין וְגוֹמְרִין וְלָא שְׁמִיעַ דְּתַמָּן אָֽמְרִין לֹא יַתְחִיל וַיֹּאמֶר וְאִם הִתְחִיל גּוֹמֵר. וְרַבָּנָן דְּהָכָא אָֽמְרִין מַתְחִיל וְאֵינוֹ גּוֹמֵר.

Rebbi Abba bar Aḥa[297] descended there and saw them start and finish; he had not heard that there they say one does not have to start but if he started he has to finish. The rabbis here[298] say one starts and does not finish.

297 An early Israeli Amora who went to study in Babylonia, probably in the Yeshivah of Rav. Hence, he did not know of the rule established by Rav before he arrived at the Yeshivah.

298 This sentence is superfluous here, it is inserted only in parallel to the previous section. This is frequent in the Yerushalmi and not a sign of dittography.

בָּעוּן קוֹמוֹי רִבִּי אֲחִייָא בֵּרִבִּי זְעִירָא הֵיךְ הֲוָה אֲבוּךְ נָהוּג עֲבִיד כְּרַבָּנָן דְּהָכָא אוֹ כְּרַבָּנָן דְּהָתָם. רִבִּי חִזְקִיָּה אָמַר כְּרַבָּנָן דְּהָכָא. רִבִּי יוֹסֵה אָמַר כְּרַבָּנָן דְּהָתָם. אָמַר רִבִּי חֲנִינָא מִסְתַּבְּרָא דְּרִבִּי יוֹסֵה דְּרִבִּי זְעִירָא מַחְמִיר וִינוּן מַחְמִירִין וְהוּא עֲבַד נְהִיג כְּוָותְהוֹן.

They asked before Rebbi Aḥiyya ben Rebbi Zeïra: How did your father do in practice, like the teachers here or the teachers there[299]. Rebbi Ḥizqiah said, like the teachers here. Rebbi Yose[300] said, like the teachers there. Rebbi Ḥanina said, it is reasonable like R. Yose, since R. Zeïra always chose the harder way[301] and they chose the harder way, so he did what he was used to, like them.

299 Since Rebbi Zeïra was a Babylonian immigrant to Galilee. Note that they speak to his son in Babylonian Aramaic.

300 Both Rebbis Ḥizqiah and Yose are from the fourth generation, students of Rebbis Jeremiah and Ilaï who in turn were students of Rebbi Zeïra. The answer of Rebbi Zeïra's son has not been recorded.

301 He tended to follow the stricter Babylonian rules, cf. later *Halakhah* 8:7, fol. 12c.

תַּנֵּי הַקּוֹרֵא אֶת שְׁמַע בַּבּוֹקֶר צָרִיךְ לְהַזְכִּיר יְצִיאַת מִצְרַיִם בֶּאֱמֶת וְיַצִּיב. רִבִּי אוֹמֵר צָרִיךְ לְהַזְכִּיר בָּהּ מַלְכוּת. אֲחֵרִים אוֹמְרִים צָרִיךְ לְהַזְכִּיר בָּהּ קְרִיעַת יַם סוּף וּמַכַּת בְּכוֹרִים. רִבִּי יְהוֹשֻׁעַ בֶּן לֵוִי אוֹמֵר צָרִיךְ לְהַזְכִּיר אֶת כּוּלָּן וְצָרִיךְ לוֹמַר צוּר יִשְׂרָאֵל וְגוֹאֲלוֹ.

We have stated[302]: "He who recites *Shema'* in the morning must mention the Exodus in *Emet veyaẓiv*. Rebbi says, he must mention

[God's] kingdom. Others say, he has to mention the splitting of the Reed Sea and the slaying of the firstborn." Rebbi Joshua ben Levi says, he has to mention all these and has to say "Rock of Israel and its Redeemer".[303]

302 This section is composed of a Tosephta (*Berakhot* 2:1) containing the statements of the anonymous first Tanna, Rebbi, and "Others" (usually: Rebbi Meïr), and then the comment by the Amora R. Joshua ben Levi. In practice, the ruling of R. Joshua ben Levi applies to both morning and evening prayers.

303 The formula was the Israeli conclusion of the benediction of redemption, in contrast to the Babylonian "He Who redeemed Israel" (Babli *Pesaḥim* 117b). This formula has survived in the poetic forms of Ashkenazic evening prayers for the holidays, while in ordinary prayers the form prescribed by the authoritative Babylonian Talmud has prevailed.

רִבִּי סִימוֹן בְּשֵׁם רִבִּי יְהוֹשֻׁעַ בֶּן לֵוִי אוֹמֵר לֹא הִזְכִּיר תּוֹרָה בָּאָרֶץ מַחֲזִירִין אוֹתוֹ. מַה טַעַם וַיִּתֵּן לָהֶם אַרְצוֹת גּוֹיִם מִפְּנֵי מַה בַּעֲבוּר יִשְׁמְרוּ חֻקָּיו וְתוֹרוֹתָיו יִנְצוֹרוּ. רִבִּי בָּא בֵּרִבִּי אָחָא בְּשֵׁם רִבִּי אִם לֹא הִזְכִּיר בְּרִית בָּאָרֶץ אוֹ שֶׁלֹּא הִזְכִּיר בְּבוֹנֵה יְרוּשָׁלַיִם מַלְכוּת בֵּית דָּוִד מַחֲזִירִין אוֹתוֹ. אָמַר רִבִּי אִילָא אִם אָמַר מְנַחֵם יְרוּשָׁלַיִם יָצָא.

Rebbi Simon in the name of Rebbi Joshua ben Levi says: If someone did not mention Torah in the benediction on the Land[304] one tells him to repeat. What is the reason? (*Ps.* 105:44) "He gave them the lands of peoples"; why? "That they should keep His decrees and preserve His teachings." Rebbi Abba ben Rebbi Aḥa in the name of Rebbi: If one did not mention the covenant in the benediction on the Land or the kingdom of David's dynasty in "Builder of Jerusalem"[305], one tells him to repeat. Rebbi Ilaï said: if he said "He Who consoles Jerusalem"[306], he did his duty.

304 Since the Talmud started discussing required topics of otherwise personal texts, they continue with a discussion of the relevant parts of

Grace. The benediction of the Land is the second benediction, and that on Jerusalem the third. The parallel in the Babli (*Berakhot* 48b) is a Tannaïtic text in different order. The Amoraïc text of the Yerushalmi is in strict chronological order: R. Joshua ben Levi of the very early second generation, R. Abba bar Aḥa of the second, and Rebbi Ilaï of the third generations. The second statement of R. Abba bar Aḥa is attributed by the printed editions and most Medieval authors of the Babli to Rebbi Eliezer but in the Munich ms. to Rebbi, as in the Yerushalmi. The first statement is attributed to an otherwise unknown Tanna Naḥum the elder. The statement of R. Joshua ben Levi is attributed to Rebbi Yose (ben Ḥalaphta) but without the verse that gives the reason. The Yerushalmi gives a statement of Amoraïm, not to claim that the required topics were introduced by Amoraïm (that is quite obvious from the mention of Rebbi), but in order to point out the Scriptural basis and to fix the exact place where Torah has to be mentioned in Grace.

305 The old doxology of the third benediction was: "Praised be You, o Eternal, Builder of Jerusalem." The final adoption of the text "He Who in His mercy builds Jerusalem" is on the authority of *Shulḥan Arukh*, cf. *The Scholar's Haggadah*, p. 357-358.

306 In the text, not in the final sentence.

בַּר קַפָּרָא אָמַר הַקּוֹרֵא לְאַבְרָהָם אַבְרָם עוֹבֵר בַּעֲשֵׂה. רִבִּי לֵוִי אָמַר בַּעֲשֵׂה וְלֹא תַעֲשֶׂה. וְלֹא (fol. 4a) יִקָּרֵא עוֹד אֶת שִׁמְךָ אַבְרָם הֲרֵי בְּלֹא תַעֲשֶׂה. וְהָיָה שִׁמְךָ אַבְרָהָם הֲרֵי בַּעֲשֵׂה. הָתִיבוּן הֲרֵי אַנְשֵׁי כְּנֶסֶת הַגְּדוֹלָה קָרְאוּ אוֹתוֹ אַבְרָם. אַתָּה הוּא יי הָאֱלֹהִים אֲשֶׁר בָּחַרְתָּ בְּאַבְרָם. שַׁנְיָא הִיא שֶׁעַד שֶׁהוּא אַבְרָם בָּחַרְתָּ בוֹ.

Bar Qappara[307] said: He who calls Abraham Abram transgresses a positive commandment. Rebbi Levi said, a positive and a negative commandment. (*Gen.* 17:4) "Your name shall not in the future be called Abram", that is the negative commandment, "But your name shall be Abraham", that is the positive commandment. They objected: But the Men of the Great Assembly called him Abram, (*Neh.* 9:7) "You are, o

Eternal, the God Who selected Abram". There is a difference, while he was still Abram You selected him.

307 Bar Qappara belongs to the generation of transfer between Tannaïm and Amoraïm. In the Yerushalmi his words are presented as those of an Amora. The place was chosen here because we discussed required language for benedictions (*Shema'* and Grace); now we turn to required language in general speech. In the Babli, the parallel (13a) appears also at the end of the first Chapter, somewhat disconnected. One may assume that it is mentioned in parallel to the Yerushalmi.

In the printed editions of the Babli, the text is: "Bar Qappara stated", a Tannaïtic statement. However, in the Munich ms. and the *Pisqe RYD* the text reads דרש בר קפרא "Bar Qappara preached", an Amoraïc statement. (It also seems that Rebbi Eliezer, who completes the statement of Bar Qappara in the Babli in parallel to Rebbi Levi in the Yerushalmi, is "Rebbi Eleazar, the son of Bar Qappara's sister".) The people who object are determined in the Babli to be Rebbi Yose bar Abin or Rebbi Yose bar Zabida, of the later generation of Galilean Amoraïm. The statements of Bar Qappara and Rebbi Levi/Rebbi Eleazar are not mentioned in any of the Medieval codes, *Halakhot Gedolot, Alfasi, Mishneh Torah*; their authors took also the text in the Babli as Amoraïc sermon.

וְדִכְוָתָהּ הַקּוֹרֵא לְשָׂרָה שָׂרַי עוֹבֵר בַּעֲשֵׂה. הוּא נִצְטַוָּה עָלֶיהָ. וְדִכְוָתָהּ הַקּוֹרֵא לְיִשְׂרָאֵל יַעֲקֹב עוֹבֵר בַּעֲשֵׂה. שֵׁינִי נִתּוֹסָף לוֹ הָרִאשׁוֹן לֹא נֶעֱקַר מִמֶּנּוּ.

Similarly, does he who calls Sarah Sarai transgress a commandment? He[308] was commanded regarding her. Similarly, does he who calls Israel Jacob transgress a commandment? The second name was given him in addition, the first was not taken away from him[309].

308 Abraham alone was commanded not to call Sarah Sarai as it is written (*Gen.* 17:15): "God said to Abraham: Your wife Sarai, do not call her name Sarai but Sarah is her name." The commandment to call Sarai Sarah was

directed to Abraham alone.

309 Since the Torah continues to call him Jacob even after he received his new name of Israel.

וְלָמָּה נִשְׁתַּנָּה שְׁמוֹ שֶׁל אַבְרָהָם וּשְׁמוֹ שֶׁל יַעֲקֹב וּשְׁמוֹ שֶׁל יִצְחָק לֹא נִשְׁתַּנָּה.
אֵילּוּ אֲבוֹתָן קָרְאוּ אוֹתָן בִּשְׁמָן. אֲבָל יִצְחָק הַקָּדוֹשׁ בָּרוּךְ הוּא קְרָאוֹ יִצְחָק
שֶׁנֶּאֱמַר וְקָרָאתָ אֶת שְׁמוֹ יִצְחָק. ד׳ נִקְרְאוּ עַד שֶׁלֹּא נוֹלְדוּ וְאֵילּוּ הֵן. יִצְחָק
וְיִשְׁמָעֵאל יֹאשִׁיָּהוּ וּשְׁלֹמֹה. יִצְחָק וְקָרָאתָ אֶת שְׁמוֹ יִצְחָק. יִשְׁמָעֵאל דִּכְתִיב
וְקָרָאת אֶת שְׁמוֹ יִשְׁמָעֵאל. יֹאשִׁיָּהוּ הִנֵּה בֵן נוֹלָד לְבֵית דָּוִד יֹאשִׁיָּהוּ שְׁמוֹ.
שְׁלֹמֹה כִּי שְׁלֹמֹה יִהְיֶה שְׁמוֹ. עַד כְּדוֹן בְּצַדִּיקִים. אֲבָל בָּרְשָׁעִים זוֹרוּ רְשָׁעִים
מֵרָחֶם.

Why were the names of Abraham and Jacob changed but Isaac's name was not changed? The former were given their names by their fathers; but Isaac was called Isaac by the Holy One, Praise to His Name, as it is said (*Gen.* 17:19) "You shall call his name Isaac".

Four were given names before they were born, and they are Isaac, Ismael, Josiah, and Solomon. Isaac, (*Gen.* 17:19) "You shall call his name Isaac". Ismael as it is written (*Gen.* 16:11): "You shall call his name Ismael". Josiah, (*1Kings* 13:2): "Behold, a son will be born to the dynasty of David; his name will be Josiah". Solomon, (*1Chr.* 22:9) "Solomon will be his name"[310]. All this for the just. But the wicked (*Ps.* 58:4) "The wicked are perverted from the womb."

310 While in *2Sam.* 12:24-25 it seems that David gave the name Solomon to his son and Nathan called him Yedidiah after his birth; it is clear from Chronicles that the name Solomon was not David's invention but prophetically pre-ordained.

בֶּן זוֹמָא אוֹמֵר עֲתִידִין הֵן יִשְׂרָאֵל שֶׁלֹּא לְהַזְכִּיר יְצִיאַת מִצְרַיִם לֶעָתִיד לָבוֹא
וּמַה טַעַם לָכֵן יָמִים בָּאִים נְאוּם יי לֹא יֵאָמֵר עוֹד חַי יי אֲשֶׁר הֶעֱלָה אֶת בְּנֵי
יִשְׂרָאֵל מֵאֶרֶץ מִצְרַיִם כִּי אִם חַי יי אֲשֶׁר הֶעֱלָה וַאֲשֶׁר הֵבִיא אֶת זֶרַע בֵּית

יִשְׂרָאֵל מֵאֶרֶץ צָפוֹן. אָמְרוּ לוֹ לֹא שֶׁיֵּעָקֵר יְצִיאַת מִצְרַיִם אֶלָּא מִצְרַיִם מוֹסָף עַל מַלְכִיּוֹת. מַלְכִיּוֹת עִיקָּר וּמִצְרַיִם טְפֵילָה. וְכֵן הוּא אוֹמֵר לֹא יִקָּרֵא שִׁמְךָ עוֹד יַעֲקֹב כִּי אִם יִשְׂרָאֵל יִהְיֶה שְׁמֶךָ. אָמְרוּ לֹא שֶׁיֵּעָקֵר שֵׁם יַעֲקֹב אֶלָּא יַעֲקֹב מוֹסָף עַל יִשְׂרָאֵל. יִשְׂרָאֵל עִיקָּר וְיַעֲקֹב טָפֵל. וְכֵן הוּא אוֹמֵר אַל תִּזְכְּרוּ רִאשׁוֹנוֹת אֵילּוּ הַמִּצְרִיִּים וְקַדְמוֹנִיּוֹת אַל תִּתְבּוֹנָנוּ אֵילּוּ הַמַּלְכִיּוֹת. הִנְנִי עוֹשֶׂה חֲדָשָׁה עַתָּה תִצְמָח זוּ שֶׁל גּוֹג. מָשְׁלוּ מָשָׁל לְמַה הַדָּבָר דּוֹמֶה לְאֶחָד שֶׁהָיָה מְהַלֵּךְ בַּדֶּרֶךְ וּפָגַע בּוֹ זְאֵב וְנִצַּל מִמֶּנּוּ. הִתְחִיל מְסַפֵּר מַעֲשֵׂה הַזְּאֵב וְאַחַר כָּךְ פָּגַע בּוֹ הָאֲרִי וְנִצַּל מִיָּדוֹ. שָׁכַח מַעֲשֵׂה הַזְּאֵב הִתְחִיל מְסַפֵּר מַעֲשֵׂה הָאֲרִי. וְאַחַר כָּךְ פָּגַע בּוֹ נָחָשׁ וְנִיצַּל מִמֶּנּוּ. שָׁכַח מַעֲשֵׂה שְׁנֵיהֶם וְהִתְחִיל מְסַפֵּר מַעֲשֵׂה הַנָּחָשׁ. כַּךְ הָיוּ יִשְׂרָאֵל הַצָּרוֹת הָאַחֲרוֹנוֹת מְשַׁכְּחוֹת אֶת הָרִאשׁוֹנוֹת.

Ben Zoma said: There will be a future time when Israel will no longer mention the Exodus. What is the reason? (*Jer*. 23:7-8) "Therefore, days will come, says the Eternal, that one no longer will say, by the Eternal Who brought the Children of Israel up from Egypt, but rather, by the Eternal Who raised and brought the descendants of the House of Israel from the Northern land . . ." They said to him, not that the Exodus will be eliminated but the Exodus will be additional to the Kingdoms[311]. The Kingdoms will be principal and the Exodus additional. And similarly it was said (*Gen*. 35:10): :Your name shall not be called Jacob anymore, but Israel shall be your name." Not that the name Jacob will be taken away but Jacob will be additional to Israel. Israel will be principal and Jacob additional. And so it says (*Is*. 43:18-19): "Do not remember the first things"; this means the Egyptians, "And what was earlier do not dwell on"; this means the Kingdoms, "Behold, I create something new, now it will grow"; this refers to Gog. They gave a simile: to what can this be compared? To someone who encountered a wolf and was saved from it. He started telling about the wolf when he encountered a lion and was saved from it. He forget about the wolf and started telling about the lion.

After that, he encountered a snake and was saved from it. He forgot about both of them and started telling about the snake. So it is with Israel, the last troubles make them forget the earlier ones.

311 "Kingdoms" is short for שעבוד מלכיות "subjugation by alien kingdoms," a general term for the sufferings of the Jewish people inflicted by Gentiles.

פרק שני היה קורא

(fol. 4a) **משנה א**: הָיָה קוֹרֵא בַתּוֹרָה וְהִגִּיעַ זְמַן הַמִּקְרָא אִם כִּוֵּן לִבּוֹ יָצָא וְאִם לָאו לֹא יָצָא. וּבִפְרָקִים שׁוֹאֵל מִפְּנֵי הַכָּבוֹד וּמֵשִׁיב. וּבְאֶמְצַע שׁוֹאֵל מִפְּנֵי הַיִּרְאָה וּמֵשִׁיב דִּבְרֵי רִבִּי מֵאִיר. רִבִּי יְהוּדָה אוֹמֵר בְּאֶמְצַע שׁוֹאֵל מִפְּנֵי הַיִּרְאָה וּמֵשִׁיב מִפְּנֵי הַכָּבוֹד. וּבִפְרָקִים שׁוֹאֵל מִפְּנֵי הַכָּבוֹד וּמֵשִׁיב שָׁלוֹם לְכָל־אָדָם.

Mishnah 1: If someone was reading in the Torah at the time of recital[1], if he read with intention[2] he fulfilled his duty, otherwise he did not fulfill his duty. Between the sections[3], one greets people out of respect and answers their greetings. In the middle of a section one may greet because of fear and answer, the words of Rebbi Meïr. Rebbi Yehudah says: in the middle of a section one may greet out of fear and answer for respect, between sections one greets for respect and answers greetings from everybody.

1 Time of the obligatory recital of *Shema'*.

2 The intention of fulfilling the commandment of reading the *Shema'*.

3 Of the *Shema'*.

הלכה א: אָמַר רִבִּי בָּא זֹאת אוֹמֶרֶת שֶׁאֵין הַבְּרָכוֹת מְעַקְּבוֹת.

Halakhah 1: Rebbi Abba said: This means that benedictions do not prevent[4].

4 Since the Mishnah allows one to concentrate on reading the Torah text as *Shema'* without requiring an interruption for recitations of the benedictions, it follows that benedictions are a separate obligation. In a number of prayer texts from the Genizah, the recitation of the *Shema'* has a separate

benediction: "Praised be You, o Eternal, King of the Universe, Who sanctified us through His commandments and commanded us about the recitation of *Shema'*, with a full heart to declare Him King over us, and willingly to declare His Unity." While these texts are from a period about 500 years later than the text of the Yerushalmi, they show that recitation of *Shema'* was then still considered an obligation separate from the benedictions mentioned in the Mishnah. The latter benedictions could then be recited before the *Amidah*. See Ezra Fleischer, תפילה ומנהגי תפילה ארץ־ישראליים בתקופת הגניזה, Jerusalem 1988.

The paragraph has been explained as parallel to the Babli (11b–12a) by R. Solomon ben Adrat (*Rashba*) in his responsa, vol. 1, no 319.

אָמַר רִבִּי יוֹסֵה אִם אוֹמֵר אַתְּ שֶׁהוּא צָרִיךְ לְבָרֵךְ. בֵּירַךְ צָרִיךְ שֶׁיְּכַוֵּין אֶת לִבּוֹ בְכוּלָּן. הָתִיבוּן וְאֵינוֹ מַפְסִיק וְלֹא תַנִּינָתָהּ וְהָכָא אַף עַל גַּב דְּלֹא תַנִּינָתָהּ צָרִיךְ לְבָרֵךְ. זֹאת אוֹמֶרֶת צָרִיךְ לְכַוֵּין אֶת לִבּוֹ בְכוּלָּן. נִישְׁמְעִינָהּ מִן הֲדָא רִבִּי אַחַי אוֹמֵר מִשּׁוּם רִבִּי יְהוּדָה אִם כִּוֵּן לִבּוֹ בְּפֶרֶק רִאשׁוֹן אַף עַל פִּי שֶׁלֹּא כִּוֵּן לִבּוֹ בְּפֶרֶק שֵׁינִי יָצָא.

Rebbi Yose said: If you say that one needs to recite the benedictions; when he recited them he must focus his attention for the entire *Shema'*[5]. They objected: Does he not interrupt and it does not appear in our statement?[6] So here also, even though it has not been stated he must recite the benedictions. That means[7], one must focus one's attention for the entire *Shema'*. We may hear it from the following: Rebbi Aḥai[8] said in the name of Rebbi Yehudah: "He has fulfilled his obligation if he focussed his attention for the first paragraph, even though he did not focus his attention during recitation of the second paragraph"[10].

5 Rebbi Yose supports the statement of Rebbi Abba: If one would require concentration on what one recites for benedictions before and after *Shema'*, certainly one requires total attention during the recitation of *Shema'*. As seen at the end of this paragraph, this is not the rule.

6 In the Mishnah, it is assumed that one may recite the several sections of the *Shema'* separately since they are written at different places in the Torah scroll. Since the Mishnah does not mention the necessary interruptions in the recital, it might be possible that the Mishnah contemplates interruptions for the recitation of the benedictions before and after *Shema'*; hence, the inference of Rebbi Abba is not justified.

7 The argument would be good only if the statement of Rebbi Yose were true.

8 Rebbi Aḥai was "Tanna", collector of *baraitot*, in the Yeshivah of Rebbi Ḥiyya. He belongs to the generation between Tannaïm and Amoraïm. His statement, *Tosephta Berakhot* 2:2 (Babli *Berakhot* 13a), shows that Rebbi Yose's argument is correct and that Rebbi Abba stated the practice correctly. (In the printed editions of the Babli, the name is Rebbi Aḥa, but in the Munich manuscript, and in all manuscripts of the Tosephta, the name is correctly Rebbi Aḥai. Rebbi Aḥa is an Amora of the fourth generation.)

9 The third paragraph is not included in the discussion since it is not recited in the evening prayers.

מַה בֵין פֶּרֶק רִאשׁוֹן וּמַה בֵין פֶּרֶק שֵׁנִי. אָמַר רִבִּי חֲנִינָא כָּל־מָה שֶׁכָּתוּב בְּזֶה כָּתוּב בְּזֶה. מֵעַתָּה לֹא יִקְרָא אֶלָּא אֶחָד. אָמַר רִבִּי אִילָּא הָרִאשׁוֹן לְיָחִיד וְהַשֵּׁנִי לְצִיבּוּר. וְהָרִאשׁוֹן לְתַלְמוּד. וְהַשֵּׁנִי לְמַעֲשֶׂה.

What is the difference between the first and second paragraphs?[10] Rebbi Ḥanina said: Everything mentioned in the first paragraph is mentioned in the second. In that case, should one have to recite only one of them? Rebbi Illa said: The first one is directed to the individual, the second one to the community; the first one concentrates on learning, the second one on doing[11].

10 A natural question following the Tosephta of Rebbi Yehudah.

11 The first paragraph is formulated in the singular, the second one in the plural. In addition, while the essence of the first paragraph is repeated in the second as a communal obligation, there are many topics in the second paragraph that are not mentioned in the first. In the language of the Babli

(14b), the first paragraph is the acceptance of the Kingdom of Heaven, the second one the acceptance of the commandments of the Torah.

בַּר קַפָּרָא אָמַר אֵין לָךְ צָרִיךְ כַּוָּנָה אֶלָּא ג פְּסוּקִים הָרִאשׁוֹנִים בִּלְבַד. וְתַנֵּי כֵן וְשִׁנַּנְתָּם עַד כַּאן לְכַוָּנָה מִיכַּן וְאֵילַךְ לְשִׁינּוּן.

Bar Qappara said: One has to focus his attention only during the first three verses[12]. It was stated thus: (*Deut.* 6:7) "You should repeat"[13] until there is the obligation of focussed attention; from there starts the obligation of repetition.

12 This is the accepted practice for the Yerushalmi with no one objecting. In the Babli (13b), the statement is given in the name of an otherwise unknown Tanna Rebbi Zutra, and, even though it exemplifies the attitude of Rebbi Aqiba, it is later replaced by the statement of Rebbi Meïr that only the first verse, *Deut.* 6:4, must be recited with focussed attention. Another difference between the more demanding Yerushalmi and the Babli is that the Yerushalmi requires the rest of *Shema'* to be "repeated", i.e., memorized, whereas in the Babli it has only to be read.

13 Meaning, "memorize".

רִבִּי חוּנָה רִבִּי אוּרִי רַב יוֹסֵף רַב יְהוּדָה בְּשֵׁם שְׁמוּאֵל צָרִיךְ לְקַבֵּל עָלָיו מַלְכוּת שָׁמַיִם מְעוּמָּד. מַה אִם הָיָה יוֹשֵׁב עוֹמֵד. לֹא אִם הָיָה מְהַלֵּךְ עוֹמֵד.

Rebbi Ḥunah, Rebbi Uri[14], Rav Joseph, Rav Yehudah[15] in the name of Samuel: One has to accept the Kingdom of Heaven standing. Does this mean that one has to get up when one is sitting? No, if one is walking he has to stand still.

14 Rebbi Uri is not known from any other source. The Rome manuscript of the Yerushalmi reads "Rebbi Ammi"; this might be a better reading but Rebbi Ammi was a student of Rebbi Yoḥanan who in the parallel in the Babli (13b) is reported to require that a person walking has to stand still during recitation of the entire first paragraph of *Shema'*, since he follows the ruling

of Rebbi Aḥai in the name of Rebbi Yehudah that the entire first paragraph requires concentrated attention.

15 The most influential of all students of Samuel.

תַּנֵּי צָרִיךְ לְהַאֲרִיךְ בְּאֶחָד. רַב נַחְמָן בַּר יַעֲקֹב אָמַר וּבִלְבַד בְּד׳. סוּמְכוֹס בַּר יוֹסֵף אוֹמֵר כָּל־הַמַּאֲרִיךְ בְּאֶחָד מַאֲרִיכִין לוֹ יָמָיו וּשְׁנוֹתָיו בְּטוֹבָה. רִבִּי יִרְמְיָה הָיָה מַאֲרִיךְ סַגִּין. אָמַר לֵיהּ רִבִּי זְעִירָא לֵית אַתְּ צָרִיךְ כָּל־הָכִין אֶלָּא כְדֵי שֶׁתַּמְלִיכֵהוּ בַשָּׁמַיִם וּבָאָרֶץ וּבְאַרְבַּע רוּחוֹת הָעוֹלָם.

It was stated: One has to prolong "is One".[16] Rav Naḥman bar Jacob said: But only at the *daleth*.[17] Symmachos bar Joseph[18] said: Anyone who prolongs "is One" has his days and years prolonged in wellbeing. Rebbi Jeremiah was prolonging very much. Rebbi Zeïra said to him: So much is unnecessary, only so long that you should think of Him as King of Heaven and Earth and the four directions of the world.

16 The last word of the first sentence of *Shema'*. The composition here is difficult to understand since one starts with a tannaïtic statement ("It was stated"), continues with the opinion of an Amora (Rav Naḥman bar Jacob), and then returns to a Tanna (Symmachos, an outstanding student of Rebbi Meïr). The parallel Babli (13b) starts with the statement of Symmachos and then continues with the statement of Rav Naḥman bar Jacob which is quoted there in the name of Rav Aḥa bar Jacob. It is possible that "Aḥa", a name without meaning, is simply a form of endearment of the formal name "Naḥman", and that in the Babli it is necessary to use the form of endearment to distinguish this Amora from Rav Naḥman, quoted without his father's name because of his exalted status, whose full name seems to have been Rav Naḥman bar Jacob.

17 The soft ד, without *dagesh*, was pronounced like an Arabic ذ, or a voiced English *th*, a sibilant sometimes close to ז. For example, the Aramaic די appears in the Elephantine papyri as זי. Hence, it really was possible to prolong the consonant *daleth* since it was not a plosive sound as it is today.

In the Babli (13b), Rav Ashi adds that one should not omit to pronounce the ח. This was because in Babylonia, as in Medieval Ashkenaz, a ח was pronounced like a stronger ה and therefore tended to be silent in the middle of a word, as ה is mostly silent in the middle of a word in modern Hebrew. (Even the masters of the Massorah tried to counteract this tendency, e. g. by punctuating יֶהְיֶה, to make the *Sheva* heard when it should be silent by grammatical rules, so that the Torah reader should be forced to pronounce the ה, but obviously to no avail.)

18 A Tanna, student of Rebbi Meïr.

רַב שָׁאֵיל לְרִבִּי חִייָא וְלֵינָא חָמֵי לרִבִּי מְקַבֵּל עָלָיו עוֹל מַלְכוּת שָׁמַיִם. אָמַר לֵיהּ כַּד תַּחְמִינֵיהּ יָהֵיב יָדֵיהּ עַל אַפּוֹהִי הוּא מְקַבֵּל עָלָיו עוֹל מַלְכוּת שָׁמַיִם. אָמַר לֵיהּ (fol. 4b) וְאֵינוֹ צָרִיךְ לְהַזְכִּיר יְצִיאַת מִצְרַיִם. אָמַר לֵיהּ לֵית אֶפְשַׁר דְּלָא יַטֵּי מִילָּה. רִבִּי טַבְיוֹמֵי שָׁאַל לְרִבִּי חִזְקִיָּה לֵית הָדָא אָמְרָה שֶׁאֵין לָךְ צָרִיךְ כַּוָּנָה אֶלָּא פָּסוּק הָרִאשׁוֹן בִּלְבַד. אָמַר לֵיהּ אָדָא יִתַנֶּה עַד וְשִׁנַּנְתָּם.

Rav asked Rebbi Ḥiyya: But I never see that Rebbi accepts upon himself the yoke of the Kingdom of Heaven. He answered him: When you will see him cover his face with his hand, at that moment he accepts the yoke of the Kingdom of Heaven.[19] He asked him back: Is it not necessary also to mention the Exodus? He answered him: It is impossible that he should not turn his words[20]. Rebbi Tavyome[21] asked Rebbi Ḥizkiah: Does this not mean that one has to focus attention only for the first verse?[22] He said to him: With that[23] he might recite until "You shall repeat."

19 The parallel is in Babli, *Berakhot* 13b. It seems that Rebbi started his Yeshivah classes early in the morning, before one could recite *Shema'*, and continued until it was too late to recite *Shema'* as "acceptance of the yoke of heaven", but only as "reading from the Torah."

20 Turn his words to the Exodus. In the Babli, Bar Qappara reports that Rebbi never gave a class in which he did not mention the Exodus.

21 An Israeli Amora of the fourth generation who otherwise is quoted only in Midrashim.

22 If Rebbi recited the relevant

portion of *Shema'* while covering his face with his hand during his morning classses, he could not have spent much time on it and, therefore, Rebbi does not accept the opinion of Bar Qappara that the first three verses have to be recited with focussed attention.

23 While he was covering his face he could have recited all three verses and there is no proof that he disagreed with the ruling that requires concentration for the first three verses.

רִבִּי מָנִי אָמַר מִשּׁוּם רִבִּי יוּדָה שֶׁאָמַר מִשּׁוּם רִבִּי יוֹסֵי הַגָּלִילִי אִם הִפְסִיק בָּהּ כְּדֵי לִקְרוֹת אֶת כּוּלָּהּ לֹא יָצָא יְדֵי חוֹבָתוֹ. רִבִּי בָּא רַב יִרְמְיָה בְּשֵׁם רַב הֲלָכָה כְּרִבִּי מִינָא שֶׁאָמַר מִשּׁוּם רִבִּי יְהוּדָה שֶׁאָמַר מִשּׁוּם רִבִּי יוֹסֵי הַגָּלִילִי.

[24]Rebbi Muna[25] said in the name of Rebbi Yehudah who said in the name of Rebbi Yose the Galilean: If one interrupted so that he would have been able to read all of it, he did not fulfill his duty. Rebbi Abba, Rav Jeremiah in the name of Rav: The practice follows Rebbi Muna who said in the name of Rebbi Yehudah who said in the name of Rebbi Yose the Galilean.

24 Here starts the discussion of the second part of the Mishnah, about the permitted interruptions in the recitation of *Shema'*. The parallel in the Babli, *Megillah* 18b, quotes both Rebbi Muna and Rav, but from a discussion of the rules of blowing the *shofar*, given below; they change the statement of Rav to "practice does not follow" and consider the statement here to be the opinion of Rebbi Yehudah only.

25 This author, whose name appears in several forms here in print and in manuscripts, is Rebbi Muna, student of Rebbi Yehudah (Judah) and Tanna of the last generation.

רִבִּי יוֹחָנָן בְּשֵׁם רִבִּי שִׁמְעוֹן בֶּן יְהוֹצָדָק אַף בְּהַלֵּל וּבִקְרִיַּת הַמְּגִילָּה כֵּן.

Rebbi Yoḥanan in the name of Rebbi Simeon ben Jehozadak: The same rule[26] applies to *Hallel* and the reading of the Esther scroll.

26 That one has to start again if the interruption is so long that one could have finished the entire text in the meantime. The Babli (*Rosh Hashanah*

34b) quotes the same statement and declares that this is only the opinion of Rebbi Yoḥanan's teacher but not his own, and, therefore, is not followed in practice, since arbitrary interruptions are allowed for blowing the *shofar*. The Yerushalmi differs from the Babli in that the principle of time limitation of interruptions in recitals is accepted without reservation; the blowing of *shofar* on Rosh Hashanah is not a recitation and, therefore, can follow different rules.

אַבָּא בַּר רַב הוּנָא וְרַב חִסְדָּא הֲווּ יָתְבִין אָמְרִין אַף בִּתְקִיעוֹת כֵּן. סָלְקוּן לְבֵית רַב וְשָׁמְעוּן רַב חוּנָא בְּשֵׁם רַב אֲפִילוּ שְׁמָעָן עַד תֵּשַׁע שָׁעוֹת יָצָא. אָמַר רִבִּי זְעִירָא עַד דַּאֲנָא תַּמָּן צְרִיכַת לִי וְכַד סָלְקִית לְהָכָא שָׁמְעִית רִבִּי יָסָא בְּשֵׁם רִבִּי יוֹחָנָן אֲפִילוּ שְׁמָעָן כָּל הַיּוֹם יָצָא. וְהוּא שֶׁשְּׁמָעָן עַל הַסֵּדֶר. רִבִּי יוֹסֵה בָּעֵי הֲוָה זֶה צָרִיךְ פְּשׁוּטָה הָרִאשׁוֹנָה. וְזֶה צָרִיךְ פְּשׁוּטָה הָאַחֲרוֹנָה. תְּקִיעָה אַחַת מוֹצִיאָה יְדֵי שְׁתֵּיהֶן.

Abba bar Rav Huna[27] and Rav Ḥisda sat together and said, the same rule applies to blowing the *Shofar*[28]. They went up to Rav's Yeshivah and heard Rav Ḥuna in the name of Rav[29]: Even if one heard it in up to nine hours he fulfilled his obligation[30]. Rebbi Zeïra said: When I was there, this was a problem for me[31]. When I came here, I heard Rebbi Yasa[32] in the name of Rebbi Yoḥanan: Even if one heard it during an entire day, one has fulfilled one's obligation[33]. But only if one heard it in the correct order[34]. Rebbi Yose investigated: If one needed to hear the first simple tone and another one the final simple tone, one blow of the *Shofar* serves the requirements of both of them[35].

27 He appears in the Babli as Rabba bar Rav Huna; he and Rav Ḥisda were the leaders of the third generation of Amoraïm in Babylonia.

26 That no interruption is allowed longer than what is needed to complete the entire ritual.

29 This must have been after the death of Rav when Rav Ḥuna was the head of the Academy. The text given here is from the Rome manuscript; the Venice print and Leyden manuscript

have רַב חוּנָא בְּשֵׁם רַב הוּנָא "Rav Ḥuna in the name of Rav Huna", which certainly is a scribal error.

30 If one heard the nine sounds precribed for Rosh Hashanah on nine different occasions during the day (but in the correct order), then he has done his duty.

31 Whether the rule of interruptions applies to the blowing of the *Shofar* or not. This shows that Rav Ḥuna's ruling was not widely accepted in Babylonia in his time.

32 He is called Rebbi Assi in the Babli, student of R. Yoḥanan, and co-head of the Academy of Tiberias with Rebbi Immi (Ammi) after R. Yoḥanan. Both were Cohanim.

33 As mentioned earlier, this is the statement quoted in the Babli (*Megillah* 18b, *Rosh Hashanah* 34b).

34 The basic obligation is to hear three times a straight note (תקיעה), followed by a broken sound, followed by a straight note. [Since there was diasgreement in practice whether the broken sound should be in three waves or in nine small variations, Rebbi Abbahu in the administrative center of Caesarea, where Jews from many different places came together, instituted the rule that one blows three times, each one of the two kinds of modulated sound and the third time the two sounds together.]

36 In fact, the benediction on Rosh Hashanah is not "to blow the *Shofar*" but "to listen to the sound of the *Shofar*"; hence, it is the personal obligation of each listener and does not depend on the intention of the blower.

רִבִּי אָבִין בַּר חִיָּיא בָּעֵי קִרְיַת שְׁמַע וּבִרְכוֹתֶיהָ הִיא וְלֹא בִרְכוֹתֶיהָ בִּרְכוֹתֶיהָ וְלֹא הִיא. הִפְסִיק שְׁלִישָׁה וְחָזַר וְהִפְסִיק שְׁלִישָׁה בְּקוֹרֵא מְשַׁעֲרִין. אוֹ בְּכָל־אָדָם מְשַׁעֲרִין. אָמַר רִבִּי מַתַּנְיָה מִסְתַּבְּרָא בְּקוֹרֵא.

Rebbi Abin bar Ḥiyya[36] investigated: The recitation of *Shema'* with its benedictions, it (the recitation of *Shema'*) without its benedictions, its benedictions without it[37]? If he interrupted after a third, interrupted after a second third[38]? Does one estimate by the reader's speed or by the average speed of all men? Rebbi Mattaniah[39] said, it seems reasonable by the reader's.

36 An outstanding student of Rebbis Yoḥanan and Zeïra who died young.

37 Since we have decided that one has to start anew if he interrupted long enough to have finished the entire recitation during the interruption, does he count the time for *Shema'* with its benedictions, or without benedictions, and does the rule of interruptions apply at all to the benedictions? The question remains unanswered.

38 Do separate interruptions count as one or is every interruption a separate count of time? The question remains unanswered.

39 A Galilean Amora of the last generation. In the parallel in *Megillah* (2:2), the reading is: Rebbi Mattaniah said: Is it not reasonable that . . ., with a rhetorical negation [interpretation of Rashba (Rebbi Shelomo ben Adrat) in his commentary to the Mishnah in *Berakhot*.]

רִבִּי אַבָּהוּ שָׁאַל לְרִבִּי יוֹחָנָן בְּגִין דַּאֲנָא קָרֵי שְׁמַע וְעָבַר בִּמְבוֹאוֹת הַמְּטוּנָּפוֹת וּמַפְסִיק נְפִיק אֲנָא יְדֵי חוֹבָתִי. אָמַר לֵיהּ אַבָּהוּ בְּנִי אִם מַפְסִיק אַתְּ כְּדֵי לִקְרוֹת אֶת כּוּלָּהּ לֹא יָצָאת יְדֵי חוֹבָתָךְ.

Rebbi Abbahu[40] asked Rebbi Yoḥanan: Assuming that I am reciting *Shema'* and interrupting while passing by stinking passage ways[41], do I fulfill my obligation? He answered him: Abbahu my son, if you interrupt enough that you could have finished all of it, you did not fulfill your obligation.

40 A student of R. Yoḥanan who became the principal defender of the Jews in Israel before the Roman authorities. His father's name is unknown. His school was at Caesarea Philippi [C. Paneas], seat of the Roman prefect for Galilee.

41 Where it is forbidden to study Torah or recite prayers, cf. Mishnah 5:3. This section is also discussed in Babli *Rosh Hashanah* 34b, where, according to the theory of the Babli mentioned above, R. Yoḥanan answers only according to the opinion of those who think that after a longer interruption one has to start anew.

רִבִּי אֶלְעָזָר סְלִיק מְבַקְּרָא לְרִבִּי שִׁמְעוֹן בַּר אַבָּא. אָמַר לֵיהּ בְּגִין דַּאֲנָא תָּשִׁישׁ וַאֲנָא קָרֵי שְׁמַע וּמִתְנַמְנֵם נְפִיק אֲנָא יְדֵי חוֹבָתִי. אָמַר לֵיהּ אִין. רִבִּי יִרְמְיָה בָּעָא קוֹמוֹי רִבִּי זְעִירָא בְּגִין דְּרִבִּי אֶלְעָזָר יָדַע דְּרִבִּי שִׁמְעוֹן בַּר אַבָּא מְדַקְדֵּק בְּמִצְוָתָא סַגִּין הוֹרֵי לֵיהּ אוֹ בְגִין דְּהוּא תָשִׁישׁ הוֹרֵי לֵיהּ. אָמַר לֵיהּ בְּפֵירוּשׁ פְּלִיגִין רִבִּי אֶלְעָזָר אוֹמֵר יָצָא. רִבִּי יוֹחָנָן אוֹמֵר לֹא יָצָא. מַה פְּלִיגִין בְּקִרְיַת שְׁמַע מִפְּנֵי שֶׁהִיא עֲשׂוּיָה פְּרָקִים פְּרָקִים. אֲבָל בְּהַלֵּל וּבִקְרִיַּאת הַמְּגִילָּה אוּף רִבִּי אֶלְעָזָר מוֹדֵי.

Rebbi Eleazar[42] went to pay a sick-bed visit to Rebbi Simeon bar Abba[43]. He said to him: Since I am weak, when I am reciting *Shema'* I tend to slumber; do I fulfill my obligation? He said to him: yes.

Rebbi Jeremiah asked before Rebbi Zeïra: Did Rebbi Eleazar give this ruling since he knew that Rebbi Simeon bar Abba is very scrupulous in the execution of his religious duties[44], or because he was so weak[45]? He answered him: They[46] disagree explicitly; Rebbi Eleazar said he fulfilled his obligation, Rebbi Yoḥanan said he did not fulfill his obligation. They disagree for the recitation of *Shema'* since that is composed of separate chapters, but for the recitation of *Hallel* and the Esther scroll, Rebbi Eleazar will agree[47].

42 A Babylonian who first was a student and then became a colleague of Rebbi Yoḥanan. Even though he was the greatest of his generation after Rebbi Yoḥanan, he never became head of a Yeshivah since he died shortly before Rebbi Yoḥanan. He often follows Babylonian positions like the one presented here, where the position of Rebbi Eleazar is that which the Babli, *Rosh Hashanah* 34b, accepts as the re-interpreted position of Rebbi Yoḥanan.

43 A fellow Babylonian who was a student of the great Amoraïm of the first generation, thus much older than Rebbi Eleazar.

44 Therefore, will make an effort that his slumber periods will not be too long.

45 Since there is no other way he could fulfill his obligation he could

claim an exemption from the general rule because of אונס, an act of God.

46 Rebbis Yoḥanan and Eleazar, concerning whether a person who interrupted a recitation for a longer period and then continued where he interrupted, did fulfill his religious duty.

47 That after a long interruption one has to start from the beginning again. This sentence is a comment by the editors of the Yerushalmi; it is not the Babylonian position.

תַּנֵּי הַשּׁוֹאֵל בִּשְׁלוֹם רַבּוֹ אוֹ בְמִי שֶׁהוּא גָדוֹל מִמֶּנּוּ בַּתּוֹרָה הָרְשׁוּת בְּיָדוֹ. הָדָא אָמְרָה שֶׁאָדָם צָרִיךְ לִשְׁאוֹל בְּמִי שֶׁהוּא גָדוֹל מִמֶּנּוּ בַּתּוֹרָה. וְעוֹד מִן הָדָא דְתַנֵּי קָרַע וְחָזְרָה נְשָׁמָה אִם עַל אֲתַר אֵינוֹ צָרִיךְ לִקְרוֹעַ. אִם לְאַחַר זְמַן צָרִיךְ לִקְרוֹעַ. וְכַמָּה הוּא עַל אֲתַר כְּדֵי דִבּוּר. וְכַמָּה הוּא כְדֵי דִבּוּר. רִבִּי סִימוֹן בְּשֵׁם רִבִּי יְהוֹשֻׁעַ בֶּן לֵוִי כְּדֵי שְׁאִילַת שָׁלוֹם בֵּין אָדָם לַחֲבֵירוֹ. אַבָּא בַּר בַּר חָנָא בְּשֵׁם רִבִּי יוֹחָנָן כְּדֵי שְׁאִילַת שָׁלוֹם בֵּין הָרַב לַתַּלְמִיד וְיֹאמַר לוֹ שָׁלוֹם עָלֶיךָ רַבִּי.

It was stated: If someone wants to greet his teacher or anybody who his greater than himself in Torah, he is permitted to do so[48]. That implies that a person has to greet anybody who is greater than himself in Torah. And also from the following[49]: If one tore his clothes and the soul returned, if it is instantaneous he does not have to tear again. If it is later, he has to tear again. How much is instantaneous? The time for speech. How much is time of speech? Rebbi Simon in the name of Rebbi Joshua ben Levi said: the time one needs to greet his friend[50]. Abba bar bar Ḥana[51] in the name of Rebbi Yoḥanan: the time for greeting between teacher and student, when he says "Peace be with you, my teacher.[52]"

48 To continue the discussion of the Mishnah, we now turn to the definition of what it means to interrupt "to greet somebody out of respect."

49 A similar but more explicit *baraita* is found in Babli *Nedarim* 87a. A person stands at the deathbed of someone for whom he would be required to mourn. He must tear his clothes after the person's death. In the case discussed here, he tore his clothes, thinking that the patient was dead but

then the dying person showed signs of life. If the final death occurs within the time needed for "speech", the first tear is sufficient. The *baraita* is quoted here only to introduce the standard for greeting, which is that the student is required to say: "Peace be with you, my teacher." This is the standard of behavior for a student.

50 The greeting of a person to his friend is שלום עליכם "Peace be with you." In the main parallel in the Babli (*Baba qama* 73b), no names are given but it is stated that there are two measurements of "speech", one from teacher to student, the same as a person to a friend, and the longer one from student to teacher.

51 He appears in the Babli as Rabba bar bar Ḥana; his father Rabba bar Ḥana was a nephew of Rav.

52 The Babli (*loc. cit.*) has the longer sentence שלום עליך מורי ורבי, "peace be with you, my instructor and teacher."

רִבִּי יוֹחָנָן הֲוָה מִסְתַּמֵּיךְ עַל רִבִּי יַעֲקֹב בַּר אִידִי וְהָיָה רִבִּי אֶלְעָזָר חָמֵי לֵיהּ וּמִטָּמָר מִן קֳדָמוֹי. אָמַר הָא תַּרְתֵּי מִילִּין הָדֵין בַּבְלָיָא עֲבִיד בִּי חָדָא דְלָא שָׁאֵל בִּשְׁלוֹמִי. וְחָדָא דְלֹא אָמַר שְׁמוּעָתָא מִשְּׁמִי. אָמַר לֵיהּ כַּךְ אִינּוּן נְהִיגִין גַּבֵּיהֶן. זְעִירָא לֹא שָׁאַל בִּשְׁלָמֵיהּ דְּרַבָּה דְאִינּוּן מְקַיְּימִין רָאוּנִי נְעָרִים וְנֶחְבָּאוּ. מִי מְהַלְּכִין חָמֵי חַד בֵּית מִדְרָשׁ. אָמַר לֵיהּ הָכָא הֲוָה רִבִּי מֵאִיר יָתִיב דָּרַשׁ וְאָמַר שְׁמוּעָתָא מִן שְׁמֵיהּ דְּרִבִּי יִשְׁמָעֵאל וְלֹא אָמַר שְׁמוּעָתָא מִן שְׁמֵיהּ דְּרִבִּי עֲקִיבָה. אָמַר לֵיהּ כָּל־עָלְמָא יָֽדְעִין דְּרִבִּי מֵאִיר תַּלְמִידוֹ דְרִבִּי עֲקִיבָה. אָמַר לוֹ כָּל־עָלְמָא יָֽדְעִין דְּרִבִּי אֶלְעָזָר תַּלְמִידֵיהּ דְּרִבִּי יוֹחָנָן. מִיהוּ מִיעֲבוֹר קוֹמֵי אַהֲדוּרֵי צִילְמָא. אָמַר לֵיהּ מַה אִיתְפַּלֵּיג לֵיהּ אִיקָר. אֶלָּא עֲבוֹר קוֹמוֹי וְסַמִּי עֵינֵיהּ. אָמַר לֵיהּ יְאוּת עָבַד רִבִּי אֶלְעָזָר דְּלָא עָבַר קוֹמֵיךְ. אָמַר רִבִּי יַעֲקֹב בַּר אִידִי יוֹדֵעַ אַתְּ לְפַיֵּס.

Rebbi Yoḥanan was leaning on Rebbi Jacob bar Idi when Rebbi Eleazar saw him and hid himself before him[53]. He said, these two things the Babylonian does to me: First, that he does not greet me, and second, that he does not teach the traditions in my name. He said to him, thus they behave among themselves; Zeïra did not greet Rabba[54] since they observe (*Job* 29:8) "Boys see me and hide themselves." As they were walking, he[55] saw a *Bet Midrash*. He[55] said to him: Here Rebbi Meïr sat and reported traditions in the name of Rebbi Ismaël but he never reported traditions in the name of Rebbi Aqiba. He[56] answered: Everybody knows that Rebbi Meïr was the student of Rebbi Aqiba. He[55] retorted, everybody knows that Rebbi Eleazar is the student of Rebbi Yoḥanan. May one pass by a cursed[57] statue? He[58] said to him, do you want to honor it? Pass it by and blind its eyes! He[59] said to him, Rebbi Eleazar did well that he did not pass before you. He said: Rebbi[60] Jacob bar Idi, you know how to pacify.

53 This story is inserted here to show that the obligation to greet one's teacher was accepted in Babylonia only when the student could not hide from his teacher. Rebbi Yoḥanan also insists that all his teachings be reported in his own name; this is discussed in the next section. A psalm is quoted there to support Rebbi Yoḥanan's position mentioning the Temple; the rôle of David in the building of the Temple is discussed in the third part of this aggadic insert.

54 The names here do not seem to be correctly transmitted. Rabba belongs to the generation after Rebbi Yoḥanan and Rebbi Zeïra studied under Rav Huna and Rav Yehudah in Babylonia. Therefore, it seems that the name is Zeïri, a Babylonian who studied under Rav and them emigrated to Israel where he became famous but did not acquire any rabbinic title. The second name, therefore, is Rav.

55 Rebbi Jacob bar Idi.

56 Rebbi Yoḥanan.

57 The word אהדורי makes no sense. In the parallel sources in the Yerushalmi, *Sheqalim* 2:6, *Moëd qaṭan* 3:2, the word is ארורי "cursed".

58 Rebbi Yoḥanan; the person who asks is Rebbi Jacob bar Idi who already knew the answer from Rebbi Joshua ben Levi, *Avodah zarah* 3:8.

59 Rebbi Jacob bar Idi points out that one avoids only important people or circumstances. One "blinds the eyes" of the idol if one passes by it without taking any notice of it and the idol sees that it is not taken seriously.

60 The title "Rebbi" is missing in the Rome ms.; this is the better reading since the teacher will not adress his student (nor his equal) by his title.

וְרִבִּי יוֹחָנָן בָּעֵי דְּיֵימְרוּן שְׁמַעְתָּא מִן שְׁמֵיהּ. אַף דָּוִד בִּקֵּשׁ עָלֶיהָ רַחֲמִים אָגוּרָה בְאָהָלְךָ עוֹלָמִים. רִבִּי פִּינְחָס רִבִּי יִרְמְיָה בְּשֵׁם רִבִּי יוֹחָנָן וְכִי עָלַת עַל לֵב דָּוִד שֶׁהוּא חַי לְעוֹלָם אֶלָּא אָמַר דָּוִד אֶזְכֶּה שֶׁיְּהוּ דְבָרַי נֶאֱמָרִין עַל שְׁמִי בְּבָתֵּי כְנֵסִיּוֹת וּבְבָתֵּי מִדְרָשׁוֹת. מְהַנְיָא לֵיהּ. לֵוִי בַּר נְזִירָא אָמַר כָּל־הָאוֹמֵר שְׁמוּעָה מִשֵּׁם אוֹמְרָהּ שִׂפְתוֹתָיו רוֹחֲשׁוֹת עִמּוֹ בַקֶּבֶר. מַה טַעַם דּוֹבֵב שִׂפְתֵי יְשֵׁנִים. כְּכוֹמֶר הַזֶּה שֶׁל עֲנָבִים שֶׁהוּא זָב מֵאֵילָיו. רִבִּי חֲנִינָה בַּר פַּפַּאי וְרִבִּי סִימוֹן חַד אָמַר כְּהָדֵין דְּשָׁתֵי קוֹנְדִּיטוֹן. וְחָרָנָה אָמַר כְּהָדֵין דְּשָׁתֵי חֲמָר עַתִּיק אַף עַל גַּב דְּהוּא שָׁתֵי לֵיהּ טַעֲמֵיהּ בְּפוּמֵיהּ.

But Rebbi Yoḥanan required that traditions should be reported in his name. Also David begged for divine mercy in this respect, (*Ps.* 61:5) "may I dwell in Your tent forever!"[61] Rebbi Phineas[62], Rebbi Jeremiah, in the name of Rebbi Yoḥanan; Could David think of living forever? Rather, David meant: May I have the merit that my words will be mentioned in my name in synagogues and houses of study. What good does that do to him? Levi, the son of the *Nazir*[63] said: If someone mentions a tradition in the name of its author, the latter's lips whisper with him in the grave. What is the reason? (*Cant.* 7:10) "Dripping from the lips of the sleeping ones." Like that bunch of grapes which drips by itself. Rebbi Ḥanina bar Pappai[64] and Rebbi Simon, one said, like one who drinks spiced wine, the other said, like one who drinks old wine, even though he consumed it, its taste remains in his mouth.

61 The context of the Psalm excludes an interpretation that would refer the verse to the Future World since it directly refers to the earthly Temple.

62 R. Pinḥas bar Ḥama Hacohen, leading preacher of the fourth generation of Galilean Amoraïm.

63 An author who is not otherwise mentioned in the Talmudim. In the parallels in the Babli (*Yebamot* 96b, *Sanhedrin* 90b, *Bekhorot* 31b) the statement is R. Yoḥanan's in the name of R. Simeon (either ben Yoḥai or ben Yehoẓadaq) and the verse is quoted in the name of several authors, one of

them Simeon Nazira who probably was the father of Levi, the son of the *Nazir* who is quoted here. (The *Nazir* may not cut his hair, drink wine, or become impure by a dead body. Since the destruction of the Temple, any vow of *nezirut* is permanent.)

64 A colleague of Rebbi Simon and Rebbi Abbahu, equally outstanding in practice and in *aggadah*. ("Spiced wine" from Latin *conditura* "condiment, spice.")

אֵין דּוֹר שֶׁאֵין בּוֹ לֵיצָנוּת. מַה הָיוּ פְּרִיצֵי הַדּוֹר עוֹשִׂין הָיוּ הוֹלְכִין אֶצֶל חֲלוֹנוֹתָיו שֶׁל דָּוִד וְאוֹמְרִין לוֹ דָּוִד אֵימַת יִבָּנֶה בֵּית הַמִּקְדָּשׁ אֵימָתַי בֵּית יי נֵלֵךְ. וְהוּא אוֹמֵר אַף עַל פִּי שֶׁמִּתְכַּוְּנִין לְהַכְעִיסֵנִי יָבוֹא עָלַי שֶׁאֲנִי שָׂמֵחַ בְּלִבִּי. שָׂמַחְתִּי בְּאוֹמְרִים לִי בֵּית יי נֵלֵךְ. וְהָיָה כִּי יִמְלְאוּ יָמֶיךָ. אָמַר רִבִּי שְׁמוּאֵל בַּר נַחְמָנִי אָמַר הַקָּדוֹשׁ בָּרוּךְ הוּא לְדָוִד דָּוִד יָמִים מְלֵאִים אֲנִי מוֹנֶה לְךָ אֵינִי מוֹנֶה לְךָ יָמִים חֲסֵרִים. כְּלוּם שְׁלֹמֹה בִנְךָ בּוֹנֶה בֵּית הַמִּקְדָּשׁ לֹא לְהַקְרִיב בּוֹ קָרְבָּנוֹת חָבִיב עָלַי מִשְׁפָּט וּצְדָקָה שֶׁאַתָּה עוֹשֶׂה יוֹתֵר מִן הַקָּרְבָּנוֹת. וּמַה טַעַם עֹשֹׂה צְדָקָה וּמִשְׁפָּט נִבְחַר לַיי מִזָּבַח.

There is no generation without scoffers. What did the hooligans of that generation do? They went to David's windows and said to him: David, when will the Temple be built, when will we go to the Lord's house? But he said, even though they intend to enrage me, it comes over me that I am happy, (*Ps.* 122:1) "I enjoy it when they say to me: let us go to the Lord's house."[65] (*2Sam.* 7:12) "[66]When your days will be complete"; Rebbi Samuel bar Naḥmani said, the Holy One, praise to Him, said to David: 'I am counting full days for you, I am not counting missing days for you[67]. Will not your son Solomon build the Temple to sacrifice? Law and justice that you are upholding is more to my liking than sacrifices.' What is the reason? (*Prov.* 21:3) "Upholding justice and law is preferred by the Lord to sacrifice".

65 Knowing that he would not build the Temple and not see it.

66 The word והיה given here is not in *2Samuel*; the quote starts with the second word.

67 This is one of the blessings bestowed at Mount Sinai on the Jewish people, *Ex.* 23:26, that the Just will live complete years; as in fact Moses died on his 120th birthday. It is asserted here that David also lived complete years; his age is never indicated in *Tanakh*.

פסקא. ובפְּרָקִים שׁוֹאֵל מִפְּנֵי הַכָּבוֹד וּמֵשִׁיב. מִפְּנֵי מַה הוּא מֵשִׁיב מִפְּנֵי הַיִּרְאָה אוֹ מִפְּנֵי הַכָּבוֹד. נִשְׁמְעִינָא מִן הָדָא וּבְאֶמְצַע שׁוֹאֵל מִפְּנֵי הַיִּרְאָה וּמֵשִׁיב (מִפְּנֵי הַכָּבוֹד)[68] דִּבְרֵי רִבִּי מֵאִיר. הָא בְקַדְמִיתָא שׁוֹאֵל מִפְּנֵי הַכָּבוֹד וּמֵשִׁיב מִפְּנֵי הַכָּבוֹד וּבְאֶמְצַע שׁוֹאֵל מִפְּנֵי הַיִּרְאָה וּמֵשִׁיב דִּבְרֵי רִבִּי מֵאִיר. מִפְּנֵי מַה הוּא מֵשִׁיב מִפְּנֵי הַיִּרְאָה אוֹ מִפְּנֵי הַכָּבוֹד. נִשְׁמְעִינָא מִן הָדָא רִבִּי יְהוּדָה אוֹמֵר בְּאֶמְצַע שׁוֹאֵל מִפְּנֵי הַיִּרְאָה וּמֵשִׁיב מִפְּנֵי הַכָּבוֹד. הָא קַדְמִיתָא שׁוֹאֵל מִפְּנֵי הַיִּרְאָה וּמֵשִׁיב מִפְּנֵי הַיִּרְאָה.

New Section. "Between the sections one greets people out of respect, and answers them."[69] Why does one answer, out of fear or to show respect? We may hear it from this: "In the middle of a section one may greet because of fear and answer (for respect), the words of Rebbi Meïr." Hence, in the prior case one may ask because of respect and answer out of respect.[71] "In the middle of a section one may greet because of fear and answer, the words of Rebbi Meïr." For what does one answer, out of fear or to show respect? We may hear it from this: "Rebbi Yehudah says: in the middle of a section one may greet out of fear and answer for respect." Hence[72], in the first case one asks because of fear and answers because of fear.

68 The words are in both the Leyden and Rome manuscripts, but missing in the Genizah fragments and in the text of R. Solomon Cirillo. Since they contradict the following discussion, they should be disregarded.

69 This is a quote from the Mishnah. The problem is that Rebbi Meïr does not indicate why one should answer. Since for Rebbi Yehudah the rules for answering are more lenient than for initiating the exchange, it follows that for Rebbi Meïr the rules for answering are not more lenient, but it is unclear whether answering and initiating have identical status or that the rules for answering are more restrictive than those for initiating a verbal exchange. The Babli (13b) explains the words of Rebbi Meïr as meaning "one may start an exchange *and it goes without saying* that one may answer", they seem to assume that it is obvious that the rules of answering cannot be stricter than those for starting. Also, the Babli takes the two parts together; it is possible that the unnecessary length in the statement of Rebbi Meïr is considered simply as a parallel to the necessary length of the statement of Rebbi Yehudah while for the Yerushalmi the two parallel statements of Rebbi Meïr represent two parallel problems which have to be solved separately. Hence the seemingly repetitous arrangement of the Yerushalmi here; but the first quote of Rebbi Meïr is in support of an argument while the second one presents the topic for further discussion; the two quotes of the identical text are of different status.

71 Since in the middle of a section certainly more restrictive rules apply than between sections.

72 Since Rebbi Meïr disagrees with Rebbi Yehudah, and from the previous discussion we know that answering does not have more restrictive rules than starting the conversation, it follows that Rebbi Meïr must hold in all cases that answering and starting have the same status.

עַד כְּדוֹן בְּאֶמְצַע הַפָּרָשָׁה וַאֲפִילוּ בְּאֶמְצַע הַפָּסוּק. רִבִּי יִרְמְיָה מְדַמֵּי. רִבִּי יוֹנָה מִשְׁתָּעֵי. רִבִּי חוּנָא רַב יוֹסֵף וְדִבַּרְתָּ בָּם מִיכַּן שֶׁיֵּשׁ לְךָ רְשׁוּת לְדַבֵּר בָּם.

So far in the middle of a section. Or even in the middle of a verse[73]? Rebbi Jeremiah gave hints[74]. Rebbi Jonah made himself understood[75]. Rebbi Ḥuna, Rav Joseph: (*Deut.* 6:7) "You may talk *in* them", from here that one is authorized to talk between them[76].

73 Do the rules given in the Mishnah apply only between verses in the middle of a section or even in the middle of a verse?

74 The text here is not uniform. The Leyden manuscript and the Genizah text are as the Venice print, מרמה, but in the quotes of this passage by Ramban, *Milḥamot Hashem*, *Berakhot* Chap. 2 and the authorities depending on him (Rashba and Rosh on Babli *Berakhot* 14a), the text reads מרמז. The meaning is in both cases that Rebbi Jeremiah did not talk but give greetings or instructions by pantomime.

75 I. e., he talked.

76 In Hebrew, future, imperative, and subjunctive may have the same form. In general, the passage ודברת בם in *Shema'* is translated "you must talk about them" (The Divine commandments), but Rebbi Ḥuna takes it to mean "you may talk in them", i. e., while reciting the verses.

משנה ב: וְאֵלּוּ הֵן בֵּין הַפְּרָקִים בֵּין בְּרָכָה רִאשׁוֹנָה לִשְׁנִיָּה. בֵּין שְׁנִיָּה לִשְׁמַע. בֵּין שְׁמַע לְוְהָיָה אִם שָׁמֹעַ. בֵּין וְהָיָה אִם שָׁמֹעַ לְוַיֹּאמֶר. בֵּין וַיֹּאמֶר לֶאֱמֶת וְיַצִּיב. רִבִּי יְהוּדָה אוֹמֵר בֵּין וַיֹּאמֶר לֶאֱמֶת וְיַצִּיב לֹא יַפְסִיק.

Mishnah 2: The following are "between the sections": between the first benediction and the second, between the second and *Shema'*, between *Shema'* and (*Deut*. 11:13) "it shall be when you will really listen", between "it shall be when you will really listen" and (*Num*. 15:37) "the Eternal spoke". Between "the Eternal spoke" and "true and outstanding[77]". Rebbi Yehudah said, between "the Eternal spoke" and "true and outstanding" one may not interrupt.

77 The benediction after *Shema'*, starting with a series of epithets of the Torah.

הלכה ב: אָמַר רִבִּי לֵוִי טַעֲמֵיהּ דְּרִבִּי יְהוּדָה אֲנִי יי אֱלֹהֵיכֶם. וּכְתִיב וַיי אֱלֹהִים אֱמֶת.

Halakhah 2: Rebbi Levi said[78], the reason of Rebbi Yehudah: (*Num*. 15:41) "I am the Eternal, your God[79]", and it is written (*Jer*. 10:10) "But the Eternal is the true God".

78 In the parallel in the Babli (14a), the explanation is by R. Abbahu in the name of R. Yoḥanan. Since Rebbi Levi was preacher in the Yeshivah of Rebbi Yoḥanan, the explanation originated in that Yeshivah. In addition, Rebbi Abbahu in the name of Rebbi Yoḥanan in the Babli declares that the practice follows Rebbi Yehudah; this decision is missing in the Yerushalmi and, hence, it seems that in Israel one used to follow the majority opinion that an interruption is permitted between the last words of the *Shema'* and "true". Hence, the question asked in the Babli, whether after reciting "the Eternal, your God. True!" one stops and starts again "true and outstanding", is irrelevant for the Yerushalmi. The question in the Babli is whether Rebbi Yehudah disagrees with the first Tanna in principle, that 'between "the Eternal spoke" and "true and outstanding"' there is no interruption allowed or whether he simply moves the end of technical *Shema'* by one word and then allows the regular interruptions there.

79 These are the concluding words of *Shema'*.

משנה ג: אָמַר רִבִּי יְהוֹשֻׁעַ בֶּן קָרְחָה לָמָּה קָדְמָה שְׁמַע לִוְהָיָה אִם שָׁמֹעַ כְּדֵי שֶׁיְּקַבֵּל עָלָיו מַלְכוּת שָׁמַיִם תְּחִילָּה וְאַחַר כָּךְ עוֹל מִצְוֹת. וְהָיָה אִם שָׁמֹעַ לְוַיֹּאמֶר שֶׁוְּהָיָה אִם שָׁמֹעַ נוֹהֵג בַּיּוֹם וּבַלַּיְלָה. וַיֹּאמֶר אֵינוֹ נוֹהֵג אֶלָּא בַיּוֹם.

Mishnah 3: Ribbi Joshua ben Qorḥah[90] said: Why does *Shema'* precede "it shall be when you will really listen"? In order that one should accept the Kingdom of Heaven before he accepts the yoke of the commandments. And "it shall be when you will really listen" to "The Eternal said"? Because "it shall be when you will really listen" is applicable day and night[81], "the Eternal said" is applicable only during daytime.

80 A Tanna who lived from the times, of R. Aqiba to those of Rebbi; he is mostly known for his aggadic interpretations.

81 The obligation to study the Torah and keep its commandments applies everywhere and at all times; the obligation to have *ẓiẓit* on one's

garment, expressed in the third section of *Shema'*, is applicable only during daytime according to most opinions.

הלכה ג: רִבִּי חִייָא בְּשֵׁם רִבִּי יוֹחָנָן מַה טַעַם אָמְרוּ אָדָם לוֹבֵשׁ תְּפִילִּין וְקוֹרֵא אֶת שְׁמַע (fol. 4c) וּמִתְפַּלֵּל כְּדֵי שֶׁיְּקַבֵּל עָלָיו מַלְכוּת שָׁמַיִם תְּחִילָּה מֻשְׁלָם. רַב אָמַר קוֹרֵא אֶת שְׁמַע וְלוֹבֵשׁ אֶת תְּפִילָּיו וּמִתְפַּלֵּל. מַתְנִיתָא דְּרַב פְּלִיגָא עָלוֹי. הֲרֵי שֶׁהָיָה עָסוּק עִם הַמֵּת בְּקֶבֶר וְהִגִּיעַ עוֹנַת קְרִיַּת שְׁמַע הֲרֵי זֶה פּוֹרֵשׁ לְמָקוֹם טָהֳרָה וְלוֹבֵשׁ תְּפִילִּין וְקוֹרֵא אֶת שְׁמַע וּמִתְפַּלֵּל. מַתְנִיתָא מְסַייְעָא לְרַב לֹא שֶׁאָדָם יְקַבֵּל עָלָיו מַלְכוּת שָׁמַיִם תְּחִילָּה וְאַחַר כָּךְ יְקַבֵּל עָלָיו עוֹל מִצְוֹות.

Halakhah 3: Rebbi Ḥiyya[80] in the name of Rebbi Yoḥanan: Why did they say, a man puts on *tefillin*, recites the *Shema'* and prays? So that he first should accept upon himself the Kingdom of Heaven completely. Rav said, one reads the *Shema'*, puts on *tefillin*, and prays[81]. A *baraita* of Rav himself[82] disagrees with him: "If somebody was occupied with a dead person in his grave and the time for the recital of *Shema'* arrived, he should move to a pure place[83], put on *tefillin*, recite the *Shema'*, and pray". Does not the Mishnah support Rav: "In order that one should accept the Kingdom of Heaven before he accepts the yoke of the commandments"[84]?

80 R. Ḥiyya bar Abba, the student of R. Yoḥanan.

81 The essential difference between the Yerushalmi and the Babli is that in the Yerushalmi Rav precribes that one should be putting on *tefillin* (phylacteries) either after reciting the entire *Shema'*, or after reciting the first paragraph of *Shema'*, whereas in the Babli (14b) he is only reported to have put on his *tefillin* after the recital of *Shema'* without giving an explanation of what he was doing. Hence, the explanation of the Babli, that Rav had to wait until his *tefillin* were brought to him while he had to recite *Shema'* at its appropriate time, is impossible in the Yerushalmi. But since the Yerushalmi quotes Rebbi Yoḥanan as explaining the generally accepted practice, there is no practical difference between the two Talmudim

and the statement of Rav can be left standing without a decision on his own opinion.

82 This is the reading of the Leyden manuscript. In both Talmudim we hear that Rav and Samuel collected *baraitot*, tannaïtic statements not made part of the Mishnah.

83 Since a dead person can no longer pray, it is explained later in this *Halakhah* that praying in a graveyard would violate the verse (*Prov.* 17:5): "He who makes fun of the poor blasphemes his Maker"; hence one has to leave the graveyard if he wants to pray. The order of prayer given in the *baraita* is the one adopted by Rebbi Yoḥanan.

84 *Tefillin*, while mentioned in the first paragraph, belong to the execution of commandments. It follows that, in the opinion of the Yerushalmi, Rav recommended to put on *tefillin* between the first and second sections of *Shema'*; otherwise, the Mishnah would not support his position. This contradicts the opinion of the Babli as quoted above; it eliminates the objection of the Babli that certainly Rav would not put off fulfilling the obligation of *tefillin* until after the recital of *Shema'*.

אָמַר רִבִּי יַנַּאי תְּפִילִּין צְרִיכִין גּוּף נָקִי.

Rebbi Yannai[85] said: *Tefillin* need a clean body[86].

85 The most important Amora of the first generation in Galilea, student of Rebbi and teacher of Rebbi Yoḥanan.

86 The same rule is quoted in Rebbi Yannai's name in the Babli (*Sabbath* 49a, 130a); there Abbai and Rava explain that one may not break wind while wearing *tefillin* and also may not sleep while wearing them. The Yerushalmi does not go into details. The connection with the previous text probably is the quote that one may not wear *tefillin* in a graveyard. This also counts as having an unclean body since on leaving the graveyard one has to wash his hands. A Mishnah in the next Chapter also implies that one may not wear *tefillin* when his body is not cleansed from an emission of semen. Some Medieval authorities imply from the statement of R. Yannai that while wearing *tefillin* one may not have unclean thoughts.

מִפְּנֵי מַה לֹא הֶחֱזִיקוּ בָהֶן. מִפְּנֵי הָרַמָּאִין. עוּבְדָּא הֲוָה בְחַד בַּר נַשׁ דְּאַפְקִיד גַּבֵּיהּ חַבְרֵיהּ וְכָפַר בֵּיהּ. אָמַר לֵיהּ לֹא לָךְ הֵימָנִית אֶלָּא לְאִילֵּין דִּבְרֵישָׁךְ הֵימָנִית.

Why does one not hold on[87] to them? Because of the impostors[88]. It happened that a man deposited something with another, and the latter then reneged on it. He said to him: Not you I thought trustworthy but those on your head I thought trustworthy.

87 There are two interpretations of this sentence. Rabbenu Yeruḥam [path 19, part 5] explains: Why does one not keep on his *tefillin* the entire day but takes them off after praying? Tosaphot [*Šabbat* 49a] explain: Why does one not consider a person wearing *tefillin* automatically as a trustworthy Jew who may be trusted to keep all *mizwot*? The explanation of Tosaphot is easier to fit into our text but the explanation of Rabbenu Yeruḥam seems to have the correct historical background. Both the Roman and the Byzantine governments from time to time forbade the wearing of *tefillin*. Therefore, from the start of the reconstruction of Jewish life after the war of Bar Kokhba, *tefillin* were not worn publicly in the Land of Israel. The reading of the Rome manuscript, "Why does one not hold on to them in the Land of Israel?" seems to explain the situation from a Babylonian point of view where *tefillin* never were a problem with the government and where, in R. Sherira Gaon's time at least, *tefillin* were worn by scholars all day long. But even in Babylonia in the first generations of Amoraïm Rav Sheshet is reported (Babli *Šabbat* 118b) of being proud that he wore *tefillin* the entire day, not just for a minimal time.

88 Hence, wearing *tefillin* outside of times of prayer may make a person suspect of being a gangster impersonating a pious person.

רִבִּי יַנַּאי הָיָה לוֹבְשָׁן אַחַר חוֹלְיוֹ ג יָמִים לוֹמַר שֶׁהַחוֹלִי מְמָרֵק. מַה טַעַם הַסּוֹלֵחַ לְכָל־עֲוֹנֵיְכִי הָרוֹפֵא לְכָל־תַּחֲלוּאָיְכִי. רִבִּי יוֹחָנָן בֶּן זַכַּאי לֹא הֲווֹן תְּפִילּוֹי זָעִין מִינֵּיהּ לֹא בְקַיְיטָא וְלֹא בְסִיתְוָא. וְכַךְ נָהַג רִבִּי אֱלִיעֶזֶר תַּלְמִידוֹ אַחֲרָיו.

Rebbi Yannai was wearing them after his sickness for three days, to show that sickness cleanses[89]. What is the reason? (*Ps.* 103:2): "He Who forgives all my sins, He Who heals all my sicknesses." Rebbi Yoḥanan ben Zakkai's *tefillin* were not coming off from him either in summer or in winter. And so did his student Rebbi Eliezer after him.[90]

89 This statement supports the interpretation that the "clean body" required from a wearer of *tefillin* is a body cleansed from sinful thoughts, since a person recovered from sickness is a person all whose sins have been forgiven. It is spelled out in *Midrash Tehillim* 103 that the first three days, R. Yannai wore his *tefillin* the entire day but after that he was putting them on only for prayer.

90 This shows that before the war of Bar Kokhba, the wearing of *tefillin* the entire day in the Land of Israel was not unheard-of.

רִבִּי יוֹחָנָן בְּסִיתְוּא דַּהֲוָה חֲזִיק רֵישֵׁיהּ הֲוָה לְבֵישׁ תְּרַוֵיהוֹן. בְּרַם בְּקַיְיְטָא דְּלָא הֲוָה חֲזִיק רֵישֵׁיהּ לָא הֲוָה לְבֵישׁ אֶלָּא דְּאַדְּרָעֵיהּ. וְאֵינוֹ אָסוּר מִפְּנֵי עֶרְוָה. אָמַר רִבִּי חִייָא בַּר אַבָּא אַפִּיקַרְסִין הָיָה לוֹבֵשׁ מִבִּפְנִים. כַּד הֲוָה אָזִיל מַסְחֵי כֵּיוָן שֶׁהָיָה מַגִּיעַ אֵצֶל הָאוֹלְיְירִין הָיָה חוֹלְצָן. אָמַר רִבִּי יִצְחָק עַד יַעֲקֹב תֶּרְמוֹסָרָא הָיָה לוֹבְשָׁן. וְכַד הֲוָה נָפִיק מַסְחֵי הֲווּ יְהָבִין לֵיהּ. וְכַד הֲווּ מַיְיתִין לֵיהּ אָמַר שְׁנֵי אֲרוֹנוֹת הָיוּ מְהַלְּכִין עִם יִשְׂרָאֵל בַּמִּדְבָּר אֲרוֹנוֹ שֶׁל חַי הָעוֹלָמִים וַאֲרוֹנוֹ שֶׁל יוֹסֵף. וְהָיוּ אוּמּוֹת הָעוֹלָם אוֹמְרִין מַה טִּיבָן שֶׁל שְׁנֵי אֲרוֹנוֹת הַלָּלוּ. וְהָיוּ יִשְׂרָאֵל אוֹמְרִין לָהֶן זֶה אֲרוֹנוֹ שֶׁל יוֹסֵף עִם אֲרוֹנוֹ שֶׁל חַי הָעוֹלָמִים. וְהָיוּ אוּמּוֹת הָעוֹלָם מוֹנִין אֶת יִשְׂרָאֵל וְאוֹמְרִין וְכִי אֶפְשַׁר לַאֲרוֹן הַמֵּת לִהְיוֹת מְהַלֵּךְ עִם אֲרוֹנוֹ שֶׁל חַי הָעוֹלָמִים. וְהָיוּ יִשְׂרָאֵל אוֹמְרִין עַל יְדֵי שֶׁשִּׁימֵּר זֶה מַה שֶּׁכָּתוּב בְּזֶה. וְלָמָּה הוּא אָמַר דָּא מִילְתָא. אָמַר רִבִּי חֲנַנְיָא בְּגִין מֵימַר מִילָּא דְאוֹרָיָא. אָמַר לֵיהּ רִבִּי מָנָא וְהָכֵין לָא הֲוָה לֵיהּ מִילָּא דְאוֹרָיָא אוֹחְרִי לְמֵימַר אֶלָּא דָא. אֶלָּא קִנְתֵּרִין הֲוֹון לוֹמַר יוֹסֵף לֹא זָכָה לְמַלְכוּת אֶלָּא עַל יְדֵי שֶׁשִּׁימֵּר מִצְווֹתָיו שֶׁל הַקָּדוֹשׁ בָּרוּךְ הוּא וְאָנוּ לֹא זָכִינוּ לְכָל הַכָּבוֹד הַזֶּה אֶלָּא עַל יְדֵי שֶׁשָּׁמַרְנוּ מִצְוֹתָיו שֶׁל הַקָּדוֹשׁ בָּרוּךְ הוּא וְאַתּוּן בָּעֵין מְבַטְּלָא מִצְווֹתֵיהּ מִינָּן.

Rebbi Yoḥanan was wearing both of them[91] in winter when his head was healthy. But in sommer when his head was not healthy he put on only that of the arm. But is not that forbidden because of nakedness[92]? Rebbi Ḥiyya bar Abba said: He wore an undershirt[93] under his clothes. When he went to bathe, he was taking them off when he came to the oil sellers[94]. Rebbi Isaac said, he was wearing them up to Jacob, the bath master[95]. When he exited the bath, they brought them to him. When they were bringing them, he used to say: [96]Two caskets were travelling with Israel in the wilderness, the ark of Him, Who is the Life of the Universe, and the casket of Joseph. The Gentiles were saying: What is the purpose of these two caskets? Israel was answering them, that is the casket of Joseph with the ark of Him, Who is the Life of the Universe. The Gentiles were taunting Israel and saying, how is it possible that the casket of a dead person is travelling with the ark of Him, Who is the Life of the Universe? But Israel were answering, because this one kept all that is written in that one.

Why did he say that? Rebbi Ḥanania[97] said, in order to speak some words of learning. Rebbi Mana said to him: Did he have no other word of learning to say but that[98]? But that was sarcasm, to say that Joseph did only attain kingdom by keeping the commandments of the Holy One, praise to Him, and we received all that glory only because we kept the commandments of the Holy One, praise to Him, but you[99] want to remove His commandments from us!

91 Both *tefillin*.

92 Since the *tefillin* on the arm are worn under the coat or shirt, there is the possibility that no garment separates the holy *tefillin* from his genitals and that is forbidden as we shall see later. [Only in recent times have *tefillin* become so large that they cannot be covered by the coat sleeves and the bad habit of praying with the

left arm uncovered has taken over Ashkenazic congregations.]

93 ἐπικάρσιον, τό, "striped garment". This must have been a large undershirt reaching at least to the upper parts of his legs.

94 Latin *olearii*.

95 Cf. Greek θερμασία, ἡ, "warmth, heat.". Rebbi Yoḥanan would trust his *tefillin* only into the hands of a reliable Jewish man.

96 This *aggadah* appears several times: Tosephta *Soṭa* 4:7, *Mekhilta Beshallaḥ* 1, Babli *Soṭa* 13a. The Hebrew verb קנתר , a few times also קנטר, is probably from Greek κεντρόω "to sting, vex, goad".

97 A late Galilean Amora from Sepphoris (Ẓipporin), colleague of R. Mana.

98 Since he went frequently, why did he have to repeat the same text over and over again?

99 For R. Yoḥanan, the Roman government under Diocletian; for R. Mana, the Roman government under the Christian emperors.

בְּאֵי זֶה צַד הוּא מְבָרֵךְ עֲלֵיהֶן. רִבִּי זְרִיקָן בְּשֵׁם רִבִּי יַעֲקֹב בְּרִבִּי אִידִי כְּשֶׁהוּא נוֹתֵן עַל יָד מַהוּ אוֹמֵר בָּרוּךְ אֲשֶׁר קִדְּשָׁנוּ בְּמִצְוֹתָיו וְצִוָּנוּ עַל מִצְוַת תְּפִילִין. כְּשֶׁהוּא נוֹתֵן עַל הָרֹאשׁ מַהוּ אוֹמֵר בָּרוּךְ אֲשֶׁר קִדְּשָׁנוּ בְּמִצְוֹתָיו וְצִוָּנוּ עַל מִצְוַת הֲנָחַת תְּפִילִין. כְּשֶׁהוּא חוֹלְצָן מַהוּ אוֹמֵר בָּרוּךְ אֲשֶׁר קִדְּשָׁנוּ בְּמִצְוֹתָיו וְצִוָּנוּ לִשְׁמוֹר חוּקָּיו. וְאַתְיָא כְּמַאן דָּמַר בְּחוּקַּת תְּפִילִין הַכָּתוּב מְדַבֵּר בְּרַם כְּמַאן דָּמַר בְּחוּקַּת הַפֶּסַח הַכָּתוּב מְדַבֵּר לֹא בְדָא.

How does one make the benedictions on them? Rebbi Zeriqan[100] in the name of Rebbi Jacob ben Rebbi Idi: When he puts *tefillin* on his arm, what does he say:[101] "Praised[102] Who sanctified us by His commandments and commanded us about the obligation of *tefillin*." When he puts them on his head, what does he say? "Praised Who sanctified us by His commandments and commanded us about the obligation of putting on *tefillin*." When he takes them off, what does he say? "Praised Who sanctified us by His commandments and commanded us to obey His laws." That follows the opinion that the verse[103] speaks about the law of *tefillin*.

However, according to those who say that the verse speaks about the law of Passover, that does not apply.

100 An Amora in the generation after R. Yoḥanan and R. Jacob bar Idi. The parallels in the Babylonian Talmud are all anonymous.

101 In the Babli (*Berakhot* 60b, *Menaḥot* 36a) the order of the first two benedictions is inverted; the third benediction never was recited in Babylonia (Babli *Berakhot* 44b). There is a disagreement in principle between the two Talmudim. It is clear that the Yerushalmi requires two separate benedictions for the two *tefillin*; therefore, the second one which completes the action is the important and complete one. In the Babli (*Menaḥot* 36a) it seems that if both *tefillin* are put on together then only one benediction is needed; the first benediction is the one that counts and has to be recited. [This is Sephardic and Oriental practice today; Ashkenazim recite the second benediction, which is strictly required only if no *tefillin* are available for one's arm, out of doubt about the situation. In any case, in the Babylonian style, the second benediction is the minor one. Ashkenazic practice is an uneasy adaptation of Yerushalmi practice to Babylonian rules.]

102 In all formulas of benedictions, one has to add after "praised": "are You, o Eternal, our God, King of the Universe".

103 *Ex.* 13:10. In that chapter, verses 1-8 speak of the laws of Passover, v. 9 introduces the commandment of *tefillin*. V. 10, the last in that paragraph, reads: "You shall keep this law in its time, מימים ימימה." If the "law" is that of *tefillin*, one has to translate "from day to day", meaning that at nighttime the law is either inoperative or that it is forbidden to wear *tefillin*. If the "law" is that of Passover, one has to translate "from year to year." The latter meaning is the usual one for the Hebrew expression, but then it would have been rational to expect that verses 9 and 10 traded places.

The Yerushalmi refrains from attaching names to the different interpretations. In the Babylonian Talmud (*Erubin* 96a), the first interpretation is that of R. Yose the Galilean, the second one that of R. Aqiba. In the Yerushalmi source *Mekhilta deR. Simeon bar Yoḥai* (p. 41), the first interpretation is that of R. Aqiba and the second one of R. Eliezer. Since R.

Aqiba belongs to the following generation, the basic disagreement can be attributed to Rebbis Yose the Galilean and Eliezer.

רִבִּי אַבָּהוּ בְּשֵׁם רִבִּי אֶלְעָזָר הַנּוֹתֵן תְּפִילִּין בַּלַּיְלָה עוֹבֵר בַּעֲשֵׂה. וּמַה טַעַם וְשָׁמַרְתָּ אֶת הַחוּקָּה הַזֹּאת לְמוֹעֲדָהּ מִיָּמִים יָמִימָה. יָמִים וְלֹא לֵילוֹת. יָמִימָה פְּרָט לְשַׁבָּתוֹת וְיָמִים טוֹבִים. וְהָא רִבִּי אַבָּהוּ יְתִיב מַתְנֵי בְּרַמְשָׁא וּתְפִילוֹי עִילוֹי. מִצְדָּדִין הֲוָה וּכְמִין פִּקָּדוֹן הָיוּ בְיָדוֹ. אִית דְּבָעֵי מֵימַר לֹא אָמַר אֶלָּא הַנּוֹתֵן אֲבָל אִם הָיוּ עָלָיו מִבְּעוֹד יוֹם מוּתָּר. אִית דְּבָעֵי מֵימַר נִשְׁמְעִינֵיהּ מִן הֲדָא וְהָיָה לְךָ לְאוֹת אֶת שֶׁהוּא לְךָ לְאוֹת פְּרָט לְיוֹם טוֹב וְשַׁבָּתוֹת שֶׁכּוּלָּן אוֹת. וְלֹא כֵן כָּתַב מִיָּמִים יָמִימָה. לֵית לָךְ אֶלָּא כַּיי דָּמַר רִבִּי יוֹחָנָן כָּל מִילָּה דְּלֹא מְחוּוְרָא מְסַמְּכִין לָהּ מִן אַתְרִין סַגִּי.

Rebbi Abbahu in the name of Rebbi Eleazar[104]: He who puts on *tefillin* in the night transgresses a positive commandment. What is the reason? (*Ex.* 13:10) ""You shall keep this law in its time, from day to day;" "days" not night, "to days"[105] to exclude Sabbaths and holidays. But Rebbi Abbahu sat studying at night with his *tefillin* on his head![106] He put them on the side[107]; they were like a deposit in his keeping. Some want to say, he only meant not to put them on, but when they were on him during daytime it would be permitted. Some want to say, let us hear it from there (*Ex.* 13:9): "It shall be for you a sign," when you need it for a sign, but not holiday or Sabbaths that are all sign. But is it not written "to days"[108]? You have only what Rebbi Yoḥanan said: Everything that is not clear one supports from many places[109].

104 Probably the Amora, student of Rebbi Yoḥanan, and not one of the Tannaïm.

105 Meaning certain days, but not all days.

106 How can he transgress his own statement?

107 Not between his eyes, so that he was not fulfilling the commandment of wearing them, but he had them on his head to keep them since *tefillin*, as holy objects, have to be deposited in

safe places.

108 We do not expect the Torah to repeat commandments needlessly.

109 Since *Ex.* 13:10 may apply to Passover, any derivation from that verse is not clear. In *Mekhilta deR. Simeon bar Yoḥai*, the first derivation is anonymous, the second one is attributed to Rebbi Aqiba. While the discussion here is of Amoraïm, the entire material is tannaïtic.

נָשִׁים מְנַיִין וְלִמַּדְתֶּם אוֹתָם אֶת בְּנֵיכֶם וְלֹא אֶת בְּנוֹתֵיכֶם. אֶת שֶׁהוּא חַיָּיב בְּתַלְמוּד תּוֹרָה חַיָּיב בִּתְפִילִין. נָשִׁים שֶׁאֵינָן חַייָבוֹת בְּתַלְמוּד תּוֹרָה אֵינָן חַיָּיבִין בִּתְפִילִין. הֵתִיבוּן הֲרֵי מִיכַל בַּת כּוּשִׁי הָיְתָה לוֹבֶשֶׁת תְּפִילִין. וְאִשְׁתּוֹ שֶׁל יוֹנָה הָיְתָה עוֹלָה לִרְגָלִים וְלֹא מִיחוּ בְּיָדֶיהָ חֲכָמִים. רִבִּי חִזְקִיָּה בְּשֵׁם רִבִּי אֲבָהוּ אִשְׁתּוֹ שֶׁל יוֹנָה הוּשְׁבָה. מִיכַל בַּת כּוּשִׁי מִיחוּ בְיָדֶיהָ חֲכָמִים.

Women from where? (*Deut.* 11:19) "And you should teach them to your sons", and not to your daughters.[110] Anyone who is obliged to study Torah is obliged for *tefillin*, women who are not obliged to study Torah are not obliged for *tefillin.*[111] They objected, but did not Michal, the daughter of the Kushi[112], wear *tefillin*, and did not the wife of Jonah make the pilgrimage to the Temple[113], and the sages did not object. Rebbi Ḥisqiah in the name of Rebbi Abbahu: Jonah's wife was turned back[114], the sages forbade it to Michal the daughter of Kushi.[115]

110 The main discussion of this point appears in Chapter 3:3.

111 The proof, explicit in the *Mekhiltot*, is really from *Ex.* 13:9: "It shall be a sign on your hand and a remembrance between your eyes, *so that the Torah of the Eternal shall be in your mouth*, because with a strong hand the Eternal led you out of Egypt." Hence, only one who is obliged to study is obliged to wear *tefillin*. Naturally, for those who declare that *Ex.* 13:10 speaks of *tefillin* and nights are not a time for *tefillin*, it follows that *tefillin* is a positive commandment bound to stated times and, as a general principle, women are not obligated. However, since that interpretation of v. 10 is in doubt, it is not used here.

112 Saul, addressed as "Kush" in the

heading of Psalm 7.

113 Obviously, everybody can go to Jerusalem anytime he wishes, and we know from many sources that entire families made the pilgrimage, in particular for Passover. What is meant here is that Jonah's wife went to Jerusalem to bring the obligatory sacrifices in her own name, either additional to those of her husband or for herself when her husband was away at sea or at Nineveh. She may bring עולת ראייה, the holocaust of appearance, as a voluntary offering, but if she insists on presenting the offering as obligatory for her pilgrimage, then there is a question of the legality of the offering and doubtful sacrifices should not be offered.

114 Not from Jerusalem, but from presenting her pilgrimage sacrifice in the Temple separately from her husband.

115 The first statement, that Michal wore *tefillin* and that the wife of Jonah made the pilgrimage, is a tannaïtic statement in the Babli (*Erubin* 96a), and the Babli concludes from it that women *may* exercise all obligations that are bound to a fixed time from which women are freed. The Yerushalmi Amoraïm and later Yerushalmi sources (*Pesiqta rabbati* Chap. 22) disagree. This disagreement is not mentioned in the Babli; i. e., the argument is rejected.

תַּנֵּי נִכְנַס לְמֶרְחָץ מָקוֹם שֶׁבְּנֵי אָדָם עוֹמְדִין לְבוּשִׁין יֵשׁ שָׁם מִקְרָא וּתְפִילָּה וְאֵין צָרִיךְ לוֹמַר שְׁאֵילַת שָׁלוֹם. נוֹתֵן תְּפִילִּין וְאֵינוֹ צָרִיךְ לוֹמַר שֶׁלֹּא יַחֲלוֹץ. מָקוֹם שֶׁרוֹב בְּנֵי אָדָם רְגִילִין לִהְיוֹת עוֹמְדִין עֲרוּמִין אֵין שָׁם שְׁאֵילַת שָׁלוֹם וְאֵין צָרִיךְ לוֹמַר מִקְרָא וּתְפִילָּה וְחוֹלֵץ תְּפִילִּין וְאֵין צָרִיךְ לוֹמַר שֶׁלֹּא יִתֵּן. מִקְצָתָן עֲרוּמִין וּמִקְצָתָן לְבוּשִׁין יֵשׁ שָׁם שְׁאֵילַת שָׁלוֹם וְאֵין שָׁם לֹא מִקְרָא וְלֹא תְפִילָּה וְאֵינוֹ חוֹלֵץ תְּפִילִּין וְאֵינוֹ נוֹתֵן. אֲבָל אֵינוֹ לוֹבְשָׁן עַד שֶׁיֵּצֵא מֵאוֹתָהּ רְשׁוּת שֶׁל כָּל־אוֹתָהּ מֶרְחָץ. וְדָא מְסַייְעָא כַּיי דָּמַר רִבִּי יִצְחָק בְּגִין רִבִּי יוֹחָנָן עַד יַעֲקֹב תּוֹרְמוֹסָרָה הָיָה לוֹבְשָׁן.

It was stated[116]: "Entering a bathhouse, in the room where everybody is fully clothed[117] one may read the Bible, pray[118], and needless to say, one may greet people[119]. One may put on *tefillin*, and needless to say, one does not remove them. In the room where most people are naked one may not exchange greetings and needless to say, there is no Bible reading or prayer; one removes one's *tefillin* and needless to say, one does not put them on. Where some are naked and some are clothed there is greeting, no Bible reading and no prayer, one does not remove *tefillin* and one does not put them on. But one does not put them on again until he has completely left the grounds of that bathhouse." This supports what Rebbi Isaac said about Rebbi Yoḥanan, that he wore them until he came to Jacob, the bath master.

116 Tosephta *Berakhot* 2:20; a slightly different version is Babli *Šabbat* 10a. One returns to the problem discussed earlier that *tefillin*, as objects of holiness, cannot be worn on an arm that is not separated from one's genitals by some clothing. Hence, *tefillin* cannot be worn when one is naked, or in the presence of naked people. Prayer and religious study go by the same rules, following the verse (*Amos* 4:12) "Israel, prepare yourself for your God".

117 A Roman bathhouse was essentially a sauna. In the hot room, everybody was naked. In the anteroom, one was cooling down after the hot steam, getting massaged by the *olearii*, and putting on one's clothes. The outer rooms were used for social affairs, especially in large cities.

118 This is the reading of the Rome manuscript, the Tosephta and R. Solomon Cirillo; the Leyden manuscript and the Venice print have תפילין "*tefillin*"; but these are separately mentioned later.

119 The problem with the greeting formula "peace with you" is that Peace is one of the names of God, *Jud.* 6:24; hence, greeting somebody with שָׁלוֹם עֲלֵיכֶם is permitted only under circumstances that would allow prayer. The prohibition does not include greetings in other languages if the name of God is not invoked.

רִבִּי יִרְמְיָה בְּעָא קוֹמוֹי רִבִּי זְעִירָא הָיְתָה מֶרְחַץ מְרַחֶצֶת בִּימוֹת הַחַמָּה וְאֵינָהּ מְרַחֶצֶת בִּימוֹת הַגְּשָׁמִים. אָמַר לֵיהּ מֶרְחַץ וְאַף עַל פִּי שֶׁאֵינָהּ מְרַחֶצֶת וּבֵית הַכִּסֵּא אַף עַל פִּי שֶׁאֵין בּוֹ צוֹאָה. מַר עוּקְבָּא אָמַר אֲהֵן חֲזִירָא בֵּית כִּסֵּא

מְטוּלְטַל הֲוָה. רִבִּי יוֹנָה בָּעֵי אֲהֵן צְרָרָה דְּעַל גֵּיף יָמָא מַהוּ. אָמַר רִבִּי אַמִּי אַסְיָא הוֹרֵי רִבִּי יִרְמְיָה מַעֲבָר לֵיהּ בְּפִילְיוּס וְלָא סָמְכִין עִילוֹי.

Rebbi Jeremiah asked before Rebbi Zeïra: If it was used as bath house in summer but not in the rainy season, what is the rule[120]? He said to him, a bath house even if it is not in use, a toilet even if it does not contain excrement[121]. Mar Uqba[122] said: a pig is a moving toilet. Rebbi Jonah[123] investigated: A pebble on the sea shore, what is the rule?[124] Rebbi Ammi the physician[125] said: Rebbi Jeremiah taught that one may pass it by *pylyvs*[126], but one does not trust this ruling[127].

120 May one pray in the room in which people are naked if the installation is in use?

121 The rules of toilets, in which all religious acts are forbidden, are explained in Chapter 3, both in Yerushalmi (fol. 6d) and Babli (*Berakhot* 26a).

122 It is questionable whether this is a statement of Mar Uqba, *Resh Galuta* (Head of the Diaspora) in the time of Rav. The author of the statement is either Rabbana Uqba, grandson of Mar Uqba and Rav, or, more likely, Rav Uqba bar Ḥama, student and son-in-law of Rav Ḥisda. In the Babli (*Berakhot* 25a), the statement is attributed to Rav Papa, student of Rav Ḥisda's student Rava (brother-in-law of Rav Uqba bar Ḥama).

123 Head of the Yeshivah of Tiberias together with the Amora Rebbi Yose, of the fourth generation of Amoraïm, and a student of Rebbi Jeremiah.

124 May one pray next to a pebble on the seashore covered with excrement, when one has to assume that some human used the pebble to cleanse himself after defecating, but in the meantime waves covered the pebble many times and it does not smell any more?

125 An Amora about whom nothing more is known.

126 Perhaps compare פיליוס to Latin *pileus, pilleus*, "bonnet, felt hat", also Greek πίλινος "of felt", πιλίον "a bandage" (E. G.). The reading of the Rome manuscript is פיליונס. The word appears as פוליוס in Mishnah *Niddah* 8:1; Rashi there explains the word by old French *orel*, a scarf; *Arukh*, in its Italian translation *ossi*, means a scarf used to cover the mouth. The meaning

therefore is that Rebbi Jeremiah counsels to cover one's face with a scarf. (Musaphia reads *pallium*, "coverlet, gown.")

127 It is not clear whether the rejection of Rebbi Jeremiah's statement is from Rebbi Ammi the physician or from the editor of the Talmud.

רִבִּי זְעִירָא בְשֵׁם אַבָּא בַר יִרְמְיָה אוֹכֵל בָּהֶן אֲכִילַת עֲרַאִי. וְאֵינוֹ אוֹכֵל בָּהֶן אֲכִילַת קֶבַע. יָשֵׁן בָּהֶן שִׁינַּת עֲרַאִי. וְאֵין יָשֵׁן בָּהֶן שִׁינַּת קֶבַע. אִית תְּנָיֵי תַנֵּי מְבָרֵךְ פַּעַם אַחַת. אִית תְּנָיֵי תַנֵּי פַּעֲמַיִן. מַאן דָּמַר פַּעַם אַחַת נִיחָא. מַאן דָּמַר מְבָרֵךְ שְׁתֵּי פְעָמִים הָא אָכַל וְאֵינָן עִילּוֹי. אָמַר רִבִּי זְעִירָא קַייְמָא אַבָּא בַר יִרְמְיָה בְּאוֹכֵל בָּהֶן אֲכִילַת עֲרַאִי.

Rebbi Zeïra in the name of Abba bar Jeremiah[128]: One may eat a snack while wearing them[129], but one may not eat a regular meal while wearing them; one may doze[130] while wearing them, but one may not sleep while wearing them. Some Tannaïm formulate: One says the benediction once; some Tannaïm formulate: One says the benediction twice[131]. He who says one says the benediction once, how can he be right? He who says, one says the benediction twice, because he ate and then they are not on him. Rebbi Zeïra said, Abba bar Jeremiah talks about one who eats only snacks.

128 A Babylonian Amora (in the Babli he has a title and is called Rabba bar Jeremiah, short for Rav Abba bar Jeremiah), a student of Rav and possibly the son of Rav's companion Rav Jeremiah bar Abba. From the following it is clear that Rabba bar Jeremiah quotes the ruling as a traditional one from Tannaïm, not a new amoraic ruling. In the Babli (*Berakhot* 23b, *Sukkah* 41b), the second part of his statement, about sleeping, is introduced as an anonymous tannaitic statement (תנו רבנן).

129 The *tefillin*. A snack is a meal which does not involve bread. The rule about eating is not mentioned in the Babli; hence, the Babli agrees with it.

130 Dozing is defined as "sleeping and not sleeping." The Babli forbids both dozing and sleeping.

131 It is also possible to read פַּעֲמַיִן

"several times" but the discussion in the next sentence mentions "two times". The entire sentence is a continuation of the first statement of Abba bar Jeremiah; he is reported by Rebbi Zeïra to have said that one may eat a snack and doze while wearing *tefillin*, R. Zeïra then reports that some Tannaïm require that one recite the benediction over *tefillin* once a day, but some others say that the benediction is recited (at least) two times a day. The objection is that (except for a fast day) one has to eat, hence one has to take off one's *tefillin* and put them on again, certainly with a benediction. The anwer is that some people eat only snacks during daytime; hence, it is proved that the Tanna agrees with Abba bar Jeremiah that for a snack one does not have to remove his *tefillin*.

רִבִּי זְעִירָא בְּשֵׁם רִבִּי אַבָּא לֹא יִכָּנֵס אָדָם לְבֵית הַמַּיִם וּסְפָרָיו וּתְפִילָּיו בְּיָדָיו. רִבִּי יוֹחָנָן כַּד הֲוָה סִיפְרָא בְּיָדֵיהּ הֲוָה יָהֵיב לֵיהּ לַחוֹרָן. כַּד הַוְייָן תְּפִילּוֹי עִילוֹי הֲוָה קָאֵי בוֹן. מַתְנִיתָא פְלִיגָא עַל אַבָּא בַּר יִרְמְיָה נִכְנַס אָדָם לְבֵית הַמַּיִם וּסְפָרָיו וּתְפִילָּיו בְּיָדוֹ. אָמַר רִבִּי זְעִירָא קַיְימָא אַבָּא בַּר יִרְמְיָה כַּאן בְּיָכוֹל לְלוֹבְשָׁן. כַּאן בְּשֶׁאֵינוֹ יָכוֹל לְלוֹבְשָׁן. דְּלָכֵן מִצְוָה לֹא עֲבֵיד בוֹן. לָמָּה הוּא מְבַזֵּי לוֹן.

Rebbi Zeïra in the name of (Rebbi) Abba [bar Jeremiah][132]: A person should not enter a urinal[133] with his books or *tefillin* in his hands. Rebbi Yoḥanan, when he had a book[134] in his hand he gave it to somebody else. When his *tefillin* were on him, he stood in them[135]. A *baraita* disagrees with Abba bar Jeremiah: A man may enter a urinal with his books or *tefillin* in his hand. Rebbi Zeïra said: Abba bar Jeremiah refers to one case where he can wear them, and to another case where he cannot wear them[136]. For if he cannot perform a *mitzwah* with them, why should he degrade them?

132 While all sources have here "Rebbi Abba", the continuation shows that one must read "(Rav) Abba bar Jeremiah". This is also required since the next statement of Rebbi Zeïra, unrelated to the subject under

discussion, is only quoted because it also is in the name of Abba bar Jeremiah.

133 R. Eleazar Askari (followed by *Pene Moshe*) wants to identify the "house of water" with a toilet since in Arabic a toilet is called בֵּית אַלְמָא "house of water", but L. Ginzburg already noted that this is impossible; in the Yerushalmi as in the Babli a toilet is called בית הכסא . In the Tosephta (*Sanhedrin* 4:8) it is stated that a king, who has to write for himself a Torah that has to accompany him everywhere (*Deut.* 17:19), may not take the Torah with him to the "house of water". This rule is quoted in Babli *Sanhedrin* 21b, in the reading of R. Ḥananel and ms. ק, in the formulation that he takes the Torah with him neither to the bathhouse, nor to the toilet, nor to urinate. Hence, the toilet and the "house of water" are two different things.

134 In the Babli (*Berakhot* 23a), a book of sermons.

135 The Babli (*loc. cit.*) reports that Rebbi Yoḥanan put the *tefillin* in a pouch which he kept in his hand , not that he was wearing them. But the Babli does not speak about a urinal (with canalization, after the Roman fashion) but of a toilet, i. e., an outhouse. Roman canalization was unknown in Babylonia. Hence, the seemingly parallel passages in reality deal with different subjects.

136 This distinction is also reported in the Babli (*loc. cit.*) in the name of Rebbi Zera (Zeïra). If one takes off the *tefillin* in the evening, when there is not time anymore to put them on afterwards, one must put the *tefillin* in a designated bag or chest so as to treat them with respect. Temporary disrespect is only authorized if *tefillin* have to be ready for immediate use.

בָּרִאשׁוֹנָה הָיוּ נוֹתְנִין אוֹתָן לַחֲבֵירֵיהֶן וְהָיוּ נוֹטְלִין אוֹתָן וּבוֹרְחִין. הִתְקִינוּ שֶׁיְּהוּ מַנִּיחִין בְּחוֹרִין. וּכְשֶׁאִירַע אוֹתוֹ מַעֲשֶׂה הִתְקִינוּ שֶׁיְּהֵא אָדָם נִכְנַס וְהֵן בְּיָדוֹ. רִבִּי יַעֲקֹב בַּר אָחָא בְשֵׁם רִבִּי זְעִירָא אָמַר וְהוּא שֶׁיְּהֵא בַּיּוֹם כְּדֵי לְלוֹבְשָׁן. אֲבָל אִם אֵין בַּיּוֹם כְּדֵי לְלוֹבְשָׁן אָסוּר. דְּלָכֵן מִצְוָה לֹא עֲבֵיד בּוֹן. לָמָּה הוּא מְבַזֵּי לוֹן. מַיְישָׁא בַּר בְּרֵיהּ דְּרִבִּי יְהוֹשֻׁעַ בֶּן לֵוִי אָמַר מַאן דַּעֲבַד טַבָאוּת עוֹשֶׂה לָהֶן כִּיס שֶׁל טֶפַח וְנוֹתְנָן עַל לִבּוֹ. מַה טַעַם שִׁוִּיתִי יי לְנֶגְדִּי תָמִיד. תַּמָּן אָמְרִין כָּל־שֶׁאֵינוֹ כֶאֱלִישָׁע בַּעַל כְּנָפַיִם לֹא יִלְבַּשׁ תְּפִילִין.

First they were giving them[137] to others; these were taking them and fleeing. They decreed that one should put them in holes in the wall. When that incident[138] happened, they decreed that a person should enter and keep them in his hand. Rebbi Jacob bar Aḥa[139] in the name of Rebbi Zeïra said: but only if there is time left during the day to put them on again. But if there is no time left in the day to put them on, it is forbidden. For if he cannot perform a *mitzwah* with them, why should he degrade them? Maisha (Moses), grandson of R. Joshua ben Levi, said: He who wants to do it right, makes for them a pouch the size of a handbreadth and puts them on his heart[140]. What is the reason? (*Ps*. 16:8): "I put the Eternal always before me." There[141] they say: He who is not like Elisha of the bird's wings should not put on *tefillin*.

137 The *tefillin*, when somebody was entering a toilet. In the parallel in the Babli (*Berakhot* 23a), it is not mentioned that first one had to hand the *tefillin*, which represent a considerable monetary worth, to other people.

138 The incident is decribed in detail in the Babli (*loc. cit.*): A prostitute found a pair of *tefillin* in a hole near a public toilet, took them, and bragged publicly that she had received them for her services from a certain holy man who then committed suicide as a consequence of the public scandal.

139 A colleague of Rebbi Zeïra. The argument here, relating to a toilet, is parallel to the preceding one, relating to a urinal.

140 A pouch with straps so that in case of need one can put the *tefillin* in the pouch and carry them hanging under his outer garment, the strap going around his neck. Since one needs the pouch anyhow for storing the *tefillin* during nighttime, the counsel of Rebbi Maishe is only to put the straps on so that the pouch can be used also during daytime. The Babli (24a) forbids expressly to have the *tefillin* hanging on its own straps (not those of a pouch).

141 In Babylonia. The parallel in the Babli (*Šabbat* 49a) reads: "Rebbi Yannai said: *Tefillin* need a clean body, like Elisha of the bird's wings." R. Z. Frankel points out that at the start of

fol. 4c, the Yerushalmi quotes that "Rebbi Yannai said: *Tefillin* need a clean body"; hence, the reference to Elisha of the bird-wings is really a Babylonian addition. The story is told only in the Babli, *loc. cit.*, that Elisha was wearing *tefillin* when, in the aftermath of the war of Bar Kokhba, wearing *tefillin* was a capital crime. But he took them off when he saw a policeman and kept them in his hands. When the policeman asked him what he held in his hands, he said: "a couple of bird's wings." When he was ordered to open his hands, two birds flew away and his life was saved. (This story shows again that *tefillin* cases were not supposed to be larger than about $^3/_8$th of an inch square.)

The implication of this Babylonian ruling is that nobody can be expected to keep his body perfectly clean for very long; hence, *tefillin* should be removed after prayers.

רִבִּי זְעִירָא בְּשֵׁם רַב אַבָּא בַּר יִרְמְיָה לֹא יִכָּנֵס אָדָם לְבֵית הַקְּבָרוֹת וְיַעֲשֶׂה צְרָכָיו שָׁם. וְאִם עָשָׂה כֵן עָלָיו הַכָּתוּב אוֹמֵר לוֹעֵג לָרָשׁ חֵרֵף עוֹשֵׂהוּ. דֵּלְמָה רִבִּי חִיָּא רוּבָּא וְרִבִּי יוֹנָתָן הָיוּ מְהַלְּכִין קוֹמֵי עַרְסֵיהּ דְּרִבִּי שִׁמְעוֹן בַּר יוֹסֵי בַּר לַקּוֹנְיָא וַהֲוָה רִבִּי יוֹנָתָן מַפְסֵעַ עַל קִבְרֵיהּ. (fol. 4d) אָמַר לֵיהּ רִבִּי חִיָּא רוּבָּא כְּדוֹן אִינּוּן מֵימַר לְמָחָר אִינּוּן גַּבָּן וְאִינּוּן מְעִיקִין לָן. אָמַר לֵיהּ וַחֲכָמִין אִינּוּן כְּלוּם לָא כֵן כְּתִב וְהַמֵּתִים אֵינָם יוֹדְעִים מְאוּמָה. אָמַר לֵיהּ לִקְרוֹת אַתְּ יוֹדֵעַ. לִדְרוֹשׁ אֵין אַתְּ יוֹדֵעַ. כִּי הַחַיִּים יוֹדְעִים שֶׁיָּמוּתוּ אֵלּוּ הַצַּדִּיקִים שֶׁאֲפִילוּ בְּמִיתָתָן קְרוּיִין חַיִּים. וְהַמֵּתִים אֵינָם יוֹדְעִים מְאוּמָה אֵלּוּ הָרְשָׁעִים שֶׁאֲפִילוּ בְחַיֵּיהֶן קְרוּיִין מֵתִים. מְנַיִין שֶׁהָרְשָׁעִים אֲפִילוּ בְחַיֵּיהֶן קְרוּיִין מֵתִים שֶׁנֶּאֱמַר כִּי לֹא אֶחְפּוֹץ בְּמוֹת הַמֵּת. וְכִי הַמֵּת מֵת. אֶלָּא אֵילוּ הָרְשָׁעִים שֶׁאֲפִילוּ בְחַיֵּיהֶן קְרוּיִין מֵתִים. וּמְנַיִין שֶׁהַצַּדִּיקִים אֲפִילוּ בְּמִיתָתָן קְרוּיִין חַיִּים. דִּכְתִיב וַיֹּאמֶר אֵלָיו זֹאת הָאָרֶץ אֲשֶׁר נִשְׁבַּעְתִּי לְאַבְרָהָם לְיִצְחָק וּלְיַעֲקֹב לֵאמֹר. מַה תַּלְמוּד לֹאמַר לֵאמֹר. אָמַר לוֹ לֵךְ וֶאֱמוֹר לָאָבוֹת כָּל־מַה שֶׁהִתְנֵיתִי לָכֶם עָשִׂיתִי לִבְנֵיכֶם אַחֲרֵיכֶם.

Rebbi Zeïra in the name of Rav Abba bar Jeremiah: A person may not enter a cemetery and relieve himself there.[142] When he did it anyway, about him the verse says (*Prov.* 17:5) "He who makes fun of the poor blasphemes his Maker."[143] Clarification: The great Rebbi Ḥiyya and Rebbi Jonathan[144] were walking before the bier of Rebbi Simeon bar Yose bar Laqonia when Rebbi Jonathan stepped over his grave. The great Rebbi Ḥiyya said to him: About that they will say, tomorrow they will be with us but they hurt us. He answered him, do they know anything? Is it not written: (*Prov.* 9:5) "But the dead do not know anything." He told him: you know how to read, you do not know how to preach. (*Prov.* 9:5) "The living know that they will die", these are the Just who even in death are considered living; "but the dead do not know anything;" these are the wicked who even in life are called dead. From where that the wicked even in life are called dead? It is said (*Ez.* 18:32) "For I have no pleasure in the death of the dead;" how can a dead person die? But these are the wicked who even in life are called dead. And from where that the Just even in death are considered living? It is written (*Deut.* 34:4) "And He said to him: This is the land I had sworn to Abraham, Isaac, and Jacob, to tell." Why does the verse say "to tell"? He said to him: go and tell the patriarchs that all I had promised I fulfilled to your descendants after you.

142 The connection with the preceding section is that this is a statement of Rebbi Zeïra in the name of Rav Abba bar Jeremiah, and it speaks about relieving oneself.

143 He who relieves himself in the cemetery makes fun of the dead twofold; first he shows his contempt for the dead and then he does something that the dead can do no more. Even graveside sermons are unacceptable in Judaism since the dead can no longer have any Torah thoughts.

144 The greatest of the preachers of the first generation of Amoraïm, student of R. Simeon bar Yose bar Laqonia, a preacher of the last generation of Tannaïm who was the brother-in-law of the son of R. Simeon bar Yoḥai.

עִירֵב אֶת הָאוֹתִיּוֹת. אִית תְּנָיֵי תַנֵּי כָּשֵׁר. וְאִית תְּנָיֵי תַנֵּי פָּסוּל. רִבִּי אִידִי בְשֵׁם רִבִּי שִׁמְעוֹן בְּשֵׁם רִבִּי יוֹחָנָן מַן דָּמַר כָּשֵׁר מִלְּמַטָּן. מַן דָּמַר פָּסוּל מִלְּמַעֲלָן. כְּגוֹן אַרְצֵינוּ תִּפְאַרְתֵּינוּ. אַרְצְךָ צְרִיכָה. תִּפְאַרְתְּךָ צְרִיכָה.

If one connected the letters[145]; there is a Tanna who stated: it is valid, and there is a Tanna who stated: it is invalid. Rebbi Idi[146] in the name of Rebbi Simeon in the name of Rebbi Yoḥanan: He who says it is valid, below; he who said it is invalid, on top. For example, **ארצנו, תפארתנו**. **ארצך** is questionable, **תפארתך** is questionable.

145 One speaks here about writing *tefillin, mezuzot* and Torah scrolls, not about wearing them. The main discussion is in Yerushalmi *Megillah* 1:9; here it is quoted since it is somehow connected with the topic of *tefillin* but mainly because it belongs to a sequence of statements by Rebbi Idi in the name of Rebbi Simeon in the name of Rebbi Yoḥanan, which belong to the topic of prayer. The explanation of this paragraph follows the interpretation of *Rashba* (Solomon ben Adrat, *Responsa*, vol. 1, #711).

The problem is the legal status of a holy text in which two letters touch one another. The Babli states (*Menaḥot* 49a) that every letter must be surrounded by white parchment. The Yerushalmi has no equivalent statement but one may assume that it subscribes to the same standard. It is also required that a letter should be written, not carved out. Hence, if a letter is completely written and its foot accidentally touches the following letter, as with a slightly too long foot of נ in נו, one may scratch off the superfluous length and has a complete acceptable letter. But when a letter has its head elongated, so that from the start the letter was not standing free, then the entire letter has to be scratched out and the writing has to start anew. The questionable case is a situation with a letter that is hanging down below the line, as in the combination תך when the small foot of ת meets the downward stroke of ך. In that case, the ת was complete but the ך was not; this case remains unsettled (i. e., for practical rulings both letters have to be erased and rewritten.)

146 A Babylonian who became a Galilean Amora in the Yeshivah of Rebbi Ammi. The Rebbi Simeon here is Rebbi Simeon ben Laqish.

רִבִּי אִידִי בְּשֵׁם רִבִּי שִׁמְעוֹן בְּשֵׁם רִבִּי יוֹחָנָן לֹא יַעֲמוֹד אָדָם בְּמָקוֹם גָּבוֹהַּ וְיִתְפַּלֵּל. מַה טַעַם אָמַר רִבִּי אַבָּא בְּרֵיהּ דְּרַב פַּפַּי מִמַּעֲמַקִּים קְרָאתִיךָ יי׳.

Rebbi Idi in the name of Rebbi Simeon in the name of Rebbi Yoḥanan[147]: No man should stand at an elevated place and pray. What is the reason? Rebbi Abba the son of R. Pappai[148] said: (*Ps.* 130:1) "From the depth I call on You, o Eternal!"

147 These are the correct names, appearing in the parallel in *Megillah* 1:9 and in the Rome ms. here. The parallel in the Babli (*Berakhot* 10) is aatributed to Rebbi Yose ben R. Ḥanina in the name of the Tanna Rebbi Eliëzer ben Jacob. Venice print: ר' אידי בר' שמעון בשם ר' יוסה.

148 It seems that the name must be "son of *Rebbi* Pappai"; the Galilean Amora Rebbi Abba lived a generation before the Babylonian Amora Rav Pappi, one of the successors of Rava.

אָמַר רִבִּי אִידִי בְּשֵׁם רִבִּי שִׁמְעוֹן בְּשֵׁם רִבִּי יוֹחָנָן לֹא יַעֲמוֹד אָדָם וְיִתְפַּלֵּל וְצָרִיךְ לִנְקָבָיו. מַה טַעַם הִכּוֹן לִקְרַאת אֱלֹהֶיךָ יִשְׂרָאֵל. אָמַר רִבִּי אֲלֶכְסַנְדְּרִי שְׁמוֹר רַגְלְךָ כַּאֲשֶׁר תֵּלֵךְ אֶל בֵּית אֱלֹהִים שְׁמוֹר עַצְמְךָ מִן הַטִּיפִּים הַיּוֹצְאוֹת מִבֵּין רַגְלֶיךָ. הָדָא דְתֵימַר בְּדַקִּין. אֲבָל בְּגַסִּין אִם יָכוֹל לִסְבּוֹל יִסְבּוֹל.

Rebbi Idi in the name of Rebbi Simeon in the name of Rebbi Yoḥanan said: No man should pray when he has an urge to go to the bathroom[149]. What is the reason? (*Amos* 4:12) "Prepare yourself before Your God, o Israel!" Rebbi Alexandri said: (*Eccl.* 4:17) "Watch you feet when you go to God's house"; watch yourself from the drops that drip from between your feet. That means, for urine. But for defecation, if he can bear it, let him bear it[150].

149 In the Babli (*Berakhot* 23a) this appears as a statement of R. Samuel ben Naḥmani in the name of Rebbi Jonathan. It is really a Tosephta (*Berakhot* 2:18).

150 The Babli disagrees and states

that prayer is only permitted when one is able to walk 4 *mil* without going to the bathroom (about a 70 minutes' walk).

רִבִּי יַעֲקֹב בַּר אַבַּיי בְּשֵׁם רִבִּי אָחָא שְׁמוֹר רַגְלְךָ כַּאֲשֶׁר תֵּלֵךְ אֶל בֵּית אֱלֹהִים שְׁמוֹר עַצְמְךָ כְּשֶׁתְּהֵא נִקְרָא אֶל בֵּית אֱלֹהִים שֶׁתְּהֵא טָהוֹר וְנָקִי. אָמַר רִבִּי אַבָּא יְהִי מְקוֹרְךָ בָרוּךְ. יְהִי מִקְרָאֵךְ לַקֶּבֶר בָּרוּךְ. אָמַר רִבִּי בֶּרֶכְיָה עֵת לָלֶדֶת וְעֵת לָמוּת. אַשְׁרֵי אָדָם שֶׁשְּׁעַת מִיתָתוֹ כִּשְׁעַת לֵידָתוֹ. מַה שְּׁעַת לֵידָתוֹ נָקִי כָּךְ בִּשְׁעַת מִיתָתוֹ.

Rebbi Jacob bar Abbai[151] in the name of Rebbi Aḥa: (*Eccl.* 4:17) "Watch you feet when you go to God's house"; watch yourself when you are called to God's house[152] that you should be pure and innocent. Rebbi Abba said: (*Prov.* 5:18) "Your fountain shall be blessed", your being called to the grave shall be blessed. Rebbi Berekhiah said (*Eccl.* 3:1): "A time to be born and a time to die", hail to the man whose hour of death is like the hour of his birth; just as at the hour of his birth he was innocent so at the hour of his death may he be innocent.

151 An Israeli Amora of the last generation. His statement is placed here since it gives a different interpretation of the last verse quoted before. In the Babli (*loc. cit.*) this is also a statement of R. Samuel bar Naḥmani in the name of Rebbi Jonathan, i. e., of the first generations of Israeli Amoraïm.

152 I. e., when you die.

משנה ד: הַקּוֹרֵא אֶת שְׁמַע וְלֹא הִשְׁמִיעַ לְאָזְנוֹ (רִבִּי יְהוּדָה אוֹמֵר) יָצָא. רִבִּי יוֹסֵי אוֹמֵר לֹא יָצָא. קָרָא וְלֹא דִקְדֵּק בְּאוֹתִיּוֹתֶיהָ רִבִּי יוֹסֵי אוֹמֵר יָצָא וְרִבִּי יְהוּדָה אוֹמֵר לֹא יָצָא. הַקּוֹרֵא לְמַפְרֵעַ לֹא יָצָא. קָרָא וְטָעָה יַחְזוֹר לְמָקוֹם שֶׁטָּעָה.

Mishnah 4: He who recited the *Shema'* and did not make his ear hear, (Rebbi Yehudah says that)[153] he has fulfilled his obligation, Rebbi Yose says that he has not fulfilled his obligation. If he recited and was not exact in its letters[154], Rebbi Yose says that he has fulfilled his obligation, Rebbi Yehudah says that he has not fulfilled his obligation. He who reads backwards has not fulfilled his obligation. If he recited and made a mistake then he should return to the place of the mistake.

153 In the separate Mishnah at the start of the chapter (fol. 4a), as well as in most Mishnah and Babli manuscripts, the words in parenthesis are missing. However, in some manuscripts both of Mishnah and Babli, the words appear. It seems from the *Halakhah* that the editors of the Yerushalmi did not read the words in parenthesis and, maybe, considered the full text as a *baraita*. A similar instance appears in the Babli (15a) where the Mishnah is presented in this form: He who recited the *Shema'* and did not make his ear hear has fulfilled his obligation, and the Gemara two lines later treats this as anonymous statement, but five lines further down quotes the Mishnah (דתנן) as: 'He who recited the *Shema'* and did not make his ear hear has fulfilled his obligation, these are the words of Rebbi Yehudah.' One of the editors of 18th Cent. editions of the Talmud, R. Joel Sirkes known as *Baḥ*, wants to cross out the last part of the quote, but the Yerushalmi shows that two versions of the Mishnah did exist and, since it is impossible to write two versions at the same place, one is quoted as a separate Mishnah and the other in the text.

154 I. e., he mispronounced or slurred.

הלכה ד: רַב אָמַר הֲלָכָה כְדִבְרֵי שְׁנֵיהֶן לְהָקֵל. דִּלָכֵן מַה כֵן אָמְרִין סְתָמָה וְרִבִּי יוֹסֵי הֲלָכָה כִסְתָמָא. רִבִּי יוֹסֵי וְרִבִּי יְהוּדָה הֲלָכָה כְרִבִּי יוֹסֵי. וּמַה צְרִיכָא לְמֵימַר רַב הֲלָכָה כְדִבְרֵי שְׁנֵיהֶן לְהָקֵל. אֶלָּא בְגִין שָׁמַע דְּתַנֵּי לָהּ רִבִּי חִיָּיא בְשֵׁם רִבִּי מֵאִיר לְפוּם כֵּן צָרִיךְ לְמֵימַר הֲלָכָה כְדִבְרֵי שְׁנֵיהֶן לְהָקֵל.

Halakhah 4: Rav said: practice follows both of them for leniency[155]. If it were not so, what could one say? An anonymous statement and Rebbi

Yose, practice follows the anonymous[156]. Rebbi Yose and Rebbi Yehudah, practice follows Rebbi Yose[157]. So why does Rav have to say, practice follows both of them for leniency? Because he had heard Rebbi Ḥiyya formulating it in the name of Rebbi Meïr[158], he has to say that practice follows both of them for leniency.

155 In the Babli (*Berakhot* 15b), this is a statement of Rebbi Ṭabi in the name of Rebbi Josiah; the latter was a student of Rebbi Yoḥanan. The statement in the Babli is accepted without discussion because, as Rav Haï Gaon points out in his commentary, the Talmud previously did establish that the first statement is Rebbi Yehudah's and, therefore, the question asked in the Yerushalmi has no place in the Babli.

One may assume that the fact that the ruling is attributed to a Babylonian in the Yerushalmi and to a Galilean in the Babli is intentional, to show that this is the universally accepted practice [necessary, because in general borrowing leniencies from opposing points of view is frowned upon.]

156 Here, the Yerushalmi uses the Mishnah without the clause which identifies Rebbi Yehudah as the author. An anonymous statement in the Mishnah gives the consensus of the Sages and therefore has the force of law.

157 This is also the position of the Babli, *Erubin* 46b. It follows that the statement of Rav seems superfluous.

158 In the Babli (*loc. cit.*), Rebbi Meïr states that the obligation of reciting *Shema'* "is in the mind"; this implies that one does not have to hear what he himself is saying. Since the Mishnah or an equivalent is never quoted in the name of Rebbi Meïr, R. Zachariah Frankel wants to correct "Rebbi Meïr" to "Rebbi Yehudah" and considers the second version of the Mishnah in both Talmudim as the Mishnah of Rebbi Ḥiyya, in contrast to the Mishnah of Rebbi that is formulated anonymously. However, there is no textual support for such a theory.

Practice follows Rebbi Yose even against Rebbi Meïr; hence, the statement of Rav is necessary for the first part of the Mishnah.

תַּנֵּי נִתְפַּלֵּל וְלֹא הִשְׁמִיעַ לְאָזְנוֹ יָצָא. לְמִי נִצְרְכָה לְרִבִּי יוֹסֵי. הַיידֵין רִבִּי יוֹסֵי הֲדָא דְתַנִּינָן הַקּוֹרֵא אֶת שְׁמַע וְלֹא הִשְׁמִיעַ לְאָזְנוֹ יָצָא. וְרִבִּי יוֹסֵי אוֹמֵר לֹא יָצָא. אָמַר רַב מַתָּנָה דְּרִבִּי יוֹסֵי הִיא. אָמַר רִבִּי יוֹסֵי הֲוֵינָן סָבְרִין מֵימַר מַה פְלִיגִין רַבָּנָן וְרִבִּי יוֹסֵי בִּשְׁמַע דִּכְתִיב בָּהּ שְׁמַע. הָא שְׁאָר כָּל־הַמִּצְוֹת לֹא. מִן דָּמַר רַב מַתָּנָה דְּרִבִּי יוֹסֵי הִיא הֲוֵי הִיא שְׁאָר כָּל הַמִּצְוֹת. מַאי טַעֲמָא דְּרִבִּי יוֹסֵי. וְהַאֲזַנְתָּ לְמִצְוֹתָיו. יִשְׁמְעוּ אָזְנֶךָ מַה שֶׁפִּיךָ מְדַבֵּר.

It was stated: "He who did pray[159] and did not make his ear hear did fulfill his obligation." For whom do we need that? For Rebbi Yose! For which statement of Rebbi Yose? For that which we have stated: "He who recites the *Shema'* and did not make his ear hear has fulfilled his obligation, Rebbi Yose says that he has not fulfilled his obligation." Rav Mattanah[160] said: That formulation is Rebbi Yose's. Rebbi Yose[161] said: We could be of the opinion that the rabbis and Rebbi Yose disagree only about *Shema'* since there it is written: "hear!", but not about any other obligations. Since Rav Mattanah said "that formulation is Rebbi Yose's", it is the same for all obligations. What is the reason of Rebbi Yose? (*Ex.* 15:26) "Bend your ear to His commandments", your ears should hear what your mouth says.

159 The thrice daily *Amidah* prayer.

160 This paragraph and the following do not really belong here, they refer to the Mishnah *Megillah* 2:4: "The insane, the deaf and dumb, and minors cannot read the *Megillah* (for others)". Rav Mattanah notes that, obviously, one does not mean a deaf and dumb person who cannot talk, but a deaf person who cannot hear. Since the Mishnah is anonymous, it must be the consensus of the Sages that one cannot fulfill the obligation of reading the *Megillah* if one does not hear what he himself is saying. Hence, the general consensus in *Megillah* is identical with the opinion of Rebbi Yose in *Berakhot*. The practice, therefore, should follow Rebbi Yose for stringency, in contrast to Rav's statement in the preceding paragraph.

161 The Amora, one of the compilers of the Jerusalem Talmud.

אָמַר רַב חִסְדָּא לֵית כַּאן חֵרֵשׁ. הַשְׁגָּרַת לָשׁוֹן הִיא. מַתְנִיתָא לְרִבִּי יְהוּדָה. אָמַר רִבִּי יוֹסֵי מִסְתַּבְּרָא דְיוֹדֵי רַב חִסְדָּא בִתְרוּמוֹת דְּהִיא דְרִבִּי יוֹסֵי. אָמַר רִבִּי חֲנִינָא בְשֵׁם רַב חִסְדָּא דְּרִבִּי יוֹסֵי הִיא. אָמַר רִבִּי יוֹסֵי בֵּרִבִּי בוּן עַל כָּרְחֵיךְ אִיתְמַר דְּהִיא דְרִבִּי יוֹסֵי דְתַנִּינָן חֲמִישְׁתָּא קַדְמִייָתָא וְלֹא תַנִּיתָא עִמָּהֶן אִם מִשּׁוּם שֶׁאֵין תְּרוּמָתָן תְּרוּמָה. וְהָא תַנִּינָן חֲמִישְׁתָּא אַחֲרָנִייָתָא וְלֹא תַנִּיתָהּ עִמָּהֶן. הָא סוֹפָךְ מֵימַר דְּרִבִּי יוֹסֵי הִיא.

Rav Ḥisda said: The deaf and dumb person is not mentioned, it is a formula.[162] Then the Mishnah might be Rebbi Yehudah's. Rebbi Yose[163] said: It is reasonable to think that Rav Ḥisda concedes that the statement from *Terumot* is from Rebbi Yose[164]. Rabbi Ḥanina said in the name of Rav Ḥisda, this one is by Rebbi Yose. Rebbi Yose bar Rebbi Abun said: It must be said that that one is Rebbi Yose's since we have stated the first five cases and did not include it[165], because their *terumah* is no *terumah*. Then we have stated the five later ones and did not include it. So in the end you must say, that one is by Rebbi Yose[166].

162 Since in all legal matters the insane, the deaf and dumb, and minors are equally incapacitated, the people who had to memorize "insane and minors" automatically changed the phrase in their memories to "insane, deaf and dumb, and minors". After this correction, the Mishnah in *Megillah* may well be Rebbi Yehudah's.

163 The Amora.

164 *Terumah*, the heave, is the first gift of grain to the Cohen from the new harvest. There is no amount fixed for *terumah* in the Pentateuch; it must be consecrated explicitly. Only a person of sound mind can consecrate *terumah*. The first Mishnah in tractate *Terumot* reads: "Five categories of people cannot consecrate *terumah* and if they did it anyhow, their actions are null and void: the deaf and dumb, the insane, minors, one who is not the owner, and a non-Jew." The sixth Mishnah then reads: "Five categories of people should not consecrate *terumah* (since *a priori* it requires the recitation of a benediction) but if they did it anyhow their actions are valid: the speechless, the drunk, the naked, the blind, those impure by emission of

semen." In between it is explained that חרש means a deaf and dumb person who is not legally capable of acting but that the deaf who can talk belongs to the same category as the second group of five.

165 The case of the deaf who is able to speak.

166 Hence, the second Mishnah in *Terumot*, explaining that the deaf who is able to speak can give *terumah*, has to be formulated separately and could not be included in the sixth Mishnah since the first and sixths Mishnayot are Rebbi Yose's who will object to the inclusion of the deaf-but-not-speechless in the second group.

אֵלּוּ צָרִיךְ דִּקְדּוּק. עַל לְבָבְךָ. עַל לְבַבְכֶם. עֵשֶׂב בְּשָׂדְךָ. וַאֲבַדְתֶּם מְהֵרָה. הַכָּנָף פְּתִיל. אֶתְכֶם מֵאֶרֶץ. רִבִּי חֲנִינָא בְשֵׁם רִבִּי אָחָא אֲשֶׁר נִשְׁבַּע יי.

These need careful attention: *al-lĕvāvĕkhā, al-lĕvavkhem, ēśev bĕśādĕkhā, waăvadîem mĕħērāh, hakkānāph pĕtīl, etkhem mēereẓ*[167]. Rebbi Ḥanina in the name of Rebbi Aḥa: *ăšer nišba' ădonay*[168].

167 In the Babli (*Berakhot* 15b) this list is an appendix by Rava to a *baraita* stating that in reciting the *Shema'* one has to differentiate between identical sounds. There is no problem with the words in *Shema'* where final and initial l and m clash. More of a problem is the clash of soft and hard ב, פ. The late Prof. Y. Kutscher pointed out that in classical Arabic there is a tendency to pronounce fb as bb [*Contemporary Studies in North-Western Semitic*, Journal of Semitic Studies 10(1965) pp. 21-51, see p. 30] but it seems clear at least for ב which, under the influence of the Greek that was the common vernacular, in Galilee both ב and בּ were pronounced "v". For example, the technical term מחוור "logically consistent" in the Babli appears as מְחוּבָּר "connected" in Yerushalmi *Peah* 2:1, fol.16d. It does not make any sense to derive מחוור from Aramaic חוור "pale". Hence, Galilean מחבר sounded מחוור in Babylonian ears. (Possibly both ב and בּ were pronounced as "b" in Babylonia, as they still are today in dialects of Jews from Arabic speaking countries.) It is less certain but still possible that פ was pronounced "p-h" rather than "f".

168 In Biblical times, ע (') was a hard glottal sound similar to Arabian Arabic ع but in Talmudic times it was either silent (see the next paragraph) or very weak so that there was (almost) a double vowel a.

רִבִּי שְׁמוּאֵל בַּר חֲנִינָא בְּשֵׁם רִבִּי הוֹשַׁעְיָא יוֹצֵר אוֹר וּבוֹרֵא חוֹשֶׁךְ. דְּלָא יֵימַר יוֹצֵר אוֹר וּבוֹרֵא נוֹגַהּ. רִבִּי חַגַּיי בְּשֵׁם רִבִּי אַבָּא בַּר זַבְדָּא שָׁם שָׁרוּ לָךְ דְּלָא יֵימַר שָׁם הַלְלוּ לָךְ. רִבִּי לֵוִי רִבִּי אֶבְדִּימָא דְחֵיפָה בְּשֵׁם רִבִּי לֵוִי בַּר סִיסִי צָרִיךְ לְהַתִּיז לְמַעַן תִּזְכְּרוּ. רִבִּי יוֹנָה בְּשֵׁם רַב חִסְדָּא צָרִיךְ לְהַתִּיז כִּי לְעוֹלָם חַסְדּוֹ. תַּנֵּי אֵין מַעֲבִירִין לִפְנֵי הַתֵּיבָה לֹא חֵיפָנִין וְלֹא בֵּישָׁנִין וְלֹא טִיבְעוֹנִין מִפְּנֵי שֶׁהֵן עוֹשִׂין חֵיתִין הֵיהִין וְעַיְנִין אָאִין. אִם הָיָה לְשׁוֹנוֹ עָרוּךְ מוּתָּר.

Rebbi Samuel bar Ḥanina in the name of Rebbi Hoshaiah[169]: "He Who forms light and creates darkness[170]"; one should not say: "He Who forms light and creates radiance."

Rebbi Ḥaggai[171] in the name of Rebbi Abba bar Zavda[172]: "There they sang for You[173]", one should not say: "There they praised You".

Rebbi Levi, Rebbi Eudaimon[174] of Haifa, in the name of Rebbi Levi bar Sisi[175]: one has to pronounce *tizkeru* voiced[176]. Rebbi Jonah in the name of Rav Ḥisda: one has to pronounce *ki lĕʿôlām ḥasdô* voiced[177]. It was stated: One does not take as reader anyone from Haifa, Beth Sheän or Tivʿon since they read ח like ה[178] and ע like א. If his pronunciation was orderly, it would be permitted[179].

169 A Babylonian, student of Rav Yehudah and Rav Huna, who later emigrated to Israel and became student of Rebbi Yoḥanan.

170 This is the beginning of the first benediction before the *Shema'*, it appears here in the context of the recitation of *Shema'*. The language is that of the verse (*Is.* 45:7) "He Who forms light and creates darkness, makes peace and creates evil." In prayer, the verse is changed to "He Who forms light and creates darkness, makes peace and creates all" to soften the language. Rebbi Hoshaiah notes that one may not go so far as to eliminate the mention of darkness, in the words of the Babli (12a) "to mention night at day and day at night", to negate any Zoroastrian dualism.

171 A Babylonian who went to study in Tiberias.

172 A Galilean who went to study temporarily in Babylonia; he was a chief authority in Galilee after the death of Rebbi Yoḥanan. Both authors

mentioned here were familiar with the Babylonian prayer ritual.

173 In Halakhah 1:9, the Yerushalmi quotes the Babylonian version of a short benediction after *Shema'*: "We thank You that You took us out of Egypt and redeemed us from the house of slavery to thank Your Name". The Babli (14b) has the corresponding Galilean version: "We thank You that You took us out of Egypt and redeemed us from the house of slavery, did for us wonders and great deeds on the sea, and we sang for You". The version "There they praised You" seems to be an alternative Babylonian form that is rejected here (since it is not a proper introduction to the required recitation of *Ex.* 15:11,19. In later times, the Israeli standard introduction to these verses was בגילה ברנה בשמחה רבה ואמרו כולם, retained in the Ashkenazic service on holiday nights.)

174 An Amora of the second generation. His name Εὐδαίμων "fortunate" shows that the pronounciation of Greek in his time was as today, that υ = f = ב.

175 Levi who usually is quoted without title or patronymic.

176 Since voiced z (ז) and voiceless s (ס,שׂ) are similar sounds, care is needed to distinguish between תזכרו (*Num.* 15:40) "you shall remember" and תסכרו "you shall dam up", תשׂכרו "you shall hire", and even, under the influence of Greek, which knows no *sh* sound, תשכרו "you will get drunk".

177 It is not clear why one should pronounce חַסְדּוֹ with a soft *s*. R. Zachariah Frankel notes that the two Aramaic verbs חֲסַד *ḥăsad* "to be loving" and חַסֵּד *ḥassad* "to insult, degrade" differ in the quality of its *s* sound; hence, one has to take care that "truly, His kindness is forever" should not sound as "truly, His insulting is forever". It seems that while *s* should not really sound like *z*, care has to be taken not to make it sound like *ss*. Maybe the same difference was once heard between Hebrew חסד I "to show kindness" and חסד II "to insult."

178 Western Ashkenazic pronunciation treated ח like *hh* until the middle of the sixteenth Century. Under the influence of Polish, which in contrast to German has only one *ch*-sound, Ashkenazic pronunciation lost the difference between ח (*ḥ*) and כ (*kh*). In all other Jewish dialects, the problem is not the identification of כ,ח but of ח,ה . ע is lost in all Ashkenazic pronunciations; it is retained in Italian and Portuguese Hebrew as *ng*.

179 If he makes an effort and tries to realize the difference, even if he does not quite succeed.

פיסקא. הַקּוֹרֵא לְמַפְרֵעַ לֹא יָצָא. רִבִּי יוֹנָה אָמַר תַּנָּא רַב נַחְמָן בַּר אָדָא רִבִּי יוֹסֵי אוֹמֵר תַּנָּא נַחְמָן סַבָּא וְהָיוּ כְּדֶרֶךְ הֲוִייָתָן יְהוּ. תַּנֵּי אַף בְּהַלֵּל וּבִקְרִיאַת הַמְּגִילָּה כֵּן.

New Section. He who reads backwards[180] has not fulfilled his obligation. Rebbi Jonah said that Rav Naḥman bar Ada[181] stated, Rebbi Yose said that Naḥman the Old stated, (*Deut.* 6:6) "They shall be", they shall be unaltered[182]. We have stated: The same holds for *Hallel* and the reading of the Esther scroll.

180 Reading sentences out of order; reading words out of order is clearly useless since it makes no sense.

181 A Babylonian, student of Samuel. He probably is identical with "Naḥman the Old", to distinguish him from later Amoraïm also called Naḥman.

182 Taking the verb היה "to be" in the sense of "to exist".

נִיחָא בִקְרִיאַת הַמְּגִילָּה דִּכְתִיב בָּהּ כִּכְתָבָם. בְּרַם בְּהַלֵּלָא בְגִין דִּכְתִיב מִמִּזְרַח שֶׁמֶשׁ עַד מְבוֹאוֹ מְהוּלָּל שֵׁם יי מַה אַתְּ שְׁמַע מִינָּהּ אָמַר רִבִּי אָבוּן עוֹד הִיא אֲמוּרָה עַל הַסֵּדֶר. בְּצֵאת יִשְׂרָאֵל מִמִּצְרַיִם לְשֶׁעָבַר. לֹא לָנוּ יי לֹא לָנוּ לְדוֹרוֹת הַלָּלוּ. אָהַבְתִּי כִּי יִשְׁמַע יי אֶת קוֹלִי לִימוֹת הַמָּשִׁיחַ. אִסְרוּ חַג בָּעֲבוֹתִים לִימוֹת גּוֹג וּמָגוֹג. אֵלִי אַתָּה לֶעָתִיד לָבוֹא.

This is fine for the Esther scroll since it is written there (*Esther* 9:27): "As they are written"[183]. But for *Hallel*, since it is written (*Ps.* 113:3): "From sunrise to sunset, may the name of the Eternal be praised?"[184] What can you understand from that? Rebbi Abun said: It also is written in order. (*Ps.* 114:1) "When Israel left Egypt" in the past. (*Ps.* 115:1) "Not for us, o Eternal, not for us" in the present[185]. (*Ps.* 116:1) "I loved, truly the Eternal listened to my voice" in the days of the Messiah. (*Ps.* 118:27) "Bind the holiday sacrifice with ropes" in the days of Gog and Magog[186]. (*Ps.* 118:28) "You are my God" in the future world.

183 The verse reads: "The Jews confirmed and accepted for themselves, not to be cancelled, that they would observe these two days *as they are written* and it its time, every single year." Hence, the scroll must be read as it is written.

184 Since there is no difference between East and West, there should be no difference between before and after.

185 In the much more detailed parallel passage in the Babli (*Pesaḥim* 118a), this sentence is applied by Rebbi Yoḥanan either to the oppression by hostile governments or to the sufferings preceding the coming of the Messiah. That may be the meaning of the sentence here also. Alternatively, the psalm is interpreted there as the song of Hananiah, Mishael and Azariah in the fiery oven.

186 In the celebration after the final defeat of the forces of evil. In *Midrash Tehillim, Ps.* 118:24 "This is the day the Eternal made, let us rejoice and be happy on it" is taken to describe the time when one can be sure that the deliverance will not be followed by another oppression.

רִבִּי אָחָא בְשֵׁם רִבִּי יְהוֹשֻׁעַ בֶּן לֵוִי אַף מִי שֶׁהִתְקִין אֶת הַתְּפִילָּה הַזֹּאת עַל הַסֶּדֶר הִתְקִינָהּ. שָׁלֹשׁ בְּרָכוֹת הָרִאשׁוֹנוֹת וְשָׁלֹשׁ בְּרָכוֹת הָאַחֲרוֹנוֹת שִׁבְחוֹ שֶׁל מָקוֹם וְהָאֶמְצָעִיּוֹת צָרְכָן שֶׁל בְּרִיּוֹת. חָנֵּנוּ דֵעָה. חֲנַנְתָּנוּ דֵעָה רְצֵה תְשׁוּבָתֵנוּ. רָצִיתָ תְשׁוּבָתֵנוּ סְלַח לָנוּ. סָלַחְתָּ לָנוּ גָּאָלֵנוּ. גְּאַלְתָּנוּ רְפָה חָלְיֵינוּ. רִיפִּיתָ חָלְיֵינוּ בָּרֵךְ שְׁנוֹתֵינוּ. בֵּירַכְתָּ שְׁנוֹתֵינוּ קַבְּצֵנוּ. קִיבַּצְתָּנוּ שָׁפְטֵנוּ בְּצֶדֶק. שְׁפַטְתָּנוּ בְּצֶדֶק הַכְנַע קָמֵינוּ. הִכְנַעְתָּ קָמֵנוּ צַדְּקֵנוּ. צִדַּקְתָּנוּ בְּנֵה בֵיתְךָ וּשְׁמַע עֲתִירָתֵינוּ וּרְצֵנוּ בְתוֹכוֹ. לֵית צוֹרְכָה דִבְנֵה בֵיתְךָ וּשְׁמַע עֲתִירָתֵינוּ וּרְצֵנוּ בְתוֹכוֹ. אֶלָּא כְמַה דְאִישְׁתָּעֵי קַרְיָיא כֵּן אִישְׁתָּעֵית מַתְנִיתָא וַהֲבִיאוֹתִים אֶל הַר קָדְשִׁי וְשִׂמַּחְתִּים בְּבֵית תְּפִילָּתִי.

Rebbi Aḥa in the name of Rebbi Joshua ben Levi: Also he who composed this prayer[187] composed it in good order. The first three and the last three are the praise of the Omnipresent, the middle ones are the needs of the creatures. Give us knowledge. You gave us knowledge[188], accept our repentance. You accepted our repentance, forgive us. You forgave us, save us. You saved us, heal our diseases. You healed our diseases, bless our years. You blessed our years, gather us in. You gathered us in, judge us in justice. You judged us in justice, subdue those who arise against us.[189] You subdued those who arise against us, justify us[190]. You justified us, build Your house, listen to our supplications, be pleased with us in it. Is it necessary after "build Your house," listen to our supplications, be pleased with us in it[191]? But as the verse is, so is the tradition (*Is.* 56:7): "I shall bring them to My holy mountain, make them happy in My house of prayer.[193]"

187 The week-day 18 benedictions of the *Amidah*. Another derivation is given in the following paragraph.

188 The entire list should be read as a conditional: Assuming that You gave us knowledge (fourth benediction), please accept our repentance (fifth benediction). This is particularly evident in the second part, starting from the prayer for good years, which is a prayer for redemption and therefore future oriented even though the formulation here is in the past tense.

189 While the benediction against apostates was introduced at Jabneh and the rest of the *Amidah* is an institution of the Men of the Great Assembly, its place was chosen in the spirit of those who first formulated the prayer.

190 This is the text of the Rome and Genizah manuscripts, not like the Leyden manuscript and the Venice print which have צדקנו במשפט "justify us in law" that belongs to the benediction before the previous one, not to the one for the elders (and all) of Israel and the converts which follows after the imprecation against apostates.

191 After a prayer for the rebuilding of Jerusalem and the Temple, the prayers for acceptance of the prayer and the hope that our service be for God's pleasure may seem superfluous since acceptance of prayer and God's pleasure are guaranteed in the Temple.

192 As usual, the main argument is the part of the verse not quoted: "I shall bring them to My holy mountain," corresponds to the prayer for Jerusalem, "make them happy in My house of prayer" corresponds to the supplication for acceptance of our prayer, "their holocausts and sacrifices for pleasure on my altar", corresponds to the prayer for God's pleasure. There

is no benediction for the restitution of the dynasty of David here since in Israeli practice this was part of the prayer for Jerusalem; see the next paragraph.

אָמַר רִבִּי יִרְמְיָה מֵאָה וְעֶשְׂרִים זְקֵנִים וּמֵהֶם שְׁמוֹנִים וְכַמָּה נְבִיאִים הִתְקִינוּ אֶת הַתְּפִילָּה הַזֹּאת. וּמַה רָאוּ לִסְמוֹךְ הָאֵל הַקָּדוֹשׁ לְחוֹנֵן הַדָּעַת עַל שֵׁם וְהִקְדִּישׁוּ אֶת קְדוֹשׁ יַעֲקֹב. מַה כְתִיב בַּתְרֵיהּ וְיָדְעוּ תוֹעֵי רוּחַ בִּינָה. דֵּיעָה לִתְשׁוּבָה הַשְׁמֵן לֵב הָעָם הַזֶּה וְאָזְנָיו הַכְבֵּד וְעֵינָיו הָשַׁע וגו׳ עַד וּלְבָבוֹ יָבִין וָשָׁב וְרָפָה לוֹ. תְּשׁוּבָה לִסְלִיחָה וְיָשׁוֹב אֶל יי וִירַחֲמֵהוּ וְאֶל אֱלֹהֵינוּ כִּי יַרְבֶּה לִסְלוֹחַ. סְלִיחָה לִגְאוּלָּה הַסּוֹלֵחַ לְכָל־עֲווֹנֵיְכִי הָרוֹפֵה לְכָל־תַּחֲלוּאָיְכִי הַגּוֹאֵל מִשַּׁחַת חַיֵּיכִי. וְיֹאמַר רוֹפֵא חוֹלִים קֳדָמוֹי. אָמַר רִבִּי אֲחָא מִפְּנֵי מַה הִתְקִינוּ גּוֹאֵל יִשְׂרָאֵל בְּרָכָה שְׁבִיעִית לְלַמְּדָךְ שֶׁאֵין יִשְׂרָאֵל נִגְאָלִין אֶלָּא בִשְׁבִיעִית. רִבִּי יוֹנָה בְּשֵׁם רִבִּי אָחָא שִׁיר הַמַּעֲלוֹת בְּשׁוּב יי אֶת שִׁיבַת (fol. 5a) צִיּוֹן שִׁירָה שְׁבִיעִית הִיא לְהוֹדִיעָךְ שֶׁאֵין יִשְׂרָאֵל נִגְאָלִין אֶלָּא בִשְׁבִיעִית. אָמַר רִבִּי חִיָּיא בַּר אַבָּא מִפְּנֵי מַה הִתְקִינוּ רוֹפֵא חוֹלִים בְּרָכָה שְׁמִינִית כְּנֶגֶד הַמִּילָה שֶׁהִיא לַשְּׁמִינִי. עַל שֵׁם בְּרִיתִי הָיְתָה אִתּוֹ הַחַיִּים. אָמַר רִבִּי אַלֶכְסַנְדְּרִי מִפְּנֵי מַה הִתְקִינוּ בִּרְכַּת הַשָּׁנִים בְּרָכָה תְשִׁיעִית כְּנֶגֶד קוֹל יי שׁוֹבֵר אֲרָזִים. שֶׁהוּא עָתִיד לִשְׁבּוֹר כָּל־בַּעֲלֵי שְׁעָרִים. רִבִּי לֵוִי בְשֵׁם רִבִּי אָחָא בַּר חֲנִינָא מַה רָאוּ לִסְמוֹךְ מְבָרֵךְ הַשָּׁנִים לִמְקַבֵּץ נִדְחֵי יִשְׂרָאֵל. עַל שֵׁם וְאַתֶּם הָרֵי יִשְׂרָאֵל עֲנַפְכֶם תִּתְּנוּ וּפֶרְיְכֶם תִּשְׂאוּ לְעַמִּי יִשְׂרָאֵל. לָמָּה כִּי קֵרְבוּ לָבוֹא. נִתְקַבְּצוּ הַגָּלִיּוֹת וְהַדִּין נַעֲשֶׂה הַזֵּדִין נִכְנָעִין וְהַצַּדִּיקִים שְׂמֵחִים. וְתַנֵּי עֲלָהּ כּוֹלֵל שֶׁל מִינִים וְשֶׁל רְשָׁעִים בְּמַכְנִיעַ זֵדִים. וְשֶׁל גֵּרִים וְשֶׁל זְקֵנִים בְּמִבְטָח לַצַּדִּיקִים. וְשֶׁל דָּוִד בְּבוֹנֵה יְרוּשָׁלַיִם. אַחַר יָשׁוּבוּ בְּנֵי יִשְׂרָאֵל וּבִקְשׁוּ אֶת יי אֱלֹהֵיהֶם וְאֵת דָּוִד מַלְכָּם.

[193]Rebbi Jeremiah said: 120 elders, among them more than 80 prophets, instituted this prayer. Why did they follow "the holy God"[194] by "He Who favors with knowledge"? Because (*Is.* 29:23-24) "they sanctify the Holy One of Jacob" is followed by "and those of erring spirit will know insight." "Knowledge" followed by "Repentance", (*Is.* 6:10) "Make

fat the heart of this people, make it hard of hearing and its eyes sticky, that it should not see with its eyes, nor hear with its ears, nor understand with its heart, because if it would repent then it would be healed." "Repentance" by "Forgiveness", (*Is*. 55:7) "He should return to the Lord that He would have mercy on him, and to our God because He forgives much." "Forgiveness" by "Redemption", (*Ps*. 103:2-3) "He Who forgives all your sins, He Who hears all your maladies, He Who redeems your soul from destruction." Then he should say "Healer of the sick" before that[195]. Rebbi Aḥa said: why did they institute "Redeemer of Israel" as the seventh benediction? To teach you that Israel will be redeemed only in a Seventh Year[196]. Rebbi Jonah in the name of Rebbi Aḥa: (*Ps*. 126) "A song of ascent. When the Eternal will return the returnees of Zion" is the seventh song, to show you that Israel will be redeemed only in a Seventh Year. Rebbi Ḥiyya bar Abba said: Why did they institute "Healer of the sick" as the eighth benediction? That is for circumcision which is done on the eighth, following (*Maleachi* 2:5) "My covenant was with him: Life"[197]. Rebbi Alexander said: Why did they institute "He Who blesses the years" as the ninth benediction? Corresponding to (*Ps*. 29:5) "The sound of the Eternal breaks cedars", since in the future He will break all market manipulators[198]. Rebbi Levi in the name of Rebbi Aḥa bar Ḥanina: Why did they follow "He Who blesses the years" by "Ingatherer of the dispersed of Israel"? Because of (*Ez*. 36:8) "you, mountains of Israel, sprout your branches and carry your fruits for my people Israel", why? "because they will soon come." When the dispersed are gathered in then justice will be done, the evildoers will succumb, and the just will be happy[199]. It was stated: One includes the apostates and the wicked in "He Who subdues the evildoers", the converts and the elders in "refuge of the just", David in

"Builder of Jerusalem"[200]. (*Hosea* 3:5) "Then the children of Israel will repent, seek the Eternal, their God, and their king David.[201]"

193 A parallel with slightly different treatment of the entire paragraph appears in Babli *Megillah* 17b-18a.

194 The third benediction of the *Amidah*. What follows is a description of the benedictions of the week-day *Amidah*.

195 Since in the verse redemption comes after healing. (Redemption here is personal redemption; redemption of the people is described by benedictions 9-14).

196 A Seventh Year (*shemiṭṭah*) in a Jubilee cycle. The "seventh song" in the next sentence is the seventh of the songs of ascent.

197 *The* Covenant refers to circumcision.

198 Manipulators of prices of basic commodities who are compared to cedars for their (financial) strength. In the Babli, R. Alexander quotes *Ps*. 10:15, which in Babylonian (and Rashi's) count was *Ps*. 9:36 and, therefore, is appropriate for the Ninth benediction. Our texts of Psalms which split an alphabetic acrostich between Psalms 9 and 10 is the Yerushalmi tradition which, therefore, cannot use the verse quoted in the Babli.

199 This describes benedictions 10-13. The wicked are Gentile governments that oppress the Jews. The evildoers are Jewish evildoers.

200 This is today the practice of Ashkenazic and Sephardic Jews. The Babylonian practice was not to mention the restoration of the Davidic dynasty in the benediction for Jerusalem, but to make it a separate benediction preceding the final benediction "He Who hears prayer". Only the Yemenite ritual follows the strict Babylonian style; the other Jewish groups pray twice for the Davidic dynasty, once in the Yerushalmi form of "Builder of Jerusalem" and then in the Babylonian form "He Who makes sprout the horn of salvation".

201 The verse concludes: "They will tremble for the Eternal and His Goodness at the End of Days", referring to Messianic times.

רַבָּנָן אָמְרֵי אָהֵן מַלְכָּא מְשִׁיחָה אִין מִן חַיָּיא הוּא דָּוִד שְׁמֵיהּ. אִין מִן דְּמָכִייָא הוּא דָּוִד שְׁמֵיהּ. אָמַר רִבִּי תַּנְחוּמָא אֲנָא אָמְרִי טַעְמָא וְעוֹשֶׂה חֶסֶד לִמְשִׁיחוֹ לְדָוִד.

The Rebbis say: This King Messiah, if he is from the living, his name is David. If he is from the dead, his name is David. Rebbi Tanḥuma said: I am declaring the reason (*Ps.* 18:51) "He gives kindness to His anointed, to David.[202]'

202 The previous discussion ended with the verse from Hosea, which indicates that in Messianic times all twelve tribes will seek their king David; it is clear that Hosea talks about the Messiah and calls him David. This gives rise to an insertion about the Messiah in this and the next paragraph.

The second argument is more explicit in the Babli, *Sanhedrin* 98b, where for the first case a verse in Jeremiah (30:9) is cited: "They shall serve the Eternal, their God, and their king David whom I shall raise for them" which also is written in the future tense. The second case, that the original David will be resurrected as Messiah, is based on a verse in Ezechiel (34:24) "I, the Eternal, shall be for them their God, and My servant David prince in their midst", seems to refer to the historical David in Messianic times. The Babylonian Talmud points out that a prince is less than a king and, therefore, the new King Messiah will have the status of a Roman Augustus whereas the resurrected David will occupy the position of Caesar, or Crown Prince. In any case, the next paragraph makes is quite clear that the Messiah was born on the day of the destruction of the Temple and that, therefore, nobody with a recorded date of birth can ever be considered as Messiah. There is no reason to believe that the Babli would disagree with this conclusion. In addition, Maimonides in his *Letter to Yemen* is quite adamant that the Messiah can only appear in the Land of Israel and must be a political figure.

רִבִּי יְהוֹשֻׁעַ בֶּן לֵוִי אָמַר צֶמַח שְׁמוֹ. רִבִּי יוּדַן בְּרֵיהּ דְּרִבִּי אַיְיבוּ אָמַר מְנַחֵם שְׁמוֹ. אָמַר חֲנִינָה בְּרֵיהּ דְּרִבִּי אַבָּהוּ וְלֹא פְלִיגֵי חוּשְׁבְּנֵיהּ דַּהֲדֵין כְּחוּשְׁבְּנֵיהּ דַּהֲדֵין הוּא צֶמַח הוּא מְנַחֵם. דָּמַר רִבִּי יוּדַן בְּרֵיהּ דְּרִבִּי אַיְיבוּ עוּבְדָּא הֲוָה בְּחַד יְהוּדָאֵי דַּהֲוָה קָאִים רְדִי בְּהָדֵי בִּקְעַת אַרְבֵּל גָּעַת תּוֹרְתֵיהּ קוּמוֹי עָבַר חַד עַרְבִיי וּשְׁמַע קָלָהּ. אָמַר לֵיהּ בַּר יוּדָאֵי בַּר יוּדָאֵי שָׁרִי תוֹרָךְ וְשָׁרִי קַנְקַנָּךְ דְּהָא חָרֵיב בֵּית מוּקְדְּשָׁא. גָּעַת זְמַן תִּנְיָינוּת. אָמַר לֵיהּ בַּר יוּדָאֵי בַּר יוּדָאֵי קְטוֹר תּוֹרָךְ וּקְטוֹר קַנְקַנָּךְ דְּהָא יְלִיד מַלְכָּא מְשִׁיחָא. אָמַר לֵיהּ מַה שְׁמֵיהּ מְנַחֵם. אָמַר לֵיהּ וּמַה שְׁמֵיהּ דְּאָבוֹי אָמַר לֵיהּ חִזְקִיָּה. אָמַר לֵיהּ מָן הֵן הוּא. אָמַר לֵיהּ מִן בִּירַת מַלְכָּא דְּבֵית לֶחֶם יְהוּדָה. אֲזַל זַבִּין תּוֹרוֹי וְזַבִּין קַנְקַנּוֹי וְאִיתְעֲבִיד זַבִּין לְבָדִין לְמֵיינוּקֵי וַהֲוָא עָיֵיל קִרְיָה וְנַפְקָא קִרְיָה. עַד דְּעָל לְהַהוּא קַרְתָּא וַהֲוָיָן כָּל־נְשַׁיָּא זָבְנָן וְאִימֵּה דִּמְנַחֵם לָא זָבְנָה. שְׁמַע קָלָן דִּנְשַׁיָּא אָמְרִין אִימֵּיהּ דִּמְנַחֵם אִימֵּיהּ דִּמְנַחֵם אַיְיתִי זוּבְנִין לִבְרָךְ. אָמְרָא בָּעֲיָא אֲנָא מֵיחְנְקוּנֵיהּ סַנְאֵיהוֹן דְּיִשְׂרָאֵל דְּבְיוֹמָא דְאִיתְיַלִּיד אִיחְרוּב בֵּית מוּקְדְּשָׁא. אָמַר לָהּ רְחִיצָא אֲנָן דִּבְרַגְלֵיהּ חֲרֵיב וּבְרַגְלֵיהּ מִתְבְּנֵיי. אָמְרָה לֵיהּ לֵית לִי פְּרִיטִין. אָמַר לָהּ וּמַה אִיכְפַּת לֵיךְ אַיְיתִי זוּבְנִין לֵיהּ אִין לֵית קוּמֵךְ יוֹמָא דֵין בָּתַר יוֹמֵי אֲנָא אָתֵי וְנָסֵיב. בָּתַר יוֹמִין עָאַל לְהַהוּא קַרְתָּא אָמַר לָהּ מַהוּ מֵיינוּקֵיךְ עֲבֵיד. אָמְרָה לֵיהּ מִן שַׁעְתָּא דַּחֲמִיתָנִי אָתוּן רוּחִין וְעַלְעוֹלֵיהּ וַחֲטְפִינֵיהּ מִן יָדַיי. אָמַר רִבִּי בּוּן מַה לָנוּ לִלְמוֹד מִן הָעַרְבִי הַזֶּה וְלֹא מִקְרָא מָלֵא הוּא וְהַלְּבָנוֹן בְּאַדִּיר יִפּוֹל. מַה כְּתִיב בַּתְרֵיהּ וְיָצָא חוֹטֶר מִגֶּזַע יִשָׁי.

Rebbi Joshua ben Levi said, his name is Zemaḥ. Rebbi Yudan, the son of Rebbi Aivu, said his name is Menaḥem[203]. Ḥanina the son of Rebbi Abbahu said: they have no disagreement since the numerical value of one is the numerical value of the other: Zemaḥ is equal to Menaḥem[204]. Since Rebbi Yudan the son of Rebbi Aivu said, it happened to a Jew who was plowing in the valley of Arbel[205] that his ox was bellowing. An Arab passed by and heard the bellowing of the ox. He said to him: Jew, Jew, unharness your ox, unharness your plow[206] because the Temple was destroyed. The ox bellowed a second time. He said: Jew, Jew, harness your ox, fix your plow because King Messiah has been born. He said to him: What is his name? Menaḥem. He said to him: What is his father's name? Ḥizqiah. He said to him: Where is he? He said to him: At the king's palace in Bethlehem in Judea. He went and sold his ox and plow and made himself a vendor of baby linens. He went to towns and left towns until he came to that town. All the women bought from him but the mother of Menaḥem did not buy. He heard the women say: Menaḥem's mother, Menaḥem's mother, come and buy for your son! She said: I would rather strangle him like a hater of Israel because he was born on the day the Temple was destroyed. He said to her: I like him, because for him it was destroyed and for him it will be rebuilt. She said to him, I have no money. He said to her, that does not bother me, come and buy for him! If you have nothing with you today, I shall return another day and I will take it then. After some time he went up to that town and said to her: How is your baby doing? She said to him: After you had seen me there came storms and raised him and tore him from my hands[207].

Rebbi Abun said: We do not need to learn from that Arab, is it not a full verse (*Is.* 10:35): "The Lebanon will fall through a noble one"?[208] And the next verse is (11:1) "A sprout will come from the stem of Jesse."

203 The parallel to the entire paragraph is in *Midrash Ekha rabbati* 1(57). The verse of R. Joshua ben Levi is *Zach.* 6:12: "Behold, a man of the name of Ẓemaḥ, he will sprout from below and build the Eternal's temple." The verse of Rebbi Yudan is *Threni* 1:16: "Behold, far from me is Menaḥem who will restore my spirit."

204 138. צמח = 90+40+8, מנחם = 40+50+8+40.

205 This is the reading of the Rome ms. and Genizah fragments; the valley of Arbel is West of Tiberias. The place name is missing in the Leyden ms. and the Venice print.

206 קנקן usually means a pitcher or a bottle, from late Latin *canna* "small vessel". However, this קנקן appears several times also in the Babli (noted in the Rabbinic dictionary *'Arukh* under קנקן ב׳) and seems to mean the central peg by which the motion of the plow is controlled; possibly from old Persian *gan*, "plow".

207 The *Zohar* (II, 7b-8b) improves on the story and asserts that the Messiah is living in Paradise at a place known as "bird's nest".

208 The use of Lebanon as a figure of speech for the Temple can be traced to the interpretation of *Deut.* 3:25, where Moses begs to see "this good mountain and the Lebanon." Since God later showed Moses all he wanted to see, but nothing North of the city of Dan, it follows that "Lebanon" here cannot mean the mountain range. The verse here was used by Rabban Joḥanan ben Zakkai to predict to Vespasian that he would be emperor before he could conquer Jerusalem because the Temple could fall only to a noble one (*Ekha rabbati* 1(32)). In Isaiah, the verse is the introduction to a description of Messianic times.

אָמַר רִבִּי תַּנְחוּמָא מִפְּנֵי מָה הִתְקִינוּ שׁוֹמֵעַ תְּפִילָּה בְּרָכָה חֲמֵשׁ עֶשְׂרֵה כְּנֶגֶד יי לַמַּבּוּל יָשָׁב שֶׁהוּא כוֹלֶה אֶת הַפּוּרְעָנוּת מִלָּבוֹא לָעוֹלָם.

[209]Rebbi Tanḥuma said: Why did they institute "He Who listens to prayer" as the fifteenth benediction? Corresponding to (*Ps.* 29:10) "The Eternal throned over the Deluge", that He avert the catastrophy, that it should not come over the world[210].

209 After the digression about the Messiah, one returs to the main theme; the final benediction of the weekday insertion is the fifteenth in the Galilean count, and the mention of God's name in the verse is the fifteenth in the Psalm.

210 God has sworn that no future Deluge will engulf the entire globe, but one has to pray that partial deluges will be averted.

עֲבוֹדָה לְהוֹדָיָיה זוֹבֵחַ תּוֹדָה יְכַבְּדָנְנִי וְשָׂם דֶּרֶךְ אַרְאֶנּוּ בְּיֵשַׁע אֱלֹהִים. וְחוֹתֵם בְּשָׁלוֹם שֶׁכָּל־בְּרָכוֹת חוֹתְמֵיהֶן שָׁלוֹם. אָמַר רִבִּי שִׁמְעוֹן בַּר חֲלַפְתָּא אֵין לְךָ כְּלִי מַחֲזִיק בְּרָכָה יוֹתֵר מִן הַשָּׁלוֹם וּמַה טַעַם יי עוֹז לְעַמּוֹ יִתֵּן יי יְבָרֵךְ אֶת עַמּוֹ בְשָׁלוֹם.

Temple service (precedes) Thanksgiving[211]: (*Ps.* 50:23) "He who brings a sacrifice of thanksgiving honors Me and shows a path; I shall make him see God's help." One finishes with Peace, since all benedictions end with peace[212]. Rebbi Simeon bar Ḥalaphta[213] said: There is no vessel that contains more blessing than peace. What is the reason? (*Ps.* 29:11) "The Eternal gives strength to His people, the Eternal blesses His people with peace."

211 Now we are back to the explanation of the sequence of benedictions in the *Amidah.* The 16th (Israeli count) prays for restoration of the Temple service and acceptance of our prayer as if performed in the Temple. The 17th benediction is Thanksgiving, the 18th is for Peace, following (in the Morning Service) the Priestly Blessings that end in "peace".

212 The Priestly Blessings end in "peace", and all other services, prayers and grace, end with "He Who makes peace in His heights, may He give peace to us and all of Israel, Amen."

213 A great preacher of the last generation of Tannaïm; his statement here is the last statement of the Mishnah (*Uqeẓin* 3:12).

קָרָא וְטָעָה יַחְזוֹר לְמָקוֹם שֶׁטָּעָה. טָעָה בֵין כְּתִיבָה רִאשׁוֹנָה לִשְׁנִייָה חוֹזֵר לִכְתִיבָה הָרִאשׁוֹנָה. טָעָה וְאֵינוֹ יוֹדֵעַ הֵיכָן טָעָה יַחְזוֹר כְּבַתְּחִילָּה לְמָקוֹם הַבָּרוּר לוֹ. דֵּלְמָה רִבִּי חִייָא רִבִּי יַסָּא רִבִּי אַמִּי סַלְקוֹן מֶעֱבַד גְּנוּנְיָה דְּרִבִּי אֶלְעָזָר. שָׁמְעוּן קָלֵיהּ דְּרִבִּי יוֹחָנָן אִי מְחַדֵּית מִילָּה. אָמְרִין מַן נָחֵית שְׁמַע לָהּ מִינֵיהּ. אָמְרִין וְיֵיחוּת רִבִּי אֶלְעָזָר דְּהוּא זָרִיז סַגִּין. נָחֵית וְסַלִּיק אֲמַר לָן כֵּן אָמַר רִבִּי יוֹחָנָן קָרָא וּמָצָא עַצְמוֹ בִּלְמַעַן חֲזָקָה כִּוֵּן.

"If he recited and made a mistake then he should return to the place of the mistake."[214] If he made a mistake between the first and second mention of "writing" he must return to the first "writing"[215]. If he made a mistake and does not know where he made the mistake, he returns to the start, to any place that he is sure about[216]. An explanation: Rebbi Ḥiyya, Rebbi Yasa, Rebbi Ammi were preparing the wedding canopy[217] for Rebbi Eleazar. They heard the voice of Rebbi Joḥanan when he explained something new. They said: Who is going down to hear that from him? They said, let Rebbi Eleazar go down since he is very careful. He descended, ascended, and said to them: So says Rebbi Joḥanan, if he recited and found himself at למען[219] one can be sure that he had the right intention.

214 Quote from the last part of the Mishnah that now will be discussed. The entire paragraph is repeated in Babli *Berakhot* 16a.

215 Both verses *Deut.* 6:9, 11:20, read: "You shall write them on the doorposts of your house and your gates." Since the verses are identical, a person who recited *Shema'* mechanically has no way of deciding between the two but must start anew from the first verse.

216 In the Babli, this is quoted in the language of the Tosephta (*Berakhot* 2:5) that one has to return to the start of the section he remembers. Since the language from the start of the paragraph to here is in pure Hebrew, it probably represents an Israeli version of that Tosephta.

217 Probably Latin *genialia, ium* (n., plur.) "marriage bed, marriage" (E. G.). Rebbi Ḥiyya mentioned here is R. Ḥiyya bar Abba; his name is missing in the Babli.

218 In the last verse of the second section of *Shema'*. Since the third section is completely different in wording and style, one may assume that he recited the first two parts correctly.

רִבִּי לִיָּא רִבִּי יָסָא בְּשֵׁם רִבִּי אָחָא רוּבָּא נִתְפַּלֵּל וְנִמְצָא עַצְמוֹ בְשׁוֹמֵעַ תְּפִילָּה חֲזָקָה כִּוֵּן. רִבִּי יִרְמְיָה בְּשֵׁם רִבִּי אֶלְעָזָר נִתְפַּלֵּל וְלֹא כִּוֵּן לִבּוֹ אִם יוֹדֵעַ שֶׁהוּא חוֹזֵר וּמְכַוֵּן יִתְפַּלֵּל וְאִם לָאו אַל יִתְפַּלֵּל. אָמַר רִבִּי חִיָּיא רוּבָּא אֲנָא מִן יוֹמַי לֹא כַוּוֹנִית אֶלָּא חַד זְמַן בָּעִי מְכַוְּנָא וְהִרְהָרִית בְּלִבִּי וְאָמְרִית מַאן עֲלֵיל קוֹמוֹי מַלְכָּא קְדָמִי אַרְקַבֶּסָא אוֹ רֵישׁ גָּלוּתָא. שְׁמוּאֵל אָמַר אֲנָא מָנִית אֶפְרוֹחַיָּא. רִבִּי בּוּן בַּר חִיָּא אָמַר אֲנָא מָנִית דֵּמוֹסִיָּא. אָמַר רִבִּי מַתַּנְיָה אֲנָא מַחֲזִיק טִיבוּ לְרֹאשִׁי דְּכַד הֲוָה מָטֵי מוֹדִים הוּא כָּרַע מִגַּרְמֵיהּ.

Rebbi Lia[219], Rebbi Yasa in the name of the great Rebbi Aḥa[220]: If he prayed and he found himself in "He Who hears prayer", he may assume that he prayed with intent[221].

Rebbi Jeremiah in the name of Rebbi Eleazar: If he prayed without intent and he knows that the second time he will pray with intent, he may pray a second time; otherwise he should not pray[222]. The great Rebbi Ḥiyya said: I never managed to pray with intent, but one time I made an effort to concentrate and I started to think and said to myself, who enters first before the king, the ἀργαπέτης[223] or the *Resh Galuta*[224]? Samuel said: I counted chicks[225]. Rebbi Abun bar Ḥiyya said: I counted stone rows[226]. Rebbi Mattaniah said: I an thankful to my head that when I come to *modim* it bends down by itself.

219 Rebbi La or Illaï, Galilean Amora of the third generation.

220 He cannot be the Amora Rebbi Aḥa since the latter belongs to the fourth generation. Probably he is the Tanna Rebbi Aḥa of the last generation of Tannaïm.

221 Since the weekday *Amidah* is a long prayer, it is probable that he lost concentration on what he was saying somewhere in between but when he realizes that he recited the last of the intermediary benedictions he may assume that he said all others in the required order.

222 It seems that the Yerushalmi requires total concentration for all 18 benedictions for somebody who is not

satisfied with the quality of his prayer. The following examples show that such a total concentration over a lengthy period of time is impossible and, hence, repetition of an imperfect prayer is excluded. The Babli [*Berakhot* 34b, a statement of Rebbi Ḥiyya (bar Abba) in the name of the Babylonian Rav Safra] requires total concentration only during the first benediction; hence, for the Babli someone who did not concentrate during the first benediction has to repeat the *Amidah*. (In the *Shulḥan Arukh* (Sec. 101,1), R. Josef Qaro follows the Babli but R. Moshe Isserles decides Ashkenazic practice according to the Yerushalmi.]

223 This Greek form was found in a Palmyrenian inscription. Following Fleischer, the title is a composition of Persian ارك *ark* "citadel", پد *pad* (old Persian *pat*) "master, overseer". So the title seems to designate the person who overseas the royal castle (Fleischer) or "commandant of a fort" (Liddell & Scott).

224 The Davidic head of Babylonian Jewry, who was a hereditary Noble under the Parthian and Persian rulers and still an important official in Moslem times.

225 When I consciously attempted total concentration for all the 19 (Babylonian) benedictions of the *Amidah*.

226 Greek δόμος, "building; rows of stones or bricks in a building." At other places in the Yerushalmi, the spelling דומדס is found; in the Babli it always is דימוס (which, however, might mean another word, δῆμος).

משנה ה: הָאוּמָנִין קוֹרִין בְּרֹאשׁ הָאִילָן אוֹ בְרֹאשׁ הַנִּדְבָּךְ מַה שֶׁאֵין רְשָׁאִין לַעֲשׂוֹת כֵּן בִּתְפִילָּה.

Mishnah 5: Professional workers[226] read[227] on top of a tree or on top of a wall in construction; they are not permitted to do this for prayer.

226 The אומן is a professional who is a contractor for his work; in contrast, the פועל is paid by the hour. The time the *uman* loses for prayer is his own.

227 The *Shema'*; since this recitation needs concentration only for the first

verse, we may assume that the professional can concentrate for that short time span without fear of falling down. The rest of *Shema'* can be recited by rote from memory. In contrast, prayer (the *Amidah*) needs concentration from beginning to end and can be recited only on the ground.

הלכה ה: כֵּינִי מַתְנִיתָא הַפּוֹעֲלִין קוֹרִין בְּרֹאשׁ הָאִילָן וְהָאוּמָנִין בְּרֹאשׁ הַנִּדְבָּךְ.

Halakhah 5: So[228] is the Mishnah: The hourly workers read on top of a tree[229] and the professionals on top of a wall in construction.

228 The Venice edition has מני which is an interrogatory particle referring to persons and does not make sense here. The Genizah fragments and the commentator of *Sefer Ḥaredim* read כיני as given here.

229 The Babli does not mention hourly workers at all. It is not clear whether the Yerushalmi is of the opinion that work on a tree is unskilled work and, therefore, a careful construction of the Mishnah requires the mention of hourly workers here or that this rule is contrary to the opinion prevalent in Babylonia.

וְתַנֵּי כֵן מִתְפַּלְלִין בְּרֹאשׁ הַזַּיִת וּבְרֹאשׁ הַתְּאֵנָה. הָא בִשְׁאָר כָּל־הָאִילָנוֹת יוֹרֵד וּמִתְפַּלֵּל לְמַטָּן. וּבַעַל הַבַּיִת לְעוֹלָם יוֹרֵד וּמִתְפַּלֵּל לְמַטָּן. וְלָמָּה בְּרֹאשׁ הַזַּיִת וּבְרֹאשׁ הַתְּאֵנָה. רִבִּי אַבָּא וְרִבִּי סִימוֹן תְּרֵוַיְהוּ אָמְרִין מִפְּנֵי שֶׁטִּירְחוֹתָן מְרוּבָּה.

It was stated[230]: "They pray on top of an olive tree or on top of a fig tree." Hence[231], on all other trees he descends and prays on the ground. "The owner descends in all cases and prays on the ground." And why on top of an olive tree or on top of a fig tree? Rebbi Abba and Rebbi Simon say both, because those are very laborious[232].

230 This is a fragment from a text similar to *Tosephta Berakhot* 2:8: "Hourly workers read on top of a tree and on top of a wall in construction; they pray on top of an olive tree and a fig tree but for all other trees they have to descend and pray. The owner descends in any case for prayer." A

similar text, only with "professionals" instead of "hourly workers". is quoted in Babli *Berakhot* 16a.

231 This looks like an inference since הא is not a tannaïtic technical term. However, given the parallels in Tosephta and Babli, the word הא "therefore", may be an interpolation and the rest of the sentence may belong to the Tosephta.

232 It is not clear whether it is very troublesome to come down from these trees and, therefore, too much time would be spent at the expense of the owner, or that olive and fig trees need great care and there is danger that the trees or their fruits would be damaged if the hourly worker would try to go down and up quickly, again to the detriment of the owner. Both explanations are found in the commentaries. Rashi in the Babli (16a) explains that these trees have so many branches that one can stand there securely and may concentrate on prayer without fear; it may be that he agrees that because of the many branches it is very troublesome to come down from the trees.

תַּנֵּי הַכַּתָּף אַף עַל פִּי שֶׁמַּשָּׂאוֹ עַל כְּתֵיפוֹ הֲרֵי זֶה קוֹרֵא אֶת שְׁמַע אֲבָל לֹא יַתְחִיל לֹא בְשָׁעָה שֶׁהוּא פוֹרֵק וְלֹא בְשָׁעָה שֶׁהוּא טוֹעֵן מִפְּנֵי שֶׁאֵין לִבּוֹ מְיוּשָּׁב. בֵּין כָּךְ וּבֵין כָּךְ אַל יִתְפַּלֵּל עַד שֶׁיִּפְרוֹק. וְאִם הָיָה עָלָיו מַשּׂאוּי שֶׁל אַרְבָּעָה קַבִּין מוּתָּר. אָמַר רִבִּי יוֹחָנָן וְהוּא שֶׁשִּׁיקֵּל. מַהוּ שֶׁשִּׁיקֵּל תְּרֵין חֲלָקִים לַחוֹרָיי וְחַד לְקוֹמוֹיי.

It was stated[233]: "The porter may recite the *Shema'* even with his load on his shoulders[234] but he should start neither when he unloads nor when he loads because he cannot then concentrate. In any case he may not pray until he unloads, but if he was carrying a load of 4 *qab*[235] it is permitted." Rebbi Joḥanan said: only if he is in equilibrium. What means that he is in equilibrium? Two parts on his back and one part in front.

233 This statement is a *Tosephta* (*Berakhot* 2:7) where, however, the exemption for the carrier of a large load is not mentioned.

234 For the same reason as that given for the workman. In the *Tosephta*, the porter is mentioned before the worker.

235 A *qab* is 4 *log*, about 2.17 liters. 4 *qab* are a Roman *modius*, about a British peck, a fourth of a bushel.

The Babli, *Baba meẓi'a* 105b, quotes a *baraita* which states that the porter may pray with his load *on his back* if the load is less than 4 *qab*, but not if the load is 4 *qab* or more. Therefore, it seems that in the Yerushalmi the meaning is that the porter may pray without unloading if his load does not exceed 4 *qab*, on condition that it be balanced. The two differences between Yerushalmi and Babylonian practice are that for the Babli, the load has to be strictly less than 4 *qab*, for the Yerushalmi it may reach 4 *qab*, and for the Babli the load has to be all on the back and not distributed fore and aft.

תַּנֵּי לֹא יְהֵא מְרַמֵּז בְּעֵינָיו וְקוֹרֵא.

It was stated[236]: "Nobody should give messages with his eyes while reciting."

236 An extended prohibition to communicate with others by movements of eyes, lips, or hands while reciting the *Shema'* is given in the Babli, *Yoma* 19b, in the name of the early Babylonian Amora Rav Isaac bar Samuel Bar Martha. However, the Biblical justification of the prohibition is there given in the name of the early Tanna Rebbi Eleazar Ḥisma. Hence, the statement of the Yerushalmi is a genuine tannaïtic one.

תַּנֵּי הַפּוֹעֲלִין שֶׁהָיוּ עוֹשִׂין מְלָאכָה אֵצֶל בַּעַל הַבַּיִת הֲרֵי אֵילּוּ מְבָרְכִין בְּרָכָה רִאשׁוֹנָה וְכוֹלְלִין שֶׁל יְרוּשָׁלַיִם וְשֶׁל הָאָרֶץ וְחוֹתְמִין בְּשֶׁל הָאָרֶץ. אֲבָל אִם הָיוּ עוֹשִׂין עִמּוֹ בִסְעוּדָן אוֹ שֶׁהָיָה בַּעַל הַבַּיִת אוֹכֵל עִמָּהֶן הֲרֵי אֵילּוּ מְבָרְכִין ד'. אָמַר רִבִּי מָנָא זֹאת אוֹמֶרֶת שֶׁאָסוּר לַעֲשׂוֹת מְלָאכָה בְּשָׁעָה שֶׁיְּבָרֵךְ. דְּלָכֵן מַה אֲנָן אָמְרִין יַעֲשֶׂה מְלָאכָה וִיבָרֵךְ.

It was stated: "The hourly workers who worked for an employer have to recite the first benediction of Grace and subsume that of Jerusalem in the benediction for the Land and close with the benediction for the Land[237]. But if they were working for him for their meals[238] or if the employer was eating with them, then they recite all four benedictions." Rebbi Mana said: This means that one may not work while reciting Grace. Otherwise, why do we have to say this[239]? Let him work and recite the benedictions!

237 The obligation of reciting Grace is biblical but the number of benedictions is a rabbinical ordinance (*Beth Yosef* on *Ṭur Oraḥ Ḥayyim* 191). In order to reduce the expense for the employer (and, hence, increase employment for the poor), the hourly workers whose lunchbreak is paid for by their employer recite an abbreviated version of Grace that still contains all required elements. Since the Yerushalmi does not mention the benedictions before the meal it seems that the hourly workers are required to recite these [this is also the reading of the *Tosephta* (5:24) and most of the manuscripts of the Babli, against the Venice text of the Babli (16a)].

238 For the food only, without cash payment to them.

239 The abbreviated version of Grace; it is necessary only if it profits the employer.

רִבִּי שְׁמוּאֵל בַּר רַב יִצְחָק בְּשֵׁם רַב חוּנָה לֹא יַעֲמוֹד אָדָם וְיִתְפַּלֵּל וּמִין מַטְבֵּעַ בְּיָדוֹ. לְפָנָיו אָסוּר לְאַחֲרָיו מוּתָּר. רִבִּי יָסָא הָיָה צוֹרְרָן וְתוֹפְשָׁן בְּיָדוֹ. וּלְמִדַּת הַדִּין וְצַרְתָּ הַכֶּסֶף בְּיָדְךָ. וּבִלְבַד בְּיָדְךָ. רִבִּי יוֹסֵי בַּר אָבוּן הוֹרֵי לְרִבִּי הִלֵּל חַתְנֵיהּ כֵּן.

Rebbi Samuel bar Rav Isaac[240] in the name of Rav Ḥuna: One should not stand and pray while he keeps a coin in his hand[241]; (having the coin) in front of him is forbidden, at his back it is allowed. Rebbi Yasa used to bind them together and grab them in his hand[242]. And for money matters, (*Deut.* 14:25) "you shall bind the money together in your hand", only in your hand[243]. Rebbi Yose bar Abun thus taught his son-in-law Rebbi Hillel[244].

240 An Israeli Amora of Babylonian origin who in his youth was a student of Rav Huna, the student of Rav.

241 That one should not come to examine it while praying; having the coin where it cannot be seen is no impediment to prayer.

242 Since bound together they cannot be examined.

243 The verse deals with money that has to be spent in Jerusalem, for which the owner is a kind of trustee. The inference, which is not a strict derivation, is that anybody who is trustee for other people's money can discharge his obligation of prudent care only by having the money tied together and in his personal control all the time.

244 Probably referring to both prayer and trusteeship.

רִבִּי חִזְקִיָּה וְרִבִּי יַעֲקֹב בַּר אָחָא הֲווֹ יָתְבִין בְּחַד אֲתַר וַהֲוָה גַּבֵּי רִבִּי יַעֲקֹב בַּר אָחָא פְּרִיטִין. אָתָת עוֹנְתָא דִצְלוֹתָא וְשָׁרְתוּן וִיהָבוּן לְרִבִּי חִזְקִיָּה. קָטַר פּוּרְתֵּיהּ לְפוּרְתֵּיהּ. וְשָׁרְתוּן וְעָרַק. אָמַר לֵיהּ וּמַה בְּיָדָךְ.

Rebbi Ḥizqiah and Rebbi Jacob bar Aḥa were sitting at one place and Rebbi Jacob bar Aḥa had coins on him. There came the time for prayer, he unbound them and gave them to Rebbi Ḥizqiah. He bound them together little by little. They became untied and lost. He asked: What have you left?[245]

245 This story is a counterexample to the prescription given before. Since coins are shown to come untied sometimes, binding them together is no remedy for the worry. Hence, the practical conclusion would be that coins have to be put in a safe place before the start of prayer.

אָמַר רִבִּי חֲנִינָא אַף מִי שֶׁהָיוּ מֵימָיו עַל כְּתֵיפוֹ הֲרֵי זֶה קוֹרֵא אֶת שְׁמַע וּמִתְפַּלֵּל. רַב חוּנָא אָמַר קִרְיַת שְׁמַע וּתְפִילָּה אֵינָן צְרִיכוֹת כַּוָּנָה. אָמַר רִבִּי מָנָא קַשִּׁיתִי קוֹמֵי רִבִּי פִּינְחָס וַאֲפִילוּ תֵּימַר קִרְיַת שְׁמַע צְרִיכָה כַּוָּנָה תְּפִילָּה אֵינָהּ צְרִיכָה כַּוָּנָה. אָמַר רִבִּי יוֹסֵי קִיַּמְתֵּיהָ כְּיֵי דָמַר רִבִּי יַעֲקֹב בַּר אַחָא בְשֵׁם רִבִּי יוֹחָנָן הִגִּיעוּךָ סוֹף מְלֶאכֶת הַמַּיִם שֶׁאֵינָם מְחוּוָרִים דְּבַר תּוֹרָה.

Rebbi Ḥanina[246] said: Also one who has his water on his shoulder may recite *Shema'* and pray. Rav Ḥuna said: So the reciting of *Shema'* and praying do not require concentration? Rebbi Mana said: I pointed out the difficulty before Rebbi Phineas that even if you say that the recitation of *Shema'* does not need concentration, does prayer not need concentration[247]? Rebbi Yose[248] said: I confirmed it following what Rebbi Jacob bar Aḥa said in the name of Rebbi Joḥanan: You got it, the completion of the works of water[249] that are not clear from the words of the Torah.

246 He refers back to the *Tosephta* that allowed praying if the carrier's load did not exceed 4 *qab*. The statement is introduced here since it is explained on the authority of R. Jacob ben Aḥa who was the main person in the preceding section.

The water referred to here is water used for the sprinkling with the ashes of the red heifer to cleanse from impurity caused by contact or closeness to the body of a dead Jew, as explained in *Num.* 19 and the Mishnah tractate *Parah*. The ashes of the red heifer have to be given into מים חיים אל כלי, virgin fresh water in a vessel. This means that after being drawn from flowing water, the water has to be watched so that no kind of work is done with it. A lapse of attention to the water makes it unfit for use in cleansing from impurity. Nevertheless, Rebbi Ḥanina states that one may recite *Shema'* and even pray while carrying such water. This statement is obviously difficult to accept. Rav Ḥuna (the second) dismisses Rebbi Ḥanina's statement as in obvious contradiction to generally accepted principles.

247 Even if one accepts Rebbi Ḥanina's statement for *Shema'*, its reference to prayer must be a mistake even though it refers to a prior statement about prayer only. The sentence is a rhetorical question. In a text from the Cairo Genizah, it is formulated as a declarative sentence: "recitation of *Shema'* does not need concentration; prayer needs concentration". The meaning is the same in both versions.

248 The Amora, one of the editors

of the Yerushalmi.

249 After the ashes have already been given into the water, when it is clear that the term "living water" no longer applies and there is no indication in the Torah that it has to be guarded as strictly as before. This also explains R. Ḥanina's expression "his water", not מי חטאת "the water of sprinkling" that is the technical term used for fresh water guarded for the ashes. It follows that as long as the ashes have not been given into the water, one may neither recite *Shema'* nor pray while guarding it.

(fol. 5b) **משנה ו**: חָתָן פָּטוּר מִקְּרִיַּת שְׁמַע לַיְלָה רִאשׁוֹן עַד מוֹצָאֵי שַׁבָּת אִם לֹא עָשָׂה מַעֲשֶׂה. מַעֲשֶׂה בְּרַבָּן גַּמְלִיאֵל שֶׁנָּשָׂא וְקָרָא לַיְלָה הָרִאשׁוֹן. אָמְרוּ לוֹ תַלְמִידָיו לִימַּדְתָּנוּ רַבֵּינוּ שֶׁחָתָן פָּטוּר. אָמַר לָהֶם אֵינִי שׁוֹמֵעַ לָכֶם לְבַטֵּל מִמֶּנִּי מַלְכוּת שָׁמַיִם אֲפִילוּ שָׁעָה אַחַת.

Mishnah 6: The bridegroom is free from reciting the *Shema'* in the first night[250]; until the end of Sabbath if he did not do the act[251]. An action: Rabban Gamliël married and recited in the first night[252]. His students said to him: Our teacher, did you not teach us that the bridegroom is free? He said to them: I will not listen to you to lift from me the Kingdom of Heaven even for one hour.

250 Since he is unable to concentrate in anticipation of his first night with his bride. The bride, as a woman, has no obligation to recite *Shema'* since this is a positive commandment occurring at stated times and does not apply to women.

251 It was common usage even in seventeenth Century Germany that couples who married Wednesday night had their first sexual relations the night following the Sabbath, cf. *Minhagim of the Community of Worms by R. Yospe Shamash*, ed. I. Zimer, I. M. Peles, vol. 2, p. 47; there the editor gives several conjectural reasons in note 16. He also indicates that this is a possible reflection of old usages from the Land of Israel, never followed in Babylonia. It seems to me that the

usage is quite understandable if it is noted that bride and bridegroom were in their low teens, the girl possibly even a pre-teen. The marriage was arranged by the parents, with minimal involvement of the parties to the wedding. Some time was needed for the parties to get acquainted enough to get intimate.

252 Since he already had the title "Rabban" and had students of his own, it is obvious that he was not a teenager and the marriage was not his first. Hence, his level of anxiety was low.

הלכה ו: רִבִּי אֶלְעָזָר בֶּן אַנְטִיגְנֹס בְּשֵׁם רִבִּי אֶלְעָזָר בֵּי רִבִּי יַנַּאִי זֹאת אוֹמֶרֶת שֶׁמּוּתָּר לִבְעוֹל בִּתְחִילָּה בְּשַׁבָּת. אָמַר רִבִּי חַגַּיי קוֹמֵיהּ רִבִּי יוֹסֵי תִּיפְתַּר בְּאַלְמָנָה שֶׁאֵינָהּ עוֹשָׂה חַבּוּרָה. אָמַר לֵיהּ וְהָא תַנִּינָן אַרְבַּע לֵילוֹת. אִית לָךְ לְמֵימַר אַרְבַּע לֵילוֹת בְּאַלְמָנָה.

Halakha 6: Rebbi Eleazar ben Antigonos[253] in the name of Rebbi Eleazar the son of Rebbi Yannai: This means that it is permitted to start sexual relations on the Sabbath[254]. Rebbi Ḥaggai said before Rebbi Yose: Explain it for a widow where he does not make a wound. He answered him: Did we not formulate "Four nights?[255]" Can you say four nights for a widow?

253 An Israeli Amora of the second generation who always reports in the name of R. Eleazar, son of R. Yannai.

254 Since the groom is free from reciting the *Shema'* Friday evening if he did not yet have intercourse with his wife, it follows that we expect him to be anxious about it also Friday night. If he were not allowed to have intercourse, then he could defer his anxiety for a day and recite *Shema'*. The problem is that he will make a wound in deflowering his wife and, in the normal case of a very young girl, the making of the wound is automatic. Now, the making of a wound is forbidden on the Sabbath but, according to Rebbi Simeon (bar Yoḥai), any work not done for its own sake is not forbidden, except in the case of an automatic consequence (פסיק רישא "cut off its head, will it not die?'). For the very young girls discussed here, the wound might be an automatic consequence.

The entire discussion belongs more

to *Niddah* X:1 where all the parallels in the Babli are found. The second part of the Yerushalmi *Niddah* is lost and it cannot be ascertained anymore whether the entire discussion of our Mishnah is taken from there.

255 This refers to the first Mishnah in the last chapter of tractate *Niddah*: "About a young girl who marries before puberty, the House of Shammai say that one allows four nights and the House of Hillel say until the wound is healed" (one does not suspect any blood to be menstrual). While it is quite possible that a very young girl can already be a widow, the Mishnah cannot apply to her since the marriage festivities of a widow are only three days (Thursday, Friday, Sabbath) while those of a virgin are seven days (*Ketubot* 1:1). Hence, we cannot talk here about a widow.

אָמַר רִבִּי יַעֲקֹב בַּר זַבְדִּי קַשִׁיתָהּ קוֹמֵי רִבִּי יוֹסֵי מַה בֵינָהּ לְבֵין שׁוֹבֵר אֶת הֶחָבִית לֶאֱכוֹל מִמֶּנָּה גְרוֹגֶרֶת. אָמַר לִי וָמַר דְּבַתְרֵיהּ וּבִלְבַד שֶׁלֹּא יִתְכַּוֵּן לַעֲשׂוֹתָהּ כֶּלִי. וְכַאן שֶׁמִּתְכַּוֵּן לַעֲשׂוֹתָהּ בְּעוּלָה כְּמִי שֶׁמִּתְכַּוֵּן לַעֲשׂוֹתָהּ כֶּלִי. רַב יִצְחָק בַּר רַב מְשִׁירְשִׁיָּא אוֹ מַקְשֵׁי מַה בֵינָהּ לְמֵפִיס מוּרְסָה בְשַׁבָּת. אָמַר לוֹ וָמַר דְּבַתְרֵיהּ וּבִלְבַד שֶׁלֹּא יִתְכַּוֵּן לַעֲשׂוֹתָהּ פֶּה. וְכַאן מִתְכַּוֵּן שֶׁהוּא מִתְכַּוֵּן לַעֲשׂוֹתָהּ בְּעוּלָה כְּמִי שֶׁהוּא מִתְכַּוֵּן לַעֲשׂוֹתָהּ כֶּלִי.

Rebbi Jacob bar Savdi[256] said: I asked the question before Rebbi Yose: What is the difference between her and him who breaks a clay amphora in order to eat a dried fig from it[257]? He said to me: But it says afterwards, "only he should have no intent to make it into a usable vessel." And here when he has the intention of making her a married woman it is as if he had the intention of making her into a vessel. Rav Isaac bar Rav Meshirshia[258] said similarly: What is the difference between her and him who opens a boil on the Sabbath[259]? He said to him, but it says afterwards: "only he should have no intention of making a permanent opening." And here when he has the intention of making her a married woman it is as if he had the intention of making her into a vessel[260].

256 An Amora of the fourth generation, probably somewhat older than Rebbi Yose.

257 This refers to Mishnah *Šabbat* XXII:3: "One may break a clay amphora (whose top has been closed off by solid clay) in order to eat a dried fig from its contents, but he may not have the intent to make it into a permanent vessel," i. e., he may not break the seal open in such a way that it needs no more action after the Sabbath to make the opening a permanent one that is easy to use. This follows the principle quoted before that according to R. Simeon, work not needed for its own sake is not forbidden on the Sabbath. Even R. Yehudah, who disagrees and states that any complete work is forbidden on Sabbath irrespective of intent, will agree that breaking off an irregular piece of the covering does not constitute complete work since it needs further regularization after the Sabbath. Rebbi Yose's answer is that breaking the hymen is a complete action in itself and, therefore, both R. Simeon and R. Yehudah will forbid it: R. Simeon because of his intent and R. Yehudah because it is a complete action.

In the Babli, the deflowered woman is called a vessel; the Yerushalmi only compares her to a vessel.

258 In the Babli, the name is Mesharshia. He is a Babylonian who was associated with the last editors of the Yerushalmi and the first editor of the Babli. In the Babli (*Ketubot* 6b), the same question is asked by Rebbi Ammi, the Galilean authority two generations earlier.

259 Which is allowed (Babli *Šabbat* 107a) for the same reason as why the top of an amphora may be broken, with the same restriction as to intent.

260 In the Rome ms. and Geniza fragments, the last statement reads: לעשות לה פה "(He has the intention) to make her a permanent opening." Our text probably is dittography.

תַּנֵּי לֹא יִבְעוֹל אָדָם בְּעִילָה לְכַתְּחִילָּה בְּשַׁבָּת מִפְּנֵי שֶׁהוּא עוֹשֶׂה חַבּוּרָה וַאֲחֵרִים מַתִּירִין. אָמַר רִבִּי יוֹסֵי בֵּי רִבִּי אָבוּן טַעֲמוֹן דַּאֲחֵרִים לִמְלַאכְתּוֹ הוּא מִתְכַּוֵּן. מֵאֵילֶיהָ נַעֲשֶׂה חַבּוּרָה. אַסִּי אָמַר אָסוּר. בִּנְיָמִן גִּנְזַכַּיָּיה נָפַק וָמַר מִשְּׁמֵיהּ דְּרַב מוּתָּר. שָׁמַע שְׁמוּאֵל וְאִיקְפִּיד עִילוֹי וּמִית וְקָרֵי עִילוֹי בָּרוּךְ שֶׁנְּגָפוֹ. וְעַל רַב קָרֵי לֹא יְאוּנֶּה לַצַּדִּיק כָּל־אָוֶן.

It was stated[261]: "A man should not have first sexual relations on the Sabbath because he makes a wound; but others allow it." Rebbi Yose bar Abun said: The reason of the others is that he is intent on his job; the wound results automatically[262]. Assi[263] said, it is forbidden. Benjamin from Ginzak[264] went out and said in the name of Rab, it is allowed. Samuel heard it and resented it, he [Benjamin] died, he [Samuel] recited for him: praised be He Who smote him[265]. About Rav, he [Samuel] recited: (*Prov.* 12:21) "The just will cause no wrong."

261 This *baraita* is also quoted in Babli *Ketubot* 5b, where it is determined that "others" means R. Simeon who states that an action not expressly intended is not forbidden on the Sabbath. It is explained there, that even though R. Simeon forbids actions which automatically imply some other action that desecrates the Sabbath, here he allows a first sex act on Sabbath since splitting the hymen is not a necessary consequence if the male partner is considerate (and, consequently, an intact hymen is no guarantee of virginity.) Since we decide on the Sabbath according to the opinion of Rebbi Simeon and since the medical statement is by Samuel, the greatest medical authority in the Babli, it is clear that the Babli decides that first sex relations on Friday night are permitted. (In the Middle Ages, poor people married on Friday afternoon in order to save expenses for a separate wedding meal.) It is seen here that the Yerushalmi is strictly of the opposite opinion; hence, the identity of "others" is not determined here.

262 Hence, the act is permitted according to R. Simeon.

263 His alter ego, Ammi, is quoted in the Babli as the first authority who allows it.

264 Ginzak ("city of the treasury") is the capital of Media, called Gazaka by Ptolemy. Another version is told in the Babli, *Niddah* 65a. According to the version which allows first sex acts on the Sabbath, Benjamin, called there "from Saqasan", tried to follow a ruling attributed to Rav to the effect that a second sex act would be permitted even without waiting the seven days of a cleansing period regularly required of a menstruating women, and applied to the newlyweds since blood from the breaking of the hymen is indistinguishable from menstrual blood,

as discussed in the following section. In the Babylonian version, Benjamin tried to act according to this ruling but he died before he could do so.

265 "קרי" means "recited a Biblical verse". There is no such verse but its intent is close to *1Sam.* 25:39.

שְׁמוּאֵל אָמַר כָּל־הַהִיא הִילְכְתָא דְּרֵישֵׁיהּ דְּפִירְקָא אַחֲרִייָא דְנִידָּה לַהֲלָכָה אֲבָל לֹא לְמַעֲשֶׂה. רִבִּי יַנַּיי עָרַק אֲפִילוּ מִתִּינוֹקֶת שֶׁלֹּא הִגִּיעַ זְמַנָּהּ וְנִשֵּׂאת. בָּעוּן קוֹמוֹי רִבִּי יוֹחָנָן מַהוּ לִבְעוֹל בְּעִילָה שְׁנִייָה. אָמְרִין לִתְלוֹת בְּדַם הַמַּכָּה לֹא הוֹרֵי וְלִבְעוֹל בְּעִילָה שְׁנִייָה הוּא מוֹרֵייא. מַה צְרִיכָה לָהּ כְּשֶׁבָּאוּ לֵיהּ יְמֵי הֶפְסֵק יְמֵי טָהֳרָה בֵּנְתַיִם. אָמַר רִבִּי אַבָּהוּ שׁוּשְׁבִינֵיהּ דְּרִבִּי שִׁמְעוֹן בַּר אַבָּא הֲוֵינָא שְׁאֵלִית לְרִבִּי אֶלְעָזָר מַהוּ לִבְעוֹל בְּעִילָה שְׁנִייָה וְשָׁרָא לֵיהּ דְּהוּא סָבַר כַּהֲדָא דִשְׁמוּאֵל. דִּשְׁמוּאֵל אָמַר פִּרְצָה דְחוּקָה נִכְנָסִין בָּהּ בְּשַׁבָּת אֲפִילוּ מְשָׁרֶת צְרוֹרוֹת. אָמַר רִבִּי חַגַּי שׁוּשְׁבִינֵיהּ דְּרִבִּי שְׁמוּאֵל קַפּוֹדְקִיָּא הֲוֵינָא שְׁאֵלִית לְרִבִּי יֹאשִׁיָּה וְשָׁרַע מִינֵיהּ. שְׁאֵלִית לְרִבִּי שְׁמוּאֵל בַּר יִצְחָק אָמַר לִי מֵעַתָּה אֵי זֶה דַם נִידָּה וְאֵי זֶה דַם בְּתוּלִים. תַּנֵּי כַּלָּה אֲסוּרָה לְבֵיתָהּ כָּל־שִׁבְעָה וְאָסוּר לִיטּוֹל מִמֶּנָּה כּוֹס שֶׁל בְּרָכָה דִּבְרֵי רִבִּי אֱלִיעֶזֶר. מַה טַעֲמָא דְּרִבִּי אֱלִיעֶזֶר אִי אֶפְשַׁר שֶׁלֹּא יֵצֵא דַם נִידָּה עִם דַּם בְּתוּלִים.

Samuel said: All the rules spelled out at the start of the last chapter of *Niddah* are theoretical and not for practical application[266]. Rebbi Yannai fled even from married pre-puberty girls[267]. They asked before Rebbi Yoḥanan: What about a second sex act? They said, he did not teach to take all for blood of the wound, how could he rule for a second sex act[268]? What we are asking about is the case when there were days of interruption, days of purity, in between[269]. Rebbi Abbahu said: I was the best man of Rebbi Simeon bar Abba and I asked Rebbi Eleazar: is it possible to have the second sex act? He permitted it, since he holds like Samuel, and Samuel said: One may enter a narrow gap[270] on the Sabbath, even if one rubs off some pebbles. Rebbi Ḥaggai said: I was the best man of Rebbi Samuel the Cappadocian[271]; I asked Rebbi Josiah and he shrank from it[272]. I asked Rebbi Samuel bar Isaac; he said: now, what is blood of a period and what is blood of virginity[273]? It was stated[274]: "The bride is forbidden for her house all seven days and he may not take from her the cup of blessings, the words of Rebbi Eliezer." What is the reason of Rebbi Eliezer? It is impossible that not some menstrual blood be mixed in the blood of virginity.

266 The rules allowing more than one sex act with newlywed virgins while either the wound is not healed or seven days had not passed since the wedding night. The same statement of Samuel is in Babli *Niddah* 65a.

267 He refrained from touching them, just as it is forbidden to touch a married woman after puberty.

268 In the wedding night, where according to him only one sex act is allowed. "He" is R. Yoḥanan.

269 That means that when a man married a virgin and the required time has passed since the wedding night it turns out that the first night in which a second sex act is permissible would be a Sabbath. This is a valid question for the Yerushalmi which forbids a first act on the Sabbath; there is some chance that a second act will again produce some minor lesion and some drops of blood.

270 In a dirt wall. The statement of Samuel is also in Babli *Ketubot* 6b and is used there for the same argument as here.

271 Like all other authorities quoted here, an Amora of the third generation, of the circle of students of Rebbi Yoḥanan.

272 He refused to give an opinion. It is not 100% clear what Rebbi Ḥaggai asked, but we may assume that his question was identical with that of Rebbi Abbahu.

273 It seems impossible to decide, since on the one hand we allow an occasional rubbing off, and, hence, in our case an occasional drop of blood, following Samuel, but on the other hand we treat every drop of blood on female genitals as menstrual and necessitating seven days of cleansing when all bodily contact between spouses is forbidden.

274 In a slightly different wording this is a *baraita* in *Massekhet Kallah* 1 (a collection in the Yerushalmi tradition.) At any meal during all seven days after the wedding, seven benedictions are said over a cup of

wine for the newlyweds after grace is recited. The bride is required to drink from the cup of which her husband drank, as a fertility rite. Rebbi Eliezer notes that the groom is not allowed to take the cup back from the bride since she has to follow all the rules of the menstruating woman.

משנה ז: רָחַץ לַיְלָה רִאשׁוֹן שֶׁמֵּתָה אִשְׁתּוֹ. אָמְרוּ לוֹ תַלְמִידָיו לִימַּדְתָּנוּ רַבֵּנוּ שֶׁאָבֵל אָסוּר לִרְחוֹץ. אָמַר לָהֶן אֵינִי כִשְׁאָר כָּל־בְּנֵי אָדָם אִיסְטְנֵיס אָנִי.

Mishnah 7: He[275] took a bath in the first night after his wife died. His students said to him: Did you, our teacher, not teach us that the mourner may not take a bath. He said to them: I am not like most other people, I am asthenic[276].

275 Rabban Gamliel.

276 Greek ἀσθενής. Medical considerations, even if no life-threatening situation is involved, always have precedence over the rules of mourning.

הלכה ז: מַאן תַּנָּא אָבֵל אָסוּר בִּרְחִיצָה כָּל־שִׁבְעָה רִבִּי נָתָן. רִבִּי אַמִּי הֲוָה לֵיהּ עוּבְדָּא וְשָׁאַל לְרִבִּי חִייָה בַּר בָּא וְהוֹרֵי לֵיהּ כָּל־שִׁבְעָה כְרִבִּי נָתָן. רִבִּי יוֹסֵי הֲוָה לֵיהּ עוּבְדָּא וְשָׁלַח לְרִבִּי בָּא בַּר כֹּהֵן לְגַבֵּי רִבִּי אָחָא אָמַר לֵיהּ וְלֹא כֵן אִלְפָּן רִבִּי. רִבִּי אַמִּי הֲוָה לֵיהּ עוּבְדָּא וְשָׁאַל לְרֵישׁ לָקִישׁ וְהוֹרֵי לֵיהּ כְּרִבִּי נָתָן כָּל־שִׁבְעָה. אָמַר לֵיהּ דִּילְמָא תְּרֵין עוּבְדִּין אִינּוּן. אֲנָן אָמְרִין לֵיהּ עַל דְּרִבִּי חִייָה בַּר בָּא. וְאַתּוּן אַמְרִיתוּן עַל דְּרֵישׁ לָקִישׁ. וְעוֹד מִן הָדָא רִבִּי חָמָא אָבוֹי דְּרִבִּי אוֹשַׁעְיָא הֲוָה לֵיהּ עוּבְדָּא שָׁאַל לְרַבָּנָן וְאָסְרוּן.

Halakha 7: Who[277] stated that the mourner is forbidden to take a bath during the entire seven days? Rebbi Nathan[278]. Something happened to Rebbi Ammi[279], he asked Rebbi Ḥiyya bar Abba who instructed him "all seven days following Rebbi Nathan". Something happened to Rebbi Yose[280]; he sent Rebbi Abba bar Cohen to Rebbi Aḥa; he said to him:

Rebbi, did you not so teach us that something happened to Rebbi Ammi, he asked Resh Laqish[281] who instructed him "all seven days following Rebbi Nathan". He said to him[282], maybe these were two separate incidents, we say it in the name of Rebbi Ḥiyya bar Abba, you say it in the name of Resh Laqish. And also from the following[283]: Something happened to Rebbi Ḥama[284], father of Rebbi Oshaya, he asked the rabbis and they forbade it.

277 This entire discussion belongs to the third chapter of tractate *Moëd Qaṭan* (*Halakhah* 5, fol. 62d). There are some textual differences between the two texts, an occurrence rare in the Yerushalmi. But in fact the deviations of the text here from its original in *Moëd Qaṭan* are all scribal or printer's errors, as is shown from the Rome ms. and the Genizah fragments. Therefore, the text here follows the *Moëd Qaṭan* text wherever there is manuscript evidence from *Berakhot* to support that version.

278 Usually known as Nathan the Babylonian, a Babylonian from the Davidic family, second in the Synhedrion under Rabban Simeon ben Gamliël.

279 A close relative of Rebbi Ammi died, for whom he had to mourn for seven days.

280 The fourth generation Amora. It seems that Rebbi Yose felt uncomfortable with the prohibition of bathing; he sent one of his students to ask Rebbi Aḥa, the greatest authority in Lydda, in Judea. In the next section, it will be seen that in the South, in Judea, one did not follow Rebbi Nathan and allowed bathing for the mourner. Nevertheless, Rebbi Aḥa did not want to interfere with the prohibition accepted in Galilee and answered not with his own opinion but with a note that Rebbi Yose himself had taught about two cases where the question had come up in Galilee and was answered in the sense of Rebbi Nathan.

281 Rebbi Simeon ben Laqish; the abbreviation "Resh Laqish" is standard in the Babli but very infrequent in the Yerushalmi. The abbreviation probably is that of a lazy copyist.

282 Rebbi Yose to Rebbi Aḥa, that maybe this was only one occasion reported under two different names and, therefore, represents only the opinion of one teacher and not a generally accepted rule that would

need at least two supporting authorities.

283 This is Rebbi Aḥa's answer: Even if you do not agree that Rebbi Ammi asked twice, for two different cases of mourning, and was given the same answer by two different authorities, I have a completely independent occurrence in which Galilean rabbis gave the same ruling and, therefore, you have to accept it.

284 He is the third generation Amora, father of Rebbi Oshaya the second.

רִבִּי יוֹסֵי בָּעֵי אִילֵּין רַבָּנָן. רַבָּנָן דְּהָכָא אוֹ רַבָּנָן דְּרוֹמַיָּא. אִין תֵּימַר רַבָּנָן דְּהָכָא נִיחָא. אִין תֵּימַר רַבָּנָן דְּרוֹמַיָּא. רַבְרְבַייָא קוֹמוֹי וְהוּא שָׁאַל לִזְעִירַייָא. אִין תֵּימַר רַבָּנָן דְּרוֹמַיָּא אִינּוּן שָׁרֵיִן וְאִינּוּן אָסְרִין. דְּתַנֵּי מָקוֹם שֶׁנָּהֲגוּ לְהַרְחִיץ אַחַר הַמִּיטָּה מַרְחִיצִין וּבְדָרוֹם מַרְחִיצִין. אָמַר רִבִּי יוֹסֵי בֵּי רִבִּי אָבוּן מִי שֶׁהוּא מַתִּיר אֶת הָרְחִיצָה הַזֹּאת עוֹשֶׂה אוֹתָהּ כַּאֲכִילָה וּשְׁתִיָּה.

Rebbi Yose asked, which rabbis[285]? The rabbis here or the rabbis in the South? If you say the rabbis of here, it is fine[286]. If you would say the rabbis from the South, would he have asked minor authorities when greater ones were before him? If you say the rabbis of the South, some of them would allow and some of them would forbid, as we have stated: "At a place where it is customary to bathe after a funeral, one may bathe; in the South one bathes." Rebbi Yose bar Abun said: He who permits that bath makes it like eating and drinking[287].

285 Rebbi Yose is not satisfied with the second source of Rebbi Aḥa since it speaks of unspecified "rabbis" whose place and importance, as a precedent in Galilee, is indeterminate.

286 This is Rebbi Aḥa's answer: Since the questioner is Galilean and all the important Academies were in Galilee at his time, it is unreasonable to assume that "the rabbis" were Southerners whose opinion, as a minority opinion, would not count as precedent.

287 According to Ramban (*Writings*, ed. Chavel, p. 175-176), Rebbi Yose bar Abun restricts the bathing to the aftermath of the funeral and says that in the same way that the mourner must

have his first meal prepared for him by his relatives and friends, so his relatives and friends must cleanse him after the funeral from dust and germs (שיבתא). Hence, where it is customary, e. g. in the South, the mourner can have one bath, prepared by others, just after the funeral but is forbidden to have another one for the rest of the period of mourning. It then is difficult to understand the question of Rabban Gamliel's students. Ramban writes that either he lived in a community where that bath was not customary or he was not satisfied with the cold bath prepared for him but took a full warm bath with following rubbing with oil for his asthenic condition.

הָדָא דְתֵימַר בִּרְחִיצָה שֶׁל תַּעֲנוּג. אֲבָל בִּרְחִיצָה שֶׁאֵינָהּ שֶׁל תַּעֲנוּג מוּתָּר. כְּהָדָא דִשְׁמוּאֵל בַּר אַבָּא עָלוּ בוֹ חַטָּטִין אָתוּן שָׁיילוּן לְרִבִּי יוֹסֵי מַהוּ דְיַסְחֵי. אָמַר לוֹן דְּלָא יַסְחֵי מַיִית הוּא. אִין בָּעֵי אֲפִילוּ בְתִשְׁעָה בְאַב. אִין בָּעֵי אֲפִילוּ בְיוֹם הַכִּיפּוּרִים.

That means, about a bath for pleasure. But a bath that is not for pleasure is permitted[288]. An example is the case of Samuel bar Abba who developed scab. They came and asked Rebbi Yose, what is the rule, may he bathe? He said to them: If he does not bathe, would he not die[289]? If he needs it, even on the Ninth of Av. If he needs it, even on Yom Kippur[290].

288 This is in keeping with Rabban Gamliel's ruling, that every medically indicated bath is permitted.

289 The author of *Sepher Ḥaredim* takes this as hyperbole since in case of danger to life everything is permitted except murder, incest, and idolatry; he does not consider the remark of Rebbi Yose a restriction on the use of any medically indicated bath.

290 On both days, formal washing is forbidden. The rule is quoted in Babli *Yoma* 77b.

רִבִּי יוֹסֵי בְּרִבִּי חֲנִינָא רָאוּ אוֹתוֹ טוֹבֵל. אִם לְקֵירוּיוֹ לֹא יָדְעִין אִם לְהָקֵר גּוּפוֹ שֶׁאֵין רְחִיצַת צוֹנֵן רְחִיצָה לֹא יָדְעִין.

They saw Rebbi Yose, son of Rebbi Ḥanina[291], immersing himself. They did not know whether it was for his emission[292], they did not know whether it was to cool down because bathing in cold water is not called bathing[293].

291 One of the first students of Rebbi Yoḥanan, preceding the other authorities mentioned up to now.

292 An emission of semen which requires immersion in a ritual bath as explained in the next chapter. Marital relations are forbidden for the mourner during the entire seven days of mourning.

293 It remains undecided whether taking a cold bath during the mourning period is permitted or not. The Babylonian authorities in the Babli (*Taänit* 13a) declare that a cold bath is forbidden to a mourner (and, therefore, on the Ninth of Av) but is allowed on fast days (in a year of draught) when the emphasis is on deprivation.

הוֹרֵי רִבִּי בָּא כְהֵין תַּנְיָא. הוֹרֵי רִבִּי אָחָא בְּבָא מִן הַדֶּרֶךְ וְהָיוּ רַגְלָיו קֵיהוֹת עָלָיו שֶׁמּוּתָּר לְהַרְחִיצָן בַּמַּיִם.

Rebbi Abba taught like that which was stated[294]. Rebbi Aḥa taught about him who comes from the road[295] and his feet ache that he is permitted to wash them with water.

294 This statement does not belong here but either in the last chapter of *Yoma* (fol. 44d) or the first chapter of *Taäniot*: "When somebody goes (on the Ninth of Av or Yom Kippur) to see his teacher and has to pass a river on the way, he crosses it without compunction." The statement is given here to show that, in fact, taking a cold bath by walking through the ford of a river, is no infringement of the prohibition of taking a bath on these fast days.

295 A family member who comes to observe the period of mourning with the family but arrives only after the funeral when the rest of the family already is in full mourning. This ruling of Rebbi Aḥa is not restricted to the place where one allows a bath for the mourner but falls under the heading of medical necessity.

This ruling introduces subsequent statements concerning a mourner on a trip, or people on a trip who meet mourners.

תַּנֵּי אָבֵל וּמְנוּדֶּה שֶׁהָיוּ מְהַלְּכִין בַּדֶּרֶךְ מוּתָּרִין בִּנְעִילַת הַסַּנְדָּל. לִכְשֶׁיָּבוֹאוּ אֶל הָעִיר יַחֲלוֹצוּ. וְכֵן בְּתִשְׁעָה בְאַב וְכֵן בְּתַעֲנִית צִיבּוּר.

It has been stated: "A mourner and one banned[296] on a trip are permitted to wear sandals[297]. When they come to town they should remove them. The same holds for the Ninth of Av and public fasts[298]."

296 One put in the ban by rabbinical authority for improper behavior, who should show the signs of mourning.

297 Even though mourners are not allowed to wear leather shoes or sandals. This again is a medical exemption.

298 The fast days proclaimed in the Land of Israel during a draught, when all the deprivations of Yom Kippur are also in force. The only fast day in the diaspora where these rules also apply is the Ninth of Av.

תַּנֵּי בְּמָקוֹם שֶׁנָּהֲגוּ לִשְׁאוֹל אֲבֵלִים בְּשַׁבָּת שׁוֹאֲלִין. וּבְדָרוֹם שׁוֹאֲלִין. רִבִּי הוֹשַׁעְיָא רוּבָּא אֲזַל לְחַד אֲתָר וַחֲזָא אֲבֵילַיָּא בְשׁוּבְתָּא וּשְׁאִיל בּוֹן. אָמַר לוֹן אֲנִי אֵינִי יוֹדֵעַ מִנְהַג מְקוֹמְכֶם. אֶלָּא שָׁלוֹם עֲלֵיכֶם כְּמִנְהַג מְקוֹמֵינוּ. רִבִּי יוֹסֵי בֵּי רִבִּי חֲלַפְתָּא מְשַׁבֵּחַ בִּדְרִבִּי מֵאִיר קוֹמֵי צִיפּוֹרָאֵי אָדָם גָּדוֹל אָדָם קָדוֹשׁ אָדָם צָנוּעַ. חַד זְמַן חֲמָא אֲבֵלַיָּא בְשׁוּבְתָּא וּשְׁאַל בּוֹן. אָמְרֵי לֵיהּ אֲהֵן דְּאַתְּ מַתְנֵי שְׁבָחֵיהּ. אֲמַר לוֹן מַה עִסְקֵיהּ. אָמְרֵי לֵיהּ חֲמָא אֲבֵלַיָּא בְשׁוּבְתָּא וּשְׁאַל בּוֹן. אֲמַר לוֹן בָּעְאֵי אַתּוּן מֵידַע מַהוּ חֵילֵיהּ בָּא לְהוֹדִיעֲכֶם שֶׁאֵין אֵבֶל בְּשַׁבָּת. הֲדָא הוּא דִכְתִיב בִּרְכַּת יי הִיא תַעֲשִׁיר זוּ בִּרְכַּת שַׁבָּת. וְלֹא יוֹסִיף עֶצֶב עִמָּהּ זוּ אֲבֵלוּת. כְּמָה דְתֵימָא נֶעֱצַב הַמֶּלֶךְ עַל בְּנוֹ.

It is stated: "In a place where one is used to greet mourners[299] on the Sabbath one may do so. In the South one does greet."

The great Rebbi Oshaya[300] went to some place, saw there mourners on the Sabbath and greeted them. He said to them: "I do not know the custom of your place, but be greeted according the custom of our place."

Rebbi Yose, son of Rebbi Ḥalaphta, praised Rebbi Meïr before the people of Sepphoris: A great, holy, and meek man. At some time, he saw mourners on the Sabbath and greeted them. They said to him[301]: Is that the one whose praise you proclaim[302]? He said to them, what are his works? They said to him, he saw mourners on the Sabbath and greeted them. He said to them: you have to recognize his strength; he comes to make you aware that there is no mourning on the Sabbath. That is what is written (*Prov.* 10:22): "The blessing of the Lord makes rich," that is the blessing of Sabbath, "He will not add grief to it," that is mourning, as it is said (*2Sam.* 19:3): "The king is grieving about his son."[303]

299 Wishing them well.

300 One of the foremost students of Rebbi, the compiler of the Mishnah, and of Rebbi Ḥiyya. He was from the region of Lod in the South, but he studied in Galilee. In his story, the Aramaic verb for "to see" is חזי in Southern (and Babylonian) Aramaic. In the following story about Rebbi Yose from Galilee, the corresponding verb is Galilean Aramaic חמי. the South was adopted also in Galilee.

301 In this entire story, the singular refers to Rebbi Yose (the Tanna) and the plural to the people of Sepphoris. We learn that in the region of Sepphoris, lower Galilee, is was not customary to console mourners on the Sabbath. From the conclusion we may infer that under the influence of Rabbis Yose and Meïr the custom of the South was adopted also in Galilee. The disagreement between the people in the South (Judea) and North (Galilee) is also discussed in the Babli (*Megillah* 23a,b); according to that source the dispute was only settled in favor of the Southern stance in the days of Rebbi Yoḥanan.

302 Because he seems to be an ignoramus.

303 This is a lexicographical note about the meaning of the root עצב, which as a verb either means "to grieve, to be pained", connected with Arabic עֹצב, or "to form, create", close to Arabic עצֹב. As a noun, one usually distinguishes עֶצֶב "pain, grief; labor, gain; vessel", עַצָּב "worker", and עֹצֶב "idol, pain". Usually, the noun in the verse in *Proverbs* is translated by

"labor", but the explanation here substitutes the more common meaning "grief".

משנה ח: וּכְשֶׁמֵּת טֶבִי עַבְדּוֹ קִיבֵּל עָלָיו תַּנְחוּמִין. אָמְרוּ לוֹ לֹא לִימַּדְתָּנוּ רַבֵּנוּ שֶׁאֵין מְקַבְּלִין תַּנְחוּמִין עַל הָעֲבָדִים. אָמַר לָהֶן אֵין טֶבִי עַבְדִּי כִּשְׁאָר עֲבָדִים כָּשֵׁר הָיָה.

Mishnah 8: And when his[304] slave Tevi died, he received condolences about him. They said to him: Our teacher, did you not teach us that one does not accept condolences for slaves? He said to them: My slave Tevi was not like other slaves, he was honest[305].

304 Rabban Gamliel's.

305 Since slaves were not liable in civil law, they could not be sued for damages of any kind, and neither could their master for their misdeeds; it was assumed that slaves were thieves, confidence men, and careless with anybody's property and, when freed, had trouble establishing themselves as trustworthy witnesses.

הלכה ח: הָא בְנֵי חוֹרִים אַחֵרִים מְקַבְּלִין תַּנְחוּמִין עֲלֵיהֶן. כֵּינִי מַתְנִיתָא אֵין מְקַבְּלִין תַּנְחוּמִין עַל הָעֲבָדִים.

Halakhah 8: Hence, about unrelated freed men one accepts condolences? So is the Mishnah: one does not accept condolences for slaves.[306]

306 There are several different explanations of this cryptic piece. The most reasonable is by R. Abraham ben Adrat (Rashba) in his commentary on Babli *Berakhot* 16b: Since the slave is not related to his master, even if he were free the master would not accept formal condolences for him since these are restricted to those close relatives for which one has to keep a period of formal mourning. The answer is that the Mishnah has to declare explicitly

that one does not accept formal condolences since the slave is a member of the household and, presumably, is treated like a family member, parallel to the case of a student for whom the teacher may accept condolences; see the section after the next.

מַעֲשֶׂה וּמֵתָה שִׁפְחָתוֹ שֶׁל רִבִּי אֱלִיעֶזֶר וְנִכְנְסוּ תַלְמִידָיו לְנַחֲמוֹ וְלֹא קִיבֵּל. נִכְנַס מִפְּנֵיהֶם לֶחָצֵר וְנִכְנְסוּ אַחֲרָיו. לְבַיִת וְנִכְנְסוּ אַחֲרָיו. אָמַר לָהֶן כִּמְדוּמֶּה הָיִיתִי שֶׁאַתֶּם נִכְוִין בְּפוֹשְׁרִין וְאִי אַתֶּם נִכְוִין אֲפִילוּ בְרוֹתְחִין. הֲלֹא אָמְרוּ אֵין מְקַבְּלִין תַּנְחוּמִין עַל הָעֲבָדִים מִפְּנֵי שֶׁהָעֲבָדִים כִּבְהֵמָה. אִם עַל בְּנֵי חוֹרִין אֲחֵרִים אֵין מְקַבְּלִין תַּנְחוּמִין כָּל־שֶׁכֵּן עַל הָעֲבָדִים. מִי שֶׁמֵּת עַבְדּוֹ אוֹ בְהֶמְתּוֹ אוֹמֵר לוֹ הַמָּקוֹם יְמַלֵּא חֶסְרוֹנָךְ.

It happened that Rebbi Eliezer's maidservant died[307] and his students came to him for condolences but he did not accept. He entered the courtyard, they followed him there. He entered the house, they followed him there. He told them: I was thinking that you would be burned by lukewarm water but you are not burned even by boiling water. Did they not say that one does not accept condolences for slaves because slaves are in this like animals? If one does not accept condolences for unrelated free persons, so much more for slaves[308]. If one's slave or animal died, people say to him: The Omnipresent may replace your loss.

307 She must have been his personal maidservant. The story is repeated in an enlarged version in Babli *Berakhot* 16b and, in the Yerushalmi version, in *Evel Rabbati* 1:9,10.

308 Rebbi Eliezer disagrees with his brother-in-law Rabban Gamliel and with the statement of the previous section in the Talmud. He will read in the Mishnah "*because* one does not accept condolences for slaves", meaning that this is a rule that cannot be waved. In the Babli, his attitude is directly contradicted by Rebbi Yose, the most authoritative of the Tannaïm of the fourth generation. Rebbi Yose even recommends eulogies for honest slaves; this represents the Galilean attitude (not shared in Babylonia) and, while not spelled out in the

Yerushalmi, is taken for granted in this passage which immediately after the present story gives examples of model eulogies for rabbis.

כַּד דָּמַךְ רִבִּי חִיָּא בַּר אָדָא בַּר אַחְתֵּיהּ דְּבַר קַפָּרָא קִבֵּיל רֵישׁ לָקִישׁ עִילוֹי דַּהֲוָה רַבֵּיהּ נֵימָא תַּלְמִידֵיהּ דְּבַר נַשָּׁא חָבִיב עֲלֵיהּ כִּבְרֵיהּ עָאַל וְאִיפְטַר עִילוֹי דּוֹדִי יָרַד לְגַנּוֹ לַעֲרוּגֹת הַבּוֹשֶׂם לִרְעוֹת בַּגַּנִּים. לֹא צוּרְכָה אֶלָּא דּוֹדִי יָרַד לְגַנּוֹ לִרְעוֹת בַּגַּנִּים. דּוֹדִי זֶה הַקָּדוֹשׁ בָּרוּךְ הוּא. יָרַד לְגַנּוֹ זֶה הָעוֹלָם. לַעֲרוּגֹת הַבּוֹשֶׂם אֵילוּ יִשְׂרָאֵל. לִרְעוֹת (fol. 5c) בַּגַּנִּים אֵילוּ אוּמּוֹת הָעוֹלָם. וְלִלְקוֹט שׁוֹשַׁנִּים אֵילוּ הַצַּדִּיקִים שֶׁמְּסַלְּקָן מִבֵּינֵיהֶן. מָשְׁלוּ מָשָׁל לְמַה הַדָּבָר דּוֹמֶה לְמֶלֶךְ שֶׁהָיָה לוֹ בֵן וְהָיָה חָבִיב עָלָיו יוֹתֵר מִדַּאי. מַה עָשָׂה הַמֶּלֶךְ נָטַע לוֹ פַּרְדֵּס. בְּשָׁעָה שֶׁהָיָה הַבֵּן עוֹשֶׂה רְצוֹנוֹ שֶׁל אָבִיו הָיָה מְחַזֵּר בְּכָל הָעוֹלָם כּוּלּוֹ וְרוֹאֶה אֵי זוֹ נְטִיעָה יָפָה בָעוֹלָם וְנוֹטְעָהּ בְּתוֹךְ פַּרְדֵּיסוֹ. וּבְשָׁעָה שֶׁהָיָה מַכְעִיסוֹ הָיָה מְקַצֵּץ כָּל־נְטִיעוֹתָיו. כַּךְ בְּשָׁעָה שֶׁיִּשְׂרָאֵל עוֹשִׂין רְצוֹנוֹ שֶׁל הַקָּדוֹשׁ בָּרוּךְ הוּא מְחַזֵּר בְּכָל־הָעוֹלָם כּוּלּוֹ וְרוֹאֶה אֵי זֶה צַדִּיק בְּאוּמּוֹת הָעוֹלָם וּמֵבִיאוֹ וּמְדַבְּקוֹ בְּיִשְׂרָאֵל. כְּגוֹן יִתְרוֹ וְרָחָב. וּבְשָׁעָה שֶׁהֵן מַכְעִיסִין אוֹתוֹ הָיָה מְסַלֵּק הַצַּדִּיקִים שֶׁבֵּינֵיהֶן.

When Rebbi Ḥiyya bar Ada[309], the nephew of Bar Qappara, died did Resh Laqish accept for him since he was his teacher and a student is beloved as a son[310]. He went and eulogized him: (*Song of Songs* 6:2) "My friend descended to his garden, to the spice patch[311], to shepherd in the gardens."[312] It would have been necessary only to say ""My friend descended to shepherd in the gardens." But "my friend" is the Holy One, praise to Him. "He descended to His garden", that is the world. "To the spice patch", that is Israel. "To shepherd in the gardens", these are the peoples of the world. "And to collect lilies", these are the just ones whom He removes from their midst. They gave a parable, to what can this be compared? To a king who had a son whom he loved very much. What did the king do? He planted a garden for him. When the son did the will of his father, the father searched in the entire world for a nice plant and planted it in his garden. When the son was making him angry, he cut down all his plants. So when Israel does the will of the Holy One, praise to Him, he searches the entire world and observes the just person, brings him and attaches him to Israel, like Jethro and Rahab. And when they are making him angry he removes the just ones from amongst them[313].

309 A second generation Amora in Galilee. He had the reputation of a saintly man. He might have been a student of the young Rav in the Academy of Rebbi, but his main teacher was R. Simeon ben Laqish.

Since the topic of condolences and eulogies is implied in the previous text, a list of sample eulogies follows. Most of these are found (with some change in names) in *Midrash Rabba, Song of Songs* on 6:2, *Ecclesiastes* on 5:11.

310 Hence, a teacher may formally mourn a student. In the Babli (*Moëd Qaṭan* 26b), only a student may formally mourn a teacher.

311 While the masoretic text has "spice patches", the consonantal spelling here seems to prefer the singular which also is appropriate to the sermon based on this verse. This does not imply that the verse in Resh Laqish's Bible had here a singular, only that the interpretation as singular is more convenient for his sermon.

312 As with most Scriptural quotes in the Talmud, the main inference is to be drawn from the part of the verse that is not quoted; the student is expected to recognize the verse and to complete it himself. The spelling is left as in the manuscripts and is not edited to conform to our masoretic texts.

313 Implying that Rebbi Ḥiyya bar Ada was collected because of the sins of his generation.

דֵּלְמָא. רִבִּי חִייָא בַּר אַבָּא וַחֲבוּרָתֵיהּ. וְאִית דְּמְרִין רִבִּי יוֹסֵי בֵּי רִבִּי חֲלַפְתָּא וַחֲבוּרָתֵיהּ. וְאִית דְּמְרִין רִבִּי יַעֲקֹב וַחֲבוּרָתֵיהּ. הֲווּ יָתְבִין לָעֵיי בְּאוֹרַיְתָא תְחוֹת חָדָא תְאֵינָה וַהֲוָא מָרָא דִתְאֵינְתָא קָרֵיץ וְלָקֵיט בְּכָל יוֹם. אָמְרֵי שֶׁמָּא הוּא חוֹשְׁדֵינוּ. נַחְלִיף אֶת מְקוֹמֵינוּ. לְמָחָר אַתְיָא מָרָהּ דִּתְאֵינְתָא גַבּוֹן אָמַר לוֹן מָרַיי אַף חָדָא מִצְוָה דַהֲוִיתֵן נְהִיגִין וְעָבְדִין עִמִּי מְנַעְתּוּנִין מִנִּי. אָמְרוּן לֵיהּ

אֲמְרִינָן דִּילְמָא דְאַחְשַׁד לוֹן. בְּצַפְרָא אֲתֵי מוֹדַע יַתְהוֹן זָרְחָה עָלָיו הַחַמָּה וְהִתְלִיעוּ תְּאֵינָתֵיהּ. בְּאוֹתָהּ שָׁעָה אָמְרוּ בַּעַל הַתְּאֵינָה יוֹדֵעַ אֵימָתַי עוֹנָתָהּ שֶׁל תְּאֵינָה לִלְקוֹט וְהָיָה לוֹקְטָהּ. כַּךְ הַקָּדוֹשׁ בָּרוּךְ הוּא יוֹדֵעַ אֵימָתַי עוֹנָתָן שֶׁל צַדִּיקִים לְסַלֵּק מִן הָעוֹלָם וְהוּא מְסַלְּקָן.

A clarification. Rebbi Ḥiyya bar Abba[314] and his group, some say Rebbi Yose bar Ḥalaphta and his group, and some say Rebbi Jacob and his group, were sitting to study Torah under a fig tree. The owner of the fig tree was coming every morning at sunrise and collected figs. They said, maybe he mistrusts us[315], let us change place. The next day, the owner of the fig tree came to them[316]; he said to them: the one *miẓwah* that you used to do with me you are withholding from me[317]. They said to him: We thought that maybe you mistrust us. During the morning he came and informed them that if the sun shines on ripe figs they get wormy[318]. At that time they said, the owner of the fig tree knows the best time to collect figs and he collects them. Likewise, the Holy One, praise to Him, knows the time of the just ones to be removed from the world and He removes them[319].

314 In the Rome manuscript, he is identified as the Great Rebbi Ḥiyya (whose full name was Ḥiyya bar Abba bar Aḥa Karsala from Kufra in Iraq), who otherwise is never referred to as "bar Abba" in the Yerushalmi. The sage here cannot be the third generation Amora R. Ḥiyya bar Abba, student of R. Yoḥanan, since not only are the alternate authors Tannaïm of the fourth generation but the story is very explicit in showing that the scholars among themselves are speaking Hebrew and only with the unlearned farmer they speak Aramaic. The Great Rebbi Ḥiyya belongs to the generation of transition between Tannaïm and Amoraïm; even his inclusion is a little late compared to the other two possible sources. This, as noted by Levi Ginzberg (following Eliezer ben Yehudah) is characteristic of Tannaïtic times.

It is possible that the author of the

Zohar identified this R. Ḥiyya bar Abba as a Tanna of the fourth generation, contemporary of Rebbi Yose, Rebbi Jacob, and, therefore, Rebbi Simeon bar Yoḥai, since he appears there as a major partner in dialogues with the latter.

315 Since he comes early every morning to check on us. (In the Leyden manuscript and the Venice print, the text is "mistrusts me" but the Rome manuscript can be read as "mistrusts us").

316 In the Midrash, it is explained that he went on a systematic search to find his scholars.

317 Since the one who provides the physical means for Torah study, not the scholar, acquires the greater merit from the study, you are depriving me of the merit of Torah study that I cannot acquire on my own.

318 Hence, he has to come early every morning to harvest all figs that are ripe because later they become worthless.

319 In contrast to the Amora Resh Laqish, the Tannaïm do not see in the premature death of a saintly man a consequence of the sins of his contemporaries.

כַּד דָּמַךְ רִבִּי בּוּן בַּר רִבִּי חִייָא עָל רִבִּי זְעִירָא וְאַפְטַר עִילוֹי מְתוּקָה שְׁנַת הָעוֹבֵד. יָשֵׁן אֵין כְּתִיב כָּאן אֶלָּא אִם מְעַט אִם הַרְבֵּה יֹאכֵל. לְמַה הָיָה רִבִּי בּוּן בַּר רִבִּי חִייָא דוֹמֶה לְמֶלֶךְ שֶׁשָּׂכַר פּוֹעֲלִים הַרְבֵּה וְהָיָה שָׁם פּוֹעֵל אֶחָד שֶׁהָיָה מִשְׂתַּכֵּר בִּמְלַאכְתּוֹ יוֹתֵר מִדַּאי. מַה עָשָׂה הַמֶּלֶךְ נְטָלוֹ וְהָיָה מְטַיֵּל עִמּוֹ אֲרוּכוֹת וּקְצָרוֹת. לְעִתּוֹתֵי עֶרֶב בָּאוּ אוֹתָם פּוֹעֲלִים לִיטּוֹל שְׂכָרָן וְנָתַן לוֹ שְׂכָרוֹ אִתָּם מֻשְׁלָם. וְהָיוּ הַפּוֹעֲלִים מִתְרַעֲמִין וְאוֹמְרִין אָנוּ יָגַעְנוּ כָל־הַיּוֹם וְזֶה לֹא יָגַע אֶלָּא שְׁתֵּי שָׁעוֹת וְנָתַן לוֹ שְׂכָרוֹ עִמָּנוּ מֻשְׁלָם. אָמַר לָהֶן הַמֶּלֶךְ יָגַע זֶה לִשְׁתֵּי שָׁעוֹת יוֹתֵר מִמָּה שֶׁלֹּא יְגַעְתֶּם אַתֶּם כָּל־הַיּוֹם כּוּלוֹ. כָּךְ יָגַע רִבִּי בּוּן בַּתּוֹרָה לְעֶשְׂרִים וּשְׁמוֹנֶה שָׁנָה מַה שֶׁאֵין תַּלְמִיד וָתִיק יָכוֹל לִלְמוֹד לְמֵאָה שָׁנָה.

When Rebbi Abun bar Rebbi Ḥiyya[320] died, Rebbi Zeïra ascended his pulpit and eulogized him: (*Eccl.* 6:11) "Sweet is the year of the worker." It does not say here "sleeps" but "whether he eats little or much." To what can Rebbi Bun bar Ḥiyya be likened? To a king who hired many workers and there was one worker who was exceptionally productive in his work.

What did the king do? He took him and walked with him the long and the short. In the evening, the workers came to receive their wages and he gave him his total wages with them. The workers complained and said: we were toiling the entire day and this one did toil only for two hours and he gave him his total wages with us! The king told them: This one produced in two hours more than what you produced all day long. So Rebbi Bun produced in Torah in 28 years what an outstanding[321] student cannot learn in a hundred years.

320 One of the frequently quoted authorities of the Jerusalem Talmud, a student of Rebbi Yoḥanan and Rebbi Zeïra; he died young as his eulogy shows.

321 Or, with the Arabic ותיק "constant, resolute".

כַּד דָּמַךְ רִבִּי סִימוֹן בַּר זְבִיד עָאַל רִבִּי לַיא וְאַפְטַר עִילוֹי אַרְבָּעָה דְּבָרִים תַּשְׁמִישׁוֹ שֶׁל עוֹלָם וְכוּלָּן אִם אָבְדוּ יֵשׁ לָהֶן חֲלִיפִין כִּי יֵשׁ לַכֶּסֶף מוֹצָא וּמָקוֹם לַזָּהָב יָזוֹקוּ בַּרְזֶל מֵעָפָר יוּקָּח וְאֶבֶן יָצוּק נְחוּשָׁה. אֵילּוּ אִם אָבְדוּ יֵשׁ לָהֶן חֲלִיפִין. אֲבָל תַּלְמִיד חָכָם שֶׁמֵּת מִי מֵבִיא לָנוּ חֲלִיפָתוֹ. מִי מֵבִיא לָנוּ תְּמוּרָתוֹ. וְהַחָכְמָה מֵאַיִן תִּמָּצֵא וְאֵי זֶה מָקוֹם בִּינָה וְנֶעֶלְמָה מֵעֵינֵי כָּל חָי. אָמַר רִבִּי לֵוִי אִם אַחֵי יוֹסֵף עַל שֶׁמָּצְאוּ מְצִיאָה יָצָא לִבָּם דִּכְתִיב וַיֵּצֵא לִבָּם. אָנוּ שֶׁאָבַדְנוּ אֶת רִבִּי סִימוֹן בַּר זְבִיד עַל אַחַת כַּמָּה וְכַמָּה.

When Rebbi Simon bar Zevid[322] died, Rebbi Illai ascended and eulogized him: Four things are used in the world and if they are lost, they have replacement, (*Job* 28:1,2) "But silver has a source, and a place is where gold is refined; iron is taken from dust, and stone is smelted into copper." Those, if they are lost, have replacement. But a scholar who died, who can bring us his replacement, who can bring us his substitute? (*Job* 28:12[323],21) "Wisdom, where can it be found, where is the place of understanding? It is hidden from the eyes of all living!" Rebbi Levi[324] said: If the brothers of Joseph lost their spirit because they found something, as it is written (*Gen.* 42:28) "they lost their spirit", we, who lost Rebbi Simon bar Zevid, so much more!

322 A Galilean Amora of the third generation, also quoted as Rebbi Simon bar Savdi, whose discussions with Rebbi Illaï (Lai) are recorded several times in the Yerushalmi. He was a teacher of the leaders of the fourth generation of Amoraïm, Rebbis Ḥizkiah, Jonah, and Phineas.

323 It seems that the preacher wanted to refer to verse 20: "Wisdom, from where does it come?"

324 Probably a scribal error for Lai. But the parallel in Yerushalmi *Horaiot* 3:8 (fol. 38b) also has Rebbi Levi.

כַּד דָּמַךְ רִבִּי לֵוִי בַּר סִיסִי עָל אֲבִיו דִּשְׁמוּאֵל וְאַפְטַר עִילוֹי סוֹף דָּבָר הַכֹּל נִשְׁמָע אֶת הָאֱלֹהִים יְרָא. לְמַה הָיָה לֵוִי בַּר סִיסִי דוֹמֶה לְמֶלֶךְ שֶׁהָיָה לוֹ כֶּרֶם וְהָיוּ בוֹ מֵאָה גְּפָנִים וְהָיוּ עוֹשׂוֹת כָּל־שָׁנָה וְשָׁנָה מֵאָה חָבִיּוֹת שֶׁל יַיִן. עָמַד עַל חֲמִשִּׁים עָמַד עַל אַרְבָּעִים עָמַד עַל שְׁלֹשִׁים עָמַד עַל עֶשְׂרִים עָמַד עַל עֶשֶׂר עָמַד עַל אֶחָד וְהָיָה עוֹשֶׂה מֵאָה חָבִיּוֹת שֶׁל יַיִן. וְהָיָה אוֹתוֹ הַגֶּפֶן חָבִיב עָלָיו כְּכָל־הַכֶּרֶם כּוּלּוֹ. כָּךְ הָיָה רִבִּי לֵוִי בַּר סִיסִי חָבִיב לִפְנֵי הַקָּדוֹשׁ בָּרוּךְ הוּא כְּכָל־אָדָם. הָדָא הוּא דִכְתִיב כִּי זֶה כָּל־הָאָדָם כִּי זֶה כְּכָל־הָאָדָם.

When Rebbi Levi bar Sisi[325] died, the father of Samuel came and eulogized him: (*Eccl.* 12:13) "Final word: Everything has been heard, fear God." To what can Rebbi Levi ben Sisi be compared? To a king who had a vineyard with a hundred vines which gave him every year a hundred barrels of wine. He reduced them to 50, to 40, to 30, to 20, to ten, to one, and this one gave him a hundred barrels of wine. This one vine was as dear to him as the entire vineyard. So Rebbi Levi bar Sisi was beloved before the Holy One, praise to Him, like all mankind. This is what is written (*loc. cit.*) "Because that is all of man," that one is like all of mankind[326].

325 One of the outstanding students of Rebbi, in the generation of transition between Tannaïm and Amoraïm. Some time after Rebbi's death he emigrated to Nahardea in Babylonia where he became an associate of Abba bar Abba, the father of Samuel, a descendant of Ḥananiah, the nephew of Rebbi Joshua, who founded the first Talmudic academy in Babylonia at the outbreak of the war of Bar Kokhba. He, like the Great Rebbi Ḥiyya, was a collector of mishnaic material (*baraitot*); his collection became the foundation of study in Nahardea.

326 A kind of pun on the possible interpretations of כל as "all" or "entire". In the Babli (*Berakhot* 6b) this is a sermon of Rebbi Abba bar Kahana, a Babylonian who became preacher of the third generation of Amoraïm in Galilee.

כַּהֲנָא הֲוָה עוּלֶם סַגִּין כַּד סְלִיק לְהָכָא חַמְתֵּיהּ חַד בַּר פַּחִין. אָמַר לֵיהּ מַה קָלָא בִשְׁמַיָּא. אָמַר לֵיהּ גְּזַר דִּינֵיהּ דְּהַהוּא גַּבְרָא מִיחְתָּם. וְכֵן הֲוָת לֵיהּ. וּמִתְפְּגַע בֵּיהּ. חַמְתֵּיהּ חַד חָרָן. אָמַר לֵיהּ מַה קָלָא בִשְׁמַיָּא. אָמַר לֵיהּ גְּזַר דִּינֵיהּ דְּהַהוּא גַּבְרָא מִיחְתָּם. וְכֵן הֲוָת לֵיהּ. אָמַר מַה סְלִיקִית מִזַּכֵּי וַאֲנָא אִיחֲטֵי. מַה סְלִיקִית לְמִיקְטְלָה בְנֵי אַרְעָא דְיִשְׂרָאֵל נֵיזוּל וְנִיחוּת לִי מִן הֵן דִּסְלִיקִית. אָתָא לְגַבֵּי רִבִּי יוֹחָנָן אָמַר לֵיהּ בַּר נַשׁ דְּאִימֵּיהּ מַסְבְּרָא לֵיהּ וְאִיתְּתֵיהּ דַּאֲבוּהִי מוֹקְרָא לֵיהּ לְהֵן יֵיזִיל לֵיהּ. אָמַר לֵיהּ יֵיזִל לֵיהּ דְּמוֹקְרִין לֵיהּ. נָחַת לֵיהּ כַּהֲנָא מִן הֵן דִּסְלִיק. אֲתוּן אָמְרִין לֵיהּ לְרִבִּי יוֹחָנָן הָא נְחִית כַּהֲנָא לְבָבֶל. אָמַר מַה הֲוָה מֵיזַל לֵיהּ דְּלָא מֵיסַב רְשׁוּתָא. אָמְרִין לֵיהּ הַהִיא מִילְּתָא דְאָמַר לָךְ הִיא הֲוָת נְטִילַת רְשׁוּת דִּידֵיהּ.

Cahana[327] was very young when he came up here. A person in rags saw him and asked him, what is new in Heaven? He answered: The judgment over this man has been sealed. This happened to him and he was stricken. Another one in rags saw him and asked, what is new in Heaven? He answered: The judgment over this man has been sealed. This happened to him. He said: Did I not go up to gain merit, but I am sinning! Did I come up to kill the people of the Land of Israel? I shall go and step down the way I came up. He came to Rebbi Yoḥanan and said to him: A man whose mother wishes him well and whose step mother[328] honors him, should he go there? He said to him, he should go there where he is honored. Cahana descended the way he came up. They came and told Rebbi Yoḥanan that Cahana had descended to Babylonia. He said, how could he go without asking permission? They told him: that question, that he asked of you, was his request for permission.

327 While the previous section dealt with a Galilean emigrating to Babylonia, we now deal with Babylonians immigrating into Israel. Cahana here is Rav Cahana II; his story can be understood only in connection with the remarks in Babli *Bava Qama* 117a,b; the interpretation is Rashi's (117b).

Rav Cahana was a young member of the Academy of Rav when Rav unsuccessfully tried to dissuade a Jew from informing against another Jew before the Persian authorities. Rav Cahana was so outraged that he slapped the would-be informer and broke his neck. Rav pointed out to him that under the new Sassanid regime the Jews had lost the criminal jurisdiction they had under the Parthians and that, therefore, he was liable to be prosecuted. Rav told him to go ("ascend") to the Land of Israel, to the Academy of Rebbi Yoḥanan, but he warned him not to ask difficult questions from Rebbi Yoḥanan for seven years. This must have happened between the Sassanid victory in 226 C.E. and Rav's death in 247 C.E. (Since the organization of the new Persian empire must have taken some time, the earliest time for Rav Cahana's flight is probably around 235 C.E. When Rav Cahana returned to Babylonia, he became a student of Rav's successors Rav Yehudah and Rav Huna; hence, he returned after 247 C.E.) In Tiberias, Cahana (whose rabbinical title is not recognized in the Yerushalmi) first kept Rav's injunction but in the end he found a way to get around it and was recognized by Rebbi Yoḥanan as a great scholar. Unfortunately, by a birth defect or an accident, Cahana had unsymmetric lips which gave his face the look of a permanent smirk and Rebbi Yoḥanan got offended. He gave him an evil eye so that Cahana died. When informed that the smirk was no smirk but a bodily feature of Cahana, he went to the cave where Cahana was buried. The entrance to the cave was guarded by a poisonous snake which let Rebbi Yoḥanan enter only after he had publicly acknowledged that he had been a student of Cahana. Then he prayed in the cave and Cahana was resurrected from the dead. This is the basis of the questions asked here by the hoodlums. According to the Babli, Rav Cahana found the presence of R. Yoḥanan too dangerous. This will explain the roundabout way in which he asked for leave from the Academy in the Yerushalmi version.

328 The land of Babylonia.

רִבִּי זְעִירָא כַּד סְלִיק לְהָכָא אָזַל אַקִּיז דָּם. אֲזַל בָּעֵי מִיזְבַּן חָדָא לִיטְרָא דְקוּפָּד מִן טַבְּחָא. אָמַר לֵיהּ בְּכַמָּה הָדֵין לִטְרְתָא אָמַר לֵיהּ בְּחַמְשִׁין מָנַיי וְחַד קוּרְסָם. אָמַר לֵיהּ סַב לָךְ שִׁיתִּין וְלָא קְבִיל עִילוֹי. סַב לָךְ ע וְלָא קְבִיל עִילוֹי. סַב לָךְ פ. סַב לָךְ צ. עַד דְּמָטָא לְמֵאָה וְלָא קְבִיל עִילוֹי. אָמַר לֵיהּ עֲבִיד כְּמִנְהָגָךְ. בְּרוּמְשָׁא נְחִית לְבֵית וַעֲדָא. אָמַר לוֹן רַבָּנָן מַה בִּישׁ מִנְהָגָא דְהָכָא דְּלָא אָכַל בַּר נַשׁ לִיטְרָא דְקוּפָּד עַד דְּמָחֵי לֵיהּ חַד קוּרְסָם. אָמְרִין לֵיהּ וּמַה הוּא דֵין. אָמַר לוֹן פְּלָן טַבְּחָא. שְׁלְחוּן בָּעֵיי מֵיתְתֵיהּ וְאַשְׁכְּחוּן אֲרוֹנֵיהּ נַפְקָא. אָמְרוּ לֵיהּ רִבִּי כָּל־הָכֵין אָמַר לָהוּ וְיֵיתֵי עָלַי דְּלָא כָעַסִית עִלוֹי מִי סְבָרִת דְּמִנְהָגָא כָּךְ.

Rebbi Zeïra went to have himself bled when he ascended here[329]. He went and wanted to buy a pound[330] of red meat from a butcher. He asked him: How much is that pound? He said to him, 50 minas and one slap[331]. He said to him: Take 60, but he did not accept. Take 70, but he did not accept. Take 80, take 90, until he came to 100 and he did not accept. Then he said: Do what is your routine. The next morning he went to the Academy and said to them: Rabbis, what is this bad practice here that nobody can eat a pound of red meat unless they slap him! They said to him: Who is that? He said, the butcher so-and-so. They sent to him to bring him but they found that his coffin was being carried out. They said to him: Our teacher, all that[332]? He said to them: That should happen to me, but I was not angry about him[333]; did I not think that this was general practice?

329 This used to be the general method to heal minor illnesses and also served as a prophylactic. Bleeding required that one must eat enough red meat afterwards to replace the lost substance.

330 A Roman pound (*libra*, λίτρα) of twelve Roman ounces, slightly more than 12 avoirdupois ounces. It seems that Rebbi Zeïra incurred the wrath of the butcher by using the correct feminine form *litrĕta* for the Greek *litra*, while common usage was *litra* which in Aramaic really should be masculine (but was not taken as such in popular use).

331 The price of meat can be taken to determine the time of R. Zeïra's arrival in Israel. A Mina (Μνᾶ) was 100 Denar. In old times, a Mina was an enormous sum. But the inflation in the later part of the military anarchy, from the failed currency reform of Aurelianus to the reorganization of the Roman state under Diocletianus, was extreme. All Midrashim telling about exorbitant sums being paid for simple objects of daily use must be dated to that period, from 274-284 C.E. Diocletian introduced new gold coinage based on a price of 50'000 old gold Denars for a Roman pound of gold. This makes one pound of gold (345 g) the equivalent of 1'250'000 old silver denars. At that time, 50 Minas, or 5'000 silver Denars, would therefore be 1.38 g = 0.04 oz of gold or at today's gold prices, $14.45. This is a very high price but not out of line in a time of extreme decline of farming and ranching. It is quite clear from this and other stories that the obligation to eat meat on holidays was a serious monetary obligation. (The so-called silver coins of that period were copper coins dipped for a second in a silver solution.)

קורסם is Greek κρουσμός, ὁ, "striking, smiting, collision".

332 Rebbi Zeïra really had acquired a Babylonian title, "Rav", before he immigrated to Galilee but, being dissatisfied with the style of Talmudic study in Babylonia, he never used it. Seeing that Heaven was giving him special protection, the members of the academy of Tiberias started giving him the Palestinian title, Rebbi, right away. They wondered that Heaven was so quick in punishing a man who had offended him.

333 Hence, I did not wish him dead and I am innocent of his death. This remark connects to the next story.

רִבִּי יָסָא כַּד סְלִיק לְהָכָא אֲזַל סְפָר. בָּעֵי מַסְחֵי בְּאַהֵן דֵּימוֹסִין דְּטִיבֵּרִייָא. פָּגַע בֵּיהּ חַד לֵיצָן וְיָהִיב לֵיהּ פּוּרְקְדָל חַד. אֲמַר לֵיהּ עַד כְּדוֹן עֲנוּבְתָּא דְּהַהוּא גַּבְרָא רַפְיָא. הֲוָה אַרְכוֹנָא קָאִים דָּאִין אֶחָד לֵיסְטֵיס וְאָזַל קָם לֵיהּ גָּחֵיךְ כָּל־קִבְלֵיהּ. אֲמַר לֵיהּ אַרְכוֹנָא מָאן הֲוָה עִמָּךְ תָּלָה עֵינוֹי וְחָמֵי דְּהַהוּא גָּחֵיךְ אֲמַר לֵיהּ הַהוּא דְּגָחֵיךְ הֲוָא עִמִּי. נְסָבֵיהּ וְדָנֵיהּ וְאוֹדֵי לֵיהּ עַל חַד קְטִיל. מִי נַפְקִין תְּרֵוֵיהוֹן טְעֵינִין תַּרְתֵּי שֵׁרִין דְּעָבַר רִבִּי יָסָא מַסְחֵי. אֲמַר לֵיהּ הַהִיא עֲנוּבְתָּא דַּהֲוָת רַפְיָא כְּבָר שְׁנִצַּת. אֲמַר לֵיהּ בִּישׁ גַּדָּא דְּהַהוּא גַּבְרָא וְלָא כְתִיב וְעַתָּה אַל תִּתְלוֹצָצוּ פֶּן יֶחְזְקוּ מוֹסְרֵיכֶם. רִבִּי פִּינְחָס רִבִּי יִרְמְיָה בְּשֵׁם רִבִּי שְׁמוּאֵל בַּר רַב יִצְחָק קָשָׁה הִיא הַלֵּיצָנוּת שֶׁתְּחִילָּתָהּ יִיסוּרִין וְסוֹפָהּ כְּלָיָה. תְּחִילָּתָהּ יִיסוּרִין דִּכְתִיב וְעַתָּה אַל תִּתְלוֹצָצוּ פֶּן יֶחְזְקוּ מוֹסְרֵיכֶם. וְסוֹפָהּ כְּלָיָה דִּכְתִיב כִּי כָלָה וְנֶחֱרָצָה שָׁמַעְתִּי מֵאֵת יי צְבָאוֹת עַל כָּל־הָאָרֶץ.

When Rebbi Yasa ascended here, he went to a barber. He wanted to bathe in a public bath of Tiberias. He met a scoffer who hit him once on his neck and said: The noose[334] of this man is loose. There was an admistrator[335] sitting who was interrogating[336] a robber[337]. He[338] went and stood there all laughing opposite him. The administrator asked him: Who was with you? He looked around and said: The one who is laughing here was with me. He[339] fetched him, interrogated him, and he confessed about one murder. When they both went out, carrying two beams[340], Rebbi Yasa passed by going to the bath. He[341] said to him: That noose which was loose you already tightened. He answered him: That is the bad luck of this man, is it not written (*Is.* 28:22): "Now do not scoff, that your fetters should not be tightened."[342] Rebbi Phineas, Rebbi Jeremiah, in the name of Rebbi Samuel bar Rav Isaac[343]: Scoffing is hard since its start is pain and its end destruction. Its start is pain since it is written "Now do not scoff, that your fetters should not be tightened," and its end is destruction as it is written (*loc. cit.*) "For destruction and finality I heard from the Lord of Hosts[344] over the entire earth."

334 This is the reading of the Rome manuscript. The Venice print has ענוקא "neck" which cannot be loose or tight, but the noose around the neck can.

335 Ἄρχων, "ruler"; in Imperial Rome a local administrator, *praefectus*.

336 Under threat or by the use of judicial torture. (Referring to a Jewish court, the word would mean "punish".)

337 Greek ληστής (also a collateral form ληιστής). The word appears in the Babylonian tradition as לְסְטִים.

338 The scoffer. The next "he, him, he" refer to the robber.

339 The archon, who fetched the scoffer who then confessed to a murder under the threat of torture.

340 The beams used for their own crucifixion.

341 The scoffer who might have laughed about the trick he played on the scholar but who was caught because the robber thought that he was laughing about the pain inflicted on himself and who took revenge by denouncing the scoffer.

342 And, therefore, Rebbi Yasa was not guilty of the scoffer's death.

343 Since he was a contemporary of Rebbis Zeïra and Yasa, it is not clear whether this is an independent aggadic interpretation, appended here because it uses the same verse that R. Yasa used, or as the source of Rebbi Yasa/Assi's interpretation.

344 The Divine Names are not correctly quoted; this relieves the scribe from the necessity of writing down a name which cannot be erased.

משנה ט: חָתָן אִם רוֹצֶא לִקְרוֹת אֶת שְׁמַע בַּלַּיְלָה הָרִאשׁוֹן קוֹרֵא. רַבָּן שִׁמְעוֹן בֶּן גַּמְלִיאֵל אוֹמֵר לֹא כָל־הָרוֹצֶא לִיטּוֹל אֶת הַשֵּׁם יִטּוֹל.

Mishnah 9: The bridegroom may recite the *Shema'* in his first night if he wishes. Rabban Simeon ben Gamliël says, not everyone who wants to grab a reputation[345] can do so.

345 Asserting that he is such a holy man that he can concentrate on his prayers under any circumstances.

הלכה ט: תַּנֵּי כָּל־דָּבָר (fol. 5d) שֶׁהוּא שֶׁל צַעַר כָּל־הָרוֹצֶא לַעֲשׂוֹת עַצְמוֹ יָחִיד עוֹשֶׂה. תַּלְמִיד חָכָם עוֹשֶׂה וְתָבוֹא עָלָיו בְּרָכָה. וְכָל־דָּבָר שֶׁהוּא שֶׁל שְׁבָח לֹא כָּל־הָרוֹצֶא לַעֲשׂוֹת עַצְמוֹ יָחִיד עוֹשֶׂה. תַּלְמִיד חָכָם עוֹשֶׂה אֶלָּא אִם כֵּן מִינּוּ אוֹתוֹ פַּרְנָס עַל הַצִּיבּוּר.

Halakhah 9: It was stated[346]: In anything that gives pain, everyone who wants to distinguish himself may do so. A scholar does and may blessing come to him. In anything that gives praise, not everyone who wants to distinguish himself may do so. A scholar does except if he has been appointed to a position of public authority.

346 This Tosephta (*Taäniot* 1:7) refers to the Mishnah (*Taänit* 1:4) that if there was no rain by the middle of the month of Ḥeshwan, distinguished people start fasting; public fasts because of the draught start only in Kislev. Rabban Simeon ben Gamliel states that in matters that bring pain, everybody can join with the distinguished persons; only in matters that bring prestige, not everyone can join and a scholar cannot join if he has been duly appointed to a position of authority since in that case he has to avoid even the appearance of being better than the people under his authority. The Yerushalmi quotes this Tosephta anonymously, hence it accepts it as valid ruling.

תַּנֵּי מִסְתַּלְּקִין לִצְדָדִין מִפְּנֵי יְתֵידוֹת הַדְּרָכִים. וּבְשָׁעָה שֶׁהוּא מִשְׁתַּקֵּעַ אֲפִילוּ בְשָׂדֶה שֶׁהִיא מְלֵאָה כוּרְכְּמִין. אָמַר רִבִּי אַבָּהוּ מַעֲשֶׂה בְּרַבָּן גַּמְלִיאֵל וְרִבִּי יְהוֹשֻׁעַ שֶׁהָיוּ בַדֶּרֶךְ וְהָיוּ מִסְתַּלְּקִין לִצְדָדִין מִפְּנֵי יְתֵידוֹת הַדְּרָכִים וְרָאוּ אֶת רִבִּי יְהוּדָה בֶן פַּפּוֹס שֶׁהָיָה מִשְׁתַּקֵּעַ וּבָא כְנֶגְדָּן. אָמַר רַבָּן גַּמְלִיאֵל לְרִבִּי יְהוֹשֻׁעַ מִי הוּא זֶה שֶׁמַּרְאֶה עַצְמוֹ בְאֶצְבַּע אָמַר לוֹ יְהוּדָה בֶן פַּפּוֹס הוּא שֶׁכָּל־מַעֲשָׂיו לְשׁוּם שָׁמַיִם. אָמַר לֵיהּ וְלָא כֵן תַּנֵּי כָּל־דָּבָר שֶׁהוּא שֶׁל שְׁבָח לֹא כָל־הָרוֹצֶא לַעֲשׂוֹת עַצְמוֹ יָחִיד עוֹשֶׂה. תַּלְמִיד חָכָם עוֹשֶׂה אֶלָּא אִם כֵּן מִינּוּ אוֹתוֹ פַּרְנָס עַל הַצִּיבּוּר. אָמַר לֵיהּ וְהָא תַנֵּי כָּל־דָּבָר שֶׁהוּא שֶׁל צַעַר כָּל־הָרוֹצֶא לַעֲשׂוֹת עַצְמוֹ יָחִיד עוֹשֶׂה. תַּלְמִיד חָכָם עוֹשֶׂה וְתָבוֹא עָלָיו בְּרָכָה. אָמַר רִבִּי זְעִירָא וּבִלְחוּד דְּלָא יְבַזֶּה חוֹרָנִין.

It was stated: One may step to one side because of obstacles on the road[347]. And when one sinks[348], even into a field full of saffron. Rebbi Abbahu said[349]: It happened that Rabban Gamliel and Rebbi Joshua were on the road and stepped on the side because of obstacles on the road when they saw Rebbi Yehudah ben Pappos, who was sinking, coming towards them. Rabban Gamliël said to Rebbi Joshua: Who is this one who makes an exhibition of himself[350]? He answered: This is Yehudah ben Pappos, all whose deeds are done for Heaven's sake. He said to him[351]: Did we not formulate "In anything that gives praise, not everyone who wants to distinguish himself may do so. A scholar does except if he has been appointed to a position of public authority." He answered him[352]: Did we not also formulate, "In anything that gives pain, everyone who wants to distinguish himself may do so. A scholar does and may blessing come to him." Rebbi Zeïra said, but only if he does not shame others[353].

347 This is one of the conditions of public use of private land which Joshua imposed on the land distributed to the Israelite tribes (Babli *Bava Qama* 81b, Yerushalmi *Bava Batra* 5:1). If a road is impassable, one may walk on the shoulder even if the field is planted up to the roadbed.

348 In the rainy season on an unpaved road.

349 A parallel to this story is quoted in the Babli (*Bava Qama* 81b) concerning Rebbi, Rebbi Ḥiyya, and Rebbi Yehudah ben Qanosa. The disapproving conclusion, given here in the name of the late Amora R. Zeïra, an immigrant from Babylonia, in the Babli is attributed to Rebbi. This shows that the note of Rebbi Zeïra is a belated accomodation of Galilean practice to Babylonian standards.

350 Showing overly great care not to infringe on other people's property. Since the possession of land is a gift of God, any property rights are from the start subject to the liens enacted by Joshua, and use of the shoulders is no infringement of other people's property. R. Yehudah ben Pappos' piety therefore is quite misplaced.

351 Rabban Gamliel to Rebbi Joshua. The implication is that R.

Yehudah ben Pappos, who otherwise is unknown, held a public position and, therefore, was prohibited from exhibiting his piety. (In *Kafṭor waperaḥ*, R. Astorre Parḥi gives the name as Pappos ben Yehudah, a man known for his extreme habits, cf. Tosephta *Soṭa* 5:9. However, of the two men of this name mentioned in Talmudic literature, one is too early, in Temple times, and the other one is mentioned in the prehistory of the revolt of Bar Kokhba, too late).

352 Rebbi Joshua to Rabban Gamliel. Since walking on a wet dirt road is exhausting and very slow, even the holder of public office is permitted to walk on the road.

353 And here, the leaders of the generation were embarrassed by his unnecessary exhibition of piety.

דֵּלְמָא. רִבִּי מִייָשָׁא וְרִבִּי שְׁמוּאֵל בַּר רַב יִצְחָק הֲווּ יָתְבִין אָכְלִין בְּחָדָא מִן אִילֵּין כְּנִישָׁתָא עִלַּייָתָא. אִתַּת עוֹנָתָא דִצְלוֹתָא וְקָם רִבִּי שְׁמוּאֵל בַּר רַב יִצְחָק מְצַלַּייָא. אֲמַר לֵיהּ רִבִּי מִייָשָׁא לָא כֵן אַלְפָן רַבִּי אִם הִתְחִילוּ אֵין מַפְסִיקִין. וְתַנֵּי חִזְקִיָּא כָּל־מִי שֶׁהוּא פָּטוּר מִדָּבָר וְעוֹשֵׂהוּ נִקְרָא הֶדְיוֹט. אֲמַר לֵיהּ וְהָא תַנִּינָן חָתָן פָּטוּר. חָתָן אִם רוֹצֶה. אֲמַר לֵיהּ וְלָא דְּרַבָּן גַּמְלִיאֵל הִיא. אֲמַר לֵיהּ יָכוֹל אֲנָא פְטַר כְּרַבָּן גַּמְלִיאֵל דְּרַבָּן גַּמְלִיאֵל אָמַר אֵינִי שׁוֹמֵעַ לָכֶם לְבַטֵּל מִמֶּנִּי מַלְכוּת שָׁמַיִם.

Clarification. Rebbi Miasha[354] and Rebbi Samuel bar Rav Isaac were sitting and eating in one of the upper synagogues[355]. There came the time of prayer and Rebbi Samuel bar Rav Isaac got up to pray. Rebbi Miasha said to him: Teacher, did you not teach us that once one started one does not interrupt[356]. And Ḥizkiah stated: Every one who is free from an obligation and does it anyway is called uneducated[357]. He answered him: Did we not state[358]: "The bridegroom is free?" The bridegroom, if he wants. He[359] answered him: Is that not from Rabban Gamliël[360]? He said to him, I can free myself as Rabban Gamliel did; Rabban Gamliel said: I shall not listen to you to lift from me the Kingdom of Heaven.

354 This is the reading of ms. Rome. The Venice print has "Rebbi Yasa". The Venice reading explains why R. Samuel is mentioned in second place, since Rebbi Miasha was a student of Rebbi Samuel ben Rav Isaac. Maybe there existed a version in which Rebbi Yasa was mentioned both times.

355 Of Tiberias. Most commentators invert the word order and explain: On the upper floor of a synagogue (since in the synagogue itself one may not eat).

356 Mishnah *Šabbat* 1:5. If the speaker is Rebbi Yasa, one would have to translate: "Did not Rebbi (the editor of the Mishnah) teach us . . .".

357 Greek ἰδιώτης "private person, individual" (as opposed to the State).

358 The two Mishnayot from this chapter, that the groom is absolved from reciting *Shema'* but that he may do so if he wishes.

359 Rebbi Miasha.

360 Mishnah 9, even though formulated anonymously, is only acceptable to Rabban Gamliel, not to those who disagree with the him. The answer is that the Mishnah is acceptable to all.

מי שמתו פרק שלשי

משנה א: מִי שֶׁמֵּתוֹ מוּטָּל לְפָנָיו פָּטוּר מִקְּרִיַּת שְׁמַע וּמִן הַתְּפִילִּין. נוֹשְׂאֵי הַמִּיטָּה וְחִילּוּפֵיהֶן וְחִילּוּפֵי חִילּוּפֵיהֶן אֶת שֶׁלִּפְנֵי הַמִּיטָּה וְאֶת שֶׁלְּאַחַר הַמִּיטָּה. אֶת שֶׁהַמִּיטָּה צוֹרֶךְ בָּהֶן פְּטוּרִין. וְאֶת שֶׁאֵין הַמִּיטָּה צוֹרֶךְ בָּהֶן חַיָּבִין. אֵילּוּ וָאֵילּוּ פְּטוּרִין מִן הַתְּפִילָּה.

Mishnah 1: Anyone whose dead is lying before him[1] is free from reciting *Shema'* and from *tefillin*.[2] The carriers of the bier, their substitutes, and the substitutes of their substitutes, in front of the bier or behind the bier, those that are needed by the bier are free, those that are not needed by the bier are obligated.[3] All of them are free from the obligation to pray.[4]

1 Any close relative who has to mourn for the dead and who has to organize the burial.

2 This is the text of the Yerushalmi and the Mishnah manuscripts. Most sources of the Babylonian Talmud add "and from all obligations of the Torah", but the commentary of *Talmid Rabbenu Yonah* to Alfassi declares that good manuscripts do not contain the addition and it also seems that the addition was not accepted by Tosaphot.

3 In the Babli: "Those behind the bier are obligated". Rashi explains that those in front of the bier await their turn to carry the bier to the cemetary but that those behind the bier already did that; they follow only to honor the dead person, but not to actively render any more services. The Yerushalmi does not know of such an organization.

4 According to Maimonides, the obligation from the Torah is only to say some prayer every day; hence, even if the participants in the burial miss one prayer they still have two others to fulfill the Biblical requirement. According to Nachmanides, the

obligation of prayer is entirely rabbinical and is eliminated before the Torah obligation to bury a fellow Jew.

הלכה א: תַּנֵּי וּמִן הַתְּפִילִּין. אָבֵל בְּיוֹם הָרִאשׁוֹן אֵינוֹ נוֹתֵן תְּפִילִּין. בַּיּוֹם הַשֵּׁנִי הוּא נוֹתֵן תְּפִילִּין. וְאִם בָּאוּ פָּנִים חֲדָשׁוֹת הוּא חוֹלְצָן כָּל־שִׁבְעָה דִּבְרֵי רִבִּי אֱלִיעֶזֶר. רִבִּי יְהוֹשֻׁעַ אוֹמֵר בָּרִאשׁוֹנָה וּבַשֵּׁנִי אֵינוֹ נוֹתֵן תְּפִילִּין בַּיּוֹם הַשְּׁלִישִׁי הוּא נוֹתֵן תְּפִילִּין וְאִם בָּאוּ פָּנִים חֲדָשׁוֹת אֵינוֹ חוֹלְצָן. אִם בַּיּוֹם הַשֵּׁינִי אֵינוֹ נוֹתֵן תְּפִילִּין צוֹרְכָה מֵימַר מִי שֶׁמֵּתוֹ מוּטָּל לְפָנָיו. אֶלָּא בְגִין דְּתַנָּא דָא תַנָּא דָא.

Halakhah 1: It was stated[5]: "And from *tefillin*." A[6] mourner may not put on *tefillin* on the first day; on the second day he puts on *tefillin* and when new faces appear during the seven days of mourning he takes them off; these are the words of Rebbi Eliezer. Rebbi Joshua says: On the first and second days he does not put on *tefillin*; on the third day he puts on *tefillin* and if new faces come he does not take them off.

If he does not put on *tefillin* even on the second day, why is it necessary to mention "anyone whose dead is lying before him"? Because he stated the one he stated the other[7].

5 In the first sentence of our Mishnah.

6 This is a *baraita* from *Moëd Qaṭan* (3:5); a similar *baraita* (with the names of Rebbis Eliezer and Joshua switched) is quoted in Babli *Moëd Qaṭan* 21a. All authorities in all sources agree that a mourner may not put on *tefillin* the entire first day of mourning, even if the burial was conducted in the preceding night. So there is no connection between *tefillin* and the necessity to attend to the burial.

7 Since it is necessary to mention that he is free from reciting *Shema'* (and from prayer, whether that is stated in the Mishnah or not), the mention of *tefillin* is added as a memory aid. Since for a long time the Mishnah was transmitted by memory, it could not have been written down. Memory aids are an important part of Mishnah composition.

רִבִּי זְעִירָא רַב יִרְמְיָה בְּשֵׁם רַב הֲלָכָה כְּרִבִּי אֱלִיעֶזֶר בִּנְתִינָה וּכְרִבִּי יְהוֹשֻׁעַ בַּחֲלִיצָה. רִבִּי זְעִירָא בָּעֵי נָתַן בְּיוֹם הַשֵּׁנִי כְּרִבִּי אֱלִיעֶזֶר מַהוּ שֶׁיַּעֲשֶׂה רִבִּי אֱלִיעֶזֶר כְּרִבִּי יְהוֹשֻׁעַ שֶׁלֹּא לַחְלוֹץ. אָמַר רִבִּי יוֹסֵי בֵּירִבִּי בּוּן וְכֵינִי נַעֲשֶׂה רִבִּי אֱלִיעֶזֶר כְּרִבִּי יְהוֹשֻׁעַ שֶׁלֹּא לַחְלוֹץ וְאִין כֵּינִי נֵימָא הֲלָכָה כְּרִבִּי אֱלִיעֶזֶר.

Rebbi Zeïra, Rav Jeremiah in the name of Rav: Practice follows Rebbi Eliezer in putting on and Rebbi Joshua in taking off[8]. Rebbi Zeïra inquired: If he put them on on the second day, following Rebbi Eliezer, would Rebbi Eliezer act like Rebbi Joshua, not to take them off? Rebbi Yose bar Abun said: Is it so that Rebbi Eliezer would act like Rebbi Joshua, not to take them off? If it were so, we should say "practice follows Rebbi Eliezer."[9]

8 The mourner puts on *tefillin* starting the second day after the funeral and does not take them off for a new visitor. In the Babli, this is a ruling of Ulla, one of the commuters between Babylonia and Galilee in the second generation of Amoraïm.

9 If on the second day, on which we follow Rebbi Eliezer, he takes off *tefillin* for new visitors, then the ruling should have been: Practice follows Rebbi Eliezer on the second day and Rebbi Joshua from the third day on. Since days are not mentioned, it is clear that Rebbi Joshua's opinion, that one does not take off *tefillin* for visits of condolence, does not depend on the day. In the Babli, this is the ruling of Rava, of the generation following Rebbi Zeïra. The Babli quotes from the early Tanna Rebbi Jehudah ben Tema that one puts on *tefillin* and takes them off even a hundred times. Since R. Jehudah ben Tema, whose time cannot be determined, precedes Rav in any case, his opinion is not of much practical value.

אָמַר רִבִּי בּוּן כְּתִיב לְמַעַן תִּזְכּוֹר אֶת יוֹם צֵאתְךָ מֵאֶרֶץ מִצְרַיִם כֹּל יְמֵי חַיֶּיךָ. יָמִים שֶׁאַתְּ עוֹסֵק בָּהֶן בַּחַיִּים. וְלֹא יָמִים שֶׁאַתְּ עוֹסֵק בָּהֶן בַּמֵּתִים.

Rebbi Abun said: It is written (*Deut.* 16:3) "So that you should remember the day of your exodus from Egypt the totality of the days of your living;" the days when you are occupied with the living, not the days that you are occupied with the dead[10].

10 The verse deals with the celebration of Passover but is used to indicate that any obligation of remembrance, and *tefillin* is one of them, are only for living and are invalid once one has to care for the dead. Rebbi Abun here follows the opponents of Ben Zoma in the first chapter who read בֹּל, "the entirety" and not "all". The verse gives a complete justification for the Mishnah, *viz.*, that the entire first day is not for *tefillin*, even after the burial.

תַּנֵּי אִם רָצָא לְהַחֲמִיר עַל עַצְמוֹ אֵין שׁוֹמְעִין לוֹ. לָמָּה מִפְּנֵי כְבוֹדוֹ שֶׁל מֵת. אוֹ מִשּׁוּם שֶׁאֵין לוֹ מִי שֶׁיִּשָּׂא מַשּׂוֹאוֹ. מַה נָפִיק מִבֵּינֵיהוֹן הָיָה לוֹ מִי שֶׁיִּשָּׂא מַשּׂוֹאוֹ. וְאִין תֵּימַר מִפְּנֵי כְבוֹדוֹ שֶׁל מֵת אָסוּר. וְאִם תֹּאמַר מִפְּנֵי שֶׁאֵין לוֹ מִי שֶׁיִּשָּׂא מַשּׂוֹאוֹ הֲרֵי יֵשׁ לוֹ מִי שֶׁיִּשָּׂא מַשּׂוֹאוֹ. וְהָתַנֵּי פָּטוּר מִנְּטִילַת לוּלָב. תִּיפְתַּר בְּחוֹל. וְהָתַנֵּי פָּטוּר מִתְּקִיעַת שׁוֹפָר. אִית לָךְ לְמֵימַר בְּחוֹל לֹא בְיוֹם טוֹב. אָמַר רִבִּי חֲנִינָא מִכֵּיוָן שֶׁהוּא זָקוּק לוֹ לְהָבִיא לוֹ אָרוֹן וְתַכְרִיכִין כְּיֵי דְתַנִּינָן תַּמָּן מַחְשִׁיכִין עַל הַתְּחוּם לְפַקֵּחַ עַל אִיסְקֵי הַכַּלָּה וְאַל עִיסְקֵי הַמֵּת לְהָבִיא לוֹ אָרוֹן וְתַכְרִיכִין חֲלִילִים וּמְקוֹנְנוֹת כְּמִי שֶׁהוּא נוֹשֵׂא מַשָּׂאוֹ.

It was stated: If he wants to be more stringent with himself[10] one does not listen to him[11]. Why? Because of the honor of the deceased or because he has nobody to carry his load[12]? What is the difference between them? If he has someone who is carrying his load; if you say because of the honor of the deceased it is forbidden, but if you say because he has nobody to carry his load, here he has somebody to carry his load. Has it not been stated: he is free from taking the *lulab*[13]? Explain that it refers to weekdays. But has it not been stated: he is free from blowing the *shofar*. Can you say on weekday? No, on holiday. Rebbi Ḥanina said[14]: Because he is obliged to bring him a casket and burial shrouds as we have stated (*Šabbat* 23:4): "One waits for nightfall at the borders of the Šabbat[15] domain to oversee matters for a bride and matters for a deceased to bring for him a casket, burial shrouds, fifes, and women mourners;" it is as if someone was carrying his load.

10 To put on *tefillin* even though he is not obligated.

11 He is forbidden to put on *tefillin*.

12 In organizing the funeral.

13 The mourner whose deceased has not yet been buried may not weave the *lulab* on Tabernacles, nor may he blow the *shofar* on New Year's Day. While the rule of *lulab* applies only to the intermediate days when burials are permitted, one never blows *shofar* as an obligation except on a holiday.

13 R. Ḥanina points out that the argument that somebody works for him is irrelevant since even if he does not do anything physical for the arrangement of the funeral, the task of overseeing and deciding cannot be delegated.

14 Even though it is forbidden to use the Sabbath to prepare for the next day, in these cases it is permitted to position oneself on the Sabbath so that one can start immediately fulfilling a *mizwah* after the end of the Sabbath. The Sabbath domain extends 2000 cubits from the last house of one's city; one may not move outside that domain on the Sabbath.

מֵאֵימָתַי כּוֹפִין אֶת הַמִּיטּוֹת מִשֶּׁיֵּצֵא הַמֵּת מִפֶּתַח הֶחָצֵר דִּבְרֵי רִבִּי אֱלִיעֶזֶר. וְרִבִּי יְהוֹשֻׁעַ אוֹמֵר מִשֶּׁיִּסָּתֵם הַגּוֹלֵל. וּכְשֶׁמֵּת רַבָּן גַּמְלִיאֵל כֵּיוָן שֶׁיָּצָא מִפֶּתַח הֶחָצֵר אָמַר רִבִּי אֱלִיעֶזֶר לְתַלְמִידָיו כְּפוּ אֶת הַמִּיטּוֹת. וּכְשֶׁנִּסְתַּם הַגּוֹלֵל אָמַר רִבִּי יְהוֹשֻׁעַ כְּפוּ אֶת הַמִּיטּוֹת. אָמְרוּ לוֹ כְּבָר כְּפִינוּם[15] עַל פִּי הַזָּקֵן. בְּעֶרֶב שַׁבָּת הוּא זוֹקֵף אֶת מִיטָּתוֹ. וּבְמוֹצָאֵי שַׁבָּת הוּא כוֹפָן.

When does one overturn the couches[16]? From the moment when the dead left the gate of the courtyard[17], the words of Rebbi Eliezer. But Rebbi Joshua says, from when the cover plate was laid on the grave[18]. And when Rabban Gamliel died, after he left the gate of the courtyard, Rebbi Eliezer said to his students: Overturn the couches[19]. And when the cover plate was laid on the grave, Rebbi Joshua said: Overturn the couches. They said to him: We already did turn them over on the orders of the old man[20]. Friday evening he rights his couch, at the end of Sabbat he overturns them[21].

15 The Venice (and Leyden) text here, בפיטם, is unintelligible. The text given here is that of the Genizah fragments and the parallel in *Śemaḥot.*

16 The mourner is not allowed to eat reclining on a couch, but has to eat sitting upright on a chair as a sign of mourning. This duty applies to all those who are required to observe the week of mourning. The *baraita* is found in *Massekhet Śemaḥot* IX. The entire discussion is taken from Yerushalmi *Moëd Qaṭan* 3:5; the *baraita* is also found Babli *Moëd Qaṭan* 27a.

17 In the Talmud it is assumed that a house has no door leading to the street outside. A number of houses was always clustered around a courtyard, the door of the house lead into the courtyard, and the courtyard had an exit gate. In that way, privacy was always assured. The statement asserts that the moment the funeral procession is on its way is not when the bier leaves the house but when it leaves the outer gate of the courtyard.

18 The dead was buried on a bier, not in a casket. Hence, the grave had to be covered by a large flat stone, the *golal.*

19 When the head of the Synhedrion dies, all are mourners.

20 Even though Rebbi Eliezer was put in the ban since he did not agree with a majority ruling when he knew that the ruling contradicted tradition, it follows from here not only that he continued to lead his Yeshivah but also that in his lifetime, his authority in matters of religious practice remained supreme.

21 Since any outward sign of mourning is forbidden on the Sabbath.

תַּנֵּי דַּרְגֵּשׁ נִזְקֶפֶת וְאֵינָהּ נִכְפֵּית. רִבִּי שִׁמְעוֹן בֶּן אֶלְעָזָר אוֹמֵר שׁוֹמֵט קלבינטרין שֶׁלָּהּ וְדַיּוֹ. רִבִּי יוֹסָה בְּשֵׁם רִבִּי יְהוֹשֻׁעַ בֶּן לֵוִי הֲלָכָה כְּרִבִּי שִׁמְעוֹן בֶּן אֶלְעָזָר. רִבִּי יַעֲקֹב בַּר אָחָא בְּשֵׁם רִבִּי יוֹסֵי מִיטָּה שֶׁנִּיקְלִיתֵיהָ עוֹלִין וְיוֹרְדִין בָּהּ שׁוֹמְטָן וְדַיּוֹ.

It was stated: "A *dargesh*[22] is put upright[23] and is not turned over. Rebbi Simeon ben Eleazar[24] says, he removes its *qlbnṭryn*[25] and that is enough[26]." Rebbi Yosa[27] in the name of Rebbi Joshua ben Levi: practice follows Rebbi Simeon ben Eleazar. Rebbi Jacob bar Aḥa in the name of Rebbi Yose, a couch whose posts[28] are upright and removed together with it, he takes them off and that is enough.

22 A kind of bed whose exact nature was unknown even in the time of the Talmud, as seen from the discussion that follows and in Babli *Nedarim* 56a. Maimonides, in his commentary to *Nedarim*, defines *dargesh* as a low couch (used for sitting only in the case of a mourner), much lower than a regular couch called *miṭṭah*. The Babli tentatively defines *dargesh* as a couch made of a frame onto which a leather mattress is attached by ropes. This definition may be compatible with the description given in the next section.

23 Most commentators explain that the *dargesh* is lifted to stand either on its front end or its foot end. But already *Rosh* (Rabbenu Asher ben Yeḥiël, 14th Century in Mayence and Toledo) has shown in his commentary to Babli *Nedarim* that this explanation is impossible and that the statement must mean: it is left standing as is. The other commentators are influenced by the version of the Babli which instead of the passive form used here have an active "he stands them up", which seems to imply an action by the mourner, not passive as is implied here.

24 In all places where this is quoted in the Babli, the name is *Rabban Simeon ben Gamliel*, the father of Rebbi and son of Rabban Gamliel. Rebbi Simeon ben Eleazar was a Tanna of the last generation who lived to see the start of the second generation of Amoraïm.

25 The spelling and, therefore, the meaning of the word are uncertain. The spelling here is קלבינטרין, that of the Genizah texts and *Śemaḥot* is קלמנטרין, the corresponding word in the Babli is קרביטין. The last word, according to Z. Frankel, is Greek τὸ κραβάτιον, Byzantine Greek κραββατάριον, "accessories to the bed"; this seems to be correct but is not very instructive. [Cf. also κράββατος "couch, mattress"; Latin *grabatus*, from Macedonian κράβατος "low couch, camp bed" (E. G.).]

26 There is a question whether the

anonymous Tanna requires more or less that Rebbi Simeon ben Eleazar. The quote in *Śemahot* XI reads: דרגש המקפת אינה נכפת. רבי שמעון בן אלעזר אומר מוריד קלמנטרין שלה ומניחה כמות שהיא "A surrounding *dargesh* is not turned over. Rebbi Simeon ben Eleazar says, he removes the accessories and leaves it as is." In this formulation, Rebbi Simeon ben Eleazar explains that while the *dargesh* is not turned over, some sign of mourning has to be made. It seems that this is also the explanation here, that Rebbi Simeon ben Eleazar adds a certain requirement to the first statement.

27 Rebbi Yasa.

28 Τὰ ἀνάκλιτα, "things to lean on"; according to both Rashi and Arukh the two posts over which the mosquito screen was hung.

אֵי זֶה הוּא מִיטָּה וְאֵי זֶהוּ דַּרְגֵּשׁ. אָמַר רִבִּי יִרְמְיָה כָּל־שֶׁמְּסָרְגִין עַל גּוּפָהּ זוֹ הִיא מִיטָּה וְכָל־שֶׁאֵין מְסָרְגִין עַל גּוּפָהּ זֶהוּ דַּרְגֵּשׁ. וְהָא תַנִּינָן הַמִּיטָּה וְהָעֲרִיסָה מִשֶּׁיְּשׁוּפֵם בְּעוֹר הַדָּג. אִם מְסָרֵג הוּא עַל גּוּפָהּ לְאֵי זֶה דָּבָר הוּא שָׁפָהּ. (fol. 6a) אָמַר רִבִּי אֶלְעָזָר תִּיפְתָּר בְּאִילֵּין עַרְסָתָה קֵיסַרְיָתָא דְּאִית לָהֶן נְקָבִין.

What is a couch and what is a *dargesh*? Rebbi Jeremiah[29] said, one that one plaits[30] on its body is a couch and one that one does not plait on its body[31] is a *dargesh*. But have we not stated (*Kelim* 16:1) "Bed and[32] crib after he rubs them with fish skin[33]." If he plaits on its body, why does he rub[34]? Rebbi Eleazar said, explain it with those Caesarean cribs that have holes[35].

29 In Babli, *Sanhedrin* 20a/b, this appears in the name of Rebbi Jeremiah in the name of Rebbi Yohanan.

30 The couch has a frame and instead of a box spring it has length- and crosswise strips that are plaited together.

31 Maybe, according to the Babli, because instead of a plaited bed of strips it has a base of leather that is fastened only in a few places to the frame.

32 Reading of the Rome and Mishnah mss. The conjunction is missing in the Venice print and Leyden ms.

33 This Mishnah deals with the moment when a wooden implement is finished. Wood in itself cannot become

ritually impure but wooden vessels and implements can. The moment when a wooden bed frame is finished so that it can become ritually unclean is the moment when it can be delivered by the carpenter to the customer, after it is polished with the classical equivalent of sand paper.

34 If the entire frame is covered by the strips forming the base of the bed, who cares how the wooden frame looks?

35 The strips are not wound around the frame but go through the holes in the frame, leaving half of it exposed.

מְנַיִין לִכְפִיַּת הַמִּיטָּה. רִבִּי קְרִיסְפָּא בְשֵׁם רִבִּי יוֹחָנָן וַיֵּשְׁבוּ אִתּוֹ לָאָרֶץ. עַל הָאָרֶץ אֵין כְּתִיב כָּאן אֶלָּא וַיֵּשְׁבוּ אִתּוֹ לָאָרֶץ. דָּבָר שֶׁהוּא סָמוּךְ לָאָרֶץ. מִיכַּן שֶׁהָיוּ יְשֵׁנִין עַל מִיטּוֹת כְּפוּפוֹת. בַּר קַפָּרָא אָמַר אֵיקוֹנִין אַחַת טוֹבָה הָיָה לִי בְּתוֹךְ בֵּיתָךְ וּגְרַמְתָּנִי לְכוֹפְפָהּ. אַף אַתְּ כְּפֵה מִיטָּתָךְ. וְאִית דְּמַפְקִין לִישְׁנָא וְיִכְפֶּה כְּפֵה הַסִּירְסוּר. רִבִּי יוֹנָה וְרִבִּי יוֹסֵי תְּרַוֵּיהוֹן בְּשֵׁם רִבִּי שִׁמְעוֹן בֶּן לָקִישׁ חַד אָמַר מִפְּנֵי מַה הוּא יָשֵׁן בְּמִיטָּה כְפוּיָה שֶׁיְּהֵא נוֹעֵר בַּלַּיְלָה וְנִזְכַּר שֶׁהוּא אָבֵל. וְחָרָנָה אָמַר מִתּוֹךְ שֶׁהוּא יָשֵׁן בְּמִיטָּה כְפוּיָה הוּא נוֹעֵר בַּלַּיְלָה וְנִזְכַּר שֶׁהוּא אָבֵל.

From where the overturning of beds[36]? Rebbi Crispus[37] in the name of Rebbi Joḥanan: (*Job* 2:13) "They sat with him towards the ground." It does not say here "on the ground" but "they sat with him towards the ground," on something close to the ground. It follows that they were sleeping[38] on overturned couches.

Bar Qappara said: A beautiful form[39] I had in your house and you caused me to overturn[40] it, you also overturn your bed! Some quote it by the expression "let him overturn; overturn[41] the agent!"

Rebbi Jonah and Rebbi Yose, both in the name of Rebbi Simeon ben Laqish. One said, why does he sleep on an overturned coach? So that he should wake up in the night and realize that he is a mourner. The other one said, since he sleeps on an overturned bed he wakes up in the night and realizes that he is a mourner.

36 Levi Ginzberg noted correctly that all the sermons here point only to the overturning of beds on which one sleeps, not couches on which one sits. The Yerushalmi does not address the question whether during the day the mourner has to sit on the ground or may sit on an overturned couch.

37 "Curly haired" (Latin, a Roman surname). A student of Rebbi Joḥanan and R. Simeon ben Laqish, and teacher of Rebbis Jonah and Yose.

38 Since the friends were sitting with Job for seven days and seven nights, they must have slept "towards the ground".

39 Greek εἰκών "image", also "phantom".

40 The parallel *Megillah* 3:5 has לכופתה "to overturn it" (Babylonian Talmudic Hebrew.) The form לכופפה has no parallel in the Yerushalmi and might be a scribal error.

Bar Qappara seems to think that persons die because of the sins of their relatives. This is appropriate only for children who cannot die for their own sins since nobody below the age of 20 is liable before the heavenly court. The following, alternate version also shows that Bar Qappara speaks about mourning for small children.

41 The imperative כפה "overturn!" is missing in the parallel *Moëd Qaṭan* 5:3. The agent is the bed on which one not only sleeps but also has sex. Hence, the couch is the agent which produces the birth of a new baby.

אָבֵל כָּל־זְמָן שֶׁמֵּתוֹ מוּטָּל לְפָנָיו אוֹכֵל אֵצֶל חֲבֵירוֹ וְאִם אֵין לוֹ חָבֵר אוֹכֵל בְּבַיִת אַחֵר. וְאִם אֵין לוֹ בַיִת אַחֵר עוֹשֶׂה מְחִיצָה וְאוֹכֵל. וְאִם אֵינוֹ יָכוֹל לַעֲשׂוֹת מְחִיצָה הוֹפֵךְ אֶת פָּנָיו לַכּוֹתֶל וְאוֹכֵל. וְלֹא מֵיסֵב וְלֹא אוֹכֵל כָּל־צוֹרְכוֹ וְלֹא שׁוֹתֶה כָּל־צוֹרְכוֹ. וְלֹא אוֹכֵל בָּשָׂר וְלֹא שׁוֹתֶה יַיִן. וְאֵין מְזַמְּנִין עָלָיו. וְאִם בֵּירַךְ אֵין עוֹנִין אַחֲרָיו אָמֵן. וַאֲחֵרִים שֶׁבֵּירְכוּ אֵינוֹ עוֹנֶה אַחֲרֵיהֶן אָמֵן. הָדָא דְתֵימַר בְּחוֹל. אֲבָל בְּשַׁבָּת מֵיסֵב וְאוֹכֵל. וְאוֹכֵל בָּשָׂר וְשׁוֹתֶה יַיִן. וְאוֹכֵל כָּל־צוֹרְכוֹ וְשׁוֹתֶה כָּל־צוֹרְכוֹ. וּמְזַמְּנִין עָלָיו. וְאִם בֵּירַךְ עוֹנִין אַחֲרָיו אָמֵן. וַאֲחֵרִים שֶׁבֵּירְכוּ עוֹנֶה אַחֲרֵיהֶן אָמֵן. אָמַר רַבָּן שִׁמְעוֹן בֶּן גַּמְלִיאֵל הוֹאִיל וְהִתַּרְתִּי לוֹ אֶת כָּל־אֵילּוּ חַיְיבֵהוּ בִשְׁאָר כָּל־הַמִּצְווֹת שֶׁל תּוֹרָה. אִם חַיֵּי שָׁעָה הִתַּרְתִּי לְךָ חַיֵּי עוֹלָם לֹא כָּל־שֶׁכֵּן. רִבִּי יוּדָה בֶּן פָּזִי בְשֵׁם רִבִּי יְהוֹשֻׁעַ בֶּן לֵוִי הֲלָכָה כְרַבָּן שִׁמְעוֹן בֶּן גַּמְלִיאֵל.

[42]All the time that his deceased in lying before him, he eats at his neighbor's, and if he has no neighbor, he eats in another room. If he has no other room, he makes a wall of separation and eats. If he is unable to make a wall of separation, he turns his face towards the wall and eats. He does not eat reclining; he does neither eat nor drink his fill. He eats neither meat nor drinks wine. One does not allow him to participate in a group to say Grace. If he recited Grace, one does not answer "amen" after him. If others recited Grace, he does not anwer "amen". That is meant on weekdays. But on the Sabbath, he does eat reclining; he eats meat and drinks wine, eats and drinks his fill. One lets him participate in a group to say Grace. If he recited Grace, one does answer "amen" after him. If others recited Grace, he answers "amen". Rabban Simeon ben Gamliel[43] said: Because I allowed all of these, oblige him for all other obligations of the Torah. If I permitted him temporary life, so much more eternal life[44]. Rebbi Judah ben Pazi in the name of Rebbi Joshua ben Levi: Practice follows Rabban Simeon ben Gamliel.

42 This *baraita* is found in almost identical form in Babli *Berakhot* 17b, *Moëd Qaṭan* 23b, and the Yerushalmi source *Śemaḥot* X.

43 In Babli sources, the author is Rabban Gamliel. The difference is essential since practice follows Rabban Simeon ben Gamliel even against a plurality of dissenters, but does not necessarily follow Rabban Gamliel. In the interpretation of the Babli, Rabban Gamliel obliges the married male mourner to fulfill his conjugal duties towards his wife. This is rejected as practice by the Babli which requires only that the enjoyment of Sabbath should not be diminished in any situation that is seen by others. The Yerushalmi makes no distinction between public and private obligations.

44 And he who does not fulfill his conjugal duties towards his wife on Sabbath transgresses a positive commandment of the Torah. [The emphasis on this probably is anti-Sadducean; for the Sadducees, any sex act on the Sabbath was a Sabbath desecration punishable by death.]

נִמְסַר לָרַבִּים אוֹכֵל בָּשָׂר וְשׁוֹתֶה יַיִן. נִמְסַר לַכַּתָּפִים כְּמִי שֶׁנִּמְסַר לָרַבִּים.

If he[45] was handed over to the public[46], he may eat meat and drink wine. If he was handed over to the carriers[47] it is as if he was handed to the public.

45 The deceased. The other "he" denotes the mourner.

46 The public body organizing funerals, the *Ḥevrah Qadishah.*

47 Paid carriers.

כַּד דָּמָךְ רִבִּי יָסָא קִבֵּיל רִבִּי חִייָא בַּר וָוה אֲבֵילוֹי וְאַייְכְלוּן בָּשָׂר וְאַשְׁקִיתוּן חֲמַר. כַּד דָּמָךְ רִבִּי חִייָא בַּר אַבָּא קִבֵּיל רִבִּי שְׁמוּאֵל בַּר רַב יִצְחָק אֲבֵילוֹי וְאַייְכְלוּן בָּשָׂר וְאַשְׁקִיתוּן חֲמַר. כַּד דָּמָךְ רִבִּי שְׁמוּאֵל בַּר רַב יִצְחָק קִבֵּיל רִבִּי זְעִירָא אֲבֵילוֹי וְאַייְכְלוּן טְלוֹפְחִין מֵימַר כְּמָה דְהוּא מִנְהָגָא. רִבִּי זְעִירָא מִידְמָךְ פָּקֵיד וָמַר לֹא תְקַבְּלוּן עֲלַי יוֹמָא הֵן אֶבְלָא לְמָחָר מַזְרְחַיָּא.

When Rebbi Yassa died, Rebbi Ḥiyya bar Abba received his mourners[48] and gave them meat to eat and wine to drink. When Rebbi Ḥiyya bar Abba died, Rebbi Samuel bar Rav Isaac received his mourners and gave them meat to eat and wine to drink. When Rebbi Samuel bar Rav Isaac died, Rebbi Zeïra received his mourners and gave them lentils to eat, saying that this was the tradition[49]. When Rebbi Zeïra was dying he commanded and said: "You should not accept mourning for me this day, tomorrow consolers.[50]"

48 I. e., Rebbi Yasa's immediate family and possibly students. A mourner returning from the burial has to receive the first meal from others; the mourners were received with food so that they could go home and prepare the next meal themselves. Rebbi Ḥiyya bar Abba did allow meat and wine for this first meal. (In Galilee, under the influence of late Greek, every ב was pronounced *v*; ווה stands for בא in Rebbi Ḥiyya's name.)

49 It is quoted in Babli *Baba batra* 16b as a Galilean tradition (transmitted by Rabba bar Mari, a student of Rebbi Joḥanan) that Jacob prepared a meal of

lentils (*Gen.* 25:29) for his father Isaac as the first meal after the burial of Abraham. The same tradition is given anonymously in the Galilean *Midrash Bereshit rabba* 63:16. The substitution of eggs used today instead of lentils is Babylonian (*Baba batra* 16b). Even though Rebbi Zeïra was Babylonian, the practice might have been that of the city of Rebbi Samuel bar Rav Isaac.

50 It is not very clear what Rebbi Zeïra was commanding to his students; also the text is quoted in very different forms by Nachmanides (*Torat Haädam*; ed. Chavel, p. 144) and those who quote from the latter. The only consistent interpretation is that of Levi Ginzberg: Rebbi Zeïra told his students not to be among the mourners the first day nor among those who arrange meals of consolation the next day. While he was a Babylonian by birth, he objected to the Babylonian practice that students mourn only one day for their teacher (Babli *Moëd Qatan* 25b) but wanted them to mourn for him the entire seven days (or not at all).

מרזחיא are those who arrange the meal for the mourners, מַרְזֵחַ ; as Levi Ginzberg points out, this meaning in Galilean (not Babylonian) Aramaic is clear from *Targum Sheni* on *Esther* 1:2, towards the end.

רִבִּי יִצְחָק בְּרֵיהּ דְּרִבִּי חִייָא[51] כָּתוֹבָה מְטָתֵיהּ אוֹנֵס. עָלוֹן לְגַבֵּיהּ רִבִּי מָנָא וְרִבִּי יוּדָן וַהֲוָה חֲמַר טָב וְאִישְׁתּוֹן סַגִּין וְגָחֲכִין. לְמָחָר אָתוֹן בָּעֲיָן מֵיעוֹל גַּבֵּיהּ. אָמַר לוֹן רַבָּנָן אָכֵן בַּר נָשׁ עֲבֵיד לְחַבְרֵיהּ. לָא הֲוֵינָן חֲסֵרִין אֶתְמֹל אֶלָּא מֵיקוּם וּמִירְקוֹד.

Rebbi Isaac the son of Rebbi Ḥiyya the Scribe suffered an accident[52]. Rebbis Mana and Yudan went to him. There was good wine, they drank a lot[53] and laughed. The next day they wanted to visit him again. He said to them: Rabbis, is that what a man does to his friend? Yesterday, the only thing that was missing for us was that we would get up and dance!

51 Reading of the Rome ms. Venice and Leyden: הוה . The text here is the only mention we have of this Amora.

52 I. e., a close relative died.

53 More than the 10 cups allowed. The entire story is an introduction to the following *baraita* about the cups to be drunk in a house of mourning. (A cup of wine consists of two thirds water and one third wine).

תַּנֵּי עֲשָׂרָה כוֹסוֹת שׁוֹתִין בְּבֵית הָאָבֵל שְׁנַיִם לִפְנֵי הַמָּזוֹן וַחֲמִשָּׁה בְתוֹךְ הַמָּזוֹן. וּשְׁלֹשָׁה לְאַחַר הַמָּזוֹן. אֵילּוּ שְׁלֹשָׁה שֶׁל אַחַר הַמָּזוֹן. אֶחָד לְבִרְכַּת הַמָּזוֹן וְאֶחָד לִגְמִילוּת חֲסָדִים. וְאֶחָד לְתַנְחוּמֵי אֲבֵילִים. וּכְשֶׁמֵּת רַבָּן שִׁמְעוֹן בֶּן גַּמְלִיאֵל הוֹסִיפוּ עֲלֵיהֶן עוֹד שְׁלֹשָׁה אֶחָד לְחַזַּן הַכְּנֶסֶת וְאֶחָד לְרֹאשׁ הַכְּנֶסֶת וְאֶחָד לְרַבָּן גַּמְלִיאֵל. וְכֵיוָן שֶׁרָאוּ בֵּית דִּין שֶׁהָיוּ מִשְׁתַּכְּרִין וְהוֹלְכִין גָּזְרוּ עֲלֵיהֶן וְהֶחֱזִירוּם לִמְקוֹמָן.

It is stated[54]: Ten cups one drinks in the house of a mourner: two before the meal[55], five during the meal, and three after the meal. These are the three after the meal: one for Grace[56], one for those who exercise charity[57], one for those who console mourners[58]. And when Rabban (Simeon ben)[59] Gamliel died, they added another three: One for the *Ḥazzan* of the community[60], one for the head of the community[61], and one for Rabban Gamliel[62]. But when the Rabbinical authorities saw that they regularly got drunk they decreed and returned it to the original status[63].

54 This is the Yerushalmi formulation, also found in *Śemaḥot* XIV. The Babli version, *Ketubot* 8b, has 3 cups before the meal, 3 during the meal, and 4 after the meal for the four benedictions of Grace.

55 As an apéritif. The next five are regular drinks to go with the solid food.

56 The regular cup over which Grace is said, as explained in later chapters. Since one may not recite Grace together in the presence of the mourner, one cup is needed for each one of the participants.

57 In honor of those who gave their time and went out in the funeral procession.

58 The outsiders who provided the meal and participate in it.

59 As is seen from the following and the parallel sources, "Simeon ben" is a scribal error.

60 The religious leader of the community who leads the services and all religious activities including the funerals. (A rabbi is only a religious judge; the *ḥazzan* was not only the reader but also the ritual slaughterer and general servant of the community.)

61 The president of the congregation, who was responsible for the establishment and upkeep of the cemetery.

62 He had himself buried in a simple linen shirt and in a plain unadorned wooden casket. Before his time, people were buried in elaborate clothing in expensive caskets. After him it became the Jewish standard that everybody has to be buried in Rabban Gamliel's way.

63 The preceding story, from later Galilean Amoras, shows that "the original way" are the prescribed 10 cups; there is no prohibition of wine at the funeral meal.

כֹּהֵן מַהוּ שֶׁיִּטַּמֵּא לִכְבוֹד רַבּוֹ. רִבִּי יַנַּאי זְעִירָא דָּמַךְ חָמוֹי. הוּא הֲוָה חָמוֹי וְהוּא הֲוָה רַבֵּיהּ. שָׁאַל לְרִבִּי יוֹסֵי וְאָסַר לֵיהּ. שָׁמַע רִבִּי אָחָא וָמַר יִטַּמְּאוּ לוֹ תַלְמִידָיו. רִבִּי יוֹסֵי נִטְמְאוּ לוֹ תַלְמִידָיו וְאָכְלוּ בָּשָׂר וְשָׁתוּ יַיִן. אָמַר לוֹן רִבִּי מָנָא חָדָא מִן תַּרְתֵּי לָא פְלָטַת לְכוֹן. אִם אֲבֵילִים אַתֶּם לָמָּה אֲכַלְתֶּם בָּשָׂר וְלָמָּה שְׁתִיתֶם יַיִן. וְאִם אֵין אַתֶּם מִתְאַבְּלִין לָמָּה נִטְמֵאתֶם.

May a Cohen defile himself[64] for the honor of his teacher? The father-in-law of Rebbi Yannai the younger[65] died. He was both his father-in-law[66] and his teacher. He asked Rebbi Yose who forbade it. Rebbi Aḥa heard it and said: His students should defile themselves for him. The students of Rebbi Yose defiled themselves for him but ate meat and drank wine[67]. Rebbi Mana told them: One of two things you cannot escape. If you are mourners, why did you eat meat and drink wine; if you are not mourners, why did you defile yourselves?

64 By touching a dead body or carrying his casket (cf. *Lev.* 21). The main place of these discussions is in Yerushalmi *Nazir* 7:1.

65 An Amora of the fourth Galilean generation; so called to distinguish him from Rebbi Yannai, the teacher of Rebbi Joḥanan. It is implied that he was a Cohen.

66 A Cohen must defile himself for his wife but may not defile himself for any of her relatives.

67 Before the burial.

מַהוּ שֶׁיִּטַּמֵּא כֹהֵן לִכְבוֹד תּוֹרָה. רִבִּי יוֹסֵי הֲוָה יָתִיב מַתְנֵי וְאָעַל מִיתָא. מָן דְּנָפַק לֵיהּ לֹא אָמַר לֵיהּ כלוּם. וּמָן דְּיָתִיב לֵיהּ לֹא אָמַר לֵיהּ כְּלוּם.

May a Cohen defile himself for the honor of Torah? Rebbi Yose was sitting and teaching when a dead body was brought in[68]. He did not say anything either to those who left or to those who remained sitting[69].

68 To be eulogized in the Yeshivah.

69 He said nothing to those who were Cohanim and did not want to stay in the same house with the dead person even though they were missing some of Rebbi Yose's lectures, nor to those Cohanim among his students who preferred to study even if it meant staying with the dead person in the same "tent". Rebbi Yose was undecided whether a Cohen should stay or leave.

רִבִּי נְחֶמְיָה בְּרֵיהּ דְּרִבִּי חִיָּיא בַּר אַבָּא אָמַר אַבָּא לֹא הָיָה עָבוֹר תְּחוֹת כִּפְּתָא דְקֵיסָרִין. רִבִּי אַמִּי רִבִּי חִזְקִיָּה וְרִבִּי כֹהֵן וְרִבִּי יַעֲקֹב בַּר אָחָא הֲווּ מְטַיְּלִין בְּאִילֵּין פְּלָטִיוּתָא דְצִיפּוֹרִי. הִגִּיעוּ לְכִיפָּה וּפִירֵשׁ רִבִּי כֹהֵן. הִגִּיעוּ לְמָקוֹם טַהֲרָה וְחָזַר אֶצְלָן. אָמַר לוֹן בְּמַה עֲסַקְתֶּם. אָמַר רִבִּי חִזְקִיָּה לְרִבִּי יַעֲקֹב בַּר אָחָא לֹא תֵימוֹר לֵיהּ כְּלוּם. אִין מִשּׁוּם דְּבָאַשׁ לֵיהּ דְּפָרַשׁ שֶׁמִּטַּמֵּא לְתַלְמוּד תּוֹרָה לָא יָדְעִין. וְאִין מִשּׁוּם דַּהֲוָה גוּוייְסָן לָא יָדְעִין.

Rebbi Nehemiah the son of Rebbi Ḥiyya bar Abba said: My father did not walk under the arch of Caesarea[70]. Rebbi Ammi, Rebbi Ḥizqiah, Rebbi Cohen and Rebbi Jacob bar Aḥa went walking on those streets[71] of Sepphoris. They came to the arch and Rebbi Cohen left[72]. They reached a place of purity and he returned to them. He asked them: "What were you discussing?" Rebbi Ḥizqiah said to Rebbi Jacob bar Aḥa: "Do not tell him anything!" We do not know whether it was because he was angry that he left since one defiles oneself for words of Torah or whether it was because he[73] was haughty[74].

70 R. Ḥiyya bar Abba was a Cohen, as is also clear from the later account of the visit of Diocletian. He did not pass under an arch attached to a building or archway under which there were graves. The Caesarea here is Caesarea Philippi, on the Jordan near Banias. Even though Caesarea Philippi was built by the Herodian family, it is unlikely that the arch belonged to a building containing a Jewish grave and it is accepted in the Babylonian Talmud (*Yebamot* 61a), following R. Simeon bar Yoḥai, that only Jewish graves defile "in a tent" but not Gentile ones. The problem is not mentioned in any of the surviving parts of the Yerushalmi; one might infer from the stories told here that the ruling of the Babli was not that accepted in Galilee. Nachmanides (תורת אדם, ענין ההוצאה, ed. Chavel, vol. 2, p. קה) adds: "but R. Ammi (who also was a Cohen) did pass under them." The rest of the paragraph supports the reading of Nachmanides.

71 Latin *platea*, Greek πλατεῖα (*scil.* ὁδός), "street".

72 Probably for the same reason that Rebbi Ḥiyya bar Abba did not pass under the arch of Caesarea.

73 Rebbi Cohen. (The first "he" refers to R. Ḥizqiah.) Since the problem is unresolved, it seems that in the opinion of the Yerushalmi, as a doubt in matters of Torah, he should not defile himself for Torah study. (This is the opinion of the Babli, *Avodah zarah* 13a, for all defilements that have a Biblical basis.)

74 The reading is that of the Leyden manuscript; the *editio princeps* of Nachmanides has גייסן. The Venice print has טייסן, "a flyer" which makes no sense. The implication seems to be that Rebbi Ḥizqiah, the Rabbinic authority, was piqued by the fact that Rebbi Cohen, a very minor figure, did not ask his opinion whether he might pass under the arc.

תַּנֵּי מְטַמֵּא כֹּהֵן וְיוֹצֵא חוּצָה לָאָרֶץ לְדִינֵי מָמוֹנוֹת וּלְדִינֵי נְפָשׁוֹת וּלְקִידּוּשׁ הַחוֹדֶשׁ וּלְעִיבּוּר שָׁנָה. לְהַצִּיל שָׂדֶה מִן הַגּוֹי וַאֲפִילוּ לִיטוֹר[75] יוֹצֵא וְעוֹרֵר עָלֶיהָ. לִלְמוֹד תּוֹרָה וְלִישָּׂא אִשָּׁה. רִבִּי יוּדָה אוֹמֵר אִם יֵשׁ לוֹ מֵאֵיכָן לִלְמוֹד אַל יִטַּמֵּא. רִבִּי יוֹסֵי אוֹמֵר אֲפִילוּ יֵשׁ לוֹ מֵאֵיכָן לִלְמוֹד תּוֹרָה יִטַּמֵּא שֶׁלֹּא מִכָּל־אָדָם זוֹכֶה לִלְמוֹד. אָמְרוּ עָלָיו עַל יוֹסֵף הַכֹּהֵן שֶׁהָיָה מִטַּמֵּא וְיוֹצֵא אַחַר רַבּוֹ לְצִידָן. אֲבָל אָמְרוּ אַל יֵצֵא כֹּהֵן לְחוּץ לָאָרֶץ אֶלָּא אִם כֵּן הִבְטִיחוּ לוֹ אִשָּׁה.

It is stated[76]: A Cohen may defile himself by leaving the Land[77] for civil and criminal suits, for the consecration of the New Moon and intercalation of a year[78], to save a field from a Gentile, and he even may leave and lodge a complaint about it[79], to study Torah and to marry a wife. Rebbi Judah says, if he has a place to study[80], he should not defile himself. Rebbi Yose says, even if he has a place to study, he may defile himself, since a man may not have the luck to learn from every teacher. They said about Joseph the Cohen[81] that he defiled himself and followed his teacher to Sidon[82]. In truth[83], they said a priest should not go abroad unless one promised him a wife.

75 The unexplained word ליטור is missing in the parallel *Nazir* 7:1 (fol. 56a). It probably is a corruption and is best disregarded. It could be from נטר "to act as watchman." R. M. Margalit assumes that a silent ע is missing, that one should read לעיטור, to annul (a document of indebtedness.) The interpretations of Z. Frankel (Latin *latro*), J. Levy (Greek ῥητώρ), and M. Jastrow ("to Iturea") have to be rejected.

76 This *baraita* is in similar form in other Yerushalmi sources, *Nazir* 7:1, *Śemaḥot* IV:25,26, Tosephta *Moëd qaṭan* 1:12, *Avodah zarah* 1:8, and in materially different Babylonian tradition in Babli *Avodah zarah* 13a, *Erubin* 47a.

77 It is not clear which verse of the Torah declares all land outside the Land of Israel ritually unclean but the fact that it is so, is obvious from *Amos* 7:17. (The Babli takes the impurity of the "land of Gentiles" to be rabbinic, but this refers to the time when no ashes of a red heifer were available anymore and every Cohen was impure from the start, whereas the Yerushalmi *baraita* might refer to earlier times, cf. Chapter 1, Note 3.) The prohibition for the Cohen to defile himself willingly derives from *Lev.* 21:1-15.

78 In the absence of a computed calendar, the last two activities may be exercised outside the Land of Israel only if political circumstances make the consecration in Israel impossible. (The statements up to this point are missing in the Babli parallels; see the preceding Note.)

79 "To lodge a complaint" about

real estate usually means to claim ownership against a squatter, in particular if there are no written documents for either party.

80 Any place to study in the Land of Israel.

81 Joseph (called Issi) ben Yehudah (or Aqabiah) from Huzal in Babylonia who immigrated to Israel and was a student of Rebbis Eleazar ben Shamua and Yose ben Ḥalaphta. He is a Tanna of the last generation and known as the "last of the pious". If such a holy man leaves Israel to follow his secondary teacher, the practice of leaving the Land for study purposes is well established.

82 Note the Talmudic vocalization Ṣīdān, in contrast to Biblical Ṣīdōn, close to modern Arabic Ṣaidā.

83 As a rule, any tannaïtic statement label אבל "in truth", represents established practice. The permission for a priest to leave the Land for marriage is only for an arranged marriage, not for a search for a possible bride.

מַהוּ שֶׁיִּטַּמֵּא כֹהֵן לִנְשִׂיאַת כַּפַּיִם. גְּדִילָה אַחֲוֵי דְּרִבִּי אַבָּא בַּר כֹּהֵן אָמַר קוֹמֵי רִבִּי יוֹסֵי בְּשֵׁם רִבִּי אָחָא מִטַּמֵּא כֹהֵן לִנְשִׂיאַת כַּפַּיִם. שָׁמַע רִבִּי אָחָא וָמַר אֲנָא לָא אֲמָרִית לֵיהּ כְּלוּם. חָזַר וְאָמַר אוֹ דִילְמָא לָא שָׁמַע מִינִּי אֶלָּא כְּיֵי דָמַר רִבִּי יוּדָה בֶּן פָּזִי בְּשֵׁם רִבִּי אֶלְעָזָר. כָּל־כֹּהֵן שֶׁהוּא עוֹמֵד בְּבֵית הַכְּנֶסֶת וְאֵינוֹ נוֹשֵׂא אֶת כַּפָּיו עוֹבֵר בַּעֲשֵׂה. וְסָבַר מֵימַר שֶׁמִּצְוַת עֲשֵׂה דוֹחֶה לְמִצְוַת לֹא תַעֲשֶׂה. אֲנָא לָא אֲמָרִית לֵיהּ כְּלוּם. אַיְתוּנֵיהּ וַאֲנָא אַלְקוּנֵיהּ.

May a Cohen defile himself for the lifting of hands[84]? Gedilah[85], the brother of Rebbi Abba bar Cohen[86] said before Rebbi Yose in the name of Rebbi Aḥa: A Cohen defiles[87] himself for the lifting of hands. Rebbi Aḥa heard it and said: I never told him anything. On second thoughts he said, maybe he heard from me that which Rebbi Jehudah ben Pazi said in the name of Rebbi Eleazar: Every Cohen who stays in the synagogue and does not lift his hands transgresses a positive commandment, and he wanted to say that a positive commandment[88] supersedes a negative commandment. I never told him anything[89]. Bring him in and I will cause him to be flogged!

84 The priestly blessing (*Num.* 6:24-26) that the Cohen has to recite during morning prayers. Since the priest has to lift his hands for the blessing, in imitation of Aaron the High Priest (*Lev.* 9:22), the entire ceremony is called "the lifting of hands".

85 This is the reading of the Rome manuscript. The names given in other sources, מגבילה, גבילה, are not otherwise attested as Semitic names.

86 An Amora of the fifth generation, student of the Amora Rebbi Yose, two generations after Rebbi Abba bar Kahana.

87 Implying that a Cohen *must* defile himself to fulfill the obligation of reciting the priestly blessing.

88 The obligation on the Cohen to recite the blessing. The negative commandment is the prohibition for the Cohen to defile himself without good cause.

89 The obligation to recite the priestly blessing is only on a Cohen who happens to be in the synagogue at the right time. But if a coffin is in the synagogue for an eulogy before the funeral, the Cohen cannot be in the synagogue when the priests are called and, hence, would have to enter the synagogue to be defiled at a moment when there is no positive commandment on him. The hypothetical argument of Rebbi Aḥa could only be resolved in favor of Gedilah in the unlikely event that someone in the synagogue dies suddenly while the priests already assemble for the priestly blessing.

רִבִּי אַבָּהוּ הֲוָא יָתִיב מַתְנֵי בִכְנִישְׁתָּא מֶרְדְּתָא בְּקֵיסָרִין וַהֲוָה תַמָּן מֵיתָא. אָתַת עָנְתָא דִנְשִׂיאוּת כַּפַּיִם וְלָא שָׁאֲלוּן לֵיהּ. אָתַת עָנְתָא דְמֵיכְלָא וְשָׁאֲלוּן לֵיהּ. אָמַר לוֹן עַל נְשִׂיאוּת כַּפַּיִם לָא שְׁאִילתּוּן לִי וּלְמֵיכְלָא שְׁאִילתּוּן לִי. כֵּיוָן דִּשְׁמָעוּן כֵּן הֲוָה כָל חַד וְחַד שָׁבַק גַּרְמֵיהּ וְעָרַק.

Rebbi Abbahu was sitting teaching in the fortified[90] synagogue in Caesarea[91]; there was a coffin there. There came the time for lifting the hands and they[92] did not ask him. There came the time for eating and they asked him. He said to them: For the lifting of hands you did not ask me, for eating you are asking me[93]? When they heard this, each one was taking himself away and fled.

90 This is the reading of the Rome ms., from Syriac מרדא, "fortified". Graetz's translation "revolutionary" is phantasy. The word could be from Greek μερίς, -ίδος, ἡ "part, region, district". In that case, the translation would be "regional synagogue" (E. G.). The reading of the Leyden ms. and the Venice print, מדדתא, "measuring" or "tripping", does not make any sense.

91 It is not quite clear whether this was Caesarea on Sea or Caesarea Philippi; the former is usually assumed but it will become clear that the latter is in fact meant.

92 The Cohanim among his students. They remained sitting for Rebbi Abbahu's lecture.

93 Since Rebbi Abbahu did not deliver a ruling, it seems that he had not formed a definite opinion on the matter. Rebbi Yose was one of the last students of Rebbi Abahu; the discussion quoted in the preceding paragraph could not have taken place if a ruling was issued by Rebbi Abbahu.

אָמַר רִבִּי יַנַּאי מִטַּמֵּא כֹּהֵן לִרְאוֹת אֶת הַמֶּלֶךְ. כַּד סְלִיק דּוֹקְלֶטִייַנוּס מַלְכָּא לְהָכָא חָמוּן לְרִבִּי חִייָא בַּר אַבָּא מַפְסַע עַל קִבְרַיָּה דְּצוֹר בְּגִין מֵיחְמָנֵיהּ. רִבִּי חִזְקִיָּה וְרִבִּי יִרְמְיָה בְּשֵׁם רִבִּי יוֹחָנָן מִצְוָה לִרְאוֹת גְּדוֹלֵי מַלְכוּת לִכְשֶׁתָּבוֹא מַלְכוּת בֵּית דָּוִד יְהֵא יֹדֵעַ לְהַפְרִישׁ בֵּין מַלְכוּת לְמַלְכוּת.

Rebbi Yannai said: A Cohen defiles himself in order to see the king. When king Diocletian visited here, Rebbi Ḥiyya bar Abba was seen stepping over graves at Tyre in order to see him[94]. Rebbi Ḥizqiah and Rebbi Jeremiah in the name of Rebbi Joḥanan: There is an obligation to see great persons of government, so that when the kingdom of the dynasty of David will return one will know how to distinguish one government from the other.

94 Since Diocletian changed the constitution of the Roman empire from a formally republican one to an absolute monarchy, it is not totally clear whether a Cohen may defile himself only for a ruler who also carries the formal title of "king" or whether he should be a ruler who has power over life and death. Since the rule appears here in the name of Rebbi Yannai who lived under the principate, the second alternative is the more

likely one. In the Babli (*Berakhot* 19b), the ruling (and the statement of Rebbi Joḥanan) is not by an early Amora but by a very early Tanna, Rebbi Eleazar bar Ẓadoq, a Cohen who mentions having seen the late Herodian rulers before the destruction of the Temple.

It was reported before that Rebbi Ḥiyya bar Abba was a Cohen. We also saw before that the Yerushalmi does not seem to exclude Gentile graves from the defilement of a "tent"; hence, it is not proven that Rebbi Ḥiyya bar Abba stepped over Jewish graves at Tyre. (The Babli, *loc. cit.*, notes that a Cohen is prohibited by Biblical commandment from stepping over a grave only if there is less than a handbreadth of space between the corpse and the upper cover of the coffin, as explained in Mishnah *Ahilot* VII; in most cases stepping over a grave is only a rabbinical prohibition which may be lifted in special circumstances.)

כַּד דָּמַךְ רִבִּי יוּדָן נְשִׂיאָה אַכְרִיז רִבִּי יַנַּאי וָמַר אֵין כְּהוּנָּה הַיּוֹם. כַּד דָּמַךְ רִבִּי יוּדָה נְשִׂיאָה בַּר בְּרֵיהּ דְּרִבִּי יוּדָה נְשִׂיאָה דָּחַף רִבִּי חִייָא בַּר אַבָּא לְרִבִּי זְעִירָא בְּכְנִישְׁתָּא דְגוּפְנָה דְצִיפּוֹרִין וּסְאָבֵיהּ. כַּד דָּמְכַת נְהוֹרַאי אַחְתֵיהּ דְּרִבִּי יְהוּדָה נְשִׂיאָה שָׁלַח רִבִּי חֲנִינָה בָּתַר רִבִּי מָנָא וְלָא סְלִיק. אָמַר לֵיהּ אִם בְּחַיֵּיהֶן אֵין מִטַּמְּאִין לָהֶן כָּל־שֶׁכֵּן בְּמִיתָתָן. אָמַר רִבִּי נַסָּא בְּמִיתָתָן עָשׂוּ אוֹתָן כְּמֵת מִצְוָה.

When Rebbi Judah the Prince[95] died, Rebbi Yannai proclaimed and said: "There is no priesthood today[96]." When Rebbi Judah the Prince, grandson of Rebbi Judah the Prince, died, Rebbi Ḥiyya bar Abba did push Rebbi Zeïra[97] in the Gufna synagogue of Sepphoris and defiled him. When Nahoraï[98], the sister of Rebbi Judah the prince, died, Rebbi Ḥanina[99] sent for Rebbi Mana but the latter did not come. He said to him, if one does not defile himself for them during their lifetime, so much less in their death. Rebbi Nassa[100] said, in their death they made them like a corpse of obligation[101].

95 Rebbi, the son of Rabban Simeon ben Gamliel and editor of the Mishnah.

96 All priests are obliged to come to the eulogy and funeral.

97 Who also was a Cohen and did

not want to defile himself. While the Prince Judah I was not only patriarch but also recognized as the greatest rabbinic authority of his day, Judah II was patriarch and a competent but not outstanding scholar. Rebbi Zeïra apparently felt that his scholarship did not merit that a Cohen should defile himself, whereas Rebbi Ḥiyya bar Abba, who like Rebbi Zeïra was a greater scholar than Judah II, insisted that the office of patriarch alone deserved this recognition.

98 Nahoraï is really a man's name. In the parallel in Nazir she is called Yehudinaï, which seems to be the better tradition. She was the sister of Judah II.

99 Rebbi Ḥananiah from Sepphoris, a colleague of Rebbi Mana; see Chap. 2, Note 97.

100 A student of Rebbi Eleazar and others; a resident of Caesarea whose name is prominent in the part of the Yerushalmi that was edited in Caesarea (*Neziqin*.)

101 A corpse of obligation is the body of a Jew who is not the known relative of anybody nearby and, therefore, has nobody who could organize his funeral. In such a situation, the first person who finds him must care for him; even the High Priest, who does not defile himself even for father and mother, *must* defile himself for a corpse of obligation.

It is not too clear who is meant. We may assume that Maimonides writes from tradition when he formulates (*Hilkhot Evel*, 3:10) "When a patriarch dies, everybody defiles himself for him, including Cohanim; they made him like a corpse of obligation for everybody because everybody is required to honor him and everybody is stunned by his death." *Hagahot Maimuniot* (*ad loc.*) note that the sentence "they made him like a corpse of obligation" is the statement of Rebbi Nassa. The discussion goes as follows:

The sister of the patriarch Judah II died after him. Rebbi Ḥanina demanded that Rebbi Mana, a Cohen, should defile himself for her. Rebbi Mana retorted that, since he would not defile himself for her during the patriarch's lifetime, when it would have constituted an honor for the patriarch, he might not do so after the patriarch's death. Rebbi Nassa, in support of Rebbi Mana, explains that the defilement of Cohanim for the patriarch is because he is considered an obligation for all of Israel.

מַהוּ שֶׁיִּטַּמֵּא כֹּהֵן לִכְבוֹד אָבִיו וְאִמּוֹ. רִבִּי יָסָא שָׁמַע דְּאָתַת אִימֵּיהּ לְבוֹצְרָה. אָתָא שָׁאַל לְרִבִּי יוֹחָנָן מַהוּ לָצֵאת. אָמַר לֵיהּ אִי מִפְּנֵי סַכָּנַת דְּרָכִים צֵא. אִי מִשּׁוּם כְּבוֹד אָבִיו וְאִמּוֹ אֵינִי יוֹדֵעַ. אָמַר רִבִּי שְׁמוּאֵל (fol. 6b) בַּר רַב יִצְחָק עוֹד הִיא צְרִיכָה לְרִבִּי יוֹחָנָן. אַטְרַח עֲלוֹי וָמַר אִם גָּמַרְתָּ לָצֵאת תָּבוֹא בְשָׁלוֹם. שָׁמַע רִבִּי אֶלְעָזָר וָמַר אֵין רְשׁוּת גְּדוֹלָה מִזֶּה.

May a Cohen defile himself in honor of his father and mother[102]? Rebbi Yasa heard that his mother had come to Bostra[103]. He went and asked Rebbi Yoḥanan, may I leave? He said to him, if it is because of danger on the road[104], leave. If it is in order to honor father and mother, I do not know. Rebbi Samuel bar Rav Isaac said, Rebbi Yoḥanan still needs to answer. He importuned him[105], so he said: If you decided to go, return in peace[106]. Rebbi Eleazar heard this and said: there is no greater permission than that.

102 As the sequel shows, the only question is whether a Cohen may leave the Holy Land doing something in honor of father or mother. The Biblical prohibitions cannot be violated for the honor of father and mother.

103 This city is South of the Hauran mountains, not far from Edreï, on the caravan route to Babylonia. It is not the Biblical Edomite Boṣra. The parallel in the Babli (*Qiddushin* 31b) is much more explicit, stating that Rebbi Assi's (Yasa's) mother was mentally disturbed and that it turned out that her coffin arrived at Bostra.

104 To accompany his mother because of the dangers of the road is clearly allowed since it is a matter of life and death.

105 Rebbi Yasa did not accept Rebbi Joḥanan's answer as final, insisting to have a definite yes or no.

106 Rebbi Joḥanan would not order any Cohen to leave the Holy Land in order to meet father or mother but neither would he hinder any one who very much wanted to go.

מַהוּ שֶׁיִּטַּמֵּא כֹּהֵן לִכְבוֹד הָרַבִּים. תַּנֵּי הָיוּ שָׁם שְׁתֵּי דְרָכִים מַתְאִימוֹת אַחַת רְחוֹקָה וּטְהוֹרָה וְאַחַת קְרוֹבָה וּטְמֵאָה. אִם הָיוּ הָרַבִּים הוֹלְכִין בָּרְחוֹקָה הוֹלֵךְ

בָּרְחוֹקָה וְאִם לָאו הוֹלֵךְ בַּקְּרוֹבָה מִפְּנֵי כְבוֹד הַצִּיבּוּר. עַד כְּדוֹן בְּטוּמְאָה שֶׁל דִּבְרֵיהֶם אֲפִילוּ טוּמְאָה שֶׁהִיא מִדִּבְרֵי תוֹרָה. מִן מַה דָּמַר רִבִּי זְעִירָא גָּדוֹל הוּא כְּבוֹד הָרַבִּים שֶׁהוּא דוֹחֶה מִצְוָה בְּלֹא תַעֲשֶׂה שָׁעָה אַחַת. אָדָא אָמְרָה אֲפִילוּ טוּמְאָה שֶׁהִיא מִדִּבְרֵי תוֹרָה.

May a Cohen defile himself in honor of the public? It is stated: When there are two acceptable roads, one long and pure, the other one short and impure: If the public was walking[107] on the long one, he goes on the long one; otherwise, he goes on the short one in honor of the public. That refers to impurity by their words[108]; also for impurity that is from the words of the Torah? From what Rebbi Zeïra said, so great is the honor of the public that it temporarily pushes aside a prohibition[109], that means even impurity that is from the words of the Torah[110].

107 In a funeral procession. The *baraita* is from *Semaḥot* 4:14. Since the following *baraita* 15 speaks about digging the grave, the text here speaks of the procession preceding the actual burial. A similar but different *baraita* in the Babli (*Berakhot* 19b) deals with people returning after the burial.

108 If the impurity is not certain but only possible, the prohibition of passage for the Cohen is only rabbinical, not biblical.

109 It is explained in *Kilaim* 9:2 that if somebody notices that his clothing is forbidden as *shaätnez*, he may keep his clothes on until he gets home and does not have to stand naked or in his underwear in public.

110 The Babli comes to the opposite conclusion but, as noted before, it deals with people returning from the funeral, not a funeral procession as here.

רִבִּי יוֹנָה רִבִּי יוֹסֵי גְלִילָיָא בְשֵׁם רִבִּי יָסָא בַּר חֲנִינָא אֵין שׁוֹאֲלִין הֲלָכָה לִפְנֵי מִיטָּתוֹ שֶׁל מֵת. וְהָא רִבִּי יוֹחָנָן שָׁאַל לְרִבִּי יַנַּאי קוֹמֵי עַרְסֵיהּ דְּרִבִּי שִׁמְעוֹן בֶּן יוֹצָדָק הִקְדִּישׁ עוֹלָתוֹ לְבֶדֶק הַבַּיִת וַהֲוָה מְגִיב לֵיהּ. נֵימַר כַּד הֲוָה רָחִיק אוֹ כַד הֲוֹון מַסְקִין לֵיהּ לְסִדְרָה. וְהָא רִבִּי יִרְמְיָה שָׁאַל לְרִבִּי זְעִירָא קוֹמֵי עַרְסֵיהּ דְּרִבִּי שְׁמוּאֵל בַּר רַב יִצְחָק. נֵימַר כַּד הֲוָה רָחִיק הֲוָה מְגִיב לֵיהּ. כַּד הֲוָה קָרִיב לָא הֲוָה מְגִיב לֵיהּ.

Rebbi Jonah, Rebbi Yose the Galilean[111], Rebbi Yasa bar Hanina: One does not ask rulings on practice before the bier of a deceased[112]. But Rebbi Yoḥanan asked Rebbi Yannai before the bier of Rebbi Simeon ben Yoẓadaq[113] about him who dedicated his holocaust sacrifice for the upkeep of the Temple, and he answered him[114]! Let us say when he was far away[115] or when they were bringing him to the study hall[116]. But Rebbi Jeremiah asked Rebbi Zeïra before the bier of Rebbi Samuel bar Rav Isaac! Let us say that he answered him when he was far away; when he was close he did not answer him.

111 A Galilean Amora of the third generation, teacher of Rebbi Jonah.

112 In the Babli (*Berakhot* 3b) it is stated more generally, in the name of R. Joshua ben Levi, that words of Torah are forbidden in presence of a coffin. According to Rashi, the reason is (*Prov.* 17:5): "He who scoffs at the poor blasphemes his Maker." Since the dead person can no longer study Torah, he is poor in this respect.

113 This is the correct reading of the Rome ms. R. Simeon bar Yoẓadaq was an Amora of the first generation, one of the teachers of Rebbi Yoḥanan. The Leyden ms. has שמואל בר יוצדק by a scribal error.

114 The Mishnah (*Temurah* 32a) states that a forbidden substitution is valid only from lesser to higher sanctity. The highest sanctity of a sacrifice is the עוֹלָה, the holocaust, which is totally burnt on the altar, whereas gifts for the upkeep of the Temple are only a monetary obligation. So it should be impossible to dedicate an *'olah* for the upkeep of the Temple. However, a *baraita* (Babli *Temurah* 32b) states that a holocaust which afterwards was dedicated for the upkeep of the Temple cannot be slaughtered unless redeemed first and the money given to the Temple. The answer given there (presumably by Rebbi Yannai) is that the obligation of redemption is purely rabbinical, a kind of fine, but that from the Torah the second dedication is invalid.

115 So that the deceased could not have heard them even were he still alive.

116 Most commentators explain that Rebbis Yoḥanan and Yannai were outside the Bet-Hamidrash. However, that would be the same as "being far away". Therefore, it seems that the

correct interpretation is given by R. Zacariah Frankel, that a eulogy of a Torah teacher in his own school by necessity must involve words of Torah.

תַּנֵּי הַכַּתָּפִים אֲסוּרִין בִּנְעִילַת הַסַּנְדָּל שֶׁמָּא יִפְסוֹק סַנְדָּלוֹ שֶׁל אֶחָד מֵהֶן וְנִמְצָא מִתְעַכֵּב מִן הַמִּצְוָה.

It is stated: The carriers[117] may not wear sandals[118] lest a shoelace of one of them break so he would be eliminated from the good deed.

117 The carriers of the bier in the funeral procession, members of the "holy society".

118 According to *Ṭure Zahav* on *Shulḥan Arukh Yore Dea* 358:3, this applies only to professional carriers, or members of a society that monopolizes the *mitzvah* of carrying the bier, who will have to walk barefooted. However, it seems that shoes without laces would be permitted by the Yerushalmi.

רִבִּי זְעִירָא שְׁרַע בְּדִיבּוּרָא אָתוּן בְּעַיִין מִיזְקְפָנֵיהּ וְאַשְׁכְּחוּנֵיהּ אִיעָנֵי. אָמְרוּ לֵיהּ מַהוּ כֵן אָמַר לוֹן דַּאֲתִינוּן עַל שֵׁם וְהַחַי יִתֵּן אֶל לִבּוֹ.

Rebbi Zeïra bent down[119] during a eulogy. They wanted to straighten him up and found that he tarried[120]. They said to him, what is this? He said to them, because we will go there, following (*Eccl.* 7:2): "Let the one who is alive take it to heart."

119 Most commentators explain that Rebbi Zeïra fell down. But the parallels quoted in Levy's dictionary show that Aramaic שרע is the parallel of biblical Hebrew סרח, "overhanging". The speaker was leaning down over the railing of his pulpit.

120 The Aramaic עני may mean 1) to become poor, 2) to take one's time, tarry, 3) to empty oneself. In Yerushalmi sources, the form איענִי is found only in meaning 2). The verse quoted reads in full: "It is better to go to a house of mourning than to go to a wedding. Since that is the end of all humanity, let the one who is alive take it to heart."

משנה ב: קָבְרוּ אֶת הַמֵּת וְחָזְרוּ אִם יְכוֹלִין לְהַתְחִיל וְלִגְמוֹר עַד שֶׁלֹּא יַגִּיעוּ לְשׁוּרָה יַתְחִילוּ וְאִם לָאו לֹא יַתְחִילוּ. הָעוֹמְדִין בְּשׁוּרָה הַפְּנִימִיִּין פְּטוּרִין וְהַחִיצוֹנִין חַיָּבִין.

Mishnah 2: When they buried the deceased and returned, if they are able to start and finish before they form the row[121] they should start, otherwise they should not start. Those who stand in the row, the innermost are exempt[122] and the outer ones are obliged.

121 Before the mourners leave for their home, the other participants of the funeral form two lines and the mourners pass in the row between them. While they pass, words of consolation are spoken to them. Today, that ceremony is performed in the cemetary so that the Mishnah becomes void. In talmudic times, the burial was in the cemetary far from the city, but the ceremony of the row took place at the entrance to the city. There may be a long enough walk from cemetary to town that the prescribed time for *Shema'* would pass. The words "start" and "finish" refer to the recitation of *Shema'*.

122 Since the mourners can see and hear them, they are doing a good deed and cannot be distracted by other obligations. The "outer ones" are those who cannot be seen by the mourners.

הלכה ב: תַּנֵּי אֵין מוֹצִיאִין אֶת הַמֵּת סָמוּךְ לִקְרִיַּת שְׁמַע אֶלָּא אִם כֵּן הִקְדִּימוּ שָׁעָה אַחַת. אוֹ אִם אִיחֲרוּ שָׁעָה אַחַת כְּדֵי שֶׁיִּקְרְאוּ וְיִתְפַּלְּלוּ. וְהָא תַנִּינָן קָבְרוּ אֶת הַמֵּת וְחָזְרוּ. תִּיפְתָּר בְּאִילֵּין דַּהֲוִין סָבְרִין דְּאִית בֵּיהּ עוֹנָה וְלֵית בֵּיהּ עוֹנָה.

Halakhah 2:[123] It is stated: "One does not take the dead for burial close to the recitation of the *Shema'* unless one does it one hour in advance or one hour afterwards, so that they may recite and pray." But did we not formulate: "When they buried the deceased and returned"[124]? Explain it for those who thought that they have a free period[125] but they did not have a free period.

123 The entire discussion of this Mishnah is repeated word by word in Yerushalmi *Sanhedrin* 2:2 (fol. 20a).

124 How can the situation dealt with in the Mishnah ever arise if the *baraita* is correct?

125 In the absence of reliable clocks. In the parallel in the Babli (*Berakhot* 19a), it is stated flatly that the restriction of the *baraita* does not apply to funerals of important persons. In the opinion of the Babli, the situation envisaged by the Mishnah can apply to previously planned funerals.

תַּנֵּי הַמְּהַסְפֵּד וְכָל הָעוֹסְקִין בְּהֶסְפֵּד מַפְסִיקִין לִקְרִיַּת שְׁמַע וְאֵין מַפְסִיקִין לִתְפִילָּה. מַעֲשֶׂה הָיָה וְהִפְסִיקוּ רִבּוֹתֵינוּ לִקְרִיַּת שְׁמַע וְלִתְפִילָּה. וְהָא תַנִּינָן אִם יְכוֹלִין לְהַתְחִיל וְלִגְמוֹר. מַתְנִיתָא בְּיוֹם הָרִאשׁוֹן. וּמָה דְתַנֵּי בְּיוֹם הַשֵּׁנִי.

It is stated[126]: The eulogizer and all who participate in a eulogy interrupt for the recitation of *Shema'* and do not interrupt for prayer. It happened that our teachers interrupted for the recitation of *Shema'* and prayer. Did we not formulate: "If they are able to start and finish"? Our Mishnah speaks of the first day, what is stated for the second day.

126 Tosephta *Berakhot* 2:11. This Tosephta comes after the one dealing with the funeral (which will be quoted later in this Halakhah.) Hence, it clearly deals with a eulogy *after* the funeral. The text of the Tosephta follows that of the Genizah fragments; it is slightly corrupted in the Venice (and Leyden) texts that have ההספד instead of the unusual המהספד (the corresponding word in the Babli would be המספיד.) [A seemingly similar *baraita* in the Babli, *Berakhot* 19a, deals with a eulogy before burial and has nothing in common with the text given here.]

אָמַר רִבִּי שְׁמוּאֵל בַּר אֶבְדּוּמָא זֶה שֶׁהוּא נִכְנַס לְבֵית הַכְּנֶסֶת וּמָצְאָן עוֹמְדִין וּמִתְפַּלְלִין. אִם יוֹדֵעַ הוּא מַתְחִיל וְגוֹמֵר עַד שֶׁלֹּא יַתְחִיל שְׁלִיחַ צִיבּוּר כְּדֵי לַעֲנוֹת אַחֲרָיו אָמֵן יִתְפַּלֵּל וְאִים לָאו אַל יִתְפַּלֵּל. בְּאֵי זֶה אָמֵן אָמְרוּ תְּרֵין אֲמוֹרָאִין חַד אָמַר בְּאָמֵן שֶׁל הָאֵל הַקָּדוֹשׁ. וְחַד אָמַר בְּאָמֵן שֶׁל שׁוֹמֵעַ תְּפִילָּה. אָמַר רִבִּי פִּינְחָס וְלֹא פְלִיגֵי. מַאן דָּמַר בְּאָמֵן שֶׁל הָאֵל הַקָּדוֹשׁ בְּשַׁבָּת. וּמַאן דָּמַר בְּאָמֵן שֶׁל שׁוֹמֵעַ תְּפִילָּה בְּחוֹל.

Rebbi Samuel ben Eudaimon[127] said: He who enters the synagogue and finds them standing and praying[128], if he knows that he could start and finish before the reader starts, so that he may answer "Amen", he may pray, otherwise he should not pray. About which "Amen" did they talk? Two Amoraïm, one says the Amen of "the holy King"[129] and the other says the Amen of "He Who listens to prayer". Rebbi Phineas said, they do not disagree. He who said: the Amen of "the holy King", on the Sabbath, and he who said: the Amen of "He Who listens to prayer" on weekdays.

127 An Amora of the fifth Galilean generation, student of Rebbi Mana. The paragraph added deals with the problem of whether to start or not; it is a kind of appendix to the first two paragraphs. After that digression, one will return to the discussion of the Mishnah.

128 The Amidah prayer.

129 The third benediction of the Amidah. "He Who hears prayer" is the last of the middle benedictions of weekday prayers (15th in Israel, 16th in Babylonia). The statement refers to the old Galilean usage that *Qedushah* was recited only on special days; it probably was not recited in the Sabbath afternoon prayers and, hence, it is not mentioned that one should be able to respond to *Qedushah.*

תַּנֵּי רִבִּי יוּדָה אוֹמֵר הָיוּ כוּלָּם בְּשׁוּרָה אַחַת הָעוֹמְדִין מִשּׁוּם כָּבוֹד חַיָּבִין. מִשּׁוּם אֵבֶל פְּטוּרִין. יָֽרְדוּ לְסֶפֶד הָרוֹאִין פָּנִים פְּטוּרִין. וּשְׁאֵינָן רוֹאִין פָּנִים חַיָּבִין. הֲוֵי הֲדָא דְתַנִּינָן הָעוֹמְדִין בַּשּׁוּרָה הַפְּנִימִיִּם פְּטוּרִין וְהַחִיצוֹנִים חַיָּבִין מִשְׁנָה אַחֲרוֹנָה. הֲדָא דְתַנֵּי הָעוֹמְדִין מִשּׁוּם כָּבוֹד חַיָּבִין. מִשּׁוּם אֵבֶל פְּטוּרִין מִשְׁנָה רִאשׁוֹנָה. וְהַיי דְתַנִּינָן תַּמָּן וּכְשֶׁהוּא מְנַחֵם אֶת אֲחֵרִים דֶּרֶךְ כָּל־הָעָם זֶה אַחַר זֶה. וְהַמְּמוּנֶּה מְמַצְּעוֹ בֵּינוֹ לְבֵין הָעָם מִשְׁנָה אַחֲרוֹנָה. ס״א ראשונה. אָמַר רִבִּי חֲנִינָא בָּרִאשׁוֹנָה הָיוּ מִשְׁפָּחוֹת עוֹמְדוֹת וַאֲבֵלִים עוֹבְרִין. מִשֶּׁרַבַּת תַּחֲרוּת בְּצִיפּוֹרִין הִתְקִין רִבִּי יוֹסֵי בֶּן חֲלַפְתָּא שֶׁיְּהוּ הַמִּשְׁפָּחוֹת עוֹבְרוֹת וְהָאֲבֵלִים עוֹמְדִין. אָמַר רִבִּי שְׁמוּאֵל תּוֹסֶפְתָּא חָֽזְרוּ הַדְּבָרִים לְיוֹשְׁנָן.

It is stated (*Tosephta Berakhot* 2:11): "Rebbi Judah says, if they all are standing in one row, those who are standing because of honor are obliged, those because of mourning are exempt[130]. When they descend for a eulogy, those who see inside are exempt, those who do not see inside are obliged[131]." It would be that what we stated: "Those who stand in the row, the innermost are exempt and the outer ones are obliged" is the last teaching[132], and what is stated: "Those who are standing because of honor are obliged, those because of mourning are exempt", is the first teaching[133]. And what we have stated there (Mishnah *Sanhedrin* 2:2): "When he[134] consoles others, all the people stand one behind the other and the executive officer becomes a partition between himself and the people", the last teaching. (Another opinion: the first.) Rebbi Ḥanina said: Originally, all families were standing still and the mourners passed between them. When competition increased in Sepphoris, Rebbi Yose ben Ḥalaphta decreed that the families should pass by and the mourners stand still. Rebbi Samuel Tosephta[135] said: Matters returned to their original state.

130 In the text of the Babli (*Berakhot* 19b), Rashi reads: "those who come because of themselves", not "because of honor", but most manuscripts and old authors have "because of honor". Also, in the Babli only the second part of the Tosephta is attributed to Rebbi Yehudah. According to Rashi, only those are obliged to read the *Shema'* who come out of curiosity whereas according to most others those who come to honor the dead and his family but do not actively console are not exempt. The Babylonian Talmud makes no comment; we have to assume that it accepts the position of R. Samuel Tosephta.

131 Since they cannot be seen by the mourners, the may recite the *Shema'* for themselves without offending anybody.

132 The question is, what is the last teaching? We are informed that the original custom was that the mourners walk between two rows of participants who greet them with words of con-

solation. When competition grew in Sepphoris, it seems because people were jostling for the best positions (those who did not make it to the front rows could not be seen or heard by the mourners), Rebbi Yose decreed that the mourners should stay put and all others march by them to greet and console them. This is the case dealt with by Rebbi Judah, that there is only one row (moving, not standing). An otherwise unknown Rebbi Samuel declares that the innovation of Rebbi Jose did not stand the test of time and in his time the consolers stand and the mourners move. Rebbi Samuel's opinion is the "last teaching", Rebbi Yose's "the first teaching". In the first teaching, there are no people in outer rows, so the Mishnah automatically has to apply to the last teaching.

133 Since the entire Tosephta is Rebbi Judah's, it speaks of the case where there is only one row. (This argument is not applicable to the text quoted in the Babli.)

134 The High Priest. When he goes out, he is accompanied by his executive officer; when he consoles mourners the executive goes first, the High Priest second, and everybody else in one orderly row after him. This is possible only in the scenario envisaged by Rebbi Yose; it is shown that the practice instituted by Rebbi Yose at Sepphoris (in the second half of the second century C. E.) is in effect an old Jerusalem practice from the time before the destruction of the Temple, as stated explicitly in Babli *Sanhedrin* 19a, where it is noted that also under that system people quarrelled in Jerusalem. Here the copyist (or the editor) seems to have doubts whether to go with the definition of "first" and "last" as above or to call "first" the first practice reported by Rebbi Ḥanina and "last" the second one. Hence, there are two opinions about the attribution but the meaning is clear. If the uncertainty is the editor's, then the note "Another opinion: the first" belongs to the text. If it is the scribe's or some reader's, then it is a gloss that has entered the text from the margin. For consistency, the hypothesis of a gloss is preferable.

135 In the Venice text, "Rebbi Simeon of the Tosephta". The name given in the text is from the Geniza fragments (Rebbi Samuel Tosephta) and similar to the parallel in Yerushalmi *Sanhedrin* 2:2 (fol. 20a) "Rebbi Samuel of Sofephta". Tosephta might be the region of Northern Armenia, called Thospitis by Ptolemy, which was the birthplace of Rabba Tosphaä, one of the later heads of the Academy of Sura in Babylonia.

משנה ג: נָשִׁים וַעֲבָדִים וּקְטַנִּים פְּטוּרִין מִקְּרִיַּת שְׁמַע וּמִן הַתְּפִילִּין וְחַיָּבִין בִּתְפִילָּה וּבִמְזוּזָה וּבְבִרְכַּת הַמָּזוֹן.

Mishnah 3: Women, slaves, and minors are exempt from reciting the *Shema'* and from phylacteries but are obliged for prayer, *mezuzah*,[136] and Grace for food.

136 While both phylacteries and *mezuzot* are based on verses in *Shema'*, their status is different.

הלכה ג: נָשִׁים מְנַיִּין וְלִמַּדְתֶּם אוֹתָם אֶת בְּנֵיכֶם. אֶת בְּנֵיכֶם וְלֹא אֶת בְּנוֹתֵיכֶם.

Halakhah 3: Women from where? (*Deut*. 11:19) "You must teach them to your sons." To your sons but not to your daughters[137].

137 The father is unconditionally obliged to teach his sons Torah; since this is an integral part of *Shema'*, the same is valid for reciting the *Shema'*. It is general practice that women *may* recite *Shema'*; it follows that in the opinion of the Yerushalmi, women may study any subjects of Torah they wish. [The Babli, *Berakhot* 20b, simply notes that *Shema'* is an obligation to be executed at stated times, of which women and slaves are automatically exempted. Since the Yerushalmi brings this argument in relation to other things later in this section, it follows that for it the recital of *Shema'* is simply an aspect of Torah study and Torah study is required "day and night", not depending on any particular time.]

עֲבָדִים מְנַיִּין שְׁמַע יִשְׂרָאֵל יי אֱלֹהֵינוּ יי אֶחָד. אֶת שֶׁאֵין לוֹ אָדוֹן אֶלָּא הַקָּדוֹשׁ בָּרוּךְ הוּא יָצָא הָעֶבֶד שֶׁיֵּשׁ לוֹ אָדוֹן אַחֵר.

Slaves from where? (*Deut*. 6:4): "Hear, o Israel, the Eternal, our Power, the Eternal is unique." He who has only one Lord, this excludes the slave who has another lord[138].

138 As explained in the preceding paragraph, the Yerushalmi does not refer to the obligation of reciting *Shema'* as an obligation to be performed at stated times; therefore, a separate argument is necessary to free from the obligation slaves who accepted Judaism.

קְטַנִּים מְנַיִין לְמַעַן תִּהְיֶה תּוֹרַת יי בְּפִיךָ בְּשָׁעָה שֶׁהוּא תָדִיר בָּהּ.

Minors from where? (*Ex.* 13:9) "So that the Torah of the Eternal should stay in your mouth", at a time when he is permanent in it[139].

139 This paragraph is exceedingly difficult for two reasons. 1) It is a generally accepted principle that minors are not obliged to do anything; it is their parents who are obliged to teach them and see to it that they perform *mizwot.* 2) The verse deals only with *tefillin.*

In the Yerushalmi tradition, the statement and the tradition are not unquestioned. Both *Mekhiltot* (*Mekhilta dR. Ismael*, ed. Horovitz-Rabin, p. 68; *Mekhilta dR. Simeon bar Iohai,* p.41), the Tannaïtic commentaries to Exodus, give the same commentary on the next verse (*Ex.* 13:10): "You must preserve this decree in its time, from year to year". "Why has this been said? Because it has been said (v.9): 'It shall be for you a sign on your hand', I might understand this to include minors. And it is logical, since *mezuzah* is a positive commandment and *tefillin* are a positive commandment; if you find that *mezuzah* applies to minors the same way it applies to adults you might think that *tefillin* apply to minors the same way they apply to adults, but the verse says 'you must preserve this decree', I spoke only about those able to watch over their *tefillin*; from here they said: If a minor knows how to watch his *tefillin*, his father makes him *tefillin.*"

The argument presupposes the statement that minors are obliged to have *mezuzot* on their doors (meaning that if they live alone, the rabbinic authorities have to see to it that they have *mezuzot* on their doors). *Mezuzah* and *tefillin* are always mentioned together in the first two paragraphs of *Shema'*. Hence, one may assume that they are identical in those details that are not spelled out. Both Yerushalmi and Mekhiltot agree that some explanation is needed to distinguish between the rules for *mezuzah* and those for *tefillin*. However, the Mekhiltot extend the obligation of *tefillin* to all school children whereas the Yerushalmi restricts it to those for whom the study of Torah is a permanent obligation, i. e., from Bar-Mizwah onwards. In itself the argument about minors is totally irrelevant; it is needed to exclude the opinion of the Mekhiltot.

וְחַייָבִין בִּתְפִילָּה כְּדֵי שֶׁיְּהֵא כָּל־אֶחָד וְאֶחָד מְבַקֵּשׁ רַחֲמִים עַל עַצְמוֹ.

They are obliged to pray so that everybody ask mercy for himself[140].

140 Here again, we have a divergence between Yerushalmi and Babli. The Yerushalmi states that prayer is an obligation not because it is a Biblical commandment but because the rabbis thought that everybody has to implore divine mercy for himself. In the Babli (*Berakhot* 20b), the argument of the Yerushalmi is repeated but then it is stated that in Psalms (*Ps.* 55:18) three times daily are stated for prayer and if that were a general obligation, women would be automatically dispensed from it. Hence, it follows that the rabbinical obligation of prayer for women cannot mean for the Babli an obligation to pray at those stated times, which it could mean in the interpretation of the Yerushalmi. The opinion of the Babli is that of Maimonides, the possible one of the Yerushalmi that of Nachmanides.

וּבִמְזוּזָה דִּכְתִיב וּכְתַבְתָּם עַל מְזוּזוֹת בֵּיתֶךָ וּבִשְׁעָרֶיךָ.

And for *mezuzah*, as it is written (*Deut.* 6:9): "You shall write them on the doorpost of your house and your gates[141].

141 This is an obligation of ownership, not of person.

וּבִרְכַּת הַמָּזוֹן דִּכְתִיב וְאָכַלְתָּ וְשָׂבָעְתָּ וּבֵרַכְתָּ אֶת יי אֱלֹהֶיךָ.

And grace after meals, as it is written (*Deut.* 8:10): "You will eat and be satiated; then you must praise the Eternal, your God.[142]"

142 According to the Yerushalmi, women and slaves are required to recite Grace from the Torah since everybody who eats must give praise. In the Babli (*loc. cit.*), this remains questionable.

תַּמָּן תַּנִּינָן כָּל־מִצְוַת עֲשֵׂה שֶׁהַזְּמָן גְּרָמָהּ אֲנָשִׁים חַייָבִין וְהַנָּשִׁים פְּטוּרוֹת. וְכָל־מִצְוַת עֲשֵׂה שֶׁלֹּא הַזְּמָן גְּרָמָהּ אֶחָד אֲנָשִׁים וְאֶחָד נָשִׁים חַייָבִין. אֵי זֶה הוּא מִצְוַת עֲשֵׂה שֶׁהַזְּמָן גְּרָמָהּ כְּגוֹן סוּכָּה לוּלָב שׁוֹפָר וּתְפִילִּין. וְאֵי זוֹ הִיא מִצְוַת עֲשֵׂה שֶׁלֹּא הַזְּמָן גְּרָמָהּ כְּגוֹן אֲבֵידָה וְשִׁלּוּחַ הַקֵּן מַעֲקֶה וְצִיצִית. רִבִּי שִׁמְעוֹן פּוֹטֵר אֶת הַנָּשִׁים מִמִּצְוַת צִיצִית שֶׁהוּא מִצְוַת עֲשֵׂה שֶׁהַזְּמָן גְּרָמָהּ. שֶׁהֲרֵי כְסוּת לַיְלָה פָּטוּר מִן הַצִּיצִית. אָמַר רִבִּי לִייָא טַעֲמוֹן דְּרַבָּנָן שֶׁכֵּן אִם הָיְתָה מְיוּחֶדֶת לוֹ לְיוֹם וּלְלַיְלָה שֶׁהִיא חַייֶבֶת בְּצִיצִית.

There (Mishnah *Qiddushin* 1:7) we have stated: "Every positive commandment that is activated by time, men are obliged by it but women are exempt. Every positive commandment that is not activated by time, both men and women are obliged by it." (Tosephta *Qiddushin* 1:10): "What is a positive commandment that is activated by time? For example *sukkah, lulab, shofar,* and *tefillin.* What is a positive commandment that is not activated by time? For example lost articles[143], sending away the nest[144], railing[145], and *ẓiẓit*[146]. Rebbi Simeon exempts women from *ẓiẓit* because it is a positive commandment activated by time." Because a nightgown is exempt from *ẓiẓit*. Rebbi Lia said: The reason of the rebbbis is that, if a garment is designated both for daytime and for night, it needs *ẓiẓit*.

143 The obligation to return found articles and stray animals to their owners in *Deut.* 22:1-3.

144 The obligation to send away the mother if eggs or chicks are taken from a nest in *Deut.* 22:6-7.

145 The obligation to make a fence around a flat roof in *Deut.* 22:8.

146 The obligation to wear *ẓiẓit* in the third section of *Shema'* where it is stated that they must be seen, so garments, worn exclusively in the night when it is dark, do not need *ẓiẓit*. The Babli (*Qiddushin* 33b-34a; *Menaḥot* 43a) mentions neither *ẓiẓit* nor the opinion of Rebbi Simeon in its quotes from the Tosephta; it assumes the position of Rebbi Simeon to be generally accepted.

תַּנֵּי כָּל־מִצְווֹת שֶׁאָדָם פָּטוּר אָדָם מוֹצִיא אֶת הָרַבִּים יְדֵי חוֹבָתָן חוּץ מִבִּרְכַּת הַמָּזוֹן. וְהָא דְתַנִּינָן שֶׁאֵינוֹ חַיָּב בַּדָּבָר אֵין מוֹצִיא אֶת הָרַבִּים יְדֵי חוֹבָתָן. הָא אִם הָיָה חַיָּב אֲפִילוּ אִם יָצָא מוֹצִיא. אָמַר רִבִּי לִייָא שַׁנְיָא הִיא בִּרְכַּת הַמָּזוֹן דִּכְתִיב בָּהּ וְאָכַלְתָּ וְשָׂבָעְתָּ וּבֵרַכְתָּ אֶת יי אֱלֹהֶיךָ. מִי שֶׁאָכַל הוּא יְבָרֵךְ. רִבִּי יוֹסֵי וְרִבִּי יוּדָה בֶּן פָּזִי הֲווּ יָתְבִין וְאָמְרִין לָא מִסְתַּבְּרָא בִקְרִיַּת שְׁמַע שֶׁיְּהֵא כָּל־אֶחָד וְאֶחָד מְשַׁנֵּן בְּפִיו. לָא מִסְתַּבְּרָא בִתְפִילָּה שֶׁיְּהֵא כָּל־אֶחָד וְאֶחָד מְבַקֵּשׁ רַחֲמִים עַל עַצְמוֹ.

It is stated: "For every obligation that a man is free of, he may help the congregation to fulfill their obligation, except for Grace." But have we not stated: "Anybody who is not obligated may not help the congregation to fulfill their obligation"? If he were obligated, he could help them to fulfill even if he himself already fulfilled it![147] Rebbi Lia said: There is a difference about Grace since it is written (*Deut*. 8:10): "You will eat and be satiated, then you must praise the Eternal, your God;" he who ate must give praise.

Rebbi Yose and Rebbi Judah ben Pazi were sitting together and saying: It would be reasonable[148] for reciting the *Shema‘* that every single person should repeat it aloud. It would be reasonable for prayer that every single person should pray for mercy by himself.

147 "To be free" does not mean the same as "not being obligated" but rather "having already acquitted himself of the obligation." The first statement means, e. g., that someone who already has heard the *shofar* on Rosh Hashanah nevertheless may blow the *shofar* and recite the appropriate benediction for somebody who did not hear the blowing. The only exception mentioned is that of saying Grace. The second statement means, e. g., that a woman, not being obligated to hear the *shofar*, may not blow the *shofar* for a man who is obligated. Since everybody is obligated to say Grace after a meal, there seems to be no reason why Grace should be exempted in the first statement.

148 The exemption mentioned for

Grace should be extended to the recital of *Shema'* and prayer. The argument for *Shema'* rests on the expression (*Deut.* 6:7) ושננתם לבניך "you should repeat it to your sons"; it implies a personal action and cannot be performed by listening to a reader. The discussion of prayer presupposes the Galilean practice that the reader recite the *Amidah* aloud, without silent prayer, and it is stated that everyone is required to say the prayer with the reader, not just to respond with "Amen". In Babylonia the question did not arise since silent prayer was always required before the repetition by the reader.

מַה בֵּין סוּכָּה וּמַה בֵּין לוּלָב. סוּכָּה אֵינָהּ טְעוּנָה בְרָכָה אֶלָּא לֵילֵי יוֹם טוֹב רִאשׁוֹן בִּלְבַד. לוּלָב טָעוּן בְּרָכָה כָּל־שִׁבְעָה. רִבִּי יוֹסֵי וְרִבִּי אָחָא הֲווּ יָתְבִין אָמְרִין מַה בֵּין סוּכָּה וּמַה בֵּין לוּלָב. סוּכָּה נוֹהֶגֶת בַּלֵּילוֹת וּבְיָמִים. לוּלָב אֵינוֹ נוֹהֵג אֶלָּא בַיּוֹם. הָתִיב רִבִּי יַעֲקֹב דְּרוֹמַיָּא הֲרֵי תַלְמוּד תּוֹרָה נוֹהֵג בַּלֵּילוֹת כְּבְיָמִים. מַיי כְדוֹן סוּכָּה אִיפְשַׁר לָהּ לִיבָּטֵל. תַּלְמוּד תּוֹרָה אִיפְשַׁר לָהּ שֶׁלֹּא לִיבָּטֵל.

What[149] is the difference between *sukkah* and *lulab? Sukkah* does not need a benediction after the first night of the holiday, *lulab* needs a benediction all seven days[150]. Rebbi Yose and Rebbi Aḥa were sitting and saying, what is the difference between *sukkah* and *lulab? Sukkah* applies both nights and days, *lulab* applies only during daytime[151]. Rebbi Jacob the Southerner objected: But the study of Torah applies by night as by day? How is this? *Sukkah* will end; the study of Torah, it is impossible that it should ever end[152].

149 It seems that this paragraph is put here because 1) *sukkah* and *lulab* were mentioned as examples of temporary obligations and 2) it was the subject of a discussion between Rebbi Yose (the Amora) and one of his colleagues.

150 This is a shortened version of a Tosephta (*Berakhot* 6:9,10) discussed more in detail later (Halakhah 9:4, fol. 14a) and in Babli *Sukkah* 46a, where Rebbi states that one makes a

benediction all seven days of Sukkoth and that Babylonian practice follows Rebbi. Galilean practice followed the rule that the benediction "Who commanded us to dwell in the *sukkah*" was recited only once during the entire holiday. About *lulab*, the Babli notes correctly that in the absence of a Temple, taking the *lulab* after the first day is a rabbinic ordinance, not a Torah commandment; hence, the obligation of the second day cannot be covered by the benediction of the first. It may be that this distinction caused Rebbi Yose to be dissatisfied with the first explanation.

151 While *sukkah* is one continuous obligation, *lulab* represents seven distinct periods of obligation of which each one merits a new benediction.

152 It is unreasonable to say that a boy on becoming Bar Mizwah should recite the benediction for the Torah once and not repeat it for his entire lifetime. *Sukkah* at least gets a new benediction every year.

תַּנֵּי אֲבָל אָֽמְרוּ אִשָּׁה מְבָרֶכֶת לְבַעְלָהּ וְעֶבֶד מְבָרֵךְ לְרַבּוֹ וְקָטָן לְאָבִיו. לֹא כֵן אָמַר רִבִּי אָחָא בְּשֵׁם רִבִּי יוֹסֵי בַּר נְהוֹרָאִי כָּל־שֶׁאָֽמְרוּ בְקָטָן כְּדֵי לְחַנְּכוֹ. תִּיפְתָּר בְּעוֹנֶה אַחֲרֵיהֶן (אמן). כְּיֵי דְתַנֵּינָן תַּמָּן מִי שֶׁהָיָה עֶבֶד אוֹ אִשָּׁה אוֹ קָטָן מַקְרִין אוֹתוֹ עוֹנֶה אַחֲרֵיהֶן מַה שֶּׁהֵן אוֹמְרִין וּתְהֵא לוֹ מְאֵירָה. אֲבָל אָֽמְרוּ תָּבוֹא מְאֵירָה לְבֶן עֶשְׂרִים שֶׁצָּרִיךְ לְבֶן עֶשֶׂר.

It is stated[153]: In truth, they said a woman may say Grace for her husband[154], a slave for his master, and a minor for his father. Did not Rebbi Aḥa say in the name of Rebbi Yose bar Nahoraï: All they said about a minor is for the latter's education[155]? Explain it that he recites after him[156], as we stated there[157]: "He for whom a slave, a woman, or a minor were reading it, repeats after them what they are saying, and may it be a curse for him. In truth, they said there should be a curse on the man of twenty years who needs the child of ten."

153 Tosephta *Berakhot* 5:17, Babli *Berakhot* 20b, *Sukkah* 38a. The entire piece is found in *Sukkah* 3:11, *Rosh Hashanah* 3:9.

154 He who does not know how to say Grace may listen to a companion

recite Grace aloud. The Yerushalmi has no problem with women or slaves but for the Babli the question remains whether women may in fact recite Grace for males who have an obligation from the Torah, i. e., who actually ate their fill.

155 The minor must be educated; there is an obligation on the father to teach him all religious obligations but the minor himself is not obligated and, by the previously mentioned principle, cannot perform any religious duty for others.

156 The adult repeats word by word what the minor says, so the adult in fact has recited all benedictions.

157 In some Tosephta collection no longer extant.

משנה ד: בַּעַל קֶרִי מְהַרְהֵר בְּלִבּוֹ וְאֵינוֹ מְבָרֵךְ לֹא לְפָנֶיהָ וְלֹא לְאַחֲרֶיהָ וְעַל הַמָּזוֹן מְבָרֵךְ לְאַחֲרֶיהָ וְאֵינוֹ מְבָרֵךְ לְפָנֶיהָ. רִבִּי יְהוּדָה אוֹמֵר מְבָרֵךְ לִפְנֵיהֶן וּלְאַחֲרֵיהֶן.

Mishnah 4: He who had *qeri*[158] thinks but does not recite any benediction before or after[159]; on his food he recites the benedictions afterwards[160] but not before. Rebbi Yehudah says, he recites benedictions before and after.

158 An emission of semen.

159 The recitation of *Shema'*.

160 Grace, which is an obligation from the Torah. He does not recite the rabbinic benedictions before the meal.

הלכה ד: מַהוּ מְהַרְהֵר בְּרָכוֹת.

Halakhah 4: What does he think of? The benedictions[161].

161 But the *Shema'*, which is an obligation from the Torah, he recites normally. But Rashi explains "he thinks the *Shema'*", and this also seems to be the opinion of Maimonides in his decision based on the Babli.

מַתְנִיתָא בְּמָקוֹם שֶׁאֵין מַיִם וּכְרִבִּי (fol. 6c) מֵאִיר דְּתַנֵּי בַּעַל קֶרִי שֶׁאֵין לוֹ מַיִם לִטְבּוֹל הֲרֵי זֶה קוֹרֵא אֶת שְׁמַע וְאֵינוֹ מַשְׁמִיעַ לְאָזְנוֹ וְאֵינוֹ מְבָרֵךְ לֹא לְפָנֶיהָ וְלֹא לְאַחֲרֶיהָ דִּבְרֵי רִבִּי מֵאִיר וַחֲכָמִים אוֹמְרִין קוֹרֵא אֶת שְׁמַע וּמַשְׁמִיעַ לְאָזְנוֹ וּמְבָרֵךְ לְפָנֶיהָ וּלְאַחֲרֶיהָ.

The Mishnah deals with a place where there is no water[162] and follows Rebbi Meïr, as it is stated (Tosephta *Berakhot* 2:13): "He who had *qeri* but no water to immerse himself reads the *Shema'* but not so that he himself can hear it, but he does not recite any benediction before or after; these are the words of Rebbi Meïr. But the Sages say, he reads so that he himself can hear it and recites benedictions before and after.[163]"

162 It will be confirmed in the next *Halakhah* that even Rebbi Yehudah agrees that after an emission one may not recite unless he washed first. So this statement is agreed to by everybody in the Yerushalmi.

163 The Babli (*Berakhot* 22a) quotes a parallel but different *baraita* in which the position of "the Sages" is in the name of R. Yehudah.

תַּנֵּי בַּעַל קֶרִי חוֹלֶה שֶׁנָּפְלוּ עָלָיו תִּשְׁעָה קַבִּין מַיִם וְטָהוֹר שֶׁנָּפְלוּ עַל רֹאשׁוֹ וְעַל רוּבּוֹ שְׁלֹשָׁה לוֹגִין מַיִם שְׁאוּבִים טָהֵר לְעַצְמוֹ אֲבָל אֵינוֹ מוֹצִיא אֶת הָרַבִּים יְדֵי חוֹבָתָן עַד שֶׁיָּבוֹא בְּאַרְבָּעִים סְאָה. רִבִּי יוּדָה אוֹמֵר אַרְבָּעִים סְאָה מִכָּל־מָקוֹם.

It is stated (Tosephta *Berakhot* 2:12): "A sick person who had *qeri* on whom fell nine *qab*[164] of water (and a pure one on whose head and body fell three *log* of drawn water)[165] is clean for himself but he cannot lead the public in their obligations until he immersed himself in 40 *seah.* Rebbi Yehudah says, 40 *seah* in all cases[166]."

164 One *qab* equals 4 *log*, one log is .533 liter or .164 gallons, so that a *qab* equals approximately .563 gallons, 9 *qab* about 5.07 U. S. gallons. One *seäh* is 6 *qab* or about 3.38 gallons, so 40 *seäh* equal about 135.2 gallons or 512 liter. In Roman measures, the *log* corresponds to the *sextarius*, and the

seäh to the *urna*. That makes 40 *seah* equal to a Roman *culleus*.

165 The parenthesis is not in the Tosephta or in the quote in the Babli 22b, and does not belong here. The impurity of the man with emission is Biblical (*Lev*. 15:16) but the prohibition of studying Torah and speaking sacred words is from the institutions of Ezra, i. e., it is pre-rabbinic. On the other hand, the impurity of a person washing himself with drawn water after an immersion in a *miqweh* belongs to the "18 ordinances" passed by the adherents of the house of Shammai before the Jewish revolt against the Romans and is purely rabbinical. It was passed because most *miqwaöt* were not built but were water holes in natural caves that were naturally muddy and people had the tendency to wash off the mud after they emerged from the *miqweh*. The rabbis of the time were afraid that in time washing would supersede immersion as (illegal) means of purification, so they decreed that washing after immersion resurrects some mild form of ritual impurity.

166 This translation is not guaranteed. The Babli (*loc. cit*.) takes the statement of Rebbi Yehudah to mean that he requires the stated amount of water but not that it should be in a *miqweh* that satisfies all rules. However, as Levi Ginzberg points out, that requires the expression בכל מקום which is found in manuscripts of the Babli; it represents the majority opinion in the Babli. The idiomatic translation of מכל מקום is "in every case", including the sick person. R. Yehudah then is more restrictive than the other sages if water is available, and this may be the meaning of the Yerushalmi. If the parenthesis is genuinely part of this *baraita*, then the latter interpretation is the only possible one since an impurity imposed to enforce immersion in a genuine *miqweh* can be removed only by such an immersion.

רִבִּי יַעֲקֹב בַּר אָחָא רִבִּי יָסָא בְשֵׁם רִבִּי יְהוֹשֻׁעַ בֶּן לֵוִי אֵין קֶרִי אֶלָּא מִתַּשְׁמִישׁ הַמִּיטָּה. רַב הוּנָא אָמַר וַאֲפִילוּ רָאָה אֶת עַצְמוֹ נֵאוֹת בַּחֲלוֹם. הֲווֹן בָּעִין מֵימַר וּבִלְבַד מֵאִשָּׁה. רִבִּי יוֹנָה וְרִבִּי יוֹסֵי אָמְרִין וַאֲפִילוּ מִדָּבָר אַחֵר. תַּמָּן תַּנִּינָן יוֹם הַכִּיפּוּרִים אָסוּר בַּאֲכִילָה וּשְׁתִיָּה וּבִרְחִיצָה וְסִיכָה וּבִנְעִילַת הַסַּנְדָּל וּבְתַשְׁמִישׁ הַמִּיטָּה. וְתַנֵּי עֲלָהּ בַּעֲלֵי קֶרָיִין טוֹבְלִין כְּדַרְכָּן בְּצִינְעָה בְּיוֹם הַכִּיפּוּרִים. וְלֵית הָדָא פְלִיגָא עַל רִבִּי יְהוֹשֻׁעַ בֶּן לֵוִי דְּרִבִּי יְהוֹשֻׁעַ בֶּן לֵוִי אוֹמֵר אֵין קֶרִי אֶלָּא

מִתַּשְׁמִישׁ הַמִּיטָּה. פְּתַר לָהּ בִּמְשַׁמֵּשׁ מִיטָּתוֹ מִבְּעוֹד יוֹם וְשָׁכַח וְלֹא טָבַל. וְהָתַנֵּי מַעֲשֶׂה בְּרִבִּי יוֹסֵה בֶּן חֲלַפְתָּא שֶׁרָאוּ אוֹתוֹ טוֹבֵל בְּצִינְעָא בְּיוֹם הַכִּיפּוּרִים. אִית לָךְ מֵימַר עַל אוֹתוֹ גוּף קָדוֹשׁ בְּשׁוֹכֵחַ.

Rebbi Jacob bar Aḥa, Rebbi Yasa in the name of Rebbi Joshua ben Levi: *Qeri* is only from sexual intercourse. Rav Huna said, even if he saw himself enjoying in his dream. They wanted to say, only from a woman. Rebbi Jonah and Rebbi Yose, both of them say, even from something else. There (Mishnah *Yoma* 8:1) we have stated: Eating, drinking, washing, anointing, wearing shoes, and sexual intercourse are forbidden on *Yom Kippur*. And it was stated in that respect: Men with *qeri* immerse themselves secretly in their normal way on *Yom Kippur*[167]. Does this not contradict Rebbi Joshua ben Levi since Rebbi Joshua ben Levi says, *qeri* is only from sexual intercourse? Explain it if he had intercourse on the previous day and forgot and did not immerse himself. But it is stated: It happened that Rebbi Yose ben Ḥalaphta was seen immersing himself secretly on *Yom Kippur*. Can you say about that holy body that he forgot[168]?

167 In Tosephta *Kippurim* 4:5 and Babli *Yoma* 88a the reading is: Men with *qeri* immerse themselves normally on *Yom Kippur;* one speaks of a full immersion and "in secret" is not mentioned. The Tosephta seems to be a Babylonian formulation. (The entire paragraph is also found in Yerushalmi *Yoma* 8:1).

168 Hence, the interpretation of Rav Huna is incorrect and that of Rebbis Yose (the Amora) and Jonah is correct.

אָמַר רִבִּי יַעֲקֹב בַּר אָבוּן כָּל־עַצְמָן לֹא הִתְקִינוּ אֶת הַטְּבִילָה הַזֹּאת אֶלָּא שֶׁלֹּא יִהְיוּ יִשְׂרָאֵל כְּתַרְנְגוֹלִין הַלָּלוּ מְשַׁמֵּשׁ מִיטָּתוֹ וְעוֹלֶה וְיוֹרֵד וְאוֹכֵל.

Rebbi Jacob bar Abun said: This immersion has only been enacted so that Jews should not be like chickens, that one would have sex: mount, descend, and eat[169].

169 This means that sexual relations should be stripped of their animal nature as much as possible; the sanctification of marital duties applies to all Jews. The parallel in the Babli (*Berakhot* 22a, in the name of R. Yose bar Abun) reads: "so that scholars should not be found near their wives like roosters." One may conclude that there are two main differences between Galilean and Babylonian practice: In the Yerushalmi, the duty of immersion applies uniformly to everybody and requires a kosher *miqweh*, in the Babli it is necessary only for study and may be done by washing.

R. Jacob bar Abun was a Galilean Amora of the third generation, colleague of R. Jeremiah.

There is no hint anywhere that one is forbidden to eat after intercourse or before immersion; the expression here is just a graphic expression of the behavior of cocks (commentary of Levi Ginzberg).

רִבִּי חֲנִינָא הֲוָה עָבַר עַל תַּרְעֵי דֵימוֹסִין בִּקְרִיצְתָּא וַאֲמַר מַה טוֹבְלֵי שַׁחֲרִית עוֹשִׂין פֹּה יֵיזְלוּן וְיִתְנוּן. בְּהַהִיא דְצַפְרָא הֲוָה אֲמַר מַאן דְּאִית לֵיהּ עֲבִידָא יֵיזִיל וַעֲבַד.

Rebbi Ḥanina passed by the gates of public baths[170] before dawn and said: What are those who have to immerse themselves in the morning doing here? They should go and study Mishnah! In the morning he said: He who has to do it shall go and do it.

170 Greek δημόσιος, α, ον, adj. "public", here understood with βαλανεῖα "baths". The public baths certainly were not open before dawn and Rebbi Ḥanina orders the people there not to waste their time but to study Torah (being from the first Amora generation, he said "to study Mishnah") since the interpretation given later to *qeri* only hinders one to pronounce the Divine name (and, hence, to pray) but not to study where the Divine name is seldom mentioned and, if mentioned at all, only by paraphrase. On the other hand, when morning came and the time for morning prayers, he told those that had intercourse to go and immerse themselves before praying.

מַהוּ לְהַרְהֵר בְּבֵית הַכִּסֵּא. חִזְקִיָּה אָמַר מוּתָּר. רִבִּי יָסָא אָמַר אָסוּר. אָמַר רִבִּי זְעִירָא כָּל־סֶבֶר קָשֶׁה שֶׁהָיָה לִי תַּמָּן סְבֵירְתֵּיהּ. אָמַר רִבִּי אֶלְעָזָר בַּר שִׁמְעוֹן כָּל־הַהוּא סְבָרָא קַשְׁיָא דִטְבוּל יוֹם תַּמָּן סְבֵירְתֵּיהּ.

What are the rules about thinking[171] in the toilet? Ḥizqiah said it is permitted; Rebbi Yasa said it is forbidden. Rebbi Zeïra said, all difficult arguments that I had became clear to me there. Rebbi Eleazar bar Simeon[172] said, the entire difficult subject of *ṭĕbūl yōm* became clear to me there.

171 About Torah subjects. While this paragraph seems to be somewhat out of place here, it is introduced because of the later discussion of the status of a man with *qeri* in the study of Torah subjects.

172 The son of Rebbi Simeon bar Yoḥai. His difficult argument is detailed in Babli *Zebaḥim* 102b. In Babylonia (Babli *Berakhot* 24b) it was accepted by everybody that thinking about Torah subjects in a toilet is forbidden except if the person cannot help doing it. In Galilee the practical rule was to allow it.

רִבִּי אָחָא בְשֵׁם תַּנְחוּם בֵּי רִבִּי חִייָא בְּיוֹמוֹי רִבִּי יְהוֹשֻׁעַ בֶּן לֵוִי בִיקְשׁוּ לַעֲקוֹר אֶת הַטְּבִילָה הַזֹּאת מִפְּנֵי נַשֵׁי הַגָּלִיל שֶׁהָיוּ נֶעֱקָרוֹת מִפְּנֵי הַצִּינָּה. אָמַר לָהֶן רִבִּי יְהוֹשֻׁעַ בֶּן לֵוִי דָּבָר שֶׁהוּא גוֹדֵר אֶת יִשְׂרָאֵל מִן הָעֲבֵירָה אַתֶּם מְבַקְשִׁים לַעֲקוֹר אוֹתוֹ. מַהוּ גוֹדֵר יִשְׂרָאֵל מִן הָעֲבֵירָה. מַעֲשֶׂה בְשׁוֹמֵר כְּרָמִים אֶחָד שֶׁבָּא לְהִזָּקֵק עִם אֵשֶׁת אִישׁ. עַד שֶׁהֵן מְתַקְּנִין מָקוֹם אֵיכַן הֵן טוֹבְלִין עָבְרוּ הָעוֹבְרִין וְהַשָּׁבִין וּבָטְלָה הָעֲבֵירָה. מַעֲשֶׂה בְּאֶחָד שֶׁבָּא לְהִזָּקֵק עִם שִׁפְחָתוֹ שֶׁל רִבִּי. אָמְרָה לוֹ אִם אֵין גְּבִירְתִּי טוֹבֶלֶת אֵינִי טוֹבֶלֶת. אָמַר לָהּ וְלֹא כִבְהֵמָה אַתְּ. אָמְרָה לוֹ וְלֹא שָׁמַעְתָּ בְּבָא עַל הַבְּהֵמָה שֶׁהוּא נִסְקָל שֶׁנֶּאֱמַר כָּל־שׁוֹכֵב עִם בְּהֵמָה מוֹת יוּמָת.

Rebbi Aḥa in the name of Tanḥum ben Rebbi Ḥiyya: In the days of Rebbi Joshua ben Levi they wanted to abolish this immersion because of the Galilean women who became sterile[173] because of the cold. Rebbi

Joshua ben Levi told them: Do you want to uproot something that fences Israel off from sin?

What means: Fences Israel off from sin? It happened that a watchman of vinyards wanted to have an affair with a married woman. By the time they were preparing a place where they could immerse themselves, passers-by came by and the sin was not committed[174].

It happened that someone wanted to have an affair with Rebbi's slave girl. She said to him: If my mistress does not immerse herself, I do not immerse myself[175]. He said to her: Are you not like an animal[176]? She said to him: Did you not hear that one who has relations with an animal will be stoned, as it is said (Ex. 22:18): "Anyone lying with an animal shall certainly be executed."

173 Since in Galilee the immersion was required for everybody, not only for Torah study as in Babylonia, it also applied to women. In winter in upper Galilee, water sometimes freezes and all *miqwaöt* were cold-water *miqwaöt*; in a parallel in Babli *Berakhot* 22a, Rav Huna notes that instead of a *miqweh* one could use a hot bath in Babylonia.

174 A parallel in Babli *Berakhot* 22a is explicitly designated as a *baraita*, dating from Mishnaic times, and applying the need for immersion only to the man. [Levi Ginzberg conjectures that the watchman was a bachelor; hence, he could not use the public *miqweh* (except on holiday eve) without drawing public attention to his unmarried sexual activities. However, it is stated explicitly at the end of this *halakhah* that a *miqweh* was not used for this immersion.]

175 Meaning that as an unmarried woman she does not frequent the *miqweh* and, therefore, cannot have sex with any man. The slave girl was quite famous for speaking better classical Hebrew than the rabbis.

186 The argument here is not perfectly clear. There is a verse in Ezechiel 23:20, speaking about the heathen, "for the flesh of donkeys is their flesh and the semen of horses is their semen" (where "flesh" as human limb here and elsewhere means the penis, the only boneless limb), but that speaks only about males and, in any case, the slave in a Jewish household is

a semi-Jew, becoming a full Jew on manumission without any formality of conversion. Hence, no verse applying to heathen is appropriate here. The real reason seems to be the command given to Adam that "a man shall leave his father and his mother and stick to his wife" (*Gen.* 2:24); since a slave is not legally able to contract a marriage, he is missing the essential human quality of having to marry. That makes questionable humans out of adults who are bachelors by choice. [The sex life of slaves is not discussed in the Yerushalmi. In the Babli (*Niddah* 47a) it is stated that slaves may have sex with anybody except a Jew (and a married Gentile woman).]

אָמַר רִבִּי חִיָּא בַּר וָוה כָּל־עַצְמָן לֹא הִתְקִינוּ אֶת הַטְּבִילָה הַזֹּאת אֶלָּא מִפְּנֵי תַלְמוּד. שֶׁאִם אַתָּה אוֹמֵר לוֹ שֶׁהוּא מוּתָּר אַף הוּא אוֹמֵר אֲנִי אֵלֵךְ וְאֶעֱשֶׂה צְרָכַי וּבָא וְשׁוֹנֶה כָּל־צוֹרְכוֹ וּמִתּוֹךְ שֶׁאַתָּה אוֹמֵר אָסוּר הוּא בָא וְשׁוֹנֶה כָּל־צוֹרְכוֹ. תַּמָּן אָמְרִין אֲפִילוּ לִשְׁמוֹעַ דִּבְרֵי תוֹרָה אָסוּר.

Rebbi Ḥiyya bar Abba[177] said: They ordered this immersion essentially only for study. For if you tell him that he is permitted, he is going to say: "I shall go, satisfy my needs, and then come and study what is needed," but since you say that it is forbidden, he will come and study all he needs[178]. There[180] they said it is even forbidden to hear words of Torah.

177 Rebbi Ḥiyya bar Abba the Babylonian quotes here the Babylonian tradition that this immersion is appropriate only for Torah scholars, in contrast to the Galilean practice shown be the preceding and the following examples that the unlearned were the most ardent practitioners of the ritual.

178 Not having sex in those nights where study starts before dawn, i. e., all week except Friday night.

179 Any תמן "there" in the Yerushalmi means Babylonia. The ruling is not mentioned in the Babli explicitly but there is a parallel to the statement attributed to Rebbi Eleazar, and a statement by the 10th century Rav Hai Gaon (*Oẓar Hageonim Berakhot* p. 56), that in his time scholars in Babylonia did not pray until they had cleansed themselves by washing.

אָמַר רִבִּי יוּדָה בַּר טִיטֵס רִבִּי אָחָא בְשֵׁם רִבִּי אֱלִיעֶזֶר בַּתְחִילָּה וְהָיוּ נְכוֹנִים בַּיּוֹם הַשְּׁלִישִׁי אַל תִּגְּשׁוּ אֶל אִשָּׁה.

Rebbi Judah bar Titus[180], Rebbi Aḥa in the name Rebbi Eliezer: as at the start (*Ex.* 19:11) "They shall be prepared on the third day, do not approach a woman[181]."

180 A Galilean Amora from Caesarea Philippi, of the fourth generation.

181 The impurity of *qeri* for the study of Torah is derived from the theophany at Sinai where the Israelites purified themselves for three days from any impurity caused by marital relations. This gives support to the opinion stated earlier by R. Joshua ben Levi that the impurity of *qeri* is only caused by sexual intercourse. The Talmud notes (Babli *Šabbat* 86a, Yerushalmi *Šabbat* 9:3, fol. 11c) that a separation of three days was needed only for the women since a woman may lose live sperm from her body up to three days after intercourse. For men a simple immersion in water the next day would be enough. This proves that women were included by Divine decree among the original recipients and students of the Torah; the inclusion of women in the Tosephta quoted in the next paragraph is intentional.

תַּנֵּי זָבִין וְזָבוֹת נִידּוֹת וְיוֹלְדוֹת קוֹרִין בַּתּוֹרָה וְשׁוֹנִין מִדְרַשׁ וַהֲלָכוֹת וְהַגָּדוֹת. וּבַעַל קֶרִי אָסוּר בְּכוּלָּן. רִבִּי אַבָּא בַּר אָחָא בְשֵׁם רִבִּי שׁוֹנֶה הֲלָכוֹת וְאֵינוֹ שׁוֹנֶה הַגָּדוֹת. תַּנֵּי בְשֵׁם רִבִּי יוֹסֵי שׁוֹנֶה הִילְכוֹת רְגִילִיּוֹת וּבִלְבַד שֶׁלֹּא יַצִּיעַ אֶת הַמִּשְׁנָה. אִית דְּבָעֵי מֵימָר וּבִלְבַד שֶׁלֹּא יַזְכִּיר אַזְכָּרוֹת. רִבִּי זְעִירָא בָּעֵי קוֹמוֹי רִבִּי יָסָא לֵית רִבִּי פָּשַׁט בֵּי עִם רִבִּי בּוּן פִּירְקֵיהּ בַּלֵּילְיָא. אֲמַר לֵיהּ אִין. רִבִּי חִיָּיא בַּר אַבָּא פָּשַׁט עִם רִבִּי נְחֶמְיָה בְרֵיהּ פִּירְקֵיהּ בַּלֵּילְיָא. בְּהַהִיא צַפְרָא הֲוָה מַר מַה דְאִית לֵיהּ עֲבִידָא יֵיזִיל עֲבֵיד.

It is stated[182]: "Males and females with discharges[183], menstruating women, and women having given birth[184] read in the Torah and study *midrash*[185], practical rules, and homiletics; the person with *qeri* is forbidden all these." Rebbi Abba bar Aḥa in the name of Rebbi[186]: He may study practical rules[187] but not homiletics. It is stated in the name of

Rebbi Yose: He may repeat known rules but he may not expound[188] the Mishnah. Some want to say, only that he may not mention the Divine Name[189]. Rebbi Zeïra asked before Rebbi Yasa: Did my teacher not prepare his lecture together with Rebbi Abun in the night? He said, yes. Rebbi Ḥiyya bar Abba prepared his lecture together with his son Rebbi Neḥemiah in the night. The next morning he said, anybody who has to do should go and do it[190].

182 Tosephta *Berakhot* 2:12. In the parallel in the Babli, *Berakhot* 22a, only males are in the list. The *baraita* in the Babli is a Babylonian formulation of material ascribed to the students of Rebbi Aqiba.

183 From their genitals, the male *zab* suffering from gonorrhea and similar diseases, the female bleeding other than menstruating, see *Lev*. Chapter 15.

184 Whose basic impurity is one week after having a son, two weeks after having a daughter; *Lev*. 12:1-8.

185 This is the derivation of practical rules from the Biblical text, as in the *Midrĕshē Hălākhăh* to the last four books of the Pentateuch.

186 Since Rebbi Abba bar Aḥa was a student of Rab in Babylonia, it is probable that the abbreviation 'ר found in manuscripts and prints should be read רַבֵּנוּ, a common title given to Rab in the Yerushalmi.

187 Which need only memorization, not independent thinking; in contrast to the construction of sermons which are supposed to be original with the preacher. In this respect, the rule of Rab would coincide with that given in the name of Rebbi Yose (the Tanna) in the next sentence.

188 Going into the details and general rules behind the simple casuistic statements of the Mishnah; that requires individual mental effort.

189 This is a problem only in prayer, not in study where the Name is never pronounced even in quotes from the Bible.

190 Note that all Amoraïm involved here are originally Babylonians, but this may be a coincidence. The point seems to be that in the night, when immersion is dangerous, the position of a *baäl qeri* is the same as one who is at a place with no water. While the sources do not discuss the position of Torah study at a place without water, it seems from here and the story about

Rebbi Yose in the paragraph following the next that in the night one never goes for the immersion required and that, therefore, all involved here may study Torah during the night and immerse themselves in the morning before prayers.

מַעֲשֶׂה בְּאֶחָד שֶׁעָמַד לִקְרוֹת בַּתּוֹרָה בְּנְצִיבִין כֵּיוָן שֶׁהִגִּיעַ לְהַזְכָּרָה הִתְחִיל מְגַמְגֵּם בָּהּ. אָמַר לֵיהּ רִבִּי יְהוּדָה בֶּן בְּתֵירָה פְּתַח פִּיךָ וְיָאִירוּ דְבָרֶיךָ שֶׁאֵין דִּבְרֵי תוֹרָה מְקַבְּלִין טוּמְאָה. אֲמַר רִבִּי יַעֲקֹב בַּר אָחָא וּנְהִיגִין תַּמָּן כְּרִבִּי אִלָּעְאִי בְּרֵאשִׁית הַגֵּז וּכְרִבִּי יֹאשִׁיָּה בְּכִלְאֵי הַכֶּרֶם וּכְרִבִּי יְהוּדָה בֶּן בְּתֵירָה בְּבַעֲלֵי קֶרִיִין. כְּרִבִּי אִלָּעְאִי בְּרֵאשִׁית הַגֵּז דְּתַנָּא רִבִּי אִלָּעְאִי אָמַר אֵין רֵאשִׁית הַגֵּז אֶלָּא בָאָרֶץ. כְּרִבִּי יֹאשִׁיָּה בְּכִלְאַיִם דְּתַנֵּי רִבִּי יֹאשִׁיָּה אוֹמֵר לְעוֹלָם אֵינוֹ חַיָּיב עַד שֶׁיִּזְרַע חִטָּה וּשְׂעוֹרָה וְחַרְצָן בְּמַפֹּלֶת יָד. כְּרִבִּי יְהוּדָה בֶּן בְּתֵירָה בְּבַעֲלֵי קֶרִיִין דְּתַנֵּי רִבִּי יְהוּדָה בֶּן בְּתֵירָה אוֹמֵר אֵין דִּבְרֵי תוֹרָה מְקַבְּלִין טוּמְאָה.

It happened that someone was reading the Torah in Nsebin[191]; when he came to the Divine Name he started to stutter. Rebbi Yehudah ben Bathyra told him: Open your mouth and let your words shine because words of the Torah cannot receive impurity.

Rebbi Jacob bar Aḥa said: There they act following Rebbi Illaï regarding the first shearing[192], following Rebbi Josiah[193] regarding *kilaim*[194] in the vineyard, and following Rebbi Yehudah ben Bathyra regarding people with *qeri*. Following Rebbi Illaï regarding the first shearing. as we have stated: "Rebbi Illaï said: The first shearing applies only in the Land." Following Rebbi Josiah regarding *kilaim* as it is stated: "One is never guilty unless one sowed wheat, barley, and grape kernels falling from the same hand." Following Rebbi Yehudah ben Bathyra regarding people with *qeri* as it is stated: "Rebbi Yehudah ben Bathyra says, words of the Torah cannot receive impurity."

191 Nisibis, a town in northern Mesopotamia, today on the border between Syria and Turkey, known as seat of the family Ben Bathyra from at least the start of the Common Era. The authority quoted here is R. Yehuda ben Bathyra II, a student of R. Aqiba. The reader was reading the Torah in the synagogue. In the parallel in the Babli (*Berakhot* 22a), the reason is given that God's word is compared to fire and fire cannot become impure.

192 It has to be given to the Cohen, *Deut*. 18:4. While it is not spelled out in the Pentateuch that this is an obligation only on sheep owners in Israel, "there" in Babylonia one did not give first shearings to the Cohen. The entire statement is quoted in the Babli (*Berakhot* 22a) in the formulation "people follow these three", in the name of Rav Naḥman bar Isaac, a Babylonian contemporary of R. Jacob bar Aḥa.

193 Tanna of the fourth generation, student of R. Ismael, from the town of Huẓal in Babylonia, a contemporary of R. Yehuda ben Bathyra II. All his traditions are from the school of R. Ismael.

194 The prohibition of planting or sowing several species together. The special rules for *kilaim* in a vineyard are based on *Deut*. 22:9: "Do not sow your vineyard *kilaim*". Usually, a vineyard is not sown but planted; R. Josiah therefore restricts the prohibition to the case where even the vines are grown from seeds sown, not planted one by one in separate places.

רִבִּי יוֹסֵי בַּר חֲלַפְתָּא הֲוָה אָתֵי בְּאִיסְמְטָא בְּלֵילְיָא וַהֲוָה חַמָּרָא מְהַלֵּךְ בַּתְרֵיהּ עַל חַד בֵּית שִׁיחַ. אֲמַר לֵיהּ הַהוּא גַבְרָא בָּעֵי מִסְחֵי. אֲמַר לֵיהּ לָא תַסְכֵּן נַפְשָׁךְ. אֲמַר לֵיהּ מִן נִידָּה וּמִן אֵשֶׁת אִישׁ הַהוּא גַבְרָא בָּעֵי לְמִיסְחֵי. אֲפִילוּ כֵן אֲמַר לֵיהּ לֹא תַסְכֵּן נַפְשָׁךְ. כֵּיוָן דְּלֹא שָׁמַע לֵיהּ אֲמַר לֵיהּ יֵיחוֹת הַהוּא גַבְרָא וְלָא יִסּוֹק. וְכֵן הֲוָות לֵיהּ.

Rebbi Yose bar Ḥalaphta came on a footpath[195] in the night and a donkey driver was walking after him along a ditch. He said to him: This man must wash. He said to him: Do not imperil yourself. He said to him: This man must wash because of a menstruating, married woman. Even so he said to him: Do not imperil yourself. Since he did not listen to him he said: May this man descend and not ascend. And that happened to him.

195 Latin *semita* (the Rome ms. has איסרטא, *strata* "a paved [street].") This story belongs to the discussion of the paragraph before the last and shows that in the minds of the people the original intention of the ordinance requiring washing was inverted, that instead of "fencing off Israel from sin" it became a ritual in the minds of the uneducated with which one could wash off even adultery with a menstruating women, combining a capital crime with one punishable by extirpation. Hence, the story supports Rebbi Yehudah ben Bathyra who negates the importance of the ritual even for public reading of the Torah, not only for Torah study.

רִבִּי יוֹסֵי בֶּן יוֹסֵי הֲוָה אָתֵי בְאִילְפָא חֲמָא חַד קָטַר גַּרְמֵיהּ בְּחַבְלָא מֵיחוֹת וּמִסְחֵי. אֲמַר לֵיהּ לָא תַסְכֵּן בְּנַפְשָׁךְ. אֲמַר לֵיהּ הַהוּא מֵיכַל בָּעֵינָא. אֲמַר לֵיהּ אֲכִיל. הַהוּא גַּבְרָא בָּעֵי מִישְׁתֵּי. אֲמַר לֵיהּ שְׁתֵי. כֵּיוָן דְּמָטוּן לְלִמֵינָה. אֲמַר לֵיהּ תַּמָּן לָא שָׁרִית לָךְ אֶלָּא בְגִין סַכַּנְתָּא דְנַפְשָׁא בְּרַם הָכָא אָסוּר לְהַהוּא גַּבְרָא לְמִיטְעַם כְּלוּם עַד שַׁעְתָּא דְיִסְחֵי.

Rebbi Yose ben Yose[196] came on a ship. He saw one who was tying a rope around himself in order to descend[197] and wash. He said to him: Do not endanger your life. He said to him: This one needs to eat. He said to him: eat! This man needs to drink. He said to him: drink! When they came to the harbor[198], he said to him: There[199] I permitted it only because of danger to your life but here this man may not taste anything before he washes.

196 One of the last Galilean Amoraïm. It is not known whether he is identical with the poet of the same name, the first of the synagogal poets known by name; neither is it clear whether his name indicates that he was a posthumous child (cf. E. and H. Guggenheimer, *Etymologisches Lexikon der jüdischen Familiennamen*, Saur, München 1996, p. xviii).

197 From the ship to the ocean in order to wash. This story makes clear that the washing after sexual intercourse was general practice in Israel down to the time of edition of the Jerusalem Talmud. Its time is six generations after the preceding story. It negates the negative moral impli-

cations of the preceding story but retains its emphasis on avoiding life-threatening situations.

198 Greek λιμήν.

199 On the high seas. The problem was not that one may not eat before washing but that one is not allowed to pronounce the Divine Name and, therefore, is unable to utter the benedictions before eating.

אָמַר רִבִּי יַנַּאי שָׁמַעְתִּי שֶׁמְּקִילִין בָּהּ וּמַחְמִירִין בָּהּ. וְכָל־הַמַּחְמִיר בָּהּ מַאֲרִיךְ יָמִים בְּטוֹבָה. מְקִילִין בָּהּ לִרְחוֹץ בְּמַיִם שְׁאוּבִין וּמַחְמִירִין בָּהּ לִטְבּוֹל בְּמַיִם חַיִּים.

Rebbi Yannai[200] said: I heard that some take it lightly and some are stringent and every one who is stringent lives a long, good life. Some take it lightly by washing in drawn water; some are stringent to immerse themselves in running water.

200 Rebbi Yannai, from the first generation of Amoraïm, makes it clear that essentially nobody uses the *miqweh* for the immersion of *qeri*; either one uses a regular bath or a running stream or the sea (whose total volume is certainly greater than 40 *sĕa*.) The parallel in the Babli (*Berakhot* 22a) has only the first part of the statement and no hint of using running water. Running water is required for the cleansing of the male with gonorrhea (*Lev.* 15:13).

משנה ה: הָיָה עוֹמֵד בִּתְפִילָּה וְנִזְכַּר שֶׁהוּא בַּעַל קֶרִי לֹא יַפְסִיק אֶלָּא יְקַצֵּר. יָרַד לִטְבּוֹל אִם יָכוֹל לַעֲלוֹת וּלְהִתְכַּסּוֹת וְלִקְרוֹת עַד שֶׁלֹּא תָנֵץ הַחַמָּה יַעֲלֶה וְיִתְכַּסֶּה וְיִקְרָא וְאִם לָאו יִתְכַּסֶּה בַּמַּיִם וְיִקְרָא. לֹא יִתְכַּסֶּה לֹא בַמַּיִם הָרָעִים וְלֹא בְמֵי הַמִּשְׁרָה עַד שֶׁיַּטִּיל לְתוֹכָן מַיִם. וְכַמָּה יַרְחִיק מֵהֶן וּמִן הַצּוֹאָה אַרְבַּע אַמּוֹת.

Mishnah 5: If someone was standing and praying[201] when he remembered that he had *qeri*, he should not stop but shorten his prayer.

If he descended to immerse himself, if he can ascend, get dressed, and recite[202] by the time of sunrise he should ascend, get dressed, and recite; otherwise, he should cover himself with water and recite. He should cover himself neither with stinking water nor with steeping water unless he diluted them with water. How much does one have to remove oneself from these and excrement? Four cubits.

201 The formal *Amidah*.

202 The *Shema'*. The leniency mentioned here is not only if otherwise the time for *Shema'* would pass but even for the usage of the very religious (Chapter 1, Note 155) even though it is totally impossible to pray the *Amidah* while immersed in the water and, therefore, one cannot completely follow the practice of the very religious.

הלכה ה: מַתְנִיתָא בְּרַבִּים אֲבָל בֵּינוֹ לְבֵין עַצְמוֹ מַפְסִיק וּכְרִבִּי מֵאִיר. בְּרַם כְּרִבִּי יְהוּדָה אֲפִילוּ בֵּינוֹ לְבֵין עַצְמוֹ אֵינוֹ מַפְסִיק. בְּשֶׁאֵין לֹא מַיִם לִטְבּוֹל. אֲבָל אִם יֵשׁ לוֹ מַיִם לִטְבּוֹל אַף רִבִּי יְהוּדָה מוֹדֵי שֶׁהוּא מַפְסִיק.

Halakhah 5: The Mishnah refers to someone in public, but if he is alone he interrupts following Rebbi Meïr[203]. But following Rebbi Yehudah he does not interrupt even when alone, on condition that he have no water to immerse himself. But if he has water to immerse himself even Rebbi Yehudah agrees that he must interrupt.

203 Since Mishnah 4 stated that he may not pronounce any benediction and the *Amidah* is composed of benedictions, it is clear that Mishnah 4 forbids formal praying. Both Mishnah 4 and Mishnah 5 are anonymous; an anonymous Mishnah is always supposed to represent the ideas of Rebbi Meïr since the latter's collection was the basis of Rebbi's edition of the Mishnah. To avoid two contradicting Mishnayot, it is spelled out here that the public embarrassment that would be caused by the rule of Mishnah 4 has to be

avoided, see *Halakhah* 1, note 119. The opinion of R. Yehudah is given in Mishnah 4.

חוֹלֶה שֶׁשִּׁמֵּשׁ מִיטָּתוֹ אָמַר רִבִּי אַמִּי אִם הוּא גָּרַם לְעַצְמוֹ יִטְבּוֹל וְיָמוּת. וְאִם בְּאוֹנֶס אֵין מַטְרִיחִין עָלָיו. רִבִּי חַגַּי בְּשֵׁם רִבִּי אַבָּא בַּר זַבְדָּא בֵּין כָּךְ וּבֵין כָּךְ אֵין מַטְרִיחִין עָלָיו. חוֹלֶה מַרְגִּיל צָרִיךְ תִּשְׁעָה קַבִּין. בָּרִיא מַרְגִּיל צָרִיךְ אַרְבָּעִים סְאָה. חוֹלֶה מֵאוֹנֶס אֵין מַטְרִיחִין עָלָיו. בָּרִיא מֵאוֹנֶס צָרִיךְ תִּשְׁעָה קַבִּין.

About a sick person who had intercourse, Rebbi Ammi said: If he caused it by himself, let him immerse himself and die[204]; if it was forced upon him one does not bother him[205]. Rebbi Ḥaggai in the name of Rebbi Abba bar Zavda: One does not bother him in any case. A sick person[206] who does it habitually[207] needs nine *qab*, a healthy person who does it habitually needs 40 *sĕah*. A sick person forced, one does not bother him. A healthy person forced needs nine *qab*.

204 Obviously, that is an exaggeration since it was shown earlier that even an adulterer should not expose himself to danger because of this immersion; it means simply: let him be inconvenienced.

205 It is difficult to know what "forced intercourse" means. Any possible interpretation depends on the problem discussed in the preceding Halakhah, whether *qeri* comes only from intercourse or also from involuntary emissions. If the second case is accepted, "forced" does not speak of intercourse but only of involuntary emissions. In the second case, one cannot say that one speaks of a sick man fulfilling his marital duties even if it hurts him since in that case he is free from these duties. Even if he was seduced by his wife, there is really no intercourse against one's will. Hence, one has to conclude that all authorities here decide that involuntary emissions require immersion in water.

206 This second paragraph clearly is independent of the previous statements since it contradicts them. It represents the consensus of the editors of the Yerushalmi. In the parallel of the Babli (*Berakhot* 22b), Rava reports that any מרגיל needs 40 *seah*. Since the

immersion was not practiced in Babylonia, this statement is purely historical or theoretical; the difference between Babylonia and Israel was in the essence of this immersion and not in little details.

207 In the Babli (22a), Rashi explains מרגיל by: "he draws *qeri* upon himself by having intercourse." A strictly grammatical explanation would be: "he causes it to be usual". However, such a translation would require three categories: 1) one who runs after sex, 2) a normal person, 3) a sick person. Since only two categories are mentioned where one would expect three, Rashi's explanation is the only consistent one even if it does not explain the particular verb form.

רִבִּי זְבַדְיָה בְּרֵיהּ דְּרִבִּי יַעֲקֹב בַּר זַבְדִּי בְּשֵׁם רִבִּי יוֹנָה (fol. 6d) עִיר שֶׁמַּעְיָינָהּ רָחוֹק הֲרֵי זֶה קוֹרֵא אֶת שְׁמַע וְיוֹרֵד וְטוֹבֵל וְעוֹלֶה וּמִתְפַּלֵּל. אִם הוּא אָדָם מְסוּיָּם עָשׂוּ אוֹתוֹ כְּמַעְיָין רָחוֹק.

Rebbi Zevadiah, the son of Rebbi Jacob bar Zavdi, in the name of Rebbi Jonah: In a city whose well is far away, he may recite the *Shema'*, then descends and immerses himself, ascends and prays. If he is blind[208] they made him like a far-away well.

208 This translation is not given by any commentator. Usually, מסוים means "definite, outstanding", from the verbal root *swm*, but this makes no sense here. In other Talmudic passages "an outstanding man" means a particularly pious one and it is unimaginable that a pious man should claim for himself exemption from some religious duty. Hence, the derivation from the root *sm'* "to blind", in the passive "to be blinded", makes much more sense.

פסקא. וְאִם לָאו יִתְכַּסֶּה בַמַּיִם וְיִקְרָא. מַתְנִיתָא בַּעֲכוּרִין אֲבָל בִּצְלוּלִין אָסוּר. וְאִם הוּא יָכוֹל לַעֲכוֹר בְּרַגְלָיו יַעֲכוֹר.

New Section. "Otherwise, he should cover himself with water and recite."[209] The Mishnah deals with opaque water, but in clear water it is forbidden[210]. And if he is able to make it opaque by stirring with his feet he may make it opaque.

209 Quote from the Mishnah.

210 Since prayer is forbidden if the genitals are uncovered. (A different tradition is given in Babli *Berakhot* 25b).

תַּנֵּי מַרְחִיקִין מִצּוֹאַת אָדָם אַרְבַּע אַמּוֹת וּמִצּוֹאַת כְּלָבִים אַרְבַּע אַמּוֹת וּבְשָׁעָה שֶׁהוּא נוֹתֵן לְעוֹרוֹת. רִבִּי יִרְמְיָה בְּשֵׁם רִבִּי זְעִירָא נְבֵילָה שֶׁנִּסְרְחָה צָרִיךְ לְהַרְחִיק מִמֶּנָּהּ אַרְבַּע אַמּוֹת. אָמַר רִבִּי אֲבִינָא וּמַתְנִיתָא אָמְרָה כֵן. וְכַמָּה יַרְחִיק מֵהֶן וּמִן הַצּוֹאָה אַרְבַּע אַמּוֹת. אָמַר רִבִּי אַמִּי אָמַר רִבִּי שַׁמַּאי תִּיפְתָּר בְּמִישְׁרָה שֶׁל כּוֹבְסִין. אָמַר לֵיהּ רִבִּי מָנִי אִם בְּמִישְׁרָה שֶׁל כּוֹבְסִין הָא תַנִּינָן לֹא בְּמַיִם הָרָעִים וְלֹא בְמֵי הַמִּשְׁרָה.

It is stated: One removes himself[211] from human excrement four cubits and from dog's excrement four cubits, the latter when it is given on skins[212]. Rebbi Jeremiah in the name of Rebbi Zeïra: One must remove hinself four cubits from a stinking carcass. Rebbi Avina said: Does not the Mishnah say all this : "How much does one have to remove himself from these and excrement? Four cubits." Rebbi Ammi in the name of Rebbi Shammai[213]: Explain it by steeping water of launderers. Rebbi Mani[214] said to him: About steeping waters of launderers, we have stated: "neither with stinking water nor with steeping water."

211 In order to pray or to recite *Shema'*.

212 Antique technology of making leather from skins required that the skins were steeped in water containing dog's excrement for a lengthy period of time. The steeping water had a horrible smell. This *baraita* explains that "steeping water" in the Mishnah refers to tanner's steeping water and not to launderer's steeping water that simply does not smell good.

This statement is from Tosephta *Berakhot* 2:16; the Babli (25a) has a different *baraita* that refers to the paragraph after the next one here.

213 The tradition of names is impossible since Rebbi Shammai was an Amora of the fifth and last generation in Galilee; he cannot be the author of a tradition of a third generation Amora. The paragraph is quoted by R. Asher

ben Yeḥiël (*Rosh Berakhot*, Chap. 3, #44) in the name of Rebbi Simlaï (without mention of Rebbi Ammi), a preacher and Amora of the first generation. Launderers' steeping water does not smell so badly that it would need a special entry in the Mishnah. He is a contemporary of Rebbi Simlaï, not Rebbi Ammi.

214 Rebbi Mani, Mana, the first.

תַּנֵּי קָטָן שֶׁהוּא יָכוֹל לֶאֱכוֹל כְּזַיִת דָּגָן פּוֹרְשִׁין מִצּוֹאָתוֹ וּמִמֵּימֵי רַגְלָיו אַרְבַּע אַמּוֹת וְאִים אֵינוֹ יָכוֹל לֶאֱכוֹל כְּזַיִת דָּגָן אֵין פּוֹרְשִׁין לֹא מִצּוֹאָתוֹ וְלֹא מִמֵּימֵי רַגְלָיו אַרְבַּע אַמּוֹת. בָּעֵי קוֹמֵי רִבִּי אַבָּהוּ מִפְּנֵי מַה פּוֹרְשִׁין מִצּוֹאָתוֹ וּמִמֵּימֵי רַגְלָיו. אָמַר לוֹן מִפְּנֵי שֶׁמַּחְשְׁבוֹתָיו רָעוֹת. אָמְרִין לֵיהּ וְלֹא קָטָן הוּא. אָמַר לוֹן וְלָא כְתִיב כִּי יֵצֶר לֵב הָאָדָם רַע מִנְּעוּרָיו. אָמַר רִבִּי יוּדָן מִנְּעָרָיו כְּתִיב. מִשָּׁעָה שֶׁהוּא נִנְעָר וְיוֹצֵא לָעוֹלָם.

It is stated: One removes himself four cubits from excrement and urine of a toddler who can eat grain the volume of an olive[215], but if he cannot yet eat grain the volume of an olive one does not need to remove himself four cubits either from his excrement or from his urine. They asked before Rebbi Abbahu: Why does one separate himself from his excrement and urine? He said to them, because his thoughts are evil. They said to him: But is not he too young? He said to them, is it not written (*Gen.* 8:21): "For the inclination of man's heart is evil from his youth?" Rebbi Yudan said, it is written "from his awakening[216]", from the moment that the awakes and enters the world.

215 In one meal, which in the Babli (*Sukkah* 42b) is defined as the time a grown-up can eat half a stuffed pitta. The Yerushalmi does not give a time limit.

216 The word בעוריו, even though it has a long vowel *ū*, is written defective in the Bible; hence, it can be vocalized נְעָרָיו "his awakenings", not only puberty, the sexual awakening usually referred to by the root נער but also the first awakening of the baby during birth. According to Rebbi Abbahu, the awakening comes only when the baby is weaned.

רִבִּי יוֹסֵי בַּר חֲנִינָא אָמַר מַרְחִיקִין מִגָּלְלֵי בְהֵמָה אַרְבַּע אַמּוֹת. רִבִּי שְׁמוּאֵל בַּר רַב יִצְחָק אָמַר בְּרַכִּים וּבִלְבַד בְּשֶׁל חֲמוֹר. רִבִּי חִייָא בַּר אַבָּא אָמַר בְּבָא מִן הַדֶּרֶךְ. לֵוִי אָמַר מַרְחִיקִין מִצּוֹאַת חֲזִיר אַרְבַּע אַמּוֹת. וְתַנֵּי כֵן מַרְחִיקִין מִצּוֹאַת חֲזִיר אַרְבַּע אַמּוֹת. וּמִצּוֹאַת הַנְּמִייָא אַרְבַּע אַמּוֹת. וּמִצּוֹאַת הַתַּרְנְגוֹלִין אַרְבַּע אַמּוֹת. רִבִּי יוֹסֵי בְּרִבִּי אָבוּן בְּשֵׁם רַב חוּנָא וּבִלְבַד בָּאֲדוּמִים.

Rebbi Yose bar Ḥanina said: One removes himself four cubits from animal dung. Rebbi Samuel bar Rav Isaac said, if it is soft, but only from donkeys. Rebbi Ḥiyya bar Abba said, if it[217] arrived from a trip. Levi said, one removes himself four cubits from the excrement of a pig. And it was stated: One removes himself four cubits from the excrement of a pig[218], four cubits from the excrement of a marten[219], four cubits from the excrement of chickens. Rebbi Yose ben Rebbi Abun in the name of Rav Huna: Only from red[220] ones.

217 The donkey. The statements of Rebbis Samuel bar Rav Isaac and Ḥiyya bar Abba restrict the general statement of Rebbi Yose bar Ḥanina to one specific case.

218 In the Babli (25a), the excrement of a pig is deemed unacceptable only if it is used in tanning. It seems that in Israel no pig excrement was used in tanning.

219 This statement is taken by Medieval commentators to apply also to excrement of cats.

220 Some commentators prefer to understand "Edomite", but the meaning "red" is preferable since red chickens are mentioned in Babli *Avodah zarah* 14b as a separate kind. All these are singled out for their obnoxious smell.

תַּנֵּי מַרְחִיקִין מֵרֵיחַ רַע אַרְבַּע אַמּוֹת. אָמַר רִבִּי אַמִּי מִסּוֹף רֵיחַ רַע אַרְבַּע אַמּוֹת. הָדָא דְאָמַר לְאַחֲרָיו אֲבָל לְפָנָיו עַד מָקוֹם שֶׁעֵינָיו רוֹאוֹת אוֹתוֹ. כְּהָדָא רִבִּי לִיָּא וַחֲבֵרַייָא הֲווּ יָתְבִין קוֹמֵי פוּנְדְּקִיָּא בְּרַמְשָׁא. אָמְרִין מַהוּ מֵימַר מִילֵּי דְאוֹרָיְתָא. אֲמַר לוֹן מִכֵּיוָן דְּאִילּוּ הֲוָה אִימְמָא הֲוֵינָן חָמֵייָן מַה קוֹמֵינָן. בְּרַם כְּדוֹן אָסוּר.

It is stated: One removes himself four cubits from a bad smell[221]. Rebbi Ammi said, four cubits from the end of the bad smell. That means behind his back, but in front of him until he can no longer see it. Like that of Rebbi Lia and his colleagues who were sitting in front of a hostelry[222] in the night. They said, may one say words of Torah? He said to them: If it were daytime, we would see what is before us. But[223] like that it is forbidden.

221 It is clear from the following that one talks of a source of bad smell which can be identified and seen. In the Babli (25a) this is called ריח רע שיש לו עיקר "a bad smell that has a material source." The opinion of the Yerushalmi corresponds in the Babli to the minority opinion of Rav Ḥisda.

222 Greek πανδοκεῖον (also πανδοκίον) "inn". It is difficult to see what is so bad about a hostelry. Maybe they were sitting close to the outhouse.

223 The text is elliptic, but we do not know what is missing. Generally, ברם means either "on the other hand" or "in addition".

תַּנֵּי גֶּרֶף אֶחָד שֶׁל רְעִי וְאֶחָד שֶׁל מַיִם צָרִיךְ לְהַרְחִיק מִמֶּנּוּ אַרְבַּע אַמּוֹת. וְשֶׁלִּפְנֵי הַמִּיטָּה נָתַן לְתוֹכוֹ מַיִם כָּל־שֶׁהוּא יִקְרָא וְאִם לָאו לֹא יִקְרָא. רִבִּי זַכַּאי אָמַר נָתַן לְתוֹכוֹ רְבִיעִית מַיִם יִקְרָא וְאִם לָאו לֹא יִקְרָא. וּמַהוּ כְּדֵי רְבִיעִית רְבִיעִית בְּתוֹךְ רְבִיעִית. אֶחָד כְּלִי קָטוֹן וְאֶחָד כְּלִי גָדוֹל. רַבָּן שִׁמְעוֹן בֶּן גַּמְלִיאֵל אוֹמֵר שֶׁלְּאַחַר הַמִּיטָּה יִקְרָא שֶׁלִּפְנֵי הַמִּיטָּה לֹא יִקְרָא. רִבִּי שִׁמְעוֹן בֶּן אֶלְעָזָר אוֹמֵר אֲפִילוּ טְרִקְלִין עֶשֶׂר עַל עֶשֶׂר לֹא יִקְרָא עַד שֶׁיְּכַסֶּנּוּ אוֹ עַד שֶׁיַּנִּיחֶנּוּ תַּחַת הַמִּיטָּה. רִבִּי יַעֲקֹב בַּר אָחָא בְּשֵׁם רִבִּי חִיָּא בַּר וָנָא הוֹרֵי רִבִּי חֲנִינָא תּוֹרְתַּיָּה כְּהַדָּא דְּרִבִּי שִׁמְעוֹן בֶּן אֶלְעָזָר.

It is stated: One must remove himself four cubits from a chamberpot, be it used for excrement or for urine[224]. If it is before the bed, if he put some water in the pot he may recite[225], otherwise he may not recite. Rebbi Zakkai[226] said, if he put a *quartarius*[227] of water in, he may recite; otherwise, he may not recite. How many corresponding *quartarii*? One *quartarius* corresponding to one *quartarius*[228], be the vessel small or large. Rabban Simeon ben Gamliel said, if it stands behind the bed he may recite, before the bed he may not recite. Rebbi Simeon ben Eleazar said, even in a dining hall[229] large ten-by-ten[230] he may not recite until he covers it up or until he puts it under the couch. Rebbi Jacob bar Aḥa in the name of Rebbi Ḥiyya bar Abba: Rebbi Ḥanina Tortayya[231] ruled following Rebbi Simeon ben Eleazar.

224 Since in the preceding paragraph one dealt with visible excrement, it follows that in this entire paragraph we are dealing with a chamberpot used at night which is empty at present but still smells from its prior use. The Tosephta (*Berakhot* 2:16) is quite explicit: "A chamberpot *with him in the house*, he has to remove himself four cubits." The Babli (25a) deals separately with full and empty chamberpots.

225 The *Shema'*.

226 Rebbi Zakkai the First, Tanna of the fifth generation, contemporary of Rebbi.

227 A quarter of a *log* of .533 liter or about 4.5 fl. oz. U.S.

228 As much water as was the volume of urine or excrement in the last use.

229 Latin *triclinium*, from Greek τρικλίνιον "dining room", a hall of three dining couches arranged in U-shape.

230 Probably 10 by 10 cubits, which gives a diagonal distance of 14 cubits, taken as an example. The Babli (25a) speaks of a "dining hall of 100 cubits" where "cubits" stands for "square cubits". [The use of "cubit" for "square cubit" is frequent in Yerushalmi *Kilaim*.]

231 A student of Rebbi Yoḥanan; his birthplace, Torta, has not been identified. His decision is also quoted in the Babli as decision of the earlier generations, later overruled by Rava (bar Joseph bar Ḥama), the leader of the fifth generation of Amoraïm in Babylonia.

רִבִּי בִנְיָמִן בַּר יֶפֶת בְּשֵׁם רִבִּי יוֹחָנָן צוֹאָה כָּל־שֶׁהוּא מְבַטְּלָהּ בְּרוֹק. רִבִּי זְעוּרָא רִבִּי יַעֲקֹב בַּר זַבְדִּי הֲווּ יָתְבִין חָמִין צוֹאָתָה. קָם רִבִּי יַעֲקֹב בַּר זַבְדִּי רָקַק עֲלָהּ. אֲמַר לֵיהּ רִבִּי זְעוּרָא מִן יַמָּא לְטֵיגְנָא.

Rebbi Benjamin ben Yephet[232] in the name of Rebbi Yoḥanan: A minute amount of excrement can be eliminated by spit. Rebbi Zeïra and Rebbi Jacob bar Zavdi were sitting; they saw some excrement. Rebbi Jacob bar Zavdi got up and spat on it. Rebbi Zeïra said to him: From the sea to the pan[233]!

232 A student of Rebbi Yoḥanan. Rebbi Zeïra is on record (Babli *Berakhot* 38b, Yerushalmi *Pesaḥim* 2:5) that R. Benjamin is not trustworthy as witness to the opinions of Rebbi Yoḥanan. His statement is quoted in the Babli (25b) as original Babylonian tradition.

233 Greek τήγανον. Rashi (Babli *Qiddushin* 44a) and *'Arukh* (טגן 1) explain this expression to mean: "immediately", like a fish that has to be fried immediately before it spoils. Most commentators explain that R. Zeïra declares the entire rule invalid since spit dries quickly and afterwards is useless. The Babli avoids the problem by allowing only thick spit, probably from the bronchiae, which does not evaporate. One may consider the treatment of the Babli as answer to R. Zeïra's criticism.

תֵּיבָה שֶׁהִיא מְלֵאָה סְפָרִים נוֹתְנָהּ מְרַאֲשׁוֹתֵי הַמִּיטָּה וְאֵינָהּ נוֹתְנָהּ מַרְגְּלוֹת הַמִּיטָּה. רִבִּי אָבוּן בְּשֵׁם רִבִּי חוּנָא וְהוּא שֶׁתְּהֵא הַמִּיטָּה גְבוֹהַּ עֲשָׂרָה טְפָחִים. וּבִלְבַד שֶׁלֹּא יְהוּ חֶבְלֵי הַמִּיטָּה נוֹגְעִין בַּתֵּיבָה. הוֹרֵי רִבִּי יָסָא בְּמְקוֹמֵיהּ דְּרִבִּי שְׁמוּאֵל בַּר רַב יִצְחָק כְּהָדָא דְּרִבִּי חוּנָה.

[234]A chest full of scrolls one may put under the head of the bed but one may not put it under the foot end of the bed. Rebbi Abun in the name of Rebbi Ḥuna: But only if the bed is 10 hand-breadths[235] high, and only if the ropes of the bed do not touch the chest. Rebbi Yasa taught the ruling of Rebbi Ḥuna in the town of Rebbi Samuel bar Rav Isaac.

234 After discussing what may or may not be put under one's bed, one continues with the case of holy scrolls in one's room, first under the bed and then in the room.

235 A *ṭefaḥ* (hand-breadth) is one-

sixth of a cubit. The basic information one has about length is that the distance one may travel from a town on Sabbath is one *mil* or 2000 cubits. If the *mil* is taken to be the traditional 1111m = 3648 feet then a cubit is 1.824 ft and a *ṭefaḥ* is 3.65 inches. (If the *mil* is taken to be an unlikely Roman mile of 1473.2m = 4833.33 ft, then a cubit is 2.417 ft and a *ṭefaḥ* is 4.836 inches.)

Another approach is based on Mishnah *Kelim* 17:11 which reports an opinion that fluid measures are Roman. The Babli (*Pesaḥim* 109 a/b) defines 40 *seah* as three cubic cubits. By the data quoted in note 164, the cubit would be 55.47 cm and the *ṭefaḥ* 9.25 cm or 3.64 in.

Anything more than 10 *ṭefaḥ* above the ground is considered to be in another domain. This reason also applies to the next paragraph.

לֹא יְשַׁמֵּשׁ אָדָם מִיטָּתוֹ וְסֵפֶר תּוֹרָה עִמּוֹ בְּבַיִת. רִבִּי יִרְמְיָה בְּשֵׁם רִבִּי אַבָּהוּ אִם הָיָה כָּרוּךְ בְּמַפָּה אוֹ שֶׁהָיָה נָתוּן בְּחַלּוֹן שֶׁהוּא גָּבוֹהַּ עֲשָׂרָה טְפָחִים מוּתָּר. רִבִּי יְהוֹשֻׁעַ בֶּן לֵוִי עוֹשֶׂה לוֹ כִּילְיוֹן.

A person should not have sexual intercourse when there is a Torah scroll with him in the room. Rebbi Jeremiah in the name of Rebbi Abbahu: it is permitted if it was wrapped in a wrapper or if it was in a window opening that is ten hand-breadths above the ground. Rebbi Joshua ben Levi made a small curtain[236] for it.

236 Diminutive of כילה "curtain". (The parallel statement in the Babli, *Berakhot* 25b, states the dangers of sexual intercourse in the presence of a Torah scroll; its connection with the preceding discussion of praying in presence of a chamberpot can be understood only as a commentary on the Yerushalmi.)

לֹא יֵשֵׁב אָדָם עַל גַּבֵּי סַפְסָל שֶׁסֵּפֶר תּוֹרָה נָתוּן עָלָיו. מַעֲשֶׂה בְּרִבִּי אֱלִיעֶזֶר שֶׁהָיָה יוֹשֵׁב עַל גַּבֵּי סַפְסָל שֶׁסֵּפֶר תּוֹרָה נָתוּן עָלָיו וְהִרְתִּיעַ מִלְּפָנָיו כְּמַרְתִּיעַ מִלִּפְנֵי נָחָשׁ. אִם הָיָה נָתוּן עַל גַּבֵּי דָּבָר אַחֵר מוּתָּר. עַד הֵיכָן. רִבִּי אַבָּא בְּשֵׁם רִבִּי חוּנָא טֶפַח. רִבִּי יִרְמְיָה בְּשֵׁם רִבִּי זְעוּרָא אֲפִילוּ כָּל־שֶׁהוּא.

A person should not sit on a low bench[237] on which a Torah scroll was placed. It happened that Rebbi Eliezer sat down on a low bench on which a Torah scroll was placed and he recoiled from it as one recoils before a snake[238]. If it was placed on something other, it is permitted. How far? Rebbi Abba in the name of Rebbi Ḥuna: One handbreadth. Rebbi Jeremiah in the name of Rebbi Zeïra: Anything.

237 Latin *subsellium* "bench".

238 Cf. *Massekhet Soferim* 3:13, and *Massekhet Sefer Torah* 3:10 (where it says "he got up as if bitten by a snake"); also quoted in Babli *Menaḥot* 32b. The reason given is the verse (*Lev.* 26:6): "You shall fear My holy things." This is then qualified that one may not sit on a bench on which there is a Torah scroll, but if the scroll is on a separate table or chair, there is no minimum distance to be kept.

דִּייסַקִּי שֶׁהִיא מְלֵאָה סְפָרִים אוֹ שֶׁהָיוּ בְתוֹכָהּ עַצְמוֹת הַמֵּת הֲרֵי זֶה מַפְשִׁילָן מֵאֲחוֹרָיו וְרוֹכֵב.

A double sack[239] full of scrolls or if there were in it bones of a dead person[240], one carries it on his back and rides.

239 Greek διcάκκιον, "saddle bag", a sack made to be carried by a donkey (or horse) hanging down on both sides of the animal. The rule is inserted here in the sequence of rules dealing with the respect due to holy things. The respect shown here is that the sack may not be put on the animal but must be carried on the person even if the latter is riding.

240 For reburial in an ossuary in a cave.

תְּפִילִין תּוֹלֶה אוֹתָן מְרַאֲשׁוֹת הַמִּיטָּה וְאֵינוֹ תוֹלֶה אוֹתָם מַרְגְּלוֹת הַמִּיטָּה. רִבִּי שְׁמוּאֵל רִבִּי אַבָּהוּ רִבִּי אֶלְעָזָר בְּשֵׁם רִבִּי חֲנִינָא רִבִּי הָיָה תוֹלֶה אֶת הַתְּפִילִין בִּמְרַאֲשׁוֹת הַמִּיטָּה. רִבִּי חִזְקִיָּה בְּשֵׁם רִבִּי אַבָּהוּ וּבִלְבַד דְּלָא יַעֲבִיד כְּהָדֵין דִּייקִלָרָא אֶלָּא תְּפִילִין מִלְמַעְלָן וּרְצוּעוֹת מִלְּמַטָּן.

Tefillin one may hang on the headboard of the bed but one may not hang them at the foot end of the bed[241]. Rebbi Samuel[242], Rebbi Abbahu, Rebbi Eleazar in the name of Rebbi Ḥanina: Rebbi did hang his *tefillin* on the headboard of his bed. Rebbi Ḥizqiah in the name of Rebbi Abbahu: But only that he should not do in the way of makers of palm leaf baskets but *tefillin* on top and the straps on the bottom[243].

241 For the same reason as before, to show respect.

242 Since he was a student of R. Abbahu and sometimes student of R. Zeïra, the chain of transmission here are four uninterrupted generations. It seems that only R. Samuel made a formal statement out of an informal tradition; however, in the Babli (24a) the statement is in the name of R. Ḥanina himself.

243 In the interpretation of J. Levy, basket makers put their wares on a rope from which they are hanging down. *Tefillin* should never hang down. [While דיקולא are palm-leaf baskets, the Latin ending *-arius* is suspect. It might be better to derive the word from Latin *collare, collarium* "neck chain, collar", with the prefix די meaning either "double" or being the Aramaic relative pronoun (E. G.). *Tefillin* should not hang as a pendant from its chain.]

In the Babli (24a), this is a rejected opinion. One requires there that the *tefillin* be put in a pouch, the pouch then may be hung at the head of the bed.

תַּנָּא רִבִּי חֲלַפְתָּא בֶּן שָׁאוּל הָעוֹטֵשׁ בִּתְפִילָּתוֹ סִימָן רַע לוֹ. הֲדָא דְאַתְּ אֲמַר מִלְּמַטָּה אֲבָל מִלְּמַעֲלָה לֹא. אַתְיָא דָּמַר רִבִּי חֲנִינָא אֲנִי רָאִיתִי אֶת רִבִּי מְפַהֵק וּמְעַטֵּשׁ וְנוֹתֵן יָדָיו עַל פִּיו אֲבָל לֹא רוֹקֵק. רִבִּי יוֹחָנָן אָמַר אֲפִילוּ רוֹקֵק כְּדֵי שֶׁיְּהֵא כוֹסוֹ נָקִי. לְפָנָיו אָסוּר לְאַחֲרָיו מוּתָּר. לִימִינוֹ אָסוּר לִשְׂמֹאלוֹ מוּתָּר. הֲדָא הוּא דִכְתִיב יִפֹּל מִצִּדְּךָ אֶלֶף. כָּל־עַמָּא מוֹדַיי בְּהָהֵין דְּרָקַק אִיצְטְלִין דְּהוּא אָסוּר. רִבִּי יְהוֹשֻׁעַ בֶּן לֵוִי אוֹמֵר הָרוֹקֵק בְּבֵית הַכְּנֶסֶת כְּרוֹקֵק בְּבָבַת עֵינוֹ. רִבִּי יוֹנָה רָקַק וְשִׁייֵף. רִבִּי יִרְמְיָה רִבִּי שְׁמוּאֵל בַּר חֲלַפְתָּא בְּשֵׁם רַב אָדָא בַּר אַחֲוָה הַמִּתְפַּלֵּל אַל יָרוֹק עַד שֶׁיְּהַלֵּךְ אַרְבַּע אַמּוֹת. אָמַר רִבִּי יוֹסֵי בֵּירִבִּי אָבוּן וְכֵן הָרוֹקֵק אַל יִתְפַּלֵּל עַד שֶׁיְּהַלֵּךְ אַרְבַּע אַמּוֹת.

Rebbi Ḥalaphta ben Shaul[244] stated: It is a bad sign if one lets wind during one's prayer. That means on one's bottom, but not on one's top. This parallels what Rebbi Ḥanina said: I saw Rebbi yawning, belching, putting his hand on his mouth, but not spitting[245]. Rebbi Yoḥanan said, one may even spit so that one's cup[246] should be clean; forward is forbidden, behind oneself is permitted[247]. To one's right is forbidden, to one's left is permitted; that is what is written (*Ps.* 91: 7): "On your left hand side will fall a thousand.[248]" Everybody agrees about one who spits toward the stele[249], that he is forbidden to do so. Rebbi Joshua ben Levi says, he who spits in the synagogue is like one who spits into his own eye[250]. Rebbi Jonah spat and rubbed out. Rebbi Jeremiah, Rebbi Samuel bar Ḥalaphta in the name of Rav Ada bar Aḥava: He who prayed should not spit until he walked four cubits. Rebbi Yose bar Rebbi Abun said, similarly he who spat should not pray until he walked four cubits.

244 An Amora of the first generation, of the collectors of *baraitot*. In the Babli, he mostly appears as Rebbi Taḥlipha ben Shaul. The section here is a continuation of the discussion of respect due to either places of holiness (the synagogue) or acts of holiness (prayer).

245 In the Babli (24a/b), R. Ḥanina reports that he saw Rebbi spitting; this is permitted in the Babli only for people who were disgusted if they had to spit into their garments.

246 I. e., one's mouth.

247 In the Babli (24b) this is reported as an act of Rav Ashi, the first editor of the Babylonian Talmud. Its theoretical justification must be sought here in the Yerushalmi.

248 As usual, the real argument is from the later part of the verse which is not quoted: "On your left hand side will fall a thousand, but ten thousand on your right hand side." Hence, the right hand side is ten times as important as the left hand side.

249 Greek στήλη. The stele in the synagogue was the pulpit on which the Torah scroll was laid for reading and was a place of particular holiness [Cf. Y. Brand, *Iẓṭelin*, Lĕšōnēnū 32 (5728), 276-277]. This passage appears in

many corrupt versions in early medieval rabbinic authors (e. g., R. Abraham bar David and the student of Rabbenu Jonah) and has given rise to many phantastic conjectures.

250 A parallel in the Babli (24b) states "he is as if he spat out before the king."

וְכֵן הַמַּטִּיל מַיִם אַל יִתְפַּלֵּל עַד שֶׁיְּהַלֵּךְ אַרְבַּע אַמּוֹת. אָמַר רִבִּי יַעֲקֹב בַּר אָחָא לֹא סוֹף דָּבָר עַד שֶׁיְּהַלֵּךְ אַרְבַּע אַמּוֹת. אֶלָּא אֲפִילוּ שָׁהָא כְּדֵי הִילּוּךְ אַרְבַּע אַמּוֹת. אָמַר רִבִּי אַמִּי אִם אוֹמֵר אַתָּה עַד שֶׁיְּהַלֵּךְ אַרְבַּע אַמּוֹת יְהֵא אָסוּר אֲנִי אוֹמֵר אַחֵר בָּא וְהִטִּיל שָׁם.

Similarly, he who urinates should not pray until he walks four cubits[251]. Rebbi Jacob bar Aḥa said: not only that he walks four cubits but even if he waits corresponding to a walk of four cubits. Rebbi Ammi said, if you say that he is forbidden until he removes himself four cubits, I say that maybe somebody else came and urinated there[252].

251 In the Tosephta (*Berakhot* 2:19), the language is more restrictive: "A person should not urinate at the place where he prays unless he removes himself four cubits. Once he urinated he should not pray unless he removed himself four cubits. If it is dry or absorbed (in the earth) it is permitted." This text is the basis of the discussion of the Babli (*Megillah* 27b) but not of the Yerushalmi.

252 And there is no place in the world where he could pray. The Babli (*Berakhot* 25a) explicitly rules out this argument and states that one is forbidden only at a place where certainly somebody urinated and the moisture is still recognizable.

רִבִּי אַבָּא בְּשֵׁם רַב צוֹאָה עַד שֶׁתִּיַּבֵּשׁ כְּעֶצֶם. מַיִם כָּל־זְמַן שֶׁהֵן מַטְפִּיחִין. גְּנִיבָא אָמַר כָּל־זְמַן שֶׁרִישׁוּמָן נִיכָּר. שְׁמוּאֵל אָמַר עַד שֶׁיִּקְרְמוּ פָּנֶיהָ. שִׁמְעוֹן בַּר וָוא בְּשֵׁם רִבִּי יוֹחָנָן עַד שֶׁיִּקְרְמוּ פָּנֶיהָ. רִבִּי יִרְמְיָה רִבִּי זְעוּרָא בְּשֵׁם רַב צוֹאָה אֲפִילוּ כְעֶצֶם אֲסוּרָה. שְׁמוּאֵל אָמַר עַד שֶׁיִּקְרְמוּ פָּנֶיהָ. שִׁמְעוֹן בַּר וָוא אָמַר בְּשֵׁם רִבִּי יוֹחָנָן עַד שֶׁיִּקְרְמוּ פָּנֶיהָ. אָמַר חִזְקִיָּה רִבִּי אַבָּא מַחְמִיר בְּמַיִם יוֹתֵר

מִן הַצּוֹאָה. אֲמַר לֵיהּ רִבִּי מָנָא מִן הֲדָא דִגְנִיבָא. אָמַר לוֹ אֲפִילוּ עֲשׂוּיָה כְעֶצֶם אֲסוּרָה שֶׁמַּמָּשָׁהּ[253] קַיָּם מַיִם אֵין מַמָּשָׁהּ קַיָּם.

Rebbi Abba in the name of Rav: Excrement until it is hardened like bone, urine all the time it makes moist[254]. Ganiva[255] said: All the time that its impression is visible. Samuel said: Until its[256] surface is hardened. Simeon bar Abba in the name of Rebbi Yoḥanan: Until its surface is hardened. Rebbi Jeremiah, Rebbi Zeïra in the name of Rav: Excrement is forbidden even if it is hard like bone. Samuel said: Until its surface is hardened. Simeon bar Abba in the name of Rebbi Yoḥanan: Until its surface is hardened[257].

Ḥizqiah said: Rebbi Abba is more restrictive for urine than for excrement? Rebbi Mana said to him: From that of Ganiva[258]; he said to him: Even if it is hard like bone it is forbidden because its matter exists; urine's matter no longer exists[259]

253 Reading of the Rome ms. Venice and Leyden: משמשה (both times).

254 This refers to the earlier statement that one has to remove himself from excrement until he no longer sees it, and from urine four cubits. The question is how long excrement legally is in its state.

In the Babli (25a), the statement of Samuel/R. Yoḥanan is attributed to Rav by Rav Yehudah and Rebbi Abba's statement about urine to Samuel/Rebbi Yoḥanan. There is no difference between the Talmudim *in praxi* for urine but the conclusion, that excrement is forbidden even if it is hard like bone, while supported there in the name of R. Yoḥanan, is finally rejected as a matter of common practice.

255 A colleague of Rav in Babylonia. He was an extreme political opponent of the then Resh Galuta and was executed by the Persian king as a trouble maker (without the intervention of the Resh Galuta.) His statement refers to urine and is quoted as such in the Babli (25a).

256 Refers to excrement only.

257 The seeming repetition shows that Rebbi Zeïra formulated the entire statement concerning the opinions of

Rav, Samuel, and R. Yoḥanan. In the first half, the statements of Rebbi Abba, Samuel, and Rebbi Yoḥanan are three independent statements.

258 "As long as it is recognizable" applies both to excrement and to urine. Since excrement is recognizable even if it is hard as bone (Rome ms.: "hard as wood"), it remains forbidden.

259 As recognizable entity.

משנה ו: זָב שֶׁרָאָה קֶרִי וְנִדָּה שֶׁפָּלְטָה שִׁכְבַת זֶרַע וְהַמְשַׁמֶּשֶׁת שֶׁרָאֲתָה נִדָּה צְרִיכָה טְבִילָה וְרִבִּי יוּדָה פּוֹטֵר.

Mishnah 6: The person with gonorrhea who had an emission of semen, as well as a menstruating woman who lost semen, and the woman who started menstruating while having intercourse, need immersion, but Rebbi Yehudah frees them[260]

260 It is explained in *Lev.* 15 that the man with gonorrhea makes everything around himself impure and cannot be become pure except by a lengthy procedure. Similarly, the menstruating woman needs at least seven days for her purification. If any of these is polluted by the minor impurity of *qeri* as explained in the preceding *halakhah*, any immersion for *qeri* has no influence on the severe impurity already existing (or the one additional in the case of the woman who notices her period while she is already impure by having intercourse). Rebbi Yehudah notes that since the immersion for *qeri* has no practical consequences, it is not needed. The other sages seem to think that since the immersion does not need *miqweh* or flowing water and since it is needed to let the persons pray it is of a completely different character and independent of the other impurities. Since the woman noticing her period during intercourse has to stop it immediately, even before emission of semen, it is clear that her impurity is not the Biblical one described in *Lev.* 15:16-18 but the rabbinic one of *qeri*.

הלכה ו: עַד כְּדוֹן זָב שֶׁרָאָה קֶרִי וַאֲפִילוּ (fol. 7a) קֶרִי שֶׁרָאָה זָב מוֹעִיל הוּא שֶׁהוּא טוֹבֵל. נִשְׁמְעִנָּהּ מִן הָדָא הַמְּשַׁמֶּשֶׁת שֶׁרָאֲתָה נִדָּה צְרִיכָה טְבִילָה. וְרִבִּי יוּדָה פּוֹטֵר.

Halakhah 6: So far the person with gonorrhea who had an emission of semen; is it good for anything if the person immerses himself who had an emission and afterwards has an episode of gonorrhea? We hear it from this: "The woman who started menstruating while having intercourse needs immersion, but Rebbi Yehudah frees her.[261]"

261 In both cases, the impurity of *qeri* preceded the severe Biblical impurity and, nevertheless, the disagreement between the majority and Rebbi Yehudah is the same as when the severe impurity precedes *qeri*. This particular case, which is not in the Mishnah, is treated in Babli 26a where it is stated explicitly not only that Rebbi Yehudah does not require immersion but that the majority require it.

מַה טַעַם דְּרִבִּי יוּדָה מִשֵּׁם מַה מוֹעִיל הוּא שֶׁהוּא טוֹבֵל שֶׁאִם שֵׁם לְטוּמְאָה קַלָּה אֵצֶל טוּמְאָה חֲמוּרָה. מַה נָפַק מִבֵּינֵיהוֹן רָאָה קֶרִי אִין תֵּימַר מַה מוֹעִיל שֶׁהוּא טוֹבֵל מוֹעִיל הוּא הֲוֵי לֵית טַעֲמֵיהּ דְּלָא מִשּׁוּם שֶׁאֵין שֵׁם לְטוּמְאָה קַלָּה אֵצֶל טוּמְאָה חֲמוּרָה.

What is Rebbi Yehudah's reason? Is it because what would one profit if he immersed himself[262] or whether there is a name for light impurity in the presence of severe impurity[263]? What is the difference between these possibilities? If he saw *qeri*, if you say what would one profit if he immersed himself, he would profit[264]! Hence, the only reason is that there is no name for light impurity in the presence of severe impurity!

262 Since the person remains impure as before.

263 Does the severe impurity eliminate the minor impurity, or does it simply add another level of impurity?

264 He eliminates the rabbinic prohibition against studying Torah and reciting *Shema'* without washing.

עַד כְּדוֹן כְּשֶׁבָּאַת לוֹ טוּמְאָה קַלָּה בְּסוֹף. אֲפִילוּ בָּאַת לוֹ טוּמְאָה חֲמוּרָה בְּסוֹף. נִשְׁמְעִינָהּ מִן הָדָא וְהַמְשַׁמֶּשֶׁת שֶׁרָאֲתָה נִדָּה צְרִיכָה טְבִילָה וְרִבִּי יוּדָה פוֹטֵר. הָדָא אָמְרָה הִיא הָדָא הִיא הָדָא.

That is if the light impurity came at the end. Is it even if the severe impurity came at the end[265]? We may understand it from this: "The woman who started menstruating while having intercourse needs immersion, but Rebbi Yehudah frees her." That means, one case is like the other case.

265 Does the severe impurity add to the minor impurity or does it supersede the minor impurity?

תפילת השחר פרק רביעי

משנה א: תְּפִילַּת הַשַּׁחַר עַד חֲצוֹת. רִבִּי יְהוּדָה אוֹמֵר עַד אַרְבַּע שָׁעוֹת. תְּפִילַּת הַמִּנְחָה עַד הָעֶרֶב. רִבִּי יְהוּדָה אוֹמֵר עַד פְּלַג הַמִּנְחָה. תְּפִילַּת הָעֶרֶב אֵין לָהּ קֶבַע. וְשֶׁל מוּסָפִין כָּל הַיּוֹם.

Mishnah 1: Morning prayers are until noon; Rebbi Yehudah says, until four hours[1]. Afternoon[2] prayers are until evening, Rebbi Yehudah says until half of' *Minḥah*. Evening prayers have no fixed time. *Musaph* prayers have all day.

1 One hour being one twelfth of the time difference between sunrise and sundown (according to some interpreters of the Babli, from dawn to dusk).

2 "*Minḥah*" prayers. This expression refers to the Temple service when the flour offering after the afternoon sacrifice signalled the end of the day. The preferred time fixed for this offering was 2h 30min. before sundown. Hence, "half of *Minḥah*" is 1h 15min. before sundown. The earliest time for the evening sacrifices (on Passover eve) was 30 minutes after noontime. *Musaph* prayers were added on days when there were additional public sacrifices between morning and afternoon sacrifices.

הלכה א: כְּתִיב לְאַהֲבָה אֶת יי אֱלֹהֵיכֶם וּלְעָבְדוֹ בְּכָל־לְבַבְכֶם וּבְכָל־נַפְשְׁכֶם וְכִי יֵשׁ עֲבוֹדָה בְּלֵב. וְאֵי זוֹ זוֹ תְּפִילָּה. וְכֵן הוּא אוֹמֵר אֱלָהָךְ דִּי אַנְתְּ פָּלַח לֵיהּ בִּתְדִירָא הוּא יְשֵׁזְבִנָּךְ. וְכִי יֵשׁ פּוּלְחָן בְּבָבֶל. וְאֵי זוֹ זוֹ תְּפִילָּה.

Halakhah 1: It is written (*Deut.* 11:13) "To love the Eternal, your God, and to work[3] for Him with all yor heart and all your soul," does there exist work in the heart? This refers to prayer. And so it says (*Dan.* 6:17):

"Your God, whom you serve permanently, may rescue you." Is there any service in Babylonia? This refers to prayer.

3 The root עבד means "to work, to serve" and implies some physical exertion. In the religious sense, עבודה without qualifier always means the Temple service, the actual offering of sacrifices and all that is connected with it. (Hence, as noted in reference to Daniel, it cannot take place in Babylonia.) In the Babli (*Taänit* 2a), prayer is explicitly qualified as "service by the heart".

יָכוֹל יְהֵא מִתְפַּלֵּל שְׁלָשְׁתָּן כְּאַחַת פֵּרֵשׁ בְּדָנִיֵּאל וְזִמְנִין תְּלָתָא בְיוֹמָא הוּא בָּרֵךְ עַל בִּרְכוֹהִי וְגוֹמֵר. יָכוֹל יְהֵא מִתְפַּלֵּל לְכָל־רוּחַ שֶׁיִּרְצֶה. תַּלְמוּד לוֹמַר וְכַוִּין פְּתִיחִין לֵיהּ נֶגֶד יְרוּשְׁלֵם. יָכוֹל מִשֶּׁבָּאוּ לַגּוֹלָה כֵן תַּלְמוּד לוֹמַר כָּל־קֳבֵל דִּי הֲוָה עָבֵד מִן קַדְמַת דְּנָא. יָכוֹל יְהֵא מִתְפַּלֵּל שְׁלָשְׁתָּן בְּכָל־שָׁעָה שֶׁיִּרְצֶה. כְּבָר פֵּירֵשׁ דָּוִד עֶרֶב וָבוֹקֶר וְצָהֳרַיִם. יָכוֹל יְהֵא מַגְבִּיהַּ קוֹלוֹ וְיִתְפַּלֵּל. פֵּירֵשׁ בְּחַנָּה וְחַנָּה הִיא מְדַבֶּרֶת עַל לִבָּהּ. יָכוֹל יְהֵא מְהַרְהֵר בְּלֵב. תַּלְמוּד לוֹמַר רַק שְׂפָתֶיהָ נָעוֹת. הָא כֵיצַד מְרַחִישׁ בִּשְׂפְתוֹתָיו.

One might think that one may pray all three[4] together - it is explained in Daniel (*Dan.* 6:11): "Three times a day he fell on his knees, etc." One might think that one may pray in any direction one wants - the verse says "slits were open for him in the direction of Jerusalem." One might think that he started after he went into captivity - the verse says "as was his wont from before that." One might think that one may pray all three at any time he wishes - already David did explain (*Ps.* 55:18): "Morning, evening, and afternoon." One might think that one may pray aloud - it was explained about Hannah (*1Sam.* 1:13): "Hannah was speaking to herself." One might assume that he might simply think - the verse says "only her lips moved." How is that? One whispers with one's lips.

4 It will be explained later that the three daily prayers were either inherited from the patriarchs or they were fashioned after the Temple service. The verse in Daniel is not discussed in the order it is written, neither is the order of the verse preserved in the Tosephta (*Berakhot* 3:6) or in the Babli (31a), whose text is close to the Tosephta. The last remarks about moving one's lips is neither in the Babli nor in the Tosephta.

אָמַר רִבִּי יוֹסֵי בַּר חֲנִינָא מִן הַפָּסוּק הַזֶּה אַתְּ לָמֵד אַרְבָּעָה דְּבָרִים. וְחַנָּה הִיא מְדַבֶּרֶת עַל לִבָּהּ. מִיכַּן שֶׁהַתְּפִילָּה צְרִיכָה כַּוָּנָה. רַק שְׂפָתֶיהָ נָעוֹת. מִיכַּן שֶׁהוּא צָרִיךְ לְהַרְחִישׁ בִּשְׂפָתָיו. וְקוֹלָהּ לֹא יִשָּׁמֵעַ. מִיכַּן שֶׁלֹּא יְהֵא אָדָם מַגְבִּיהַּ קוֹלוֹ וְיִתְפַּלֵּל. וַיַּחְשְׁבֶהָ עֵלִי לְשִׁכּוֹרָה. מִיכַּן שֶׁהַשִּׁכּוֹר אָסוּר לְהִתְפַּלֵּל.

Rebbi Yose bar Ḥanina said: From this verse (*1Sam.* 1:13) you may learn four things. "Hannah was speaking to her heart," from here that prayer needs attention. "Only her lips moved," from here that one must whisper with one's lips. "Her voice was not heard," from here that nobody should pray at high voice. "And Eli thought that she was drunk," from here that a drunk is forbidden to pray.[5]

5 This paragraph is given in the Babli (31a) in the name of Rav Hamnuna, a Babylonian contemporary of Rebbi Yose bar Ḥanina.

מִילְּתָא דְּחָנָן בַּר בָּא פְּלִיגָא דְּחָנָן בַּר בָּא אָמַר לַחֲבֵרַיָּא נֵימוֹר לְכוֹן מִילְּתָא טָבָא דַּחֲמִית לְרַב עֲבִיד וְאַמְרִיתָהּ קוֹמֵי שְׁמוּאֵל וְקָם וְנָשַׁק עַל פּוּמִי. בָּרוּךְ אַתָּה שׁוֹחֵחַ. בָּא לְהַזְכִּיר אֶת הַשֵּׁם זוֹקֵף. שְׁמוּאֵל אָמַר אֲנִי אֲמְרִית טַעֲמָא יי זוֹקֵף כְּפוּפִים. אָמַר רִבִּי אַמִּי לֹא מִסְתַּבְּרָא אֶלָּא מִפְּנֵי שְׁמִי נִיחַת הוּא. אָמַר רִבִּי אָבוּן אִלּוּ הֲוָא כְתִיב בִּשְׁמִי נִיחַת הוּא יֵאוּת. לֵית כְּתִיב אֶלָּא מִפְּנֵי שְׁמִי נִיחַת הוּא. קוֹדֶם עַד שֶׁלֹּא הִזְכִּיר אֶת הַשֵּׁם כְּבָר נִיחַת הוּא.

The word of Ḥanan bar Abba[6] disagrees since Ḥanan bar Abba said to the colleagues: I shall tell you one of the good things that I saw Rav do and, when I told it before Samuel he got up and kissed me on my mouth. At "praised are You", he bows down. When he comes to mention *Hashem*, he straightens up. Samuel said: I shall give the reason (*Ps.* 35:10): "The Lord straightens the bent ones." Rebbi Ammi said: It is not reasonable, but (*Mal.* 2:5): "Before My Name he is low." Rebbi Abun said: If it were written "at My Name he is low" then you would be right, but it is written "before My Name he is low", before he mentions *Hashem* he is low.

6 The entire paragraph does not belong here but is taken word by word from Chapter 1, Halakhah 8, at note 265 ff.

רִבִּי אַבָּא בַּר זַבְדָּא מַצְלֵי בְקָלָא. רִבִּי יוֹנָה כַּד הֲוָא מַצְלֵי בִכְנִישְׁתָּא הֲוָה מַצְלֵי בִלְחִישָׁה. כַּד הֲוָא מַצְלֵי בְּבֵיתָא הֲוָא מַצְלֵי בְקָלָא עַד דְּיַלְפּוּן בְּנֵי בֵיתֵיהּ צְלוּתָא מִינֵּיהּ. אָמַר רִבִּי מָנָא וּבְנֵיהּ בֵּיתֵיהּ דְּאַבָּא יָֽלְפָא צְלוּתָא מִינֵּיהּ.

Rebbi Abba bar Zavda prayed aloud[7]. Rebbi Jonah prayed whispering in the synagogue; he prayed aloud in his house so that the people in his house[8] should learn prayer from him. Rebbi Mana[9] said: Really, the people in my father's house learned prayer from him.

7 He opposes the generalization from Hannah's prayer to general rule. As a student of Rav, he represents Babylonian practice; the following example of Rebbi Jonah shows that two generations later his opinion was accepted in Galilee.

8 His wife and children.

9 Rebbi Mana II, son of Rebbi Jonah.

מֵאֵיכָן לָמְדוּ ג תְּפִילּוֹת. רִבִּי שְׁמוּאֵל בַּר נַחְמָנִי אָמַר כְּנֶגֶד ג פְּעָמִים שֶׁהַיּוֹם מִשְׁתַּנֶּה עַל הַבְּרִיּוֹת. בְּשַׁחַר צָרִיךְ אָדָם לוֹמַר מוֹדֶה אֲנִי לְפָנֶיךָ יי אלדי ואלדי אֲבוֹתַי שֶׁהוֹצֵאתָנִי מֵאֲפֵילָה לְאוֹרָה. בְּמִנְחָה צָרִיךְ אָדָם לוֹמַר מוֹדֶה אֲנִי לְפָנֶיךָ יי אלדי ואלדי אֲבוֹתַי כְּשֵׁם שֶׁזִּכִּיתָנִי לִרְאוֹת הַחַמָּה בְּמִזְרָח כַּךְ זָכִיתִי לִרְאוֹת

בְּמַעֲרָב. בָּעֶרֶב צָרִיךְ לוֹמַר יְהִי רָצוֹן מִלְּפָנֶיךָ יי אלדי ואלדי אֲבוֹתַי כְּשֵׁם שֶׁהָיִיתִי בָּאֲפֵילָה וְהוֹצֵאתָנִי לְאוֹרָה כַּךְ תּוֹצִיאֵנִי מֵאֲפֵילָה לְאוֹרָה.

From where did they learn the three prayers? Rebbi Samuel bar Naḥmani said[10]: According to the three times that the day changes for man. In the morning, one must say: I thank you, o Eternal, my God and God of my fathers, that you led me from darkness to light. At *Minḥah*, one must say: I thank you, o Eternal, my God and God of my fathers, that just as You let me see the sun in the East, so I could see it in the West. In the evening, one must say: May it be Your pleasure, o Eternal, my God and God of my fathers, that just as I was in darkness and You led me into light, so may You lead me from darkness into light.

10 This paragraph is found *in extenso*, the next two pragraphs very shortened, in *Midrash Bereshit Rabba* 68(11). There, the order of prayers is evening, morning, afternoon, and the afternoon prayer is: "just as You let me see the sun in the East, so may You let me see it in the West." The form of the Midrash is appropriate for early *Minḥah* (half an hour after noon), the form of the Talmud is appropriate for the standard *Minḥah*, close to evening. Neither of the two texts is a corruption of the other.

רִבִּי יְהוֹשֻׁעַ בֶּן לֵוִי אָמַר תְּפִילּוֹת מֵאָבוֹת לְמֵדוּם. תְּפִילַּת הַשַּׁחַר מֵאַבְרָהָם אָבִינוּ וַיַּשְׁכֵּם אַבְרָהָם בַּבּוֹקֶר אֶל הַמָּקוֹם אֲשֶׁר עָמַד שָׁם אֶת פְּנֵי יי. וְאֵין עֲמִידָה אֶלָּא תְפִילָּה כְּמָה דְתֵימַר וַיַּעֲמוֹד פִּינְחָס וַיְפַלֵּל. תְּפִלַּת הַמִּנְחָה מִיִּצְחָק אָבִינוּ. וַיֵּצֵא יִצְחָק לָשׂוּחַ בַּשָּׂדֶה וְאֵין שִׂיחָה אֶלָּא תְפִלָּה. כְּמָה דְתֵימַר תְּפִילָּה לְעָנִי כִי יַעֲטוֹף וְלִפְנֵי יי יִשְׁפּוֹךְ שִׂיחוֹ. תְּפִילַּת הָעֶרֶב מִיַּעֲקֹב אָבִינוּ וַיִּפְגַּע (fol. 6b) בַּמָּקוֹם וַיָּלֶן שָׁם. וְאֵין פְּגִיעָה אֶלָּא תְפִילָּה כְּמָה דְתֵימַר יִפְגְּעוּ נָא בַּיי צְבָאוֹת. וְאוֹמֵר אַל תִּשָּׂא בַעֲדָם רִינָּה וּתְפִילָּה וְאַל תִּפְגַּע בִּי.

Rebbi Joshua ben Levi[11] said: They[12] learned prayers from the patriarchs. Morning prayer from our father Abraham (*Gen.* 19:27): "Abraham got up early to the place where he had stood there in the presence of the Eternal." Standing means praying, as it says (*Ps*. 106:30) "Phineas stood and prayed[13]." *Minḥah* prayers from our father Isaac. (*Gen*. 24:63) "Isaac went out to speak on the field[14]." Speaking means praying, as it says (*Ps*. 102:1) "A prayer of the deprived one when he faints and pours out his speech before the Eternal." Evening prayer from our father Jacob. (*Gen*. 28:11) "He entreated at the Place[15]." Entreaty means prayer, as it is said (*Jer*. 27:18) "Please, let them entreat the Eternal of hosts." And it says (*Jer*. 7:16): "Do not lift for them (your voice in) a cry and do not entreat me."

11 In the parallel in the Babli (26b), the opinion of Rebbi Joshua ben Levi is ascribed to R. Yose bar Ḥanina and the opinion of "the rabbis" in the following paragraph to R. Joshua ben Levi. The detailed derivation in both cases is declared to be a *baraita*, meaning that the two Amoraïm quoted do not claim originality, they simply adopt pre-existing ideas.

12 The Men of the Great Assembly who instituted formal prayers and benedictions.

13 Usually translated as "judged".

14 The essential proof is from the part of the verse that is not quoted: "To speak on the field towards evening." [The Arabic שׂוח, corresponding to Hebrew שׂוח, means "to run, or fly, with outstretched arms".]

15 Usually translated "came suddenly upon the place." For the meaning of "Place", see H. Guggenheimer, *The Scholar's Haggadah*, pp. 268-269.

וְרַבָּנָן אָמְרוּ תְּפִילּוֹת מִתְּמִידִין גָּמְרוּ. תְּפִילַּת הַשַּׁחַר מִתָּמִיד שֶׁל שַׁחַר. אֶת הַכֶּבֶשׂ הָאֶחָד תַּעֲשֶׂה בַבֹּקֶר. תְּפִילַּת הַמִּנְחָה מִתָּמִיד שֶׁל בֵּין הָעַרְבַּיִם. וְאֵת הַכֶּבֶשׂ הַשֵּׁנִי תַּעֲשֶׂה בֵּין הָעַרְבָּיִם. תְּפִילַּת הָעֶרֶב לֹא מָצְאוּ בַּמֶּה לִתְלוֹתָהּ וְשָׁנוּ אוֹתָהּ סְתָם. הֲדָא הוּא דְתַנִּינָן תְּפִילַּת הָעֶרֶב אֵין לָהּ קֶבַע וְשֶׁל מוּסָפִין כָּל־הַיּוֹם. אָמַר רִבִּי תַּנְחוּמָא עוֹד הִיא קָבְעוּ אוֹתָהּ כְּנֶגֶד אִיכּוּל אֵיבָרִים וּפְדָרִים שֶׁהָיוּ מִתְאַכְּלִין עַל גַּבֵּי הַמִּזְבֵּחַ כָּל־הַלַּיְלָה.

The rabbis said, they inferred prayers from daily sacrifices. The morning prayer from the perpetual sacrifice of the morning (*Num.* 28:4): "The first lamb you should present in the morning." *Minḥah* prayer from the perpetual sacrifice of the evening: "And the second lamb you should present in the evening." They did not find anything to peg evening prayers onto it and simply stated it; that is what we have stated: Evening prayers have no fixed time. *Musaph* prayers are all day. Rebbi Tanḥuma[16] said: In fact, they fixed it corresponding to the consumption of limbs and fat which were consumed on the altar during the entire night.

16 In the Babli (26b), this statement of a late Amora also is quoted as Tannaïtic.

מִדִּבְרֵי תוֹרָה לָמַד רִבִּי יְהוּדָה. דְּתַנֵּי רִבִּי יִשְׁמָעֵאל וְחַם הַשֶּׁמֶשׁ וְנָמָס בְּאַרְבַּע שָׁעוֹת. אַתָּה אוֹמֵר בְּאַרְבַּע שָׁעוֹת אוֹ אֵינוֹ אֶלָּא בְּשֵׁשׁ שָׁעוֹת. כְּשֶׁהוּא אוֹמֵר כְּחוֹם הַיּוֹם הֲרֵי שֵׁשׁ אָמוּר. הָא מַה אֲנִי מְקַיֵּם וְחַם הַשֶּׁמֶשׁ וְנָמָס בְּאַרְבַּע שָׁעוֹת. וְאַתְּ דָּרֵשׁ בַּבֹּקֶר בַּבֹּקֶר. מַה בַּבֹּקֶר שֶׁנֶּאֱמַר לְהַלָּן בְּאַרְבַּע שָׁעוֹת. אַף בַּבֹּקֶר שֶׁנֶּאֱמַר כַּאן בְּאַרְבַּע שָׁעוֹת. בְּאַרְבַּע שָׁעִין שִׁמְשָׁא חֲמִין וְטוּלָא קָרִיר. בְּשִׁית שָׁעִין שִׁמְשָׁא חֲמִין וְטוּלָא חֲמִין. אָמַר רִבִּי תַּנְחוּמָא מַהוּ כְּחוֹם הַיּוֹם. בְּשָׁעָה שֶׁאֵין צֵל לְכָל־בְּרִיָּה.

Rebbi Yehudah[17] learned from words of the Torah, since Rebbi Ismael stated: (*Ex.* 17:21) "The sun was hot and it melted," four hours into the day. You say four hours or should it be six hours? When it says (*Gen.* 18:1): "In the heat of the day", that means at six hours. Therefore, how can I interpret: "The sun was hot and it melted," four hours into the day[18]!

You derive it from (*Ex.* 17:21): "In the morning," (*Num.* 28:4) "in the morning." Since the first "morning" meant "four hours", "morning" mentioned there also means "four hours." At four hours the sun is warm and the shadow is cool. At six hours both sun and shadow are hot. Rebbi

Tanḥuma said (*Gen.* 18:1): "In the heat of the day", at an hour when there is no shadow for any creature.

17 This paragraph is found also in the Babli (27a) and in both Mekhiltot (to *Ex.* 17:21). The second paragraph which connects the derivation to the previous association with sacrifices, and hence, with prayer, is found only in the Yerushalmi.

18 Here and in the next paragraph, one supposes, as in most Talmudic derivations, that the vocabulary of the Torah is uniquely fixed and that different expressions must have different meanings. [The only Bible translation that can be clearly dated to Tannaïtic times, the fragments of Aquilas's Greek translation from the school of Rebbis Eliezer and Joshua, systematically has one-on-one correspondence between Hebrew and Greek words.]

רִבִּי יָסָא מְצַלֵּי בִּתְלַת שָׁעִין. רִבִּי חִייָא בַּר וָוא מְצַלֵּי בִּתְלַת שָׁעִין. רִבִּי בְּרֶכְיָה חֲמוּנֵיהּ קָרֵי קִרְיַת שְׁמַע וּמְצַלֵּי בָּתָר תְּלַת שָׁעִין. וְהָא תַנִּינָן הַקּוֹרֵא מִיכָּן וְאֵילָךְ לֹא הִפְסִיד כְּאָדָם הַקּוֹרֵא בַּתּוֹרָה. נֵימַר כְּבָר קִיבֵּל מַלְכוּת שָׁמַיִם בְּעוֹנָתָהּ.

Rebbi Yasa prayed at three hours[19]. Rebbi Ḥiyya bar Abba prayed at three hours. They saw Rebbi Berekhiah that he recited *Shema'* and prayed after three hours. But did we not formulate (*Berakhot* 1:5): "He who reads after that did not lose, he is like a man reading in the Torah." We may say that he accepted the yoke of heaven in its time[20].

19 While in theory in Mishnaic times the recitation of *Shema'* and prayer were separate activities, the practice in Amoraic times was to unite them. It is stated in the Babli (9b) in the name of Israeli authorities that it is preferable to pray immediately after the last benediction of *Shema'*. All authorities quoted here subscribe to this usage; the first two pray at the correct time for the recitation of *Shema'*, the last one recites *Shema'* at the time of prayer according to Rebbi Yehudah.

20 It is current practice to recite the first verse of *Shema'* during the preliminary benedictions recited immediately after one gets dressed in

the morning. Then the remainder of *Shema'* is just recitation of verses of Torah and may be delayed, in particular on Sabbath and holidays.

אִי מֵעֵדוּת לָמַד רִבִּי יוּדָה דָּמַר רִבִּי סִימוֹן בְּשֵׁם רִבִּי יְהוֹשֻׁעַ בֶּן לֵוִי בִּימֵי מַלְכוּת יָוָן הָיוּ מְשַׁלְשְׁלִין לָהֶן שְׁתֵּי קוּפּוֹת שֶׁל זָהָב וְהָיוּ מַעֲלִין לָהֶן שְׁנֵי טְלָיִים. פַּעַם אַחַת שִׁילְשְׁלוּ לָהֶן שְׁתֵּי קוּפּוֹת שֶׁל זָהָב וְהָיוּ מַעֲלִין לָהֶן שְׁנֵי גְדָיִים. בְּאוֹתָהּ שָׁעָה הֵאִיר הַקָּדוֹשׁ בָּרוּךְ הוּא עֵינֵיהֶם וּמָצְאוּ שְׁנֵי טְלָיִים מְבוּקָּרִים בְּלִשְׁכַּת הַטְּלָאִים. עַל אוֹתָהּ שָׁעָה הֵעִיד רִבִּי יְהוּדָה בַּר אַבָּא עַל תָּמִיד שֶׁל שַׁחַר שֶׁקָּרֵב בְּאַרְבַּע שָׁעוֹת.

Or Rebbi Yehudah learned from testimony[21] since Rebbi Simon said in the name of Rebbi Joshua ben Levi: In the time of the hellenistic government[22] they[23] lowered them two boxes with gold and they gave them two lambs to pull up. Once they lowered them two boxes with gold and they gave them two kid goats[24] to pull up. At that moment the Holy One, praise to Him, enlightened their eyes and they found two certified lambs in the hall of lambs[25]. About that time did Rebbi Yehudah bar Abba[26] testify that the perpetual morning sacrifice was brought at four hours.

21 Since we said that the rules of prayer are imitations of the rules of sacrifices and we do not find that the perpetual sacrifice was ever brought later than four hours in the day. Usually it is brought at first dawn.

22 The Babli (*Menaḥot* 64b) telescopes this story and the next into one and dates it at the civil war of the two Hasmonean brothers Hyrkanos and Aristobulos.

23 The officials of the Temple lowered the boxes from the wall of besieged Jerusalem; in each box was payment for the lamb to be placed in it for the daily sacrifice.

24 Which cannot be used for the perpetual sacrifice.

25 Since the verse (*Num.* 28:3) requires that the perpetual sacrifice be "a yearling sheep without blemish", the sheep were usually held in a separate "hall of lambs" and were inspected three times before being used as

sacrifice.

26 In the Babli (27a), the name is Rebbi Yehudah ben Baba. Levi Ginzberg points out that the name Yehudah bar Abba is found instead of Yehudah ben Baba is some Mishnah manuscripts at *Idiut* 6:1, 8:2, *Yebamot* 16:7 and that R. Yehudah ben Baba, who was killed in the aftermath of the war of Bar Kokhba, is much too late to testify about occurrences in the Temple. Hence, the name "bar Abba" should not be changed.

אָמַר רִבִּי לֵוִי אַף בִּימֵי מַלְכוּת רִשְׁעָא הַזֹּאת הָיוּ מְשַׁלְשְׁלִין לָהֶן שְׁתֵּי קוּפּוֹת שֶׁל זָהָב וְהָיוּ מַעֲלִין לָהֶן שְׁנֵי כְבָשִׂים. וּבְסוֹף שִׁלְשְׁלוּ לָהֶם שְׁתֵּי קוּפּוֹת שֶׁל זָהָב וְעָלוּ לָהֶן שְׁנֵי חֲזִירִין. לֹא הִסְפִּיקוּ לְהַגִּיעַ לַחֲצִי חוֹמָה עַד שֶׁנָּעַץ הַחֲזִיר בַּחוֹמָה וְנִזְדַּעְזְעָה הַחוֹמָה וְקָפַץ מ׳ פַּרְסָה מֵאֶרֶץ יִשְׂרָאֵל. בְּאוֹתָהּ שָׁעָה גָּרְמוּ הָעֲווֹנוֹת וּבָטֵל הַתָּמִיד וְחָרֵב הַבַּיִת.

Rebbi Levi said: Also in the days of the present evil government[27] they lowered them two boxes with gold and they gave them two sheep to pull up. Once they lowered them two boxes with gold and they let them pull up two swine[28]. They did not manage to get to half the height of the wall when the swine clawed the wall; the wall trembled, and [the swine] jumped 40 parasangs from the Land of Israel. At that time the sins caused that the perpetual sacrifice was stopped and the Temple destroyed.

27 In both Talmudim, the "evil government" or simply "government" is the Roman government.

28 In the Babli (*Menaḥot* 64b), there was only one swine and not only the wall but the entire Land of Israel trembled. (The civil war was at the time when Pompey conquered the East for Rome but the story here clearly speaks of the war of Titus. However, it seems that the Babli tradition in this case is more correct.)

מַה טַעֲמוֹן דְּרַבָּנָן. שְׁנַיִם לַיּוֹם. חֲלוֹק אֶת הַיּוֹם. טַעְמָא דְּרִבִּי יְהוּדָה שְׁנַיִם לַיּוֹם. שְׁנֵי פְּרַקְלֵיטִין לַיּוֹם. שְׁנַיִם לַיּוֹם. שֶׁתְּהֵא שְׁחִיטָתָן לְשֵׁם הַיּוֹם.

What is the reason of the rabbis? (*Num.* 28:3) "Two for the day", split the day in two. The reason of Rebbi Yehudah[30]: "two for the day", two advocates[31] per day; "two for the day" that they should be slaughtered expressly for the day[32].

30 Not the reason why prayer and sacrifice has to be finished at four hours but the reason why the verse is written as it is, "two for the day" and not "two in the day".

31 Greek παράκλητος (also meaning "intercessor".).

32 The slaughterer must keep in mind that he slaughters for the perpetual sacrifice of that particular day. A sacrifice becomes invalid if it is slaughtered with the wrong intention.

שְׁנַיִם לַיּוֹם. שֶׁתְּהֵא שְׁחִיטָתָן כְּנֶגֶד הַיּוֹם. הֲדָא הִיא דְתַנִּינָן תַּמָּן תָּמִיד שֶׁל שַׁחַר הָיָה נִשְׁחָט עַל קֶרֶן מַעֲרָבִית צְפוֹנִית עַל טַבַּעַת שְׁנִיָּה כְּנֶגֶד הַיּוֹם וְשֶׁל בֵּין הָעַרְבַּיִם הָיָה נִשְׁחָט עַל קֶרֶן צְפוֹנִית מִזְרָחִית עַל טַבַּעַת שְׁנִיָּה כְּנֶגֶד הַיּוֹם. וְהוּא שֶׁיְּהֵא יוֹדֵעַ אֵי זֶה מֵהֶן נִשְׁחַט בְּשַׁחֲרִית וְאֵי זֶה מֵהֶן נִשְׁחַט בָּעֲרָבִים.

"Two for the day", that their slaughtering should be facing the day. That is what we have stated[33]: The perpetual morning sacrifice was slaughtered at the Northwest corner at the second ring[34], facing the day[35], and the evening one was slaughtered at the Northeast corner at the second ring, facing the day. And[36] that he should know which one was to be slaughtered in the morning and which one in the evening.

33 Mishnah *Tamid* 4:1. The entire passage is in *Sifra Num.* 142, in changed form Babli *Yoma* 62a, *Tamid* 31b.

34 In the wall of the Temple enclosure, where the sacrifice is hung to be skinned and cut into pieces.

35 I. e., the sun. Every holocaust sacrifice has to be slaughtered North of the altar (*Lev.* 1:11).

36 This is not a continuation of the previous argument but another interpretation of "two for the day", that the victims should be selected separately for the sacrifices of the day.

רִבִּי חִייָא בְשֵׁם רִבִּי יוֹחָנָן תְּפִילַּת הַמִּנְחָה וּתְפִילַּת הַמּוּסָף תְּפִילַּת הַמִּנְחָה קוֹדֶמֶת. הֲוֹון בָּעֵין מֵימַר כְּשֶׁאֵין בַּיּוֹם כְּדֵי לְהִתְפַּלֵּל שְׁנֵיהֶן אֲבָל אִם יֵשׁ בַּיּוֹם כְּדֵי לְהִתְפַּלֵּל שְׁנֵיהֶן תְּפִילַּת מוּסָף קוֹדֶמֶת. רִבִּי זְעִירָא בְשֵׁם רִבִּי יוֹחָנָן וַאֲפִילוּ יֵשׁ בַּיּוֹם כְּדֵי לְהִתְפַּלֵּל שְׁתֵיהֶן תְּפִילַּת הַמִּנְחָה קוֹדֶמֶת. רִבִּי נָתָן בַּר טוֹבִי בְשֵׁם רִבִּי יוֹחָנָן וַאֲפִילוּ יֵשׁ בַּיּוֹם כְּדֵי לְהִתְפַּלֵּל שְׁתֵיהֶן תְּפִילַּת הַמִּנְחָה קוֹדֶמֶת. וְהָתַנִּי הִקְדִּים תְּפִילַּת הַמִּנְחָה לִתְפִילַּת הַמּוּסָפִין יָצָא. לְשֶׁעָבַר הָא בַּתְּחִילָּה לָא בְדָא. פָּתַר לָהּ בְּשֶׁלֹּא הִגִּיעַ זְמַן הַתְּפִילָּה. כַּהֲדָא רִבִּי יְהוֹשֻׁעַ בֶּן לֵוִי מְפַקֵּד לְתַלְמִידָיו אִין הֲוָה לְכוֹן אֲרִיסְטוֹן וּמָטָא יוֹמָא לְשִׁית שָׁעִין עַד דְּלָא תִסְקוּן לַאֲרִסְטוֹן תְּהֲווֹן מַצְלוֹן דְּמִנְחָתָא עַד דְּלָא תִסְקוּן.

Rebbi Ḥiyya[37] in the name of Rebbi Yoḥanan: *Minḥah* and *Musaph* prayers[38], the *Minḥah* prayer has precedence. They wanted to say, that is if there is no time in the day to pray both of them; but if there is time in the day to pray both of them then the *Musaph* prayer has precedence. Rebbi Zeïra in the name of Rebbi Yoḥanan: Even if there is time in the day to pray both of them, the *Minḥah* prayer has precedence[39]. Rebbi Nathan bar Ṭobi[40] in the name of Rebbi Yoḥanan: Even if there is time in the day to pray both of them, the *Minḥah* prayer has precedence. But did we not state: "If somebody made *Minḥah* prayer precede *Musaph* prayer, he has done his duty." Retrospectively, but from the start, not so[41]. Explain it if the time for prayer has not yet arrived, as in the following: Rebbi Joshua ben Levi commanded his students: If you have lunch[42] and the day progressed to six hours before you entered, then pray *Minḥah* before you enter[43].

37 Rebbi Ḥiyya bar Abba. In the Babli (28a), the statement is R. Yoḥanan's own.

38 If on a day that requires a *Musaph* prayer, a person has not prayed *Musaph* before 12:30 pm local time and now he is obligated for two prayers.

39 Following the general principle: "If a frequent duty and an infrequent

one collide, the frequent one has precedence" (Babli *Pesaḥim* 114a, Yerushalmi *Berakhot* 8:1). It is reported in the Babli (28a) that Rebbi Zeïra learned the rule not from R. Yoḥanan directly but from R. Nathan bar Ṭobi.

40 A student of R. Yoḥanan, whose house was close to the Academy.

41 Meaning: If somebody did, we let him get away with it. But if somebody comes to ask, we tell him not to do it.

42 Greek ἄριστον ("breakfast", later also "main meal").

43 Even though one should not pray before 12:30 pm, it is preferable to pray too early than not to pray at all. In contrast to the recital of *Shema'* which is bound to rigid times, prayer may be said too early as explained later in this *Halakhah*.

וְכַמָּה הוּא פְּלַג הַמִּנְחָה אַחַת עֶשְׂרֵה שָׁעוֹת חָסֵר רְבִיעַ.

(Tosephta *Berakhot* 3:1) How much is half of *Minḥah*? Eleven hours minus a quarter[44].

44 The Babli (26b) has a parallel statement in the name of Rebbi Yehudah which is not from the Tosephta.

תַּמָּן תַּנִּינָן תָּמִיד נִשְׁחַט בִּשְׁמוֹנֶה וּמֶחֱצָה וְקָרֵב בְּתֵשַׁע וּמֶחֱצָה. עֶרֶב פְּסָחִים נִשְׁחַט בְּשֶׁבַע וּמֶחֱצָה וְקָרֵב בִּשְׁמוֹנֶה וּמֶחֱצָה בֵּין בְּחוֹל בֵּין בְּשַׁבָּת. רִבִּי יִרְמְיָה בָּעֵי הָכָא אַתְּ עֲבַד מִנְחָה שְׁתֵּי שָׁעוֹת וּמֶחֱצָה וְהָכָא אַתְּ עֲבַד מִנְחָה שָׁלֹשׁ שָׁעוֹת וּמֶחֱצָה. אָמַר רִבִּי יוֹסֵי לֹא הוּקְשָׁה תְּפִילַּת הַמִּנְחָה לְתָמִיד שֶׁל הָעַרְבַּיִם אֶלָּא לִקְטוֹרֶת. מַה טַעַם תִּכּוֹן תְּפִילָּתִי קְטוֹרֶת לְפָנֶיךָ מַשְׂאַת כַּפַּי מִנְחַת עָרֶב. צֵא שָׁעָה אַחַת לְעִיסוּקוֹ וְאַתְּ עֲבַד מִנְחָה שְׁתֵּי שָׁעוֹת וּמֶחֱצָא.

There (*Pesaḥim* 5:1) we have stated: "The perpetual sacrifice is slaughtered at 8:30 hours[45] and brought at 9:30 hours. On Passover Eve days[46] it is sacrificed at 7:30 hours and brought at 8:30 hours, whether it be weekday or Sabbath." Rebbi Jeremiah asked: Here[47] you make *Minḥah* at two and a half hours and here you make *Minḥah at* three and a half hours? Rebbi Yose said, *Minḥah* prayer was not bound to the perpetual sacrifice of evening but to incense burning[48]. What is the reason? (*Ps.* 141:2): "May my prayer be prepared as incense before You, the lifting up of my hands as the gift of evening." Take one hour for its[49] preparation and you make *Minḥah* at two and one half hours.

45 The count starts at sunrise. At the equinox, 8:30 in the day is 2:30 pm (14:30).

46 The afternoons of the 14th of Nisan and of the 14th of Iyar.

47 Regarding prayer, the Mishnah states that *Minḥah* is $2^1/_2$ hours before night. The next "here" refers to the evening sacrifice which on ordinary days is slaughtered at 8:30 hours, $3^1/_2$ hours before sundown. If the rules of prayer are derived from the rules of sacrifice then the time of *Minḥah* prayers should be fixed at $3^1/_2$ hours before sundown!

48 The evening portion of incense was burned at the time of lighting the candelabra, after all sacrifices had been offered (*Ex.* 30:8).

49 The perpetual sacrifice's.

רִבִּי יוֹסֵי בֶּן חֲנִינָא הָיָה מִתְפַּלֵּל עִם דִּמְדוּמֵי חַמָּה כְּדֵי שֶׁיְּהֵא עָלָיו מוֹרָא שָׁמַיִם כָּל־הַיּוֹם. אָמַר רִבִּי יוֹסֵי בֶּן חֲנִינָא וִיהֵא חֶלְקִי עִם הַמִּתְפַּלְלִים עִם דִּמְדוּמֵי חַמָּה מַה טַעַם עַל זֹאת יִתְפַּלֵּל כָּל־חָסִיד אֵלֶיךָ לְעֵת מְצוֹא. לְעֵת מִיצּוּיוֹ שֶׁל יוֹם.

Rebbi Yose ben Ḥanina used to pray when the sun set so that the fear of Heaven should be on him the entire day long. Rebbi Yose ben Ḥanina said: May my lot be with those who pray at sunset[50]. What is the reason? (*Ps.* 32:6) "For that, every pious person should pray to You at the time of מצא", at the time when the day is pushed out[51].

50 In the Babli (29b), the statement is attributed to Rebbi Ḥiyya bar Abba in the name of Rebbi Yoḥanan, also Galilean sages. Nevertheless, it is stated there that in "the West", i. e., the Land of Israel, one curses those who pray at sunset since if anything happens at that time, the time of prayer will have passed whereas if one plans for earlier prayer, one always has space to accomodate emergencies. This opinion must be dated to the time after the work on the Jerusalem Talmud had stopped.

The root דמדם appears only in the expression דמדומי חמה. While in the Babli this means "dawn or dusk", in the Yerushalmi it means only "sunset" as is clear from *Pesaḥim* 5:1 (fol. 31c), where דמדומי חמה is the opposite of הנץ החמה "sunrise". The same verbal stem in Arabic means "to eliminate by force."

51 Replacing the verb מצא "to find" by מצה "to squeeze dry, suck dry".

אַחֲוֵיהּ דְּאִימֵּיהּ דְּרִבִּי אָדָא הֲוָא מְצַיֵּיץ גּוּלְתֵיהּ דְּרַב בְּצוֹמָא רַבָּא. אֲמַר לֵיהּ כַּד תִּחְמִי שִׁימְשָׁא בְּרֵישׁ דִּקְלֵי תִּיהַב לִי גּוּלְתִי דְנַצְלֵי דְּמִנְחָתָא. וְשִׁמְשָׁא בְּרֵישׁ דִּיקְלֵי אַיְמָמָא הוּא. הכא דָּמַר רִבִּי יוֹחָנָן הָאוֹמֵר לְצוּלָה חֳרָבִי זוּ בָּבֶל שֶׁהִיא זוּטוֹ שֶׁל עוֹלָם. אָמַר רִבִּי יוֹחָנָן לָמָּה נִקְרָא שְׁמָהּ צוּלָה שֶׁשָּׁם צָֽלְלוּ מֵיתֵי דוֹר הַמַּבּוּל. גַּם בְּבָבֶל לִנְפּוֹל חַלְלֵי יִשְׂרָאֵל גַּם בְּבָבֶל נָֽפְלוּ חַלְלֵי כָל־הָאָרֶץ. כְּתִיב וַיִּמְצְאוּ בִקְעָה בְּאֶרֶץ שִׁנְעָר וַיֵּשְׁבוּ שָׁם. אָמַר רֵישׁ לָקִישׁ לָמָּה נִקְרָא שְׁמָהּ שִׁנְעָר שֶׁשָּׁם נִנְעֲרוּ מֵיתֵי דוֹר הַמַּבּוּל. דָּבָר אַחֵר שֶׁהֵם מֵתִים בְּתַשְׁנוּק בְּלֹא נֵר בְּלֹא מֶרְחָץ. דָּבָר אַחֵר שִׁנְעָר שֶׁהֵם מְנוּעָרִים מִן הַמִּצְוֹות בְּלֹא תְרוּמָה וּבְלֹא מַעֲשֵׂר. דָּבָר אַחֵר שִׁנְעָר שֶׁשָּׂרֶיהָ מֵתִים נְעָרִים. דָּבָר אַחֵר שִׁנְעָר שֶׁהֶעֱמִידָה שׂוֹנֵא וָעָר לְהַקָּדוֹשׁ בָּרוּךְ הוּא וְאֵי זֶה זֶה נְבוּכַדְנֶצַּר הָרָשָׁע.

The maternal uncle of Rebbi Ada[52] had rolled up the kaftan of Rav on the Great Fastday[53]. He said to him: When you see the sun on top of the date palms[54], give me my kaftan so that we may pray *Minḥah*. And when the sun is on top of the date palms it is daytime. As[55] Rebbi Yoḥanan said (*Is*. 44:27): "He Who said to the deep: dry up!", that is Babylonia, the filth[56] of the world.

Rebbi Yoḥanan said[57]: Why is it called "the deep", because there the dead of the Deluge were submerged, (*Jer*. 51:49) "Also in Babylonia the slain of Israel will fall, also in Babylonia the corpses of all the earth[58] did fall." It is written (*Gen*. 11:2) "They found a valley in the land Shinear and dwelt there." Rebbi Simeon ben Laqish said, why is it called Shinear? Because there the dead of the Deluge were thrown[59]. Another explanation: Because they die in strangulation[60], without light[61] or public baths. Another explanation: Shinear, because they are stripped of *miẓwot*, without *terumah* and without tithes[62]. Another explanation: Shinear, because its rulers die as youths. Another explanation: Shinear, because it produced a hater and enemy of the Holy One, praise to Him. Who is that? That is Nebuchadnezzar the evil one.

52 Rav Ada bar Ahava.

53 Yom Kippur. The Babylonian scholars never prayed without wearing the kaftan with the precribed belt. It seems that the Yeshivah of Rav had an intermission between *Musaph* and *Minḥah* on Yom Kippur.

54 Since their synagogues were outside the cities in the fields, the sun on top of the date palms may indicate a rather early hour but probably inside the timeframe admitted by Rebbi Yehudah.

55 The text הכא makes no sense. In the absence of manuscript evidence, the text has been left unchanged but the translation follows Levi Ginzberg's conjecture that one has to read כְּהָא "As to that", by a simple metathesis of two letters. The argument is that in a deep valley running N-S, the sun on the top of trees on the slopes of the valley designates a rather early time.

56 Latin *situs* "situation; filth".

57 This paragraph is an aggadic interruption about Babylonia; the discussion of Rav's action is continued in the following paragraph. This group of sermons is also found three times in *Midrash rabba*: *Gen. rabba 37:4, Threni rabba, Petiḥta* 23, *Eccl. rabba* 12:7. In the first two, there is an additional explanation of Shinear: A land whose (Jewish) rulers study Torah as youths (but do not continue studying as adults.)

58 Only in the Deluge the slain were of all mankind.

59 Taking שנער as *shaf'el* of the root נער "to pour out"; a later explanation refers to נער "to be a youth".

60 In the Targumim, חשנוק means "strangulation." However, in Syriac the words means "suffering", which makes sense here.

61 Since they had no olive oil, they had to use sesame oil which does not adhere well to wicks. Public hot baths were a characteristic institution of the provinces of the Roman empire.

62 While in old times the exiles tried to fulfill the "obligations that are

incumbent on the Land of Israel" also in Babylonia, in Talmudic times they were no longer observed there.

רַב כְּרִבִּי יוּדָה. אִין תַּעַבְדִּינֵיהּ כְּרַבָּנָן לֵית רִבִּי יוּדָה מוֹדֵי. אִין תַּעַבְדִּינֵיהּ כְּרִבִּי יוּדָה אַף רַבָּנָן מוֹדוּ.

Rav acted according to Rebbi Yehudah. If you do it following the rabbis, Rebbi Yehudah will not agree. If you do it following Rebbi Yehudah, the rabbis also will agree[63].

63 The previous questionable interpretation based on the topography of Babylonia (which is a double valley, but a very flat one) is unnecessary: Since the time frame of Rebbi Yehudah is more restrictive than that of the majority, if one follows Rebbi Yehudah one prays in a time frame acceptable to everybody.

מְנַיִין לִנְעִילָה. אָמַר רִבִּי לֵוִי גַּם כִּי תַרְבּוּ תְפִלָּה. מִכַּאן שֶׁכָּל־הַמַּרְבֶּה בִתְפִילָּה נֶעֱנֶה. מְחַלְּפָא שִׁיטָּתֵיהּ דְּרִבִּי לֵוִי תַּמָּן אָמַר רִבִּי אַבָּא בְּרֵיהּ דְּרִבִּי פַּפֵּי רִבִּי יְהוֹשֻׁעַ דְּסִיכְנִין בְּשֵׁם רִבִּי לֵוִי בְּכָל־עֶצֶב יִהְיֶה מוֹתָר וּדְבַר שְׂפָתַיִם אַךְ לְמַחְסוֹר. חַנָּה עַל יְדֵי שֶׁרִיבְתָה בִתְפִילָּה קִצְּרָה בְיָמָיו שֶׁל שְׁמוּאֵל שֶׁאָמְרָה וְיָשַׁב שָׁם עַד עוֹלָם וַהֲלֹא אֵין עוֹלָמוֹ שֶׁל לֵוִי אֶלָּא חֲמִשִּׁים שָׁנָה. דִּכְתִיב וּמִבֶּן חֲמִשִּׁים שָׁנָה יָשׁוּב מִצְּבָא הָעֲבוֹדָה. וְהַוְיָן לֵיהּ חַמְשִׁין וְתַרְתֵּין. אָמַר רִבִּי יוֹסֵי בֵּירִבִּי בּוּן שְׁתַּיִם שֶׁגְּמָלַתּוּ. (fol. 6c) וְכָא אָמַר הָכֵין. אִי אָמְרָהּ כֵּן לְיָחִיד הֵן לְצִיבּוּר. רִבִּי חִייָא בְּשֵׁם רִבִּי יוֹחָנָן רִבִּי שִׁמְעוֹן בֶּן חֲלַפְתָּא בְּשֵׁם רִבִּי מֵאִיר וְהָיָה כִּי הִרְבְּתָה לְהִתְפַּלֵּל לִפְנֵי יי. מִיכַּן שֶׁכָּל־הַמַּרְבֶּה בִתְפִילָּה נֶעֱנֶה.

From where about *Neïlah*[64]? Rebbi Levi said: (*Is.* 1:15) "Even if you prolong your prayers.[65]" From here that everyone who increases his prayers will be answered.

The argument of Rebbi Levi is inverted. There says Rebbi Abba, the son of Rebbi Pappai[66], Rebbi Joshua of Sikhnin in the name of Rebbi Levi (*Prov.* 14:23) "In all excitement there is something superfluous; and the word of the lips is but for deficit." Hannah, because she prayed too long, reduced the years of Samuel because she said (*1Sam.* 1:22) "He shall dwell there forever" but "forever" for a Levite is only 50 years, as it is written (*Num.* 8:25): "At age fifty he should return from the worshipping hosts[67]". But in fact it was 52[68]. Rebbi Yose ben Rebbi Abun said two years until she weaned him. And here you say so[69]? If he ever said it, one for private the other for public prayers.

Rebbi Ḥiyya[70] in the name of Rebbi Yoḥanan, Rebbi Simeon bar Ḥalaphta in the name of Rebbi Meïr (*1Sam.* 1:12): "When she prayed very long before the Eternal," it follows that everyone who extends his prayers will be answered.

64 The additional, fifth prayer close to the end of Yom Kippur and the major fasts in a draught.

65 The argument is from the full sentence: "Even if you augment your prayers, I shall not hear." Since Isaiah presents this as a particular curse, it follows that, otherwise, if the people increase their prayers they will be heard.

66 Amora of the fourth generation, student of Rebbi Joshua from Sikhnin (Suknin in Lower Galilee), a student of Rebbi Levi. Only aggadic material is transmitted by these two sages.

67 In fact, Hannah gave that detailed dedication not in her prayer but only when she explained to her husband that she would not come with him to Shiloh until she had weaned the baby, so that the boy could stay in the Tabernacle for the rest of his life. A Levite could serve (as carrier) only to age 50.

68 There is no Biblical source that gives Samuel 52 years; this Yerushalmi tradition is the result of a computation detailed in *Midrash Seder Olam*, Chap.13, and is based on the assertion (*1Sam.* 13:1) that Saul ruled only for two years, and on certain not obvious principles of interpretation of the Bible. Shiloh was destroyed when Samuel was still relatively young and afterwards he never lived near the Tabernacle again.

69 That additional prayer is always good. The answer is that additional prayers are guaranteed to be heard only if the entire congregation prays together.

70 R. Ḥiyya bar Abba. In the Babli (32b) he supports the negative opinion of Rebbi Levi in the name of R. Yoḥanan, at least in the case that somebody prays with the certain idea that he must be heard. The Yerushalmi clearly accepts the first statement of R. Levi but not the second one.

אֵימָתַי הִיא נְעִילָה רַבָּנָן דְּקֵיסָרִין אָמְרִין אִיתְפַּלְּגוּן רַב וְרִבִּי יוֹחָנָן. רַב אָמַר בְּנְעִילַת שַׁעֲרֵי שָׁמַיִם. וְרִבִּי יוֹחָנָן אָמַר בִּנְעִילַת שַׁעֲרֵי הֵיכָל. אָמַר רִבִּי יוּדָן אַנְתּוֹרְדָּיָא מַתְנִיתִין מְסַייְעָא לְרִבִּי יוֹחָנָן. בִּשְׁלוֹשָׁה פְרָקִים הַכֹּהֲנִים נוֹשְׂאִין אֶת כַּפֵּיהֶם אַרְבַּע פְּעָמִים בַּיּוֹם. בְּשַׁחֲרִית. בְּמוּסָף. בְּמִנְחָה. וּבִנְעִילַת שְׁעָרִים. בְּתַעֲנִיּוֹת. וּבְמַעֲמָדוֹת. וּבְיוֹם הַכִּיפּוּרִים. אִית לָךְ מֵימַר נְעִילַת שַׁעֲרֵי שָׁמַיִם בַּיּוֹם.

When is *Neïlah*? The rabbis of Caesarea say: Rav and Rebbi Yoḥanan disagree. Rav said, when the gates of Heaven are locked[71]. And Rebbi Yoḥanan said, when the gates of the Temple are locked. Rebbi Yudan Antordaya[72] said: A Mishnah supports Rebbi Yoḥanan (*Taäniot* 4:1): "On three occasions do the Cohanim lift their hands four times in one day, mornings, *Musaph, Minḥah*, and at the locking of the gates: on fastdays[73], at support services[74], and on Yom Kippur. May you say that the gates of heaven are locked while it is still daytime[75]?

71 It is not clear when the Gates of Heaven are locked. Maybe it is at sundown when the sun disappears, but it is more likely sometime after that when on a very clear day one may notice a sudden darkening of the sky in the middle of the gradual dusk. The gates of the Temple were locked for the public at the time of the lighting of the candelabra in the Sanctuary, which must be before sundown.

72 An Amora of the later generations who must be younger than the Amora R. Yose. His name appears variously as אנתורדיא, אנתודריא, ענתודריא, ענתוריא. The name probably is a toponymic [from Antarados, on the Phoenician coast opposite the island city of Arados (Arwad). Antarados is mentioned in an old commentary to Pliny (V 20). (E. G.)]

73 Publicly declared additional

fastdays in case of a draught.

74 Since the perpetual sacrifices were offered from public money and in the name of the public, some public representatives had to be present at the sacrifice. For this purpose, the Land of Israel was divided into districts and each district sent a few representatives to Jerusalem for the week to which it was appointed. During that week, the people of that district conducted special services with prayers that the sacrifices should be accepted by God; at these prayers the Cohanim recited the priestly blessing an additional time before nightfall, to coincide with an additional prayer for that purpose. It follows that the additional prayer was said year round on weekdays but every week at another district.

75 Since the priestly blessing may be recited only during daytime, the "locking of the gates" mentioned in the Mishnah must have been during daytime and cannot have been in the night, maybe not after sundown.

אַחֲוֵיהּ דְּאִימֵּיהּ דְּרִבִּי אָדָא הֲוָא צַיֵּיר גּוּלְתֵיהּ דְּרַב בְּצוֹמָא רַבָּא. אֲמַר לֵיהּ כַּד תֵּיחְמֵי שִׁימְשָׁא בְּרֵישׁ דִּקְלֵי תֵּיהַב לִי גּוּלְתִי דְּנַצְלֵי נְעִילַת שְׁעָרִים. מְחַלְּפָא שִׁיטָּתֵיהּ דְּרַב תַּמָּן הוּא אָמַר בִּנְעִילַת שַׁעֲרֵי שָׁמַיִם. וְכֹה אָמַר בִּנְעִילַת שַׁעֲרֵי הֵיכָל. אֲמַר רַב מַתָּנָה אַל יְדֵי דַּהֲוָה מַאֲרִיךְ רַב סַגִּין הֲוָה מַגִּיעַ לִנְעִילַת שַׁעֲרֵי שָׁמַיִם.

The maternal uncle of Rebbi Ada had rolled up the kaftan of Rav on the great fast. He said to him: When you see the sun on the top of the date palms, give me my kaftan so that we may pray the Locking of the Gates. The argument of Rav is inverted. There he says "the locking of the Gates of Heaven" and here he says "the locking of the gates of the Temple.[76]" Rav Mattanah said: Since Rav needed a lot of time to pray, he reached the Locking of the Gates of Heaven[77].

76 Since the sun is on the top of the date palms quite some time before sunset, Rav cannot possibly pray at the Locking of the Gates of Heaven. Hence, his deeds contradict his teachings.

77 It is clear from here that prayer may start before the closing of any gates, it just may not end earlier. This is the interpretation of Maimonides.

[Levi Ginzberg explains that Rav, in whose Yeshivah the Galilean *Minhag* of reciting poetic inserts was accepted, did spend the time until sundown in reciting prayers before the *Amidah* of *Neïlah*. This interpretation is impossible since "prayer" always means "the *Amidah*."]

נְעִילָה מַהוּ שֶׁתִּפְטוֹר שֶׁל עֶרֶב. רִבִּי אַבָּא וְרַב חוּנָא בְּשֵׁם רַב נְעִילָה פּוֹטֶרֶת שֶׁל עֶרֶב. אָמַר לֵיהּ רִבִּי אַבָּא לְרַב חוּנָא הֵיאַךְ הוּא מַזְכִּיר שֶׁל הַבְדָּלָה. אָמַר רִבִּי יוֹנָה לְרִבִּי אַבָּא הֵיאַךְ יְהוּא שֶׁבַע פּוֹטֶרֶת שְׁמוֹנֶה עֶשְׂרֵה. אֲמַר לֵיהּ וְלֹא כְּבָר אִיתְתִּיבַת. אֲמַר לֵיהּ בְּגִין דְּאִיתְתִּיבַת תִּיבְטִיל. אָמַר רִבִּי יוֹסֵי מַה דְּאַקְשֵׁי רִבִּי אַבָּא קָשֶׁה יְאוּת. מַה דְּאַקְשֵׁי רִבִּי יוֹנָה לָא קָשֶׁה יְאוּת. קַל הֵקִילוּ עָלָיו מִפְּנֵי תַעֲנִיתוֹ שֶׁיְּהוּא שֶׁבַע פּוֹטְרוֹת שְׁמוֹנֶה עֶשְׂרֵה. רִבִּי אַבָּא בַּר מָמָל אָמַר לַחֲבֵרַיָּא מָרַיי מִן כּוּלְּהוֹן שַׁמְעִית שֶׁאֵין נְעִילָה פּוֹטֶרֶת שֶׁל עֶרֶב. רִבִּי סִימוֹן בְּשֵׁם רִבִּי יְהוֹשֻׁעַ בֶּן לֵוִי אֵין נְעִילָה פּוֹטֶרֶת שֶׁל עֶרֶב. אָמַר רִבִּי יוֹסֵי בֵּרִבִּי בּוּן וְתַנֵּי רִבִּי חִייָא כֵן בְּכָל־יוֹם אָדָם מִתְפַּלֵּל שְׁמוֹנֶה עֶשְׂרֵה בְּמוֹצָאֵי שַׁבָּת וּבְמוֹצָאֵי יוֹם הַכִּיפּוּרִים וּבְמוֹצָאֵי תַעֲנִית צִיבּוּר.

May *Neïlah* free one from evening prayers? Rebbi Abba[78], Rav Ḥuna in the name of Rav: *Neïlah* frees one from evening prayers[79]. Rebbi Abba said to Rav Ḥuna: How may he mention *havdalah*[80]? Rebbi Jonah said to Rebbi Abba[81]: How may seven[82] free one from eighteen? He said to him, did I not already contradict it? He said to him: Because you contradicted it, should it be abandoned[83]? Rebbi Yose[84] said, what Rebbi Abba asked is truly difficult. What Rebbi Jonah asked is not at all difficult, they made it easy on people because of the fast, that seven should free one from eighteen. Rebbi Abba bar Mamal[85] said to his colleagues: From all of them I understand that *Neïlah* does not free one from evening prayers. Rebbi Simon in the name of Rebbi Joshua ben Levi: *Neïlah* does not free one from evening prayers. Rebbi Yose bar Abun said: Did not Rebbi Ḥiyya state this: "Every day one prays eighteen benedictions, including the end of Sabbath, end of Yom Kippur, and end of public fast days[86]."

78 Rebbi Abba, the student of Rav Huna, taught the statement in the name of Rav Huna when he came to Galilee and mentioned his own objection to Rav Huna's teaching.

79 According to Rav's original opinion that one prays at the Locking of the Gates of Heaven, *Neïlah* may be started only when evening prayers may already be said. It does not make sense to recite two prayers at one time.

80 It will be explained in Mishnah 5:2 that at the end of Sabbath or holiday work is permitted only if *havdalah* ("distinction") was recited in the evening *Amidah*. Hence, Rav's decision seems to be impossible. (Even though it is possible, but undesirable, to recite *havdalah* only on a cup of wine, in particular after Yom Kippur when no fire is lit for *havdalah*.)

81 Rebbi Jonah, of the fifth generation of Galilean Amoraïm, apparently knew Rebbi Abba of the third generation.

82 The seven benedictions of the holiday *Amidah*.

83 If somebody could find a satisfactory answer to your question, there would be no reason to abandon the ruling of Rav.

84 The Amora, contemporary of Rebbi Jonah.

85 Or, from Mamal (Khirbet Mamleh in the valley of Genezareth), Amora of the second/third generation. He seems to refer to the decision of Babylonian scholars, reported by Rebbi Abba the Babylonian. This contradicts the position of the Babli (*Yoma* 87b) which reports the opinion of Rav that *Neïlah* does free one from evening prayers and explains that, in the opinion of Rav, the evening *Amidah* is not really obligatory (and, hence, is eliminated by the contemporaneous *Neïlah*.) *Havdalah* is said over a cup of wine.

The next statement in the name of Rebbi Joshua ben Levi is strictly from the Land of Israel.

86 This *baraita* is a commentary on Mishnah 3; it explains the opinion of Rabban Gamliel that a full 18 benedictions have to be prayed three times every day (see the end of this Halakhah), including the end of Sabbath and Yom Kippur (against the opinion of Rebbi Aqiba that on those occasions there are 19 benedictions, including a separate benediction for *havdalah)*, and the end of public fasts for rain, to

exclude the opinion that *Neïlah* eliminates the evening prayer. The Israeli position is thus supported by a tannaïtic statement.

רִבִּי יִצְחָק בַּר נַחְמָן בְּשֵׁם רִבִּי יְהוֹשֻׁעַ בֶּן לֵוִי יוֹם הַכִּיפּוּרִים שֶׁחָל לִהְיוֹת בְּשַׁבָּת אַף עַל פִּי שֶׁאֵין נְעִילָה בְּשַׁבָּת מַזְכִּיר שֶׁל שַׁבָּת בִּנְעִילָה. אוֹסְפוּן עָלֵיהּ רֹאשׁ חֹדֶשׁ שֶׁחָל לִהְיוֹת בְּתַעֲנִית צִיבּוּר אַף עַל פִּי שֶׁאֵין נְעִילָה בְּרֹאשׁ חֹדֶשׁ מַזְכִּיר שֶׁל רֹאשׁ חֹדֶשׁ בִּנְעִילָה. רִבִּי סִימוֹן בְּשֵׁם רִבִּי יְהוֹשֻׁעַ בֶּן לֵוִי שַׁבָּת שֶׁחָלָה לִהְיוֹת בַּחֲנוּכָּה אַף עַל פִּי שֶׁאֵין מוּסָף בַּחֲנוּכָּה מַזְכִּיר שֶׁל חֲנוּכָּה בְּמוּסָף. אוֹסְפוּן עָלֵיהּ רֹאשׁ חֹדֶשׁ שֶׁחָל לִהְיוֹת בְּתוֹכָהּ אַף עַל פִּי שֶׁאֵין מוּסָף בַּחֲנוּכָּה מַזְכִּיר שֶׁל חֲנוּכָּה בְּמוּסָף.

Rebbi Isaac bar Naḥman in the name of Rebbi Joshua ben Levi[87]: If Yom Kippur happens to be on the Sabbath, one mentions Sabbath in *Neïlah* even though there is no *Neïlah* for Sabbath. They added to it: If the New Moon happens to be on a public fast-day, one mentions the New Moon in *Neïlah* even though there is no *Neïlah* for the New Moon[88]. Rebbi Simon in the name of Rebbi Joshua ben Levi: On a Sabbath that falls on Ḥanukkah, one mentions Ḥanukkah for *Musaph* even though there is no *Musaph* for Ḥanukkah. They added to it the New Moon that happens to be in it, one mentions Ḥanukkah for *Musaph* even though there is no *Musaph* for Ḥanukkah[89].

87 These rules are inserted here because they are about statements of Rebbi Joshua ben Levi in the order of *Amidah* prayers.

88 In general, fasting is forbidden on the days of the New Moon. The one exception is in the case of a prolonged draught when one fasts while praying for rain. In such a case, once they started the severe fasts, they continue Mondays and Thursdays without interruptions as explained in Tractate *Taäniot*.

89 The parallel in the Babli (*Šabbat* 34b) is in the name of Rebbi Joshua ben Levi only; there the reason is stated that "the day requires four (or five) prayers", and since the addition is required for some of the prayers it is required for all of them.

רֹאשׁ חֹדֶשׁ שֶׁחָל לִהְיוֹת בְּתַעֲנִית הֵיאַךְ מַזְכִּיר הוּא שֶׁל רֹאשׁ חֹדֶשׁ. רִבִּי זְעִירָא אָמַר בְּהוֹדָיָה. רִבִּי אַבָּא בַּר מָמָל אָמַר בַּעֲבוֹדָה. רִבִּי אֲבִינָא אָמַר אוֹמֵר בְּרָכָה רְבִיעִית. אָמַר רִבִּי אַבָּא מַה מָצִינוּ בְּכָל־מָקוֹם אוֹמְרָהּ בְּרָכָה רְבִיעִית. אַף כַּאן אוֹמְרָהּ בְּרָכָה רְבִיעִית. וְכֵן נָפַק עֲבְדָא כַּהֲדָה דְרִבִּי אַבָּא.

When the New Moon falls on a fast day, how does one mention the New Moon[90]? Rebbi Zeïra said, in "thanksgiving". Rebbi Abba bar Mamal said, in "Temple service". Rebbi Avina said, he says it as the fourth benediction. Rebbi Abba said, how do we find everywhere that he says it as the fourth benediction, here also as the fourth benediction. And so it was acted upon according to Rebbi Abba[91].

90 This paragraph is extremely difficult to understand and the greatest authorities of the Middle Ages, Rashba (R. Abraham ben Adrat, on Babli *Berakhot* 32b) and Rosh (R. Asher ben Yeḥiël, to Chap. 5, #10) felt compelled to emend the text. Since three of the four prayers of the New Moon are weekday prayers with an addition added in "Temple service" (רצה, the 16th benediction in the Yerushalmi version) as given later in Chapter 5, Halakhah 2, the only question can be about *Musaph*. However, we never hear that the particular inserts in the morning prayers of a fast day were recited also for *Musaph*. On the other hand, as Rosh points out, the previous paragraph certainly implies that the one benediction recited on *all* fast-days except Yom Kippur, not only on those for rain, known as עננו, must be recited also for *Musaph* since the day requires that the benediction be inserted in all prayers. One may at least understand the position of Rebbi Abba that on a fast day for rain which coincides with a day of the New Moon, one recites the usual *Musaph* with an additional fifth benediction which deals with the fast day, after the fourth for the New Moon. The dissenting opinions of Rebbis Zeïra and Abba bar Mamal seem to imply that *Musaph* on a fast day consisted of the introductory and final benedictions that are common to all prayers and the additional benedictions for the fast day, whereas the section on the New Moon, for which *Musaph* is recited in the first place, is moved from its regular place to an insert in either the 16th or the

17th (מודים, "thanksgiving", a place usually reserved for thanksgiving for past miracles) benediction.

91 A reported action on an opinion is the best proof that this is accepted practice, see Chap. 1, Note 125.

בְּמַה קוֹרְאִין. רִבִּי יוֹסֵי אוֹמֵר קוֹרִין בְּרָכוֹת וּקְלָלוֹת. אָמַר לֵיהּ רִבִּי מָנָא כְּגוֹן מוֹדַעְתּוֹן בּוֹ תַּעֲנִית רְבִיעִין עַל מֵעֵיהוֹן וְלֹא יָדְעִין דְּהִיא תַעֲנִיתָא. אָמַר לֵיהּ לְהוֹדִיעָךְ שֶׁקּוֹרִין בְּרָכוֹת וּקְלָלוֹת. רִבִּי יוּדָן קַפּוֹדָקִיָּא אָמַר קוֹמֵי רִבִּי יוֹסֵי בְּשֵׁם רִבִּי יוּדָה בֶּן פָּזִי קוֹרִין בְּרֹאשׁ חֹדֶשׁ. קָם רִבִּי יוֹסֵי עִם רִבִּי יוּדָה בֶּן פָּזִי. אָמַר לֵיהּ אַתְּ שְׁמַעְתְּ מֵאָבוּךְ הָדָא מִילְּתָא. אָמַר לֵיהּ אַבָּא לֹא הָיָה אוֹמֵר כֵּן אֶלָּא בְּעֵינְטָב עַל יְדֵי דְּאִינּוּן יָדְעִין דְּהוּא רֵישׁ יַרְחָא קוֹרִין בְּרֹאשׁ חֹדֶשׁ. הָא שְׁאָר כָּל־הַמְּקוֹמוֹת קוֹרִין בְּרָכוֹת וּקְלָלוֹת.

What does one read? Rebbi Yose said, one reads blessings and curses[92]. Rebbi Mana said to him: For example to tell them about the fast day? They are lying on their bellies[93] and should not know that it is a fast day? He said to him: To tell you that one reads blessings and curses[94]. Rebbi Yudan the Kappadokian[95] said before Rebbi Yose in the name of Rebbi Yehudah ben Pazi: One reads about the New Moon. Rebbi Yose met Rebbi Yehudah ben Pazi. He asked him: Did you hear that from your father? He said to him: My father did not say so, except that at Eyn Ṭab[96], since they know for sure that it is the New Moon, they read about the New Moon. Hence, at all other places one reads blessings and curses.

92 Both on the day of the New Moon and on fast days one reads in the Torah. The readings are explained in Mishnah *Megillah* 3:6. On the day of the New Moon, one reads abouts its sacrifices, *Num.* 28:11-15 (in Babylonia, 28:1-15), and on fast days for rain, blessings and curses, *Lev.* 26:3-46. (In Babylonia on other fast days, *Ex.* 32:11-14, 34:1-10). In Babylonia there would be no problem since there two Torah scrolls were used to read both portions, giving each person a larger share to read. However, in Israel the Torah was not read in the Babylonian one-year cycle but in an irregular three-year

cycle with shorter readings and where the regular reading was postponed for any special one. For example, on Sabbath Ḥanukkah, in Israel *only* the corresponding part of the dedication sacrifices (*Num.* 7) was read, whereas in Babylonia that was simply the reading from the second Torah scroll. Similarly, for a Sabbath New Moon one read in Israel only *Num.* 28:1-15 and not the regular Torah reading. Hence, there is a serious question which portion to read on the New Moon which is also a fast day.

93 Meaning, falling on their faces for private prayer after the *Amidah*, a penitential service (נפילת אפים) that is forbidden on semi-holidays like the day of the New Moon.

94 Not that the reading is to proclaim a fast day, but it is the reading appropriate for a fast day. If one already eliminates the prohibition of fasting on the New Moon, the occasion is so serious that the Torah reading also is eliminated.

95 A scholar from Kappadokia in Anatolia; he is always mentioned in connection with the Amora Rebbi Yose.

96 After the destruction of the Academy of Jabneh and the move of the Patriarchate to Galilee, the declaration of New Moons and New Years (before the publication of the permanent calendar) did always take place at Eyn Ṭab "beautiful spring", known in Greek as *Kallirrhoë* (καλλιρρόη "the beautifully flowing one"); it possibly is Ḥamat Gader. Since the sequence of 30 day and 29 day months was not determined beforehand, only at Eyn Ṭab was the day of the New Moon fixed. Everywhere else one knew that it was certainly a fast day and probably a day of the New Moon; the certain has precedence over the probable.

יִרְמְיָה סַפְרָא שָׁאַל לְרִבִּי יִרְמְיָה רֹאשׁ חֹדֶשׁ שֶׁחָל לִהְיוֹת בְּשַׁבָּת בְּמָה קוֹרִין. אָמַר לֵיהּ קוֹרִין בְּרֹאשׁ חֹדֶשׁ. אָמַר רִבִּי חֶלְבּוֹ קוֹמֵי רִבִּי אַמִּי וּמַתְנִיתָא אָמְרָה כֵן בַּכֹּל מַפְסִיקִין לְרָאשֵׁי חֳדָשִׁים לַחֲנוּכָּה וּלְפוּרִים.

Jeremiah the Scribe[97] asked before Rebbi Jeremiah: What does one read if the day of the New Moon is a Sabbath? He said to him: One reads about the New Moon. Rebbi Ḥelbo said before Rebbi Ammi: The Mishnah says so (*Megillah* 3:6), "One interrupts for everything, for New Moons, for Ḥanukkah, and for Purim."

97 A scholar not otherwise known. As explained before, in Israel one interrupted the regular sequence of Torah reading, not just the reading for the *maphtir* as in Babylonia. The parallel discussion of this and the next paragraph is in Babli *Megillah* 29b.

יִצְחָק סְחוֹרָא שָׁאַל לְרִבִּי יִצְחָק רֹאשׁ חֹדֶשׁ שֶׁחָל לִהְיוֹת בַּחֲנוּכָּה בְּמַה קוֹרִין. אָמַר לֵיהּ קוֹרִין שְׁלֹשָׁה בְּרֹאשׁ חֹדֶשׁ וְאֶחָד בַּחֲנוּכָּה. רִבִּי פִּינְחָס וְרִבִּי סִימוֹן רִבִּי אַבָּא בַּר זְמִינָא מָטוּ בָהּ בְּשֵׁם רִבִּי אֶבְדִּימִי דְּמִן חֵיפָה קוֹרִין שְׁלֹשָׁה בַּחֲנוּכָּה וְאֶחָד בְּרֹאשׁ חֹדֶשׁ. לְהוֹדִיעָךְ שֶׁלֹּא בָּא הָרְבִיעִי אֶלָּא מֵחֲמַת רֹאשׁ חֹדֶשׁ. בַּר שֶׁלֶמְיָה סַפְרָא שָׁאַל לְרִבִּי מָנָא הַגַּע עַצְמָךְ שֶׁחָל רֹאשׁ חֹדֶשׁ שֶׁל חֲנוּכָּה לִהְיוֹת בְּשַׁבָּת וְלֹא שִׁבְעָה אִינּוּן קוֹרִין. אִית לָךְ מֵימַר שֶׁלֹּא בָּא הָרְבִיעִי אֶלָּא מֵחֲמַת רֹאשׁ חֹדֶשׁ. שְׁאִילְתִּינְהוּ לְסַפְרָא אָמַר לֵיהּ וַהֲדָא שְׁאִילְתָא דְּסָפָר.

Isaac the trader asked Rebbi Isaac: What does one read on a New Moon that falls in Ḥanukkah? He said to him: Three for the New Moon and one for Ḥanukkah. Rebbi Phineas and Rebbi Simon, Rebbi Abba bar Zamina[98] brought it in the name of Rebbi Eudaimon of Haifa[99]: Three read of Ḥanukka and one of the New Moon, to tell you that the fourth one comes only because of the New Moon[100]. Bar Shelemiah the scribe asked Rebbi Mana: Think of it, if the New Moon of Ḥanukkah falls on a Sabbath, do not seven read? How can you say, to tell you that the fourth one comes only because of the New Moon? They asked the scribe[101]; he said to him: That is a true question of a scribe.

98 A student of Rebbi Zeïra.

99 A teacher of Rebbi Zeïra, Amora of the second/third generation. In the Babli (*Megillah* 29b) he is called Rebbi Dimi.

100 Usually on Ḥanukkah only three people read from the Torah, since it is a regular workday. On the day of the New Moon, four persons read since it is a day with a *Musaph* sacrifice in the Temple. On the Sabbath, seven read (and the *maphtir* reads one additional portion). Hence, it seems impossible that the fourth person should read

about Ḥanukkah.

101 This phrase is missing in the parallels (Yerushalmi *Taäniot* 4:1, *Megillah* 3:4) but it may be justified to assume that the question was not his, but that he was asked by others on his authority as scribe to the rabbi. Most probably, as conjectured by Levi Ginzberg, it is a second version of Rebbi Mana's answer, that this is a really stupid question from a scribe who has not learned to think by himself: Since one interrupts for the Sabbath, it is clear that the reading of the New Moon, which occurs at least 16 times a year, has precedence over Ḥanukkah which occurs only 8 times.

רִבִּי מִיפְקֵד לְאַבְדָּן אֲמוֹרֵיהּ אַכְרִיז קוֹמֵי צִיבּוּרָא מַאן דְּמַצְלִי יַצְלִי דְּרַמְשָׁא עַד יוֹמָא קָאִים. רִבִּי חִיָּא בַּר וָוא מְפַקֵּד לַאֲמוֹרֵיהּ אַכְרִיז קוֹמֵי צִיבּוּרָא מַאן דְּמַצְלִי יַצְלִי דְּרַמְשָׁא עַד יוֹמָא קָאִים. אָמַר רִבִּי חֲנִינָא מָשְׁכֵנִי רִבִּי יִשְׁמָעֵאל בֵּי רִבִּי יוֹסֵי אֵצֶל פּוּנְדּוּק אֶחָד אָמַר לִי כַּאן נִתְפַּלֵּל אַבָּא שֶׁל לֵילֵי שַׁבָּת בְּעֶרֶב שַׁבָּת. אָמַר רִבִּי אַמִּי רִבִּי יוֹחָנָן פְּלִיג וְלָא הֲוָה צְרִיךְ מִפְלְגָה עַל הָדָא לָמָּה שֶׁכֵּן מוֹסִיפִין מֵחוֹל עַל הַקּוֹדֶשׁ. וְעוֹד דְּסַלְקוּן חַמָּרַיָּא מִן עֲרָב לְצִיפּוֹרִין וְאָמְרִין כְּבַר שַׁבָּת רִבִּי חֲנִינָא בֶּן דּוֹסָא בְּעִירוֹ. וִידָה אָמְרָה דָא דְּאָמַר רִבִּי חֲנִינָא מָשְׁכֵנִי רִבִּי יִשְׁמָעֵאל בֵּי רִבִּי יוֹסֵי אֵצֶל פּוּנְדּוּק אֶחָד אָמַר לִי כַּאן נִתְפַּלֵּל אַבָּא שֶׁל מוֹצָאֵי שַׁבָּת בְּשַׁבָּת וְאַף עֲלָהּ לָא הֲוָה צְרִיךְ מִפְלְגָה דְּרִבִּי מִיפְקֵד לְאַבְדָּן אֲמוֹרֵיהּ אַכְרִיז קוֹמֵי צִיבּוּרָא מַאן דְּמַצְלִי יַצְלִי דְּרַמְשָׁא עַד יוֹמָא קָאִים. רִבִּי חִיָּא בַּר וָוא מְפַקֵּד לַאֲמוֹרֵיהּ אַכְרִיז קוֹמֵי צִיבּוּרָא מַאן דְּמַצְלִי יַצְלִי דְּרַמְשָׁא עַד יוֹמָא קָאִים. דְּבֵית רִבִּי יַנַּאי אָמְרִין עָלָה אָדָם עַל מִיטָּתוֹ אֵין מַטְרִיחִין אוֹתוֹ לֵירֵד. אֲמַר רִבִּי זְעִירָא כָּל מַאן דַּהֲוֵינָא עֲבַד כֵּן הֲוֵינָא מְפָחֵד בַּלֵּילְיָא. לֵית לָךְ אֶלָּא כַּהָדָא דְּרִבִּי מִיפְקֵד לְאַבְדָּן אֲמוֹרֵיהּ אַכְרִיז קוֹמֵי צִיבּוּרָא מַאן דְּמַצְלִי יַצְלִי עַד יוֹמָא קַיָּם. רִבִּי חִיָּא בַּר וָוא מְפַקֵּד לַאֲמוֹרֵיהּ כו'.

Rebbi[102] commanded his speaker Abdan[103]: Proclaim before the congregation that he who wants to pray, should pray evening prayers as long as it is still daylight. Rebbi Ḥiyya bar Abba[104] commanded his speaker: Proclaim before the congregation that he who wants to pray should pray evening prayers as long as it is still daylight. Rebbi Ḥanina said: Rebbi Ismael ben Rebbi Yose[105] drew me to an inn and said to me: Here my father prayed Saturday (Friday night) prayers on Friday. Rebbi Ammi said: Rebbi Yoḥanan disagrees[106] but he should not have disagreed since one adds from the profane to the holy time[107]; in addition, donkey drivers come from Arab[108] to Sepphoris and say, Rebbi Ḥanina ben Dosa already did consecrate the Sabbath in his town. But so it has been said, that Rebbi Ḥanina said: Rebbi Ismael ben Rebbi Yose drew me to an inn and said to me, here my father prayed Saturday night prayers on the Sabbath. But even with that he should not have disagreed, since Rebbi commanded his speaker Abdan: Proclaim before the congregation that he who wants to pray should pray evening prayers as long as it is still daylight. Rebbi Ḥiyya bar Abba commanded his speaker: Proclaim before the congregation that he who wants to pray should pray evening prayers as long as it is still daylight. In the house of Rebbi Yannaï they said: If a man went to bed, one does not bother him to get up[109]. Rebbi Zeïra said, all the time that I followed this rule, I was afraid in the night[110]. You have only what Rebbi commanded his speaker Abdan: Proclaim before the congregation that he who wants to pray should pray evening prayers as long as it is still daylight. Rebbi Ḥiyya bar Abba commanded etc.

102 After the discussion of the side issues introduced by the mention of *Neïlah* and fast days, the discussion returns to the last part of the Mishnah. The text appears in modified form also in *Bereshit rabba* 8:10, *Pesiqta rabbati* 23; the parallel in Babli *Berakhot* 27b disagrees fundamentally with the practice explained here.

According to the Mishnah, the time of *Minḥah* is until $^5/_4$ hours before sundown for Rebbi Yehudah and until sundown for the other sages. As a corollary, the time of evening prayers starts at $^5/_4$ hours before sundown for Rebbi Yehudah and at sundown for the others. Since Rebbi was a student of Rebbi Yehudah, it is possible that he simply followed his teacher and himself was followed by his own student R. Ḥiyya. Perhaps it is assumed here that we already know the result of the next paragraph, that evening prayer is not obligatory (this is also accepted in the Babli), and that because of this one permits evening prayer before sundown because it is a minor obligation and in Galilee apparently was not recited in the synagogue. This is the medieval Ashkenazic tradition. [The Babli states that evening prayers should be said in the night, that this is also Rebbi's position, but that in case of error, under very dark clouds, one does not have to repeat the prayer which in Babylonia was recited in the synagogue.]

103 It seems that his name was Abba Yudan. In the talmudic academies, the head of the academy never raised his voice to speak to a large class; he explained what he had to say to one or more speakers, *Amoraïm*, who spoke in a loud voice. It is probable that the situation described here is that of Sabbath afternoon when everybody came to listen to the sermon, since the audience is called "congregation" and not "students", who were the weekday audience.

104 He is Rebbi Ḥiyya the Great, in Rebbi's Academy, not the student of R. Yoḥanan.

105 Ben Ḥalaphta, the Tanna.

106 And insists that Evening prayers may be said only after sundown.

107 It is an obligation to start the Sabbath (and holidays) before sundown and end it after sundown, not exactly at sundown. This obligation is not spelled out in the Babli; its source is here in the Yerushalmi.

108 The village of Arrabeh, North of Kafr Kanah in lower Galilee.

109 If one forgot to recite evening prayers. R. Yannai certainly agrees that evening prayers are not obligatory.

110 Even though evening prayers are not obligatory, it is the practice to recite them for peace of mind, subject to the leniencies of Rebbi and Rebbi Ḥiyya.

אָמַר רִבִּי יַעֲקֹב בַּר אַבָּא תַּנֵּיי תַּמָּן תְּפִילַּת הָעֶרֶב מַהוּ. רַבָּן גַּמְלִיאֵל אָמַר חוֹבָה. רִבִּי יְהוֹשֻׁעַ אָמַר רְשׁוּת. אָמַר רִבִּי חֲנִינָא אַתְיָן אִילֵּין פַּלְגְּוָתָא כְּאִינּוּן פַּלְגְּוָתָא מָאן דָּמַר חוֹבָה אֵין נְעִילָה פוֹטֶרֶת שֶׁל עֶרֶב. וּמָאן דָּמַר רְשׁוּת נְעִילָה פוֹטֶרֶת שֶׁל עֶרֶב.

Rebbi Jacob bar Abba[111] said: There, they did state, what is the status of evening prayer? Rabban Gamliel said, it is obligatory. Rebbi Joshua[112] said, it is voluntary. Rebbi Ḥanina said, this difference parallels the other difference: He who holds that evening prayer is obligatory, holds that *Neïlah* does not free one from evening prayers. He who holds that it is voluntary, holds that *Neïlah* frees one from evening prayers[113].

111 An Israeli Amora of the second generation, student of Rav in Babylonia. His tradition from "there" (Babylonia) and the following story are reported at great length in Babli 27b.

112 In a dispute between Rebbi Joshua and Rabban Gamliel, practice always follows Rebbi Joshua. There is never a doubt that the recitation of *Shema'* is obligatory.

113 But, as stated before, evening prayers are still needed for mental health.

מַעֲשֶׂה בְּתַלְמִיד אֶחָד שֶׁבָּא וְשָׁאַל אֶת רִבִּי יְהוֹשֻׁעַ תְּפִילַּת הָעֶרֶב מַהוּ. אָמַר לֵיהּ רְשׁוּת. בָּא וְשָׁאַל אֶת רִבִּי גַּמְלִיאֵל תְּפִילַּת הָעֶרֶב מַהוּ. אָמַר לֵיהּ חוֹבָה. אָמַר לוֹ וְהָא רִבִּי יְהוֹשֻׁעַ אָמַר לִי רְשׁוּת. אָמַר לוֹ מָחָר כְּשֶׁאֶכָּנֵס לְבֵית הַוַּעַד עֲמוֹד וּשְׁאוֹל אֶת הַהֲלָכָה (fol. 7d) הַזֹּאת. לְמָחָר עָמַד אוֹתוֹ הַתַּלְמִיד וְשָׁאַל אֶת רַבָּן גַּמְלִיאֵל תְּפִילַּת הָעֶרֶב מַהוּ. אָמַר לוֹ חוֹבָה. אָמַר לוֹ וְהָא רִבִּי יְהוֹשֻׁעַ אָמַר לִי רְשׁוּת. אָמַר רַבָּן גַּמְלִיאֵל לְרִבִּי יְהוֹשֻׁעַ אַתְּ הוּא אוֹמֵר רְשׁוּת אָמַר לֵיהּ לָאו. אָמַר לוֹ עֲמוֹד עַל רַגְלֶיךָ וְיָעִידוּךָ. וְהָיָה רַבָּן גַּמְלִיאֵל יוֹשֵׁב וְדוֹרֵשׁ וְרִבִּי יְהוֹשֻׁעַ עוֹמֵד עַל רַגְלָיו עַד שֶׁרִנְּנוּ כָּל הָעָם וְאָמְרוּ לְרִבִּי חֻצְפִּית הַתּוּרְגְּמָן הַפְטֵר אֶת הָעָם. אָמְרוּ לְרִבִּי זֵינוֹן הַחַזָּן אֱמוֹר הַתְחֵיל וְאָמַר הַתְחִילוּ. וְעָמְדוּ כָּל־הָעָם עַל רַגְלֵיהֶם וְאָמְרוּ לוֹ כִּי עַל מִי לֹא עָבְרָה רָעָתְךָ תָּמִיד. הָלְכוּ וּמִינּוּ אֶת רִבִּי אֶלְעָזָר בֶּן עֲזַרְיָה בִּישִׁיבָה בֶּן שֵׁשׁ עֶשְׂרֵה שָׁנָה וְנִתְמַלֵּא כָּל־רֹאשׁוֹ שֵׂיבָה. וְהָיָה רִבִּי עֲקִיבָא יוֹשֵׁב וּמִצְטָעֵר וְאָמַר לֹא שֶׁהוּא בֶּן תּוֹרָה יוֹתֵר מִמֶּנִּי אֶלָּא שֶׁהוּא בֶּן גְּדוֹלִים יוֹתֵר מִמֶּנִּי. אַשְׁרֵי אָדָם שֶׁזָּכוּ לוֹ אֲבוֹתָיו אַשְׁרֵי אָדָם שֶׁיֵּשׁ לוֹ יָתֵד בְּמִי לְהִתָּלוֹת בָּהּ. וְכִי מַה הָיְתָה יְתֵידָתוֹ שֶׁל רִבִּי אֶלְעָזָר בֶּן עֲזַרְיָה שֶׁהָיָה דוֹר עֲשִׂירִי לְעֶזְרָא. וְכַמָּה סַפְסָלִין הָיוּ שָׁם. רִבִּי יַעֲקֹב בֶּן סִיסִי אָמַר שְׁמוֹנִים סַפְסָלִים הָיוּ

שָׁם שֶׁל תַּלְמִידֵי חֲכָמִים חוּץ מִן הָעוֹמְדִין לַאֲחוֹרֵי הַגֶּדֶר. רִבִּי יוֹסֵי בֵּירִבִּי אָבוּן אָמַר שְׁלֹשׁ מֵאוֹת הָיוּ שָׁם חוּץ מִן הָעוֹמְדִין לַאֲחוֹרֵי הַגֶּדֶר. כְּיֵי דְּתַנִּינָן תַּמָּן בְּיוֹם שֶׁהוֹשִׁיבוּ אֶת רִבִּי אֶלְעָזָר בֶּן עֲזַרְיָה בִישִׁיבָה. תַּמָּן תַּנִּינָן זֶה דָרַשׁ רִבִּי אֶלְעָזָר בֶּן עֲזַרְיָה לִפְנֵי חֲכָמִים בְּכֶרֶם בְּיַבְנֶה. וְכִי כֶּרֶם הָיָה שָׁם אֶלָּא אֵלוּ תַּלְמִידֵי חֲכָמִים שֶׁהָיוּ עֲשׂוּיִין שׁוּרוֹת שׁוּרוֹת כְּכֶרֶם. מִיַּד הָלַךְ לוֹ רַבָּן גַּמְלִיאֵל אֵצֶל כָּל אֶחָד וְאֶחָד לְפַייְסוֹ בְּבֵיתוֹ. אֲזַל גַּבֵּי רִבִּי יְהוֹשֻׁעַ אַשְׁכְּחֵיהּ יְתִיב עֲבֵד מְחָטִין. אֲמַר לֵיהּ אִילֵּין אַתְּ חַיֵּי. אֲמַר לֵיהּ וְעַד כְּדוֹן אַתְּ בָּעֵי מִידְעֵי. אוֹי לְדוֹר שֶׁאַתָּה פַּרְנָסוֹ. אָמַר לוֹ נַעֲנֵיתִי לָךְ. וְשָׁלְחוּן גַּבֵּי רִבִּי אֶלְעָזָר בֶּן עֲזַרְיָה חַד קַצָּר. וְאִית דְּאָמְרִין רִבִּי עֲקִיבָא הֲוָה. אָמַר לוֹ מִי שֶׁהוּא מַזֶּה בֶּן מַזֶּה יַזֶּה מִי שֶׁאֵינוֹ לֹא מַזֶּה וְלֹא בֶּן מַזֶּה יֵימַר לְמַזֶּה בֶּן מַזֶּה מֵימֶיךָ מֵי מְעָרָה וְאֶפְרָךְ אֵפֶר מַקְלֶה. אָמַר לוֹ נִתְרַצִּיתֶם אֲנִי וְאַתֶּם נַשְׁכִּים לְפִתְחוֹ שֶׁל רַבָּן גַּמְלִיאֵל. אַף עַל פִּי כֵן לֹא הוֹרִידוּ אוֹתוֹ מִגְּדוּלָּתוֹ אֶלָּא מִינּוּ אוֹתוֹ אַב בֵּית דִּין.

It happened that one student came and asked Rebbi Joshua: What is about evening prayer? He said to him: It is voluntary. He asked Rabban Gamliel: What is about evening prayer? He said to him: It is obligatory. He said to him: But Rebbi Joshua told me that it was voluntary. He said to him: Tomorrow, when I enter the assembly hall, stand up and ask me about this practice. The next day, this student stood up and asked Rabban Gamliel: What is about evening prayer? He said to him: It is obligatory. He said to him: But Rebbi Joshua told me that it was voluntary. Rabban Gamliel said to Rebbi Joshua: Are you the one who says it is voluntary? He answered him: No[114]. He said to him: Stand up on your feet so that they may testify against you. Then Rabban Gamliel was sitting down and lecturing while Rebbi Joshua was standing up until the people started talking and said to Rebbi Ḥuẓpit the interpreter[115]: Send the people home. They said to Rebbi Zenon the *ḥazan*[116]: Start! He said: Start! All the people stood up and said to him (*Nahum* 3:19): "Certainly, on whom did your evil not pass always?" They went and appointed[117] Rebbi Eleazar ben Azariah to the Yeshivah when he was 16 years old[118]; his head became all white. Rebbi Aqiba sat and was sad; he said, not that he is a greater Torah scholar than I am, but he comes from a greater family than I do; hail to the man whose forefathers created merit for him, hail to the man who has a peg to hang on to. What was Rebbi Eleazar ben Azariah's peg? He was the tenth generation after Ezra[119].

How many seats were there[120]? Rebbi Jacob ben Sisi[121] said: Eighty seats were there of accomplished scholars, not to count those standing behind the railing. Rebbi Yose ben Rebbi Abun said 300 were there, not to count those standing behind the railing. As we have stated there (Mishnah *Zebaḥim* 1:3) "On the day Rebbi Eleazar ben Azariah was appointed to the Academy."[122] There (Mishnah *Ketubot* 4:6) we have stated: "This inference did Rebbi Eleazar ben Azariah present before the sages at the vineyard of Jabneh." Was there a vineyard? It means that the scholars sat there in rows like vines in a vineyard.

Rabban Gamliel went immediately to pacify each one in his house. He came to Rebbi Joshua and found him occupied with the making of needles[123]. He asked him: This is how you earn your living? He answered him: Until now you did not know? Woe to the generation whose caretaker you are! He said to him: I humble myself before you. They sent a washerman to Rebbi Eleazar ben Azariah, but some say that it was Rebbi Aqiba. He told him: The sprinkler, son of a sprinkler, should sprinkle. Should anyone who is neither a sprinkler nor the son of a sprinkler say to the sprinkler: your water is water from a cave and your ashes are ashes from a fireplace[124]? He said to him: You made your peace with him! I and you shall go in the morning to Rabban Gamliel's door. Nevertheless they did not remove him from his dignity but made him head of the court.

114 Since Rabban Gamliel went to great lengths to insist on uniformity, not only of practice, but also of doctrine, Rebbi Joshua, the most important member of the generation preceding Rabban Gamliel, did not want to start a quarrel.

115 The "Amora" of Rabban Gamliel, one of the "Ten Martyrs".

116 The *ḥazan* was not only the reader in congregational prayers, but also the general organizer of religious affairs. In outlying communities he was the ritual slaughterer and the conduit through whom questions of religious practice were addressed to the Academies. Here it seems that he had to recite the prayer at the end of a study session discussed in the next Halakhah, that it was customary to start with a Bible verse and that the people spontaneously chose one which was a curse on the speaker.

117 In the Yerushalmi, "appoint" (מנה) is the equivalent of the Babli's "ordain" (סמך). Rebbi Eleazar ben Azariah was ordained the same day he was appointed head of the Synhedrion.

118 In pre-war Poland, that was the usual age for *sĕmikha.* (In the Babli, the age is given as 18 years.) The difficulty of this age determination is discussed at length by the author in *The Scholar's Haggadah*, p. 265-266.

119 His family was of equal rank with that of the Patriarch. In the Rome manuscript, there is an addition that he alone was as rich as the Patriarch (and, hence, had the money to deal with the Roman government).

120 This insertion is more detailed in the Babli (28a), where the question is discussed how many seats *were added* when, with the deposition of Rabban Gamliel, also his elitistic exclusionary policies of admission to the Yeshivah were scrapped. The insertion is Amoraïc, as is shown by the names of the authorities and the quotes from the Mishnah. The previous paragraph and the following one are Tannaïtic.

121 A Galilean Amora of the fourth generation, contemporary of the Amora R. Yose, older than R. Yose ben R. Abun.

122 In the tradition of the Babli, all of tractate *Idiut* was presented on that day.

123 In the Babli, his profession is given as charcoal-burner.

124 The argument is taken from the ritual of the ashes of the red heifer. The ashes have to be given into "living" water, drawn from a stream. Sprinkling the water was not a reserved profession, but it may be assumed that the care of the ashes, and

supervision of the cleansing ritual, was in the hands of the priests, of whom R. Eleazar ben Azariah was one. Hence, it was intimated to him that just as a non-Cohen should not presume upon his duties, so an outsider should not presume upon the duties of the Patriarch.

משנה ב: רִבִּי נְחוּנְיָה בֶּן הַקָּנָה הָיָה מִתְפַּלֵּל בִּכְנִיסָתוֹ לְבֵית הַמִּדְרָשׁ וּבִיצִיאָתוֹ תְּפִילָּה קְצָרָה. אָמְרוּ לוֹ מַה טִיבָהּ שֶׁל תְּפִילָּה זוֹ. אָמַר לָהֶן בִּכְנִיסָתִי אֲנִי מִתְפַּלֵּל שֶׁלֹּא תֶאֱרַע תְּקָלָה עַל יָדִי וּבִיצִיאָתִי אֲנִי נוֹתֵן הוֹדָיָה עַל חֶלְקִי.

Mishnah 2: Rebbi Neḥoniah ben Haqqanah[125] used to recite a short prayer when he entered and when he left the house of study. They asked him, what kind of prayer is this? He told them: When I enter, I pray that no mishap should come through me and when I leave I give thanks for my lot.

125 A Tanna of the second generation, teacher of Rebbi Ismael. In Medieval mysticism he is credited with authorship of *Sefer Habahir* and many mystical teachings.

הלכה ב: בִּכְנִיסָתוֹ מַהוּ אוֹמֵר יְהִי רָצוֹן מִלְּפָנֶיךָ יי אֱלֹהַי וֵאלֹהֵי אֲבוֹתַי שֶׁלֹּא אַקְפִּיד כְּנֶגֶד חֲבֵרַי וְלֹא חֲבֵרַי יַקְפִּידוּ כְנֶגְדִּי. שֶׁלֹּא נְטַמֵּא אֶת הַטָּהוֹר וְלֹא נְטָהֵר אֶת הַטָּמֵא. שֶׁלֹּא נֶאֱסוֹר אֶת הַמּוּתָּר וְלֹא נַתִּיר אֶת הָאָסוּר. וְנִמְצֵאתִי מִתְבַּיֵּשׁ לְעוֹלָם הַזֶּה וּלְעוֹלָם הַבָּא. וּבִיצִיאָתוֹ מַהוּ אוֹמֵר מוֹדֶה אֲנִי לְפָנֶיךָ יי אֱלֹהַי וֵאלֹהֵי אֲבוֹתַי שֶׁנָּתַתָּ חֶלְקִי מִיּוֹשְׁבֵי בֵית הַמִּדְרָשׁ וּבָתֵּי כְנֵסִיּוֹת וְלֹא נָתַתָּ חֶלְקִי בְּבָתֵּי תֵּרַטִּיּוֹת וּבְבָתֵּי קִרְקְסִיּוֹת שֶׁאֲנִי עָמֵל וְהֵן עֲמֵלִין. אֲנִי שׁוֹקֵד וְהֵן שׁוֹקְדִין. אֲנִי עָמֵל לִירֵשׁ גַּן עֵדֶן. וְהֵן עֲמֵלִין לִבְאֵר שַׁחַת שֶׁנֶּאֱמַר כִּי לֹא תַעֲזוֹב נַפְשִׁי לִשְׁאוֹל לֹא תִתֵּן חֲסִידְךָ לִרְאוֹת שָׁחַת.

Halakhah 2: What does he say when he enters[126]? May it be Your pleasure, o Eternal, my God and God of my fathers, that I should not be offended by my colleagues and my colleagues should not be offended by me; that we should not declare impure that which is pure, nor declare pure what is impure; that we should not forbid that which is permitted, nor permit what is forbidden and I would be ashamed in this world and the world to come.

What does he say when he leaves? I thank You, o Eternal, my God and God of my fathers, that You ordained my lot with those who sit in the house of study and in synagogues and You did not ordain my lot in theaters and circuses[127]. For I toil and they toil, I am diligent and they are diligent. I toil to inherit the Garden of Eden, but they toil for the pit of destruction as it is said (*Ps.* 16:10): "Certainly, You will not abandon my soul to the pit, You will not let Your pious ones see destruction."

126 The text in the Babli (28b) is similar in content but different in formulation. The manuscripts of the Babli and the quotes in Medieval authors differ widely in language.

127 This does *not* imply that Rebbi Neḥonia accepted the doctrine of predestination as conjectured by L. Finkelstein (מבוא לפרקי אבות ואבות דרבי נתן, ניו יורק תשי״א, נספח ב).

רִבִּי פְּדָת בְּשֵׁם רִבִּי יַעֲקֹב בַּר אִידִי רִבִּי אֶלְעָזָר הָיָה מִתְפַּלֵּל שָׁלֹשׁ תְּפִילּוֹת. לְאַחַר תְּפִילָּתוֹ מַהוּ אוֹמֵר. יְהִי רָצוֹן מִלְּפָנֶיךָ יי אֱלֹהַי וֵאלֹהֵי אֲבוֹתַי שֶׁלֹּא תַעֲלֶה שִׂנְאָתֵינוּ עַל לֵב אָדָם וְלֹא שִׂנְאַת אָדָם תַּעֲלֶה עַל לִבֵּנוּ. וְלֹא תַעֲלֶה קִנְאָתֵינוּ עַל לֵב אָדָם וְלֹא קִנְאַת אָדָם תַּעֲלֶה עַל לִבֵּנוּ. וּתְהֵא תוֹרָתְךָ מְלַאכְתֵּנוּ כָּל־יְמֵי חַיֵּינוּ וְיִהְיוּ דְּבָרֵינוּ תַחֲנוּנִים לְפָנֶיךָ. רִבִּי חִיָּיא בַּר אַבָּא מוֹסִיף וּתְיַחֵד לְבָבֵינוּ לְיִרְאָה אֶת שְׁמֶךָ וּתְרַחֲקֵנוּ מִכָּל־מַה שֶּׁשָּׂנֵאתָ וּתְקָרְבֵנוּ לְכָל מַה שֶּׁאָהַבְתָּ וְתַעֲשֶׂה עִמָּנוּ צְדָקָה לְמַעַן שְׁמֶךָ.

Rebbi Pedat in the name of Rebbi Jacob bar Idi[128]: Rebbi Eleazar used to recite three prayers. What did he say after his prayer? May it please You, o Eternal, my God and God of my fathers, that nobody should come to hate us in his heart nor should we hate anybody in our hearts, that nobody should be envious of us nor we envious of anybody. May Your Torah be our occupation all the days of our life and may our words be supplications before You. Rebbi Ḥiyya bar Abba added: Make our hearts singleminded in the fear of Your name, remove us from all You hate and bring us close to all You love, and deal with us in charity for Your name's sake.

128 A list of similar prayers after the *Amidah* is given in the Babli, 16b-17a, where a different text appears in the name of Rebbi Eleazar. It is remarkable that Rebbi Pedat, son of Rebbi Eleazar (ben Pedat), gives his father's text in the name of Rebbi Jacob bar Idi, student of Rebbi Yoḥanan and colleague of Rebbi Eleazar, rather than from his own knowledge of his father's practices. He also emphasizes that his father prayed three times, including evening prayers, as noted in the previous Halakhah.

דְּבֵית רִבִּי יַנַּאי אָמְרִין הַנֵּעוֹר מִשְּׁנָתוֹ צָרִיךְ לוֹמַר בָּרוּךְ אַתָּה יי מְחַיֵּה הַמֵּתִים. רִבּוֹנִי חָטָאתִי לָךְ יְהִי רָצוֹן מִלְּפָנֶיךָ יי אֱלֹהַי שֶׁתִּתֵּן לִי לֵב טוֹב חֵלֶק טוֹב יֵצֶר טוֹב סֵבֶר טוֹב שֵׁם טוֹב עַיִן טוֹבָה וְנֶפֶשׁ טוֹב וְנֶפֶשׁ שְׁפֵלָה וְרוּחַ נְמוּכָה. אַל יִתְחַלֵּל שִׁמְךָ בָּנוּ אַל תַּעֲשֵׂינוּ שִׂיחָה בְּפִי כָל הַבְּרִיּוֹת וְאַל תְּהִי אַחֲרִיתֵנוּ לְהַכְרִית וְלֹא תִקְוָתֵינוּ לְמַפַּח נֶפֶשׁ. וְאַל תַּצְרִיכֵנוּ לִידֵי מַתְּנַת בָּשָׂר וָדָם וְאַל תִּמְסוֹר מְזוֹנוֹתֵינוּ בִּידֵי בָשָׂר וָדָם שֶׁמַּתְּנָתָם מְעוּטָה וְחֶרְפָּתָם מְרוּבָּה. וְתֵן חֶלְקֵנוּ בְּתוֹרָתָךְ עִם עוֹשֵׂי רְצוֹנָךְ. בְּנֵה בֵיתָךְ הֵיכָלָךְ עִירָךְ מִקְדָּשָׁךְ בִּמְהֵרָה בְיָמֵינוּ.

In the house of Rebbi Yannai they say: He who awakes from his sleep must say "Praised are You, o Eternal, Who resurrects the dead. My Lord, I sinned before You. May it please You, o Eternal, my God, that You might give me a good heart, good part, good inclinations, good hope, good repute, benevolent eye, good soul, meek soul and meek spirit. Your Name should not be desecrated by us; do not make us a byword in the mouths of all creatures; our future should not end in destruction, nor our hope in sorrow. Do not let us need the gifts of flesh and blood, do not deliver our subsistence into the hands of flesh and blood, for their gifts are small but the shame is big. Give our part in Your Torah with those who do Your will, build Your house, Your Temple, Your city, Your Sanctuary quickly, in our days[129].

129 This paragraph appears among the morning benedictions in the *Siddur* of Rav Amram Gaon. In modern prayer rites, the corresponding Babylonian prayer (Babli 60b) is universally accepted.

רִבִּי חִייָא בַּר וָוא מַצְלִי יְהִי רָצוֹן מִלְּפָנֶיךָ יי אֱלֹהֵינוּ וֵאלֹהֵי אֲבוֹתֵינוּ שֶׁתִּתֵּן בְּלִבֵּינוּ לַעֲשׂוֹת תְּשׁוּבָה שְׁלֵימָה לְפָנֶיךָ שֶׁלֹּא נֵבוֹשׁ מֵאֲבוֹתֵינוּ לְעוֹלָם הַבָּא. רִבִּי יוּדָן בֵּי רִבִּי יִשְׁמָעֵאל קָבַע לָהּ לַאֲמוֹרֵיהּ דְּיֵימַר בָּתַר פִּרְשָׁתֵיהּ כֵּן.

Rebbi Ḥiyya bar Abba prayed[130]: May it please You, o Eternal, our God and God of our fathers, that You may put into our hearts to do complete repentance before You so that we should not be ashamed before our forefathers in the World to Come. Rebbi Yudan ben Rebbi Ismael[131] made it permanent that his Amora should say this after his explanations.

130 This is Rebbi Ḥiyyȧ bar Abba's personal prayer. The previous text mentioned in his name was his version of Rebbi Eleazar's prayer.

131 Galilean Amora of the third generation who was known for his great piety and assiduous study.

רִבִּי תַּנְחוּם בַּר אִיסְכוֹלַסְטִיקָא מַצְלִי יְהִי רָצוֹן מִלְּפָנֶיךָ יי אֱלֹהַי וֵאלֹהֵי אֲבוֹתַי שֶׁתִּשְׁבּוֹר וְתַשְׁבִּית עוּלּוֹ שֶׁל יֵצֶר הָרַע מִלִּבֵּינוּ שֶׁכָּךְ בְּרָאתָנוּ לַעֲשׂוֹת רְצוֹנָךְ וְאָנוּ חַייָבִים לַעֲשׂוֹת רְצוֹנָךְ אַתְּ חָפֵץ וְאָנוּ חֲפֵיצִים וּמִי מְעַכֵּב שְׂאוֹר שֶׁבְּעִיסָּה גָּלוּי וְיָדוּעַ שֶׁאֵין בָּנוּ כֹּחַ לַעֲמוֹד בּוֹ. אֶלָּא יְהִי רָצוֹן מִלְּפָנֶיךָ יי אֱלֹהַי וֵאלֹהֵי אֲבוֹתַי שֶׁתַּשְׁבִּיתֵהוּ מֵעָלֵינוּ וְתַכְנִיעֵהוּ וְנַעֲשֶׂה רְצוֹנָךְ כִּרְצוֹנֵנוּ בְּלֵבָב שָׁלֵם.

Rebbi Tanḥum the scholar[132] prayed: May it please You, o Eternal, my God and God of my fathers, that You may break and remove the yoke of evil inclinations from our hearts since so You created us to do Your will, and we are required to do Your will. You desire it and we desire it, who obstructs? The sour matter in the dough! It is obvious and known that we have no power to resist. But may it be Your pleasure, o Eternal, my God and God of my fathers, that You may remove it from us, subdue it, so that we may do Your will as our own with a willing heart.

132 A title, σχολαστικός "scholar", also found in ancient synagogue inscriptions. The prayer, with minor variations, is reported in the Babli (17a) in the name of Rebbi Alexandri. בר may mean "son of"; it also may mean "endowed with the quality of".

רִבִּי יוֹחָנָן הֲוָה מַצְלֵי יְהִי רָצוֹן מִלְּפָנֶיךָ יי אֱלֹהַי וֵאלֹהֵי אֲבוֹתַי שֶׁתַּשְׁכֵּן בְּפוּרְיֵינוּ אַהֲבָה וְאַחֲוָה שָׁלוֹם וְרֵעוּת וְתַצְלִיחַ סוֹפֵינוּ אַחֲרִית וְתִקְוָה וְתַרְבֶּה גְּבוּלֵינוּ בְּתַלְמִידִים וְנָשִׂישׂ בְּחֶלְקֵינוּ בְּגַן עֵדֶן וְתַקְנֵנוּ לֵב טוֹב וְחָבֵר טוֹב וְנַשְׁכִּים וְנִמְצָא וְתָבֹא לְפָנֶיךָ קוֹרַת נַפְשֵׁינוּ לְטוֹבָה.

Rebbi Yoḥanan prayed[133]: May it please You, o Eternal, my God and God of my fathers, that You may make dwell in our marriage couches love and understanding, peace and friendship. Let our end suceed in future and hope, increase the students in our boundaries. May we enjoy our part in paradise; grant us a good heart and a good colleague; may we get up and find[134], and may the quiet of our minds come before You in kindness.

133 The prayer of Rebbi Yoḥanan in the Babli (16b) is completely different. The first prayer uses the wording of the last benediction at a wedding; the meaning seems to be that he prays for a marriage that always retains the feelings of the wedding day. "Future and hope" means "existence in the

Future World."

134 Find the solutions of all problems that remained unsolved the previous evening.

וּבִיצִיאָתִי אֲנִי נוֹתֵן הוֹדָיָה עַל חֶלְקִי. אָמַר רִבִּי אָבוּן לָאֵל שֶׁחָלַק לִי דֵּעָה וּמַעֲשֶׂה טוֹב.

"When I leave I give thanks for my lot[135]." Rebbi Abun said, to God Who alotted me knowledge and good works.

135 Quote of the last clause in the Mishnah. Rebbi Abun seems to free the mindless from responsibility if they do not live a religious life.

משנה ג: רַבָּן גַּמְלִיאֵל אוֹמֵר בְּכָל־יוֹם אָדָם מִתְפַּלֵּל שְׁמוֹנֶה עֶשְׂרֵה. וְרִבִּי יְהוֹשֻׁעַ אוֹמֵר מֵעֵין שְׁמוֹנֶה עֶשְׂרֵה. רִבִּי עֲקִיבָא אוֹמֵר אִם שְׁגוּרָה[136] תְפִילָּתוֹ בְּפִיו מִתְפַּלֵּל שְׁמוֹנֶה עֶשְׂרֵה וְאִם לָאו מֵעֵין שְׁמוֹנֶה עֶשְׂרֵה.

Mishnah 3: Rabban Gamliel says: Every day one prays[137] eighteen benedictions; Rebbi Joshua says, similar to eighteen benedictions. Rebbi Aqiba says, if he is fluent in his prayer then he prays eighteen benedictions, otherwise similar to eighteen benedictions.

136 In the Kaufmann manuscript of the Mishnah, the vocalization is שְׁגֵירָה, a reading not found in other traditions.

137 For the *Amidah*. The shortened version of Rebbi Joshua will be discussed in the Halakhah.

הלכה ג: וְלָמָּה שְׁמוֹנֶה עֶשְׂרֵה. רִבִּי יְהוֹשֻׁעַ בֶּן לֵוִי אוֹמֵר כְּנֶגֶד שְׁמוֹנָה עָשָׂר הַמִּזְמוֹרוֹת שֶׁכָּתוּב מֵרֹאשׁוֹ שֶׁל (fol. 8a) תְּילִים עַד יַעַנְךָ יי בְּיוֹם צָרָה. אִם יֹאמַר לָךְ תְּשַׁע עֶשְׂרֵה הֵן אֱמוֹר לוֹ לָמָּה רָגְשׁוּ גוֹיִם לֵית הוּא מִינּוֹן. מִכָּן אָמְרוּ הַמִּתְפַּלֵּל וְלֹא נֶעֱנֶה צָרִיךְ תַּעֲנִית. אָמַר רִבִּי מָנָא רֶמֶז לְתַלְמִיד חָכָם שֶׁאָדָם צָרִיךְ לוֹמַר לְרַבּוֹ תִּשְׁמַע תְּפִילָּתָךְ.

Halakhah 3: And why 18[138]? Rebbi Joshua ben Levi says, corresponding to the 18 psalms that are written from the start of Psalms to (*Ps*. 20:2): "May the Lord listen to you on the day of need." If somebody would say to you they are 19, tell him (*Ps*. 2:1) "Why are the Gentiles in upheaval" is not in the count[139]. From here they said that one who prayed and was not answered needs to fast. Rebbi Mana said, a hint that a Torah student must say to his teacher: May your prayers be answered[140].

138 The list of the Yerushalmi is quoted at length in *Tanḥuma Wayyera* 1, and from there in other Midrashim. The Babli (28b) has a shorter list with different names; many allusions given here are not in that list.

139 In most of Talmudic sources, Psalms 1 and 2 form one song. To compensate, *Ps*. 116 is divided in two.

140 Since *Ps*. 20:2 is adressed to David by his students (or the Synhedrion).

אָמַר רִבִּי סִימוֹן כְּנֶגֶד שְׁמוֹנֶה עֶשְׂרֵה חוּלְיוֹת שֶׁבְּשִׁדְרָה שֶׁבְּשָׁעָה שֶׁאָדָם עוֹמֵד וּמִתְפַּלֵּל צָרִיךְ לָשׁוּחַ בְּכוּלָּן. מַה טַעַם כָּל עַצְמוֹתַי תֹּאמַרְנָה יי מִי כָמוֹךָ.

Rebbi Simon said, corresponding to the 18 bones in the spine since when a person prays he has to bend all of them bowing down. What is the reason? (*Ps*. 35:10) "All my bones shall say, o Eternal, who is like You?[141]"

141 In the Babli (28b), this reason for the number 18 is given by Rebbi Tanḥum in the name of R. Joshua ben Levi who notes that, when bowing down in prayer, all joints must be moved.

אָמַר רִבִּי לֵוִי כְּנֶגֶד שְׁמוֹנֶה עֶשְׂרֵה הַזְּכָּרוֹת שֶׁכָּתוּב בְּהָבוּ לַיי בְּנֵי אֵלִים. אָמַר רִבִּי חוּנָה אִם יֹאמַר לָךְ אָדָם שֶׁבַע עֶשְׂרֵה אִינּוּן. אֱמוֹר לוֹ שֶׁל מִינִין כְּבָר קָבְעוּ חֲכָמִים בְּיַבְנֶה. הָתִיב רִבִּי אֶלְעָזָר בֵּי רִבִּי יוֹסֵי קוֹמֵי רִבִּי יוֹסֵי וְהָכְתִיב אֵל הַכָּבוֹד הִרְעִים. אָמַר לֵיהּ וְהָתַנֵּי כּוֹלֵל שֶׁל מִינִין וְשֶׁל פּוֹשְׁעִים בְּמַכְנִיעַ זֵדִים.

וְשֶׁל זְקֵנִים וְשֶׁל גֵּרִים בְּמִבְטָח לַצַּדִּיקִים וְשֶׁל דָּוִד בְּבוֹנֵה יְרוּשָׁלַיִם. אִית לָךְ מַסְפְּקָא לְכָל־חָדָא וְחָדָא מִינְהוֹן אַדְכָּרָה.

Rebbi Levi[142] said, corresponding to the 18 Divine Names written in (*Ps.* 29) "Give to the Eternal, o sons of the mighty." Rebbi Ḥuna said: If it were said that they are 17, tell him the one against sectarians the Sages fixed already at Jabneh[143]. Rebbi Eleazar ben Rebbi Yose objected before Rebbi Yose, but is it not written (*Ps.* 29:3) "the God of Glory thundered[144]"? He said to him: Has it not been stated: He takes together the one against sectarians and sinners in "He Who subdues offenders"[145], the one for elders and proselytes in "Assurance to the righteous", and the one for David in "He Who builds Jerusalem."[146] Then you have enough to have a Divine name[147] for each one of them.

142 In the Babli, this is a statement of Rebbi Hillel, the son of Rebbi Samuel bar Naḥmani. Also the following discussion has a parallel in the Babli.

143 Rebbi Ḥuna's question is an attack against all who try to find a reason for the eighteen benedictions by pointing out that in the 500 years between the institution of formalized prayer by the Men of the Great Assembly and the Synhedrion of Rabban Gamliel, the *Amidah* prayer consisted of only 17 benedictions. Rebbi Ḥuna's answer, not very satisfactory, is that the eighteenth benediction is also an institution of the Synhedrion, the legal successor of the Great Assembly, and, therefore, all eighteen benedictions have the same status.

144 The mention of God introduces a nineteenth Divine name.

145 This implies that the benediction containing the curse upon apostates and sectarians (i. e., Christians) was not newly introduced at Jabneh but that it was a modification of an old benediction directed at those who wantonly transgress the commandments of the Torah. Hence, the original number of benedictions instituted by the Great Assembly was 18. The benediction has been changed in Christian surroundings beyond recognition. The text of Jabneh must have been close to today's Yemenite version: למשומדים אל תהי תקוה, כל המינים

והמוסרים כרגע יאבדו ומלכות זדון תעקור ותשבור מהרה בימינו. ברוך אתה יי שובר אויבים ומכניע זדים.

146 This is the Israeli version which has no separate benediction asking for the return of the Davidic rulers. The Babylonian version has no mention of the Davidic dynasty in the prayer for rebuilding Jerusalem; it is retained in today's Yemenite prayerbook. Current Ashkenazic and Sephardic versions combine the Israeli prayer, for Jerusalem and the Davidic dynasty in benediction 14, with the Babylonian one for the Davidic dynasty alone in benediction 15. Hence, Psalm 29 accomodates both the Galilean (18) benedictions based on the number of mentions of the Tetragrammaton, and the Babylonian (19) versions, based on all invocations of the Deity in the Psalm.

147 The parallels הזכרות, אדכרה in this paragraph show that in the times of the Yerushalmi the sounds of ז /z/ and soft ד /ð/ (voiced *th*) were almost indistinguishable.

רִבִּי חֲנִינָה בְשֵׁם רִבִּי פִינְחָס כְּנֶגֶד שְׁמוֹנֶה עֶשְׂרֵה פְעָמִים שֶׁאָבוֹת כְּתוּבִין בַּתּוֹרָה. אַבְרָהָם יִצְחָק יַעֲקֹב. אִם יֹאמַר לָךְ אָדָם תְּשַׁע עֶשְׂרֵה הֵן אֱמוֹר לוֹ וְהִנֵּה יי נִצָּב עָלָיו לֵית הוּא מִינְהוֹן. אִם יֹאמַר לָךְ אָדָם שְׁבַע עֶשְׂרֵה הֵן אֱמוֹר לוֹ וְיִקָּרֵא בָהֶם שְׁמִי וְשֵׁם אֲבוֹתַי אַבְרָהָם וְיִצְחָק מִינְהוֹן.

Rebbi Ḥanina in the name of Rebbi Phineas: Corresponding to the eighteen times the Patriarchs are mentioned together in the Torah, Abraham, Isaac, Jacob. If somebody will tell you that there are nineteen, tell him that (*Gen.* 23:13) "Behold, the Eternal was standing over him" is not counted[148]. If somebody will tell you that there are seventeen, tell him that (*Gen.* 48:16) "My name should be called over them, as well the names of my fathers Abraham and Isaac" is counted[149].

148 Since Jacob is not mentioned in that verse.

149 Since Jacob is mentioned implicitly; he speaks about "my name".

רִבִּי שְׁמוּאֵל בַּר נַחְמָנִי בְּשֵׁם רִבִּי יוֹחָנָן כְּנֶגֶד שְׁמוֹנֶה עֶשְׂרֵה צִיוּוּיִין שֶׁכָּתַב בְּפָרָשַׁת מִשְׁכָּן שֵׁנִי. אַמַר רִבִּי חִיָּיא בַּר וָוא וּבִלְבַד מִן וְאִתּוֹ אָהֳלִיאָב בֶּן אֲחִיסָמָךְ עַד סוֹפֵיהּ דְּסִפְרָא.

Rebbi Samuel bar Naḥmani in the name of Rebbi Yoḥanan: Corresponding to the eighteen times "commandment" is mentioned in the second description of the tabernacle[150]. Rebbi Ḥiyya bar Abba said, only from (*Ex*. 38:23) "And with him Aholiab ben Aḥisamakh" to the end of the book[151].

150 The description of the actual construction of the tabernacle.

151 Since from the start of the section, v. 21, there would be 19 times mentioned that "the Eternal commanded Moses".

שֶׁבַע שֶׁל שַׁבָּת מְנַיִין. אָמַר רִבִּי יִצְחָק כְּנֶגֶד שֶׁבַע קוֹלוֹת שֶׁכָּתוּב בְּהָבוּ לַיי בְּנֵי אֵלִים. אָמַר רִבִּי יוּדָן עַנְתּוֹרַיָא כְּנֶגֶד שֶׁבַע אַזְכָּרוֹת שֶׁכָּתוּב בְּמִזְמוֹר שִׁיר לְיוֹם הַשַּׁבָּת.

The seven[152] of Sabbath, from where? Rebbi Isaac[153] said, corresponding to the seven "voices" written in (*Ps*. 29) "Give to the Eternal, o sons of the mighty." Rebbi Yudan Antoraya said, corresponding to the seven Divine Names in (*Ps*. 92) "Psalm, Song for the Sabbath Day."

152 Benedictions of the *Amidah*. There is no need to ask for a reason for the seven benedictions of a holiday since holidays in everything imitate the Sabbath. In the Babli (29a) only the first reason is given, in the name of R. Ḥalaphta ben Shaul. In a *Midrash Yelamdenu* quoted in *Yalqut Shim'oni Psalms* #863, the seven voices are said to refer to the seven kinds of voices heard at the theophany at Sinai, which was on a Sabbath.

153 An Amora from the circle of Rebbi Yoḥanan.

תֵּשַׁע שֶׁל רֹאשׁ הַשָּׁנָה מְנַיִין. אָמַר רִבִּי אַבָּא קַרְטִיגְנַיָא כְּנֶגֶד תֵּשַׁע אַזְכָּרוֹת שֶׁכָּתוּב בְּפָרָשַׁת חַנָּה. וּכְתִיב בְּסוֹפָהּ יי יָדִין אַפְסֵי אָרֶץ.

Nine of New Year's Day, from where? Rebbi Abba from Carthage[154] said: Corresponding to the nine Divine Names in Hanna's prayer; there it is written at the end: (*1Sam* 2:10) "The Eternal will judge the ends of the earth[155]."

154 An Israeli Amora of the circle of Rebbi Yoḥanan and Resh Laqish. He is either from Carthage in North Africa or from Cartagena in Spain.

155 This is reported in shortened form in Babli 29a. The entire series of analogous numbers is given only by Israeli Amoraïm; the Yerushalmi is the source for all abbreviated statements in the Babli. The verse from Hannah's prayer, not quoted in the Babli, is the reason that Hannah's prayer forms the Haphtarah of the first day of the New Year.

עֶשְׂרִים וְאַרְבַּע שֶׁל תַּעֲנִיּוֹת מְנַיִין. רִבִּי חֶלְבּוֹ וְרִבִּי שְׁמוּאֵל בַּר רַב נַחְמָן תְּרַוֵּיהוֹן אָמְרִין כְּנֶגֶד עֶשְׂרִים וְאַרְבַּע פְּעָמִים שֶׁכָּתוּב בְּפָרָשָׁה שֶׁל שְׁלֹמֹה רִינָּה וּתְפִילָּה וּתְחִינָּה.

The twenty-four of fast days[156], from where? Rebbi Ḥelbo and Rebbi Samuel bar Rav Naḥman both say, corresponding to the twenty-four times that entreaty, prayer, and supplication are mentioned in Solomon's prayer (*1Kings* 8).

156 Public fasts for rain in a year of draught. The argument is quoted in the Babli (29a) in the name of Rebbi Ḥelbo alone.

רִבִּי זְעִירָא בְּשֵׁם רַב יִרְמְיָה יָחִיד בְּתַעֲנִית צִיבּוּר צָרִיךְ לְהַזְכִּיר מֵעֵין הַמְּאוֹרָה. אֵיכָן הוּא אוֹמְרָהּ בֵּין גּוֹאֵל יִשְׂרָאֵל לְרוֹפֵא חוֹלִים. וּמַהוּ אוֹמֵר עֲנֵנוּ יי עֲנֵנוּ בָּעֵת וּבְעוֹנָה הַזֹּאת כִּי בְצָרָה גְדוֹלָה אֲנָחְנוּ אַל תַּסְתֵּר פָּנֶיךָ מִמֶּנּוּ וְאַל תִּתְעַלֵּם מִתְּחִינָּתֵנוּ כִּי אַתָּה יי עוֹנֶה בְעֵת צָרָה פּוֹדֶה וּמַצִּיל בְּכָל עֵת מְצוּקָה וַיִּצְעֲקוּ אֶל יי בַּצַּר לָהֶם מִמְּצוּקוֹתֵיהֶם יוֹצִיאֵם. בָּרוּךְ אַתָּה יי עוֹנֶה בְעֵת צָרָה. רִבִּי יַנַּיי בֵּרִבִּי יִשְׁמָעֵאל בְּשֵׁם בֵּית רִבִּי יַנַּיי אוֹמֵר בְּשׁוֹמֵעַ תְּפִילָּה.

Rebbi Zeïra in the name of Rav Jeremiah, a private person has to mention the occasion on a public fast day[157]. Where does he say it? Between "Redeemer of Israel" and "Healer of the sick."[158] What does he say? "Answer us, o Eternal, answer us in this time and season because we are in great trouble, do not hide Your presence from us, do not be oblivious to our supplications, because You, o Eternal, will answer in time of trouble, redeem and save in any time of distress. (*Ps*. 107.6) "They cried to the Eternal in their trouble, He led them out from their distress."[159] Praise to You, o Eternal, Answering in times of trouble.

Rebbi Yannai ben Rebbi Ismael[160] in the name of the House of Rebbi Yannai[161] says: In "He Who hears prayer.[162]"

157 The following discussions belong to tractate *Taäniot* (fol. 65c). They are inserted here because the 24 benedictions of fast days were mentioned. On the other hand, the correspondences to the 18, 7, and 9 benedictions on other days belong here and are repeated in *Taäniot* only because of the following text.

The 24 benedictions are recited by the reader in public prayer. In the Babli (*Taänit* 13b-14a) the opinion quoted here in the name of Rav Jeremiah (bar Abba, one of the most important students of Rav in Babylonia) is attributed to Rav himself.

158 Between the Seventh and Eighth benedictions, as a separate benediction.

159 The Galilean practice was to end every benediction in prayer or Grace with a verse from the Bible. This practice has survived only sporadically. Even though this prayer text is given only in the Yerushalmi, (the Babli usually assumes that all texts are known) there are many variants already in the extant prayer manuals from the 8th to the 10th centuries.

160 This is the reading of the Rome ms. here and the Venice text in the parallel version in *Taäniot* 65c. Rebbi Yannai ben R. Ismael was a student of R. Yoḥanan and a colleague of R. Zeïra. (The Venice text here has בשם instead of בר.)

161 The Yeshivah established by Rebbi Yannai in the first generation of Amoraïm; it continued after its founder's death.

162 In the 15th benediction. In the

Babylonian rite we never find that a private person adds a benediction to his prayer. The House of Rebbi Yannai omitted the final benediction in Rav Jeremiah's text.

רִבִּי יוֹנָה בְּשֵׁם רַב אֲפִילוּ יָחִיד שֶׁגָּזַר עַל עַצְמוֹ תַּעֲנִית צָרִיךְ לְהַזְכִּיר מֵעֵין הַמְּאוֹרָע. אֵיכָן הוּא אוֹמְרָהּ. רִבִּי זְעוּרָא בְּשֵׁם רַב חוּנָא כְּלֵילֵי שַׁבָּת וּכְיוֹמוֹ. אָמַר רִבִּי מָנִי אֲנָא דְּלָא בְדַקְתָּהּ אִין כְּהָדָא דְּרַב יִרְמְיָה. אִין כְּהָדָא דְּרִבִּי יַנַּאי בְּרִבִּי יִשְׁמָעֵאל סָלְקִית לְסִדְרָה וְשָׁמְעִית רַב חוּנָה בְּשֵׁם רַב אֲפִילוּ יָחִיד שֶׁגָּזַר עַל עַצְמוֹ תַּעֲנִית צָרִיךְ לְהַזְכִּיר מֵעֵין הַמְּאוֹרָע. הָתִיב רִבִּי יוֹסֵי וְהָא מַתְנִיתָא פְלִיגָא. בְּכָל יוֹם אָדָם מִתְפַּלֵּל שְׁמוֹנֶה עֶשְׂרֵה בְּמוֹצָאֵי שַׁבָּת וּבְמוֹצָאֵי יוֹם הַכִּיפּוּרִים וּבְמוֹצָאֵי תַעֲנִית צִיבּוּר. מִן מַה דָּמַר רִבִּי יוֹסֵי מַתְנִיתָא פְּלִיגָא. הֲוָה כֵן אִתְתָּבַת בֵּין גּוֹאֵל יִשְׂרָאֵל לְרוֹפֵא חוֹלִים.

Rebbi Jonah in the name of Rav: Even an individual who decreed a fast day on himself has to mention the occasion[163]. Where does he say it? Rebbi Zeïra in the name of Rav Ḥuna: Similar to Friday night and Sabbath day[164].

Rebbi Mani said: I, who did not check whether one follows Rav Jeremiah or Rebbi Yannai the son of Rebbi Ismael, went to the study hall and I heard: "Rav Ḥuna in the name of Rav: Even an individual who decreed a fast day on himself has to mention the occasion. Rebbi Yose objected that a *baraitha* disagrees: Every day one prays eighteen benedictions, including the night after Sabbath and the nights after Yom Kippur and after Public Fasts[165]." Since Rebbi Yose said, this *baraita* disagrees[166], it contradicts the statement: between "Redeemer of Israel" and "Healer of the sick."

163 He also has to recite עננו. [In practice, the fastdays of the 3rd of Tishre, 10th of Tevet, 13th of Adar, and 17th of Tammuz, follow the rules of private fast days.]

164 During every prayer he has to

recite that day.

165 See Halakhah 1, Note 86.

166 Rebbi Mani's argument goes as follows: Since R. Yose stated that the *baraita* contradicts Rav, he takes the *baraita* to mean that a private person *always* recites 18 benedictions on weekdays, *never* 19, even on fast days. The additional days are mentioned to point out that insertions for a private person are always accomodated in an existing benediction, never as an additional one, in contrast to the opinion of R. Aqiba who states in Mishnah 5:2 that *Havdalah* Saturday nights is a separate benediction. In addition, it is stated that on those days when *Neïlah* is recited, Yom Kippur and fast days for a severe draught, the *Neïlah* prayer does not replace the following night's prayer as discussed in Halakhah 1. The Yerushalmi does not address the question what the reader says on a public fast day which is not a fast for rain; the Babli decides that the reader will recite עננו as a separate benediction between "Redeemer of Israel" and "Healer of the sick." This decision does not go against R. Mani's argument.

אָמַר רִבִּי אָחָא בַּר יִצְחָק בְּשֵׁם רִבִּי הוּנָה רַבָּא דְצִיפּוֹרִין יָחִיד בְּתִשְׁעָה בְּאַב צָרִיךְ לְהַזְכִּיר מֵעֵין הַמְּאוֹרָע. מַהוּא אוֹמֵר. רַחֵם יי אֱלֹהֵינוּ בְּרַחֲמֶיךָ הָרַבִּים וּבַחֲסָדֶיךָ הַנֶּאֱמָנִים עָלֵינוּ וְעַל עַמְּךָ יִשְׂרָאֵל וְעַל יְרוּשָׁלַיִם עִירָךְ וְעַל צִיּוֹן מִשְׁכַּן כְּבוֹדָךְ וְעַל הָעִיר הָאֲבֵילָה וְהַחֲרֵיבָה וְהֶהָרוּסָה וְהַשּׁוֹמְמָה הַנְּתוּנָה בְּיַד זָרִים הָרְמוּסָה בְּיַד עָרִיצִים וַיִּירָשׁוּהָ לִגְיוֹנוֹת וַיְחַלְּלוּהָ עוֹבְדֵי פְסִילִים וּלְיִשְׂרָאֵל עַמְּךָ נְתַתָּהּ נַחֲלָה וּלְזֶרַע יְשׁוּרוּן יְרוּשָּׁה הוֹרַשְׁתָּהּ כִּי בְאֵשׁ הִיצַּתָּהּ וּבָאֵשׁ אַתָּה עָתִיד לִבְנוֹתָהּ כָּאָמוּר וַאֲנִי אֶהְיֶה לָהּ נְאֻם יי חוֹמַת אֵשׁ סָבִיב וּלְכָבוֹד אֶהְיֶה בְתוֹכָהּ.

Rebbi Aḥa bar Isaac[167] in the name of the older Rebbi Huna of Sepphoris[168]: An individual must mention the occasion on the Ninth of Av. What does he say? "Have mercy, o Eternal, our God, in Your great mercy and your trusted kindness, towards us, Your people Israel, Your city Jerusalem, Zion the dwelling place of Your glory, and on the mourning, ruined, destroyed, and desolate city that is given into the hand of strangers, trampled down by haughty peoples, that was inherited by legions and desecrated by idol worshippers, when You had given her to

Your people Israel as property, and let her be inherited by the seed of Yeshurun, for in fire You set her on fire and with fire You will build her in the future as it has been said (*Zach.* 2:9): "But I shall be for her, says the Eternal, a wall of fire around, and Glory I shall be in her midst.[169]"

167 An Israeli Amora of the third generation, companion of Rebbi Abba bar Mamal and contemporary of Rebbi Zeïra.

168 A student of R. Yoḥanan whose sayings are reported by several sages of the third and fourth generations in Galilee. The name is correctly given in the Rome ms. and in the Venice text in *Taäniot*.

169 This is the only text of the prayer in Talmudic sources; it is quoted in the manuals of Rif (R. Isaac Fassi) and Rosh (R. Asher ben Yehiël). However, Maimonides has a different text from Gaonic sources and the currently used versions are derived from his. Also, most rituals have replaced רחם "have mercy" by נחם "console" as more appropriate in a prayer for Jerusalem.

רִבִּי אֶבְדֵּימָא דְּצִיפּוֹרִין בְּעָא קוֹמֵי רִבִּי מָנָא אֵיכַן אוֹמְרָהּ. אָמַר לוֹ וְאֲדַיִין אֵין אַתְּ לְזוֹ. כָּל־דָּבָר שֶׁהוּא לָבוֹא אוֹמְרָהּ בָּעֲבוֹדָה. וְכָל־דָּבָר שֶׁהוּא לְשֶׁעָבַר אוֹמְרָהּ בְּהוֹדָאָה. וּמַתְנִיתָא אָמְרָה וְנוֹתֵן הוֹדָאָה לְשֶׁעָבַר וְצוֹעֵק לְעָתִיד לָבוֹא.

Rebbi Eudaimon of Sepphoris[170] asked before Rebbi Mana: Where does one say this? He said to him: You still do not understand? Anything for the future one says in "Service"[171] and anything about the past one says in "Thanksgiving"[172]. The Mishnah (*Berakhot* 9:6) says as much: "One gives thanks for the past and cries about the future."

170 An Amora of the fifth generation, student of R. Mana.

171 The 16th benediction in the Galilean service, a prayer for the restitution of the Temple service. In the opinion of the Yerushalmi, that is the correct place for the insertion of the prayer for the Ninth of Ab. However, in all historical documents we have from Gaonic times and later, the insertion is made in the 14th benediction, which is a prayer for the

rebuilding of Jerusalem. This is either a popular custom or a Gaonic institution. It is justified since the place is fitting and the later discussion will show that occasional variations in the prayer text are welcomed.

172 The 17th benediction, the natural place for the mention of the miracles of Ḥanukkah and Purim.

אֵי זוּ הִיא שֶׁבַע מֵעֵין שְׁמוֹנֶה עֶשְׂרֵה. רַב אָמַר סוֹף כָּל־בְּרָכָה וּבְרָכָה. וּשְׁמוּאֵל אָמַר רֹאשׁ כָּל־בְּרָכָה וּבְרָכָה. אִית תְּנָיֵי תַנֵּי שֶׁבַע מֵעֵין שְׁמוֹנֶה עֶשְׂרֵה. וְאִית תְּנָיֵי תַנֵּי שְׁמוֹנֶה עֶשְׂרֵה מֵעֵין שְׁמוֹנֶה עֶשְׂרֵה. מָאן דָּמַר שֶׁבַע מֵעֵין שְׁמוֹנֶה עֶשְׂרֵה מְסַייֵעַ לִשְׁמוּאֵל וּמָאן דָּמַר שְׁמוֹנֶה עֶשְׂרֵה מֵעֵין שְׁמוֹנֶה עֶשְׂרֵה מְסַייֵעַ לְרַב.

[173]What are "seven similar to eighteen"? Rav says the end of each benediction[174] and Samuel says the head of each benediction[175]. Some formulate "seven similar to eighteen" and some formulate "eighteen similar to eighteen."[176] He who says "seven similar to eighteen" supports Samuel, he who says "eighteen similar to eighteen" supports Rav.

173 After the digression about prayers on special days one returns to the discussion of the Mishnah and the statement of Rebbi Joshua that a private prayer on weekdays is "similar to the eighteen benedictions" recited by the reader in public service.

174 Rav requires the first three and the last three benedictions in full and of the twelve benedictions in between only the final doxology of each: Praise to You, o Eternal, Who bestows knowledge as a favor. Praise to You, o Eternal, Who desires repentance, etc., without any other text.

175 Samuel also requires the first and last three benedictions in full but of the text of the intermediate ones only a few words, as explained in full in the next paragraph. The statements of Rav and Samuel are in Babli 29a, the following connection with tannaïtic statements appears only in the Yerushalmi.

176 The disagreement of Rav and Samuel did not originate with them, but they follow different tannaïtic traditions.

רִבִּי זְעִירָא שָׁלַח לְרִבִּי נָחוּם גַּבֵּי רִבִּי יַנַּיי בֵּירִבִּי יִשְׁמָעֵאל אָמַר לֵיהּ אֵי זוּ הִיא שֶׁבַע מֵעֵין שְׁמוֹנֶה עֶשְׂרֵה דִשְׁמוּאֵל. אָמַר לֵיהּ הֲבִינֵנוּ רְצֵה תְשׁוּבָתֵינוּ סְלַח לָנוּ גּוֹאֲלֵינוּ רְפָא חָלְיֵינוּ בָּרֵךְ שְׁנוֹתֵינוּ. אָמַר רִבִּי חַגַּיי אִם הָיוּ גְשָׁמִים אוֹמְרִים בְּגִשְׁמֵי בְרָכָה. אִם הָיוּ טְלָלִים אוֹמְרִים בְּטַלְלֵי בְרָכָה. כִּי מְפוּזָרִים אַתָּה מְקַבֵּץ וְתוֹעִים עָלֶיךָ לִשְׁפּוֹט וְעַל הָרְשָׁעִים תָּשִׁית יָדֶךָ וְיִשְׂמְחוּ כָּל־חוֹסֵי בָךְ בְּבִנְיַן עִירָךְ וּבְחִידּוּשׁ בֵּית מִקְדָּשָׁךְ וּבְצֶמַח דָּוִיד עַבְדָּךְ כִּי טֶרֶם נִקְרָא אַתָּה תַעֲנֶה כָּאָמוּר וְהָיָה טֶרֶם יִקְרָאוּ וַאֲנִי אֶעֱנֶה עוֹד הֵם מְדַבְּרִים וַאֲנִי אֶשְׁמָע בָּרוּךְ אַתָּה יי שׁוֹמֵעַ תְּפִילָּה. וְאוֹמֵר שָׁלֹשׁ בְּרָכוֹת רִאשׁוֹנוֹת וְשָׁלֹשׁ אַחֲרוֹנוֹת. וְאוֹמֵר בָּרוּךְ יי כִּי שָׁמַע קוֹל תַּחֲנוּנָי.

Rebbi Zeïra sent Rebbi Naḥum[177] to Rebbi Yannai ben Rebbi Ismael and said to him: What are the "seven similar to eighteen" of Samuel? He said to him:[178] Give us understanding, have pleasure in our repentance, forgive us, redeem us, heal our sicknesses, bless our years [Rebbi Ḥaggai said, in the rainy season one says: with blessed rains, in the season of dew one says: with blessed dew[179]], for You gather in the dispersed, Yours it is to judge the misguided, put down Your hand on the wicked, but in You may rejoice all who hope for You to rebuild Your city, to renew Your Temple with the offspring of Your servant David, because before we call You will answer as it is said[180] (*Is.* 65:24): "It shall be before they call that I shall answer, they still shall be talking while I will listen." Praise to You, o Eternal, Who hears prayer. And he says the first three and the last three benedictions. And he says[181] (*Ps.* 28:6): Praised be the Eternal, Who certainly hears the voice of my supplications.

177 Probably identical with Rebbi Naḥum, the organizer of the Yeshivah of Rebbi Abbahu.

178 The text in the Babli (29a) is different but based on the same principles.

179 The Babli (29a) forbids the recitation of the shortened prayer in winter time because the change would disturb the memory of the person who

prays. It seems that in Babylonia the text of the prayer for blessed agricultural years was similar to today's Sephardic and Oriental versions where the summer prayer is short (in Rabbenu Saadia's *siddur* 19 words) and the winter prayer is long (in Rabbenu Saadia's *siddur* 48 words) and this change is not adaptable to the short prayer. In contrast, in the Ashkenazic tradition based on Yerushalmi sources, the difference between summer and winter prayer is just two words. One may note that the French *Maḥzor Vitry* from the school of Rashi combines the Babylonian text of הבינני with the Israeli versions for summer and winter and, hence, allows the short prayer for the entire year following the Jerusalem Talmud.

180 The obligatory verse before the end of a longer benediction in the Israeli tradition. This verse is used in the middle of the currently used text of עננו on fast days.

181 As private prayer after all seven required prayers.

רִבִּי אֱלִיעֶזֶר אוֹמֵר הָעוֹשֶׂה תְּפִילָּתוֹ קֶבַע אֵין תְּפִילָּתוֹ תַחֲנוּנִים. רִבִּי אַבָּהוּ בְשֵׁם רִבִּי אֶלְעָזָר וּבִלְבַד שֶׁלֹּא יְהֵא כְקוֹרֵא בְאִיגֶּרֶת. רִבִּי אָחָא בְשֵׁם רִבִּי יוֹסֵי צָרִיךְ לְחַדֵּשׁ בָּהּ דָּבָר בְּכָל־יוֹם. אֲחִיתוֹפֶל הָיָה מִתְפַּלֵּל שָׁלֹשׁ תְּפִילוֹת חֲדָשׁוֹת בְּכָל־יוֹם. אֲמַר רִבִּי זְעִירָא כָּל זְמַן דַּהֲוֵינָא עֲבִיד כֵּן הֲוֵינָא טָעֵי. וְלֵית לָךְ אֶלָּא כַּיי דָּמַר רִבִּי אַבָּהוּ בְשֵׁם רִבִּי אֶלְעָזָר וּבִלְבַד שֶׁלֹּא יְהֵא כְקוֹרֵא בְאִיגֶּרֶת. רִבִּי אֶלְעָזָר הָיָה מִתְפַּלֵּל תְּפִילָּה חֲדָשָׁה בְּכָל־יוֹם. רִבִּי אַבָּהוּ הָיָה מְבָרֵךְ בְּרָכָה חֲדָשָׁה בְּכָל־יוֹם.

"Rebbi Eliezer says: If one makes his prayer fixed, his prayer is not supplication[182]." Rebbi Abbahu in the name of Rebbi Eleazar: Only that one should not be like one who reads a letter[183]. Rebbi Aḥa in the name of Rebbi Yose: One has to say something new every day[184]. Aḥitophel[185] used to say three new prayers every day. Rebbi Zeïra said: Any time that I was trying to do that, I was committing errors. Therefore, one has only what Rebbi Abbahu said in the name of Rebbi Eleazar: Only that one should not be like one who reads a letter. Rebbi Eleazar used to say a new prayer every day. Rebbi Abbahu used to recite a new benediction every day[186].

182 This belongs to the next Mishnah; the paragraph explains this statement. Most newer editions of the Yerushalmi move the section from here to the end of Halakhah 3 or to Halakhah 4. However, it seems that the error is not with the copyists of the Yerushalmi but with the copyists of the Mishnah and that the statement of Rebbi Eliezer belongs to Mishnah 3 where Rabban Gamliel says that everybody always prays 18 fixed benedictions. R. Joshua says everybody prays a shortened but fixed version, and R. Aqiba notes that one should follow either course depending on one's knowledge. But Rebbi Eliezer insists that the appropriate form of prayer depends only on intent. In the first prints of the Babli, Soncino and Venice 5280, the statement of R. Eliezer belongs to Mishnah 3.

183 In the Babli (29b), it is the opinion of the anonymous rabbis that one should pronounce the prayers in form and intent of supplication.

184 While this explanation seems to fit best the standard Hebrew אין קבע, it appears in the Babli only as an opinion of the third generation Amoraïm Rabba and Rav Joseph, and here as an opinion of the fourth generation R. Yose; hence, it is not acceptable as original intention of R. Eliezer. R. Zera (= R. Zeïra) is also the one in the Babylonian Talmud who points out the practical impossibility of finding a new formulation in a fixed framework of 18 benedictions every day. One may also note that the statement of R. Simeon ben Nethanael (*Abot* 2:13) "do not make your prayer קבע" appears in *Abot deR. Nathan A* 17:8 as "do not make your prayer (idle) talk"; this agrees with the interpretation of Rebbi Eleazar.

185 In Agadah, he is the paradigm of a person who knows everything.

186 While Rebbis Eleazar and Aḥa are the authors of the lenient interpretation, that the use of a formulaic text is accepted by all sages, they did not want to use this leniency for themselves, R. Eleazar for the *Amidah* prayer and R. Aḥa for any of the permanent benedictions, possibly those to be recited in the morning before prayer.

רִבִּי יוֹסֵי צַיידָנָיָא בְּשֵׁם רִבִּי יוֹחָנָן לִפְנֵי תְפִילָּתוֹ הוּא אוֹמֵר יי שְׂפָתַי תִּפְתָּח וּפִי יַגִּיד תְּהִילָּתֶךָ. לְאַחַר תְּפִילָּתוֹ הוּא אוֹמֵר יִהְיוּ לְרָצוֹן אִמְרֵי פִי וְהֶגְיוֹן לִבִּי לְפָנֶיךָ יי צוּרִי וְגוֹאֲלִי. רִבִּי יוּדָן הֲוָה אוֹמֵר תְּרֵוֵיהוֹן קוֹמֵי צְלוֹתֵיהּ.

Rebbi Yose from Sidon[187] in the name of Rebbi Yoḥanan: Before one's prayer one says (*Ps.* 51:17) "Master, open my lips that my mouth may proclaim Your praise." After one's prayer, one says (*Ps.* 19:15): "May the sayings of my mouth be agreeable and the thoughts of my heart, before You, my Rock and my Redeemer." Rebbi Yudan used to say both of them before his prayer.

187 A student of Rebbi Jeremiah, from the city of Sidon. The statements of R. Yoḥanan are in Babli 9b. There the requirement of recitation of these verses is noted as "institutions of the Rabbis"; the Babli would not tolerate the action of Rebbi Yudan.

הָיָה עוֹמֵד וְנִזְכַּר שֶׁהִתְפַּלֵּל רַב אָמַר חוֹתֵךְ. וּשְׁמוּאֵל אָמַר אֵינוֹ חוֹתֵךְ. שִׁמְעוֹן בַּר וָוא בְּשֵׁם רִבִּי יוֹחָנָן וּלְוַאי שֶׁיִּתְפַּלֵּל (fol. 8b) אָדָם כָּל־הַיּוֹם. לָמָּה שֶׁאֵין תְּפִילָּה מַפְסֶדֶת. רִבִּי זְעִירָא בְּעָא קוֹמֵי רִבִּי יוֹסֵי לֵית מִילְתֵיהּ דְּרִבִּי יוֹחָנָן אָמְרָה סָפֵק נִתְפַּלֵּל סָפֵק לֹא נִתְפַּלֵּל אַל יִתְפַּלֵּל. וְלֹא אֲגִיבֵיהּ. אָתָא רִבִּי אַבָּהוּ בְּשֵׁם רִבִּי יוֹחָנָן סָפֵק נִתְפַּלֵּל סָפֵק לֹא נִתְפַּלֵּל אַל יִתְפַּלֵּל. רִבִּי חֲנִינָא לֹא אָמַר כֵּן אֶלָּא בְּעַיין קוֹמֵי רִבִּי יוֹחָנָן סָפֵק נִתְפַּלֵּל סָפֵק לֹא נִתְפַּלֵּל אֲמַר לוֹן וּלְוַאי שֶׁיִּתְפַּלֵּל אָדָם כָּל־הַיּוֹם. לָמָּה שֶׁאֵין תְּפִילָּה מַפְסֶדֶת.

If one was praying and remembered that he already had prayed, Rav says, he cuts short, and Samuel says, he does not cut short. Simeon bar Abba in the name of Rebbi Yoḥanan[188]: If only one would pray the whole day long, why, because prayer is never in vain. Rebbi Zeïra asked before Rebbi Yose[189]: Did not Rebbi Yoḥanan say that if one is in doubt whether he did pray or not, that he should not pray? He did not give him an answer. Rebbi Abbahu came in the name of Rebbi Yoḥanan: If one is in doubt whether he did pray or not, he should not pray. Rebbi Ḥanina did not say so but: They asked before Rebbi Yoḥanan, if one is in doubt whether he did pray or not? He told them, if only one would pray the whole day long, why, because prayer is never in vain.

188 The statement of Rebbi Yoḥanan and his problem have been explained in Chapter One, Notes 16 ff. The shortened parallel to this and the following paragraph appear in Babli 21a.

189 He is Rebbi Yasa (Assi).

הָיָה עוֹמֵד וּמִתְפַּלֵּל בְּשַׁבָּת וְשָׁכַח שֶׁל שַׁבָּת וְהִזְכִּיר שֶׁל חוֹל. רִבִּי חוּנָא אֲמַר אִיתְפַּלְּגוּן רַב נַחְמָן בַּר יַעֲקֹב וְרַב שֵׁשֶׁת. חַד אָמַר חוֹתֵךְ אֶת הַבְּרָכָה. וְחָרָנָה אָמַר גוֹמֵר אֶת הַבְּרָכָה. הַכֹּל מוֹדִים בְּחוֹנֵן הַדַּעַת שֶׁהוּא גוֹמְרָהּ. וְתָא כְּרִבִּי דְּרִבִּי אָמַר תְּמִיָּה אֲנִי הֵיאַךְ בִּטְּלוּ חוֹנֵן הַדַּעַת בְּשַׁבָּת. אִם אֵין דֵּיעָה מְנַיִן תְּפִילָּה. אָמַר רִבִּי יִצְחָק גְּדוֹלָה הִיא הַדֵּיעָה שֶׁהִיא מְמוּצַּעַת בֵּין שְׁתֵּי הַזְּכָּרוֹת שֶׁנֶּאֱמַר כִּי אֵל דֵּעוֹת יי. אִית דְּבָעֵי מַשְׁמְעִינָהּ מִן הָדָא אָז תָּבִין יִרְאַת יי וְדַעַת אֱלֹהִים תִּמְצָא.

If one was standing praying on the Sabbath; he forgot about the Sabbath and prayed for weekday. Rebbi Ḥuna said, Rav Naḥman bar Jacob[190] and Rav Sheshet[191] disagree, one says he cuts the benediction short and the other says, he finishes the benediction. All agree that he finishes "Gracious Giver of knowledge"[192]. This follows Rebbi, since Rebbi said: I wonder why they eliminated "Gracious Giver of knowledge" on Sabbath; if there is no knowledge, from where comes prayer? Rebbi Isaac said: Knowledge is great because it is in the middle between two mentions of divine names as it is said (*1Samuel* 2:3): "Certainly, a God of knowledge is the Eternal". Some want to understand from here (*Prov.* 2:5): "Then you will understand the fear of the Eternal and the knowledge of God you will find."

190 He appears as Rav Naḥman in the Babli, a student of Samuel and of the *Resh Galuta* Rabba bar Abuh, who became his father-in-law and appointed Rav Naḥman as chief judge of the Jews in Babylonia. Hence, the opinions of Rav Naḥman have the weight of Supreme Court decisions in all money matters. He is reported in the Babli (21a) to require that the benediction that was started must be finished. The contrary opinion, which therefore must be attributed to Rav Sheshet, is not mentioned in the Babli.

191 Rav Sheshet was a contemporary of Rav Naḥman, a student of Rav. He was blind and the greatest expert in Tannaïtic literature in his time. In the Babli, it is a Gaonic tradition that in disagreements between Rav Sheshet and Rav Naḥman, practice follows Rav Sheshet in all matters that do not involve money. Hence, it is clear that the Babli, which wants to establish the rule that one must finish the benediction, cannot mention Rav Sheshet.

192 The first of the weekday benedictions, a prayer for knowledge and insight.

משנה ד: רִבִּי אֱלִיעֶזֶר אוֹמֵר הָעוֹשֶׂה תְּפִילָּתוֹ קֶבַע אֵין תְּפִילָּתוֹ תַּחֲנוּנִים. רִבִּי יְהוֹשֻׁעַ אוֹמֵר הַמְּהַלֵּךְ בְּמָקוֹם הַסַּכָּנָה מִתְפַּלֵּל תְּפִילָּה קְצָרָה מֵעֵין שְׁמוֹנֶה עֶשְׂרֵה וְאוֹמֵר הוֹשִׁיעָה יי אֶת עַמְּךָ אֶת יִשְׂרָאֵל בְּכָל־פָּרָשַׁת הָעִיבּוּר יִהְיוּ צָרְכֵיהֶם לְפָנֶיךָ. בָּרוּךְ אַתָּה יי שׁוֹמֵעַ תְּפִילָּה וְתַחֲנוּנִים.

Mishnah 4: Rebbi Eliezer says: If one makes his prayers fixed, his prayer is not a supplication[193]. Rebbi Joshua says: He who passes through a place of danger recites a short prayer (similar to eighteen prayers)[194] and says: Help, o Eternal, your people Israel; in all passing situations may their needs be before You. Praised are You, o Eternal, Who hears prayer (and entreaties)[195].

193 The Gemara to this statement is found in the preceding Halakha.

194 This phrase is only found in Mishnah codices of the Israeli tradition, never in the Babylonian Mishnah. It seems that for R. Joshua in the

Yerushalmi the short prayer is a replacement for Samuel's text of the middle part of the short *Amidah* as explained here later by (the Babylonian!) Rav Ḥisda, but in Babylon it is interpreted as an independent prayer that must be complemented by a full *Amidah* once the danger has passed.

195 This is only in the Mishnah text in the Yerushalmi Halakhah (not in the Mishnah preceding the Chapter) and in a few Mishnah manuscripts.

הלכה ד: רִבִּי שִׁמְעוֹן בַּר אַבָּא בְּשֵׁם רִבִּי חֲנִינָא כָּל־הַדֶּרֶךְ בְּחֶזְקַת סַכָּנָה. רִבִּי יַנַּיי כַּד הֲוָה נְפִיק לָאַכְסֶנְיָא הֲוָה מְפַקֵּד גֵּו בֵּיתֵיהּ. רִבִּי מָנָא כַּד הֲוָה אָזִיל מַסְחֵי בְּמֶרְחָץ שֶׁהִיא נִיסוֹקֶת הֲוָה מְפַקֵּד גֵּו בֵּיתֵיהּ. רִבִּי חֲנִינָא בְּרֵיהּ דְּרִבִּי אַבָּהוּ רִבִּי שִׁמְעוֹן בַּר אַבָּא בְּשֵׁם רִבִּי יְהוֹשֻׁעַ בֶּן לֵוִי כָּל־הַחוֹלִי בְּחֶזְקַת הַסַּכָּנָה.

Halakhah 4: Rebbi Simeon bar Abba in the name of Rebbi Ḥanina: Any travel is presumed to be dangerous[196]. Rebbi Yannai, when he went abroad[197], commanded his household[198]. Rebbi Mana commanded his household when he went to a bathhouse that was heated[199]. Rebbi Ḥanina the son of Rebbi Abbahu[200], Rebbi Simeon bar Abba in the name of Rebbi Joshua ben Levi: Every sickness is presumed to be dangerous.

196 And an occasion for the prayer of Rebbi Joshua.

197 Greek ξενία "hospitality; guest chamber".

198 Made his will and settled his affairs as if he expected to die.

199 In Roman thermal baths, the water was heated in a room directly below the sauna room. If the floor was falling down, the people in the sauna would be in danger of being burned to death. This does not apply to geothermal bathhouses as in Tiberias; he made his will only when he went to thermal baths that were artificially heated.

200 Son of Rebbi Abbahu of Caesarea; studied in Tiberias and became his father's successor in Caesarea.

רִבִּי אָחָא בְּשֵׁם רִבִּי אַסָּא כָּל־מַה שֶׁשְּׁלִיחַ צִיבּוּר עוֹבֵר לִפְנֵי הַתֵּיבָה וְתוֹבֵעַ צָרְכֵי עַמְּךָ לְפָנֶיךָ. רִבִּי פִּינְחָס רִבִּי לֵוִי רִבִּי יוֹחָנָן בְּשֵׁם מְנַחֵם דְּגַלְיָיא זֶה שֶׁעוֹבֵר לִפְנֵי

הַתֵּיבָה אֵין אוֹמֵר לוֹ בּוֹא וְהִתְפַּלֵּל אֶלָּא בּוֹא וְקָרֵב קָרְבֵּינוּ עֲשֵׂה צָרְכֵינוּ עֲשֵׂה מִלְחֲמוֹתֵינוּ. פַּיֵּיס בַּעֲדֵינוּ.

[201]Rebbi Aḥa in the name of Rebbi Assi: Everything that the representative of the congregation passes by before the Ark and requests the needs of Your people before You. Rebbi Phineas, Rebbi Levi, Rebbi Yoḥanan, in the name of Menaḥem from Gallia[202]: He[203] does not say to the one who steps before the Ark "come and pray for us" but "come and present our presentation[204], work our needs, wage our wars, pacify for us."

201 Here starts the discussion of R. Joshua's text, in particular the meaning of בכל שעת העיבור. The explanations of the Babli (29b) of this cryptic expression are varied and totally different. In Galilee, the reader passes (עובר) before the ark, in Babylonia he descends (יורד) before the ark. Hence, only in Galilee can the prayer of R. Joshua refer to the prayer of the cantor in the synagogue.

202 A Tanna of the last generation. His sayings are usually transmitted by R. Yoḥanan.

203 The person in charge of organizing services.

204 קרב may mean "battle" (explained here by "wars") or "to come near" (explained by "pacify for us") but in the liturgic sense, used here as main sense, it means a poem either inserted in the regular *Amidah* or replacing the *Amidah* prayer, as recognized by L. Ginzberg. Religious poetry was very important in Israel in these times; in Babylonia it was banned from synagogues except in the Yeshivah of Rav who was trained in Galilee. Hence, the Babylonian Talmud could not accept the interpretation given here.

אֲחֵרִים אָמְרוּ צוֹרְכֵי עַמְּךָ מְרוּבִּין וְדַעְתָּן קְצָרָה אֶלָּא יְהִי רָצוֹן מִלְּפָנֶיךָ יי אֱלֹהֵינוּ וֵאלֹהֵי אֲבוֹתֵינוּ שֶׁתִּתֵּן לְכָל־בְּרִיָּה וּבְרִיָּה צְרָכֶיהָ וּלְכָל־גְּוִיָּה וּגְוִיָּה דֵּי מַחְסוֹרָהּ. בָּרוּךְ יי כִּי שָׁמַעְתָּ[205] קוֹל תַּחֲנוּנָי. בָּרוּךְ אַתָּה יי שׁוֹמֵעַ תְּפִילָּה. רַב חִסְדָּא אָמַר הֲלָכָה כַּאֲחֵרִים. רַב חִסְדָּא אָמַר שָׁלֹשׁ בְּרָכוֹת הָרִאשׁוֹנוֹת וְשָׁלֹשׁ הָאַחֲרוֹנוֹת.

Others say[206]: "The needs of Your people are many and their minds are dull. May it be pleasure before You, o Eternal, our God and God of our fathers, that You may give every single creature its needs and to every single body according to his want. (*Ps.* 28:6) Praised be the Eternal, certainly He heard the sound of my supplications. Praised are You, o Eternal, Who hears prayer." Rav Ḥisda said: Practice follows "others". Rav Ḥisda said, the first and last three benedictions[207].

205 A scribal error for שְׁמַע in the verse. The entire sentence is missing in the Rome ms.

206 This prayer is reported in Babylonian style (without the Biblical verse preceding the doxology) together with the prayers formulated by other rabbis in Babli 29b and Tosephta *Berakhot* 3:7. The statement that practice follows this text is Rav Huna's in the Babli.

207 The "short prayer" is the middle one between the first and the last three of the *Amidah*; see the commentary to the Mishnah.

אִית תַּנָּיֵי תַּנֵּי מִתְפַּלֵּל וְאַחַר כַּךְ תּוֹבֵעַ צְרָכָיו. אִית תַּנָּיֵי תַּנֵּי תּוֹבֵעַ צְרָכָיו וְאַחַר כַּךְ מִתְפַּלֵּל. מַאן דָּמַר מִתְפַּלֵּל וְאַחַר כַּךְ תּוֹבֵעַ צְרָכָיו תְּפִילָּה לְעָנִי כִּי יַעֲטוֹף וְאַחַר כַּךְ וְלִפְנֵי יי יִשְׁפּוֹךְ שִׂיחוֹ. וּמַאן דָּמַר תּוֹבֵעַ צְרָכָיו וְאַחַר כַּךְ מִתְפַּלֵּל לִשְׁמוֹעַ אֶל הָרִינָּה וְאַחַר כַּךְ עַל הַתְּפִילָּה. דִּבְרֵי חֲכָמִים. רִבִּי זְעִירָא בְּשֵׁם רַב חוּנָא יָחִיד תּוֹבֵעַ צְרָכָיו בְּשׁוֹמֵעַ תְּפִילָּה.

Some Tannaïm have stated: One should first pray and then ask for one's personal needs. Some Tannaïm have stated: One should first ask for one's personal needs and then pray.[208] He who says, one should first pray and then ask for one's personal needs (*Ps.* 102:1) "Prayer of the deprived one who wraps himself up[209]" and afterwards "and before the Eternal he pours out his speech." But he who says, one should first ask for one's personal needs and then pray, (*1Kings* 8:28) "To listen to lamentation[210]" and after that "and to prayer." The opinion of the sages[211]: Rebbi Zeïra in the name of Rav Ḥuna, the private person asks for his personal needs in "He Who hears prayer"[212].

208 In Babli *Avodah zarah* 7b, the first opinion is R. Joshua's, the second one R. Eliezer's. [If the Yerushalmi had mentioned the names, the order of the *baraitot* would have been inverted.] R. Joshua, whose opinion always prevails against R. Eliezer, requires that private prayers be said following completion of the prescribed 18 benedictions. This is accepted as a possible practice in Babli *Avodah zarah* 8a.

209 Usually translated: "who faints", but used here in the sense of "who wraps himself in his prayer coat or shawl." The Babli uses the verse for the opposite argument since "prayer" is mentioned first.

210 The Babli (*Berakhot* 31a) is forced to re-interpret רנה as "prayer".

211 The consensus of the Amoraïm.

212 But public entreaties are said either in the form of extra benedictions for rain fasts, or as penitential prayers in the sixth benediction "Merciful, Who forgives much."

רִבִּי אַבָּא רִבִּי חִיָּיא בְּשֵׁם רִבִּי יוֹחָנָן צָרִיךְ אָדָם לְהִתְפַּלֵּל בְּמָקוֹם שֶׁהוּא מְיוּחָד לִתְפִילָּה. וּמַה טַעַם בְּכָל־הַמָּקוֹם אֲשֶׁר אַזְכִּיר אֶת שְׁמִי. אֲשֶׁר תַּזְכִּיר אֶת שְׁמִי אֵין כָּתוּב כַּאן אֶלָּא בְּכָל־הַמָּקוֹם אֲשֶׁר אַזְכִּיר. אָמַר רִבִּי תַנְחוּם בַּר חֲנִינָא צָרִיךְ אָדָם לְיַחֵד לוֹ מָקוֹם בְּבֵית הַכְּנֶסֶת לְהִתְפַּלֵּל. וּמַה טַעַם וַיְהִי דָוִד בָּא עַד הָרֹאשׁ אֲשֶׁר הִשְׁתַּחֲוֶה שָׁם לֵאלֹהִים אֵין כָּתוּב כָּאן אֶלָּא אֲשֶׁר יִשְׁתַּחֲוֶה שָׁם לֵאלֹהִים.

Rebbi Abba, Rebbi Ḥiyya[213], in the name of Rebbi Yoḥanan: A person has to pray at a place that is dedicated for prayer. What is the reason? (*Ex.* 20:24) "At every place where I shall let My name be mentioned[214]." It does not say "where you will mention" but "at every place where I shall let My name be mentioned." Rebbi Tanḥum bar Ḥanina[215] said: A person has to select a fixed place in the synagogue where he prays. What is the reason? (*2Sam.* 15:32) "David came to the top", it does not say "where he prostrated himself before God" but "where he was used to prostrate himself before God."

213 R. Ḥiyya bar Abba.

214 The verse ends: "I shall come there and bless you." One has to pray in the synagogue because only there is God's blessing guaranteed for one's prayers.

215 Probably identical with Rebbi Tanḥum bar Ḥanilaï, a specialist in Aggadah in the second generation who was in contact both with R. Yoḥanan and with R. Joshua ben Levi, as well as with R. Ḥiyya bar Abba of the following generation. A statement similar to his, but not restricted to a synagogue, is attributed in the Babli (6b) to R. Ḥelbo in the name of Rav Huna.

רִבִּי יָסָא רִבִּי חֶלְבּוֹ. רִבִּי בֶּרֶכְיָה רִבִּי חֶלְבּוֹ מָטִי בָהּ בְּשֵׁם רִבִּי אֶבְדּוּמָה דְמִן חֵיפָה צָרִיךְ אָדָם לְהָסֵב פָּנָיו לַכּוֹתֶל לְהִתְפַּלֵּל. מַה טַעַם וַיַּסֵּב חִזְקִיָּהוּ פָּנָיו אֶל הַקִּיר. בְּאֵיזֶה קִיר נָשָׂא עֵינָיו. רִבִּי יְהוֹשֻׁעַ בֶּן לֵוִי אָמַר בְּקִירָהּ שֶׁל רָחָב נָשָׂא עֵינָיו כִּי בֵיתָהּ בְּקִיר הַחוֹמָה. אָמַר לְפָנָיו רִבּוֹנוֹ שֶׁל עוֹלָם רָחָב הַזּוֹנָה שְׁתֵּי נְפָשׁוֹת הִצִּילָה לָךְ רְאֵה כַּמָּה נְפָשׁוֹת הִצַּלְתָּ לָהּ. הֲדָא הוּא דִכְתִיב וַיָּבוֹאוּ הַנְּעָרִים וְגוֹמֵר. תַּנֵּי רִבִּי שִׁמְעוֹן בַּר יוֹחַי אֲפִילוּ הָיְתָה בְמִשְׁפַּחְתָּהּ מָאתַיִם אֲנָשִׁים וְהָלְכוּ וְדָבְקוּ בְּמָאתַיִם מִשְׁפָּחוֹת כּוּלְּהֶם נִיצּוֹלוּ בִזְכוּתָהּ. אֲבוֹתַי שֶׁקִּירְבוּ לָךְ כָּל־הַגֵּרִים הָאֵילוּ עַל אַחַת כַּמָּה וְכַמָּה. רִבִּי חֲנַנְיָא בַּר פַּפָּא אָמַר בְּקִירוֹת בֵּית הַמִּקְדָּשׁ נָשָׂא עֵינָיו. בְּתִתָּם סִפָּם אֶת סִיפִּי וּמְזוּזָתָם אֵצֶל מְזוּזָתִי וְהַקִּיר בֵּינִי וּבֵינֵיהֶם. בְּנֵי אָדָם גְּדוֹלִים הָיוּ וְלֹא הָיוּ יְכוֹלִין לַעֲלוֹת וּלְהִתְפַּלֵּל בְּבֵית הַמִּקְדָּשׁ בְּכָל־שָׁעָה וְהָיוּ מִתְפַּלְלִין בְּתוֹךְ בָּתֵּיהֶן. וְהַקָּדוֹשׁ בָּרוּךְ הוּא מַעֲלֶה עֲלֵיהֶם כְּאִילּוּ מִתְפַּלְלִין בְּבֵית הַמִּקְדָּשׁ. אֲבוֹתַי שֶׁעָשׂוּ לָךְ כָּל־הַשֶּׁבַח הַזֶּה עַל אַחַת כַּמָּה וְכַמָּה. רִבִּי שְׁמוּאֵל בַּר נַחְמָן אָמַר בְּקִירָהּ שֶׁל שׁוּנָמִית נָשָׂא עֵינָיו שֶׁנֶּאֱמַר נַעֲשֶׂה נָּא עֲלִיַּת קִיר קְטַנָּה. אָמַר לְפָנָיו רִבּוֹנוֹ שֶׁל עוֹלָם הַשּׁוּנָמִית קִיר אַחַת עָשְׂתָה לֶאֱלִישָׁע וְהֶחֱיֵיתָ אֶת בְּנָהּ. אֲבוֹתַי שֶׁעָשׂוּ לָךְ כָּל־הַשֶּׁבַח הַזֶּה עַל אַחַת כַּמָּה וְכַמָּה תִּתֵּן לִי נַפְשִׁי. וְרַבָּנָן אָמְרֵי בְּקִירוֹת לִבּוֹ נָשָׂא עֵינָיו. מֵעַיי מֵעַיי אוֹחִילָהּ קִירוֹת לִבִּי הוֹמֶה לִּי. אָמַר לְפָנָיו רִבּוֹנוֹ שֶׁל עוֹלָם חִיזַּרְתִּי עַל רמ״ח אֵיבָרִים שֶׁנָּתַתָּ בִּי וְלֹא מָצָאתִי שֶׁהִכְעַסְתִּיךָ בְּאַחַת מֵהֶן אַחַת כַּמָּה וְכַמָּה תִּינָּתֶן לִי נַפְשִׁי.

Rebbi Yasa, Rebbi Ḥelbo. Rebbi Berekhiah, Rebbi Ḥelbo comes to it in the name of Rebbi Eudaimon from Ḥaifa: A person has to turn his face to the wall in order to pray. What is the reason? (*Is*. 38:2) "Hezekiah turned his face to the wall." Which wall did he lift his eyes to? Rebbi Joshua ben Levi said, he lifted his eyes to Raḥab's wall, (*Jos*. 2:15) "For her house was on the wall of the fortification." He said before Him: Master of the world, Raḥab the inn-keeper saved two souls for You, and see how many souls You saved for her. [That is what is written (*Jos*. 6:23): "The youths came, etc." Rebbi Simeon bar Yoḥai said, even if her family was 200 persons strong and they furthermore were related to another 200 families, all of these were saved by her merit[216].] My forefathers who brought to You all these proselytes, so much more[217].

Rebbi Ḥananiah bar Pappus[218] said, he lifted his eyes to the wall of the Temple. (*Ez*. 43:8) "When they put their lintel next to My lintel, their doorposts next to My doorpost, with the wall between Me and them[219]." They were important people, they could not go and pray in the Temple every time, so they prayed in their house and the Holy One, praise to Him, considers it as if they had prayed in the Temple. My fathers who built for You all this glory, so much more.

Rebbi Samuel bar Naḥman[220] said, he lifted his eyes to the wall of the woman from Sunem, as it was said (*2Kings* 4:10): "Let us make a small upper storey on the wall". He said before Him: Master of the world, the woman from Sunem made one wall for Elisha and You revived her son. My forefathers who built for You all this glory, so much more that You should give me my life.

The rabbis say, he lifted his eyes to the walls of his heart. (*Jer*. 4:19) "My innards, my innards I make tremble, the walls of my heart are in uproar." He said before Him: Master of the world, I checked all my 248 limbs[221] that You gave me and I did not find one of them I offended You with; so much more that You should give me my life.

216 The argument, as usual, refers to the part of the verse not quoted in the text: "The youths, the spies, came and removed Raḥab, her father, her mother, her brothers, and all her belongings; and they removed *all her families* and deposited them outside of the camp of Israel." One would have expected "all her family" but it says "all her families".

217 This expression is elliptic, see the last two paragraphs.

218 In the Babli, he is called Rebbi Ḥanina bar Pappus. He belongs to the circle of the students of R. Yoḥanan, but it is not known whether he was himself one of the latter's students. His authority was accepted by Abbaie and Rava, the undisputed leaders of the fourth generation of Amoraïm in Babylonia.

219 This verse ends with a curse upon the people addressed, the bad kings of Judea. But since the royal palace and the Temple were designed by David and built by Solomon, one must assume that the layout and use were done by praiseworthy kings.

220 In the Babli (10b), this sermon is by Rebbi Levi and the following one by R. Simeon ben Laqish.

221 This number is given in Mishnah *Ahilut* 1:8 where they are all enumerated in anatomic detail.

משנה ה: הָיָה רוֹכֵב עַל הַחֲמוֹר יֵרֵד וְאִם אֵינוֹ יָכוֹל לֵירֵד יַחֲזִיר אֶת פָּנָיו וְאִם אֵינוֹ יָכוֹל לְהַחֲזִיר אֶת פָּנָיו יְכַוֵּין אֶת לִבּוֹ כְּנֶגֶד בֵּית קָדְשֵׁי הַקֳּדָשִׁים. הָיָה רוֹכֵב בִּסְפִינָה אוֹ בְּאַסְדָּא יְכַוֵּין אֶת לִבּוֹ כְּנֶגֶד בֵּית קָדְשֵׁי הַקֳּדָשִׁים.

Mishna 5: If one was riding on a donkey[222], he should descend. If he cannot descend[223], he should turn his head; if he cannot even turn his head, he should focus his intent towards the Holiest of Holies[224]. If he was riding in a ship or on a raft, he should focus his intent towards the Holiest of Holies.

222 If it is close to the end of the time alotted for the prayer, so that he must pray now.

223 Either because of danger or because he is in a caravan that would not stop.

224 In praying, he should imagine himself praying in the direction of the Temple.

הלכה ה: תַּנֵּי הָיָה רוֹכֵב עַל הַחֲמוֹר אִם יֵשׁ לוֹ מִי לֶאֱחוֹז בַּחֲמוֹרוֹ. יֵרֵד וּמִתְפַּלֵּל לְמַטָּן. וְאִם לַאו מִתְפַּלֵּל בִּמְקוֹמוֹ. רִבִּי אוֹמֵר בֵּין כָּךְ וּבֵין כָּךְ מִתְפַּלֵּל בִּמְקוֹמוֹ שֶׁכָּךְ לִבּוֹ מְיוּשָּׁב. רִבִּי יוּדָה בֶּן פָּזִי בְּשֵׁם רִבִּי יְהוֹשֻׁעַ בֶּן לֵוִי הֲלָכָה כְּרִבִּי.

Halakhah 5: It has been stated[225]: One who was riding on a donkey, if he has somebody to hold his donkey, he should descend and pray on the ground, otherwise he should pray where he is. Rebbi says, in any case he should pray where he is because then his mind will be at peace[226]. Rebbi Judah ben Pazi in the name of Rebbi Joshua ben Levi: Practice follows Rebbi[227].

225 Tosephta *Berakot* 3:18, Babli 30a (in slightly changed wording).

226 This is explained in *Midrash Tanḥuma, Ḥayye Śarah* 1: He should not descend because he will be worried about valuables he has on the donkey or because of Gentiles.

227 This ruling is given in the Babli in the names of Rebbi Joshua ben Levi and Rava. Since the Babylonian Rava (son of Rav Joseph bar Ḥama, the last Babylonian mentioned in the Yerushalmi) lived about 100 years after R. Joshua ben Levi, it appears that it took about 100 years for this Israeli practice to be accepted in Babylonia.

אָמַר רִבִּי יַעֲקֹב בַּר אָחָא תְּנָיי תַּמָּן לְכָל־הָרוּחוֹת אֵין מַחְזִירִין אוֹתוֹ חוּץ מֵרוּחַ מִזְרָחִית. אֲמַר רִבִּי יוֹסֵי בַּר אָבוּן בַּתְּחִילָּה אֲחוֹרֵיהֶם אֶל הֵיכַל יי וּפְנֵיהֶם קֵדְמָה וְהֵמָּה מִשְׁתַּחֲוִים קֵדְמָה לַשֶּׁמֶשׁ.

Rebbi Jacob bar Aḥa: It has been stated there[228], in all directions one does not stop him except in the Eastern direction[229]. Rebbi Yose bar Abun said, as of old (*Ez.* 8:16)[230]: "Their backs to the Temple of the Eternal and their faces turned East, they were prostrating themselves Eastwards before the sun."

228 In Babylonia, where the direction towards the Temple in Jerusalem would be to the West.

229 When somebody turns his back to Jerusalem, he cannot pray. This formulation is not mentioned in the Babli except that the blind Rav Sheshet ordered his servant not to let him pray in an Eastern direction because that was a Christian custom (*Bava Batra* 25a).

230 In Ezechiel's vision of all the abominations for which Jerusalem will be destroyed.

תַּנֵּי סוּמָא וּמִי שֶׁאֵינוֹ יָכוֹל לְכַוֵּין אֶת הָרוּחוֹת הֲרֵי אֵילוּ מִתְפַּלְלִין כְּלַפֵּי לְמַעֲלָן שֶׁנֶּאֱמַר וְהִתְפַּלְלוּ אֶל יי. הָעוֹמְדִין וּמִתְפַּלְלִין בְּחוּצָה לָאָרֶץ הוֹפְכִין אֶת פְּנֵיהֶן כְּלַפֵּי אֶרֶץ יִשְׂרָאֵל. וּמַה טַעַם וְהִתְפַּלְלוּ אֵלֶיךָ דֶּרֶךְ אַרְצָם אֲשֶׁר נָתַתָּ לַאֲבוֹתָם. הָעוֹמְדִין וּמִתְפַּלְלִין בְּאֶרֶץ יִשְׂרָאֵל הוֹפְכִין אֶת פְּנֵיהֶן כְּלַפֵּי יְרוּשָׁלַיִם. וּמַה טַעַם וְהִתְפַּלְלוּ (fol. 8d) אֵלֶיךָ דֶּרֶךְ הָעִיר אֲשֶׁר בָּחַרְתָּ בָּהּ. הָעוֹמְדִין וּמִתְפַּלְלִין בִּירוּשָׁלַיִם הוֹפְכִין פְּנֵיהֶן כְּלַפֵּי הַר הַבַּיִת. שֶׁנֶּאֱמַר וְהַבַּיִת אֲשֶׁר בָּנִיתִי לִשְׁמֶךָ. הָעוֹמְדִין וּמִתְפַּלְלִין בְּהַר הַבַּיִת הוֹפְכִין פְּנֵיהֶן כְּלַפֵּי בֵּית קָדְשֵׁי הַקֳּדָשִׁים. וּמַה טַעַם וְהִתְפַּלְלוּ אֶל הַמָּקוֹם הַזֶּה וְאַתָּה תִשְׁמַע אֶל מְקוֹם שִׁבְתְּךָ אֶל הַשָּׁמַיִם וְשָׁמַעְתָּ וְסָלַחְתָּ. נִמְצְאוּ הָעוֹמְדִין בַּצָּפוֹן פְּנֵיהֶן לְדָרוֹם. הָעוֹמְדִין בַּדָּרוֹם פְּנֵיהֶן לְצָפוֹן. הָעוֹמְדִין בַּמִּזְרָח פְּנֵיהֶן לְמַעֲרָב. לְמַעֲרָב פְּנֵיהֶן לְמִזְרָח. נִמְצְאוּ כָל־יִשְׂרָאֵל מִתְפַּלְלִין אֶל מָקוֹם אֶחָד. הַהוּא דִכְתִיב כִּי בֵיתִי בֵּית תְּפִלָּה יִקָּרֵא לְכָל־הָעַמִּים.

It has been stated[231]: One who is blind and one who cannot determine directions should have in mind to pray to Heaven as it is said (*1Kings* 8:44) "They shall pray to the Eternal". Those who are praying outside the Land turn their faces towards the Land of Israel. What is the reason?

(*1Kings* 8:48) "They will pray to You through their Land that You gave to their forefathers." Those who are praying in the Land of Israel turn their faces towards Jerusalem. What is the reason? (*2Chr.* 6:34) "They shall pray to You by way of this city that You chose." Those who are praying in Jerusalem turn their faces towards the Temple Mount, as it is said (*1Kings* 8:48): "And the Temple that I built for Your Name." Those who are praying on the Temple Mount turn their faces towards the Holiest of Holies. What is the reason? (*1Kings* 8:30) "They will pray to this place and You will hear at Your dwelling place in Heaven, You will hear and forgive." Those who stand North will be facing South, those who stand South will be facing North, those who stand East will be facing West, those who stand West will be facing East. It turns out that all of Israel pray towards one place. That is what is written (*Is.* 56:7) "For My house will be called a house of prayer for all people."

231 Shortened versions are in Tosephta *Berakhot* 3:13-16 and Babli *Berakhot* 30a; the entire text to the end of the Halakhah is in *Shir rabba* 4:11 with minor deviations. The tradition of the verses is somewhat garbled in order to make the point of the derivation clearer.

אָמַר רִבִּי יְהוֹשֻׁעַ בֶּן לֵוִי הוּא הַהֵיכָל לִפְנָי לִפְנִים. הֵיכָל שֶׁכָּל־הַפָּנִים פּוֹנִין לוֹ. עַד כַּאן בְּבִנְיָנוֹ. בְּחוּרְבָּנוֹ מְנַיִין. אָמַר רִבִּי אָבוּן בָּנוּי לְתַלְפִּיּוֹת. תֵּל שֶׁכָּל־הַפִּיּוֹת מִתְפַּלְלִין עָלָיו. בִּבְרָכָה בְּקִרְיַת שְׁמַע וּבִתְפִילָּה. בִּבְרָכָה בּוֹנֵה יְרוּשָׁלַיִם. בִּתְפִילָּה אֱלֹהֵי דָוִד וּבוֹנֵה יְרוּשָׁלַיִם. בְּקִרְיַת שְׁמַע פּוֹרֵשׂ סוּכַּת שָׁלוֹם עָלֵינוּ וְעַל עַמּוֹ יִשְׂרָאֵל מְנַחֵם צִיּוֹן וּבוֹנֵה יְרוּשָׁלַיִם.

Rebbi Joshua ben Levi said: (*1Kings* 6:17) "That is the Temple 'לִפְנָי', Inside[232]. A Temple towards which all turn. So far when it[233] is standing. In its destruction, from where? Rebbi Abun said (*Cant.* 4:4): "Built for *talpiot*", a mound (תל) on which all mouths (פיות) pray, in Grace, recitation of *Shema*, and *Amidah*. In Grace, "Builder of Jerusalem". In *Amidah*, "God of David Who builds Jerusalem[235]". In the recitation of *Shema'*, "He Who spreads a hut of peace over us and His people Israel, Consoler of Zion and Builder of Jerusalem.[236]"

232 The word לפנים is missing in the Rome manuscript and in the quotes in Yalqut; it seems to be a marginal gloss that found its way into the text, to explain the unintelligible term לִפְנַי that in *1Kings* really seems to mean what Rabbinic לִפְנִים "inside" expresses. [There is an expression in the Babylonian Talmud for the Holiest of Holies, לפני ולפנים, which probably should be vocalized לִפְנַי וְלִפְנִים, based on this Yerushalmi.] The explanation here suggests to read לִפְנַי as shorthand for לְפָנִים פּוֹנִים, "for faces to turn."

234 The Temple. The problem is, how do we know to pray in the direction of the Temple after its destruction.

235 The standard Yerushalmi ending for benediction 14, see above Note 146.

236 The first part of this blessing is the Babylonian (current) version of the second benediction after the *Shema'* on Sabbaths and holidays. The entire benediction was the Yerushalmi version for everyday. The phrase "Consoler of Zion" is missing in the Leyden manuscript and Venice print but it is in the Rome manuscript and Genizah fragments and is supported by what is known of the Israeli prayer rites in the times of the Cairo Genizah.

כָּתוּב אֶחָד אוֹמֵר אֵלֵךְ אָשׁוּבָה אֶל מְקוֹמִי. וְכָתוּב אֶחָד אוֹמֵר וְהָיוּ עֵינַי וְלִבִּי שָׁם כָּל־הַיָּמִים. הָא כֵּיצַד פָּנָיו לְמַעְלָה וְעֵינָיו וְלִבּוֹ לְמַטָּה.

One verse says (*Hosea* 5:19) "I shall go, I shall return to My place". Another verse says (*1Kings* 9:3) "My eyes and attention shall be there forever." How is that? One's face upwards, one's eyes and attention downwards[237].

237 (The parallel in the Babli, *Yebamot* 105b, replaces the verse from Hosea by one from Threni. The ruling here is credited there to R. Yose the Tanna.) The two verses speak of God. The first asserts that God has left the

earth and is found only in Heaven, the second that God's attention is always given to the Temple here on earth. Since prayer adresses God, it is necessary to adress it in the correct direction and how can one pray in two distinct directions?

וְאִם לָאו יְכַוֵּין אֶת לִבּוֹ כְּנֶגֶד בֵּית קָדְשֵׁי הַקֳּדָשִׁים. לְאֵי זֶה בֵּית קָדְשֵׁי הַקֳּדָשִׁים. רִבִּי חִיָּא רַבָּא כְּנֶגֶד בֵּית קָדְשֵׁי הַקֳּדָשִׁים שֶׁל מַעְלָן. רִבִּי שִׁמְעוֹן בֶּן חֲלַפְתָּא אָמַר כְּנֶגֶד בֵּית קָדְשֵׁי הַקֳּדָשִׁים שֶׁל מַטָּן. אָמַר רִבִּי פִּינְחָס לָא פְּלִיגֵי בֵּית קָדְשֵׁי הַקֳּדָשִׁים שֶׁלְּמַטָּן מְכוּוָּן כְּנֶגֶד בֵּית קָדְשֵׁי הַקֳּדָשִׁים שֶׁלְּמַעְלָן. מָכוֹן לְשִׁבְתְּךָ. מְכוּוָּן כְּנֶגֶד שִׁבְתְּךָ.

"And if not he should focus his intent towards the Holiest of Holies.[238]" Toward which Holiest of Holies? The Great Rebbi Ḥiyya: towards the Heavenly Holiest of Holies. Rebbi Simeon ben Ḥalaphta said, towards the earthly Holiest of Holies. Rebbi Phineas said, they do not disagree, the earthly Holiest of Holies corresponds to the Heavenly Holiest of Holies. (*Ex.* 15:16) "A base for Your throne", corresponding to Your throne[239].

238 This is a shortened quote from the Mishnah, about the person who cannot stand and pray in the direction of the Temple.

239 Rebbi Phineas takes מכון to be derived not from the Biblical Hebrew root כון "to be based, solid", but from Aramaic/Rabbinic Hebrew כון "to direct".

בְּהַר הַמּוֹרִיָּה. רִבִּי חִיָּא רוּבָּא וְרִבִּי יַנַּיי חַד אָמַר שֶׁמִּשָּׁם הוֹרָיָה יוֹצְאָה לָעוֹלָם. וְחָרָנָה אָמַר שֶׁמִּשָּׁם יִרְאָה יוֹצְאָה לָעוֹלָם. אָרוֹן רִבִּי חִיָּא רוּבָּא וְרִבִּי יַנַּאי חַד אָמַר שֶׁמִּשָּׁם אוֹרָה יוֹצְאָה לָעוֹלָם. .וְחָרָנָה אָמַר שֶׁמִּשָּׁם אֲרִירָה יוֹצְאָה לָעוֹלָם. דְּבִיר[240] רִבִּי חִיָּא וְרִבִּי יַנַּאי חַד אָמַר שֶׁמִּשָּׁם דִּבֵּר יוֹצֵא לָעוֹלָם. וְחָרָנָה אָמַר שֶׁמִּשָּׁם דִּיבְּרוֹת יוֹצְאוֹת לָעוֹלָם.

(*2Chr.* 3:1) On Mount Moriah[241]. The Great Rebbi Ḥiyya and Rebbi Yannai, one of them said that from there teaching goes out to the world, the other one said that from there fear goes out to the world. Ark. The Great Rebbi Ḥiyya and Rebbi Yannai, one of them said that from there light goes out to the world, the other one said that from there curse goes out to the world. Temple Hall. Rebbi Ḥiyya and Rebbi Yannai, one of them said that from there inspiration goes out to the world, the other one said that from there the commandments go out to the world.

240 Reading of the Rome ms. and *Berešit rabba*. The Venice print has דברי, from a scribal error in the Leyden ms.

241 This Aggadah is a continuation of the previous discussion about the place of the Holiest of Holies, which was on Mount Moriah. An enlarged parallel is in *Berešit rabba* 55(9); a very shortened version is in Babli *Taänit* 16a.

מוריה is taken either from the root הורה "to teach, direct" or from מוֹרָא "fear". ארון is taken either as abstractum from אוֹר "light" or from ארה "to curse" (the unbelievers). The use of דִּבֵּר "Divine inspiration" in the explanation of דביר is from *Jer*. 5:13. דבר denoting one of the Ten Commandments is found in *Deut*. 4:13.

הִיא אַסָּדָה הִיא אִסְכַּדְיָה[242] הִיא רַפְסוֹדוֹת. וּנְבִיאֵם לְךָ רַפְסוֹדוֹת.

Assada is the same as σχεδία, which is the same as *raphsodot*.[243] (*2Chr*. 2:15) "We shall bring them to you as rafts."

242 The Yerushalmi text has אסכריה; the word is missing in ms. Rome. Musaphia in *Arukh*, s. v. אסדא, reads אסכדיה, as does the Gaonic Commentary to Mishnah *Negaïm* 13:1. The other commentaries of *Negaïm* 13:1 read the word as אִסְקַרְיָא, Greek κεραία "beam; horn; projection", which does not make sense here. σχεδία means "raft." {The technical term רפסודה in late Biblical Hebrew might be a Phoenician term derived from Greek ῥάπτω "string or link together" (E. G.).}

243 The end of the Halakhah explains the unusual word used for "raft" at the end of the Mishnah. The verse refers to the logs of cedar delivered by Hiram of Tyre to Solomon for the building of the Temple.

משנה ו: רִבִּי אֶלְעָזָר בֶּן עֲזַרְיָה אוֹמֵר אֵין תְּפִילַּת הַמּוּסָפִים אֶלָּא בְּחֶבֶר עִיר. וַחֲכָמִים אוֹמְרִים בְּחֶבֶר עִיר וּשֶׁלֹּא בְּחֶבֶר עִיר. רִבִּי יְהוּדָה אוֹמֵר מִשְּׁמוֹ כָּל־מָקוֹם שֶׁיֵּשׁ בּוֹ חֶבֶר עִיר הַיָּחִיד פָּטוּר מִתְּפִילַּת הַמּוּסָפִין.

Mishnah 6: Rebbi Eleazar ben Azariah says, *Musaph* prayer is said only in an organized community, but the Sages say, with and without an organized community. Rebbi Yehudah says in his name[244], at any place where there is an organized community a private person is free from reciting *Musaph* prayers.

244 Rebbi Eleazar ben Azariah's name. He disputes the tradition in the name of R. Eleazar that *Musaph* cannot be recited outside an organized community. According to Rebbi Yehudah, *Musaph* has to be recited everywhere, but in a town with an organized synagogue it is enough to listen to the public prayer of the reader that he recited without a corresponding silent prayer of the congregation.

הלכה ו: רִבִּי בִּיבִי בְּשֵׁם רִבִּי חָנָה אָמַר הֲלָכָה כְּרִבִּי יוּדָה שֶׁאָמַר מִשּׁוּם רִבִּי אֶלְעָזָר בֶּן עֲזַרְיָה. מִילְּתֵיהּ דִּשְׁמוּאֵל אָמַר כֵּן דִּשְׁמוּאֵל אָמַר אֲנָא מִן יוֹמוֹי לָא צַלִּית דְּמוּסָפָא אֶלָּא חַד זְמַן דְּמִית בְּרֵיהּ דְּרֵישׁ גָּלוּתָא וְלָא צַלּוּ צִיבּוּרָא וּצְלִית.

Halakhah 6: Rebbi Bibi[245] in the name of Rebbi Ḥana: Practice follows Rebbi Yehudah who said in the name of Rebbi Eleazar ben Azariah. What we know of Samuel means the same; for Samuel said: I never prayed *Musaph* except once when the son of the *Resh Galuta* died and there was no public prayer, then I prayed[246].

245 Probably his name was Vivianus, an Amora of the third generation. Rebbi Ḥana's name appears twice in the Talmudim; he seems to have been a student of Rebbi Jeremiah. Neither Rebbi Bibi nor Rebbi Ḥana are great authorities. In the Babli (30a-b), the author of the ruling is Ḥiyya, the son of Rav.

246 The story of Samuel in the Babli refers to a time when there was a military occupation of Nahardea.

מִילֵּיהוֹן דְּרַבָּנָן פְּלִיגִן. דָּמַר רִבִּי יַעֲקֹב בַּר אִידִי בְּשֵׁם רִבִּי שִׁמְעוֹן חֲסִידָא בְּרוֹעִים וּבְקַייָצִים. הָא מַתְנִיתִין לָא אֲמַר אֶלָּא[247] בְּרוֹעִים וּבְקַייָצִים הָא שְׁאָר כָּל־אָדָם חַייָבִין. מִילְתֵיהּ דְּרִבִּי יוֹחָנָן אֲמַר כֵּן דָּמַר רִבִּי יוֹחָנָן אֲנִי רָאִיתִי אֶת רִבִּי יַנַּאי עוֹמֵד וּמִתְפַּלֵּל בְּשׁוּק שֶׁל צִיפּוֹרִין וּמְהַלֵּךְ ד׳ אַמּוֹת וּמִתְפַּלֵּל מוּסָף. וְאֵין חֶבֶר עִיר בְּצִיפּוֹרִין. אַתְּ שְׁמַע מִינֵּיהּ תְּלָת. אַתְּ שְׁמַע מִינֵּיהּ שֶׁשּׁוּקֵי שֶׁל צִיפּוֹרִין כְּצִיפּוֹרִין. אַתְּ שְׁמַע מִינֵּיהּ חֲלוּקִין עַל רִבִּי יְהוּדָה שֶׁאָמַר מִשּׁוּם רִבִּי אֶלְעָזָר בֶּן עֲזַרְיָה. אַתְּ שְׁמַע מִינֵּיהּ שֶׁאָדָם מִתְפַּלֵּל וּמְהַלֵּךְ ד׳ אַמּוֹת וּמִתְפַּלֵּל שֶׁל מוּסָף. אָמַר רִבִּי אַבָּא לֹא סוֹף דָּבָר שֶׁיְּהַלֵּךְ ד׳ אַמּוֹת אֶלָּא אֲפִילוּ שָׁהָא כְּדֵי הִילּוּךְ ד׳ אַמּוֹת.

The words of the rabbis disagree since Rebbi Jacob bar Idi said in the name of Rebbi Simeon the pious[248]: For shepherds and field guards[249]. Hence, the Mishnah spoke only for shepherds and field guards; therefore, everybody else is obliged. The words of Rebbi Yoḥanan agree since Rebbi Yoḥanan said: I saw Rebbi Yannai standing in the market of Sepphoris praying; then he walked four cubits and prayed *Musaph*[250]. Is there no organized community in Sepphoris? You infer from this three conclusions. You infer that the markets of Sepphoris have the status of Sepphoris[251]. You infer that one disagrees with Rebbi Yehudah who spoke in the name of Rebbi Eleazar ben Azariah. You infer that a person may pray, walk four cubits, and then pray *Musaph*. Rebbi Abba said, not necessarily four cubits but even if he waited the time necessary to walk four cubits[252].

247 Reading of the Rome manuscript. The word is missing in the Venice text.

248 An Amora of the first Galilean generation.

249 Persons whose occupation prevents them from going to the synagogue. They probably were unable to pray *Musaph* by themselves since they were uneducated and prayerbooks were unknown at the time. Other uneducated people can attend the

synagogue and fulfill their duty by attentively follow the reader's repetition of the prayer word-by-word, but not shepherds and watchmen; hence a way has to be found to help them.

250 A shortened version, speaking only about the *Musaph* prayer, is in Babli 30b. In both Talmudim, it is clear that the sages who reject R. Yehudah's tradition are Galilean in the tradition of R. Yannai.

251 "Organized community" refers to the whole town and not only to the buildings that are the property of the Jewish community.

252 The parallel in the Babli (30b) requires time to concentrate one's attention without giving a numerical estimate; that tradition is in the name of the Babylonian Rav Huna and the Babylonian-born Rebbi Ḥiyya. One may assume that the statement of Rebbi Abba reflects the opinions of his teacher Rav Huna.

רַב אָמַר צָרִיךְ לְחַדֵּשׁ בָּהּ דָּבָר. וּשְׁמוּאֵל אָמַר אֵין צָרִיךְ לְחַדֵּשׁ בָּהּ דָּבָר. רִבִּי זְעִירָא בְּעֵי קוֹמֵי רִבִּי יוֹסֵי מַהוּ לְחַדֵּשׁ בָּהּ דָּבָר. אָמַר לֵיהּ אֲפִילוּ אָמַר וְנַעֲשֶׂה לְפָנֶיךָ אֶת חוֹבוֹתֵינוּ תְּמִידֵי יוֹם וְקָרְבַּן מוּסָף יָצָא.

Rav says, one must change the text[253], but Samuel says, one does not have to change the text. Rebbi Zeïra asked before Rebbi Yose: What is the practice, to change the text? He said to him: even if one said only: "And we shall bring before You what is our duty, the perpetual sacrifice of the day and the *Musaph* sacrifices[254]", he has satisfied his duty.

253 Since the *Musaph* sacrifices are distinct for every holiday, the prayer must accomodate this distinction.

254 Every holiday has its own set of *Musaph* sacrifices but the language is uniform for all holidays. A *Musaph* prayer is acceptable if the sentence quoted here is the only addition to the *Amidah* prayer for holidays, cf. Ezra Fleischer, תפילה ומנהגי תפילה ארץ־ישראליים בתקופת הגניזה, Jerusalem 1988.

רִבִּי שִׁילָא בְּשֵׁם רַב חֲנַנְאֵל נִתְפַּלֵּל וּמָצָא י בְּנֵי אָדָם מִתְפַּלְלִין מִתְפַּלֵּל עִמָּהֶן. רִבִּי זְעִירָא וְרַב נַחְמָן בַּר יַעֲקֹב הֲווּ יָתְבִין. מִן דְּמַצְלוּן אִתַּת צְלוּתָא קָם רַב נַחְמָן בַּר יַעֲקֹב מַצְלִיא. אֲמַר לֵיהּ רִבִּי זְעִירָא וְלָא כְבָר צְלִינָן. אֲמַר לֵיהּ אֲנָא

מַצְלִי וַחֲזַר וּמַצְלִי. דָּמַר רִבִּי שִׁילָא בְּשֵׁם רַב חֲנַנְאֵל נִתְפַּלֵּל וּמָצָא עֲשָׂרָה בְּנֵי אָדָם מִתְפַּלְלִין מִתְפַּלֵּל עִמָּהֶן.

Rebbi Shila[255] in the name of Rav Ḥananel[256]: If he had prayed and found ten people who were praying, he prays with them. Rebbi Zeïra and Rav Naḥman bar Jacob were sitting. After they had prayed there came prayer[257]. Rav Naḥman bar Jacob got up and prayed. Rebbi Zeïra said to him: Did we not pray already? He said to him: I pray and pray again, since Rebbi Shila said in the name of Rav Ḥananel: If he had prayed and found ten people who were praying, he would pray with them.

255 The head of the Yeshivah of Nahardea at the end of the Mishnaic period. His title shows that he must have studied and obtained ordination in the Land of Israel.

256 He appears in both Talmudim as a student of Rav, who was younger than Rebbi Shila. The tradition here is difficult to accept but is not impossible; it might be that Rebbi Shila accepted the position of the school of Rav in this matter. The Babli (21a/b) quotes only the position of Samuel that one may repeat prayer with the community only if one is able to pray a new text, different from the one already used. The tradition here seems to be based on the opinion, rejected in the Babli, that private prayer is considered nonexistent if compared to prayer in public with a quorum of ten adult males.

257 The congregation assembling for public prayer. The entire story happens in Babylonia; Rebbi Zeïra represents the opinion of Samuel and Rav Naḥman that of Rav.

רִבִּי אָחָא רִבִּי יוֹנָה בְּשֵׁם רִבִּי זְעִירָא נִתְפַּלֵּל שֶׁל שַׁחֲרִית וּבָא וּמְצָאָן מִתְפַּלְלִין שֶׁל מוּסָף מִתְפַּלֵּל עִמָּהֶן. לֹא נִתְפַּלֵּל שֶׁל שַׁחֲרִית וּבָא וּמְצָאָן מִתְפַּלְלִין שֶׁל מוּסָף. אִם יוֹדֵעַ הוּא שֶׁהוּא מַתְחִיל וְגוֹמֵר עַד שֶׁלֹּא יַתְחִיל שְׁלִיחַ צִיבּוּר כְּדֵי לַעֲנוֹת אַחֲרָיו אָמֵן יִתְפַּלֵּל וְאִם לָאו אַל יִתְפַּלֵּל. בְּאֵי זֶה אָמֵן אָמְרוּ. תְּרֵין אֲמוֹרָאִין חַד אָמַר בְּאָמֵן שֶׁל הָאֵל הַקָּדוֹשׁ. וְחָרְנָה אָמַר בְּאָמֵן שֶׁל שׁוֹמֵעַ תְּפִילָּה. אָמַר רִבִּי פִּינְחָס וְלֹא פְלִיגֵי. מַאן דָּמַר בְּאָמֵן שֶׁל הָאֵל הַקָּדוֹשׁ בְּשַׁבָּת. וּמַאן דָּמַר בְּאָמֵן שֶׁל שׁוֹמֵעַ תְּפִילָּה בְּחוֹל.

Rebbi Aḥa, Rebbi Jonah, in the name of Rebbi Zeïra: If one had said the morning prayers and came and found them praying *Musaph*, he prays with them. If he did not pray the morning prayers and came and found them praying *Musaph*, if he knows that he may start and finish[258] before the reader begins and he can answer "Amen", he may start, otherwise he may not start. About[259] which "Amen" did they talk? Two Amoraïm, one says the Amen of "the holy King" and the other says the Amen of "He Who listens to prayer". Rebbi Phineas said, they do not disagree. He who said: the Amen of "the holy King", on Sabbath, and he who said: the Amen of "He Who listens to prayer", on weekdays.

258 The morning prayer that has to precede *Musaph*.

259 Since one speaks about *Musaph* prayer that has only seven benedictions, the paragraph is out of place. It is copied word by word from Halakhah 3:2.

תַּמָּן תַּנִּינָן רַבָּן גַּמְלִיאֵל אוֹמֵר שְׁלִיחַ צִיבּוּר מוֹצִיא אֶת הָרַבִּים יְדֵי חוֹבָתָן. רִבִּי הוּנָא רַבָּא דְצִיפּוֹרִין בְּשֵׁם רִבִּי יוֹחָנָן הֲלָכָה כְּרַבָּן גַּמְלִיאֵל בְּאִילֵּין תְּקִיעָתָא. רִבִּי זְעִירָא וְרַב חִסְדָּא הֲווּ יָתְבִין תַּמָּן בְּאִילֵּין תְּקִיעָתָא. מִן דִּצְלוֹן אֶת צְלוֹתָא קָם רַב חִסְדָּא מַצְלִיא. אֲמַר לֵיהּ רִבִּי זְעִירָא וְלָא כְּבָר צְלִינָן. אֲמַר לֵיהּ מַצְלִי אֲנָא וַחֲזַר וּמַצְלִי. דְּנַחְתּוּן מַעֲרָבָאֵי לְתַמָּן וְאָמְרִין בְּשֵׁם רִבִּי יוֹחָנָן הֲלָכָה כְּרַבָּן גַּמְלִיאֵל בְּאִילֵּין תְּקִיעָתָא. וַאֲנָא דְּלָא כְּוָנִית הָא אִלּוּ כְּוָנִית הֲוֵינָא נְפִיק יְדֵי חוֹבָתִי. אֲמַר רִבִּי זְעִירָא וְיֵאוּת כָּל־תְּנָאֵי תַּנֵּי בְּשֵׁם רַבָּן גַּמְלִיאֵל. וְרִבִּי הוֹשַׁעְיָא תַּנֵּי לָהּ בְּשֵׁם חֲכָמִים. רִבִּי אָדָא דְקֵיסָרִין בְּשֵׁם רִבִּי יוֹחָנָן וְהוּא שֶׁיְּהֵא שָׁם מֵרֹאשׁ. אָמַר רִבִּי תַּנְחוּם וּמַתְנִיתָא אָמְרָה כֵן סֵדֶר בְּרָכוֹת אוֹמֵר אָבוֹת וּגְבוּרוֹת וּקְדוּשַּׁת הַשֵּׁם.

There[260] we have stated: Rabban Gamliel says, the reader frees the public from their obligation[261]. The older Rebbi Huna from Sepphoris in the name of Rebbi Yoḥanan: Practice follows Rabban Gamliel for the prayer accompanying the blowing of the Shofar[262]. Rebbi Zeïra and Rav Ḥisda were sitting there[263] for the blowing of the Shofar. After they finished the prayer[264], Rav Ḥisda got up and prayed. Rebbi Zeïra said to him: Did we not pray just now? He said to him, I prayed and I am repeating the prayer, because Westerners came down and said in the name of Rebbi Yoḥanan: Practice follows Rabban Gamliel for the prayer accompanying the blowing of the Shofar, but I was inattentive. If I had been attentive, I would have fulfilled my duty. Rebbi Zeïra said, that is fine[265]. All Tannaïm[266] state it in the name of Rabban Gamliel, Rebbi Hoshaia states it in the name of the Sages[267]. Rebbi Ada from Caesarea[268] in the name of Rebbi Yoḥanan: This is only if he attended from the start. Rebbi Tanḥum said, the Mishnah[269] expresses this: The order of benediction, one says "Forefathers", "Greatness", and "Sanctification of the Name".

260 In the last Mishnah of *Rosh Hashanah.* The entire piece is from the end of tractate *Rosh Hashanah*; at two places where the text of the Venice print here deviates from the one in *Rosh Hashanah*, the text follows the latter version. (The first, "Rabban Simeon ben Gamliel" instead of "Rabban Gamliel" is a clear scribal error, the second אתת for את is an echo of the previous story of R. Zeïra and Rav Naḥman.)

261 The Mishnah deals with the *Musaph* prayer of New Year's day which contains nine benedictions; each of the middle benedictions requires the quoting of at least 10 verses from the Bible. In the absence of prayerbooks, that prayer was possible only for learned specialists. In the time of later Gaonim (*Oẓar Hagĕonim Rosh Hashanah*, p. 68-69), two different Babylonian practices are reported. One, which seems to be alluded to in Babli *Rosh Hashanah* 35a, is that individuals first prayed a silent *Musaph* prayer of the usual seven benedictions for holidays and then listened to the nine benedictions of the reader (with shofar blowing) from beginning to end. The second, which

seems to be alluded to here, was that there was no silent *Musaph* prayer at all on *Rosh Hashanah.*

262 The Mishnah of Rabban Gamliel deals only with *Musaph* of Rosh Hashanah. From the statement of Rebbi Huna it seems that Rabban Gamliel held that a private person, even if educated, never needs to pray *Musaph* if he listens attentively to the reader in the synagogue. This remains a conjecture in the Babli (*Rosh Hashanah* 34b-35a).

263 In Babylonia. Perhaps "staying" would be better than "sitting".

264 From the following, it seems clear that they did not pray *Musaph* for themselves but listened to the reader from start to end.

265 Since Rav Ḥisda, the head of a Yeshivah, certainly is competent to recite his own nine benedictions for *Rosh Hashanah* from memory.

266 These *Tannaïm* are not the teachers of the Mishnaic period but the people who memorize Mishnah and *baraitot* to recite them in the Yeshivah when they are needed.

267 Most Tannaïm imply that in the days of Rabban Gamliel his opinion was a minority opinion, which became generally accepted only through the decision of Rebbi Yoḥanan. Rebbi Hoshaiah implies that Rabban Gamliel's was the generally accepted practice already in Mishnaic times.

268 Another student of R. Yoḥanan, of the third generation of Galilean Amoraïm.

269 *Rosh Hashanah* 4:5, implying that the prayer is valid only if it is recited in the correct order. Hence, it is valid for the listener only if he listened in the correct order, starting from the very first word.

אין עומדין פרק חמישי

משנה א: אֵין עוֹמְדִין לְהִתְפַּלֵּל אֶלָּא מִתּוֹךְ כּוֹבֶד רֹאשׁ. חֲסִידִים הָרִאשׁוֹנִים הָיוּ שׁוֹהִין שָׁעָה אַחַת וּמִתְפַּלְּלִין כְּדֵי שֶׁיְּכַוְּנוּ אֶת לִבָּם. אֲפִילוּ הַמֶּלֶךְ שׁוֹאֵל בִּשְׁלוֹמוֹ לֹא יְשִׁיבֶנּוּ. וַאֲפִילוּ נָחָשׁ כָּרוּךְ עַל עֲקֵבוֹ לֹא יַפְסִיק.

Mishnah 1: One starts to pray only in a serious frame of mind. The first *Ḥasidim* waited one hour[1] before praying in order to be able to concentrate. Even if the king greets one, he should not respond. Even if a snake is wound around one's heel[2], he should not interrupt.

1 In preparation, reciting Psalms.

2 As explained in the Halakhah, if one sees a snake attacking from a distance one must interrupt and flee, or kill the snake. The Mishnah speaks only about the snake already being wound around his leg without biting; probably that is a nonpoisonous snake.

(fol. 8d) **הלכה א**: רִבִּי יִרְמְיָה בְּשֵׁם רִבִּי אַבָּא הַבָּא מִן הַדֶּרֶךְ אָסוּר לוֹ לְהִתְפַּלֵּל. וּמַה טַעַם לָכֵן שִׁמְעִי נָא זֹאת עֲנִיָּה וּשְׁכוּרַת וְלֹא מִיָּיִן. רִבִּי זְרִיקָן רִבִּי יוֹחָנָן בְּשֵׁם רִבִּי אֱלִיעֶזֶר בְּנוֹ שֶׁל רִבִּי יוֹסֵי הַגְּלִילִי הַמֵּיצַר אָסוּר לְהִתְפַּלֵּל לֹא קְרָיָין לָכֵן שִׁמְעִי נָא זֹאת עֲנִיָּה וּשְׁכוּרַת וְלֹא מִיָּיִן.

Halakhah 1: Rebbi Jeremiah in the name of Rebbi Abba: Prayer is forbidden to him who comes from a trip. What is the reason? (*Is.* 51:21) "Listen to that, poor woman, drunk and not from wine.[3]" Rebbi Zeriqan, Rebbi Yoḥanan in the name of Rebbi Eliezer, son of Rebbi Yose the Galilean[4]: Prayer is forbidden to one in pain; is that not our verse: "Listen to that, poor woman, drunk and not from wine"?

3 This proves that there is drunkenness not induced by alcohol. Formal prayer, the *Amidah*, is forbidden to a drunk. The parallel in the Babli (*Eruvin* 65a) even notes that after a lengthy caravan trip one needs three days to get one's thoughts together.

4 Tanna of the fourth generation, active in the aftermath of the war of Bar Kokhba. He tried to systematize aggadic interpretation of the Bible.

תַּנֵּי לֹא יַעֲמוֹד אָדָם וְיִתְפַּלֵּל לֹא מִתּוֹךְ שִׂיחָה וְלֹא מִתּוֹךְ שְׂחוֹק וְלֹא מִתּוֹךְ קַלּוּת רֹאשׁ וְלֹא מִתּוֹךְ דְּבָרִים בְּטֵלִין אֶלָּא מִתּוֹךְ דָּבָר שֶׁל תּוֹרָה וְכֵן אַל יִפָּטֵר אָדָם מִתּוֹךְ חֲבֵירוֹ[5] לֹא מִתּוֹךְ שִׂיחָה וְלֹא מִתּוֹךְ שְׂחוֹק וְלֹא מִתּוֹךְ קַלּוּת רֹאשׁ וְלֹא מִתּוֹךְ דְּבָרִים בְּטֵלִין אֶלָּא מִתּוֹךְ דָּבָר שֶׁל תּוֹרָה. שֶׁכֵּן מָצִינוּ בִּנְבִיאִים הָרִאשׁוֹנִים שֶׁהָיוּ חוֹתְמִין אֶת דִּבְרֵיהֶן בְּדִבְרֵי שֶׁבַח וּבְדִבְרֵי נְחָמָה. אָמַר רִבִּי אֶלְעָזָר חוּץ מִיִּרְמְיָהוּ שֶׁחָתַם בְּדִבְרֵי תוֹכָחוֹת. אָמַר לוֹ רִבִּי יוֹחָנָן עוֹד הוּא בְּדִבְרֵי נְחָמוֹת חָתַם וְאָמַר כָּכָה תִּשְׁקַע בָּבֶל. לְפִי שֶׁהָיָה יִרְמְיָה חוֹזֵר וּמִתְנַבֵּא עַל בֵּית הַמִּקְדָּשׁ. יָכוֹל בְּחוּרְבַּן בֵּית הַמִּקְדָּשׁ חָתַם. תַּלְמוּד לוֹמַר עַד הֵנָּה דִּבְרֵי יִרְמְיָה בְּמַפּוֹלֶת שֶׁל מַחֲרִיבָיו חָתַם. לֹא חָתַם בְּדִבְרֵי תוֹכָחוֹת. וְהָכְתִיב וְהָיוּ דֵרָאוֹן לְכָל־בָּשָׂר. בְּגוֹיִים הִיא עֲסִיקִינָן. וְהָכְתִיב כִּי מָאוֹס מְאַסְתָּנוּ. הֲשִׁיבֵנוּ תַּחַת כִּי מָאוֹס מְאַסְתָּנוּ. אַף אֱלִיָּהוּ לֹא נִפְטַר מֵאֱלִישָׁע אֶלָּא מִתּוֹךְ דָּבָר שֶׁל תּוֹרָה. וַיְהִי הֵמָּה הוֹלְכִים הָלוֹךְ וְדַבֵּר. בְּמַה הָיוּ עוֹסְקִין רִבִּי אַחֲוָה בְּרִבִּי זְעִירָא אָמַר בִּקְרִיַּת שְׁמַע הָיוּ עוֹסְקִין. הֵיךְ מַה דְּאָמַר אָמַר וְדִבַּרְתָּ בָּם. רִבִּי יוּדָה בֶּן פָּזִי אָמַר בִּבְרִיאַת עוֹלָם הָיוּ עוֹסְקִין. הֵיךְ מַה דְּאָמַר בִּדְבַר יי שָׁמַיִם נַעֲשׂוּ. רִבִּי יוּדָן בְּרֵיהּ דְּרִבִּי אַיְבוּ אָמַר בְּנֶחָמוֹת יְרוּשָׁלַיִם הָיוּ עוֹסְקִין. כְּמַה דְאָמַר דַּבְּרוּ עַל לֵב יְרוּשָׁלַיִם. וְרַבָּנָן אָמְרִין בַּמֶּרְכָּבָה הָיוּ עוֹסְקִין. הֵיךְ מַה דְּאַתְּ אָמַר וְהִנֵּה רֶכֶב אֵשׁ וְסוּסֵי אֵשׁ וגו'.

It is stated[6]: "One should pray neither out of conversation, nor out of jokes, nor out of frivolities, nor out of idle occupations, but out of words of Torah. Similarly, one should not take leave from one's friend either out of conversation, or out of jokes, or out of frivolities, or out of idle occupations, but out of words of Torah, since we find that the earlier prophets were closing their words with expressions of praise and consolation." Rebbi Eleazar said, except for Jeremiah who closed with words of reprobation. Rebbi Yoḥanan said to him, still he closed with words of consolation and said *(Jer.* 51:64) "So Babylon shall sink." Because Jeremiah continued to prophesy about the Temple. One could think that he closed with the destruction of the Temple, but the verse states (*Jer.* 51:64) "So far the words of Jeremiah," he finished with the downfall of its destroyers, he did not close with words of reprobation[7]. But is it not written (*Is.* 66:24): "They will be a horror for all flesh?[8]" That verse deals with Gentiles. But is it not written (*Lament.* 5:22): "But You much despised us[9]"? (*Lament.* 5:21) "Make us return" replaces "But You much despised us". Also Elijah did take leave from Elisha only out of words of Torah, (*2Kings* 2:11) "they walked talking." What did they talk of? Rebbi Aḥawa the son of Rebbi Zeïra[10] said, they discussed the recitation of *Shema'*, (*Deut.* 6:7) "you should talk about them." Rebbi Judah ben Pazi said, they were discussing Creation, (*Ps.* 33:6) "through the word of the Eternal the heavens were made." Rebbi Yudan, the son of Rebbi Ayvu[11], said, they were occupied with the consolations of Jerusalem, as you say (*Is.* 40:2) "Speak to Jerusalem's heart." But the rabbis say, they were occupied with the Divine Chariot, as you say (*2Kings* 2:11) "behold, a chariot of fire and horses of fire, etc."

5 Probably a scribal error for מְחַבֵּירוֹ.

6 We have three versions of this formulation, in the Yerushalmi, the Babli (*Berakhot* 31a), and the Tosephta (3:21). The main difference in formulation is between the Tosephta and the Talmudim, since the Tosephta requires that one start prayer מתוך דברים של חכמה. In Mishnaic Hebrew, as in Modern Sephardic Hebrew usage, the *Ḥakham* is the rabbi, and *dibrē ḥokhmāh* are halakhic rulings; as in the following paragraph, practices universally accepted and not subject to

doubt or discussion. From the order of the Yerushalmi it seems that in practice the text of the Yerushalmi should be interpreted as implying the statement of the Tosephta. The tradition of the Babli is uncertain; see *Diqduqe Soferim, Berakhot*, p. 160, note ר. The Venice print of the Babli requires that one start prayer "out of joy over commandments". Rashi, the Munich manuscript of the Babli, Halakhot Gedolot and the students of Rabbenu Jonah have simply "out of joy." The Koronel manuscript and *Menorat Hamaör* have "out of joy of Torah", parallel to the Yerushalmi. A Florence manuscript that is typically Sephardic has "out of joy of Halakhah", directly parallel to the Tosephta. Rabbenu Asher ben Yeḥiel (Rosh) has "out of words of joy"; the insistence on "words" is parallel to Yerushalmi and Tosephta. While the Babli in the printed version would refer to the state of mind required for the *Amidah*, as implied in the two rulings preceding this Tosephta in the Yerushalmi, the Tosephta and the Yerushalmi require the correct state of mind before one starts with the preparatory sections of prayer, even preceding the recitation of *Shema'*. This seems also to be confirmed by the preparatory prayer reported later by R. Ḥizqiah in the name of R. Abbahu. Most of the variants of the Babli text would demand an interpretation similar to that of the Tosephta. All three versions agree that one should start afternoon prayers with a word of Torah or Halakhah directly before the *Amidah.*

7 The last chapter of the book of Jeremiah is not attributed by the Talmud to Jeremiah; it is a historical addition by the editor, Barukh ben Neriah.

8 Last verse in Isaiah.

9 Last verse of Lamentations. A possible interpretation of the statement is that the last two verses of the book, chapter 5, were considered as one; then the book ends with a prayer.

10 In the Babli, his name is R. Ahavah, son of Rebbi Zera, son of the famous Rebbi Zeïra. He was *Tanna*, a memorizer of tannaitic material, in his father's Yeshivah. The entire section is a digression induced by the ancillary statements of the Tosephta.

11 Rebbi Ayvu was one of the main promoters of *Aggadah* in the third generation of Amoraïm. He learned from all Galilean Amoraïm of the second generation. His son Rebbi Yudan might be the Rebbi Yudan who otherwise is quoted without mention of his father's name.

ר׳ יִרְמְיָה אָמַר לֹא יַעֲמוֹד אָדָם וְיִתְפַּלֵּל אֶלָּא מִתּוֹךְ דִּין שֶׁל הֲלָכָה. רַב יִרְמְיָה אָמַר הָעוֹסֵק בְּצוֹרְכֵי צִיבּוּר כְּעוֹסֵק בְּדִבְרֵי תוֹרָה. רַב הוּנָא אָמַר הָרוֹאָה טִיפָּה כְּעֵין חַרְדָּל יוֹשֶׁבֶת וּמְשַׁמֶּרֶת עָלָיו שִׁבְעָה נְקִיִּים וְקָאִים וּמְצַלִּי. זְעִירָא בַּר חִינְנָא אָמַר הַמֵּקִיז דָּם בְּקֳדָשִׁים מָעַל. עוֹד הִיא מֵהֲלָכוֹת קְצוּבוֹת. תַּנֵּי בַּר קַפָּרָא אָמַר אַחַד עָשָׂר יוֹם שֶׁבֵּין נִידָּה לְנִידָּה הֲלָכָה לְמֹשֶׁה מִסִּינַי. תַּנֵּי רַבִּי הוֹשַׁעְיָא מַרְבֶּה אָדָם דָּגָן וְתֶבֶן וּמַעֲרִים עָלָיו לְפוֹטְרוֹ מִן הַמַּעְשְׂרוֹת. אַבְדָּן שָׁאַל לְרַבִּי כַּמָּה מַעֲלוֹת בְּקוֹדֶשׁ. וְהוּא אָמַר לֵיהּ אַרְבַּע. וְכַמָּה מַעֲלוֹת בִּתְרוּמָה. וְהוּא אָמַר שָׁלֹשׁ וְקָאִים וּמְצַלִּי.

Rav Jeremiah said, one should start to pray only from a practical rule[12]. Rav Jeremiah said, he who deals with public needs is like him who studies Torah[13]. Rav Ḥuna said: a woman who saw a spot like a mustard seed sits and watches seven days of purification because of it[14]; then he stood up and prayed. Zeïra bar Ḥinena[15] said: He who draws blood from a dedicated animal committed larceny[16]; that is one of the decided practices. Bar Qappara stated: Eleven days between periods is a practice taught to Moses at Sinai[17]. Rebbi Hoshaiah stated: One may add produce on the stalk and be tricky in order to free it from tithes[18]. Abdan asked Rebbi: How many levels[19] are there for dedicated things? He answered him: four. And how many levels for *Terumah*? He answered: three, then he stood up and prayed.

12 In the Babli (31a), this is a *baraita* and is considered a contrast to, not an explanation of, the requirement of the Mishnah that one pray only in a serious frame of mind. In the Yerushalmi it is considered to be the genuine interpretation of the Mishnah. דין של הלכה means a practical ruling that is well established, that gives no cause for discussion which could interfere with the concentration needed for prayer. The Babli and the personalities whose practices in preparation of prayer are reported are so early that the name here must be Rav Jeremiah and not Rebbi Jeremiah.

13 This Halakhah is not found in the Babli, so it is accepted there.

14 This appears in the Babli (31a) in the name of Rav Huna's student Rebbi Zeïra. A menstruating woman is ritually unclean and prohibited from having sexual contact until seven days have passed. On the other hand, a woman having a discharge looking like blood is subject to quite different rules that are more lenient for an occasional occurence and much more strict for recurrent discharges. A decision about the character of the discharge can be made only by a competent rabbi. In theory all women should show their discharges to a rabbi. Even in the time of the Temple, that was a practice only of wives of Cohanim who had to minimize their time of impurity by all means. It may be assumed that all other women chose to follow the method described here, to consider any discharge as a recurrent discharge and to wait seven days after the last day of discharge. In that way, no problems arise that would require a rabbi in intimate matters. Since this is a stringency adopted by Jewish women in excess of the strict Biblical law, there cannot be any rabbinic discussion about limits or details.

15 Galilean Amora of the second generation. He was once imprisoned by Zenobia, queen of Palmyra, and saved by the intervention of Rebbi Ammi and Rebbi Samuel. The parallel in the Babli (31a) is ascribed to Zeïri, a contemporary of Zeïra and student of Rav.

16 An animal dedicated as sacrifice in the Temple cannot be used for any other purpose whatsoever, not even to draw blood from it.

17 If a woman has a discharge between the 8th and the 19th day of the begin of her last period, that discharge cannot be menstrual blood and must be treated by the rules of זבה-discharge. This is a tradition ascribed to Moses and, therefore, is a fact not subject to discussion.

18 Grain is subject to *Terumah* and tithes after the harvest, when it is separated from the stalk and collected in heaps or silos. By a rabbinic ordinance, it is forbidden to eat grain on the stalk as a meal, once it has been transported from the field to the farmhouse or barn. However, eating it as snack from the grain on the stalk is still permitted. Now Rebbi Hoshaiah approves of setting aside as much of the produce for animal feed as one desires, without incurring an obligation for *Terumah* and tithes. This is also quoted as beyond doubt in Babli 31a.

19 Of derivative impurity. If originally impure matter (אב הטומאה "father of impurity") touches something

that can become impure, the latter becomes "first in impurity". If a "first in impurity" touches other secular matter, nothing happens except if that matter is food, it will become "second in impurity". If "second in impurity" touches anything secular, nothing happens, but if it touches either *terumah* or sacrificial meat, these become "third in impurity". Sacrifial meat only can become "fourth in impurity" which will make it unusable either for the altar or for consumption by Cohanim. (Mishnah *Ḥagigah* 2:3, *Tahorot* 2:1). The additional levels of impurity are a rabbinic institution, not subject to discussion.

רִבִּי חִזְקִיָּה רִבִּי יַעֲקֹב בַּר אָחָא רִבִּי יָסָא בְּשֵׁם רִבִּי יוֹחָנָן לְעוֹלָם אַל יְהֵא הַפָּסוּק הַזֶּה זָז מִתּוֹךְ פִּיךָ יי צְבָאוֹת עִמָּנוּ מִשְׂגָּב לָנוּ אֱלֹהֵי יַעֲקֹב סֶלָה. רִבִּי יוֹסֵי בֵּי רִבִּי אָבִין רִבִּי אַבָּהוּ בְּשֵׁם רִבִּי יוֹחָנָן וַחֲבֵרַיָּיא יי צְבָאוֹת אַשְׁרֵי אָדָם בּוֹטֵחַ בָּךְ.

Rebbi Ḥizqiah, Rebbi Jacob bar Aḥa, Rebbi Yasa in the name of Rebbi Yoḥanan: The following verse should never leave your lips[20]: (*Ps.* 46:12) "The Eternal of hosts is with us, the God of Jacob is a refuge to us, Selah". Rebbi Yose ben Rebbi Abin, Rebbi Abbahu in the name of Rebbi Yohanan and the colleagues: (*Ps.* 84:13) "O Eternal of hosts, hail to the man who trusts in You".

20 Meaning, they should be mentioned in every prayer service. However, in current rituals, the verses are used only in the morning service and the קדושה דסדרא.

רִבִּי חִזְקִיָּה בְּשֵׁם רִבִּי אַבָּהוּ יְהִי רָצוֹן מִלְּפָנֶיךָ יי אֱלֹהֵינוּ וֵאלֹהֵי אֲבוֹתֵינוּ שֶׁתַּצִּילֵנוּ מִשָּׁעוֹת הַחֲצוּפוֹת הַקָּשׁוֹת הָרָעוֹת הַיּוֹצְאוֹת הַמִּתְרַגְּשׁוֹת לָבוֹא לָעוֹלָם.

Rebbi Ḥizqiah in the name of Rebbi Abbahu: May it be please You, o Eternal, our God and God of our fathers, that You may save us from agressive, hard, evil hours that organize to come upon the world[21].

21 This is clearly a supplication to be recited before the start of formal prayers, see the discussion above; in our prayerbooks its equivalent is a modification of a prayer of Rav (Babli *Berakhot* 16b).

אֵין עוֹמְדִין לְהִתְפַּלֵּל אֶלָּא מִתּוֹךְ כּוֹבֶד רֹאשׁ. רִבִּי יְהוֹשֻׁעַ בֶּן לֵוִי אָמַר הִשְׁתַּחֲווּ לַיי בְּהַדְרַת קֹדֶשׁ בְּחֶרְדַּת קֹדֶשׁ. רִבִּי יוֹסֵי בֶּן חֲנִינָא אָמַר עִבְדוּ אֶת יי בְּיִרְאָה וְגִילוּ בִּרְעָדָה. אָמַר רִבִּי אָחָא לִכְשֶׁיָּבוֹא יוֹם רָעָה תָּגִילוּ.

"One starts to pray only in a serious frame of mind."[22] Rebbi Joshua ben Levi said, (*Ps*. 29:2) "Bow down before the Eternal in the splendor of the sanctuary," in fear of the holy[23]. Rebbi Yose ben Ḥanina said, (*Ps*. 2:11) "Serve the Eternal in fear, rejoice in trembling." Rebbi Aḥa said, when an evil day should come, you may rejoice[24].

22 With this quote from the Mishnah, the detailed discussion starts. The following verses seek to prove that a serious state of mind is required in a place of holiness (Babli 30b).

23 In some Galilean and all Babylonian dialects, ה and ח sounded the same and were not distinguished. In other dialects, the sounds were close.

24 The person to rejoice even in bad times is the Just, who has nothing to fear. In the opinion of Tosaphot (*Berakhot* 31a, s. v. במקום), R. Aḥa gives the simple sense of the verse, in contrast to the homiletics of R. Yose ben R. Ḥanina.

אָמַר רִבִּי יְהוֹשֻׁעַ בֶּן לֵוִי זֶה שֶׁהוּא עוֹמֵד וּמִתְפַּלֵּל צָרִיךְ לֵישֵׁב שְׁתֵּי יְשִׁיבוֹת. אַחַת עַד שֶׁלֹּא יִתְפַּלֵּל וְאַחַת מִשֶּׁיִּתְפַּלֵּל. עַד שֶׁלֹּא יִתְפַּלֵּל אַשְׁרֵי יוֹשְׁבֵי בֵיתֶךָ. וְאַחַת מִשֶּׁיִּתְפַּלֵּל אַךְ צַדִּיקִים יוֹדוּ לִשְׁמֶךָ יֵשְׁבוּ יְשָׁרִים אֶת פָּנֶיךָ.

Rebbi Joshua ben Levi said, he who is about to pray has to sit down twice. Once before he prays and once after he prays. Before he prays, (*Ps*. 84:5) "Hail to those who sit in Your house." Once after he prays, (*Ps*. 140:14) "But the righteous will thank Your name, the upright ones will sit before You.[25]"

25 Under the influence of the tradition given in the next paragraph, the parallel of the Babli (32b) requires in the name of R. Joshua ben Levi that one sit in the synagogue one hour each before and after prayer. "One hour" probably means "some time." The argument given here is that in Ps. 84 there is no qualification for those in God's house, but in Ps. 140 this is restricted to the righteous, those who have fulfilled their obligation in praying.

חֲסִידִים הָרִאשׁוֹנִים הָיוּ שׁוֹהִין שָׁעָה אַחַת וּמִתְפַּלְלִין שָׁעָה וְשׁוֹהִין שָׁעָה אַחַת אַחַר תְּפִילָּתָן. אֵימָתַי עוֹסְקִין בַּתּוֹרָה. אֵימָתַי עוֹסְקִין בִּמְלַאכְתָּן. אָמַר רִבִּי יִצְחָק בֵּי רִבִּי אֶלְעָזָר עַל יְדֵי שֶׁהָיוּ חֲסִידִים הָיְתָה בְרָכָה נִיתֶּנֶת בְּתוֹרָתָן וּבְרָכָה נִיתֶּנֶת בִּמְלַאכְתָּן.

"The first *Ḥasidim* waited one hour before praying,[26]" they prayed for one hour and waited an hour after their prayer. When did they study Torah? When did they work? Rebbi Isaac ben Rebbi Eleazar[27] said, because they were pious, their study was blessed and their work was blessed.

26 Quote from the Mishnah.

27 The explanation of R. Isaac ben R. Eleazar is part of the *baraita* in the Babli (32b); this may indicate that the author here is the earlier of two Amoraïm of that name, a student of R. Yoḥanan. The Babli, which notes explicitly that the pious were spending 9 hours in prayer, must take "an hour" in its exact sense; the Yerushalmi may accept "an hour" as "some time". On the other hand, the replacement of "sitting down" by "waiting" may indicate that in this paragraph ישב has its original Biblical meaning of "being occupied, being at one's regular place of business."

חוּנָה אָמַר הַמִּתְפַּלֵּל אֲחוֹרֵי בֵּית הַכְּנֶסֶת נִקְרָא רָשָׁע. שֶׁנֶּאֱמַר סָבִיב רְשָׁעִים יִתְהַלֵּכוּן. רַב חוּנָה אָמַר כָּל־מִי שֶׁאֵינוֹ נִכְנַס בְּבֵית הַכְּנֶסֶת בָּעוֹלָם הַזֶּה אֵינוֹ נִכְנַס לְבֵית הַכְּנֶסֶת לֶעָתִיד לָבוֹא. מַה טַּעַם סָבִיב רְשָׁעִים יִתְהַלֵּכוּן.

Ḥuna[28] said, he who prays behind the synagogue is called criminal as it is said (*Ps.* 12:9) "Criminals walk around." Rav Ḥuna[29] said, one who does not enter a synagogue in this world will not enter the synagogue in the future world. What is the reason? (*Ps.* 12:9) "Criminals walk around."

28 The parallel in the Babli (6b) shows that this is Rav Huna, the Babylonian. Authors of later generations in the Babli attenuate this statement to label as criminals only those who pray behind the synagogue facing away from the building; this is not accepted in the Yerushalmi.

29 In the (Yerushalmi) *Midrash Tehillim* the parallel statement is one of R. Joshua ben Levi, the author of the preceding homiletics, and is part of his homiletics on *Ps.* 84:5.

אָמַר רִבִּי יוֹחָנָן הַמִּתְפַּלֵּל בְּתוֹךְ בֵּיתוֹ כְּאִילּוּ מַקִּיפוֹ חוֹמָה שֶׁל בַּרְזֶל. מְחַלְּפָה שִׁיטָּתֵיהּ דְּרִבִּי יוֹחָנָן. תַּמָּן אָמַר רִבִּי אַבָּא אָמַר רִבִּי חִייָא בְּשֵׁם רִבִּי יוֹחָנָן צָרִיךְ לְאָדָם לְהִתְפַּלֵּל בְּמָקוֹם שֶׁהוּא מְיוּחָד לִתְפִילָּה. וְכָה אָמַר הָכִין. כַּאן בְּיָחִיד כַּאן בְּצִיבּוּר.

Rebbi Yoḥanan said: He who prays in his own house is as if he were surrounded by an iron wall[30]. The argument of Rebbi Yoḥanan is inverted. There[31] Rebbi Abba said, Rebbi Ḥiyya said in the name of Rebbi Yoḥanan, one has to pray at a place that is dedicated to prayer[32]. And here he says that? One is about a single person, the other about the public[33].

30 I. e., his prayer is not heard because he is enclosed by such a wall. (Interpretation of R. Solomon Cirillo.)

31 Chapter 4, Halakhah 4.

32 Not necessarily in the synagogue, but in one's own house only at a place that is dedicated to prayer. Hence, private prayer is acceptable and no wall will hinder the prayer from being heard.

33 A person living at a place where there is no synagogue has to pray at a dedicated place in his house. If, however, there is public prayer at his

place of residence then private prayer in one's house will not be heard. However, that statement is relativized by the statement of Rebbi Abbahu below that a place of Torah study is equal (or superior) to a synagogue.

רִבִּי פִּינְחָס בְּשֵׁם רִבִּי הוֹשַׁעְיָא הַמִּתְפַּלֵּל בְּבֵית הַכְּנֶסֶת כְּאִילּוּ מַקְרִיב מִנְחָה טְהוֹרָה. מַה טַעַם כַּאֲשֶׁר יָבִיאוּ בְּנֵי יִשְׂרָאֵל אֶת הַמִּנְחָה בִּכְלִי טָהוֹר בֵּית יי. רִבִּי יִרְמְיָה[34] בְּשֵׁם רִבִּי אַבָּהוּ דִּרְשׁוּ אֶת יי בְּהִמָּצְאוֹ. אֵיכַן הוּא מָצוּי. בְּבָתֵּי כְּנֵסִיּוֹת וּבְבָתֵּי מִדְרָשׁוֹת. קְרָאוּהוּ (fol. 9a) בִּהְיוֹתוֹ קָרוֹב. אֵיכַן הוּא קָרוֹב. בְּבָתֵּי כְּנֵסִיּוֹת וּבְבָתֵּי מִדְרָשׁוֹת.[35] אָמַר רִבִּי יִצְחָק בֵּי רִבִּי אֶלְעָזָר וְלֹא עוֹד אֶלָּא שֶׁאֱלֹהֵיהֶן עוֹמֵד עַל גַּבָּן. מַאי טַעְמָא אֱלֹהִים נִצָּב בַּעֲדַת אֵל בְּקֶרֶב אֱלֹהִים יִשְׁפּוֹט.

Rebbi Phineas in the name of Rebbi Hoshaiah: He who prays in the synagogue is as if he had sacrificed a pure flour offering. What is the reason? (*Is.* 66:20) "As the children of Israel bring flour offering in a pure vessel in the Eternal's House.[36]" Rebbi Jeremiah in the name of Rebbi Abbahu: (*Is.* 55:6) "Seek the Eternal where He is to be found". Where is He to be found? In synagogues and houses of study. "Call on Him when He is close." Where is He close? In synagogues and houses of study. Rebbi Isaac ben Rebbi Eleazar said, not only that but their God stands over them. What is the reason? (*Ps.* 81:1) "God stands in the assembly of the mighty; from the inside God will judge."

34 This is the reading of *Yalqut Shim'oni Isaiah* §481. The Venice-Leyden version "R. Abbahu" is certainly corrupt.

35 Text of the Rome manuscript; the sentence is missing in the Leyden ms. and the Venice print.

36 Since the actual flour offering was brought by the Cohanim, the prophet speaks here of a symbolic act.

רַב חִסְדָּא אָמַר זֶה שֶׁנִּכְנַס לְבֵית הַכְּנֶסֶת צָרִיךְ לְהִכָּנֵס לִפְנִים מִשְּׁנֵי דְלָתוֹת. מַה טַעַם אַשְׁרֵי אָדָם שׁוֹמֵעַ לִי לִשְׁקוֹד עַל דַּלְתוֹתַי תָּמִיד. דַּלְתוֹתַי וְלֹא דְלָתִי. מְזוּזוֹת וְלֹא מְזוּזַת. אִם עָשָׂה כֵן מַה כְתִיב תַּמָּן כִּי מוֹצְאִי מָצָא חַיִּים.

Rav Ḥisda said: He who enters the synagogue must enter inside two doors. What is the reason (*Prov.* 8:34) "Hail to the man who listens to Me, always to be diligent at My doors[37]." My doors and not my door. Doorposts and not doorpost[38]. If he did that, what is written there? (*Prov.* 8:35) "Because he who found Me found life.[39]"

37 The verse is spoken by Wisdom (or the Torah) but is interpreted as God's word.

38 This refers to the end of the verse which is omitted here: "To guard the doorposts of my entrances always."

39 In the Babli (8b), the statement of Rav Ḥisda appears without justification, but it follows a statement of R. Joshua ben Levi that he who frequents the synagogue will live long and which is supported by the two verses quoted here. Hence, the Babli is dependent on the Yerushalmi in this case.

רַב חוּנָא אָמַר זֶה שֶׁהוּא הוֹלֵךְ לְבֵית הַכְּנֶסֶת צָרִיךְ לְהָקֵל אֶת רַגְלָיו. מַה טַעַם נֵדְעָה נִרְדְּפָה לָדַעַת אֶת יי. וּכְשֶׁהוּא יוֹצֵא צָרִיךְ לְהַלֵּךְ קִמְעָא. מַה טַעַם כִּי אַתָּה[40] צְעָדַי תִּסְפּוֹר.

Rav Ḥuna said: He who goes to the synagogue must be light-footed. What is the reason? (*Hos.* 6:3) "We shall know, let us run to know the Eternal." But when one leaves, one has to go in small steps. What is the reason? (*Job* 14:16) "For now You will count my steps.[41]"

40 In the Biblical text עַתָּה "now".

41 In the Babli (6b), Rav Ḥuna is credited only with the second statement (without supporting verse). The first statement, with the supporting verse, is given by Abbaye, two generations later; clearly under the influence of the Yerushalmi tradition.

אָמַר רִבִּי יוֹחָנָן בְּרִית כְּרוּתָה הִיא הַיָּגֵעַ תַּלְמוּדוֹ בְּבֵית הַכְּנֶסֶת לֹא בִמְהֵרָה הוּא מְשַׁכֵּחַ. אָמַר רִבִּי חֲנִינָא עֵינְתּוֹנַיָא בְּרִית כְּרוּתָה הִיא הַיָּגֵעַ תַּלְמוּדוֹ בְּצִנְעָה לֹא בִמְהֵרָה הוּא מְשַׁכֵּחַ. מַה טַעַם וְאֶת צְנוּעִים חָכְמָה. אָמַר רִבִּי יוֹחָנָן בְּרִית

כְּרוּתָה הִיא הַלָּמֵד אֲגָדָה מִתּוֹךְ הַסֵּפֶר לֹא בִמְהֵרָה הוּא מְשַׁכֵּחַ. אָמַר רִבִּי תַּנְחוּם הַסּוֹבֵר תַּלְמוּדוֹ לֹא בִמְהֵרָה הוּא מְשַׁכֵּחַ. מַה טַעַם פֶּן תִּשְׁכַּח אֶת הַדְּבָרִים אֲשֶׁר רָאוּ עֵינֶיךָ.

Rebbi Yoḥanan said: A covenant is sealed that he who labors at his studies in the synagogue will not quickly forget. Rebbi Ḥanina from Ein Tana said: A covenant is sealed that he who labors at his studies in modesty will not quickly forget. What is the reason? (*Prov*. 11:2) "Wisdom is with the modest." Rebbi Yoḥanan said: A covenant is sealed that he who studies homiletics from a book will not quickly forget. Rebbi Tanḥum said: He who understands what he has learned will not quickly forget. What is the reason? (*Deut*. 4:9) "That you shall not forget the things your eyes understood.[42]"

42 The order of the items is not correct; it is better in the Rome manuscript and the fragments of the Yerushalmi from the Genizah: First come the two statements of the second generation Rebbi Yoḥanan. The first one is a continuation of the description of good behavior in the synagogue; the synagogue is a good place for study between times for prayer. The second statement appears here because it is from R. Yoḥanan; it is a polemic against the opinion of R. Joshua ben Levi (Yerushalmi *Šabbat* 16:1) that homiletics is a part of "oral Torah" that may not be written down. Next comes the statement of R. Ḥanina of Ein Tana, Amora of the fourth generation and student of R. Zeïra. (His name is corrupted in the Venice print to R. Yoḥanan of Ein Tana; it is correct in the Rome ms. Ein Tana was a place near Sepphoris.) At the end comes the statement of the fifth generation Rebbi Tanḥum (Tanḥuma bar Abba, the first known author of a collection of *Midrashim* and greatest of the preachers of the period of the Talmud Yerushalmi).

רִבִּי יוֹנָה בְשֵׁם רִבִּי תַּנְחוּם בֵּי רִבִּי חִייָא זֶה שֶׁהוּא רוֹאֶה חֲלוֹם קָשֶׁה צָרִיךְ לוֹמַר יְהִי רָצוֹן מִלְּפָנֶיךָ יי אֱלֹהַי וֵאלֹהֵי אֲבוֹתַי שֶׁיְּהוּ כָּל־חֲלוֹמוֹתַי שֶׁחָלַמְתִּי בֵּין

בַּלַּיְלָה הַזֶּה בֵּין בִּשְׁאָר הַלֵּילוֹת בֵּין שֶׁחָלַמְתִּי אֲנִי וּבֵין שֶׁחָלְמוּ לִי אֲחֵרִים. אִם טוֹבִים הֵם יִתְקַיְּימוּ עָלַי לְשָׂשׂוֹן וּלְשִׂמְחָה לִבְרָכָה וּלְחַיִּים. וְאִם לְדָבָר אַחֵר כְּשֵׁם שֶׁהָפַכְתָּ אֶת מֵי הַמָּרָה לְמְתִיקָה וּמֵי יְרִיחוֹ עַל יְדֵי אֱלִישָׁע לִמְתִיקָה. וְאֶת קִלְלַת בֶּן בְּעוֹר לִבְרָכָה כֵּן תַּהֲפוֹךְ אֶת כָּל חֲלוֹמוֹת הַקָּשִׁין. וּמַה שֶּׁחָלְמוּ אֲחֵרִים לְטוֹבָה לִבְרָכָה וְלִרְפוּאָה וּלְחַיִּים לְשִׂמְחָה וּלְשָׂשׂוֹן וּלְשָׁלוֹם. הָפַכְתָּ מִסְפְּדִי לְמָחוֹל לִי פִּתַּחְתָּ שַׂקִּי וַתְּאַזְּרֵנִי שִׂמְחָה. לְמַעַן יְזַמֶּרְךָ כָּבוֹד וְלֹא יִדּוֹם יי אֱלֹהַי לְעוֹלָם אוֹדֶךָּ. וְלֹא אָבָה יי אֱלֹהֶיךָ לִשְׁמוֹעַ אֶל בִּלְעָם וַיַּהֲפוֹךְ יי אֱלֹהֶיךָ אֶת הַקְּלָלָה לִבְרָכָה כִּי אֲהֵבְךָ יי אֱלֹהֶיךָ. אָז תִּשְׂמַח בְּתוּלָה בְּמָחוֹל וּבַחוּרִים וּזְקֵנִים יַחְדָּיו וְהָפַכְתִּי אֶבְלָם לְשָׂשׂוֹן וְנִיחַמְתִּים וְשִׂימַּחְתִּים מִיגוֹנָם.

Rebbi Jonah in the name of Rebbi Tanḥum ben Rebbi Hiyya[43], He who sees a disquieting dream must say: "May it be Your pleasure. o Eternal, my God and God of my fathers, that all my dreams that I dreamed, in this night or in any other night, whether I dreamed or others dreamed about me, if they are good they should be fulfilled for me in enjoyment and joy, blessing and life. If they are something else then, just as You turned bitter water to sweet waters, the waters of Jericho to sweet ones through Elisha, and the curse of the son of Beör to a blessing, so may You turn all bad dreams, including what others dreamed about me, to good, blessing, healing, life, joy and enjoyment, and peace. (*Ps*. 30:12-13) 'You turned my wailing into a dance, you opened my sackcloth and girded me with joy. So that the liver may sing to You and never be silent; o Eternal, my God, I shall eternally thank You! (*Deut*. 23:6) The Eternal, your God, refused to listen to Bileam, the Eternal, your God, turned curse into blessing since the Eternal, your God, loves you. (*Jer*. 31:12) Then the maiden will rejoice in dance, young and old men together; I shall turn their mourning to enjoyment and I shall console them and give them joy out of their hurt."'

43 The parallel in the Babli (55b) contains two traditions. The first one, attributed to the earlier R. Yoḥanan, is that one should assemble three people (a court of law) and declare before them: I saw a good dream. They should answer: It is good, should be good, the All-Merciful shall turn it into a good one sevenfold; may they decree from heaven that it should be good. Then they should recite the verses given here at the end, add three verses of peace and three of redemption. The second one, of Rav Ashi, Amemar, and Mar Zuṭra, two generations later than the authors in the Yerushalmi, has a text similar to the one given here but without the verses. Hence, the Yerushalmi represents an intermediate stage in the development of this prayer. The Babli requires, in contrast to the Yerushalmi, that the prayer be said during the priestly blessing given at morning prayers.

אֲפִילוּ הַמֶּלֶךְ שׁוֹאֵל בִּשְׁלוֹמוֹ לֹא יְשִׁיבֶנּוּ. אָמַר רִבִּי אָחָא הָדָא דְאָמַר בְּמַלְכֵי יִשְׂרָאֵל. אֲבָל בְּמַלְכֵי אוּמּוֹת הָעוֹלָם מֵשִׁיב שְׁאֵילַת שָׁלוֹם. תַּנֵּי הָיָה כּוֹתֵב אֶת הַשֵּׁם אֲפִילוּ מֶלֶךְ שׁוֹאֵל בִּשְׁלוֹמוֹ לֹא יְשִׁיבֶנּוּ. הָיָה כּוֹתֵב שְׁנַיִם אוֹ שְׁלֹשָׁה שֵׁמוֹת כְּגוֹן אֵל אֱלֹהִים יי הֲרֵי זֶה גוֹמֵר אֶת אֶחָד מֵהֶן וּמֵשִׁיב שְׁאֵילַת שָׁלוֹם.

"Even if the king greets one, he should not respond.[44]" Rebbi Aḥa said, that is, if the greeter is a king of Israel. But one returns greeting from a Gentile king. It was stated[45]: If one is writing a Divine name, then even if the king greets him, he should not respond. If he is writing two or three Names, e. g. (*Jos.* 22:22) "Powerful, God, Eternal", he finishes one of them[46] and then responds to the greeting.

44 Quote from the Mishnah, title of the following discussion. The statement of R. Aḥa is quoted in the Babli (32b) in the name of the slightly earlier Rav Joseph.

45 Slightly different versions appear in Tosephta *Berakhot* 3:22, *Massekhet Soferim* 5:6.

46 The one he is currently writing.

רִבִּי יוֹחָנָן הֲוָה יְתִיב קְרֵי קוֹמֵי כְּנִישְׁתָּא דְבָבֶל בְּצִיפּוֹרִין עָבַר אַרְכוֹנָא וְלָא קָם לֵיהּ קוֹמוֹי אָתוּן בְּעַיָּן מִימְחוּנֵיהּ. אֲמַר לוֹן אַרְפּוּנֵיהּ בְּנִימוֹסָא דִבְרֵייֵהּ הוּא

עֲסִיק. רִבִּי חֲנִינָא וְרִבִּי יְהוֹשֻׁעַ בֶּן לֵוִי עָלוּן קוֹמֵי אַנְטִיפּוּטָא דְקֵיסָרִין חֲמָתוּן וְקָם מִן קוֹמֵיהוֹן. אָֽמְרוּ לֵיהּ מִן קוֹמוֹי אִילֵּין יְהוּדָאֵי אַתְּ קָאִים. אָמַר לוֹן אַפֵּיהוֹן דְּמַלְאָכִין חֲמִית. רִבִּי יוֹנָה וְרִבִּי יוֹסֵי עָלוּן קוֹמוֹי אֻרְסְקִינָס בְּאַנְטוֹכִיָא חֲמָתוּן וְקָם מִן קוֹמֵיהוֹן. אָֽמְרִין לֵיהּ מִן קוֹמוֹי אִילֵּין יְהוּדָאֵי אַתְּ קָאִים. אָמַר לוֹן אַפֵּיהוֹן דְּהַנֵּי אֲנָא חֲזֵי בִקְרָבָא וּנְצַח. רִבִּי אָבוּן עַל קוֹמוֹי מַלְכוּתָא כִּי נְפַק הָפַךְ קְדָל. אֲתוּן בְּעַיּוֹן מִיקְטְלִינֵיהּ וַחֲמוֹן תְּרֵין זִיקוּקִין דְּנוּר נָֽפְקִין מִקְּדָלֵיהּ וְשָֽׁבְקוּהּ. לְקַיֵּם מַה שֶּׁנֶּאֱמַר וְרָאוּ כָּל־עַמֵּי הָאָרֶץ כִּי שֵׁם יי נִקְרָא עָלֶיךָ וְיָֽרְאוּ מִמֶּךָּ.

Rebbi Yoḥanan[47] was sitting and reciting in front of the Babylonian synagogue of Sepphoris. The prefect passed by and he did not get up before him. They wanted to whip him; he said to them: Let him, he is occupied in the laws of his Creator. Rebbi Ḥanina and Rebbi Joshua ben Levi appeared before the proconsul[48] of Caesarea. He saw them and rose before them. They said to him, you get up before these Jews? He said to them, I saw faces of angels. Rebbi Jonah and Rebbi Jose appeared before Ursicinus[49] in Antiochia. He saw them and rose before them. They said to him, you get up before these Jews? He said, I win in battle if I see the faces of these. Rebbi Abun appeared before the king[50]. When he left, he turned his neck. They came and wanted to kill him but they saw two sparks of fire emanating from his neck, so they let him go, to affirm what is said (*Deut.* 28:10): "All peoples of the earth will see that the Name of the Eternal is called over you and they will be afraid of you.[51]"

47 The following notes show that the permission to accomodate Gentile rulers is not prescriptive but can be disregarded by genuinely holy men (though not by any other Jew.) The stories are ordered by rank of the Gentile involved. Rebbi Yoḥanan was reciting *Shema'* when the ἄρχων, the prefect of the district, passed by. He was in danger to be beaten up by prefect's bodygard but, as ruler of a city with an important Jewish popu

lation, he was acquainted with their behavior and their adherence to the νόμος, "the law" of the Torah.

48 Ἀνθύπατος "proconsul", the Roman governor of an entire province. Both prefect and proconsul were also the local military commanders.

49 The general in charge of all of Syria and Palestine under the Caesar Gallus, around 350 C. E.

50 The "king" is either the emperor Diocletian or one of his immediate successors, so probably R. Abun here is R. Abun II. Diocletian changed the formally republican Roman principate into an absolute monarchy in which the sacred person of the emperor required veneration as a godlike person (this was not abolished by his Christian successors.) In particular, after an audience the visitor was supposed to walk backwards with his face always towards the throne. R. Abun's act was one of denial of the godlike nature of the king. After this incident, R. Abun escaped to Babylonia, as noted in Babli *Hulin* 106a, "when Rabin came, it was because he was in danger of being killed."

51 This is a reference to a statement in Babli 6a: "All peoples of the earth will see that the name of the Eternal is called over you and they will be afraid of you;" the great Rebbi Eliezer said: These are the *tefillin* on the head. It can be safely assumed that this statement of an Israeli Tanna was known to the editors of the Yerushalmi, so they had no need for an explicit statement that the sparks came from the straps of R. Abun's *tefillin*.

תַּנֵּי רִבִּי שִׁמְעוֹן בֶּן יוֹחַי וְרָאוּ כָּל־עַמֵּי הָאָרֶץ כִּי שֵׁם יי נִקְרָא עָלֶיךָ. כֹּל אֲפִילוּ רוּחוֹת אֲפִילוּ שֵׁדִים. רִבִּי יַנַּיי וְרִבִּי יוֹנָתָן הֲווּ מְטַייְלִין בְּאִסלטין חַמְתּוֹן חַד וְשָׁאַל בְּהוֹן אֲמַר לְהוֹן שְׁלַמְכוֹן רִבַּייָא. אָמְרִין אֲפִילוּ תּוֹאַר חֲבֵרוּת אֵין עָלֵינוּ לְרָעָה.

Rebbi Simeon ben Yoḥai stated: "All peoples of the earth will see that the name of the Eternal is called over you", all - even spirits and demons. Rebbi Yannai and Rebbi Jonathan were promenading in a forest[52]. One saw them, greeted them, and said: "Peace upon you, rabbis." They said, even the religious title does not harm us.

52 The hapax אסלטין seems to be Latin *saltus*, "forest". The Rome ms. reading is אסרטין , Latin *strata*, "street", Genizah fragments read אסטדין "stadion." The forest is a more likely place to find promenading rabbis greeted by a demon.

רִבִּי שִׁמְעוֹן בֶּן לָקִישׁ מִיהֲגֵי בְּאוֹרַיְיתָא סַגִּין הֲוָה נְפִיק לְבַר מִתְּחוּמָא דְּשַׁבָּתָא וְהוּא לָא יְדַע לְקַיֵּם בְּאַהֲבָתָהּ תִּשְׁגֶּה תָמִיד. רִבִּי יוּדָן בֵּי רִבִּי יִשְׁמָעֵאל מִיהֲגֵי בְּאוֹרַיְיתָא סַגִּין הֲוָת גּוּלְתֵיהּ שְׁרָעָה מִינֵיהּ [וְהוּא לָא יְדַע לְקַיֵּם בְּאַהֲבָתָהּ תִּשְׁגֶּה תָמִיד. רִבִּי אֶלְעָזָר בֵּירִבִּי שִׁמְעוֹן מִיהֲגֵי בְּאוֹרַיְיתָא סַגִּין הֲוָת גּוּלְתֵיהּ שְׁרָעָה מִינֵיהּ][53] וַהֲוָת חֲכִינָא מִזְהֲרָה לָהּ. אָמְרִין לֵיהּ תַּלְמִידוֹי רִבִּי הָא גּוּלְתֵיךְ שְׁרִיעָה. אָמַר לוֹן וְלֵית הַהִיא רְשִׁיעָתָא זְהִירָה לָהּ.

Rebbi Simeon ben Laqish[54] was thinking very hard about Torah. He overstepped the Sabbath boundary without noticing it, to confirm (*Prov.* 5:19): "In its love you will always err." Rebbi Yudan ben Rebbi Ismael was thinking very hard about Torah. His toga slipped off from him and he did not notice it, to confirm : "In its love you will always err." Rebbi Eleazar ben Rebbi Simeon was thinking very hard about Torah. His toga slipped off from him but a viper was caring for it. His students told him: Teacher, your toga has slipped off. He said to them, does this evil one not care for it?

53 The text here is that of the Yerushalmi from the Genizah and, partially, from the Rome manuscript; the Leyden/Venice text is shortened by omission of the words in parenthesis.

54 This paragraph is a connection between the preceding and the following ones. First, it shows that great scholars are apt to be absent-minded (and, hence, may not notice the presence of potentially dangerous men or situations) and, second, to show that even snakes can be helpful to Torah sages.

אֲפִילוּ נָחָשׁ כָּרוּךְ עַל עֲקֵבוֹ לֹא יַפְסִיק. רִבִּי חוּנָא בְּשֵׁם רִבִּי יוֹסֵי לֹא שָׁנוּ אֶלָּא נָחָשׁ. אֲבָל עַקְרָב מַפְסִיק. לָמָּה דְּמָחְיָיא וְחָזְרָה וּמָחְיָיא. רִבִּי אִילָא אָמַר לֹא

אָמְרוּ אֶלָּא כָּרוּךְ אֲבָל אִם הָיָה מַרְתִּיעַ כְּנֶגְדּוֹ הֲרֵי זֶה מַסְתִּיר מִלְּפָנָיו. וּבִלְבַד שֶׁלֹּא יַפְסִיק אֶת תְּפִילָּתוֹ. תַּנֵּי הָיָה עוֹמֵד בְּאִסְרָטִיָּא אוֹ בִּפְלָטֵיָּא הֲרֵי זֶה מַעֲבִיר מִפְּנֵי הַחֲמוֹר וּמִפְּנֵי הַקָּרוֹן וּבִלְבַד שֶׁלֹּא יַפְסִיק אֶת תְּפִילָּתוֹ.

"Even if a snake is wound around one's heel, one should not interrupt." Rebbi Ḥuna in the name of Rebbi Yose: They mentioned only a snake, but for a scorpion he interrupts[55]. Why, because it stings repeatedly. Rebbi Ilaï said: They stated only "wound around", but if a snake is attacking him, he hides before him but he should not interrupt his prayer. It is stated: If he was praying in a thoroughfare or on a square[56] he removes himself from before a donkey or before a cart but he should not interrupt his prayer[57].

55 In the Babli (33a), the statement is in the name of the earlier Rav Sheshet; no reason is given there.

56 Greek πλατεῖα (ὁδός) "wide open" (road). "Cart" is from Greek κάῤῥος, κάῤῥον. "Thoroughfare" is also found in Arabic as צְרַאט صِراط.

57 The Babli (32a) states that one should shorten his prayer (by reciting only the final doxologies of all the remaining benedictions). R. Isaac Alfassi's version is: "If he can shorten, he should shorten, and if not, he should interrupt." In the Yerushalmi, one is permitted in an emergency to change his place and then continue with prayer at another place, but in the Babli the prayer is interrupted automatically if one moves.

אָמְרִין עָלָיו עַל רִבִּי חֲנִינָא בֶּן דוֹסָא שֶׁהָיָה עוֹמֵד וּמִתְפַּלֵּל וּבָא חֲבַרְבָּר וְהִכִּישׁוֹ וְלֹא הִפְסִיק אֶת תְּפִילָּתוֹ וְהָלְכוּ וּמָצְאוּ אוֹתוֹ חֲבַרְבָּר מֵת מוּטָל עַל פִּי חוֹרוֹ. אָמְרוּ אִי לוֹ לְאָדָם שֶׁנְּשָׁכוֹ חֲבַרְבָּר. וְאִי לוֹ לַחֲבַרְבָּר שֶׁנָּשַׁךְ אֶת רִבִּי חֲנִינָא בֶּן דוֹסָא. מַה עִיסְקֵיהּ דְּהָדֵין חֲבַרְבָּרְיָא כַּד הֲוָה נְכִית לְבַר נַשָּׁא אִין בַּר נַשָּׁא קָדִים לְמַיָּא חֲבַרְבָּרָא מָיִית. וְאִין חֲבַרְבָּרְיָא קָדִים לְמַיָּא בַּר נַשָּׁא מָיִית. אָמְרוּ לוֹ תַּלְמִידָיו רִבִּי לֹא הִרְגַּשְׁתָּ. אָמַר לָהֶן יָבֹא עָלַי מִמָּה שֶׁהָיָה לִבִּי מִתְכַּוֵּן בִּתְפִילָּה אִם הִרְגַּשְׁתִּי. אָמַר רִבִּי יִצְחָק בַּר אֶלְעָזָר בָּרָא לוֹ הַקָּדוֹשׁ בָּרוּךְ הוּא

מַעְיָן תַּחַת כַּפּוֹת רַגְלָיו לְקַיֵּם מַה שֶׁנֶּאֱמַר רְצוֹן יְרֵאָיו יַעֲשֶׂה וְאֶת שַׁוְעָתָם יִשְׁמַע וְיוֹשִׁיעֵם.

They said about Rebbi Ḥanina ben Dosa[58] that he was standing in prayer when a brightly dotted snake[59] came and bit him. He did not interrupt his prayer. The went and found that dotted snake lying dead at the entrance of its hole. They said, woe to the human who is bitten by a dotted snake, but woe to the dotted snake that bites Rebbi Ḥanina ben Dosa. [What is the nature of that dotted snake? If it bites a human and the human reaches water first, the dotted snake dies, but if the dotted snake reaches water first, the human dies.] His students asked him: Rabbi, did you not notice? He said to them: There should happen to me these things[60]; I was concentrating on my prayer and did not notice! Rebbi Isaac ben Eleazar[61] said, the Holy One, praise to Him, created a well under his foot soles, to confirm what has been said (*Ps.* 145: 19): "He will do the will of those who fear Him, He will hear their entreaties and save them."

58 Tanna of the first generation, from lower Galilee, companion of Rabban Yoḥanan ben Zakkai. He is the perfectly holy man who never committed a single sin. All his traditions are about ethical maxims. A text close to the present one [without the Aramaic insert] appears in Tosephta *Berakhot* 3:30; a very different version is in Babli 33a.

59 In Biblical Hebrew, חברבורות are the spots of a leopard. The root חבר "to shine" appears once more in the Bible (*Job* 16:4); in Arabic the parallel root is חבר "to be richly ornamented" [distinguished from Hebrew חבר, Arabic ח̇בר, "to be joined".] The word could also denote a brightly striped snake. The more brightly a snake is colored, the more poisonous it is.

60 A formula of affirmation, taking the place of an oath.

61 This Amoraic addition belongs to the explanation given in the insert and is not part of the *baraita* tradition.

משנה ב: מַזְכִּירִין גְּבוּרוֹת גְּשָׁמִים בִּתְחִיַּת הַמֵּתִים וְשׁוֹאֲלִין גְּשָׁמִים בְּבִרְכַּת הַשָּׁנִים וְהַבְדָּלָה בְּחוֹנֵן הַדָּעַת. רִבִּי עֲקִיבָה אוֹמֵר אוֹמְרָהּ בְּרָכָה רְבִיעִית בִּפְנֵי עַצְמָהּ. רִבִּי אֱלִיעֶזֶר אוֹמֵר בְּהוֹדָאָה.

Mishnah 2: One mentions the power of rains in "resurrection of the dead[62]"; one prays for rain in the benediction "of years" and *Havdalah*[62] in "He Who by His grace grants knowledge;" Rebbi Aqiba said: it is recited as separate fourth benediction; Rebbi Eliezer says, in "thanksgiving".

62 The second benediction of the *Amidah*. The benediction "for years" is the ninth, a prayer for a plentiful harvest. *Havdalah* is the required declaration of a "difference" between Sabbath (or holiday) and weekday, after the end of the Sabbath or holiday. No work may be performed before some form of *Havdalah*. The benediction for being granted knowledge is the fourth, the one for thanksgiving the 17th.

הלכה ב: כְּשֵׁם שֶׁתְּחִיַּת הַמֵּתִים חַיִּים לָעוֹלָם כַּךְ יְרִידַת גְּשָׁמִים חַיִּים לָעוֹלָם. רִבִּי חִיָּיא בַּר אַבָּא שָׁמַע לָהּ מִן הָדָא יְחַיֵּינוּ מִיּוֹמָיִם בַּיּוֹם הַשְּׁלִישִׁי יְקִימֵנוּ וְנִחְיֶה לְפָנָיו. נֵדְעָה נִרְדְּפָה לָדַעַת אֶת יי כְּשַׁחַר נָכוֹן מוֹצָאוֹ.

Halakhah 2: Just as the resurrection of the dead brings life to the world, so rains bring life to the world[63]. Rebbi Ḥiyya bar Abba understood it from here (*Hos.* 6:2-3): "He will resurrect us after two days, on the third day He will raise us up and we shall live before Him. We shall know, we shall pursue to know the Eternal, like morning his appearance is well-based[64]."

63 These are all arguments that God has to be praised for rain in the prayer for resurrection during the rainy season. The first verse of Hosea clearly speaks of resurrection, the second one ends: "it (knowing God) will come like rain to us, like late rains that pour on the Land."

64 These verses are further discussed in Yerushalmi *Taäniot* 1:1 (fol. 63d), *Sanhedrin* 11:8 (fol. 30c), Babli *Roš Haššanah* 31a, *Sanhedrin* 97a.

כְּתִיב וַיֹּאמֶר אֵלִיָּהוּ הַתִּשְׁבִּי מִתֹּשָׁבֵי גִלְעָד אֶל אַחְאָב חַי יי אֱלֹהֵי יִשְׂרָאֵל אֲשֶׁר עָמַדְתִּי לְפָנָיו אִם יִהְיֶה הַשָּׁנִים הָאֵלֶּה טַל וּמָטָר כִּי אִם לְפִי דְבָרִי. רִבִּי בֶּרֶכְיָה אָמַר רִבִּי יָסָא וְרַבָּנָן חַד אָמַר בֵּין עַל הַטַּל וּבֵין עַל הַמָּטָר נִשְׁמַע לוֹ וְחָרָנָא אָמַר עַל הַמָּטָר נִשְׁמַע לוֹ וְעַל הַטַּל (fol. 9b) לֹא נִשְׁמַע לוֹ. מִן הָדָא לֵךְ הֵרָאֵה אֶל אַחְאָב וְאֶתְּנָה מָטָר וְגוֹמֵר. וּמַן דָּמַר בֵּין עַל הַטַּל וּבֵין עַל הַמָּטָר נִשְׁמַע לוֹ. אֵיכַן הוּתַּר נִדְרוֹ שֶׁל טַל. אָמַר רִבִּי תַּנְחוּמָא עֶדְרֶעִיָּא סָבְרִין מֵימַר נֶדֶר שֶׁהוּתַּר מִכְּלָלוֹ הוּתַּר כּוּלּוֹ. אִית דְּבָעֵי מֵימַר בִּבְנָהּ שֶׁל צָרְפִית וַיִּקְרָא אֶל יי וַיֹּאמַר יי אֱלֹהָי וְגוֹמֵר. אָמַר רִבִּי יוּדָה בֶּן פָּזִי לְאֶחָד שֶׁגָּנַב נַרְתִּיקוֹ שֶׁל רוֹפֵא. עִם כְּשֶׁהוּא יוֹצֵא נִפְצַע בְּנוֹ. חָזַר עֶצְלוֹ אָמַר לוֹ אֲדוֹנִי הָרוֹפֵא רְפָא אֶת בְּנִי. אָמַר לוֹ לֵךְ וְהַחְזֵר אֶת הַנַּרְתִּק שֶׁכָּל־מִינֵי רְפוּאוֹת נְתוּנִין בּוֹ וַאֲנִי מְרַפֶּה אֶת בְּנְךָ. כַּךְ אָמַר לוֹ הַקָּדוֹשׁ בָּרוּךְ הוּא לְאֵלִיָּהוּ לֵךְ וְהַתֵּר נִדְרוֹ שֶׁל טַל שֶׁאֵין הַמֵּתִים חַיִּים אֶלָּא בְטְלָלִים וַאֲנִי מְחַיֶּה אֶת בְּנָהּ שֶׁל הַצָּרְפִית. וּמְנַיִּין שֶׁאֵין הַמֵּתִים חַיִּין אֶלָּא בִטְלָלִים. יִחְיוּ מֵיתֶיךָ נְבֵלָתִי יְקוּמוּן הָקִיצוּ וְרַנְּנוּ שׁוֹכְנֵי עָפָר כִּי טַל אוֹרוֹת טַלֶּךָ וָאֶרֶץ רְפָאִים תַּפִּיל. אֲמַר רִבִּי תַּנְחוּם עֶדְרֶעִיָּא וְאַרְעָה תַּפְקִידֶיהָ תְּפַלֵּט.

It is written (*1Kings* 17:1) "Elijah the Tisbite, from the inhabitants of Gilead, said to Aḥab: By the Living Eternal One, the God of Israel, before Whom I stood, there will not be dew nor rain these years except by my word." Rebbi Berekhia said, Rebbi Yasa and the rabbis. One of them said, he was heard both for dew and for rain; the other one said, he was heard for rain but was not heard for dew, from (*1Kings* 18:1): "Go, appear before Aḥab and I shall give rain[65], etc." And he who said, he was heard both for dew and for rain, where was the vow of dew dissolved? Rebbi Tanḥuma from Edreï[66] said, they are of the opinion that a vow that was dissolved partially is dissolved totally. Some want to say, on the occasion of the son of the woman from Sarepta, (*1Kings* 17:20) "He called on the Eternal and said, o Eternal, my God, etc." Rebbi Judah ben Pazi said, about one who stole a doctor's bag[67]. When he left, his son was injured.

He returned to him and said: Please, sir doctor, heal my son. He said to him: Go and return my bag because it is full of medicines, and I shall heal your son. So the Holy One, praise to Him, said to Elijah: Go and lift the vow of dew because the dead are resurrected only by dew, then I shall resurrect the son of the Sareptan. And from where that the dead will live only by dew? (*Is.* 26:19) "Your dead will live, the corpses will arise. Wake up and jubilate, those who dwell in dust! For a dew of light is Your dew, וְאֶרֶץ רְפָאִים תַּפִּיל." Rebbi Tanḥum from Edreï said, "the earth will give up those that are deposited in it.[68]"

65 But dew is not mentioned. The entire piece, whose main place is in *Taäniot* 1:1, is included to explain the connection of the (summer) praise for dew in the benediction on "resurrection". The praise for dew was included in the Yerushalmi prayer rite.

66 He is mentioned only here (and in the parallel in *Taäniot*). Since he appears together with Rebbi Berekhiah, he must belong to the last generation of Amoraïm in Israel.

It is the minority opinion of Rebbi Aqiba (*Nedarim* 9:6) that if in an earthly court part of a vow is annulled because it was executed under false intent, then the entire vow is annulled. This is not the majority opinion, hence, it is not the practice and does not imply Heavenly standards.

67 Greek νάρθηξ, a plant (*Ferula communis*), word also used for "casket for unguents", and title of medical works. Hesiod has Prometheus carry off the fire in the stalk of a νάρθηξ.

68 Rebbi Tanḥum from Edreï explains the difficult phrase וְאֶרֶץ רְפָאִים תַּפִּיל "it will fell Netherworlds" by taking תַּפִּיל in the sense of Rabbinic Hebrew, "having a miscarriage", the Netherworld will expel what is in it.

רִבִּי יַעֲקֹב דִּכְפַר חָנָן בְּשֵׁם רֵישׁ לָקִישׁ בְּשָׁעָה שֶׁעָשָׂה אַבְרָהָם זְקֵינָן רְצוֹנִי נִשְׁבַּעְתִּי לוֹ שֶׁאֵינִי זָז טַל מִבָּנָיו לְעוֹלָם מַה טַעַם לְךָ טַל יַלְדוּתֶךָ. וּכְתִיב בָּתְרֵיהּ נִשְׁבַּע יי וְלֹא יִנָּחֵם. אָמַר רִבִּי יוּדָה בֶּן פָּזִי בְּדִיַיתֵּיקִי נְתַתִּיו לְאַבְרָהָם בְּמַתָּנָה נְתַתִּיו לוֹ. וְיִתֶּן לְךָ הָאֱלֹהִים מִטַּל הַשָּׁמַיִם. אָמַר רִבִּי שְׁמוּאֵל בַּר נַחְמָנִי בְּשָׁעָה

שֶׁיִּשְׂרָאֵל בָּאִין לִידֵי עֲבֵירָה וּמַעֲשִׂים רָעִים הַגְּשָׁמִים נֶעֱצָרִין הֵן מְבִיאִין לָהֶן זָקֵן אֶחָד כְּגוֹן רִבִּי יוֹסֵי הַגָּלִילִי וְהוּא מַפְגִּיעַ בַּעֲדָם וְהַגְּשָׁמִים יוֹרְדִין אֲבָל הַטַּל אֵינוֹ יוֹרֵד בִּזְכוּת בְּרִיָּה מַה טַעַם כְּטַל מֵאֵת יי׳ כִּרְבִיבִים עֲלֵי עֵשֶׂב אֲשֶׁר לֹא יְקַוֶּה לְאִישׁ וְלֹא יְיַחֵל לִבְנֵי אָדָם.

Rebbi Jacob from Kefar Ḥanan[69] in the name of Resh Laqish: When Abraham their forefather did My will, I swore to him that dew will never move away from his descendants forever; what is the reason? (*Ps.* 110:3) "You have the dew of your youth." And it is written after that (*Ps.* 110:4) "The Eternal swore and He will not change His intention." Rebbi Judah ben Pazi said, by a will[70] I gave it to Abraham, as a gift I gave it to him. (Gen. 27:28) "God may give you from the dew of heaven." Rebbi Samuel ben Naḥmani said, when Israel sin and do evil the rains are arrested. They bring an old man like Rebbi Yose the Galilean, he prays for them and the rains come. But dew does not descend by the merit of any creature, what is the reason? (*Micah* 5:6) "Like dew from the Eternal, like light showers on grass, that do not listen to anybody nor wait for humans."

69 This paragraph explains the reason of those who say that Elijah's prediction that there would be no dew never came true. The homily belongs to the school of R. Simeon ben Laqish (Resh Laqish). R. Jacob from Kefar Ḥanan was his student in homiletics.

70 Greek διαθήκη "will, permanent disposition."

רִבִּי זְעִירָא בְשֵׁם רִבִּי חֲנִינָא הָיָה עוֹמֵד בְּגֶשֶׁם וְהִזְכִּיר שֶׁל טַל אֵין מַחֲזִירִין אוֹתוֹ. בְּטַל וְהִזְכִּיר שֶׁל גֶּשֶׁם מַחֲזִירִין אוֹתוֹ. וְהָתַנֵּי בְּטַל וּבְרוּחוֹת לֹא חִייְבוּ חֲכָמִים לְהַזְכִּיר וְאִם רָצָה לְהַזְכִּיר מַזְכִּיר. לֹא דָמֵי לְהַהוּא דְמֵיקַל וְהַהוּא דְּלָא מַצְלִי וְלָא מֵיקַל. בְּגֶשֶׁם וְהִזְכִּיר שֶׁל טַל אֵין מַחֲזִירִין אוֹתוֹ. וְהָתַנֵּי אִם לֹא שָׁאַל בְּבִרְכַּת הַשָּׁנִים אוֹ שֶׁלֹּא הִזְכִּיר גְּבוּרוֹת גְּשָׁמִים בִּתְחִייַת הַמֵּתִים מַחֲזִירִין אוֹתוֹ. בְּהַהוּא דְּלָא אִדְכַּר לָא טַל וְלָא מָטָר.

Rebbi Zeïra in the name if Rebbi Ḥanina: When someone stood [praying] in the rainy season and mentioned dew one does not make him repeat. In the season of dew and he mentioned rain one makes him repeat. But is it not stated[71]: The sages did not oblige one to mention dew and winds but if he wants to mention them, he may mention? One cannot compare one who takes it easy[72] to one who does not pray and does not take it easy[73]. "When he stood in the rainy season and mentioned dew one does not make him repeat." But is it not stated: If he did not ask for it in the benediction "for years", or he did not mention the power of rains in "resurrection of the dead", one makes him repeat? That is about one who mentioned neither dew nor rain.

71 The discussion follows the general pattern: If a statement contains statements A and then B, the discussion will discuss first B, then A. Hence, the first clause of the *baraita* will be repeated before the discussion turns to it. The statement of Rebbi Ḥanina and the discussion of its last part is quoted in Alfassi *Taänit* 1:1 where it is added to the tradition of the same Rebbi Ḥanina in the Babylonian Talmud (*Taänit* 3b): "In summertime, one who says 'He Who makes the wind blow' does not have to repeat; if he says 'He Who makes rain descend,' he has to repeat. In wintertime, one who omits 'He Who makes the wind blow' does not have to repeat; if he omits 'He Who makes rain descend,' he has to repeat." Alfassi gives no interpretation of the Yerushalmi he quotes but the early Medieval authorities R. Zeraḥia Halevi, R. Abraham ben David, Nachmanides, and R. Nissim Gerondi all have different interpretations (mutually contradictory) and most of them also have different readings. Among manuscripts, the expression דְלָא מַצְלִי וְלָא מֵיקַל appears with or without one or both לָא. The following interpretation follows Nachmanides closely. [Most commentaries agree with R. Nissim Gerondi in taking מיקל as a *Pa'el* form of a contracted form of קלל "to curse"; such a form קול is nowhere attested, but קיל "to take, make easy" is frequent.]

72 And does not mention the dew which he needs, but mentions the rain out of season.

73 Who prays neither for dew, nor for rain, nor for winds, and therefore does not slight anything.

רִבִּי זְעוּרָא בְּשֵׁם רִבִּי חוּנָא אִם לֹא שָׁאַל בְּבִרְכַּת הַשָּׁנִים אוֹמְרָהּ בְּשׁוֹמֵעַ תְּפִילָּה. וּדְכְוָתָהּ אִם לֹא הִזְכִּיר גְּבוּרוֹת גְּשָׁמִים בִּתְחִייַת הַמֵּתִים אוֹמְרָהּ בְּשׁוֹמֵעַ תְּפִילָּה. מַה אִם שְׁאֵלָה שֶׁהִיא מִדּוֹחָק אוֹמְרָהּ בְּשׁוֹמֵעַ תְּפִילָּה. אַזְכָּרָה שֶׁהִיא מֵרֵיוַח לֹא כָּל־שֶׁכֵּן. וְהָתַנֵּי אִם לֹא שָׁאַל בְּבִרְכַּת הַשָּׁנִים אוֹ שֶׁלֹּא הִזְכִּיר גְּבוּרוֹת גְּשָׁמִים בִּתְחִייַת הַמֵּתִים מַחֲזִירִין אוֹתוֹ. אָמַר רִבִּי אֶבְדֵּימִי אַחֲוֵי דְּרִבִּי יוֹסֵי בְּשֶׁלֹּא אָמַר בְּשׁוֹמֵעַ תְּפִילָּה.

Rebbi Zeïra in the name of Rebbi Ḥuna: If he did not ask[74] in the benediction "for years" he says it in "He Who hears prayer". Similarly, if he did not mention the power of rains in "resurrection of the dead" he says it in "He Who hears prayer". If the request, made under duress, may be recited in "He Who hears prayer," the mention, made under easy circumstances, so much more! But is it not stated: If he did not ask in the benediction "for years" or that he did not mention the power of rains in "resurrection of the dead", one makes him repeat[75]? Rebbi Eudaimon the brother of Rebbi Yose[76] said, if he did not say it in "He Who hears prayer"!

74 The request for rain is made only in the rainy season, "under duress" when rain is urgently needed. The mention of rain in the second benediction already starts "under easy circumstances" around the time of the fall equinox, some weeks before rain is needed. The benediction "He Who hears prayer" is the last of the middle benedictions, #15 on weekdays.

75 As a tannaïtic statement, this has precedence over the statement of Rebbi Ḥuna. How can R. Ḥuna present his statement about power of rains? [The Babli, *Berakhot* 29a, has the statement formulated here in the name of Rav Assi from the Yeshivah of Rav in Babylonia; the Babli mentions neither the statement of Rebbi Ḥuna nor the explanation of Rebbi Eudaimon.]

76 Brother of the Amora R. Yose of the fourth generation.

אֵיכַן הוּא חוֹזֵר. כִּדְמַר רִבִּי שִׁמְעוֹן בַּר וָוא בְּשֵׁם רִבִּי יוֹחָנָן בְּרֹאשׁ חוֹדֶשׁ אִם עָקַר אֶת רַגְלָיו חוֹזֵר לָרֹאשׁ וְאִם לָאו חוֹזֵר לַעֲבוֹדָה. אַף הָכָא אִם עָקַר אֶת רַגְלָיו חוֹזֵר לְכַתְּחִילָּה.

Where does he return to[77]? Just as Rebbi Simeon bar Abba said in the name of Rebbi Yoḥanan: On the day of the New Moon[78], if he had moved his feet[79] he repeats from the start, otherwise from "Temple service". Here also, if he had moved his feet he repeats from the start[80].

77 If he forgot either prayer for or mention of rain, and realizes his omission at the end of the *Amidah.*

78 When the day has to be mentioned in "Temple service", the first of the last three benedictions; cf. Chapter 3, Halakhah 1.

79 During *Amidah* it is forbidden to move one's feet since the angels do not move their feet. Hence, moving after prayer is the outward sign that prayer is finished.

80 Otherwise, he returns to "He Who hears prayer."

בְּנִינְוֶה צְרְכוּן מִיעֲבֵד תַּעֲנִית בָּתַר פִּסְחָא. אֲתוּן שַׁיְילוּן לְרִבִּי אָמַר לוֹן רִבִּי לְכוּ וַעֲשׂוּ וּבִלְבַד שֶׁלֹּא תְשַׁנּוּ מַטְבֵּיעָהּ שֶׁל תְּפִילָּה. אֵיכַן הוּא אוֹמְרָהּ. רִבִּי יִרְמְיָה סָבַר מֵימַר אוֹמְרָהּ בְּשׁוֹמֵעַ תְּפִילָּה. אֲמַר לֵיהּ רִבִּי יוֹסֵי לֹא כֵן אָמַר רִבִּי זְעִירָא בְּשֵׁם רַב חוּנָא אִם לֹא שָׁאַל בְּבִרְכַּת הַשָּׁנִים אוֹ שֶׁלֹּא הִזְכִּיר גְּבוּרוֹת גְּשָׁמִים בִּתְחִייַת הַמֵּתִים מַחֲזִירִין אוֹתוֹ בְּשׁוֹמֵעַ תְּפִילָּה. וָמַר לוֹן רִבִּי לְכוּ וַעֲשׂוּ וּבִלְבַד שֶׁלֹּא תְשַׁנּוּ מַטְבֵּיעָהּ שֶׁל תְּפִילָּה. עַל דַּעְתֵּיהּ דְּרִבִּי יוֹסֵי אֵיכַן הוּא אוֹמְרָהּ. בְּשֵׁשׁ שֶׁהוּא מוֹסִיף. עַד כְּדוֹן צִיבּוּר שֶׁיֵּשׁ לוֹ שֵׁשׁ. יָחִיד שֶׁאֵין לוֹ שֵׁשׁ מְנַיִין אָמַר רִבִּי חֲנִינָא לֹא כֵן אָמַר רִבִּי זְעִירָא בְּשֵׁם רַב חוּנָא יָחִיד שׁוֹאֵל צְרָכָיו בְּשׁוֹמֵעַ תְּפִילָּה וְאֵילוּ צְרָכָיו הֵן.

At Nineveh[81] they needed to make a fast-day after Passover[82]. They came to ask Rebbi. He told them, go ahead and make one but do not change the form of prayer[83]. Where may he say it? Rebbi Jeremiah thought to say that he says it in "He Who hears prayer." Rebbi Yose said to him: Did not Rebbi Zeïra say in the name of Rebbi Ḥuna: If he did not ask in the benediction "for years", or that he failed to mention the power of rains in "resurrection of the dead", one makes him repeat at "He Who hears prayer[84]?" But Rebbi said to them, go ahead and make one but do not change the form of prayer! According to the opinion of Rebbi Yose, where does one say it? In the six that he adds[85]. That works for the public which has six. A private person who does not have six, where? Rebbi Ḥanina said, did not Rebbi Zeïra say in the name of Rav Ḥuna[86], a private person asks for his personal needs in "He Who hears prayer," and these are his needs.

81 This is not Biblical Niniveh but Naveh in the center of the Bashan plateau, see *Demay* 2:1. (Eusebius mentions that the Jews call it Nineveh.) On the Golan plain, one needs spring rains if the winter was relatively dry.

82 This again is a text from *Taäniot* 1:1; the question and the answer, without the discussion, are mentioned succinctly in Babli *Taänit* 14b.

83 Do not mention the power of rain in "Resurrection" nor a prayer for rain in "years." On the other hand, if one already fasts for rain one must pray for rain in one's *Amidah*.

84 In the parallel in *Taäniot* the text is easier to understand; there it says "he says" instead of "one makes him repeat"; meaning that a prayer for rain at "He Who hears prayer" belongs to the regular form of prayer in winter and, therefore, by Rebbi's statement is excluded from summer prayer.

85 Six additional benedictions that the reader inserts in the public prayer of fast days for rain, as explained in the second chapter of Mishnah *Taänit*. Rebbi Yose must imply that even a local fast for rain is a public fast.

86 In Halakhah 4:4.

וְהַבְדָּלָה בְחוֹנֵן הַדָּעַת. שִׁמְעוֹן בַּר וָוָה בְּעָא קוֹמֵי רִבִּי יוֹחָנָן דָּבָר שֶׁהוּא נוֹהֵג וּבָא חֲכָמִים חוֹלְקִין עָלָיו. אָמַר לוֹ עַל יְדֵי שֶׁעִיקָּרָהּ בְּכוֹס שְׁכָחוּהָ בִתְפִילָּה. מִילְתֵיהּ אָמְרָה שֶׁעִיקָּרָהּ בְּכוֹס. רִבִּי יַעֲקֹב בַּר אִידִי בְּשֵׁם רִבִּי יִצְחָק רוֹבָא אָמְרָהּ בְּכוֹס אָמְרָהּ בִּתְפִילָּה בִּשְׁבִיל לְזַכּוֹת אֶת הַתִּינוֹקוֹת. מִילְתֵיהּ אָמְרָה שֶׁעִיקָּרָהּ בִּתְפִילָּה. רִבִּי זְעוּרָא רַב יְהוּדָה בְשֵׁם שְׁמוּאֵל אָמְרָהּ בְּכוֹס אָמְרָהּ בִּתְפִילָּה אָמְרָהּ בְּכוֹס. מִילְתֵיהּ אָמְרָה שֶׁעִיקָּרָהּ כַּאן וְכַאן.

"And *Havdalah* in 'He Who by His grace grants knowledge'"[87]. Simeon bar Abba asked before Rebbi Yoḥanan: Something that one does all the time, and the Sages differ about it? He said to him: Since its main place is over a cup they forgot it in prayer[88]. His statement means that its main place is over a cup[89]. Rebbi Jacob bar Idi in the name of the old Rebbi Isaac[90]: If he said it over a cup he must repeat it in prayer; it was[91] in order to let children participate. His statement means that its main place is in prayer[92]. Rebbi Zeïra, Rav Yehudah in the name of Samuel: If he said it over a cup he must repeat it in prayer, if he said it in prayer he must repeat it over a cup. His statement means that its main place is here as well as there[93].

87 Quote from the Mishnah to indicate the text to be discussed now.

88 The discussion is quoted more in detail in Babli 33a: "Rebbi Simeon bar Abba asked Rebbi Yoḥanan: Since the Men of the Great Assembly instituted the forms of benedictions, prayers, *Qiddush* and *Havdalah*, why does one not check and see what they instituted? He answered him: Originally, they instituted *Havdalah* in prayer. When they got rich, they instituted it over a cup of wine. When they became poor again, they went back and instituted it back in prayer." This implies that the differences of opinion expressed in the Mishnah refer to the second institution of prayer and that the order of the first institution therefore is irrelevant. In the Yerushalmi, the question is, how can there arise a difference of usage in something that every Jew has been doing every week since the times of the Great Assembly? The answer also here is that there was a time where only *Havdalah* over a cup of wine was practiced.

89 Since *Havdalah* over a cup was not disestablished, the mention in prayer is additional.

90 His full name was Rebbi Isaac bar Eudaimon, a Tanna of the first generation, a member of Rebbi's Academy. He is called "old" to distinguish him from Rav Isaac bar Eudaimon, a Babylonian Amora of the third generation.

91 *Havdalah* was said over the cup only to teach children.

92 In the Babli (33a), this is a

statement of the Babylonian Rav Naḥman bar Isaac.

93 In contrast to Rebbi Yoḥanan, Samuel insists that the later institution did not replace the benediction over a cup of wine by a benediction inserted in prayer, but that prayer is additional to the benediction over a cup of wine. In the Babli (33b) this is the final statement of the later Amora Rava. In the Yerushalmi also, the last statement has to be taken as the final one.

רִבִּי אֱלִיעֶזֶר אוֹמֵר בְּהוֹדָיָיה. רִבִּי יוֹחָנָן בְּשֵׁם רִבִּי מַטִּין כְּרִבִּי אֱלִיעֶזֶר בְּיוֹם טוֹב שֶׁחָל לִהְיוֹת בְּמוֹצָאֵי שַׁבָּת מִיַּד. רִבִּי יִצְחָק רֵבָה בְּשֵׁם רִבִּי הֲלָכָה כְּרִבִּי אֱלִיעֶזֶר בְּיוֹם טוֹב שֶׁחָל לִהְיוֹת בְּמוֹצָאֵי שַׁבָּת. רִבִּי יִצְחָק בַּר נַחְמָן בְּשֵׁם רִבִּי חֲנִינָא בֶּן גַּמְלִיאֵל הֲלָכָה כְּרִבִּי אֱלִיעֶזֶר לְעוֹלָם. רִבִּי אַבָּהוּ בְּשֵׁם רִבִּי אֶלְעָזָר הֲלָכָה כְּרִבִּי אֱלִיעֶזֶר לְעוֹלָם. אָמַר רִבִּי יַעֲקֹב בַּר אָחָא לָאו בְּגִין דְּאָתוֹן תַּרְתֵּיי שְׁמוּעִין אֶלָּא בְּגִין דְּרִבִּי יִצְחָק בַּר נַחְמָן וְרִבִּי אֶלְעָזָר תְּרַוֵּיהוֹן בְּשֵׁם רִבִּי חֲנִינָא בֶּן גַּמְלִיאֵל הֲלָכָה כְּרִבִּי אֱלִיעֶזֶר לְעוֹלָם.

"Rebbi Eliezer says, in 'thanksgiving'". Rebbi Yoḥanan in the name of Rebbi: One is inclined toward Rebbi Eliezer's opinion on a holiday that falls immediately after the Sabbath[94]. The old Rebbi Isaac in the name of Rebbi: Practice follows Rebbi Eliezer on a holiday that falls after the Sabbath. Rebbi Isaac bar Naḥman in the name of Rebbi Ḥanina ben Gamliel[95]: Practice follows Rebbi Eliezer at all times. Rebbi Abbahu in the name of Rebbi Eleazar: Practice follows Rebbi Eliezer at all times. Rebbi Jacob bar Aḥa, not because because there are two traditions, but because Rebbi Isaac bar Naḥman and Rebbi Eleazar both say in the name of Rebbi Ḥanina ben Gamliel: Practice follows Rebbi Eliezer at all times.

94 Privately, one prefers to act in the sense of Rebbi Eliezer but one does not declare it publicly. The first two statements of this paragraph are quoted in the Babli (33b) as Israeli practice, whereas in Babylonia one follows Rav and Samuel in an insertion in the middle benediction of the *Amidah* for the holiday. The last two statements are quoted in Babli *Niddah* 8a.

95 The oldest son of Rabban Gamliel I of Jabneh, brother of Rabban Simeon ben Gamliel. It seems that he died before the Patriarchate was reestablished after a long interruption in the aftermath of the war of Bar Kokhba.

וְאַבְדָּלָה בְּחוֹנֵן הַדַּעַת דִּבְרֵי[96] חֲכָמִים רִבִּי עֲקִיבָה אוֹמֵר אוֹמְרָהּ בְּרָכָה רְבִיעִית בְּעַצְמָהּ. רִבִּי יַעֲקֹב בַּר אָחָא בְּשֵׁם שְׁמוּאֵל אוֹמֵר בְּרָכָה רְבִיעִית. אָמַר רִבִּי יוּדָן אוֹמֵר מַטְבֵּעַ בְּרָכָה וְאַחַר כַּךְ מַבְדִּיל. וַתְיָיא כְּרִבִּי דְּרִבִּי אָמַר תְּמְהָנִי הֵיאַךְ בִּטְּלוּ חוֹנֵן הַדַּעַת בְּשַׁבָּת אִם אֵין דֵּעָה תְּפִילָּה מְנַיִין. וְכֹה אִם אֵין דֵּעָה הַבְדָּלָה מְנַיִין. אָמַר רִבִּי יִצְחָק בַּר אֶלְעָזָר מַבְדִּיל וְאַחַר כַּךְ אוֹמֵר מַטְבֵּעַ בְּרָכָה.

"And *Havdalah* in "He Who in His grace grants knowledge", the words of the Sages. Rebbi Aqibah said: one says it as separate fourth benediction[97]" Rebbi Jacob bar Aḥa in the name of Samuel: He says it as fourth benediction. Rebbi Yudan says, the text of the benediction[98] and after that he says *Havdalah*. His version agrees with Rebbi[99], since Rebbi said: I wonder why they eliminated "He Who in His grace grants knowledge" on Sabbath; if there is no knowledge, where is prayer? And here, if there is no knowledge, where is *Havdalah*? Rebbi Isaac ben Eleazar said, he says *Havdalah* and afterwards adds the text of the benediction.

96 Text of the Rome ms., in place of דרבי in the Venice print.

97 Almost a quote from the Mishnah, to introduce discussion on the way *Havdalah* has to be recited according to Rebbi Aqiba, even though his way of doing it is not accepted as practice. Hence, the discussion in this paragraph is purely theoretical.

98 The text of the regular fourth benediction, "He Who in His grace grants knowledge". This is the meaning of the phrase also in the statement of Rebbi Isaac bar Eleazar.

99 His opinion parallels that of Rebbi. [A slightly different version is in Babli 33a in the name of Rav Joseph: "Since *Havdalah* presupposes knowledge, it was incorporated in the benediction for knowledge."]

רִבִּי אֶלְעָזָר בֶּן רִבִּי הוֹשַׁעְיָא וּבִלְבַד שֶׁלֹּא יִפְחוֹת מִשָּׁלֹשׁ אַבְדָּלוֹת. אָמַר רִבִּי יוֹחָנָן אָמְרוּ הַפּוֹחֵת לֹא יִפְחוֹת מִשָּׁלֹשׁ וְהַמּוֹסִיף לֹא יוֹסִיף יוֹתֵר מִשִּׁבְעָה אַבְדָּלוֹת. לֵוִי אָמַר וּבִלְבַד מֵאַבְדָּלוֹת הָאֲמוּרוֹת בַּתּוֹרָה. נָחוּם בֵּירִבִּי סִימַאי נְפַק וָמַר בְּשֵׁם אָבוֹי וַאֲפִילוּ אַבְדָּלָה אַחַת. וְאָמַר רִבִּי אַבָּהוּ וְצָרִיךְ לַחְתּוֹם בְּהַבְדָּלָה. רִבִּי מָנָא בְעִי מֵעַתָּה אֲפִילוּ פָּתַח בְּמַבְדִּיל בֵּין קוֹדֶשׁ לְחוֹל וְחוֹזֵר וְחוֹתֵם בְּמַבְדִּיל בֵּין קוֹדֶשׁ לְחוֹל. אָמַר רִבִּי יוֹסֵי בֵּי רִבִּי בוּן וְלֹא מִבְּרָכוֹת שֶׁפּוֹתְחִין בָּהֶן בְּבָרוּךְ וְחוֹתְמִין בְּבָרוּךְ הֵן.

Rebbi Eleazar ben Rebbi Hoshaiah[100]: Only one should not mention less than three separations. Rebbi Yoḥanan said, they said that he who says little should not say less than three and he who adds should not add more than seven separations. Levi said, but only separations mentioned in the Torah[101]. Naḥum[102] ben Rebbi Simai went out and said in his father's name: even one separation. But Rebbi Abbahu said, one must seal with "separation". Rebbi Mana objected, even if he started by "He Who separates between holy and worldly" and ends, seals by "He Who separates between holy and worldly"[103]? Rebbi Yose ben Rebbi Abun said, is it not from the benedictions that one starts with "praised" and ends with "praised"[104]?

100 Son of Rebbi Hoshaiah (see Chap. 2, Note 169). The statement is in the Babli (*Pesaḥim* 103b-104a) in the name of Rebbi Oshaya (Babylonian form of Hoshaiah). The entire paragraph has the appearance of being written by a person unable to pronounce an "h".

101 For example, He Who separates between holy and private (*Lev.* 10:10), between light and darkness (*Gen.* 1:4), between Israel and the Gentiles (*Lev.* 20:26). There are no more than seven separations mentioned in the Torah. [The other four are between upper and lower waters, between day and night, between pure and impure, between Levites and other Israelites.]

102 Also called Menaḥem ben R. Simai, an Amora of the first generation who was renowned for his holiness.

103 Would Rebbi Abbahu agree

with R. Naḥum ben R. Simai that a benediction would be: "Praise to You, o Eternal, our God, King of the universe, Who separates between holy and wordly. Praise to You, Eternal, Who separates between holy and wordly"? That text looks too silly to be acceptable.

104 As stated in Halakhah 1:4. However, Rebbi Abbahu is more specific and requires the final benediction to contain the word המבדיל. In the Babli (*Pesaḥim* 104a) there is a discussion whether the separation referred to in the concluding benediction is the first or the last one of the list. In any case, it is clear that R. Abbahu cannot agree with R. Naḥum bar Simai to produce the meaningless formula of R. Mana. Hence, the opinion of R. Naḥum must be rejected.

רִבִּי אֶלְעָזָר בֶּן אַנְטִיגְנוֹס בְּשֵׁם רִבִּי אֶלְעָזָר בֵּירִבִּי יַנַּאי זֹאת אוֹמֶרֶת שֶׁאָסוּר לַעֲשׂוֹת מְלָאכָה עַד שֶׁיַּבְדִּיל. כְּמַה (fol. 9c) דְּאָמַר אָמַר אָסוּר לַעֲשׂוֹת מְלָאכָה עַד שֶׁיַּבְדִּיל. וְדִכְוָתָהּ אָסוּר לוֹ לְאָדָם לִתְבּוֹעַ צְרָכָיו עַד שֶׁיַּבְדִּיל.

Rebbi Eleazar ben Antigonos in the name of Rebbi Eleazar ben Rebbi Yannai[105]: That means[106] that one is forbidden from doing any work before one recites *Havdalah*. As he said, he said that one is forbidden from doing any work before one recites *Havdalah*, and similarly one is forbidden to pray for one's needs before one recites *Havdalah*.

105 Tanna of the last generation; his only known student is R. Eleazar ben Antigonos. In the Babli (*Sabbath* 150b), the statement is in the name of Rebbi Eliezer ben Jacob, one of the last students of Rebbi Aqiba and a major authority. In the Babli, the statement is relativized to mean that one does not even have to pray but just to recite "Praise to Him Who separates between holy and wordly" to be able to do any work. There is no such relativization in the Yerushalmi; however, it is implied by the next paragraph.

106 Refers to the majority opinion in the Mishnah, that *Havdalah* has to be inserted in the first weekday benediction of the *Amidah*. Hence, it is the first thing that one has to do. The argument in this paragraph takes this up: Since it was ordained that *Havdalah* precedes the weekday prayer with its supplications for wordly needs, it also must precede worldly

deeds. [The first weekday benediction also contains a supplication but, as Rebbi is quoted in an earlier paragraph, a prayer for knowledge is acceptable also for the Sabbath.]

רִבִּי זְעִירָא רִבִּי אֶלְעָזָר בֶּן אַנְטִיגְנוֹס בְּשֵׁם רִבִּי אֶלְעָזָר[107] בֵּירִבִּי יַנַּאי בְּשֵׁם רִבִּי יוּדָה בְּרִיבִּי אִם לֹא הִבְדִּיל בְּמוֹצָאֵי שַׁבָּת מַבְדִּיל אֲפִילוּ בַּחֲמִישִׁי בְּשַׁבָּת. הָדָא דְאַתְּ אָמַר בְּמַבְדִּיל בֵּין קוֹדֶשׁ לְחוֹל. אֲבָל בּוֹרֵא מְאוֹרֵי הָאֵשׁ אוֹמְרָהּ מִיַּד.

Rebbi Zeïra, Rebbi Eleazar ben Antigonos in the name of Rebbi Eleazar ben Rebbi Yannai in the name of the important Rebbi Yehudah[108]: If he did not recite *Havdalah* at the end of Sabbath, he recites even on Thursday. That is restricted to *Havdalah* proper, but "illuminating fire" he may say only immediately[109].

107 Reading of the Rome manuscript; "Rebbi Eleazar ben" is missing from the Venice text but R. Yannai is later than R. Eleazar ben R. Antigonos.

108 He is Rebbi Yehudah bar Illaï. In the Babli (*Pesaḥim* 106a), R. Zeïra is quoted as permitting the recitation of *Havdalah* only until Wednesday afternoon.

109 At nightfall one is permitted to light a new fire. The benediction has been formulated because at the end of the first Sabbath of Creation, Adam invented artificial fire as the first engineering feat of newly created man (Yerushalmi *Berakhot* 12b (8:6), Babli *Pesaḥim* 54a). Hence, it makes no sense to recite the benediction at any other time. The rule proclaimed here is attributed in the Babli (*Pesaḥim* 54a) to R. Jacob ben Idi.

רִבִּי זְעוּרָא בְּשֵׁם רַב יְהוּדָה רִבִּי אַבָּא בְּשֵׁם אַבָּא בַּר יִרְמְיָה אֲפִילוּ יוֹם טוֹב שֶׁחָל לִהְיוֹת בְּאֶמְצַע שַׁבָּת אוֹמֵר בֵּין יוֹם הַשְּׁבִיעִי לְשֵׁשֶׁת יְמֵי הַמַּעֲשֶׂה. אָמַר רִבִּי זְעוּרָא לְרַב יְהוּדָה וְכִי שֵׁשֶׁת יְמֵי מַעֲשֶׂה לְפָנָיו. אָמַר לֵיהּ וְכִי יֵשׁ טוּמְאָה וְטָהֳרָה לְפָנָיו.

Rebbi Zeïra in the name of Rav Yehudah, Rebbi Abba in the name of Abba bar Jeremiah: Even if a holiday falls in the middle of the week one recites "He Who separates between Sabbath and the six workdays[110]" Rebbi Zeïra said to Rav Yehudah: Has one six workdays before him? He said to him: Has one impurity and purity before him[111]?

110 This is the last "separation" in *Havdalah* before the final doxology. That "separation" is not in the Torah and not in the list of 3 - 7 separations, but necessitated by the circumstances. The statement really means that the text of *Havdalah* for holidays is identical with that for the Sabbath. In the Babli (*Ḥulin* 26b) the statement is attributed to R. Zeïra only, without discussion.

111 This is one of the seven "separations" mentioned in the Torah but today purity is impossible for us.

רִבִּי יִרְמְיָה רִבִּי זְעִירָא בְּשֵׁם רַב חִיָּא בַּר אַשִׁי צָרִיךְ לוֹמַר הָחֵל עָלֵינוּ אֶת הַיָּמִים שֵׁשֶׁת יְמֵי הַמַּעֲשֶׂה הַבָּאִים לִקְרָאתֵינוּ לְשָׁלוֹם. רִבִּי אַבָּא מוֹסִיף וְהַשְׁמִיעֵנוּ בָּהֶן שָׂשׂוֹן וְשִׂמְחָה. רִבִּי חִזְקִיָּה בְּשֵׁם רִבִּי יִרְמְיָה הֲבִינֵנוּ וְלַמְּדֵינוּ. רִבִּי חִזְקִיָּה בְּשֵׁם רִבִּי יִרְמְיָה הָעוֹנִין אָמֵן צְרִיכִין לִיתֵּן עֵינֵיהֶן בַּכּוֹס וְעֵינֵיהֶן בַּנֵּר. רִבִּי חִזְקִיָּה בְּשֵׁם רִבִּי יִרְמְיָה אַרְבַּעַת מִינִין שֶׁבְּלוּלָב נִיטָּלִין דֶּרֶךְ גִּידוּלֵיהֶן.

Rebbi Jeremiah, Rebbi Zeïra in the name of Rav Ḥiyya bar Ashi: One must say, "start the days, the six coming workdays[112], for peace." Rebbi Abba adds: "And let us hear in them rejoicing and joy." Rebbi Ḥizqiah in the name of Rebbi Jeremiah: "Let us understand and teach us." Rebbi Ḥizqiah in the name of Rebbi Jeremiah: Those who answer Amen[113] have to look at the cup and the candle. Rebbi Ḥizqiah in the name of Rebbi Jeremiah[114]: The four kinds of the *lulav* must be taken in the direction of their growth.

112 "The six coming workdays" is missing in the Rome ms. and might be superfluous. It is not in the received Ashkenazic prayer texts of *Havdalah*. Sephardic and Oriental rites do not have the phrase.

113 Since they want to discharge their own obligation by listening to another person making *Havdalah* over a cup, they must see what he is doing.

114 In order to complete the list of traditions of Rebbi Ḥizqiah in the name of Rebbi Jeremiah regarding holidays, this extraneous tradition is included. In the parallel in Babli *Sukkah* 35b, it is stated that no obligation connected with things that grow can be executed other than using them in the way they grew (bottom down, head up). [In the Babli, "Ḥizqiah" should be "Rebbi Ḥizqiah" since "Ḥizqiah" without title refers to the son of Rebbi Ḥiyya, older than Rebbi Zeïra.]

משנה ג: הָאוֹמֵר עַל קַן צִפּוֹר יַגִּיעוּ רַחֲמֶיךָ וְעַל טוֹב יִזָּכֵר שִׁמְךָ מוֹדִים מוֹדִים מְשַׁתְּקִין אוֹתוֹ. הָעוֹבֵר לִפְנֵי הַתֵּיבָה וְטָעָה יַעֲבוֹר אַחֵר תַּחְתָּיו וְלֹא יְהֵא סַרְבָּן בְּאוֹתָהּ שָׁעָה. וּמֵאַיִן הוּא מַתְחִיל מִתְּחִילַּת בְּרָכָה שֶׁטָּעָה זֶה.

Mishnah 3: One silences someone[115] who says "Your mercy will reach over a bird's nest,[116]" "Your name shall be remembered on good things," "we thank, we thank.[117]" [118]If the one standing before the arc[119] makes a mistake, another person should replace him and he should not refuse at that moment[120]. Where does he start? From the start of the benediction where the other person made the mistake.

115 The reader in public prayer.

116 Probably in the benediction "He Who hears prayer" where one prays for Divine mercy. The reference is to *Deut*. 22:6-8.

117 In the benediction "Thanksgiving."

118 In the separate Mishnah, this is the start of Mishnah 4. Hence, in the Gemara text, the next Mishnah will be #5.

119 The "emissary of the congregation", שליח צבור, in English texts usually called "the reader" but who in Talmudic times was not a reader but leader of the congregation in prayers recited by heart or prayers of his own composition. If he stumbled, there was no way to correct him from a written text and one had to try another person.

120 Usually, if a nonprofessional is asked to perform as "emissary of the congregation", he is supposed to point out his unworthiness and accede to the

summons only at the third call. In an emergency, if he knows that he can do the job, he has to agree immediately.

הלכה ג: רִבִּי פִּינְחָס[121] בְּשֵׁם רִבִּי סִימוֹן כְּקוֹרֵא תִּיגָּר עַל מִדּוֹתָיו שֶׁל הַקָּדוֹשׁ בָּרוּךְ הוּא. עַל קַן צִפּוֹר הִגִּיעוּ רַחֲמֶיךָ וְעַל אוֹתוֹ הָאִישׁ לֹא הִגִּיעוּ רַחֲמֶיךָ. רִבִּי יוֹסֵי בְּשֵׁם רִבִּי סִימוֹן כְּנוֹתֵן קִצְבָּא לְמִדּוֹתָיו שֶׁל הַקָּדוֹשׁ בָּרוּךְ הוּא. עַד קַן צִפּוֹר הִגִּיעוּ רַחֲמֶיךָ. אִת תְּנַיֵּי תַּנֵּי עַל. וְאִית תְּנַיֵּי תַּנֵּי עַד. מַאן דָּמַר עַל מְסַיֵּיעַ לְרִבִּי פִּינְחָס. וּמַאן דָּמַר עַד מְסַיֵּיעַ לְרִבִּי יוֹסֵי. אָמַר רִבִּי יוֹסֵי בֵּי רִבִּי בּוּן לָא עָבְדִּין טָבוּת שֶׁעוֹשִׂין לְמִדּוֹתָיו שֶׁל הַקָּדוֹשׁ בָּרוּךְ הוּא רַחֲמִים. וְאִילֵּין דִּמְתַרְגְּמִין עַמִּי בְּנֵי יִשְׂרָאֵל כְּמָה דַּאֲנָא רַחֲמָן בִּשְׁמַיִם כַּךְ תֶּהֱווּן רַחֲמָנִין בְּאַרְעָא. תּוֹרְתָא אוֹ רְחֵילָה יָתָהּ וְיַת בְּרָהּ לָא תִיכְסוּן תְּרַוֵּיהוֹן בְּיוֹמָא חַד לָא עָבְדִּין טָבָאוּת שֶׁהֵן עוֹשִׂין מִדּוֹתָיו שֶׁל הַקָּדוֹשׁ בָּרוּךְ הוּא רַחֲמִים.

Halakhah 3: Rebbi Phineas in the name of Rebbi Simeon: He is like one who quarrels with the measures of the Holy One, praise to Him: Your mercies reached[122] over a bird's nest but did not reach this man[123]! Rebbi Yose in the name of Rebbi Simeon: He is like one who makes finite the measures of the Holy One, praise to Him: Your mercies reach down to the bird's nest[124]. Some Tannaïm formulate "over", some Tannaïm formulate "to". He who says "over" supports Rebbi Phineas, he who says "to" supports Rebbi Yose. Rebbi Yose bar Abun said[125]: They do not act well who declare the measures of the Holy One, praise to Him, to be mercy. And those[126] who translate (*Lev.* 22:21) "My people Israel, just as I am merciful in Heaven so you should be merciful on earth. A cow or a mother sheep, it and its young you should not slaughter together on one day," they do not act well because they declare the measures of the Holy One, praise to Him, to be mercy.

121 This is the reading in the Rome manuscript and the Genizah fragments. The Venice print has "Rebbi Isaac" which is impossible because Rebbi

Isaac is older than Rebbi Simon and because later the Talmud text refers to Rebbi Phineas.

122 All Mishnah manuscripts, all Yerushalmi sources of the Mishnah, and all Babli sources (*Berakhot* 33b, *Megillah* 25a) have יגיעו but all texts in the discussion have הגיעו.

123 "This man" in Talmudic speech means "me". {The same usage is found in Greek (ὅδε) and Latin (*hic*), (E. G.).}

124 His mercies reach down to a bird's nest but not to insects and worms.

125 In Babli sources (*Berakhot* 33b, *Megillah* 25a), the statement is attributed either to R. Yose bar Abun or to R. Yose bar Zabida.

126 Targum Yerushalmi (Pseudo-Jonathan) to *Lev.* 22:28, with minor changes.

מוֹדִים מוֹדִים מְשַׁתְּקִין אוֹתוֹ. אָמַר רִבִּי שְׁמוּאֵל בַּר רַב יִצְחָק כִּי יִסָּכֵר פִּי דוֹבְרֵי שָׁקֶר. הֲדָא דְאָמַר בְּצִיבּוּר. אֲבָל בְּיָחִיד תַּחֲנוּנִים הֵן.

"One silences one who says 'we thank, we thank.'[127]" Rebbi Samuel bar Rav Isaac said (*Ps.* 63:12): "For the mouth of those who speak lies will be dammed up.[128]" That is, in public. But in private it is supplication.

127 Quote from the Mishnah, to be discussed.

128 This verse explains that it is an obligation to "dam up, wall in" the mouths of those who speak lies. Its is not explained what the lies are of those who repeat "we thank." In the Babli (*loc. cit.*) it is explained that the one who says so, like the one who wants to mention God's name only on good things, gives the impression that there are two independent forces, God for the good and Satan-Ahriman for the bad. The Babli objects to the opinion expressed here that any repetition of sections of prayer texts is permitted in private for emphasis.

הלכה ד: **הָעוֹבֵר לִפְנֵי הַתֵּיבָה וְטָעָה. רִבִּי יוֹסֵי בֶּן חֲנִינָא בְּשֵׁם רִבִּי חֲנַנְיָה בֶּן גַּמְלִיאֵל טָעָה בְּשָׁלֹשׁ בְּרָכוֹת הָרִאשׁוֹנוֹת חוֹזֵר בַּתְּחִילָּה. אָדָא בַּר בַּר חָנָה גְּנִיבָה בְּשֵׁם רַב טָעָה בְּשָׁלֹשׁ בְּרָכוֹת הָאַחֲרוֹנוֹת חוֹזֵר לָעֲבוֹדָה. רִבִּי חֶלְבּוֹ רַב חוּנָה**

בְּשֵׁם רַב טָעָה בְּשָׁלֹשׁ בְּרָכוֹת הָרִאשׁוֹנוֹת חוֹזֵר בַּתְּחִילָּה. בְּשָׁלֹשׁ בְּרָכוֹת הָאַחֲרוֹנוֹת חוֹזֵר לָעֲבוֹדָה. טָעָה וְאֵינוֹ יוֹדֵעַ אֵיכַן טָעָה חוֹזֵר לְמָקוֹם הַבָּרוּר לוֹ.

Halakhah 4: "If the one standing before the arc makes a mistake.[129]" Rebbi Yose ben Ḥanina in the name of Rebbi Ḥananiah[130] ben Gamliel: If one erred in one of the first three benedictions, he starts anew[131]. Ada bar bar Ḥana[132], Ganiva in the name of Rav: If one erred in one of the last three benedictions, he returns to "Temple Service." Rebbi Ḥelbo, Rav Huna in the name of Rav[133]: If one erred in one of the first three benedictions, he starts anew; in one of the last three benedictions, he returns to "Temple Service"; if he erred and he cannot remember where he erred he returns to the place that is clear to him.

129 Quote from the Mishnah. However, the following statements apply mainly to one who errs in his private prayer.

130 A/k/a R. Ḥanina ben Gamliel.

131 Even though the Mishnah states that one returns to the start of the incorrect benediction, this does not apply to the first and last three benedictions, which are an obligatory part of any *Amidah*. Each one of these groups has the status of a single benediction in this respect.

132 There exists no Babylonian Amora of that name. The name is similarly corrupt in the Rome manuscript and the Genizah fragments. It must be either Abba bar bar Ḥana, cousin of Rav, or his father Abba bar Ḥana.

133 There is no discrepancy between this statement and the prior ones, except that Rebbi Ḥelbo insists that the entire statement is Rav's and that he adds the prescription how to behave if the error is committed in the middle benedictions. The last rule is parallel to the one given for errors in the recitation of *Shema'* in Halakhah 2:4.

רִבִּי אָחָא וְרִבִּי יוּדָה בֶּן פָּזִי יָתְבִין בְּחַד כְּנִישְׁתָּא אָתִי עֲבַר חַד קוֹמֵי תֵיבוּתָא וְאַשְׁגַּר חַד בְּרָכָה. אֲתוּן וְשָׁיְילוּן לְרִבִּי סִימוֹן. אָמַר לוֹן רִבִּי סִימוֹן בְּשֵׁם רִבִּי יְהוֹשֻׁעַ בֶּן לֵוִי שְׁלִיחַ צִיבּוּר שֶׁהִשְׁגִּיר שְׁתַּיִם שָׁלֹשׁ בְּרָכוֹת אֵין מַחֲזִירִין אוֹתוֹ.

אַשְׁכַּח תְּנַיי וּפְלִיג. לַכֹּל אֵין מַחֲזִירִין אוֹתוֹ חוּץ מִמִּי שֶׁלֹּא אָמַר מְחַיֵּה הַמֵּתִים וּמַכְנִיעַ זֵדִים וּבוֹנֶה יְרוּשָׁלַיִם. אֲנִי אוֹמֵר מִין הוּא. שְׁמוּאֵל הַקָּטָן עֲבַר קוֹמֵי תֵיבוּתָא וְאַשְׁגַּר מַכְנִיעַ זֵדִים בְּסוֹפָהּ שָׁרֵי מַשְׁקִיף עֲלֵיהוֹן. אָמְרִין לֵיהּ לֹא שִׁיעֲרוּ חֲכָמִים בָּךְ.

Rebbi Aḥa and Rebbi Judah ben Pazy were sitting in a synagogue. One came and stood before the arc and forgot one benediction. They went and asked Rebbi Simon. Rebbi Simon said to them in the name of Rebbi Joshua ben Levi: One does not remove an emissary of the congregation who forgot two or three benedictions[134]. They found a formulation that made a difference: One does not remove him for anything except if he did not say "He Who revives the dead", "He Who subdues evildoers", "He Who builds Jerusalem;" I say that he is a sectarian[135]. Samuel Minor[136] stood before the ark and forgot "He Who subdues evildoers." At the end he started looking at them[137]. They said to him, the Sages did not take you as a yardstick.

134 But an individual has to repeat following the standards of the Mishnah.

135 If he does not believe in resurrection of the body, he is a Sadducee. If he refrains from uttering the deprecation against Christians or expressing the hope that Jerusalem will be rebuilt before a Second Coming, he is a Christian.

136 A Tanna of the second generation. He was the person who formulated the prayer against Christians in the first place (Babli 28b-29a), but after that he forgot what he himself had formulated. He is called "minor" because his stature was not as great as that of the prophet Samuel, but greater than everybody else in his generation.

137 When at the end he realized that he had forgotten the benediction and also remembered that with the introduction of his formulation came the order to remove any "emissary of the congregation" who omitted that benediction, he started wondering about the reaction of his audience which according to the Babli was the Synhedrion at Jabneh. The Babli goes into a lengthy discussion why they did

not remove him under suspicion of a belated sympathy with Christians. One answers that he started the benediction and only got lost in the middle; one removes only an emissary who leaves it out altogether. This is clearly in contradiction to the version of the Yerushalmi.

In Israel, the holy ark was movable and for prayer it was transported in front of the congregation; the emissary of the congregation then stood in front of the ark. Therefore, removal of the reader is denoted in the Yerushalmi by מחזירין "one returns him (to his seat in the synagogue)". In Babylonia, the ark was built-in and the place of the reader was lower than the floor of the synagogue; hence removal of the reader in the Babli is expressed by מעלין "one moves him up (from the low place of the reader)".

רִבִּי יַעֲקֹב בַּר אָחָא רִבִּי שִׁמְעוֹן בַּר אַבָּא בְּשֵׁם רִבִּי אֶלְעָזָר סָפֵק הִזְכִּיר שֶׁל רֹאשׁ חוֹדֶשׁ סָפֵק לֹא הִזְכִּיר מַחֲזִירִין אוֹתוֹ. לְאֵיכַן הוּא חוֹזֵר. שִׁמְעוֹן בַּר וָוא בְּשֵׁם רִבִּי יוֹחָנָן אִם עָקַר אֶת רַגְלָיו חוֹזֵר לְכַתְּחִילָּה. וְאִם לָאו חוֹזֵר לָעֲבוֹדָה. אָמַר רִבִּי יוּדָה בֶּן פָּזִי הִסִּיעַ דַּעַת כְּמִי שֶׁעָקַר אֶת רַגְלָיו. וְאִילֵּין תַּחֲנוּנַיָּא צְרִיכָה.

Rebbi Jacob bar Aḥa, Rebbi Simeon bar Abba in the name of Rebbi Eleazar: If one is in doubt whether he mentioned the New Moon or not, one makes him repeat. Where does he return to? Simeon bar Abba in the name of Rebbi Yoḥanan, if he had moved his feet, he repeats from the start, otherwise from "Temple Service."[138] Rebbi Judah ben Pazi said, if he let his thoughts wander that is as if he had moved his feet[139]. The private supplications[140] are a problem.

138 All this has been explained earlier in this chapter, Halakhah 2, Notes 79-80.

139 If the person praying did not move his feet but started thinking of other things, it is as if he had moved his feet.

140 Private prayers said after the conclusion of the official 18 benedictions of the *Amidah*, as exemplified in the texts presented in Halakhah 4:2. They are certainly part of prayer and recited while standing still, but not part of official prayers. Hence, their status in respect to repetition is unclear.

רִבִּי אַבָּא בְּרֵיהּ דְּרִבִּי חִייָא בַּר אַבָּא בְּשֵׁם רִבִּי יוֹחָנָן הָיָה קוֹרֵא בַּתּוֹרָה וְנִשְׁתַּתֵּק זֶה שֶׁהוּא עוֹמֵד תַּחְתָּיו יַתְחִיל מִמָּקוֹם שֶׁהִתְחִיל הָרִאשׁוֹן. אִם אֹמֵר אַתְּ מִמָּקוֹם שֶׁפָּסַק הָרִאשׁוֹנִים נִתְבָּרְכוּ לִפְנֵיהֶן וְלֹא נִתְבָּרְכוּ לְאַחֲרֵיהֶן. וְהָאַחֲרוֹנִים נִתְבָּרְכוּ לְאַחֲרֵיהֶן וְלֹא נִתְבָּרְכוּ לִפְנֵיהֶן וּכְתִיב תּוֹרַת יי תְּמִימָה מְשִׁיבַת נָפֶשׁ. שֶׁתְּהֵא כוּלָּהּ תְּמִימָה.

Rebbi Abba the son of Rebbi Ḥiyya bar Abba in the name of Rebbi Yoḥanan[141]: If one became paralyzed while reading in the Torah[142], the one who steps in for him should start from the place the first one started. For if you say from the place he stopped, the first verses would have been blessed before them but not after them, the last ones after them but not before them, but it is written (*Ps.* 19:8): "The Torah of the Eternal is perfect, restores the soul", that it should be totally perfect.

141 Torah reading is discussed in tractate *Megillah*. The main place of this paragraph is in *Megillah* Halakhah 4:5.

142 In public, where every section read in public needs a benediction before and one after the reading. [Ezra Fleischer has recently published Genizah texts which might imply that private Bible readings also need benedictions before and after the reading: קטעים מקובצי תפילה ארץ־ישראליים מן הגניזה, קובץ על יד יג (כג) תשנ״ו.]

תַּנֵּי לֹא יְהוּ שְׁנַיִם קוֹרִין בַּתּוֹרָה וְאֶחָד מְתַרְגֵּם. אָמַר רִבִּי זְעִירָא מִפְּנֵי הַבְּרָכָה. וְהָתַנֵּי לֹא יְהוּ שְׁנַיִם מְתַרְגְּמִין וְאֶחָד קוֹרֵא אִית לָךְ מֵימַר מִפְּנֵי הַבְּרָכָה אֶלָּא מִשּׁוּם שֶׁאֵין שְׁנֵי קוֹלוֹת נִכְנָסִין לְתוֹךְ אוֹזֶן אַחַת.

It has been stated[143]: Two should not read the Torah[144] and one translate[145]. Rebbi Zeïra said, because of the benedictions[146]. But has it not been stated: Two should not translate and one read; could you say that is because of the benedictions? But it is because two voices do not enter into one ear.

143 Tosephta *Megillah* 3:20. The parallel to this discussion is found in Yerushalmi *Megillah* 4:1. The Babli (*Rosh Hashanah* 27a) quotes only the result of the present discussion.

144 Simultaneously, in public.

145 It was the usage, as it is still today in some Yemenite congregations, that someone read one verse in the Torah and then another person, the *meturgeman*, translated the verse into Aramaic (Onkelos for Eastern, Yerushalmi for Western congregations). In Greek speaking congregations, the Greek text (Septuagint, later Aquila, Symmachos, or Theodotion) was used.

146 On one text, only one set of benedictions is admissible.

תַּנֵּי שְׁנַיִם קוֹרִין בַּתּוֹרָה וְאֵין שְׁנַיִם מַפְטִירִין בְּנָבִיא. אָמַר רִבִּי עוּלָּא קְרוּיוֹת בַּתּוֹרָה וְאֵין קְרוּיוֹת בְּנָבִיא.

It has been stated: "Two may read in the Torah but two may not read the *haphtarah* in the prophets." Rebbi Ulla[147] said, one calls several people to the Torah[148] but one does not call several people for the prophets.

147 A student of Rebbis Yoḥanan and Eleazar who used to commute between Babylonia and Galilee.

148 The *baraita* does not speak of simultaneous, but of successive readers. It asserts that the *haphtarah* after the Torah reading on Sabbaths, holidays, and fastdays, cannot be split between different readers, but the Torah reading should be split among different people for different sections.

אָמַר רִבִּי יְהוֹשֻׁעַ דְּרוֹמָיָא שְׁלֹשָׁה דְּבָרִים רוּבָּן וּמִיעוּטָן רַע וּבֵינוֹנִתָן יָפֶה הַשְּׂאוֹר וְהַמֶּלַח וְהַסֵּרוּב. בַּתְּחִילָּה מְסָרֵב שְׁנִיָּיה מְעַמְעֵם. וּבַשְּׁלִישִׁית רָץ וּבָא. רִבִּי חוּנָא הֲוָה יְתִיב בְּחַד כְּנִשְׁתָּא עֲאַל חֲזָנָא וְאַטְרַח עַל חַד דְּיֵיעוֹל וְלָא קְבִיל עִילוֹי. בְּסוֹפָא אֲתָא לְגַבֵּי רִבִּי אֶלְעָזָר אֲמַר לֵיהּ לָא יִכְעוֹס מָרִי עֲלַי בְּגִין דְּלָא הֲוֵינָא מִיתְעַר לָא עֲלִית. אֲמַר לֵיהּ עֲלָךְ לָא כְּעַסִית אֶלָּא עַל הַדֵּין דְּאַטְרַח.

Rebbi Joshua the Southerner[149] said: There are three things of which too little or too much is bad and average is good: sour dough, salt, and refusal[150]. The first time he refuses, the second time he hesitates, the third time he runs and comes. Rebbi Ḥuna[151] was sitting in a synagogue. The organizer came and importuned one[152] to go up and he did not accept it. At the end, that one came to Rebbi Eleazar and said to him: My master should not be angry with me; I did not go up because I was not fully awake. He said to him: I am not mad at you but at the one who importuned.

149 A Galilean Amora of the fourth generation, student of R. Jonah and R. Aḥa. A similar statement is quoted in the Babli (34a) as tannaïtic text.

150 This refers to the part of the Mishnah which declares that in an emergency, if a reader has to be removed, his replacement should not refuse. It follows that without an emergency one should refuse; the rules are spelled out here.

151 In the Rome ms.: Rebbi Eleazar, the better reading.

152 Asked him more than three times and did not realize that if somebody refuses three times, he must have a valid reason not to be "emissary of the congregation."

בְּטִיטַיי אִשְׁתַּתַּק בְּאוֹפַנַּייָא אֲתוּן וְשַׁיילוּן לְרִבִּי אָבוּן. אֲמַר לוֹן רִבִּי אָבוּן בְּשֵׁם רִבִּי יְהוֹשֻׁעַ בֶּן לֵוִי זֶה שֶׁעוֹבֵר תַּחְתָּיו יַתְחִיל מִמָּקוֹם שֶׁפָּסַק. אָֽמְרִין לֵיהּ וְהָא תַנִּינָן מַתְחִיל הַבְּרָכָה שֶׁטָּעָה זֶה. אֲמַר לוֹן מִכֵּיוָן דַּעֲנִיתוּן קְדוּשְׁתָּא כְּמוֹ שֶׁהוּא תְּחִילַּת בְּרָכָה.

Batitay was paralized at *ophanim*[153]. They went and asked Rebbi Abun. Rebbi Abun said to them in the name of Rebbi Joshua ben Levi: His replacement should start at the place where he interrupted. They said to him: But did we not state: "He starts from the start of the benediction where the other person made the error?" He said to them: Since you answered *Qedušah,* it is as if you started a new benediction.

153 The second part of the *Qedušah*, the recitation of *Is*. 6:3 and *Ez*. 3:12 in the middle of the first benediction of *Shema'*. [The paragraph cannot deal

with *Qedušah* in the *Amidah* since there *ophanim* are not mentioned in the introductory sentence and any error in the first three benedictions requires restarting anyhow.] Rebbi Abun's answer shows that Baṭiṭai the reader was paralyzed not during, but after his recitation of the sentence connecting *Is.* 6:3 and *Ez.* 3:12 since the congregation already had answered the second verse.

The first part of the benediction speaks of the creation of the world and leads up to *Qedušah;* the second part after *Qedušah* is a hymn to God in His relation to man; it has a different subject. The Yerushalmi here assumes that the *Qedušah* before the *Shema'* could not be recited in private prayers. Hence, the two parts of the benediction, both of which can be recited in private prayer, in public service have the status of two distinct benedictions in the sense of the Mishnah.

משנה ה: הָעוֹבֵר לִפְנֵי הַתֵּיבָה לֹא יַעֲנֶה אַחַר הַכֹּהֲנִים אָמֵן מִפְּנֵי הַטֵּירוּף. וְאִם אֵין שָׁם כֹּהֵן אֶלָּא הוּא לֹא יִשָּׂא אֶת כַּפָּיו. וְאִם הִבְטַחְתּוֹ שֶׁהוּא נוֹשֵׂא אֶת כַּפָּיו וְחוֹזֵר לִתְפִילָּתוֹ רַשַּׁאי.

Mishnah 5: He who stands before the arc should not answer Amen after the Cohanim because of the distraction[154]. If there is no Cohen there but him, he should not lift his hands. But if he is sure that he can lift his hands and return to his prayer, he may do so[155].

154 The "emissary of the congregation" who stands before the arc and has to recite the priestly blessing (between the last two benedictions) so that the Cohanim may repeat the blessing aloud should not say "Amen" after each sentence of the priesly blessing because he must go on reciting the appropriate words (and the following last benediction) without the help of a prayer book.

155 *Midrash Rabba Devarim* 7(1), an early Israeli *Yelammedenu* Midrash, extends the last sentence, "but if he is sure that he can return to his prayer, he may do so," also to answering Amen

after the Cohanim, "because there is nothing greater before the Holy One, praise to Him, than the Amen which Israel answer." It is very likely that when this Midrash was composed, the flowering of synagogal poetry already had led to the writing of prayer books for the reader.

הלכה ה: תַּנֵּי הַפּוֹרֵס אֶת שְׁמַע וְהָעוֹבֵר לִפְנֵי הַתֵּיבָה וְהַנּוֹשֵׂא אֶת כַּפָּיו וְהַקּוֹרֵא בַתּוֹרָה וְהַמַּפְטִיר בְּנָבִיא וְהַמְבָרֵךְ עַל אַחַת מִכָּל־מִצְוֹת הָאֲמוּרוֹת בַּתּוֹרָה לֹא יַעֲנֶה אַחַר עַצְמוֹ אָמֵן. וְאִם עָנָה הֲרֵי זֶה בּוּר. אִית תְּנָיֵי תַּנֵּי הֲרֵי זֶה בּוּר. וְאִית תְּנָיֵי תַּנֵּי הֲרֵי זֶה חָכָם. אָמַר רַב חִסְדָּא מַאן דָּמַר הֲרֵי זֶה חָכָם בְּעוֹנֶה בְסוֹף. וּמַאן דָּמַר הֲרֵי זֶה בוּר בְּעוֹנֶה עַל בְּרָכָה וּבְרָכָה.

Halakhah 5: It was stated[156]: He who recites the blessings for the *Shema'*[157], he who stands before the ark, he who lifts his hands, he who reads in the Torah, he who recites *Haphtarah* from the prophets, and he who recites any blessing for obligations spelled out in the Torah, should not recite Amen after his own benediction. If he answered, he is uncivilized. Some Tannaïm have stated: he is uncivilized; and some Tannaïm have stated: he is wise. Rav Ḥisda said: He who said "he is wise" refers to him who answers at the end[158], but he who says "he is uncivilized" refers to him who answers every single benediction.

156 Tosephta *Megillah* 3:27 is similar to this text.

157 The Hebrew expression meant different things at different times. The translation follows the consensus of the Gaonic responsa that פורס means "recites the benediction" on basis of *Targum Jonathan* to *1Sam.* 9:13 where הוא יברך הזבח is rendered by הוּא פָּרֵיס מְזוֹנָא. The Gaonic interpretation is that, even though at the end of a full prayer one may recite Amen on his own prayer, this does not apply to the benedictions after the *Shema'*. Most Medieval commentators take פורס to mean "to parcel out" and apply the term to a group of people who prayed with less than a quorum and after the *Amidah* found themselves with 10 adult males; they then may appoint a reader who recites half *Kaddish*, ברכו, possibly the first benediction for the *Shema'*,

and the repetition of the *Amidah* with *Qedushah* and the priestly blessings. The Ashkenazic interpretation is supported by the reading of the Tosephta (*loc. cit.*) where פורס clearly means "breaking, parcel out".

158 In Sephardic and Oriental interpretation, this refers to all prayers, when one recites "Amen" after one's own benediction at the end of a well defined unit of several benedictions which form a whole that can stand for itself (except the benedictions for the recitation of *Shema'*). This is the reasonable interpretation of the Yerushalmi here. In the Babli, the parallel discussion is *Berakhot* 45b on reciting Grace after the meal, where Amen separates the part which is a Biblical obligation from the rest which is purely rabbinic. Hence, Ashkenazic interpretation restricts "Amen" after one's own benediction to the third benediction of Grace.

(fol. 9d) אָמַר רִבִּי חֲנִינָא שְׁנַיִם יִשְׂרָאֵל וְאֶחָד כֹּהֵן מְמַצְּעִין אֶת הַכֹּהֵן. אֵימָתַי בִּזְמַן שֶׁכּוּלָּם שָׁוִין. אֲבָל אִם הָיָה אֶחָד מֵהֶן תַּלְמִיד חָכָם מְמַצְּעִין אֶת הֶחָבֵר.

Rebbi Ḥanina said[159]: Two Israel[160] and one Cohen, one takes the Cohen in the middle[161]. That is, when they are all equal. But if one of them is learned, one takes the one with a title[162] in the middle.

159 Since the Mishnah speaks about the priestly blessing, some rules are added here about the preference given to Cohanim in the society of Non-Cohanim. The parallel to the second statement of R. Ḥanina is in Babli *Yoma* 37a.

160 Jews who are not Cohanim. Levites seem to be included in the general denomination of "Israel".

161 To give the place of honor to the Cohen.

162 A rabbinic title. A compacted version of the Yerushalmi is quoted in *Raviah* #577.

אָמַר רִבִּי יְהוֹשֻׁעַ בֶּן לֵוִי מִיָּמַי לֹא בֵּרַכְתִּי לִפְנֵי כֹהֵן וְלֹא הִנַּחְתִּי יִשְׂרָאֵל לְבָרֵךְ לְפָנַי.

Rebbi Joshua ben Levi said: I never recited Grace[163] in the presence of a Cohen and I never let an Israel say Grace before me[164].

163 Reciting Grace aloud for all the participants in a meal. Rebbi Joshua ben Levi was the greatest authority in his generation; nevertheless he refused for himself the precedence granted the rabbinical authority by Rebbi Ḥanina. In the Babli, *Megillah* 28a, that is rather vehemently opposed by R. Yoḥanan.

164 In the parallel, Yerushalmi *Giṭṭin* 5:9, the reading is "before him", meaning the Cohen. In that version, R. Joshua ben Levi negates the entire ruling of R. Ḥanina and states that the Cohen always has precedence. Nevertheless, since his statement is formulated as a personal act, not as a precept for everybody, the Yerushalmi *Giṭṭin* proves by this statement that the precedence given the Cohen is a Rabbinic ordinance, not a Torah law. [R. Eliahu Fulda and R. Z. Frankel hold that R. Joshua was a Levite and extends the rule of R. Ḥanina to place the Levite between Cohen and Israel in order of precedence.]

רִבִּי יוּדָה בֶּן פָּזִי בְּשֵׁם רִבִּי אֶלְעָזָר כָּל־כֹּהֵן שֶׁהוּא עוֹמֵד בְּבֵית הַכְּנֶסֶת וְאֵינוֹ נוֹשֵׂא אֶת כַּפָּיו עוֹבֵר בַּעֲשֵׂה. רִבִּי יוּדָה בֶּן פָּזִי כַּד הֲוָה תָּשִׁישׁ הֲוָה חֲזִיק רֵישֵׁיהּ וְקָאִים לֵיהּ אֲחוֹרֵי עֲמוּדָה. רִבִּי אֶלְעָזָר נְפִיק לֵיהּ לְבָרָא.

Rebbi Judah ben Pazi in the name of Rebbi Eleazar: Every Cohen who stays in the synagogue and does not lift his hands transgresses a positive commandment[165]. When Rebbi Judah ben Pazi was weak he supported his head[166] and stood behind a pillar. Rebbi Eleazar went outside.

165 This statement has been discussed in Halakha 3:1, Notes 84-89. The two tradents here were both Cohanim and they had different ways to evade their duty if they felt sick or weak. [In the Babli (*Soṭah* 38b) three positive commandments are enumerated that the Cohen transgresses by his inaction.]

166 Possibly he bandaged his head so that is was clear to everybody that he was not well.

רִבִּי אָחָא רִבִּי תַּנְחוּמָא בֵּרִבִּי חִיָּא בְּשֵׁם רִבִּי שִׂמְלַאי עִיר שֶׁכּוּלָּהּ כֹּהֲנִים נוֹשְׂאִין אֶת כַּפֵּיהֶן. לְמִי הֵן מְבָרְכִין לַאֲחֵיהֶן שֶׁבְּצָפוֹן לַאֲחֵיהֶן שֶׁבְּדָרוֹם לַאֲחֵיהֶן שֶׁבְּמִזְרָח לַאֲחֵיהֶן שֶׁבְּמַעֲרָב. וּמִי עוֹנֶה אַחֲרֵיהֶן אָמֵן הַנָּשִׁים וְהַטַּף.

Rebbi Aḥa, Rebbi Tanḥuma ben Rebbi Ḥiyya in the name of Rebbi Simlai: They lift their hands in a town where all are Cohanim[167]. Whom do they bless? Their brethren in North, South, East, and West. Who answers Amen after them? Women and small children.

167 And there is nobody left in the men's section of the synagogue whom they could bless. In the parallel in the Babli (*Soṭa* 38b) it is required that 10 Cohanim remain in their places in order to answer Amen after the blessings. The Babli is everywhere opposed to giving women a place in services or study. From here to the end of the Halakhah, the text is found (almost) word by word in Yerushalmi *Giṭṭin* 5:9.

תַּנָּא אַבַּיי בֵּי רִבִּי בִּנְיָמִן הָעוֹמְדִין לַאֲחוֹרֵי הַכֹּהֲנִים אֵינָן בִּכְלַל בְּרָכָה. הָעוֹמְדִין לִפְנֵי הַכֹּהֲנִים אָמַר רִבִּי חִיָּיא בַּר וָוא אֲפִילוּ חוֹמָה שֶׁל בַּרְזֶל הַבְּרָכָה מַפְסֶקֶת. הָעוֹמְדִין מִן הַצְּדָדִים נִשְׁמְעִינָהּ מִן הֲדָא נִתְכַּוֵּן לְהַזּוֹת לְפָנָיו וְהִזָּה לַאֲחוֹרָיו. לַאֲחוֹרָיו וְהִזָּה לְפָנָיו הַזָּייָתוֹ פְּסוּלָה. לְפָנָיו וְהִזָּה עַל הַצְּדָדִין שֶׁלְּפָנָיו הַזָּייָתוֹ כְּשֵׁירָה. הֲדָא אָמְרָה אַף הָעוֹמְדִין מִן הַצְּדָדִים מִכְּלַל בְּרָכָה הֵן.

Abbaye ben Rebbi Benjamin[168] stated: Those who stand behind the Cohanim are not included in their blessing. Those who stand before the Cohanim; Rebbi Ḥiyya bar Abba said the blessing even cuts through an iron wall[169]. About those who stand on the side, we may understand from the following[170]: If he wanted to sprinkle before him and he sprinkled behind him, behind him and he sprinkled before him, his sprinkling is invalid. Before him and he sprinkled on his sides, his sprinkling is valid. This implies that those who stand on the side are included in the blessing[171].

168 In the Babli (*Soṭah* 38b) he is called Abba the son of Rav Minyamin bar Ḥiyya, a Babylonian Amora of the third generation.

169 In the Babli (*loc. cit.*) this is a tradition of R. Joshua ben Levi.

170 Mishnah *Parah* 12:2, dealing with a man who wants to sprinkle from the water mixed with ashes from the red heifer on a person impure by contact with a dead body. It is a general rule that the water used for this purpose becomes invalid if, after it was taken from a flowing source, the person in charge of the water lets it slip from his mind. An action that contradicts the intention has the status of a slip of mind.

171 Since the Cohanim intend to bless the people before them, this intention automatically includes those who stand on their sides and excludes only those behind their backs. (The same reason is given in the Babli, *loc. cit.*)

אָמַר רַב חִסְדָּא וְצָרִיךְ שֶׁיְּהֵא הַחַזָּן יִשְׂרָאֵל. רַב נַחְמָן בַּר יַעֲקֹב אָמַר אִם הָיָה כֹהֵן אֶחָד אוֹמֵר כֹּהֵן אִם הָיוּ שְׁנַיִם אוֹמְרִים כֹּהֲנִים. אָמַר רַב חִסְדָּא אֲפִילוּ כֹהֵן אֶחָד אוֹמֵר כֹּהֲנִים שֶׁאֵינוֹ קוֹרֵא אֶלָּא לַשֵּׁבֶט.

Rav Ḥisda said, the organizer[172] must be an Israel[173]. Rav Naḥman bar Jacob said, if there was one Cohen he calls "Cohen"[174], if there are two they call "Cohanim". Rav Ḥisda[175] said, even if there was only one Cohen he says "Cohanim", because he only calls the tribe.

172 In old sources, the חזן is not the person who sings in the service but the organizer of the community. The statement of the Yerushalmi implies that the call "Cohanim" to alert the priests to recite the benediction preceding the priestly blessing is not pronounced by the reader (who has to pronounce every word of the priestly blessing before it is recited aloud by the Cohanim) but by the organizer (or the servant) of the community.

173 In the Babli (*Soṭah* 38a), Rav Ḥisda is quoted to the opposite effect that only a Cohen may call "Cohanim". However, in one manuscript (Rome) of the Babli, the reading is not "a Cohen may call 'Cohanim'" but "one Cohen calls 'Cohanim'" and then the statement would be parallel to the Yerushalmi. This reading of the Babli is the basis of the interpretation of (the Italian) *Shibbole Halleqet*.

174 In the Babli (*loc. cit.*), Abbaye declares that one Cohen is not called at all but he starts by himself.

175 In Yerushalmi *Giṭṭin*, the author of this statement is Rav Ḥuna.

משנה ו: הַמִּתְפַּלֵּל וְטָעָה סִימָן רַע הוּא לוֹ. וְאִם שְׁלִיחַ צִיבּוּר הוּא סִימָן רַע לְשׁוֹלְחָיו שֶׁשְּׁלוּחוֹ שֶׁל אָדָם כְּמוֹתוֹ. אָמְרוּ עָלָיו עַל רִבִּי חֲנִינָא בֶּן דּוֹסָא שֶׁהָיָה מִתְפַּלֵּל עַל הַחוֹלִים וְאוֹמֵר זֶה חַי וְזֶה מֵת. אָמְרוּ לוֹ מְנַיִין אַתָּה יוֹדֵעַ. אָמַר לָהֶן אִם שְׁגוּרָה תְפִילָּתִי בְּפִי יוֹדֵעַ אֲנִי שֶׁהוּא מְקוּבָּל. וְאִם לָאו יוֹדֵעַ אֲנִי שֶׁהוּא מְטוֹרָף.

Mishnah 6: It is a bad sign for him who prays when he makes a mistake. And if he is an emissary of the congregation, it is a bad sign for those who sent him because the emissary of somebody is like that person. They said about Rebbi Ḥanina ben Dosa that he was praying for sick people and saying that this one was going to live and that one was dying. They asked him, how do you know? He said to them, if my prayer comes easily from my lips I know that he has been accepted; otherwise, I know that he is being torn.

הלכה ו: רַב אַחָא בַּר יַעֲקֹב אָמַר וּבִלְבַד בְּאָבוֹת.

Halakha 6: Rav Aḥa bar Jacob said, only at "Forefathers.[176]"

176 Is it a bad omen if he errs there. The tradent here is Babylonian. In the Babli (*Berakhot* 34b), the parallel statement is attributed to the Babylonian-born Rebbi Ḥiyya (bar Abba) in the name of (the third generation) Babylonian Rav Safra. The statement must be Babylonian since the Yerushalmi requires attention for the entire *Amidah*.

מַעֲשֶׂה בְּרַבָּן גַּמְלִיאֵל שֶׁחָלָה בְנוֹ וְשָׁלַח שְׁנֵי תַלְמִידֵי חֲכָמִים אֵצֶל רִבִּי חֲנִינָא בֶּן דּוֹסָא בְּעִירוֹ. אָמַר לוֹן הַמְתִּינוּ לִי עַד שֶׁאֶעֱלֶה לַעֲלִיָּיה וְעָלָה לַעֲלִיָּיה וְיָרַד אָמַר לָהֶן בָּטוּחַ אֲנִי שֶׁנִּינוֹחַ בְּנוֹ שֶׁל רַבָּן גַּמְלִיאֵל מֵחָלְיוֹ וְסִיְּימוּ בְּאוֹתָהּ שָׁעָה תָּבַע מָזוֹן. אָמַר רִבִּי שְׁמוּאֵל בְּרִבִּי נַחְמָנִי אִם כּוֹוַנְתָּ אֶת לִבְּךָ בִּתְפִילָּה תְּהֵא מְבוּשָּׂר שֶׁנִּשְׁמְעָה תְפִילָּתָךְ. וּמַה טַעַם תָּכִין לִבָּם תַּקְשִׁיב אָזְנֶיךָ. אָמַר רִבִּי יְהוֹשֻׁעַ בֶּן לֵוִי אִם עָשׂוּ שְׂפָתוֹתָיו שֶׁל אָדָם תְּנוּבָה יְהֵא מְבוּשָּׂר שֶׁנִּשְׁמְעָה תְפִילָּתוֹ. מַה

טַעַם בּוֹרֵא נִיב שְׂפָתַיִם שָׁלוֹם שָׁלוֹם לָרָחוֹק וְלַקָּרוֹב אָמַר יי וּרְפָאתִיו.

It happened that the son of Rabban Gamliel fell ill and he sent two scholars to Rebbi Ḥanina ben Dosa in the latter's city. He said to them, wait until I go to the upper floor. He went to the upper floor, came back, and said to them: I am sure that Rabban Gamliel's son will get respite from his sickness. They noted that at this hour he asked for food[177]. Rebbi Samuel ben Rebbi Naḥmani said: If you were able to concentrate your attention on your prayer, you are told that your prayer was heard. What is the reason? (*Ps.* 10:17) "You prepare their hearts, You will listen with Your ears.[178]"

Rebbi Joshua ben Levi said: If a person's lips bore fruit[179] he is told that his prayer was heard. What is the reason? (*Is.* 57:19) "He Who created the fruit of lips: peace, peace to the far and the near said the Eternal, I shall heal him."

177 In the Babli (34b) he is reported to have asked for water.

178 The first "you" refers to the person, the others to God.

179 Not only that he concentrated his attention as required by R. Samuel ben Naḥmani, but that his lips produced a well-formed result.

כיצד מברכין פרק ששי

משנה א: כֵּיצַד מְבָֽרְכִין עַל הַפֵּירוֹת עַל פֵּירוֹת הָאִילָן הוּא אוֹמֵר בּוֹרֵא פְּרִי הָעֵץ. חוּץ מִן הַיַּיִן שֶׁעַל הַיַּיִן הוּא אוֹמֵר בּוֹרֵא פְּרִי הַגֶּפֶן. וְעַל פֵּירוֹת הָאָרֶץ הוּא אוֹמֵר בּוֹרֵא פְּרִי הָאֲדָמָה. חוּץ מִן הַפַּת שֶׁעַל הַפַּת הוּא אוֹמֵר הַמּוֹצִיא לֶחֶם מִן הָאָרֶץ. וְעַל הַיְּרָקוֹת הוּא אוֹמֵר בּוֹרֵא פְּרִי הָאֲדָמָה. רִבִּי יְהוּדָה אוֹמֵר בּוֹרֵא מִינֵי דְשָׁאִים.

Mishnah 1: Which benedictions are recited on produce[1]? On tree-grown fruits one says "Creator of the fruit of the tree" except for wine, because on wine one says "Creator of the fruit of the vine." But on fruits of the land one says "Creator of the fruit of the soil" except for bread, because on bread[2] one says "He Who produces bread from the earth." On vegetables one says "Creator of the fruit of the soil", Rebbi Yehudah says: "Creator of kinds of vegetables[3]."

1 Before one eats of these fruits, as will be explained in the Halakhah. All benedictions start with "Praise to You, Eternal, our God, King of the Universe". This formula is understood and does not have to be repeated.

2 The words "because on bread" are not in the Venice print but since they appear in the Leyden manuscript the omission seems to be a printer's error.

3 Rebbi Yehudah insists that benedictions should be exact and vegetables without seeds do not qualify as "fruits".

הלכה א: כְּתִיב לַיי הָאָרֶץ וּמְלוֹאָהּ תֵּבֵל וְיוֹשְׁבֵי בָהּ. הַנֶּהֱנֶה כְּלוּם מִן הָעוֹלָם מָעַל עַד שֶׁיַּתִּירוּ לוֹ הַמִּצְוֹת. אָמַר רִבִּי אַבָּהוּ כְּתִיב פֶּן תִּקְדַּשׁ הַמְלֵאָה הַזֶּרַע אֲשֶׁר תִּזְרָע וּתְבוּאַת הַכָּרֶם. הָעוֹלָם כּוּלּוֹ וּמְלוֹאוֹ עָשׂוּי כְּכֶרֶם. וּמַהוּ פִּדְיוֹנוֹ

בְּרָכָה. רִבִּי חִזְקִיָּה רִבִּי אָבוּן בְּשֵׁם רִבִּי שִׁמְעוֹן בֶּן לָקִישׁ אָמַרְתְּ לַיי יי אַתָּה טוֹבָתִי בַּל עָלֶיךָ. אִם אָכַלְתָּ וּבֵירַכְתָּ כִּבְיָכוֹל כְּאִילוּ מִשֶּׁלְּךָ אָכַלְתָּ. דָּבָר אַחֵר טוֹבָתִי בַּל עָלֶיךָ מְבַלֶּה אֲנִי טוֹבָתִי בְּגוּפָךְ. דָּבָר אַחֵר טוֹבָתִי בַּל עָלֶיךָ. (fol. 10a) יְבַלְלוּ כָּל הַטּוֹבוֹת וְיָבוֹאוּ עָלֶיךָ. אָמַר רִבִּי אָחָא מַהוּ בַּל עָלֶיךָ. שֶׁאֵינִי מֵבִיא טוֹבָה עַל הָעוֹלָם מִבַּלְעָדֶיךָ. כְּמָה דְּאַתְּ אָמַר וּמִבַּלְעָדֶיךָ לֹא יָרִים אִישׁ אֶת יָדוֹ. תַּנֵּי רִבִּי חִיָּא קוֹדֶשׁ הִילּוּלִים מְלַמֵּד שֶׁטָּעוּן בְּרָכָה לְפָנָיו וּלְאַחֲרָיו. מִיכַּן הָיָה רִבִּי עֲקִיבָה אוֹמֵר לֹא יִטְעוֹם אָדָם כְּלוּם עַד שֶׁיְּבָרֵךְ.

Halakhah 1: It is written (*Ps.* 24:1): "The Eternal's are the earth and what is in it, the dry land and its inhabitants." He who profits from the world commits larceny[4] until good deeds will permit him[5]. Rebbi Abbahu said, it is written (*Deut.* 22:9) "Lest the fullness of the seed that you sow and the yield of the vineyard should be forbidden." The entire world and its contents are like a vineyard. What is its redemption? The benediction[6]. Rebbi Ḥizqiah, Rebbi Abun in the name of Rebbi Simeon ben Laqish: (*Ps.* 16:2) "Say to the Eternal, You are my Master[7], my good is only with You." If you ate and recited the benedictions then it is as if you ate from your own. Another explanation[8]: "My good is בל with you", I am feeding My goodness to your body. Another explanation: "My good is בל with you", all good things may be mixed together and come to you. Rebbi Aḥa said, what is "only with you?" I shall not bring any good things to the world without you. As it is said (*Gen.* 41:44) "Without you nobody may lift his hand.[9]" Rebbi Ḥiyya stated: (*Lev.* 19:24) "Holy for praises", this shows that it needs benediction before and after. From here did Rebbi Aqiba say that nobody should taste anything before he gives praise[10].

4 Since he uses God's property, not his own.

5 The obligation to say Grace after a meal is spelled out in *Deut.* 8:10. The

obligation to recite blessings before one eats is not mentioned explicitly in the Torah. Since Grace is only treated in the next Chapter, one has to find here Biblical allusions to this duty and (in the next section) to the duty of reciting a benediction before fulfilling specified commandments.

The verse appears in the Babli (35a) in the name of Samuel. R. Levi compares the verse (*Ps.* 115:16) "Heaven is the Eternal's heaven but the earth He gave to mankind", explaining that before a benediction everything is the Eternal's property but after a benediction it becomes human property. While Rebbi Levi is a Galilean teacher, the Yerushalmi rejects his combination since in the third paragraph earthly enjoyment is only "*as* if one ate from one's own". The text of the Yerushalmi is from Tosephta *Berakhot* 4:1 which is identical with the Talmudic text except that there it says "until all good deeds will permit him", meaning that only if the preparation of food is completely within the commandments of the Torah then the last step of the preparation, the recitation of the benediction, will allow the food to be given to man as his own.

6 This argument is very difficult to understand and the commentators either chose to ignore it or give very incongruous explanations. The best explanation is that of R. Eliahu Fulda who in his Yerushalmi edition suppresses the word פֶּן "lest". One would have to assume that Rebbi Abbahu's text did not have the word but that later scribes added it from memory. By it the negative implication of the verse (which speaks about growing different kinds of plants in a vineyard) are changed to a positive one which now should be translated: "That you shall sanctify the fullness of the seed that you sow and the yield of the vineyard." Since the sanctity is not that of sacrifices, the sanctity may be removed by redemption (*Lev.* 27:11). However, there can be no monetary redemption of anything not explicitly authorized in the Torah. Hence, the redemption is non-monetary and is the traditional praise given to God in benedictions. [The simple sense of the verse is that produce grown in a vineyard becomes forbidden for private use as if it were dedicated for sacrifice.]

7 The translation follows the Biblical text, not the text written here.

8 The verse is extremely hard to understand; the next two interpretations have nothing to do with the topic on hand; they are only added to indicate translations that might be

considered if בל is not a negation but a verb form derived from בלל, which may mean either "to give food" (*Jud*. 19:24) or, more frequently, "mixed with fluid, moistened."

9 Taking בל as shorthand for בִּלְעֲדֵי "without".

10 This is also quoted in the Babli (35a); the source of both Talmudim is *Sifra* on the verse. The verse speaks of the fruits of a vineyard in its fourth year when the grapes can be used for the first time after having been forbidden for the first three years. This is only a hint for any other food.

רִבִּי חַגַּיי וְרִבִּי יִרְמְיָה סָלְקוּן לְבֵי חַנְוָתָא קָפַץ רִבִּי חַגַּיי וּבֵירַךְ עֲלֵיהֶן. אָמַר לֵיהּ רִבִּי יִרְמְיָה יְאוּת עֲבַדַת שֶׁכָּל הַמִּצְוֹת טְעוּנוֹת בְּרָכָה. וּמְנַיִין שֶׁכָּל הַמִּצְוֹת טְעוּנוֹת בְּרָכָה. רִבִּי תַּנְחוּמָא רִבִּי אַבָּא בַּר כַּהֲנָא בְּשֵׁם רִבִּי אֶלְעָזָר וְאֶתְּנָה לְךָ אֶת לוּחוֹת הָאֶבֶן הַתּוֹרָה וְהַמִּצְוָה. הִקִּישׁ תּוֹרָה לְמִצְוָה. מַה תּוֹרָה טְעוּנָה בְּרָכָה אַף מִצְוָה טְעוּנָה בְּרָכָה.

Rebbi Ḥaggai and Rebbi Jeremiah went to the Bazaar[11]. Rebbi Ḥaggai was quick to recite a blessing. Rebbi Jeremiah said to him: You acted correctly because all commandments need a benediction. And from where that all commandments[12] need a benediction? Rebbi Tanḥuma, Rebbi Abba bar Cahana in the name of Rebbi Eleazar: (*Ex*. 24:12) "I want to give you the stone tablets, the Torah and the commandment[13]." It brackets Torah and commandment. Just as Torah needs a benediction, a commandment also needs benediction.

11 The translation is tentative; בית חנוותא means "the house of stores", which might be a description of a *shuq* even though it is difficult to explain why the word שׁוּקָא was not used. It is not clear what kind of *mizwah* the two rabbis performed in the market. In the opinion of R. Eleazar Askari they were *agoranomoi*, overseers of weights and measures, and Rebbi Ḥaggai recited a benediction before starting to go from stall to stall and checking the balances for correctness since that is a Biblical commandment repeated several times in the Pentateuch (*Deut*. 25:15, *Lev*. 19:36) in addition to the prohibition of

fraudulent business practices.

The Rome manuscript has instead of בית חנותא the expression לְמֵי חַטָּאתָה "the water for the ashes of the read heifer", the drawing of which certainly would need a benediction. The Talmud reports that Rebbi Ḥaggai finished his Talmud studies with Rav Ḥuna I at age 18 and lived to be 160 years old; so, as shown in the commentary to Mishnah 1:1, he still could have seen ashes of the read heifer, but these could not have been preserved at the time of Rebbi Jeremiah who lived during the third and fourth generations of Amoraïm, even if these ashes were uniquely reserved for Cohanim eating *Terumah.*

R. Zachariah Frankel wants to emend to בֵּית חַתְנוּתָא "place of a wedding" but his reading has no basis in antique or medieval sources.

12 After establishing benedictions before the consumption of food one establishes now the need for benedictions before the execution of positive commandments (by tradition, only those to be performed at specific times or occasions, not those that are always valid).

13 The verse really reads: "both Torah and Commandments". The double *vaw* in the verse is essential for R. Eleazar's argument.

רִבִּי יוֹחָנָן נְסַב זֵיתָא וּבֵירַךְ לְפָנָיו וּלְאַחֲרָיו וַהֲוָה רִבִּי חִיָּיא בַּר וָוא מִסְתַּכֵּל בֵּיהּ. אֲמַר לֵיהּ רִבִּי יוֹחָנָן בַּבְלָיָא לָמָּה אַתְּ מִסְתַּכֵּל בִּי. לֵית לָךְ כָּל־שֶׁהוּא מִמִּין שִׁבְעָה טָעוּן בְּרָכָה לְפָנָיו וּלְאַחֲרָיו. אִית לֵיהּ. וּמַה צְרִיכָא לֵיהּ. מִפְּנֵי שֶׁגַּלְעִינָתוֹ מְמַעֲטוֹ. וְלֵית לֵיהּ לְרִבִּי יוֹחָנָן שֶׁגַּלְעִינָתוֹ מְמַעֲטוֹ. מַה עֲבַד לֵיהּ רִבִּי יוֹחָנָן מִשּׁוּם בִּירְיָיה. מִלְתֵיהּ דְּרִבִּי יוֹחָנָן אָמְרָה שֶׁכֵּן אֲפִילוּ אָכַל פְּרִידָה אַחַת שֶׁל רִימּוֹן שֶׁהוּא טָעוּן בְּרָכָה לְפָנֶיהָ וּלְאַחֲרֶיהָ.

Rebbi Yoḥanan took an olive[14] and recited a benediction before and after. Rebbi Ḥiyya bar Abba was looking at him. Rebbi Yoḥanan said to him: Babylonian, why are you looking at me? Don't you agree that everything from the Seven Kinds[15] needs a benediction before and after? He agrees. What is his problem? Because its pit reduces it[16]. Does Rebbi Yoḥanan agree that its pit reduces it? What Rebbi Yoḥanan did was because of a creature[17]. The word of Rebbi Yoḥanan implies that even one berry from a pomegranate needs a benediction before and after[18].

14 Here starts the actual discussion of the rules given in the Mishnah. R. Ḥiyya bar Abba's report on the story appears also in the Babli (38b-39a) but there the argument and the inferences drawn are totally different. In the Babli, R. Ḥiyya bar Abba reports that the olive was salted, which seems natural since raw olives are bitter. The discussion in the Babli is whether pickling or cooking changes the applicable benediction; it is clear from this paragraph that at least for the "Seven Kinds" the Yerushalmi does not contemplate any change in benedictions.

15 The Seven Kinds are "the fruits for which the Land of Israel is praised", enumerated in *Deut.* 8:8: "A land of wheat and barley, vine and fig, and pomegranate; a land of oil olive and (date) honey." Since in v. 10 it is stated "when you will eat and be satiated, you must praise the Eternal, your God, for the good land that He gave you," it follows that these kinds need a benediction afterwards that contains praise for food, land, (and Jerusalem.) This is called "one benediction in the kind of three"; the three benedictions are reserved for grain eaten in the form of bread. The benediction before is the applicable one of those mentioned in the Mishnah.

16 In general, anything smaller than the volume of an average olive is too insignificant to require a benediction. The edible part of an olive is much smaller than the volume of an average olive.

17 The Babli (*loc. cit.*) conjectures that R. Yoḥanan ate a large olive which even if pitted still has the size of an average olive. The Yerushalmi here is emphatic that any complete edible fruit needs a benediction before and after it is eaten, irrespective of size.

18 A pomegranate is full of seeds; each seed is surrounded by fruit flesh encased in a membrane. One such cell containing the seed and the fruit flesh is a berry. Without the seed it would not be a creature and without the fruit flesh it would not be edible but with both it needs benediction before and after if the membrane is untouched.

יַיִן בִּזְמַן שֶׁהוּא כְּמוֹת שֶׁהוּא אוֹמֵר עָלָיו בּוֹרֵא פְּרִי הָעֵץ וְאֵין נוֹטְלִין מִמֶּנּוּ לַיָּדַיִם. בִּזְמַן שֶׁהוּא מָזוּג אוֹמֵר עָלָיו בּוֹרֵא פְּרִי הַגֶּפֶן וְנוֹטְלִין מִמֶּנּוּ לַיָּדַיִם דִּבְרֵי רִבִּי אֱלִיעֶזֶר. וַחֲכָמִים אוֹמְרִים בֵּין חַי בֵּין מָזוּג אוֹמְרִים עָלָיו בּוֹרֵא פְּרִי הַגֶּפֶן וְנוֹטְלִין מִמֶּנּוּ לַיָּדַיִם. אָמַר רִבִּי אַבָּא אֵין בּוֹ מִשּׁוּם אָבְדַּן אוֹכְלִין.

[19]"Wine in its natural state[20], one says for it 'Creator of the fruit of the tree'[21] and one may not use it to wash his hands[22]; when it is mixed[23], one says for it 'Creator of the fruit of the vine' and one may use it to wash his hands; these are the words of Rebbi Eliezer. But the Sages say, both pure and mixed one says over it 'Creator of the fruit of the vine' and one may use it to wash his hands[24]." Rebbi Abba said, it is not forbidden because of wasting food[25].

19 Parallel texts in Tosephta *Berakhot* 4:3 and Babli 50b.

20 A heavy subtropical wine with an alcohol content of close to 15%, unmixed with any water.

21 R. Eliezer holds that no human will want to drink such a heavy dose of alcohol or at least it is not admissible to have such unmixed wine at a formal dinner.

22 Hands must be washed with water and while fruit juice is considered water, in the opinion of R. Eliezer pure wine is not.

23 Standard mixing is one part wine to two parts water for an alcohol content of about 5%, Mishnah *Niddah* 2:7.

24 All sources of the Tosephta read everywhere "one may not" where the Yerushalmi has "one may", and "one may" where the Yerushalmi has "one may not". In the Babli, all sources read "one may" the first and last time but in the second instance some manuscripts and authorities follow readings of the Tosephta and some (Munich manuscript and some Medieval authorities) the readings of the Yerushalmi.

25 In general, wilful spoiling of food is a sin. It seems that the Yerushalmi restricts the use of fruit juice for washing of the hands to the ritual washing before eating bread, since that is part of the meal, but that washing with fruit juice just for cleansing is forbidden. The Gaonic *Halakhot Gedolot* explains that the prohibition of the Sages (in the version of the Babli) refers to the sin of wasting food.

רִבִּי יַעֲקֹב בַּר זַבְדִּי בְּשֵׁם רִבִּי אַבָּהוּ שֶׁמֶן זַיִת אוֹמֵר עָלָיו בּוֹרֵא פְּרִי הָעֵץ. אָמַר רִבִּי חִיָּא בַּר פַּפָּא קוֹמֵי רִבִּי זְעִירָא וּמַתְנִיתָא אָמְרָה כֵן. חוּץ מִן הַיַּיִן שֶׁעַל

הַיַּיִן הוּא אוֹמֵר בּוֹרֵא פְּרִי הַגֶּפֶן. וְיַיִן לָאו שָׁחוּק הוּא. לָא מַר אֶלָּא חוּץ מִן הַיַּיִן הָא שְׁאָר כָּל־הַדְּבָרִים אַף עַל פִּי שֶׁשְּׁחוּקִין בְּעֵינָן הֵן.

Rebbi Jacob bar Zavdi in the name of Rebbi Abbahu[26]: On olive oil one recites "Creator of the fruit of the tree." Rebbi Ḥiyya bar Pappus[27] said before Rebbi Zeïra: The Mishnah says so. "Except for wine because on wine one says 'Creator of the fruit of the vine'." Is wine not mashed[28]? But it says only "except for wine", hence all other things even if they are mashed are recognizable in their state.

26 In the Babli (35b) this is a statement of R. Yoḥanan. The argument of R. Ḥiyya bar Pappus is purely Yerushalmi.

27 An otherwise unknown Galilean Amora. In the Rome manuscript, his name is Rebbi Ḥinena bar Pappus.

28 Grape juice is really pressed, but so is olive oil, and only second and third pressings of oil are from ground olives. In any case, wine goes through a fermentation process and cannot be described as being "recognizable in its state."

רִבִּי אַבָּא אָמַר רַב וּשְׁמוּאֵל תְּרֵוַיְהוֹן אָמְרִין יֶרֶק שָׁלוּק אוֹמֵר עָלָיו שֶׁהַכֹּל נִהְיֶה בִּדְבָרוֹ. רִבִּי זְעוּרָא בְּשֵׁם שְׁמוּאֵל רָאשֵׁי לִפְתּוֹת שֶׁשְּׁלָקָן אִם בְּעֵינָן הֵן אוֹמֵר עֲלֵיהֶן בּוֹרֵא פְּרִי הָאֲדָמָה. שְׁחָקָן אוֹמֵר עֲלֵיהֶן שֶׁהַכֹּל נִהְיֶה בִּדְבָרוֹ. אָמַר רִבִּי יוֹסֵי וּמַתְנִיתָא אָמְרָה כֵן. חוּץ מִן הַפַּת שֶׁעַל הַפַּת הוּא אוֹמֵר הַמּוֹצִיא לֶחֶם מִן הָאָרֶץ. וּפַת לָאו שָׁחוּק הוּא. לָא מַר אֶלָּא חוּץ מִן הַפַּת הָא שְׁאָר כָּל־הַדְּבָרִים אַף עַל פִּי שֶׁשְּׁחוּקִין בְּעֵינָן הֵן.

Rebbi Abba[29] said: Rav and Samuel both say, on cooked vegetable one says "that everything was created by His word." Rebbi Zeïra in the name of Samuel: Large cooked[30] pieces of *liftan*[31], if they are recognizable one says on them "Creator of the fruit of the earth;" if one mashed them one says "He, by Whose word everything was created." Rebbi Yose said, does the Mishnah say so? "Except for bread because on bread one says 'He Who produces bread from the earth.'." Is bread not mashed[32]? But it says only "except for bread", hence all other things even if they are mashed are recognizable in their state[33].

29 In the Babli (38b), Samuel is said to hold a different opinion. The Galilean authorities quoted there are those of the next paragraph. The interpretations of Babli and Yerushalmi differ.

30 שלוק "cooked in water" in contrast to מבושל "cooked in broth".

31 As a plant, לפתן means "beets", but generally it means cooked vegetables served as main dish with bread (pitta bread to be used as fork and spoon in the absence of tableware except knives.) Meat was only eaten on special occasions, such as Sabbath, holidays, visits of important people, and after bleeding.

32 Flour is ground ("mashed") grain, one of the Seven Kinds.

33 Hence, the statement of Rebbi Abba is superior to that of Rebbi Zeïra. This conclusion is the opposite of that of the Babli.

רִבִּי חִייָא בַּר וָוא בְּשֵׁם רִבִּי יוֹחָנָן זַיִת כָּבוּשׁ אוֹמֵר עָלָיו בּוֹרֵא פְּרִי הָעֵץ. רִבִּי בִּנְיָמִן בַּר יֶפֶת בְּשֵׁם רִבִּי יוֹחָנָן יָרָק שָׁלוּק אוֹמֵר עָלָיו שֶׁהַכֹּל נִהְיֶה בִּדְבָרוֹ. אָמַר רִבִּי שְׁמוּאֵל בַּר רַב יִצְחָק מַתְנִיתָא מְסַייְעָא לְרִבִּי בִּנְיָמִן בַּר יֶפֶת. אֲבָל לֹא כְבוּשִׁין וְלֹא שְׁלוּקִין וְלֹא מְבוּשָּׁלִין אִם בְּעֵייָנָן הֵן אָדָם יוֹצֵא בָּהֶן יְדֵי חוֹבָתוֹ בַּפֶּסַח. אָמַר רִבִּי זְעִירָא מַאן יְדַע מַשְׁמַע מִן רִבִּי יוֹחָנָן יֵאוּת רִבִּי חִייָא בַּר וָוא אוֹ רִבִּי בִּנְיָמִן בַּר יֶפֶת. לֹא רִבִּי חִייָא בַּר וָוא. וְעוֹד מִן הֲדָא מִן מַה דַּאֲנָן חֲמִייָן רַבָּנָן רַבְרְבַיָּא עָלוּן לְאַבְרִייְתָא וְנָסְבִין תּוּרְמוּסִין וּמְבָרְכִין עֲלֵיהֶן בּוֹרֵא פְּרִי הָאֲדָמָה. וְתוּרְמוּסִין לָאו שְׁלוּקִין הֵן. אִין תֵּימַר שַׁנְיָיא הִיא שֶׁאֲמָרָה הַתּוֹרָה מְרוֹרִין תּוּרְמוּסִין כֵּיוָן שֶׁשְּׁלָקָן בָּטְלָה מָרָתָן. אָמַר רִבִּי יוֹסֵי בֵּי רִבִּי אָבוּן וְלֹא פְלִיגִין. זַיִת עַל יְדֵי שֶׁדַּרְכּוֹ לֵאָכֵל חַי אַף עַל פִּי שֶׁכָּבוּשׁ בְּעֵינוֹ הוּא. יָרָק כֵּיוָן שֶׁשְּׁלָקוֹ נִשְׁתַּנֶּה.

[34]Rebbi Ḥiyya bar Abba in the name of Rebbi Yoḥanan: One says "Creator of the fruit of the tree" on marinated[35] olives. Rebbi Benjamin bar Jephet in the name of Rebbi Yoḥanan: One says "By Whose word

everything was created[36]" on water-cooked vegetables. Rebbi Samuel bar Rav Isaac said: a Mishnah supports Rebbi Benjamin bar Yephet: (*Pesaḥim* 2:6) "but not marinated or cooked in water or cooked in broth[37]"; if they were recognizable in their state one could fulfill his duty with them on Passover. Rebbi Zeïra said, who understands well what Rebbi Yoḥanan said, Rebbi Ḥiyya bar Abba or Rebbi Benjamin bar Yephet? Not Rebbi Ḥiyya bar Abba?[38] And in addition from the fact that we see great rabbis going to a mourner's meal, eat lupines[39] and recite on them "Creator of the fruit of the earth;" Are not lupines certainly cooked? If you want, you may say there is a difference, since the Torah said "bitter herbs", and cooked lupines have lost their bitterness. Rebbi Yose ben Rebbi Abun said, they[40] have no disagreement. Since olives usually are eaten fresh, they are recognizable in their state even if they are marinated. Vegetables are changed once they are cooked[41].

34 The entire paragraph is also found in *Pesaḥim* 2:5. One word in the current text has been corrected following that Yerushalmi text.

35 This is the exact meaning of the corresponding Arabic כבס.

36 The general benediction on everything not expressly mentioned in the Mishnah.

37 The Mishnah enumerates all herbs which qualify as "bitter herbs" on Passover, adding that these herbs are not usable if cooked or marinated. The implication is that after treatment they are no longer herbs but general food.

38 R. Ḥiyya bar Abba studied much more intensively than R. Benjamin bar Yephet. This is the argument and conclusion of the Babli (38b). The refutation of Rebbi Zeïra's argument is not in that Talmud.

39 Greek θέρμος. Raw lupines are cattle feed, too bitter for human consumption. They become edible only after long cooking. This statement supports R. Ḥiyya bar Abba.

40 R. Ḥiyya bar Abba and R. Benjamin bar Yephet.

41 One must assume that roots of lupine keep their shape and general appearance in cooking just as olives do. The rule that vegetables which are

inedible unless cooked require the blessing "Creator of the fruit of the earth" is the opinion of Rav Ḥisda in the Babli (*loc. cit.*).

רִבִּי יַעֲקֹב בַּר אָחָא אִיתפַּלְגוּן רִבִּי נְחֶמְיָה וְרַבָּנָן. רִבִּי נְחֶמְיָה[42] אָמַר הַמּוֹצִיא לֶחֶם מִן הָאָרֶץ. וְרַבָּנָן אָמְרֵי מוֹצִיא לֶחֶם מִן הָאָרֶץ .אַתְיָיא אִילֵּין פְּלוּגְוָותָא כְּאִינּוּן פְּלוּגְוָותָא. לֶפֶת רִבִּי חִינְנָא בַּר יִצְחָק וְרִבִּי שְׁמוּאֵל בַּר אִימִּי חַד אָמַר לֶפֶת לָא פַּת הָיְתָה. וְחָרָנָא אָמַר לֶפֶת לָא פַּת הִיא עֲתִידָה לִהְיוֹת. יְהִי פִיסַּת בַּר בָּאָרֶץ בְּרֹאשׁ הָרִים. רִבִּי יִרְמְיָה בְּרִיךְ קוֹמֵי רִבִּי זְעִירָא הַמּוֹצִיא לֶחֶם מִן הָאָרֶץ וְקַלְּסֵיהּ. מַה כְּרִבִּי נְחֶמְיָה שֶׁלֹּא לְעָרֵב רָאשֵׁי אוֹתִיּוֹת. מֵעַתָּה הַמֵּין הָאָרֶץ. עַל דַּעְתֵּיהּ רִבִּי נְחֶמְיָה הַבּוֹרֵא פְּרִי הַגֶּפֶן. וְעַל דַּעְתְּהוֹן דְּרַבָּנָן בּוֹרֵא פְּרִי הַגֶּפֶן.

Rebbi Jacob bar Aḥa: Rebbi Neḥemiah and the rabbis disagree. Rebbi Neḥemiah said: "Who produced bread from the earth." But the rabbis say, "Who produces bread from the earth.[43]" This disagreement is like that disagreement: לפת, Rebbi Ḥinena bar Isaac[44] and Rebbi Samuel bar Immi[45]; one said "*lefet*, was it not bread?[45]" and the other one said "*lefet*, will it not be bread"? (*Ps*. 72:16) "There will be a piece of flour on the land, on mountain tops.[47]" Rebbi Jeremiah recited before Rebbi Zeïra "Who produced bread from the earth" and the latter praised him. Following Rebbi Neḥemiah[48]? Not to amalgamate the letters[49]! If it is so, הַמֵּין הָאָרֶץ [50]? In the opinion of Rebbi Neḥemiah[51], "He Who created the fruit of the vine"; in the opinion of the rabbis "Who creates the fruit of the vine."

42 Reading of the Rome ms., Genizah fragments, and the parallel to this paragraph in *Midrash Bereshit rabba*. The Leyden ms. and Venice print have רב נחמן. The name of an Amora is impossible in a tannaïtic disgreement.

43 In the Babli (38a), the opinion ascribed here to the rabbis is that of Rebbi Neḥemiah and vice versa. This eliminates the question which the Yerushalmi raises about the current text of the benediction. In the opinion

of the Babli, the preferred version (R. Neḥemiah here, the rabbis in the Babli) takes the present participle in an atemporal sense.

44 A preacher of the third generation of Galilean Amoraïm. The name of his teacher is unknown.

45 A Galilean Amora of the third generation who also appears as R. Samuel bar Ammi. His father and father-in-law also were rabbis.

46 While the traditional vocalization is לֶפֶת which corresponds to Arabic לפת "beets, kohlrabi", it is clear from the homilies that the vocalization was לְפַת. This is extended to לָא פַּת "not bread" since writing an *aleph* is optional in the spelling of the Yerushalmi. The entire paragraph is copied in *Midrash Bereshit rabba* 15(8) to prove that the fruit of the tree that Adam and Eve ate was bread.

47 Since flour cannot form a loaf until it is baked, this means that bread will grow on mountain tops. This is a homily of R. Yoḥanan in *Midrash Tehillim* 92(6), which appears in the name of several other Amoraïm in Babli *Šabbat* 30b, *Ketubot* 111b.

48 One is not supposed to follow a minority of one, much less to be praised for it.

49 So that הָעוֹלָם מוֹצִיא should not be pronounced *ha'ôlāmôẓî*, but clearly be said in two distinct words.

50 Since לֶחֶם מִן also has two consecutive *mem* and could be read together. However, the change proposed here makes no sense; nobody wants to pronounce a meaningless benediction that would be close to blasphemy. The question does not merit an answer.

51 One wonders why they disagree only about the language for bread and not for wine.

רִבִּי זְרִיקָן אָמַר רִבִּי זְעוּרָא בָּעֵי אֲהֵן דִּנְסַב תּוּרְמוּסָא וּמְבָרֵךְ עִילוֹי וְנָפַל מִינֵיהּ מַהוּ מְבָרְכָה עִילוֹי זְמָן תִּנְיָינוּת. מַה בֵּינוֹ לְבֵין אַמַּת הַמַּיִם. אָמְרִין תַּמָּן לְכַךְ כִּיוֵן דַּעְתּוֹ מִתְּחִילָּה. בְּרַם הָכָא לֹא לְכַךְ כִּיוֵן דַּעְתּוֹ מִתְּחִילָּה. תַּנֵּי רִבִּי חִייָא אֵין מְבָרְכִין עַל הַפַּת אֶלָּא בְשָׁעָה שֶׁהוּא פּוֹרֵס. אָמַר רִבִּי חִייָא בַּר וָוא הָדָא אָמְרָה אֲהֵן דִּנְסַב עִיגוּלָא וּמְבָרֵךְ עִילוֹי וְהָכָא לֹא אָתֵי בְיָדֵיהּ צָרִיךְ מְבָרְכָה עִילוֹי זְמָן תִּנְיָינוּת. אָמַר רִבִּי תַּנְחוּם בַּר יוּדָן צָרִיךְ לוֹמַר בָּרוּךְ שֵׁם כְּבוֹד מַלְכוּתוֹ לְעוֹלָם וָעֶד. שֶׁלֹּא לְהַזְכִּיר שֵׁם שָׁמַיִם לְבַטָּלָה.

Rebbi Zeriqan said: Rebbi Zeïra asked: He who took a lupine and was reciting the benediction over it when it fell from his hand, does he have to recite a second benediction[52]? What is the difference between that and a water canal[53]? They said, there he intended it from the start, but here he did not intend it from the start. Rebbi Ḥiyya stated: One recites the benediction on bread only when one breaks it[54]. Rebbi Ḥiyya bar Abba said: This means that he who took a loaf[55] and pronounced the benediction on it before it came to his hand, must recite a second benediction. Rebbi Tanḥum bar Yudan[56] said, he must say "Praised be the Name of the Glory of His kingdom forever and ever," in order not to utter the Name of Heaven in vain[57].

52 Since the cooked lupine root becomes inedible when it falls into the dust, he has to take another one, not the one for which the benediction was intended.

53 Since one has to say the benediction on water before one starts to drink, the water drops one drinks are not those that were in the same place at the moment of the benediction.

54 The formulation in the Babli (39a) is: Rebbi Ḥiyya said, the benediction and the breaking of the bread must be finished simultaneously. This is accepted practice in the Yerushalmi, but is rejected in the Babli in favor of a ruling of the much later, fourth generation Babylonian Amora Rava who requires that the benediction be completely recited before one starts to break the bread.

55 The usual expression פַּת for bread designates a pittah; עִיגּוּל here is a loaf of bread; it might be a round cake of pressed figs. R. Asher ben Yeḥiel copies the passage (Chapter 6, #20) which has פוּגְלָא "a radish" instead of "a loaf". That reading seems to be a copyist's error.

56 A Galilean Amora whose time cannot be determined.

57 By a statement of R. Yoḥanan and R. Simeon ben Laqish in the Babli (33a), any unnecessary benediction is a violation of the Fifth Commandment.

עַד כַּמָּה יִפְרוֹס. רִבִּי חִנְנָא וְרִבִּי מָנָא חַד אָמַר עַד כְּזַיִת. וְחָרָנָא אָמַר עַד פָּחוֹת מִכְּזַיִת. מַאן דָּמַר כְּזַיִת. כְּיֵי דְתַנִּינָן תַּמָּן וְכוּלָּן פְּתִיתִין כְּזַיִת. מַאן דָּמַר עַד פָּחוֹת מִכְּזַיִת תַּנֵּי רִבִּי יִשְׁמָעֵאל אֲפִילוּ מַחֲזִירָהּ לְסוֹלְתָהּ. תַּנֵּי כָּל־שֶׁאוֹמֵר אַחֲרָיו שְׁלֹשָׁה בְּרָכוֹת אוֹמֵר לְפָנָיו הַמּוֹצִיא לֶחֶם מִן הָאָרֶץ. וְכָל־שֶׁאֵין אַחֲרָיו שָׁלֹשׁ בְּרָכוֹת אֵין אוֹמֵר לְפָנָיו הַמּוֹצִיא לֶחֶם מִן הָאָרֶץ. הֲתִיבוּן הֲרֵי פָּחוֹת מִכְּזַיִת הֲרֵי אֵין אוֹמֵר לְאַחֲרָיו שָׁלֹשׁ בְּרָכוֹת. מֵעַתָּה לֹא יֹאמְרוּ לְפָנָיו הַמּוֹצִיא לֶחֶם מִן הָאָרֶץ. רִבִּי יַעֲקֹב בַּר אַחָא אָמַר לִשְׁאָר הַמִּינִין נִצְרְכָה.

How far may he break[58]? Rebbi Ḥinena and Rebbi Mana, one says down to the size of an olive, the other says even smaller than the size of an olive. He who says down to the size of an olive, as it is stated "all[59] are crumbled into olive-size pieces." He who says, smaller than the size of an olive: "Rebbi Ismael stated, even if he reduced it[60] to its original form of fine flour." It has been stated[61]: "On everything that needs three benedictions at the end one says 'He Who produces bread from the earth' at the start, but on everything that does not need three benedictions at the end one does not say 'He Who produces bread from the earth' at the start." They objected: But if it is less than the size of an olive, one does not say three benedictions at the end. Does this mean that one should not say "He Who produces bread from the earth" at the start? Rebbi Jacob bar Aḥa said, it is needed for other kinds[62].

58 There are two connected problems here. The first one, what is the minimum size of a piece of bread (or any other food) that requires a benediction beforehand; the second, if one person makes a benediction over bread for an entire company (with the other participants answering "Amen" instead of reciting their own benedictions), what is the minimal size of a piece of bread that every participant has to receive and eat after the benediction. For Grace after meals, the situation is clear. The requirement from the Torah (*Deut.* 8:10) is "when you will have eaten and will be satiated then you must praise the Eternal . . ."; the Biblical obligation

applies only after a full meal. The rabbinic obligation explicitly applies to food that fills at least the volume of an olive; smaller amounts do not require Grace and, according the preceding paragraph, one may not recite Grace for such minute amounts. But since benedictions before eating are all rabbinic institutions, the problem is whether food in an amount less than the volume of an average olive must (or may) have a benediction and, if a benediction is recited on a larger loaf, whether the piece eaten immediately after the recitation of the benediction must be the size of an olive or not.

The Babli (37b) has another angle to the problem. Since bread has a separate benediction from cereal and cakes, how small may the recognizable pieces of bread in cereal or soup be so that it still falls under the category of bread rather than cereal or soup?

59 This refers to Mishnah *Menaḥot* 7:4 that all flour offerings prepared in a vessel (baked or fried) must be broken into pieces before a handful of them is burned on the altar. There are two opinions on the size of admissible pieces (also reported Babli *Berakhot* 37a).

60 The baked or fried flour-offering.

61 The first half of this statement appears in Tosephta *Berakhot* 4:7.

62 The statement does not refer to size, but to kinds of food; if it is not bread it does not receive the benediction for bread. Hence, no conclusion as to the correct practice can be drawn.

רִבִּי אַבָּא בְּשֵׁם רַב מְסוּבִּין אֲסוּרִין לִטְעוֹם כְּלוּם עַד שֶׁיִּטְעוֹם הַמְבָרֵךְ. רִבִּי יְהוֹשֻׁעַ בֶּן לֵוִי אָמַר שׁוֹתִין אַף עַל פִּי שֶׁלֹּא שָׁתָה. מַה פְּלִיג. מַה דָּמַר רַב כְּשֶׁהָיוּ כּוּלָּם זְקוּקִין לְכִכָּר אֶחָד מַה דָּמַר רִבִּי יְהוֹשֻׁעַ כְּשֶׁהָיָה כָּל אֶחָד וְאֶחָד כּוֹסוֹ בְּיָדוֹ.

Rebbi Abba in the name of Rav: Those assembled may not taste anything before the one who recited the benediction did taste. Rebbi Joshua ben Levi said: They may drink even if he did not drink. Do they disagree? Rav said in case all need the same loaf[63] but Rebbi Joshua said when each one had his own cup in his hand.

63 Which is the normal case if there is a real loaf of bread and not pittot. But wine everybody drinks from his own glass that was filled beforehand. The question whether the one who recites the benediction should eat first

and then distribute the bread or vice versa is addressed in the next paragraph. [The parallel in the Babli (47a) has only the statement of Rav; there it is explained that לטעום "to taste", usually applied to drinking, here means "eating" as is clear from the Yerushalmi.]

תַּנֵּי הַמְבָרֵךְ פּוֹשֵׁט יָדוֹ תְחִילָּה אֶלָּא אִם רָצָה לַחֲלוֹק לוֹ כָּבוֹד לְרַבּוֹ אוֹ לְמִי שֶׁגָּדוֹל מִמֶּנּוּ בַּתּוֹרָה הָרְשׁוּת בְּיָדוֹ. רַב כַּד הֲוָה קְצִי הֲוָה טְעִים בִּשְׂמָאלֵיהּ וּמַפְלִיג בִּימִינֵיהּ. רַב הוּנָא אֲמַר אֲהֵן דָּמַר סַב וּבְרִיךְ סַב וּבְרִיךְ אֵין בּוֹ מִשּׁוּם הֶפְסֵק בְּרָכָה. הַב אַחֲוָנָא לְתוֹרַיָּא יֵשׁ בּוֹ מִשּׁוּם הֶפְסֵק בְּרָכָה.

It has been stated: The one who recited the benediction takes first[64] but if he wants to honor his teacher or someone who is greater than himself in Torah, he has the right to do so. When Rav was breaking bread he was eating with his left hand and distributing with his right hand[65]. Rav Huna said: "Take and recite a benediction, take and recite a benediction" is not an interruption for the benediction[66]; "give hay to the oxen" is an interruption for the benediction[67].

64 From the food on his plate (Babli 47a).

65 To minimize the time between the benediction and the actual eating by the other participants in the meal.

66 Since it is needed for the other person's benediction, it will not cause the person who made the original benediction to forget that he made the benediction in order to eat.

67 In the Babli (40a) this is the opinion of R. Yoḥanan (i. e., the Yerushalmi), but there practice follows R. Sheshet who quotes Rav to the effect that nobody may eat as long as his animals are hungry; hence, the order to feed the oxen is a necessary step in preparing to eat.

רַב חוּנָא אֲמַר הָדָא שְׁתִיתָא וַהֲדָא מוֹרֶתָּא שְׁחִיקְתָּא (fol. 10b) אוֹמֵר עָלָיו שֶׁהַכֹּל נִהְיֶה בִּדְבָרוֹ.

Rab Ḥuna said: On *shatita*[68], which is ground *moretum*, one recites "that everything was created by His word".

68 The Aramaic *shatita* is the same as Latin *moretum*, a dish made by mixing pounded roasted flour or pounded roasted pea meal with water or vinegar (and other ingredients.) Its preparation is described in the Babli *Avodah zarah* 36b and in great detail in the poem *Moretum* in *Appendix Vergiliana* [cf. E. and H. Guggenheimer, לשוננו vol. 36 (5733) pp. 105-112]. In the Babli (*Berakhot* 31a), the rule of R. Huna applies only to watery *moretum.* This and the following rule are placed here to collect all formal statements of Rav Huna on benedictions for food. [An intermediate between *šĕtîtā* and *moretum* may be Greek μυττωτός "dish composed of pounded ingredients", title of a poem by Virgil's teacher Parthenios and model of Virgil's *moretum* (E. G.).]

רַב הוּנָא אָמַר הֲרֵי שֶׁנָּתַן לְתוֹךְ פִּיו וְשָׁכַח וְלֹא בֵּירַךְ אִם הָיוּ מַשְׁקִין פּוֹלְטָן. אִם הָיוּ אוֹכְלִין מְסַלְּקָן לִצְדָדִין. רִבִּי יִצְחָק בַּר מָרִי קוֹמוֹי רִבִּי יוֹסֵי בֵּי רִבִּי אָבוּן בְּשֵׁם רִבִּי יוֹחָנָן אֲפִילוּ אוֹכְלִין פּוֹלְטָן דִּכְתִיב יִמָּלֵא פִי תְּהִילָּתֶךָ כָּל־הַיּוֹם תִּפְאַרְתֶּךָ.

Rav Huna said: If one put something into his mouth and forgot to recite the benediction, if it is fluid he spits it out, if it is food he puts it to one side[69]. Rebbi Isaac bar Mari[70] before Rebbi Yose ben Rebbi Abun in the name of Rebbi Yoḥanan even if it is food he takes it out since it is written (*Ps.* 71:8) "May my mouth be full of Your praise[72], all day long of Your glory."

69 In the Babli (50b-51a), Rav Yehudah, a student of Rav but mainly of Samuel, has three categories: Fluids he swallows, food that can be taken out he takes out, food that one cannot touch once it is in the mouth he puts into one cheek. In the Babli, the verse of R. Yoḥanan is quoted to prove that food which can be taken out without problems must be taken out. While the Yerushalmi states a clear difference between Babylonian and Israeli practice, the Babli harmonizes both practices.

70 His name appears only here. In the Babli (*loc. cit.*) he is called רִבִּי יִצְחָק קַסְקְסָאָה , cf. Latin *cascus* "old, old-fashioned" (E. G.). [The word קסקסים

that appears in Tosephta and Babli is explained by Rashi as weeds, by S. Lieberman as rock outcrops in a field, from קשקשים "fins", by J. Levy as clumps of earth or stones hewn from a rock.]

71 It should not be half full of food and half of praise.

הַכּוֹסֵס אֶת הַחִיטִּים אוֹמֵר עֲלֵיהֶן בּוֹרֵא מִינֵי זְרָעוֹנִים. אֲפִייָן וּבִשְּׁלָן בִּזְמַן שֶׁהַפְּרוּסוֹת קַיָּימוֹת אוֹמֵר עֲלֵיהֶן הַמּוֹצִיא לֶחֶם מִן הָאָרֶץ וּמְבָרֵךְ לְאַחֲרָיו שָׁלֹשׁ בְּרָכוֹת. אִם אֵין הַפְּרוּסוֹת קַיָּימוֹת אוֹמֵר עֲלֵיהֶן בּוֹרֵא מִינֵי מְזוֹנוֹת וּמְבָרֵךְ אַחֲרָיו בְּרָכָה אַחַת מֵעֵין שָׁלֹשׁ. עַד כַּמָּה יְהוּא פְרוּסוֹת. רִבִּי יוֹסֵי בֵּי רִבִּי אָבוּן כַּהֲנָא בַּר מַלְכִּיָּה בְּשֵׁם רַב עַד כְּזֵיתִים.

He who chews wheat kernels says on them "Creator of kinds of seeds." If he baked or cooked them, as long as pieces are recognizable he recites on them "He Who produces bread from the earth" and afterwards three benedictions. If the pieces are not recognizable, he recites "Creator of kinds of food" and afterwards one benediction in the kind of three[72]. Down to which size are there pieces? Rebbi Yose bar Rebbi Abun, Cahana bar Malkiah[73] in the name of Rav: down to olive-sized bits.

72 This text is also in Tosephta *Berakhot* 4:6. It is quoted in Babli 37a where, however, the formula "Creator of kinds of seeds" is replaced by "Creator of the fruit of the earth" since the Babli does not recognize any benediction for produce not mentioned by the majority opinion in the Mishnah.

73 Rav Cahana bar Malkio in the Babli, whose quote of a statement of Rav is quoted by Rebbi Jeremiah. Hence, his time has to be fixed between Rav and the emigration of Rebbi Jeremiah from Babylonia. The statement here is not identical with the earlier one that dealt with pieces of bread eaten by themselves. In the interpretation of Tosaphot (37b), his statement is rejected by the Babli.

הַכּוֹסֵס אֶת הָאוֹרֶז אוֹמֵר עָלָיו בּוֹרֵא מִינֵי זְרָעוֹנִים. אֲפִייָן וּבִשְּׁלָן אַף עַל פִּי שֶׁהַפְּרוּסוֹת קַיָּימוֹת אוֹמֵר עָלָיו בּוֹרֵא מִינֵי מְזוֹנוֹת וְאֵינוֹ צָרִיךְ אַחֲרָיו לְבָרֵךְ.

רִבִּי יִרְמְיָה אָמַר בּוֹרֵא פְּרִי הָאֲדָמָה. בַּר מְרִינָה בְּרִיךְ קוֹמֵי רִבִּי זְעוּרָא וְקוֹמֵי רִבִּי חִיָּיא בַּר אַבָּא שֶׁהַכֹּל נִהְיֶה בִּדְבָרוֹ. רִבִּי שִׁמְעוֹן חֲסִידָה אוֹמֵר בּוֹרֵא מִינֵי מַעֲדָנִים. אָמַר רִבִּי יוֹסֵי בֵּי רִבִּי אָבוּן וְלָא פְלִיגוֹן מַאן דָּמַר בּוֹרֵא מִינֵי מְזוֹנוֹת בְּהַהוּא דַּעֲבִיד בּוּל. מַאן דָּמַר בּוֹרֵא פְּרִי הָאֲדָמָה בְּהַהוּא דִּבְרִיר. מַאן דָּמַר שֶׁהַכֹּל נִהְיֶה בִּדְבָרוֹ בְּהַהוּא דִּשְׁלִיק. מַאן דָּמַר בּוֹרֵא מִינֵי מַעֲדָנִים בְּהַהוּא דִּטְרִיף.

He who chews rice[74] says for it: "Creator of kinds of seeds." If he baked or cooked it, even if there are recognizable pieces he says for it: "Creator of kinds of food" and he does not have to recite a benediction afterwards[75]. Rebbi Jeremiah said, "Creator of the fruit of the earth." Bar Marina recited before Rebbi Zeïra and Rebbi Ḥiyya bar Abba "By Whose word everything was created.[76]" Rebbi Simeon the pious said "Creator of all sorts of delicacies." Rebbi Yose bar Rebbi Abun said: They do not disagree. He who says "Creator of kinds of food", if he made it into a ball. He who said "Creator of the fruit of the earth", if it is separated[77]. He who said "By Whose word everything was created", if it is cooked in water a long time[78]. He who said "Creator of all sorts of delicacies", if it is torn[79].

74 Greek ὄρυζα.

75 Tosephta *Berakhot* 4:7. Rebbi Jeremiah quotes the Tosephta in the Babli (37a) which also disagrees about the concluding benediction. The next paragraph will show that "no benediction afterwards" really means "no lengthy benediction afterwards", only the short form.

76 From their silence one may infer that they agreed.

77 If the individual kernels are still recognizable, in contrast to the ball (Latin *bulla*) in which no individual kernels are visible.

78 If it is a mash.

79 If one bakes any kind of rice product with spices, except whole grains. [The Babli does not admit different benedictions for different cases.]

עַד כְּדוֹן בַּתְּחִילָּה. בְּסוֹף רִבִּי יוֹנָה בְּשֵׁם רִבִּי שִׁמְעוֹן חֲסִידָא אֲשֶׁר בָּרָא מִינֵי מַעֲדָנִים לְעַדֵּן בָּהֶן נֶפֶשׁ כָּל חַי בָּרוּךְ אַתָּה יי עַל הָאָרֶץ וְעַל מַעֲדָנֶיהָ.

That is beforehand. Afterwards, Rebbi Jonah in the name of Rebbi Simeon the pious: "He Who created all sorts of delicacies to delight with them the souls of all living. Praise to You, Eternal, for the Land and its delicacies."[80]

80 It is implied that the four admissible benedictions for baked or cooked rice (and all other food not covered otherwise) requires a final benediction adapted to the corresponding intial benediction. [Again, the Babli has only one form of the short final benediction, the one given in the Yerushalmi for meat.]

רִבִּי אַבָּא בַּר יַעֲקֹב בְּשֵׁם רִבִּי יִצְחָק רוּבָּא רִבִּי כְּשֶׁהָיָה אוֹכֵל בָּשָׂר אוֹ בֵיצָה הָיָה אוֹמֵר בּוֹרֵא נְפָשׁוֹת רַבּוֹת לְהַחֲיוֹת בָּהֶן נֶפֶשׁ כָּל חַי. בָּרוּךְ אַתָּה יי חַי הָעוֹלָמִים.

Rebbi Abba bar Jacob in the name of the great Rebbi Isaac[81]: When Rebbi was eating meat or an egg he used to say: "Creator of many living things to sustain with them all living souls. Praise to You, Eternal, Life of the worlds.[82]

81 He is Rebbi Isaac (Nappaḥa), Amora of the second generation. His formula is quoted in the Babli (37a) for cooked cereal but without the final doxology. [Current practice is to include the doxology without invoking the Name, cf. Tosaphot 37a, s. v. בורא.]

82 If the vocalization is חֵי הָעוֹלָמִים (rejected by Maimonides), the translation would be: "Eternally living."

עַד כְּדוֹן בְּסוֹף. בִּתְחִילָּה אָמַר רִבִּי חַגַּיי בּוֹרֵא מִינֵי נְפָשׁוֹת. הָתִיב רִבִּי יוֹסֵי מַתְנִיתָא פְלִיגָא. עַל הַחוֹמֶץ וְעַל הַגּוֹבַיי וְעַל הַנּוֹבְלוֹת הוּא אוֹמֵר שֶׁהַכֹּל נִהְיֶה בִּדְבָרוֹ. וְהָדֵין גּוֹבַיי לֹא מִין נֶפֶשׁ הוּא.

That is at the end. At the start? Rebbi Ḥaggai said: "Creator of kinds of living things." Rebbi Yose objected, does not the Mishnah (6:4) disagree? "On vinegar, on locusts, and on fallen fruits he says: "By Whose word everything was created." And is a locust not a living thing[83]?

83 The Mishnah states explicitly that "on everything that is not growing from the earth one says 'By Whose word everything was created.'" The mention of vinegar (soured wine) and fallen fruits is meant to show that even produce that has become almost worthless needs this benediction; (edible) locusts are a scourge and the emphasis is that nevertheless they need a benediction if roasted and eaten. Hence, the statement of Rebbi Ḥaggai has no justification. In Hebrew and Aramaic, "living" applies only to animals but not to plants.

אַתְיָא דְרִבִּי שִׁמְעוֹן חֲסִידָא כְּרִבִּי וְדִבְרֵי שְׁנֵיהֶן כְּרַבָּן גַּמְלִיאֵל. דְּתַנֵּי זֶה הַכְּלָל שֶׁהָיָה רִבִּי יְהוּדָה אוֹמֵר מִשּׁוּם רַבָּן גַּמְלִיאֵל כָּל־שֶׁהוּא מִמִּין שֶׁבַע וְאֵינוֹ מִמִּין דָּגָן מִין דָּגָן וְלֹא אָפָאוֹ פַּת רַבָּן גַּמְלִיאֵל אוֹמֵר מְבָרֵךְ לְאַחֲרָיו שָׁלֹשׁ בְּרָכוֹת. וַחֲכָמִים אוֹמְרִים בְּרָכָה אַחַת. וְכָל־שֶׁאֵינוֹ מִמִּין שִׁבְעָה וְלֹא מִמִּין דָּגָן רַבָּן גַּמְלִיאֵל אוֹמֵר מְבָרֵךְ לְפָנָיו וּלְאַחֲרָיו. וַחֲכָמִים אוֹמְרִים לְפָנֶיהָ וְלֹא לְאַחֲרֶיהָ.

The statement of Rebbi Simeon the pious[84] turns out like that of Rebbi[85] and both of them like Rabban Gamliel[86], as it was stated: "The following is the principle: Rebbi Yehudah said in the name of Rabban Gamliel that on everything that is of the Seven Kinds but is not flour, or flour[87] but not baked as bread, Rabban Gamliel says that he recites afterwards three benedictions; but the Sages say, one benediction. On everything that is neither from the Seven Kinds nor a kind of flour, Rabban Gamliel says he recites benedictions before and after, but the sages say before, but not after[88]."

84 He requires a formal "benediction in the kind of three" for delicacies made from any kind of flour. We now return to the main topic after the digression about non-vegetable food.

85 He requires a final doxology from "Creator of many living things."

86 The second statement of his is in Tosephta *Berakhot* 4:7. The first part of this Tosephta is quoted in Babli 37a.

87 Including grain flour that is not enumerated in the verse, e. g., rye and spelt.

88 Meaning "Creator of all kinds of living things" without the final doxology; it is not considered a formal benediction. Rebbi Simeon the Pious and Rebbi follow Rabban Gamliel who in this case does not spell out which benediction he requires at the end.

רִבִּי יַעֲקֹב בַּר אִידִי בְּשֵׁם רִבִּי חֲנִינָא כָּל־שֶׁהוּא כְּעֵין סוֹלֶת וּכְעֵין חֲלִיטָה וּמֵחֲמֵשֶׁת הַמִּינִין אוֹמֵר עָלָיו בּוֹרֵא מִינֵי מְזוֹנוֹת וּמְבָרֵךְ לְאַחֲרֶיהָ בְּרָכָה אַחַת מֵעֵין שָׁלֹשׁ. וְכָל־שֶׁהוּא כְּעֵין סוֹלֶת וּכְעֵין חֲלִיטָה וְאֵינוֹ מֵחֲמֵשֶׁת הַמִּינִין. אָמַר רִבִּי יוֹנָה שָׁלַח רִבִּי זְעִירָא גַּב אִילֵין דְּבֵית רִבִּי יַנַּאי וְאָמְרוּן לֵיהּ לֵית אֲנָא יְדַע מַה אָמְרוּן לֵיהּ. מִי כְדוֹן. אָמַר רִבִּי יוֹסֵי מִסְתַּבְּרָא שֶׁהַכֹּל נִהְיֶה בִּדְבָרוֹ. רִבִּי יִרְמְיָה בָּעֵי הָדֵין דְּאָכַל סוֹלֶת מַהוּ לְמִיבְרְכָה בְּסוֹפָהּ. אָמַר רִבִּי יוֹסֵי וְהָכֵן לָא אֲכַל רִבִּי יִרְמְיָה סוֹלֶת מִן יוֹמוֹי. לֵית צוֹרְכָה דְּאִי לֹא.

Rebbi Jacob bar Idi in the name of Rebbi Ḥanina: Everything that is cereal and like dough put in boiling water and is of the Five Kinds[89], over it one says "Creator of kinds of foods", and one recites after it one benediction imitating three. And everything that is cereal and like dough put in boiling water, but is not of the Five Kinds, Rebbi Jonah said that Rebbi Zeïra sent to those of the Yeshivah of Rebbi Yannai[90] and they told him, but I do not know what they told him. What is it? Rebbi Yose said, it is reasonable to assume "That everything was created by His word.[91]" Rebbi Jeremiah inquired: He who ate cereal, what does he recite at the end[93]? Rebbi Yose said, and therefore Rebbi Jeremiah never ate any cereal[94]. That is the only one thing about which he was in doubt[95].

89 The five kinds of flour that are admissible for *matzot* on Passover because they can become sour: Wheat, barley, oats, rye, and spelt. Only these produce bread that needs full Grace and pastries that need "one benediction imitating three (or, in our text today, four) benedictions," i. e., its text contains one sentence each for each benediction of full Grace.

90 Still existing two generations after the death of Rebbi Yannai.

91 The catch-all for all food not covered by anything else and that will allow one to eat all foods.

93 "One benediction imitating three" or "Creator of many living things."

94 Except in a meal that was covered by the benediction over bread at the start and Grace afterwards.

95 צורכא, a technical expression, frequent in the Yerushalmi in this sense, and difficult to translate verbally.

לָמָּה הוּא חוֹתֵם בָּהּ בָּאָרֶץ. נַעֲשִׂית כְּבִרְכַּת פּוֹעֲלִים. דְּתַנֵּי הַפּוֹעֲלִים שֶׁהָיוּ עוֹשִׂין מְלָאכָה עִם בַּעַל הַבַּיִת הֲרֵי אֵלּוּ מְבָרְכִין בְּרָכָה רִאשׁוֹנָה וְכוֹלְלִין שֶׁל יְרוּשָׁלַיִם בְּשֶׁל הָאָרֶץ וְחוֹתְמִין בְּשֶׁל הָאָרֶץ. אֲבָל אִם הָיוּ עוֹשִׂין עִמּוֹ בִּסְעוּדָן אוֹ שֶׁהָיָה בַּעַל הַבַּיִת אוֹכֵל עִמָּהֶן הֲרֵי אֵלּוּ מְבָרְכִין אַרְבַּע. דְּבֵית רִבִּי יַנַּאי עָבְדִין לָהּ כְּמַטְבֵּעַ בְּרָכָה.

Why does one finish[96] with "the Land"? It is similar to Grace for day laborers. As has been stated[97]: "Workers who were doing work with the owner shall recite the first benediction, include Jerusalem in the benediction for the Land and finish with 'the Land.' But if they were working for their food[98] or if the employer was eating with them, then they recite four benedictions." In the school of Rebbi Yannai they treated it as a formula of benediction[99].

96 The "benediction imitating three" is recited for wine, the Seven Fruits, and baked goods other than bread. That benediction first gives praise for the food, then for the Land of Israel, then prays for the rebuilding of Jerusalem (and adds a sentence for the Rabbinic fourth benediction of Grace, praising God as source of all good.) The question is why only the first two themes are repeated at the end since the final doxology reads in all cases:

"Praise to You, Eternal, for the Land and . . . (here the specific food is named)."

97 Tosephta *Berakhot* 5:24, Babli 16a. Day laborers who are paid by the hour and whose lunch break counts as worked time have the obligation to spend as little time as possible on their lunch and, in any case, their worship of God should not be paid by the employer except for the legal minimum.

98 Without any cash payments the employer is legally required to give them time for full standard Grace.

99 They formulated the fixed "benediction imitating three" and did not tolerate any deviation.

מַהוּ לְהַזְכִּיר בָּהּ מֵעֵין הַמְּאוֹרָע. אָמַר רִבִּי אַבָּא בַּר זְמִינָא רִבִּי זְעִירָא הָיָה מַזְכִּיר בָּהּ מֵעֵין הַמְּאוֹרָע. אָמַר רִבִּי יִרְמְיָה הוֹאִיל וְחָשׁ לָהּ רִבִּי זְעִירָא צְרִיכִין אָנוּ מֵיחוּשׁ.

Does one have to mention in it the occasion[100]? Rebbi Abba bar Zamina said that Rebbi Zeïra used to mention the occasion in it. Rebbi Jeremiah said: Since Rebbi Zeïra took notice of it, so we have to take notice[101].

100 Does one have to mention the Sabbath, holidays, and the days of the New Moon in the "benediction imitating three"?

101 Hence, one has to mention Sabbath and holidays. (This was adopted as formal practice by Maimonides from the Yerushalmi, cf. Babli 39a, Tosaphot s. v. על העץ).

תַּנֵּי מְבָרְכִין עַל הַדָּגָן כְּשֶׁהוּא מִן הַמּוּבְחָר. קָלוּסְקִין וּשְׁלֵמָה שֶׁל בַּעַל הַבַּיִת אוֹמֵר עַל הַקָּלוּסְקִין. פְּרוּסָה שֶׁל קָלוּסְקִין וּשְׁלֵמָה שֶׁל בַּעַל הַבַּיִת אוֹמֵר הַשְּׁלֵמָה שֶׁל בַּעַל הַבַּיִת. פַּת חִיטִּין וּפַת שְׂעוֹרִין אוֹמֵר עַל שֶׁל חִטִּין. פְּרוּסָה שֶׁל חִטִּים וּשְׁלֵמָה שֶׁל שְׂעוֹרִים אוֹמֵר עַל הַפְּרוּסָה שֶׁל חִטִּין. פַּת שְׂעוֹרִין וּפַת כּוּסְמִין אוֹמֵר עַל שֶׁל שְׂעוֹרִין. וַהֲלֹא שֶׁל כּוּסְמִין יָפָה מִמֶּנּוּ. אֶלָּא שֶׁזּוּ מִמִּין שִׁבְעָה וְזוּ אֵין מִמִּין שִׁבְעָה. רִבִּי יַעֲקֹב בַּר אָחָא בְּשֵׁם רִבִּי זְעִירָא דְּרִבִּי יוּדָה הִיא דְּרִבִּי יוּדָה אָמַר אִם יֵשׁ בֵּינֵיהֶן מִמִּין שִׁבְעָה עָלָיו הוּא מְבָרֵךְ. פַּת טְמֵאָה

וּפַת טְהוֹרָה רִבִּי חִייָא בַּר וָוא אָמַר אוֹמֵר עַל הַטְּהוֹרָה. פַּת נְקִייָה טְמֵאָה וּפַת קִיבָר טְהוֹרָה. רִבִּי חִייָא בַּר אָדָא בְּשֵׁם רִבִּי אָחָא עַל אֵיזֶה מֵהֶן שֶׁיִּרְצֶה מְבָרֵךְ.

It has been stated[102]: "One recites the benediction on the better kind of flour. Rolls[103] and a full home baked loaf, one recites over a roll. A broken roll and a full home baked loaf, one recites on the full home baked loaf. Wheat bread and barley bread, one recites on wheat bread. A broken loaf of wheat bread and a full loaf of barley bread, one recites on the broken wheat bread. Barley bread and spelt bread, one recites on barley bread. But is not spelt bread better? But this is from one of the Seven Kinds, that one is not of the Seven Kinds." Rebbi Jacob bar Aḥa in the name of Rebbi Zeïra: This is from Rebbi Yehudah, since Rebbi Yehudah said (Mishnah 4), "if there is[104] among them a fruit of the Seven Kinds, on it he recites the benediction." Impure bread and pure bread, Rebbi Ḥiyya bar Abba said, he recites on the pure one[105]. Impure white bread and pure coarse[106] bread, Rebbi Ḥiyya bar Ada in the name of Rebbi Aḥa: He may recite on the one that he prefers[107].

102 Tosephta *Berakhot* 4:15; a small part of it is quoted in Babli 39b as statement of Amoraïm. The problem is that only the first bread of a meal needs a benediction; all other foods of that meal can then be eaten without additional benedictions. The food that is chosen for benediction should be distinguished.

103 Greek, singular κόλλιξ, "roll".

104 On a fruit plate; one has to choose one fruit to eat first for a benediction, on the strength of which one may then eat all other fruits without additional benediction. The sages opposing Rebbi Yehudah assert that one makes the benediction over the fruit (or here, bread) one prefers, to let God's praise come from a full heart. The Babli in practice follows the Sages but the Yerushalmi follows Rebbi Yehudah.

105 In the time of Rebbi Ḥiyya bar Abba, this was a theoretical question only, since at that time nobody was free from the impurity associated with the dead. It must be assumed that the food in question is secular and impure

by transfer from something that is the source of impurity; in that case, it cannot pollute the person who touches and eats it with due care.

106 Levy declares it to be from Greek κυρηβία, τά (plur.) "bran, shells of grain kernels," Krauss and Löw from *cibarius* (*panis*) "coarse bread."

107 Since each one has good and bad qualities.

קוֹרָא רִבִּי יַעֲקֹב בַּר אָחָא בְּשֵׁם שְׁמוּאֵל אוֹמֵר עָלָיו בּוֹרֵא פְּרִי הָעֵץ. תַּנָּא רִבִּי חֲלַפְתָּא בֶּן שָׁאוּל שֶׁהַכֹּל נִהְיֶה בִּדְבָרוֹ. תַּנֵּי רִבִּי יְהוֹשֻׁעַ בּוֹרֵא מִינֵי דְשָׁאִים. מַתְנִיתָא דְרִבִּי אוֹשַׁעְיָא פְלִיגָא עִילוֹי וְאֵלוּ הֵן מִינֵי דְשָׁאִים הַקִּינָרֵס וְהַחֲלִימָה וְהַדְּמוּעַ וְהָאָטָד.

Young palm shoots. Rebbi Jacob bar Aḥa in the name of Samuel: He recites on it "Creator of the fruit of the tree[108]." Rebbi Ḥalaphta ben Saul stated, "By Whose word everything was created[109]." Rebbi Joshua stated: "Creator of kinds of grasses.[110]" The *baraita* of Rebbi Oshaiah disagrees: "The following are the kinds of grasses: artichoke[111], *ḥalimah*[112], *demua*[113], and lycium[114].

108 In the Babli (36a), the opinion of Rav Yehudah, accepted by his teacher Samuel, is to say "Creator of the fruit of the earth" since it is a vegetable growth but cannot qualify as "fruit" of the tree, since it will turn into inedible wood.

109 This is the original opinion of Samuel in the Babli, since nobody grows date palms for the few shoots one can eat each spring. Hence, it does not qualify as "fruit" of anything.

110 This is the only genuinly old tradition quoted, but it is rejected even by the Yerushalmi which admits a variety of formulas of benedictions, since young palm shoots cannot qualify as grasses. As the following list shows, thistles and thorny plants may qualify as grasses.

While it is clear that in the Babli קורא means "heart of the palm", in the statement of R. Joshua the word might refer to Arabic קֻרַּה "cardamine, meadow cress"

111 Greek κυνάρα, κινάρα.

112 This plant is defined by *Arukh*, the talmudic dictionary of 11th cent. R. Nathan of Rome, as mallow or okra. However, the Syriac dictionaries define

the word as equivalent of Latin *anchusa*, "ox tongue".

113 An otherwise unknown grassy plant; the corresponding Arabic word دناع is explained in classical Arabic dictionaries as "seemingly the name of a plant."

115 A spiny plant frequent in the Jordan valley.

משנה ב: בֵּירַךְ עַל פֵּירוֹת הָאִילָן בּוֹרֵא פְּרִי הָאֲדָמָה יָצָא. עַל פֵּירוֹת הָאֲדָמָה בּוֹרֵא פְּרִי הָעֵץ לֹא יָצָא. וְעַל כּוּלָּם אִם אָמַר שֶׁהַכֹּל יָצָא.

Mishnah 2: If he pronounced the benediction "Creator of the fruit of the soil" on fruits of the tree, he has fulfilled his obligation, on fruits of the soil "Creator of the fruit of the tree", he has not fulfilled his obligation. On all of them if he pronounced "everything was created[116]", he has fulfilled his obligation.

116 "By Whose word everything was created." While this is not the preferred benediction, the statement is true and therefore admissible.

הלכה ב: רִבִּי חִזְקִיָּה בְּשֵׁם רִבִּי יַעֲקֹב בַּר אָחָא דְּרִבִּי יוּדָה הִיא דְּרִבִּי יוּדָה עֲבִיד אֶת הָאִילָנוֹת כְּקַשִּׁים. אָמַר רִבִּי יוֹסֵי דִּבְרֵי הַכֹּל הִיא פֵּירוֹת הָאִילָן בִּכְלַל פֵּירוֹת הָאֲדָמָה. וְאֵין פֵּירוֹת הָאֲדָמָה בִּכְלַל פֵּירוֹת הָעֵץ. רַב הוּנָא אָמַר חוּץ מִן הַיַּיִן וּמִן הַפַּת. מַתְנִיתָא אָמְרָה כֵן חוּץ מִן הַיַּיִן שֶׁעַל הַיַּיִן הוּא אוֹמֵר בּוֹרֵא פְּרִי הַגֶּפֶן. חוּץ מִן הַפַּת שֶׁעַל הַפַּת הוּא אוֹמֵר הַמּוֹצִיא לֶחֶם מִן הָאָרֶץ.

Halakhah 2: Rebbi Ḥizqiah in the name of Rebbi Jacob bar Aḥa: This is Rebbi Yehuda's since Rebbi Yehudah makes trees like straws[117]. Rebbi Yose said, it is everybody's opinion since fruits of a tree are also fruits of the soil but fruits of the soil are not fruits of the tree[118]. Rav Huna said[119], except for bread and wine. The Mishnah (6:1) says so: Except for wine because on wine one says "Creator of the fruit of the vine;" except for bread because on bread one says "He Who produces bread from the earth."

117 In the Babli (40a) this is the accepted opinion, in the name of Rav Naḥman. The proof is from Mishnah *Bikkurim* 1:8 which states that if a tree was felled, its owner may not bring the first fruits of that tree to the Temple, but Rebbi Yehudah insists that he may. Since everybody agrees that grain may be offered as first-fruits, and grain can be brought only after it was cut and separated from the straw, it follows that Rebbi Yehudah treats trees simply as stalks for their fruits.

118 In contrast to the opinion of the Tanna R. Yose quoted in the next paragraph, every true statement about food is acceptable.

119 Babli 40b. His opinion is rejected in the Babli in favor of a dissenting one of Rebbi Yoḥanan not mentioned in the Yerushalmi. The next paragraph, which relativizes the statement of Rav Huna, requires a separate benediction for bread even if it is not the one formulated by the Men of the Great Assembly.

תַּנֵּי רִבִּי יוֹסֵי אוֹמֵר כָּל־הַמְּשַׁנֶּה עַל הַמַּטְבֵּעַ שֶׁטָּבְעוּ חֲכָמִים לֹא יָצָא יְדֵי חוֹבָתוֹ. רִבִּי יוּדָה אוֹמֵר כָּל־שֶׁנִּשְׁתַּנֶּה מִבְּרִייָתוֹ וְלֹא שִׁינָּה בִּרְכָתוֹ לֹא יָצָא. רִבִּי מֵאִיר אוֹמֵר אֲפִילוּ אָמַר בָּרוּךְ שֶׁבָּרָא הַחֵפֶץ הַזֶּה. מַה נָּאֶה הוּא זֶה יָצָא. רִבִּי יַעֲקֹב בַּר אָחָא בְּשֵׁם שְׁמוּאֵל הֲלָכָה כְּרִבִּי מֵאִיר. מִילְּתֵיהּ דְּרַב אָמְרָה כֵן. חַד פָּרְסוֹי אָתָא לְגַבֵּי רַב בְּגִין דַּאֲנָא אֲכַל פִּיסָּתִי וְלָא אֲנָא חֲכִים מְבָרְכָה עָלֵיהּ וַאֲנָא אֲמַר בָּרוּךְ דְּבָרָא הָדֵין פִּיסָּא נְפִיק אֲנָא יְדֵי חוֹבָתִי. אֲמַר לֵיהּ אִין.

It has been stated[120]: Rebbi Yose says, anyone who changes the formula established by the Sages did not fulfill his duty. Rebbi Yehudah says, everything that has been changed from the way it was created but one did not change its benediction, he did not fulfill his duty[121]. Rebbi Meïr says, even if he says: "Praised be He Who created this property, how beautiful it is," he has fulfilled his duty. Rebbi Jacob bar Aḥa in the name of Samuel: practice follows Rebbi Meïr. The words of Rav also say so. A Persian[122] came before Rav: "Since I am eating my piece of bread, but I do not know how to recite the benediction over it, I use to say: 'Praise to Him Who created this piece of bread,' did I fulfill my duty?" He said to him: yes.

120 Tosephta *Berakhot* 4:5.

121 Rebbi Yose accepts only the formulas established by the Men of the Great Assembly. Rebbi Yehudah accepts these formulas as guidelines which have to be adapted to varying circumstances and this adaptation is more important than using the approved formulas. The great number of different formulas of benediction in the Yerushalmi and fragments of Yerushalmi rite prayer books show that the opinion of Rebbi Yehudah was the dominant one in the Land of Israel. In staying with this attitude, it was even discussed at the start of this *halakhah* that the anonymous Mishnah should present the opinion of Rebbi Yehudah. In the parallel in the Babli (40b), Rebbi Yehudah's opinion is not even quoted; in Babylonia only the opinions of Rebbi Yose (for those who know Hebrew) and of Rebbi Meïr (for the illiterate) are accepted.

122 A Persian Jew. In the Babli (40b), he is called Benjamin the shepherd.

רַב יְהוּדָה בְשֵׁם אַבָּא בַּר בַּר חָנָה בַּר קַפָּרָא וּתְרֵין תַּלְמִידוֹי נִתְאָֽרְחוּ אֵצֶל בַּעַל הַבַּיִת בְּהָדֵין פּוּנְדָּקָא דְּבִרְכָתָא אַפִּיק קוֹמֵיהוֹן פְּרָגִין וְאַחְוָנִייָא (fol. 10c) וְקֵפַּלוֹטִין. אָֽמְרֵי נְבָרֵךְ עַל קֵפַּלוֹטָה דּוּ פָּטַר אַחְוָנִיתָא וְלֹא פָּטַר פְּרָגִיתָא. נְבָרֵךְ עַל אַחְוָנִייָתָא לָא פָּטַר לָא דֵין וְלָא דֵין. קָפַץ חַד וּבֵירַךְ עַל פְּרָגִיתָא שֶׁהַכֹּל נִהְיֶה בִּדְבָרוֹ. גִּחִיךְ לֵיהּ חֲבֵרִים. אָמַר לֵיהּ בַּר קַפָּרָא לֹא לְזֶה גוֹרְגְּרָן אֶלָּא לָךְ לוֹגְלָן. זֶה עָשָׂה בְּגַרְגְּרָנוּתוֹ אַתָּה לָמָּה לִגְלַגְתָּ. וְלָזֶה אָמַר חָכָם אֵין כַּאן זָקֵן אֵין כַּאן. אָֽמְרוּ לֹא יָֽצְאָה שְׁנָתָן עַד שֶׁמֵּתוּ. אָמַר רִבִּי יוֹסֵי הָא אָֽזְלִינָן תְּרֵין וְלֹא שְׁמָעִינָן מִינָּהּ כְּלוּם. מַיי כְדוֹן מִסְתַּבְּרָא מְבָרֵךְ עַל הַקֵּפַּלוֹט שֶׁהַכֹּל נִהְיֶה בִּדְבָרוֹ טְפֵילָה לְיֶרֶק[123].

Rav Yehudah in the name of Abba bar bar Ḥana[124]: Bar Qappara and two of his students were with the innkeeper at the "inn of blessings". He brought before them partridge, orach[125], and leeks[126]. They said, if we recite the benediction on leeks[127], it will serve also for orach but not for the partridge[128]. If we recite on orach, it will not serve for anything else. One of them jumped the gun and recited "by Whose word everything was created" on the partridge. His colleague[129] laughed at him. Bar Qappara said to that one, not about that glutton but about you scoffer[130]. This one acted in his gluttony, why did you laugh? And to the other one he said, is there no rabbi here, is there no old man here? They said, within a year they both died. Rebbi Yose said, there two are gone and we did not learn anything from the incident. What is it? It is reasonable that one recites the benediction on leeks because "By Whose word everything was created" is secondary for vegetables[131].

123 Reading of the Rome manuscript. The Venice text has לו.

124 He is Rabba bar bar Ḥana. A slightly different version is in Babli 39a as a tannaïtic statement.

125 A salty plant, *Atriplex rosea*, growing mainly in salt marshes, that was used as (relatively cheap) vegetable. [The identification of the plant (and of the bird species) is Rashi's in the Babli, reported in the name of R. Isaac ben R. Yehudah of Worms.] The vegetable cannot be eaten raw, but must be cooked and, therefore, must have a changed benediction according to Rebbi Yehudah.

126 Greek κεφαλωτός, "having a head". The identification as leeks is from Rashi in Babli *Yom Ṭov* and the use of the word in Syriac.

127 It seems that these leeks were raw; hence, their benediction is "Creator of the fruit of the soil" and that will serve also for the cooked vegetable by the reasoning given in the Mishnah; however, a benediction over the cooked vegetable, which is a changed one following Rebbi Yehudah, cannot serve for raw leeks.

128 The benediction for patridge is "everything." The story makes two points. First, that in benedictions one did follow Rebbi Yehudah in frequently changing the wording of benedictions. [This principle, absent in the Babli, is the cause that the reports about and conclusions from this story in the two Talmudim are not comparable.] The second, more important one, is that the language of

the Mishnah, "On all of them if he pronounced 'everything', he has fulfilled his obligation" does *not* mean that one may recite that benediction on anything that specifically needs it and then extend it to fruits and vegetables, only that if one recited the benediction on agricultural produce it also is valid, but not preferred.

129 The Aramaic text seems to have a scribal error for חַבְרֵיה.

130 I am angry.

131 The meaning of the statement is that one should not start with the benediction over the quail because that benediction is also applicable to vegetables and, hence, cannot be recited a second time for the same meal without taking God's name in vain. But, as explained earlier, the benediction "everything" is not valid for vegetables if recited on meat and, in any case, is undesirable for plants that have their own more specific benediction. Hence, the person reciting the benediction first on partridge cannot eat of the vegetables. On the other hand, if he makes the first benediction "Creator of the fruit of the soil" for the vegetables, then he can make a second benediction "that all was by His word" for the bird and all is fine.

משנה ג: עַל דָּבָר שֶׁאֵין גִּידּוּלָיו מִן הָאָרֶץ אוֹמֵר שֶׁהַכֹּל נִהְיֶה בִּדְבָרוֹ. עַל הַחוֹמֶץ וְעַל הַגּוֹבָיי וְעַל הַנּוֹבְלוֹת הוּא אוֹמֵר שֶׁהַכֹּל נִהְיֶה בִּדְבָרוֹ. רִבִּי יְהוּדָה אוֹמֵר כָּל־שֶׁהוּא מִין קְלָלָה אֵין מְבָרְכִין עָלָיו.

Mishnah 3: On food that is not grown on the soil one recites "that all was by His word." On vinegar[132], on locusts, and on wind-fall fruit one recites "that all was by His word." Rebbi Yehudah says, one does not recite a benediction on a kind that comes from a curse.

132 Vinegar which came from wine turned sour, not vinegar that was produced as such from the start.

הלכה ג: הֶחְמִיץ יֵינוֹ אוֹמֵר בָּרוּךְ דַּייָן אֱמֶת. בָּא לְאֹכְלוֹ אוֹמֵר שֶׁהַכֹּל נִהְיֶה בִּדְבָרוֹ. רָאָה גוֹבַיי אוֹמֵר בָּרוּךְ דַּייָן אֱמֶת. בָּא לְאֹכְלָן אוֹמֵר שֶׁהַכֹּל נִהְיֶה בִּדְבָרוֹ. רָאָה נוֹבְלוֹת שֶׁנֶּשְׁרוּ אוֹמֵר בָּרוּךְ דַּייָן אֱמֶת. בָּא לְאֹכְלָן אוֹמֵר שֶׁהַכֹּל נִהְיֶה בִּדְבָרוֹ

Halakha 3: If his wine turned sour, he recites "praise to the True Judge"[133]. When he consumes it, he recites "that all was by His word." If he sees a locust[134], he recites "praise to the True Judge". When he consumes it, he recites "that all was by His word." If he sees fallen fruit, he recites "praise to the True Judge". When he consumes it, he recites "that all was by His word."

133 The standard benediction on bad news, cf. Mishnah 9:6.

134 The edible locusts come in swarms which destroy crops. Hence seeing one presages disaster.

משנה ד: הָיוּ לְפָנָיו מִינִין הַרְבֶּה רִבִּי יְהוּדָה אוֹמֵר אִם יֵשׁ בֵּינֵיהֶן מִמִּין שִׁבְעָה עָלָיו הוּא מְבָרֵךְ. וַחֲכָמִים אוֹמְרִים עַל אֵי זֶה מֵהֶן שֶׁיִּרְצֶה.

Mishnah 4: If there were many kinds before him[135], Rebbi Yehudah said, if among them is one of the Seven Kinds[15] that is the one over which he recites the benediction. But the Sages say, on any one that he wishes[136].

135 He wants to eat of all of them, they all require the same benediction, and he may recite one benediction only.

136 The Babli (41a) interprets the Sages to mean that the fruit to be chosen for benediction should be the one that he likes best personally. It seems that the Yerushalmi means quite literally "any one that he wants".

הלכה ד: רִבִּי יְהוֹשֻׁעַ בֶּן לֵוִי אָמַר מַה פְּלִיגִין רִבִּי יְהוּדָה וְרַבָּנָן. כְּשֶׁהָיָה בְדַעְתּוֹ לֶאֱכֹל פַּת. אֲבָל אֵין בְּדַעְתּוֹ לֶאֱכֹל פַּת כָּל־עַמָּא מוֹדוּיי שֶׁאִם יֵשׁ בֵּינֵיהֶן מִמִּין שִׁבְעָה עָלָיו הוּא מְבָרֵךְ. אָמַר רִבִּי אַבָּא צָרִיךְ לְבָרֵךְ בְּסוֹף. אָמַר רִבִּי יוֹסֵי הָדָא דְּרִבִּי בָּא פְּלִיגָא עַל דְּרִבִּי יְהוֹשֻׁעַ בֶּן לֵוִי דְּרִבִּי יְהוֹשֻׁעַ בֶּן לֵוִי אָמַר מַה פְּלִיגִין רִבִּי יוּדָה וְרַבָּנָן בְּשֶׁהָיָה בְדַעְתּוֹ לֶאֱכֹל פַּת אֲבָל אֵין בְּדַעְתּוֹ לֶאֱכֹל פַּת כָּל־עַמָּא מוֹדֵיי שֶׁאִם יֵשׁ בֵּינֵיהֶן מִמִּין שִׁבְעָה עָלָיו הוּא מְבָרֵךְ. וָמַר רִבִּי אַבָּא וְצָרִיךְ לְבָרֵךְ בְּסוֹף לֹא בֵּירַךְ נַעֲשָׂה טְפֵילָה. דְּתַנִּינָן תַּמָּן כָּל־שֶׁהוּא עִיקָר וְעִמּוֹ טְפֵילָה מְבָרֵךְ עַל הָעִיקָּר וּפוֹטֵר אֶת הַטְּפֵילָה.

Halakhah 4: Rebbi Joshua ben Levi said, Rebbi Yehudah and the rabbis disagree only when he intended afterwards to eat bread[137], but if he did not intend to eat bread afterwards, everybody agrees that if among them one is of the Seven Kinds, that is the one over which he recites the benediction. Rebbi Abba said, he has to recite a benediction at the end[138]. Rebbi Yose said, the statement of Rebbi Abba disagrees with Rebbi Joshua ben Levi since Rebbi Joshua ben Levi said, Rebbi Yehudah and the rabbis disagree only when he intended afterwards to eat bread, but if he did not intend to eat bread afterwards everybody agrees that if among them is one of the Seven Kinds, that is the one over which he recites the benediction; but Rebbi Abba said, he has to recite a benediction at the end. If he did not recite a benediction at the end it[139] became an accessory and we have stated there (Mishna 7): "In every situation where there is a main course and side dishes, one recites the benediction for the main course and thereby frees the side dishes.[140]"

137 If the fruits are eaten as appetizers to be followed by a meal, then the benediction over bread for the main meal is a benediction over one of the Seven Kinds, even over the most important of the Seven Kinds. Hence, a benediction on some other fruit is no slight for the Land of Israel. But if the snack of fruits is not followed by bread and Grace after the meal then the

fruits of the Land of Israel take precedence since they require at the end a "benediction imitating three benedictions" whereas other fruits only require the short benediction "Creator of living things" that earlier was considered to be "nothing".

138 Even if Grace is recited afterwards.

139 The fruit eaten as appetizer.

140 Hence, bread being the most important food and requiring recitation of full Grace, any fruit eaten beforehand becomes a side dish for the bread and should be covered by Grace. The Yerushalmi takes Mishnah 7 to apply also to benedictions after the meal, not only before the meal.

הֲדָא גְּרִיזְמָתָא רִבִּי יִרְמְיָה בְּשֵׁם רִבִּי אַמִּי מְבָרֵךְ עַל הַתּוּרְמוּסָא. אָמַר רִבִּי לֵוִי עַל שֵׁם אַל תִּגְזוֹל דָּל כִּי דַל הוּא.

Garizmata[141]. Rebbi Jeremiah in the name of Rebbi Ammi, he recites the benediction over the lupine[142]. Rebbi Levi said, because of (*Prov.* 22:22) "do not rob a poor one[143] because he is poor."

141 The exact meaning of the word, its vocalization and etymology are unknown. It is clear from Midrashim (*Lev. rabba* 9, *Thr. rabba* introduction) that it refers to a dessert. The *Arukh* translates the word by Italian קוציאי which Perles misread as *guscio* "trestle; shell, hull". Even *coccio* "potsherd" does not make much sense. The older commentaries to the Yerushalmi were misled by a scribal "correction" in the *Arukh* that identified *gryzmth* with lupines, which refers to the next word in the text. Levy's dictionary, following Perles, derives the word from a non-existing Greek word γαρίσμη [but compare γαρισκός, ὁ, "an unknown fish", γάρος, ὁ "paste of brine and small fish", γάρον, τό "fish sauce".] Jastrow considers the word as Par'el from (Hebrew and Arabic) גזם "to cut in pieces". From the usage in the next Halakhah it seems that one speaks of baked, in contrast to cooked, goods. It is possible to connect the word with Arabic جرذم, גרדם "to devour voraciously" (said of worms and other pests.)

The background of the remark is that this kind of dessert at a formal dinner, being extraordinary and not part of a regular meal, is not covered by the benediction over the bread at the start of the meal and, hence, needs its own benediction.

142 He may make the benediction even on lupines even though they probably are the cheapest dish on the plate.

143 Of its benediction.

עַד כְּדוֹן כְּשֶׁיֵּשׁ בְּדַעְתּוֹ לֶאֱכֹל פַּת. אֵין בְּדַעְתּוֹ לֶאֱכֹל פַּת לָא בְדָא. רַבָּן גַּמְלִיאֵל זוּגָא סְלַק גַּבֵּי אִילֵּין דְּבֵית רִבִּי יַנַּאי חַמְתּוּן נָסְבִין זֵיתָא וּמְבָרְכִין לְפָנָיו וּלְאַחֲרָיו. אֲמַר לוֹן וַעֲבְדִין כְּדוֹן. רִבִּי זְעִירָא שָׁלַח שָׁאַל לְרִבִּי שְׁמוּאֵל בַּר נַחְמָן רִבִּי כֲּהָנָא בְּשֵׁם רִבִּי אֲבִינָא כָּל־עַמָּא מוֹדֵיי שֶׁאִם יֵשׁ בֵּינֵיהֶן מִמִּין שִׁבְעָה עָלָיו הוּא מְבָרֵךְ. אָמַר רִבִּי זֵירָא וְיֵאוּת. מִן מַאן דַּאֲנָן חֲמִייָן רַבָּנָן סָלְקִין לְרֵישׁ יַרְחָא וְאָכְלִין עֲנָבִין וְלָא מְבָרְכִין בְּסוֹפָהּ. לֹא בְשֶׁיֵּשׁ בְּדַעְתּוֹ לֶאֱכֹל פַּת.

That is if it is his intention to eat bread[144]. But if it is not his intention to eat bread, that does not apply. (Rabban) Gamliel the twin[145] went to those of the house of Rebbi Yannai. He saw them eat an olive[146] and recite the benediction before and afterwards. He said to them: Does one do that? Rebbi Zeïra sent and asked Rebbi Samuel bar Nahman. Rebbi Cahana[147] in the name of Rebbi Avina[148]: Everybody agrees that if among them was one of the Seven Kinds, that is the one over which he recites the benediction. Rebbi Zeïra said, that must be correct, since we see the rabbis assembling for the proclamation of the New Moon and eat grapes but they do not recite a benediction afterwards. That is because it is his[149] intention to eat bread.

144 One returns to the opinion of the Sages in the Mishnah and the interpretation given by R. Joshua ben Levi.

145 The name of his twin brother was Hillel. He was an Amora of the third generation who usually appears asking questions from his contemporaries, not formulating his own rules. The title "Rabban" was given to him here by a thoughtless scribe; everywhere else his name appears without title.

146 As an appetizer before a meal with bread.

147 Rebbi Cohen at other places in

the Talmud.

148 A student of Ganiva, also of Rav Huna and Rav Yehudah, who immigrated into Israel and was ordained in the Yeshivah of Rebbi Ammi.

149 It is their intention to have a full meal after the formal proclamation of the New Moon.

הָיוּ לְפָנָיו מִינִין שִׁבְעָה עַל אֵי זֶה מֵהֶן הוּא מְבָרֵךְ. תַּמָּן אָמְרִין כָּל הַקּוֹדֵם לַמִּקְרָא קוֹדֵם לִבְרָכָה וְכָל הַסָּמוּךְ לָאָרֶץ קוֹדֵם לַכֹּל.

If there were before him of the Seven Kinds, on which one does he recite the benediction? There[150] they say: Everything that has precedence in the verse has precedence for benediction and everything that is close to "the Land" has precedence over everything else[151].

150 In Babylonia; Babli 41a.

151 Hence, the orders of preference are (*Deut*. 8:6): "A land of (1) wheat and (2) barley, (3) grapes, and (4) figs, and (5) pomegranates; a land of (1) oil olives and (2) date honey.

משנה ה: בֵּירַךְ עַל הַיַּיִן שֶׁלִּפְנֵי הַמָּזוֹן פָּטַר אֶת הַיַּיִן שֶׁלְּאַחַר הַמָּזוֹן. בֵּירַךְ עַל הַפַּרְפֶּרֶת שֶׁלִּפְנֵי הַמָּזוֹן פָּטַר אֶת הַפַּרְפֶּרֶת שֶׁלְּאַחַר הַמָּזוֹן. בֵּירַךְ עַל הַפַּת פָּטַר אֶת הַפַּרְפֶּרֶת. בֵּירַךְ עַל הַפַּרְפֶּרֶת לֹא פָּטַר אֶת הַפַּת. בֵּית שַׁמַּאי אוֹמְרִים אַף לֹא מַעֲשֶׂה קְדֵירָה.

Mishnah 5: If one recited the benediction on wine before the meal[152], he also covers wine after the meal. If one recited the benediction on little pieces[153] before the meal, he also covers little pieces after the meal. If one recited the benediction on bread, he also covers little pieces; if one recited the benediction on little pieces, he did not cover bread; the House of Shammai say, neither did he cover cooked food.

152 Given as an appetizer. They drank wine after the main meal but before Grace was recited. Since Grace covers all food, it is obvious that anything consumed after Grace needs a new benediction. Both wine and cookies were served before and after the meal only on festive dinners as explained in Chapter 8; they do not belong to everyday meals. Their rules need to be spelled out.

153 The verb פרר means "to break into little pieces, crumble". It is possible that פרפר is a *pilpel* form of פרר. This is the opinion of the dictionaries. It is more likely that פרפרת is derived from παραφέρω "to serve, bring to one's side" (food), or the passive "set on table, served" (definitions of Liddell & Scott). The correct translation then is "side dish before or after meal; appetizer or dessert, snacks." The vocalization should be פָּרָפֶּרֶת (E. G.).

הלכה ה: אָמַר רַב חִסְדָּא לֹא תַנִּינָן אֶלָּא בֵּירַךְ עַל הַיַּיִן שֶׁלִּפְנֵי הַמָּזוֹן פָּטַר אֶת הַיַּיִן שֶׁלְּאַחַר הַמָּזוֹן. אֲבָל אִם בֵּירַךְ עַל הַיַּיִן שֶׁבְּתוֹךְ הַמָּזוֹן לֹא פָטַר אֶת הַיַּיִן שֶׁלְּאַחַר הַמָּזוֹן. תַּמָּן אָמְרִין אֲפִילוּ בֵּירַךְ עַל הַיַּיִן שֶׁלִּפְנֵי הַמָּזוֹן לֹא פָטַר אֶת הַיַּיִן שֶׁלְּאַחַר הַמָּזוֹן. וְהָא תַנִּינָן בֵּירַךְ עַל הַיַּיִן שֶׁלִּפְנֵי הַמָּזוֹן פָּטַר אֶת הַיַּיִן שֶׁלְּאַחַר הַמָּזוֹן. רַב הוּנָא וְרִבִּי יְהוֹשֻׁעַ בֶּן לֵוִי. חַד אָמַר בְּהָדֵין[154] דְּשָׁתֵי קוֹנְדִּיטוֹן. וְחָרָנָא אָמַר בְּהָדֵין דְּשָׁתֵי חֲמַר אַחַר בֵּילְנֵי.

Halakhah 5: Rav Ḥisda said, we stated only "if one recited the benediction on wine before the meal, he also covers wine after the meal", but if one recited the benediction for wine during the meal[155], he did not cover the wine after the meal. There[156] they say, even if one recited the benediction on wine before the meal, he did not cover wine after the meal. But did we not state "if one recited the benediction on wine before the meal, he also covers wine after the meal"? Rav Huna and Rebbi Joshua ben Levi, one of them said, if he drank spiced wine[157], the other one said, if he drank wine after the bath[158].

154 Reading of the Rome manuscript. Venice print: בהדין.

155 When wine serves only to wash down the food. But wine after the

meal is consumed for its own sake.

156 In Babylonia, where wine was a rarity and only used on Sabbath and holidays. Their usual drink was beer made from date syrup. The entire discussion is Babylonian, cf. Babli 42b.

157 Latin *conditum* (scil., *vinum*); this wine cannot be compared to regular wine and therefore needs an extra benediction.

158 Latin *balnea, -orum* (plur.), a sauna. Since the first wine after return from the sauna is taken for medical reasons, its benediction does not cover wine consumed as food.

רִבִּי חֶלְבּוֹ רַב הוּנָא רַב בְּשֵׁם רִבִּי חִייָא רוּבָּא פַּת הַבָּאָה כִּיסְנִין אַחַר הַמָּזוֹן טְעוּנָה בְּרָכָה לְפָנֶיהָ וּלְאַחֲרֶיהָ. אָמַר רִבִּי אַמִּי רִבִּי יוֹחָנָן פְּלִיג. אָמַר רִבִּי מָנָא לְרִבִּי חִזְקִיָּה בְּמַה הוּא פְלִיג. כְּשֶׁאָכַל מֵאוֹתוֹ הַמָּזוֹן בְּאֶמְצַע הַמָּזוֹן. אָמַר לֵיהּ אֲפִילוּ לֹא אָכַל מֵאוֹתוֹ הַמִּין בְּאֶמְצַע הַמָּזוֹן. אָתָא רַב חַגַּי בְּשֵׁם רִבִּי זְעִירָא אֲפִילוּ לֹא אָכַל מֵאוֹתוֹ הַמִּין בְּאֶמְצַע הַמָּזוֹן.

Rebbi Ḥelbo, Rav Huna, Rav, in the name of the great Rebbi Ḥiyya: Bread that comes *kisnīn*[159] needs a benediction before and after. Rebbi Ammi said that Rebbi Yoḥanan disagrees. Rebbi Mana asked Rebbi Ḥizqiah, in what does he disagree? When one ate from the same food[160] during the meal? He said to him, even if one did not eat from the same kind during the meal. Rav Ḥaggai came in the name of Rebbi Zeïra: Even if one did not eat from the same kind during the meal[161].

159 Rav Hai Gaon explains that *kisnīn*-bread is called כעכ in Arabic. This is "pastry, small baked goods" in common Arabic, "donuts" in Syrian dialect. Rabbenu Ḥananel and Rashi explain that it is a baked shell filled with candied almonds and other nuts. Since it is baked it needs a benediction, but since it is not baked as bread it is not covered by the benediction over bread. The Babli (42a) quotes only the opinion of Samuel who seems to agree with Rebbi Yoḥanan here.

160 The Rome ms. has here המין, conforming to the next two sentences.

161 Any baked goods eaten after the benediction over bread and before Grace are covered by these two benedictions.

רִבִּי חֲנִינָא בַּר סִיסַיי הֲוּון אִילֵּין דִּנְשִׂייָא מְשַׁלְּחִין לֵיהּ נִקְלַווְסִין וַהֲוָה שְׁבַק לוֹן בָּתָר מְזוֹנֵיהּ וּמְבָרֵךְ עֲלֵיהֶן תְּחִילָּה וְסוֹף. רַב חוּנָא אָכַל תְּמָרִין עִם פִּיסְתֵּיהּ. אָמַר לֵיהּ רַב חִיָּיא בַּר אַשִׁי פְּלִיג אַתְּ עַל רַבָּךְ שׁוֹבְקִין בָּתָר מְזוֹנָךְ וְאַתְּ מְבָרֵךְ עֲלֵיהֶן תְּחִילָּה וְסוֹף. אֲמַר לֵיהּ אִינּוּן אִינּוּן עִיקָּר נְגִיסָתִי. רִבִּי יוֹנָה וְרִבִּי יוֹסֵי סָלְקוּן לְמִשְׁתִּיתֵיהּ דְּרִבִּי חֲנִינָא עֵנְתָּנָייָה אַפִּיק קוֹמֵיהוֹן פַּת הַבָּאָה בְּכִיסְנִין לְאַחַר הַמָּזוֹן. אָמְרִין נִישְׁבּוֹק אוּלְפָּנָא וְנֵיתֵי לָן לְמַתְנִיתָא. דְּתַנֵּי רִבִּי מָנָא מִשּׁוּם רִבִּי יוּדָה שֶׁאָמַר מִשּׁוּם רִבִּי יוֹסֵי הַגְּלִילִי פַּת הַבָּאָה כִּיסְנִין לְאַחַר הַמָּזוֹן טְעוּנָה בְרָכָה לְפָנֶיהָ וּלְאַחֲרֶיהָ. אָמְרֵי מִכֵּיוָן דְּהֵן יְחִידָיֵי וְרַבָּנָן פְּלִיגִין עֲלוֹי נַעֲבֵד כְּרַבָּנָן.

From the Patriarch they sent Nicolaus dates[162] to Rebbi Ḥanina bar Sisai[163]. He left them for dessert after his meal and recited a benediction over them before and after. Rav Ḥuna ate dates with his bread. Rav Ḥiyya bar Ashi said to him, are you disagreeing with your teacher[164]? Leave them for dessert after your meal and you may recite a benediction over them before and after. He said to him, they are the main thing my teeth get to bite. Rebbi Jonah and Rebbi Yose went to the marriage feast of Rebbi Ḥanina Eyntanaya. They brought before them *kisnīn* bread after the meal. They said, let us leave our learning and let us bring a *baraita*: Rebbi Mana stated in the name of Rebbi Yehudah, who said in the name of Rebbi Yose the Galilean: Bread that comes *kisnīn* after the meal needs a benediction before and after. They said, since they are the minority and the rabbis disagree with them, let us act following the rabbis[165].

162 A kind of large Syrian dates, in Arabic אַנקִילָא.

163 He is also called Ininai bar Sisai (in the Yerushalmi) and Anani bar Sason (in the Babli); Amora of the second generation and student of Rebbi Ḥanina.

164 Rav, who said that food eaten after the main meal, without bread, needs separate benedictions.

165 That bread covers all food which comes regularly with a meal,

whether during the main course or as a dessert. This, as report of an action, is the final decision in the matter.

אֲמַר מָרִינוֹס בֵּי רִבִּי יְהוֹשֻׁעַ אֵהֵן אֲכַל גָּרִיזְמִי וְסָלִית אַף עַל גַּב דְּהוּא מְבָרֵךְ עַל גָּרִיזְמָתָא בְּסוֹפָהּ לֹא פָּטַר סוּלְתָא. מַה כְּבֵית שַׁמַּאי דְּבֵית שַׁמַּאי אוֹמֵר אַף לֹא מַעֲשֶׂה קְדֵרָה. אָמַר רִבִּי יוֹסֵי דִּבְרֵי הַכֹּל הִיא. בֵּירַךְ עַל הַפַּת פָּטַר אֶת הַפַּרְפֶּרֶת וְאֶת מַעֲשֵׂה קְדֵרָה. בֵּית שַׁמַּאי אוֹמְרִים לֹא פָּטַר אֶת מַעֲשֵׂה קְדֵירָה. אֲבָל אִם בֵּירַךְ עַל הַפַּרְפֶּרֶת תְּחִילָּה כָּל־עַמָּא מוֹדוֹי דְּלֹא פָּטַר אֶת הַפַּת וְלֹא מַעֲשֵׂה קְדֵירָה. רִבִּי אַבָּא בְּרֵיהּ דְּרִבִּי פַּפֵּי בְּעֵי. אֵהֵן דְּאָכַל סוֹלֶת וּבְדַעְתֵּיהּ מֵיכוֹל פִּיתָּא מַהוּ מְבָרְכָה עַל סוּלְתָא בְּסוֹפָהּ. רַבָּנָן דְּקֵיסָרִין פַּשְׁטִין לָהּ צָרִיךְ לְבָרֵךְ בְּסוֹף.

Marinos, the son of Rebbi Joshua[166] said: He who ate dessert[141] and cereal[167], even though he recites a benediction on the dessert at the end, he did not cover cereal[168]. Is he like the House of Shammai, since the House of Shammai say[169], "neither cooked food?" Rebbi Yose said, this is everybody's opinion. If one recited the benediction on bread, he also covers little pieces and cooked food; the House of Shammai say, neither did he cover cooked food. But if one first recited the benediction over little pieces, everybody agrees that he covered neither bread nor cooked food[170]. Rebbi Abba, the son of Rebbi Ḥaggai asked: He who ate cereal and he has the intention of later eating bread, does he have to recite a separate benediction for cereal at the end? The rabbis of Caesarea find it obvious that he has to recite a separate benediction at the end[171].

166 At other places in the Yerushalmi, he is called Marinos, the son of the great Rebbi Oshayah; an Israeli Amora between the first and second generations.

167 Cereal made from flour or flakes of grain that can be used to make bread.

168 Since vegetable dessert needs only a short benediction afterwards but cereal needs a "benediction imitating three."

169 In the Mishnah. Except if it is explicitly stated, practice never follows the House of Shammai; Marinos should not follow it.

170 They need the "benediction imitating three." The Yerushalmi takes it as obvious that the remark on the House of Shammai refers to the sentence just preceding their remark. In the Babli (42b) it remains undecided whether the House of Shammai refer to the first or the second clause in the Mishnah.

171 In Israel, one never ate cereal with bread. R. Zeïra (himself a native Babylonian) is quoted in the Babli (*Beẓa* 16a) as making fun of "those stupid Babylonians who eat bread with bread" because they eat bread with cereal. Hence, in Caesarea, someone eating cereal is not presumed to have the intention to eat bread.

משנה ו: הָיוּ יוֹשְׁבִין כָּל־אֶחָד וְאֶחָד מְבָרֵךְ לְעַצְמוֹ. הֵיסֵיבוּ אֶחָד מְבָרֵךְ לְכוּלָּן. בָּא לָהֶן יַיִן בְּתוֹךְ הַמָּזוֹן כָּל־אֶחָד מְבָרֵךְ לְעַצְמוֹ לְאַחַר הַמָּזוֹן אֶחָד מְבָרֵךְ לְכוּלָּן. וְאוֹמֵר עַל הַמּוּגְמָר.

Mishnah 6: If they were sitting[172], every one makes the benediction for himself[173]. If they were lying on couches[174], one would make the benediction for everybody[175]. If wine were served to them in the middle of the meal, everyone would make the benediction for himself[176]; after the meal one person makes the benediction for everybody, and he makes the benediction on *mugmar*[177].

172 In a sitting room, not in a dining room, either for talk or before a meal. (Some Mishnah manuscripts have "sitting before a meal" but the addition seems irrelevant.) In Mishnaic times, a formal meal was always taken lying down on couches, supporting oneself with one's left arm and eating with the right hand.

173 For wine, pastries, or fruit.

174 Assembled to eat a meal as a company.

175 On bread and/or wine. The other participants must answer "Amen" so that the benediction is counted also for them.

176 Since people may be eating, their mouth is not free to answer "Amen".

177 The Hebrew verb גמר, Arabic גַּמַּר, means "to roast on burning coals". *Mugmar* are spices or incense roasted on burning coals, used as air-freshener after a meal and also to perfume garments.

הלכה ו: רִבִּי יְהוֹשֻׁעַ בֶּן לֵוִי אָמַר בִּשְׁבוּעַ הַבֵּן הִיא מַתְנִיתָא. הָא בַּעַל הַבַּיִת בְּתוֹךְ בֵּיתוֹ לֹא. תַּנֵּי רִבִּי חִייָא אֲפִילוּ בַּעַל הַבַּיִת בְּתוֹךְ בֵּיתוֹ.

Halakhah 7: Rebbi Joshua ben Levi said, the Mishnah deals with a party for circumcision[178]. Hence, it does not apply to a man in his own house[179]. Rebbi Ḥiyya stated[180], even a man in his own house.

178 And similar festive occasions when a formal dinner takes place.

179 Since all members of the household look to the head of the house to start the meal, he should make the benediction for all of them even if they are sitting and not reclining, since not every apartment has a formal dining room.

180 In one of his *baraitot*. He allows a common benediction only in a formal dining room. The disagreement between him and R. Joshua ben Levi is not resolved; both are authorities of equal standing.

תַּנֵּי (fol. 10d) סֵדֶר סְעוּדָה אוֹרְחִין נִכְנָסִין וְיוֹשְׁבִין עַל הַסַּפְסָלִין וְעַל הַקַּתֶדְרָיוֹת עַד שֶׁכּוּלָּן מִתְכַּנְּסִין. הֵבִיאוּ לָהֶן יַיִן כָּל־אֶחָד וְאֶחָד מְבָרֵךְ לְעַצְמוֹ. הֵבִיאוּ לָהֶן לְיָדַיִם כָּל־אֶחָד וְאֶחָד נוֹטֵל יָדוֹ אַחַת. הֵבִיאוּ לָהֶן פַּרְפֶּרֶת כָּל־אֶחָד וְאֶחָד מְבָרֵךְ לְעַצְמוֹ. עָלוּ וְהֵסֵיבוּ הֵבִיאוּ לָהֶן יַיִן אַף עַל פִּי שֶׁבֵּירַךְ עַל הָרִאשׁוֹן צָרִיךְ לְבָרֵךְ עַל הַשֵּׁנִי. וְאֶחָד מְבָרֵךְ עַל יְדֵי כוּלָּם. הֵבִיאוּ לָהֶן לְיָדַיִם אַף עַל פִּי שֶׁנָּטַל יָדוֹ אַחַת צָרִיךְ לִיטּוֹל שְׁתֵּי יָדָיו. הֵבִיאוּ לָהֶן פַּרְפֶּרֶת אֶחָד מְבָרֵךְ עַל יְדֵי כוּלָּן. וְאֵין רְשׁוּת לְאוֹרֵחַ לִיכָּנֵס אַחַר שָׁלֹשׁ פַּרְפְּרָאוֹת.

It was stated[181]: The order of a formal meal: Guests enter and sit on low benches[182] or on chairs[183] until all of them are assembled. They are served wine; everyone makes the benediction for himself. They bring them water, everyone washes one hand. They bring them snacks, everyone makes the benediction for himself. When they entered[184] and lie down on couches they are served wine; even though one made the benediction on the first one, he must now make the benediction on the second one; one of them makes the benediction for all of them. They bring them water; even though one had washed one hand, he now has to wash both hands. When they are served snacks, one makes the benediction for all of them. No guest may enter after three servings of snacks.

181 Tosephta *Berakhot* 4:8; Babli 43a. This Tosephta explains the background of the Mishnah.

182 Latin *subsellium.*

183 Greek καθέδρα.

184 The dining room. הסב means "to lie on couches" in Mishnaic Hebrew.

תַּמָּן תַּנִּינָן סוּכָּה שִׁבְעָה כֵּיצַד. גָּמַר מִלֶּאֱכוֹל לֹא יַתִּיר אֶת סוּכָּתוֹ אֲבָל מוֹרִיד הוּא אֶת הַכֵּלִים מִן הַמִּנְחָה וּלְמַעְלָה בִּשְׁבִיל כְּבוֹד יוֹם טוֹב הָאַחֲרוֹן. רִבִּי אַבָּא בַּר כַּהֲנָא רַב חִייָא בַּר אַשִׁי בְּשֵׁם רַב צָרִיךְ אָדָם לִפְסוֹל סוּכָּתוֹ מִבְּעוֹד יוֹם. רִבִּי יְהוֹשֻׁעַ בֶּן לֵוִי אָמַר צָרִיךְ לְקַדֵּשׁ בְּתוֹךְ בֵּיתוֹ. רִבִּי יַעֲקֹב בַּר אָחָא בְּשֵׁם שְׁמוּאֵל קִידֵּשׁ בְּבַיִת זֶה וְנִמְלַךְ לֶאֱכוֹל בְּבַיִת אַחֵר צָרִיךְ לְקַדֵּשׁ. רִבִּי אָחָא רִבִּי חִינְנָא בְּשֵׁם רִבִּי הוֹשַׁעְיָא מִי שֶׁסּוּכָּתוֹ עֲרֵיבָה עָלָיו מְקַדֵּשׁ לֵילֵי יוֹם טוֹב הָאַחֲרוֹן בְּתוֹךְ בֵּיתוֹ וְעוֹלֶה וְאוֹכֵל בְּתוֹךְ סוּכָּתוֹ. אָמַר רִבִּי אָבִין וְלֹא פְלִיגִין. מַה דָּמַר רַב כְּשֶׁלֹּא הָיָה בְדַעְתּוֹ לֶאֱכוֹל בְּבַיִת אַחֵר. וּמַה דָּמַר שְׁמוּאֵל כְּשֶׁהָיָה בְדַעְתּוֹ לֶאֱכוֹל בְּבַיִת אַחֵר. אָמַר רִבִּי מָנָא אַתְיָא דִשְׁמוּאֵל כְּרִבִּי חִייָא וּדְרִבִּי הוֹשַׁעְיָא כְּרִבִּי יְהוֹשֻׁעַ בֶּן לֵוִי.

There (Mishnah *Sukkah* 4:5) we have stated: "Sukkah seven days, how is this[185]? If he finished to eat he should not take down his *sukkah*[186], but he takes out the vessels starting from the time of afternoon prayers because of the honor due to the last holiday." Rebbi Abba bar Cahana,

Rav Ḥiyya bar Ashi in the name of Rav: A person must make his *sukkah* invalid[187] as long as it is still day. Rebbi Joshua ben Levi said, a person must make *Qiddush*[188] inside his house[189]. Rebbi Jacob bar Aḥa in the name of Samuel: If one made *Qiddush* in one house and changed his mind to eat in another house he must make *Qiddush*[190]. Rebbi Aḥa, Rebbi Ḥinena in the name of Rebbi Hoshaiah[191]: He who loves his *sukkah* makes *Qiddush* of the last holiday in his house and goes to eat in his *sukkah*[192]. Rebbi Abun said, they do not disagree. What Rav said was, if he did not have the intention to eat in another house[193]. But what Samuel said was if he had the intention to eat in another house. Rebbi Mana said[194], Samuel comes like Rebbi[195] Ḥiyya and Rebbi Hoshaiah like Rebbi Joshua ben Levi[196].

185 The holiday of Sukkot is seven days; the eighth day, *Shemini Aẓeret*, is an additional festive day, where the obligation to live in a *sukkah* does not apply. Since one may not add to the commandments of the Torah (*Deut.* 13:1), in Israel, where holidays are only one day, one may not live in the *sukkah* on the eighth day.

186 The obligation to live in the *sukkah* extends until nightfall of the eighth day.

187 That it would no longer qualify as *sukkah*. At the end of the discussion, the interpretation is that one must make the *sukkah* invalid as *sukkah* only if one intends to eat in the *sukkah* during the holiday of *Shemini Aẓeret*. One makes the *sukkah* invalid either by removing some of the roofing, or by putting up a sheet of cloth under the roofing, or in a similar way.

188 The sanctification of (Sabbath and) holidays, pronounced over a cup of wine.

189 On *Shemini Aẓeret*, irrespective of the place of the meal.

190 This parallels the statement of Samuel in Babli *Pesaḥim* 101a that "there cannot be *Qiddush* except at the place of the holiday meal."

191 The Venice text reads: Rebbi Joshua; the text here is from the Rome manuscript. The correct text is in the parallel in *Sukkah* 4:5: Rebbi Hoshaiah in the name of Rav. In the sequel, this statement will be referred to either as

Rebbi Hoshaiah's or Rav's.

192 Contradicting the statement of Samuel, that *Qiddush* must be said at the place of the meal.

193 So that at the moment of recitation of *Qiddush*, his intention was valid; a valid benediction cannot be voided retroactively.

194 The explanation of R. Abun is impossible since then we would have two contradictory statements in the name of Rav. Rav Ḥiyya bar Ashi said in his name that one must make the *sukkah* invalid before the start of the eighth day if one wants to use it during that day; hence, if Rebbi Hoshaiah requires in Rav's name that one make *Qiddush* in the house it is obvious that he had the prior intention to eat in the *sukkah*. Hence, Rav must disagree with Samuel. If Rav Ḥiyya bar Ashi made his statement without reference to Rav we may refer to the Babli (*Pesaḥim* 100b) that Rav disagrees explicitly with Samuel but that Rav Huna, Rav's foremost student, agrees with Samuel. Rav Huna would not have gone against Rav if not at least one of the latter's colleagues in his Yeshivah, e. g., Rav Ḥiyya bar Ashi, had supported Samuel. Hence, the attribution of the statement of Rav Ḥiyya bar Ashi to Rav seems to be in error, even though it is supported by both manuscripts of the Yerushalmi.

195 Scribal error for "Rav". Since Rav Ḥiyya bar Ashi requires that one eat in an invalid *sukkah* he must require that *Qiddush* be in that invalid *sukkah*.

196 This seemingly unrelated topic is discussed here because it has an implicit relationship with the foregoing Tosephta and the Mishnah. According to R. Joshua ben Levi, one may make *Qiddush* in the house and then continue eating and drinking wine in the *sukkah*. This means that one may start drinking wine at one place and then continue drinking at another place without reciting a new benediction. This contradicts the previous Tosephta that the benediction over wine in the sitting room does not free one from reciting a new benediction in the dining room. Samuel (seconded by Rebbi Yoḥanan in Babli *Pesaḥim* 101a/b) will agree to the conclusion from the Tosephta.

שְׁאֲלוּ אֶת בֶּן זוֹמָא מִפְּנֵי מַה בָּא לָהֶן יַיִן בְּתוֹךְ הַמָּזוֹן כָּל־אֶחָד מְבָרֵךְ לְעַצְמוֹ. אָמַר לָהֶן מִפְּנֵי שֶׁאֵין בֵּית הַבְּלִיעָה פָּנוּי. אָמַר רִבִּי מָנָא הֲדָא אָמְרָה אֲהֵן דְּעָטִישׁ גַּו מֵיכְלָא אֲסִיר לְמֵימַר יַיַּס בְּגִין סַכַּנְתָּא דְנַפְשָׁא.

They asked Ben Zoma[197]: Why, if wine was served to them in the middle of the meal, everyone makes the benediction for himself? He said to them, because the place of swallowing is not empty[198]. Rebbi Mana said, this means that if someone sneezes during the meal one may not say to him "for health[199]" because of danger to one's life.

197 Tosephta *Berakhot* 4:12, Babli 43a.

198 Talking during swallowing may bring food into one's windpipe and cause one's death by asphyxiation.

199 Greek ἴασις. The *Arukh* reads here זט, Greek ζήτω "for life!" The Tosephta (*Šabbat* 7:5) declares this to be a non-Jewish custom.

מַה בֵּין מוּגְמָר וּבֵין יַיִן. מוּגְמָר כּוּלָּן מְרִיחִין. יַיִן אֶחָד הוּא טוֹעֵם. רִבִּי זְעִירָא בְּשֵׁם רַב יִרְמְיָה מוּגְמָר כֵּיוָן שֶׁהֶעֱלָה עָשָׁן צָרִיךְ לְבָרֵךְ. רִבִּי יִרְמְיָה בְּעָא מִיבְדּוֹק לְרִבִּי זְעִירָא. אֲמַר לֵיהּ כֵּיצַד הוּא אוֹמֵר עַל שֶׁמֶן עָרֵב. אֲמַר לֵיהּ אֲשֶׁר נָתַן רֵיחַ טוֹב בְּשֶׁמֶן עָרֵב. אָמַר לֵיהּ אֲשֶׁר נָתַן רֵיחַ טוֹב בַּעֲצֵי בְשָׂמִים. יִצְחָק בַּר אַבָּא בַּר מְחַסְיָה וְרַב חֲנַנְאֵל הֲווֹן יָתְבִין חַד אֲמַר בָּרוּךְ שֶׁנָּתַן רֵיחַ טוֹב בַּעֲצֵי בְשָׂמִים. וְחָרָנָא אֲמַר בָּרוּךְ שֶׁנָּתַן רֵיחַ טוֹב בְּעֵשֶׂב הָאָרֶץ. מָתִיב מַן דָּמַר בְּעֵשֶׂב הָאָרֶץ לְמָן דָּמַר בַּעֲצֵי בְשָׂמִים. וְכִי עֵצִים הֵן. אָמַר לֵיהּ וְהָכְתִיב וַתִּיטְמְנֵם בְּפִשְׁתֵּי הָעֵץ. וְכִי עֵצִים הֵן. סָלְקִין לְבֵית רַב וְשָׁמְעוֹן רַב חוּנָא בְּשֵׁם רַב אֲשֶׁר נָתַן רֵיחַ טוֹב בַּעֲצֵי בְשָׂמִים. גְּנִיבָא אָמַר שֶׁמֶן לְזוּהֲמָה אֵינוֹ צָרִיךְ לְבָרֵךְ. אָמַר רִבִּי יוּדָן אֲפִילוּ קָווּי לְתוֹךְ יָדוֹ. רִבִּי חֶלְבּוֹ רַב חוּנָא בְּשֵׁם רַב הַמְּרַבֵּץ אֱלֵינְתִּית בְּתוֹךְ בֵּיתוֹ אֵינוֹ צָרִיךְ לְבָרֵךְ. אָמַר רַב חִסְדָּא עַל כּוּלָּן הוּא אוֹמֵר אֲשֶׁר נָתַן רֵיחַ טוֹב בַּעֲצֵי בְשָׂמִים. בַּר מִן אִהֵן מוּסְכִין דְּיֵימַר אֲשֶׁר נָתַן רֵיחַ טוֹב בְּמִינֵי בְשָׂמִים.

What is the difference between *mugmar* and wine? Everybody smells *mugmar*, each person tastes wine. Rebbi Zeïra in the name of Rav Jeremiah[200]: One has to recite the benediction for *mugmar* as soon as the smoke rises. Rav[201] Jeremiah wanted to examine Rebbi Zeïra. He said to him, which benediction does one recite on perfumed oil? He said, "He

Who gave pleasant fragrance in perfumed oil." He said to him, "He Who gave pleasant fragrance in spice wood." Isaac bar Abba from Meḥasiah[202] and Rav Ḥananel were sitting. One said, "Praise to Him Who gave pleasant fragrance in spice wood." The other one said, "Praise to Him Who gave pleasant fragrance in the plants of the earth." He who said "in the plants of the earth" objected to him who said "in spice wood": are they wood? He answered him, is it not written (*Jos.* 2:6) "She hid them in the hemp of wood", are these wood? They went to the Yeshivah of Rav and heard Rav Huna[203] in the name of Rav: "He Who gave pleasant fragrance in spice wood." Ganiva said, he who uses oil for dirt[204] does not have to recite a benediction. Rebbi Yudan said, even if he collects it into his hand. Rebbi Ḥelbo, Rav Huna in the name of Rav: He who sprinkles *olentia*[205] in his house[206] does not have to recite a benediction. Rav Ḥisda said, on everything he recites "He Who gave pleasant fragrance in spice wood" except for musk on which he recites "He who gave pleasant fragrance in all kinds of spices.[207]"

200 The entire discussion is paralleled in Babli 43a/b.

201 The text, "Rebbi", is in error since Rebbi Zeïra was the student of Rav Jeremiah in Babylonia and the teacher of Rebbi Jeremiah in Galilee.

202 A Babylonian; twice mentioned as associate of Rav Ḥananel. Mata ("City of") Meḥasia was the place of Rav's Yeshivah.

203 Head of the Yeshivah of Rav after Rav's death.

204 If the oil is used primariiy for cleaning and it does not matter that it is perfumed This applies to all other cleaning fluids also.

205 Latin *olens, olentis* "sweet smelling" (E. G.). Most authors equate the word with *oleamentum*, "ointment made from olive oil"; this fits neither the spelling of the word nor the context.

206 If the main intent is to either bind the dirt or to get rid of bad odors, not to produce the pleasant fragrance.

207 Musk is of animal, not vegetable, origin. The statement of Rav Ḥisda in the Babli is quoted in the

name of Rav; but there the benediction for musk is accepted for everything except for balsamum.

משנה ז: הֶבִיאוּ לְפָנָיו מְלִיחַ וּפַת עִמּוֹ מְבָרֵךְ עַל הַמְּלִיחַ וּפוֹטֵר אֶת הַפַּת שֶׁהַפַּת טְפֵילָה לוֹ. זֶה הַכְּלָל כָּל־שֶׁהוּא עִיקָּר וְעִמּוֹ טְפֵילָה מְבָרֵךְ עַל הָעִיקָּר וּפוֹטֵר אֶת הַטְּפֵילָה.

Mishnah 7: If salted fish[208] was brought before him with bread, one recites the benediction over the salted fish and frees the bread[209] because the bread is accessory. The following is the principle: Anything that is the main dish and comes with a side dish, one recites the benediction on the main dish and this frees the side dish.

208 This is the usual interpretation of "salted" and is the correct interpretation of Mishnah and Yerushalmi by the testimony of the *Arukh* who quotes the Mishnah *Nedarim* 6:3: "He who makes a vow not to eat any salted foods, is forbidden only salted fish."

209 From having to recite the benediction because salted fish cannot be eaten without bread; hence, the bread would not have been eaten were it not for the salted fish.

הלכה ז: רִבִּי שְׁמוּאֵל בַּר נַחְמָן בְּשֵׁם רִבִּי יוֹנָתָן מַתְנִיָּיתָא עַד שֶׁלֹּא לָמְדוּ סְעוּדַת מְלָכִים וּבִמְקוֹם שֶׁעוֹשִׂין אֶת הַמְּלִיחַ עִיקָּר. אֲבָל בְּמָקוֹם שֶׁאֵין עוֹשִׂין אֶת הַמְּלִיחַ עִיקָּר לָא בְדָא. רִבִּי יִרְמְיָה בְשֵׁם רַב פִּיתָּא וּפֵירוּר אוֹמֵר עַל הַפֵּירוּר בְּמָקוֹם שֶׁעוֹשִׂין אֶת הַפֵּירוּר עִיקָּר. אֲבָל בְּמָקוֹם שֶׁאֵין עוֹשִׂין אֶת הַפֵּירוּר עִיקָּר לָא בְדָא. רִבִּי סִימוֹן בְּשֵׁם רִבִּי שִׁמְעוֹן בֶּן לָקִישׁ שְׁקִיזְמִי וּפִיתָּא אוֹמֵר עַל הַשְּׁקִיזְמִי בְּמָקוֹם שֶׁעוֹשִׂין אֶת הַשְּׁקִיזְמִי עִיקָּר. אֲבָל בְּמָקוֹם שֶׁאֵין עוֹשִׂין אֶת הַשְּׁקִיזְמִי עִיקָּר לָא בְדָא.

Halakhah 7: Rebbi Samuel bar Naḥman in the name of Rebbi Jonathan[210]: The Mishnah was from before they learned royal meals and at a place where the salted fish is the main food, but at a place where salted fish is not the main food that does not apply[211]. Rav[212] Jeremiah in the name of Rav, *pitta* bread and morsels, one recites on the morsels at a place where the morsels are the main food[213]. But at a place where morsels are not the main food that does not apply. Rebbi Simon in the name of Rebbi Simeon ben Laqish, *šeqizmi*[214] and bread, one recites on the *šeqizmi* at a place where the *šeqizmi* are the main food. But at a place where *šeqizmi* are not the main food that does not apply.

210 Israeli Amora of the first generation, close to R. Joshua ben Levi, Rebbi Ḥiyya the Great and R. Ḥanina.

211 Hence, for the Babli (44a) it no longer applies.

212 Again, "Rebbi" is scribal error.

213 This does not contradict the stament in Halakhah 1 that one makes the benediction on a complete loaf of bread if at all possible since the morsels here are not eaten as morsels, but are collected and milk is poured over them; the whole is left standing until it gets moldy. The result was considered in Babylonia to be an exquisite delicacy called "Babylonian *kutaḥ*". The authorities involved here are all Babylonian.

214 An unidentified word. [*Pne Mosheh* (Margalit), followed by Levy in his dictionary, takes the word to mean a delicacy made from almonds (שקד) with ז replacing soft ד. *Pne Mosheh* (Ben Ḥabib) identifies *šeqizmi* as kinds of fruit.]

משנה ח: אָכַל תְּאֵנִים וַעֲנָבִים וְרִמּוֹנִים מְבָרֵךְ עֲלֵיהֶן שָׁלֹשׁ בְּרָכוֹת דִּבְרֵי רַבָּן גַּמְלִיאֵל. וַחֲכָמִים אוֹמְרִים בְּרָכָה אַחַת מֵעֵין שָׁלֹשׁ. רִבִּי עֲקִיבָא אוֹמֵר אֲפִילוּ אָכַל שֶׁלֶק וְהוּא מְזוֹנוֹ מְבָרֵךְ עָלָיו שָׁלֹשׁ בְּרָכוֹת. הַשּׁוֹתֶה מַיִם לִצְמָאוֹ אוֹמֵר שֶׁהַכֹּל נִהְיֶה בִּדְבָרוֹ. רִבִּי טַרְפוֹן אוֹמֵר בּוֹרֵא נְפָשׁוֹת רַבּוֹת.

Mishna 8: One who ate figs, grapes, or pomegranates[215] recites for them three benedictions[216], the words of Rabban Gamliel; but the Sages say, one benediction imitating three. Rebbi Aqiba says, even if one ate cooked food and that is his meal he recites for it three benedictions[217]. He who drinks water for his thirst[218] says "By Whose word everything was created." Rebbi Tarphon[219] said, "Creator of many living things"[220].

215 Or any other of the "Seven Fruits" that has not been made into bread; see note [15].

216 Full grace; this Mishnah is the introduction to the subject of Grace which will occupy the next two chapters.

217 Since the verse says: (*Deut.* 8:10) "When you will eat and will have been satiated then you must praise the Eternal, your God, for the good land that He has given you." There is no mention of bread. The three benedictions are (1) for the food, (2) for the Land, (3) for Jerusalem.

218 He drinks water for itself and not to accompany or wash down food.

219 Probably the Greek name Τρυφῶν. He was old enough to have served as a priest in the Temple before its destruction. The text of the Yerushalmi in the Halakhah, a manuscript of the Babli, and some quotes from Medieval authorities have "R. Yehudah" instead of "R. Tarphon". Since the main thrust of the Mishnah is about concluding benedictions, it is not clear whether R. Tarphon/Yehudah speaks of a first benediction, contradicting R. Aqiba, or about the concluding benediction for food that needs neither "three benedictions" nor "one benediction imitating three."

220 Some Mishnah manuscripts have here the full text of the minor benediction after food.

הלכה ח: רִבִּי סִימוֹן רִבִּי תַּדַּאי בְּשֵׁם רִבִּי הוֹשַׁעְיָא[221] אָכַל בְּמִזְרָחָהּ שֶׁל תְּאֵינָה וּבָא לֶאֱכֹל בְּמַעֲרָבָהּ צָרִיךְ לְבָרֵךְ. אַבָּא בַּר רַב חוּנָא אָמַר יַיִן יָשָׁן יַיִן חָדָשׁ צָרִיךְ לְבָרֵךְ. שִׁינּוּי יַיִן אֵין צָרִיךְ לְבָרֵךְ. שִׁינּוּי מָקוֹם צָרִיךְ לְבָרֵךְ. הִסִּיעַ דַּעְתּוֹ כְּמִי שֶׁהוּא שִׁינּוּי מָקוֹם. רִבִּי עַל כָּל־חָבִית וְחָבִית שֶׁהָיָה פוֹתֵחַ הָיָה מְבָרֵךְ עָלֶיהָ. וּמַה הָיָה אוֹמֵר. רִבִּי יִצְחָק רוּבָּא בְּשֵׁם רִבִּי בָּרוּךְ הַטּוֹב וְהַמֵּטִיב. מַעֲשֶׂה בְּרִבִּי עֲקִיבָה שֶׁעָשָׂה מִשְׁתֶּה לְשִׁמְעוֹן בְּנוֹ עַל כָּל־חָבִית וְחָבִית שֶׁהָיָה פוֹתֵחַ הָיָה מְבָרֵךְ עָלֶיהָ וְאוֹמֵר חַמְרָא טָבָא לְרַבָּנָן וּלְתַלְמִידֵיהוֹן.

Halakhah 8: Rebbi Simon, Rebbi Thaddeus[222], in the name of Rebbi Hoshaia: If one ate East of a fig tree and then changed to West of it[223] to eat, he must make a benediction. Abba bar Rav Huna said: old wine, new wine, he has to recite a benediction[224]. Change of wine he does not have to make a benediction. Change of place he has to make a benediction. If he took his mind off[225] it is equal to change of place. Rebbi was reciting a benediction on any wine amphora that he was opening. What did he say? The old Rebbi Isaac in the name of Rebbi: "He Who is good and does good[226]." When Rebbi Aqiba was making a marriage feast for his son Simeon, he said a benediction over every wine amphora that he opened and said: "Good wine for the rabbis and their students."

221 Reading of the Rome manuscript. The Leyden manuscript and Venice print have again "R. Joshua".

222 Israeli Amora of the second generation. His sayings are reported either by R. Simon or by R. Abba.

223 Assuming that the fig tree is very old and large enough so that he cannot see his old place from the new one.

224 Since the benediction, as explained later in this Halakhah, is for the quality of the wine, one would expect that the change from new to old wine should require a benediction rather than the other way around. However, one has to assume that one deals with wine stored in cheap pottery amphoras rather than in extremely expensive glass bottles. The amphoras are porous and most of the alcohol will have vanished by the time the amphora is opened and also the flavor will have deteriorated under the influence of the air seeping in from the outside. Hence, the text here is justified.

225 After some time has passed. If one then returns to drink, it is a new activity.

226 Benediction on getting good news.

הַשּׁוֹתֶה מַיִם לִצְמָאוֹ אוֹמֵר שֶׁהַכֹּל נִהְיֶה בִּדְבָרוֹ. אָמַר רִבִּי יוֹנָה חוּץ מִמֵּי דְקָרִים. אָמַר רִבִּי יוֹסֵי וּלְכָל־מַיִם שֶׁהוּא צָמֵא לָהֶן. אָמַר רִבִּי אָבוּן הַשּׁוֹתֶה מֵי

דְּקָרִים מַהוּ אוֹמֵר בָּרוּךְ שֶׁבָּרָא מֵי רְפוּאוֹת. אִית תְּנָיֵי תַנֵּי מֵי דְקָרִים. אִית תְּנָיֵי תַנֵּי מֵי דְקָלִים. מַאן דָּמַר מֵי דְקָרִים שֶׁהֵן דּוֹקְרִין אֶת הַמָּרָה. וּמַא דָמַר מֵי דְקָלִים שֶׁהֵן יוֹצְאִין מִבֵּין שְׁנֵי דְקָלִים.

"[227]He who drinks water for his thirst says 'That everything was created by His word."' Rebbi Jonah said, except pick-axe water[228]. Rebbi Yose said, on any water that he thirsts for[229]. Rebbi Abun said, he who drinks pick-axe water, what does he say? "Praise to Him Who created medicinal waters."[230] Some Tannaïm state "*deqarim* water", other Tannaïm state "*deqalim* waters". He who said *deqarim* (pick-axe) waters, because they pierce the gall bladder. And he who says *deqalim* (date palm) waters, because they gush forth between two palm trees[231].

227 Quote from the Mishnah.

228 As is clear from the text, this is water drunk only for medicinal purposes.

229 If somebody drinks medicinal waters for his thirst, he has to recite the benediction for water, not that for medicinal waters. If he drinks water not for his thirst (in the language of the Babli, 44b, if a piece of food is stuck in his esophagus,) he does not have to recite any benediction.

230 The fact that a benediction is due is also noted in the Babli (38a), but the text is given only here.

231 Compare Latin *decalicator* "hard drinker" , one who is able to empty a *calix*, a goblet, at one draught (E. G.).

שלשה שאכלו פרק שביעי

משנה א: שְׁלֹשָׁה שֶׁאָכְלוּ כְּאַחַת חַיָּבִין לְזַמֵּן. אָכַל דְּמַאי וּמַעֲשֵׂר רִאשׁוֹן שֶׁנִּיטְּלָה תְרוּמָתוֹ וּמַעֲשֵׂר שֵׁנִי וְהֶקְדֵּשׁ שֶׁנִּיפְדּוּ וְהַשַּׁמָּשׁ שֶׁאָכַל כְּזַיִת וְהַכּוּתִי מְזַמְּנִין עֲלֵיהֶן. אֲבָל אִם אָכַל טֶבֶל וּמַעֲשֵׂר רִאשׁוֹן שֶׁלֹּא נִיטְּלָה תְרוּמָתוֹ וּמַעֲשֵׂר שֵׁנִי וְהֶקְדֵּשׁ שֶׁלֹּא נִיפְדּוּ וְהַשַּׁמָּשׁ שֶׁאָכַל פָּחוֹת מִכְּזַיִת וְהַנָּכְרִי אֵין מְזַמְּנִין עֲלֵיהֶן.

Mishnah 1: Three persons who ate together are required to "invite"[1]. If one ate *demai*[2], or first tithe of which the heave was taken[3], or second tithe[4] or dedicated foods[5] that were redeemed, or the waiter who ate the volume of an olive[6], or a Samaritan[7], these can be invited. But if one ate untithed produce, or first tithe of which the heave was not taken, or the second tithe[8] or dedicated foods that were not redeemed[9], or the waiter who ate less than the volume of an olive, or a Gentile[10], these cannot be invited.

1 Three adult males who ate together are obliged to recite Grace as a group and start with a special invitation to all participants to join in the praise of the Lord by Whose kindness we live. The text of the "invitation" is given in Mishnah 3.

2 Newly harvested produce is subject to several obligatory gifts and tithes. The first one is the heave, תְּרוּמָה, that can be given to any Cohen. This *terumah* must be eaten by a Cohen's family in ritual purity. There is no rate set for *terumah* in the Torah but in times when ritual purity can be observed, the rabbinically established rate was 2 percent. Next, the tithe of 10% must be given to a Levite. This *maäser* again is subject to a 10% *terumah of the tithe* to be given to the Cohen. The remainder of this *first tithe* is secular private property of the Levite and need not be kept in purity. However, consumption by a non-Cohen

of any food containing still *terumah* (and of impure *terumah* by a Cohen) is a deadly sin. In Temple times it was established that all Jews, educated and uneducated, observant and nonobservant alike, did separate *terumah* and give it to a Cohen. However, the first tithe was not given by a substantial minority of uneducated and nonobservant. Since untithed produce still contains the *terumah of the tithe* and its consumption would be a deadly sin, it was instituted that observant Jews have to separate at least the *terumah of the tithe* for produce bought from unreliable sources. Since a majority of all agricultural producers did give the tithe, the obligation to tithe is conditional and is waved for the poor. Produce sold by unreliable persons is called *demai*; the rules under which *demai* has to be given are spelled out in a separate Tractate. In any case, since any person might give away all his property and then become poor and eat *demai* without tithing, *demai* is potentially permitted food for everybody and the person who eats it does not commit blasphemy in reciting Grace.

3 The Babli explains, even if the heave was taken somewhat irregularly. There is no mention of that in the Yerushalmi.

4 The second tithe remains the property of the farmer but either it must be eaten in Jerusalem or it must be redeemed and the proceeds taken to Jerusalem and spent there for food. Second tithe that was redeemed is normal food permitted to everybody.

5 This is food from an animal not of the kind that may be sacrificed, or vegetables that may not be sacrificed, but were given to support the upkeep of the Temple. These gifts are then sold and the money used for the Temple. After the sale, the food is profane, for everybody to eat. Also, an animal dedicated for the altar that develops a blemish before it is sacrificed, can be redeemed and then becomes secular food which, however, must be consumed in a dignified manner.

6 Nobody may recite Grace who did not eat at least food of the volume of an average olive. The waiter is acceptable even though he did not sit down with the guests he served.

7 The descendants of the people settled in Samaria by the king of Assyria (*2Kings* 17) who accepted the written Torah but not the oral law. [Since they did not resist the effort made by Diocletian to unify the Roman Empire in pagan rite, this statement of

the Mishnah no longer applies. It does apply, however, to Karaites.]

8 Outside of Jerusalem.

9 Except for the second tithe, the consumption of the foods mentioned here is a deadly sin; hence, pronouncing a benediction over that food would be the additional sin of blasphemy.

10 He is not obliged to recite Grace and has no part in the Land for which we give praise.

(fol. 11a) **הלכה א**: הָכָא אִיתְמַר אֵין רְשָׁאִין לְחַלֵּק. וְכָא אִיתְמַר חַייָבִין לְזַמֵּן. שְׁמוּאֵל אָמַר כַּאן בִּתְחִילָּה כַּאן בְּסוֹף. אֵי זֶהוּ בִּתְחִילָּה וְאֵי זֶהוּ בְּסוֹף. תְּרֵין אֲמוֹרָיִן חַד אָמַר נָֽתְנוּ דַּעַת לֶאֱכֹל זֶהוּ בִּתְחִילָּה. אָֽכְלוּ כְזַיִת זֶהוּ בְּסוֹף. וְחָרָנָא אָמַר אָֽכְלוּ כְזַיִת זֶהוּ בִּתְחִילָּה. גָּֽמְרוּ אֲכִילָתָן זֶהוּ בְּסוֹף.

Halakha 1: Here[11] it has been said "they are not allowed to split" and here it has been said "they are required to 'invite'"[12]. Samuel said, one is at the start and one is at the end. What means "beginning" and what means "end"? Two Amoraïm; one said if they decided to eat together that is the start[13], when they ate the volume of an olive that is the end[14]. But the other one said, if they ate the volume of an olive that is the start[15], when they finished their meal that is the end[16].

11 Mishnah 5: Three who ate together are not allowed to split. [There the emphasis is on the fact that six people who ate together may split into two groups of three.] The Yerushalmi is discussed at length by *Tosaphot Berakhot* 45a and *Talmid Rabbenu Jonah*, *Rosh* on Mishnah 5.

12 The two Mishnayot seem to say the same thing, so one of them would be superfluous.

13 They are no longer allowed to split.

14 They are required to recite Grace together with the formal "invitation."

15 They are no longer allowed to eat each one for himself.

16 They must recite Grace together; if one of them finishes early he is not allowed to recite Grace for himself and then leave.

רִבִּי אַבָּא בְּשֵׁם רַב הוּנָא רִבִּי זְעִירָא בְּשֵׁם אַבָּא בַּר יִרְמְיָה שְׁלֹשָׁה חוֹבָה שְׁנַיִם רְשׁוּת. אֲמָרָהּ רִבִּי זְעִירָא קוֹמֵי רִבִּי יָסָא. אָמַר לֵיהּ אֲנִי אֵין לִי אֶלָּא מִשְׁנָה שְׁלֹשָׁה שֶׁאָכְלוּ כְּאַחַת חַייָבִין לְזַמֵּן. רַבָּנָן דְּהָכָא כְּדַעְתּוֹן. רַבָּנָן דְּהָתָם כְּדַעְתּוֹן. שְׁמוּאֵל אָמַר שְׁנַיִם שֶׁדָּנוּ דִּינָן דִּין אֶלָּא שֶׁהוּא נִקְרָא בֵּית דִּין חָצוּף. רִבִּי יוֹחָנָן וְרִבִּי שִׁמְעוֹן בֶּן לָקִישׁ תְּרַוֵּיהוֹן אָמְרִין אֲפִילוּ שְׁנַיִם שֶׁדָּנוּ אֵין דִּינָן דִּין.

Rebbi Abba in the name of Rav Huna, Rebbi Zeïra in the name of Abba bar Jeremiah: Three are required, two have permission. Rebbi Zeïra said this before Rebbi Yasa. He said to him: I have only the Mishnah, three who ate together are required to "invite"[17]. The rabbis of here stick by their opinion, the rabbis of there[18] stick by their opinion. Samuel said, two who judged, their judgment is valid but they are called an insolent court. Rebbi Yoḥanan and Rebbi Simeon ben Laqish both say, two who judged, their judgment is invalid.

17 But two may not recite Grace together with the formula of invitation. The Babli (45a/b) comes to the same conclusion that the old tradition of Babylonia was that two may say Grace together but three must do it, but the Israeli tradition was always to exclude two if three are required.

18 Babylonia. The disagreement between Samuel and R. Yoḥanan / R. Simeon ben Laqish belongs to tractate *Sanhedrin*; in Babli *Sanhedrin* (5b/6a) this is a disagreement between Samuel and Rebbi Abbahu, student of R. Simeon ben Laqish and R. Yoḥanan. The Babli (*Berakhot* 45b) only hints that the difference has its roots in different local traditions.

רַב הוּנָא אָמַר שְׁלֹשָׁה שֶׁאָכְלוּ זֶה בִּפְנֵי עַצְמוֹ וְזֶה בִּפְנֵי עַצְמוֹ וְזֶה בִּפְנֵי עַצְמוֹ וְנִתְעָרְבוּ מְזַמְּנִין. רַב חִסְדָּא אָמַר וְהֵן שֶׁבָּאוּ מִשָּׁלֹשׁ חֲבוּרוֹת. עַל דַּעְתֵּיהּ דְּרִבִּי זְעִירָא וַחֲבוּרָתֵיהּ וְהֵן שֶׁאָכְלוּ שְׁלֹשָׁה כְּאַחַת. רִבִּי יוֹנָה עַל הֲדָא דְּרַב הוּנָא הִטְבִּיל שָׁלֹשׁ אֵיזוֹבוֹת זֶה בִּפְנֵי עַצְמוֹ וְזֶה בִּפְנֵי עַצְמוֹ וְנִתְעָרְבוּ מַזֶּה בָּהֶן. רַב חִסְדָּא אָמַר וְהֵן שֶׁבָּאוּ מִשָּׁלֹשׁ חֲבִילוֹת. עַל דַּעְתֵּיהּ דְּרִבִּי זְעִירָא וַחֲבוּרָתֵיהּ וְהֵן שֶׁהִטְבִּיל שְׁלָשְׁתָּן כְּאַחַת. אִין תֵּימַר אֵין לְמֵידִין אֵזוֹב מִבְּרָכָה.

וַאֲנָן חֲזִינָן רַבָּנָן קַיְימִין בְּסוּכָּה וְיַלְפִין מִטִּיט הַנָּרוּק. כְּיֵי דְתַנִּינָן תַּמָּן הִרְחִיק אֶת הַסִּיכּוּךְ מִן הַדְּפָנוֹת שְׁלֹשָׁה טְפָחִים פְּסוּלָה. הָא פָחוֹת מִיכֵּן כְּשֵׁירָה. מַהוּ לִישָׁן תַּחְתָּיו. הָתִיב רִבִּי יִצְחָק בֶּן אֶלְיָשׁוּב הֲרֵי טִיט הַנָּרוּק מַשְׁלִים בְּמִקְוֶה וְאֵין מַטְבִּילִין בּוֹ. אַף הָכָא מַשְׁלִים בְּסוּכָּה וְאֵין יְשֵׁינִין תַּחְתָּיו.

Rav Huna said, three who ate each one by himself[19] and then came together[20] do "invite". Rav Ḥisda said, only if they came from three groups[21]. According to the opinion of Rebbi Zeïra[22] and his group, only if all three ate together[23]. Rebbi Jonah on that of Rav Huna: If he dipped three stalks of hyssop each one by himself and then took them together, he may sprinkle with it[24]. Rav Ḥisda said, only if they came from three bundles. According to the opinion of Rebbi Zeïra and his group, only if all three were dipped together. If you want to say that we do not infer rules of hyssop from rules of benedictions, do we not see the rabbis deal with *sukkah* and learn from pourable mud?[25]. As we have stated (Mishnah *Sukkah* 1:10): "If the roofing was three hand-breadths away from the walls it is invalid.[26]" Hence less than that is acceptable. May one sleep under that[27]? Rebbi Isaac ben Elyashib[28] answered, pourable mud completes a *miqweh*[29] but one may not immerse in it, here also it completes the *sukkah* but one may not sleep under it.

19 Different food at different tables, or at one table but they are strangers to one another and each one eats his own food that he brought with him. The disagreement between Rav Huna and Rav Ḥisda is explained differently in the Babli, 50a.

20 At one table (or on one group of couches) befor they recited Grace.

21 Every one of the three was required to recite Grace with "invitation"; he may fulfill his obligation even in another group. But if three people were not obligated to "invite" during their meal they cannot become subject to "inviting" after they had finished eating.

22 Here he is called by his Babylonian name זירא since, under the influence of Accadic, the Jews in

Babylonia early on had lost the sound of ע. While his Israeli name appears in the list of R. Jonah, the entire piece seems to have had a Babylonian editor; so it uses the Babylonian Aramaic חזי "to see" instead of the usual Israeli חמי.

23 From the start. (In the Babli, 50a, this is the opinion of Samuel, but here it is the opinion only of the rabbis in Israel). Connected with this is the *Tosephta* (*Berakhot* 5:23, cf. end of Halakhah 5) that people in a caravan, if they eat while walking, cannot recite Grace together even if they all ate from the same food, but if they sit together at a rest stop, they must recite Grace together even if everyone ate his own provisions. In contrast to the Babli, the Yerushalmi never entertains the thought that for common Grace one would have to lie down on couches.

24 Used for cleansing a person or utensils impure by contact with a corpse; cleansing needs sprinkling with a bunch of hyssop that was dipped in water in which some of the ashes of a red heifer were dissolved (*Num.* 19, Mishnah *Parah*). A "bunch" is a minimum of three stalks. The opinions here are attributed to the older authorities by Rebbi Jonah.

25 This proof that one requires logical consistency even in fields that are rather remote from each other is also a belated justification of the previous comparison of the rules of Grace with the composition of a court of law.

26 The essence of the *sukkah* is that its roof must be botanical (but only materials that cannot become ritually unclean). The branches or other material must be arranged so that there is more shadow than sun inside the *sukkah*. If there is a place where that condition is not satisfied for three hand-breadths horizontally from a wall, the *sukkah* cannot be used to fulfill the commandment "to dwell" in it (*Lev.* 23:42).

27 The place, less than two hand-breadths wide, under which there is more sun than shadow. Instead of sleeping, the question could have been asked about eating.

28 An Israeli Amora of the fourth generation, colleague of Rebbi Mana; a holy man and worker of miracles.

29 A ritual bath can be used for cleansing impurities only if it contains 40 *seäh*, about 135 gallons. If there is not enough clear water, the desired volume can be obtained by adding mud that is so moist that it can be poured from a bucket (Mishnah *Miqwaöt* 7:1). The complete argument is in Yerushalmi *Sukkah* 1:10, Babli *Sukkah* 19a.

שְׁלֹשָׁה שֶׁאָכְלוּ כְּאַחַת וּבִקֵּשׁ אֶחָד מֵהֶן לֵילֵךְ לוֹ רַב אָמַר יְבָרֵךְ בְּרָכָה רִאשׁוֹנָה וְיֵלֶךְ לוֹ. אֵי זוּ הִיא בְּרָכָה רִאשׁוֹנָה. דְּבֵית רַב אָמְרוּ זוּ בִּרְכַּת הַזִּימּוּן. רִבִּי זְעִירָא בְּשֵׁם רַב יִרְמְיָה זוּ הַזָּן אֶת הַכֹּל. רִבִּי חֶלְבּוֹ רַב חָנָן בְּשֵׁם רַב זוּ הַזָּן אֶת הַכֹּל. הָתִיב רַב שֵׁשֶׁת וְהָא מַתְנִיתָא פְלִיגָא שְׁנַיִם שְׁלֹשָׁה חַייָבִין בְּבִרְכַּת הַזִּימּוּן. אִין תֵּימַר בִּרְכַּת זִימּוּן רִאשׁוֹנָה נִתְנֵי אַרְבָּעָה. אַשְׁכְּחָן תַּנֵּי אַרְבָּעָה. אִין תֵּימַר זוּ הַזָּן אֶת הַכֹּל קַשְׁיָא. אִין תֵּימַר זוּ הַטּוֹב וְהַמֵּטִיב. לֵית אַתְּ יָכִיל. שַׁנְייָא דְּאָמַר רַב חוּנָא מִשֶּׁנִּיתְּנוּ הֲרוּגֵי בֵיתָר לִקְבוּרָה נִקְבְּעָא הַטּוֹב וְהַמֵּטִיב. הַטּוֹב שֶׁלֹּא נִסְרְחוּ וְהַמֵּטִיב שֶׁנִּיתְּנוּ לִקְבוּרָה. אָמַר רַב חוּנָא תִּיפְתָּר כְּרִבִּי יִשְׁמָעֵאל דְּרִבִּי יִשְׁמָעֵאל אָמַר הַטּוֹב וְהַמֵּטִיב דְּבַר תּוֹרָה דִּכְתִיב וְאָכַלְתָּ וְשָׂבָעְתָּ וּבֵרַכְתָּ זוּ בִּרְכַּת הַזִּימּוּן. אֶת יי אֱלֹהֶיךָ זוּ הַזָּן אֶת הַכֹּל. עַל הָאָרֶץ זוּ בִּרְכַּת הָאָרֶץ. הַטּוֹבָה זוּ בִּרְכַּת בּוֹנֵה יְרוּשָׁלַיִם. וְכֵן הוּא אוֹמֵר הָהָר הַטּוֹב הַזֶּה וְהַלְּבָנוֹן. אֲשֶׁר נָתַן לָךְ זֶה הַטּוֹב וְהַמֵּטִיב.

Three who ate together and one wants to leave, Rav said he should recite the first benediction, then he may leave. What is the first benediction? In the Yeshivah of Rav[30] they said, the benediction of invitation. Rebbi Zeïra in the name of Rav Jeremiah: that is "He Who feeds all."[31] Rebbi Ḥelbo, Rav Ḥanan in the name of Rav: that is "He Who feeds all." Rav Sheshet objected, but a *baraita* disagrees: "Two, three are obliged to recite Grace.[32]" If you want to say the benediction of invitation is the first one, one should state "four." They found stated "four." If you want to say this is "He Who feeds all", it is difficult. If you want to say that it[33] is "He Who is good and does good", you cannot do that, there is a difference[34] because Rav Huna said that "He Who is good and does good" was fixed[35] after permission was received to bury the slain of Betar[36], "He Who is good" because the dead did not decompose and "He Who does good" that they could be buried. Rav Huna said, you may explain it following Rebbi Ismael since Rebbi Ismael said[37], "He Who is good and does good" is an obligation from the Torah as it is written (*Deut.*

8:10): *You will eat and be satiated, then you must praise*, that is the benediction of invitation; *the Eternal, your God,* that is "He Who feeds all"[38]; *for the Land*, that is the benediction over the Land; *the good one*, that is the benediction "builder of Jerusalem" [and so it says (*Deut.* 3:25) "this good mountain and the Lebanon[39]"]; *that He gave you*, that is "He Who is good and does good".

30 After Rav's death.

31 The first benediction of Grace when recited without "invitation". It seems that Rebbi Zeïra also agrees that the one who wants to leave has to recite the benediction "of invitation" aloud so that the other two may answer and fulfill their duty to recite Grace with "invitation"; the disagreement is only about how much he has to recite aloud, whether only the "invitation" or also the first benediction of Grace proper. [If all three recite Grace together, the one who recites the "invitation" has to recite all of Grace aloud; this custom has disappeared in Eastern European Ashkenazic Jewry after the invention of printing and the availability of inexpensive prayer books for everyone.]

32 It is generally agreed that ברכת הזימון is a scribal error and that the correct reading is that of Alfassi ברכת המזון "Grace". The explanation of the elliptic *baraita* is according to Alfassi: If two or three people sit together and neither of them knows how to recite the entire Grace but each of them knows one or two benedictions that the others do not, then they take turns in reciting the benedictions and they all have fulfilled their obligations, the one reciting by pronouncing the benediction and the others by listening and answering "Amen". The numbers are important to show that we require one person to recite an entire benediction; it is not permissible to split one benediction among several people. Hence, the maximal number of people who can share in reciting Grace is the number of benedictions in Grace.

33 The fourth benediction according to him who requires the first benediction to include "He Who feeds all."

34 Between the first three benedictions that are Torah obligations and the fourth one who seems to be Rabbinic in character.

35 It says "fixed", not "instituted" as in the parallel in the Babli (48b). According to the Yerushalmi, the

fourth benediction is old, probably Biblical, but it was not permanently required in earlier times; the problem is discussed in the author's *The Scholar's Haggadah* (Northvale NJ, 1995) p. 358-359.

36 Roman law did not allow the burial of rebels against the government. Hence, the dead of Betar, the last of Bar Kokhba's fortresses, could certainly not be buried during Hadrian's lifetime. It is not known which of his successors gave permission to bury the dead. We may assume that it was the same emperor who permitted the re-establishment of the Synhedrion.

37 *Mekhilta deR. Ismael* Ba 16.

38 Since the name "God" represents God as Creator of the physical world.

39 "Lebanon" means the Temple; this identification goes back at least to the time of Rabban Yoḥanan ben Zakkai who predicted to Vespasian that he would become emperor, since he would destroy the Temple and it is written (*Is.* 10:34) "the Lebanon will fall through a powerful one" (Babli *Giṭṭin* 56b; Yerushalmi sources: *Abot deR. Nathan* 4, *Midrash Ekha rabba* 1).

כָּתוּב בַּתּוֹרָה בְּרָכָה לְפָנֶיהָ וְאֵין כָּתוּב בַּתּוֹרָה בְּרָכָה לְאַחֲרֶיהָ. מַה כָּתוּב בָּהּ לְפָנֶיהָ כִּי שֵׁם יי אֶקְרָא הָבוּ גוֹדֶל לֵאלֹהֵינוּ. כְּתִיב בְּמָזוֹן בְּרָכָה לְאַחֲרֶיהָ וְאֵין כָּתוּב לְפָנָיו. מַה כְּתִיב לְאַחֲרָיו וְאָכַלְתָּ וְשָׂבָעְתָּ וּבֵרַכְתָּ. וּמְנַיִין לִיתֵּן אֶת הָאָמוּר בְּזֶה בְּזֶה וְאֶת הָאָמוּר בְּזֶה בְּזֶה. רִבִּי שְׁמוּאֵל בַּר נַחְמָנִי בְּשֵׁם רִבִּי יוֹנָתָן אַתְיָא שֵׁם שֵׁם לִגְזֵרָה שָׁוָה. מַה שֵּׁם שֶׁנֶּאֱמַר בַּתּוֹרָה בְּרָכָה לְפָנָיו אַף שֵׁם שֶׁנֶּאֱמַר בְּמָזוֹן בְּרָכָה לְפָנָיו. וּמַה שֵּׁם שֶׁנֶּאֱמַר בְּמָזוֹן בְּרָכָה לְאַחֲרָיו. אַף שֵׁם שֶׁנֶּאֱמַר בַּתּוֹרָה בְּרָכָה לְאַחֲרֶיהָ. עַד כְּדוֹן כְּרִבִּי עֲקִיבָה כְּרִבִּי יִשְׁמָעֵאל. רִבִּי יוֹחָנָן בְּשֵׁם רִבִּי יִשְׁמָעֵאל קַל וָחוֹמֶר. מַה אִם מָזוֹן שֶׁאֵין טָעוּן בְּרָכָה לְפָנָיו טָעוּן בְּרָכָה לְאַחֲרָיו תּוֹרָה שֶׁהִיא טְעוּנָה בְּרָכָה לְפָנֶיהָ. אֵינוֹ דִין שֶׁתְּהֵא טְעוּנָה בְּרָכָה לְאַחֲרֶיהָ. עַד כְּדוֹן תּוֹרָה. מָזוֹן מַה. אִם תּוֹרָה שֶׁאֵינָהּ טְעוּנָה בְּרָכָה לְאַחֲרֶיהָ טְעוּנָה בְּרָכָה לְפָנֶיהָ. מָזוֹן שֶׁהוּא טָעוּן בְּרָכָה לְאַחֲרָיו. אֵינוֹ דִין שֶׁטָּעוּן בְּרָכָה לְפָנָיו. רִבִּי יִצְחָק וְרִבִּי נָתָן אָמַר כִּי הוּא יְבָרֵךְ אֶת הַזֶּבַח אַחֲרֵי כֵן יֹאכְלוּ הַקְּרוּאִים. רִבִּי נָתָן אוֹמֵר וַעֲבַדְתֶּם אֶת יי אֱלֹהֵיכֶם וּבֵרַךְ אֶת לַחְמְךָ וְאֶת מֵימֶיךָ. אֵימָתַי הוּא קָרוּי לַחְמְךָ וְאֶת מֵימֶיךָ. עַד שֶׁלֹּא אָכַלְתָּ. רִבִּי אוֹמֵר מַה אִם בְּשָׁעָה שֶׁאָכַל וְשָׂבַע צָרִיךְ לְבָרֵךְ בְּשָׁעָה שֶׁהוּא תָאֵב לֶאֱכֹל לֹא כָל־שֶׁכֵּן.

עַד כְּדוֹן מָזוֹן. תּוֹרָה מַה. אִם מָזוֹן שֶׁאֵינוֹ אֶלָּא חַיֵּי שָׁעָה טָעוּן בְּרָכָה לְפָנָיו וּלְאַחֲרָיו. תּוֹרָה שֶׁהִיא חַיֵּי עַד לֹא כָּל־שֶׁכֵּן.

For Torah[40] there is written a benediction before, but no benediction is written after. What is written before it? (*Deut.* 32:3) "For I am invoking the name of the Eternal, attribute greatness to our God." For food there is written a benediction after, but no benediction is written before. What is written after it? (*Deut.* 8:10): "You will eat and be satiated, then you must praise". From where that which is said about one on the other and vice-versa? Rebbi Samuel bar Naḥmani in the name of Rebbi Jonathan: The Name is mentioned in both verses as parallel expressions[41]. Just as the Name that is mentioned concerning Torah implies a benediction before, so the Name that is mentioned concerning food implies a benediction before. And just as the Name that is mentioned concerning food implies a benediction after, so the Name that is mentioned concerning Torah implies a benediction after. That follows Rebbi Aqiba[42]. What following Rebbi Ismael? Rebbi Yoḥanan in the name of Rebbi Ismael, an inference from the lesser to the greater[43]. If food that needs no explicit benediction before, needs a benediction afterwards, regarding Torah that needs a benediction before, it is only logical that it should need a benediction afterwards. That works for Torah; what about food? If Torah that needs no benediction afterwards, needs a benediction before, regarding food that needs a benediction afterwards, it is only logical that it should need a benediction before. Rebbi Isaac and Rebbi Nathan say, (*1Sam.* 9:13): "For he will recite the benediction over the sacrifice and after that the invited guests will eat."[44] Rebbi Nathan[45] said, (*Ex.* 23:24) "you shall serve the Eternal, your God and give praise for your bread and your water"; when is it called your bread and your water, before you eat[46]. Rebbi said, if he has to give praise when he ate and is satiated, so much more at a time when he is hungry for food. That is for food, what about Torah? If food, which sustains only temporary life, needs a benediction before and after, Torah, which sustains eternal life, so much more[47].

40 Torah study, including Torah reading.

41 In general, it is assumed in the system of Rebbi Aqiba that a word can have only one meaning. A stronger implication, agreed to by all tannaïtic authorities, is a "parallel expression". The formal definition of the school of R. Ismael is that *if* one has a tradition that two equal or synonymous expressions are written in the Torah for purposes of comparison and *if* these two words are not used for any other inference, *then* all laws connected with one word apply to the other and vice-versa. The derivation here does not fulfill these conditions; hence, it is labelled to follow the rules of R. Aqiba who is not known to require too much formality in case the verse is used to give a biblical base to an old tradition.

42 Who is an exponent of intensional interpretation, whereas R. Ismael is an exponent of extensional interpretation. The rules of R. Ismael are systematized in his "13 rules" given in the introduction to the halakhic Midrash *Sifra* on *Leviticus*. The problem of both Rebbi Aqiba and Rebbi Ismael is that in its mishnaic-talmudic form, the rules of Jewish conduct form a logically consistent whole. It was shown earlier in this chapter, Notes 24 - 29, that rules must be consistent from one application to the next, such as rules of Grace and forming a court of law. But the basis of these laws, the words of the Torah, are unsystematic, fragmentary, and sometimes appear contradictory. Hence, one needs a method of translating the aphoristic text of the Torah in a legally consistent new language; cf. the author's *Logical problems in Jewish tradition*, in: Confrontations with Judaism, ed. P. Longworth, Blond, London 1966, 171-196. The rules are discussed in the medieval texts *Introduction to the Talmud* by R. Samuel Hanaggid and *Sefer Keritut* of R. Simson of Sens.

43 קל וחומר, the first rule of R. Ismael. If there are two commandments, A and B, and if every rule for A is no more stringent than the corresponding rule for B, then a rule expressed for A that has no equivalent for B is valid also for

B. The Babli (21a) quotes the following *qal wahomer* in the name of R. Yoḥanan only and points out that the application here is not justified since it is self-contradictory. The Yerushalmi seems to be of the opinion that in the formulation given here, with "not more stringent" instead of "less stringent", the argument is logically admissible.

44 In the Babli (48b) and in the *Mekhilta* (*loc. cit.*) this is given in the name of R. Nathan only. A verse from Samuel (Biblical but not Pentateuchal) cannot prove a commandment but can prove a practice.

45 In the Babli and the Mekhilta, this appears in the name of Rebbi Isaac.

46 The full verse seems to read: "You shall serve the Eternal, your God, then He will bless your bread and your water and I will remove sickness from your midst." The switch from third to first person is awkward in any case. In the Babli (in particular, in the Sephardic incunabula print) it is spelled out: Do not read וּבֵרַךְ "He will bless" but וּבָרֵךְ "and praise". However, the Bible Concordance of G. Lisowsky (Stuttgart 1958) takes the verse, as it stands, to mean "You shall serve the Eternal, your God, and praise for your bread and your water, then I will remove sickness from your midst." One may recite a benediction one one's bread and one's water only before it is consumed; afterwards one may speak only of nourishment and sustenance.

47 In the Babli and the *Mekhilta* this is a קל וחומר of Rebbi Ismael.

רִבִּי זְעוּרָא בְּעִי (fol. 11b) אִילֵּין שְׁלֹשׁ קְרוּיוֹת מַה אַתְּ עֲבִיד לוֹן. כִּשְׁלֹשָׁה שֶׁאָכְלוּ כְּאַחַת. אוֹ כִשְׁלֹשָׁה שֶׁאָכְלוּ זֶה בִפְנֵי עַצְמוֹ וְזֶה בִּפְנֵי עַצְמוֹ וְזֶה בִּפְנֵי עַצְמוֹ. אִין תַּעַבְדִּינוּן כִּשְׁלֹשָׁה שֶׁאָכְלוּ כְּאַחַת. הָרִאשׁוֹן מְבָרֵךְ בְּרָכָה רִאשׁוֹנָה. וְהָאַחֲרוֹן בְּרָכָה אַחֲרוֹנָה. וְהָאֶמְצָעִי אֵינוֹ מְבָרֵךְ כָּל־עִיקָּר. אִין תַּעַבְדִּינוּן כִּשְׁלֹשָׁה שֶׁאָכְלוּ זֶה בִפְנֵי עַצְמוֹ וְזֶה בִּפְנֵי עַצְמוֹ וְזֶה בִּפְנֵי עַצְמוֹ. אֲפִילוּ הָאֶמְצָעִי מְבָרֵךְ לְפָנָיו וּלְאַחֲרָיו. אָמַר רִבִּי שְׁמוּאֵל בַּר אֶבְדֵּימִי לֹא לָמְדוּ בִּרְכַּת הַתּוֹרָה מִבִּרְכַּת הַמָּזוֹן אֶלָּא לְרַבִּים. וְאִם לְרַבִּים אֲפִילוּ בֵינוֹ לְבֵין עַצְמוֹ לֹא יְבָרֵךְ. אָמַר רִבִּי אַבָּא מָרִי אַחֲוֵי דְּרִבִּי יוֹסֵי עֲשָׂאוּהָ כִּשְׁאָר כָּל־הַמִּצְוֹת שֶׁל תּוֹרָה. מַה שְּׁאָר כָּל־הַמִּצְוֹת טְעוּנוֹת בְּרָכָה. אַף זוֹ טְעוּנָה בְרָכָה.

Rebbi Zeïra asked: These three that are called[48], how are you treating them? As three who ate together or as three who ate each one for himself? If you treat them as three who ate together then the first one recites the benediction before, the last one recites the benediction after, and the middle one does not recite any benediction at all. If you treat them as three who ate each one for himself then even the middle one recites benedictions before and after. Rebbi Samuel ben Eudaimon said, they did learn the benedictions for the Torah from Grace[49] only in public[50]. If in public, then in private one should not recite any benediction! Rebbi Abba Mari, the brother of Rebbi Yose[51], said: They made it equal to other commandments of the Torah. Just as other commandments of the Torah need benedictions, this also needs a benediction[52].

48 For reading the Torah in public. Since the preceding arguments tied benedictions over Torah reading to Grace, one has to ask in which way they are comparable. In the Babli *Megillah* 21b there is a *baraita*: "(In reading the Torah) he who starts recites the benediction before and he who finishes recites the benediction after." On that, the Gemara notes: But today, all recite benedictions before and after. This "today" may be long after the work on the Yerushalmi stopped. In any case, the *baraita* seems to represent the early Babylonian practice; we do not know of any direct Yerushalmi source that let people read the Torah without benediction. Rebbi Zeïra, the Galilean head of academy who had come from Babylonia, is the right person to ask for the reasons and the correct practice. Since his questions remain without answers, both practices might be acceptable. Both the preceding paragraph and R. Zeïra's question presuppose that private Torah reading requires benedictions before and after, cf. מסכת סופרים Chap. 13 and Ezra Fleischer, קטעים מקובצי תפילה ארץ־ישראליים מן הגניזה, קובץ על יד יג (כג) 139-141, 188-189.

49 Text of the parallel in *Megillah* 4:1; the Venice print has here "benediction of 'invitation'", a scribal error הזימון for המזון.

50 R. Samuel ben Eudaimon seems to object to reciting a benediction after Torah study. Also, since Torah study is a permanent obligation (*Jos*. 1:8), one benediction in the morning is enough to

cover all Torah study during the day and evening; one does not have to recite a new benediction for study after an interruption. The prayer manuals of Yerushalmi type (see Note 48) which have benedictions after the reading of Pentateuch, Prophets, and Hagiographs require these only for reading the Bible, not oral Torah study.

51 An Amora of the fourth generation who is never mentioned in the Babli.

52 Most commandments need only a benediction before, not after their execution. Thus, the benediction for the Torah in private study follows the general rule of benedictions over commandments. The quote for benediction for the Torah before the reading, *Deut.* 32:3, is clearly addressed to the public and, therefore, not applicable to private study.

אָכַל דְּמַאי. הֲדָא אָמְרָה אָכַל פֵּירוֹת סָפֵק נִיתַקְּנוּ סָפֵק לֹא נִיתַקְּנוּ מְזַמְּנִין. אָמַר רִבִּי שִׁמְעוֹן אַחֲוֵי דְּרִבִּי בֶּרֶכְיָה. בְּשָׁעָה שֶׁגָּזְרוּ עַל הַדְּמַאי רוֹב עַמֵּי הָאָרֶץ הָיוּ מַכְנִיסִין לְבָתֵּיהֶן. וַיי דָא אָמְרָה דָא כּוּתִי מְזַמְּנִין עָלָיו. וְאָהֵן כּוּתִי לָאו סָפֵק הוּא. אָמַר רִבִּי אַבָּא תִּיפְתָּר כְּמַן דָּמַר כּוּתִי כְּגוֹי דִּבְרֵי רִבִּי. רַבָּן שִׁמְעוֹן בֶּן גַּמְלִיאֵל אוֹמֵר כּוּתִי כְּיִשְׂרָאֵל לְכָל־דָּבָר.

"If one ate *demay*."[53] This means that, if one ate produce which perhaps was tithed[54] and perhaps was not tithed, one invites him. Rebbi Simeon, the brother of Rebbi Berekhiah[55]: At the time when they were instituting *demai*, most of the unlearned brought the harvest into their houses[56]. Which one says that[57]? "One invites the Samaritan." And is that Samaritan not doubtful[58]? Rebbi Abba said, explain it following what is said[59]: A Samaritan is like a Gentile, the words of Rebbi. Rabban Simeon ben Gamliel says, a Samaritan is like a Jew in all respects.

53 Quote from the Mishnah.

54 Food of which *terumah* and *terumah of the tithe* were taken so that it may be consumed without incurring guilt

55 He is not otherwise mentioned in the Talmud.

56 The obligation to give *terumah* and tithe starts when produce is brought through the door of the house

(or barn). The expression here implies that most of the unlearned followed the rules and ate only produce that was in order; only because of the severity of the offense of eating *ṭevel* was the rule of *demai* decreed since a minority of uneducated did not follow the rules for produce sold; in that case the probablity of having produce that was not in order was less than 50%. There is therefore no inference possible for the problem under discussion, where the probability of things being wrong is 50%.

57 Which part of the Mishnah does speak to our problem?

58 Since Samaritans do not follow rabbinic rules, we cannot check on the status of their produce.

59 Referring to the opinion of Rabban Simeon ben Gamliel in the *baraita;* for him the Mishnah simply declares that Samaritans are counted as Jews and no inference is possible for our case. The question is left without answer.

משנה ב: נָשִׁים וַעֲבָדִים וּקְטַנִּים אֵין מְזַמְּנִין עֲלֵיהֶן. עַד כַּמָּה מְזַמְּנִין עַד כְּזַיִת. רִבִּי יְהוּדָה אוֹמֵר עַד כְּבֵיצָה.

Mishnah 2: One does not 'invite'[60] women, slaves, and minors. What is the minimum to 'invite'? Down to the size of an olive, Rebbi Yehudah says to the size of an egg[61].

60 To recite the invitation aloud and to count them for a group of three. [The Babli notes that women for themselves and slaves for themselves may recite Grace with "invitation"; we cannot know what was the position of the Yerushalmi in that matter.]

61 That the total food consumed by each person is at least the volume of an average olive or chicken egg.

הלכה ב: רִבִּי סִימוֹן בְּשֵׁם רִבִּי יְהוֹשֻׁעַ בֶּן לֵוִי רִבִּי יוֹסֵי בֶּן שָׁאוּל בְּשֵׁם רִבִּי קָטָן עוֹשִׂין אוֹתוֹ סְנִיף לַעֲשָׂרָה. וְהָתַנֵּי אֵין מְדַקְדְּקִין בְּקָטָן. אָמַר רִבִּי יוֹסֵי קַיְּימָא רִבִּי סִימוֹן רִבִּי חֲנִינָא רִבִּי סִימוֹן בְּשֵׁם רִבִּי יְהוֹשֻׁעַ בֶּן לֵוִי לִשְׁנֵי קְטַנִּים נִצְרְכָה. שֶׁאִם הָיָה קָטָן עוֹשִׂין אוֹתוֹ וַדַּאי. סָפֵק עוֹשִׂין אוֹתוֹ סָפֵק. רִבִּי יְהוּדָה בַּר פָּזִי

בְּשֵׁם רִבִּי יוֹסֵי תִּשְׁעָה נִרְאִין כַּעֲשָׂרָה מַה מְזַמְּנִין מְסוּיְּימִין. אֶלָּא אֲפִילוּ קָטָן בֵּינֵיהֶן.

Halakhah 2: Rebbi Simon in the name of Rebbi Joshua ben Levi, Rebbi Yose ben Shaul in the name of Rebbi: One makes a minor an appendix for ten[62]. But did we not state: One does not investigate a minor[63]? Rebbi Yose said, one confirms Rebbi Simon, Rebbi Ḥanina, Rebbi Simon in the name of Rebbi Joshua ben Levi[64]: it[65] is needed for two minors; if he is a minor, one considers him doubtful, if he is doubtful[66], one considers him certain. Rebbi Yehudah ben Pazi in the name of Rebbi Yose: nine that look like ten[67], does one "invite" only those that are certain? Also if a minor was among them?

62 The next Mishnah explains that the formula of "invitation" for three is "let us praise Him of Whose bounty we ate" whereas for ten it is "let us praise our God of Whose bounty we ate". The question is whether the ten all have to be male adults or whether they have to be just ten males (of which nine are certain adults and the tenth possibly a minor as "appendix".) In the Babli (47b/48a), R. Joshua ben Levi is quoted as permitting the tenth (for reciting Grace) even to be a baby lying in a crib. However, from the continuation of the discussion here it seems that the Yerushalmi does not even consider allowing a minor to join for the long form of "invitation" but only for Torah reading or other *public* services.

Rebbi Yose ben Shaul was a student of Rebbi. He transmits sayings of Rebbi only.

63 One version of the full *baraita* is quoted in Babli 47b: "A minor who grew two pubic hairs may take part in 'invitation', a minor who did not grow two pubic hairs may not take part in 'invitation' but one does not investigate a minor." The other version is in Tosephta *Berakhot* 5:18: "A minor who can eat an olive may take part in 'invitation', a minor who cannot eat an olive may not take part in 'invitation'; one does not investigate a minor." Most commentators refer the Yerushalmi to the version in Berakhot but it seems clear that the Yerushalmi is based on a text close to the Tosephta and

emphatically disagrees with the Babli, cf. *Tosephta Kifshutah, ad loc.*

64 The entire text is also in *Bereshit rabba* 91; there it says correctly "Rebbi Yose said, one confirms Rebbi Simon in the name of Rebbi Joshua ben Levi".

The last part of the Tosephta implies that if a boy is on the threshhold of manhood (*bar mizwah*), one can make him take part in any ceremony that needs ten adults by simply asking him if he is of age; one does not have to investigate if what he says is true. The implication here is that if one has a boy who looks younger than the age of puberty, one certainly cannot take him as tenth man.

65 The Tosephta which insists that one does not investigate but that the boy should not look too young.

66 If he has reached the age, but we do not know whether he started growing pubic hair. The sentence speaks of all other occasions where one needs ten adult males, such as public prayer and Torah reading, but not of Grace which depends only on whether the child is able to eat an olive-size piece made of grain (in a country and time where children were usually nursed for between three and five years.)

67 Where the Babli (47b) agrees that one may recite the invitation formula for ten adults.

רִבִּי בֶּרֶכְיָה אָמַר רִבִּי יַעֲקֹב בַּר זַבְדִּי בְּעָא קוֹמֵי רִבִּי יוֹסֵי בְּמַה דְּבָרִים אֲמוּרִים תַּמָּן קָטָן עוֹשִׂין אוֹתוֹ סְנִיפִין לַעֲשָׂרָה. וָמַר אַף הָכָא עוֹשִׂין אוֹתוֹ סְנִיף לִשְׁלֹשָׁה. מַה תַּמָּן שֶׁמַּזְכִּירִין אֶת הַשֵּׁם עוֹשִׂין אוֹתוֹ סְנִיף. כַּאן שֶׁאֵין מַזְכִּירִין אֶת הַשֵּׁם לֹא כָּל־שֶׁכֵּן. אָמַר לֵיהּ וְהָא אֵינוֹ כָּל־שֶׁכֵּן. תַּמָּן עַל יְדֵי שֶׁהֵן אוֹמְרִים אֶת הַשֵּׁם עוֹשִׂין אוֹתוֹ סְנִיף. וְכַאן שֶׁאֵין קוֹרִין אֶת הַשֵּׁם אֵין עוֹשִׂין אוֹתוֹ סְנִיף.

Rebbi Berekhiah said that Rebbi Jacob bar Zavdi asked before Rebbi Yose: "What are we dealing with? There[68] one makes him an appendix for ten, one should say that here[69] one should make him an appendix for three. Since there one makes him an appendix for the mention of the Divine Name, here, when one does not mention the Divine Name, *a fortiori* should one make him an appendix." He answered him: "It is not *a fortiori*! There, since they must mention the Name[70], one makes him an appendix; here, since one does not recite the Name[71], there is no need to make him an appendix!"

68 In the case of public reading of the Torah, as given in the next paragraph.

69 Reciting Grace.

70 In an obligatory public service.

71 In private.

תַּנֵּי קָטָן וְסֵפֶר תּוֹרָה עוֹשִׂין אוֹתוֹ סְנִיף. אָמַר רִבִּי יוּדָן כֵּינִי מַתְנִיתָא קָטָן לְסֵפֶר תּוֹרָה עוֹשִׂין אוֹתוֹ סְנִיף.

It has been stated: One may take a minor and a Torah scroll as appendix. Rebbi Judan said: So is the *baraita*: One may take a minor as appendix for the purpose of Torah reading[72].

72 But the Torah scroll is not a human and one never will get by with only eight adult males. The original *baraita* is close to a statement of Rav Huna in the Babli (47b) which there is corrected differently.

מֵאֵימָתַי עוֹשִׂין אוֹתוֹ סְנִיף. רִבִּי אֲבִינָא אֲמַר אִיתְפַּלְּגוּן רַב חוּנָא וְרַב יְהוּדָה תְּרֵוַיְהוֹן בְּשֵׁם שְׁמוּאֵל. חַד אָמַר כְּדֵי שֶׁהוּא יוֹדֵעַ טִיב בְּרָכָה. וְחָרָנָא אָמַר שֶׁיְּהֵא יוֹדֵעַ לְמִי הוּא מְבָרֵךְ. אֲמַר רִבִּי נָסָא כַּמָּה זִימְנִין אֲכָלִית עִם רִבִּי תַּחְלִיפָא אַבָּא וְעִם אֲנִינְיָא בַּר סִיסַיי חֲבִיבִי וְלָא זַמְּנִין עָלַי עַד שֶׁהֵבֵאתִי שְׁתֵּי שְׂעָרוֹת.

When does one start to make him an appendix? Rebbi Avina said: Rab Ḥuna and Rav Yehudah disagreed, both in the name of Samuel. One said, that he has to understand the nature of a benediction; the other one said that he has to understand to Whom one has to recite the benediction[73]. Rebbi Nassa said, many times did I eat with my father Taḥlipha and my uncle Aninia bar Sisai and they did not recite the 'invitation' with me until I grew two pubic hairs[74].

73 In the Babli (48a), this is the opinion of Rav Naḥman, another student of Samuel.

74 Since report of an action is the best proof, it is shown that one never uses a minor as appendix for reciting Grace with 'invitation'.

שְׁמוּאֵל בַּר שִׁילַת בְּעָא קוֹמֵי רַב. וְאִית דְּאָֽמְרִין בְּעוֹן קוֹמֵי רִבִּי שְׁמוּאֵל בַּר שִׁילַת. תִּשְׁעָה פַּת וְאֶחָד יֶרֶק. אָמַר לָהֶן מְזַמְּנִין. שְׁמוֹנֶה פַּת וּשְׁתַּיִם יֶרֶק אָמַר לוֹן מְזַמְּנִין. שִׁבְעָה פַּת וּשְׁלֹשָׁה יֶרֶק אָמַר לוֹן מְזַמְּנִין. רִבִּי אֲבִינָא בְּעֵי מֶחְצָה לְמֶחְצָה מַהוּ. אֲמַר רִבִּי זְעִירָא עַד דַּאֲנָא תַּמָּן אִצְרְכַת לִי מֵיצְרִי לִי מִינָךְ לָא שַׁלְתֵּיהּ.

Samuel bar Shilat[75] asked before Rav, but some say that it was asked before Rav Samuel bar Shilat: Nine ate bread and one ate vegetable[76]? He said to them: One 'invites'. Eight ate bread and two ate vegetable? He said to them: One 'invites'. Seven ate bread and two ate vegetable? He said to them: One 'invites'. Rebbi Avina asked: What is the rule for half and half[77]? Rebbi Zeïra said, as long as I was there, I would have needed that. I regret that I did not ask.

75 A student of Rav who is regarded as the ideal teacher in the Babli. For nine years he did not have time to tend his garden because he was caring about the children in his school. The title "Ribbi" given him in the next sentence is a scribal error.

76 Nine are required to recite Grace. The tenth is only required to recite the short formula but he is there to form a quorum of ten adult males for the invocation of the Name.

77 Does one need a majority of those who are required to recite Grace or is it enough to have ten adult males present. In the Babli (48a), Rebbi Zeïra is of the opinion that not only does one need a majority but one even needs a qualified majority and seven is the minimal number for reciting the 'invitation' with the Name.

רִבִּי יִרְמְיָה בְּעֵי אוֹתוֹ שֶׁאָכַל יֶרֶק מַהוּ שֶׁיְּבָרֵךְ. מְחֻלְּפָא שִׁיטָּתֵיהּ דְּרִבִּי יִרְמְיָה. תַּנֵּי שְׁלֹשׁ מֵאוֹת נְזִירִין עָלוּ בִימֵי רִבִּי שִׁמְעוֹן בֶּן שֶׁטַח מֵאָה וַחֲמִשִּׁים מָצָא לָהֶן פֶּתַח. וּמֵאָה וַחֲמִשִּׁים לֹא מָצָא לָהֶן פֶּתַח. אֲתָא גַבֵּי יַנַּאי מַלְכָּא. אֲמַר לֵיהּ אִית הָכָא תְּלַת מְאָה נְזִירִין בְּעְיָין תְּשַׁע מְאוֹת קָרְבָּנִין. אֶלָּא יְהַב אַתְּ פַּלְגָּא מִן דִּידָךְ וַאֲנָא פַּלְגָּא מִן דִּידִי. שְׁלַח לֵיהּ אַרְבַּע מְאָה וְחַמְשִׁין. אֲזַל לִשְׁנָא בִישָׁא וָמַר לֵיהּ לָא יְהַב מִן דִּידֵיהּ כְּלוּם. שָׁמַע יַנַּאי מַלְכָּא וְכָעַס. דְּחַל שִׁמְעוֹן בֶּן שֶׁטַח וְעָרַק. בָּתַר יוֹמִין סָלְקוּן בְּנֵי נַשׁ רַבְרְבִין מִן מַלְכוּתָא דְפָרַס גַּבֵּי יַנַּאי מַלְכָּא. מִן דְּיָתְבִין אָכְלִין אָמְרִין לֵיהּ נְהִירִין אֲנָן דַּהֲוָה אִית הָכָא חַד גְּבַר סָב וַהֲוָה אֲמַר קוֹמִין מִילִּין דְּחָכְמָה. תַּנֵּי לוֹן עוּבְדָא. אָמְרִין לֵיהּ שְׁלַח וְאַיְיתִיתֵיהּ שְׁלַח וִיהִיב לֵיהּ מִילָּא וַאֲתָא וְיָתֵיב בֵּין מַלְכָּא לְמַלְכְּתָא. אֲמַר לֵיהּ לָמָּה אַפְלַיְיָת לִי. אֲמַר לֵיהּ לָא אַפְלָיִית בָּךְ אַתְּ מִמָּמוֹנָךְ וַאֲנָא מִן אוֹרַיְיתִי. דִּכְתִיב כִּי בְּצֵל חָכְמָה בְּצֵל הַכֶּסֶף. אֲמַר לֵיהּ וְלָמָּה עָרַקְתְּ. אֲמַר לֵיהּ שְׁמָעִית דְּמָרִי כָּעַס עָלַי וּבְעִית מְקַיְּימָה הָדֵין קִרְיָיא חֲבִי כִמְעַט רֶגַע עַד יַעֲבָר זָעַם. וּקְרָא עִלּוֹי וְיִתְרוֹן דַּעַת הַחָכְמָה תְּחַיֶּה בְעָלֶיהָ. אֲמַר לֵיהּ וְלָמָּה יָתַבְתְּ בֵּין מַלְכָּא וּמַלְכְּתָא. אֲמַר לֵיהּ בְּסִפְרָא דְּבֶן סִירָא כְּתִיב סַלְסְלֶהָ וּתְרוֹמְמֶךָּ וּבֵין נְגִידִים תּוֹשִׁיבֶךָּ. אֲמַר הָבוּ לֵיהּ כַּסָּא דְּלִיבְרִיךְ. נְסַב כַּסָּא וָמַר נְבָרֵךְ עַל הַמָּזוֹן שֶׁאָכַל יַנַּאי וַחֲבֵירָיו. אֲמַר לֵיהּ עַד כְּדוֹן אַתְּ בְּקַשְׁיוּתָךְ. אֲמַר לֵיהּ וּמַה נֹּאמַר עַל הַמָּזוֹן שֶׁלֹּא אָכַלְנוּ. אֲמַר הָבוּן לֵיהּ דְּלֵיכוּל. יְהָבוּ לֵיהּ וְאָכַל. וָמַר נְבָרֵךְ עַל הַמָּזוֹן שֶׁאָכַלְנוּ. אָמַר רִבִּי יוֹחָנָן חוֹלְקִין עַל רִבִּי שִׁמְעוֹן בֶּן שֶׁטַח. רִבִּי יִרְמְיָה אָמַר עַל הָרִאשׁוֹנָה. רִבִּי אָבָּא אָמַר עַל הַשְּׁנִיָּה. מְחֻלְּפָא שִׁיטָּתֵיהּ דְּרִבִּי יִרְמְיָה. הָתָם צְרִיכָה לֵיהּ. וְהָכָה פְשִׁיטָא לֵיהּ. הֵן דִּצְרִיכָא לֵיהּ כְּרַבָּן הֵן דִּפְשִׁיטָא לֵיהּ כְּרַבָּן שִׁמְעוֹן בֶּן גַּמְלִיאֵל. תַּנֵּי עָלָה הֵיסֵב וְאָכַל עִמָּהֶן אַף עַל פִּי שֶׁלֹּא אָכַל כְּזַיִת דָּגָן מְזַמְּנִין דִּבְרֵי חֲכָמִים. רִבִּי יַעֲקֹב בַּר אַחָא בְּשֵׁם רִבִּי יוֹחָנָן לְעוֹלָם אֵין מְזַמְּנִין עָלָיו עַד שֶׁיֹּאכַל כְּזַיִת דָּגָן. וְהָתַנֵּי שְׁנַיִם פַּת וְאֶחָד יֶרֶק מְזַמְּנִין. מַתְנִיתָה כְּרַבָּן שִׁמְעוֹן בֶּן גַּמְלִיאֵל.

Rebbi Jeremiah asked: May he who ate vegetable recite Grace? Rebbi Jeremiah seems to contradict himself[78]! It has been stated: 300 *nezirim*[79] came in the days of Simeon ben Shetaḥ[80]. For 150 of them he found an opening[81], for 150 of them he did not find an opening. He came to king Yannai and said to him: There are here 300 *nezirim* who need 900 sacrifices. You should give half of them from your side, I shall give half from my side. The king sent him 450 animals. An informer went around and said that the other one had not given anything from his own money. King Yannai heard about it and got angry. Simeon ben Shetaḥ feared and fled[82]. After some time, important people from the Persian empire came to king Yannai[83]. At the meal, they said to him: We remember that there was here an old man who gave us a rabbinic discourse. He told them what had happened. They said to him, send and bring him! He sent and gave him his word[84]; he came and sat between king and queen. He said to him, why did you trick me? He said, I did not trick you; you with your money and I with my learning, as it is written (*Eccl.* 7:12) "In the shadow of wisdom, in the shadow of money[85]." He said to him, why did you disappear? He said to him, I heard that my lord was angry with me and I wanted to fulfill the verse (*Is.* 26:20) "Hide a little bit until the rage passes;" he used about himself (*Eccl.* 7:12): "Knowledge is an advantage, wisdom lets its possessor live." He said to him, why did you sit between king and queen? He said to him, it is written in the book of Ben Sirach[86]: "Esteem it and it will raise you and set you between princes." He said, bring him a cup that he may recite Grace. He took the cup and said: "Let us give praise for the food that Yannai and his company ate." He said to him, are you still obstinate as ever? He said to him, what should I say, "for the food that we did not eat?" He said, bring him something that he may eat. They brought, he ate and recited: "For the food that we ate."

Rebbi Yoḥanan said, his colleagues disagree with Simeon ben Shetaḥ. Rebbi Jeremiah said, about the first action[87]; Rebbi Abba said, about the second action. Rebbi Jeremiah seems to contradict himself! There he wondered about it and here[88] it is obvious for him! He wondered following the Sages; it is obvious for him following Rabban Simeon ben Gamliel. We have stated about this: If one was lying on a couch and ate[89] with them, even if he did not eat grain the volume of an olive one 'invites' with him, the words of the Sages. Rebbi Jacob bar Aḥa in the name of Rebbi Yoḥanan: One never 'invites' anyone unless he had eaten grain the volume of an olive[90]. But did we not formulate, "two bread and one vegetable, then one 'invites'?" This *baraita* follows Rabban Simeon ben Gamliel.

78 The contradiction will be explained in the following lengthy story.

79 People who made a vow to abstain from all grape products, let their hair grow, and kept themselves in strict ritual purity for a certain amount of time. At the end of that time, the *nazir* could terminate his vow only if he offered a sheep as holocaust sacrifice, a female sheep for a sin-offering, and a goat for a family sacrifice (*Num.* 6). Most of these *nezirim* were poor people who relied on charity to fulfill their obligations in the Temple.

80 President of the Synhedrion in the times of the Hasmonean king Alexander Yannai and brother of queen Shlomẓion (Salome Alexandra).

81 An "opening of regrets", an argument that made the *nazir* regret his original decision to become a *nazir*; this invalidates the vow retroactively so that no sacrifice may be brought.

82 In the parallel in the Babli (48ab), Simeon ben Shetaḥ went into hiding because Alexander Yannai sided with the Sadducees when it was reported to him that some Pharisees thought him to be unfit as priest.

83 During all of the Second Commonwealth and certainly during the reign of Alexander Yannai, the Jewish state relied on contributions from the Jews in the diaspora, both from Rome and from Persia (then, Parthia). It may be assumed that the delegation brought the yearly subsidy and, therefore, was in a position to enforce their will.

84 That it was safe and nothing would happen to him. In the Babli, it was the queen, Simeon's sister, who

arranged matters.

85 Wisdom and money are equivalent to give protection.

86 This verse cannot be reconstructed with confidence, since the manuscripts of the Babli and parallel sources all have different versions.

87 That he tricked Yannai to give the animals for sacrifices under false pretenses, even though formally Simeon ben Shetaḥ was correct. The second action was that he refused to recite Grace without having eaten at least a minimal meal.

The text here is clearly corrupt since by the statement of the Talmud, Rebbi Jeremiah disagrees with Simeon ben Shetaḥ about the recitation of Grace. The correct text, that R. Abba refers to the first action and R. Jeremiah to the second, is in the Yerushalmi source *Midrash Bereshit rabba* 51. [In the Babli, 48a, it is R. Abba the son of R. Ḥiyya bar Abba in the name of R. Yoḥanan who declares that Grace cannot be recited by someone who did not eat bread. But the Babli cannot be used for the text of the Yerushalmi.]

88 In his theoretical question he wonders, in his critique of Simeon ben Shetaḥ following R. Yoḥanan he is certain.

89 In the Midrash, the Rome manuscript, the Tosephta, (and the Babli) "dipped (some vegetable in broth)". Both in the Yerushalmi, here and *Nazir* 5:5, and the prints of the Midrash, this is labelled "words of the Sages." But in the Tosephta (5:20) and manuscripts of the Midrash (and in the Babli 48a), the statement is attributed to Rabban Simeon ben Gamliel. It seems that the attribution here to the Sages is a scribal error since the opinion attributed to Rabban Simeon ben Gamliel in the last *baraita* is the one given in the Tosephta and R. Jeremiah is reported as following the latter's opinion in the interpretation of the story of Simeon ben Shetaḥ.

90 In the restrictive spirit of the Yerushalmi as explained earlier.

(fol. 11a) **משנה ג:** כֵּיצַד מְזַמְּנִין בִּשְׁלֹשָׁה אוֹמֵר נְבָרֵךְ. בִּשְׁלֹשָׁה וְהוּא אוֹמֵר בָּרְכוּ. בַּעֲשָׂרָה אוֹמֵר נְבָרֵךְ לֵאלֹהֵינוּ. בַּעֲשָׂרָה וְהוּא אוֹמֵר בָּרְכוּ. אֶחָד עֲשָׂרָה וְאֶחָד עֶשֶׂר רִבּוֹא. בְּמֵאָה אוֹמֵר נְבָרֵךְ לַיי אֱלֹהֵינוּ. בְּמֵאָה וְהוּא אוֹמֵר בָּרְכוּ.

בְּאֶלֶף אוֹמֵר נְבָרֵךְ לַיי אֱלֹהֵינוּ אֱלֹהֵי יִשְׂרָאֵל. בְּאֶלֶף וְהוּא אוֹמֵר בָּרְכוּ. בְּרִבּוֹא אוֹמֵר נְבָרֵךְ לַיי אֱלֹהֵינוּ אֱלֹהֵי יִשְׂרָאֵל אֱלֹהֵי הַצְּבָאוֹת יֹשֵׁב הַכְּרוּבִים עַל הַמָּזוֹן שֶׁאָכַלְנוּ. רִבִּי יוֹסֵי הַגְּלִילִי אוֹמֵר לְפִי רוֹב הַקָּהָל מְבָרְכִין שֶׁנֶּאֱמַר בְּמַקְהֵלוֹת בָּרְכוּ אֱלֹהִים יי מִמְּקוֹר יִשְׂרָאֵל.

Mishnah 3: How does one 'invite'? If there are three, he says: let us praise[91]. If there are three in addition to himself, he says: praise![92] If there are ten, he says: let us praise our God. If there are ten in addition to himself, he says: praise! There is no difference between ten and ten myriads[93]. If there are a hundred, he says: let us praise the Eternal, our God. If there are a hundred in addition to himself, he says: praise! If there are a thousand, he says: let us praise the Eternal, our God, the God of Israel. If there are a thousand in addition to himself, he says: praise! If there are ten thousand, he says: let us praise the Eternal, our God, the God of Israel, God of Hosts, Who thrones over the Cherubim, for the food that we ate. Rebbi Yose the Galilean says, the praise has to be according to the multitude of the assembled, as it is said (*Ps*. 68:27): "In assemblies[94] praise God, the Lord, from the root of Israel."

91 The changes apply only to the start of the invitation; in all cases one continues with "Him, Whose food we ate".

92 Since there are three without him, he may address them without including himself.

93 This is the majority opinion; the rest of the Mishnah is Rebbi Yose the Galilean's, as explained at the end of the Mishnah.

94 It will be clear in the Halakhah that the difference between the Sages and R. Yose the Galilean is in the interpretation of this word, whether it means "assemblies", i. e., different assemblies recite different praises, or "choirs" that all sing together.

(fol. 11b) **הלכה ג**: דִּלְמָה. רִבִּי זְעִירָא וְרִבִּי יַעֲקֹב בַּר אָחָא וְרִבִּי חִיָּיא בַּר בָּא וְרִבִּי חֲנִינָא חֲבֵרוֹן דְּרַבָּנָן הֲווּ יָתְבִין אָכְלִין. נְסַב רִבִּי יַעֲקֹב בַּר אָחָא כַּסָּא

וּבֵירַךְ וַאֲמַר נְבָרֵךְ וְלָא אֲמַר בָּרְכוּ. אֲמַר לֵיהּ רִבִּי חִייָא בַּר בָּא. וְלָמָּה לֹא אָמַרְתָּ בָּרְכוּ. אֲמַר לֵיהּ וְלֹא כֵן תַּנֵּי אֵין מְדַקְדְּקִין בַּדָּבָר. בֵּין שֶׁאָמַר נְבָרֵךְ בֵּין שֶׁאָמַר בָּרְכוּ אֵין (fol. 11c) תּוֹפְסִין אוֹתוֹ עַל כָּךְ. וְהַנּוֹקְדָנִין תּוֹפְסִין אוֹתוֹ עַל כָּךְ. וּבְאִישׁ לְרִבִּי זְעִירָא בְּגִין דִּצְוַוח רִבִּי יַעֲקֹב בַּר אָחָא לְרִבִּי חִייָא בַּר בָּא נוֹקְדָנָא.

Halakhah 3: Clarification. Rebbi Zeïra, Rebbi Jacob bar Aḥa, Rebbi Ḥiyya bar Abba, and Rebbi Ḥanina the colleague of the rabbis, were sitting and eating together. Rebbi Jacob bar Aḥa took the cup[95] and said "let us praise", he did not say: "praise!". Rebbi Ḥiyya bar Abba asked him, why did you not say "praise!" He said to him, did we not state[96]: "One does not insist on the formulation. Whether he says 'let us praise'. or he says 'praise!', one does not criticize him, but the pedants[97] criticize him for that." Rebbi Zeïra felt badly that Rebbi Jacob bar Abba had called Rebbi Ḥiyya bar Abba a pedant.

95 The cup of wine over which Grace is recited. Since there were four sages eating together, the Mishnah would require that he start with "praise!".

96 Tosephta *Berakhot* 5:18, Babli 50a.

97 The reading of the *Arukh* is נקרנין "nitpickers." The Babli (50a) interprets the Tosephta to mean that "praise!" is acceptable but not preferred; the Yerushalmi seems to accept Samuel's statement (also Babli 49b) at face value that "praise!" should not be used in practice.

שְׁמוּאֵל אָמַר אֵינִי מוֹצִיא אֶת עַצְמִי מִן הַכְּלָל. הֵיתִיבוּן הֲרֵי בִּרְכַּת הַתּוֹרָה הֲרֵי הוּא אוֹמֵר בָּרְכוּ. אָמַר רִבִּי אָבוּן מִכֵּיוָן דְּיֵימַר הַמְּבוֹרָךְ אַף הוּא אֵינוֹ מוֹצִיא אֶת עַצְמוֹ מִן הַכְּלָל.

Samuel said: I do not want to exclude myself from the group[98]. They objected: look at the benediction for the Torah where he says "praise!" Rebbi Abun said, since he will conclude by "the Praised One", he does not exclude himself from the group.[99]

98 In the Babli, Samuel is quoted as saying "nobody should exclude himself from the group" as obligatory ruling, whereas here he is quoted as stating his personal preference for נברך against the Mishnah.

99 It is explained in the next Mishnah that the benediction for reading the Torah starts with "Praise the Eternal" according to Rebbi Aqiba, and "Praise the Eternal, the Praised One" according to Rebbi Ismael. Rebbi Abun indicates that practice follows Rebbi Ismael. The Babli (50a) indicates that in Torah reading, the people forced adherence to the opinion of R. Ismael, apparently against the resistance of some rabbis (called "black vessels" by Rava) who preferred to follow Rebbi Aqiba. It seems that R. Ḥiyya bar Abba, a native Babylonian, felt that R. Jacob bar Aḥa was following the uneducated, but in Galilee everybody followed Samuel and popular opinion.

רִבִּי אַבָּא בַּר זְמִינָא הֲוָה מְשַׁמֵּשׁ קוֹמֵי זְעִירָא. מְזַג לֵיהּ כַּסָּא. אֲמַר לֵיהּ סָב בְּרִיךְ. אֲמַר לֵיהּ[100] וְהַב דַּעְתָּךְ דְּאַתְּ מִישְׁתֵּי חָרָנָה. דְּתַנֵּי הַשַּׁמָּשׁ מְבָרֵךְ עַל כָּל־כּוֹס וְכוֹס. וְאֵינוֹ מְבָרֵךְ עַל כָּל־פְּרוּסָה וּפְרוּסָה. אֲמַר לֵיהּ כְּהָא דַּאֲנָא יְהַב דַּעְתִּי מַפְקָא יָתָךְ יְדֵי חוֹבָךְ בְּבִרְכָתָה. כֵּן יְהַב דַּעְתָּךְ מַפְקָא יְדֵי חוֹבָתִי בְּאָמֵן. אָמַר רִבִּי תַּנְחוּם בַּר יִרְמְיָה מַתְנִיתָא אָמְרָה כֵן הַמִּתְעַסֵּק לֹא יָצָא וְהַשּׁוֹמֵעַ מִן הַמִּתְעַסֵּק לֹא יָצָא.

Rebbi Abba bar Zamina waited upon Zeïra and mixed him a cup. He[100] said to him: Old man, make the benediction, and have the intention of drinking another one, as we have stated: The waiter makes a benediction for every single cup[101] but not for every morsel. He answered him: Just as I have the intention of absolving you of your obligation by the benediction so you must have the intention of absolving me of my obligation[102] by "Amen". Rebbi Tanḥum bar Jeremiah[103] said, a Mishnah (*Rosh Hashanah* 4:8) states this: The absent-minded[104] did not fulfill his obligation and he who heard from the absent-minded did not fulfill his obligation.

100 The last two words are not in the Rome manuscript and are probably dittography.

101 Since he cannot expect to get another cup, he cannot have the intention to make one benediction for more than one cup. On the other hand, in the opinion of the Yerushalmi the waiter will always have occasion to eat some food from the kitchen, hence he may make a benediction for the future. In the Babli (*Ḥulin* 107b), this *baraita* is a statement of Rav and is restricted there to formal dinners. The Babli also quotes an opinion of the Galilean R. Yoḥanan that for solid food also the waiter cannot make a benediction for the uncertain future; since this is not mentioned here one has to conclude that the Yerushalmi rejects the distinction made in the Babli.

102 All commentators except R. Moshe Margalit declare this passage to be corrupt and that it should read מַפְקָא יְדֵי חוֹבָתָךְ "fulfill your obligation"; this seems to be required by the following quote (which is formulated for sounding the *shofar* but is valid for all obligations that may be fulfilled by listening.)

103 A student of R. Mana II of the fifth generation.

104 The word means usually "absent-minded" but can also mean "practicing" and that probably is the primary meaning in this Mishnah, that one who blows the *shofar* in order to learn the technique cannot by the same act fulfill his obligation, neither can anyone who hears him. But in our application, the intended meaning is "absent-minded." R. Abba bar Zamina's implication is that in hearing a benediction one must answer "Amen" in order to make sure that the listener is not absent-minded either. This explains the placing of this paragraph here, following another one where also one person recites Grace in order for all others (even a hundred thousand) to be freed from their obligation.

במאה אומר וכו׳. אָמַר רִבִּי יוֹחָנָן זוּ דִבְרֵי רִבִּי יוֹסֵי הַגְּלִילִי אֲבָל דִּבְרֵי חֲכָמִים אֶחָד עֶשֶׂר וְאֶחָד עֶשֶׂר רִבּוֹא. רָבָא אָמַר הֲלָכָה כְּמִי שֶׁאוֹמֵר אֶחָד עֶשֶׂר וְאֶחָד עֶשֶׂר רִבּוֹא.

"If there are a hundred" etc. Rebbi Yoḥanan said, these are the words of Rebbi Jose the Galilean, but the Sages say "there is no difference between ten and ten myriads". Rava[105] said, practice follows him who states that there is no difference between ten and ten myriads.

105 It seems that here an apostrophe is missing and the name is R. Abba who is frequently mentioned in the Yerushalmi, rather than Rava (Rav Abba), one of the architects of dialectics in the Babli who lived at the time when the work on the Yerushalmi came to an end. The latter is mentioned only once in the Yerushalmi [*Beẓa* 1:3 (fol. 60b)] as Rebbi (!) Abba bar Josef [in the parallel in the Babli, based on the Yerushalmi, his full name is given as Rava bar Rav Josef bar Ḥama in contrast to Babylonian material where his name consistently is only Rava]. In the Babli, (50a) Rava is quoted as saying that "the people follow R. Ismael", i. e., there is no binding ruling in the matter but a silent consensus, whereas the statement in the Yerushalmi indicates a rabbinic ruling.

מְנַיִין לְעֵדָה שֶׁהִיא עֲשָׂרָה. רִבִּי בָּא וְרִבִּי יָסָא בְשֵׁם רִבִּי יוֹחָנָן נֶאֱמַר כָּאן עֵדָה וְנֶאֱמַר לְהַלָּן עֵדָה. מַה עֵדָה שֶׁנֶּאֱמַר לְהַלָּן עֲשָׂרָה. אַף עֵדָה שֶׁנֶּאֱמַר כָּאן עֲשָׂרָה. אָמַר רִבִּי סִימוֹן נֶאֱמַר כָּאן תּוֹךְ וְנֶאֱמַר לְהַלָּן תּוֹךְ וַיָּבוֹאוּ בְּנֵי יִשְׂרָאֵל לִשְׁבּוֹר בְּתוֹךְ הַבָּאִים. מַה תּוֹךְ הָאָמוּר לְהַלָּן עֲשָׂרָה. אַף כָּאן עֲשָׂרָה. אֲמַר לֵיהּ רִבִּי יוֹסֵי בֵּי רִבִּי בּוּן כִּי אִם מִתּוֹךְ אַתְּ יְלִיף סַגִּין אִינוּן. אֶלָּא נֶאֱמַר כָּאן בְּנֵי יִשְׂרָאֵל וְנֶאֱמַר לְהַלָּן בְּנֵי יִשְׂרָאֵל. מַה בְּנֵי יִשְׂרָאֵל הָאָמוּר לְהַלָּן עֲשָׂרָה. אַף כָּאן עֲשָׂרָה.

From where that "congregation" means ten people[106]? Rebbi Abba and Rebbi Yasa in the name of Rebbi Yoḥanan: It is said here "congregation" and it says there[107] "congregation". Since "congregation" mentioned there means ten, so also "congregation" mentioned here must mean ten. Rebbi Simon said, it is said here "in the midst" and it is said there "in the midst" (*Gen.* 42:5): "The sons of Israel came to buy grain in the midst of those who came." Since "in the midst" said there means ten, so also here it must mean ten. Rebbi Yose ben Rebbi Abun said to him, if you deduce from "in the midst", there are too many of them[108]. But it is said here "the children of Israel" and it is said there "the children of Israel." Since "children of Israel" said there means ten, so here it also must mean ten.

106 The discussion here is to prove that for a public invocation of the Name one needs a congregation of at least ten adult males. The relevant verses are *Lev.* 19:2 "Speak to the entire congregation of the children of Israel and tell them: conduct yourselves in holiness because I, The Eternal, your God, Am Holy" and *Lev.* 22:32 "I shall be sanctified in the midst of the children of Israel." The same discussion is reported *Megillah* 4:4, *Sanhedrin* 1:4. The parallel discussion in the Babli, *Megillah* 23a, in the name of the first generation Rebbi Ḥiyya, is based on the second verse and is intelligible only if it is understood as reference to the derivation in the Yerushalmi.

107 "Here" refers to *Lev.* 19:2, "there" to *Num.* 14:27: "How long for this evil congregation", speaking of the ten spies who argued against entering the Land. There were twelve spies in all; Joshua and Caleb were in the opposition; accordingly there were ten evil persons who formed the congregation.

108 In particular, in *Lev.* 22:32, "in the midst" must mean 600'000 adult males. In the Babli, *Lev.* 22:32 is used to establish a formal parallel, known as *gezerah shawah*, between this verse and the one from Genesis. The latter verse is then used to arrive at the number ten (since of the twelve tribes, Joseph and Benjamin were missing). From the Babli it seems that there was a tradition linking the two verses (since in its opinion, *gezerah shawah* must be based on a tradition) and, therefore, R. Simon is forced to quote a verse that in itself seems to be less adequate than the one used before.

מַה מְקַייְמִין רַבָּנָן טַעְמָא דְרַבִּי יוֹסֵי הַגָּלִילִי בְּמַקְהֵלוֹת בְּכָל־קְהִילָּה וּקְהִילָּה. אָמַר רַבִּי חֲנִינָא בְּרֵיהּ דְּרַבִּי אַבָּהוּ במקהלת כְּתִיב.

How do the Sages use the reason of Rebbi Yose the Galilean? "In assemblies", in each separate congregation. Rebbi Ḥanina the son of Rebbi Abbahu said, it is written במקהלת[109].

109 The opinion of the sages is that the plural "assemblies" points to different assemblies at different places and not to different categories of the same assembly. R. Ḥanina notes that in R. Yose the Galilean's tradition, the word was written defective and could be read as a singular מַקְהֶלֶת "assembly".

Hence, if the word is vocalized as a plural, it is an ideal plural that refers to different stages of the same assembly. In all our sources, the word in Psalms is written *plene* to support the position of the Sages; the Masorah to *Num.* 32:25/26 (composed several centuries after the conclusion of the Talmudim) notes that מקהלת appears as geographical name only in *Num.* and that in Psalms, מקהלות is a *hapax legomenon*. The parallel Babli (50a) refers the verse in Psalms, in the name of R. Meir, to the choir of children at the Red Sea, a tradition more justly attributed to Rabban Gamliel in Yerushalmi *Soṭa* 5:6.

(fol. 11a) **משנה ד:** אָמַר רִבִּי עֲקִיבָה מַה מָצִינוּ בְּבֵית הַכְּנֶסֶת אֶחָד מְרוּבִּין וְאֶחָד מוּעָטִין אוֹמֵר בָּֽרְכוּ אֶת יי. רִבִּי יִשְׁמָעֵאל אוֹמֵר בָּֽרְכוּ אֶת יי הַמְבוֹרָךְ.

Mishnah 4: Rebbi Aqiba said, do we not find in the synagoge that one recites "Praise the Eternal" whether there are many or few? Rebbi Ismael says, "Praise the Eternal, the Praised One!"[110]

110 This Mishnah is sequel to the preceding one and presents the argument of the Sages against Rebbi Yose the Galilean. The difference in text between the two authorities already was discussed in the preceding Halakhah.

(fol. 11c) **הלכה ד:** רִבִּי חִייָא בַּר אַשִׁי קָם מִקְרֵי בְּאוֹרַייְתָא וְאָמַר בָּֽרְכוּ וְלֹא אָמַר הַמְבוֹרָךְ. בְּעִין מִישְׁתְּקוּנֵיהּ אֲמַר לְהֶן רַב אַרְפּוּנֵיהּ. דְּנְהִיג כְּרִבִּי עֲקִיבָה. רִבִּי זְעִירָא קָם מִקְרֵי כֹּהֶן בִּמְקוֹם לֵוִי וּבֵירַךְ לְפָנֶיהָ וּלְאַחֲרֶיהָ וּבְעִין מִישְׁתְּקוּנֵיהּ אֲמַר לְהֶן רִבִּי חִייָא בַּר אַשִׁי אַרְפּוּנֵיהּ. דְּכֵן אִינּוּן נְהִיגִין גַּבֵּייְהוּ.

Halakhah 4: Rav Ḥiyya bar Ashi rose to read in the Torah and said "Praise the Eternal," he did not add "the Praised One!" They wanted to silence him. Rav said to them, let him, because he follows Rebbi Aqiba[111].

Rebbi Zeïra rose to read as Cohen in place of a Levite and recited the benediction before and after. They wanted to silence him. Rav Hiyya bar Ashi said to them, let him, because that is their way of doing it[112].

111 The title "Rebbi" found twice in the text is a scribal error; Rav Ḥiyya Bar Ashi never went to Israel.

It seems that Rav, when he returned to Babylonia from his studies in Galilee, followed the Galilean order of prayers. [Even centuries later, we still find that Rav's Yeshivah in Surah followed the *minhag Eretz Israel* in reciting liturgical poems in the prayers, whereas the autochthonous Yeshivah of Pum Beditha (Nahardea) never recited them.] Rav Ḥiyya Bar Ashi became a member of Rav's Yeshivah but kept the old Babylonian *minhag* following Rebbi Aqiba. Rav had to explain to his students that this way also is acceptable. The parallel in the Babli (50a) tells a similar story about Rafrem bar Papa, a student of Rav's student Rav Huna; there, Rava notes that even in Babylonia "the people follow Rebbi Ismaël." This shows that common practice was settled only three generations after Rav. (The Rome ms. has "Rav Ada" instead of "Rav". Since Rav Ada was one of Rav's students, ranking much below Rav Ḥiyya bar Ashi, the reading has to be rejected.)

112 This second story deals with another subject. The original practice, as spelled out in the Mishnah *Megillah* 3:1, was that the first to read in the Torah pronounced the benediction before the reading and the last one the benediction after the reading. Even in Mishnaic times it became customary that every reader recited his own benediction. Here, Rebbi Zeïra had read his portion as Cohen; in the absence of a Levite he was called a second time to read and he started by reciting the benedictions again. It is reported in the Babli (*Avodah Zarah* 16b) that R. Zeïra studied some time in the Yeshivah of R. Ḥiyya bar Ashi after having been ordained by Rav Yehudah and before his immigration to Galilee. The action of R. Zeïra, therefore, reflects the practice of the Yeshivah of Nahardea.

כְּתִיב וַיְבָרֶךְ עֶזְרָא אֶת יי אֱלֹהִים הַגָּדוֹל. בְּמַה הוּא גוֹדְלוֹ. גּוֹדְלוֹ בְּשֵׁם הַמְפוֹרָשׁ. רַב מַתָּנָה אָמַר גּוֹדְלוֹ בִּבְרָכָה. רִבִּי סִימוֹן בְּשֵׁם רִבִּי יְהוֹשֻׁעַ בֶּן לֵוִי לָמָּה נִקְרוּ אַנְשֵׁי כְנֶסֶת הַגְּדוֹלָה שֶׁהֶחֱזִירוּ הַגְּדוּלָּה לְיוֹשְׁנָהּ. אָמַר רִבִּי פִּינְחָס מֹשֶׁה הִתְקִין מַטְבְּעָהּ שֶׁל תְּפִילָּה הָאֵל הַגָּדוֹל הַגִּיבּוֹר וְהַנּוֹרָא. יִרְמְיָה אָמַר הָאֵל הַגָּדוֹל הַגִּיבּוֹר וְלֹא אָמַר הַנּוֹרָא. לָמָּה אָמַר הַגִּיבּוֹר לְזֶה נָאֶה לִקְרוֹת גִּיבּוֹר שֶׁהוּא רוֹאֶה חוּרְבָּן וְשׁוֹתֵק. וְלָמָּא לֹא אָמַר נוֹרָא אֶלָּא שֶׁאֵין נוֹרָא אֶלָּא בֵית הַמִּקְדָּשׁ שֶׁנֶּאֱמַר נוֹרָא אֱלֹהִים מִמִּקְדָּשֶׁךָ. דָּנִיֵּאל אָמַר הָאֵל הַגָּדוֹל וְהַנּוֹרָא וְלֹא אָמַר הַגִּיבּוֹר בָּנָיו מְסוּרִין בְּקוֹלָרִין הֵיכָן הִיא גְבוּרָתוֹ. וְלָמָּה אָמַר וְהַנּוֹרָא. לְזֶה נָאֶה לִקְרוֹת נוֹרָא בְּנוֹרָאוֹת שֶׁעָשָׂה לָנוּ בְּכִבְשָׁן הָאֵשׁ. וְכֵיוָן שֶׁעָמְדוּ אַנְשֵׁי כְנֶסֶת הַגְּדוֹלָה הֶחֱזִירוּ אֶת הַגְּדוּלָּה לְיוֹשְׁנָהּ. הָאֵל הַגָּדוֹל הַגִּיבּוֹר וְהַנּוֹרָא. וּבָשָׂר וָדָם יֵשׁ בּוֹ כּוֹחַ לִיתֵּן קִצְבָה לַדְּבָרִים הַלָּלוּ. אָמַר רִבִּי יִצְחָק בֶּן אֶלְעָזָר יוֹדְעִין הֵן הַנְּבִיאִים שֶׁאֱלֹהֵיהֶן אֱמֶת וְאֵינָן מַחֲנִיפִין לוֹ.

It is written (*Neh.* 8:6): "Ezra praised the Eternal, the great God." In what did he declare Him great? He declared Him great by the Explicit Name[113]. Rav Mattanah said, he declared Him great by a benediction. Rebbi Simon in the name of Rebbi Joshua ben Levi: Why are they called the Men of the Great Assembly[114]? Because they returned the Crown to its former status. Rebbi Phineas said, Moses fixed the formula of benediction, (*Deut.* 10:17) "the Great, Strong, and Awesome God." Jeremiah said (*Jer.* 32:18): "the Great, Strong God," but he left out "Awesome." Why did he say "the Strong"? He may rightly be called strong because He sees the destruction and is silent. And why did he not say "the Awesome"? Awesome is only the Temple, as it is said (*Ps.* 68:36): "Awesome is the Eternal from Your holy place." Daniel said (*Dan.* 9:4)[115]: "the Great and Awesome God," he did not say "the Strong"; His sons are put in neck-irons[116], where is His strength? Why did he say: "the Awesome?" He may well be called "the Awesome" by the wonders He did for us in the fiery oven. But when the Men of the Great Assembly came, they restituted Greatness to its former place, "the Great, Strong, and Awesome God." Does flesh and blood have power to set limits in these matters? Rebbi Isaac ben Eleazar[117] said, the prophets know that their God is Truth and they will not fawn before him.

113 The name YHWH pronounced with the correct vocalization that is unknown to us.

114 The parallel is in *Megillah* 3:8; in Babli *Yoma* 69b it is spelled out that Rav Mattanah means the first benediction of the *'Amidah* that contains the sentence "the Great, Strong, and Awesome God" chosen by the Men of the Great Assembly, and the observation of R. Joshua ben Levi is intended to buttress the argument of Rav Mattanah.

115 The same expression is used by Nehemiah, *Neh.* 1:5.

116 Latin *collare* "neck-iron."

117 There were two sages of this name, one a student of R. Yoḥanan and the other in the fourth generation, a colleague of R. Mana. In the Babli, the statement is attributed to R. Eleazar.

(fol. 11a) **משנה ה**: שְׁלוֹשָׁה שֶׁאָכְלוּ כְּאַחַת אֵינָן רְשָׁאִין לֵיחָלֵק וְכֵן אַרְבָּעָה וְכֵן חֲמִשָּׁה. שִׁשָּׁה נֶחְלָקִין עַד עֲשָׂרָה. וַעֲשָׂרָה אֵינָן נֶחֱלָקִין עַד שֶׁיְּהוּ עֶשְׂרִים.

Mishnah 5: Three who ate together are not permitted to split[118], neither are four or five. Six may split and so on up to ten. Ten may not split and so on unless they are twenty.

118 Since three together are required to recite the "invitation" whereas two or one do not recite it; the minimum number required for two separate recitations of Grace is six. Nine may form three groups, but ten are required to recite the "invitation" with an invocation of the Name. Hence, 10 to 19 people in a group may not split in the recitation of Grace.

(fol. 11c) **הלכה ה**: תַּנֵּי הָיָה אוֹכֵל וְיוֹשֵׁב בְּשַׁבָּת וְשָׁכַח וְלֹא הִזְכִּיר שֶׁל שַׁבָּת. רַב אָמַר חוֹזֵר. וּשְׁמוּאֵל אָמַר אֵינוֹ חוֹזֵר.

Halakhah 5: It was stated: If one was eating sitting down on Sabbath and forgot and did not mention Sabbath, Rav said: he must repeat, and Samuel said: he need not repeat[119].

119 In the parallel in the Babli, 49b, the opinion of Samuel is not mentioned; even Rav Naḥman, the student of Samuel, is reported to follow the ruling of Rav. Later commentators state that, since on the Sabbath one may not fast, eating on the Sabbath is a consequence of it being Sabbath and the Sabbath has to be mentioned in reciting Grace. Samuel might be of the opinion that anything not mentioned in the verse *Deut*. 8:10 cannot be a reason for repeating Grace.

שִׁמְעוֹן בַּר בָּא בְּשֵׁם רִבִּי יוֹחָנָן סָפֵק הִזְכִּיר שֶׁל רֹאשׁ חוֹדֶשׁ. סָפֵק לֹא הִזְכִּיר אֵין מַחֲזִירִין אוֹתוֹ. אַשְׁכַּח תַּנֵּי וּפְלִיג. כָּל־יוֹם שֶׁיֵּשׁ בּוֹ קָרְבַּן מוּסָף כְּגוֹן רֹאשׁ חוֹדֶשׁ וְחוֹלוֹ שֶׁל מוֹעֵד צָרִיךְ לְהַזְכִּיר מֵעֵין הַמְּאוֹרָע וְאִם לֹא הִזְכִּיר מַחֲזִירִין אוֹתוֹ. וְכָל־שֶׁאֵין בּוֹ קָרְבַּן מוּסָף כְּגוֹן חֲנוּכָּה וּפוּרִים צָרִיךְ לְהַזְכִּיר מֵעֵין הַמְּאוֹרָע וְאִם לֹא הִזְכִּיר אֵין מַחֲזִירִין אוֹתוֹ.

Simeon bar Abba in the name of Rebbi Yoḥanan: If one is in doubt whether he mentioned the New Moon or did not mention it, one does not make him repeat[120]. They found a dissenting statement: On every day that has a *Musaph* sacrifice (e. g., the day of the new moon and the intermediate days of holidays,) he must mention the occasion and if he did not mention it, one makes him repeat. But on every day that has no *Musaph* sacrifice (e. g., Hanukkah and Purim,) he must mention the occasion but if he did not, one does not make him repeat.

120 In the Babli (49b) there is a similar statement by Rav Naḥman in the name of Samuel that, if someone forgot the day of the New Moon in

Grace, one does not make him repeat. According to the Yerushalmi, that seems obvious as the opinion of Samuel. However, the mention of Samuel is not in the Munich manuscript of the Babli, and the Spanish incunabula prints of *Berakhot* Babli have "Rav" instead of "Samuel"; this seems to be the correct reading. According to the Babli, one does not have to repeat even if he is sure that he did not mention the day; according to the way the Yerushalmi quotes the formulation, one has to repeat even if there was only a doubt that he did not mention the day.

חָנָן בַּר אַבָּא וַחֲבֵרָיָיא הֲווּ אָכְלִין בְּשַׁבָּתָא. מִן דְּאָכְלִין וּבָרְכִין קָם אָזַל לֵיהּ. חֲזַר לְגַבָּן אַשְׁכַּחְנוּן בָּרְכִין. אֲמַר וְלֹא כְּבָר בָּרַכְנוּ. אָמְרִין לֵיהּ מְבָרְכִין וְחוֹזְרִין וּמְבָרְכִין דַּאֲשְׁכְּחָן מַדְכְּרָא דְשַׁבָּתָא. לָא אֲמַר כֵּן רִבִּי בָּא בְשֵׁם רִבִּי חוּנָא וְרִבִּי יִרְמְיָה מָטוּ בָהּ בְּשֵׁם רַב שָׁכַח וְלֹא הִזְכִּיר שֶׁל שַׁבָּת אוֹמֵר אֲשֶׁר נָתַן מְנוּחָה לְעַמּוֹ יִשְׂרָאֵל. כַּן בְּשֶׁהִסִּיעַ דַּעְתּוֹ וְכַן בְּשֶׁלֹּא הִסִּיעַ דַּעְתּוֹ.

Ḥanan bar Abba and the colleagues were eating on Sabbath. After they had eaten and recited Grace he got up and left. When he returned, he found them reciting Grace. He said, did we not recite Grace already? They said to him, we recited, but now we recite again because we forgot to mention the Sabbath. Rebbi Abba in the name of Rav[121] Huna (Rav Jeremiah extends it in the name of Rav) did not say so: If he forgot to mention the Sabbath, he says: He[122] Who gave rest to His people Israel. Here[123] if he turned[124] his mind away, there if he did not turn his mind away.

121 The titles of Huna and Jeremiah must be Rav, not Rebbi as in the Hebrew text, since the entire discussion is between students of Rav.

122 The full benediction would be: Praised are You, Eternal, our God, King of the universe, Who gave . . . .

123 One has to repeat if he turned from reciting Grace to other activities; one recites an addtional benediction if he realizes the omission before he has finished. The Babli (49a/b) gives the full text of this benediction and the corresponding one for holidays, but

there it is authorized only (in the name of Rav) if one realizes the omission before one starts the next benediction. This certainly is not the position of the Yerushalmi.

124 הסיע "he moved away", appears in the Babli as הסיח ; ע or ח were inaudible in Babylonian speech.

תַּנֵּי עֲשָׂרָה בְּנֵי אָדָם שֶׁהָיוּ מְהַלְּכִין בַּדֶּרֶךְ אַף עַל פִּי שֶׁכּוּלָּם אוֹכְלִין מִכִּכָּר אֶחָד כָּל־אֶחָד וְאֶחָד מְבָרֵךְ לְעַצְמוֹ. יָשְׁבוּ וְאָכְלוּ אַף עַל פִּי שֶׁכָּל־אֶחָד וְאֶחָד אוֹכֵל מִכִּכָּר עַצְמוֹ אֶחָד מְבָרֵךְ עַל יְדֵי כוּלָּם. רִבִּי יִרְמְיָה זְמִין לַחֲבֵרָיָא בְּפוּנְדָּקָא.

It is stated[125] : Ten people walking on the road, even if all of them eat from the same loaf, each one recites Grace for himself. If they sat down and ate, even though each one eats his own loaf, one recites Grace for all of them. Rebbi Jeremiah "invited" his colleagues at an inn[126].

125 A similar text appears in Babli 42a and Tosephta *Berakhot* 5:23. In both these texts, the second sentence reads "if they sat down to eat"; this is interpreted in the Babli to mean that they are sitting together by a common decision. Hence, they form a group and have to recite Grace together. The language of the Yerushalmi, "they sat down and ate," points to a spontaneous act that would not require Grace to be recited in common in the opinion of the Babli.

126 It is assumed that everybody pays for his own meal (or, if the hostelry has no restaurant, eats from his own provisions) in an inn and, also, that the formation of the group is casual rather than planned. Nevertheless, they have to recite Grace together; see the preceding note.

(fol 11a) **משנה ו:** שְׁתֵּי חֲבוּרוֹת שֶׁהָיוּ אוֹכְלִין בְּבַיִת אֶחָד בִּזְמַן שֶׁמִּקְצָתָן רוֹאִין אֵילּוּ אֶת אֵילּוּ הֲרֵי אֵילּוּ מִצְטָרְפִין לְזִימּוּן. וְאִם לָאו אֵילּוּ מְזַמְּנִין לְעַצְמָן וְאֵילּוּ מְזַמְּנִין לְעַצְמָן. וְאֵין מְבָרְכִין עַל הַיַּיִן עַד שֶׁיִּתֵּן לְתוֹכוֹ מַיִם דִּבְרֵי רִבִּי אֱלִיעֶזֶר. וַחֲכָמִים אוֹמְרִים מְבָרְכִין.

Mishnah 6: Two groups that ate in one house, if some of one group saw some of the other group they join in "invitation"; otherwise, each group recites the "invitation" for itself. One does not recite a benediction over wine[126] unless he added water; these are the words of Rebbi Eliezer. But the Sages say, one may recite the benediction.

126 Instead, one uses the benediction "Creator of the fruit of the tree," appropriate for fruit juice.

(fol. 11c) **הלכה ו**: רִבִּי יוֹנָה וְרִבִּי אַבָּא בַּר זָמִינָא בְּשֵׁם רִבִּי זְעִירָא לִשְׁנֵי בָתִּים נִצְרְכָה.

Halakha 6: Rebbi Jonah and Rebbi Abba bar Zamina in the name of Rebbi Zeïra: For two houses, there is a problem[127].

127 The Mishnah gives the rule for two groups assembled at different places in one house. The problem of two groups which eat in different houses but see one another is not treated and one may make arguments both ways. {Tosaphot in *Babli* 50b read the statement as : "[The Mishnah] is only needed for two houses," the inference being that if they see one another they can join in saying Grace. This transfers the meaning of Babylonian צריכא ("it is necessary") to the Palestinian expression נצרכה ("it is problematic") used here!}

אָמַר רִבִּי יוֹחָנָן וְהֵן שֶׁנִּכְנְסוּ מִשָּׁעָה רִאשׁוֹנָה עַל מְנָת כֵּן.

Rebbi Yoḥanan said, it applies only if they entered with that in mind[128].

128 R. Yoḥanan refers to the Mishnah: Two groups not in the same room may recite common Grace only if they started the meal with that intention. This corresponds to the opinion of Babli and Tosephta in the case of the caravan travelling together, discussed at the end of the previous Halakhah. However, since it is necessary to state this rule for people in two different rooms, it follows that the Yerushalmi does not require common intent for

people in one room; R. Yoḥanan agrees with his student's student R. Jeremiah in the preceding Halakhah.

אֵילֵּין בֵּית נְשִׂיאֵי מַה אַתְּ עֲבֵד לוֹן כְּבַיִת אֶחָד אוֹ כִּשְׁנֵי בָתִּים. נֹאמַר אִם דַּרְכָּן לַעֲבוֹר אֵילוּ עַל אֵילוּ מְזַמְּנִין. וְאִם לָאו אֵין מְזַמְּנִין. רִבִּי בֶּרֶכְיָה מוֹקִים לַאֲמוֹרֵיהּ עַל תַּרְעָא מְצִיעָיָא דְּבֵי מִדְרָשָׁא וְהוּא מְזַמֵּן עַל אִילֵּין וְעַל אִילֵּין.

What do you do with those at the house of the patriarch, like one house or like two houses[129]? Let us say that if they usually walk over from one group to the other then they "invite" together; otherwise they do not "invite" together. Rebbi Berekhiah used to place his speaker in the middle of the door of the house of study and he recited the "invitation" together with both groups[130].

129 The Babli (50a) notes that at a dinner in the house of the Resh Galuta, the head of the Jews of Babylonia, one recites Grace in small groups since the place is so noisy that one could not hear a person at the dais reciting Grace. Here it seems that the Patriarch held his formal dinners in a very large hall with several groups forming circles and not communicating with one another. The question is whether the room acts as a common enclosure for all these groups or not.

130 The meals in the Yeshivah were taken in two adjacent rooms. A similar note in the Babli (50b) states that if the same waiter waits upon several groups in a very large room, the waiter makes them one group.

אֵין מְבָרְכִין עַל הַיַּיִן עַד שֶׁיִּתֵּן לְתוֹכוֹ מַיִם דִּבְרֵי רִבִּי אֱלִיעֶזֶר. וַחֲכָמִים אוֹמְרִים מְבָרְכִין: רִבִּי זְרִיקָא בְּשֵׁם רִבִּי יוֹסֵי בֶּן חֲנִינָא מוֹדִים חֲכָמִים לְרִבִּי אֱלִיעֶזֶר בְּכוֹס שֶׁל בְּרָכָה שֶׁהוּא נוֹתֵן לְתוֹכוֹ מַיִם כָּל־שֶׁהוּא. נְהִיגִין רַבָּנָן בְּהָהֵן כַּסָּא דְקִידּוּשָׁא. מִילְּתָא דְּרִבִּי יוֹסֵה פְּלִיגָא אַדְּרִבִּי יוֹנָה. דְּרִבִּי יוֹנָה טָעַם כַּסָּא וּמְתַקֵּן לָהּ. אִין תֵּימַר דְּהוּא מָזוּג. וְהָתַנֵּי הַשּׁוֹתֶה מַשְׁקִין מְזוּגִין שֶׁעָבַר עֲלֵיהֶן הַלַּיְלָה דָּמוֹ בְּרֹאשׁוֹ. אָמַר רִבִּי יוֹחָנָן וְהוּא שֶׁלָּנוּ בִּכְלֵי מַתָּכוֹת.

"One does not recite a benediction over wine unless he added water; these are the words of Rebbi Eliezer. But the Sages say, one may recite the benediction." Rebbi Zeriqa in the name of Rebbi Yose ben Ḥanina: The Sages agree with Rebbi Eliezer that one has to add a small amount of water into the cup used for Grace[131]. The rabbis do so for the *Qiddush* cup. The statement of Rebbi Yose disagrees with Rebbi Jonah, for Rebbi Jonah tasted it and restored it[132]. If you imply that it was mixed, did we not formulate: He who drinks mixed drinks that were standing through the night, his blood is on his head. Rebbi Yoḥanan said, that is only if it was standing in metal vessels[133].

131 Because that is the civilized way of acting and religious obligations should be executed with dignity.

132 Rebbi Jonah tasted from the cup for *Qiddush* of Friday evening, then left the rest standing in the cup and "repaired" it the next morning by filling it again with more wine. As will be explained later in this Halakhah, a cup that has been drunk from cannot be used for another benediction; hence, it has to be replenished. The question is, if R. Jonah put water into his *Qiddush* cup, how could he leave it standing half full through the night?

133 The last two statements are also in the Babli (*Niddah* 17a); the *baraita* is very close to the text in *Derekh Ereẓ Rabba*, Chapter 11. Both of these sources give a list of things that are dangerous to one's health. In the Yerushalmi, the statement of R. Yoḥanan answers the question raised: R. Jonah might add water to his wine as long as his cup was not of metal.

רִבִּי יִרְמְיָה בְּשֵׁם רִבִּי יוֹחָנָן רִאשׁוֹנִים הָיוּ שׁוֹאֲלִין שְׂמֹאל מַהוּ שֶׁתְּסַייֵעַ לְיָמִין בְּכוֹס שֶׁל בְּרָכָה. אַתְּ שְׁמַע מִינֵּיהּ תְּלָת. אַתְּ שְׁמַע שֶׁהוּא צָרִיךְ לְתוֹפְסוֹ בְּיָמִין. וְצָרִיךְ שֶׁתְּהֵא יָדוֹ (fol. 11d) גְּבוֹהָה מִן הַשֻּׁלְחָן טֶפַח. וְצָרִיךְ שֶׁנּוֹתֵן עֵינָיו בּוֹ.

Rebbi Jeremiah[134] in the name of Rebbi Yoḥanan: The first generations asked whether the left hand may help the right hand with the cup used for reciting Grace. You may infer from this three things. You infer that one must hold the cup with his right hand[135], that one's hand must be lifted from the table at least a hand-breadth[136], and that one has to look at the cup[137].

134 The parallel statement in the Babli (51a) is in the name of R. Ḥiyya bar Abba. The inferences are not given there but they follow from the parallel to the next statement.

135 If the left hand only is required to help, the main action is done by the right hand.

136 For a lesser height than a hand-breadth (one sixth of a cubit), no help would be necessary.

137 Otherwise, it would not be necessary to lift the cup during recital of the benedictions.

אָמַר רִבִּי אָחָא שְׁלֹשָׁה דְּבָרִים נֶאֶמְרוּ בְּכוֹס שֶׁל בְּרָכָה מָלֵא. עִיטּוּר. וּמוּדָּח. וּשְׁלָשְׁתָּן בְּפָסוּק אֶחָד נַפְתָּלִי שְׂבַע רָצוֹן וּמָלֵא בִּרְכַּת יי. שְׂבַע עִיטּוּר. רָצוֹן מוּדָּח. מָלֵא כְּמַשְׁמָעוֹ. אָמַר רִבִּי חֲנִינָא אִם עָשִׂיתָה כֵן מַה כְּתִיב תַּמָּן יָם וְדָרוֹם יְרָשָׁה. אַתְּ זוֹכֶה לִירַשׁ הָעוֹלָם הַזֶּה וְהָעוֹלָם הַבָּא.

Rebbi Aḥa said: Three things were said about the cup of Grace: full, decorated, and washed. All three come from one verse (*Deut*. 33:23): "Naphtali is satiated with goodwill, full of the blessings of the Eternal." Satiated - decorated[138], goodwill - washed[139], full as its acception. Rebbi Ḥanina said, if you did so, what is written there: "West and South his inheritance," you merit to inherit this world and the world to come[140].

138 There are different lists in the Babli (51a); one also mentions "decorated" and different interpretations are given. Rav Yehudah is reported to have surrounded himself with his students when he recited Grace over a cup of wine; Rav Ḥisda surrounded the (larger) cup of benediction with smaller cups that presumably were filled with wine. This second interpretation seems to be the one original with the Yerushalmi which identifies satiated with decorated, i. e., more than enough wine to fulfill every desire.

139 So that everybody would willingly take the cup and drink from it. The Babli is a little more explicit and requires "rinsed and dried."

140 This homily is given in the Babli in the name of R. Yose ben R. Ḥanina; R. Yoḥanan says that he is given boundless property. Both seem to note the incongruence of Naphtali inheriting West and South when in fact his territory was the North-Eastern corner of the Land of Israel. Hence, the allusion cannot be meant to describe his territory but is either a geographic amplification or refers to another world.

אָמַר רִבִּי אֶלְעָזָר כּוֹס פָּגוּם אֵין מְבָרְכִין עָלָיו. טָעֲמוֹ פְּגָמוֹ. אַתְּ שְׁמַע מִינָּהּ תְּלָת. שְׁמַע מִינָּהּ כּוֹס פָּגוּם אֵין מְבָרְכִין עָלָיו. וְצָרִיךְ שֶׁיְּהֵא בוֹ כְּשִׁיעוּר. וְטָעֲמוֹ פְּגָמוֹ.

Rebbi Eleazar said: One does not recite benedictions on a damaged cup. If one tasted from it, he damaged it. You may infer from this three things. You infer that one does not recite benedictions on a damaged cup. And that it must contain a measure. And if one tasted from it, he damaged it[141].

141 Two of the three statements are exactly what Rebbi Eleazar said. The only inference to be drawn from the fact that the cup should not be "damaged" is that it must contain a minimum measure (a *reviït*, a quarter *log*) to be valid. In the Babli (*Pesaḥim* 105b/106 a), the derivation is both from the argument given here and from a *baraita* about *Havdalah* after the Sabbath. The parallel argument would have been to derive the necessity of a minimal volume of wine from the next paragraph which implies that if one does not have enough wine for *Qiddush* both Friday night and Sabbath morning one leaves all the wine for the morning. Otherwise, one simply could divide the wine and drink the volume of a liquor glass each time. The order of topics here does not exclude that this also is the Yerushalmi reasoning.

אָמַר רִבִּי תַּנְחוּם בַּר יוּדָן כְּבוֹד הַיּוֹם קוֹדֵם לִכְבוֹד הַלַּיְלָה. קְדוּשַּׁת הַלַּיְלָה קוֹדֶמֶת לִקְדוּשַּׁת הַיּוֹם. אֵי זֶהוּ כְּבוֹד הַיּוֹם רִבִּי יוֹסֵה בְשֵׁם רִבִּי יַעֲקֹב בַּר אָחָא וְרִבִּי אֶלְעָזָר בַּר יוֹסֵף בְּשֵׁם רַב בּוֹרֵא פְּרִי הַגֶּפֶן.

Rebbi Tanḥum bar Yudan said: The honor of the day takes precedence over the honor of the night. The *Qiddush* of the night takes precedence over the *Qiddush* of the day. What is the honor of the day? Rebbi Yosi in the name of Rebbi Jacob bar Aḥa, and Rebbi Eleazar bar Joseph[142] in the name of Rav: "He Who created the fruit of the vine.[143]"

142 An otherwise unknown student of Rav.

143 This means that the primary obligation of reciting *Qiddush* is in the night. The obligation of honoring the Sabbath is mainly during the day. Hence, if there is only one cup of wine, *Qiddush* of the night should be recited over bread. The *honor* of the day, referred to in the Babli euphemistically as "great *Qiddush*," consists in reciting the benediction over wine only, without any additions, over a specially dedicated cup of wine. This is reported and endorsed in the Babli (*Pesaḥim* 106a) as the action "of an old man," confirming a Yerushalmi practice.

רִבִּי זְרִיקָן בַּר חָמוֹי דְּרִבִּי זְרִיקָן הִזְכִּיר שֶׁל חֲנוּכָּה בָּאָרֶץ וְקִילְּסוּ אוֹתוֹ. רִבִּי בָּא בְּרֵיהּ דְּרִבִּי חִיָּא בַּר בָּא הִזְכִּיר דַּיָּין אֱמֶת בְּהַטּוֹב וְהַמֵּטִיב וְקִלְּסוּ אוֹתוֹ.

Rebbi Zeriqan, son of the father-in-law of Rebbi Zeriqan, mentioned Ḥanukkah in "the Land" and they praised him[144]. Rebbi Abba, son of Rebbi Ḥiyya bar Abba, mentioned "the true Judge[145]" in "He Who is good and does good" and they praised him.

144 It was stated in an earlier *baraita* in Halakhah 5 that Ḥanukkah should be mentioned. Here, the place of the mention is fixed in the second benediction of Grace. The Babli (*Šabbath* 24a) concurs, but notes that the mention is not obligatory.

145 The prayer in a house of mourning. The Babli (*Berakhot* 46b) quotes a *baraita* in the name of Rebbi Aqiba which seems to imply that in a house of mourning the benediction "He Who is good" is replaced by "the True Judge"; the Talmud then reinterprets the *baraita* to mean that "the True Judge" is inserted in "He Who is good." The Yerushalmi here gives a date for the re-interpretation.

רִבִּי בָּא בְּרֵיהּ דְּרִבִּי חִיָּיא בַּר בָּא אוֹכֵל מְהַלֵּךְ עוֹמֵד וּמְבָרֵךְ. אוֹכֵל עוֹמֵד יוֹשֵׁב וּמְבָרֵךְ. אוֹכֵל יוֹשֵׁב מֵיסָב וּמְבָרֵךְ. אוֹכֵל מֵיסָב מִתְעַטֵּף וּמְבָרֵךְ. אִם עָשָׂה כֵן הֲרֵי הוּא כְמַלְאֲכֵי הַשָּׁרֵת. מַה טַעֲמָא בִּשְׁתַּיִם יְכַסֶּה פָנָיו וּבִשְׁתַּיִם יְכַסֶּה רַגְלָיו.

Rebbi Abba, son of Rebbi Ḥiyya bar Abba: If one eats walking, he stands still for Grace. If one eats standing, he sits down for Grace. If one eats sitting, he reclines[146] for Grace. If one eats reclining, he wraps himself in his toga[147] for Grace. If one acts in this fashion, he is like an Angel of Service[148]. What is the reason? (*Is.* 6:2) "With two [wings] he would cover his face, and with two [wings] he would cover his feet."

146 On a couch, as for a formal dinner. The statement, that for Grace one always increases one step in dignity, is reported in the Babli (51b) as a *baraita* but is rejected. There it is declared that one always recites Grace sitting upright. There as here, this is the end of the Chapter; one has to see in the Babli an intentional answer to the Yerushalmi.

147 The *tallit* with *tzitzit*.

148 The angels who serve the Divine Presence.

אלו דברים פרק שמיני

משנה א: אֵילוּ דְּבָרִים שֶׁבֵּין בֵּית שַׁמַּאי וּבֵית הִלֵּל בִּסְעוּדָה. בֵּית שַׁמַּאי אוֹמְרִים מְבָרֵךְ עַל הַיּוֹם וְאַחַר כָּךְ מְבָרֵךְ עַל הַיַּיִן. וּבֵית הִלֵּל אוֹמְרִים מְבָרֵךְ עַל הַיַּיִן וְאַחַר כָּךְ מְבָרֵךְ עַל הַיּוֹם.

Mishnah 1: These are the matters between the House of Shammai and the House of Hillel about meals. The House of Shammai say, one pronounces the benediction of the day[1] and then the one over wine. But the House of Hillel say, one pronounces the benediction over wine and aftewards the one of the day.

1 The *Qiddush* of Friday night and holidays that has to precede the meal.

הלכה א: מַה טַעֲמְהוֹן דְּבֵית שַׁמַּאי שֶׁקְּדוּשַּׁת הַיּוֹם גָּרְמָה לְיַיִן שֶׁיָּבוֹא וּכְבָר נִתְחַיֵּב בִּקְדוּשַּׁת הַיּוֹם עַד שֶׁלֹּא בָא הַיַּיִן. מַה טַעֲמְהוֹן דְּבֵית הִלֵּל שֶׁהַיַּיִן גּוֹרֵם לִקְדוּשַּׁת הַיּוֹם שֶׁתֵּאָמֵר. דָּבָר אַחֵר הַיַּיִן תָּדִיר וּקְדוּשָּׁה אֵינָהּ תְּדִירָה.

Halakhah 1: What[2] is the reason of the House of Shammai? The Sanctification of the Day causes the wine to be served; he was obligated for the Sanctification of the Day[3] before the wine was served. What is the reason of the House of Hillel? The wine causes the Sanctification of the Day to be recited[4]. Another explanation: The wine is frequent, Sanctification is less frequent[5].

2 The entire section is paralleled in Yerushalmi *Pesaḥim* 10:2 (with a slightly better text). The content of this paragraph is paralleled in Babli *Berakhot* 51b and, in language very close to the Babli, in Tosephta *Bera-*

khot 5:25. Both Babli and Tosephta add that "practice follows the House of Hillel," a seemingly unnecessary statement since practice always follows the House of Hillel (except if noted otherwise.) It seems that the Tosephta is very old, from before the times of Rabban Gamliel. The Yerushalmi either suppressed the note that was no longer relevant or quotes another source which never had that statement.

3 Since there is a Biblical injunction (*Ex.* 20:8): "Remember the Sabbath Day to declare it holy" and this obligation starts immediately at nightfall, whereas the meal is held later for technical reasons. The laws of *Qiddush* are discussed in Chapter 10 of *Pesaḥim* and reviewed in the author's *The Scholar's Haggadah*, pp. 209-227.

4 The Sanctification cannot be recited without food especially designated for the Sabbath. (However, *Qiddush* may also be recited over the Sabbath bread but this is not the preferred way, at least not in the Land of Israel where wine was and is abundant.)

5 The principle of sacral actions is: The more frequent action (or benediction) has precedence. This is spelled out by the Babli here; Yerushalmi sources are: *Yoma* 2:3, *Šeqalim* 8:6, *Sukkah* 5:6. *Taäniot* 4:5. The principle is implied by the Yerushalmi here. Both Houses have two reasons for their positions. Wine is more frequent since it is also used during weekdays and it may also be used for *Havdalah.*

אָמַר רִבִּי יוֹסֵה מִדִּבְרֵי שְׁנֵיהֶן יַיִן וְהַבְדָּלָה הַיַּיִן קוֹדֵם. כְּלוּם טַעֲמְהוֹן דְּבֵית שַׁמַּאי אֶלָּא שֶׁקְּדוּשַּׁת הַיּוֹם גָּֽרְמָה לְיַיִן שֶׁיָּבוֹא. וְכַאן הוֹאִיל וְלֹא אַבְדָּלָה גָּֽרְמָה לְיַיִן שֶׁיָּבוֹא הַיַּיִן קוֹדֵם. כְּלוּם טַעֲמְהוֹן דְּבֵית הִלֵּל אֶלָּא שֶׁהַיַּיִן תָּדִיר וּקְדוּשָּׁה אֵינָהּ תְּדִירָה. וְכֵן הוֹאִיל וְהַיַּיִן תָּדִיר וְאַבְדָּלָה אֵינָהּ תְּדִירָה הַיַּיִן קוֹדֵם. אָמַר רִבִּי מָנָא מִדִּבְרֵי שְׁנֵיהֶן יַיִן וְאַבְדָּלָה אַבְדָּלָה קוֹדֶמֶת. כְּלוּם טַעֲמְהוֹן דְּבֵית שַׁמַּאי אֶלָּא שֶׁכְּבָר נִתְחַייֵב בִּקְדוּשַּׁת הַיּוֹם עַד שֶׁלֹּא בָּא הַיַּיִן. וְכָאן הוֹאִיל וְנִתְחַייֵב בְּהַבְדָּלָה עַד שֶׁלֹּא בָּא הַיַּיִן אַבְדָּלָה קוֹדֶמֶת. כְּלוּם טַעֲמְהוֹן דְּבֵית הִלֵּל אֶלָּא שֶׁהַיַּיִן גּוֹרֵם לִקְדוּשַּׁת הַיּוֹם שֶׁתֵּאָמֵר. וְכָאן הוֹאִיל וְאֵין הַיַּיִן גּוֹרֵם לְאַבְדָּלָה שֶׁתֵּאָמֵר אַבְדָּלָה קוֹדֶמֶת.

Rebbi Yose[6] said: From the words of both of them[7] it follows that for wine and *Havdalah*[8], the wine comes first. Is not the reason of the House of Shammai that the Sanctification of the Day causes the wine to be served? But here, *Havdalah* does not cause the wine to be served[9]; wine therefore has precedence. Is not the reason of the House of Hillel that the wine is frequent, Sanctification of the Day is less frequent? Also here, wine is frequent and *Havdalah* is less frequent: the wine has precedence. Rebbi Mana said: From the words of both of them it follows that for wine and *Havdalah*, *Havdalah* comes first. Is not the reason of the House of Shammai that he was obligated for the Sanctification of the Day before the wine came? Also here, since he is obligated for *Havdalah* before the wine came, *Havdalah* has precedence. Is not the reason of the House of Hillel that the wine causes the Sanctification of the Day to be recited? But here, the wine does not cause *Havdalah* to be recited: *Havdalah* has precedence[9].

6 He is R. Yasa (Assi), colleague of R. Mana I.

7 The Houses of Hillel and Shammai.

8 The "separation" between Sabbath and weekdays that has to be recited at the end of Sabbath. The obligation of reciting *Havdalah* starts at the very moment of nightfall.

9 *Havdalah* may be recited over any alcoholic beverage (in the opinion of the Babli, over any beverage, other than water, that is common in the country.) *Qiddush* may be recited only over wine or possibly the Sabbath bread.

10 Hence, the problem is undecided and both practices, that of R. Yose and that of R. Mana, are possible, since the two reasons given by each of the two Houses lead to contradictory results if applied to *Havdalah*.

אָמַר רִבִּי זְעִירָא מִדִּבְרֵי שְׁנֵיהֶן מַבְדִּילִין בְּלֹא יַיִן וְאֵין מְקַדְּשִׁין בְּלֹא יַיִן. הִיא דַעְתֵּיהּ דְּרִבִּי זְעִירָא. דְּרִבִּי זְעִירָא אָמַר מַבְדִּילִין עַל הַשֵּׁכָר וַאֲזְלִין מִן אֲתָר לַאֲתָר מִשּׁוּם קִדּוּשָׁה.

Rebbi Zeïra said: One infers from the words of both of them[11] that one may make *Havdalah* without wine but one may not make *Qiddush* without wine[12]. That is the opinion of Rebbi Zeïra since Rebbi Zeïra said: One makes *Havdalah* on alcoholic beverages[13] but one goes from one place[14] to another to hear *Qiddush*.

11 Rebbi Yose and Rebbi Mana.

12 Whereas the Babli (*Pesaḥim* 106b) allows one to make *Qiddush* over bread, at least in Babylonia where wine is hard to come by.

13 Any alcoholic beverage, including low grade beer. The opinion of the Babli is not clearly stated (*Pesaḥim* 107a), but the practice there is spelled out that any alcoholic beverage common in a country may be used for *Havdalah*. Current practice allows even non-alcoholic beverages, except water, as long as they are commonly used (*Oraḥ Ḥayyim* 296(2)).

14 The physical exertion of the walk may interfere with one's Sabbath rest but the duty to hear *Qiddush* recited over wine has precedence.

אָמַר רִבִּי יוֹסֵי בְּרִיבִּי נְהִיגִין תַּמָּן בְּמָקוֹם שֶׁאֵין יַיִן שְׁלִיחַ צִיבּוּר עוֹבֵר לִפְנֵי הַתֵּיבָה וְאוֹמֵר בְּרָכָה אַחַת מֵעֵין שֶׁבַע וְחוֹתֵם בִּמְקַדֵּשׁ יִשְׂרָאֵל וְאֶת יוֹם הַשַּׁבָּת.

The Great Rebbi Yose said: Over there[15], they have the custom that at a place without wine, the reader stands before the Ark[16], recites one benediction that contains seven[17], and closes by "He Who sanctifies Israel and the Sabbath Day[18]."

15 In Babylonia.

16 For a formal prayer, a kind of shortened repetition of the *'Amidah*. Normally, evening prayers are communal without a reader.

17 The middle portion of the prayer by the reader contains allusions to all seven benedictions of the Sabbath *'Amidah*: "(1) Shield of the Patriarch, (2) He Who revives the dead by His command, (3) the Holy God, (4) Who gives rest to His people, (5) before Him we shall serve (6) and give thanks to His name, God of thanksgiving, (7) Master of peace." Today, the benediction is recited always except the

first night of Passover when everybody is required to drink four cups of wine; thus, there is no reason to replace *Qiddush* by public prayer. In Babylonian sources, the benediction is not mentioned explicitly; in Medieval sources, a different reason is given for the benediction.

18 This is the Israeli formula. The Babylonian one has only "He Who sanctifies the Sabbath," probably because the Sabbath is a cosmic day of rest in contrast to holidays that exist only in Jewish history.

וְקַשְׁיָא עַל דְּבֵית שַׁמַּאי בְּלֵילֵי שַׁבָּת הֵיאַךְ עֲבִידָא. הָיָה יוֹשֵׁב וְאוֹכֵל בְּעֶרֶב שַׁבָּת וְחָשְׁכָה לֵילֵי שַׁבָּת וְאֵין שָׁם אֶלָּא אוֹתוֹ הַכּוֹס אַתְּ אָמַר מֵנִיחוֹ לְאַחַר הַמָּזוֹן וּמְשַׁלְשֵׁל כּוּלָּם עָלָיו. מַה נַפְשֵׁךְ יְבָרֵךְ עַל הַיּוֹם הַמָּזוֹן קוֹדֵם. יְבָרֵךְ עַל הַיַּיִן הַיּוֹם קוֹדֵם. נִשְׁמְעִינָהּ מִן הֲדָא. בָּא לָהֶן יַיִן אַחַר הַמָּזוֹן וְאֵין שָׁם אֶלָּא אוֹתוֹ הַכּוֹס. אָמַר רִבִּי בָּא עַל יְדֵי שֶׁהִיא בְּרָכָה קְטַנָּה שֶׁמָּא יִשְׁכַּח וְיִשְׁתֶּה. בְּרַם הָכָא מְשַׁלְשְׁלָהּ עַל יְדֵי הַכּוֹס אֵינוֹ שׁוֹכֵחַ. כֵּיצַד יַעֲשׂוּ עַל דִּבְרֵי בֵית שַׁמַּאי יְבָרֵךְ עַל הַמָּזוֹן תְּחִילָּה וְאַחַר כַּךְ מְבָרֵךְ עַל הַיּוֹם וְאַחַר כַּךְ עַל הַיַּיִן.

It is difficult in the opinion of the House of Shammai, how to proceed on Friday evening if someone was sitting and eating on Friday afternoon, it got dark, and there was only one cup of wine[19]? You must say that he reserves the cup until after the recitation of Grace and includes all other benedictions. Obviously, if he would want to pronounce the benediction for the day, Grace has precedence[20]. If he wants to recite the benediction over wine, the day has precedence[21]. One may infer this from the following (*Mishnah* 8:9): "If wine was brought to them after the meal and there was only one cup.[22]" Rebbi Abba said: Because it is a very short benediction, he might forget and drink[23]. But here, he connects everything with the cup of wine and he will not forget. How should he proceed according to the House of Shammai? He should recite Grace first, after that he makes *Qidddush*, and only after that he recites the benediction over the wine.

19 One returns to the discussion of the Mishnah. One may not start a meal Friday afternoon close to the Sabbath (Mishnah *Shabbat* 1:2) but one may start earlier and continue until nightfall. The Talmud (Babli *Pesaḥim* 100a, Yerushalmi *Pesaḥim* 10:1, fol. 37b) reports that R. Yehudah bar Illai requires one to stop before nightfall, but R. Yose bar Ḥalaphta lets him continue, and practice follows R. Yose. It is assumed here that even the House of Shammai will accept the position of R. Yose.

20 Even if one continues, the Sabbath meal must be separate since eating on Sabbath is a religious obligation. Hence, Grace must be said for the preceding meal and, if one has wine, it must be recited over a cup of wine.

21 According to the House of Shammai.

22 In that situation, the House of Shammai say that one starts Grace with the benediction over wine while the House of Hillel require the benediction for wine after Grace. It would seem that in our situation also, the wine could come before *Qiddush*.

23 He might inadvertently drink from the wine after Grace without a benediction. This is a special situation and the House of Shammai will not agree to apply that Mishnah to it.

וְקַשְׁיָא עַל דִּבְרֵי בֵית הִלֵּל בְּמוֹצָאֵי שַׁבָּת הֵיאַךְ עֲבִידָא. הָיָה יוֹשֵׁב וְאוֹכֵל בְּשַׁבָּת וְחָשְׁכָה מוֹצָאֵי שַׁבָּת וְאֵין שָׁם אֶלָּא אוֹתוֹ הַכּוֹס אַתְּ אָמַר מֵנִיחוֹ לְאַחַר הַמָּזוֹן וּמְשַׁלְשֵׁל כּוּלָּם עָלָיו. מַה נַפְשֵׁךְ יְבָרֵךְ (fol. 12a) עַל הַיַּיִן הַמָּזוֹן קוֹדֵם. יְבָרֵךְ עַל הַמָּזוֹן הַנֵּר קוֹדֵם. יְבָרֵךְ עַל הַנֵּר אַבְדָּלָה קוֹדֶמֶת. נִשְׁמְעִינָהּ מִן הֲדָא. אָמַר רִבִּי יְהוּדָה לֹא נֶחְלְקוּ בֵית שַׁמַּאי וּבֵית הִלֵּל עַל בִּרְכַּת הַמָּזוֹן שֶׁהִיא בַּתְּחִילָּה וְלֹא עַל הַבְדָּלָה שֶׁהִיא בַּסּוֹף. עַל מַה נֶחְלְקוּ עַל הַנֵּר וְעַל הַבְּשָׂמִים שֶׁבֵּית שַׁמַּאי אוֹמְרִים בְּשָׂמִים וְאַחַר כַּךְ נֵר. וּבֵית הִלֵּל אוֹמְרִים מָאוֹר וְאַחַר כַּךְ בְּשָׂמִים. רָבָא וְרַב יְהוּדָה הֲלָכָה כְּמִי שֶׁהוּא אוֹמֵר בְּשָׂמִים וְאַחַר כַּךְ נֵר. כֵּיצַד יַעֲשׂוּ עַל דִּבְרֵי בֵית הִלֵּל. יְבָרֵךְ עַל הַמָּזוֹן תְּחִילָּה וְאַחַר כַּךְ יְבָרֵךְ עַל הַיַּיִן וְאַחַר כַּךְ עַל הַנֵּר.

It is difficult in the opinion of the House of Hillel, how may one proceed at the end of the Sabbath if someone was sitting and eating on Sabbath, it got dark, and there was only one cup of wine? You say, he reserves it[24] until after the meal and connects everything to it. What can you say? Shall he recite the benediction for the wine, Grace has precedence. Shall he recite Grace, the light has precedence[25]. Shall he recite for the light, *Havdalah* has precedence. We may infer from the following[26]: "Rebbi Yehudah said, the house of Shammai and the house of Hillel do not disagree that Grace comes first and *Havdalah* at the end. They disagree only over light and spices because the House of Shammai say spices and afterwards light, but the house of Hillel say light and afterwards spices." Rebbi Abba and Rav Jehudah[27]: Practice follows him who says spices and afterwards light. What should he do following the opinion of the House of Hillel? He should say Grace first, afterwards he should recite the benediction over wine and afterwards *Havdalah.*

24 The cup of wine that should follow Grace and precede *Havdalah.*

25 After the end of the Sabbath, one has to recite not only *Havdalah* but with it a benediction for man-made fire (that was forbidden on the Sabbath and now can be kindled anew) and spices (to make up for the loss of the intensified pleasure one derives from the Sabbath that now is being lost.) The invention of man-made fire is traditionally attributed to Adam at the end of his first Sabbath, see Halakhah 6. The problem here is that one must make the benediction for the light as soon as one profits from newly lit fire.

26 Tosephta *Berakhot* 5:30, Babli *Berakhot* 52a. In both of these sources, the House of Shammai is reported to require light before spices and the House of Hillel spices before light. R. Arieh Leib Yellin in his *Yephe Enayim* points out that the text of the Yerushalmi is consistent with all the inferences drawn here and in Halakhah 5. Hence, there is a genuine difference in tradition between Galilee and Babylonia.

27 Two Babylonians, one an authority in Galilee, the other in Babylonia. They are responsible for enforcing uniformity in Jewish custom in both countries.

יוֹם טוֹב שֶׁחָל לִהְיוֹת בְּמוֹצָאֵי שַׁבָּת. רִבִּי יוֹחָנָן אָמַר יק״נה יַיִן קִידּוּשׁ נֵר הַבְדָּלָה. חָנִין בַּר בָּא אָמַר בְּשֵׁם רַב יַיִן קִידּוּשׁ נֵר הַבְדָּלָה סוּכָּה וּזְמָן. רִבִּי חֲנִינָא אָמַר [28]נהי״ק. אַתְיָא דִשְׁמוּאֵל כַּהֲדָא דְרִבִּי חֲנִינָא דְּאָמַר רִבִּי אָחָא בְשֵׁם רִבִּי יְהוֹשֻׁעַ בֶּן לֵוִי מֶלֶךְ יוֹצֵא וְשִׁלְטוֹן נִכְנָס מְלַוִּין אֶת הַמֶּלֶךְ וְאַחַר כָּךְ מַכְנִיסִין אֶת הַשִּׁלְטוֹן. לֵוִי אָמַר ינה״ק. מִסְתַּבְּרָא דְּלֵוִי אָמַר מֵעֵין שְׁנֵיהֶם. [29]רִבִּי זְעִירָא בְּעָא קוֹמֵי רִבִּי יוֹסֵי הֵיךְ עָבְדִין עוּבְדָּא. אָמַר לֵיהּ כְּרַב וּכְרִבִּי יוֹחָנָן. וְכֵן נְפַק עוּבְדָּה כְּרַב וּכְרִבִּי יוֹחָנָן.

A holiday that starts at the end of Sabbath. Rebbi Yoḥanan said YQNH, wine, *Qiddush*, light, *Havdalah*. Ḥanan bar Abba said in the name of Rav: Wine, *Qiddush*, light, *Havdalah, sukkah*, time[30]. Rebbi Ḥanina said, NHYQ[31]. Samuel follows the opinion of Rebbi Ḥanina since Rebbi Aḥa said in the name of Rebbi Joshua ben Levi[32]: A king[33] leaves and a prefect comes. One accompanies the king and only afterwards does one receive the prefect. Levi said YNHQ[34]. It seems that Levi says it both ways[35]. Rebbi Zeïra asked before Rebbi Yose[36]: What does one do in practice? He said to him: one follows Rav and Rebbi Yoḥanan. And so it became the practice following Rav and Rebbi Yoḥanan.

28 The Venice text here is self-contradictory: י״נהיק. שמואל לא אמר. Hence, the text chosen for the next three words is that of the Rome manuscript.

29 The Venice text has here a superfluous אמר that is not found in the Rome ms.

30 He agrees with Rebbi Yoḥanan but includes all possibilities that may be appropriate for a holiday. The benediction for time is: "He Who let us live, kept us, and let us reach this time." This benediction is not recited on the last day of Passover. Hence, Rebbi Yoḥanan gives the minimal formula as pointed out in the Babli (*Pesaḥim* 101b).

31 Light, *Havdalah*, wine, *Qiddush*. In the Babli (*Pesaḥim* 102a), this order is attributed to R. Joshua, the early highest authority who is given his full name, R. Joshua ben Ḥananiah. It is possible that this led to the substitution of "R. Joshua ben Levi" for "Samuel" in the following parable. However, Rashbam (R. Samuel ben Meïr), in his

commentary to Babli *Pesaḥim*, quotes R. Ḥanina as requiring YNHQ, wine, light, *Havdalah, Qiddush*. But this is the undisputed order of Levi here who is described as taking a middle road between R. Ḥanina and R. Yoḥanan. The Venice print of the Yerushalmi has the impossible reading YNHYQ which is a confluence of the codes attributed to R. Ḥanina in the Babli and the Yerushalmi.

32 Rashbam quotes "in the name of Samuel". In the Babli, as mentioned earlier, this parable is from "R. Ḥanina illustrating the words of R. Joshua ben Ḥananiah."

33 The king is the Sabbath and the subordinate prefect is the holiday; the Sabbath has to be mentioned first, including the light that belongs to the ceremony of Sabbath end, before making *Qiddush* for the holiday. Since holidays also give one spiritual ease, spices are not added at the end of a Sabbath that is the start of a holiday.

34 Wine, light, *Havdalah, Qiddush*; first the full *Havdalah* and then an appended *Qiddush*. In the Babli (*Pesaḥim* 102a), Levi is reported as requiring QNYH, in opposition to everybody mentioned here.

35 He puts wine first following R. Yoḥanan and *Havdalah* before *Qiddush* following R. Ḥanina.

36 R. Yasa (Assi) elsewhere. The Babylonian R. Zeïra inquired from the Tiberian R. Assi whether the practice in Galilee was identical with the Babylonian.

רִבִּי אַבָּהוּ כַּד הֲוָה אָזִיל לִדְרוֹמָה הֲוָה עֲבִיד כְּרִבִּי חֲנִינָא. וְכַד הֲוָה נָחִית לְטִיבֵּרְיָא הֲוָה עֲבִיד כְּרִבִּי יוֹחָנָן. דְּלָא מִפְלַג עַל בַּרְנַשׁ בְּאַתְרֵיהּ.

When Rebbi Abbahu went to the South[37], he followed Rebbi Ḥanina. When he descended[38] to Tiberias, he followed Rebbi Yoḥanan in order not to disagree with anybody in his home town.

37 The region of Lod, the only remaining Jewish settlement in Judea and the Southern plain. R. Abbahu lived in Caesarea and personally followed the rule of R. Ḥanina who always speaks in the name of the authority of Rebbi.

38 Tiberias is below sea level. From Caesarea Philippi (Banias) one has to descend, from Caesarea Maritima via Bet Sheän one would ascend.

עַל דַּעְתֵּיהּ דְּרִבִּי חֲנִינָא נִיחָא. וְקַשְׁיָא עַל[39] רִבִּי יוֹחָנָן אִילּוּ בִשְׁאַר יְמוֹת הַשָּׁנָה אֵינוֹ מְבָרֵךְ עַל הַנֵּר שֶׁלֹּא יִכְבֶּה. וְכָא מְבָרֵךְ עַל הַנֵּר שֶׁלֹּא יִכְבֶּה. מַה עֲבַד לֵיהּ רִבִּי יוֹחָנָן מִכֵּיוָן שֶׁיֵּשׁ לוֹ יַיִן אֵין נֵרוֹ כוֹבֶה. וִיבָרֵךְ עַל הַנֵּר בְּסוֹף. שֶׁלֹּא לַעֲקוֹר זְמָן מִן הַשַּׁבָּתוֹת הַבָּאוֹת.

The opinion of Rebbi Ḥanina is understandable. It is difficult to understand Rebbi Yoḥanan: Does one not pronounce the benediction over the light at all other days that one should extinguish it[40]? And here, he makes the benediction over the light so that he should not extinguish it[41]. How does Rebbi Yoḥanan handle this? Since he has wine[42], his light will not go out. Then he might say the benediction over the light at the end[43]. In order not to disturb its timing from other Sabbaths[44].

39 Reading of the Rome ms. The Venice print has יוחנן על.

40 Since the light is for celebration only; it is extinguished after *Havdalah*. The light for *Havdalah* is preferably a torch, but the light for a meal is from a lamp.

41 On a holiday, one may light a fire (from an existing one) but one may not extinguish it. Hence, the light in our case is a light for the meal, not for *Havdalah*, and should precede *Qiddush* irrespective of the order of *Qiddush* and *Havdalah*. [In current practice, the wife lights the candles first with her own benediction and the husband then recites his benediction (after *Qiddush*) over the same lights. That does not seem to be reasonable. It may be assumed that R. Ḥanina requires either husband or wife to recite the first benediction over light.]

42 For a full meal for which the light is needed.

43 When the light is really needed for the food.

44 To keep the order wine - (spices) - light - *Havdalah* as a matter of course.

(fol. 11d) **משנה ב:** בֵּית שַׁמַּאי אוֹמְרִים נוֹטְלִין לְיָדַיִם וְאַחַר כָּךְ מוֹזְגִין אֶת הַכּוֹס. וּבֵית הִלֵּל אוֹמְרִים מוֹזְגִין הַכּוֹס תְּחִילָּה וְאַחַר כָּךְ נוֹטְלִין לְיָדַיִם.

Mishnah 2: The House of Shammai say that one washes his hands and after that he mixes the cup, but the House of Hillel say that one mixes the cup first and then he washes his hands[45].

45 The cup here is the *Qiddush* cup. *Qiddush* is followed by a meal with bread for which one must wash his hands. The details and reasons are spelled out in the Halakhah. This disagreement has nothing to do with the question whether one washes his hands before (following R. Moses Isserls) or after (following R. Joseph Caro) *Qiddush*; in both cases, the cup is filled before one washes his hands.

(fol. 12a) **הלכה ב**: מַה טַעֲמוֹן דְּבֵית שַׁמַּאי שֶׁלֹּא יִטָּמְאוּ מַשְׁקִין שֶׁאֲחוֹרֵי הַכּוֹס מִיָּדָיו וְיַחְזְרוּ וִיטַמְּאוּ אֶת הַכּוֹס.

Halakhah 2: What is the reason of the House of Shammai? The fluids on the back of the cup should not become impure from his hands and in their turn defile the cup[46].

46 The Biblical principles on ritual impurity are spelled out in the book of *Leviticus*. A Biblical source of impurity is called אב הטומאה "father of impurity". The only possible objects of impurity are humans, vessels, and food. Any object that becomes impure secondarily, usually by contact, is "first in impurity." For profane objects, the two stages are the only ones. However, by rabbinic tradition there exists a "second in impurity" for profane and "third, fourth" for certain holy objects. The general principle is that any transmitted impurity decreases by one degree. There is one important exception. Since body fluids of a person with gonorrhea are "fathers of impurity", it was decreed that any impurity involving fluids is at least "first in impurity." Also, unwashed hands are always assumed to be "second in impurity." If one touches a dry cup with unwashed hands, nothing happens. But if there should be drops of wine on the outside of the cup, these drops will become "first in impurity" and defile the contents of the cup. It is the characteristic of Rabbinic (pharisaic) Judaism that one tries to eat one's profane meals in a way reasonably consistent with rules of

ritual purity. It seems that the House of Shammai assumes that a "full cup" required for *Qiddush* is full to the rim, kept together only by surface tension, and, hence, it is unlikely that the back of the cup will be dry. (For pottery vessels, other rules apply.)

The text of the explanation is from the Tosephta (*Berakhot* 5:26).

מַה טַעֲמוֹן דְּבֵית הִלֵּל לְעוֹלָם אֲחוֹרֵי הַכּוֹס טְמֵאִין. דָּבָר אַחֵר אֵין נְטִילַת יָדַיִם אֶלָּא סָמוּךְ לִבְרָכָה.

What is the reason of the House of Hillel? The back of the cup is always impure[47]. Another explanation: Washing of the hands should be as close as possible to the benediction[48].

47 The back of the cup is impure ("second in impurity") by Rabbinic decree, as explained in the next paragraph. If one washes his hands first and does not dry them very thorougly, then the hands will become "first in impurity" by holding the cup, as explained in the previous note, and one is worse off than with unwashed hands. (This is also the explanation of the Babli, 52a.) The House of Hillel assume that a "full cup" is one filled close to the rim but leaving a reasonable safety margin as hedge against a spill.

48 It is not clear whether the benediction in question is that over bread (R. Joseph Caro) or the wine for *Qiddush* (R. Moshe Isserls). Here also both explanations are from the Tosephta (*loc. cit.*)

רִבִּי בִּיבָן בְּשֵׁם רִבִּי יוֹחָנָן אַתְיָא דְּבֵית שַׁמַּאי כְּרִבִּי יוֹסֵי וּדְבֵית הִלֵּל כְּרִבִּי מֵאִיר. דְּתַנִּינָן תַּמָּן רִבִּי מֵאִיר אוֹמֵר לְיָדַיִם טְמֵאוֹת וּטְהוֹרוֹת. אָמַר רִבִּי יוֹסֵי לֹא אָמְרוּ אֶלָּא לְיָדַיִם טְהוֹרוֹת בִּלְבָד.

Rebbi Vivan[49] in the name of Rebbi Yoḥanan: It turns out that the House of Shammai is consistent with Rebbi Yose and the House of Hillel with Rebbi Meïr[50], since we have stated there (Mishnah *Kelim* 25:7)[51]: "Rebbi Meïr said, for impure and pure hands. Rebbi Yose said, they spoke only about pure hands."

49 A Galilean Amora of the third generation, student of all the great Amoraïm of R. Johanan's generation. His name probably was Vivianus. In other quotes, his name is shortened to Bibi, Vivi.

50 This is paradoxical since practice follows the House of Hillel and Rebbi Yose. The Babli (52a/b) explains otherwise, that the Houses of Shammai and Hillel disagree on whether one may use a cup which is impure outside at all if one cares about consuming food in purity.

51 Chapter 25 starts: "All vessels have an inside and an outside." For earthenware vessels, it is a decree of the Torah that they become impure only if an impure "father of impurity" is found in the volume enclosed by the vessel (even without touching the walls,) never from the outside (even if the "father of impurity" touches the wall.) From this is derived a Rabbinic decree that also all other vessels, e. g. metal vessels that become impure from a biblical "father of impurity" by simple touch, cannot become impure inside if a Rabbinic impurity touches from the outside (but not vice versa.) Mishnah 7 then reads: "All vessels have an outside, an inside, and a rim. Rebbi Tarphon said, [one speaks of] a large wooden trough, Rebbi Aqiba said, of cups. Rebbi Meïr said for impure and pure hands, R. Yose said, they spoke only about pure hands." Since inside and outside have been discussed before, the opinions of Rabbis Meïr and Yose, students of R. Aqiba, deal with the rim, the part of the outside of the cup that is slightly bent outward or otherwise distinguished as place for the lips when one drinks from the cup. The explanation of the Mishnah is given in Tosephta *Kelim Baba bathra* 3:9-10: "R. Meïr said: How is it for impure hands? If one's hands are impure, the outside of the cup is pure; if it has moist spots then he may hold the cup by its rim without worry. R. Yose said: How is it for pure hands? If his hands were pure and moist, but the outside of the cup impure, then he may hold the cup at the rim without worrying that the moisture of his hand should become impure from the outside and then defile his hand." It follows that for R. Yose, the hands have to be pure (i. e., washed) and for R. Meïr they may be impure.

רִבִּי יוֹסֵי בְשֵׁם רִבִּי שַׁבְּתַי וְרִבִּי חִייָא בְשֵׁם רִבִּי שִׁמְעוֹן בֶּן לָקִישׁ לְחַלָּה וְלִנְטִילַת יָדַיִם אָדָם מְהַלֵּךְ אַרְבַּע מִיל. רִבִּי אַבָּהוּ בְשֵׁם רִבִּי יוֹסֵי בֵּי רִבִּי חֲנִינָא הֲדָא דַאֲמַר לְפָנָיו אֲבָל לַאֲחָרָיו אֵין מַטְרִיחִין עָלָיו.

Rebbi Yose[52] in the name of Rebbi Sabbatai[53] and Rebbi Ḥiyya[54] in the name of Rebbi Simeon ben Laqish: For *ḥallah*[55] and for washing one's hands[56], he has to walk[57] up to four *mil*. Rebbi Abbahu in the name of Rebbi Yose ben Rebbi Ḥanina: That is, going forward; but one does not bother him to return on his way[58].

52 He is R. Yasa (Assi).

53 An Israeli Amora of the first generation, student of Ḥizqiah the son of Rebbi Ḥiyya.

54 He is Rebbi Ḥiyya bar Abba.

55 *Ḥallah* is the gift for the Cohen from newly kneaded dough. It has the status of holiness of *Terumah*; hence, it has to be separated from the dough in purity which, in all cases, means also that in the Land of Israel one has to wash his hands before taking it. (All other countries are impure anyhow and their *ḥallah* must be burned.)

56 For any action for which the washing of one's hands is required.

57 If no water is available one has to wait, e. g., to eat bread, until he has washed his hands. If the distance to water is greater than 4 *mil* then the Babli declares in the name of the Galilean sages that one should clean his hands with sand or any other cleaning material.

58 The Babli (15a) has a different rule, that one has to return if the distance required is less than one *mil*.

שׁוֹמְרֵי גַּנּוֹת וּפַרְדֵּסִים מַה אַתְּ עֲבַד לָהֶן כִּלְפְנֵיהֶן כִּלְאַחֲרֵיהֶן. נִשְׁמְעִינָהּ מִן הֲדָא הָאִשָּׁה יוֹשֶׁבֶת וְקוֹצָה לָהּ חַלָּתָהּ עֲרוּמָה מִפְּנֵי שֶׁהִיא יְכוֹלָה לְכַסּוֹת אֶת עַצְמָהּ אֲבָל לֹא הָאִישׁ. וַהֲדָא אִשָּׁה לֹא בְתוֹךְ הַבַּיִת הִיא יוֹשֶׁבֶת וְאַתְּ אֲמַר אֵין מַטְרִיחִין עָלֶיהָ. וְכַאן אֵין מַטְרִיחִין עָלָיו.

How does one treat watchmen in gardens and orchards, as before them, as after them[59]? Let us hear it from this (Mishnah *Ḥallah* 2:3): "A woman may sit down naked and separate her *ḥallah*[60] because she can cover herself, but a man may not." Is that woman not sitting inside her house[61] and you say that one does not bother her? Also here, one does not bother him[62].

59 Do they have to go up to four *mil* in search of water or may they clean their hands with sand or other cleansers?

60 Since the separation of *ḥallah* needs a benediction, it may not be done if one's genitals are visible. A woman may hide her genitals by sitting down but a man cannot do that.

61 And, presumably, has some clothes there that she could put on. The entire argument is possible only for the Yerushalmi which does not require any retracing of one's steps at all in the search for water; it is impossible for the Babli which requires retracing one's steps, if only for a reduced distance.

62 One does not bother him at all and if there is no water at his place, he need not leave it in his search for water.

תַּנֵּי מַיִם שֶׁלִּפְנֵי הַמָּזוֹן רְשׁוּת וְשֶׁל אַחַר הַמָּזוֹן חוֹבָה. אֶלָּא שֶׁבָּרִאשׁוֹנִים נוֹטֵל וּמַפְסִיק. וּבַשְּׁנִיִּים נוֹטֵל וְאֵינוֹ מַפְסִיק. מַה הוּא נוֹטֵל וּמַפְסִיק. רִבִּי יַעֲקֹב בַּר אָחָא אָמַר נוֹטֵל וְשׁוֹנֶה. רִבִּי שְׁמוּאֵל בַּר יִצְחָק אָמַר בְּעִי נוֹטֵל וְשׁוֹנֶה וְאַתְּ אָמַרְתְּ רְשׁוּת.

It has been stated[63]: "Water before the meal is conditional[64], after the meal it is obligatory. Only that for the first one he takes and interrupts[65]; for the second he takes and may not interrupt[66]." What is: "He takes and interrupts"? Rebbi Jacob bar Aḥa said, he takes[67] and repeats. Rebbi Samuel bar Isaac said[68], I asked: "He takes and interrupts[69]" and you say it is conditional?

63 The language is close to Tosephta *Berakhot* 5:13. Since the Mishnah introduces laws of washing one's hands, the details are discussed from here on.

64 In the language of the Babli, רשות means "permitted." However, in the language of the Mishnah and the Yerushalmi, i. e., the language of the Land of Israel, רשות means "a minor obligation" as shown by S. Lieberman

[תיקוני ירושלמי, *Tarbiẓ* 5 (5694), pp. 97-110]. The same language is found in the Tosephta, in *Tanḥuma Balaq* 15, and in other Galilean Midrashim. The *Tanḥuma* explains the expression "conditional" for something that is required, by "it is optional in the sense that if one decides not to eat bread with his meal, he does not have to wash his hands."

65 Most commentators explain this expression from the Mishnah *Yadayim* 2:1-3 that rules, if one washed his hands with less than a *revi'it* of water for each hand then he has to wash each hand twice. However, in that case it is not true that one may interrupt the washing because if he does not keep his mind concentrated on watching his hands they become impure again. As S. Lieberman points out, one might follow the interpretation of R. Isaiah I of Trani (*Pisqe RYD* on *Berakhot* 52a) that the Yerushalmi here stays with the previous topic of *Qiddush* and speaks of washing one's hands twice, once for *Qiddush* for cleanliness and after that for food for ritual purity. This agrees with Tosephta *Berakhot* 4:8, which requires the washing of one hand for the wine drunk as appetizer before a formal dinner.

66 Washing one's hands after the meal is not a ritual requirement. Since spoons and forks were not used, the hands were dirty by necessity. Washing one's hands after any meal involving sauces was a necessity for cleanliness (in the opinion of the Yerushalmi, later in this Halakhah) or for health reasons (in the opinion of the Babli). In any case, since no ritual impurity is involved, there is no required minimum volume of water and one does not have to repeat the washing.

67 Takes water and pours it over his hands.

68 In the parallel in *Ḥallah* it reads: "Rebbi *Jacob* bar Isaac asked: . . ." This language is somewhat easier but the reading R. *Samuel* bar Isaac is better; since it refers to an Amora also otherwise known, there is no reason to cross out the word "said" here. In the Rome ms., the reading is: רבי שמואל בר יצחק את מימר דבעי ואת אמרת רשות "R. Samuel bar Isaac: You say that it is needed and you say that it is conditional?"

69 In peremptory language.

אָמַר רִבִּי יַעֲקֹב בַּר אִידִי עַל הָרִאשׁוֹנִים נֶאֱכַל בְּשַׂר חֲזִיר. עַל הַשְּׁנִיִּים יָצְאָה אִשָּׁה מִבֵּיתָהּ. וְיֵשׁ אוֹמְרִים שֶׁנֶּהֶרְגוּ עָלֶיהָ שְׁלֹשָׁה נְפָשׁוֹת.

Rebbi Jacob bar Idi said: Because of the first[70], pork was eaten. Because of the second[71], a woman had to leave her house; some say, three persons were killed.

70 The water used for washing one's hands before the meal. The text is given in the name of Rav Dimi in Babli *Ḥulin* 106a, the opinion of "some say" is ascribed there to Ravin (Rebbi Abin). The full story is in *Tanḥuma Buber Balaq* 24 [quoted also in *Tanḥuma Balaq* 15, *Bemidbar rabba Balaq* 2(20)]: In a time of persecution, when one could not show one's Jewishness openly, a shopkeeper had both kosher and non-kosher food prepared. Since he could not ask his customers whether they were Jewish, he gave the kosher food to people who washed before eating bread and pig's meat to customers who did not wash. When a man came in who did not wash his hands, he was taken for a Gentile and served non-kosher food. [For halakhic consequences of this story, see *Šulḥan 'Arukh Yore Deä* 178, Note #4 of *Šifte Cohen.*]

71 The washing of one's hands after the meal. The story is told in Babli *Yoma* 83b of a man who unlawfully kept a money-pouch that was deposited with him. He did not wash his hands, so the victimized person saw that he had eaten peas, went to the wife of the thief and told her that her husband wanted her to give him the pouch and as sign of recognition he told him to tell her that their last meal was peas. The wife then gave him back the money pouch. When the husband came back, he was so incensed that he killed his wife. It seems that the Yerushalmi has a first version in which the husband simply divorced his wife and in the second version he killed his wife, the intended victim, and himself. In the Yerushalmi source, *Tanḥuma Buber*, quoted above, the husband was not a thief, but he was the victim of a man who tricked the wife out of a precious ring by the identification of the food of his last meal.

שְׁמוּאֵל סְלַק לְגַבֵּי רַב. חָמָא יָתֵיהּ אֲכַל בְּחָתָה יָדֵיהּ.[72] אֲמַר לֵיהּ מַהוּ כֵן. אֲמַר לֵיהּ אִסְתְּנֵיס אֲנִי. רִבִּי זְעִירָא כַּד סְלֵיק לְהָכָא חָמָא כֹּהֲנַיָּא אָכְלִין בְּחָתָה יָדֵיהּ. אֲמַר לוֹן הָא אֲזִילָא הַהִיא דְּרַב וּשְׁמוּאֵל. אָתָא רִבִּי יוֹסֵי בַּר בַּר כַּהֲנָא בְשֵׁם שְׁמוּאֵל נְטִילַת יָדַיִם לְחוּלִּין אֵין נְטִילַת יָדַיִם לִתְרוּמָה. רִבִּי יוֹסֵי אוֹמֵר לִתְרוּמָה וּלְחוּלִּין.

Samuel went to visit Rav and saw him eating with his hands covered by cloth. He asked him, what is that[73]? He answered him, I am asthenic[74]. When Rebbi Zeïra immigrated here, he saw Cohanim eating with their hands covered by cloth[75]. He told them, was not that of Rav and Samuel explained away? Rebbi Yose bar bar Cahana[76] came in the name of Samuel: Handwashing is for profane food[77], not for *terumah*. Rebbi Yose[78] says, for *terumah* and for profane food.

72 In the Venice print and Leyden manuscript, the reading is כחתם "as there", which makes no sense. The reading here is from the Rome manuscript; Yerushalmi חתה is parallel to Babylonian חייתא "sack, sackcloth."

73 He thought that Rav did not wash his hands and used the cloth, which cannot become impure from one's hands, to eat bread without incurring an obligation to wash. Samuel wondered, since that subterfuge is permitted only for people who would have to walk more than four *mil* to the next water source. The parallel in the Babli is *Ḥulin* 107a.

74 I washed my hands but am unable to eat without gloves.

75 Without washing their hands.

76 In the Rome manuscript, the name is R. Yose bar Huna Cahana. Neither of these names appears a second time; it is impossible to decide between the readings. In the Babli (*Ḥullin* 107a/b), the name is Rav Taḥlifa bar Abime, a known student of Samuel.

77 If someone wants to eat profane food "in the discipline of *terumah*," he must wash his hands. While this washing is taken from the discipline of *terumah*, one opinion allows Cohanim to eat *terumah* without washing but wearing gloves since a Cohen knows that eating impure *terumah* is a deadly sin, so he will avoid any contact between his hands and the food. But for profane food where washing is simply a matter of discipline (although taken from the rules of *terumah*,) it cannot be circumvented, cf. Babli *Ḥullin* 106a.

78 He seems to be the Tanna R. Yose (ben Ḥalaphta.)

רִבִּי יוֹסֵה בְּשֵׁם רִבִּי חִייָא בַּר אַבָּא וְרִבִּי יוֹנָה וְרַב חִייָא בַּר אַשִׁי בְּשֵׁם רַב נְטִילַת יָדַיִם לִתְרוּמָה עַד הַפֶּרֶק. וּבְחוּלִּין עַד קִשְׁרֵי אֶצְבְּעוֹתָיו. מַיישָׁא בַּר בְּרֵיהּ דְּרִבִּי יְהוֹשֻׁעַ בֶּן לֵוִי אָמַר מָן דַּהֲוָה אֲכַל עִם סַבִּי וְלָא מַשְׁטַף יָדוֹי עַד הַפֶּרֶק לָא הֲוָה אֲכַל עִימֵּיהּ.

Rebbi Yose in the name of Rebbi Ḥiyya bar Abba, and Rebbi Jonah, and Rav Ḥiyya bar Ashi in the name of Rav: Handwashing for *terumah* is to the wrist but for profane food it is to the finger joints. Maisha, the grandson of Rebbi Joshua ben Levi said: If someone wanted to eat with my grandfather and he did not rinse his hands to the wrist, he would not eat with him[79].

79 The parallel is in Babli *Ḥullin* 106a/b. Since R. Joshua ben Levi is a higher authority than Rav, practice in both Talmudim requires washing to the wrist also for profane food. The identification of פרק as wrist and קשרי אצבעות as the joint of fingers to the hand follows *Raviah* (R. Eliezer ben Joel Halevi), not Rashi and Tosaphot in their commentaries on the Babli.

רַב הוּנָא אָמַר אֵין נְטִילַת יָדַיִם אֶלָּא לְפַת בִּלְבָד. תַּנֵּי רִבִּי הוֹשַׁעְיָא כָּל־דָּבָר שֶׁיֵּשׁ בּוֹ לִכְלוּךְ מַשְׁקֶה. רִבִּי זְעִירָא אָמַר אֲפִילוּ מְקַצֵּץ תּוּרְמוּסִין הֲוָה נְטַל יָדֵיהּ.

Rav Huna said: Handwashing is only for bread. Rebbi Hoshaya stated: For anything getting dirty by a fluid[80]. Rebbi Zeïra said: Even when cutting lupines[81], he used to wash his hands.

80 This is also reported in Babli *Pesaḥim* 115a to explain why at the *Seder* ceremony one has to wash his hands before touching the vegetable that is to be dipped in fluid. For any sacred food like *terumah* or the Passover sacrifice, it is obvious that one has to wash his hands before touching fluids since the secondary impurity of hands causes primary impurity for the fluid. Hence, for the *Seder* it is only a question whether one should pronounce a benediction, as in the times of the Temple, or whether one washes his hands as a remembrance of Temple times. Here, the question is posed for

everyday food, since handwashing for profane food comes from the "discipline of *terumah*." Rav is of the opinion that the Rabbinic institution of handwashing applies only to bread whereas Rebbi Hoshaya requires handwashing for profane food in all situations where it would be required for *terumah*. In Antiquity, in the absence of spoons most foods in sauce were scooped up with pitta bread. Hence, the real difference between Rav and R. Hoshaya was in food handling as explained by R. Zeïra.

81 They do not contain much sap.

רַב אָמַר נָטַל יָדָיו שַׁחֲרִית אֵין מַטְרִיחִין עָלָיו בֵּין הָעַרְבַּיִם. רִבִּי אֲבִינָא מְפַקֵּד לְחַמָּרַיָּה הֵן דְּאַתּוּ מַשְׁכְּחוּן מִיסְתְּהוֹן מַיָּא נַסְבִּין יְדֵיכוֹן וּמַתְנֵי עַל כָּל־יוֹמָא.

Rav[82] said: If one washed his hands in the morning, one does not bother him in the evening. Rebbi Avina commanded the donkey drivers: If you find water to wash, wash your hands and condition them for the entire day.

82 In the Babli (*Ḥullin* 106b/107a), Rav is quoted as requiring an explicit declaration to make the washing of the hands valid for the entire day and Rebbi Avina seems to restrict this to desert-like conditions where water is not easily found. The latter interpretation is then rejected by the Talmud. In the Yerushalmi it seems that Rav is reported to require only one washing per day and Rebbi Avina restricts it to people like donkey drivers who cannot easily find water. Since he is the Israeli authority, it may be presumed that the Yerushalmi prefers the interpretation that is rejected in the Babli.

רִבִּי זְעִירָא סְלִיק גַּבֵּיהּ רִבִּי אַבָּהוּ לְקֵיסָרִין אַשְׁכְּחֵיהּ אָמַר אֲזַל לְמֵיכוֹל יְהַב לֵיהּ עֲגוּלָה דְּקַצֵּי. אֲמַר לֵיהּ סָב בְּרִיךְ אֲמַר לֵיהּ בַּעַל הַבַּיִת יוֹדֵעַ כֹּחוֹ שֶׁל כִּכָּרוֹ. מִן דְּאָכְלִין אֲמַר לֵיהּ סָב בְּרִיךְ. אֲמַר לֵיהּ חֲכַם רִבִּי לְרַב הוּנָא אֱנָשָׁא רַבָּא. וְהוּא הֲוָה אֲמַר הַפּוֹתֵחַ הוּא הַחוֹתֵם. מַתְנִיתָא פְלִיגָא עַל רַב הוּנָא. דְּתַנֵּי סֵדֶר נְטִילַת יָדַיִם עַד חֲמִשָּׁא מַתְחִילִין מִן הַגָּדוֹל. יוֹתֵר מִיכֵּן מִן הַקָּטוֹן. בְּאֶמְצַע הַמָּזוֹן מַתְחִילִין מִן הַגָּדוֹל. לְאַחַר הַמָּזוֹן מַתְחִילִין מִן הַמְבָרֵךְ לֹא שֶׁיַּתְקִין עַצְמוֹ

לִבְרָכָה. אִין תֵּימַר הַפּוֹתֵחַ הוּא חוֹתֵם כְּבָר מְתוּקָּן הוּא. אָמַר רִבִּי יִצְחָק תִּיפְתַּר בְּאִילֵין דַּהֲווּ עָלִין קִטְעִין קִטְעִין וְלָא יָדְעִין מַה מְבָרְכָה.

Rebbi Zeïra went up to Rebbi Abbahu in Caesarea. When he met him he said: Come to eat. He [R. Abbahu] gave him a loaf to break and told him: Take it and recite the benediction. He [R. Zeïra] said to him: The householder knows best the qualities of his loaf. After they had eaten, he [R. Abbahu] said to him: Start and recite Grace. He [R. Zeïra] said to him: The rabbi knows Rav Huna who is a great man and he used to say that he who starts is the one who finishes[83]. A *baraita* disagrees with Rav Huna, as it was stated[84]: "The order of washing of the hands[95]. Up to five persons, one starts with the most important personality. More than that, one starts with the least important one[86]. In the middle of the meal one starts with the most important one[87]. After the meal one starts with him who will recite Grace." Does that not mean that he may prepare himself for reciting Grace[88]? If you say that the one who starts is the one who finishes, he already is prepared! Rebbi Isaac said, explain it for those who come separately and do not know who will recite Grace.

83 The parallel to this story is in the Babli, *Berakhot* 46a. There, the Babli adds that practice follows R. Joḥanan (in the name of R. Simeon bar Yoḥai) who declares that the head of the household should recite the benediction for the bread since he is the host but that the guest should recite Grace and add to it a public blessing for the host. Even though the two authors quoted are Israeli, it follows from the Yerushalmi here that the public blessing for the host was never accepted practice in Galilee.

84 A similar formulation is in Tosephta *Berakhot* 5:6 and a different one in Babli *Berakhot* 46b. It seems that the three texts represent three different traditions.

85 When people are reclining on couches, the servants have to bring them pitchers of water and a basin for the used water. Hence, rules of good order are necessary.

86 Since one cannot ask the V.I.P. to wait a long time between washing and breaking the bread. Once the hands are washed, one may not let his attention be diverted from them, otherwise he has to wash again.

87 In the Tosephta, this sentence does not refer to washing one's hands at all, but to pouring wine. The Babli (*Ḥullin* 105a/b) quotes a *baraita* that declares washing of hands in the middle of the meal (between courses) to be voluntary; the exact halakhic meaning of this statement is in doubt.

88 The Babli (46b) brings a story that Rebbi asked Rav to wash his hands first, meaning that he should recite Grace aloud for the entire company. It follows that Rebbi emphatically denies the rule of Rav Huna that, as noted earlier, was never accepted in Babylonia.

(fol. 11d) **משנה ג**: בֵּית שַׁמַּאי אוֹמְרִים מְכַבְּדִין אֶת הַבַּיִת וְאַחַר כַּךְ נוֹטְלִין לְיָדַיִם. וּבֵית הִלֵּל אוֹמְרִים נוֹטְלִין לְיָדַיִם וְאַחַר כַּךְ מְכַבְּדִין אֶת הַבַּיִת.

Mishnah 3: The House of Shammai say, one sweeps the house and after that one washes his hands[89]. But the House of Hillel say, one washes his hands and after that he sweeps the house.

89 One sweeps the house if he ate sitting on the floor, or the table if he ate reclining on a couch. The washing of hands here is that after the meal; the problem of the House of Shammai is that spilled water from washing may spoil bits of food still lying around. The rule of the House of Hillel is optional; that of the House of Shammai is obligatory.

(fol. 12a) **הלכה ג**: מַה טַעֲמְהוֹן דְּבֵית שַׁמַּאי מִפְּנֵי אוֹבְדָּן אוֹכְלִין. וּמַה טַעֲמְהוֹן דְּבֵית הִלֵּל אִם הַשַּׁמָּשׁ פִּיקֵּחַ הֲרֵי זֶה מַעֲבִיר פֵּירוּרִין פָּחוֹת מִכְּזַיִת וְנוֹטְלִין לְיָדַיִם וְאַחַר כַּךְ מְכַבְּדִין אֶת הַבַּיִת.

Halakha 3: What[90] is the reason of the House of Shammai? Because of loss of food. But what is the reason of the House of Hillel? If the waiter is intelligent he removes the leftovers, even less than the volume of an olive; then one may wash his hands and after that sweep the house[91].

90 The Babli (52b) and the Tosephta (5:28) speak only about morsels the size of an olive. The Tosephta also includes the reason given here for the House of Shammai in its text.

91 The Babli and the Tosephta are unanimous that morsels smaller than the size of an olive may be deliberately spoiled; only larger morsels count as food and fall under the Biblical prohibition to destroy usable things. A second difference between Yerushalmi and Babli is that the Yerushalmi permits washing first if the waiter is intelligent; in Babli and Tosephta it is required that the waiter be learned.

(fol. 11d) **משנה ד:** בֵּית שַׁמַּאי אוֹמְרִים מְקַנֵּחַ יָדָיו בְּמַפָּה וּמְנִיחָהּ עַל הַשּׁוּלְחָן. וּבֵית הִלֵּל אוֹמְרִים עַל הַכֶּסֶת.

Mishnah 4: The House of Shammai say, one dries his hands[92] with a towel and puts the latter on the table; the House of Hillel say, on the pillow.

92 After washing one's hands for the meal.

(fol. 12a) **הלכה ד:** מַתְנִיתָא בְּשׁוּלְחָן שֶׁל שַׁיִשׁ וְשֶׁל פְּרָקִים שֶׁאֵינוֹ מְקַבֵּל טוּמְאָה. מַה טַעֲמוֹן דְּבֵית שַׁמַּאי שֶׁלֹּא יִטָּמְאוּ מַשְׁקִין שֶׁבְּמַפָּה מִן הַכֶּסֶת וְיַחְזְרוּ וִיטַמְּאוּ אֶת יָדָיו.

Halakhah 4: The Mishnah deals with a table of marble or one of parts screwed together that cannot become impure[93]. What is the reason of the House of Shammai? That the fluids on the towel should not become impure from the pillow[94] and in turn defile his hands.

93 The House of Shammai can prefer the table over the pillow only if the table cannot become impure and, hence, not impart any impurity to the fluids on the towel. No vessel made of stone can become impure; that includes marble tables. The Tosephta *(Kelim Bava bathra* 1:10) even states that a wooden table that contains a frame into which a marble table top is put cannot become impure since wooden implements become impure only if they enclose a volume and in this case the frame is filled with material that cannot become impure. The table whose legs are screwed in and can be unscrewed without tools is covered by the Tosephta (*loc. cit.* 1:11): "Restaurant chairs, even those having holes, that have their legs screwed in are permanently pure; if legs are fixed with a nail then they may become impure." The parallel in the Babli (52b) states that the House of Shammai will forbid the use of a table that is ritually unclean; both Babli and Tosephta (5:27) note that the House of Hillel will never allow one to put the towel on the table because the fluid on the towel might touch the food and render it impure in the second degree (and by eating from it an amount greater than the volume of two eggs one's body becomes impure in the second degree, Mishnah *Ṭahorot* 2:2). The arguments of the Babli are incompatible with those of the Yerushalmi.

94 Since fluids in contact with primary or secondary impurity become a primary source of impurity and, while a human can become impure only from a "father of impurity", his hands become secondarily impure from contact with primary impurity. The arrangement would be more logical if the order of these two sentences were inverted.

וּמָה טַעֲמוֹן דְּבֵית הִלֵּל לְעוֹלָם סָפֵק מַשְׁקִין לְיָדַיִם טָהוֹר. דָּבָר אַחֵר אֵין יָדַיִם לְחוּלִּין.

What is the reason of the House of Hillel? In case of doubt, fluids and hands are considered pure[95]. Another explanation: "Hands" are not for profane food[96].

95 Mishnah *Ṭahorot* 4:11: "In doubtful cases involving hands to become impure, to transmit impurity, or to be pure, they are declared pure."

Hence, since the House of Shammai agree that the entire matter is one of doubt, there is no problem since the hands of the person eating remain pure.

96 The entire institution of secondary impurity for hands has no Biblical basis for profane food; it has been instituted following "the discipline of *terumah*." Hence, there is no reason to follow strict rules in case of doubt since it is a principle that doubts regarding Rabbinic institutions must be resolved leniently.

וּכְבֵית שַׁמַּאי יֵשׁ יָדַיִם לחוּלִּין. תִּיפְתָּר אוֹ כְּרִבִּי שִׁמְעוֹן בֶּן אֶלְעָזָר אוֹ כְּרִבִּי אֶלְעָזָר בֵּי רִבִּי צָדוֹק. כְּרִבִּי שִׁמְעוֹן בֶּן אֶלְעָזָר דְּתַנֵּי רִבִּי שִׁמְעוֹן בֶּן אֶלְעָזָר אוֹמֵר מִשּׁוּם רִבִּי מֵאִיר הַיָּדַיִם תְּחִילָּה לְחוּלִּין וּשְׁנִיּוֹת לִתְרוּמָה. אוֹ כְּרִבִּי אֶלְעָזָר בֵּי רִבִּי צָדוֹק דְּתַנִּינָן תַּמָּן חוּלִּין שֶׁנַּעֲשׂוּ עַל טָהֳרַת הַקּוֹדֶשׁ הֲרֵי אֵילוּ כְּחוּלִּין. רִבִּי אֶלְעָזָר בֵּי רִבִּי צָדוֹק אוֹמֵר הֲרֵי אֵילוּ כִּתְרוּמָה לְטַמֵּא שְׁנַיִם וְלִפְסוֹל אֶחָד.

Do the House of Shammai hold that "hands" are for profane food[97]? Explain it either following Rebbi Simeon ben Eleazar or following Rebbi Eleazar, son of Rebbi Ẓadoq. Following Rebbi Simeon ben Eleazar as it has been stated[98]: "Rebbi Simeon ben Eleazar said in the name of Rebbi Meïr, hands are primarily impure for profane food and secondarily for *terumah*." Or following Rebbi Eleazar, son of Rebbi Ẓadoq, as we have stated there[99]: "Profane food that was prepared under the rules of purity of sacrifices is still profane food. Rebbi Eleazar, the son of Rebbi Ẓadoq said, it is like *terumah* becoming impure in two stages and unusable in a third."

97 Given the explanation of the House of Hillel, they seem to presuppose that the secondary impurity of hands has a Biblical root. This is incredible.

98 Tosephta *Tahorot* 1:6 in the reading of Rabbenu Simson of Sens. In the printed editions and the Vienna manuscript, the reading is "hands are of primary impurity for sacrifices." That reading is rejected by R. David Pardo in his commentary on the Tosephta. The statement is quoted several times in the Yerushalmi and also in Babli

Ḥulin 33b. The interpretation here is that profane food can become impure only from the source of impurity or primary impurity. Hence, unwashed hands must be of primary impurity in order to influence profane food. In contrast, *terumah* becomes unusable if it was in contact with secondary impurity; hence, primary impurity causes the same result for profane food as secondary impurity for *terumah*. This seems to be the opinion of Maimonides (הלכות אבות הטומאה יא:ט), who often is influenced by the Yerushalmi, also in *Ḥulin*; it is incompatible with Rashi's interpretation of the text in *Ḥulin*. There it is stated that hands can become primarily impure only if held into the windows of a house afflicted with leprosy. That would not make a good reason for the House of Shammai.

99   Mishnah *Tahorot* 2:8, quoted in Babli *Ḥagigah* 20a, *Ḥulin* 35b. Profane food can receive only primary impurity. *Terumah* can receive both primary and secondary impurity; the third stage is called "unusable" since it cannot be eaten, but it does not transmit the impurity further. Sacrifices become impure also in a tertiary way; only the fourth stage is "unusable."

תַּמָּן תַּנִּינָן הַסָּךְ שֶׁמֶן טָהוֹר נִטְמָא וְיָרַד וְטָבַל. בֵּית שַׁמַּאי אוֹמְרִים אַף עַל פִּי מְנַטֵּף טָהוֹר. וּבֵית הִלֵּל אוֹמְרִים (fol. 12b) טָמֵא[100]. וְאִם הָיָה שֶׁמֶן טָמֵא מִתְּחִילָּתָן בֵּית שַׁמַּאי אוֹמְרִים כְּדֵי סִיכַת אֵבֶר קָטָן. וּבֵית הִלֵּל אוֹמְרִים מַשְׁקֶה טוֹפֵחַ. רִבִּי יְהוּדָה אוֹמֵר מִשּׁוּם בֵּית הִלֵּל טוֹפֵחַ וּמַטְפִּיחַ. מוּחְלֶפֶת שִׁיטָתְהוֹן דְּבֵית הִלֵּל תַּמָּן אָמְרִין טָמֵא וְהָכָא אָמְרִין טָהוֹר. תַּמָּן בְּעֵינוֹ הוּא. וְהָכָא בָּלוּעַ בְּמַפָּה הוּא.

There (Mishnah *Idiut* 4:6) we have stated: "Someone who rubbed himself with pure oil, then he became impure, he descended[101] and immersed himself. The House of Shammai say, he is pure even if it[102] drips, but the House of Hillel say impure[103]. But if the oil was impure to start out with, the House of Shammai say, up to the anointing of a small limb[104]; but the House of Hillel say, moist fluid[105]. Rebbi Yehudah says in the name of the House of Hillel, moist and making moist." The opinions of the House of Hillel are reversed! There they say "impure" and here they say "pure." There it is visible, here it is absorbed in the towel.

100 The Rome ms. has here an insert: מחלפה שיטתהון דבית שמאי תמן אמרין טהור והכא אמרין טמא תמן (מאוס) [מסוס] ברם הכא בעינו הוא. The word in parenthesis has been corrected following the text of the commentary of R. Abraham ben David (*Ravad*) to Idiut. "The opinions of the House of Shammai are reversed, there (*Idiut*) they say it is pure, here (*Berakhot*) they say it is impure. There it is melted into the body, here it is visible." Since a similar discussion is given for the House of Hillel, the insertion is part of the Yerushalmi that was lost from the Leyden ms. by oversight.

101 He descended into the *miqweh* for purification.

102 The oil was not washed off but is still on his body. Since his body is pure, so is the rubbing oil which became part of his body.

103 It seems that they declare only the oil to remain impure, but one can also make the argument that the person remains impure since the water of the *miqweh* cannot touch his skin where it is covered by oil.

104 Both Talmudim (Yerushalmi *Šabbat* 8:1, Babli *Šabbat* 77a) agree that "a small limb" is a small limb of a newborn. This is the maximum amount that can become pure by immersion of one's body.

105 It feels moist but does not transfer moisture to anything that touches it.

(fol. 11d) **משנה ה**: בֵּית שַׁמַּאי אוֹמְרִים נֵר וּמָזוֹן בְּשָׂמִים וְהַבְדָּלָה. וּבֵית הִלֵּל אוֹמְרִים נֵר וּבְשָׂמִים וּמָזוֹן וְהַבְדָּלָה.

Mishnah 5: The House of Shammai say: Light, Grace, spices and *Havdalah*[106]. But the House of Hillel say, Light, spices, Grace, and *Havdalah.*

106 Order of benedictions if the Sabbath meal extended until after nightfall when *Havdalah* is required in addition to Grace.

(fol. 12b) **הלכה ה**: תַּנֵּי אָמַר רִבִּי יְהוּדָה לֹא נֶחְלְקוּ בֵּית שַׁמַּאי וּבֵית הִלֵּל עַל בִּרְכַּת הַמָּזוֹן שֶׁהִיא בַּתְּחִילָּה וְלֹא עַל הַבְדָּלָה שֶׁהִיא בַסּוֹף. עַל מַה נֶחְלְקוּ עַל

הַנֵּר וְעַל הַבְּשָׂמִים שֶׁבֵּית שַׁמַּאי אוֹמְרִים בְּשָׂמִים וְאַחַר כָּךְ נֵר. וּבֵית הִלֵּל אוֹמְרִים מָאוֹר וְאַחַר כָּךְ בְּשָׂמִים. רִבִּי בָּא וְרַב יְהוּדָה הֲלָכָה כְּמִי שֶׁהוּא אוֹמֵר בְּשָׂמִים וְאַחַר כָּךְ מָאוֹר.

Halakhah 5: It was stated: "Rebbi Yehudah said, the house of Shammai and the house of Hillel did not disagree that Grace comes first and *Havdalah* at the end. They disagree only over light and spices because the House of Shammai say spices and afterwards light, but the house of Hillel say light and afterwards spices." Rebbi Abba and Rav Yehudah: Practice follows him who says spices and afterwards light[107].

107 The entire paragraph was discussed in Halakha 1, fol. 11d.

בֵּית שַׁמַּאי אוֹמְרִים כּוֹס בִּימִינוֹ וְשֶׁמֶן עָרֵב בִּשְׂמֹאלוֹ אוֹמֵר עַל הַכּוֹס וְאַחַר כָּךְ עַל שֶׁמֶן עָרֵב. בֵּית הִלֵּל אוֹמְרִים שֶׁמֶן עָרֵב בִּימִינוֹ וְכוֹס בִּשְׂמֹאלוֹ אוֹמֵר עַל שֶׁמֶן עָרֵב וְטָחוֹ עַל רֹאשׁ הַשַּׁמָּשׁ. אִם הָיָה שַׁמָּשׁ תַּלְמִיד חָכָם טָחוֹ בְּכוֹתֶל. שֶׁאֵין שִׁבְחוֹ שֶׁל תַּלְמִיד חָכָם לִהְיוֹת יוֹצֵא מְבוּשָּׂם.

The[108] House of Shammai say, the cup in his right hand and perfumed oil[109] in his left hand; first he says the benediction over the cup and then over the perfumed oil. The House of Hillel say, perfumed oil in his right hand and the cup in his left hand, he recites the benediction over the perfumed oil and rubs it on the head of the waiter[110]. But if the waiter was learned, he would rub it on the wall because it does no credit[111] to the learned to walk around perfumed.

108 Tosephta *Berakhot* 5:29, Babli 43b. The text of the Tosephta manuscripts is close to the Yerushalmi. In the Babli and the traditional printed text of the Tosephta, the rôles of the Houses of Shammai and Hillel are reversed. The Babli starts: "When they brought to them oil and wine . . ." meaning that it was brought in the middle of the dinner for enjoyment. This is the opinion of R. Abraham ben David. According to Maimonides

(*Berakhot* 7:14), wine and spiced oil were brought after dinner, to recite Grace over them. According to Rashi, this wine was brought after Grace had already been recited.

109 As an air freshener.

110 To have some use for it since he must get rid of the perfumed oil in order not to walk around perfumed.

111 The Babli is more explicit and calls it "a shame."

אַבָּא בַּר בַּר חָנָא וְרַב חוּנָא הֲוון יָתְבִין אָכְלִין. וַהֲוָה רִבִּי זְעִירָא קָאִים מְשַׁמֵּשׁ קוֹמֵיהוֹן עָל וְטָעִין תְּרֵוֵיהוֹן בְּחָדָא יָדָא. אֲמַר לֵיהּ אַבָּא בַּר בַּר חָנָא מַה יָדֵיךְ חוֹרִיתָא קְטָעִין. וְכָעַס עִילוֹי אָבוֹי. אֲמַר לֵיהּ לָא מִיסְתָּךְ דְּאַתְּ רְבִיעַ וְהוּא קָאִים מְשַׁמֵּשׁ. וְעוֹד דְּהוּא כֹּהֵן וְאָמַר שְׁמוּאֵל הַמִּשְׁתַּמֵּשׁ בִּכְהוּנָּה מָעַל אַתְּ מֵיקַל לֵיהּ. גְּזֵירָה דְּהוּא רְבַע וְאַתְּ קָאִים וּמְשַׁמֵּשׁ תַּחְתָּיו. מְנַיִן הַמִּשְׁתַּמֵּשׁ בִּכְהוּנָּה מָעַל. רִבִּי אָחָא בְּשֵׁם שְׁמוּאֵל אָמַר וְאוֹמְרָה לָהֶם אַתֶּם קוֹדֶשׁ לַיי וְהַכֵּלִים קוֹדֶשׁ. מַה כֵּלִים הַמִּשְׁתַּמֵּשׁ בָּהֶן מָעַל. אַף הַמִּשְׁתַּמֵּשׁ בִּכְהוּנָּה מָעַל.

Abba[112] bar bar Ḥana and Rav Ḥuna were sitting down and eating and Rebbi Zeïra was standing and serving them. He came and carried both in one hand[113]. Abba bar bar Ḥana said to him: Is your other hand cut off? His father got angry with him and said to him: "Is it not enough for you that you are reclining and he stands and serves? But in addition, he is a Cohen and you make fun of him when Samuel said that he who uses a Cohen commits larceny[114]. I order that he should recline and you get up and serve in his stead." From where that he who uses a Cohen commits larceny? Rebbi Aḥa in the name of Samuel said (*Ezra* 8:28): "I said to them, you are holy and the vessels are holy." Since one who uses the Temple vessels commits larceny, also one who uses a Cohen commits larceny!

112 There is a parallel to this story in *Yalquṭ Šim'oni Ezra* 1089(8); there the names are Rebbi Abba and Rav Ḥuna. This is more reasonable, but there the names do not fit either since it says that Rav Huna insulted Rebbi

Zeïra and Rebbi Abba told him to get up and serve. This is totally impossible since both Rebbis Abba and Zeïra were students of Rav Huna. On the other hand, the reading אבוי "his father" is impossible in the Yerushalmi since R. Abba bar bar Ḥana's full name was R. Abba bar R. Abba bar Ḥana, which shows that he was a posthumous child and his father could not get angry with him. The most reasonable scenario is that R. Abba insulted the much younger R. Zeïra and R. Huna ordered them to switch places; but this has no manuscript evidence.

113 It seems that Rebbi Zeïra knew the diverging traditions about the sayings of the Houses of Hillel and Shammai in this matter, as explained in the preceding paragraph, and, therefore, decided to circumvent all problems (since practice has to follow the House of Hillel) by carrying both wine and perfumed oil in one hand.

114 *Meïlah*, the particular larceny committed in using Temple property for profane ends (*Lev.* 5:14-16).

(fol. 11d) **משנה ו:** בֵּית שַׁמַּאי אוֹמְרִים שֶׁבָּרָא מְאוֹר הָאֵשׁ. וּבֵית הִלֵּל אוֹמְרִים בּוֹרֵא מְאוֹרֵי הָאֵשׁ.

Mishnah 6: The House of Shammai say: "He Who created illumination by fire." But the House of Hillel say, "He Who is creating illuminations by fire.[115]"

115 There are two differences between the formulas of the two Houses for the benediction over the light at the end of Sabbath. For the House of Shammai, the creation is complete and in the past. For the House of Hillel, creation is a continuous process and comprises many kinds of light, including light created by human engineering that in the Babli (*Pesaḥim* 54a) is called "divine inspiration."

(fol. 12b) **הלכה ו:** עַל דַּעְתְּהוֹן דְּבֵית שַׁמַּאי אֲשֶׁר בָּרָא פְּרִי הַגֶּפֶן. עַל דַּעְתְּהוֹן דְּבֵית הִלֵּל בּוֹרֵא פְּרִי הַגֶּפֶן. יַיִן מִתְחַדֵּשׁ בְּכָל־שָׁנָה וְשָׁנָה. הָאֵשׁ אֵינוֹ מִתְחַדֵּשׁ בְּכָל־שָׁעָה.

Halakha 6: According to the opinion of the House of Shammai, should one not say: "He Who created the fruit of the vine?" According to the opinion of the House of Hillel, one should say: "Creator of the fruit of the vine."[116] Wine is new[117] every year; fire is not different every hour.

116 There is no source that would even hint at the proposed formula of the House of Shammai. Hence, the House of Shammai will not insist on using the past in the benediction for wine.

117 With a different taste. Hence, the past would be inappropriate here.

הָאֵשׁ וְהַכִּלְאַיִם אַף עַל פִּי שֶׁלֹּא נִבְרְאוּ מִשֵּׁשֶׁת יְמֵי בְרֵאשִׁית אֲבָל עָלוּ בְּמַחְשָׁבָה מִשֵּׁשֶׁת יְמֵי בְרֵאשִׁית. הַכִּלְאַיִם וּבְנֵי צִבְעוֹן וְאַיָּא וַעֲנָה הוּא עֲנָה אֲשֶׁר מָצָא אֵת הַיֵּמִים בַּמִּדְבָּר. מַהוּ יֵימִים. רִבִּי יְהוּדָה בֶּן סִימוֹן אוֹמֵר הֶמִיוֹנֹס וְרַבָּנָן אָמְרִין הֵיימִיס. חֶצְיוֹ סוּס וְחֶצְיוֹ חֲמוֹר. וְאֵילוּ הֵן הַסִּימָנִין. אָמַר רִבִּי יְהוּדָה כָּל שֶׁאָזְנָיו קְטָנוֹת אִמּוֹ סוּס וְאָבִיו חֲמוֹר. גְּדוֹלוֹת אִמּוֹ חֲמוֹרָה וְאָבִיו סוּס. רִבִּי מָנָא מְפַקֵּד לְאִילֵּין דִּנְשִׂיאָה אִין בְּעִיתוּן מִיזְבּוֹן מוּלְיוֹן תְּהוֹן זָבְנִין אִילֵּין דְּאוּדְנֵיהוֹן דְּקִיקִין שֶׁאִמּוֹ סוּסָה וְאָבִיו חֲמוֹר.

Fire and hybrids were not created in the six days of Creation but they were in the Divine plan of the six days of Creation[118]. Hybrids (*Gen.* 36:24): "These are the sons of Ẓiv'on, Ayyah and Anah. He is the Anah who invented the *yemim* in the prairie." What is *yemim*? Rebbi Yehudah[119] ben Simon said ἡμίονος ("Half she-ass, mule") and the rabbis say ἥμισυς ("half"), half horse and half donkey. These[120] are its signs: Rebbi Jonah says, if it has small ears, its mother is a horse and its father a donkey. If they are large, its mother is a donkey and its father a horse. Rebbi Mana ordered those of the patriarch's estate: If you want to buy a mule[121], you should buy one with small ears whose mother is a horse and whose father is a donkey.

118 Tosephta *Berakhot* 5:31, as reason for the benediction over fire as will be explained later. In the Tosephta, R. Yose disagrees and says the fire of hell was created on the Second Day; in the opinion of the Babli (*Pesaḥim* 54a) hell and its fire precede the Creation. The Yerushalmi takes no position on this. The text of this and the following two sections are also in *Bereshit rabba* 82(17); there is a parallel in Babli *Pesaḥim* 54a.

As is normal in the Talmudim, a proposition of subjects A B is discussed in order B A.

119 Son of Rebbi Simon, an Amora of the third/fourth generation in Galilee, known as preacher.

120 This and the following sentence are redundant. The sentences are copied here from *Kil'aim* 8:3. The reading "R. Jonah" is from the Venice print in *Kil'aim*, the Rome manuscript here, and *Bereshit rabba*. There is no Amora who is called Rebbi Jehudah (reading of the Venice print and Leyden ms.) without mention of his father's name. In the Babli (*Ḥullin* 79a), the criterion is ascribed to Rav Papa, fifth generation Babylonian Amora.

121 Latin *mulus, i, m.* "mule".

מַה עָשָׂה צִבְעוֹן וַעֲנָה. זִימֵּן חֲמוֹרָה וְהֶעֱלָה עָלֶיהָ סוּס זָכָר וְיָצָא מֵהֶן פִּרְדָּה. אָמַר הַקָּדוֹשׁ בָּרוּךְ הוּא לָהֶם. אַתֶּם הֲבֵאתֶם לְעוֹלָם דָּבָר שֶׁהוּא מַזִּיקָן אַף אֲנִי מֵבִיא עַל אוֹתוֹ הָאִישׁ דָּבָר שֶׁהוּא מַזִּיקוֹ. מַה עָשָׂה הַקָּדוֹשׁ בָּרוּךְ הוּא זִימֵּן חֲכִינָה וְהֶעֱלָה עָלֶיהָ חַרְדּוֹן וְיָצָא מִמֶּנָּה חֲבַרְבָּר. מִיָּמָיו לֹא יֹאמַר לְךָ אָדָם שֶׁעֲקָצוֹ חֲבַרְבָּר וְחָיָה. נְשָׁכוֹ כֶּלֶב שׁוֹטֶה וְחָיָה. שֶׁבְּעָטוֹ פִּרְדָּה וְחָיָה. וּבִלְבַד פִּירְדָּה לְבָנָה.

What did[22] Ẓiv'on and Anah do? He prepared a female donkey and mated her with a male horse; a mule came out from them. The Holy One, praise to Him, said to them: You brought into the world a harmful thing, I shall bring over that man something that will harm him. What did the Holy One, praise to Him, do? He prepared a snake and mated her with a Ḥardaun[123]; a brightly colored snake[124] came out of them. Nobody will ever tell you that he was bitten by a brightly colored snake and survived, bitten by a rabid dog and survived, hit by a mule and survived (but only by a white female mule[125].)

122 The text here is difficult. The parallel in *Bereshit rabba* has only "Anah" and is in the singular throughout, but here it starts with two persons but then in the middle of God's speech switches from plural to singular. One has to assume that there were two texts, one dealing only with Anah and the other with Ẓiv'on and Anah and that our text here is a confluence of both of them.

123 Arabic name of a large kind of lizard.

124 Arabic حبر "embellish, decorate".

125 The Babli (*Ḥulin* 7b) adds that the only mule that kills with its hoof is a white one even whose hoofs are white.

רִבִּי לֵוִי בְּשֵׁם רִבִּי נָזִירָה[126] שְׁלֹשִׁים וְשֵׁשׁ שָׁעוֹת שִׁימְּשָׁה אוֹתָהּ הָאוֹרָה שֶׁנִּבְרָאת בַּיּוֹם הָרִאשׁוֹן. שְׁתֵּים עֶשְׂרֵה בְּעֶרֶב שַׁבָּת וּשְׁתֵּים עֶשְׂרֵה בְּלֵילֵי שַׁבָּת וּשְׁתֵּים עֶשְׂרֵה בְּשַׁבָּת. וְהָיָה אָדָם הָרִאשׁוֹן מַבִּיט בּוֹ מִסּוֹף הָעוֹלָם וְעַד סוֹפוֹ. כֵּיוָן שֶׁלֹּא פָסְקָה הָאוֹרָה הִתְחִיל כָּל־הָעוֹלָם כּוּלּוֹ מְשׁוֹרֵר שֶׁנֶּאֱמַר תַּחַת כָּל־הַשָּׁמַיִם יִשְׁרֵהוּ. לְמִי שְׁאוֹרוֹ עַל כַּנְפוֹת הָאָרֶץ. כֵּיוָן שֶׁיָּצָת שַׁבָּת הִתְחִיל מְשַׁמֵּשׁ הַחוֹשֶׁךְ וּבָא. וְנִתְיָירֵא אָדָם וְאָמַר אִלּוּ הוּא שֶׁכָּתוּב בּוֹ הוּא יְשׁוּפְךָ רֹאשׁ וְאַתָּה תְּשׁוּפֶנּוּ עָקֵב. שֶׁמָּא בָא לְנַשְּׁכֵנִי וְאָמַר אַךְ חוֹשֶׁךְ יְשׁוּפֵנִי. אָמַר רִבִּי לֵוִי בְּאוֹתָהּ הַשָּׁעָה זִמֵּן לוֹ הַקָּדוֹשׁ בָּרוּךְ הוּא שְׁנֵי רַעֲפִין וְהֶקִּישָׁן זֶה לָזֶה וְיָצָא מֵהֶן הָאוֹר. הָדָא הוּא דִכְתִיב וְלַיְלָה אוֹר בַּעֲדֵנִי. וּבֵירַךְ עָלֶיהָ בּוֹרֵא מְאוֹרֵי הָאֵשׁ. שְׁמוּאֵל אָמַר לְפִיכָךְ מְבָרְכִין עַל הָאֵשׁ בְּמוֹצָאֵי שַׁבָּתוֹת שֶׁהִיא תְחִילַּת בְּרִייָתָהּ.

R. Levi in the name of Bar Nazira[126]: Thirty-six hours did Man enjoy the light that was created on the First Day of Creation[127], twelve on Friday, twelve in the night of Sabbath, and twelve during the day of Sabbath; in this light Adam saw from one end of the world to the other. In this unending light, the entire Creation started singing God's praise as it is said (*Job* 37:2), "All under the heavens sing to Him, His light is on the corners of the world." When the Sabbath ended, darkness came. Adam was afraid that this was what was said (*Gen.* 3:15): "You will crush its head and it will crush your heel;" certainly it will crush me, so he said (*Ps.* 139:11), "But the darkness will crush me." R. Levi said: At this moment the Holy One, praised be He, let him find two flintstones that he knocked against each other[128] and made fire; that is what is said (*Ps*. 139:11), "Now the night is light for me," and he praised the Creator of the illuminating fire. Samuel says: Therefore we give praise for the [man-made] fire at the end of Sabbath because that was the time of its first production.

126 Name from the parallel in the Midrash. The text here has ר' בזירה, an otherwise unknown person.

127 The vanished light of the Creation is reserved for the just in the future world (Babli *Ḥagigah* 12a). Psalm 139 is ascribed to David in the Book of Psalms, but in all of talmudic literature it is taken to describe the experiences of Adam.

128 In the Babli (*Pesaḥim* 54a), the discovery of man-made fire is called "a heavenly inspiration."

רַב הוּנָא בְשֵׁם [רַב][129] רִבִּי אַבָּהוּ בְשֵׁם רִבִּי יוֹחָנָן אַף בְּמוֹצָאֵי יוֹם הַכִּיפּוּרִים מְבָרֵךְ עָלֶיהָ שֶׁכְּבָר שָׁבַת הָאוֹר כָּל אוֹתוֹ הַיּוֹם.

Rav Huna in the name of Rav, Rebbi Abbahu in the name of Rebbi Yoḥanan: At the end of Yom Kippur one also recites the benediction since the light had rested all that day long[130].

129 Insert following the text on *Bereshit rabba*. The omission in the other sources makes no sense since Rav Huna preceded Rebbi Abbahu. The note "Rav Huna in the name of Rav" is missing in the parallel (Babli *Pesaḥim* 54a).

130 But, as noted in the Babli (*loc. cit.*), one does not recite the benediction over *newly lit* fire.

(fol. 11d) **משנה ז**: אֵין מְבָרְכִין עַל הַנֵּר וְעַל הַבְּשָׂמִים שֶׁל גּוֹיִם וְעַל הַנֵּר וְעַל הַבְּשָׂמִים שֶׁל מֵתִים וְעַל הַנֵּר וְעַל הַבְּשָׂמִים שֶׁלִּפְנֵי עֲבוֹדָה זָרָה. וְאֵין מְבָרְכִין עַל הַנֵּר עַד שֶׁיֵּאוֹתוּ לְאוֹרוֹ.

Mishnah 7: One does not recite a benediction[131] over a lamp and spices of Gentiles, or over lamp and spices for the dead[132], or over lamp and spices set before an idol. Also, one does not recite the benediction over a lamp unless he has profited from its light.

131 For *Havdalah.*

132 Light and perfumes set before a casket.

(fol. 12b) **הלכה ז**: תַּנָּא רִבִּי יַעֲקֹב קוֹמֵי רִבִּי יִרְמְיָה מְבָרְכִין עַל הַבְּשָׂמִים שֶׁל גּוֹיִם. מַהוּ פְלִיג. קַיּוֹמוּנָהּ בִּמְעַשֵּׁין[133] לִפְנֵי חֲנוּתוֹ.

Halakha 7: Rebbi Jacob stated[134] before Rebbi Jeremiah: One recites a benediction over spices of Gentiles. How can he disagree? Uphold it for someone who burns spices in front of his store[135].

133 Reading of the Rome ms. Venice and Leyden: במעשיו.

134 Not that he formulated it, but he quoted the tannaïtic formulation in the Yeshivah of R. Jeremiah.

135 He does it to attract customers, not for idolatrous practices. The reason of the original prohibition is that any perfuming by Gentiles is done for their idols.

עַשָּׁשִׁית אַף עַל פִּי שֶׁלֹּא כָבַת מְבָרְכִין עָלֶיהָ. נֵר בְּתוֹךְ חֵיקוֹ אוֹ בְתוֹךְ פַּנָּס אוֹ בְתוֹךְ סְפֶקְלַרְיָא רוֹאֶה אֶת הַשַּׁלְהֶבֶת וְאֵינוֹ מִשְׁתַּמֵּשׁ לְאוֹרָהּ. מִשְׁתַּמֵּשׁ לְאוֹרָהּ וְאֵינוֹ רוֹאֶה אֶת הַשַּׁלְהֶבֶת. לְעוֹלָם אֵין מְבָרְכִין עַד שֶׁיְּהֵא רוֹאֶה אֶת הַשַּׁלְהֶבֶת וּמִשְׁתַּמֵּשׁ לְאוֹרָהּ.

One may make the benediction over a lantern even if it did not go out[136]. A lamp in his bosom or in a lantern[137] or in glass[138], if he sees the flame and does not use its light, or uses the light but does not see the flame, one never recites the benediction until one sees the flame and uses the light.

136 This is the language of the Tosephta (5:31) following the Erfurth manuscript. The Babli (53a) has a slightly different formulation for the same statement. Since one permits a benediction over light that was burning at nightfall, the Tosephta must deal with the benediction after *Yom Kippur*.

137 Greek φανός, "torch, light".

138 Latin *specularia* "transparence; window panes, window (adj., plur. n.)". This term is missing in the Tosephta (5:31) and the parallel in the Babli (53b).

חֲמִשָּׁה דְּבָרִים נֶאֶמְרוּ בְּגַחֶלֶת וַחֲמִשָּׁה בְּשַׁלְהֶבֶת. גַּחֶלֶת שֶׁל הֶקְדֵּשׁ מוֹעֲלִין בָּהּ. וְהַשַּׁלְהֶבֶת לֹא נֶהֱנִין וְלֹא מוֹעֲלִין. גַּחֶלֶת שֶׁל עֲבוֹדָה זָרָה אֲסוּרָה וְשַׁלְהֶבֶת מוּתֶּרֶת. הַמּוּדָּר הֲנָאָה מֵחֲבֵירוֹ אָסוּר בְּגַחַלְתּוֹ וּמוּתָּר בְּשַׁלְהַבְתּוֹ. הַמּוֹצִיא אֶת הַגַּחֶלֶת לִרְשׁוּת הָרַבִּים חַיָּיב וְהַשַּׁלְהֶבֶת פָּטוּר. מְבָרְכִין עַל הַשַּׁלְהֶבֶת וְאֵין מְבָרְכִין עַל הַגַּחֶלֶת. רִבִּי חִיָּיא בַּר אַשִׁי בְּשֵׁם רַב אִם הָיוּ הַגְּחָלִים לוֹחֲשׁוֹת מְבָרְכִין. רִבִּי יוֹחָנָן דְּקַרְצִיוֹן בְּשֵׁם רִבִּי נָחוּם בַּר סִימַאי בִּלְבַד הַנִּקְטֶפֶת.

Five[139] things were said about burning charcoal and five about the flame. One commits larceny with the burning charcoal of the Temple; one may not use its flame but one cannot commit larceny with the latter[140]. Burning charcoal of idolatry is forbidden, its flame is allowed. He who makes a vow not to use anything of another person may not use his burning charcoal but is allowed his flame. He who carries out burning charcoal into the public domain[141] is guilty but for the flame he is free of punishment. One makes the benediction over the flame but not over glowing charcoal. Rav Ḥiyya bar Ashi in the name of Rav[142]: If the charcoal was crackling one makes the benediction. Rebbi Yoḥanan from Karẓion[143] in the name of Rebbi Naḥum bar Simai: Only if [the flame] is jumping off[144].

139 Tosephta *Beẓah* 4:7. There is a similar *baraita* in Babli *Beẓah* 29a but it has no reference to *Havdalah*.

140 Coal is a material, so if one takes it for unauthorized use he commits larceny. A flame is essentially

immaterial; the Babli (*Beẓah* 29a) declares the prohibition of its use as Rabbinic decree. The following cases all derive from the same principle.

141 On the Sabbath. The Babli (*Beẓah* 29a) discusses how one could possibly move the flame without the underlying coal.

142 In the Babli (53b) this is a *baraita* which specifies explicitly that glowing but not crackling coals are not to be used for the benediction. [The title "Rebbi" in the text is again a scribal error.]

143 An Amora whose time cannot be determined since he appears only here. Karẓion is today's Kaẓion in Upper Galilee; the reading קייציון of the Rome ms. might be better.

144 More or less this is the definition of "crackling."

תַּנֵּי גּוֹי שֶׁהִדְלִיק מִיִּשְׂרָאֵל וְיִשְׂרָאֵל שֶׁהִדְלִיק מִגּוֹי. נִיחָא גּוֹי שֶׁהִדְלִיק מִיִּשְׂרָאֵל. מֵעַתָּה אֲפִילוּ גּוֹי מִגּוֹי. אַשְׁכַּח תַּנֵּי גּוֹי מִגּוֹי אֵין מְבָרְכִין.

It was stated "A Gentile who lit from a Jew and a Jew who lit from a Gentile.[145]" One understands a Gentile who lit from a Jew[146], but then even a Gentile who lit from a Gentile? It was found that it was stated: "One does not recite the benediction if a Gentile [lit] from a Gentile."

145 Tosephta *Berakhot* 5:31. The text continues: "One recites the benediction." In the Babli (53a) there is a *baraita* that combines the two formulations of the Yerushalmi.

146 Since the Jew made new fire after the end of Sabbath. Similarly, one considers the act of lighting a fire from the existing fire of a Gentile as creation of a new light by a Jew after the end of Sabbath. But a Gentile lighting from a Gentile cannot do this since he never had a moment when making a fire was forbidden to him.

רִבִּי אַבָּהוּ בְּשֵׁם רִבִּי יוֹחָנָן מָבוֹי שֶׁכּוּלּוֹ גוֹיִם וְיִשְׂרָאֵל אֶחָד דָּר בְּתוֹכוֹ וְיָצָא מִשָּׁם הָאוֹר. מְבָרְכִין עָלֶיהָ בִּשְׁבִיל אוֹתוֹ יִשְׂרָאֵל שֶׁשָּׁם. רִבִּי אַבָּהוּ בְּשֵׁם רִבִּי יוֹחָנָן אֵין מְבָרְכִין לֹא עַל הַבְּשָׂמִים שֶׁל לֵילֵי שַׁבָּת בְּטִבֵּרְיָא וְלֹא עַל הַבְּשָׂמִים שֶׁל מוֹצָאֵי שַׁבָּת בְּצִפּוֹרִין וְלֹא עַל הַנֵּר וְלֹא עַל הַבְּשָׂמִים שֶׁל אוֹר עֶרֶב שַׁבָּת בְּצִפּוֹרִין שֶׁאֵינָן אֶלָּא לְדָבָר אַחֵר.

Rebbi Abbahu in the name of Rebbi Yoḥanan: A dead end street of Gentiles and one Jew lives in it, if light comes from there one recites the benediction because of the one Jew who is there[147]. Rebbi Abbahu in the name of Rebbi Yoḥanan: One does not recite the benediction on the spices[148] of Friday afternoon in Tiberias, nor on the spices of Sabbath night of Sepphoris, nor on light[149] and spices of Friday Eve in Sepphoris, because they are for other purposes.

147 If the one who sees the light knows the Jew living there.

148 Obviously, here one does not speak about *Havdalah* but about the benediction that is required for the enjoyment of perfume. In the Babli (53a), R. Joḥanan is more explicit and says that these perfumes are burned to disinfect clothes; hence, they are not produced for human enjoyment.

149 The mention of light here makes no sense, but it is found in both mss.

וְעַל הַנֵּר וְעַל הַבְּשָׂמִים שֶׁל מֵתִים. רִבִּי חִזְקִיָּה וְרִבִּי יַעֲקֹב בַּר אָחָא בְּשֵׁם רִבִּי יוֹסֵי בֵּי רִבִּי חֲנִינָא הָדָא דְאַתְּ אָמַר בִּנְתוּנִין לְמַעֲלָה מִמִּיטָּתוֹ שֶׁל מֵת. אֲבָל אִם הָיוּ נְתוּנִין לִפְנֵי מִיטָּתוֹ שֶׁל מֵת מְבָרְכִין. אֲנִי אוֹמֵר לִכְבוֹד הַחַיִּים הֵן עֲשׂוּיִן.

"Nor over lamp and spices for the dead.[150]" Rebbi Ḥizqiah and Rebbi Jacob bar Aḥa in the name of Rebbi Yose, son of Rebbi Ḥanina: That is, if they are put at the head of the bier. But if they are put in front of the bier one may recite the benediction; I say they are put there for the honor of the living[151].

150 Quote from the Mishnah.

151 The reason that one may not recite the benediction over perfumes and light arranged for the deceased is that one may not have any use from things given to the dead. But if they are arranged for the convenience of the living who are paying their respects, one may use them for a benediction. The parallel in the Babli (53a) has another definition: Light burning only in the night is acceptable; that which burns day and night is not.

וְלֹא עַל הַנֵּר וְעַל הַבְּשָׂמִים שֶׁל עֲבוֹדָה זָרָה. וְלֹא הִיא שֶׁל גּוֹיִם (fol. 12c) הִיא שֶׁל עֲבוֹדָה זָרָה. תִּיפְתָּר בַּעֲבוֹדָה זָרָה שֶׁל יִשְׂרָאֵל.

"Nor over lamp and spices set before an idol.[150]" Is not that of Gentiles identical[152] with that of idolatry? Explain it with the idol of a Jew.

152 Why are light of idolatry and light of Gentiles mentioned as separate items in the Mishnah?

וְאֵין מְבָרְכִין עַל הַנֵּר עַד שֶׁיֵּאוֹתוּ לְאוֹרוֹ. דָּרַשׁ רִבִּי זְעִירָה בְּרֵיהּ דְּרִבִּי אַבָּהוּ וַיַּרְא אֱלֹהִים אֶת הָאוֹר כִּי טוֹב וְאַחַר כַּךְ וַיַּבְדֵּל אֱלֹהִים בֵּין הָאוֹר וּבֵין הַחוֹשֶׁךְ. אָמַר רִבִּי בֶּרֶכְיָה כַּךְ דָּרְשׁוּ שְׁנֵי גְּדוֹלֵי עוֹלָם רִבִּי יוֹחָנָן וְרִבִּי שִׁמְעוֹן בֶּן לָקִישׁ וַיַּבְדֵּל אֱלֹהִים אַבְדָּלָה וַדַּאי. רִבִּי יְהוּדָה בֵּי רִבִּי סִימוֹן אָמַר הִבְדִּילוֹ לוֹ. וְרַבָּנִין אָמְרִין הִבְדִּילוֹ לַצַּדִּיקִים לֶעָתִיד לָבוֹא. מָשְׁלוּ מָשָׁל לְמַה הַדָּבָר דּוֹמֶה לְמֶלֶךְ שֶׁהָיוּ לוֹ שְׁנֵי אִיסְטְרַטֵיגִין זֶה אוֹמֵר אֲנִי מְשַׁמֵּשׁ בַּיּוֹם וְזֶה אוֹמֵר אֲנִי מְשַׁמֵּשׁ בַּיּוֹם. קָרָא לָרִאשׁוֹן וְאָמַר לוֹ הַיּוֹם יְהֵא תְחוּמָךְ. קָרָא לְשֵׁנִי וְאָמַר לוֹ הַלַּיְלָה יְהֵא תְחוּמָךְ. הֲדָא הוּא דִכְתִיב וַיִּקְרָא אֱלֹהִים לָאוֹר יוֹם וְגוֹמֵר. לָאוֹר אָמַר לוֹ הַיּוֹם יְהֵא תְחוּמָךְ וְלַחוֹשֶׁךְ אָמַר לוֹ הַלַּיְלָה יְהֵא תְחוּמָךְ. אָמַר רִבִּי יוֹחָנָן הוּא שֶׁאָמַר לוֹ הַקָּדוֹשׁ בָּרוּךְ הוּא לְאִיּוֹב הֲמִיָּמֶיךָ צִוִּיתָ בֹּקֶר יִדַּעְתָּ הַשַּׁחַר מְקוֹמוֹ. יָדַעְתָּ אֵי זֶה מְקוֹמוֹ שֶׁל אוֹר שֵׁשֶׁת יְמֵי בְרֵאשִׁית אֵיכָן נִגְנָז. אָמַר רִבִּי תַנְחוּמָא אֲנָא אֲמָרִית טַעֲמָא יוֹצֵר אוֹר וּבוֹרֵא חוֹשֶׁךְ עוֹשֶׂה שָׁלוֹם מִשֶּׁיָּצָא עוֹשֶׂה שָׁלוֹם בֵּינֵיהֶן.

"Also, one does not recite the benediction over a lamp unless one has profited from its light.[150]" Rebbi Zeïra, the son of Rebbi Abbahu, preached: (*Gen.* 1:4) "God saw the light that it was good" and after that, "God separated between the light and the darkness.[153]". Rebbi Berekhiah said: The following was preached by the two greats of the world, Rebbi Yoḥanan and Rebbi Simeon ben Laqish: "God separated," a true separation. Rebbi Yehudah, the son of Rebbi Simon, said: He separated it for Himself[154]. But the rabbis say, He separated it for the just in the future world. They gave a parable, to what can this situation be compared? To a king who had two generals[155]; both of them said: "I want to command during the day." He called the first one and told him: day shall be your domain. He called the second one and told him: night shall be your domain. That is what is written: (*Gen.* 1:5) "God called the light 'day', etc." To the light he said: day shall be your domain; but to the darkness he said: night shall be your domain. Rebbi Yoḥanan said, that it is which the Holy One, praise to Him, said to Job: (*Job* 38:12) "Did you ever command the morning, did you inform the morning of its place?" Do you know the place where the light of the Six Days of Creation was hidden? Rebbi Tanḥuma said: I shall give its reason. (*Is.* 45:7) "He Who fashioned the light and created darkness, He makes peace." When it left[156], it made peace between them.

153 In *imitatio Dei*, one should not make *Havdalah* until he saw the light and that it is useful. The same paragraph is found in *Bereshit rabba* 3(7) in slightly more explicit language.

154 That this is the light of the *Shekhinah.*

155 Greek (sing.) στρατηγός.

156 In *Bereshit rabba*: "From the moment that they were created, He is making peace."

אֵין מְבָרְכִין עַל הַנֵּר עַד שֶׁיֵּאוֹתוּ לְאוֹרוֹ. רַב אָמַר יְאוּתוּ. וּשְׁמוּאֵל אָמַר יְעוּתוּ. מַאן דָּמַר יְאוּתוּ אַךְ בְּזֹאת נֵאוֹת לָכֶם. מַאן דָּמַר יְעוּתוּ לָדַעַת לָעוּת אֶת עָיֵף דָּבָר. תַּמָּן תַּנִּינָן כֵּיצַד מְאַבְּרִין אֶת הֶעָרִים. רַב אָמַר מְאַבְּרִין. וּשְׁמוּאֵל אָמַר מְעַבְּרִין. מַאן דָּמַר מְאַבְּרִין מוֹסִיפִין לָהּ אֵבֶר. וּמַאן דָּמַר מְעַבְּרִין כְּאִשָּׁה עוּבָּרָה. תַּמָּן תַּנִּינָן לִפְנֵי אֵידֵיהֶן שֶׁל גּוֹיִם. רַב אָמַר עֵידֵיהֶן וּשְׁמוּאֵל אָמַר אֵידֵיהֶן. מַאן דָּמַר אֵידֵיהֶן כִּי קָרוֹב יוֹם אֵידָם. וּמַאן דָּמַר עֵידֵיהֶן וְעֵידֵיהֶם הֵמָּה בַּל יִרְאוּ וּבַל יֵדְעוּ לְמַעַן יֵבוֹשׁוּ. מַאן מְקַיֵּים שְׁמוּאֵל טַעֲמֵי דְּרַב וְעֵידֵיהֶם הֵמָּה שֶׁהֵן עֲתִידִין לְבַיֵּשׁ אֶת עוֹבְדֵיהֶן לְיוֹם הַדִּין.

"One does not recite the benediction over a lamp unless one has profited from its light." Rav says *yeʼutu*, and Samuel says *yeʻutu*[157]. He who says *yeʼutu*, (*Gen.* 34:15) "But with this we shall be agreeable (*nēʼôt*) to you." He who says *yeʻutu*, (*Is.* 50:4) "To know, to inform (*lāʻût*) the weary of wisdom." There (Mishnah *Erubin* 5:1) we have stated: How does one complete cities[158]? Rav says *meʼabberin*, and Samuel says *meʻabberin*. He who says *meʼabberin*, one adds a limb (אבר) to it. And he who says *meʻabberin*, like a pregnant (עוברה) woman. There (Mishnah *Avodah zarah* 1:1) we have stated: Before the holidays of the Gentiles[159]. Rav says *ʻêdêhen* and Samuel says *ʼêdêhen*. He who says *ʼêdêhen*, (*Deut*. 32:35) "For the day of their misfortune (אידם) is near." He who says *ʻêdêhen*, (*Is*. 44:9) "They[160] are their witnesses (עידיהם), may they neither see nor know, so that they may come to naught." How does Samuel deal with Rav's reason? They are their witnesses, in the future they will bring to naught their worshippers on the day of judgment.

157 Under the influence of Accadic, Babylonian Jews early on had lost the difference between *aleph* (ʼ) and *ayin* (ʻ) (and *he*, *ḥet*); they re-acquired the differences only later under the influence of Arabic. Similarly, under the influence of Greek, in the speech of most Galileans also *aleph* and *ayin* had become silent. Since the Mishnah was transmitted orally, there was no difference in pronunciation between the two silent consonants and the interpretation of the words depended on whether one was imagining one or the other.

The particular case here is not discussed in the Babli. The examples from *Eruvin* and *Avodah zarah* are discussed following these Mishnayot in the Babli where at other places one also finds examples of a silent ח (*Beẓah* 35b) and switches between ס (s) and צ (ss) (*Bava qama* 116b). In most cases, roots of Rabbinic expressions are sought in Biblical Hebrew.

158 "Completion" is the determination of a rectangle oriented NS, EW whose edges are distant 2000 cubits from the last house of the city in that direction.

159 One may not trade with them.

160 The idols. In the Babli (*Avodah zarah* 2a), the interpretation of this verse takes up several pages.

אֵין מְבָרְכִין עַל הַנֵּר עַד שֶׁיֵּאוֹתוּ לְאוֹרוֹ. רַב יְהוּדָה בְּשֵׁם שְׁמוּאֵל כְּדֵי שֶׁיְּהוּ הַנָּשִׁים טָווֹת לְאוֹרוֹ. אָמַר רִבִּי יוֹחָנָן כְּדֵי שֶׁעֵינוֹ רוֹאָה מַה בְכוֹס וּמַה שֶׁבִּקְעָרָה. אָמַר רַב חִינְנָא כְּדֵי שֶׁיְּהֵא יוֹדֵעַ לְהַבְחִין בֵּין מַטְבֵּעַ לְמַטְבֵּעַ.

"One does not recite the benediction over a lamp unless he has profited from its light." Rav Yehudah in the name of Samuel: So that women would be able to spin by its light. Rebbi Yoḥanan said: So that his eye should see what is in the cup or in the bowl. Rav Ḥinena said, so that he should be able to distinguish between two coins[161].

161 Rav Yehudah is the most restrictive, following the old Babylonian custom. In the Babli (53b) there are two opinions, both by early Galilean authorities; so it seems that R. Ḥinena, the student of R. Yoḥanan, is referring to earlier statements. In the opinion of Ulla, one must be able to distinguish between an *as* ($^1/_{24}$ *denarius*) and a *dupondius* ($^1/_{12}$ *denarius*); in the opinion of Ḥizqiah, one has to distinguish between local coins of the same weight and value but different mints. Since R. Ḥinena is the student of R. Yoḥanan, it seems that he is following Ulla's opinion.

תַּנֵּי רִבִּי אוֹשַׁעְיָא אֲפִילוּ טְרַקְלִין עֶשֶׂר עַל עֶשֶׂר מְבָרְכִין. רִבִּי זְעִירָא מַקְרִיב קוֹמֵי בוּצִינָא. אָמְרוּ לוֹ תַּלְמִידָיו רַבֵּנוּ מַה אַתְּ מַחְמִיר עָלֵינוּ. וְהָתַנֵּי רִבִּי אוֹשַׁעְיָא אֲפִילוּ טְרַקְלִין עֶשֶׂר עַל עֶשֶׂר מְבָרְכִין.

Rebbi Oshaia stated: Even if it was a banquet hall of ten by ten[162], one recites the benediction. Rebbi Zeïra went close to the light. His students told him: Why does our teacher make it so difficult for us, did not Rebbi Oshaya formulate: "even if it was a banquet hall of ten by ten, one recites the benediction[163]?"

162 Since the *triclinium* is a banquet hall in the Roman style, the "ten" probably are not Jewish cubits but Roman *passus*, of 4.5 feet each. Then the distance from a light kindled in one corner to the observer in the corner diagonally opposed would be about 67 feet; based on cubits it would be 48 feet, still a great distance in an otherwise dark room.

163 In the Babli (53a), R. Zeïra is quoted that originally he insisted on making the benediction over his own light (following an old Babylonian custom), but that he changed his opinion after hearing that great authorities allow one to make the benediction even over fire lit by other people in their houses, as explained earlier in this Halakhah. That report must date from the time when he visited Babylonia after becoming head of his own Yeshivah in Galilee.

(fol. 11d) **משנה ח**: מִי שֶׁאָכַל וְשָׁכַח וְלֹא בֵּירַךְ. בֵּית שַׁמַּאי אוֹמְרִים יַחְזוֹר לִמְקוֹמוֹ וִיבָרֵךְ. וּבֵית הִלֵּל אוֹמְרִים יְבָרֵךְ בְּמָקוֹם שֶׁנִּזְכָּר. וְעַד מָתַי מְבָרֵךְ עַד כְּדֵי שֶׁיִּתְאַכֵּל הַמָּזוֹן שֶׁבְּמֵעָיו.

Mishnah 8: He who ate, forgot, and did not recite Grace. The House of Shammai say, he should return to his place[164] and recite. The House of Hillel say, he should recite at the place where he remembers it. How long[165] may he recite? Until the food is digested in his bowels.

164 The place of the meal.

165 After the end of the meal, so that he should not by guilty of disregarding a biblical commandment.

(fol. 12c) **הלכה ח**: רִבִּי יוֹסְטָא בַּר שׁוּנֶם אֲמַר תְּרֵין אֲמוֹרִין חַד אֲמַר טַעֲמוֹן דְּבֵית שַׁמַּאי וְחַד אֲמַר טַעֲמוֹן דְּבֵית הִלֵּל. מַאן דָּמַר טַעֲמוֹן דְּבֵית שַׁמַּאי אִילּוּ שָׁכַח שָׁם כִּיס אֲבָנִים טוֹבוֹת וּמַרְגָּלִיּוֹת שֶׁמָּא לֹא הָיָה חוֹזֵר וְנוֹטֵל כִּיסוֹ. אַף הָכָא יַחְזוֹר לִמְקוֹמוֹ וִיבָרֵךְ. מַאן דָּמַר טַעֲמוֹן דְּבֵית הִלֵּל אִלֵּן פּוֹעֵל עוֹשֶׂה בְּרֹאשׁ הַדֶּקֶל אוֹ בְּתוֹךְ הַבּוֹר שֶׁמָּא מַטְרִיחִין שֶׁיַּחְזוֹר לִמְקוֹמוֹ וִיבָרֵךְ. אֶלָּא מְבָרֵךְ בְּמָקוֹם שֶׁנִּזְכָּר. אַף הָכָא מְבָרֵךְ בְּמָקוֹם שֶׁנִּזְכָּר.

Halakha 8: Rebbi Justus bar Shunem[166] said: Two Amoraïm, one proposed the reason of the House of Shammai and the other proposed the reason of the House of Hillel. He who proposed the reason of the House of Shammai: If he had forgotten there a wallet full of precious stones and pearls, would he not go back and retrieve his wallet? Here also, let him return to his place and recite Grace. He who proposed the reason of the House of Hillel: A worker who worked at the top of a date palm or at the bottom of a cistern, would one bother him to return and recite Grace? No, he should recite at the place where he remembers. So here also, he should recite at the place where he remembers[167].

166 A late Amora, student of Rebbi Mana II.

167 In the formulation here, it is agreed that a worker at a dangerous place does not have to return (a) to expose himself to unnecessary danger and (b) to spend unproductive time at the expense of his employer who is required to pay his entire day. In the Babli (53b), the entire discussion is a *baraita* and the argument of the House of Hillel precedes that of the House of Shammai. Hence, its implication is that the House of Shammai require the worker to return to his dangerous place and his employer to pay for the time lost. In this case, it seems that the Yerushalmi reports a deliberate change from earlier practice in order to embody a change in labor law.

עַד מָתַי מְבָרֵךְ רִבִּי חִייָא בְּשֵׁם שְׁמוּאֵל עַד שֶׁיִּתְעַכֵּל הַמָּזוֹן בְּמֵעָיו וַחֲכָמִים אוֹמְרִים כָּל זְמַן שֶׁהוּא צָמֵא מֵחֲמַת אוֹתָהּ סְעוּדָה. רִבִּי יוֹחָנָן אָמַר עַד שֶׁיִּרְעַב.

How long may he recite? Rebbi Ḥiyya in the name of Samuel, until the food in his bowels is digested. But the sages say, all the time that he is thirsty because of that meal[168]. Rebbi Yoḥanan says, until he gets hungry again[169].

168 Presumably, if he did not drink during the meal.

169 The Babli (53b) quotes R. Yoḥanan as is he quoted here and

attributes the statement of the Sages (that would guide practice here) to R. Simeon ben Laqish, whose opinion carries less weight than that of R. Yoḥanan. Another statement of R. Simeon ben Laqish, who gives as maximum the time it would take to walk four *mil*, 1 hour 12 min., has no parallel in the Yerushalmi. The difference between the Galilean יתאכל and the Babylonian יתעכל is dialectal; the Babylonian Mishnah has יתעכל. Since Samuel was a medical doctor, his explanation "until the food was digested" may have been practical for him; it certainly is not practical for everybody else. It is therefore not necessary to say that R. Yoḥanan is more restrictive than the Mishnah (as is the opinion of the student of Rabbenu Jonah in his commentary on Alfassi.)

(fol. 11d) **משנה ט**: בָּא לָהֶן יַיִן אַחַר הַמָּזוֹן וְאֵין שָׁם אֶלָּא אוֹתוֹ הַכּוֹס. בֵּית שַׁמַּאי אוֹמְרִים מְבָרֵךְ עַל הַיַּיִן וְאַחַר כַּךְ מְבָרֵךְ עַל הַמָּזוֹן. וּבֵית הִלֵּל אוֹמְרִים מְבָרֵךְ עַל הַמָּזוֹן וְאַחַר כַּךְ מְבָרֵךְ עַל הַיַּיִן. עוֹנִין אָמֵן אַחַר יִשְׂרָאֵל מְבָרֵךְ וְאֵין עוֹנִין אָמֵן אַחַר כּוּתִי מְבָרֵךְ עַד שֶׁיִּשְׁמַע כָּל־הַבְּרָכָה.

Mishnah 9: If wine was brought to them after the meal and there was only one cup. The House of Shammai say, he recites the benediction over wine and afterwards says Grace, but the House of Hillel say, he recites Grace and afterwards the benediction over wine. One answers "Amen" after a Jew but one does not answer "Amen" after a Samaritan unless one has heard the entire benediction[170].

170 Since the Samaritan follows a non-standard form of Judaism, one may not answer after his benediction unless one has ascertained that his benediction is compatible with our rules.

(fol. 12c) **הלכה ט**: אָמַר רִבִּי בָּא עַל יְדֵי שֶׁהִיא בְּרָכָה קְטַנָּה שֶׁמָּא יִשְׁכַּח וְיִשְׁתֶּה. בְּרַם הָכָא מְשַׁלְּשָׁהּ עַל יְדֵי הַכּוֹס אֵינוֹ שׁוֹכֵחַ.

Halakha 9: Rebbi Abba said: Because it is a very short benediction, he might forget and drink[170]. But here, he connects everything with the cup of wine and will not forget.

170 While Grace should be recited over an untouched cup of wine, in the opinion of the House of Shammai this does not apply here; see the start of Halakhah 1. The next sentence belongs only there (Note 23); it was copied here by mistake.

הָא אַחַר יִשְׂרָאֵל עוֹנִין אָמֵן אַף עַל פִּי שֶׁלֹּא שָׁמַע. לֹא כֵן תַּנֵּי שָׁמַע וְלֹא עָנָה יָצָא. עָנָה וְלֹא שָׁמַע לֹא יָצָא. חִייָה בְּרֵיהּ דְּרַב אָמַר בְּשֶׁלֹּא אָכַל עִמָּהֶן כְּזַיִת.

Hence[171], one answers "Amen" after a Jew even though one did not hear. Did we not formulate: If he heard[172] but did not answer, he did his duty. If he answered but did not hear, he did not do his duty. Ḥiyya, the son of Rav[173], said: when he did not eat with them the volume of an olive[174].

171 This is implied by the last sentence of the Mishnah.

172 Any of the obligatory prayers (if he himself is unable to recite them, or under the conditions discussed in the next paragraph) or benedictions may be performed by listening to an equally obliged person.

173 The only known son of Rav, who had the best of Rav's students as teachers; hence, he must have been born to Rav rather late in his life. After the death of Rav, he was a student of Samuel. He is usually quoted without any title (maybe he did not want to be addressed with a title that was the commonly used nickname of his father) but it is known that he acted in a Rabbinical capacity. He had a son who also was a scholar.

174 He answers "Amen" for the benediction but not in order to fulfill his own obligation. The parallel, without the question asked, appears in Babli 53b.

הָכָא מַתְנִיתָא תַנֵּי שָׁמַע וְלֹא עָנָה יָצָא. עָנָה וְלֹא שָׁמַע לֹא יָצָא. רַב בְּשֵׁם אַבָּא בַּר חָנָה וְאִית דְּאָמְרֵי לָהּ אַבָּא בַּר חָנָה בְּשֵׁם רַב וְהוּא שֶׁעָנָה רָאשֵׁי פְרָקִים. רִבִּי זְעִירָא בְּעִי הֵי אִינּוּן רָאשֵׁי פְרָקִים. הַלְלוּ יָהּ הַלְלוּ עַבְדֵי יי הַלְלוּ אֶת שֵׁם יי בְּעוּן קוֹמֵי רִבִּי חִיָּא בַּר אַבָּא מְנַיִין שֶׁאִים שָׁמַע וְלֹא עָנָה יָצָא. אֲמַר מִן מַה דַּאֲנָן חָמֵי רַבָּנָן רַבְרְבָיָא עָבְדִין כֵּן. אִינּוּן קַיְימִין בְּצִיבּוּרָא דְּאִילֵין אָמְרִין דֵּין בָּרוּךְ הַבָּא וְאִילֵין אָמְרִין בְּשֵׁם יי. וְאִילֵין וְאִילֵין יוֹצְאִין יְדֵי חוֹבָתָן.

Here[175], a *baraita* states: "If he heard but did not answer, he did his duty. If he answered but did not hear, he did not do his duty." Rav in the name of Abba bar Ḥana[176], or, as some say, Abba bar Ḥana in the name of Rav, that is only if he answered the beginnings of chapters. Rebbi Zeïra inquired, what are beginnings of chapters? (*Ps.* 113:1) "Hallelujah, praise, you servants of the Eternal, praise the name of the Eternal.[177]" They asked before Rebbi Ḥiyya bar Abba, from where do we know that if somebody heard but did not answer, that he fulfilled his duty? He said, because we see great rabbis acting accordingly. They stand in the congregation where some say (*Ps.* 118:26): "Blessed he who comes," and the others say: "in the name of the Eternal," and all have fulfilled their duty[178].

175 This paragraph is a copy of the corresponding one in *Sukkah* 3:12; "here" refers to the discussion of *Hallel* in that tractate. The entire paragraph deals with the recitation of *Hallel*; the parallel in the Babli is *Sukkah* 38b.

176 A cousin of Rav who studied with him under their common uncle R. Ḥiyya. In contrast to Rav, Rebbi Abba bar Ḥana did not return to Babylonia permanently. In the Babli, the statement is reported in the name of Rav's son-in-law Rav Ḥanan bar Abba.

177 Neither here nor in the Babli is it clear whether "headings" means only the first sentence of *Hallel* or the first sentence of every Psalm to be recited; cf. Tosaphot *Sukkah* 38b, *s. v.* מכאן.

178 Hence, it is unnecessary in the recitation of Psalms or synagogal poetry that in responsively recited pieces everyone should pronounce

everything; the practice given here is also endorsed by the Babli (*Sukkah* 38b) and is accepted in most Jewish groups.

תַּנָּא רִבִּי אוֹשַׁעְיָא עוֹנֶה הוּא אָדָם אָמֵן אֲפִילוּ לֹא אָכַל. וְאֵינוֹ אוֹמֵר נְבָרֵךְ שֶׁאָכַלְנוּ מִשֶּׁלּוֹ אֶלָּא אִם כֵּן אָכַל.

Rebbi Oshaya stated: One answers "Amen" even if he did not eat[179], but he may not say: "Let us bless Him, of Whose bounty we ate," except if he did eat.

179 This is the rule formulated by Ḥiyya bar Rav. The second rule was illustrated by R. Simeon ben Shetaḥ and king Yannai, Halakhah 7:2.

תַּנֵּי אֵין עוֹנִין אָמֵן יְתוֹמָה וְלֹא אָמֵן קְטוּפָה וְלֹא אָמֵן חֲטוּפָה. בֶּן עֲזַאי אוֹמֵר כָּל הָעוֹנֶה אָמֵן יְתוֹמָה יִהְיוּ בָנָיו יְתוֹמִים. חֲטוּפָה יִתְחַטְּפוּ יָמָיו. קְטוּפָה תִּקָּטֵף נִשְׁמָתוֹ. אֲרוּכָה מַאֲרִיכִין לוֹ יָמָיו וּשְׁנוֹתָיו בְּטוֹבָה: אֵי זוֹ הִיא אָמֵן יְתוֹמָה אָמַר רַב הוּנָא דֵּין דְּיָתִיב לְמִיבְרְכָה וְהוּא עָנָה וְלֹא יָדֵע לְמָה הוּא עָנָה.

It is stated[180]: "One answers neither an orphan Amen, nor a plucked[181] Amen, nor a hurried Amen. Ben Azai said, if one answered an orphan Amen, may his children be orphans; hurried, may the end of his days be hurried; plucked, may his soul be plucked off. For a long Amen, they lengthen his days and years in a good way." What is an orphan Amen? Rav Huna said, that is one who sits to recite a blessing, he answers Amen, and is not conscious for what he answered Amen.

180 Tosephta *Megillah* 3:27, also Babli *Berakhot* 47a.

181 Amen not completely pronounced.

תַּנָּא גּוֹי שֶׁבֵּירַךְ אֶת הַשֵּׁם עוֹנִין אַחֲרָיו אָמֵן בַּשֵּׁם אֵין עוֹנִין אַחֲרָיו אָמֵן. אָמַר רִבִּי תַנְחוּמָא אִם בֵּירַכָךְ גּוֹי עֲנֵה אַחֲרָיו אָמֵן דִּכְתִיב בָּרוּךְ תִּהְיֶה מִכָּל הָעַמִּים. גּוֹי אֶחָד פָּגַע אֶת רִבִּי יְהוֹשֻׁעַ וּבֵרְכוֹ. אָמַר לוֹ כְּבָר מִילָּתָךְ אֲמוּרָה. פָּגַע

אַחֲרִינָא וְקִלְלוֹ אָמַר לוֹ כְּבָר מִילָּתָךְ אֲמוּרָה. אָמְרוּ לוֹ תַלְמִידָיו רִבִּי כְּמַה דְּאָמַרְתָּ לְהָדֵין אָמַרְתָּ לְהָדֵין. אֲמַר לוֹן כֵּן כָּתוּב אוֹרְרֶיךָ אָרוּר וּמְבָרְכֶיךָ בָּרוּךְ.

It is stated: One answers Amen after a Gentile who recited a benediction for the Eternal, [but if he recited a benediction with the Name one does not answer[182].] Rebbi Tanḥuma said, if a Gentile blesses you, answer after him Amen since it is written (*Deut.* 7:14) "You shall be blessed by all peoples." A Gentile met Rebbi Joshua and blessed him. He answered: The word about you has already been said. He met a second one who cursed him; he answered: The word about you has already been said. His students said to him: Rebbi, did you say to the one what you said to the other? He said to them, so it is written (*Gen.* 27:29): "Those who curse you are cursed, but those who bless you are blessed."

182 The text in parenthesis is from the Rome manuscript; it seems that it is missing from the Leyden manuscript and the Venice print because here also, the final clause "one answers only if one heard the entire benediction" is missing since it is implied by the Mishnah. The complete text is that of most sources of the Tosephta (*Berakhot* 5:21). The correct interpretation seems to be that given by R. Saul Lieberman in *Tosephta kifshutah*: Since the Gentile is not subject to our rules, if he praises the Eternal, one answers after him Amen. But if he uses a Jewish formula, one may not answer after him Amen unless one has ascertained that he conformed with our rules.

הרואה פרק תשיעי

משנה א: הָרוֹאֶה מָקוֹם שֶׁנַּעֲשׂוּ בוֹ נִסִּים לְיִשְׂרָאֵל אוֹמֵר בָּרוּךְ שֶׁעָשָׂה נִסִּים לַאֲבוֹתֵינוּ בַּמָּקוֹם הַזֶּה.

Mishnah 1: He who sees a place where wonders were done for Israel, says: Praise to Him[1] Who did wonders for our forefathers at this place.

1 In all these Mishnayot, "Praise to Him" stands for "Praised are You, Eternal, our God, King of the Universe, Who . . .

(fol. 12d) **הלכה א:** מַתְנִיתִין בְּנִסֵּי יִשְׂרָאֵל. אֲבָל בְּנִסֵּי יְחִידִי שֶׁנַּעֲשׂוּ לוֹ אֵינוֹ צָרִיךְ לְבָרֵךְ.

Halakhah 1: The Mishnah deals with wonders of Israel[2]. But for wonders of a single person that happened to him[3], one does not have to recite a benediction.

2 *Pne Mosheh* (Margalit) notes that probably "Israel" here means "more than 50% of all of Israel" as in other circumstances.

3 Happened to that single person, not to the person who passes by the place.

מַהוּ שֶׁיְּבָרֵךְ אָדָם עַל נִסֵּי אָבִיו וְעַל נִסֵּי רַבּוֹ. וְאִם הָיָה אָדָם מְסוּיָּם כְּגוֹן יוֹאָב בֶּן צְרוּיָה וַחֲבֵירָיו. וְאָדָם שֶׁנִּתְקַדֵּשׁ בּוֹ שֵׁם שָׁמַיִם כְּגוֹן חֲנַנְיָה מִישָׁאֵל וַעֲזַרְיָה. וְנִסֵּי שְׁבָטִים מַהוּ שֶׁיְּבָרֵךְ. מַאן דְּאָמַר כָּל שֵׁבֶט וְשֵׁבֶט אִיקְרֵי קָהָל צָרִיךְ לְבָרֵךְ. מַאן דְּאָמַר כָּל הַשְּׁבָטִים קְרוּיִין קָהָל אֵין צָרִיךְ לְבָרֵךְ.

Does one have to recite a benediction for the wonders that were done for his father or his teacher[4]? Or if he was a famous person like Joab ben Ẓeruiah and his companions? Or a man through whom the Name of

Heaven was sanctified, for example Ḥananiah, Mishael, and Azariah[5]? About wonders done for one of the tribes? According to him who said[6] that each tribe is called "assembly", one has to recite the benediction; but according to him who said that only all tribes together are called "assembly", one does not have to recite the benediction.

4 From the question it follows that a person who had a miraculous escape from danger must recite the benediction ("Who did wonders for me at this place.") This is explicit in the Babli (54a).

5 This is the text of the Leyden manuscript and the Venice print; in this version, only the last question has an answer, all others are left dangling. However, *Rosh* [Rabbenu Asher ben Yeḥiel] has a different reading: "Does one have to recite a benediction for the wonders that were done for his father or his teacher? Or if he was a famous person like Joab ben Ẓeruiah and his companions? Or a man through whom the Name of Heaven was sanctified, for example Daniel and his companions? He recites a benediction." In this version, all questions are being answered and the next sentence starts a new paragraph. *Rosh* also quotes from Rav Hai Gaon a reading in the Babli, referring to the previous paragraph, that for a miraculous escape a man, his son, and his grandson have to recite the (appropriate) benediction.

6 Rebbi Yehudah and Rebbi Simeon in *Horayot* (Yerushalmi 1:6, fol. 46a; Babli 5b). The opposite opinion is that of Rebbi Meïr.

הָרוֹאֶה בָּבֶל צָרִיךְ לְבָרֵךְ חָמֵשׁ בְּרָכוֹת: רָאָה פְּרָת אוֹמֵר בָּרוּךְ עוֹשֵׂה בְרֵאשִׁית. רָאָה מֶרְקוּלִיס אוֹמֵר בָּרוּךְ אֶרֶךְ אַפַּיִם. רָאָה בֵּיתוֹ שֶׁל נְבוּכַדְנֶצַּר אוֹמֵר בָּרוּךְ שֶׁהֶחֱרִיב בֵּיתוֹ שֶׁל אוֹתוֹ רָשָׁע. רָאָה מְקוֹם כִּבְשַׁן הָאֵשׁ וְגוֹב הָאֲרָיוֹת אוֹמֵר בָּרוּךְ שֶׁעָשָׂה נִיסִּים לַאֲבוֹתֵינוּ בַּמָּקוֹם הַזֶּה. רָאָה מָקוֹם שֶׁנּוֹטְלִין מִמֶּנּוּ עָפָר אוֹמֵר בָּרוּךְ אוֹמֵר וְעוֹשֶׂה בָּרוּךְ גּוֹזֵר וּמְקַיֵּים. רָאָה בָּבֶל אוֹמֵר וְטֵאטֵאתִיהָ בְּמַטְאֲטֵא הַשְׁמֵד.

He who sees Babylon has to recite five benedictions[7]. If he sees the Euphrates, he says: "Praise to Him Who made the Creation." If he sees a (statue of) Mercury[8], he says: "Praise to Him, Who is patient." If he sees the house of Nabucadnezzar, he says: "Praise to Him, Who destroyed the house of that evil one." If he sees the fiery oven[9] or the lions' den, he says: "Praise to Him, Who did wonders for our forefathers at this place." If he sees a place from which one takes dust[10], he says: "Praise to Him, Who pronounces and does, decrees and upholds." If one sees Babylon, he says (*Is.* 14:23): "I shall sweep her out with the broom of destruction[11]."

7 In the Babli (57b), this is a sermon of Rav Hamnuna, in a slightly different order. In travel reports of Medieval travelers, it is reported that the ruin labelled "house of Nabucadnezzar" is outside of the ruins of the main wall, confirming the order of the Yerushalmi against the Babli.

8 According to both Talmudim, in the Eastern provinces of the Roman Empire, a Hermes (or Mercury) could be simply a heap of stones to which passers-by added in order to show their respect. [Note Greek ἑρμολογέω (τάφον) "build with loose stones (grave)" (E. G.)]. The benediction refers to the fact that God allows idols to exist; the Hermes is singled out since it was ubiquitous at intersections of roads.

9 Traditionally shown at Babylon even though the story in Daniel is set in the valley of Dura. This sentence confirms the reading of the Rome manuscript in the previous paragraph, that all questions asked were answered positively.

10 I. e., uses old Babylon as a quarry. The decrees referred to which are upheld are the prophecies of doom pronounced over Babylon in the books of Isaiah and Jeremiah.

11 In the Babli it is told that Mar, son of Ravina, a colleague of Rava in the fourth generation, when he visited the ruins of Babylon, collected some dust and recited the verse from Isaiah. It seems that he followed a Yerushalmi custom.

רִבִּי זְעִירָא וְרִבִּי יְהוּדָה בְשֵׁם רַב כָּל־בְּרָכָה שֶׁאֵין עִמָּהּ מַלְכוּת אֵינָהּ בְּרָכָה. אָמַר רִבִּי תַּנְחוּמָא אֲנָא אֲמַר טַעֲמָא אֲרוֹמִמְךָ אֱלֹהַי הַמֶּלֶךְ. רַב אָמַר צָרִיךְ לוֹמַר אַתָּה וּשְׁמוּאֵל אָמַר אֵינוֹ צָרִיךְ לוֹמַר אַתָּה.

Rebbi Zeïra and Rebbi Yehudah[12] in the name of Rav[13]: Any benediction without mention of the Kingdom is no benediction. Rebbi Tanḥuma said, I shall give the reason (*Ps*. 145:1): "I shall elevate You, my God, o King!" Rav said, one has to say "You," but Samuel said, one does not have to say "You[14]."

12 Since he is mentioned after Rebbi Zeïra, he must be Rebbi Yehudah Neśia, Patriarch and grandson of Rebbi.

13 In the Babli (40b), Rav is reported to have said that no benediction is valid without mention of the Name (YHWH), and Rebbi Yoḥanan notes that, in addition, the Kingdom must be mentioned. [The formula for the Kingdom: "our God, King of the Universe," probably was introduced to counter Christian ideas that God's kingdom is not of this world.] In addition, Abbaye notes in the Babli that Rav will not require R. Yoḥanan's addition. The formulation of the Yerushalmi shows that in Galilee, they interpreted the statement of Rav that one is required to say "You" to mean that one has to say "You, o Eternal," since in adressing somebody in the second person one must specify the adressee. Hence, the statement of R. Yoḥanan in the Babli was meant as clarification of Rav's statement, not a new requirement; it does not have to be mentioned since Rebbi Yoḥanan would disclaim any originality. Only in Babylonia they adopted a narrow interpretation of Rav's words. [In practice, reference to the Kingdom is required only for benedictions that either stand alone or start a series of benedictions.]

14 A practical reminder of Samuel's opinion is the formula of Grace for people who are too ignorant to pray in Hebrew: "Praised be the All-merciful, Owner of this bread."

רִבִּי יוֹחָנָן וְרִבִּי יוֹנָתָן אֲזָלִין מִיעֲבֵד שְׁלָמָא בְּאִילֵּין קִרְיָיתָא דְּדָרוֹמָה עָלוֹן לְחָד אֲתַר וְאַשְׁכְּחוֹן לְחַזָּנָא דַּאֲמַר הָאֵל הַגָּדוֹל הַגִּבּוֹר וְהַנּוֹרָא הָאַבִּיר וְהָאַמִּיץ וְשִׁיתְּקוּ אוֹתוֹ. אָמְרוּ לוֹ אֵין לְךָ רְשׁוּת לְהוֹסִיף עַל מַטְבֵּעַ שֶׁטָּבְעוּ חֲכָמִים בִּבְרָכוֹת. רַב הוּנָא בְּשֵׁם רַב שַׁדַּי לֹא מְצָאנוּהוּ שַׂגִּיא כֹחַ. לֹא מָצִינוּ כֹּחוֹ וּגְבוּרָתוֹ שֶׁל הַקָּדוֹשׁ בָּרוּךְ הוּא. רִבִּי אַבָּהוּ בְּשֵׁם רִבִּי יוֹחָנָן הַיְסוּפַּר לוֹ כִּי אֲדַבֵּר

אִם אָמַר אִישׁ כִּי יְבוּלָּע. אִם בָּא אָדָם לְסַפֵּר גְּבוּרוֹתָיו שֶׁל הַקָּדוֹשׁ בָּרוּךְ הוּא נִתְבַּלֵּעַ מִן הָעוֹלָם. אָמַר רִבִּי שְׁמוּאֵל בַּר נַחְמָן מִי יְמַלֵּל גְּבוּרוֹת יי כְּגוֹן אֲנִי וַחֲבֵרָי. אָמַר רִבִּי אָבוּן מִי יְמַלֵּל גְּבוּרוֹת יי. תִּרְגֵּם יַעֲקֹב כְּפַר נָבוֹרָיָא בְּצוֹר לְךָ דוּמִיָּה תְהִילָּה אֱלֹהִים בְּצִיּוֹן. סַמָּא דְכוּלָּא מַשְׁתּוּקָא. לְמַרְגָּלִית דְּלֵית לָהּ טִימֵי כָּל־שֶׁמִּשְׁתַּבֵּחַ בָּהּ פָּגְמָהּ.

Rebbi Yoḥanan[15] and Rebbi Jonathan went to make peace in the Southern settlements. They came to a place where they found the reader saying[16]: "The great God, the strong and awe-inspiring, the noble and overpowering;" they stopped him and told him: you are not permitted to add to the formula the Sages coined for benedictions. Rav Huna in the name of Rav: (*Job* 37:23) "The All-powerful, we did not find for Him the fullness of His might," we did not find out the might and strength of the Holy One, praise to Him[17]! Rebbi Abbahu in the name of Rebbi Yoḥanan: (*Job* 37:20) "Can it be told to Him if I should speak, if a man tells, he certainly will be swallowed up." If a man comes to tell the strengths of the Holy One, praise to Him, he sets himself up to be swallowed away from the world. Rebbi Samuel bar Naḥman said (*Ps.* 106:2) "Who can tell the strengths of the Eternal?" For example, I and my colleagues[18]. Rebbi Abun said: "Who can ever tell the strengths of the Eternal?" Jacob[19] of Kefar Naburaia explained in Tyre: (*Ps.* 65:2) "Silence is praise for You, God in Zion!" The medicine for everything is silence; like a priceless[20] jewel: everyone who adorns himself with it, diminishes it.

15 The Rome ms. has "R. Ḥanina" and that must be the correct reading since R. Yoḥanan belongs to the generation after R. Jonathan but R. Ḥanina (the Amora) was an older colleague of R. Jonathan and should be mentioned first.

16 In the first benediction of the *'Amidah*. The parallel in the Babli (33b) is in the name of R. Ḥanina only who notes there that the three attributes we mention are only permitted because Moses used them in the Torah

and the Men of the Great Assembly adopted them for prayer.

In the Babli, R. Ḥanina let the reader finish and only afterwards asked him: Did you finish all that can be said about your Creator? This argument also is accepted by the Yerushalmi since the explanations of the verses that follow are based on the principle that God's infinity cannot be expressed in finite words. In the Yerushalmi tradition, anyone who deviates from the pattern instituted by the Sages has to be stopped in the middle of his prayer.

17 It is too much for finite man.

18 Not Rebbi Samuel bar Naḥman but King David, meaning that Psalms cannot be composed without inspiration. This side remark is only brought as preliminary to Rebbi Abun's interpretation.

19 In the parallel in the Babli (*Megillah* 18a) he is called Rebbi Yehudah from Kefar Giboraia. His birthplace is a village North of Safed. He is mentioned as being in Tyre, where Rebbi Ḥaggai had him whipped because he proposed the principle of patrilineal descent for Jews [*Midrash Qohelet rabba* 7(44), *Bereshit rabba* 7(3), *Bemidbar rabba* 19].

20 Greek τιμή "value, price".

תַּנֵּי הַפּוֹתֵחַ בְּיוּ״ד הֵ״א וְחוֹתֵם בְּיוּ״ד הֵ״א הֲרֵי זֶה חָכָם. בְּאָלֶ״ף לָמֶ״ד וְחוֹתֵם בְּאָלֶ״ף לָמֶ״ד הֲרֵי זֶה בּוּר. בְּאָלֶ״ף לָמֶ״ד וְחוֹתֵם בְּיוּ״ד הֵ״א הֲרֵי זֶה בֵּינוֹנִי. בְּיוּ״ד הֵ״א וְחוֹתֵם בְּאָלֶ״ף לָמֶ״ד הֲרֵי זֶה דֶּרֶךְ אַחֶרֶת.

It was stated[21]: He who starts[22] with YH and closes with YH is wise, with 'L[23] and closes with 'L is ignorant, with 'L and closes with YH is average[24], with YH and closes with 'L is not Jewish[25].

21 Tosephta *Berakhot* 6:20; an older source dealing with a different set of circumstances; see the last note in this paragraph.

22 A longer benediction, that should start with the formula: "Praise to You, o Eternal, our God, King of the universe . . ." and ends: "Praise to You, o Eternal." In the normal form, there are two invocations of the Name, YHWH, one at the start and one at the end. Anyone following this format is wise.

23 If instead of the Name *ădōnāy*, standing in for the unpronounceable YHWH, he uses *ĕlōhīm* "God"; he fails to specify God's name.

24 Since he specifies that God's name is YHWH.

25 Since he starts with the Name YHWH and ends with the plural form *ĕlōhīm*, he asserts that YHWH is a name common to a trinity. Hence, he is not Jewish but a Christian. This statement introduces the following discussions of Rebbi Simlai with Jewish Christians. [R. Saul Liebermann points out that the Tosephta may deal with a different period in Jewish history. In the Tosephta, the sequence 'L-'L is termed "not Jewish" and YH-'L as "ignorant." He conjectures that the Tosephta is directed against sects similar to the Dead Sea sect in whose "Discipline of the community", 1QS, one finds a formula: ברוך אתה אלי "Praise to You, my God (singular form)." (The prayer manual of the sect, 1QH, always uses the *ădônāi* as replacement for YHWH.) In the time of the Yerushalmi, such sects no longer existed.]

הַמִּינִין שָׁאֲלוּ אֶת רִבִּי שִׂמְלַאי כַּמָּה אֱלֹהוּת בָּֽרְאוּ אֶת הָעוֹלָם. אָמַר לָהֶן לִי אַתֶּם שׁוֹאֲלִין. לְכוּ וְשַׁאֲלוּ אֶת אָדָם הָרִאשׁוֹן שֶׁנֶּאֱמַר כִּי שְׁאַל נָא לְיָמִים הָרִאשׁוֹנִים וְגוֹמֵר. אֲשֶׁר בָּֽרְאוּ אֱלֹהִים אָדָם עַל הָאָרֶץ אֵין כְּתִיב כָּאן אֶלָּא לְמִן הַיּוֹם אֲשֶׁר בָּרָא אֱלֹהִים אָדָם עַל הָאָרֶץ. אָֽמְרוּ לוֹ וְהָֽכְתִיב בְּרֵאשִׁית בָּרָא אֱלֹהִים. אָמַר לָהֶן וְכִי בָּֽרְאוּ כְתִיב אֵין כְּתִיב אֶלָּא בָּרָא. אָמַר רִבִּי שִׂמְלַאי כָּל־מָקוֹם שֶׁפָּֽרְקוּ[26] הַמִּינִין תְּשׁוּבָתָן בְּצִידָּן.

(Jewish) Christians asked Rebbi Simlai: How many aspects of divinity created the world? He answered them: Are you asking me? Go and ask the first Adam, as it is said (*Deut.* 4:32): "Please ask the first days etc[27]." It does not say there "when gods created man on the earth" but "from the day that God created man on the earth". They said to him, but it is written (*Gen.* 1:1): "In the beginning, *ĕlōhīm* created . . ." He said to them: Is it written "they created" (plural)? It says "he created" (singular). Rebbi Simlai said, every place where the Christians read heretic meanings[28], their answer is at that place.

26 Probably a scribal error for פקרו, but there is no manuscript evidence. In the parallel, *Bereshit rabba* 8(8), the text reads: כל מקום שאתה מוצא פתחון פה למינין "any place where you find that herectics can open their mouth". There, the entire sequence is found.

27 "Please ask the first days that were before you, starting from the day that God created man on the earth . . . "

28 That *ĕlōhīm* is a genuine plural, not one of majesty.

חָזְרוּ וְשָׁאֲלוּ אוֹתוֹ. מַה אָהֵן דִּכְתִיב נַעֲשֶׂה אָדָם בְּצַלְמֵנוּ כִּדְמוּתֵנוּ. אָמַר לָהֶן וַיִּבְרְאוּ אֱלֹהִים אֶת הָאָדָם בְּצַלְמָם אֵין כְּתִיב כָּאן אֶלָּא וַיִּבְרָא אֱלֹהִים אֶת הָאָדָם בְּצַלְמוֹ. אָמְרוּ לוֹ תַלְמִידָיו לְאֵלּוּ דָּחִיתָה בְּקָנֶה לָנוּ מַה אַתָּה מֵשִׁיב. אָמַר לָהֶן לְשֶׁעָבַר אָדָם נִבְרָא מִן הֶעָפָר וְחַוָּה נִבְרָאת מִן הָאָדָם. מֵאָדָם וָאֵילַךְ בְּצַלְמֵנוּ כִּדְמוּתֵנוּ. אִי אֶפְשַׁר לָאִישׁ בְּלֹא אִשָּׁה. וְאִי אֶפְשַׁר לְאִשָּׁה בְּלֹא אִישׁ. אִי אֶפְשַׁר לִשְׁנֵיהֶן בְּלֹא שְׁכִינָה.

They came back and asked him: What is that which is written (*Gen.* 1:26): "Let us make a human in our image, as in our pattern." He answered them, it is not written: "*ĕlōhīm* created man in their image" but (*Gen.* 1:27): "God created man in His image." His students told him: these you pushed away with a stick, what can you answer us[29]? He said to them: Adam was created from dust, Eve was created from Adam. After Adam "in our image, like our pattern;" it is impossible for a man without a woman, or for a woman without a man, and for both of them without the *Shekhinah*[30].

29 The verse presents a real difficulty, not for the plural, which is one of majesty, but for shape and form which cannot be attributes of God.

30 In the Babli (*Niddah* 31a) this is formulated as: There are three partners in the creation of a child: Father, mother, and the Holy One, praise to Him (who gives soul and intelligence.)

חָזְרוּ וְשָׁאֲלוּ אוֹתוֹ. מַה הָהֵן דִּכְתִיב אֵל אֱלֹהִים יי אֵל אֱלֹהִים יי הוּא יוֹדֵעַ. אָמַר לָהֶן הֵם יוֹדְעִים אֵין כְּתִיב כָּאן אֶלָּא הוּא יוֹדֵעַ כְּתִיב. אָמְרוּ לוֹ תַלְמִידָיו

רִבִּי לְאֵלּוּ דָּחִיתָה בְּקָנֶה לָנוּ מַה אַתָּה מֵשִׁיב. אָמַר לָהֶן שְׁלָשְׁתָּן שֵׁם אֶחָד כְּאֵינָשׁ דַּאֲמַר בַּסִילֵיוּס קֵיסַר אַוגוּשְׂתּוֹס.

They came back and asked him: What is that which is written (*Jos.* 22:22): "God, *ĕlōhīm*, Eternal, God, *ĕlōhīm*, Eternal[31], He knows." He answered them, it is not written: "they know", but "He knows." His students told him: Teacher, these you pushed away with a stick, what can you answer us? He said to them: All three are one name, as if a man would say "King[32], Caesar, Augustus."

31 Three names for the Divinity, twice repeated.

32 Greek βασιλεύς.

חָזְרוּ וְשָׁאֲלוּ אוֹתוֹ. מַהוּ דִּכְתִיב אֵל (fol. 13a) אֱלֹהִים יי דִּבֶּר וַיִּקְרָא אָרֶץ. אָמַר לָהֶן וְכִי דִּיבְּרוּ וַיִּקְרְאוּ כְּתִיב כָּאן אֶלָּא דִּבֶּר וַיִּקְרָא אָרֶץ. אָמְרוּ לוֹ תַלְמִידָיו רִבִּי לְאֵלּוּ דָּחִיתָה בְּקָנֶה לָנוּ מַה אַתָּה מֵשִׁיב. אָמַר לָהֶן שְׁלָשְׁתָּן שֵׁם אֶחָד כְּאִינַשׁ דַּאֲמַר אוּמָנוֹן בְּנָיֵין אַרְכִיטֶקְטָנָן.

They came back and asked him: What is that which is written (*Ps.* 50:2): "God, *ĕlōhīm*, Eternal, He spoke and called the earth." He answered them, it is not written: "they spoke and called", but "He spoke and called." His students told him: Teacher, these you pushed away with a stick, what can you answer us? He said to them: All three are one name, as if a man would say "professional, builder, architect[33]."

33 Greek ἀρχιτέκτων. The first נ probably should be a ו. This paragraph is missing in *Bereshit rabba*.

חָזְרוּ וְשָׁאֲלוּ אוֹתוֹ. מַהוּ דִכְתִיב כִּי אֱלֹהִים קְדוֹשִׁים הוּא. אָמַר לָהֶן קְדוֹשִׁים הֵם אֵין כְּתִיב כַּאן אֶלָּא הוּא אֵל קַנּוֹא הוּא. אָמְרוּ לוֹ תַלְמִידָיו רִבִּי לְאֵלּוּ דָּחִיתָה בְּקָנֶה לָנוּ מַה אַתָּה מֵשִׁיב. אָמַר רִבִּי יִצְחָק קָדוֹשׁ בְּכָל־מִינֵי קְדוּשׁוֹת. דְּאָמַר רִבִּי יוּדָן בְּשֵׁם רִבִּי אָחָא הַקָּדוֹשׁ בָּרוּךְ הוּא דְּרָכוֹ בִקְדוּשָּׁה. דִּיבּוּרוֹ

בְקְדוּשָּׁה. וְיִישּׁוּבוֹ בִקְדוּשָּׁה. חֲשִׂיפַת זְרוֹעוֹ בִקְדוּשָּׁה. אֱלֹהִים נוֹרָא וְאַדִּיר בִּקְדוּשָּׁה. דַּרְכּוֹ בִּקְדוּשָּׁה. אֱלֹהִים בַּקּוֹדֶשׁ דַּרְכֶּךָ. הִילּוּכוֹ בִּקְדוּשָּׁה. הֲלִיכוֹת אֵלִי מַלְכִּי בַקּוֹדֶשׁ. מוֹשָׁבוֹ בִקְדוּשָּׁה. אֱלֹהִים יָשַׁב עַל כִּסֵּא קָדְשׁוֹ. דִּיבּוּרוֹ בִקְדוּשָּׁה. אֱלֹהִים דִּבֶּר. חֲשִׂיפַת זְרוֹעוֹ בִקְדוּשָּׁה. חָשַׂף יי אֶת זְרוֹעַ קָדְשׁוֹ. נוֹרָא וְאַדִּיר בִּקְדוּשָּׁה. מִי כָמוֹכָה נֶאְדָּר בַּקּוֹדֶשׁ.

They came back and asked him: What is that which is written (*Jos.* 24:19): "For He is a holy God." He answered them, it is not written: "they", but "He," "He is a jealous God." His students told him: Teacher, these you pushed away with a stick, what can you answer us? Rebbi Isaac said, He is holy in all kinds of holiness, as Rebbi Yudan said in the name of Rebbi Aḥa: The Holy One, praise to Him, is holy in all kinds of holiness. His speech is in holiness, His throning is in holiness, the baring of His arm is in holiness, God is awesome and majestic in holiness. His way is in holiness, (*Ps.* 77:14) "God, Your way is in holiness." His walking is in holiness, (*Ps.* 68:25) "the course of my God, my King, in holiness." His throning is in holiness, (*Ps.* 47:9) "God throned on His holy throne." His speech is in holiness, (*Ps.* 60:8) "God spoke [in His holiness]." The baring of His arm is in holiness, (*Is.* 52:10) "The Eternal bared His holy arm." He is awesome and glorious in holiness, (*Ex.* 15:11) "Who is like You, glorious in holiness!"

חָזְרוּ וְשָׁאֲלוּ אוֹתוֹ. מַה אָהֵן דִּכְתִיב מִי גוֹי גָּדוֹל אֲשֶׁר לוֹ אֱלֹהִים קְרוֹבִים אֵלָיו. אָמַר לָהֶן כַּיי אֱלֹהֵינוּ בְּכָל־קָרְאֵינוּ אֲלֵיהֶם אֵין כְּתִיב כָּאן אֶלָּא בְּכָל־קָרְאֵינוּ אֵלָיו. אָמְרוּ לוֹ תַלְמִידָיו רִבִּי לְאֵלּוּ דָּחִיתָה בְקָנֶה לָנוּ מַה אַתָּה מֵשִׁיב. אָמַר לָהֶן קָרוֹב בְּכָל מִינֵי קֵרִיבוֹת. דְּאָמַר רִבִּי פִינְחָס בְּשֵׁם רִבִּי יְהוּדָה בַּר סִימוֹן עֲבוֹדָה זָרָה נִרְאֵית קְרוֹבָה וְאֵינָהּ אֶלָּא רְחוֹקָה. מַה טַעֲמָא יִשָּׂאוּהוּ עַל כָּתֵף יִסְבְּלוּהוּ וְגוֹמֵר. סוֹף דָּבָר אֱלוֹהוֹ עִמּוֹ בַּבַּיִת וְהוּא צוֹעֵק עַד שֶׁיָּמוּת וְלֹא יִשְׁמַע וְלֹא יוֹשִׁיעַ מִצָּרָתוֹ. אֲבָל הַקָּדוֹשׁ בָּרוּךְ הוּא נִרְאֶה רָחוֹק וְאֵין קָרוֹב מִמֶּנּוּ.

דְּאָמַר לֵוִי מֵהָאָרֶץ וְעַד לָרָקִיעַ מַהֲלַךְ ה׳ מֵאוֹת שָׁנָה. וּמֵרָקִיעַ לָרָקִיעַ מַהֲלַךְ ת״ק שָׁנָה. וְעָבְיוֹ שֶׁל רָקִיעַ ת״ק שָׁנָה וְכֵן לְכָל־רָקִיעַ וְרָקִיעַ. וְאָמַר רִבִּי בֶּרֶכְיָה וְרִבִּי חֶלְבּוֹ בְּשֵׁם רִבִּי אַבָּא סְמוּקָה אַף טַלְפֵי הַחַיּוֹת מַהֲלַךְ ה׳ מֵאוֹת שָׁנָה וַחֲמֵשׁ עֶשְׂרֵה מִנְיָין ישׁר״ה. רְאֵה כַּמָּה הוּא גָבוֹהַּ מֵעוֹלָמוֹ. וְאָדָם נִכְנַס לְבֵית הַכְּנֶסֶת וְעוֹמֵד אַחוֹרֵי הָעַמּוּד וּמִתְפַּלֵּל בִּלְחִישָׁה וְהַקָּדוֹשׁ בָּרוּךְ הוּא מַאֲזִין אֶת תְּפִילָּתוֹ. שֶׁנֶּאֱמַר וְחַנָּה הִיא מְדַבֶּרֶת עַל לִבָּהּ רַק שְׂפָתֶיהָ נָעוֹת וְקוֹלָהּ לֹא יִשָּׁמֵעַ. וְהֶאֱזִין הַקָּדוֹשׁ בָּרוּךְ הוּא אֶת תְּפִילָּתָהּ. וְכֵן כָּל־בְּרִיּוֹתָיו שֶׁנֶּאֱמַר תְּפִילָּה לְעָנִי כִּי יַעֲטוֹף. כְּאָדָם הַמֵּשִׂיחַ בְּאוֹזֶן חֲבֵירוֹ וְהוּא שׁוֹמֵעַ. וְכִי יֵשׁ לְךָ אֱלוֹהַּ קָרוֹב מִזֶּה. שֶׁהוּא קָרוֹב לִבְרִיּוֹתָיו כְּפֶה לָאוֹזֶן.

They[34] came back and asked him: What is that which is written (*Deut.* 4:8): "Where is a great people that has *ĕlōhīm* close[35] to them?" He answered them, it is not written: "Like the Eternal, our *ĕlōhīm*, always when we call on them", but "always when we call on Him." His students told him: Teacher, these you pushed away with a stick, what can you answer us? He said to them, he is close in all kinds of closeness, as Rebbi Phineas said in the name of Rebbi Yehudah bar Simon: Idolatry seems close but is very far. What is the reason? (*Is.* 46:7) "They take it on the shoulder, carry it, etc." Finally, his god is with him in the house and he cries until he dies but that one will not hear and not save him from his distress. But the Holy One, praise to Him, seems to be far away when there is no one closer than Him[36], as Levi said[37]: From the earth to the (first) heaven is a distance of 500 years' walk. From one heaven to the next is a distance of 500 years' walk. The thickness of each heaven is a distance of 500 years' walk. And Rebbi Berekhiah and Rebbi Ḥelbo in the name of Red Rebbi Abba[38] said, also the toes of the heavenly *Ḥayot*[39] are a length of 515 years' walk, the number YŠRH[40]. See how much higher He is than His world! But a person enters the synagogue, stands behind a pillar, prays in a whisper, and the Holy One, praise to Him, listens to his prayer, as it has been said (*1Sam.* 1:13): "Hannah spoke to herself, only her lips were moving, but her voice was not heard." But the Holy One, praise to Him, listened to her prayer. And so it is with all His creatures, as it has been said (*Ps.* 102:1): "Prayer of the poor when he wraps himself up[41]," just like a man whispering into the ear of his friend and the latter understands. Can you have a God who is closer than that to His creatures, from mouth to ear?"

34 This is the start of a lengthy sermon that continues to the end of the Halakhah. It has been subdivided for the benefit of the reader. Since the name of Rebbi Berekhiah, one of the authors and collectors of *Midrash Bereshit rabba*, is mentioned in this sermon, one may take it as a proof that *Midrash Shemot rabba*, which in the middle switches from a style identical to that of *Midrash Bereshit rabba* to extended sermons based on the starting verses of the weekly portions, does not necessarily have two different collectors or editors.

35 Plural.

36 The following argument is in disagreement with the generally accepted doctrine of R. Yose bar Ḥalaphta that God is the place of the world but the world is not His place [*Bereshit rabba* 68(8), *Shemot rabba* 45(6), *Midrash Tehillim* 90, *Tanḥuma Ki Tissa* 27, *Tanḥuma Buber Ki Tissa* 16, *Yalqut Shim'oni* 117, 563, 841]. The piece is a homily and not a theological essay.

37 Without attribution of a name, the statement has been quoted in Chapter 1, Halakhah 1.

38 A third generation Galilean Amora whose sermons were collected by Rebbi Berekhiah.

39 They carry the Throne of Heavenly Glory in the vision of Ezechiel (*Ez.* 1).

40 The homily disregards the conclusion drawn from the verse in Halakhah 1:1 (fol. 2c), that one has to pray with feet parallel one to the other. The numerical value of ישרה is 10+300+200+5 = 515.

41 Usually, יעטף is translated "he faints." But here, it is taken in the Mishnaic sense of "wrapping oneself in a garment," a toga or prayer shawl, to exclude the world from one's prayers.

רִבִּי יוּדָן בְּשֵׁם רִבִּי יִצְחָק אָמַר בָּהּ אַרְבַּע שִׁיטִין. בָּשָׂר וָדָם יֵשׁ לוֹ פַּטְרוֹן. אָמְרוּ לוֹ נִתְפַּס בֶּן בֵּיתְךָ אָמַר לָהֶן אֲנִי מְקַיֵּים עָלָיו. אָמְרוּ לוֹ הֲרֵי יוֹצֵא לִידוֹן. אָמַר לָהֶן אֲנִי מְקַיֵּים עָלָיו. אָמְרוּ לוֹ הֲרֵי הוּא יוֹצֵא לִיתָּלוֹת. הֵיכַן הוּא וְאֵיכַן פַּטְרוֹנוֹ. אֲבָל הַקָּדוֹשׁ בָּרוּךְ הוּא הִצִּיל אֶת מֹשֶׁה מֵחֶרֶב פַּרְעֹה. אָמַר רִבִּי יַנַּאי כְּתִיב וַיִּבְרַח מֹשֶׁה מִפְּנֵי פַרְעֹה. וְאֶפְשַׁר לְבָשָׂר וָדָם לִבְרוֹחַ מִן הַמַּלְכוּת. אֶלָּא בְשָׁעָה שֶׁתָּפַס פַּרְעֹה אֶת מֹשֶׁה חִייְבוֹ לְהַתִּיז אֶת רֹאשׁוֹ וְקָהֲת הַחֶרֶב מֵעַל צַוָּרוֹ שֶׁל מֹשֶׁה וְנִשְׁבְּרָה. הֲדָא הוּא דִכְתִיב צַוָּארֵךְ כְּמִגְדַּל הַשֵּׁן. זֶה צַוָּארוֹ שֶׁל מֹשֶׁה. רִבִּי אָמַר רִבִּי אֶבְיָתָר וְלֹא עוֹד אֶלָּא שֶׁנָּתַן הַחֶרֶב מֵעַל צַוָּארוֹ שֶׁל מֹשֶׁה עַל צַוָּארוֹ שֶׁל קוּצְנְטֵר[42] וְהָרַגְתּוֹ. הֲדָא הוּא דִכְתִיב וַיַּצִּילֵנִי מֵחֶרֶב פַּרְעֹה. לִי הִצִּיל וְקוּסְנְטֵר נֶהֱרַג. רִבִּי בֶּרֶכְיָה קָרָא עָלָיו כּוֹפֶר לַצַּדִּיק רָשָׁע. רִבִּי אָבוּן קָרָא עָלָיו צַדִּיק מִצָּרָה נֶחֱלָץ וַיָּבֹא רָשָׁע תַּחְתָּיו. תַּנֵּי בַּר קַפָּרָא מַלְאָךְ יָרַד וְנִדְמֶה לָהֶן כִּדְמוּת מֹשֶׁה וְתָפְסוּ אֶת הַמַּלְאָךְ וּבָרַח מֹשֶׁה. אָמַר רִבִּי יְהוֹשֻׁעַ בֶּן לֵוִי בְּשָׁעָה שֶׁבָּרַח מֹשֶׁה מִפְּנֵי פַרְעֹה נַעֲשׂוּ כָּל־אוֹכְלוֹסִין שֶׁלּוֹ אִילְּמִין וּמֵהֶן חֵרְשִׁין וּמֵהֶן סוּמִין. אָמַר לְאִילְּמִין הֵיכַן הוּא מֹשֶׁה וְלֹא הָיוּ מְדַבְּרִים. אָמַר לְחֵרְשִׁים וְלֹא הָיוּ שׁוֹמְעִין. אָמַר לְסוּמִין וְלֹא הָיוּ רוֹאִין. הוּא שֶׁהַקָּדוֹשׁ בָּרוּךְ הוּא אָמַר לוֹ לְמֹשֶׁה מִי שָׂם פֶּה לָאָדָם אוֹ מִי יָשׂוּם אִלֵּם וְגוֹמֵר. תַּמָּן קָמַת לָךְ וְהָכָא לֵית אֲנָא קָאִים. הֲהוּא דִכְתִיב מִי כַּיי אֱלֹהֵינוּ בְּכָל־קָרְאֵינוּ אֵלָיו.

Rebbi Yudan in the name of Rebbi Isaac said it in four versions. Flesh and blood has a protector[43]. When they tell him, your client was arrested, he will say: I will protect him. When they tell him, he is going before a court, he will say: I will protect him. When they tell him, he is taken to be hanged, where is he and where is his protector? But the Holy One, praise to Him, saved Moses from the sword of Pharao; that is what is written (*Ex.* 18:4): "He saved me from the sword of Pharao." Rebbi Yannai said[44], it is written (*Ex.* 2:15): "Moses fled from before Pharao." Is it possible for flesh and blood to flee from the government?[45] But at the moment when Pharao arrested Moses, he sentenced him to have him beheaded. The sword slipped off the neck of Moses and broke. That is what is written (*Songs* 7:5): "Your neck is like the ivory tower," that is Moses's neck. Rebbi[46] said, Rebbi Eviathar: Not only that, but He moved the sword from the neck of Moses on the neck of the executioner and killed him. That is what is written: "He saved me from the sword of Pharao." He saved *me*, but killed the executioner. Rebbi Berekhiah quoted on this (*Prov*. 21:18) "The evil one is ransom for the just one." Rebbi Abun quoted on this (*Prov*. 11:8): "The just will be extricated from distress, the evil one will take his place." Bar Qappara stated: An angel came down and appeared to them in the shape of Moses. They arrested the angel and Moses fled. Rebbi Joshua ben Levi said: when Moses fled from before Pharao, all his troops[47] became dumb, deaf, or blind. He asked the dumb, where is Moses? But they could not speak. He asked the deaf, they could not hear. He asked the blind, they could not see. That is what the Holy One, praise to Him, said to Moses (*Ex*. 4:11): "Who gave man a mouth, or who makes dumb?" There it upheld you and here you do not want to uphold. That is what is written (*Deut*. 4:8): "Who is like the Eternal, our *ĕlōhīm*, always when we call on Him!"

42 Reading of the Rome ms. Venice: קוסנתירו, *Arukh* reads קוסטינר. Late Latin *quaestionarius*, "torturer, executioner."

43 Latin *patronus*, who was obliged to protect his *clients*.

44 Most of the following is also in *Exodus rabba* 1(37).

45 R. Yannai takes the sentence to mean that "Moses fled from before the face of Pharao," as translated here, and not "Moses fled because of Pharao," as usually understood.

46 The name of the tradent is missing; he cannot be Rebbi since R. Eviathar belongs to the second generation of Amoraïm and exchanged letters with Rav Ḥisda and Rav Sheshet. The sentence is missing in *Shemot rabba*.

47 Semitic plural of Greek ὄχλος, "multitude" (of people, troops).

רִבִּי יוּדָן בְּשֵׁם רִבִּי יִצְחָק שִׁיטָּה אוֹחְרִי. בָּשָׂר וְדָם יֵשׁ לוֹ פַּטְרוֹן. אָֽמְרוּ לוֹ נִתְפַּס בֶּן בֵּיתְךָ אָמַר לָהֶן אֲנִי מְקַיֵּים עָלָיו. אָֽמְרוּ לוֹ הֲרֵי יוֹצֵא לִידוֹן. אָמַר לָהֶן אֲנִי מְקַיֵּים עָלָיו. אָמְרוּ לוֹ הֲרֵי הוּא מוּשְׁלָךְ לַמַּיִם. הֵיכַן הוּא וְאֵיכַן פַּטְרוֹנוֹ. אֲבָל הַקָּדוֹשׁ בָּרוּךְ הוּא הִצִּיל אֶת יוֹנָה מִמְּעֵי הַדָּגָה. הֲרֵי הוּא אוֹמֵר וַיֹּאמֶר יי לַדָּג וַיָּקֵא אֶת יוֹנָה.

Rebbi Yudan in the name of Rebbi Isaac in another version. Flesh and blood has a protector. When they tell him, your client was arrested, he will say: I will protect him. When they tell him, he is going before a court, he will say: I will protect him. When they tell him, he is being thrown into the water, where is he and where is his protector? But the Holy One, praise to Him, saved Jonah from inside the fish, since it says (*Jonah* 2:11): "The Eternal commanded the fish and it threw Jonah up."

רִבִּי יוּדָן בְּשֵׁם רִבִּי יִצְחָק אָמַר בְּשִׁיטָּה אוֹחְרִי. בָּשָׂר וְדָם יֵשׁ לוֹ פַּטְרוֹן. אָֽמְרוּ לוֹ נִתְפַּס בֶּן בֵּיתְךָ אָמַר לָהֶן אֲנִי מְקַיֵּים עָלָיו. אָֽמְרוּ לוֹ הֲרֵי יוֹצֵא לִידוֹן. אָמַר לָהֶן אֲנִי מְקַיֵּים עָלָיו. אָֽמְרוּ לוֹ הֲרֵי הוּא מוּשְׁלָךְ לָאֵשׁ. הֵיכַן הוּא וְאֵיכַן פַּטְרוֹנוֹ. אֲבָל הַקָּדוֹשׁ בָּרוּךְ הוּא הִצִּיל לַחֲנַנְיָה מִישָׁאֵל וַעֲזַרְיָה מִכִּבְשַׁן הָאֵשׁ. הָהוּא דִּכְתִיב עָנֵה נְבוּכַדְנֶצַּר וְאָמַר בְּרִיךְ אֱלָהֲהוֹן דִּי שַׁדְרַךְ מֵישַׁךְ וַעֲבֵד נְגוֹ וְגוֹמֵר.

Rebbi Yudan in the name of Rebbi Isaac said in another version: Flesh and blood has a protector. When they tell him, your client was arrested, he will say: I will protect him. When they tell him, he is going before a court, he will say: I will protect him. When they tell him, he is being thrown into fire, where is he and where is his protector? But the Holy One, praise to Him, saved Ḥananiah, Mishael, and Azariah from the fiery oven; this is what is written (*Dan.* 3:14): "Nebucadnezzar declared and said, praised be the God of Shadrakh, Meshakh, and Abed Nego, etc."

רִבִּי יוּדָן בְּשֵׁם רִבִּי יִצְחָק אָמַר בָּהּ שִׁיטָּה אוֹחְרִי. בָּשָׂר וְדָם יֵשׁ לוֹ פַּטְרוֹן כו' עַד הֲרֵי הוּא מוּשְׁלָךְ לַחַיּוֹת. אֲבָל הַקָּדוֹשׁ בָּרוּךְ הוּא הִצִּיל אֶת דָּנִיֵּאל מִגּוֹב הָאֲרָיוֹת. הָהוּא דִכְתִיב אֱלָהִי שְׁלַח מַלְאֲכֵיהּ וּסְגַר פּוּם אַרְיָוָתָא. וגו'.

Rebbi Yudan in the name of Rebbi Isaac said in another version: Flesh and blood has a protector, etc. until: he is being thrown to the wild beasts. But the Holy One, praise to Him, saved Daniel from the lions' den. That is what is written (*Dan.* 6:23): "My God sent his angel who closed the mouth of the lions, etc."

רִבִּי יוּדָן אָמַר מִשְׁמֵיהּ דִּידֵיהּ בָּשָׂר וְדָם יֵשׁ לוֹ פַּטְרוֹן. אִם בָּאת לוֹ עֵת צָרָה אֵינוֹ נִכְנַס אֶצְלוֹ פִּתְאוֹם. אֶלָּא בָּא וְעָמַד עַל פִּתְחוֹ שֶׁל פַּטְרוֹנוֹ וְקוֹרֵא לְעַבְדּוֹ אוֹ לְבֶן בֵּיתוֹ וְהוּא אוֹמֵר אִישׁ פְּלוֹנִי עוֹמֵד עַל פֶּתַח חֲצֵירָךְ. שֶׁמָּא מַכְנִיסוֹ וְשֶׁמָּא מַנִּיחוֹ. אֲבָל הַקָּדוֹשׁ בָּרוּךְ הוּא אֵינוֹ כֵן אִם בָּאָה עַל אָדָם צָרָה לֹא יְצַוַּח לֹא לְמִיכָאֵל וְלֹא לְגַבְרִיאֵל אֶלָּא לִי יְצַוַּח וַאֲנִי עוֹנֶה לוֹ מִיַּד הָהוּא דִכְתִיב כָּל אֲשֶׁר יִקְרָא בְּשֵׁם יי יְמַלֵּט.

Rebbi Judan said in his own name[48]: Flesh and blood has a protector. If someone is in trouble, he does not enter the protector's place suddenly but rather stands at his door and calls his slave or familiar and that one will say: the man X is standing at the door of your courtyard. Maybe he will make him enter, maybe he will let him stand. But the Holy One, praise to Him, is not like this: If a human is in trouble, he should cry neither to Michael nor to Gabriel, rather he should cry to Me and I shall answer him immediately; that is what is written (*Joel* 3:5): "Every one who calls on[49] the name of the Eternal will escape."

48 In *Yalqut Shim'oni Joel* (#537), the paragraph and the next one are quoted in a shortened form in the name of Rebbi Yehudah in the name of Rebbi Jeremiah.

49 The sentence is slightly ambiguous; one could also translate "who invokes the Name"; that is the meaning given to the verse in the next paragraph.

אָמַר רִבִּי פִּינְחָס עוּבְדָא הֲוָה בְּרַב דַּהֲוָה עָיֵיל מֵחֲמָתָה דְטִיבֵּרִיָּא פָּגְעוֹן בֵּיהּ רוֹמָאֵי. אָמְרוּן לֵיהּ מִן דְּמַאן אַתְּ. אֲמַר לוֹן מִן דְּסוֹפִיינוּס וּפְנִיְיֵיהּ. בְּרַמְשָׁא אָתוּ לְגַבֵּיהּ אָמְרוּ לֵיהּ עַד אֵימָתַי אַתְּ מְקַיֵּים אִילֵּין יְהוּדָאֵי אֲמַר לוֹן לָמָּה. אָמְרוּ לֵיהּ פְּגָעִינָן בְּחַד אֲמַר לוֹן יְהוּדָאִי וַאֲמָרִין לֵיהּ מִן דְּמָאן אַתְּ אֲמַר לוֹן דְּסוֹפִיינוּס. אֲמַר לוֹן וּמַה עֲבַדִיתוּן לֵיהּ. אָמְרוּ לֵיהּ דַּיּוֹ פְּנִינָן (fol. 13b) יָתֵיהּ. אֲמַר לוֹן יְאוּת עֲבַדִיתוּן. וּמַה מִי שֶׁהוּא נִתְלָה בְּבָשָׂר וְדָם נִיצּוֹל. מִי שֶׁהוּא נִתְלָה בְּהַקָּדוֹשׁ בָּרוּךְ הוּא לֹא כָּל שֶׁכֵּן. הָהוּא דִּכְתִיב כָּל אֲשֶׁר יִקְרָא בְּשֵׁם יי יִמָּלֵט.

Rebbi Phineas said: It happened to Rav[50] that he was ascending from the hot springs of Tiberias[51] that he met Romans. They asked him, of whose party are you? He said, of Sophianus[52]; they let him go. The next morning, they came to him and asked him, how long did you carry on with these Jews? He asked them, why? They said to him, we met a Jew and asked him, of whose party are you? He said, of Sophianus. He asked them, what did you do to him? They said to him, it was enough, we let him go. He said to them, you did well. And if a person who attaches himself on to the party of a human is saved, someone who attaches himself to the Holy One, praise to Him, so much more. That is what is written (*Joel* 3:5): "Every one who calls on[53] the name of the Eternal will escape."

50 In the parallel in *Yalqut Joel*, the story is told of "some man." This seems to be a more correct version, since Rav spent his time in the Yeshivah of Rebbi in Shephar'am and Beth She'arim in Western Galilee. Also, the setting fits much more the time of the military anarchy after the murder of Alexander Severus when Rav had long since returned to Babylonia.

51 "Of Tiberias" is missing in the Rome manuscript.

52 In *Yalqut Joel*, the name is Popianus. The name is unidentifiable [could be Pompeianus (E. G.)]. [Z. Frankel wants to emend the name to (Septimius) Severus; but this identification is impossible for many

reasons (it would require that Rav stayed at the Yeshiva of Rebbi at least 25 years, that Severus should have ever been in Galilee, and that in Galilee one spoke Hebrew with a German pronunciation that identified *waw* and *phe*, *v* and *f*.)] The setting looks much more like that of a local conflict that was possible only during the military anarchy. The history of that period is not detailed enough to enumerate all local rulers. (There is a Roman surname Sophus.)

53 The sentence is slightly ambiguous; one could also translate "who invokes the Name"; that is the meaning given to the verse in the next paragraph.

אָמַר רִבִּי אֲלֶכְסַנְדְּרִי עוּבְדָּא בְחַד אַרְכוֹן דַּהֲוָה שְׁמֵיהּ אֲלֶכְסַנְדְּרוֹס וַהֲוָה קַייֵם דַּיֵּין חַד לֵיסְטֵיס. אֲמַר לֵיהּ מַה שְׁמָךְ אֲלֶכְסַנְדְּרוֹס. אֲמַר אֲלֶכְסַנְדְּרוֹס פְּנֵה לַאֲלֶכְסַנְדְּרִיָּאה. וּמַה מִי שֶׁהוּא שֶׁשְּׁמוֹ כִּשְׁמוֹ שֶׁל בְּבָשָׂר וְדָם הוּא נִיצּוֹל. מִי שֶׁשְּׁמוֹ כִּשְׁמוֹ שֶׁל הַקָּדוֹשׁ בָּרוּךְ הוּא לֹא כָּל שֶׁכֵּן. הָהוּא דִכְתִיב כָּל אֲשֶׁר יִקְרָא בְּשֵׁם ה' יִמַּלֵּט.

Rebbi Alexandri said, it happened that a prefect by the name of Alexander sat and judged a robber[54]. He asked him, what is your name? Alexander! He said, Alexander, go to Alexandria[55]. And if a person whose name is the name of a human is saved, someone whose name is that of the Holy One, praise to Him, so much more. That is what is written (*Joel* 3:5): "Every one who is called by the name of the Eternal will escape."

54 Note the exact transliteration of Greek ληστής.

55 So that people should not say, Alexander was executed. Alexandria was a very big city in which one more robber would not make a difference.

רִבִּי פִּינְחָס אָמַר בָּהּ תַּרְתֵּי חָדָא בְשֵׁם רִבִּי זְעִירָא וְחַד בְּשֵׁם רִבִּי תַּנְחוּם בַּר חֲנִילָאי. רִבִּי פִּינְחָס בְּשֵׁם רִבִּי זְעִירָא אָמַר בָּשָׂר וְדָם יֵשׁ לוֹ פַּטְרוֹן. אִם הִטְרִיחַ אָלָיו בְּיוֹתֵר הוּא אוֹמֵר אַשְׁכַּח פְּלָן דְּקָא מַטְרְחָא לִי. אֲבָל הַקָּדוֹשׁ בָּרוּךְ הוּא אֵינוֹ כֵן. אֶלָּא כָּל־מַה שֶׁאַתְּ מַטְרִיחַ עָלָיו הוּא מְקַבְּלָךְ. הָהוּא דִכְתִיב הַשְׁלֵךְ עַל

יי יְהָבְךָ וְהוּא יְכַלְכְּלֶךָ. רִבִּי פִּינְחָס בְּשֵׁם רִבִּי תַנְחוּם בַּר חֲנִילָאִי אָמַר בָּשָׂר וְדָם יֵשׁ לוֹ פַּטְרוֹן. וּבָאוּ שׂוֹנְאִים וְתָפְשׂוּ אוֹתוֹ עַל פֶּתַח חֲצֵירוֹ שֶׁל פַּטְרוֹנוֹ. עַד דְּצָוַח לֵיהּ עַד דְּהוּא נְפַק עֲבָרַת חַרְבָּא עַל קָדְלֵיהּ וְקָטְלָה יָתֵיהּ. אֲבָל הַקָּדוֹשׁ בָּרוּךְ הוּא הִצִּיל אֶת יְהוֹשָׁפָט מֵחֶרֶב אֲרָם. דִּכְתִיב וַיִּזְעַק יְהוֹשָׁפָט וַיי עֲזָרוֹ וַיְסִיתֵם אֱלֹהִים מִמֶּנּוּ. מְלַמֵּד שֶׁלֹּא הָיָה חָסֵר אֶלָּא חִיתּוּךְ הָרֹאשׁ וַיְסִיתֵם אֱלֹהִים מִמֶּנּוּ.

Rebbi Phineas gave on this subject two sermons, one in the name of Rebbi Zeïra, the other in the name of Rebbi Tanḥum bar Ḥanilai. Rebbi Phineas said in the name of Rebbi Zeïra, flesh and blood has a protector. If he bothers him too much, he will say: "There is X who will bother me." But the Holy One, praise to Him, is not like that; He will receive you with all that you might bother him with. That is what is written (*Ps.* 55:23) "Throw on the Eternal your burden and He will provide for you!" Rebbi Phineas said in the name of Rebbi Tanḥum bar Ḥanilai, flesh and blood has a protector. Enemies come and grab him at the door of his protector's courtyard. While he is crying and before someone could come out, the sword already passes over his neck and kills him. But the Holy One, praise to Him, saved Jehoshaphat from the sword of the Syrians as it is written (*2Chr.* 18:34): "Jehoshaphat cried, the Eternal helped him and God turned them away from him." That shows that only the cutting off of the head was missing, but God deflected them from him.

רִבִּי זְעִירָא בְּרֵיהּ דְּרִבִּי אַבָּהוּ רִבִּי אַבָּהוּ בְּשֵׁם רִבִּי אֶלְעָזָר אַשְׁרֵי שֶׁאֵל יַעֲקֹב בְּעֶזְרוֹ וגו'. מַה כְתִיב בַּתְרֵיהּ עֹשֶׂה שָׁמַיִם וָאָרֶץ. וְכִי מַה עִנְיָן זֶה לָזֶה. אֶלָּא מֶלֶךְ בָּשָׂר וָדָם יֵשׁ לוֹ פַּטְרוֹן שׁוֹלֵט בְּאֵיפַּרְכִיָּא אַחַת וְאֵינוֹ שׁוֹלֵט בְּאֵיפַּרְכִיָּא אַחֶרֶת. קוֹזְמוֹקְלָטוֹר שׁוֹלֵט בַּיַּבָּשָׁה שֶׁמָּא שׁוֹלֵט בַּיָּם. אֲבָל הַקָּדוֹשׁ בָּרוּךְ הוּא שׁוֹלֵט בַּיָּם וְשׁוֹלֵט בַּיַּבָּשָׁה. וּמַצִּיל בַּיָּם מִן הַמַּיִם וּבַיַּבָּשָׁה מִן הָאֵשׁ. הוּא שֶׁהִצִּיל אֶת מֹשֶׁה מֵחֶרֶב פַּרְעוֹ. הִצִּיל אֶת יוֹנָה מִמְּעֵי הַדָּגָה. חֲנַנְיָה מִישָׁאֵל וַעֲזַרְיָה

מִכִּבְשָׁן הָאֵשׁ. לְדָנִיֵּאל מִבּוֹר הָאֲרָיוֹת. הָהוּא דִכְתִיב עוֹשֶׂה שָׁמַיִם וָאָרֶץ אֶת הַיָּם וְאֶת כָּל־אֲשֶׁר בָּם.

Rebbi Zeīra, son of Rebbi Abbahu, Rebbi Abbahu in the name of Rebbi Eleazar (*Ps.* 146:5): "Happy is he whom the God of Jacob helps." What is written after that (*Ps.* 146:6): "He makes Heaven and Earth." What has one to do with the other? But a king of flesh and blood needs a protector[56], he rules over one district[57] but not over another district. A universal ruler[58] rules over dry land; does he rule over the ocean? But the Holy One, praise to Him, rules over ocean and dry land. He saves in the ocean from the water and on the dry land from the fire. He saved Moses from Pharao's sword. He saved Jonah from inside the fish, Ḥananiah, Mishael, and Azariah, from the fiery oven, Daniel from the lions' den. That is what is written (*Ps.* 146:6) "He makes Heaven and Earth, the oceans and all that is in them."

56 "King" was a title forbidden in Rome; a 'king' is a small local potentate who needs a Roman (or, possibly, a Persian) emperor as a protector.

57 Greek ἐπαρχία.

58 Greek κοσμοκράτωρ. In the parallel, *Avodah zarah* 1:1, the word is written קוזמוקרטור. There, the universal ruler is Alexander the Great.

אָמַר רִבִּי תַּנְחוּמָא מַעֲשֶׂה בִּסְפִינָה אַחַת שֶׁל גּוֹיִם שֶׁהָיְתָה פוֹרֶשֶׁת בְּיָם[59] הַגָּדוֹל וְהָיָה בָּהּ תִּינוֹק אֶחָד יְהוּדִי. עָמַד עֲלֵיהֶן סַעַר גָּדוֹל בַּיָּם וְעָמַד כָּל־אֶחָד וְאֶחָד מֵהֶן וְהִתְחִיל נוֹטֵל יִרְאָתוֹ בְּיָדוֹ וְקוֹרֵא וְלֹא הוֹעִיל כְּלוּם. כֵּיוָן שֶׁרָאוּ שֶׁלֹּא הוֹעִילוּ כְּלוּם אָמְרוּ לְאוֹתוֹ הַיְּהוּדִי. בְּנִי קוּם קְרָא אֶל אֱלֹהֶיךָ שֶׁשָּׁמַעְנוּ שֶׁהוּא עוֹנֶה אֶתְכֶם כְּשֶׁאַתֶּם צוֹעֲקִים אֵלָיו וְהוּא גִיבּוֹר. מִיַּד עָמַד הַתִּינוֹק בְּכָל לִבּוֹ וְצָעַק וְקִיבֵּל מִמֶּנּוּ הַקָּדוֹשׁ בָּרוּךְ הוּא תְפִילָּתוֹ וְשָׁתַק הַיָּם. כֵּיוָן שֶׁיָּרְדוּ לַיַּבָּשָׁה יָרְדוּ כָּל־אֶחָד וְאֶחָד לִקְנוֹת צְרָכָיו. אָמְרוּ לוֹ לְאוֹתוֹ תִינוֹק לֵית אַתְּ בְּעִי מִזְבִּין לָךְ כְּלוּם. אֲמַר לְהוֹן מַה אַתּוּן בְּעוּ מִן הָהֵן אַכְסֶנָיָא עֲלוּבָה. אָמְרוּ לוֹ אַתְּ

אַכְסֶנָיָא עֲלוּבָה. אִינּוּן אַכְסֶנָיָא עֲלוּבָה אִינּוּן הָכָא וְטַעֲוָתְהוֹן בְּבָבֶל. אִינּוּן הָכָא וְטַעֲוָתְהוֹן בְּרוֹמֵי. וְאִינּוּן הָכָא וְטַעֲוָתְהוֹן עִמָּהוֹן וְלָא מְהַנּוּן לְהוֹן כְּלוּם. אֲבָל אַתְּ כָּל־אָהֵן דְּאַתְּ אֲזַל אֱלָהֵיךְ עִמָּךְ. הָהוּא דִיכְתִיב כַּיי אֱלֹהֵינוּ בְּכָל־קָרְאֵינוּ אֵלָיו.

Rebbi Tanhuma said: A happening with a ship of Gentiles that sailed the great sea and on it was a Jewish child. There came upon them a big storm; each one got up, took his idol in his hand and called upon it, without result. When they saw that it was of no use, they said to that Jew: Son, get up, call on your God, for we heard that He answers you when you cry and He is strong. The child immediately got up with a full heart and cried; the Holy One, praise to Him, received his prayer and the sea quited down. When they came to dry land, each one descended to buy his needs. They said to that child, do you not want to buy anything for yourself? He said to them, what do you want from that unhappy stranger[60]. They said to him: Are you an unhappy stranger? They are an unhappy stranger; they are here and their errors[61] are in Babylonia, they are here and their errors are in Rome, they are here and their errors are with them, but are of no use to them. But you, everywhere you go, your God is with you. That is what is written (*Deut.* 4:7): "Like the Eternal, our God, always when we call on Him!"

59 Reading of the Rome manuscript; Venice print מים.

60 At other places in the Yerushalmi, the spelling is אכסניי, Greek ξένος "stranger, guest", with prothetic א.

61 Their idols.

רִבִּי שִׁמְעוֹן בֶּן לָקִישׁ אָמַר בָּשָׂר וָדָם יֵשׁ לוֹ קָרוֹב. אִם הָיָה עָשִׁיר הוּא מוֹדֶה בוֹ. וְאִם הָיָה עָנִי כּוֹפֵר בּוֹ. אֲבָל הַקָּדוֹשׁ בָּרוּךְ הוּא אֵינוֹ כֵן אֶלָּא אֲפִילוּ יִשְׂרָאֵל נְתוּנִין בִּירִידָה הַתַּחְתּוֹנָה הוּא קוֹרֵא אוֹתָם אַחַי וְרֵעָי. וּמַה טַעַם לְמַעַן אַחַי וְרֵעָי. רִבִּי אָבוּן וְרִבִּי אָחָא וְרִבִּי שִׁמְעוֹן בֶּן לָקִישׁ בָּשָׂר וָדָם יֵשׁ לוֹ קָרוֹב. אִם

הָיָה פִילוֹסוֹפוֹס הוּא אוֹמֵר הָהֵן פַּלָּן מִתְקָרֵב לוֹן. אֲבָל הַקָּדוֹשׁ בָּרוּךְ הוּא קוֹרֵא לְכָל־יִשְׂרָאֵל קְרוֹבִים הָהוּא דִּכְתִיב וַיָּרֶם קֶרֶן לְעַמּוֹ.

Rebbi Simeon bar Laqish said, flesh and blood has a relative. If he is rich, he acknowledges him. If he is poor, he disawovs him. But the Holy One, praise to Him, is not like this; even if Israel is in deepest distress, He calls them My brothers and My friends. What is the reason (*Ps.* 122:8): "For My brothers and friends." Rebbi Abun, Rebbi Aḥa, and Rebbi Simeon ben Laqish: flesh and blood has a relative. If he is a philosopher, he says: "This X is related to us." But the Holy One, praise to Him, calls all of Israel relatives; that is what is written (*Ps.* 148:14): "He raises the fortunes of His people.[62]"

62 While there are numerous verses declaring Israel as His people, it belongs to the style of a sermon to close with a verse promising a better future. The quote may indicate that **עם** should be translated as "relative"; this is the meaning attributed to the root in theophorous names.

(fol. 12c) **משנה ב**: מָקוֹם שֶׁנֶּעֶקְרָה מִמֶּנּוּ עֲבוֹדָה זָרָה אוֹמֵר בָּרוּךְ שֶׁעָקַר עֲבוֹדָה זָרָה מֵאַרְצֵנוּ.

Mishnah 2: At a place from which paganism was uprooted[62], one says: Praise to Him Who uprooted paganism from our Land.

62 A place where a pagan temple was destroyed or converted to profane use.

(fol. 13b) **הלכה ב**: מַתְנִיתָא כְּשֶׁנֶּעֶקְרָא מִכָּל־מְקוֹמוֹת אֶרֶץ יִשְׂרָאֵל אֲבָל אִם נֶעֶקְרָא מִמָּקוֹם אֶחָד אוֹמֵר בָּרוּךְ שֶׁעָקַר עֲבוֹדָה זָרָה מִן הַמָּקוֹם הַזֶּה. נֶעֶקְרָה מִמָּקוֹם אֶחָד וְנִקְבְּעָה בְּמָקוֹם אַחֵר. מָקוֹם שֶׁנִּיתְּנָה בוֹ אוֹמֵר בָּרוּךְ אֶרֶךְ אַפַּיִם. וּמָקוֹם שֶׁנֶּעֶקְרָה מִמֶּנּוּ אוֹמֵר בָּרוּךְ שֶׁעָקַר עֲבוֹדָה זָרָה מִן הַמָּקוֹם הַזֶּה. יְהִי

רָצוֹן מִלְּפָנֶיךָ יי אֱלֹהֵינוּ וֵאלֹהֵי אֲבוֹתֵינוּ כְּשֵׁם שֶׁעֲקַרְתָּה אוֹתָהּ מִן הַמָּקוֹם הַזֶּה כַּךְ תַּעֲקוֹר אוֹתָהּ מִן הַמְּקוֹמוֹת כּוּלָּם וְתַחֲזִיר לֵב עוֹבְדֶיהָ לְעוֹבְדָךְ. וְלֹא נִמְצָא מִתְפַּלֵּל עַל עוֹבְדֵי עֲבוֹדָה זָרָה. תַּנֵּי רִבִּי שִׁמְעוֹן בֶּן גַּמְלִיאֵל אוֹמֵר אַף בְּחוּצָה לָאָרֶץ צָרִיךְ לוֹמַר כֵּן.

Halakhah 2: Our Mishnah if it was uprooted from all places of the Land of Israel, but if it was uprooted only from one place, he says: "Praise to Him Who uprooted paganism from this place.[63]" If it was uprooted from one place but established at another place, there where it was reestablished he says: "Praise to Him Who is patient." Where it was uprooted from, he says: "Praise to Him Who uprooted paganism from this place. May it be Your pleasure, our God and God of our fathers, that just as You uprooted it from this place, so uproot it from all other places and turn the heart of its worshippers to worship You." Does he not pray for pagan worshippers[64]? It was stated: Rebbi Simeon[65] ben Gamliel says, also outside of the Land he must say this.

63 This version is not found in the parallels, Babli 57b, Tosephta *Berakhot* 6:2, *Ruth rabba* 3(2); they all apply the text of the Mishnah to a single destroyed temple, even though *Ruth rabba* is a (later) text in the Galilean tradition. The following three sentences appear in the version of the Mishnah in these three sources.

64 The answer to this question is given piecemeal in the next paragraphs.

65 Reading of the Rome manuscript; the Venice print has "R. Ismael ben Gamliel" who otherwise is unknown. In the Babli, the name is R. Simeon ben Eleazar and it is explained that even the first Tanna requires the benediction to be recited, only without the following prayer. There, R. Simeon's reason is that at the End of Days all peoples will abandon paganism.

אָמַר רִבִּי יוֹחָנָן כִּי מִי אֲשֶׁר יְחוּבָּר. יבחר כְּתִיב. אֶלָּא כָּל־הַחַיִּים יֵשׁ בִּטָּחוֹן שֶׁכָּל־זְמַן שֶׁאָדָם חַי יֵשׁ לוֹ תִקְוָה. מֵת עָבְדָה תִקְוָתוֹ. מַה טַעֲמָא בְּמוֹת אָדָם רָשָׁע תֹּאבֵד תִּקְוָה.

Rebbi Yoḥanan[66] said (*Eccl.* 9:4): "Who is it that has been connected?" It is written: "may choose." All living beings have the certitude that as long as a human is alive, he has hope. When he dies, his hope is lost. What is the reason (*Prov.* 11:7): "When an evil man dies, hope becomes lost."

66 In the parallel in *Ruth rabba*, this paragraph and the one after the next are taken together; the insertion of the next paragraph is difficult to understand.

The argument of R. Yoḥanan refers mostly to the parts of this and the preceding verses that are not quoted. "That is evil in all which is done under the sun, that the same happens to all; also, the heart of humans is full of evil, hooliganism is in their thoughts during their lifetime, but their end is with the dead. Who *is being joined*, all living beings have confidence; truly a living dog is better than a dead lion." *Is being joined* is the *qere*, the way the word is read, but "may choose" is the *ketib*, the way it is written. The interpretation given the *ketib* here is: All the living can have confidence that they may choose (the way of virtue), but death is final; nothing can be changed after death. Hence, a living dog (a living sinner) is better (might by repentance attain a higher state of holiness) than a dead lion (a good person.)

תַּנֵּי רִבִּי יְהוּדָה אוֹמֵר שְׁלֹשָׁה דְבָרִים צָרִיךְ אָדָם לוֹמַר בְּכָל יוֹם בָּרוּךְ שֶׁלֹּא עָשַׂנִי גוֹי. בָּרוּךְ שֶׁלֹּא עָשַׂנִי בוּר. בָּרוּךְ שֶׁלֹּא עָשַׂנִי אִשָּׁה. בָּרוּךְ שֶׁלֹּא עָשַׂנִי גוֹי שֶׁאֵין הַגּוֹיִם כְּלוּם כָּל הַגּוֹיִם כְּאַיִן נֶגְדוֹ. בָּרוּךְ שֶׁלֹּא עָשַׂנִי בוּר שֶׁאֵין בוּר יְרֵא חֵטְא. בָּרוּךְ שֶׁלֹּא עָשַׂנִי אִשָּׁה שֶׁאֵין הָאִשָּׁה מְצוּוָּה עַל הַמִּצְוֹת.

It has been stated: Rebbi Yehudah[67] says, three things a man has to recite every day: Praise to Him Who did not make me a Gentile. Praise to Him Who did not make me uncivilized[68]. Praise to Him Who did not make me a woman. "Praise to Him Who did not make me a Gentile," because Gentiles are not considered to be anything, (*Is.* 40:17) "all Gentiles are nothing before Him." "Praise to Him Who did not make me uncivilized," because an uncivilized person cannot fear sin[69]. "Praise to Him Who did not make me a woman," because women are not commanded about benedictions[70].

67 In the print of the Babli, *Menaḥot* 43b, "R. Meïr." However, R. Rabbinowitz notes a German and an Egyptian manuscript of the Babli that have "R. Yehudah", as well R. Isaac Fasi and *Rosh*, in line with the Yerushalmi and the Tosephta, *Berakhot* 6:17. The entire paragraph is from R. Yehudah in the Tosephta.

68 The uncivilized person is one who knows no Bible, no Mishnah, and no trade. Since he cannot know what is forbidden, he cannot fear sin. In the Babli (*Menaḥot* 43b-44a) it is reported that R. Jacob bar Aḥa changed this benediction to "Who did not make me a slave," since an uncivilized person can become civilized; his state of ignorance is not God-given.

69 Mishnah *Pirqe Avot* 2:6.

70 Here מצוות cannot mean "commandments", not even "positive commandments tied to a fixed time" that do not apply to women, but "benedictions", as in Chapter 6, Halakhah 1, first paragraph.

אָמַר רִבִּי אָחָא כִּי מִי אֲשֶׁר יְחוּבַּר. אֲפִילוּ אוֹתָם שֶׁפָּשְׁטוּ יְדֵיהֶם בִּזְבוּל יֵשׁ לָהֶם בִּטָּחוֹן. לְקָרְבָן אִי אֶפְשַׁר שֶׁבְּבָר פָּשְׁטוּ יְדֵיהֶם בִּזְבוּל. לְרַחֲקָן אִי אֶפְשַׁר שֶׁעָשׂוּ תְשׁוּבָה. עֲלֵיהֶן הוּא אוֹמֵר וְיָשְׁנוּ שְׁנַת עוֹלָם וְלֹא יָקִיצוּ. רַבָּנָן דְּקֵיסָרִין אָמְרִין קְטַנֵּי גוֹיִם וְחַיָּלוֹתָיו שֶׁל נְבוּכַדְנֶצַּר אֵין חַיִּין וְאֵין נִדּוֹנִין. עֲלֵיהֶן הַכָּתוּב אוֹמֵר וְיָשְׁנוּ שְׁנַת עוֹלָם וגו׳.

Rebbi Aḥa said, "Who is it that has been connected[71]?" Even those that stretched out their arms against the Sanctuary[72] have certitude. It is impossible to bring them near since they stretched out their arms against the Sanctuary. It is impossible to keep them far since they repented. On them it says (*Jer.* 51:39): "They will sleep eternal sleep and never awake." The rabbis of Caesarea say, Gentile minors[73] and the armies of Nebuchadnezzar[74] will not live, but never will they be judged. On them Scripture says: "They will sleep eternal sleep, etc."

71 Rebbi Aḥa explains the verse such as it is written, who is the one who is connected to God and the future world? Every human, as long as he is alive, has this possibility. The paragraph is inserted here because the verse was mentioned.

72 Tried to destroy the Temple or helped in destroying it. By necessity, these are Gentiles.

73 Who, as minors, are incapable of sin, but who, growing up as idolators, cannot have merit. [In Tosephta *Sanhedrin* 13:1, the opinion of Rabban Gamliel is quoted that children of (Jewish) evil doers (who die in infancy) have no part in the Future World, against the (prevailing) opinion of R. Joshua that all who die as children have part in the Future World, as it is written (*Ps.* 116:6): "The Eternal is the guardian of the simple ones."]

74 Who destroyed the Temple but who, in contrast to the Romans, did not do so out of hatred of Jews and Judaism. In Tosephta *Sanhedrin* 13:5 it is said that "for those who stretched out their arms against the Sanctuary, the gates of hell will be locked and they will be punished there for all eternity." It is explained here that this is valid only if they did not repent.

הָעוֹבֵר לִפְנֵי בֵּית עֲבוֹדָה זָרָה אוֹמֵר בֵּית גֵּאִים יִסַּח יי. רִבִּי יוֹסֵי בֵּי רִבִּי בּוּן בְּשֵׁם רִבִּי לֵוִי רָאָה אוֹתָם מְזַבְּחִין לַעֲבוֹדָה זָרָה אוֹמֵר זוֹבֵחַ לָאֱלֹהִים יָחֳרָם.

He who passes by a pagan temple says (*Prov.* 15:25): "The Eternal will tear down the house of the haughty." Rebbi Yose, son of Rebbi Abun, in the name of Rebbi Levi: "If he saw them sacrificing[75] to an idol, he says (*Ex.* 22:19): He who sacrifices to gods shall be devoted to destruction."

75 This is the reading of the Rome manuscript. The Venice print has מזבלין "bringing manure," meaning the same, but using language of contempt.

הָרוֹאֶה אֶת הַכּוּשִׁי וְאֶת הַגִּיחוֹר וְאֶת הַלֶּוְוקָן וְאֶת הַכִּיפֵּח וְאֶת הַנַּנָּס אוֹמֵר בָּרוּךְ מְשַׁנֶּה אֶת הַבְּרִיּוֹת. אֶת הַקָּטוּעַ וְאֶת הַסּוּמָא וְאֶת מוּכֵּי שְׁחִין אוֹמֵר בָּרוּךְ דַּיָּין אֱמֶת. מַתְנִיתִין כְּשֶׁהָיוּ שְׁלֵמִים וְנִשְׁתַּנּוּ. אֲבָל אִם הָיָה כֵן מִמְּעֵי אִמּוֹ בָּרוּךְ מְשַׁנֶּה אֶת הַבְּרִיּוֹת.

He who sees a black man[76], a red man, an albino[77], a beanstalk[78], or a dwarf, says: Praise to Him who makes unusual creatures; the amputee, the blind, or a person covered with boils, he says: Praise to the True Judge. This *baraitha* if they were whole and then changed. But if they were so from the mother's womb: Praise to Him who makes unusual creatures.

76 "Black man" here does not mean a Negro but a Caucasian with a swarthy complexion since it is stated in Babli *Bekhorot* 45b that a "black" man should not marry a "black" woman lest their children would be genuinely "black".

77 Greek λευκός "white".

78 In the Babli (58b), written קפח, in the Tosephta ביפיח. Rashi gives two explanations: 1) a potbelly, 2) a tall person with a bloated face. However, the Babli *Bekhorot* 45b defines קפח as a tall person whose frame is much too thin; the Mayence commentary ascribed to Rabbenu Gershom is the source of Rashi's second explanation.

הָרוֹאֶה אִילָנוֹת נָאִים וּבְנֵי אָדָם נָאִים אוֹמֵר בָּרוּךְ שֶׁכֵּן בָּרָא בְּרִיּוֹת נָאוֹת בְּעוֹלָמוֹ. מַעֲשֶׂה בְּרַבָּן גַּמְלִיאֵל שֶׁרָאָה גוֹיָה אִשָּׁה נָאָה וּבֵירֵךְ עָלֶיהָ. לֹא כֵן אָמַר רִבִּי זְעִירָא (fol. 13c) בְּשֵׁם רִבִּי יוֹסֵי בַּר חֲנִינָא בְּשֵׁם רִבִּי יוֹחָנָן לֹא תְחָנֵּם לֹא תִתֵּן עֲלֵיהֶן חֵן. מַה אָמַר. אַבַּסְקַנְטָא[79] לֹא אָמַר. אֶלָּא שֶׁכַּךְ בָּרָא בְּרִיּוֹת נָאוֹת בְּעוֹלָמוֹ. שֶׁכֵּן אֲפִילוּ רָאָה סוּס נָאֶה חֲמוֹר נָאֶה אוֹמֵר בָּרוּךְ שֶׁכֵּן בָּרָא בְּרִיּוֹת נָאוֹת בְּעוֹלָמוֹ. זוּ דַּרְכּוֹ שֶׁל רַבָּן גַּמְלִיאֵל לְהִסְתַּכֵּל בַּנָּשִׁים. אֶלָּא דֶּרֶךְ עֲקָמוּמִיתָא הָיְתָה. כְּגוֹן הָהֵן פּוֹפסדס. וְהִבִּיט בָּהּ שֶׁלֹּא בְטוֹבָתוֹ.

He who sees beautiful trees or beautiful people says: Praise to Him Who created beautiful creatures in His world[80]. It happened that Rabban Gamliel saw a beautiful Gentile woman and recited a benediction over her. Did not say Rebbi Zeïra in the name of Rebbi Yose bar Ḥanina in the name of Rebbi Yoḥanan (*Deut.* 7:2): "Do not favour them," do not ascribe charm to them? He did not say "may there be no harm" but "Who created beautiful creatures in His world," since even if one sees a beautiful horse or a beautiful donkey, one says: Praise to Him Who created beautiful creatures in His world. Does Rabban Gamliel usually look at women? It was a curved road, like a *pwpsdws*[81]; he looked at her because he could not avoid her.

79 Reading of the Rome ms. Venice: אבסקטא, but in *Avodah zarah* 1:9, the Venice text is equal to the Rome text here. Greek ἀβάσκαντα, "secure against witchcraft, free from harm" (D. de Lara in כתר כהונה). In the Babli, *Avodah zarah* 20a/b, Rabban (Simeon ben) Gamliel is reported to have quoted a verse (*Ps.* 104:24): "How great are Your works, o Eternal!"

80 In the Babli (58b) and the Tosephta (6:4), the formula is "Who has beautiful creatures in His world," without reference to Creation.

81 This word is unexplained. In the parallel in *Avodah zarah* and in *Arukh*, the spelling is פסוורוס, R. Salomon Cirillo has פיוסרס. R. J. Levy conjectures Greek σπεῖρα "a spiral (road)". R. M. Margalit (פני משה) thinks the word is Latinate, similar to Italian *passavia* "passageway; bridge." It could be Greek περίοδος, ἡ "way around, circuit, circular path" (E. G.).

קָרָא הַגֶּבֶר אוֹמֵר בָּרוּךְ חֲכַם הָרָזִים מִי שָׁת בַּטּוּחוֹת חָכְמָה. אָמַר רִבִּי לֵוִי בְּעֲרַבְיָא קוֹרִין לְאִימְרָא יוֹבְלָא. וְהָיָה בִּמְשׁוֹךְ בְּקֶרֶן הַיּוֹבֵל. בְּאַפְרִיקִיָּא קוֹרִין לְנִידָּה גַּלְמוּדָה. וַאֲנִי שְׁכוּלָה וְגַלְמוּדָה. בְּרוֹמֵי צוֹוְחִין לְתַרְנְגוֹלָא שֶׂכְוִי. אוֹ מִי נָתַן לַשֶּׂכְוִי בִּינָה.

If the cock crowed, one says: Praise to Him Who is wise in secrets; (*Job* 38:36) "Who put wisdom in kidneys?[82]". Rebbi Levi said, in Arabia one calls sheep *yovel*[83]; (*Jos.* 6:5) "it will be when the ram's horn is blown." In Africa[84], the menstruating woman is called *galmudah*, (*Is.* 49:21) "I am childless and barren." In Rome[85], one calls a chicken *śekhwi* (*Job* 38:36) "who gave understanding to the *śekhwi*?"

82 The full verse is: Who put wisdom into kidneys, who gave insight to the *śekhwi*?" The insight of the *śekhwi* is compared to the hidden knowledge of the kidneys, only accessible to God. The verse lends itself better to the Babylonian version (60b): "Praise to Him Who gave insight to the

śekhwi to distinguish between day and night." The text of the Galilean benediction is a disapproved version of a benediction to be recited if one sees a great scholar, Babli *Berakhot* 58b. The following explanation of words, parallel to one given in Babli *Rosh Hashanah* 26a, refers to the determination of the meaning of the word *śekhwi* (that is not quoted, only understood, at this moment.)

83 The same identification is given by R. Aqiba in Babli *Rosh Hashanah* 26a; it must refer to the Hebrew usage of Jewish tribes in Arabia, not to Arabic. [There is an Arabic word יַבַּל "giving lots of milk".]

84 In the Babli, the place referred to is Gallia (or Galatia). The etymology of the word has connections with Arabic גַּלְמַד, גֻלְמוּד "rock."

85 In the Babli, on the authority of R. Simeon ben Laqish, the place is Greek-speaking *Kenisrin*, near Aleppo.

הָרוֹאֶה אוֹכְלֹסִין אוֹמֵר בָּרוּךְ חֲכַם הָרָזִים. כְּשֵׁם שֶׁאֵין פַּרְצוּפֵיהֶן דּוֹמִין זֶה לָזֶה. כָּךְ אֵין דַּעְתָּן דּוֹמֶה זֶה לָזֶה: בֶּן זוֹמָא כְּשֶׁהָיָה רוֹאֶה אוֹכְלוֹסִין בִּירוּשָׁלַיִם אוֹמֵר בָּרוּךְ שֶׁבָּרָא כָּל־אֵילוּ לְשַׁמְּשֵׁנִי. כַּמָּה יָגַע אָדָם הָרִאשׁוֹן עַד שֶׁלֹּא אָכַל פְּרוּסָה. חָרַשׁ זָרַע נִיכֵּשׁ עִידֵּר קָצַר עִימֵּר דָּשׁ זָרָה בֵּירֵר טָחַן הִרְקִיד לָשׁ וְקִיטֵּף וְאָפָה וְאַחַר כָּךְ אָכַל פְּרוּסָה וַאֲנִי עוֹמֵד בְּשַׁחֲרִית וּמוֹצֵא כָּל־אֵלּוּ לְפָנַי. רְאֵה כַּמָּה יְגִיעוֹת יָגַע אָדָם הָרִאשׁוֹן עַד שֶׁמָּצָא חָלוּק לִלְבּוֹשׁ. גָּזַז וְלִיבֵּן וְנִיפֵּס וְצָבַע וְטָוָה וְאָרַג כִּבֵּס וְתָפַר וְאַחַר כָּךְ מָצָא חָלוּק לִלְבּוֹשׁ. וַאֲנִי עוֹמֵד בְּשַׁחֲרִית וּמוֹצֵא כָּל־אֵלּוּ מְתוּקָּן לְפָנַי. כַּמָּה בַּעֲלֵי אוּמָנִיּוֹת מַשְׁכִּימִים וּמַעֲרִיבִים. וַאֲנִי עוֹמֵד בְּשַׁחֲרִית וּמוֹצֵא כָּל־אֵלּוּ לְפָנַי. וְכֵן הָיָה בֶן זוֹמָא אוֹמֵר אוֹרֵחַ רָע מַהוּ אוֹמֵר וְכִי מָה אָכַלְתִּי מִשֶּׁל בַּעַל הַבַּיִת וְכִי מַה שָׁתִיתִי מִשֶּׁל בַּעַל הַבַּיִת חֲתִיכָה אַחַת אָכַלְתִּי לוֹ. כּוֹס יַיִן שָׁתִיתִי לוֹ. וְכָל־טוֹרַח שֶׁטָּרַח לֹא טָרַח אֶלָּא בִּשְׁבִיל אִשְׁתּוֹ וּבָנָיו. אֲבָל אוֹרֵחַ טוֹב אוֹמֵר בָּרוּךְ בַּעַל הַבַּיִת זָכוּר בַּעַל הַבַּיִת לְטוֹבָה. כַּמָּה יַיִן הֵבִיא לְפָנַי. כַּמָּה חֲתִיכוֹת הֵבִיא לְפָנַי. כַּמָּה טוֹרַח טָרַח לְפָנַי. כָּל־מַה שֶׁטָּרַח לֹא טָרַח אֶלָּא בִּשְׁבִילִי. וְכֵן הוּא אוֹמֵר זְכוֹר כִּי תַשְׂגִּיא פָעֳלוֹ אֲשֶׁר שׁוֹרְרוּ אֲנָשִׁים:

He[86] who sees multitudes says: Praise to Him Who is wise in secrets! Just as their faces are not similar one to the other, so the opinions of one are not similar to another's. When ben Zoma saw multitudes in Jerusalem, he said: Praise to Him Who created all these to serve me. How much did Adam toil until he could eat one piece of bread! He plowed, sowed, harrowed, weeded, harvested, bound sheaves, threshed, winnowed, selected, milled, sifted, made dough, split it, baked, and only after that could he eat a piece of bread. But I get up in the morning and find everything before me. See, how much toil Adam had to expend until he obtained a garment to wear! He sheared, bleached, separated the fibers, dyed, spun, weaved, washed, sewed, and after that he obtained a garment to wear. But I get up in the morning and find all before me. How many professionals work mornings and evenings! But I get up in the morning and find all before me. Similarly, ben Zoma said: What does a bad guest say? What did I eat from the householder, what did I drink from the householder? One piece I ate from him, one cup of wine I drank from him. All the effort he put in he did only for his wife and children! But a good guest says, praised be the householder, may the householder be remembered in a good way! How much wine did he bring before me, how many cuts did he bring before me! How much work did he do for me! All that effort he did only for me! And so it says (*Job.* 36:24): "Remember to magnify his work that people saw!"

86 All three sections are in almost identical form also in the Babli (58a) and the Tosephta (6:2). In both Babli and Tosephta, the good guest appears before the bad one; then for the quote from Job one has to return to the good guest. Hence, the version of the Yerushalmi looks more original.

משנה ג: עַל הַזִּיקִים וְעַל הַזְּוָעוֹת וְעַל הַבְּרָקִים וְעַל הָרְעָמִים וְעַל הָרוּחוֹת הוּא אוֹמֵר בָּרוּךְ שֶׁכּוֹחוֹ מָלֵא הָעוֹלָמִים.[87] עַל הֶהָרִים וְעַל הַגְּבָעוֹת וְעַל הַיַּמִּים וְעַל הַנְּהָרוֹת וְעַל הַמִּדְבָּרוֹת הוּא אוֹמֵר בָּרוּךְ עוֹשֵׂה בְרֵאשִׁית. רִבִּי יְהוּדָה אוֹמֵר הָרוֹאֶה אֶת הַיָּם הַגָּדוֹל אוֹמֵר בָּרוּךְ שֶׁעָשָׂה אֶת הַיָּם הַגָּדוֹל בִּזְמַן שֶׁהוּא רוֹאֵהוּ לִפְרָקִים. עַל הַגְּשָׁמִים וְעַל בְּשׂוֹרוֹת טוֹבוֹת הוּא אוֹמֵר בָּרוּךְ הַטּוֹב וְהַמֵּטִיב. וְעַל שְׁמוּעוֹת הָרָעוֹת הוּא אוֹמֵר בָּרוּךְ דַּיַּן הָאֱמֶת. בָּנָה בַיִת חָדָשׁ וְקָנָה כֵלִים חֲדָשִׁים אוֹמֵר בָּרוּךְ שֶׁהִגִּיעָנוּ לַזְּמַן הַזֶּה. מְבָרֵךְ עַל הָרָעָה מֵעֵין הַטּוֹבָה וְעַל הַטּוֹבָה מֵעֵין הָרָעָה.

Mishnah 3: On *ziqin*[88], earthquakes, lightning, thunder, and hurricanes, one says: Praise to Him Whose power[89] fills the world. On mountains, hills, seas, rivers, and deserts, one says: Praise to the Maker of Creation[90]. Rebbi Yehudah says, he who sees the ocean says: Praise to Him Who made the ocean; if he sees it at intervals[91]. On rains[92] and good tidings one says: Praise to Him Who is good and does good. On bad news, one says: Praise to the True Judge. [93]If one built a new house or bought new garments, he says: Praise to Him Who let us reach this time. One recites the benediction for bad news containing good and for good ones containing bad[94].

87 This is the text of the Mishnah in the Halakhah, fol. 14c. In the separate Mishnah, fol. 13c: שכחו וגבורתו מלא עולם.

88 The Yerushalmi does not define זיקא. In the Babli (58b), Samuel defines it as "star with a tail", which may mean either a comet (*Arukh* s. v. כבב) or a meteorite (Rashi). *Arukh* s. v. זק quotes Rav Hai Gaon as defining זיקא as thunderless lightning that illuminates an entire cloud. The latter determination is probably the correct one since it fits the context of the Mishnah and its author has the highest authority among those who explain difficult words in the Talmudim.

89 In the Rome manuscript and in many (mostly Ashkenazic) manuscripts of the Babli and the Mishnah, one adds וּגְבוּרָתוֹ "and His strength."

90 The same manuscripts that add "His strength" in the first sentence, add

"the work of Creation" here.

91 This is the reading of all manuscripts of Yerushalmi, Babli, and Mishnah, except the Leyden manuscript and the Venice print who have this language only in the Mishnah, but the quote in the Halakhah reads: "Rebbi Yehudah says, he who sees the ocean says: Praise to Him Who made the ocean; if he sees it at intervals, he says: Praise to the Maker of Creation." However, from the discussion in the Talmud it is clear that this is a scribal error.

92 In Israel, where there is only one rainy season.

93 In the Mishnah, this is Mishnah 4. However, in the Halakhah, the discussion belongs to Halakhah 3; Halakhot 4,5,6,7 belong to Mishnayot 5,6,7,8, respectively. The numbering of Mishnayot has been changed to correspond to that of the Halakhot.

94 This sentence is not commented on in the Halakhah; hence, the translation follows the interpretation of the Babli: If his crop was ruined by a flood that deposited a layer of new earth on his field, it is bad news now and requires the benediction for bad news, even though he will gain an advantage when it is time to plant next year's crop.

הלכה ג: תַּנֵּי בַּר קַפָּרָא מַתְרִיעִין עַל הַזְּוָעוֹת.

Halakhah 3: Bar Kappara stated: One blows the *shofar* because of an earthquake[95].

95 Blowing the *shofar* on days other than Rosh Hashanah was only done on public fast days. This means that Bar Qappara declares an earthquake a catastrophy which requires repentance; hence, he disagrees with the Mishnah and requires the benediction "the True Judge" for an earthquake.

שְׁמוּאֵל אֲמַר אִין עֲבַר הָהֵן זִיקָא בְּכְסִיל מַחֲרִיב הָעוֹלָם. מֵתִיבוּן לִשְׁמוּאֵל וַאֲנָן חֲמִיָן לֵיהּ עֲבַר. אֲמַר לְהוֹן לֵית אֶפְשַׁר אוֹ לְעֵיל מִינָּהּ אוֹ לְרַע מִינָּהּ. שְׁמוּאֵל אֲמַר חַכִּים אֲנָא בִשְׁקָקֵי שְׁמַיָּא כִּשְׁקָקֵי נְהַרְדְּעָא קַרְתִּי. בַּר מִן הָהֵן זִיקָא לֵית אֲנָא יְדַע מַה הוּא. וְכִי שְׁמוּאֵל עָלָה לַשָּׁמַיִם. אֶלָּא עַל שֵׁם מִי יְסַפֵּר שָׁמַיִם בְּחָכְמָה.

Samuel said: If that *ziqa* would pass by *Kesil*[96], it would destroy the world. They objected to Samuel: Do we not see that it passes by it? He said to them: It is impossible; either above or below it. Samuel said: I know the places[97] of heaven like the places of my city Nahardea; except for that *ziqa*, I do not know what that is. Did Samuel ascend to heaven? No, following (*Job*. 38:37): "Who may discourse about heaven in wisdom[98]?"

96 Ibn Janaḥ defines *kesil* as the star that in Arabic is called *suhail*, "Canopus". Ibn Ezra identifies the word as meaning "Pleiades". Since the Pleiades are seen only during summertime in the Northern Hemisphere, this might justify the characterization of *kesil* as "hot" in the Babli (58b).

The statement of Samuel and his qualifications are also quoted in the Babli (58b). The text of the Yerushalmi is quoted in slightly changed form in *Arukh*, s. v. ככב.

97 Derivative of שוק "market place," [maybe a pun on שחקים "skies" (E. G.)].

98 I. e., be an astronomer.

אֱלִיָּהוּ זָכוּר לַטּוֹב שָׁאַל לְרִבִּי נְהוֹרַיי מִפְּנֵי מַה בָּאִין זְוָעוֹת לָעוֹלָם. אָמַר לֵיהּ בְּעָוֹן תְּרוּמָה וּמַעְשְׂרוֹת. כָּתוּב אֶחָד אוֹמֵר תָּמִיד עֵינֵי יי אֱלֹהֶיךָ בָּהּ. וְכָתוּב אֶחָד אוֹמֵר הַמַּבִּיט לָאָרֶץ וַתִּרְעָד יִגַּע בֶּהָרִים וְיֶעֱשָׁנוּ. הָא כֵיצַד יִתְקַיְּימוּ שְׁנֵי כְתוּבִין הַלָּלוּ. בְּשָׁעָה שֶׁיִּשְׂרָאֵל עוֹשִׂין רְצוֹנוֹ שֶׁל מָקוֹם וּמוֹצִיאִין מַעְשְׂרוֹתֵיהֶן כְּתִיקְנָן תָּמִיד עֵינֵי יי אֱלֹהֶיךָ בָּהּ מֵרֵאשִׁית הַשָּׁנָה וְעַד אַחֲרִית שָׁנָה וְאֵינָן נִזּוֹקִין כְּלוּם. בְּשָׁעָה שֶׁאֵין יִשְׂרָאֵל עוֹשִׂין רְצוֹנוֹ שֶׁל מָקוֹם וְאֵינָן מוֹצִיאִין מַעְשְׂרוֹתֵיהֶן כְּתִיקְנָן הַמַּבִּיט לָאָרֶץ וַתִּרְעָד. אָמַר לֵיהּ בְּנִי חַיֶּיךָ כַּךְ הִיא סְבָרָא דְּמִילְתָא. אֲבָל כֵּן עִיקָּרוֹ שֶׁל דָּבָר אֶלָּא בְשָׁעָה שֶׁהַקָּדוֹשׁ בָּרוּךְ הוּא מַבִּיט בְּבָתֵּי תֵיָטְרִיּוֹת וּבְבָתֵּי קִרְקְסָאוֹת יוֹשְׁבוֹת בֶּטַח וְשַׁאֲנָן וְשַׁלְוָה וּבֵית מִקְדָּשׁוֹ חָרֵב הוּא אַפֵּילוֹן לְעוֹלָמוֹ לְהַחֲרִיבוֹ. הָהוּא דִכְתִיב שָׁאוֹג יִשְׁאַג עַל נָוֵהוּ. בִּשְׁבִיל נָוֵהוּ. אָמַר רִבִּי אָחָא בְּעָוֹן מִשְׁכַּב זָכוּר. אָמַר הַקָּדוֹשׁ בָּרוּךְ הוּא אַתָּה זִיעֲזַעְתָּ אֵיבָרָךְ עַל דָּבָר שֶׁאֵינוֹ שֶׁלָּךְ. חַיֶּיךָ שֶׁאֲנִי מְזַעְזֵעַ עוֹלָמִי עַל אוֹתוֹ הָאִישׁ. וְרַבָּנָן אָמְרֵי בִּשְׁבִיל הַמַּחְלוֹקֶת. וְנַסְתֶּם גֵּיא הָרַי כִּי יַגִּיעַ גֵּיא הָרִים אֶל אָצַל. אָמַר רִבִּי שְׁמוּאֵל אֵין

רַעַשׁ אֶלָּא הֶפְסֵק מַלְכוּת. כְּמַה דְּאַתְּ אֲמַר וַתִּרְעַשׁ הָאָרֶץ וַתָּחֹל. מִפְּנֵי מַה. כִּי קָמָה עַל בָּבֶל מַחְשְׁבוֹת יי.

Elijah, may he be well remembered[99], asked Rebbi Nehorai[100]: Why do earthquakes occur in the world? He said to him, because of sin concerning heave and tithes. One verse says (*Deut*. 11:12): The eyes of the Eternal, your God, are permanently on it. Another verse says (*Ps*. 104:32): He who gazes on the Earth and it trembles, He touches mountains and they smoke. How can these two verses coexist? If Israel fulfill the will of the Omnipresent and separate their tithes following the rules, "the eyes of the Eternal, your God, are permanently on it from the start to the end of the year" and they will not be hurt by anything. If Israel do not fulfill the will of the Omnipresent and do not separate their tithes following the rules, "He gazes on the Earth and it trembles." He said to him, my son, that is the reasonable explanation. But the main thing is that if the Holy One, praise to Him, sees theatres and circuses existing in safety and quiet, but His temple is destroyed, He is menacing[101] His world to destroy it; that is what is written (*Jer*. 25:30): "He will roar on His Place," about His place. Rebbi Aḥa[102] said, because of homosexual activity. The Holy One, praise to Him, said: You made your member tremble for something that is not for you; by your life, I shall make My world tremble because of that man. But the rabbis said, because of quarrels (Zach. 14:5): "You will flee by the valley of the mountains, for the valley of the mountains will reach Aẓel[103]." Rebbi Samuel said, an earthquake presages a change of government, as one says (*Jer*. 51:29): "The earth quaked and trembled," why? "for the intentions of the Eternal overtake Babylon."

99 This is the regular honorific given to Elijah when he is mentioned in his dealings with men. One cannot say "his remembrance for a blessing" as is done for people who died, since he did not die.

100 A student of Rebbis Joshua and Tarphon, of the fourth generation of Tannaïm; his statements are mostly aggadic.

101 Greek ἀπειλῶν.

102 This shows that in homilies, precedents (even from such an authority as the prophet Elijah) do not count.

103 The relevant part of the verse is the one not quoted: "You shall flee as you fled because of the earthquake in the days of Uzziah, king of Judah." Uzziah quarreled with the priests and wanted to usurp their functions in the Temple. The earthquake was on that day, when Isaiah saw the Seraphim flying in the Temple (*Seder Olam* Chap. 20).

אֱלִיָּהוּ זָכוּר לַטּוֹב שָׁאַל לְרִבִּי נְהוֹרַיי מִפְּנֵי מַה בָּרָא הַקָּדוֹשׁ בָּרוּךְ הוּא שְׁקָצִים וּרְמָשִׂים בְּעוֹלָמוֹ. אָמַר לוֹ לְצוֹרֶךְ נִבְרְאוּ בְּשָׁעָה שֶׁהַבְּרִיּוֹת חוֹטְאִין הוּא מַבִּיט בָּהֶן וְאוֹמֵר מַה אֵלוּ שֶׁאֵין בָּהֶן צוֹרֶךְ הֲרֵי אֲנִי מְקַייְמָן אֵלוּ שֶׁיֵּשׁ בָּהֶן צוֹרֶךְ לֹא כָּל שֶׁכֵּן. אָמַר לֵיהּ עוֹד יֵשׁ בָּהֶן צוֹרֶךְ זְבוּב לְצִרְעָה. פִּשְׁפֵּשׁ לָעֲלוּקָה. שַׁבְּלוּל לְחַזִּיוֹן. סְמָמִית לְעַקְרָב.

Elijah, may he be well remembered, asked Rebbi Nehorai: Why did the Holy One, praise to Him, create abominable and crawling animals in His world? He said to him, they fill a need because, when men sin, He gazes at those and says, if I am keeping those who have no utility, certainly I shall keep these who might have utility. He said to him, still they have utility[104]: a fly for wasps[105], bedbugs for a leech, snail for skin rash[106], *semamit*[107] for the scorpion.

104 A similar statement is found in Babli *Šabbat* 77b, by Rav Yehudah in the name of Rav.

105 Rashi in Babli *Šabbat* 77b explains that as antidote for the poison of the sting of a wasp, one grinds up some flies and puts them as ointment on the sting. He explains the same for the use of *semamit* for the sting of a scorpion, but the Babli (*loc. cit.*) notes

that the scorpion is afraid of the *semamit*. Hence, it seems more likely that flies carry diseases into wasp's nests and therefore curb their numbers, and *semamiot* eat scorpions.

106 The last two must certainly be explained as medical uses.

107 *Arukh* gives two Italian explanations of this word, the first *ragnatello* "spider" is also given by Rashi (*araignée*) in Babli *Šabbat*, the second *lucertola* "lizard" is more probable, in particular the gecko, Arabic סָאם אַבְּרַץ, which is known to eat scorpions. Arabic סַאמָּה "poisonous animal", but cf. Accadic *summatu* "pidgeon", *simmatu* "poisoning".

עַל הַבְּרָקִים. רִבִּי יִרְמְיָה וְרִבִּי זְעִירָא בְּשֵׁם רַב חַסְדַּאי דַּיּוֹ פַּעַם אַחַת בְּכָל־יוֹם. אָמַר רִבִּי יוֹסֵי מַה אֲנָן קַיָּימִין אִם בְּטוֹרְדִין דַּיּוֹ פַּעַם אַחַת בַּיּוֹם. אִם בְּמַפְסִיקִין מְבָרֵךְ עַל כָּל אַחַת וְאַחַת. חֵיילֵיהּ דְּרִבִּי יוֹסֵי מִן הָדָא. הָיָה יוֹשֵׁב בַּחֲנוּתוֹ שֶׁל בַּשָּׂם כָּל־הַיּוֹם אֵינוֹ מְבָרֵךְ אֶלָּא אַחַת. אֲבָל אִם הָיָה נִכְנָס וְיוֹצֵא נִכְנָס וְיוֹצֵא מְבָרֵךְ עַל כָּל פַּעַם וּפַעַם. אָתָא אָמַר רִבִּי אָחָא וְרִבִּי חֲנִינָא בְּשֵׁם רִבִּי יוֹסֵי אִם בְּטוֹרְדִין דַּיּוֹ פַּעַם אַחַת בַּיּוֹם. אִם בְּמַפְסִיקִין מְבָרֵךְ עַל כָּל אַחַת וְאַחַת.

"On lightning." Rebbi Jeremiah, Rebbi Zeïra in the name of Rav Ḥasdai[108]: It is enough once a day. Rebbi Yose[109] said, what are we talking about? If it is permanent[110], once a day is enough. If it is intermittent, one recites the benediction for each occurrence. The force of Rebbi Yose from the following[111]: If he was sitting in the perfumer's store all day long, he would recite the benediction only once. But if he enters and leaves, enters and leaves, he recites a benediction every time. It came[112], it was said by Rebbi Aḥa (and)[113] Rebbi Ḥanina in the name of Rebbi Yose[114]: If it is permanent, once a day is enough. If it is intermittent, one recites the benediction for each occurrence.

108 He is Rav Ḥisda.

109 From the following, it is clear that this is Rebbi Yose II, colleague of R. Jonah.

110 From Biblical דלף טורד "unceasing downpour".

111 Tosephta *Berakhot* 5:32, Babli 53a.

112 Somebody came with a collection of older formulations and showed that the discussion was already settled in earlier generations.

113 This is a scribal error; R. Aḥa cannot be concurrent with his teacher's father.

114 He is either the Amora R. Yasa (Assi) or the Tanna R. Yose.

הָיָה יוֹשֵׁב בְּבֵית הַכִּסֵּא אוֹ בְּבֵית סְפֵיקַרְיָא אִם יָכוֹל לָצֵאת וּלְבָרֵךְ בְּתוֹךְ כְּדֵי דִיבּוּר יֵצֵא וְאִם לָאו לֹא יֵצֵא. רִבִּי יִרְמְיָה בְּעִי הָיָה יוֹשֵׁב בְּתוֹךְ בֵּיתוֹ עָרוֹם מַהוּ שֶׁיֵּעָשֶׂה בֵּיתוֹ כְּמוֹ מַלְבּוּשׁ וְיוֹצִיא רֹאשׁוֹ חוּץ לַחֲלוֹן וִיבָרֵךְ. הָיָה יוֹשֵׁב בְּמִגְדָּל עָרוֹם מַהוּ שֶׁיֵּעָשֶׂה לוֹ כְּמוֹ מַלְבּוּשׁ וְיוֹצִיא רֹאשׁוֹ חוּץ לַחֲלוֹן וִיבָרֵךְ.

If one was sitting in the bathroom or the room of filth[115], if he can exit and recite the benediction in time for one sentence[116], he should exit, but if not, he should not exit[117]. Rebbi Jeremiah asked: If he was sitting naked in his house, should he make the house a garment[118], lean his head out of the window and recite the benediction? If he was sitting naked in a "tower"[119], should he make it a garment, lean his head out of the window and recite the benediction?

115 And he sees lightning while there.

It seems that the second word is simply a Latinate form of the first, the bathroom or it may mean "garbage room". In the Rome manuscript and the text of R. S. Cirillo, the reading is ספיקלריא, with change of liquids *r* - *l*. The Latin would be *faecaria*, "dregs, filthy matter"; Kohut compares Greek σφέκλη "dregs".

116 Defined earlier as time to say: "Peace on you, my teacher."

117 This implies that the benediction over lightning must be recited within this time span after the lightning was observed.

118 Since one may not mention the Divine Name with one's genitals uncovered.

119 The "tower" is no tower, but one kind of sedan chair. Mishnah and Talmudim always speak of three kinds of sedan chairs, שידה תיבה ומגדל, the

exact definitions of these are unknown. But in any case, the "tower" is a wooden chest-like implement. The new question implies that the first question was answered in the negative (it is noted so in Babli *Sukkah* 10b), that a house, or any "tent", can never be a garment. The substitute question now is whether a wooden movable cover can take the place of a textile cover. A similar question is asked in Babli *Sukkah* 10b for somebody lying naked in bed and covered by a mosquito net; the answer is that it is possible only if the bed assembly does not qualify as a "tent." The question here goes unanswered because, characteristic for R. Jeremiah, it is asked in a totally unrealistic form. [In contrast to the Babli, the Yerushalmi never requires that heart and genitals should be covered by separate garments.]

עַל הָרוּחוֹת מַהוּא אוֹמֵר. בָּרוּךְ שֶׁכֹּחוֹ מָלֵא עוֹלָם. מַתְנִיתָא כְּשֶׁבָּאִין בְּסַעַף. אֲבָל שֶׁבָּאִים בְּנַחַת אוֹמֵר בָּרוּךְ שֶׁעָשָׂה בְרֵאשִׁית.

"On winds what does he say? Praise to Him, Whose power and might fill the world." The Mishnah if they come destructively. But if they come quietly, one says: Praise to the Maker of Creation.

אָמַר רִבִּי יְהוֹשֻׁעַ בֶּן חֲנַנְיָה בְּשָׁעָה שֶׁהָרוּחַ יוֹצֵא לָעוֹלָם הַקָּדוֹשׁ בָּרוּךְ הוּא מְשַׁבְּרוֹ בֶּהָרִים וּמְכַשְּׁלוֹ בִּגְבָעוֹת וְאוֹמֵר תֵּן דַּעְתָּךְ שֶׁלֹּא תַזִּיק בְּרִיּוֹתָי. מַה טַעַם כִּי רוּחַ מִלְּפָנַי יַעֲטוֹף. מְשַׁלְהֵי לֵיהּ. כְּמַה דְּאַתְּ אֲמַר בְּהִתְעַטֵּף עָלַי רוּחִי. כָּל־כַּךְ לָמָּה. רִבִּי חוּנָא בְּשֵׁם רִבִּי אָחָא וּנְשָׁמוֹת אֲנִי עָשִׂיתִי. בִּשְׁבִיל נְשָׁמוֹת שֶׁעָשִׂיתִי.

Rebbi Joshua ben Ḥananiah said: When the wind goes out into the world, the Holy One, praise to Him, breaks it on mountains, lets it stumble on hills, and tells it: Be careful not to hurt my creatures. What is the reason? (*Is.* 57:16) "The wind becomes faint before Me." He makes it tired, as one says (*Jonah* 2:8): "When I am fainting." All that why? Rebbi Ḥuna in the name of Rebbi Aḥa (*Is.* 57:16): "And I made souls;" because of the souls that I made.

אָמַר רִבִּי חוּנָא בִּשְׁלֹשָׁה מְקוֹמוֹת יָצָא הָרוּחַ שֶׁלֹּא בְמִשְׁקָל וּבִיקֵּשׁ לְהַחֲרִיב אֶת הָעוֹלָם כּוּלּוֹ. אַחַת בִּימֵי יוֹנָה. וְאַחַת בִּימֵי אֱלִיָּהוּ. וְאַחַת בִּימֵי אִיּוֹב. בִּימֵי יוֹנָה וַיי הֵטִיל רוּחַ גְּדוֹלָה. בִּימֵי אִיּוֹב וְהִנֵּה רוּחַ גְּדוֹלָה בָּאָה מֵעֵבֶר הַמִּדְבָּר. בִּימֵי אֱלִיָּהוּ מְנַיִן וְהִנֵּה יי עוֹבֵר וְרוּחַ גְּדוֹלָה וְחָזָק מְפָרֵק הָרִים. אָמַר רִבִּי יוּדָן בַּר שָׁלוֹם נֵימַר אוֹתוֹ שֶׁל אִיּוֹב בִּשְׁבִילוֹ הָיָה. וְשֶׁל יוֹנָה בִּשְׁבִילוֹ הָיָה. אֵין לָךְ אֶלָּא שֶׁל אֱלִיָּהוּ שֶׁהָיָה קוֹסְמִיקוֹן. וְהִנֵּה יי עוֹבֵר וכו'. וְאַחַר כַּךְ רַעַשׁ וְאַחַר הָרַעַשׁ אֵשׁ לֹא בָאֵשׁ יי.

Rebbi Ḥuna said, in three places did the wind come out without measure and desired to destroy the entire world; once in the time of Jonah, once in the time of Elijah, and once in the time of Job. In the time of Jonah (*Jonah* 1:4): "The Eternal sent a strong wind." In the time of Job (*Job* 1:19): "A great wind came across the desert." In the time of Elijah, from where? (*1K*. 19: 19:11) "Lo, the Eternal passes, and a great, strong wind, shattering mountains." Rebbi Yudan ben Shalom[120] said, let us say that the one of Job was for him only[121], that of Jonah was for him only. You have only that of Elijah which was worldwide[122] "Lo, the Eternal passes, etc. After that an earthquake[123] and after the earthquake fire , but the Eternal was not in the fire."

120 A late Galilean Amora, also called Rebbi Yehudah Halevi, infrequently appearing in halakhic discussions; he is a major source of the early *Tanḥuma* Midrash.

121 It took place just around the house it destroyed.

122 Greek κοσμικόν.

123 The earthquake by its nature is felt at great distances.

רִבִּי יְהוּדָה אוֹמֵר הָרוֹאֶה אֶת הַיָּם הַגָּדוֹל אוֹמֵר בָּרוּךְ שֶׁעָשָׂה אֶת הַיָּם הַגָּדוֹל בִּזְמַן שֶׁהוּא רוֹאֵהוּ לִפְרָקִים. וְכַמָּה הוּא פֶּרֶק אֶחָד לִשְׁלֹשִׁים יוֹם. שִׁמְעוֹן קָמְטֵרָיָא שְׁאַל לְרִבִּי חִייָא בַּר בָּא בְּגִין דַּאֲנָא חַמָּר וּסְלִיק לִירוּשָׁלַיִם בְּכָל שָׁעָה מַהוּ שֶׁנִּקְרַע. אָמַר לֵיהּ אִם בְּתוֹךְ שְׁלֹשִׁים יוֹם אִי אַתָּה צָרִיךְ לִקְרוֹעַ לְאַחַר שְׁלֹשִׁים יוֹם צָרִיךְ אַתָּה לִקְרוֹעַ.

"Rebbi Yehudah says, he who sees the ocean says: Praise to Him Who made the ocean, if he sees it at intervals." What is an interval? Once in thirty days[124]. Simeon the hard-working man[125] asked Rebbi Ḥiyya bar Abba: Since I am a donkey driver and go up to Jerusalem all the time[126], how do I have to tear[127]? He said to him: If it is within thirty days, you do not have to tear, after thirty days you have to tear.

124 In the Babli (59b), this is a statement of the Palestinian Rebbi Isaac; it seems that he brought the Galilean tradition to Babylonia.

125 Greek καματηρός "laborious, hardworking" (E. G.). This person is mentioned only here and in the following *Aggadah* (which appears here because it mentions Simeon Qamateria.) As a learned man, he is addressed in Hebrew, not in Aramaic.

126 This is the reading of the Rome manuscript. The Venice print has בכל שנה "every year", which does not fit the context.

127 Just as one has to tear one's clothes upon hearing of the death of a close relative, so one has to tear one's clothes when seeing Jerusalem in a state of destruction.

רִבִּי חוּנָא וְשִׁמְעוֹן קָמָטֵרִיָּא בְשֵׁם רִבִּי שְׁמוּאֵל בַּר נַחְמָן וִיהוֹנָתָן בֶּן גֵּרְשֹׁם בֶּן מְנַשֶּׁה נוּן תְּלוּיָה. אִם זָכָה בֶּן מֹשֶׁה. וְאִם לָאו בֶּן מְנַשֶּׁה. חֲבֵרַיָּא בְּעוֹן קוֹמֵי רִבִּי שְׁמוּאֵל בַּר נַחְמָן כּוֹמֶר הָיָה לַעֲבוֹדָה זָרָה וְהֶאֱרִיךְ יָמִים. אֲמַר לוֹן עַל יַד שֶׁהָיָה עֵינוֹ צָרָה בַּעֲבוֹדָה זָרָה שֶׁלּוֹ. כֵּיצַד הָיְתָה עֵינוֹ צָרָה בַּעֲבוֹדָה זָרָה שֶׁלּוֹ. הֲוָה בַּר נַשׁ אָתֵי לְמִקְרְבָה תוֹר אוֹ אִימֵּר אוֹ גְדִי לַעֲבוֹדָה זָרָה וַאֲמַר לֵיהּ פַּייְסֵיהּ עָלַי. וְהוּא אֲמַר לֵיהּ מַה זוּ מוֹעִילָה לָךְ לֹא רוֹאָה וְלֹא שׁוֹמַעַת לֹא אוֹכֶלֶת וְלֹא שׁוֹתָה לֹא מֵטִיבָה וְלֹא מְרֵיעָה וְלֹא מְדַבֶּרֶת. אֲמַר לֵיהּ חַיֶּיךָ וּמָה נַעֲבִיד. וַאֲמַר לֵיהּ אֲזִיל עֲבִיד וְאַיְיתִי לִי חַד פִּינָךְ דְּסוֹלֶת וְאַתְקִין עֲלוֹי עֶשֶׂר בֵּיעִין וְאַתְקִין קוֹמוֹי וְהוּא אֲכַל מִכָּל־מַה דְּאָתֵי וַאֲנָא מְפַייֵס לָהּ עָלָךְ. מִכֵּיוָן דַּאֲזִיל לֵיהּ הָיָה אֲכִיל לוֹן. זִימְנָא חָדָא אֲתָא חַד בַּר נַשׁ בַּר פָּחִין אֲמַר לֵיהּ כֵּן. אֲמַר לֵיהּ אִם אֵין מוֹעִילָה כְּלוּם אַתְּ מַה אַתְּ עֲבִיד הָכָא. אֲמַר לֵיהּ בְּגִין חַיָּי. כֵּיוָן שֶׁעָמַד דָּוִד הַמֶּלֶךְ שָׁלַח וְהֵבִיאוֹ. אָמַר לֵיהּ אַתְּ בֶּן בְּנוֹ שֶׁל אוֹתוֹ צַדִּיק וְאַתְּ

עוֹבֵד עֲבוֹדָה זָרָה. אָמַר לֵיהּ כַּךְ אֲנִי מְקוּבָּל מִבֵּית אֲבִי אַבָּא מְכוֹר עַצְמְךָ לַעֲבוֹדָה זָרָה וְאַל תִּצְטָרֵךְ לַבְּרִיּוֹת. אָמַר לֵיהּ חַס וְשָׁלוֹם לֹא אָמַר כֵּן אֶלָּא מְכוֹר עַצְמְךָ לַעֲבוֹדָה שֶׁהִיא זָרָה לָךְ וְאַל תִּצְטָרֵךְ לַבְּרִיּוֹת. כֵּיוָן שֶׁרָאָה דָּוִד כָּךְ שֶׁהָיָה אוֹהֵב מָמוֹן מַה עָשָׂה הֶעֱמִידוֹ קוֹמוֹס עַל תֵּיסַבְרִיּוֹת שֶׁלּוֹ. הַהוּא דִכְתִיב וּשְׁבוּאֵל בֶּן גֵּרְשֹׁם בֶּן מֹשֶׁה נָגִיד עַל הָאוֹצָרוֹת. שְׁבוּאֵל שֶׁשָּׁב אֶל אֵל בְּכָל־לִבּוֹ וּבְכָל־כֹּחוֹ. נָגִיד עַל הָאוֹצָרוֹת שֶׁמִּינֵּהוּ עַל תֵּיסַבְרִיּוֹת שֶׁלּוֹ. מְתִיבִין לְרִבִּי שְׁמוּאֵל בַּר נַחְמָן וְהָא כְתִיב עַד יוֹם גְּלוֹת הָאָרֶץ. אֲמַר לוֹן כֵּיוָן שֶׁמֵּת דָּוִד עָמַד שְׁלֹמֹה וְחִילֵּף סֶנְקְלֵיטִין שֶׁלּוֹ. חָזַר לְקִילְקוּלוֹ הָרִאשׁוֹן. הָהוּא דִכְתִיב וְנָבִיא אֶחָד זָקֵן יוֹשֵׁב בְּבֵית אֵל וגו׳. אָמְרִין הוּא הֲוָה.

Rebbi Ḥuna and Simeon Qamateria in the name of Rebbi Samuel ben Naḥman (*Jud.* 18:30): "Jonathan ben Gershom ben Manasseh," a hanging נ[128]. If he merits it, ben Mosheh. If he does not merit it, ben Manasseh. The colleagues asked before Rebbi Samuel bar Naḥman: He was a priest of idol worship and lived so long[129]? He said to them, because *he* [Jonathan] was grudging to his idol. How was he grudging to his idol? If a man came to sacrifice an ox, a sheep, or a goat to the idol and told him: Make it favorably inclined towards me, *he* would say: What use does it have for you? It neither sees, nor hears, nor eats, nor drinks, nor does good or evil, and does not talk. He said to him, by your life, what should we do? *He* said to him, go, make, and bring me a wooden vessel[130] full of fine flour and put on it ten eggs, then *I* shall prepare it before that one and *it* will eat from all that comes and *I* shall make *it* favorably inclined towards you! After he left, *he* would eat it. One day, a son of pashas came and *he* said that to him. He said to *him*, if it is of no use, what are you doing here? *He* said to him, because of my livelihood. When David became king, he sent and brought *him*. He said to *him*, you are the grandson of that righteous man and you worship idols? *He* said to him: *I* have a tradition from my grandfather's house: Sell yourself to idol worship[131] rather than need other people[132]. He said to *him*: Heaven forbid! He did not say so, but sell yourself to work that is strange to you rather than to need other people. When David saw that he loved money, he made him count[133] of his treasuries. That is what is written (*1Chr.* 26:24): "Shabuel ben Gershom ben Moshe, overseer of the treasuries." "Shabuel" because he returned to God with all his heart and all his might. "Overseer of the treasuries," that he made him count of the treasuries. They objected to Rebbi Samuel bar Naḥman: (*Jud.* 18:30): "Until the day the land went into exile." He said to them, when David died, Shelomo rose and exchanged all his counselors[134]. *He* returned to his former bad ways. That is what is written: (*1K*. 13:11) "An old prophet[135] was dwelling at Beth El;" they say that this was *he*.

128 In Bible manuscripts and prints, the name is יהונתן בן גרשם בן מ^נשה, to hide the fact that a grandson of Moses was priest of the idol at Dan. Manasseh is the bad king of Judah, son of king Hezekiah. The parallels to this paragraph are Yerushalmi *Sanhedrin* 11:5, Babli *Bava Batra* 110a.

129 The verse reads: "Jonathan ben Gershom ben Mo(n)sheh, he and his sons, were priests for the tribe of Dan, until the day the land was exiled. They put up for themselves the idol of Micah, that the latter had made, all the days that the House of God was at Shiloh." There are several interpretations of "the day the land was exiled." Rashi takes it to mean the exile of Dan by the Assyrians, Babylonian tradition (*Seder Olam* Chapter 24) takes it as the time of captivity of king Manasse in Babylon; most later Medieval commentators (Ibn Ezra, Gersonides, R. Isaiah of Trani) take it to refer to the destruction of Shiloh (since Jeroboam put up a new Golden Calf at Dan, the original idol can no longer have survived.) However, as Y. Yadin has pointed out, already in the Song of Deborah there is a reference to the tribe of Dan who "went to dwell on ships." Rashi's interpretation is that of the Talmudim (the parallel in the Babli is *Bava Bathra* 110a), since both have Jonathan (not just one of his descendants) alive and active at the time of David, about 300 years after the conquest of Laish by the tribe of

Dan.

130 Greek πίναξ, "wooden platter".

131 In Hebrew, "strange work".

132 To take money from charity.

133 Latin *comes*, a high official in post-Diocletian Rome. "Treasury" from Greek θησαυρός.

134 Greek singular σύγκλητος (βουλή) "summoned (council, senate)", also συγκλητικός "of senatorial rank", with Aramaic plural ending. *Seder Olam*, quoted earlier, seems to assume that he stayed in Jerusalem after that.

135 Since prophets are usually experienced people, this one must have been very old.

הָרוֹאֶה אֶת הַחַמָּה בִּתְקוּפָתָהּ וְאֶת הַלְּבָנָה בִּתְקוּפָתָהּ וְאֶת הָרָקִיעַ בְּטִיהֲרוֹ אוֹמֵר בָּרוּךְ עוֹשֵׂה בְּרֵאשִׁית. אָמַר רִבִּי חוּנָה הָדָא דְתֵימַר בִּימוֹת הַגְּשָׁמִים בִּלְבַד לְאַחַר שְׁלֹשָׁה יָמִים. וְהָהוּא דִכְתִיב וְעַתָּה לֹא רָאוּ אוֹר וגו'.

He who sees the sun at its turning point[136], the moon at its turning point, and the sky in its purity, says: Praise to the Maker of Creation. Rebbi Ḥuna says, that means in the rainy season and only after three days. That is what is written (*Job* 37:21): "Now they do not see light, etc.[137]"

136 According to the Babli (59b), this is the moment when the sun would stand at the point where it was created if the Julianic calendar could be extrapolated backwards. It is not permissible to read the Yerushalmi by the interpretations of the Babli. Usually, a "turning point" of the sun is either a solstice or an equinox; it also could just mean "the sun turning". The latter meaning is implied by the Tosephta (6:6): "He who sees sun, moon, fixed stars, planets, says: Praise to the Maker of Creation. Rebbi Yehudah says, he who recites a benediction over the sun is on the way of heretics. Similarly, Rebbi Yehudah used to say, he who sees the ocean frequently has to recite a benediction if it has changed." Here it is clear that the entire statement refers to weather-related phenomena; the following statement of R. Ḥuna therefore should not be taken to refer to the clear sky only (as it is taken in the Babli) but for all celestial phenomena when they are observed in an unpolluted sky. The coastline of the ocean may have changed during a storm; after the clearing of the sky R. Jehudah requires a new benediction.

137 The end of the verse: "He is

lucent in the skies, a wind passed by and purified them," shows that the sky is really radiant only if the sun comes out after a long rain.

A parallel Yerushalmi source, Midrash *Wayiqra rabba* 23(8) reads: "'Now they do not see light,' we have formulated: He who sees the sun at its turning point, the moon in its spherical shape, the stars in their paths, the planets in their order, says: Praise to the Maker of Creation. Rebbi Ḥuna says, that means in the rainy season and only after three days." Rabbenu Ḥananel, in his commentary to the Babli, takes sun, moon, stars, and planets all together and requires a benediction if any of them has not been seen for a prolonged time.

הָרוֹאֶה אֶת הַלְּבָנָה בְּחִידּוּשָׁהּ אוֹמֵר בָּרוּךְ מְחַדֵּשׁ חֳדָשִׁים. עַד אֵיכָן. רִבִּי יַעֲקֹב בַּר אָחָא בְּשֵׁם רִבִּי יוֹסֵי עַד שֶׁתֵּרָאֶה כַּחֲצִי הַמַּטֶּה. רִבִּי אָחָא וְרִבִּי חִינְנָא בְּשֵׁם רִבִּי יוֹסֵי עַד שֶׁתִּתְמַלֵּא פְּגִימָתָהּ. רַבָּנָן דְּקֵיסָרִין אָמְרִין עַד אַרְבָּעָה עָשָׂר יוֹם. אָמַר רִבִּי יוֹסֵי בֵּי רִבִּי בּוּן וְיֵאוּת. כְּלוּם מִתְמַלְּאֵת פְּגִימָתָהּ אֶלָּא עַד אַרְבָּעָה עָשָׂר יוֹם. הָא כָּל־אַרְבָּעָה עָשָׂר יוֹם צָרִיךְ לְבָרֵךְ.

He who sees the moon in its renewal says: Praise to Him Who renews months[138]. Until when? Rebbi Jacob bar Aḥa in the name of Rebbi Yose[139]: Until it is seen like half a stick. Rebbi Aḥa and Rebbi Ḥinena in the name of Rebbi Yose: Until its missing part is filled. The rabbis of Caesarea say, until the fourteenth day. Rebbi Yose bar Abun said, that is correct; the missing part is never filled before the fourteenth day. Hence, all fourteen days one needs to recite the benediction.

138 The Babli (*Sanhedrin* 42a) notes that in Galilee one recites simply: "Praised are You, Eternal, our God, King of the Universe, Who renews months," and that this is the formula used by women in Babylonia, but men in Babylonia use the formula "Praised are You, Eternal, our God, King of the Universe, Who renews months" only as conclusion of a longer prayer.

139 He is Rebbi Assi; in the Babli (*loc. cit.*) he is reported to have said in the name of R. Yoḥanan that one recites the benediction "until its (the moon's) missing part is filled" and Rebbi Jacob bar Idi interprets this to

mean that the appearance of the moon is no longer concave, i. e. that its visible circumference looks like a semicircle with its diameter (ascribed here to R. Jacob bar Aḥa). The people of Nehardea say, until after the 15th of the month, an interpretation which is more lenient than any opinion expressed here.

בְּתְפִילָּה רִבִּי יוֹסֵי בַּר נְהוֹרַיָּא אָמַר מְקַדֵּשׁ יִשְׂרָאֵל מְחַדֵּשׁ חֳדָשִׁים. רִבִּי חִיָּיא בַּר אַשִׁי אָמַר מְקַדֵּשׁ יִשְׂרָאֵל וְרָאשֵׁי חֳדָשִׁים. שְׁמוּאֵל אָמַר צָרִיךְ לוֹמַר וְהַשִּׂיאֵנוּ. רַב אָמַר צָרִיךְ לְהַזְכִּיר בָּהּ זְמָן. תַּנֵּי רִבִּי הוֹשַׁעְיָא וְהָיוּ לְאוֹתוֹת וּמוֹעֲדִים וּלְיָמִים וְשָׁנִים.

In prayer[140], Rebbi Yose bar Nahorai said: "He Who sanctifies Israel, renews months." Rav Ḥiyya bar Ashi said: "He Who sanctifies Israel and the New Moon.[141]" Samuel said, one must say "bestow on us[142]." Rav said, one must mention "time.[143]" Rebbi Hoshaya stated: (*Gen.* 1:14) "They should be for signs and appointed times, days and years.[144] "

140 The *Musaph* prayer of the day of the New Moon.

141 This is the Babylonian version, given by a Babylonian.

142 The formula used on holidays to introduce the final paragraph of the middle benediction of the *Amidah*: "Bestow on us, o Eternal, our God, the blessing of Your holiday." There is no mention of this and the following statement of Rav in any Babylonian source. Even though this might indicate concurrence of the Babli, the requirements of Samuel and Rav are not followed. [The Yerushalmi prayer texts from the Cairo Genizah show the *Musaph* Amidah of the days of the New Moon following the text of the holiday Amidah.]

143 Recite on the day of New Moon the benediction: "Praise to You, Eternal, our God, King of the Universe, Who made us live, sustained us, and let us reach this time."

144 The explanation is given in *Bereshit rabba* 6(3): "They shall be for signs", these are the Sabbaths, "and appointed times," these are the holidays of pilgrimage, "days," these are the days of the New Moon, "and years," that is the sanctification of years. [The Sabbath is called a sign in *Ex.* 31:13,17.

The sanctification of years is the solemn declaration of a Jubilee year by the Synhedrion.] In this interpretation, the days of the New Moon are on the same level as holidays.

הָעוֹבֵר בֵּין הַקְּבָרוֹת מַהוּ אוֹמֵר בָּרוּךְ אַתָּה יי מְחַיֵּה הַמֵּתִים. רִבִּי חִיָּא בְשֵׁם רִבִּי יוֹחָנָן נֶאֱמָן בִּדְבָרוֹ וּמְחַיֵּה הַמֵּתִים. רִבִּי חִיָּא בְשֵׁם רִבִּי יוֹחָנָן הַיּוֹדֵעַ מִסְפַּרְכֶם הוּא יְעוֹרֵר אֶתְכֶם הוּא יְגַלֶּה אֶת הֶעָפָר מֵעַל עֵינֵיכֶם. בָּרוּךְ אַתָּה יי מְחַיֵּה הַמֵּתִים. רִבִּי אֶלְעָזָר בְּשֵׁם רִבִּי חֲנִינָא אֲשֶׁר יָצַר אֶתְכֶם בַּדִּין וְכִלְכֵּל אֶתְכֶם בַּדִּין. וְסִילֵּק אֶתְכֶם בַּדִּין. וְעָתִיד לְהַחֲיוֹתְכֶם בַּדִּין. הַיּוֹדֵעַ מִסְפַּרְכֶם הוּא יְגַלֶּה עָפָר מֵעֵינֵיכֶם. בָּרוּךְ מְחַיֵּה הַמֵּתִים: הַהוּא דְאָמַר בְּמֵתֵי יִשְׂרָאֵל. אֲבָל בְּמֵתֵי אוּמּוֹת הָעוֹלָם אוֹמֵר בּוֹשָׁה אִמְּכֶם מְאֹד חָפְרָה יוֹלַדְתְּכֶם וגו':

What says he who passes between graves[145]? Praised are You, Eternal, Who makes the dead live. Rebbi Ḥiyya[146] in the name of Rebbi Yoḥanan: Who is true to His word and makes the dead live. Rebbi Ḥiyya in the name of Rebbi Yoḥanan: He Who knows your number will wake you up and remove the dust from upon your eyes. Praised are You, Eternal, Who makes the dead live. Rebbi Eleazar in the name of Rebbi Ḥanina: Who created You by judgment, fed you by judgment, and removed you by judgment, He will in the future make you live by judgment. He Who knows your number will remove the dust from upon your eyes. Praised be He Who makes the dead live. That is, for Jewish dead. But for the dead of the Gentiles, he says (*Jer.* 50:12): Your mother is very shameful, the one who bore you is ashamed[147] . . . .

145 The parallel in the Babli (58a) quotes a *baraita* that parallels the statement of R. Ḥanina here. An addition in the name of Rav Naḥman gives the second text of R. Yoḥanan here. The conclusion is simply "He Who makes the dead live." In the Tosephta (6:6), the text is that of R. Yoḥanan with the longer conclusion of R. Yoḥanan. The medieval quotes of these texts differ widely, cf. *Diqduqe Soferim Berakhot* p. 330, *Tosefta*

kifshutah Berakhot p. 109. It seems that the original benediction was simply: Praised are You, Eternal, Who makes the dead live. The longer texts are additions of Tannaïm of the last and Amoraïm of the first generations.

146 Here and in the following it is always R. Ḥiyya bar Abba.

147 The end of the verse is: "Lo, the future of the Gentiles is desert, wilderness and steppe," not the blissful afterlife. The Babli quotes the same verse.

הָרוֹאֶה הַקֶּשֶׁת בֶּעָנָן אוֹמֵר בָּרוּךְ אַתָּה יי זוֹכֵר הַבְּרִית. רִבִּי חִייָא בְשֵׁם רִבִּי יוֹחָנָן נֶאֱמָן בִּבְרִיתוֹ וְזוֹכֵר הַבְּרִית.

He who sees the rainbow in the clouds says: Praised are You, Eternal, Who remembers the Covenant. Rebbi Ḥiyya in the name of Rebbi Yoḥanan: Who is faithful to His Covenant and remembers the Covenant[148].

148 This is the formulation of the Tosephta (6:5); the Babli (59a) has a different formulation from a *baraita*. The formula is not original with R. Yoḥanan; he simply chose one among several that were current.

רִבִּי חִזְקִיָּה בְשֵׁם רִבִּי יִרְמְיָה כָּל־יָמָיו שֶׁל רִבִּי שִׁמְעוֹן בֶּן יוֹחַי לֹא נִרְאֲתָה הַקֶּשֶׁת בֶּעָנָן. רִבִּי חִזְקִיָּה בְשֵׁם רִבִּי יִרְמְיָה כֵּן הֲוָה רִבִּי שִׁמְעוֹן בֶּן יוֹחַי אוֹמֵר בִּקְעָה בִקְעָה הִתְמַלְּאִי דִּינָרֵי זָהָב וְהָיְתָה מִתְמַלֵּאת. רִבִּי חִזְקִיָּה בְשֵׁם רִבִּי יִרְמְיָה כֵּן הֲוָה רִבִּי שִׁמְעוֹן בֶּן יוֹחַי אוֹמֵר אֲנִי רָאִיתִי בְּנֵי הָעוֹלָם הַבָּא וּמוּעָטִים הֵן. אִין תְּלָתָא אִינּוּן אֲנָא וּבְרִי מִנְּהוֹן. אִין תְּרֵין אִינּוּן אֲנָא וּבְרִי אִינּוּן. רִבִּי חִזְקִיָּה בְשֵׁם רִבִּי יִרְמְיָה כֵּן הֲוָה רִבִּי שִׁמְעוֹן בֶּן יוֹחַי אוֹמֵר יְקָרֵב אַבְרָהָם מִן גַּבֵּיהּ וְעַד גַּבֵּיי. וַאֲנָא מִיקָרֵב מִן גַּבֵּיי וְעַד סוֹף כָּל־דָּרֵי. וְאִין לָא יְצָרֵף אֲחִיָּה הַשִּׁילוֹנִי עִמִּי וַאֲנָא מְקָרֵב כָּל־עַמָּא.

Rebbi Ḥizqiah in the name of Rebbi Jeremiah: No rainbow was seen all the days of Rebbi Simeon ben Yoḥai[149]. Rebbi Ḥizqiah in the name of Rebbi Jeremiah: Rebbi Simeon bar Yoḥai used to say, "Valley, valley, get filled with gold denars," and it got filled[150]. Rebbi Ḥizqiah in the name of Rebbi Jeremiah: Rebbi Simeon bar Yoḥai used to say, I saw the people of the Future World and they are few[151]. If they are three, I and my son are of them. If they are two, they are me and my son. Rebbi Ḥizqiah in the name of Rebbi Jeremiah: Rebbi Simeon bar Yoḥai used to say, Abraham should bring near from his back to my back[152]; I shall bring near from my back to the end of all generations. Otherwise, Aḥiya from Shiloh[153] should join me and I shall bring everybody near.

149 Since the rainbow is a sign that God will not bring a deluge over humankind even though their misdeeds would justify it; one single perfectly just person does by his existence exclude the possibility of a deluge and, therefore, the rainbow does not have to appear in his lifetime. It follows that a person in whose lifetime (probably meaning, from age 20 and onward) a rainbow is sighted cannot be perfect. This paragraph is inserted as addition to the topic of the rainbow.

150 Rebbi Simeon is the only Tanna (except Simeon ben Azai who died very young) about whom it is reported positively that he spent *all* his time in the study of Torah and did not earn money. Since it has been shown in the story of Jonathan ben Gershom that one may not take money from charity or contributions if one can avoid it at all, it is clear that he must have lived off his own money; otherwise he could not have been a just person.

151 The Babli (*Sukkah* 45b, *Sanhedrin* 97b) explains that this refers only to the highest state attainable in the Future World. This is also implied by the rest of the paragraph where R. Simeon declares that he can bring practically everybody to the Future World. [It is obvious that in both places in the Babli, one has to read "Rebbi Ḥizqiah" instead of "Ḥizqiah" (in the current text), who would be the son of Rebbi Ḥiyya, preceding R. Jeremiah by two generations.]

152 Rescue everybody from punishment and bring him to the Future world.

153 Cf. *Seder Olam*, Chapter 1, end.

וְכִי מַה רָאוּ לִסְמוֹךְ בְּשׂוּרוֹת טוֹבוֹת לִגְשָׁמִים. רִבִּי בֶּרֶכְיָה בְּשֵׁם רִבִּי לֵוִי עַל שֵׁם מַיִם קָרִים עַל נֶפֶשׁ עֲיֵפָה שְׁמוּעָה טוֹבָה מֵאֶרֶץ מֶרְחָק.

What reason did they have to take together[154] good news and rains? Rebbi Berekhiah in the name of Rebbi Lewi: Because of (*Pr.* 25:25) "cold water on a weary person and good news from a distant land."

154 In the Mishnah, having the same formula of thanks for good news and winter rain.

וְכַמָּה גְשָׁמִים יֵרְדוּ וִיהֵא אָדָם צָרִיךְ לְבָרֵךְ. רִבִּי חִיָּא בְּשֵׁם רִבִּי יוֹחָנָן בִּתְחִילָּה כְּדֵי רְבִיעָה. וּבַסּוֹף כְּדֵי שֶׁיּוּדְחוּ פָנֶיהָ. רִבִּי יַנַּאי בַּר יִשְׁמָעֵאל בְּשֵׁם רִבִּי שִׁמְעוֹן בֶּן לָקִישׁ בִּתְחִילָּה כְּדֵי רְבִיעָה. וּבַסּוֹף כְּדֵי שֶׁתִּשְׁרֶה הַמְּגוּפָה. וְיֵשׁ מְגוּפָה נִשְׁרֵית. אֶלָּא רוֹאִין אוֹתָהּ כְּאִילּוּ הִיא שְׁרוּיָה. רִבִּי יוֹסֵי בְּשֵׁם רַב יְהוּדָה וְרִבִּי יוֹנָה וְרַב יְהוּדָה בְּשֵׁם שְׁמוּאֵל בִּתְחִילָּה כְּדֵי (fol. 14a) רְבִיעָה. וּבַסּוֹף אֲפִילוּ כָּל־שֶׁהוּא. רִבִּי יוֹסָה בְּשֵׁם רִבִּי זְעִירָא לְהַפְסִיק תַּעֲנִית נֶאֶמְרָה. רִבִּי חִזְקִיָּה וְרִבִּי נָחוּם וְרַב אָדָא בַּר אֲבִימִי הֲווֹן יָתְבִין. אָמַר רִבִּי נָחוּם לְרַב אָדָא בַּר אֲבִימִי לֹא מִסְתַּבְּרָא לִבְרָכָה נֶאֶמְרָה. אָמַר לֵיהּ אִין. אָמַר רִבִּי חִזְקִיָּה לְרַב אָדָא בַּר אֲבִימִי לֹא מִסְתַּבְּרָא לְהַפְסִיק תַּעֲנִית נֶאֶמְרָה. אָמַר לֵיהּ אִין. אָמַר לֵיהּ לָמָּה אָמַרְתְּ לֵיהּ הִין הָכִין. אָמַר לֵיהּ בְּשִׁיטַּת רִבִּי. אָמַר רִבִּי מָנָא לְרִבִּי חִזְקִיָּה מָנִי רַבֵּיהּ. אָמַר לֵיהּ רִבִּי זְעִירָא. אָמַר לֵיהּ וַאֲנָן אָמְרִינָן רִבִּי יוֹסָה בְּשֵׁם רִבִּי זְעִירָא לְהַפְסִיק תַּעֲנִית נֶאֶמְרָה.

How[155] much rain should fall that a man is required to recite a benediction? Rebbi Ḥiyya in the name of Rebbi Yoḥanan: At the start[156], that it should fertilize[157], at the end that the surface should be wet[158]. Rebbi Yannai ben Ismael in the name of Rebbi Simeon ben Laqish: At the start, that it should fertilize, at the end that the seal of the amphora should be soaked[159]. Is the seal ever soaked? But it is as if it were soaked. Rebbi Yose in the name of Rav Yehudah, Rebbi Jonah, Rav Yehudah in the name of Samuel: At the start, that it should fertilize, at the end even a minimal amount. Rebbi Yose in the name of Rebbi Zeïra: It was said for fast days[160]. Rebbi Ḥizqiah, Rebbi Naḥum, and Rav Ada bar Abimi[161] were sitting. Rebbi Naḥum said to Rav Ada bar Abimi: Is it not reasonable that this was said for the benediction; he answered: Yes. Rebbi Ḥizqiah said to Rav Ada bar Abimi: Is it not reasonable that this was said for fast days; he answered: Yes. He said to him, why did you say "yes" here? He said to him, it is the argumentation of my teacher. Rebbi Mana asked Rebbi Ḥizqiah, who is his teacher? He said to him, Rebbi Zeïra. He said to him, but we say: Rebbi Yose in the name of Rebbi Zeïra: It was said for fast days[162].

155 The almost exact parallel is in *Taäniot* 1:3, *Bereshit rabba* 13(16). The text here follows the one in Taänit where it is supported by the Rome manuscript.

156 After it was dry for at least thirty days (in the Middle East, usually for six months.)

157 The definition is discussed in the second paragraph after this one.

158 In *Taänit* and *Bereshit rabba*, "that a brick should be wet."

159 Wine and oil were kept in clay amphoras (חבית) that were closed with clumps of clay. The measure is that the clay should become wet inside.

160 If there was a draught and a fast-day was decreed, when it has started to rain in the night before services begin in the synagogue, one stops and eats if there was enough rain to fertilize the earth. If they already started to recite the liturgy for fast days during daytime, then one stops according to one of the rules given above. [The Babli, *Taänit* 25b, knows only of the rule of fertilizing.]

161 He is mentioned only here.

162 The rules have been formulated for fast days only.

רַב יְהוּדָה בַּר יְחֶזְקְאֵל אָמַר אַבָּא מְבָרֵךְ עַל יְרִידַת גְּשָׁמִים יִתְגַּדַּל וְיִתְקַדַּשׁ וְיִתְבָּרַךְ וְיִתְרוֹמַם שִׁמְךָ מַלְכֵּנוּ עַל כָּל־טִיפָּה וְטִיפָּה שֶׁאַתְּ מוֹרִיד לָנוּ שֶׁאַתְּ מַמְנִיעָן זוֹ מִזּוֹ. כִּי יְגָרַע נִטְפֵי מָיִם. כְּדַאַתְּ אֲמַר וְנִגְרַע מֶעֶרְכֶּךָ. אָמַר רִבִּי יוּדָן וְלֹא עוֹד אֶלָּא שֶׁהוּא מוֹרִידָן בְּמִידָּה. שֶׁנֶּאֱמַר וּמַיִם תִּיכֵּן בְּמִידָּה. רִבִּי יוֹסֵי בַּר

יַעֲקֹב סְלַק מְבַקְּרָא רִבִּי יוּדָן מִגְדָּלָיָא. עַד דַּהֲוָה תַּמָּן נָחַת מִיטְרָא וְשָׁמַע קָלֵיהּ אָמַר אֶלֶף אֲלָפִין וְרִיבֵּי רִיבְוָון חַיָּבִין לְהוֹדוֹת לִשְׁמָךְ מַלְכֵּינוּ עַל כָּל־טִיפָּה וְטִיפָּה שֶׁאַתְּ מוֹרִיד לָנוּ שֶׁאַתְּ גּוֹמֵל טוֹבָה לַחַיָּבִים. אֲמַר לֵיהּ הֲדָא מְנָא לָךְ. אֲמַר לֵיהּ הָכֵין הֲוָה רִבִּי סִימוֹן מְבָרֵךְ עַל יְרִידַת גְּשָׁמִים.

Rav Yehudah bar Ezechiel[163] said, my father used to recite for rainfall: May Your Name be magnified, sanctified, praised, and elevated, our King, for every drop that You bring down to us, and you make them refrain one from the other. (*Job.* 36:27) "For He reduces water drippings;" as one says (*Lev.* 27:18): "Your value will be reduced." Rebbi Yudan said, not only that, but He brings them down in measure, as it is said (*Job* 28:25): "Water He determined by measure." Rebbi Yose bar Jacob[164] went to visit Rebbi Yudan from Migdal[165]. While he was there, rain started to come down and he heard his (R. Yudan's) voice saying: Thousands of thousands and myriads of myriads we are obliged to thank Your Name, our King, for every drop that You bring down to us, for You do good things for the guilty ones. He said to him: From where do you have this? He said to him: This is the benediction that Rebbi Simon recited for rainfall.

163 He is Rav Yehudah who is frequently quoted in both Talmudim. The texts given are only an introduction to the doxology required by the Mishnah, "He Who is good and does good." In the Babli (*Taänit* 6b), Rav Yehudah quotes a shorter text in the name of Rav. A longer text, patterned on the benediction after the recitation of Psalms on Sabbath and holidays with a different final doxology, is reported there in the name of R. Yoḥanan. It seems that long texts were never accepted in Galilee.

164 He always is quoted together with R. Yudan of Migdal; he might be R. Yose bar Jacob bar Idi mentioned in Midrashim.

165 An Amora of the fourth generation, living in Migdal Nunia North of Tiberias.

וְכַמָּה גְשָׁמִים יֵרְדוּ וִיהֵא בָּהֶן כְּדֵי רְבִיעָה מְלֹא כְלִי מַחֲזִיק שְׁלֹשָׁה טְפָחִים דִּבְרֵי רִבִּי מֵאִיר. רִבִּי יְהוּדָה אוֹמֵר בַּתְּחִילָּה טֶפַח וּבַשְּׁנִיָּה שְׁנֵי טְפָחִים וּבַשְּׁלִישִׁית שְׁלֹשָׁה טְפָחִים. תַּנֵּי רִבִּי שִׁמְעוֹן בֶּן אֶלְעָזָר אוֹמֵר אֵין לְךָ טֶפַח יוֹרֵד מִלְּמַעֲלָה שֶׁאֵין הָאָרֶץ מַעֲלָה כְּנֶגְדּוֹ שְׁנֵי טְפָחִים מַאי טַעֲמָא תְּהוֹם אֶל תְּהוֹם קוֹרֵא לְקוֹל צִינּוֹרֶיךָ.

How[166] much rain should fall that it is considered fertilizing? If it fills a vessel of three hand-breadths, the words of Rebbi Meïr. Rebbi Yehudah says, the first rainfall one hand-breadth, the second one two hand breadths, and the third one three hand-breadths. It has been stated: Rebbi Simeon ben Eleazar says, there is no hand-breadth that falls from above that the earth does not raise two hand-breadths towards it. What is the reason? (*Ps*. 42:8) "The deep calls to the deep[167] by the sound of Your water spouts."

166 There are two parallel traditions, both of Galilean origin. The text here is almost identical with Tosephta *Taäniot* 1:4. In the Babli (*Taänit* 25b) and the Yerushalmi source *Bereshit rabba* 13(13), Rebbi Meïr is reported to require that the rains penetrate the depth of the penetration of the plough-share (which is assumed to be three hand-breadths,) whereas R. Yehudah says that for dry earth, one hand-breadth was enough, for average ground two hand-breadths, and for well worked ground, three hand-breadths. If these are two equivalent formulations, then the text here has to be interpreted in the light of the text in Babli/Midrash: Not that R. Meïr requires a rainfall of three hand-breadths (10.8 inches) in one storm (or R. Yehudah rainfalls of 3.6, 7.2, 10.8 inches, respectively) but that the moisture has to penetrate the earth to the depth indicated. In that case, "dry earth" is simply the earth after the rainless summer months, average earth is the earth after the first winter storms, and well worked ground is the earth after an uninterrupted rain of seven days (the first, second, and third fertilizing periods in the language of Tosephta *Taäniot* 1:4). R. Simeon ben Eleazar seems to object to both R. Meïr and R. Yehudah because rain will make

the ground water level rise by twice the amount of rain water; hence, moisture in the ground can come from below as well as from above. One must assume that in the Yerushalmi also the measurements are those of moist spots in the earth and not of rainfall in the modern sense.

167 Rashi explains in Babli *Taänit* that clouds also are called "deep".

וְאָמַר רִבִּי לֵוִי הַמַּיִם הָאֶלְיוֹנִים זְכָרִים וְהַתַּחְתּוֹנִים נְקֵבוֹת. מַה טַעַם תִּפְתַּח אֶרֶץ. כִּנְקֵבָה הַזֹּאת שֶׁהִיא פוֹתַחַת לִפְנֵי הַזָּכָר. וְיִפְרוּ יֶשַׁע. זוֹ פְּרִיָּה וְרִבְיָה. וּצְדָקָה תַצְמִיחַ יַחַד. זוֹ יְרִידַת גְּשָׁמִים. כִּי אֲנִי יי בְּרָאתִיו. לְכָךְ בְּרָאתִיהָ לְתִיקּוּנוֹ שֶׁל עוֹלָם. רִבִּי אָחָא תַּנֵּי לָהּ בְּשֵׁם רִבִּי שִׁמְעוֹן בֶּן גַּמְלִיאֵל וְלָמָּה נִקְרָא שְׁמָהּ רְבִיעָה שֶׁהִיא רוֹבַעַת אֶת הָאָרֶץ.

And Rebbi Levi said: The upper waters are male and the lower ones female. What is the reason? (*Is.* 45:8)[168] "The earth shall open," like a female who opens before a male; "they should bear fruit of help," that is being fruitful and multiplying; "and justice shall sprout together," that is rainfall; "I, the Eternal, did create it," for that I created it, for the well-being of the world. Rebbi Aḥa stated it in the name of Rebbi Simeon ben Gamliel[169]: Why is it called "fertilizing," because it impregnates the earth.

168 The verse starts: "The heavens should pour down from high, and the skies should flow with justice," speaking of rain. The Babli has two contradictory sermons in this matter. Rav Yehudah is reported in *Taänit* 6b that rain is the earth's husband because in *Is.* 55:10 it is said that rain makes the earth give birth, while Rebbi Abbahu (there and *Berakhot* 59b) says that a benediction is recited only if "the bridegroom goes towards the bride," meaning that drops jump up from the earth towards the descending rain. [This is the traditional interpretation, given by Ashkenazic Rabbenu Gershom and Sephardic Rabbenu Ḥanan'el. Rashi, sensing the apparent contradiction, has a prosaic interpretation, that on both sides of the street the gutters will spout water one towards the other.]

169 This is the end of Rebbi Simeon ben Eleazar's text in Tosephta *Taäniot*. In the Babli (*Taänit* 6b), this passage appears as a statement of the Amora Rebbi Abbahu.

רִבִּי חֲנִינָא בַּר יַקָּא בְּשֵׁם רַב יְהוּדָה שׁוֹרְשֵׁי חִיטָּה בּוֹקְעִין בָּאָרֶץ שָׁלֹשׁ אַמָּה. שׁוֹרְשֵׁי תְּאֵינָה רַכִּים בּוֹקְעִין בַּצּוּר. תַּנֵּי רִבִּי יִשְׁמָעְאֵל בֶּן אֶלְעָזָר אוֹמֵר אֵין הָאָרֶץ שׁוֹתָה אֶלָּא לְפִי חִיסוּמָהּ. אִם כֵּן מַה יַּעֲשֶׂה שׁוֹרְשֵׁי חָרוּב. מָה יַעֲשׂוּ שׁוֹרְשֵׁי שִׁקְמָה. אָמַר רִבִּי חֲנִינָא אַחַת לִשְׁלֹשִׁים יוֹם תְּהוֹם עוֹלֶה וּמַשְׁקֶה אוֹתָם. וּמַה טַּעַם אֲנִי יי נוֹצְרָהּ לִרְגָעִים אַשְׁקֶנָּהּ.

Rebbi Ḥanina bar Yaqqa[170] in the name of Rav Yehudah: The roots of wheat split the earth to a depth of three cubits. The soft roots of a fig tree split rock. It has been stated: Rebbi Ismael ben Eleazar[171] says, the earth drinks only according to its hardness[172]. If this is so, what do the roots of the carob do? What do the roots of the sycamore do[173]? Rebbi Ḥanina said, once every thirty days the abyss wells up and drenches them. What is the reason? (*Is*. 27:3) "I, the Eternal, watch over it[174] and water it in moments."

170 A Galilean Amora of the third generation who studied under Rav Yehudah in Babylonia and only reports sayings of Rav Yehudah. The paragraph has three parallels, Yerushalmi *Taäniot* 1:3, *Avodah zarah* 3:6, Midrash *Bereshit rabba* 13(19). In *Taäniot*, the name is R. Ḥanania bar Yaqqa, in *Avodah zarah* it is R. Ḥaninah bar Yasa, and in the Midrash it is R. Ḥanina ben R. 'Izqa in the name of Rebbi (!) Yehudah.

171 In *Taäniot* and *Avodah zara*, as well as here in the Rome ms., correctly R. Simeon ben Eleazar; in the printed Midrash R. Eleazar ben R. Simeon, R. Simeon ben Eleazar in manuscripts.

172 The harder the soil, the less it is penetrated by moisture.

173 These trees grow mainly wild, mostly in places unsuited for more delicate fruit trees because of the hardness of the soil. Their roots are very deep.

174 The desirable vineyard.

אָמַר רִבִּי זְעִירָא תַּנֵּי תַּמָּן רָאָה זוֹל בָּא לָעוֹלָם וְשׂוֹבַע בָּא לָעוֹלָם נָהָר מַסְפִּיק לַמְּדִינָה אוֹמֵר בָּרוּךְ הַטּוֹב וְהַמֵּטִיב.

Rebbi Zeïra[175] said, it is stated there[176]: If one notices cheapness[177] coming to the world, plenty coming to the world, or a river supplying[178] a city, one recites: He Who is good and does good.

175 Here starts the discussion of the last part of the Mishnah, what to recite for good news and what for bad news. One has first to define good and bad news.

176 In Babylonia.

177 Falling prices for consumers, disinflation.

178 A river (or, in Babylonian terms, an arm of a river) changing its course and now suppliying a town with flowing water when before they had to draw water from wells. In Israel, rivers are not fed by melting snow, so this kind of spring flood does not happen there; it is truly a Babylonian formulation.

אָמְרוּ לוֹ מֵת אָבִיו. אוֹמֵר בָּרוּךְ דַּיָּין הָאֱמֶת. מֵת וְהוֹרִישׁוֹ אוֹמֵר בָּרוּךְ הַטּוֹב וְהַמֵּטִיב.

If he was told that his father had died, he says: "Praise to the True Judge." He died and made him an heir, he says: "Praise to Him Who is good and does good[180]."

179 The sentence is also quoted in the Babli (*Berakhot* 59b) where it is noted that the benediction for the inheritance is only appropriate if there are several heirs but that the sole heir recites "Who has made us live, preserved us, and let us reach this time." This distinction is absent in the Yerushalmi which requires the benediction "Who is good and does good" for all gifts, as explained in the next Halakhah.

בָּנָה בַּיִת חָדָשׁ וְקָנָה כֵּלִים חֲדָשִׁים כו'. אָמַר רִבִּי חִייָא בַּר בָּא לֹא סוֹף דָּבָר חֲדָשִׁים אֶלָּא אֲפִילוּ שְׁחָקִים כְּאִילוּ הֵם חֲדָשִׁים לוֹ. רִבִּי יַעֲקֹב בַּר זַבְדִּי בְּשֵׁם רִבִּי חִייָא בַּר אַבָּא אָמַר קָנָה אוֹמֵר בָּרוּךְ שֶׁהֶחֱיָנוּ וְקִייְמָנוּ וְהִגִּיעָנוּ לַזְּמַן הַזֶּה.

נִיתַּן לוֹ אוֹמֵר הַטּוֹב וְהַמֵּטִיב. רִבִּי בָּא אֲבוּהּ דְּרִיבִּי בָּא מָארִי בְּשֵׁם רִבִּי אָחָא קָנָה אוֹמֵר בָּרוּךְ שֶׁהִגִּיעָנוּ לַזְּמַן הַזֶּה. נִיתַּן לוֹ אוֹמֵר הַטּוֹב וְהַמֵּטִיב. לָבַשׁ בְּגָדִים אוֹמֵר בָּרוּךְ מַלְבִּישׁ עֲרוּמִים.

"If one built a new house or bought new garments, etc.[180]" Rebbi Ḥiyya bar Abba said: Not only new ones, but even used ones if they are new for him[181]. Rebbi Jacob bar Zavdi said in the name of Rebbi Ḥiyya bar Abba: If he bought [a garment], he says: "Praise to Him Who made us live, preserved us, and let us reach this time." If it was given to him, he says: "Praise to Him Who is good and does good." Rebbi Abba, father of Rebbi Abba Mari, in the name of Rebbi Aḥa: If he bought, he says: "Praise to Him Who let us reach this time." If it was given to him, he says: "Praise to Him Who is good and does good." If he wears the garment, he says: "Praise to Him Who clothes the naked."

180 Here starts the discussion of the last part (in the Mishnah collection, Mishnah 4).

181 If he cannot afford to buy new ones, second hand clothes have the same status for him as new ones for a richer person. [In the Babli, 59b-60a, the Babylonian opinion is that (for rich Babylonians) one only makes a benediction for genuinely new articles, not for a new set of what he already has, whereas the opinion of the less wealthy Galileans is that any new garment deserves a benediction.]

הָעוֹשֶׂה סוּכָּה לְעַצְמוֹ. אוֹמֵר בָּרוּךְ אֲשֶׁר קִידְּשָׁנוּ בְּמִצְוֹתָיו וְצִיוָּנוּ לַעֲשׂוֹת סוּכָּה. לַאֲחֵרִים לַעֲשׂוֹת לוֹ[182] סוּכָּה לִשְׁמוֹ. נִכְנַס לֵישֵׁב בָּהּ אוֹמֵר בָּרוּךְ אֲשֶׁר קִידְּשָׁנוּ בְּמִצְוֹתָיו וְצִיוָּנוּ לֵישֵׁב בְּסוּכָּה. מִשֶּׁהוּא מְבָרֵךְ עָלֶיהָ לֵילֵי יוֹם טוֹב הָרִאשׁוֹן אֵינוֹ צָרִיךְ לְבָרֵךְ עָלֶיהָ עוֹד מֵעַתָּה. הָעוֹשֶׂה לוּלָב לְעַצְמוֹ. אוֹמֵר בָּרוּךְ אֲשֶׁר קִידְּשָׁנוּ בְּמִצְוֹתָיו וְצִיוָּנוּ לַעֲשׂוֹת לוּלָב. לְאַחֵר לַעֲשׂוֹת לוּלָב לִשְׁמוֹ. כְּשֶׁהוּא נוֹטְלוֹ אוֹמֵר עַל נְטִילַת לוּלָב. וַאֲשֶׁר הֶחֱיָינוּ. וּמְבָרֵךְ בְּכָל־שָׁעָה וְשָׁעָה שֶׁהוּא נוֹטְלוֹ.

He[183] who makes a *sukkah* for himself, says: "He Who sanctified us by His commandments and commanded us to make a *sukkah*." For others:

"to make a *sukkah* in that one's name[184]." If he enters it, he says: "Praise to Him Who sanctified us by His commandments and commanded us to dwell in a *sukkah*." After he recited the benediction in the first night of the holiday he does not have to recite it again[185]. He who makes a *lulav* for himself, says: "He Who sanctified us by His commandments and commanded us to make a *lulav*." For others: "to make a *lulav* in that one's name." If he uses it, he says: "Praise to Him Who sanctified us by His commandments and commanded us to take a *lulav*," and "He Who let us live." He recites the benediction every time that he takes it[186].

182 This word is missing in the parallel *Sukkah* 1:2 and is superfluous.

183 There is a similar statement in Tosephta *Berakhot* 6:9 which is quoted in Babli *Sukkah* 46a; the note about the benediction when making a *sukkah* or *lulav* for somebody else is found only here. Hence, the source here is not the Tosephta which also starts with a general declaration that: "A person performing any *mizwah* recites a benediction over it." The practice of the Babli does not follow the discussion in *Sukkah* 46a but a statement in *Menaḥot* 42b that no benediction is due for a preparatory action, such as making the *sukkah* or the *lulav*, but only for the required act itself such as living in the *sukkah* or taking the *lulav*.

184 The usual interpretation is that one makes the benediction: "To make a *sukkah*" and that the person has in mind the name of the person for whom he is doing it. It seems rather that one has to pronounce the recipient's name at the place reserved for לשמו.

185 In the Babli (*loc. cit.*), this is the opinion of the Babylonian Samuel, supported by the Tosephta. In the name of the Galilean R. Yoḥanan, it is reported that one has to recite the benediction every day. Since R. Yohanan is a higher authority than Samuel, Babylonian practice followed what there is declared to be Galilean.

186 The difference between *sukkah* and *lulav* has been explained in Halakhah 3:3.

הָעוֹשֶׂה מְזוּזָה לְעַצְמוֹ. אוֹמֵר לַעֲשׂוֹת מְזוּזָה. לְאַחֵר לַעֲשׂוֹת מְזוּזָה לִשְׁמוֹ. כְּשֶׁהוּא קוֹבְעָהּ אוֹמֵר בָּרוּךְ אֲשֶׁר קִידְּשָׁנוּ בְּמִצְוֹתָיו וְצִיוָּנוּ עַל מִצְוַת מְזוּזָה.

הָעוֹשֶׂה תְּפִילִין לְעַצְמוֹ כו'. לְאַחֵר כו'. כְּשֶׁהוּא לוֹבֵשׁ אוֹמֵר עַל מִצְוַת תְּפִילִין. הָעוֹשֶׂה צִיצִית לְעַצְמוֹ כו'. לְאַחֵר כו'. נִתְעַטֵּף כו'. הַתּוֹרֵם וְהַמְעַשֵּׂר אוֹמֵר בָּרוּךְ אֲשֶׁר קִידְּשָׁנוּ בְּמִצְוֹתָיו וְצִיוָּנוּ לְהַפְרִישׁ תְּרוּמָה וּמַעֲשֵׂר. לְאַחֵר לְהַפְרִישׁ תְּרוּמָה וּמַעֲשֵׂר לִשְׁמוֹ. הַשּׁוֹחֵט צָרִיךְ לוֹמַר בָּרוּךְ אַתָּה יי אֱלֹהֵינוּ מֶלֶךְ הָעוֹלָם אֲשֶׁר קִידְּשָׁנוּ בְּמִצְוֹתָיו וְצִיוָּנוּ עַל הַשְּׁחִיטָה. הַמְכַסֶּה אוֹמֵר עַל כִּיסּוּי הַדָּם.

He who makes a *mezuzah* for himself, says "to make a *mezuzah*." For somebody else, "to make a *mezuzah* for his name." When he nails it to the doorpost, he recites: "Praise to Him Who sanctified us by His commandments and commanded us to about *mezuzah*." He who makes *tefillin* for himself[187], etc. For somebody else, etc. When he puts them on, he says "about the commandment of *tefillin*.[188]" He who makes *ẓiẓit* for himself, etc. For somebody else etc. When he wraps himself in them, etc.[189]. He who separates *terumah* and tithes says: "Praise to Him Who sanctified us by His commandments and commanded us to separate *terumah* and tithes." For somebody else, "to separate *terumah* and tithes for his name." He who slaughters must say: "Praise to You, Eternal, our God, King of the Universe, Who sanctified us by His commandments and commanded us about *šeḥitah*[190]." He who covers [the blood[191]] says, "about covering the blood."

187 "Praise to You, o Eternal, our God, King of the Universe, Who has sanctified us by His commandments and commanded us to make *tefillin*."

188 The tannaïtic text of the Yerushalmi here clearly requires only one benediction when both *tefillin* are put on, in contrast to the amoraïc text of Halakhah 2:3, that requires two benedictions, one for *tefillin* on the arm and one for the head. Similarly, the discussion below on the timing of benedictions is based on having only one benediction. The Tosephta (6:10), representing the Babylonian text as always, does not have the notes on working for somebody else and requires here the formula "to put on *tefillin*," which is the main benediction in the Babli (*Menaḥot* 42b), followed in

Sephardic practice.

189 He says, "Who sanctified us by His commandments and commanded us about the commandment of *ẓiẓit*." The Babylonian formula is "to wrap ourselves in *ẓiẓit*."

190 It seems that the Yerushalmi chooses the wording "about", על, if the action must be done by the person who pronounces the benediction, but "to", ל, if the action is done in delegation.

191 Of slaughtered fowl and wild animals, *Lev*. 17:13.

הַמָּל צָרִיךְ לוֹמַר בָּרוּךְ אֲשֶׁר קִידְּשָׁנוּ בְּמִצְוֹתָיו וְצִיוָּנוּ עַל הַמִּילָה. אֲבִי הַבֵּן אוֹמֵר בָּרוּךְ אֲשֶׁר קִידְּשָׁנוּ בְּמִצְוֹתָיו וְצִיוָּנוּ לְהַכְנִיסוֹ בִּבְרִיתוֹ שֶׁל אַבְרָהָם אָבִינוּ. הָעוֹמְדִים שָׁם צְרִיכִין לוֹמַר כְּשֵׁם שֶׁהִכְנַסְתּוֹ לַבְּרִית כֵּן תַּכְנִיסֵיהוּ לְתוֹרָה וּלְחוּפָּה. הַמְבָרֵךְ צָרִיךְ לוֹמַר בָּרוּךְ אֲשֶׁר קִידֵּשׁ יְדִיד מִבֶּטֶן וְחוֹק בִּשְׁאֵרוֹ שָׂם וְצֶאֱצָאָיו חָתַם בְּאוֹת בְּרִית קוֹדֶשׁ עַל כֵּן בִּשְׂכַר זֹאת אֵל חַי חֶלְקֵינוּ צוּרֵינוּ צַוֵּה לְהַצִּיל יְדִידוּת שְׁאֵירֵינוּ מִשַּׁחַת. בָּרוּךְ אַתָּה יי כּוֹרֵת הַבְּרִית.

He[192] who circumcizes must say: "Praised Who sanctified us by His commandments and commanded us about circumcision." The child's father says: "Praised Who sanctified us by His commandments and commanded us to induce him into the covenant of our forefather Abraham." Those who are standing there must say: "Just as you made him enter the covenant, so make him enter Torah and the marriage canopy[193]." He who recites the benediction must say: "Praised Who sanctified the beloved[194] from the womb, Who put a statute in his flesh, and sealed his descendants with a holy sign of covenant; therefore, as a reward for this, o living God, our part, our rock, command to save the beloved of our flesh from destruction. Praised are You, o Eternal, Who seals the covenant."

192 A similar text is in Tosephta 6:12 and in Babli *Sabbath* 127b. The text of the Tosephta is closer to the Babli than to the Yerushalmi.

193 Tosephta and Babli add: "and good deeds." The Rome manuscript has

only "the marriage canopy."

194 The commentators of the Babli have identified the "beloved" as either Abraham, Isaac, or Jacob. The text of the Babli is slightly longer than that of Yerushalmi and Tosephta.

מִצְוֹת אֵימָתַי מְבָרֵךְ עֲלֵיהֶן. רִבִּי יוֹחָנָן אָמַר עוֹבֵר לַעֲשִׂיָּתָן. רַב הוּנָא אָמַר בִּשְׁעַת עֲשִׂיָּתָן. אַתְיָא דְּרַב הוּנָא כִשְׁמוּאֵל דְּאָמַר רִבִּי יוֹסֵי בֵּי רִבִּי בוּן בְּשֵׁם שְׁמוּאֵל כָּל־הַמִּצְוֹת טְעוּנוֹת בְּרָכָה בִשְׁעַת עֲשִׂיָּתָן חוּץ מִתְּקִיעָה וּטְבִילָה. וְיֵשׁ אוֹמְרִים קִידּוּשִׁין בִּבְעִילָה. אָמַר רִבִּי יוֹנָה אִית לָךְ חוֹרָניי תְּפִילִין שֶׁל יַד עַד שֶׁלֹּא יַחְלוֹץ. וְשֶׁל רֹאשׁ עַד שֶׁלֹּא יִיבָּה. לֹא יִיבָּה מִן דְּיִיבְּה הוּא יִיבָּה.

When does one recite the benediction for commandments? Rebbi Yoḥanan said, just before he starts doing them[195]. Rav Huna said, when he does it. Rav Huna agrees with Samuel, since Rebbi Yose bar Abun said in the name of Samuel: All commandments need a benediction while one is doing them except blowing[196] and immersion[197], and, some say, *qiddušin* by sexual relations[198]. Rebbi Jonah said, you have others: *Tefillin* on the hand before he takes them off, and on the head before he puts[199] them on[200]. Before he puts them on? When he puts on[201], he puts them on!

195 The Babylonian tradition (*Pesaḥim* 7b) is: "Everybody agrees that one makes the benediction beforehand, as Rav Yehudah said in the name of Samuel: On all commandments one recites the benediction just before he starts doing them." This tradition must be later when the authority of R. Yoḥanan overrode earlier Babylonian practices.

196 The shofar on *Rosh Hashanah*, since obviously one cannot blow and recite the benediction at the same time.

197 In the *miqweh*, when one is naked and forbidden to recite a benediction. The Yerushalmi requires a benediction before immersion. In the Babli (*Pesaḥim* 7b), the statement about blowing and immersion is an addition to the statement that all benedictions must precede the action. It is clear that the mention of blowing in that context makes no sense; that statement is then dropped and only immersion is left for

a benediction *after* the act. The Yerushalmi shows that in the Babli we have a later confluence of older (Rav Huna) Babylonian tradition with the adoption of Galilean (R. Yoḥanan) practice by the editors of the Talmud.

198 *Qiddušin* is the first stage of a marriage in which the bride becomes bound to the husband, in preparation for *ḥuppah*, which lets the couple live together. Usually, *qiddušin* is effected by the groom giving a valuable gift (usually a gold ring) to the bride. But the Mishnah (*Qiddušin* 1:1) lists sexual relations (in front of two witnesses) as a possible form of *qiddušin*. One may assume that in Israel this option was never used. In Babylonia it seems to have been used since the Babli (*Qiddušin* 12b) reports that Rav had people whipped (for indecent exposure) who married by public sex act. In any case, the required benediction cannot be pronounced while the parties are naked.

199 The spelling ייבה is dialectal for יהבה, root *yhb* "to give."

200 As noted before, the text presumes that only one benediction is required for the two *tefillin* and, as explained earlier (2:3), in Galilee a benediction was recited when *tefillin* were taken off. Since the Torah mentions *ṭoṭaphot* (*tefillin*) on the hand always before those on the head, one must put on first those for the arm and take off first those for the head. Even Rav Huna agrees that the benediction for removal was recited before *tefillin* were removed from the arm and the one for putting them on was recited before those of the head were put on.

201 Since *tefillin* on the arm and on the head are always mentioned together in one verse, the putting on (or taking off) of both is one act and the recitation of the benediction covers both *tefillin*.

שְׁחִיטָה אֵימָתַי הוּא מְבָרֵךְ עָלֶיהָ. רִבִּי יוֹחָנָן אוֹמֵר עוֹבֵר לִשְׁחוֹט. יוֹסֵי בֶּן נְהוֹרַאי אוֹמֵר מִשֶּׁיִּשְׁחוֹט. לָמָּה שֶׁמָּא תִתְנַבֵּל שְׁחִיטָתָהּ. מֵעַתָּה מִשֶּׁיִּבְדּוֹק הַסִּימָנִין. חֶזְקַת בְּנֵי מֵעַיִים כְּשֵׁרִים. תַּנֵּי שְׁחָטָהּ וְנָטְלוּ הַזְּאֵיבִים מֵעֶיהָ כְּשֵׁרָה. וְחוֹשֵׁשׁ שֶׁמָּא נִקְבוּ. רִבִּי בָּא בְשֵׁם רַבָּנָן דְּתַמָּן בְּנֵי מֵעַיִם בְּחֶזְקַת כּוֹשֶׁר.

When does one recite the benediction for *šeḥiṭah*[202]? Rebbi Yoḥanan says, if he prepares to slaughter. Yose ben Nehorai[203] says, after he slaughtered. Why? Maybe its slaughtering is producing a carcass[204].

Now, should he not first check the signs[205]? The *ḥazaqah* of intestines is that they are in order[206]. It was stated: If it was slaughtered and the wolves took its innards, it is in order[207]. Should one question whether they were pierced[208]? Rebbi Abba in the name of the rabbis from there[209]: Intestines have *ḥazaqah* that they are in order[210].

202 Since ritual slaughter is a commandment, its execution requires a benediction.
203 A Palestinian authority of the first generation of Amoraïm, one of the teachers of R. Joḥanan.
204 If during the act of slaughter, one of the technical rules was violated (for example, if pressure was exerted on the knife), the animal was not slaughtered but killed in a way that makes its meat unfit for consumption; then the benediction would have been in vain.
205 In the Babli, only esophagus and windpipe are called "signs"; the tiniest of holes in the esophagus makes an animal *terepha*, "torn" and unfit for consumption. The Yerushalmi seems to extend the meaning of "signs" to all internal organs, especially lungs and the digestive system, holes of which render an animal unfit for consumption. The question here is: why not wait with the benediction until the entire animal has been dissected and checked for possible *terepha*?
206 Since we do not have a Yerushalmi on tractate *Ḥulin*, the interpretation here by necessity has to follow the Babylonian tradition. The position of the latter has been formulated by Rav Huna: A living animal is in the continuing state (*ḥazaqah*) of being forbidden until it has been ascertained that it was correctly slaughtered; once it has been correctly slaughtered, it is in the continuing state (*ḥazaqah*) of being permitted food until it has been ascertained whether and why it is *terepha*. If the slaughter was ascertained to be correct and inner parts were then taken by an animal before they were checked, the meat remains permitted food.
207 As kosher food.
208 If the intestines were later retrieved in a torn state, could it not be that the intestines of the living animal had a hole there where the wolves bit, and this *terepha* cannot now be ascertained?
209 It is reported in Babli *Ḥulin* 9a that Rebbi Abba asked precisely this

question from Rav Huna.

210 The entire discussion seems to suggest that the Yerushalmi follows Yose ben Nehorai. The problem is not mentioned in the Babli, but it is assumed there and in the halakhic literature that one follows Rebbi Yoḥanan (except in the case of an emergency slaughter when the opinion of Yose ben Nehorai is considered.)

(fol 12d) **משנה ד**: וְהַזּוֹעֵק לְשֶׁעָבַר הֲרֵי זֶה תְּפִילַּת שָׁוְא. כֵּיצַד הָיְתָה אִשְׁתּוֹ מְעוּבֶּרֶת וְאָמַר יְהִי רָצוֹן שֶׁתֵּלֵד אִשְׁתִּי זָכָר הֲרֵי זוֹ תְּפִילַּת שָׁוְא. הָיָה בָא בַדֶּרֶךְ וְשָׁמַע קוֹל צְוָחָה בָּעִיר אָמַר יְהִי רָצוֹן שֶׁלֹּא יִהְיֶה בְתוֹךְ בֵּיתִי הֲרֵי זוֹ תְּפִילַּת שָׁוְא.

Mishnah 4: But if one cries about the past, that is a vain prayer. How is that? If his wife was pregnant and he said: May it be (God's) pleasure that my wife would give birth to a male, that is a vain prayer. If he came from a trip, heard wailing in town, and said: May it be (God's) pleasure that this should not be in my house, that is a vain prayer.

(fol. 14a) **הלכה ד**: דְּבֵית יַנַּאי אָמַר בְּיוֹשֶׁבֶת עַל הַמַּשְׁבֵּר. הָא קוֹדֶם כֵּן יַצְלִי. עַל שֵׁם הִנֵּה כַחוֹמֶר בְּיַד הַיּוֹצֵר. רִבִּי יְהוּדָה בֶּן פָּזִי בְּשֵׁם דְּבֵית יַנַּאי עִיקָּר עִיבּוּרָהּ שֶׁל דִּינָה זָכָר הָיָה. מֵאַחַר שֶׁנִּתְפַּלְלָה רָחֵל נַעֲשִׂית נְקֵבָה. הֲדָא הִיא וְאַחַר יָלְדָה בַּת וַתִּקְרָא אֶת (fol. 14b) שְׁמָהּ דִּינָה. מֵאַחַר שֶׁנִּתְפַּלְלָה רָחֵל נַעֲשִׂית נְקֵבָה. וְאָמַר רִבִּי יְהוּדָה בֶּן פָּזִי בְּשֵׁם דְּבֵית רִבִּי יַנַּאי אִימֵּנוּ רָחֵל מִנְּבִיאוֹת הָרִאשׁוֹנוֹת הָיְתָה. אָמְרָה עוֹד אֶחָד יִהְיֶה מִמֶּנִּי. הֲדָא הוּא דִכְתִיב יוֹסֵף יי לִי בֵּן אַחֵר. בָּנִים אֲחֵרִים לֹא אָמְרָה אֶלָּא עוֹד אַחֵר יִהְיֶה מִמֶּנִּי.

Halakhah 4: In the house of Yannai they said, if she is sitting on the birthing stool. Hence, before that he should pray, because of (*Jer*. 18:6) "Lo, like clay in the potter's hand[212] . . ." Rebbi Yehudah ben Pazi[213] in the name of the house of Yannai: The main pregnancy of Dinah was as a male. After the prayer of Rachel, she became a female. That is (*Gen.* 30:21): "Afterwards, she gave birth to a daughter and called her name Dinah." After the prayer of Rachel, she became a female. And Rebbi Yehudah ben Pazi in the name of the house of Rebbi Yannai: Our mother Rachel was of the early prophetesses[214]. She said, another one will be from me. That is what is written (*Gen.* 30:24): "May the Eternal add me another son." She did not say *other sons*, but *another son* will be from me.

212 ". . . Are you in My hand, House of Israel." This seems to imply, in the opinion of the Yerushalmi, that for Gentiles the laws of nature will not be changed and the sex of the child is determined at conception, or, in the opinion of the Babli (60a), in extraordinary cases at least during the first 40 days of pregnancy when the fetus is not yet a living being. The Babli declares that in all cases, the laws of nature prevail and that the sex change of Dinah is no proof since "one does not bring a proof from miracles." It would be presumptuous for anybody to assume that he is on the level of the Patriarchs for whom God used to perform wonders.

213 The name is missing here in the Venice print and the Leyden manuscript. It is given in the Rome manuscript and the parallel *Bereshit rabba* 72(6). In the latter source, R. Jehudah ben Pazi is in opposition to the house of Rebbi Yannai and says that even if labor has started, as long as the baby is not born one may pray because of the verse from Jeremiah.

214 In both versions of the *Tanḥuma* (Buber *Wayeẓe* 19, Standard *Wayeẓe* 8), Leah was the prophetess who knew that Jacob would have 12 sons and if she had 7 sons then her sister would be left with only one son, less than any of the maids. She therefore prayed that her pregnancy should be that of a girl. All Midrashim derive the name of Dinah not from דין "law, lawsuit", but from די "enough", meaning "we already have enough boys."

הָיָה בָא בַדֶּרֶךְ מַהוּ אוֹמֵר בָּטוּחַ אֲנִי שֶׁאֵין אֵלּוּ בְתוֹךְ בֵּיתִי. הִלֵּל הַזָּקֵן אוֹמֵר מִשְּׁמוּעָה רָעָה לֹא יִירָא.

If he returns from a trip, what does he say[215]: I am sure that these are not in my house. Hillel the elder said (*Ps.* 112:7): "He will not be afraid of bad news."

215 When he hears wailing in town and cannot pray that it should not be in his house.

(fol. 12d) **משנה ה**: נִכְנַס לְכָרָךְ מִתְפַּלֵּל שְׁתַּיִם אַחַת בִּכְנִיסָתוֹ וְאַחַת בִּיצִיאָתוֹ. בֶּן עֲזַאי אוֹמֵר אַרְבַּע שְׁתַּיִם בִּכְנִיסָתוֹ וּשְׁתַּיִם בִּיצִיאָתוֹ. וְנוֹתֵן הוֹדָאָה לְשֶׁעָבַר וְצוֹעֵק לְעָתִיד לָבוֹא.

Mishnah 5: He who enters a fortified place[216] prays two prayers, one when he enters and one when he leaves. Ben Azai said four, two when he enters and two when he leaves. He gives thanks for the past and implores for the future.

216 Greek χάραξ "palisade". A Roman fortified camp with soldiers and police not under the control of the local authorities.

(fol. 14b) **הלכה ה**: נִכְנַס לְכָרָךְ מִתְפַּלֵּל שְׁתַּיִם אַחַת בִּכְנִיסָתוֹ וְאַחַת בִּיצִיאָתוֹ. בִּכְנִיסָתוֹ מַהוּ אוֹמֵר. יְהִי רָצוֹן מִלְּפָנֶיךָ יי אֱלֹהַי וֵאלֹהֵי אֲבוֹתַי שֶׁתַּכְנִיסֵנִי לְכָרָךְ זֶה לְשָׁלוֹם. בִּיצִיאָתוֹ אוֹמֵר מוֹדֶה אֲנִי לְפָנֶיךָ יי אֱלֹהַי וֵאלֹהֵי אֲבוֹתַי כו'. בֶּן עֲזַאי אוֹמֵר אַרְבַּע שְׁתַּיִם בִּכְנִיסָתוֹ וּשְׁתַּיִם בִּיצִיאָתוֹ. בִּכְנִיסָתוֹ הוּא אוֹמֵר יְהִי רָצוֹן מִלְּפָנֶיךָ יי אֱלֹהַי וֵאלֹהֵי אֲבוֹתַי שֶׁתַּכְנִיסֵנִי לְכָרָךְ זֶה לְשָׁלוֹם. נִכְנַס אוֹמֵר מוֹדֶה אֲנִי לְפָנֶיךָ יי אֱלֹהַי וֵאלֹהֵי אֲבוֹתַי שֶׁנִּכְנַסְתִּי לְשָׁלוֹם כֵּן יְהִי רָצוֹן מִלְּפָנֶיךָ שֶׁתּוֹצִיאֵנִי מִתּוֹכוֹ לְשָׁלוֹם. כְּשֶׁיֵּצֵא אוֹמֵר יְהִי רָצוֹן מִלְּפָנֶיךָ יי אֱלֹהַי וֵאלֹהֵי אֲבוֹתַי שֶׁתּוֹצִיאֵנִי מִכְּרָךְ זֶה לְשָׁלוֹם. יָצָא אוֹמֵר מוֹדֶה אֲנִי לְפָנֶיךָ יי אֱלֹהַי שֶׁהוֹצֵאתַנִי לְשָׁלוֹם כֵּן יְהִי רָצוֹן מִלְּפָנֶיךָ שֶׁתּוֹלִיכֵנִי לְבֵיתִי לְשָׁלוֹם אוֹ לְמָקוֹם פְּלוֹנִי לְשָׁלוֹם. הָדָא דְאָמַר בִּמְדוּרוֹת גּוֹיִם אֲבָל בְּיִשְׂרָאֵל אֵין צָרִיךְ לְבָרֵךְ. אִם הָיָה מָקוֹם שֶׁהוֹרְגִין שָׁם אֲפִילוּ בִּמְדוּרוֹת יִשְׂרָאֵל צָרִיךְ לְבָרֵךְ.

Halakhah 5: "He who enters a fortified place says two prayers, one when he enters and one when he leaves." What does he say when he enters? May it be Your pleasure, o Eternal, my God and God of my fathers, that You will bring me into this fortress for peace. When he leaves, he says: May it be Your pleasure, o Eternal, my God and God of my fathers, etc. "Ben Azai said four, two when he enters and two when he leaves." When he is about to enter, he says: May it be Your pleasure, o Eternal, my God and God of my fathers, that You will bring me into this fortress for peace. After he entered, he says: I thank You, o Eternal, my God and God of my fathers, that I entered in peace; so may it be Your pleasure that You will lead me out of it for peace. When he wants to leave, he says: May it be Your pleasure, o Eternal, my God and God of my fathers, that You will lead me out from this fortress in peace. When he left, he says: I thank You, o Eternal, my God and God of my fathers, that You made me leave in peace; so may it be Your pleasure that You will lead me to my house for peace (or, to place X for peace.)[217] That means[218], if it is inhabited by Gentiles, but if it is inhabited by Jews, he does not have to recite the benedictions. But if it was a place where they kill, even in a Jewish dwelling he must recite the benediction.

217 There are parallels to these prayers in the Tosephta (6:16) and the Babli (60a). The Tosephta has only three prayers: Before entry, after entry and after exit. It is to be noted that in the version of the Yerushalmi, the prayer after entry really is also a prayer for safe exit and the third prayer repeats the second part of the prayer after safe entry. The printed version of the Babli has four prayers; the prayer after safe entry only gives thanks for that and is not a prospective prayer for safe exit. This would best be described by the words of Ben Azai. The Spanish print in *Śeridei Bavli* (Dimitrovsky) fol. 49 has only two prayers, corresponding to the opinion of the first Tanna in the Mishnah, which is disregarded in the other

versions: "What does he say when he enters? May it be Your pleasure, o Eternal, my God, that you will let me leave this fortress for peace. When he left, he says: I thank You that You guided me out of this fortress for peace, and just as You led me out in peace, so let me travel in peace, lead me in peace, and save me from the hand of any enemy or ambush on the road. Praise to You, Eternal, Who listens to prayer." The doxology that makes this a benediction is found only in the Spanish incunabula print and in *Kolbo* §87; it is expressly denied, in the tradition of the Babli, by Ravad (R. Abraham ben David of Posquières) in his critique of R. Zeraḥiah Halevi in *Alfassi*.

218 This is an editorial note; in the Babli (60a) a slightly different version is attributed to Rav Mattanah. The prayer has to be said only if there is an actual danger in entering the fortress. The difference between Gentile and Jewish populations is not in the Babli; there the problem is the question whether "one judges and kills" in the fortress. In the first version, one does not have to recite the benediction if there are courts that enforce the laws by executing criminals; in the second version one has to recite the prayer anyhow since the police, when confronted with an unsolved crime, might be tempted to frame a stranger who, not knowing any good local lawyer, is in grave danger of being convicted. By contrast, so the interpretation of R. Abraham al-Ashbili, the Yerushalmi recommends the prayer even at a Jewish place if lawless and criminal elements there can kill with impunity.

נִכְנַס לְבֵית הַכִּסֵּא מְבָרֵךְ שְׁתַּיִם אַחַת בִּכְנִיסָתוֹ וְאַחַת בִּיצִיאָתוֹ. בִּכְנִיסָתוֹ מַהוּ אוֹמֵר כָּבוֹד לָכֶם הַמְּכוּבָּדִים מְשָׁרְתֵי קוֹדֶשׁ דֶּרֶךְ אֶרֶץ הוּא פַּנּוּ דֶּרֶךְ בָּרוּךְ אֵל הַכָּבוֹד. כְּשֶׁהוּא יוֹצֵא מַהוּ אוֹמֵר בָּרוּךְ אֲשֶׁר יָצַר אֶת הָאָדָם בְּחָכְמָה.

If one enters the toilet, he recites two benedictions[219], one before and one after. When he enters, what does he say? Honor[220] to you, honored, holy servants, this is the way of the world, let me go. Praise to the God of glory! When he leaves, what does he say? Praise to Him Who created man in wisdom[221].

219 It really means "two prayers."

220 This is not a prayer but an address to the guardian angels who accompany everybody (*Ps.* 91:11) that they should let him go alone to a place unworthy of their presence. In the Babli (60b), Abbai objects to a similar version since it might imply permanent dismissal of the guardian angels.

221 The Babli (60b) has a much enlarged version. It may be that the version of the Yerushalmi is the complete text that was recited originally, but the Rome manuscript has a text similar to the Babylonian one: ברוך אשר יצר את האדם בחכמה ועשיתה אותו נקבים נקבים חלולים חלולים כניניות כניניות שאם יפתח אחד מהן אפשר לו להחיות ברוך רופא כל בשר ומפליא לעשות. "Praised Who created man in wisdom and You made him many orifices, many cavities, many secret places. If one of them were be opened it would be impossible to continue living. Praised Who heals all flesh and does wonders."

The word כניניות appears only here; in the form כונניות it is in Babli *Ḥulin* 56b. For the translation it was derived from Arabic كِنّ "hiding places". [Also compare Latin *cannula* "reed, pipe". Since חלולים can mean "round pipes", חלולים כניניות would be Semitic-Latinate synonyms "pipes-pipes" (E. G.).]

נִכְנַס לְמֶרְחָץ מִתְפַּלֵּל שְׁתַּיִם אַחַת בִּכְנִיסָתוֹ וְאַחַת בִּיצִיאָתוֹ. בִּכְנִיסָתוֹ אוֹמֵר יְהִי רָצוֹן מִלְּפָנֶיךָ יי אֱלֹהַי שֶׁתַּצִּילֵנִי מִשְּׂרֵיפַת הָאֵשׁ וּמֵהֶיזֵּק הַחַמִּין וּמִן הַמַּפּוֹלֶת. וְאַל יֶאֱרַע דָּבָר בְּנַפְשִׁי. וְאִם יֶאֱרַע תְּהֵא מִיתָתִי כַּפָּרָה עַל כָּל־עֲוֹנוֹתַי וְתַצִּילֵנִי מִזּוֹ וּמִכְּיוֹצֵא בוֹ לֶעָתִיד לָבוֹא. כְּשֶׁהוּא יוֹצֵא אוֹמֵר מוֹדֶה אֲנִי לְפָנֶיךָ יי אֱלֹהַי שֶׁהִצַּלְתָּנִי מִן הָאוּר. אָמַר רִבִּי אַבָּהוּ הָדָא אֲמָרָה בְּמֶרְחָץ שֶׁהִיא נִיסּוֹקֶת. אֲבָל בְּמֶרְחָץ שֶׁאֵינוֹ נִיסּוֹקֶת אֵינוֹ אוֹמֵר אֶלָּא מֵהֶיזֵּק חַמִּין בִּלְבַד. רִבִּי חִלְקִיָּה וְרִבִּי סִימוֹן בְּשֵׁם רִבִּי יְהוֹשֻׁעַ בֶּן לֵוִי תְּפִילַּת הַמֶּרְחָץ אֵינָהּ טוֹעֶנֶת עֲמִידָה.

When one enters the thermal bath[222], he prays twice; once on entering and once on leaving. When he enters, he says: "May it be Your pleasure, o Eternal, my God, that You may save me from being burned in fire, damaged by hot water or from collapse. Nothing should happen to me, but if it happens let my death be atonement for all my sins; save me from this and from the similar one[223] in the future world." When he leaves, he says: "I thank You, o Eternal, my God, that You saved me from fire[224]." Rebbi Abbahu said, that is for a thermal bath which is heated. But in a thermal bath that is not[225] heated, he says only "from damage by hot water". Rebbi Ḥilqiah[226] and Rebbi Simon in the name of Rebbi Joshua ben Levi: The prayer at a bathhouse does not require standing[227].

222 A Roman thermal bath had a sauna room whose water was heated in a boiler room below. Sometimes the floor caved in from the continuous exposure to steam and hot water, and the bathers might fall into the open fire below.

223 The fire of hell.

224 There are parallels in the Babli (60a) and Tosephta (6:17); the manuscripts of the Babli have widely diverging texts. The later Amoraïm in the Babli disapproved of the text of the prayer when entering, since one should not mention accidents lest they happen. This attitude is unknown to the Yerushalmi and mishnaic sources.

225 A geothermal bath, as in Tiberias.

226 An Amora of the fourth generation, student of R. Simon, from the region of Lod.

227 It is not clear whether it does not require standing up (i. e., not sitting) or not even standing still (i. e., not walking).

(fol. 12d) **משנה ו:** חַייָב לְבָרֵךְ עַל הָרָעָה כְּשֵׁם שֶׁמְּבָרֵךְ עַל הַטּוֹבָה שֶׁנֶּאֱמַר וְאָהַבְתָּ אֶת יי אֱלֹהֶיךָ בְּכָל־לְבָבְךָ וּבְכָל־נַפְשְׁךָ וּבְכָל־מְאֹדֶךָ. בְּכָל־לְבָבְךָ בִּשְׁנֵי יְצָרֶיךָ בְּיֵצֶר הַטּוֹב וּבְיֵצֶר הָרָע. בְּכָל־נַפְשְׁךָ אֲפִילוּ הוּא נוֹטֵל אֶת נַפְשְׁךָ. בְּכָל־מְאֹדֶךָ בְּכָל־מָמוֹנְךָ. דָּבָר אַחֵר בְּכָל־מְאֹדֶךָ בְּכָל־מִידָּה וּמִידָּה שֶׁהוּא מוֹדֵד לָךְ בַּכֹּל הֱוֵי מוֹדֶה לוֹ מְאֹד מְאֹד.

Mishnah 6: One is required to recite a benediction for bad things the same way[228] it is said for good things, as it is written (*Deut*. 6:5): "You must love the Eternal, your God, with all your heart, all your soul, and all your force." "With all your heart," with your two instincts, the good instinct and the bad instinct. "With all your soul," even if He takes your soul. "With all your force," with all your money. Another explanation: "With all your force," for every measure[229] that He measures for you, for everything thank him very much.

228 The Babli (60b) points out that the Mishnah cannot mean that one has to use the same formula for bad news as for good since the opposite was declared in Mishnah 3. Here one talks only about the spirit in which the benedictions should be recited.

229 This sermon identifies the roots מאד "power, plenty", מדד "measure," ידה, מדה "thanking." It supports the early grammarians who reduced Semitic roots to two letters.

(fol. 14b) **הלכה ו**: רִבִּי בֶּרֶכְיָה בְּשֵׁם רִבִּי לֵוִי עַל שֵׁם וְאַתָּה מָרוֹם לְעוֹלָם יי. לְעוֹלָם יָדְךָ עַל הָעֶלְיוֹנָה. בְּנוֹהַג שֶׁבְּעוֹלָם מֶלֶךְ בָּשָׂר וָדָם יוֹשֵׁב וְדָן כְּשֶׁהוּא נוֹתֵן דִימוּס הַכֹּל מְקַלְּסִין אוֹתוֹ. וּכְשֶׁהוּא נוֹתֵן סְפְקוּלָה הַכֹּל מְרַנְנִין אַחֲרָיו. לָמָּה שֶׁשָּׁטַף בְּדִינוֹ. אֲבָל הַקָּדוֹשׁ בָּרוּךְ הוּא אֵינוֹ כֵן אֶלָּא וְאַתָּה מָרוֹם לְעוֹלָם יי. לְעוֹלָם יָדְךָ עַל הָעֶלְיוֹנָה.

Halakhah 6: Rebbi Berekhia in the name of Rebbi Levi: [230]Because of (*Ps.* 92:5) "You are always exalted, o Eternal!" Your position is always the strongest[231]. Usually in the world, if a king of flesh and blood sits in judgment, if he dismisses[232], everybody acclaims him; if he sentences to execution[233], everybody says bad things about him since he is sweeping in his sentences. But the Holy One, praise to Him, is not so, rather: "You are always exalted, o Eternal!" Your position is always the strongest.

230 One is required to recite a benediction for bad things the same way it is said for good things.

231 This is a term from civil law; the person whose position is strongest is the one who does not have to prove his point, but the adversary has to. An example is a case in which one party bases its position on a written contract; the contract makes his position strongest.

232 Latin *dimissio*, throwing out the

indictment.

233 Latin *spiculum* "thorn, dart, pointed instrument; arrow".

רִבִּי חוּנָא בְשֵׁם רִבִּי אָחָא לְדָוִד מִזְמוֹר חֶסֶד וּמִשְׁפָּט אָשִׁירָה לְךָ יי אֲזַמֵּרָה. אָמַר דָּוִד לִפְנֵי הַקָּדוֹשׁ בָּרוּךְ הוּא. אִם חֶסֶד אַתָּה עוֹשֶׂה עִמִּי אָשִׁירָה. וְאִם מִשְׁפָּט אַתָּה עוֹשֶׂה עִמִּי אָשִׁירָה. בֵּין כָּךְ וּבֵין כָּךְ לַיי אֲזַמֵּרָה.

Rebbi Ḥuna in the name of Rebbi Aḥa[234]: (*Ps.* 101:1) "A song of David. Kindness and justice I shall sing, to You, o Eternal, I shall chant." David said before the Holy One, praise to Him: If You act in kindness towards me, I shall sing. If You act in judgment towards me, I shall sing. In any case, I shall chant.

234 In the printed edition of the Babli (60b), this homily of R. Aḥa is described as having R. Levi as first author. There are many other names given in manuscripts of the Babli.

אָמַר רִבִּי תַּנְחוּמָא בֶּן יְהוּדָה בֵּאלֹהִים אֲהַלֵּל דָּבָר בַּיי אֲהַלֵּל דָּבָר. בֵּין עַל מִדַּת הַדִּין בֵּין עַל מִדַּת רַחֲמִים אֲהַלֵּל דָּבָר.

Rebbi Tanḥuma ben Yehudah[234] said, (*Ps.* 56:11) "In God I will praise words, in the Eternal[235] I will praise words." On measures of judgment as on measures of mercy I shall praise words.

234 He is R. Tanḥum bar Yudan. In the Babli (60b) this homily is attributed to many different authors, all from the school of R. Yoḥanan and his successors.

235 The name "God", majestic plural of *ēl* "power", is always interpreted in the Talmud as "the measure of justice" acting by the immovable laws of the Creation. "Eternal" is traditionally interpreted as designating God the Merciful, Whose mercy is not subject to natural law.

וְרַבָּנָן אָמְרִין כּוֹס יְשׁוּעוֹת אֶשָּׂא וּבְשֵׁם יי אֶקְרָא צָרָה וְיָגוֹן אֶמְצָא וּבְשֵׁם יי אֶקְרָא בֵּין כָּךְ וּבֵין כָּךְ וּבְשֵׁם יי אֶקְרָא. אָמַר רִבִּי יוּדָן בֶּן פְּלָיָה הוּא שֶׁאִיּוֹב אָמַר יי נָתַן וַיי לָקַח יְהִי שֵׁם יי מְבוֹרָךְ כְּשֶׁנָּתַן בְּרַחֲמִים נָתַן. וּכְשֶׁלָּקַח בְּרַחֲמִים לָקַח. וְלֹא עוֹד אֶלָּא כְשֶׁנָּתַן לֹא נִמְלַךְ בִּבְרִיָּיה. וּכְשֶׁלָּקַח נִמְלַךְ בְּבֵית דִּינוֹ. אָמַר רִבִּי אֶלְעָזָר כָּל־מָקוֹם שֶׁנֶּאֱמַר וַיי הוּא וּבֵית דִּינוֹ. בִּנְיַן אָב שֶׁבְּכוּלָּם וַיי דִּבֶּר עָלֶיךָ רָעָה.

But the sages[236] say (*Ps*. 116:13): "I lift the cup of salvation, I call on the Name of the Eternal, trouble and sorrow I will find, but on the Name of the Eternal I shall call." Whatever may happen to me, I shall call on the Name of the Eternal. Rebbi Yudan bar Pelaya[237] said: This is what Job said (*Job* 1:21): "The Eternal gave, and the Eternal took, may the Name of the Eternal be praised!" When He gave, He gave in mercy; when He took, He took in mercy. In addition, when He gave, He did not consult anybody, but when He took, He consulted His Court[238]. Rebbi Eleazar said, everwhere it says "*and* the Eternal" it means Him and His Court. The paradigm[239] of this is (*1K*. 22:23): "And the Eternal spoke woe over you[240]."

236 In the Babli (60b) this is ascribed to R. Tanḥum, the following statement of R. Yudan bar Pelaiah is attributed to "rabbis".

237 A late Amora, student of R. Jonah, whose name is frequently corrupted in Talmud and Midrashim.

238 The proof is in the next sentence. The text is elliptic and one has to add: "As R. Eleazar said" (three generations before R. Yudan; otherwise the homilies are arranged chronologically.) The court is the Heavenly Court of Law.

239 Literally "Father's building." The theory behind this expression is that each word in the Torah has a unique meaning. If the meaning of a term is clear in one verse, "this built a father for all occurrences of this word," one of the hermeneutical rules of R. Ismael for the understanding of the Torah. Its validity is extended to all of the Bible as rule #8 of the 32 rules of

R. Eliezer, son of R. Yose the Galilean.

240 The prophecy of Michaihu starts with his vision of the Eternal surrounded by all the Hosts of Heaven.

עֲשֵׂה מֵאַהֲבָה וַעֲשֵׂה מִיִּרְאָה. עֲשֵׂה מֵאַהֲבָה שֶׁאִם בָּאָת לִשְׂנוֹא דַּע כִּי אַתָּה אוֹהֵב וְאֵין אוֹהֵב שׂוֹנֶה. עֲשֵׂה מִיִּרְאָה שֶׁאִם בָּאָת לִבְעוֹט דַּע שֶׁאַתָּה יָרֵא. וְאֵין יָרֵא מְבָעֵט.

[241]Act from love and act from fear. Act from love, because if you are tempted to hate[242], know that you must love and a lover is no hater. Act from fear, because if you are tempted to rebel, know that you must fear and one who fears does not rebel.

241 This and the next paragraphs are from *Soṭa* 5:5; in the transcription the introductory sentences were lost. There, the question is raised that one verse in Deuteronomy says: "You must love the Eternal, your God," as quoted in our Mishnah, but another verse declares: "The Eternal, your God, you must fear." How does one square these two verses? The answer is that both are required, as explained in the following.

242 The obligations that the Jewish religion puts upon you.

שִׁבְעָה פְרוּשִׁין הֵן פָּרוּשׁ שִׁכְמִי. וּפָרוּשׁ נִקְפִּי. וּפָרוּשׁ קִיזָּאִי פָּרוּשׁ מַה הַנְּכִיָּה. פָּרוּשׁ אֵדַע חוֹבָתִי וְאֶעֱשֶׂנָּה. פָּרוּשׁ יִרְאָה . פָּרוּשׁ אַהֲבָה. פָּרוּשׁ שִׁכְמִי. טְעִין מִצְווֹתָא עַל כֵּיתְפָּא. פָּרוּשׁ נִיקְפִּי. אֲקִיף לִי וַאֲנָא עֲבִיד מִצְוָה. פָּרוּשׁ קִיזָּאִי. עֲבַד חָדָא חוֹבָה וְחָדָא מִצְוָה וּמְקַזֵּז חָדָא בְחָדָא. פָּרוּשׁ מַה הַנְּכִיָּיה. מַאן דְּאִית לִי מְהָנָא מְנַכֵּי עֲבַד מִצְוָה. פָּרוּשׁ אֵדַע חוֹבָתִי וְאֶעֱשֶׂנָּה. הֵי דָא חוֹבְתָה עֲבְדִית דְּאַעֲבִיד מִצְוָה כְּוָותָהּ. פָּרוּשׁ יִרְאָה כְּאִיּוֹב. פָּרוּשׁ אַהֲבָה כְּאַבְרָהָם. אֵין לָךְ חָבִיב מִכּוּלָּם אֶלָּא פָּרוּשׁ אַהֲבָה כְּאַבְרָהָם.

There are seven kinds of religious people[243]: Religious on the shoulder, religious on credit, religious balancing, religious "what is the deduction," religious "I shall do it when I realize my guilt," religious from fear, religious from love. Religious on the shoulder, he carries his deeds[244] on his shoulder. Religious on credit, "give me credit that I can perform commandments.[245]" Religious balancing, he commits one sin and observes one commandment and balances one against the other. Religious "what is the deduction," what I have that is what I am using to deduct for doing a commandment. Religious "I shall do it when I realize my guilt," I committed that sin and therefore I shall do this good deed to counteract it[246]. Religious from fear, like Job. Religious from love, like Abraham. No one is beloved as much as the religious from love, like Abraham.

243 The same list appears in Yerushalmi *Soṭa* 5:5; a slightly different list with completely different interpretations in Babli *Soṭa* 22b declares explicitly that the first five are "destroyers of the world." In the Yerushalmi, it is clear that the first five are considered in a negative light but they are still considered better than one who performs no commandments whatsoever.

פרוש "Pharisee" is the designation of anybody who separates himself from impurity; in particular, one who follows the teachings of the rabbis.

244 Openly, for everybody to see.

245 Every commentator has a different interpretation: One who asks for a loan pretending he needs it for a *mizẉah*, while he only wants the money and has no intention of performing the *mizẉah* (*Qorban haëdah, Eliahu Fulda*); I cannot pay now because I am occupied with a *mizẉah* (*Pne Mosheh*); give me money because I am so holy that I cannot go and earn money (*Z. Frankel*).

246 While this is clearly disapproved of here, it is approved in the Babli and also in Medieval catalogues of "actions of penitence" which, under the influence of Catholic practices, prescribed just such a course of action.

אַבְרָהָם אָבִינוּ עָשָׂה יֵצֶר הָרַע טוֹב דִּכְתִיב וּמָצָאתָ אֶת לְבָבוֹ נֶאֱמָן לְפָנֶיךָ. אָמַר רִבִּי אָחָא וְהִפְשִׁיר[247] אֶלָּא וְכָרוֹת עִמּוֹ הַבְּרִית (והחסד וגומר). אֲבָל דָּוִד לֹא הָיָה יָכוֹל לַעֲמוֹד בּוֹ וְהָרְגוֹ בְּלִבָּבוֹ. מַאי טַעֲמָא וְלִבִּי חָלַל בְּקִרְבִּי.

Our forefather Abraham turned the evil instincts into good ones as it is written (*Neh.* 9:8): "You found his heart trustworthy before You." Rebbi Aḥa said, he compromised, from "concluding a covenant with him[248]." But David could not stand them and killed them in his heart. What is the reason? (*Ps.* 109:22) "But my heart is slain[249] in me."

247 Reading of the text in *Soṭa* and the Rome manuscript here. The Venice print has an unintelligible והפסיד "he lost".

248 Abraham compromised with his evil instincts, taking "him" to refer to the evil instincts residing in the heart, not to Abraham.

249 Taking חלל from the noun חָלָל "corpse" (or from Rabbinic Hebrew "empty space"), not from Biblical חיל "to tremble."

רִבִּי עֲקִיבָה הֲוָה קַייָם מִתְדַּיֵּין קוֹמֵי טוּנְסְרוּפוּס[250] הָרָשָׁע. וַאֲתָה[251] עֲנְתָא דִּקְרִיַּת שְׁמַע. שְׁרֵי קְרֵי קִרְיָה וְגָחֵךְ. אָמַר לֵיהּ סַבָּא אִי חָרָשׁ אַתְּ אִי מְבָעֵט בִּיסוּרִין אַתְּ. אָמַר לֵיהּ תִּיפַּח רוּחֵיהּ דְּהַהוּא גַּבְרָא. לָא חָרָשׁ אֲנָא וְלָא מְבָעֵט בִּיסוּרִין אֲנָא. אֶלָּא כָּל־יוֹמַי קָרִיתִי פָּסוּק זֶה. וְהָיִיתִי מִצְטָעֵר וְאוֹמֵר. אֵימָתַי יָבוֹאוּ שְׁלָשְׁתָּן לְיָדִי. וְאָהַבְתָּ אֵת יי אֱלֹהֶיךָ בְּכָל־לְבָבְךָ וּבְכָל־נַפְשְׁךָ וּבְכָל־מְאֹדֶךָ. רְחַמְתֵּיהּ בְּכָל־לִבִּי. וּרְחַמְתֵּיהּ בְּכָל־מָמוֹנִי. וּבְכָל־נַפְשִׁי לָא הֲוָה בְדִיקָה לִי. וּכְדוֹן דְּמָטַת בְּכָל־נַפְשִׁי וְהִגִּיעָה זְמַן קִרְיַת שְׁמַע וְלָא אַפְלְגָא דַּעְתִּי. לְפוּם כֵּן אֲנָא קְרֵי וְגָחֵיךְ. לֹא הִסְפִּיק לוֹמַר עַד שֶׁפָּרְחָה נִשְׁמָתוֹ.

Rebbi Aqiba was tortured before the evil Tineius Rufus[252]. There came the time for reciting the *Shema'*. He started to read and laughed. He said to him: Old man, you are either a sorcerer or one contemptuous of suffering. He said to him: The spirit of this man should be blown away; I am neither a sorcerer nor contemptuous of sufferings. But all my life I read this verse and said, when will I have occasion for these three (*Deut.* 6:5): "You must love the Eternal, your God, with all your heart, all your soul, and all your force." I loved Him with all my heart. I loved Him with all my money. But whether with all my soul I could not test. But now, when "with all your soul" came, the time of reciting the *Shema'* has arrived and my mind has not wavered, therefore I am reciting and laughing. He had not finished speaking when his soul flew away.

250 Reading of the Rome manuscript. The Venice print has טונוס טרופוס.

251 Reading of the Rome manuscript. The Venice print has רחחת, an otherwise unknown word that cannot be derived from Rabbinic רחת "winnowing shovel."

252 Governor of Palestine under the emperor Hadrian. The form of the name Tinejus is accepted by Mommsen, Renan and Schürer. (Graetz writes Tinnius or Titus Annius.) Babylonian sources give the name as טורנוס רופוס; this can be read as Turianus Rufus, traditionally interpreted as "Tyrant Rufus." According to the Babli (*Nedarim* 50b), Rufus's rich wife had divorced him, converted to Judaism, and married Rebbi Aqiba. A story closely similar to the one given here is told in the Babli (61a).

נְחֶמְיָה עֵימְּסוֹנִי שִׁימֵּשׁ אֶת רִבִּי עֲקִיבָא עֶשְׂרִים שָׁנָה וְלָמְדוֹ אִתִּים וְגַמִּים רִיבּוּיִין. אַכִין וְרַקִּין מִיעוּטִין. אָמַר לֵיהּ מַה הוּא הָהֵן דִּכְתִיב אֶת יי אֱלֹהֶיךָ תִּירָא. אָמַר לֵיהּ אוֹתוֹ וְאֶת תּוֹרָתוֹ.

Neḥemiah from Emmaus[253] served Rebbi Aqiba for 20 years and he taught him "את and גם mean additions, אך and רק mean exclusions[254]." He asked him: What means that which is written (*Deut.* 6:13) "את the Eternal, your God, you must fear." He said to him, Him and His Torah[255].

253 In Babylonian sources, Naḥum from Gimzo (*Shevuöt* 26a) or Neḥemiah from Emmaus (*Pesaḥim* 22b) was the teacher of Rebbi Aqiva; Naḥum is also quoted as teacher in Yerushalmi sources (*Bereshit rabba* 22, 53) but in a very critical sense. Hence, it seems that Naḥum was the developer of a rudimentary method of explaining the Torah by looking at expressions that mean inclusions or exclusions, that the method was made satisfactory only by R. Aqiba, and that Neḥemia was R. Aqiba's student. (The tradition of the

name in *Pesaḥim* 22b is doubtful.)

The method of inclusions and exclusions is much more general than the limited use made here in identifying particles which have extending or limiting character; its use is always called "the method of R. Aqiba", in contrast to the "method of R. Ismael", which is based on generalities and specifications.

254 The particles denoting exclusion are רַק "only", אַךְ "but only". Those denoting inclusion are גַּם "also", and אֶת, which either is the particle of the accusative or means "and". In R. Aqiba's theory, all accusative particles also have the meaning of "and." This is not original with him; in the Greek translation of Aquila, a student of Rebbis Eliezer and Joshua, every את is translated as καί "and", whether it makes sense or not. In the verse in question, it is the accusative participle used as "and" that seems to result in a meaning unacceptable to pure monotheism.

255 This is the reason that R. Aqiba was willing to be tortured to death because he could not obey Hadrian's decree that forbade the teaching of Torah. The interpretation given in Babli *Pesaḥim* 22b, "Him and the Torah Sages", is weak and inappropriate when compared with the statement here.

(fol. 12d) **משנה ז**: לֹא יָקֵל אָדָם אֶת רֹאשׁוֹ כְּנֶגֶד שַׁעַר הַמִּזְרָח שֶׁהוּא מְכוּוָּן כְּנֶגֶד בֵּית קָדְשֵׁי הַקֳּדָשִׁים. וְלֹא יִכָּנֵס לְהַר הַבַּיִת בְּמַקְלוֹ וּבְמִנְעָלוֹ וּבַאֲפוּנְדָּתוֹ וּבְאָבָק שֶׁעַל רַגְלָיו. וְלֹא יַעֲשֶׂנּוּ קַפַּנְדְּרִיָּה. וּרְקִיקָה מִקַּל וָחוֹמֶר. כָּל־חוֹתְמֵי הַבְּרָכוֹת שֶׁהָיוּ בַּמִּקְדָּשׁ הָיוּ מִן הָעוֹלָם. וּמִשֶּׁקִּלְקְלוּ הַמִּינִין וְאָמְרוּ אֵין עוֹלָם אֶלָּא אֶחָד. הִתְקִינוּ שֶׁיְּהוּ אוֹמְרִים מִן הָעוֹלָם וְעַד הָעוֹלָם. וְהִתְקִינוּ שֶׁיְּהֵא אָדָם שׁוֹאֵל אֶת שְׁלוֹם חֲבֵרוֹ בַּשֵּׁם שֶׁנֶּאֱמַר וְהִנֵּה בוֹעַז בָּא מִבֵּית לֶחֶם. וַיֹּאמֶר לַקּוֹצְרִים יי׳ עִמָּכֶם. וְאוֹמֵר אַל תָּבוּז כִּי זָקְנָה אִמֶּךָ. עֵת לַעֲשׂוֹת לַיי׳. לַיי׳ הֵפֵרוּ תוֹרָתֶךָ. רִבִּי נָתָן אוֹמֵר הֵפֵרוּ תוֹרָתֶךָ עֵת לַעֲשׂוֹת לַיי׳.

Mishnah 7: A person should not behave improperly before the Eastern gate, which lies in a straight line with the Holiest of Holies[256]. And one should not enter the Temple Mount with his walking stick, sandals[257], money belt[258], or dust on his feet[259]. Also one should not use it as a short cut[260], and certainly not spit there. All endings of benedictions in the Temple were "from eternity[261]." When heretics did err and said that there was only one world, they ordained that one should say "from eternity to eternity." They also instituted that one should greet his friend by the Name, as it was said (*Ruth* 2:4): "Lo, Boaz came from Bethlehem and said to the harvesters: The Eternal be with you!" And it says (*Pr.* 23:22): "Be not contemptuous because your mother got old.[262]" (*Ps.* 119:126) "It is time to work for the Eternal; they violated Your Torah." Rebbi Nathan says, they[263] violated Your Torah, it is time to work for the Eternal.

256 The Eastern gate in the wall of the Temple Mount (which at the same time was the city wall) was in a straight line with the Eastern gate of the Temple courtyard, the Temple gate, and the Holiest of Holies, because the priest who was burning the red heifer on the Mount of Olives had to see the Temple door through the gate of the wall and the gate of the Temple court. One must assume that in Mishnaic times, the Temple itself was totally obliterated (since, after the war of Bar Kochba, Hadrian had constructed a temple of Jupiter on its site) but that the original Eastern gate was still there and the place of the Temple could be determined on a line perpendicular to the wall at that gate.

257 All service by priests in the Temple had to be performed barefoot. Hence, also laymen entering the Temple precinct had to be barefoot. [To show the difference between the Temple and a synagogue, shoes may not be removed in a synagogue.]

258 Latin *funda*.

259 One may not enter with unwashed feet.

260 Latin *compendiaria* (*via*), cf. Chapter 1, Note 36.

261 Instead of "Amen", the answer to a benediction was "Praised be the Eternal, the God of Israel, from eternity". This is the answer asserted to be given during the existence of the first Temple. When the second Temple was inaugurated, the formula was (*Neh.* 9:5): "Praised be the Eternal, the God of Israel, from eternity to eternity," to emphasize the two worlds, the existing one and the one to come. The heretics

here cannot be Sadducees who started about three hundred years later; the Qumran documents show that it is totally false to impute a denial of the future world to Sadducees. [That "heretics" are called "Sadducees" in many editions of the Babli here is due to Christian censors who misunderstood the use of the word מין which in general, but not here, means "Christians."]

262 Rashi in the Babli explains: Even though the action of Boaz looks wrong, since God's name is used for wordly greeting, one should follow him since he is one of the elders of the people. In the verse, the harvesters answered: "May the Eternal bless you," following Boas's example.

263 The men of the Great Assembly, who instituted the response to the benedictions in the Temple and the way of greeting in the Name of God, violated the prescription of the Torah that God's name may not be taken in vain (i. e., for secular purposes) in order to further God's work and to instill religious feelings in the people.

(fol. 14b) **הלכה ז**: תַּנֵּי הַמַּטִּיל מַיִם הֲרֵי זֶה הוֹפֵךְ פָּנָיו כְּלַפֵּי צָפוֹן. הַמֵּיסֵךְ אֶת רַגְלָיו הֲרֵי זֶה הוֹפֵךְ פָּנָיו כְּלַפֵּי דָּרוֹם. אָמַר רִבִּי יוֹסֵי בֵּי רִבִּי בוּן הָדָא דַאֲמַר מַתְנִיתָא מִן הַצּוֹפִים וְלִפְנִים. רִבִּי עֲקִיבָה אוֹמֵר בְּכָל־מָקוֹם. וּבִלְבַד מָקוֹם שֶׁאֵין שָׁם כּוֹתֶל. תַּנֵּי הַמֵּיסֵךְ אֶת רַגְלָיו לֹא יִתֵּן פָּנָיו לְמִזְרָח וַאֲחוֹרָיו לְמַעֲרָב אֶלָּא לִצְדָדִין. רִבִּי יְהוּדָה אוֹמֵר בְּשְׁעַת הַמִּקְדָּשׁ. רִבִּי יוֹסֵי אוֹמֵר מִן הַצּוֹפִים וְלִפְנִים. רִבִּי עֲקִיבָה אוֹמֵר בְּכָל־מָקוֹם. וּבִלְבַד בְּמָקוֹם שֶׁאֵין שָׁם כּוֹתֶל.

Halakha 7: It was stated: He who urinates turns his face towards North[264]. He who spreads his feet[265] turns his face towards South. Rebbi Yose bar Abun[266] said, this *baraita* is from Mount Scopus towards the interior. Rebbi Aqiba says, everywhere[267] but only where there is no wall[268]. If was stated: He who spreads his feet should not face East with his back facing West but at an angle[269]. Rebbi Yehudah says, when the Temple exists. Rebbi Yose said, from Mount Scopus towards the interior. Rebbi Aqiba says, everywhere but only where there is no wall.

264 In post-Hadrianic Jerusalem, situated North of the Temple Mount. He will face a direction pointing away from the Temple.

265 To defecate; then his face is towards the Temple and his back away from it.

266 Both R. Eleazar Askari and R. Zacharias Frankel prefer to cross out the words "bar Abun said, this *baraita* deals with" since in the next formulation, and in the parallel to that in the Babli (61b), R. Yose the Tanna is quoted that these rules hold only if one can see Jerusalem. But one should hesitate to follow them since in the comment of the Babli (61b) on the prohibitions of the Mishnah, the statement attributed here to the fifth generation R. Yose bar Abun is there credited to the fourth generation R. Abba, son of R. Ḥiyya bar Abba, in the name of R. Yoḥanan; it is clearly Amoraic. But R. Abba adds that all the rules apply only when the Temple exists (following R. Yehudah in the next *baraita)*, and this is emphatically negated by the Yerushalmi.

267 Even outside of the Land of Israel, in the interpretation of the Babli. The Babli also takes the rules of the *baraita* quite strictly, E-W and N-S, not the direction towards Jerusalem. They seem to suggest that everybody has to feel himself to be in Jerusalem everywhere in the world. It is impossible to say what the opinion of the Yerushalmi would be in this question.

268 Separating between him and the forbidden direction.

269 Here in the Yerushalmi, צדדין denotes a position that is not in one of the four cardinal directions. In the parallel in the Babli, the same word means a place that is not N, E, S, W from Jerusalem!

(fol. 14c) אָמַר רִבִּי עֲקִיבָה נִכְנַסְתִּי אַחֲרֵי רִבִּי יְהוֹשֻׁעַ לִרְאוֹת הַמַּעֲשֶׂה. אָֽמְרוּ לוֹ מַה רָאִיתָה. אָמַר לְהוֹן רְאִיתִיו יוֹשֵׁב וְצִידוֹ כְּלַפֵּי מַעֲרָב וְלֹא פָּרַע עַד שֶׁיָּשַׁב. וְלֹא יָשַׁב עַד שֶׁשִּׁפְשֵׁף. וְלֹא קִינֵּחַ בְּיָמִין אֶלָּא בִשְׂמֹאל. אַף שִׁמְעוֹן בֶּן עַזַּאי הָיָה אוֹמֵר כֵּן. נִכְנַסְתִּי אַחֲרֵי רִבִּי עֲקִיבָה לִרְאוֹת הַמַּעֲשֶׂה. אָֽמְרוּ לוֹ מַה רָאִיתָה וכו'.

Rebbi Aqiba said, I entered once after Rebbi Joshua to see the action[270]. They asked him, what did you see? He said to them, I saw him sitting and his side was towards the West[271]; he did not undress until he was sitting, he did not sit down before he rubbed[272], and he did not cleanse himself with his right hand but with his left hand[273]. Simeon ben Azai also said so: I entered once after Rebbi Aqiba to see the action. They asked him, what did you see? Etc.

270 How he behaves in the bathroom.

271 At Jabneh, East of Jerusalem, he was facing either North or South.

272 He cleaned the place before he sat down. There is an alternative explanation given in the Babli (62a, bottom) that is impossible here.

273 The Babli and the Yerushalmi source *Derekh Ereẓ* 7 explain that R. Eliezer says, because one eats with his right hand; R. Joshua says, because one writes (words of Torah) with the right hand; R. Aqiba says, because one uses the right hand to show the musical signs when reciting the Torah.

תַּנֵּי לֹא יִכָּנֵס אָדָם בְּהַר הַבַּיִת בְּמִנְעָלוֹ וּבְאָבָק שֶׁעַל רַגְלָיו וּמָעוֹתָיו צְרוּרִין בְּסַדִּינוֹ וַאֲפוּנְדָּתוֹ עָלָיו מִבְּחוּץ. מַה טַעַם שְׁמוֹר רַגְלְךָ כַּאֲשֶׁר תֵּלֵךְ אֶל בֵּית הָאֱלֹהִים. רִבִּי יוֹסֵי בַּר יְהוּדָה אוֹמֵר וַיָּבֹא עַד לִפְנֵי שַׁעַר הַמֶּלֶךְ כִּי אֵין לָבֹא אֶל שַׁעַר הַמֶּלֶךְ בִּלְבוּשׁ שָׂק. אָמַר לִפְנֵי לֵיחָה סְרוּחָה כֵּן. עַל אַחַת כַּמָּה וְכַמָּה לִפְנֵי שַׁעַר הַמָּקוֹם.

It was stated[274]: Nobody should enter the Temple Mount in shoes, with dust on his feet, or his coins tied up in his head-scarf, or his money belt on him outside. What is the reason? (*Eccl.* 4:17) "Watch your feet when you go to God's house." Rebbi Yose ben Yehudah says (*Esth.* 4:2): "He came as far as the king's gate because nobody may enter the king's gate in sackcloth." He said, if it is so for a foul smelling drop[275], so much more for the gate of the Omnipresent!

274 Tosephta *Berakhot* 6:19.

275 The semen from which the king was conceived.

לֹא יַעֲשֶׂנּוּ קַפֶּנְדְּרִיָּה. וּרְקִיקָה מִקַּל וָחוֹמֶר. מַה אִם נְעִילָה שֶׁהִיא שֶׁל כָּבוֹד אַתְּ אוֹמֵר אָסוּר. רְקִיקָה שֶׁהִיא שֶׁל בִּזָּיוֹן לֹא כָּל־שֶׁכֵּן.

"[276]One should not use it as a short cut, and certainly one should not spit there[277]." If you say that wearing shoes, which is a respectful way, is forbidden, spitting, which is disrespectful, so much more.

276 Except for the quote from the Mishnah, this is the continuation of the previous Tosephta.

277 This is quoted here to explain the expression "certainly", or "so much more".

תַּנֵּי לֹא הָיוּ עוֹנִין אָמֵן בַּמִּקְדָּשׁ. מַה הָיוּ אוֹמְרִים בָּרוּךְ שֵׁם כְּבוֹד מַלְכוּתוֹ לְעוֹלָם וָעֶד. מְנַיִן שֶׁלֹּא הָיוּ עוֹנִין אָמֵן בַּמִּקְדָּשׁ תַּלְמוּד לוֹמַר קוּמוּ בָּרְכוּ אֶת יי וְגוֹמֵר. מְנַיִן עַל כָּל בְּרָכָה וּבְרָכָה תַּלְמוּד לוֹמַר וּמְרוֹמָם עַל כָּל־בְּרָכָה וּתְהִילָּה.

If was stated: One did not say "Amen" in the Temple. What did they say[278]? "Praised be His glorious name forever and ever." From where[279] that one did not say "Amen" in the Temple? The verse says (*Neh.* 9:5): "Rise up and praise the Eternal, etc." From where that this is for every single benediction, the verse says: "And Elevated for every benediction and praise.[280]"

278 In the second Temple.

279 A formulaic word meaning: "From which verse do we know that such and such is true?"

280 The full verse is: Rise up and praise the Eternal, your God, *from eternity to eternity* they shall praise Your glorious name and Elevated *for every benediction* and praise. The Tosephta (6:22), quoted Babli 63a, explains that this means: For every single benediction and every single praise.

אָמַר רִבִּי יְהוֹשֻׁעַ דְּרוֹמַיָּא שְׁלֹשָׁה דְּבָרִים גָּזְרוּ בֵית דִּין שֶׁלְּמַטָּן וְהִסְכִּימוּ בֵית דִּין שֶׁלְּמַעְלָן עִמָּהֶן. וְאֵילּוּ הֵן חֶרְמָהּ שֶׁל יְרִיחוֹ. וּמְגִילַּת אֶסְתֵּר. וּשְׁאֵילַת שָׁלוֹם בַּשֵּׁם. חֶרְמָהּ שֶׁל יְרִיחוֹ. חָטָא יִשְׂרָאֵל. וְלֹא יְהוֹשֻׁעַ גָּזַר. אֶלָּא מְלַמֵּד שֶׁהִסְכִּימוּ

בֵּית דִּין שֶׁלְּמַעֲלָן עִמָּהֶן. מְגִילַּת אֶסְתֵּר. קִיְּמוּ וְקִיבְּלוּ וְגוֹמֵר. רַב אָמַר וְקִבֵּל כְּתִיב מְלַמֵּד שֶׁהִסְכִּימוּ. וּשְׁאֵילַת שָׁלוֹם בְּשֵׁם. וְהִנֵּה בוֹעַז בָּא מִבֵּית לֶחֶם. וּמְנַיִן שֶׁהִסְכִּימוּ בֵּית דִּין שֶׁלְּמַעֲלָן עִמָּהֶן. תַּלְמוּד לוֹמַר וַיֹּאמֶר אֵלָיו יי עִמְּךָ גִּבּוֹר הַחַיִל. רִבִּי אָבוּן בְּשֵׁם רִבִּי יְהוֹשֻׁעַ בֶּן לֵוִי אַף הַמַּעְשְׂרוֹת שֶׁנֶּאֱמַר הָבִיאוּ אֶת כָּל הַמַּעֲשֵׂר וגו׳. מַהוּ עַד בְּלִי דַּיי. רִבִּי יוֹסֵי בַּר שִׁמְעוֹן בַּר בָּא בְּשֵׁם רִבִּי יוֹחָנָן דָּבָר שֶׁאִי אֶפְשַׁר לוֹ לוֹמַר דַּיי הוּא בְּרָכָה. רִבִּי בֶּרֶכְיָה וְרִבִּי חֶלְבּוֹ וְרַב אַבָּא בַּר עִילָּאִי בְּשֵׁם רַב עַד שֶׁיִּבְלוּ שִׂפְתוֹתֵיכֶם מִלּוֹמַר דַּיֵּינוּ בְּרָכוֹת דַּיֵּינוּ בְּרָכוֹת.

Rebbi Joshua the Southerner[281] said: Three things did the earthly court decree and the Heavenly Court agreed with them, and they are the following: The ban on Jericho, the Esther scroll, and greeting people using the Name. The ban on Jericho (*Jos.* 7:11): "Israel sinned[282]." But was not Joshua the one who decreed it? This certainly implies that the Heavenly Court agreed with them. The Esther scroll (*Esth.* 9:27): "They confirmed and accepted, etc." Rav said, "accepted" is written in singular[283]; this implies that they[284] accepted. Greeting people using the Name (*Ruth* 2:4): "Lo, Boaz came from Bethlehem." And from where that the Heavenly court agreed with them? The verse says (*Jud.* 6:12): "The Eternal is with you, o hero![285]" Rebbi Abun in the name of Rebbi Joshua ben Levi: Also tithes, as it is said (*Mal.* 3:10): "Bring all tithes[286], etc." What is: "[287]Until 'without enough?'" Rebbi Yose bar[288] Simeon bar Abba in the name of Rebbi Yoḥanan: The thing about which it is impossible to say "enough", that is blessing. Rebbi Berekhiah and Rebbi Ḥelbo and Rebbi Abba bar Ilaï in the name of Rav: Until your lips will wear out[290] saying, we have enough blessings, we have enough blessings.

281 Rebbi Joshua ben Levi.

282 Joshua decreed a ban on all property of the city of Jericho as *ḥērem* for the Eternal. After Akhan had taken property for himself, Israel was defeated at the Ai and Joshua was informed that "Israel sinned," i. e., a transgression of his command was

equated with a transgression of a divine command. Hence, Heaven accepted his human decree in the Heavenly Court. [While everybody can declare his own possession *ḥērem* or *qorbān* whereby its use is forbidden by a divine command (*Lev.* 27), Joshua here forbade the use of things that did not belong to him and, under usual circumstances, his decree would be invalid in a court of law.]

283 It is written קבל and read קִבְּלוֹ.

284 In fact, He (God) accepted it.

285 This is the greeting of the angel to Gideon, telling him to fight the Midianites. This shows that heavenly beings adapted the human manner of greeting as exemplified by Boaz. The argument implies that Gideon, who was quite early in the time of Judges, came after Boaz. This is explicit in *Midrash Seder Olam* Chap. 12 (in the author's edition and commentary, Northvale N.J. 1998, p. 121-123.) Boaz was the grandson of Naḥshon ben Aminadav, prince of Judah during the wanderings in the desert (*Ruth* 4:20-21.)

286 The problem alluded to here is discussed in Yerushalmi *Shevi'it* 6:1, *Qiddushin* 1:9 and Babli *Arakhin* 32b, referring to the obligations of the farmer regarding the produce of the Holy Land. It is spelled out in the Torah many times that these obligations (the heave for the priests, tithes for the Levites and the poor, the Sabbatical Year, etc.) come into force "when you come to the Land and inherit it," as duties on the land distributed as family heritage to the tribes by Moses and Joshua. These commandments became obsolete when the tribes were led into captivity, including the obligations of the remaining Israelite population of Galilee who, according to our sources, were never exiled and who reappear in history at the time of the Hasmonean revolt without any record of resettlement in Galilee. The continued obligation to observe the Laws that depend on the Land therefore is derived only from the voluntary covenant enacted by the people in the time of Ezra and Nehemia (*Shevi'it* 6:1): "Rebbi Lezer says: they voluntarily accepted the duties of the tithes. Why do I say this? (*Neh.* 10:1) 'With all this, we enact a written trust and covenant signed by our princes, Levites, and priests.' How does R. Lezer explain the inclusion (*Neh.* 10:37) of 'the firstborn of our cattle and flocks' [an obligation that does not depend on the Land and therefore is universal]? Since they accepted the obligations (of heave and tithes) that they could have avoided, Scripture gives them credit for those

obligations which they had to fulfill anyhow as if they had accepted these also voluntarily." The same idea is also expressed by an opponent of rabbinic Judaism who is reported (*Shevi'it* 9:9) to have said: "*Ḥallah* (the heave to be taken from bread dough) is a biblical obligation (*Num.* 15:20) but the Sabbatical year is now an obligation only by the authority of Rabban Gamliel and his colleagues." [Cf. the author's *The Scholar's Haggadah*, p. 280-281, and *Seder Olam* p. 248-250.]

287 *Mal.* 3:10: "Bring the full tithe into the (Temple) storehouse, so that there may be food in My House, test Me in this," said the Eternal of Hosts, "if I will not open for you the skylights of heaven, and I shall pour out for you blessing until 'without enough.'" The obligation accepted by the people on Earth without Heavenly Command gives Divine Reward. Hence, the obligation was accepted as Divine Command of human origin.

288 The Rome manuscript does not have the words "Yose bar". A son of R. Simeon bar Abba is otherwise unknown but the attribution is possible. R. Shelomo Cirillo has the reading "R. Yose in the name of R. Simeon bar Abba."

289 Identifying the negation בלי with the root בלה "to wear out."

אַל תָּבוּז כִּי זָֽקְנָה אִמֶּךָ. אָמַר רִבִּי יוֹסֵי בַּר בּוּן אִם נִתְיַישְּׁנוּ דִּבְרֵי תוֹרָה בְּפִיךָ אַל תִּבְזֶה עֲלֵיהֶן. מַה טַעֲמָא וְאַל תָּבוּז כִּי זָֽקְנָה אִמֶּךָ. אָמַר רִבִּי זְעִירָא אִם נִזְדַּקְנָה אוּמָּתְךָ עֲמוֹד וְגוֹדְרָהּ כְּשֵׁם שֶׁעָשָׂה אֶלְקָנָה שֶׁהָיָה מַדְרִיךְ אֶת יִשְׂרָאֵל לְפַעֲמֵי רְגָלִים. הָהוּא דִכְתִיב וְעָלָה הָאִישׁ הַהוּא מֵעִירוֹ וְגוֹמֵר.

(*Pr.* 23:22): "Be not contemptuous because your mother got old." Rebbi Yose bar Abun said, if words of Torah become old in your mouth, do not become contemptuous about them. What is the reason? "Be not contemptuous because your mother got old." Rebbi Zeïra said, when your people got old, get up and repair it the way Elkanah did who instructed Israel in the pilgrimage for holidays. That is what is written: (*1Sam.* 1:2) "This man went up from his town[290], etc."

290 This is explained in detail in *Midrash Samuel* 1:1 (which contains an enlarged version of the Yerushalmi here to the end of the tractate) that

Elkanah went to Siloh four times a year, three times for the three holidays of pilgrimage and once for his private vow as explained in *1Sam.* 1:2, and that every year he chose a different road to tell people to go to Shiloh for the holidays. A similar version is in *Tanna dbe Eliahu* I:8.

עֵת לַעֲשׂוֹת לַיי הֵפֵרוּ תוֹרָתֶךָ. רִבִּי נָתָן מְסָרֵס (fol. 14d) קְרָאֵי הֵפֵרוּ תוֹרָתֶךָ עֵת לַעֲשׂוֹת לַיי. רִבִּי חִלְקִיָּה בְשֵׁם רִבִּי סִימוֹן הָעוֹשֶׂה תוֹרָתוֹ עִתִּים הֲרֵי זֶה מֵיפֵר בְּרִית. מַה טַעֲמָא הֵפֵרוּ תוֹרָתֶךָ עֵת לַעֲשׂוֹת לַיי. תַּנֵּי רִבִּי שִׁמְעוֹן בֶּן יוֹחָי אוֹמֵר אִם רָאִיתָ אֶת הַבְּרִיוֹת שֶׁנִּתְיַיאֲשׁוּ יְדֵיהֶן מִן הַתּוֹרָה עֲמוֹד וְהִתְחַזֵּק בָּהּ וְאַתָּה מְקַבֵּל שְׂכַר כּוּלָּם. מַה טַעֲמָא הֵפֵרוּ תוֹרָתֶךָ עֵת לַעֲשׂוֹת לַיי.

(*Ps.* 119:126) "It is time to work for the Eternal, they violated Your Torah." Rebbi Nathan inverts the verse: "They violated Your Torah, it is time to work for the Eternal." Rebbi Ḥilqiah in the name of Rebbi Simon: He who restricts his Torah to fixed times breaches the covenant. What is the reason? "They violated Your Torah, it is time to work for the Eternal." It was stated: Rebbi Simeon ben Yoḥai says: If you see that people have given up on Torah, get up and strengthen yourself in it and you will receive the reward of all of them. What is the reason? "They violated Your Torah, it is time to work for the Eternal!"

הִלֵּל הַזָּקֵן הָיָה אוֹמֵר בְּשָׁעָה דִּמְכַנְּשִׁין בְּדַר. וּבְשָׁעָה דִּמְבַדְּרִין כְּנוֹשׁ. וְכֵן הָיָה הִלֵּל אוֹמֵר אִם רָאִיתָ אֶת הַתּוֹרָה שֶׁהִיא חֲבִיבָה עַל יִשְׂרָאֵל וְהַכֹּל שְׂמֵחִין בָּהּ בְּדַר. וְאִם לָאו כְּנוֹשׁ. אָמַר רִבִּי אֶלְעָזָר מַה הַתִּינּוֹק הַזֶּה צָרִיךְ לֵינֵק בְּכָל־שָׁעָה שֶׁבְּיוֹם. כֵּן כָּל־אָדָם שֶׁבְּיִשְׂרָאֵל צָרִיךְ לְיַגֵּעַ בַּתּוֹרָה בְּכָל־שָׁעוֹת שֶׁבְּיוֹם. רִבִּי יוֹנָה בְשֵׁם רִבִּי יוֹסֵי בֶּן גְּזֵירָה כָּל־פִּיטְטָיָא בִּישִׁין וּפִיטְטָיָא דְּאוֹרַיְתָא טָבִין. כָּל־כְּדָבַיָּא טָבִין וּכְדָבַיָּא דְּאוֹרַיְתָא בִּישִׁין.

Hillel the elder[291] used to say: When they collect, spread[292]. And when they spread, collect. So Hillel used to say, if you see that the Torah is beloved by Israel and everybody enjoys it, spread. And if not, collect.

Rebbi Eleazar said, just as the baby needs to suckle at all times of the day, so every Jew needs to exert himself in Torah all all times of the day. Rebbi Jonah in the name of Rebbi Yose ben Gezirah[293], all small talk is bad but small talk of Torah is good. All lies are good and the lies of Torah are bad[294].

291 This is Hillel, contemporary of Shammai and ancestor of the house of the Patriarchs. The same sayings appear in Hebrew in Babli 63a and Tosephta 6:24.

292 If people teach the select few, you should teach only large masses, and vice-versa.

293 An otherwise unknown Amora, but he might be identical with R. Yose Quẓira, son-in-law of R. Yose ben Yose, of the fourth/fifth generation of Amoraim in Galilee. [A similar statement appears in Babli *Ḥulin* 89a in the name of the earlier Galilean R. Isaac.]

294 This sentence is unintelligible. In the quotes of the sentence in works of medieval authors, one finds many different versions. In the commentary of Rabbenu Jonah to *Pirqe Avot*, the reading is Aramaic כרבייא "plowings" instead of כדבייא "lies." This has support in the introduction of R. Zeraḥiah Halevi to his *Maör haqaṭan*, who reads Hebrew חרשיא "plowings." Since the roots חרש (Arabic חרת) "to plow" and חרש (Arabic ח̇רש) "to be silent" are identical in Hebrew, both authors give the interpretation" silence" also to the Aramaic equivalent ברב. The author of *'En Yaaqob* reads ברכייא, "blessings." All these authors read first "bad" then "good" as in the preceding sentence; Rabbenu Jonah even quotes the sentence about silence as alternative reading for "small talk." Many commentators write here that the sentence should be: All lies are bad and the lies of Torah are good, referring to lies such as Eliezer's when he met Rebecca, first gave her gold rings and then inquired after her family but in his recital to them pretended to first having asked about her family and only afterwards given her the heavy gold jewelry, to keep within accepted norms of behavior.

אָמַר רִבִּי שִׁמְעוֹן בֶּן לָקִישׁ בִּמְגִילַּת חֲסִידִים מָצְאוּ כָתוּב יוֹם תַּעַזְבֵנִי יוֹמַיִם אֶעֶזְבֶךָּ. לִשְׁנַיִם שֶׁיָּצְאוּ אֶחָד מִטִּיבֵּרְיָא וְאֶחָד מִצִּיפּוֹרִין וּפָגְעוּ זֶה בָזֶה בְּהָדָא

מִשְׁכְּנָא. לֹא הִסְפִּיקוּ לִפְרוֹשׁ זֶה מִזֶּה עַד שֶׁהָלַךְ זֶה מִיל וְזֶה מִיל נִמְצְאוּ רְחוֹקִין זֶה מִזֶּה שְׁנֵי מִילִין. וְאִשָּׁה שֶׁהָיְתָה יוֹשֶׁבֶת וּמַמְתֶּנֶת לְאִישׁ. כָּל זְמַן שֶׁהָיְתָה בְּדַעְתּוֹ לְהִנָּשֵׂא לָהּ הָיְתָה יוֹשֶׁבֶת וּמַמְתֶּנֶת לוֹ. כֵּיוָן שֶׁהִפְלִיג דַּעְתּוֹ מִמֶּנָּהּ הִיא הָיְתָה הוֹלֶכֶת וְנִישֵּׂאת לְאַחֵר.

Rebbi Simeon ben Laqish said: In a scroll of the pious[295] they found written: If you abandon me[296] for one day, I shall abandon you for two days. An example of two people who went, one from Tiberias and one from Sepphoris, and met at a certain shelter. As soon as they parted and each one went one *mil*, they were separated two *mil*. Or a woman who sat and waited for a man. All the time that he intended to marry her, she sat and waited for him. When he put her out of his mind, she went and married another.

295 This kind of literature has not been identified. It might be similar to some of the Sadducee Qumran scrolls.

296 The Torah.

תַּנֵּי בְשֵׁם רִבִּי מֵאִיר אֵין לְךָ אֶחָד מִיִּשְׂרָאֵל שֶׁאֵינוֹ עוֹשֶׂה מֵאָה מִצְוֹת בְּכָל־יוֹם. קוֹרֵא אֶת שְׁמַע וּמְבָרֵךְ לְפָנֶיהָ וּלְאַחֲרֶיהָ וְאוֹכֵל אֶת פִּתּוֹ וּמְבָרֵךְ לְפָנֶיהָ וּלְאַחֲרֶיהָ וּמִתְפַּלֵּל שְׁלֹשָׁה פְּעָמִים שֶׁל שְׁמוֹנֶה עֶשְׂרֵה וְחוֹזֵר וְעוֹשֶׂה שְׁאָר מִצְוֹת וּמְבָרֵךְ עֲלֵיהֶן. וְכֵן הָיָה רִבִּי מֵאִיר אוֹמֵר אֵין לְךָ אָדָם מִיִּשְׂרָאֵל שֶׁאֵין הַמִּצְוֹת מַקִּיפוֹת אוֹתוֹ תְּפִילִּין בְּרֹאשׁוֹ וּתְפִילִּין בִּזְרוֹעוֹ וּמְזוּזָה בְּפִתְחוֹ מִילָה בִּבְשָׂרוֹ וְאַרְבַּע צִיצִיּוֹת בְּטַלִּיתוֹ מַקִּיפִין אוֹתוֹ. הוּא שֶׁדָּוִד אָמַר שֶׁבַע בַּיּוֹם הִלַּלְתִּיךָ עַל מִשְׁפְּטֵי צִדְקֶךָ. וְכֵן הוּא אוֹמֵר חוֹנֶה מַלְאַךְ יי סָבִיב לִירֵאָיו וַיְחַלְּצֵם. נִכְנַס לְמֶרְחָץ רָאָה אֶת עַצְמוֹ עָרוֹם. אָמַר אוֹי לִי שֶׁאֲנִי עָרוֹם מִן הַמִּצְוֹת. כֵּיוָן שֶׁהִבִּיט בְּמִילָה שֶׁלּוֹ. הִתְחִיל מְקַלֵּס לְהַקָּדוֹשׁ בָּרוּךְ הוּא לַמְנַצֵּחַ עַל הַשְּׁמִינִית מִזְמוֹר לְדָוִד.

It was stated[297] in the name of Rebbi Meïr: There is no one in Israel who does not perform 100 commandments every day. He recites the *Shema'* and benedictions before and after, eats his bread and recites benedictions before and after, prays 18 benedictions three times and then he performs other commandments and recites benedictions after them. Similarly, Rebbi Meïr used to say: There is no man in Israel who is not surrounded by commandments: *Tefillin* on his head, *tefillin* on his arm, a *mezuzah* on his door, circumcision in his flesh, and the four *ẓiẓiot* of his *tallit* surround him. That is what David said (*Ps*. 119:164): I praised You sevenfold every day for Your just laws[298]. And so it says (*Ps*. 34:8): The angel of the Eternal camps around those that fear Him and rescues them[299]. When he[300] entered the bath house, he saw himself naked. He said, woe to me that I am stripped of commandmends. When he looked at his circumcision, he started to acclaim the Holy One, praise to Him (*Ps*. 12:1): For the director, on the eighth[301], a song from David.

297 Tosephta Menaḥot 6:24-25, a parallel to the entire paragraph in slightly different language. A parallel in the Babli (*Menaḥot* 43b) has the formulation that "every man in Israel is obliged to recite 100 benedictions every day." In the Yerushalmi and the Tosephta, not only benedictions are counted but all religious deeds, and it is asserted that the number 100 is reached automatically.

298 In order to end up with a count of seven, the Yerushalmi (and the Yerushalmi source *Midrash Tehillim* 12) must consider *tefillin* as one commandment. In Babli and Tosephta, circumcision is not counted, probably because the fact of circumcision goes to the credit of the parents, not the baby, and, therefore, *tefillin* must count for two commandments.

299 The implication being that the angel is created by the good deeds of the person protected.

300 David.

301 Taken not as an eight-stringed harp but the commandment performed on the eighth day.

אָמַר רִבִּי אֶלְעָזָר בְּשֵׁם רִבִּי חֲנִינָא תַּלְמִידֵי חֲכָמִים מַרְבִּים שָׁלוֹם בָּעוֹלָם. מַה טַעַם וְכָל בָּנַיִךְ לִמּוּדֵי יי וְרַב שְׁלוֹם בָּנָיִךְ.

Rebbi Eleazar said in the name of Rebbi Ḥanina[302]: The students of the Sages increase peace in the world. What is the reason? (*Is.* 54:13) "All your sons are students of the Eternal, and ample peace is for your sons."

302 A similar homily is in Babli 64a as conclusion of the tractate; there, the expression "students of the sages" means "rabbis" but here it genuinely means "students."

Indices

Index of Biographical Notes

Abba bar Abba 18
Abbaye ben Rebbi Benjamin 451
Abdan 356

Bar Qappara 135, 152
Ben Zoma 147

Gamliel the twin 489
Ganiva 323
Gedilah 274

Ḥananiah ben Ḥananiah 5
Hillel 685
Ḥizqiah 130
Ḥiyya, son of Rav 595
House of Rebbi Yannai 372

Isaac bar Abba from Meḥasia 501

Jacob from Kefar Naburaia 604
Jeremiah the scribe 353
Joseph (Issi) ben Yehudah (Aqabiah) 274
Joseph Hacohen 274

Levi, cf. R. Levi bar Sisi 203
Levi, the son of the Nazir 170

Mar Uqba 101
Menaḥem from Gallia 384

Rabba bar Mari 267
Rabban Simeon bar Gamliel 267
Rav 9
Rav Abba bar Abimi 648
Rav Abba bar Ḥana 86
(Rav) Abba bar Jeremiah 188
Rav Ada bar Ahava (Aḥawa) 103
Rav Aḥa bar Jacob 135
Rav Cahana (II) 247
Rav Hamnuna 103
(Rav) Ḥanan bar Abba 137
Rav Ḥananel 399
Rav Ḥisda 99
Rav Ḥiyya bar Ashi 122
Rav Huna 126
Rav Jehudah 160
Rav Jeremiah (bar Abba) 44
Rav Joseph 81
Rav Mattanah 123
Rav Meshirshia (Mesharshia) 227
Rav Naḥman bar Ada 204
Rav Naḥman (bar Jacob) 160
Rav Samuel bar Shilat 525
Rav Sheshet 382
Rav Uqba bar Ḥama 187
(R)Abba bar bar Ḥana 168, 596
(R)Abba bar Rav Huna 163
Rebbi 53
Rebbi Abba 59
Rebbi Abba bar Aḥa 149
Rebbi Abba bar Cohen 275
Rebbi Abba bar Ḥana 578
Rebbi Abba bar Jeremiah 82
Rebbi Abba bar Kahana 246
Rebbi Abba bar Mamal 348
Rebbi Abba bar Pappus 46
Rebbi Abba bar Rebbi Pappaios 195

Rebbi Abba bar Zamina 352
Rebbi Abba bar Zavda 135, 202
Rebbi Abba from Carthage 371
Rebbi Abbahu 165
Rebbi Abba Mari 108
Rebbi Abba Mari,
brother of R. Yose 520
Rebbi Abba the red 610
Rebbi Abin bar Ḥiyya 165
Rebbi Abin, Rabin 73
Rebbi Abun 122, 137
Rebbi Abun bar Rebbi Ḥiyya 244
Rebbi Ada from Caesarea 402
Rebbi Aḥa 57
Rebbi Aḥa bar Isaac 375
Rebbi Aḥai 158
Rebbi Aḥawa
the son of Rebbi Zeïra 406
Rebbi Ammi the physician 187
Rebbi Ammi, Immi 76, 85
Rebbi Aqiba 317
Rebbi Assi, Yasa 79
Rebbi Avina 490
Rebbi Ayvu 406
Rebbi Azariah 72
Rebbi Benjamin bar Yephet 232
Rebbi Berekhiah 125
Rebbi Bibi 116
Rebbi Cahana bar Malkiah 472
Rebbi Cohen 272
Rebbi Crispus 265
Rebbi Eleazar 166
Rebbi Eleazar bar Avina 131
Rebbi Eleazar ben Antigonos 225
Rebbi Eleazar ben Azariah 146
Rebbi Eleazar bar Joseph 548
Rebbi Eleazar ben Rebbi Hoshaia 434
Rebbi Eleazar ben Rebbi Menaḥem 77
Rebbi Eleazar ben Rebbi Simeon 300
Rebbi Eleazar ben Rebbi Yannai 435
Rebbi Eleazar bar Ẓadoq 277
Rebbi Eliezer (ben Hyrkanos) 40
Rebbi Eliezer,
son of Rebbi Yose the Galilean 404
Rebbi Eudaimon,
brother of Rebbi Yose 428
Rebbi Eudaimon of Haifa 203, 353
Rebbi Eudaimon of Sepphoris 375
Rebbi Ḥaggai 202
Rebbi Ḥalaphta ben Shaul 134, 321
Rebbi Ḥama bar Ḥanina 138
Rebbi Ḥama,
father of Rebbi Oshaiah 233
Rebbi Ḥana 396
Rebbi Ḥanania 181
Rebbi Ḥananiah bar Pappus 389
Rebbi Ḥananiah (Ḥanina)
ben Rebbi Ada 114
Rebbi Ḥanina 53
Rebbi Ḥanina bar Andrei 62
Rebbi Ḥanina bar Ḥama 71
Rebbi Ḥanina bar Pappai 171
Rebbi Ḥanina bar Sisai 493
Rebbi Ḥanina bar Yaqqo 652
Rebbi Ḥanina ben Dosa 422
Rebbi Ḥanina (Ḥananiah)
ben Gamliel 433
Rebbi Ḥanina ben Rebbi Abbahu 383
Rebbi Ḥanina Eyntanaya 415
Rebbi Ḥanina (Ḥananiah)
the colleague of the Rebbis 59
Rebbi Ḥanina Tortayya 316
Rebbi Ḥelbo 125
Rebbi Ḥilqiah 667
Rebbi Ḥinnena 64
Rebbi Ḥinena bar Isaac 466
Rebbi Ḥiyya (the Great) 41, 66
Rebbi Ḥiyya bar Abba 142, 272
Rebbi Ḥiyya bar Ada 241
Rebbi Ḥiyya bar Josef 57
Rebbi Ḥiyya bar Pappos 462
Rebbi Ḥiyya of Sepphoris 375
Rebbi Ḥizqiah 57
Rebbi Hoshaiah 202
Rebbi Huna 61, 94
Rebbi Huna the older of Sepphoris 375
Rebbi Ḥuẓpit 360
Rebbi Idi 103, 194

Rebbi Ilaï, cf. Rebbi Lia 216
Rebbi Isaac 370
Rebbi Isaac bar Eudaimon the old 431
Rebbi Isaac bar Mari 471
Rebbi Isaac bar Naḥman 131
Rebbi Isaac ben Elyashiv 512
Rebbi Isaac ben Rebbi Eleazar 539
Rebbi Isaac Nappaḥa 474
Rebbi Isaac, son of Rebbi Ḥiyya 268
Rebbi Ismael 60
Rebbi Jacob bar Abba 357
Rebbi Jacob bar Abbai 196
Rebbi Jacob bar Abun 299
Rebbi Jacob bar Aḥa 191
Rebbi Jacob bar Idi 397
Rebbi Jacob ben Sisi 360
Rebbi Jacob bar Zavdi 227
Rebbi Jacob from Kefar Ḥanan 426
Rebbi Jacob the Southerner 51
Rebbi Jehudah 69
Rebbi Jehudah ben Bathyra (II) 306
Rebbi Jehudah ben Tema 303
Rebbi Jehudah
ben R. Simon ben Pazi 70
Rebbi Jehudah ben Rebbi Illaï 68
Rebbi Jehudah ben Simon 31
Rebbi Jeremiah 135
Rebbi Jonah 103
Rebbi Jonathan 181, 193
Rebbi Joshua (ben Ḥananiah) 5, 71
Rebbi Joshua ben Levi 83
Rebbi Joshua ben Qorḥah 175
Rebbi Joshua from Sikhnin 344
Rebbi Joshua the Southerner 446
Rebbi Josia 306
Rebbi Judah bar Titus 303
Rebbi Justus ben Shunem 593
Rebbi Levi 62
(Rebbi) Levi bar Sisi 203, 246
Rebbi Lia, La, Illaï 216
Rebbi Mana 77, 119
Rebbi Mani (Mana II) 119
Rebbi Marinos, Son of R. Oshaiah 494
Rebbi Mattaniah 165
Rebbi Meir 6
Rebbi Miasha 135, 255
Rebbi Muna (Mana) 162
Rebbi Naḥum 377
Rebbi Naḥum ben Rebbi Simai 434
Rebbi Nasa 278
Rebbi Nathan bar Ṭobi 339
Rebbi Nathan (the Babylonian) 232
Rebbi Neḥemiah 7
Rebbi Neḥemiah from Emmaus 674
Rebbi Neḥoniah bar Haqanah 351
Rebbi Nehorai 633
Rebbi Oshaiah (the Great) 237
Rebbi Phineas 77
Rebbi Pinḥas Hakohen bar Ḥama 46, 170
Rebbi Sabbatai 563
Rebbi Samuel 287
Rebbi Samuel bar Eudaimon 285
Rebbi Samuel bar Immi 466
Rebbi Samuel bar Inia 135
Rebbi Samuel bar Naḥmani (Naḥman) 81
Rebbi Samuel bar Nathan 138
Rebbi Samuel bar Rav Isaac 221
Rebbi Samuel bar Soṭar, Sosarṭa 63
Rebbi Samuel the Cappadocian 230
Rebbi Samuel Tosephta 286
Rebbi Shammai 312
Rebbi Shila 399
Rebbi Simai 133
Rebbi Simeon (bar Iohai) 83
Rebbi Simeon bar Abba 113, 166
Rebbi Simeon bar Ḥalaphta 66
Rebbi Simeon bar Zevid 245
Rebbi Simeon ben Rebbi Eleazar 262
Rebbi Simeon ben Laqish 72
Rebbi Simeon ben Yoẓadaq 281
Rebbi Simeon,
brother of R. Berekhiah 520
Rebbi Simeon, son of the Nazir 583
Rebbi Simeon the pious 397
Rebbi Simlai 313
Rebbi Simon 62

Rebbi Tanḥum (Tanḥuma bar Abba) 417
Rebbi Tanḥuma 55
Rebbi Tanḥuma Edreya 425
Rebbi Tanḥum bar Ḥanina (Ḥanilaï) 387
Rebbi Tanḥum bar Jeremiah 533
Rebbi Tanḥum bar Yudan 467
Rebbi Tanḥum ben Ḥiyya 186
Rebbi Tanḥum ben Rebbi Ḥiyya 114
Rebbi Tarphon 112
Rebbi Ṭavyome 161
Rebbi Thaddeus 505
Rebbi Ulla 445
Rebbi Uri 159
Rebbi Vivian 562
Rebbi Yannai 177
Rebbi Yannai ben Rebbi Ismael 372
Rebbi Yannai the younger 270
Rebbi Yasa, Assi 164
Rebbi Yehudah bar Abba 335
Rebbi Yehudah ben Baba 335
Rebbi Yehudah bar Zebidah 124
Rebbi Yehudah bar Simon 581
Rebbi Yehudah Nesia 602
Rebbi Yirmeiah 44
Rebbi Yoḥanan 44
Rebbi Yoḥanan ben Zakkai 3
Rebbi Yoḥanan from Karẓion 586
Rebbi Yose (bar Ḥalaphta) 55
Rebbi Yose (ben Zabida) 42
Rebbi Yose bar bar Cahana 567
Rebbi Yose bar Abun 49
Rebbi Yose bar Jacob 649
Rebbi Yose bar Simon bar Abba 683
Rebbi Yose ben Nahorai 660
Rebbi Yose ben Gezira (Quẓira) 685
Rebbi Yose ben Rebbi Ḥalaphta 7, 237
Rebbi Yose ben Rebbi Ḥanina 235
Rebbi Yose ben Shaul 522
Rebbi Yose ben Yose 307
Rebbi Yose from Sidon 380
Rebbi Yose the Galilean 281, 404
Rebbi Yudan 108
Rebbi Yudan Antordiyya 345
Rebbi Yudan bar Rebbi Ismael 364
Rebbi Yudan bar Pelaiah 670
Rebbi Yudan bar Shalom 637
Rebbi Yudan from Cappadocia 352
Rebbi Yudan Migdalaio 640
Rebbi Yudan, son of Rebbi Ayvu 406
Rebbi Zakkai (I) 316
Rebbi Zeïra 44
Rebbi Zeriqan 182
Rebbi Yasa (Assi) 164

Samuel 123
Samuel Minor 442
Samuel bar Shilat 525
Simeon ben Shetaḥ 528
Simon Kamataria 638
Symmachos bar Joseph 160

Tanna 86

Yehudah ben Pappos 253

Zakkai (I) 315
Zeïra ben Ḥinena 408
Zeiri 169

Index of Biblical Quotations

Gen. 1:1 605
1:6 69
1:14 643
1:26-27 606
2:1-4 72
2:10 69

Gen. 16:11 153
11:2 341
17:15 152
17:19 153
18:1 333
19:15 64
19:23 59,64
23:13 369
24:63 332
28:11 332
30:21,24 662
35:10 154
41:44 456
42:5 534
43:3 59
48:16 369

Ex. 2:15 611
4:11 612
12:8 93
12:10 59
12:29 93
13:9-10 183, 289
15:10 608
15:16 393
17:21 333
18:4 6:11
20:24 386
22:18 301
22:19 624
23:2 87
23:24 516
24:12 458
38:23 370
39:3 69

Lev. 1:4-5 82
5:2-4 50
5:17-19 48
19:24 456
22:6 40
22:7 40,59
27:18 649
32:5 90

Num. 15:37 174
15:39 97
15:41 174
28:3 337
28:4 333

Deut. 4:7 619
4:8 609,612
4:32 605
6:4 39,289
6:5 39
6:6 39
6:7 39,109,159, 173,405
6:8 39
6:9 39.290
7:2 625
8:10 290,516
10:17 538
11:13 174
11:19 184,288
11:20 632
11:21 69
13:2 114
16:3 146
17:11 114
22:1-3,6-8 291
22:9 456
23:6 416
32:3 516
33:23 546

Jos. 6:5 626
6:23 388
7:11 681
22:22 607
24:19 608

Jud. 6:12 681
6:24 186
7:19 75
18:30 639,640

1Sam. 1:13 328, 329, 610
2:10 371
9:13 516

2Sam. 7:12 171
15:32 371
17:27 18

1K. 6:17 392
8:28 385
8:30 392
8:44 391,392
8:54 132
9:3 393
13:1 640
13:2 153
17:1 424
17:20 424
18:1 424

2K. 2:11 405
3:15 76
4:10 388

Is. 6:2 549
6:10 207
10:34 515
10:35 212
11:1 212
14:23 601
26:19 425
27:3 652
29:23-24 207
38:2 388
40:2 405
40:17 620
40:22 67,72
43:18-19 154
44:27 341
458 651
46:7 609
52:10 608
54:13 688

Is. 55:6 413
56:7 392
57:16 636
65:24 377
66:20 413
66:24 405

Jer. 4:19 388
10:10 121,174
18:6 661
23:7-8 154
27:16,18 332
25:30 632
31:12 416
32:18 538
50:12 644
51:29 632
51:39 623
51:49 341
51:64 405

Ez. 1:7 63
8:16 391
18:32 193
43:8 388
44:20 20

Hosea 5:19 393

Joel 3:5 614,615,616

Micah 2:11 114
7:8 63

Jonah 2:8 636
2:11 613

Zach. 6:12 212
14:5 632

Mal. 2:5 137,330
3:10 681

Ps. 2:1 367
2:11 4:10
16:2 456
19:5 82
20:2 82
20:20 367
24:21 456
28:6 377,385
29:1 368
29:2 410
29:3 368
29:10-11 213
30:12-13 416
33:6 405
35:10 330,367
42:8 650
47:9 608
50:23 214
55:18 328
57:9 76
58:4 153
60:8 608
65:2 603
68:25 608
68:27 530
68:36 538
77:14 608
81:1 413
102:1 332,385,610
103:20-21 63
104:32 632
105:44 150
106:2 603
106:30 332
112:2 663
113:3 204
114:1 204
115:1 204
116:1 204
118:27-28 204
119:62 75
119:126 684
119:148 75
122:1 171
122:8 620
134:1-3 63
134:2 82
145:1 602
146:5-6 618
148:14 620

Prov. 8:27 67
8:34-35 414
9:5 193
11:7 622
11:8 612
15:25 624
17:5 177,192
21:3 171
21:18 612
23:26 121

Job 21:14 67
29:8 168
36:27 649
37:18 71,72
37:20 603
37:23 603
38:36 626

Cant. 7:5 612
7:10 170

Lament. 5:21 405

Eccl. 4:17 679
9:4 622
10:6 90

Esther 2:21 66
4:2 679
6:11-12 66
8:15-16 66
9:27 204,681

Dan. 3:14 613
6:11 328
6:23 614
7:16 63

Dan 9:4	538	7:63-65	19	1Chr. 22:9	153
9:5	680	8:6	538		
		9:14	120	2Chr. 6:34	392
Neh. 4:15	45,46			18:34	617

Index of Greek and Latin Words

ἀβάσκαντα 626
Ἀλέξανδρος 616
ἀνάκλιτα 263
ἀνθύπατος 419
ἀπειλῶν 633
ἀργαπέτης 216
ἄριστον 331
ἀρχιτέκτων 607
ἄρχων 251
ἀσθενής 231

βασιλεύς 607

δήλωμα 66
δημόσιος 299
διαθήκη 426
δισάκκιον 319
δόμος 217

εἰκών 265
ἐπαρχία 618
ἐπικάρσιον 181
Εὐδαίμων 203

ἡμίονος 580
ἥμισυς 580

ζήτω 500

θέατρον 631
θερμασία 181
θέρμος 464
θεσαυρός 641

ἴασις 500
ἰδιώτης 255

καθέδρα 497
Καλλιρρόη 352
καματηρός 638
κάρρον, κάρρος 421
κεντρόω 181
κεφαλωτός 484
κινάρα 480
κόλλιξ 479
κοσμικός 637
κοσμοκράτωρ 618
κραβάτιον 262
κρουσμός 249
κυρηβία 480

λευκός 625
ληστής 251,616
λιμήν 308
λίτρα 249

μερίς 276

νάρθηξ 425
νεκρός 132
νόμος 419

ξενία 383
ξένος 619

ὄρυζα 473
ὄχλος 612

πανδοκεῖον 315
παράκλητος 337
περίοδος 626
πίλινος 187
πίναξ 641
πλατεῖα 421

ῥάπτω 395

σημαντήριον 115
στήλη 321
στρατηγός 589
σύγκλητος 641
σφέκλη 635
σχεδία 395
σχολαστικός 365

τήγανον 317
τιμή 604
Τρυφῶν 504
τύπος 143

φανός 585
φιλόσοφος 620

χάραξ 663

Augustus 607

balnea 492
bulla 473

Caesar 607
Caesarea 569
cannula 666
cascus 471
cibarius 480
circus 631
collare 320,539
comes 641
compendiarium 54
conditum 492
conditura 171
Crispus 264

decalicator 506
delatorius 107
dimissio 668
diplomatarius 115
dupondius 591

faecaria 635
funda 676

Justus 593

legiones 373

Marinus 494
Mercurius 600
moretum 471
mulus 591

olearii 181
olens 501
olentia 87,501

patronus 612
pileus 187

quaestionarius 612

saltus 420
semita 307
situs 342
specularia 585
spiculum 669
strata 54
subsellium 319,497

Tiberias 558
Titus 303
triclinium 316

General Index

Abegg, M. G. 2
Abraham ben David, R. 427,576,577, 665
Albeck, H. 27
Alexander Severus 9,10
Alfassi 21,22,427,514,623
Arukh 115,480,488,502,531,629,631, 634
Ascari, R. E. 30,104,145,190,218, 234,458,678
Ashkenazi Hebrew 36
Ashkenazi, R. S. Y. 30

Ben Ḥabib, R. M. 100,104,145, 148,502
Ben Jehudah, E. 242
Ben-Asher, M. 37
Benvenist, R. J. 30
Brand, Y. 321
Brüll, J. 66

Caro, R. J. 561
Cirillo, R. S. 29,145,172,412,683
Constantine 11
Cubit 99,318

Demai 508
Dialectics 16
Diocletian 10
Diqduqe Soferim 406
Dmdm 341
Dor, Z. M. 27
Dusk 57

Eiger, R. A. 83
Eliahu Wilna, R. 30,98
Eliezer ben Joel, R. 51,80,449, 568
Elijah, Prophet 58
Epstein, J. N. 27
Ettinger, R. M. Z. 31
Eusebius 430

Finkelstein, L. 362
Five Kinds 477
Fleischer, E. 145,157,398,444 ,519
Fleischer, H. L. 217
Fraenkel, R. D. 30,672
Frankel, Z. 27,30,35,37,51,66, 95,191,198,203,262,273,450,459, 672 678
Fulda, R. E. 29,450,672

Gaonim 401
Gershom, Rabbenu 21
Gezerah Šawah 65
Ginzberg, L. 32,35,135,190,242, 265,268,297,299,347,354,384

Hagahot Maimuniot 51
Haî Gaon, R. 21,45,198,302, 492,600,629
Halakhot Gedolot 97,406,461
Ḥallah 563
Ḥananel, Rabbenu 21,51,74,492
Hand-breadth 317
Havdalah 423
Ḥazzan 269,452
Hermes 601

Ibn al Haytham 53
Ibn Ezra, A. 631
Ibn Janaḥ 631
Impurity 560,562,571
Impurity, derivative 408
Isserles, R. M. 561

Jabneh 4
Jacob David of Sluck, R. 31
Jastrow, M. 273

Jonah Gerondi, R. 130,256,406, 509,685
Josephus Flavius 8

Kohut, A. 101,115
Kolbo 665
Krasilščikov, R. I. E. 31
Krauss, S. 480
Kutscher, Y. 201

Levy, D. (*Ṭaz*) 282
Levy, J. 66,273,320,472,480,488
Lewy, R. I. 31
Lieberman, S. 14,31,35,146,472, 523,565,598,605,642
Livorno Standard 36
Log 296
Löw, I. 480
Lisowsky, G. 518

Maämad 127
Maharsha 23
Maharshal 23
Maḥzor Vitry 6,378
Maimonides 21,92,104,138,152, 210,256,262,290,474,478,575
Mantel, H. 2
Marcus Aurelius 5
Margalit, R. M. 30,100,503,533,599
Mekhilta 7,8
Menorat Hammaör 406
Mil 55,56,68
Minḥah, half of 327
Moon, Orbit 53
Morag, S. 36,141
Morning Hind 64
Mussaphia 115

Nachmanides 53,233,256,268,290, 427
Nahardea 5
Nathanson, R. J. S. 31
Nazir 528
Neïlah 343
Niniveh 430
Nisibis 306
Nissim Gerondi, R. 51,427

Odenathus 10
Oppenheimer, R. D. 294

Parasang 55,68
Pardo, R. D. 574
Parthenios 471
Peles, I. M. 224
Perles, J. 488
Pharisees 2
Philo 8
Place 332

Qab 89.220,296
Qéri 295
Qeroba 135
Quartarius 315

Rabbinowicz, R. 23,623
Rashba (R. Shelomo ben Adrat) 104, 121,157,194,238,350
Rashbam (R. Šemuel ben Meïr) 557, 558
Rashed, R. 53
Rashi 21,92,114,286,311,406,472, 484,492,568,575
Ratner, D. B. 31
Red Heifer 40
Rosh (R. Asher ben Yeḥiel) 24, 97,262,312,350,509,600,623

Saadia Gaon, R. 378
Sadducees 2
Salted 502
Samaritans 507
Samuel Hannagid 517
Savoraë 17
Schwab, M. 31
Seah 296
Seder Olam 7
Seder Tannaïm waAmoraïm 6

Sefer Hamanhig 129
Septimius Severus 5
Seven Kinds 460,490
Shechter, E. 27,32
Sherira Gaon, Letter 9
Shofar blowing 164
Šibbole Halleqeṭ 452
Sifra 7
Sifry 7
Simson of Sens, R. 517,574
Small *Minḥah* 43
Šurah 283

Tanna 86
Theodosius I 11
Tithe 507
Tosaphot 21
Tosephta 7

Ursacinus 419

Vergil 471

Wacholder, B. Z. 2

Yadin, Y. 117
Yalquṭ (Shim'oni) 578,615
Yelin, A. L. 31,556
Yeruḥam ben Meshullam, R. 178
Yerushalmi book 28
YHWH 44
Yospe Shammash, R. 224

Zeraḥiah Halevi, R. 427,685
Ziani, R. E. 27
Zimer, I. 224
Zohar 213

www.ingramcontent.com/pod-product-compliance
Lightning Source LLC
Chambersburg PA
CBHW031841220426
43663CB00006B/461

* 9 7 8 3 1 1 0 6 8 1 3 2 1 *